Principles of Economics
Version 3.0

Libby Rittenberg and Timothy Tregarthen

9781453384862

Principles of Economics
Version 3.0

Libby Rittenberg and Timothy Tregarthen

Published by:

FlatWorld
175 Portland Street
Boston, MA 02114

Brief Contents

Contents

About the Authors

Libby Rittenberg

Libby Rittenberg began teaching economics at Colorado College in Colorado Springs in 1989. She taught principles of economics (always her favorite course to teach), intermediate macroeconomic theory, comparative economic systems, and international political economy. She received her B. A. in economics-mathematics and Spanish from Simmons College and her Ph.D. in economics from Rutgers University.

Prior to joining the faculty at Colorado College, she taught at Lafayette College and at the Rutgers University Graduate School of Management. She served as a Fulbright Scholar in Istanbul, Turkey, and as a research economist at Mathematica, Inc., in Princeton, New Jersey.

Dr. Rittenberg specializes in the internationally oriented areas of economics, with numerous articles in journals and books on comparative and development economics. Much of her work focuses on development and transition, and on the Turkish economy.

Throughout her career, she was very involved in study abroad education and directed programs in central Europe and Turkey.

She recently became professor emeritus.

Tim Tregarthen

There is one word that captures the essence of Dr. Timothy Tregarthen—inspiring. Tim was first diagnosed with multiple sclerosis (MS) in 1975. Yet, he continued a remarkable academic career of teaching and research. In 1996, he published the first edition of his principles of economics textbook to great acclaim, and it became widely used in colleges around the country. That same year, MS made him wheelchair-bound. The disease forced his retirement from teaching at the University of Colorado at Colorado Springs in 1998. He lost the use of his arms in 2001 and has been quadriplegic ever since. In 2002, Tim's doctor expected him to die.

He was placed in the Pikes Peak Hospice program and was twice given his last rites by his priest. UCCS Chancellor Shockley-Zalabak says, "I really thought that Tim would die in hospice. That's what the doctors told me, and I really believed that. I remember one day they called me and told me to try to come see him. They didn't expect him to live through the night."

Not only did he live through the night, but he eventually recovered to the point that he moved from hospice to a long-term care facility. There, he never let his disease get him down. In fact, he turned back to his love of writing and teaching for inspiration. He obtained a voice-activated computer, recruited a coauthor, Libby Rittenberg of Colorado College, and turned his attention to revising his principles of economics book. FlatWorld was honored to publish a new, first-edition relaunch of this wonderful book a few years ago, and is proud to bring Tim's incredible talents as a teacher back to life for future generations of students to learn from.

In addition to completing the rewrite of his textbook, Tim recently completed an autobiography about the 32 years he has had MS, titled *Suffering, Faith, and Wildflowers*. He is nearing completion of a novel, *Cool Luck*, based on the life of a friend. It is the story of a young couple facing the husband's diagnosis of ALS—Lou Gehrig's disease. Remarkably, in 2007, he was able to return for a semester to the classroom at UCCS, where he had taught economics for 27 years. In 2009, Tim returned to California to be closer to his supportive extended family. He now lives in Pasadena.

Perhaps Tim's approach to life is best summed up by an observation by UCCS English Professor Thomas Naperierkowski: "One of the remarkable things is, heck, I can wake up with a headache and be a pretty grouchy character, but given his physical trials, which he faces every minute of his life these days, I've never seen him grouchy, I've never seen him cranky." Carry on, Tim.

Acknowledgments

The authors would like to thank to the following individuals who reviewed the text and whose contributions were invaluable in shaping the final product:

Carlos Aguilar	El Paso Community College
Jeff Ankrom	Wittenberg University
Lee Ash	Skagit Valley Community College
Randall Bennett	Gonzaga University
Joseph Calhoun	Florida State University
Richard Cantrell	Western Kentucky University
Gregg Davis	Flathead Valley Community College
Kevin Dunagan	Oakton Community College
Mona El Shazly	Columbia College
Jose Esteban	Palomar College
Maurita Fawls	Portland Community College
Fred Foldvary	Santa Clara University
Richard Fowles	University of Utah
Doris Geide-Stevenson	Weber State University
Sarmila Ghosh	University of Scranton, Kania School of Management
David Gordon	Illinois Valley Community College
Clinton Greene	University of Missouri-St. Louis
James Holcomb	University of Texas at El Paso
Phil Holleran	Mitchell Community College
Yu Hsing	Southeastern Louisiana University
Thomas Hyclak	Lehigh University
Bruce Johnson	Centre College
James Kahiga	Georgia Perimeter College
Andrew Kohen	James Madison University
Monaco Kristen	California State University–Long Beach
Mark Maier	Glendale Community College
David McClough	Bowling Green State University
Ann McPherren	Huntington University
John Min	Northern Virginia Community College
Shahriar Mostashari	Campbell University, Lundy-Fetterman School of Business
Francis Mummery	Fullerton College
Robert Murphy	Boston College
Kathryn Nantz	Fairfield University

Paul Okello	Tarrant County College-South Campus
Nicholas Peppes	St. Louis Community College
Ramoo Ratha	Diablo Valley College
Teresa Riley	Youngstown State University
Michael Robinson	Mount Holyoke College
Anirban Sengupta	Texas A&M University
John Solow	The University of Iowa
John Somers	Portland Community College
Charles Staelin	Smith College
Richard Stratton	The University of Akron
Kay E. Strong	Bowling Green State University–Firelands
Della Sue	Marist College
John Vahaly	University of Louisville
Robert Whaples	Wake Forest University
Mark Wheeler	Western Michigan University
Leslie Wolfson	The Pingry School
Sourushe Zandvakili	University of Cincinnati

We would like to extend a special thank you to the following instructors whose class tested the text in their courses:

Johnathan Millman	University of Massachusetts–Boston
John Min	Northern Virginia Community College
Kristen Monaco	California State University–Long Beach
Steve Skinner	Western Connecticut State University
Richard Stratton	University of Akron

Special thanks to Eric Malm, Cabrini University, for his assistance on this edition.

Preface

Greek philosopher Heraclitis said more than 2,500 years ago that "Nothing endures but change." Forecasting is a tricky business, but this sentiment strikes us as being as safe a bet as one can make. Change—rapid change—underlies all our lives. As we were completing the previous version of this textbook, the world had entered a period of marked economic uncertainty, now referred to as the Great Recession, that led many students, and indeed people from all walks of life, to tune into economic events as never before to try to understand the economic world around them. As we worked on this new version, it was political uncertainty that had taken center stage. Two electoral outcomes—first, the decision by citizens of the United Kingdom to pull out of the European Union (known as the Brexit vote) and the decision by citizens of the United States to select Donald J. Trump as president—were not widely predicted. How would these political outcomes affect economic policies and economic outcomes? The last decade has certainly given economists the public's attention, and we see an opportunity to share economics principles and the economic way of thinking in a way that emphasizes their relevance to today's world.

We use applications from sports, politics, campus life, current events, and other familiar settings to illustrate the links between theoretical principles and common experiences. Because of the increasingly global nature of economic activity and the current backlash to it, we also recognize the need for a clear and consistent international focus throughout an economics text. In addition, we have tried to provide a sense of the intellectual excitement of the field and an appreciation for the gains it has made, as well as an awareness of the challenges that lie ahead. Always trying to help students to see the relevance of economic ideas, in this new edition in the microeconomics section, we have incorporated, for example, research on technological change and the wage gap, the future of jobs, carbon-neutral tax schemes, and the controversy around increasing the minimum wage. In the macroeconomics section, we have analyzed how the recovery from the Great Recession played out, bringing in the extraordinary tools that the Federal Reserve used as well as the fiscal stimulus response and the Dodd-Frank legislation. We have also discussed the unprecedented growth of the Chinese economy and predictions concerning the pace of future growth in advanced economies. As in previous editions, we have provided a balance between current issues and historical context.

At the same time, in this new edition we have stayed true to what we believe are the elements that make this text effective. To begin with, to ensure students realize that economics is a unified discipline and not a bewildering array of seemingly unrelated topics, we develop the presentation of microeconomics and of macroeconomics around integrating themes.

The integrating theme for microeconomics is the marginal decision rule, a simple approach to choices that maximize the value of some objective. Following its presentation in an early microeconomics chapter, the marginal decision rule becomes an integrating device throughout the discussion of microeconomics. Instead of a hodgepodge of rules for different market conditions, we give a single rule that can be applied within any market setting.

The integrating theme for macroeconomics is the model of aggregate demand and aggregate supply. Following its presentation in an early macroeconomics chapter, this model allows us to look at both short-run and long-run concepts and to address a variety of policy issues and debates.

Recognizing that a course in economics may seem daunting to some students, we have tried to make the writing clear and engaging. Clarity comes in part from the intuitive presentation style, but we have also integrated a number of pedagogical features that we believe make learning economic concepts and principles easier and more fun. These features are very student-focused.

The chapters themselves are written using a "modular" format. In particular, chapters generally consist of three main content sections that break down a particular topic into manageable parts. Each content section contains not only an exposition of the material at hand but also learning objectives, summaries, examples, and problems. Each chapter is introduced with a story to motivate the material and each chapter ends with a wrap-up and additional problems. Our goal is to encourage active learning by including many examples and many problems of different types.

A tour of the features available for each chapter may give a better sense of what we mean:

- Start Up— Chapter introductions set the stage for each chapter with an example that we hope will motivate readers to study the material that follows. These essays, on topics such as the value of a college degree in the labor market or how policy makers reacted to a particular economic recession, lend themselves to the type of analysis explained in the chapter. We often refer to these examples later in the text to demonstrate the link between theory and reality.

- Learning Objectives— These succinct statements are guides to the content of each section. Instructors can use them as a snapshot of the important points of the section. After completing the section, students can return to the learning objectives to check if they have mastered the material.

- Heads Up!— These notes throughout the text warn of common errors and explain how to avoid making them. After our combined teaching experience of more than 50 years, we have seen the same mistakes made by many students. This feature provides additional clarification and shows students how to navigate possibly treacherous waters.

- Key Takeaways— These statements review the main points covered in each content section.

- Key Terms— Defined within the text, students can review them in context, a process that enhances learning.

- Try It! questions— These problems, which appear at the end of each content section and which are answered completely in the text, give students the opportunity to be active learners. They are designed to give students a clear signal as to whether they understand the material before they go on to the next topic.

- Cases in Point— These essays included at the end of each content section illustrate the influence of economic forces on real issues and real people. Unlike other texts that use boxed features to present interesting new material or newspaper articles, we have written each case ourselves to integrate them more clearly with the rest of the text.

- Summary— In a few paragraphs, the information presented in the chapter is pulled together in a way that allows for a quick review of the material.

- End-of-chapter concept and numerical problems— These are bountiful and are intended to check understanding, to promote discussion of the issues raised in the chapter, and to engage students in critical thinking about the material. Included are not only general review questions to test basic understanding but also examples drawn from the news and from results of economics research. Some have students working with real-world data.

- Chapter quizzes— Each chapter also includes online, supplementary multiple choice questions that provide students with feedback on both correct and incorrect responses. These provide yet another way for students to test themselves on the material.

Additional Material for Instructors

The authors have been personally involved in the generation of a huge *Test Bank* that includes multiple choice, true/false, and short essays questions. These questions are scored in terms of level of difficulty and include multiple ways of testing the material.

The *Solutions Manual*, with which the authors were also involved, contains answers for all concept and numerical problems found at the end of each text chapter.

The *PowerPoint Slides* include all the exhibits contained in the text to allow ease of use in class.

We hope that users will find this text an engaging and enjoyable way of becoming acquainted with economics principles and that mastery of the material will lead to looking at the world in a deeper and more meaningful way. We welcome all feedback.

Libby Rittenberg

Timothy Tregarthen

CHAPTER 1
Economics: The Study of Choice

1.1 Start Up: Economics in the News

Economic issues dominated the news in 2016, just as they dominate news in most years. What happens to economic phenomena such as growth, unemployment, gasoline and food prices, house values, and the national debt can affect the overall well being of society as well as many individuals.

What causes the prices of some goods to rise while the prices of other goods fall? Price determination is one of the things that we will study in this book. We will consider factors that lead an economy to grow more or less rapidly, the determination of unemployment rates, and even the process through which governments make choices that can lead to the kind of dilemma the United States faced in 2011 as the national debt soared past the nation's debt limit.

While the investigation of these problems surely falls within the province of economics, economics encompasses a far broader range of issues. Ultimately, economics is the study of choice. Because choices range over every imaginable aspect of human experience, so does economics. Economists have investigated the nature of family life, the arts, education, crime, sports, law—the list is virtually endless because so much of our lives involves making choices.

Consider some of the choices you face. Would you like better grades? More time to relax? More time watching movies? Getting better grades probably requires more time studying, and perhaps less relaxation and entertainment. Not only must we make choices as individuals, we must make choices as a society. Do we want a cleaner environment? Faster economic growth? Both may be desirable, but efforts to clean up the environment may conflict with faster economic growth. Society must make choices.

Economics is defined less by the subjects economists investigate than by the way in which economists investigate them. Economists have a way of looking at the world that differs from the way scholars in other disciplines look at the world. It is the *economic way of thinking*; this chapter introduces that way of thinking.

1.2 Defining Economics

Learning Objectives

1. Define economics.
2. Explain the concepts of scarcity and opportunity cost and how they relate to the definition of economics.
3. Understand the three fundamental economic questions: What should be produced? How should goods and services be produced? For whom should goods and services be produced?

Economics is a social science that examines how people choose among the alternatives available to them. It is social because it involves people and their behavior. It is a science because it uses, as much as possible, a scientific approach in its investigation of choices.

Scarcity, Choice, and Cost

All choices mean that one alternative is selected over another. Selecting among alternatives involves three ideas central to economics: scarcity, choice, and opportunity cost.

Scarcity

Our resources are limited. At any one time, we have only so much land, so many factories, so much oil, so many people. But our wants, our desires for the things that we can produce with those resources, are unlimited. We would always like more and better housing, more and better education—more and better of practically everything.

If our resources were also unlimited, we could say yes to each of our wants—and there would be no economics. Because our resources are limited, we cannot say yes to everything. To say yes to one thing requires that we say no to another. Whether we like it or not, we must make choices.

Our unlimited wants are continually colliding with the limits of our resources, forcing us to pick some activities and to reject others. **Scarcity** is the condition of having to choose among alternatives. A **scarce good** is one for which the choice of one alternative use of the good requires that another be given up.

Consider a parcel of land. The parcel presents us with several alternative uses. We could build a house on it. We could put a gas station on it. We could create a small park on it. We could leave the land undeveloped in order to be able to make a decision later as to how it should be used.

Suppose we have decided the land should be used for housing. Should it be a large and expensive house or several modest ones? Suppose it is to be a large and expensive house. Who should live in the house? If the Lees live in it, the Nguyens cannot. There are alternative uses of the land both in the sense of the type of use and also in the sense of who gets to use it. The fact that land is scarce means that society must make choices concerning its use.

Virtually everything is scarce. Consider the air we breathe, which is available in huge quantity at no charge to us. Could it possibly be scarce?

The test of whether air is scarce is whether it has alternative uses. What uses can we make of the air? We breathe it. We pollute it when we drive our cars, heat our houses, or operate our factories. In effect, one use of the air is as a garbage dump. We certainly need the air to breathe. But just as certainly, we choose to dump garbage in it. Those two uses are clearly alternatives to each other. The more garbage we dump in the air, the less desirable—and healthy—it will be to breathe. If we decide we want to breathe cleaner air, we must limit the activities that generate pollution. Air is a scarce good because it has alternative uses.

Not all goods, however, confront us with such choices. A **free good** is one for which the choice of one use does not require that we give up another. One example of a free good is gravity. The fact that gravity is holding you to the earth does not mean that your neighbor is forced to drift up into space! One person's use of gravity is not an alternative to another person's use.

There are not many free goods. Outer space, for example, was a free good when the only use we made of it was to gaze at it. But now, our use of space has reached the point where one use can be an alternative to another. Conflicts have already arisen over the allocation of orbital slots for communications satellites. Thus, even parts of outer space are scarce. Space will surely become scarcer as we find new ways to use it. Scarcity characterizes virtually everything. Consequently, the scope of economics is wide indeed.

Scarcity and the Fundamental Economic Questions

The choices we confront as a result of scarcity raise three sets of issues. Every economy must answer the following questions:

1. **What should be produced?** Using the economy's scarce resources to produce one thing requires giving up another. Producing better education, for example, may require cutting back on other services, such as health care. A decision to preserve a wilderness area requires giving up other uses of the land. Every society must decide what it will produce with its scarce resources.

2. **How should goods and services be produced?** There are all sorts of choices to be made in determining how goods and services should be produced. Should a firm employ a few skilled or a lot of unskilled workers? Should it produce in its own country or should it use foreign plants? Should manufacturing firms use new or recycled raw materials to make their products?

3. **For whom should goods and services be produced?** If a good or service is produced, a decision must be made about who will get it. A decision to have one person or group receive a good or service usually means it will not be available to someone else. For example, representatives of the poorest nations on earth often complain that energy consumption per person in the United States is many *times* greater than energy consumption per person in the world's scores of poorest countries. Critics argue that the world's energy should be more evenly allocated. Should it? That is a "for whom" question.

Every economy must determine what should be produced, how it should be produced, and for whom it should be produced. We shall return to these questions again and again.

Opportunity Cost

It is within the context of scarcity that economists define what is perhaps the most important concept in all of economics, the concept of opportunity cost. **Opportunity cost** is the value of the best alternative forgone in making any choice.

The opportunity cost to you of reading the remainder of this chapter will be the value of the best other use to which you could have put your time. If you choose to spend $20 on a potted plant, you have simultaneously chosen to give up the benefits of spending the $20 on pizzas or a paperback book or a night at the movies. If the book is the most valuable of those alternatives, then the opportunity cost of the plant is the value of the enjoyment you otherwise expected to receive from the book.

The concept of opportunity cost must not be confused with the purchase price of an item. Consider the cost of a college or university education. That includes the value of the best alternative use of money spent for tuition, fees, and books. But the most important cost of a college education is the value of the forgone alternative uses of time spent studying and attending class instead of using the time in some other endeavor. Students sacrifice that time in hopes of even greater earnings in the future or because they place a value on the opportunity to learn. Or consider the cost of going to the doctor. Part of that cost is the value of the best alternative use of the money required to see the doctor. But the cost also includes the value of the best alternative use of the time required to see the doctor. The essential thing to see in the concept of opportunity cost is found in the name of the concept. Opportunity cost is the value of the best opportunity forgone in a particular choice. It is not simply the amount spent on that choice.

The concepts of scarcity, choice, and opportunity cost are at the heart of economics. A good is scarce if the choice of one alternative requires that another be given up. The existence of alternative uses forces us to make choices. The opportunity cost of any choice is the value of the best alternative forgone in making it.

opportunity cost

The value of the best alternative forgone in making any choice.

Key Takeaways

- Economics is a social science that examines how people choose among the alternatives available to them.
- Scarcity implies that we must give up one alternative in selecting another. A good that is not scarce is a free good.
- The three fundamental economic questions are: What should be produced? How should goods and services be produced? For whom should goods and services be produced?
- Every choice has an opportunity cost and opportunity costs affect the choices people make. The opportunity cost of any choice is the value of the best alternative that had to be forgone in making that choice.

Try It!

Identify the elements of scarcity, choice, and opportunity cost in each of the following:

1. The Environmental Protection Agency is considering an order that a 500-acre area on the outskirts of a large city be preserved in its natural state, because the area is home to a rodent that is considered an endangered species. Developers had planned to build a housing development on the land.

2. The manager of an automobile assembly plant is considering whether to produce cars or sport utility vehicles (SUVs) next month. Assume that the quantities of labor and other materials required would be the same for either type of production.

3. A young man who went to work as a nurses' aide after graduating from high school leaves his job to go to college, where he will obtain training as a registered nurse.

Case in Point: Voters in the U.S. Make a Choice

Source: © Shutterstock, Inc.

The U.S. presidential campaign of 2016 seemed to many to be one of the bitterest and most contentious on record. On the Democratic side, there were two main contenders, Hillary Clinton and Bernie Sanders. On the Republican side, the primaries started with more than fifteen candidates, one of whom was long-shot candidate Donald Trump. The primary battles were a slog, with personal insults flying, especially on the Republican side. The final battle between Trump and Clinton continued at a feverish pace. The general election offered voters a clear choice of economic and social policies.

For example, Clinton largely promised a continuation of the policies of Barack Obama. One main area where she differed from Obama was on the ratification of a trade agreement that the Obama administration had negotiated with 12 countries in the Asian-Pacific area. She was against it, as was Trump. She was supportive of the Affordable Care Act (often called Obamacare), though talked about improving it. She generally supported the steps he had taken on environmental, financial, and labor regulation. She did not say who she would name to the Supreme Court but did state that she would look for judges who would uphold Roe v Wade, the Supreme Court case that legalized abortion.

Trump argued not just against the new trade agreement but also against the North American Free Trade Agreement (NAFTA) that had gone into effect under former President Bill Clinton. He also talked about the U.S. having been taken advantage of by China and threatened to impose tariffs on goods imported from China. He argued that he would "repeal and replace" Obamacare with something much better. He wanted a rollback of regulations in general. As for Supreme Court nominees, he presented a list of potential candidates who are considered conservative and thus less likely to support a right to abortion.

There were many other areas on which the two candidates disagreed. We all know the outcome and the choice that voters made in the end. Elections do have consequences.

Answers to Try It! Problems

1. The 500-acre area is scarce because it has alternative uses: preservation in its natural state or a site for homes. A choice must be made between these uses. The opportunity cost of preserving the land in its natural state is the forgone value of the land as a housing development. The opportunity cost of using the land as a housing development is the forgone value of preserving the land.

2. The scarce resources are the plant and the labor at the plant. The manager must choose between producing cars and producing SUVs. The opportunity cost of producing cars is the profit that could be earned from producing SUVs; the opportunity cost of producing SUVs is the profit that could be earned from producing cars.

3. The man can devote his time to his current career or to an education; his time is a scarce resource. He must choose between these alternatives. The opportunity cost of continuing as a nurses' aide is the forgone benefit he expects from training as a registered nurse; the opportunity cost of going to college is the forgone income he could have earned working full-time as a nurses' aide.

1.3 The Field of Economics

Learning Objectives

1. Explain the distinguishing characteristics of the economic way of thinking.
2. Distinguish between microeconomics and macroeconomics.

We have examined the basic concepts of scarcity, choice, and opportunity cost in economics. In this section, we will look at economics as a field of study. We begin with the characteristics that distinguish economics from other social sciences.

The Economic Way of Thinking

Economists study choices that scarcity requires us to make. This fact is not what distinguishes economics from other social sciences; all social scientists are interested in choices. An anthropologist might study the choices of ancient peoples; a political scientist might study the choices of legislatures; a psychologist might study how people choose a mate; a sociologist might study the factors that have led to a rise in single-parent households. Economists study such questions as well. What is it about the study of choices by economists that makes economics different from these other social sciences?

Three features distinguish the economic approach to choice from the approaches taken in other social sciences:

1. Economists give special emphasis to the role of opportunity costs in their analysis of choices.
2. Economists assume that individuals make choices that seek to maximize the value of some objective, and that they define their objectives in terms of their own self-interest.
3. Individuals maximize by deciding whether to do a little more or a little less of something. Economists argue that individuals pay attention to the consequences of small changes in the levels of the activities they pursue.

The emphasis economists place on opportunity cost, the idea that people make choices that maximize the value of objectives that serve their self-interest, and a focus on the effects of small changes are ideas of great power. They constitute the core of economic thinking. The next three sections examine these ideas in greater detail.

Opportunity Costs Are Important

If doing one thing requires giving up another, then the expected benefits of the alternatives we face will affect the ones we choose. Economists argue that an understanding of opportunity cost is crucial to the examination of choices.

As the set of available alternatives changes, we expect that the choices individuals make will change. A rainy day could change the opportunity cost of reading a book; we might expect more reading to get done in bad than in good weather. A high income can make it very costly to take a day off; we might expect highly paid individuals to work more hours than those who are not paid as well. If individuals are maximizing their level of satisfaction and firms are maximizing profits, then a change in the set of alternatives they face may affect their choices in a predictable way.

The emphasis on opportunity costs is an emphasis on the examination of alternatives. One benefit of the economic way of thinking is that it pushes us to think about the value of alternatives in each problem involving choice.

Individuals Maximize in Pursuing Self-Interest

What motivates people as they make choices? Perhaps more than anything else, it is the economist's answer to this question that distinguishes economics from other fields.

Economists assume that individuals make choices that they expect will create the maximum value of some objective, given the constraints they face. Furthermore, economists assume that people's objectives will be those that serve their own self-interest.

Economists assume, for example, that the owners of business firms seek to maximize profit. Given the assumed goal of profit maximization, economists can predict how firms in an industry will respond to changes in the markets in which they operate. As labor costs in the United States rise, for example, economists are not surprised to see firms moving some of their manufacturing operations overseas.

Similarly, economists assume that maximizing behavior is at work when they examine the behavior of consumers. In studying consumers, economists assume that individual consumers make choices aimed at maximizing their level of satisfaction. In the next chapter, we will look at the results of the shift from skiing to snowboarding; that is a shift that reflects the pursuit of self-interest by consumers and by manufacturers.

In assuming that people pursue their self-interest, economists are not assuming people are selfish. People clearly gain satisfaction by helping others, as suggested by the large charitable contributions people make. Pursuing one's own self-interest means pursuing the things that give one satisfaction. It need not imply greed or selfishness.

Choices Are Made at the Margin

Economists argue that most choices are made "at the margin." The **margin** is the current level of an activity. Think of it as the edge from which a choice is to be made. A **choice at the margin** is a decision to do a little more or a little less of something.

Assessing choices at the margin can lead to extremely useful insights. Consider, for example, the problem of curtailing water consumption when the amount of water available falls short of the amount people now use. Economists argue that one way to induce people to conserve water is to raise its price. A common response to this recommendation is that a higher price would have no effect on water consumption, because water is a necessity. Many people assert that prices do not affect water consumption because people "need" water.

But choices in water consumption, like virtually all choices, are made at the margin. Individuals do not make choices about whether they should or should not consume water. Rather, they decide whether to consume a little more or a little less water. Household water consumption in the United States totals about 105 gallons per person per day. Think of that starting point as the edge from which a choice at the margin in water consumption is made. Could a higher price cause you to use less water brushing your teeth, take shorter showers, or water your lawn less? Could a higher price cause people to reduce their use, say, to 104 gallons per person per day? To 103? When we examine the choice to consume water at the margin, the notion that a higher price would reduce consumption seems much more plausible. Prices affect our consumption of water because choices in water consumption, like other choices, are made at the margin.

The elements of opportunity cost, maximization, and choices at the margin can be found in each of two broad areas of economic analysis: microeconomics and macroeconomics. Your economics course, for example, may be designated as a "micro" or as a "macro" course. We will look at these two areas of economic thought in the next section.

Microeconomics and Macroeconomics

The field of economics is typically divided into two broad realms: microeconomics and macroeconomics. It is important to see the distinctions between these broad areas of study.

margin
The current level of an activity.

choice at the margin
A decision to do a little more or a little less of something.

microeconomics

The branch of economics that focuses on the choices made by consumers and firms and the impacts those choices have on individual markets.

macroeconomics

The branch of economics that focuses on the impact of choices on the total, or aggregate, level of economic activity.

Microeconomics is the branch of economics that focuses on the choices made by individual decision-making units in the economy—typically consumers and firms—and the impacts those choices have on individual markets. **Macroeconomics** is the branch of economics that focuses on the impact of choices on the total, or aggregate, level of economic activity.

Why do tickets to the best concerts cost so much? How does the threat of global warming affect real estate prices in coastal areas? Why do women end up doing most of the housework? Why do senior citizens get discounts on public transit systems? These questions are generally regarded as microeconomic because they focus on individual units or markets in the economy.

Is the total level of economic activity rising or falling? Is the rate of inflation increasing or decreasing? What is happening to the unemployment rate? These are the questions that deal with aggregates, or totals, in the economy; they are problems of macroeconomics. The question about the level of economic activity, for example, refers to the total value of all goods and services produced in the economy. Inflation is a measure of the rate of change in the average price level for the entire economy; it is a macroeconomic problem. The total levels of employment and unemployment in the economy represent the aggregate of all labor markets; unemployment is also a topic of macroeconomics.

Both microeconomics and macroeconomics give attention to individual markets. But in microeconomics that attention is an end in itself; in macroeconomics it is aimed at explaining the movement of major economic aggregates—the level of total output, the level of employment, and the price level.

We have now examined the characteristics that define the economic way of thinking and the two branches of this way of thinking: microeconomics and macroeconomics. In the next section, we will have a look at what one can do with training in economics.

Putting Economics to Work

Economics is one way of looking at the world. Because the economic way of thinking has proven quite useful, training in economics can be put to work in a wide range of fields. One, of course, is in work as an economist. Undergraduate work in economics can be applied to other careers as well.

Careers in Economics

Economists generally work in three types of organizations: government agencies, business firms, and colleges and universities.

Economists working for business firms and government agencies sometimes forecast economic activity to assist their employers in planning. They also apply economic analysis to the activities of the firms or agencies for which they work or consult. Economists employed at colleges and universities teach and conduct research.

Look at the website of your college or university's economics department. Chances are the department will discuss the wide variety of occupations that their economics majors enter. Unlike engineering and accounting majors, economics and other social science majors tend to be distributed over a broad range of occupations.

Applying Economics to Other Fields

Suppose that you are considering something other than a career in economics. Would choosing to study economics help you?

The evidence suggests it may. Suppose, for example, that you are considering law school. The study of law requires keen analytical skills; studying economics sharpens such skills. Economists have traditionally argued that undergraduate work in economics serves as excellent preparation for law school. Economist Michael Nieswiadomy of the University of North Texas collected data on Law School Admittance Test (LSAT) scores for the 16 undergraduate majors listed most often by students hoping to enter law school in the class of 2012–13. Table 1.1 gives the scores, as well as the ranking for each of these majors in 2008. Economics majors narrowly edged out philosophy majors for the highest average score.

TABLE 1.1 LSAT Scores for Students Taking the Exam in 2012-13
Here are the average LSAT scores and rankings for the 12 undergraduate majors with more than 1,900 students taking the test to enter law school in the 2012–2013 academic year.

Rank	Major	Average LSAT Score	# of Students
1	Economics	159.1	2,468
2	Philosophy	158.8	1,879
3	Engineering	157.3	1,127
4	History	156.7	3,323
5	English	155.8	3,728
6	Finance	154.6	1,817
7	Political Science	154.3	12,215
8	Psychology	153.3	3,335
9	Accounting	153.1	1,106
10	Marketing	152.2	1,024
11	Liberal Arts	151.9	1,177
12	Communications	151.6	1,729
13	Sociology	151.3	1,520
14	Business Administration	150.6	1,555
15	Business Management	150.2	1,371
16	Criminal Justice	146.3	2,878

Source: Based on data from Michael Nieswiadomy, "LSAT Scores of Economics Majors, The 2012-13 Class Update," The Journal of Economic Education 45:1 (January-March 2014).

Did the strong performance by economics and philosophy majors mean that training in those fields sharpens analytical skills tested in the LSAT, or that students with good analytical skills are more likely to major in them? Both were probably at work. Economics and philosophy clearly attract students with good analytical skills—and studying economics or philosophy helps to develop those skills.

Of course, you may not be interested in going to law school. One consideration relevant to selecting a major is potential earnings in that field. The National Association of Colleges and Employers conducts regular surveys of salary projections by college major . The results for the winter 2017 survey for selected majors are given in Table 1.2. If you are going for the big bucks, the best strategy is to major in engineering. But as the table suggests, economics majors (singled out for our purposes from the other social sciences) as a group did quite well in 2017.

TABLE 1.2 Average Annual Salary Projections, Class of 2017 College Graduates

Major	Average Offer
Engineering	$66,097
Computer Science	65,540
Math and Sciences	59,368
Economics	56,678
Business	54,803
Agricultural and Natural Resources	54,364
Social Sciences	53,459
Communications	51,925
Humanities	48,733

Source: Based on data from National Association of Colleges and Employers, Engineering Majors Top Class of 2017 Salary Projections, press release at http://www.naceweb.org/job-market/compensation/engineering-majors-top-class-of-2017-salary-projections/.

One's choice of a major is not likely to be based solely on considerations of potential earnings or the prospect of landing a spot in law school. You will also consider your interests and abilities in making a decision about whether to pursue further study in economics. And, of course, you will consider the expected benefits of alternative courses of study. What is *your* opportunity cost of pursuing study of economics? Does studying more economics serve your interests and will doing so maximize your satisfaction level? These considerations may be on your mind as you begin to study economics at the college level and obviously students will make many different choices. But, should you decide to pursue a major in economics, you should know that a background in this field is likely to serve you well.

Key Takeaways

- Economists focus on the opportunity costs of choices, they assume that individuals make choices in a way that maximizes the value of an objective defined in terms of their own self-interest, and they assume that individuals make those choices at the margin.
- Economics is divided into two broad areas: microeconomics and macroeconomics.
- A wide range of career opportunities is open to economics majors. Empirical evidence suggests that students who enter the job market with a major in economics tend to earn more than do students in many other majors. Further, economics majors do particularly well on the LSAT.

Try It!

The Department of Agriculture estimated that the expenditures a middle-income, husband–wife family of three would incur to raise one additional child from birth in 2005 to age 17 would be $250,530. In what way does this estimate illustrate the economic way of thinking? Would the Department's estimate be an example of microeconomic or of macroeconomic analysis? Why?

Case in Point: Opportunity Cost with *The Simpsons*

Source: © Thinkstock

In the animated television comedy *The Simpsons*, Homer's father, Grampa Simpson, faced a classic problem in the allocation of a scarce resource—his time. He wanted to spend the day with his girlfriend, Bea—it was, after all, her birthday. His alternative was to spend the day with Homer and the family, which he did not really want to do, partly because they never visited him anyway.

Homer and his family prevailed, however, and insisted on taking Grampa to "Discount Lion Safari," a local amusement park. The cost of Grampa's day with his family is the enjoyment he anticipated from spending time with Bea. It all ends up badly for Grampa anyway—Homer's car breaks down on the way to the park. As for the forgone alternative, Bea dies that day, possibly because of a broken heart from not being able to spend the day with Grampa.

Sources: Based on R. Andrew Luccasen and M. Kathleen Thomas, "Simpsonomics: Teaching Economics Using Episodes of The Simpsons," The Journal of Economic Education, 41(2), Spring 2010, 136–149. The Simpsons, Episode no. 30, first broadcast 28 March 1991 by Fox, directed by David Silverman and written by Jay Kogen and Wallace Wolodarsky.

Answer to Try It! Problem

The information given suggests one element of the economic way of thinking: assessing the choice at the margin. The estimate reflects the cost of one more child for a family that already has one. It is not clear from the information given how close the estimate of cost comes to the economic concept of opportunity cost. The Department of Agriculture's estimate included such costs as housing, food, transportation, clothing, health care, child care, and education. An economist would add the value of the best alternative use of the additional time that will be required for the child. If the couple is looking far ahead, it may want to consider the opportunity cost of sending a child to college. And, if it is looking *very* far ahead, it may want to consider the fact that nearly half of all parents over the age of 50 support at least one child over the age of 21. This is a problem in microeconomic analysis, because it focuses on the choices of individual households.

1.4 The Economists' Tool Kit

Learning Objectives

1. Explain how economists test hypotheses, develop economic theories, and use models in their analyses.
2. Explain how the all-other-things unchanged (ceteris paribus) problem and the fallacy of false cause affect the testing of economic hypotheses and how economists try to overcome these problems.
3. Distinguish between normative and positive statements.

Economics differs from other social sciences because of its emphasis on opportunity cost, the assumption of maximization in terms of one's own self-interest, and the analysis of choices at the margin. But certainly much of the basic methodology of economics and many of its difficulties are common to every social science—indeed, to every science. This section explores the application of the scientific method to economics.

variable

Something whose value can change.

constant

Something whose value does not change.

scientific method

A systematic set of procedures through which knowledge is created.

hypothesis

An assertion of a relationship between two or more variables that could be proven to be false.

Researchers often examine relationships between variables. A **variable** is something whose value can change. By contrast, a **constant** is something whose value does not change. The speed at which a car is traveling is an example of a variable. The number of minutes in an hour is an example of a constant.

Research is generally conducted within a framework called the **scientific method**, a systematic set of procedures through which knowledge is created. In the scientific method, hypotheses are suggested and then tested. A **hypothesis** is an assertion of a relationship between two or more variables that could be proven to be false. A statement is not a hypothesis if no conceivable test could show it to be false. The statement "Plants like sunshine" is not a hypothesis; there is no way to test whether plants like sunshine or not, so it is impossible to prove the statement false. The statement "Increased solar radiation increases the rate of plant growth" is a hypothesis; experiments could be done to show the relationship between solar radiation and plant growth. If solar radiation were shown to be unrelated to plant growth or to retard plant growth, then the hypothesis would be demonstrated to be false.

If a test reveals that a particular hypothesis is false, then the hypothesis is rejected or modified. In the case of the hypothesis about solar radiation and plant growth, we would probably find that more sunlight increases plant growth over some range but that too much can actually retard plant growth. Such results would lead us to modify our hypothesis about the relationship between solar radiation and plant growth.

theory

A hypothesis that has not been rejected after widespread testing and that wins general acceptance.

law

A theory that has been subjected to even more testing and that has won virtually universal acceptance.

If the tests of a hypothesis yield results consistent with it, then further tests are conducted. A hypothesis that has not been rejected after widespread testing and that wins general acceptance is commonly called a **theory**. A theory that has been subjected to even more testing and that has won virtually universal acceptance becomes a **law**. We will examine two economic laws in the next two chapters.

Even a hypothesis that has achieved the status of a law cannot be proven true. There is always a possibility that someone may find a case that invalidates the hypothesis. That possibility means that nothing in economics, or in any other social science, or in any science, can ever be *proven* true. We can have great confidence in a particular proposition, but it is always a mistake to assert that it is "proven."

Models in Economics

All scientific thought involves simplifications of reality. The real world is far too complex for the human mind—or the most powerful computer—to consider. Scientists use models instead. A **model** is a set of simplifying assumptions about some aspect of the real world. Models are always based on assumed conditions that are simpler than those of the real world, assumptions that are necessarily false. A model of the real world cannot *be* the real world.

model

A set of simplifying assumptions about some aspect of the real world.

We will encounter an economic model in Chapter 2. For that model, we will assume that an economy can produce only two goods. Then we will explore the model of demand and supply. One of the assumptions we will make there is that all the goods produced by firms in a particular market are identical. Of course, real economies and real markets are not that simple. Reality is never as simple as a model; one point of a model is to simplify the world to improve our understanding of it.

Economists often use graphs to represent economic models. The appendix to this chapter provides a quick, refresher course, if you think you need one, on understanding, building, and using graphs.

Models in economics also help us to generate hypotheses about the real world. In the next section, we will examine some of the problems we encounter in testing those hypotheses.

Testing Hypotheses in Economics

Here is a hypothesis suggested by the model of demand and supply: an increase in the price of gasoline will reduce the quantity of gasoline consumers demand. How might we test such a hypothesis?

Economists try to test hypotheses such as this one by observing actual behavior and using empirical (that is, real-world) data. The average retail price of gasoline in the United States rose from an average of $2.12 per gallon on May 22, 2005 to $2.88 per gallon on May 22, 2006. The number of gallons of gasoline consumed by U.S. motorists rose 0.3% during that period.

The small increase in the quantity of gasoline consumed by motorists as its price rose is inconsistent with the hypothesis that an increased price will lead to a reduction in the quantity demanded. Does that mean that we should dismiss the original hypothesis? On the contrary, we must be cautious in assessing this evidence. Several problems exist in interpreting any set of economic data. One problem is that several things may be changing at once; another is that the initial event may be unrelated to the event that follows. The next two sections examine these problems in detail.

The All-Other-Things-Unchanged Problem

The hypothesis that an increase in the price of gasoline produces a reduction in the quantity demanded by consumers carries with it the assumption that there are no other changes that might also affect consumer demand. A better statement of the hypothesis would be: An increase in the price of gasoline will reduce the quantity consumers demand, ceteris paribus. **Ceteris paribus** is a Latin phrase that means "all other things unchanged."

ceteris paribus

A Latin phrase that means, "all other things unchanged."

But things changed between May 2005 and May 2006. Economic activity and incomes rose both in the United States and in many other countries, particularly China, and people with higher incomes are likely to buy more gasoline. Employment rose as well, and people with jobs use more gasoline as they drive to work. Population in the United States grew during the period. In short, many things happened during the period, all of which tended to increase the quantity of gasoline people purchased.

Our observation of the gasoline market between May 2005 and May 2006 did not offer a conclusive test of the hypothesis that an increase in the price of gasoline would lead to a reduction in the quantity demanded by consumers. Other things changed and affected gasoline consumption. Such problems are likely to affect any analysis of economic events. We cannot ask the world to stand still while we conduct experiments in economic phenomena. Economists employ a variety of statistical methods to allow them to isolate the impact of single events such as price changes, but they can never be certain that they have accurately isolated the impact of a single event in a world in which virtually everything is changing all the time.

In laboratory sciences such as chemistry and biology, it is relatively easy to conduct experiments in which only selected things change and all other factors are held constant. The economists' laboratory is the real world; thus, economists do not generally have the luxury of conducting controlled experiments.

The Fallacy of False Cause

dependent variable

A variable that responds to change.

independent variable

A variable that induces a change.

Hypotheses in economics typically specify a relationship in which a change in one variable causes another to change. We call the variable that responds to the change the **dependent variable**; the variable that induces a change is called the **independent variable**. Sometimes the fact that two variables move together can suggest the false conclusion that one of the variables has acted as an independent variable that has caused the change we observe in the dependent variable.

Consider the following hypothesis: People wearing shorts cause warm weather. Certainly, we observe that more people wear shorts when the weather is warm. Presumably, though, it is the warm weather that causes people to wear shorts rather than the wearing of shorts that causes warm weather; it would be incorrect to infer from this that people cause warm weather by wearing shorts.

fallacy of false cause

The incorrect assumption that one event causes another because the two events tend to occur together.

Reaching the incorrect conclusion that one event causes another because the two events tend to occur together is called the **fallacy of false cause**. The accompanying essay on baldness and heart disease suggests an example of this fallacy.

Because of the danger of the fallacy of false cause, economists use special statistical tests that are designed to determine whether changes in one thing actually do cause changes observed in another. Given the inability to perform controlled experiments, however, these tests do not always offer convincing evidence that persuades all economists that one thing does, in fact, cause changes in another.

In the case of gasoline prices and consumption between May 2005 and May 2006, there is good theoretical reason to believe the price increase should lead to a reduction in the quantity consumers demand. And economists have tested the hypothesis about price and the quantity demanded quite extensively. They have developed elaborate statistical tests aimed at ruling out problems of the fallacy of false cause. While we cannot prove that an increase in price will, ceteris paribus, lead to a reduction in the quantity consumers demand, we can have considerable confidence in the proposition.

Normative and Positive Statements

positive statement

A statement of fact or a hypothesis.

Two kinds of assertions in economics can be subjected to testing. We have already examined one, the hypothesis. Another testable assertion is a statement of fact, such as "It is raining outside" or "Microsoft is the largest producer of operating systems for personal computers in the world." Like hypotheses, such assertions can be demonstrated to be false. Unlike hypotheses, they can also be shown to be correct. A statement of fact or a hypothesis is a **positive statement**.

normative statement

A statement that makes a value judgment.

Although people often disagree about positive statements, such disagreements can ultimately be resolved through investigation. There is another category of assertions, however, for which investigation can never resolve differences. A **normative statement** is one that makes a value judgment. Such a judgment is the opinion of the speaker; no one can "prove" that the statement is or is not correct. Here are some examples of normative statements in economics: "We ought to do more to help the poor." "People in the United States should save more." "Corporate profits are too high."

The statements are based on the values of the person who makes them. They cannot be proven false.

Because people have different values, normative statements often provoke disagreement. An economist whose values lead him or her to conclude that we should provide more help for the poor will disagree with one whose values lead to a conclusion that we should not. Because no test exists for these values, these two economists will continue to disagree, unless one persuades the other to adopt a different set of values. Many of the disagreements among economists are based on such differences in values and therefore are unlikely to be resolved.

Key Takeaways

- Economists try to employ the scientific method in their research.
- Scientists cannot prove a hypothesis to be true; they can only fail to prove it false.
- Economists, like other social scientists and scientists, use models to assist them in their analyses.
- Two problems inherent in tests of hypotheses in economics are the all-other-things-unchanged problem and the fallacy of false cause.
- Positive statements are factual and can be tested. Normative statements are value judgments that cannot be tested. Many of the disagreements among economists stem from differences in values.

Try It!

Look again at the data in Table 1.1. Now consider the hypothesis: "Majoring in economics will result in a higher LSAT score." Are the data given consistent with this hypothesis? Do the data prove that this hypothesis is correct? What fallacy might be involved in accepting the hypothesis?

Case in Point: Does Baldness Cause Heart Disease?

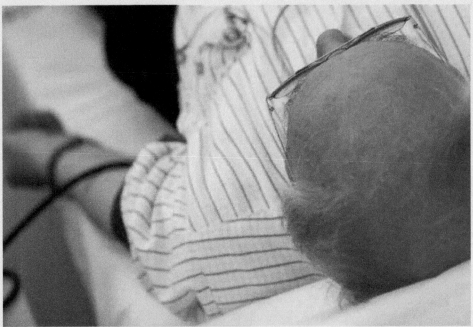

Source: © 2010 Jupiterimages Corporation

A patient walks into his doctor's office and presents the doctor with the following:

> *"I seem to be going bald. I've read that this means I'm more likely to have a heart attack. If I take a drug to prevent hair loss, will it reduce my risk of a heart attack?"*

How might the doctor reply? It is very unlikely that the doctor would recommend taking drugs to treat baldness, because doctors do not think that the baldness causes the heart disease. A more likely explanation for the association between baldness and heart disease is that both conditions are affected by underlying factors, such as hypertension, high cholesterol, and smoking, though the research establishing those connections is ongoing.

The good news for people with balding (in particular male balding of the type that starts at the top or back of the head rather with a receding hairline) is that they have a signal that might lead them to be checked for heart disease.

Source: Based on Nicholas Bakalar, "Risks: Male Baldness and Heart Disease," The New York Times, April 9, 2013, p. D4.

Answer to Try It! Problem

The data are consistent with the hypothesis, but it is never possible to prove that a hypothesis is correct. Accepting the hypothesis could involve the fallacy of false cause; students who major in economics may already have the analytical skills needed to do well on the exam.

1.5 Review and Practice

Summary

Choices are forced on us by scarcity; economists study the choices that people make. Scarce goods are those for which the choice of one alternative requires giving up another. The opportunity cost of any choice is the value of the best alternative forgone in making that choice.

Some key choices assessed by economists include what to produce, how to produce it, and for whom it should be produced. Economics is distinguished from other academic disciplines that also study choices by an emphasis on the central importance of opportunity costs in evaluating choices, the assumption of maximizing behavior that serves the interests of individual decision makers, and a focus on evaluating choices at the margin.

Economic analyses may be aimed at explaining individual choice or choices in an individual market; such investigations are largely the focus of microeconomics. The analysis of the impact of those individual choices on such aggregates as total output, the level of employment, and the price level is the concern of macroeconomics.

Working within the framework of the scientific method, economists formulate hypotheses and then test them. These tests can only refute a hypothesis; hypotheses in science cannot be proved. A hypothesis that has been widely tested often comes to be regarded as a theory; one that has won virtually universal acceptance is a law. Because of the complexity of the real world, economists rely on models that rest on a series of simplifying assumptions. The models are used to generate hypotheses about the economy that can be tested using real-world data.

Statements of fact and hypotheses are positive statements. Normative statements, unlike positive statements, cannot be tested and provide a source for potential disagreement.

Concept Problems

1. Why does the fact that something is scarce require that we make choices?
2. Does the fact that something is abundant mean it is not scarce in the economic sense? Why or why not?
3. In some countries, such as Cuba and North Korea, the government makes most of the decisions about what will be produced, how it will be produced, and for whom. Does the fact that these choices are made by the government eliminate scarcity in these countries? Why or why not?
4. Explain what is meant by the opportunity cost of a choice.
5. What is the approximate dollar cost of the tuition and other fees associated with the economics course you are taking? Does this dollar cost fully reflect the opportunity cost to you of taking the course?
6. Indicate whether each of the following is a topic of microeconomics or macroeconomics:
    1. The impact of higher oil prices on the production of steel
    2. The increased demand in the last 15 years for exotic dietary supplements
    3. The surge in aggregate economic activity that hit much of Asia late in the early 2000s

4. The sharp increases in U.S. employment and total output that occurred between 2003 and 2007

5. The impact of preservation of wilderness areas on the logging industry and on the price of lumber

7. Determine whether each of the following raises a "what," "how," or "for whom" issue. Are the statements normative or positive?

1. A requirement that aluminum used in cars be made from recycled materials will raise the price of automobiles.

2. The federal government does not spend enough for children.

3. An increase in police resources provided to the inner city will lower the crime rate.

4. Automation destroys jobs.

5. Efforts to improve the environment tend to reduce production and employment.

6. Japanese firms should be more willing to hire additional workers when production rises and to lay off workers when production falls.

7. Access to health care should not be limited by income.

8. Your time is a scarce resource. What if the quantity of time were increased, say to 48 hours per day, and everyone still lived as many days as before. Would time still be scarce?

9. Most college students are under age 25. Give two explanations for this—one based on the benefits people of different ages are likely to receive from higher education and one based on the opportunity costs of a college education to students of different ages.

10. Some municipal water companies charge customers a flat fee each month, regardless of the amount of water they consume. Others meter water use and charge according to the quantity of water customers use. Compare the way the two systems affect the cost of water use at the margin.

11. How might you test each of the following hypotheses? Suggest some problems that might arise in each test due to the ceteris paribus (all-other-things-unchanged) problem and the fallacy of false cause.

1. Reducing the quantity of heroin available will increase total spending on heroin and increase the crime rate.

2. Higher incomes make people happier.

3. Higher incomes make people live longer.

12. Many models in physics and in chemistry assume the existence of a perfect vacuum (that is, a space entirely empty of matter). Yet we know that a perfect vacuum cannot exist. Are such models valid? Why are models based on assumptions that are essentially incorrect?

13. Suppose you were asked to test the proposition that publishing students' teacher evaluations causes grade inflation. What evidence might you want to consider? How would the inability to carry out controlled experiments make your analysis more difficult?

14. Referring to the Case in Point "Baldness and Heart Disease," explain the possible fallacy of false cause in concluding that baldness makes a person more likely to have heart disease.

15. In 2005 the Food and Drug Administration ordered that Vioxx and other popular drugs for treating the pain of arthritis be withdrawn from the market. The order resulted from a finding that people taking the drugs had an increased risk of cardiovascular problems. Some researchers criticized the government's action, arguing that concluding that the drugs caused the cardiovascular problems represented an example of the fallacy of false cause. Can you think of any reason why this might be the case?

CHAPTER 2
Confronting Scarcity: Choices in Production

2.1 Start Up: An Attempt to Produce Safer Air Travel

In the wake of the terrorist attacks on the United States on September 11, 2001, American taxpayers continue to give up a great deal of money, and airline passengers continue to give much of their time—and a great deal of their privacy—in an effort to ensure that other terrorists will not turn their flights into tragedies.

The U.S. effort is run by the Transportation Security Administration (TSA), a federal agency created in response to the 2001 attacks. TSA requirements became a bit more onerous after Richard Reid, an Englishman and member of al-Qaeda, tried in December of that same year to blow up an American Airlines flight with a bomb he had concealed in his shoe. Reid was unsuccessful, but passengers must now remove their shoes so TSA agents can check them for bombs.

TSA restrictions became dramatically more stringent after Umar Farouk Abdulmutallab, a jihadist from Nigeria, tried—again without success—to blow up a plane flying from Amsterdam to Detroit on Christmas Day, 2009, using a bomb concealed in his underwear. The subsequent tightening of TSA regulations, and the introduction of body-scan machines and "patdown inspections," were quick to follow. Each new procedure took additional money and time and further reduced passenger privacy. It was a production choice that has created many irate passengers but has also been successful, to date, in preventing subsequent terrorist attacks.

While the TSA procedures represent an unusual production choice, it is still a production choice—one that is being made all over the world as countries grapple with the danger of terrorist attacks. In this chapter we introduce our first model, the **production possibilities model**, to examine the nature of choices to produce more of some goods and less of others. As its name suggests, the production possibilities model shows the goods cand services that an economy is capable of producing—its possibilities—given the factors of production and the technology it has available. The model specifies what it means to use resources fully and efficiently and suggests some important implications for international trade. We can also use the model to illustrate economic growth, a process that expands the set of production possibilities available to an economy.

We then turn to an examination of the type of economic system in which choices are made. An **economic system** is the set of rules that define how an economy's resources are to be owned and how decisions about their use are to be made. We will see that economic systems differ—primarily in the degree of government involvement—in terms of how they answer the fundamental economic questions. Many of the world's economic systems, including the systems that prevail in North America, Europe, much of Asia, and parts of Central and South America, rely on individuals operating in a market economy to make those choices. Other economic systems rely principally on government to make these choices. Different economic systems result in different choices and thus different outcomes; that market economies generally outperform the others when it comes to providing more of the things that people want helps to explain the dramatic shift from government-dominated toward market-dominated economic systems that occurred throughout the world in the last two decades of the 20th century. The chapter concludes with an examination of the role of government in an economy that relies chiefly on markets to allocate goods and services.

production possibilities model

A model that shows the goods and services that an economy is capable of producing – its opportunities – given the factors of production and the technology it has available.

economic system

The set of rules that define how an economy's resources are to be owned and how decisions about their use are to be made.

2.2 Factors of Production

factors of production

The resources available to the economy for the production of goods and services.

utility

The value, or satisfaction, that people derive from the goods and services they consume and the activities they pursue.

labor

The human effort that can be applied to the production of goods and services.

capital

A factor of production that has been produced for use in the production of other goods and services.

natural resources

The resources of nature that can be used for the production of goods and services.

human capital

The skills a worker has as a result of education, training, or experience that can be used in production.

Choices concerning what goods and services to produce are choices about an economy's use of its **factors of production**, the resources available to it for the production of goods and services. The value, or satisfaction, that people derive from the goods and services they consume and the activities they pursue is called **utility**. Ultimately, then, an economy's factors of production create utility; they serve the interests of people.

The factors of production in an economy are its labor, capital, and natural resources. **Labor** is the human effort that can be applied to the production of goods and services. People who are employed—or are available to be—are considered part of the labor available to the economy. **Capital** is a factor of production that has been produced for use in the production of other goods and services. Office buildings, machinery, and tools are examples of capital. **Natural resources** are the resources of nature that can be used for the production of goods and services.

In the next three sections, we will take a closer look at the factors of production we use to produce the goods and services we consume. The three basic building blocks of labor, capital, and natural resources may be used in different ways to produce different goods and services, but they still lie at the core of production. We will then look at the roles played by technology and entrepreneurs in putting these factors of production to work. As economists began to grapple with the problems of scarcity, choice, and opportunity cost more than two centuries ago, they focused on these concepts, just as they are likely to do two centuries hence.

Labor

Labor is the human effort that can be applied to production. People who work to repair tires, pilot airplanes, teach children, or enforce laws are all part of the economy's labor. People who would like to work but have not found employment—who are unemployed—are also considered part of the labor available to the economy.

In some contexts, it is useful to distinguish two forms of labor. The first is the human equivalent of a natural resource. It is the natural ability an untrained, uneducated person brings to a particular production process. But most workers bring far more. Skills a worker has as a result of education, training, or experience that can be used in production are called **human capital**. Students are acquiring human capital. Workers who are gaining skills through experience or through training are acquiring human capital.

The amount of labor available to an economy can be increased in two ways. One is to increase the total quantity of labor, either by increasing the number of people available to work or by increasing the average number of hours of work per time period. The other is to increase the amount of human capital possessed by workers.

Capital

Long ago, when the first human beings walked the earth, they produced food by picking leaves or fruit off a plant or by catching an animal and eating it. We know that very early on, however, they began shaping stones into tools, apparently for use in butchering animals. Those tools were the first capital because they were produced for use in producing other goods—food and clothing.

Modern versions of the first stone tools include saws, meat cleavers, hooks, and grinders; all are used in butchering animals. Tools such as hammers, screwdrivers, and wrenches are also capital. Transportation equipment, such as cars and trucks, is capital. Facilities such as roads, bridges, ports, and airports are capital. Buildings, too, are capital; they help us to produce goods and services.

Capital does not consist solely of physical objects. The score for a new symphony is capital because it will be used to produce concerts. Computer software used by business firms or government agencies to produce goods and services is capital. Capital may thus include physical goods and intellectual discoveries. Any resource is capital if it satisfies two criteria:

1. The resource must have been produced.
2. The resource can be used to produce other goods and services.

One thing that is not considered capital is money. A firm cannot use money directly to produce other goods, so money does not satisfy the second criterion for capital. Firms can, however, use money to acquire capital. Money is a form of financial capital. **Financial capital** includes money and other "paper" assets (such as stocks and bonds) that represent claims on future payments. These financial assets are not capital, but they can be used directly or indirectly to purchase factors of production or goods and services.

financial capital

Includes money and other "paper" assets (such as stocks and bonds) that represent claims on future payments.

Natural Resources

There are two essential characteristics of natural resources. The first is that they are found in nature—that no human effort has been used to make or alter them. The second is that they can be used for the production of goods and services. That requires knowledge; we must know how to use the things we find in nature before they become resources.

Consider oil. Oil in the ground is a natural resource because it is found (not manufactured) and can be used to produce goods and services. However, 250 years ago oil was a nuisance, not a natural resource. Pennsylvania farmers in the eighteenth century who found oil oozing up through their soil were dismayed, not delighted. No one knew what could be done with the oil. It was not until the mid-nineteenth century that a method was found for refining oil into kerosene that could be used to generate energy, transforming oil into a natural resource. Oil is now used to make all sorts of things, including clothing, drugs, gasoline, and plastic. It became a natural resource because people discovered and implemented a way to use it.

Defining something as a natural resource only if it can be used to produce goods and services does not mean that a tree has value only for its wood or that a mountain has value only for its minerals. If people gain utility from the existence of a beautiful wilderness area, then that wilderness provides a service. The wilderness is thus a natural resource.

The natural resources available to us can be expanded in three ways. One is the discovery of new natural resources, such as the discovery of a deposit of ore containing titanium. The second is the discovery of new uses for resources, as happened when new techniques allowed oil to be put to productive use or sand to be used in manufacturing computer chips. The third is the discovery of new ways to extract natural resources in order to use them. New methods of discovering and mapping oil deposits have increased the world's supply of this important natural resource.

Technology and the Entrepreneur

technology

The knowledge that can be applied to the production of goods and services.

entrepreneur

A person who, operating within the context of a market economy, seeks to earn profits by finding new ways to organize factors of production.

Goods and services are produced using the factors of production available to the economy. Two things play a crucial role in putting these factors of production to work. The first is **technology**, the knowledge that can be applied to the production of goods and services. The second is an individual who plays a key role in a market economy: the entrepreneur. An **entrepreneur** is a person who, operating within the context of a market economy, seeks to earn profits by finding new ways to organize factors of production. In non-market economies the role of the entrepreneur is played by bureaucrats and other decision makers who respond to incentives other than profit to guide their choices about resource allocation decisions.

The interplay of entrepreneurs and technology affects all our lives. Entrepreneurs put new technologies to work every day, changing the way factors of production are used. Farmers and factory workers, engineers and electricians, technicians and teachers all work differently than they did just a few years ago, using new technologies introduced by entrepreneurs. The music you enjoy, the books you read, the athletic equipment with which you play are produced differently than they were five years ago. The book you are reading was written and manufactured using technologies that did not exist ten years ago. We can dispute whether all the changes have made our lives better. What we cannot dispute is that they have made our lives different.

Key Takeaways

- Factors of production are the resources the economy has available to produce goods and services.
- Labor is the human effort that can be applied to the production of goods and services. Labor's contribution to an economy's output of goods and services can be increased either by increasing the quantity of labor or by increasing human capital.
- Capital is a factor of production that has been produced for use in the production of other goods and services.
- Natural resources are those things found in nature that can be used for the production of goods and services.
- Two keys to the utilization of an economy's factors of production are technology and, in the case of a market economic system, the efforts of entrepreneurs.

Try It!

Explain whether each of the following is labor, capital, or a natural resource.

1. An unemployed factory worker
2. A college professor
3. The library building on your campus
4. Yellowstone National Park
5. An untapped deposit of natural gas
6. The White House
7. The local power plant

Case in Point: Technology Cuts Costs, Boosts Productivity, Profits, and Utility

Source: © 2010 Jupiterimages Corporation

Technology can seem an abstract force in the economy—important, but invisible.

It is not invisible to the 130 people who work on a Shell Oil Company oil rig called Mars, located in the deep waters of the Gulf of Mexico, about 160 miles southwest of Pensacola, Florida. The name Mars reflects its otherworld appearance—it extends 300 feet above the water's surface and has steel tendons that reach 3,000 feet down to extract the Gulf's oil deposits. This facility would not exist if it were not for the development of better oil discovery methods that include three-dimensional seismic mapping techniques, satellites that locate oil from space, and drills that can make turns as drilling foremen steer them by monitoring them on computer screens from the comfort of Mars. "We don't hit as many dry holes," commented Shell manager Miles Barrett. As a result of these new technologies, over the past two decades, the cost of discovering a barrel of oil dropped from $20 to under $5. And the technologies continue to improve. Three-dimensional surveys are being replaced with four-dimensional ones that allow geologists to see how the oil fields change over time.

The Mars project was destroyed by Hurricane Katrina in 2005. Royal Dutch Shell completed repairs in 2006, at a cost of $200 million. But the facility is again pumping. Shell announced a new Mars-like project, Mars B Olympus, in 2010. The second Mars hub, located about 100 miles south of New Orleans, began production in 2014. The two are expected to ultimately deliver a billion barrels of oil equivalent.

Technology is doing more than helping energy companies track oil deposits. It has changed the way soft drinks and other grocery items are delivered to retail stores. For example, when a PepsiCo delivery driver arrives at a 7-Eleven, the driver keys into a handheld computer the store's inventory of soft drinks, chips, and other PepsiCo products. The information is transmitted to a main computer at the warehouse that begins processing the next order for that store. The result is that the driver can visit more stores in a day and PepsiCo can cover a given territory with fewer drivers and trucks.

New technology has even helped to produce more milk from cows. Ed Larsen, who owns a 1,200-cow dairy farm in Wisconsin, never gets up before dawn to milk the cows, the way he did as a boy. Rather, the cows are hooked up to electronic milkers. Computers measure each cow's output, and cows producing little milk are sent to a "hospital wing" for treatment. With the help of such technology, as well as better feed, today's dairy cows produce 50% more milk than did cows roughly 20 years ago. Even though the number of dairy cows in the United States in the last 20 years has fallen 17%, milk output has increased 25%.

And there are so many more innovations we could mention. When will drones deliver packages to our homes? When will truly driverless cars dominate our highways?

Who benefits from technological progress? Consumers gain from lower prices and better service. Workers gain: Their greater ability to produce goods and services translates into higher wages. And firms gain: Lower production costs mean higher profits. Of course, some people lose as technology advances. Some jobs are eliminated, and some firms find their services are no longer needed. One can argue about whether particular technological changes have improved our lives, but they have clearly made—and will continue to make—them far different.

Sources: Based on "Mars B/Olympus Deep Water Project" available at http://www.shell.us/ energy-and-innovation/energy-from-deepwater/shell-deep-water-portfolio-in-the-gulf-of-mexico/ mars-b-olympus.html. David Ballingrud, "Drilling in the Gulf: Life on Mars," St. Petersburg Times (Florida), August 5, 2001, p. 1A; Barbara Hagenbaugh, "Dairy Farms Evolve to Survive," USA Today, August 7, 2003, p. 1B; Del Jones and Barbara Hansen, "Special Report: A Who's Who of Productivity," USA Today, August 30, 2001, p. 1B; Christopher Helman, Shell Shocked, Forbes Online, July 27, 2006; "Shell Plans Second Deep Water Production Hub," September 9, 2010 at http://www.investorvillage.com/smbd.asp?mb=4288&mn=59408&pt=msg&mid=9575777.

Answers to Try It! Problems

1. An unemployed factory worker could be put to work; he or she counts as labor.
2. A college professor is labor.
3. The library building on your campus is part of capital.
4. Yellowstone National Park. Those areas of the park left in their natural state are a natural resource. Facilities such as visitors' centers, roads, and campgrounds are capital.
5. An untapped deposit of natural gas is a natural resource. Once extracted and put in a storage tank, natural gas is capital.
6. The White House is capital.
7. The local power plant is capital.

2.3 The Production Possibilities Curve

Learning Objectives

1. Explain the concept of the production possibilities curve and understand the implications of its downward slope and bowed-out shape.
2. Use the production possibilities model to distinguish between full employment and situations of idle factors of production and between efficient and inefficient production.
3. Understand specialization and its relationship to the production possibilities model and comparative advantage.

An economy's factors of production are scarce; they cannot produce an unlimited quantity of goods and services. A **production possibilities curve** is a graphical representation of the alternative combinations of goods and services an economy can produce. It illustrates the production possibilities model. In drawing the production possibilities curve, we shall assume that the economy can produce only two goods and that the quantities of factors of production and the technology available to the economy are fixed.

production possibilities curve

A graphical representation of the alternative combinations of goods and services an economy can produce.

Constructing a Production Possibilities Curve

To construct a production possibilities curve, we will begin with the case of a hypothetical firm, Alpine Sports, Inc., a specialized sports equipment manufacturer. Christie Ryder began the business 15 years ago with a single ski production facility near Killington ski resort in central Vermont. Ski sales grew, and she also saw demand for snowboards rising—particularly after snowboard competition events were included in the 2002 Winter Olympics in Salt Lake City. She added a second plant in a nearby town. The second plant, while smaller than the first, was designed to produce snowboards as well as skis. She also modified the first plant so that it could produce both snowboards and skis. Two years later she added a third plant in another town. While even smaller than the second plant, the third was primarily designed for snowboard production but could also produce skis.

We can think of each of Ms. Ryder's three plants as a miniature economy and analyze them using the production possibilities model. We assume that the factors of production and technology available to each of the plants operated by Alpine Sports are unchanged.

Suppose the first plant, Plant 1, can produce 200 pairs of skis per month when it produces only skis. When devoted solely to snowboards, it produces 100 snowboards per month. It can produce skis and snowboards simultaneously as well.

The table in Figure 2.1 gives three combinations of skis and snowboards that Plant 1 can produce each month. Combination A involves devoting the plant entirely to ski production; combination C means shifting all of the plant's resources to snowboard production; combination B involves the production of both goods. These values are plotted in a production possibilities curve for Plant 1. The curve is a downward-sloping straight line, indicating we have assumed that there is a linear, negative relationship between the production of the two goods.

Neither skis nor snowboards is an independent or a dependent variable in the production possibilities model; we can assign either one to the vertical or to the horizontal axis. Here, we have placed the number of pairs of skis produced per month on the vertical axis and the number of snowboards produced per month on the horizontal axis.

The negative slope of the production possibilities curve reflects the scarcity of the plant's capital and labor. Producing more snowboards requires shifting resources out of ski production and thus producing fewer skis. Producing more skis requires shifting resources out of snowboard production and thus producing fewer snowboards.

The slope of Plant 1's production possibilities curve measures the rate at which Alpine Sports must give up ski production to produce additional snowboards. Because the production possibilities curve for Plant 1 is linear, we can compute the slope between any two points on the curve and get the same result. Between points A and B, for example, the slope equals -2 pairs of skis/snowboard (equals -100 pairs of skis/50 snowboards). (Many students are helped when told to read this result as "-2 pairs of skis *per* snowboard.") We get the same value between points B and C, and between points A and C.

FIGURE 2.1 A Production Possibilities Curve

The table shows the combinations of pairs of skis and snowboards that Plant 1 is capable of producing each month. These are also illustrated with a production possibilities curve. Notice that this curve is linear.

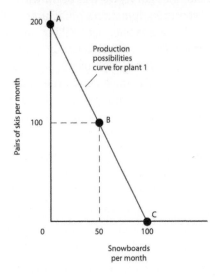

	Pairs of skis per month	Snowboards per month
A	200	0
B	100	50
C	0	100

To see this relationship more clearly, examine Figure 2.2. Suppose Plant 1 is producing 100 pairs of skis and 50 snowboards per month at point B. Now consider what would happen if Ms. Ryder decided to produce 1 more snowboard per month. The segment of the curve around point B is magnified in Figure 2.2. The slope between points B and B′ is -2 pairs of skis/snowboard. Producing 1 additional snowboard at point B′ requires giving up 2 pairs of skis. We can think of this as the opportunity cost of producing an additional snowboard at Plant 1. This opportunity cost equals the absolute value of the slope of the production possibilities curve.

FIGURE 2.2 The Slope of a Production Possibilities Curve
The slope of the linear production possibilities curve in Figure 2.1 is constant; it is −2 pairs of skis/snowboard. In the section of the curve shown here, the slope can be calculated between points B and B′. Expanding snowboard production to 51 snowboards per month from 50 snowboards per month requires a reduction in ski production to 98 pairs of skis per month from 100 pairs. The slope equals −2 pairs of skis/snowboard (that is, it must give up two pairs of skis to free up the resources necessary to produce one additional snowboard). To shift from B′ to B″, Alpine Sports must give up two more pairs of skis per snowboard. The absolute value of the slope of a production possibilities curve measures the opportunity cost of an additional unit of the good on the horizontal axis measured in terms of the quantity of the good on the vertical axis that must be forgone.

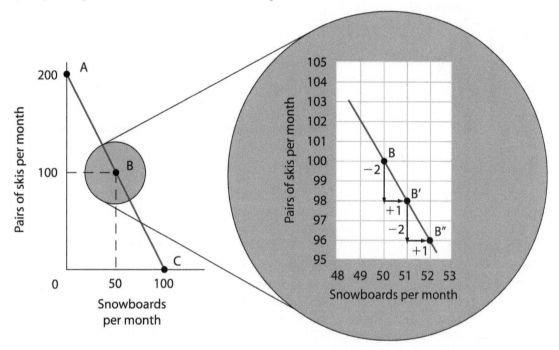

The absolute value of the slope of any production possibilities curve equals the opportunity cost of an additional unit of the good on the horizontal axis. It is the amount of the good on the vertical axis that must be given up in order to free up the resources required to produce one more unit of the good on the horizontal axis. We will make use of this important fact as we continue our investigation of the production possibilities curve.

Figure 2.3 shows production possibilities curves for each of the firm's three plants. Each of the plants, if devoted entirely to snowboards, could produce 100 snowboards. Plants 2 and 3, if devoted exclusively to ski production, can produce 100 and 50 pairs of skis per month, respectively. The exhibit gives the slopes of the production possibilities curves for each plant. The opportunity cost of an additional snowboard at each plant equals the absolute values of these slopes (that is, the number of pairs of skis that must be given up per snowboard).

FIGURE 2.3 Production Possibilities at Three Plants

The slopes of the production possibilities curves for each plant differ. The steeper the curve, the greater the opportunity cost of an additional snowboard. Here, the opportunity cost is lowest at Plant 3 and greatest at Plant 1.

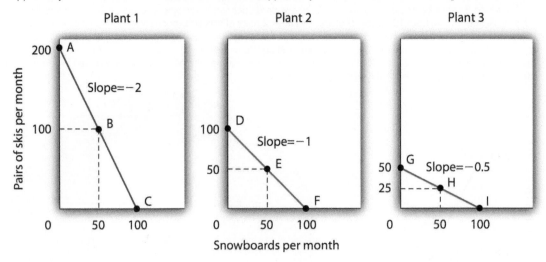

The exhibit gives the slopes of the production possibilities curves for each of the firm's three plants. The opportunity cost of an additional snowboard at each plant equals the absolute values of these slopes. More generally, the absolute value of the slope of any production possibilities curve at any point gives the opportunity cost of an additional unit of the good on the horizontal axis, measured in terms of the number of units of the good on the vertical axis that must be forgone.

The greater the absolute value of the slope of the production possibilities curve, the greater the opportunity cost will be. The plant for which the opportunity cost of an additional snowboard is greatest is the plant with the steepest production possibilities curve; the plant for which the opportunity cost is lowest is the plant with the flattest production possibilities curve. The plant with the lowest opportunity cost of producing snowboards is Plant 3; its slope of -0.5 means that Ms. Ryder's firm must give up half a pair of skis in that plant to produce an additional snowboard. In Plant 2, she must give up one pair of skis to gain one more snowboard. We have already seen that an additional snowboard requires giving up two pairs of skis in Plant 1.

Comparative Advantage and the Production Possibilities Curve

To construct a combined production possibilities curve for all three plants, we can begin by asking how many pairs of skis Alpine Sports could produce if it were producing only skis. To find this quantity, we add up the values at the vertical intercepts of each of the production possibilities curves in Figure 2.3. These intercepts tell us the maximum number of pairs of skis each plant can produce. Plant 1 can produce 200 pairs of skis per month, Plant 2 can produce 100 pairs of skis at per month, and Plant 3 can produce 50 pairs. Alpine Sports can thus produce 350 pairs of skis per month if it devotes its resources exclusively to ski production. In that case, it produces no snowboards.

Now suppose the firm decides to produce 100 snowboards. That will require shifting one of its plants out of ski production. Which one will it choose to shift? The sensible thing for it to do is to choose the plant in which snowboards have the lowest opportunity cost—Plant 3. It has an advantage not because it can produce more snowboards than the other plants (all the plants in this example are capable of producing up to 100 snowboards per month) but because it is the least productive plant for making skis. Producing a snowboard in Plant 3 requires giving up just half a pair of skis.

Economists say that an economy has a **comparative advantage** in producing a good or service if the opportunity cost of producing that good or service is lower for that economy than for any other. Plant 3 has a comparative advantage in snowboard production because it is the plant for which the opportunity cost of additional snowboards is lowest. To put this in terms of the production possibilities curve, Plant 3 has a comparative advantage in snowboard production (the good on the horizontal axis) because its production possibilities curve is the flattest of the three curves.

comparative advantage

In producing a good or service, the situation that occurs if the opportunity cost of producing that good or service is lower for that economy than for any other.

FIGURE 2.4 The Combined Production Possibilities Curve for Alpine Sports

The curve shown combines the production possibilities curves for each plant. At point A, Alpine Sports produces 350 pairs of skis per month and no snowboards. If the firm wishes to increase snowboard production, it will first use Plant 3, which has a comparative advantage in snowboards.

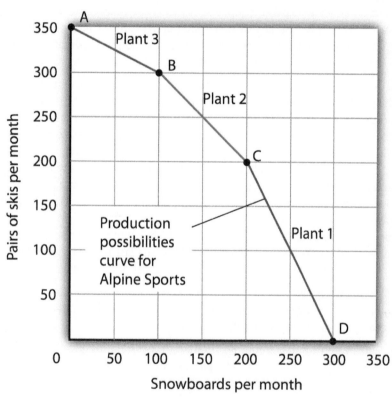

Plant 3's comparative advantage in snowboard production makes a crucial point about the nature of comparative advantage. It need not imply that a particular plant is especially good at an activity. In our example, all three plants are equally good at snowboard production. Plant 3, though, is the least efficient of the three in ski production. Alpine thus gives up fewer skis when it produces snowboards in Plant 3. Comparative advantage thus can stem from a lack of efficiency in the production of an alternative good rather than a special proficiency in the production of the first good.

The combined production possibilities curve for the firm's three plants is shown in Figure 2.4. We begin at point A, with all three plants producing only skis. Production totals 350 pairs of skis per month and zero snowboards. If the firm were to produce 100 snowboards at Plant 3, ski production would fall by 50 pairs per month (recall that the opportunity cost per snowboard at Plant 3 is half a pair of skis). That would bring ski production to 300 pairs, at point B. If Alpine Sports were to produce still more snowboards in a single month, it would shift production to Plant 2, the facility with the next-lowest opportunity cost. Producing 100 snowboards at Plant 2 would leave Alpine Sports producing 200 snowboards and 200 pairs of skis per month, at point C. If the firm were to switch entirely to snowboard production, Plant 1 would be the last to switch because the cost of each snowboard there is 2 pairs of skis. With all three plants producing only snowboards, the firm is at point D on the combined production possibilities curve, producing 300 snowboards per month and no skis.

Notice that this production possibilities curve, which is made up of linear segments from each assembly plant, has a bowed-out shape; the absolute value of its slope increases as Alpine Sports produces more and more snowboards. This is a result of transferring resources from the production of one good to another according to comparative advantage. We shall examine the significance of the bowed-out shape of the curve in the next section.

The Law of Increasing Opportunity Cost

law of increasing opportunity cost

As an economy moves along its production possibilities curve in the direction of producing more of a particular good, the opportunity cost of additional units of that good will increase.

We see in Figure 2.4 that, beginning at point A and producing only skis, Alpine Sports experiences higher and higher opportunity costs as it produces more snowboards. The fact that the opportunity cost of additional snowboards increases as the firm produces more of them is a reflection of an important economic law. The **law of increasing opportunity cost** holds that as an economy moves along its production possibilities curve in the direction of producing more of a particular good, the opportunity cost of additional units of that good will increase.

We have seen the law of increasing opportunity cost at work traveling from point A toward point D on the production possibilities curve in Figure 2.4. The opportunity cost of each of the first 100 snowboards equals half a pair of skis; each of the next 100 snowboards has an opportunity cost of 1 pair of skis, and each of the last 100 snowboards has an opportunity cost of 2 pairs of skis. The law also applies as the firm shifts from snowboards to skis. Suppose it begins at point D, producing 300 snowboards per month and no skis. It can shift to ski production at a relatively low cost at first. The opportunity cost of the first 200 pairs of skis is just 100 snowboards at Plant 1, a movement from point D to point C, or 0.5 snowboards per pair of skis. We would say that Plant 1 has a comparative advantage in ski production. The next 100 pairs of skis would be produced at Plant 2, where snowboard production would fall by 100 snowboards per month. The opportunity cost of skis at Plant 2 is 1 snowboard per pair of skis. Plant 3 would be the last plant converted to ski production. There, 50 pairs of skis could be produced per month at a cost of 100 snowboards, or an opportunity cost of 2 snowboards per pair of skis.

The bowed-out shape of the production possibilities curve illustrates the law of increasing opportunity cost. Its downwards slope reflects scarcity.

Figure 2.5 illustrates a much smoother production possibilities curve. This production possibilities curve in Panel (a) includes 10 linear segments and is almost a smooth curve. As we include more and more production units, the curve will become smoother and smoother. In an actual economy, with a tremendous number of firms and workers, it is easy to see that the production possibilities curve will be smooth. We will generally draw production possibilities curves for the economy as smooth, bowed-out curves, like the one in Panel (b). This production possibilities curve shows an economy that produces only skis and snowboards. Notice the curve still has a bowed-out shape; it still has a negative slope. Notice also that this curve has no numbers. Economists often use models such as the production possibilities model with graphs that show the general shapes of curves but that do not include specific numbers.

FIGURE 2.5 Production Possibilities for the Economy

As we combine the production possibilities curves for more and more units, the curve becomes smoother. It retains its negative slope and bowed-out shape. In Panel (a) we have a combined production possibilities curve for Alpine Sports, assuming that it now has 10 plants producing skis and snowboards. Even though each of the plants has a linear curve, combining them according to comparative advantage, as we did with 3 plants in Figure 2.4, produces what appears to be a smooth, nonlinear curve, even though it is made up of linear segments. In drawing production possibilities curves for the economy, we shall generally assume they are smooth and "bowed out," as in Panel (b). This curve depicts an entire economy that produces only skis and snowboards.

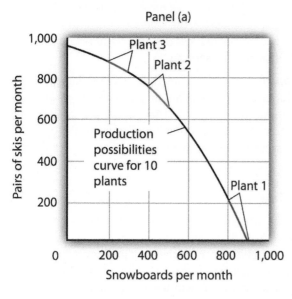

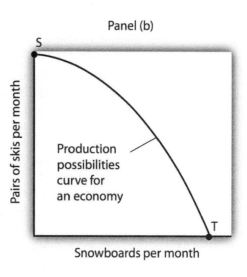

Movements Along the Production Possibilities Curve

We can use the production possibilities model to examine choices in the production of goods and services. In applying the model, we assume that the economy can produce two goods, and we assume that technology and the factors of production available to the economy remain unchanged. In this section, we shall assume that the economy operates on its production possibilities curve so that an increase in the production of one good in the model implies a reduction in the production of the other.

We shall consider two goods and services: national defense and security and a category we shall call "all other goods and services." This second category includes the entire range of goods and services the economy can produce, aside from national defense and security. Clearly, the transfer of resources to the effort to enhance national security reduces the quantity of other goods and services that can be produced. In the wake of the 9/11 attacks in 2001, nations throughout the world increased their spending for national security. This spending took a variety of forms. One, of course, was increased defense spending. Local and state governments also increased spending in an effort to prevent terrorist attacks. Airports around the world hired additional agents to inspect luggage and passengers.

The increase in resources devoted to security meant fewer "other goods and services" could be produced. In terms of the production possibilities curve in Figure 2.6, the choice to produce more security and less of other goods and services means a movement from A to B. Of course, an economy cannot really *produce* security; it can only attempt to provide it. The attempt to provide it requires resources; it is in that sense that we shall speak of the economy as "producing" security.

FIGURE 2.6 Spending More for Security

Here, an economy that can produce two categories of goods, security and "all other goods and services," begins at point A on its production possibilities curve. The economy produces S_A units of security and O_A units of all other goods and services per period. A movement from A to B requires shifting resources out of the production of all other goods and services and into spending on security. The increase in spending on security, to S_A units of security per period, has an opportunity cost of reduced production of all other goods and services. Production of all other goods and services falls by O_A - O_B units per period.

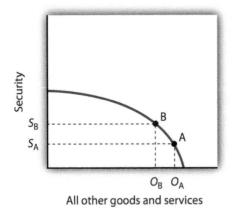

At point A, the economy was producing S_A units of security on the vertical axis—defense services and various forms of police protection—and O_A units of other goods and services on the horizontal axis. The decision to devote more resources to security and less to other goods and services represents the choice we discussed in the chapter introduction. In this case we have categories of goods rather than specific goods. Thus, the economy chose to increase spending on security in the effort to defeat terrorism. Since we have assumed that the economy has a fixed quantity of available resources, the increased use of resources for security and national defense necessarily reduces the number of resources available for the production of other goods and services.

The law of increasing opportunity cost tells us that, as the economy moves along the production possibilities curve in the direction of more of one good, its opportunity cost will increase. We may conclude that, as the economy moved along this curve in the direction of greater production of security, the opportunity cost of the additional security began to increase. That is because the resources transferred from the production of other goods and services to the production of security had a greater and greater comparative advantage in producing things other than security.

The production possibilities model does not tell us where on the curve a particular economy will operate. Instead, it lays out the possibilities facing the economy. Many countries, for example, chose to move along their respective production possibilities curves to produce more security and national defense and less of all other goods in the wake of 9/11. We will see in the chapter on demand and supply how choices about what to produce are made in the marketplace.

Producing on Versus Producing Inside the Production Possibilities Curve

An economy that is operating inside its production possibilities curve could, by moving onto it, produce more of all the goods and services that people value, such as food, housing, education, medical care, and music. Increasing the availability of these goods would improve the standard of living. Economists conclude that it is better to be on the production possibilities curve than inside it.

Two things could leave an economy operating at a point inside its production possibilities curve. First, the economy might fail to use fully the resources available to it. Second, it might not allocate resources on the basis of comparative advantage. In either case, production within the production possibilities curve implies the economy could improve its performance.

Idle Factors of Production

Suppose an economy fails to put all its factors of production to work. Some workers are without jobs, some buildings are without occupants, some fields are without crops. Because an economy's production possibilities curve assumes the full use of the factors of production available to it, the failure to use some factors results in a level of production that lies inside the production possibilities curve.

full employment

Situation in which all the factors of production that are available for use under current market conditions are being utilized.

If all the factors of production that are available for use under current market conditions are being utilized, the economy has achieved **full employment**. An economy cannot operate on its production possibilities curve unless it has full employment.

FIGURE 2.7 Idle Factors and Production

The production possibilities curve shown suggests an economy that can produce two goods, food and clothing. As a result of a failure to achieve full employment, the economy operates at a point such as B, producing F_B units of food and C_B units of clothing per period. Putting its factors of production to work allows a move to the production possibilities curve, to a point such as A. The production of both goods rises.

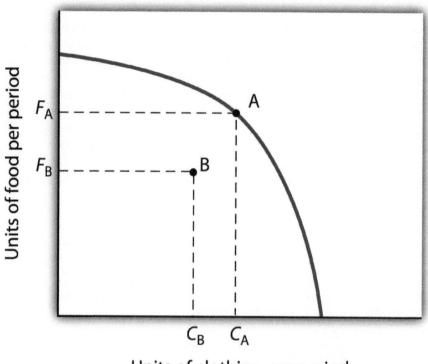

Units of clothing per period

Figure 2.7 shows an economy that can produce food and clothing. If it chooses to produce at point A, for example, it can produce F_A units of food and C_A units of clothing. Now suppose that a large fraction of the economy's workers lose their jobs, so the economy no longer makes full use of one factor of production: labor. In this example, production moves to point B, where the economy produces less food (F_B) and less clothing (C_B) than at point A. We often think of the loss of jobs in terms of the workers; they have lost a chance to work and to earn income. But the production possibilities model points to another loss: goods and services the economy could have produced that are not being produced.

Inefficient Production

Now suppose Alpine Sports is fully employing its factors of production. Could it still operate inside its production possibilities curve? Could an economy that is using all its factors of production still produce less than it could? The answer is "Yes," and the key lies in comparative advantage. An economy achieves a point on its production possibilities curve only if it allocates its factors of production on the basis of comparative advantage. If it fails to do that, it will operate inside the curve.

efficient production

When an economy is operating on its production possibilities curve.

inefficient production

Situation in which the economy is using the same quantities of factors of production but is operating inside its production possibilities curve.

Suppose that, as before, Alpine Sports has been producing only skis. With all three of its plants producing skis, it can produce 350 pairs of skis per month (and no snowboards). The firm then starts producing snowboards. This time, however, imagine that Alpine Sports switches plants from skis to snowboards in numerical order: Plant 1 first, Plant 2 second, and then Plant 3. Figure 2.8 illustrates the result. Instead of the bowed-out production possibilities curve ABCD, we get a bowed-in curve, AB'C'D. Suppose that Alpine Sports is producing 100 snowboards and 150 pairs of skis at point B'. Had the firm based its production choices on comparative advantage, it would have switched Plant 3 to snowboards and then Plant 2, so it could have operated at a point such as C. It would be producing more snowboards and more pairs of skis—and using the same quantities of factors of production it was using at B'. Had the firm based its production choices on comparative advantage, it would have switched Plant 3 to snowboards and then Plant 2, so it would have operated at point C. It would be producing more snowboards and more pairs of skis—and using the same quantities of factors of production it was using at B'. When an economy is operating on its production possibilities curve, we say that it is engaging in **efficient production**. If it is using the same quantities of factors of production but is operating inside its production possibilities curve, it is engaging in **inefficient production**. Inefficient production implies that the economy could be producing more goods without using any additional labor, capital, or natural resources.

FIGURE 2.8 Efficient Versus Inefficient Production

When factors of production are allocated on a basis other than comparative advantage, the result is inefficient production. Suppose Alpine Sports operates the three plants we examined in Figure 2.3. Suppose further that all three plants are devoted exclusively to ski production; the firm operates at A. Now suppose that, to increase snowboard production, it transfers plants in numerical order: Plant 1 first, then Plant 2, and finally Plant 3. The result is the bowed-in curve AB'C'D. Production on the production possibilities curve ABCD requires that factors of production be transferred according to comparative advantage.

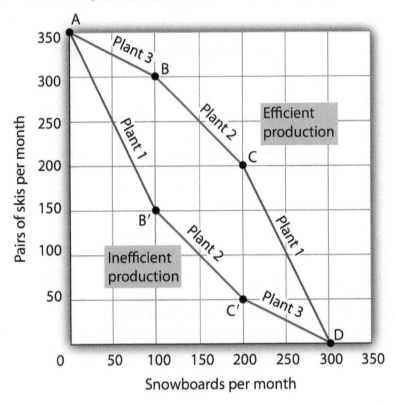

Points on the production possibilities curve thus satisfy two conditions: the economy is making full use of its factors of production, and it is making efficient use of its factors of production. If there are idle or inefficiently allocated factors of production, the economy will operate inside the production possibilities curve. Thus, the production possibilities curve not only shows what can be produced; it provides insight into how goods and services should be produced. It suggests that to obtain efficiency in production, factors of production should be allocated on the basis of comparative advantage. Further, the economy must make full use of its factors of production if it is to produce the goods and services it is capable of producing.

Specialization

The production possibilities model suggests that specialization will occur. **Specialization** implies that an economy is producing the goods and services in which it has a comparative advantage. If Alpine Sports selects point C in Figure 2.8, for example, it will assign Plant 1 exclusively to ski production and Plants 2 and 3 exclusively to snowboard production.

Such specialization is typical in an economic system. Workers, for example, specialize in particular fields in which they have a comparative advantage. People work and use the income they earn to buy—perhaps import—goods and services from people who have a comparative advantage in doing other things. The result is a far greater quantity of goods and services than would be available without this specialization.

Think about what life would be like without specialization. Imagine that you are suddenly completely cut off from the rest of the economy. You must produce everything you consume; you obtain nothing from anyone else. Would you be able to consume what you consume now? Clearly not. It is hard to imagine that most of us could even survive in such a setting. The gains we achieve through specialization are enormous.

Nations specialize as well. Much of the land in the United States has a comparative advantage in agricultural production and is devoted to that activity. Hong Kong, with its huge population and tiny endowment of land, allocates virtually none of its land to agricultural use; that option would be too costly. Its land is devoted largely to nonagricultural use.

specialization

Situation in which an economy is producing the goods and services in which it has a comparative advantage.

Key Takeaways

- A production possibilities curve shows the combinations of two goods an economy is capable of producing.
- The downward slope of the production possibilities curve is an implication of scarcity.
- The bowed-out shape of the production possibilities curve results from allocating resources based on comparative advantage. Such an allocation implies that the law of increasing opportunity cost will hold.
- An economy that fails to make full and efficient use of its factors of production will operate inside its production possibilities curve.
- Specialization means that an economy is producing the goods and services in which it has a comparative advantage.

Try It!

Suppose a manufacturing firm is equipped to produce radios or calculators. It has two plants, Plant R and Plant S, at which it can produce these goods. Given the labor and the capital available at both plants, it can produce the combinations of the two goods at the two plants shown.

Output per day, Plant R		
Combination	Calculators	Radios
A	100	0
B	50	25
C	0	50

Output per day, Plant S		
Combination	Calculators	Radios
D	50	0
E	25	50
F	0	100

Put calculators on the vertical axis and radios on the horizontal axis. Draw the production possibilities curve for Plant R. On a separate graph, draw the production possibilities curve for Plant S. Which plant has a comparative advantage in calculators? In radios? Now draw the combined curves for the two plants. Suppose the firm decides to produce 100 radios. Where will it produce them? How many calculators will it be able to produce? Where will it produce the calculators?

Case in Point: The Cost of the Great Depression

Source: © 2010 Jupiterimages Corporation

The U.S. economy looked very healthy in the beginning of 1929. It had enjoyed seven years of dramatic growth and unprecedented prosperity. Its resources were fully employed; it was operating quite close to its production possibilities curve.

In the summer of 1929, however, things started going wrong. Production and employment fell. They continued to fall for several years. By 1933, more than 25% of the nation's workers had lost their jobs. Production had plummeted by almost 30%. The economy had moved well within its production possibilities curve.

Output began to grow after 1933, but the economy continued to have vast numbers of idle workers, idle factories, and idle farms. These resources were not put back to work fully until 1942, after the U.S. entry into World War II demanded mobilization of the economy's factors of production.

Between 1929 and 1942, the economy produced 25% fewer goods and services than it would have if its resources had been fully employed. That was a loss, measured in today's dollars, of well over $3 trillion. In material terms, the forgone output represented a greater cost than the United States would ultimately spend in World War II. The Great Depression was a costly experience indeed.

Answer to Try It! Problem

The production possibilities curves for the two plants are shown, along with the combined curve for both plants. Plant R has a comparative advantage in producing calculators. Plant S has a comparative advantage in producing radios, so, if the firm goes from producing 150 calculators and no radios to producing 100 radios, it will produce them at Plant S. In the production possibilities curve for both plants, the firm would be at M, producing 100 calculators at Plant R.

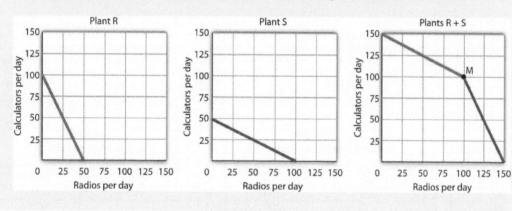

2.4 Applications of the Production Possibilities Model

Learning Objectives

1. Understand the argument for unrestricted international trade in terms of economic specialization and comparative advantage.
2. Define economic growth in terms of the production possibilities model and discuss factors that make such growth possible.
3. Explain the classification of economic systems, the role of government in different economic systems, and the strengths and weaknesses of different systems.

The production possibilities curve gives us a model of an economy. The model provides powerful insights about the real world, insights that help us to answer some important questions: How does trade between two countries affect the quantities of goods available to people? What determines the rate at which production will increase over time? What is the role of economic freedom in the economy? In this section we explore applications of the model to questions of international trade, economic growth, and the choice of an economic system.

Comparative Advantage and International Trade

One of the most important implications of the concepts of comparative advantage and the production possibilities curve relates to international trade. We can think of different nations as being equivalent to Christie Ryder's plants. Each will have a comparative advantage in certain activities, and efficient world production requires that each nation specialize in those activities in which it has a comparative advantage. A failure to allocate resources in this way means that world production falls inside the production possibilities curve; more of each good could be produced by relying on comparative advantage.

If nations specialize, then they must rely on each other. They will sell the goods in which they specialize and purchase other goods from other nations. Suppose, for example, that the world consists of two continents that can each produce two goods: South America and Europe can produce food and computers. Suppose they can produce the two goods according to the tables in Panels (a) and (b) of Figure 2.9. We have simplified this example by assuming that each continent has a linear production possibilities curve; the curves are plotted below the tables in Panels (a) and (b). Each continent has a separate production possibilities curve; the two have been combined to illustrate a world production possibilities curve in Panel (c) of the exhibit.

FIGURE 2.9 Production Possibilities Curves and Trade
Suppose the world consists of two continents: South America and Europe. They can each produce two goods: food and computers. In this example, we assume that each continent has a linear production possibilities curve, as shown in Panels (a) and (b). South America has a comparative advantage in food production and Europe has a comparative advantage in computer production. With free trade, the world can operate on the bowed-out curve GHI, shown in Panel (c). If the continents refuse to trade, the world will operate inside its production possibilities curve. If, for example, each continent were to produce at the midpoint of its production possibilities curve, the world would produce 300 computers and 300 units of food per period at point Q. If each continent were to specialize in the good in which it has a comparative advantage, world production could move to a point such as H, with more of both goods produced.

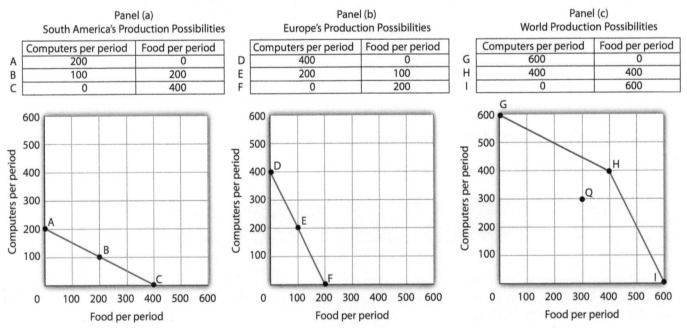

The world production possibilities curve assumes that resources are allocated between computer and food production based on comparative advantage. Notice that, even with only two economies and the assumption of linear production possibilities curves for each, the combined curve still has a bowed-out shape. At point H, for example, South America specializes in food, while Europe produces only computers. World production equals 400 units of each good. In this situation, we would expect South America to export food to Europe while Europe exports computers to South America.

But suppose the regions refuse to trade; each insists on producing its own food and computers. Suppose further that each chooses to produce at the midpoint of its own production possibilities curve. South America produces 100 units of computers and 200 units of food per period, while Europe produces 200 units of computers and 100 units of food per period. World production thus totals 300 units of each good per period; the world operates at point Q in Figure 2.9. If the two continents were willing to move from isolation to trade, the world could achieve an increase in the production of both goods. Producing at point H requires no more resources, no more effort than production at Q. It does, however, require that the world's resources be allocated on the basis of comparative advantage.

The implications of our model for trade are powerful indeed. First, we see that trade allows the production of more of all goods and services. Restrictions on trade thus reduce production of goods and services. Second, we see a lesson often missed in discussions of trade: a nation's trade policy has nothing to do with its level of employment of its factors of production. In our example, when South America and Europe do not engage in trade and produce at the midpoints of each of their respective production possibilities curves, *they each have full employment*. With trade, the two nations still operate on their respective production possibilities curves: *they each have full employment*. Trade certainly redistributes employment in the two continents. In South America, employment shifts from computer production to food production. In Europe, it shifts from food production to computer production. Once the shift is made, though, there is no effect on employment in either continent.

Of course, this idealized example would have all of South America's computer experts becoming farmers while all of Europe's farmers become computer geeks! That is a bit much to swallow, but it is merely the result of assuming linear production possibilities curves and complete specialization. In the real world, production possibilities curves are concave, and the reallocation of resources required by trade is not nearly as dramatic. Still, free trade can require shifts in resources from one activity to another. These shifts produce enormous benefits, but they do not come without costs.

Nearly all economists agree that largely unrestricted trade between countries is desirable; restrictions on trade generally force the world to operate inside its production possibilities curve. In some cases restrictions on trade could be desirable, but in the main, free trade promotes greater production of goods and services for the world's people. The role of international trade is explored in greater detail in subsequent chapters of this book.

Economic Growth

An increase in the physical quantity or in the quality of factors of production available to an economy or a technological gain will allow the economy to produce more goods and services; it will shift the economy's production possibilities curve outward. The process through which an economy achieves an outward shift in its production possibilities curve is called **economic growth**. An outward shift in a production possibilities curve is illustrated in Figure 2.10. In Panel (a), a point such as N is not attainable; it lies outside the production possibilities curve. Growth shifts the curve outward, as in Panel (b), making previously unattainable levels of production possible.

economic growth

The process through which an economy achieves an outward shift in its production possibilities curve.

FIGURE 2.10 Economic Growth and the Production Possibilities Curve
An economy capable of producing two goods, A and B, is initially operating at point M on production possibilities
curve OMR in Panel (a). Given this production possibilities curve, the economy could not produce a combination such
as shown by point N, which lies outside the curve. An increase in the factors of production available to the economy
would shift the curve outward to SNT, allowing the choice of a point such as N, at which more of both goods will be
produced.

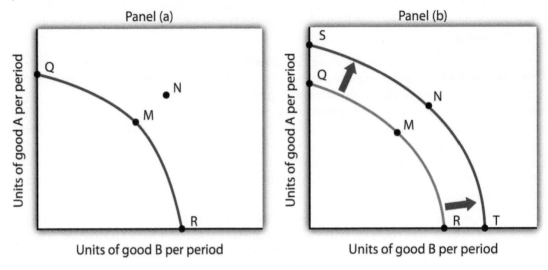

The Sources of Economic Growth

Economic growth implies an outward shift in an economy's production possibilities curve. Recall
that when we draw such a curve, we assume that the quantity and quality of the economy's factors
of production and its technology are unchanged. Changing these will shift the curve. Anything
that increases the quantity or quality of the factors of production available to the economy or that
improves the technology available to the economy contributes to economic growth.

Consider, for example, the dramatic gains in human capital that have occurred in the United
States since the beginning of the past century. In 1900, about 3.5% of U.S. workers had completed a
high school education. Today, that percentage is above 90. Fewer than 1% of the workers in 1900 had
graduated from college; as late as 1940 only 3.5% had graduated from college. Today over 30% have.
In addition to being better educated, today's workers have received more and better training on the
job. They bring far more economically useful knowledge and skills to their work than did workers
a century ago.

Moreover, the technological changes that have occurred within the past 100 years have greatly
reduced the time and effort required to produce most goods and services. Automated production
has become commonplace. Innovations in transportation (automobiles, trucks, and airplanes) have
made the movement of goods and people cheaper and faster. A dizzying array of new materials is
available for manufacturing. And the development of modern information technology—including
computers, software, and communications equipment—that seemed to proceed at breathtaking
pace especially during the final years of the last century and continuing to the present has transformed the way we live and work.

Look again at the technological changes of the last few years described in the Case in Point
on advances in technology. Those examples of technological progress through applications of
computer technology—from new ways of mapping oil deposits to new methods of milking
cows—helped propel the United States and other economies to dramatic gains in the ability to
produce goods and services. They have helped shift the countries' production possibilities curve
outward. They have helped fuel economic growth.

Table 2.1 summarizes the factors that have contributed to U.S. economic growth from 1947-2012.
The first two sources reflect increases in quantities of factors of production, the second two reflect

increases in quality of factors of production, and the last reflects technological improvements. For the 65-year period, roughly 60% of economic growth stemmed from increases in the quantities of capital and labor (calculated by adding the % contribution from increases in quantities of the factors of production, 0.58 and 1.24, dividing that by the overall growth rate of 3.05, and multiplying by 100), 20% from increases in qualities of those factors, and 20% from improvements in technology or innovation.

TABLE 2.1 Sources of U.S. Economic Growth, 1947-2012

Sources of Growth	% Contribution of Growth of Factor to Overall Growth rate of 3.05%
Increase in quantity of labor	0.58%
Increase in quantity of capital	1.24%
Increase in quality of labor	0.24%
Increase in quality of capital	0.38%
Improved technology	0.61%

Source: Dale W. Jorgenson, Mun Ho, and Jon Samuels, "U.S. Economic Growth Retrospect and Prospect: Lessons from a Prototype Industry-Level Production Account from the United States, 1947 - 2012," in Dale W. Jorgenson, Kyoji Fukao, and Marcel P. Timmer, The World Economy: Growth or Stagnation? (Cambridge: Cambridge University Press:2017). Table based on Fig. 2.17, p. 58, underlying detail supplied by authors.

Waiting for Growth

One key to growth is, in effect, the willingness to wait, to postpone current consumption in order to enhance future productive capability. When Stone Age people fashioned the first tools, they were spending time building capital rather than engaging in consumption. They delayed current consumption to enhance their future consumption; the tools they made would make them more productive in the future.

Resources society could have used to produce consumer goods are being used to produce new capital goods and new knowledge for production instead—all to enhance future production. An even more important source of growth in many nations has been increased human capital. Increases in human capital often require the postponement of consumption. If you are a college student, you are engaged in precisely this effort. You are devoting time to study that could have been spent working, earning income, and thus engaging in a higher level of consumption. If you are like most students, you are making this choice to postpone consumption because you expect it will allow you to earn more income, and thus enjoy greater consumption, in the future.

Think of an economy as being able to produce two goods, capital and consumer goods (those destined for immediate use by consumers). By focusing on the production of consumer goods, the people in the economy will be able to enjoy a higher standard of living today. If they reduce their consumption—and their standard of living—today to enhance their ability to produce goods and services in the future, they will be able to shift their production possibilities curve outward. That may allow them to produce even more consumer goods. A decision for greater growth typically involves the sacrifice of present consumption.

Arenas for Choice: A Comparison of Economic Systems

Under what circumstances will a nation achieve efficiency in the use of its factors of production? The discussion above suggested that Christie Ryder would have an incentive to allocate her plants efficiently because by doing so she could achieve greater output of skis and snowboards than would be possible from inefficient production. But why would she want to produce more of these two goods—or of any goods? Why would decision makers throughout the economy want to achieve such efficiency?

Economists assume that privately owned firms seek to maximize their profits. The drive to maximize profits will lead firms such as Alpine Sports to allocate resources efficiently to gain as much production as possible from their factors of production. But whether firms will seek to maximize profits depends on the nature of the economic system within which they operate.

Classifying Economic Systems

market capitalist economy

Economy in which resources are generally owned by private individuals who have the power to make decisions about their use.

command socialist economy

Economy in which government is the primary owner of capital and natural resources and has broad power to allocate the use of factors of production.

mixed economies

Economy that combine elements of market capitalist and of command socialist economic systems.

Each of the world's economies can be viewed as operating somewhere on a spectrum between market capitalism and command socialism. In a **market capitalist economy**, resources are generally owned by private individuals who have the power to make decisions about their use. A market capitalist system is often referred to as a free enterprise economic system. In a **command socialist economy**, the government is the primary owner of capital and natural resources and has broad power to allocate the use of factors of production. Between these two categories lie **mixed economies** that combine elements of market capitalist and of command socialist economic systems.

No economy represents a pure case of either market capitalism or command socialism. To determine where an economy lies between these two types of systems, we evaluate the extent of government ownership of capital and natural resources and the degree to which government is involved in decisions about the use of factors of production.

Figure 2.11 suggests the spectrum of economic systems. Market capitalist economies lie toward the left end of this spectrum; command socialist economies appear toward the right. Mixed economies lie in between. The market capitalist end of the spectrum includes countries such as the United States, the United Kingdom, and Chile. Hong Kong, though now part of China, has a long history as a market capitalist economy and is generally regarded as operating at the market capitalist end of the spectrum. Countries at the command socialist end of the spectrum include North Korea and Cuba.

FIGURE 2.11 Economic Systems

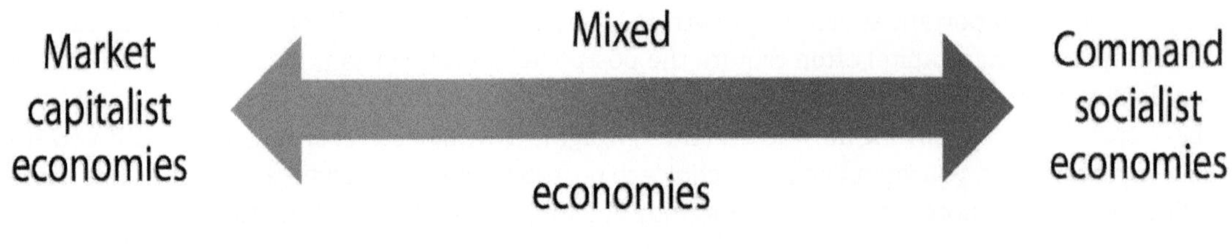

Some European economies, such as France, Germany, and Sweden, have a sufficiently high degree of regulation that we consider them as operating more toward the center of the spectrum. Russia and China, which long operated at the command socialist end of the spectrum, can now be considered mixed economies. Most economies in Latin America once operated toward the right end of the spectrum. While their governments did not exercise the extensive ownership of capital and natural resources that are one characteristic of command socialist systems, their governments did impose extensive regulations. Many of these nations are in the process of carrying out economic reforms that will move them further in the direction of market capitalism.

The global shift toward market capitalist economic systems that occurred in the 1980s and 1990s was in large part the result of three important features of such economies. First, the emphasis on individual ownership and decision-making power has generally yielded greater individual freedom than has been available under command socialist or some more heavily regulated mixed economic systems that lie toward the command socialist end of the spectrum. People seeking political, religious, and economic freedom have thus gravitated toward market capitalism. Second, market economies are more likely than other systems to allocate resources on the basis of comparative advantage. They thus tend to generate higher levels of production and income than do other economic systems. Third, market capitalist-type systems appear to be the most conducive to entrepreneurial activity.

Suppose Christie Ryder had the same three plants we considered earlier in this chapter but was operating in a mixed economic system with extensive government regulation. In such a system, she might be prohibited from transferring resources from one use to another to achieve the gains possible from comparative advantage. If she were operating under a command socialist system, she would not be the owner of the plants and thus would be unlikely to profit from their efficient use. If that were the case, there is no reason to believe she would make any effort to assure the efficient use of the three plants. Generally speaking, it is economies toward the market capitalist end of the spectrum that offer the greatest inducement to allocate resources on the basis of comparative advantage. They tend to be more productive and to deliver higher material standards of living than do economies that operate at or near the command socialist end of the spectrum.

FIGURE 2.12 Economic Freedom and Income
The graph shows the relationship between economic freedom and per capita income. Countries with higher degrees of economic freedom tended to have higher per capita incomes.

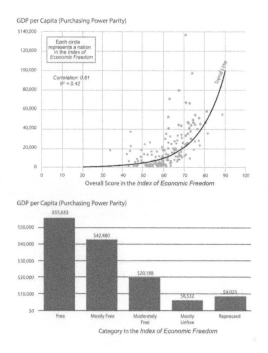

Source: Terry Miller and Kim R. Holmes, 2016 Index of Economic Freedom (Washington, D.C.: The Heritage Foundation and Dow Jones & Company, Inc., 2016), at www.heritage.org/index.

Market capitalist economies rely on economic freedom. Indeed, one way we can assess the degree to which a country can be considered market capitalist is by the degree of economic freedom it permits. Several organizations have attempted to compare economic freedom in various countries. One of the most extensive comparisons is a joint annual effort by the Heritage Foundation and the *Wall Street Journal*. The 2016 rating was based on policies in effect in 178 countries from mid-2014 to mid-2015. The report ranks these nations on the basis of such things as the degree of regulation of firms, tax levels, and restrictions on international trade. Hong Kong ranked as the freest economy in the world. North Korea received the dubious distinction of being the least free.

It seems reasonable to expect that the greater the degree of economic freedom a country permits, the greater the amount of income per person it will generate. This proposition is illustrated in Figure 2.12. The study also found a direct association between the degree of economic freedom and economic growth and an inverse association between the degree of economic freedom and poverty and food insecurity. We must be wary of slipping into the fallacy of false cause by concluding from this evidence that economic freedom generates higher incomes. It could be that higher incomes lead nations to opt for greater economic freedom. But in this case, it seems reasonable to conclude that, in general, economic freedom does lead to higher incomes.

Government in a Market Economy

The production possibilities model provides a menu of choices among alternative combinations of goods and services. Given those choices, which combinations will be produced?

In a market economy, this question is answered in large part through the interaction of individual buyers and sellers. As we have already seen, government plays a role as well. It may seek to encourage greater consumption of some goods and discourage consumption of others. In the United States, for example, taxes imposed on cigarettes discourage smoking, while special treatment of property taxes and mortgage interest in the federal income tax encourages home ownership. Government may try to stop the production and consumption of some goods altogether, as many governments do with drugs such as heroin and cocaine. Government may supplement the private consumption of some goods by producing more of them itself, as many U.S. cities do with golf courses and tennis courts. In other cases, there may be no private market for a good or service at all. In the choice between security and defense versus all other goods and services outlined at the beginning of this chapter, government agencies are virtually the sole providers of security and national defense.

All nations also rely on government to provide defense, enforce laws, and redistribute income. Even market economies rely on government to regulate the activities of private firms, to protect the environment, to provide education, and to produce a wide range of other goods and services. Government's role may be limited in a market economy, but it remains fundamentally important.

Key Takeaways

- The ideas of comparative advantage and specialization suggest that restrictions on international trade are likely to reduce production of goods and services.
- Economic growth is the result of increasing the quantity or quality of an economy's factors of production and of advances in technology.
- Policies to encourage growth generally involve postponing consumption to increase capital and human capital.
- Market capitalist economies have generally proved more productive than mixed or command socialist economies.
- Government plays a crucial role in any market economy.

Try It!

Draw a production possibilities curve for an economy that can produce two goods, CD players and jackets. You do not have numbers for this one—just draw a curve with the usual bowed-out shape. Put the quantity of CD players per period on the vertical axis and the quantity of jackets per period on the horizontal axis. Now mark a point A on the curve you have drawn; extend dotted lines from this point to the horizontal and vertical axes. Mark the initial quantities of the two goods as CD_A and J_A, respectively. Explain why, in the absence of economic growth, an increase in jacket production requires a reduction in the production of CD players. Now show how economic growth could lead to an increase in the production of both goods.

Case in Point: Economic Growth: What to Expect

Source: © Shutterstock, Inc.

The message Robert Gordon delivered in his recent book, *The Rise and Fall of American Growth*, is not one that many Americans want to hear. The Northwestern University professor uses the term "secular stagnation" to describe the future of economic growth. Secular stagnation does not mean that we will not see any economic growth. Rather he predicts that growth will be sluggish compared to what it was in the not-too-distant past. And he does not see a world without technological innovation. It is just that the innovations of today and into the future do not have the same punch that ones from the past did. He sums up his argument as follows:

"Some treat the recent slowdown as an anomaly and assume we can get back to our 'normal' high-growth mode. But a closer look at history suggests that the real anomaly is how fast things grew for much of the 20th century. The reason is not that we've stopped innovating. Instead, the basic explanation is that some inventions are more important than others—and the most important ones happened decades ago."

He argues that when you look at long periods of time, you notice that the pace of economic growth has never been steady. It was virtually nil, he states, until the Industrial Revolution and then it began to slowly pick up. For the period 1870 to 1970, it skyrocketed by historical standards due to what he calls the "Great Inventions," such as the internal combustion engine and electricity. During this 100-year period, people's lives were truly transformed as we began to live and work in lighted, clean and climate-controlled environments; life spans, spurred by modern plumbing and modern medicine, markedly increased; and the drudgery of manual labor was replaced by machines of various kinds.

Since then, innovations have been mostly in the areas of information, communications, and entertainment. And, while these advances did lead to a spurt of growth in the late 1990s and early 2000s, and while we do certainly enjoy our smartphones and the like, our lives did not really change all that much. The cars and appliances (with the addition of the microwave as a notable exception) of the 2000s are just not that different from those of the 1970s. Yes, there will continue to be improvements in technology that will contribute to growth but, he argues, their impact will not be as great, despite the hype coming from Silicon Valley.

As for solutions, he thinks research is already well funded and that more spending on roads and bridges will be helpful but not transformative in the way that the development of the interstate highway system was. He sees improving the quality of the workforce through more spending on pre-school and educational reform as more promising.

"Growth has been our American mantra, but it might just prove to be an elusive slogan. So beware politicians bearing promises of a return to a vanished past."

Not all economists agree with Professor Gordon. For example, Erik Brynjolfsson, an economist at Massachusetts Institute of Technology, thinks that it takes time for some of the current innovations, such as those related to artificial intelligence, to show their impact on the economy but that they will eventually. Others have argued that it simply takes more spending on research and innovation today to maintain growth for a variety of reasons. For example, society is more concerned about the risks of innovations. Think about rules that the Federal Aviation Administration has instituted for flying drones or rules concerning car emissions. Such rules may have another worthy purpose but they do not speed up innovation.

Sources: Based on Robert Gordon, "American Growth Has Slowed Down. Get Used to it," Politico Magazine, September/October 2016, p. 78 – 80; Greg Ip, "Are We Out of Big Ideas?" The Wall Street Journal, December 7, 2016, p. A1 and A12.

Answer to Try It! Problem

Your first production possibilities curve should resemble the one in Panel (a). Starting at point A, an increase in jacket production requires a move down and to the right along the curve, as shown by the arrow, and thus a reduction in the production of CD players. Alternatively, if there is economic growth, it shifts the production possibilities curve outward, as in Panel (b). This shift allows an increase in production of both goods, as suggested by the arrow.

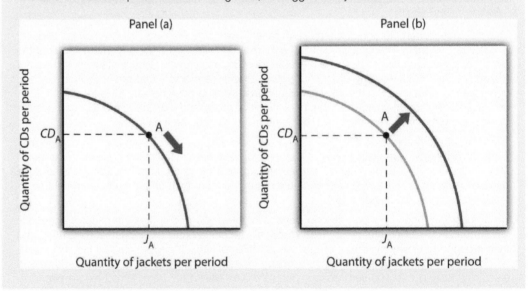

2.5 Review and Practice

Summary

Economics deals with choices. In this chapter we have examined more carefully the range of choices in production that must be made in any economy. In particular, we looked at choices involving the allocation of an economy's factors of production: labor, capital, and natural resources.

In addition, in any economy, the level of technology plays a key role in determining how productive the factors of production will be. In a market economy, entrepreneurs organize factors of production and act to introduce technological change.

The production possibilities model is a device that assists us in thinking about many of the choices about resource allocation in an economy. The model assumes that the economy has factors of production that are fixed in both quantity and quality. When illustrated graphically, the production possibilities model typically limits our analysis to two goods. Given the economy's factors of production and technology, the economy can produce various combinations of the two goods. If it uses its factors of production efficiently and has full employment, it will be operating on the production possibilities curve.

Two characteristics of the production possibilities curve are particularly important. First, it is downward sloping. This reflects the scarcity of the factors of production available to the economy; producing more of one good requires giving up some of the other. Second, the curve is bowed out. Another way of saying this is to say that the curve gets steeper as we move from left to right; the absolute value of its slope is increasing. Producing each additional unit of the good on the horizontal axis requires a greater sacrifice of the good on the vertical axis than did the previous units produced. This fact, called the law of increasing opportunity cost, is the inevitable result of efficient choices in production—choices based on comparative advantage.

The production possibilities model has important implications for international trade. It suggests that free trade will allow countries to specialize in the production of goods and services in which they have a comparative advantage. This specialization increases the production of all goods and services.

Increasing the quantity or quality of factors of production and/or improving technology will shift the production possibilities curve outward. This process is called economic growth. In the last 50 years, economic growth in the United States has resulted chiefly from increases in human capital and from technological advance.

Choices concerning the use of scarce resources take place within the context of a set of institutional arrangements that define an economic system. The principal distinctions between systems lie in the degree to which ownership of capital and natural resources and decision making authority over scarce resources are held by government or by private individuals. Economic systems include market capitalist, mixed, and command socialist economies. An increasing body of evidence suggests that market capitalist economies tend to be most productive; many command socialist and mixed economies are moving in the direction of market capitalist systems.

The presumption in favor of market-based systems does not preclude a role for government. Government is necessary to provide the system of laws on which market systems are founded. It may also be used to provide certain goods and services, to help individuals in need, and to regulate the actions of individuals and firms.

Concept Problems

1. How does a college education increase one's human capital?
2. Why does the downward-sloping production possibilities curve imply that factors of production are scarce?

3. In what ways are the bowed-out shape of the production possibilities curve and the law of increasing opportunity cost related?

4. What is the relationship between the concept of comparative advantage and the law of increasing opportunity cost?

5. Suppose an economy can produce two goods, A and B. It is now operating at point E on production possibilities curve RT. An improvement in the technology available to produce good A shifts the curve to ST, and the economy selects point E'. How does this change affect the opportunity cost of producing an additional unit of good B?

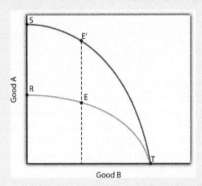

6. Could a nation's production possibilities curve ever shift inward? Explain what such a shift would mean, and discuss events that might cause such a shift to occur.

7. Suppose blue-eyed people were banned from working. How would this affect a nation's production possibilities curve?

8. Evaluate this statement: "The U.S. economy could achieve greater growth by devoting fewer resources to consumption and more to investment; it follows that such a shift would be desirable."

9. Two countries, Sportsland and Foodland, have similar total quantities of labor, capital, and natural resources. Both can produce two goods, figs and footballs. Sportsland's resources are particularly well suited to the production of footballs but are not very productive in producing figs. Foodland's resources are very productive when used for figs but are not capable of producing many footballs. In which country is the cost of additional footballs generally greater? Explain.

10. Suppose a country is committed to using its resources based on the reverse of comparative advantage doctrine: it first transfers those resources for which the cost is greatest, not lowest. Describe this country's production possibilities curve.

11. The U.S. Constitution bans states from restricting imports of goods and services from other states. Suppose this restriction did not exist and that states were allowed to limit imports of goods and services produced in other states. How do you think this would affect U.S. output? Explain.

12. By 1993, nations in the European Union (EU) had eliminated all barriers to the flow of goods, services, labor, and capital across their borders. Even such things as consumer protection laws and the types of plugs required to plug in appliances have been standardized to ensure that there will be no barriers to trade. How do you think this elimination of trade barriers affected EU output?

13. How did the technological changes described in the Case in Point "Technology Cuts Costs, Boosts Productivity and Profits" affect the production possibilities curve for the United States?

Numerical Problems

1. Nathan can mow four lawns in a day or plant 20 trees in a day.

   a. Draw Nathan's production possibilities curve for mowing lawns and planting trees. Assume the production possibilities curve is linear and put the quantity of lawns mowed per day on the horizontal axis and the quantity of trees planted per day on the vertical axis.

   b. What is Nathan's opportunity cost of planting trees?

   c. What is Nathan's opportunity cost of mowing lawns?

2. David can mow four lawns in a day or plant four trees in a day.

   a. Draw David's production possibilities curve for mowing lawns and planting trees. Again, assume a linear production possibilities curve and put the quantity of lawns mowed per day on the horizontal axis.

   b. What is David's opportunity cost of planting trees?

   c. What is David's opportunity cost of mowing lawns?

3. Given the production information in problems 1 and 2 above, who has the comparative advantage in planting trees? Mowing lawns?

4. The exhibits below describe the production possibilities for Germany and Turkey.

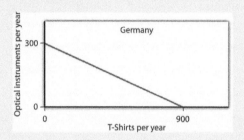

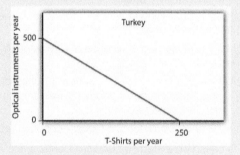

   a. What is the slope of Germany's production possibilities curve?

   b. What is the slope of Turkey's production possibilities curve?

   c. What is the opportunity cost of producing T-shirts in Germany?

   d. What is the opportunity cost of producing T-shirts in Turkey?

   e. What is the opportunity cost of producing optical instruments in Germany?

   f. What is the opportunity cost of producing optical instruments in Turkey?

   g. In which good does Germany have a comparative advantage?

   h. In which good does Turkey have a comparative advantage?

5. The nation of Leisureland can produce two goods, bicycles and bowling balls. The western region of Leisureland can, if it devotes all its resources to bicycle production, produce 100 bicycles per month. Alternatively, it could devote all its resources to bowling balls and produce 400 per month—or it could produce any combination of bicycles and bowling balls lying on a straight line between these two extremes.

   a. Draw a production possibilities curve for western Leisureland (with bicycles on the vertical axis).

   b. What it is the opportunity cost of producing an additional bowling ball measured in terms of forgone bicycles in western Leisureland?

   c. Suppose that eastern Leisureland can, if it devotes all its resources to the production of bicycles, produce 400. If it devotes all its resources to bowling ball production, though, it can produce only 100. Draw the production possibilities curve for eastern Leisureland (again, assume it is linear and put bicycles on the vertical axis).

   d. What is the opportunity cost of producing an additional bowling ball measured in terms of forgone bicycles in eastern Leisureland?

   e. Explain the difference in opportunity cost between western and eastern Leisureland. Which region has a comparative advantage in producing bowling balls? Bicycles?

   f. Draw the production possibilities curve for Leisureland, one that combines the curves for western and eastern Leisureland.

   g. Suppose it is determined that 400 bicycles must be produced. How many bowling balls can be produced?

   h. Where will these goods be produced?

6. The table below shows the production possibilities schedule for an economy.

Production Alternatives	Capital goods per period	Consumer goods per period
A	0	40
B	1	36
C	2	28
D	3	16
E	4	0

   a. Putting capital goods per period on the horizontal axis and consumer goods per period on the vertical axis, graph the production possibilities curve for the economy.

   b. If the economy is producing at alternative B, what is the opportunity cost to it of producing at alternative C instead?

   c. If the economy is producing at alternative C, what is the opportunity cost to it of producing at alternative D instead?

   d. Is it possible for this economy to produce 30 units of consumer goods per period while producing 1 unit of capital goods? Would this combination of goods represent efficient or inefficient production? Explain.

   e. Which point, B or C, would lead to higher economic growth? Explain your answer.

7. The table below is based on a study by Edward Denison analyzing the sources of growth in the United
States between 1929 and 1982 and for various subperiods. The numbers in the first row show the average annual rate of growth for the period and subperiods and those in the subsequent rows show the contribution of each factor to the overall rate of growth. Note that the numbers are percentage points and they do not add up to the average annual rate of growth due to a variety of other factors not shown. [1]

	1929-1982	1929-1948	1948-1973	1973-1982
Growth rate for the period	2.92	2.54	3.70	1.55
Increase in quantity of labor	0.94	1.04	1.00	0.66
Increase in quantity of capital	0.56	0.11	0.77	0.69
Increase in human capital	0.40	0.38	0.40	0.47
Technological improvement	0.66	0.50	1.09	-0.05

   a. Approximately what percentage of U.S. growth between 1929 and 1982 was due to increases in the quantities of factors of production?

   b. Approximately what percentage of U.S. growth between 1929 and 1982 was due to increases in quality of factors of production and technological improvement?

c. In which of the subperiods shown did the increase in the quantity of labor make the largest percentage contribution to the overall average annual growth rate?

d. In which of the subperiods shown did technological change make the largest contributor to the overall average annual growth rate?

Endnotes

1. Edward Denison, Trends in American Growth, 1929-1982 (Washington, D.C.: Brookings Institution, 1985). Data from Table 8.1 Sources of Growth of Total Actual nation Income, Selected periods, 1929 – 1982, p. 111.

CHAPTER 3
Demand and Supply

3.1 Start Up: Crazy for Coffee

Starbucks Coffee Company has revolutionized the coffee-drinking habits of millions of people all over the world. Starbucks, whose bright green-and-white logo is almost as familiar as the golden arches of McDonald's, began in Seattle in 1971. Fifteen years later it had grown into a chain of four stores in the Seattle area. Then in 1987 Howard Schultz, a former Starbucks employee, who had become intrigued by the culture of Italian coffee bars, bought the company from its founders for $3.8 million. In 2016, Americans were willingly paying $5 or more for a cappuccino or a latté, and Starbucks had grown to become an international chain, with approximately 24,000 stores in more than 70 countries .

The change in American consumers' taste for coffee and the profits raked in by Starbucks lured other companies to get into the game. Retailers such as Seattle's Best Coffee and Gloria Jean's Coffees entered the market, and today there are thousands of coffee bars, carts, drive-throughs, and kiosks in downtowns, malls, and airports all around the country. Even McDonald's began selling specialty coffees.

The price of the coffee beans themselves can be quite volatile. For example, over the last decade, the price per pound has been as low as $1 per pound and as high as $2.80 per pound. Factors such as good and bad harvests and consumer preferences influence how expensive or cheap coffee prices may be. Of course, the price of the coffee beans is only one component of the price of a cup of coffee at your favorite coffee shop.

Markets, the institutions that bring together buyers and sellers, are always responding to events, such as bad harvests and changing consumer tastes that affect the prices and quantities of particular goods. The demand for some goods increases, while the demand for others decreases. The supply of some goods rises, while the supply of others falls. As such events unfold, prices adjust to keep markets in balance. This chapter explains how the market forces of demand and supply interact to determine equilibrium prices and equilibrium quantities of goods and services. We will see how prices and quantities adjust to changes in demand and supply and how changes in prices serve as signals to buyers and sellers.

> **markets**
>
> The institutions that bring together buyers and sellers.

The model of demand and supply that we shall develop in this chapter is one of the most powerful tools in all of economic analysis. You will be using it throughout your study of economics. We will first look at the variables that influence demand. Then we will turn to supply, and finally we will put demand and supply together to explore how the model of demand and supply operates. As we examine the model, bear in mind that demand is a representation of the behavior of buyers and that supply is a representation of the behavior of sellers. Buyers may be consumers purchasing groceries or producers purchasing iron ore to make steel. Sellers may be firms selling cars or households selling their labor services. We shall see that the ideas of demand and supply apply, whatever the identity of the buyers or sellers and whatever the good or service being exchanged in the market. In this chapter, we shall focus on buyers and sellers of goods and services.

3.2 Demand

Learning Objectives

1. Define the quantity demanded of a good or service and illustrate it using a demand schedule and a demand curve.
2. Distinguish between the following pairs of concepts: demand and quantity demanded, demand schedule and demand curve, movement along and shift in a demand curve.
3. Identify demand shifters and determine whether a change in a demand shifter causes the demand curve to shift to the right or to the left.

How many pizzas will people eat this year? How many doctor visits will people make? How many houses will people buy?

Each good or service has its own special characteristics that determine the quantity people are willing and able to consume. One is the price of the good or service itself. Other independent variables that are important determinants of demand include consumer preferences, prices of related goods and services, income, demographic characteristics such as population size, and buyer expectations. The number of pizzas people will purchase, for example, depends very much on how much they like pizza. It also depends on the prices for alternatives such as hamburgers or spaghetti. The number of doctor visits is likely to vary with income—people with higher incomes are likely to see a doctor more often than people with lower incomes. The demands for pizza, for doctor visits, and for housing are certainly affected by the age distribution of the population and its size.

While different variables play different roles in influencing the demands for different goods and services, economists pay special attention to one: the price of the good or service. Given the values of all the other variables that affect demand, a higher price tends to reduce the quantity people demand, and a lower price tends to increase it. A medium pizza typically sells for $5 to $10. Suppose the price were $30. Chances are, you would buy fewer pizzas at that price than you do now. Suppose pizzas typically sold for $2 each. At that price, people would be likely to buy more pizzas than they do now.

We will discuss first how price affects the quantity demanded of a good or service and then how other variables affect demand.

Price and the Demand Curve

Because people will purchase different quantities of a good or service at different prices, economists must be careful when speaking of the "demand" for something. They have therefore developed some specific terms for expressing the general concept of demand.

quantity demanded

The quantity buyers are willing and able to buy of a good or service at a particular price during a particular period, all other things unchanged.

The **quantity demanded** of a good or service is the quantity buyers are willing and able to buy at a particular price during a particular period, all other things unchanged. (As we learned, we can substitute the Latin phrase "ceteris paribus" for "all other things unchanged.") Suppose, for example, that 100,000 movie tickets are sold each month in a particular town at a price of $8 per ticket. That quantity—100,000—is the quantity of movie admissions demanded per month at a price of $8. If the price were $12, we would expect the quantity demanded to be less. If it were $4, we would expect the quantity demanded to be greater. The quantity demanded at each price would be different if other things that might affect it, such as the population of the town, were to change. That is why we add the qualifier that other things have not changed to the definition of quantity demanded.

A **demand schedule** is a table that shows the quantities of a good or service demanded at different prices during a particular period, all other things unchanged. To introduce the concept of a demand schedule, let us consider the demand for coffee in the United States. We will ignore differences among types of coffee beans and roasts, and speak simply of coffee. The table in Figure 3.1 shows quantities of coffee that will be demanded each month at prices ranging from $9 to $4 per pound; the table is a demand schedule. We see that the higher the price, the lower the quantity demanded.

demand schedule

A table that shows the quantities of a good or service demanded at different prices during a particular period, all other things unchanged.

FIGURE 3.1 A Demand Schedule and a Demand Curve

The table is a demand schedule; it shows quantities of coffee demanded per month in the United States at particular prices, all other things unchanged. These data are then plotted on the demand curve. At point A on the curve, 25 million pounds of coffee per month are demanded at a price of $6 per pound. At point B, 30 million pounds of coffee per month are demanded at a price of $5 per pound.

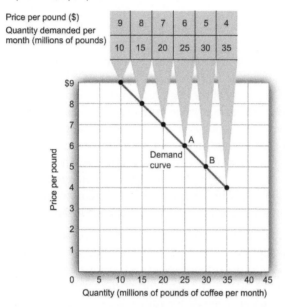

The information given in a demand schedule can be presented with a **demand curve**, which is a graphical representation of a demand schedule. A demand curve thus shows the relationship between the price and quantity demanded of a good or service during a particular period, all other things unchanged. The demand curve in Figure 3.1 shows the prices and quantities of coffee demanded that are given in the demand schedule. At point A, for example, we see that 25 million pounds of coffee per month are demanded at a price of $6 per pound. By convention, economists graph price on the vertical axis and quantity on the horizontal axis.

demand curve

A graphical representation of a demand schedule.

Price alone does not determine the quantity of coffee or any other good that people buy. To isolate the effect of changes in price on the quantity of a good or service demanded, however, we show the quantity demanded at each price, assuming that those other variables remain unchanged. We do the same thing in drawing a graph of the relationship between any two variables; we assume that the values of other variables that may affect the variables shown in the graph (such as income or population) remain unchanged for the period under consideration.

A change in price, with no change in any of the other variables that affect demand, results in a movement *along* the demand curve. For example, if the price of coffee falls from $6 to $5 per pound, consumption rises from 25 million pounds to 30 million pounds per month. That is a movement from point A to point B along the demand curve in Figure 3.1. A movement along a demand curve that results from a change in price is called a **change in quantity demanded**. Note that a change in quantity demanded is not a change or shift in the demand curve; it is a movement *along* the demand curve.

change in quantity demanded

A movement along a demand curve that results from a change in price.

law of demand

For virtually all goods and services, a higher price leads to a reduction in quantity demanded and a lower price leads to an increase in quantity demanded.

The negative slope of the demand curve in Figure 3.1 suggests a key behavioral relationship in economics. All other things unchanged, the **law of demand** holds that, for virtually all goods and services, a higher price leads to a reduction in quantity demanded and a lower price leads to an increase in quantity demanded.

The law of demand is called a law because the results of countless studies are consistent with it. Undoubtedly, you have observed one manifestation of the law. When a store finds itself with an overstock of some item, such as running shoes or tomatoes, and needs to sell these items quickly, what does it do? It typically has a sale, expecting that a lower price will increase the quantity demanded. In general, we expect the law of demand to hold. Given the values of other variables that influence demand, a higher price reduces the quantity demanded. A lower price increases the quantity demanded. Demand curves, in short, slope downward.

Changes in Demand

change in demand

A shift in a demand curve.

Of course, price alone does not determine the quantity of a good or service that people consume. Coffee consumption, for example, will be affected by such variables as income and population. Preferences also play a role. The story at the beginning of the chapter illustrates how Starbucks "turned people on" to coffee. We also expect other prices to affect coffee consumption. People often eat doughnuts or bagels with their coffee, so a reduction in the price of doughnuts or bagels might induce people to drink more coffee. An alternative to coffee is tea, so a reduction in the price of tea might result in the consumption of more tea and less coffee. Thus, a change in any one of the variables held constant in constructing a demand schedule will change the quantities demanded at each price. The result will be a *shift* in the entire demand curve rather than a movement along the demand curve. A *shift* in a demand curve is called a **change in demand**.

Suppose, for example, that something happens to increase the quantity of coffee demanded at each price. Several events could produce such a change: an increase in incomes, an increase in population, or an increase in the price of tea would each be likely to increase the quantity of coffee demanded at each price. Any such change produces a new demand schedule. Figure 3.2 shows such a change in the demand schedule for coffee. We see that the quantity of coffee demanded per month is greater at each price than before. We show that graphically as a shift in the demand curve. The original curve, labeled D_1, shifts to the right to D_2. At a price of $6 per pound, for example, the quantity demanded rises from 25 million pounds per month (point A) to 35 million pounds per month (point A').

FIGURE 3.2 An Increase in Demand

An increase in the quantity of a good or service demanded at each price is shown as an increase in demand. Here, the original demand curve D_1 shifts to D_2. Point A on D_1 corresponds to a price of $6 per pound and a quantity demanded of 25 million pounds of coffee per month. On the new demand curve D_2, the quantity demanded at this price rises to 35 million pounds of coffee per month (point A').

Price	Old quantity demanded	New quantity demanded
$9	10	20
8	15	25
7	20	30
6	25	35
5	30	40
4	35	45

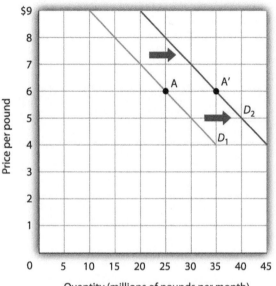

Just as demand can increase, it can decrease. In the case of coffee, demand might fall as a result of events such as a reduction in population, a reduction in the price of tea, or a change in preferences. For example, a definitive finding that the caffeine in coffee contributes to heart disease, which is currently being debated in the scientific community, could change preferences and reduce the demand for coffee.

A reduction in the demand for coffee is illustrated in Figure 3.3. The demand schedule shows that less coffee is demanded at each price than in Figure 3.1. The result is a shift in demand from the original curve D_1 to D_3. The quantity of coffee demanded at a price of $6 per pound falls from 25 million pounds per month (point A) to 15 million pounds per month (point A″). Note, again, that a change in quantity demanded, ceteris paribus, refers to a movement *along* the demand curve, while a change in demand refers to a *shift* in the demand curve.

FIGURE 3.3 A Reduction in Demand

A reduction in demand occurs when the quantities of a good or service demanded fall at each price. Here, the demand schedule shows a lower quantity of coffee demanded at each price than we had in Figure 3.1. The reduction shifts the demand curve for coffee to D_3 from D_1. The quantity demanded at a price of $6 per pound, for example, falls from 25 million pounds per month (point A) to 15 million pounds of coffee per month (point A″).

Price	Old quantity demanded	New quantity demanded
$9	10	0
8	15	5
7	20	10
6	25	15
5	30	20
4	35	25

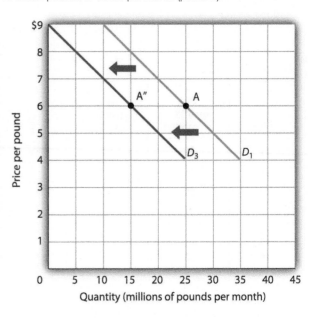

demand shifter

A variable that can change the quantity of a good or service demanded at each price.

A variable that can change the quantity of a good or service demanded at each price is called a **demand shifter**. When these other variables change, the all-other-things-unchanged conditions behind the original demand curve no longer hold. Although different goods and services will have different demand shifters, the demand shifters are likely to include (1) consumer preferences, (2) the prices of related goods and services, (3) income, (4) demographic characteristics, and (5) buyer expectations. Next we look at each of these.

Preferences

Changes in preferences of buyers can have important consequences for demand. We have already seen how Starbucks supposedly increased the demand for coffee. Another example is reduced demand for cigarettes caused by concern about the effect of smoking on health. A change in preferences that makes one good or service more popular will shift the demand curve to the right. A change that makes it less popular will shift the demand curve to the left.

Prices of Related Goods and Services

Suppose the price of doughnuts were to fall. Many people who drink coffee enjoy dunking doughnuts in their coffee; the lower price of doughnuts might therefore increase the demand for coffee, shifting the demand curve for coffee to the right. A lower price for tea, however, would be likely to reduce coffee demand, shifting the demand curve for coffee to the left.

In general, if a reduction in the price of one good increases the demand for another, the two goods are called **complements**. If a reduction in the price of one good reduces the demand for another, the two goods are called **substitutes**. These definitions hold in reverse as well: two goods are complements if an increase in the price of one reduces the demand for the other, and they are substitutes if an increase in the price of one increases the demand for the other. Doughnuts and coffee are complements; tea and coffee are substitutes.

Complementary goods are goods used in conjunction with one another. Tennis rackets and tennis balls, eggs and bacon, and stationery and postage stamps are complementary goods. Substitute goods are goods used instead of one another. iPODs, for example, are likely to be substitutes for CD players. Breakfast cereal is a substitute for eggs. A file attachment to an e-mail is a substitute for both a fax machine and postage stamps.

complements
Two goods for which an increase in price of one reduces the demand for the other.

substitutes
Two goods for which an increase in price of one increases the demand for the other.

Complements (coffee and doughnuts)	
↓ *Reducing* the price of one...	↑ *increases* the demand for the other.
↑ *Increasing* the price of one...	↓ *reduces* the demand for the other.
Substitutes (coffee and tea)	
↑ *Increasing* the price of one...	↑ *increases* the demand for the other.
↓ *Reducing* the price of one...	↓ *reduces* the demand for the other.

Income

As incomes rise, people increase their consumption of many goods and services, and as incomes fall, their consumption of these goods and services falls. For example, an increase in income is likely to raise the demand for gasoline, ski trips, new cars, and jewelry. There are, however, goods and services for which consumption falls as income rises—and rises as income falls. As incomes rise, for example, people tend to consume more fresh fruit but less canned fruit.

A good for which demand increases when income increases is called a **normal good**. A good for which demand decreases when income increases is called an **inferior good**. An increase in income shifts the demand curve for fresh fruit (a normal good) to the right; it shifts the demand curve for canned fruit (an inferior good) to the left.

normal good
A good for which demand increases when income increases.

inferior good
A good for which demand decreases when income increases.

Demographic Characteristics

The number of buyers affects the total quantity of a good or service that will be bought; in general, the greater the population, the greater the demand. Other demographic characteristics can affect demand as well. As the share of the population over age 65 increases, the demand for medical services, ocean cruises, and motor homes increases. The birth rate in the United States fell sharply between 1955 and 1975 but has gradually increased since then. That increase has raised the demand for such things as infant supplies, elementary school teachers, soccer coaches, in-line skates, and college education. Demand can thus shift as a result of changes in both the number and characteristics of buyers.

Buyer Expectations

The consumption of goods that can be easily stored, or whose consumption can be postponed, is strongly affected by buyer expectations. The expectation of newer TV technologies, such as high-definition TV, could slow down sales of regular TVs. If people expect gasoline prices to rise tomorrow, they will fill up their tanks today to try to beat the price increase. The same will be true for goods such as automobiles and washing machines: an expectation of higher prices in the future will lead to more purchases today. If the price of a good is expected to fall, however, people are likely to reduce their purchases today and await tomorrow's lower prices. The expectation that computer prices will fall, for example, can reduce current demand.

Heads Up!

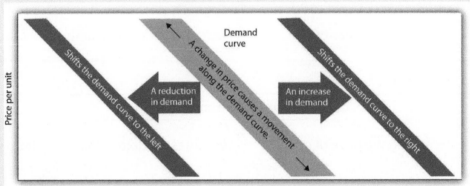

It is crucial to distinguish between a change in quantity demanded, which is a movement along the demand curve caused by a change in price, and a change in demand, which implies a shift of the demand curve itself. A change in demand is caused by a change in a demand shifter. An increase in demand is a shift of the demand curve to the right. A decrease in demand is a shift in the demand curve to the left. This drawing of a demand curve highlights the difference.

Key Takeaways

- The quantity demanded of a good or service is the quantity buyers are willing and able to buy at a particular price during a particular period, all other things unchanged.
- A demand schedule is a table that shows the quantities of a good or service demanded at different prices during a particular period, all other things unchanged.
- A demand curve shows graphically the quantities of a good or service demanded at different prices during a particular period, all other things unchanged.
- All other things unchanged, the law of demand holds that, for virtually all goods and services, a higher price induces a reduction in quantity demanded and a lower price induces an increase in quantity demanded.
- A change in the price of a good or service causes a change in the quantity demanded—a movement *along* the demand curve.
- A change in a demand shifter causes a change in demand, which is shown as a *shift* of the demand curve. Demand shifters include preferences, the prices of related goods and services, income, demographic characteristics, and buyer expectations.

- Two goods are substitutes if an increase in the price of one causes an increase in the demand for the other. Two goods are complements if an increase in the price of one causes a decrease in the demand for the other.

- A good is a normal good if an increase in income causes an increase in demand. A good is an inferior good if an increase in income causes a decrease in demand.

Try It!

All other things unchanged, what happens to the demand curve for DVD rentals if there is (a) an increase in the price of movie theater tickets, (b) a decrease in family income, or (c) an increase in the price of DVD rentals? In answering this and other "Try It!" problems in this chapter, draw and carefully label a set of axes. On the horizontal axis of your graph, show the quantity of DVD rentals. It is necessary to specify the time period to which your quantity pertains (e.g., "per period," "per week," or "per year"). On the vertical axis show the price per DVD rental. Since you do not have specific data on prices and quantities demanded, make a "free-hand" drawing of the curve or curves you are asked to examine. Focus on the general shape and position of the curve(s) before and after events occur. Draw new curve(s) to show what happens in each of the circumstances given. The curves could shift to the left or to the right, or stay where they are.

Case in Point: Solving Campus Parking Problems Without Adding More Parking Spaces

Source: © 2010 Jupiterimages Corporation

Unless you attend a "virtual" campus, chances are you have engaged in more than one conversation about how hard it is to find a place to park on campus. Indeed, according to Clark Kerr, a former president of the University of California system, a university is best understood as a group of people "held together by a common grievance over parking."

Clearly, the demand for campus parking spaces has grown substantially over the past few decades. In surveys conducted by Daniel Kenney, Ricardo Dumont, and Ginger Kenney, who work for the campus design company Sasaki and Associates, it was found that 7 out of 10 students own their own cars. They have interviewed "many students who confessed to driving from their dormitories to classes that were a five-minute walk away," and they argue that the deterioration of college environments is largely attributable to the increased use of cars on campus and that colleges could better service their missions by not adding more parking spaces.

Since few universities charge enough for parking to even cover the cost of building and maintaining parking lots, the rest is paid for by all students as part of tuition. Their research shows that "for every 1,000 parking spaces, the median institution loses almost $400,000 a year for surface parking, and more than $1,200,000 for structural parking." Fear of a backlash from students and their parents, as well as from faculty and staff, seems to explain why campus administrators do not simply raise the price of parking on campus.

While Kenney and his colleagues do advocate raising parking fees, if not all at once then over time, they also suggest some subtler, and perhaps politically more palatable, measures—in particular, shifting the demand for parking spaces to the left by lowering the prices of substitutes.

Two examples they noted were at the University of Washington and the University of Colorado at Boulder. At the University of Washington, car poolers may park for free. This innovation has reduced purchases of single-occupancy parking permits by 32% over a decade. According to University of Washington assistant director of transportation services Peter Dewey, "Without vigorously managing our parking and providing commuter alternatives, the university would have been faced with adding approximately 3,600 parking spaces, at a cost of over $100 million…The university has created opportunities to make capital investments in buildings supporting education instead of structures for cars." At the University of Colorado, free public transit has increased use of buses and light rail from 300,000 to 2 million trips per year over the last decade. The increased use of mass transit has allowed the university to avoid constructing nearly 2,000 parking spaces, which has saved about $3.6 million annually.

Sources: Based on Daniel R. Kenney, "How to Solve Campus Parking Problems Without Adding More Parking," The Chronicle of Higher Education, March 26, 2004, Section B, pp. B22-B23.

Answer to Try It! Problem

Since going to the movies is a substitute for watching a DVD at home, an increase in the price of going to the movies should cause more people to switch from going to the movies to staying at home and renting DVDs. Thus, the demand curve for DVD rentals will shift to the right when the price of movie theater tickets increases [Panel (a)].

A decrease in family income will cause the demand curve to shift to the left if DVD rentals are a normal good but to the right if DVD rentals are an inferior good. The latter may be the case for some families, since staying at home and watching DVDs is a cheaper form of entertainment than taking the family to the movies. For most others, however, DVD rentals are probably a normal good [Panel (b)].

An increase in the price of DVD rentals does not shift the demand curve for DVD rentals at all; rather, an increase in price, say from P_1 to P_2, is a movement upward to the left along the demand curve. At a higher price, people will rent fewer DVDs, say Q_2 instead of Q_1, ceteris paribus [Panel (c)].

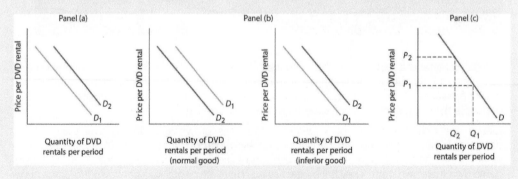

3.3 Supply

Learning Objectives

1. Define the quantity supplied of a good or service and illustrate it using a supply schedule and a supply curve.
2. Distinguish between the following pairs of concepts: supply and quantity supplied, supply schedule and supply curve, movement along and shift in a supply curve.
3. Identify supply shifters and determine whether a change in a supply shifter causes the supply curve to shift to the right or to the left.

What determines the quantity of a good or service sellers are willing to offer for sale? Price is one factor; ceteris paribus, a higher price is likely to induce sellers to offer a greater quantity of a good or service. Production cost is another determinant of supply. Variables that affect production cost include the prices of factors used to produce the good or service, returns from alternative activities, technology, the expectations of sellers, and natural events such as weather changes. Still another factor affecting the quantity of a good that will be offered for sale is the number of sellers—the greater the number of sellers of a particular good or service, the greater will be the quantity offered at any price per time period.

Price and the Supply Curve

The **quantity supplied** of a good or service is the quantity sellers are willing to sell at a particular price during a particular period, all other things unchanged. Ceteris paribus, the receipt of a higher price increases profits and induces sellers to increase the quantity they supply.

In general, when there are many sellers of a good, an increase in price results in an increase in quantity supplied, and this relationship is often referred to as the law of supply. We will see, though, through our exploration of microeconomics, that there are a number of exceptions to this relationship. There are cases in which a higher price will not induce an increase in quantity supplied. Goods that cannot be produced, such as additional land on the corner of Park Avenue and 56th Street in Manhattan, are fixed in supply—a higher price cannot induce an increase in the quantity supplied. There are even cases, which we investigate in microeconomic analysis, in which a higher price induces a reduction in the quantity supplied.

Generally speaking, however, when there are many sellers of a good, an increase in price results in a greater quantity supplied. The relationship between price and quantity supplied is suggested in a **supply schedule**, a table that shows quantities supplied at different prices during a particular period, all other things unchanged. Figure 3.4 gives a supply schedule for the quantities of coffee that will be supplied per month at various prices, ceteris paribus. At a price of $4 per pound, for example, producers are willing to supply 15 million pounds of coffee per month. A higher price, say $6 per pound, induces sellers to supply a greater quantity—25 million pounds of coffee per month.

quantity supplied

The quantity sellers are willing to sell of a good or service at a particular price during a particular period, all other things unchanged.

supply schedule

A table that shows quantities supplied at different prices during a particular period, all other things unchanged.

FIGURE 3.4 A Supply Schedule and a Supply Curve

The supply schedule shows the quantity of coffee that will be supplied in the United States each month at particular prices, all other things unchanged. The same information is given graphically in the supply curve. The values given here suggest a positive relationship between price and quantity supplied.

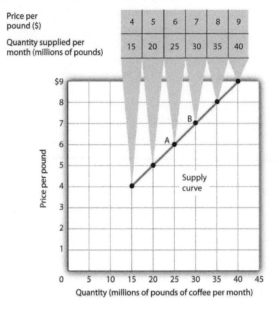

Price per pound ($)	4	5	6	7	8	9
Quantity supplied per month (millions of pounds)	15	20	25	30	35	40

supply curve

A graphical representation of a supply schedule.

A **supply curve** is a graphical representation of a supply schedule. It shows the relationship between price and quantity supplied during a particular period, all other things unchanged. Because the relationship between price and quantity supplied is generally positive, supply curves are generally upward sloping. The supply curve for coffee in Figure 3.4 shows graphically the values given in the supply schedule.

change in quantity supplied

Movement along the supply curve caused by a change in price.

A change in price causes a movement *along* the supply curve; such a movement is called a **change in quantity supplied**. As is the case with a change in quantity demanded, a change in quantity supplied does not shift the supply curve. By definition, it is a movement along the supply curve. For example, if the price rises from $6 per pound to $7 per pound, the quantity supplied rises from 25 million pounds per month to 30 million pounds per month. That's a movement from point A to point B along the supply curve in Figure 3.4.

Changes in Supply

change in supply

A shift in the supply curve.

When we draw a supply curve, we assume that other variables that affect the willingness of sellers to supply a good or service are unchanged. It follows that a change in any of those variables will cause a **change in supply**, which is a shift in the supply curve. A change that increases the quantity of a good or service supplied at each price shifts the supply curve to the right. Suppose, for example, that the price of fertilizer falls. That will reduce the cost of producing coffee and thus increase the quantity of coffee producers will offer for sale at each price. The supply schedule in Figure 3.5 shows an increase in the quantity of coffee supplied at each price. We show that increase graphically as a shift in the supply curve from S_1 to S_2. We see that the quantity supplied at each price increases by 10 million pounds of coffee per month. At point A on the original supply curve S_1, for example, 25 million pounds of coffee per month are supplied at a price of $6 per pound. After the increase in supply, 35 million pounds per month are supplied at the same price (point A′ on curve S_2).

FIGURE 3.5 An Increase in Supply

If there is a change in supply that increases the quantity supplied at each price, as is the case in the supply schedule here, the supply curve shifts to the right. At a price of $6 per pound, for example, the quantity supplied rises from the previous level of 25 million pounds per month on supply curve S_1 (point A) to 35 million pounds per month on supply curve S_2 (point A′).

Price	Old quantity supplied	New quantity supplied
$4	15	25
5	20	30
6	25	35
7	30	40
8	35	45
9	40	50

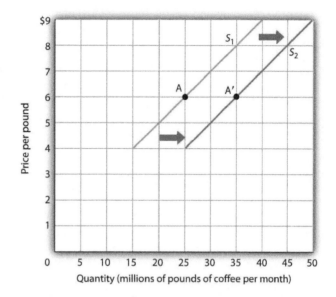

An event that reduces the quantity supplied at each price shifts the supply curve to the left. An increase in production costs and excessive rain that reduces the yields from coffee plants are examples of events that might reduce supply. Figure 3.6 shows a reduction in the supply of coffee. We see in the supply schedule that the quantity of coffee supplied falls by 10 million pounds of coffee per month at each price. The supply curve thus shifts from S_1 to S_3.

FIGURE 3.6 A Reduction in Supply

A change in supply that reduces the quantity supplied at each price shifts the supply curve to the left. At a price of $6 per pound, for example, the original quantity supplied was 25 million pounds of coffee per month (point A). With a new supply curve S_3, the quantity supplied at that price falls to 15 million pounds of coffee per month (point A″).

Price	Old quantity supplied	New quantity supplied
$4	15	5
5	20	10
6	25	15
7	30	20
8	35	25
9	40	30

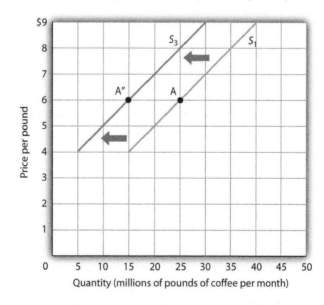

A variable that can change the quantity of a good or service supplied at each price is called a **supply shifter**. Supply shifters include (1) prices of factors of production, (2) returns from alternative activities, (3) technology, (4) seller expectations, (5) natural events, and (6) the number of sellers. When these other variables change, the all-other-things-unchanged conditions behind the original supply curve no longer hold. Let us look at each of the supply shifters.

supply shifter

A variable that can change the quantity of a good or service supplied at each price.

Prices of Factors of Production

A change in the price of labor or some other factor of production will change the cost of producing any given quantity of the good or service. This change in the cost of production will change the quantity that suppliers are willing to offer at any price. An increase in factor prices should decrease the quantity suppliers will offer at any price, shifting the supply curve to the left. A reduction in factor prices increases the quantity suppliers will offer at any price, shifting the supply curve to the right.

Suppose coffee growers must pay a higher wage to the workers they hire to harvest coffee or must pay more for fertilizer. Such increases in production cost will cause them to produce a smaller quantity at each price, shifting the supply curve for coffee to the left. A reduction in any of these costs increases supply, shifting the supply curve to the right.

Returns from Alternative Activities

To produce one good or service means forgoing the production of another. The concept of opportunity cost in economics suggests that the value of the activity forgone is the opportunity cost of the activity chosen; this cost should affect supply. For example, one opportunity cost of producing eggs is not selling chickens. An increase in the price people are willing to pay for fresh chicken would make it more profitable to sell chickens and would thus increase the opportunity cost of producing eggs. It would shift the supply curve for eggs to the left, reflecting a decrease in supply.

Technology

A change in technology alters the combinations of inputs or the types of inputs required in the production process. An improvement in technology usually means that fewer and/or less costly inputs are needed. If the cost of production is lower, the profits available at a given price will increase, and producers will produce more. With more produced at every price, the supply curve will shift to the right, meaning an increase in supply.

Impressive technological changes have occurred in the computer industry in recent years. Computers are much smaller and are far more powerful than they were only a few years ago—and they are much cheaper to produce. The result has been a huge increase in the supply of computers, shifting the supply curve to the right.

While we usually think of technology as enhancing production, declines in production due to problems in technology are also possible. Outlawing the use of certain equipment without pollution-control devices has increased the cost of production for many goods and services, thereby reducing profits available at any price and shifting these supply curves to the left.

Seller Expectations

All supply curves are based in part on seller expectations about future market conditions. Many decisions about production and selling are typically made long before a product is ready for sale. Those decisions necessarily depend on expectations. Changes in seller expectations can have important effects on price and quantity.

Consider, for example, the owners of oil deposits. Oil pumped out of the ground and used today will be unavailable in the future. If a change in the international political climate leads many owners to expect that oil prices will rise in the future, they may decide to leave their oil in the ground, planning to sell it later when the price is higher. Thus, there will be a decrease in supply; the supply curve for oil will shift to the left.

Natural Events

Storms, insect infestations, and drought affect agricultural production and thus the supply of agricultural goods. If something destroys a substantial part of an agricultural crop, the supply curve will shift to the left. The terrible cyclone that killed more than 50,000 people in Myanmar in 2008 also destroyed some of the country's prime rice growing land. That shifted the supply curve for rice to the left. If there is an unusually good harvest, the supply curve will shift to the right.

The Number of Sellers

The supply curve for an industry, such as coffee, includes all the sellers in the industry. A change in the number of sellers in an industry changes the quantity available at each price and thus changes supply. An increase in the number of sellers supplying a good or service shifts the supply curve to the right; a reduction in the number of sellers shifts the supply curve to the left.

The market for cellular phone service has been affected by an increase in the number of firms offering the service. Over the past decade, new cellular phone companies emerged, shifting the supply curve for cellular phone service to the right.

Heads Up!

There are two special things to note about supply curves. The first is similar to the Heads Up! on demand curves: it is important to distinguish carefully between changes in supply and changes in quantity supplied. A change in supply results from a change in a supply shifter and implies a shift of the supply curve to the right or left. A change in price produces a change in quantity supplied and induces a movement along the supply curve. A change in price does not shift the supply curve.

The second caution relates to the interpretation of increases and decreases in supply. Notice that in Figure 3.5 an increase in supply is shown as a shift of the supply curve to the right; the curve shifts in the direction of increasing quantity with respect to the horizontal axis. In Figure 3.6 a reduction in supply is shown as a shift of the supply curve to the left; the curve shifts in the direction of decreasing quantity with respect to the horizontal axis.

Because the supply curve is upward sloping, a shift to the right produces a new curve that in a sense lies "below" the original curve. It is easy to make the mistake of thinking of such a shift as a shift "down" and therefore as a reduction in supply. Similarly, it is easy to make the mistake of showing an increase in supply with a new curve that lies "above" the original curve. But that is a reduction in supply!

To avoid such errors, focus on the fact that an increase in supply is an increase in the quantity supplied at each price and shifts the supply curve in the direction of increased quantity on the horizontal axis. Similarly, a reduction in supply is a reduction in the quantity supplied at each price and shifts the supply curve in the direction of a lower quantity on the horizontal axis.

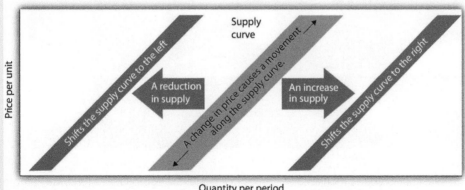

Key Takeaways

- The quantity supplied of a good or service is the quantity sellers are willing to sell at a particular price during a particular period, all other things unchanged.
- A supply schedule shows the quantities supplied at different prices during a particular period, all other things unchanged. A supply curve shows this same information graphically.
- A change in the price of a good or service causes a change in the quantity supplied—a movement *along* the supply curve.
- A change in a supply shifter causes a change in supply, which is shown as a *shift* of the supply curve. Supply shifters include prices of factors of production, returns from alternative activities, technology, seller expectations, natural events, and the number of sellers.
- An increase in supply is shown as a shift to the right of a supply curve; a decrease in supply is shown as a shift to the left.

Try It!

If all other things are unchanged, what happens to the supply curve for DVD rentals if there is (a) an increase in wages paid to DVD rental store clerks, (b) an increase in the price of DVD rentals, or (c) an increase in the number of DVD rental stores? Draw a graph that shows what happens to the supply curve in each circumstance. The supply curve can shift to the left or to the right, or stay where it is. Remember to label the axes and curves, and remember to specify the time period (e.g., "DVDs rented per week").

Case in Point: The Monks of St. Benedict's Get Out of the Egg Business

Source: © 2010 Jupiterimages Corporation

It was cookies that lured the monks of St. Benedict's out of the egg business, and now private retreat sponsorship is luring them away from cookies.

St. Benedict's is a Benedictine monastery, nestled on a ranch high in the Colorado Rockies, about 20 miles down the road from Aspen. The monastery's 20 monks operate the ranch to support themselves and to provide help for poor people in the area. They lease out about 3,500 acres of their land to cattle and sheep grazers, produce cookies, and sponsor private retreats. They used to produce eggs.

Attracted by potential profits and the peaceful nature of the work, the monks went into the egg business in 1967. They had 10,000 chickens producing their Monastery Eggs brand. For a while, business was good. Very good. Then, in the late 1970s, the price of chicken feed started to rise rapidly.

"When we started in the business, we were paying $60 to $80 a ton for feed—delivered," recalls the monastery's abbot, Father Joseph Boyle. "By the late 1970s, our cost had more than doubled. We were paying $160 to $200 a ton. That really hurt, because feed represents a large part of the cost of producing eggs."

The monks adjusted to the blow. "When grain prices were lower, we'd pull a hen off for a few weeks to molt, then return her to laying. After grain prices went up, it was 12 months of laying and into the soup pot," Fr. Joseph says.

Grain prices continued to rise in the 1980s and increased the costs of production for all egg producers. It caused the supply of eggs to fall. Demand fell at the same time, as Americans worried about the cholesterol in eggs. Times got tougher in the egg business.

"We were still making money in the financial sense," Fr. Joseph says. "But we tried an experiment in 1985 producing cookies, and it was a success. We finally decided that devoting our time and energy to the cookies would pay off better than the egg business, so we quit the egg business in 1986."

The mail-order cookie business was good to the monks. They sold 200,000 ounces of Monastery Cookies in 1987.

By 1998, however, they had limited their production of cookies, selling only locally and to gift shops. Since 2000, they have switched to "providing private retreats for individuals and groups—about 40 people per month," according to Fr. Micah Schonberger.

The monks' calculation of their opportunity costs revealed that they would earn a higher return through sponsorship of private retreats than in either cookies or eggs. This projection has proved correct.

And there is another advantage as well.

"The chickens didn't stop laying eggs on Sunday," Fr. Joseph chuckles. "When we shifted to cookies we could take Sundays off. We weren't hemmed in the way we were with the chickens." The move to providing retreats is even better in this regard. Since guests provide their own meals, most of the monastery's effort goes into planning and scheduling, which frees up even more of their time for other worldly as well as spiritual pursuits.

Source: Based on personal interviews and the monastery's website at http://www.snowmass. org.

Answer to Try It! Problem

DVD rental store clerks are a factor of production in the DVD rental market. An increase in their wages raises the cost of production, thereby causing the supply curve of DVD rentals to shift to the left [Panel (a)]. (*Caution*: It is possible that you thought of the wage increase as an increase in income, a demand shifter, that would lead to an increase in demand, but this would be incorrect. The question refers only to wages of DVD rental store clerks. They may rent some DVD, but their impact on total demand would be negligible. Besides, we have no information on what has happened overall to incomes of people who rent DVDs. We do know, however, that the cost of a factor of production, which is a supply shifter, increased.)

An increase in the price of DVD rentals does not shift the supply curve at all; rather, it corresponds to a movement upward to the right along the supply curve. At a higher price of P_2 instead of P_1, a greater quantity of DVD rentals, say Q_2 instead of Q_1, will be supplied [Panel (b)].

An increase in the number of stores renting DVDs will cause the supply curve to shift to the right [Panel (c)].

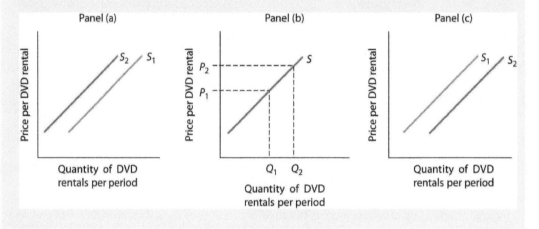

3.4 Demand, Supply, and Equilibrium

Learning Objectives

1. Use demand and supply to explain how equilibrium price and quantity are determined in a market.
2. Understand the concepts of surpluses and shortages and the pressures on price they generate.
3. Explain the impact of a change in demand or supply on equilibrium price and quantity.
4. Explain how the circular flow model provides an overview of demand and supply in product and factor markets and how the model suggests ways in which these markets are linked.

model of demand and supply

Model that uses demand and supply curves to explain the determination of price and quantity in a market.

In this section we combine the demand and supply curves we have just studied into a new model. The **model of demand and supply** uses demand and supply curves to explain the determination of price and quantity in a market.

The Determination of Price and Quantity

The logic of the model of demand and supply is simple. The demand curve shows the quantities of a particular good or service that buyers will be willing and able to purchase at each price during a specified period. The supply curve shows the quantities that sellers will offer for sale at each price during that same period. By putting the two curves together, we should be able to find a price at which the quantity buyers are willing and able to purchase equals the quantity sellers will offer for sale.

Figure 3.7 combines the demand and supply data introduced in Figure 3.1 and Figure 3.4 Notice that the two curves intersect at a price of $6 per pound—at this price the quantities demanded and supplied are equal. Buyers want to purchase, and sellers are willing to offer for sale, 25 million pounds of coffee per month. The market for coffee is in equilibrium. Unless the demand or supply curve shifts, there will be no tendency for price to change. The **equilibrium price** in any market is the price at which quantity demanded equals quantity supplied. The equilibrium price in the market for coffee is thus $6 per pound. The **equilibrium quantity** is the quantity demanded and supplied at the equilibrium price. At a price above the equilibrium, there is a natural tendency for the price to fall. At a price below the equilibrium, there is a tendency for the price to rise.

> **equilibrium price**
>
> The price at which quantity demanded equals quantity supplied.
>
> **equilibrium quantity**
>
> The quantity demanded and supplied at the equilibrium price.

FIGURE 3.7 The Determination of Equilibrium Price and Quantity
When we combine the demand and supply curves for a good in a single graph, the point at which they intersect identifies the equilibrium price and equilibrium quantity. Here, the equilibrium price is $6 per pound. Consumers demand, and suppliers supply, 25 million pounds of coffee per month at this price.

With an upward-sloping supply curve and a downward-sloping demand curve, there is only a single price at which the two curves intersect. This means there is only one price at which equilibrium is achieved. It follows that at any price other than the equilibrium price, the market will not be in equilibrium. We next examine what happens at prices other than the equilibrium price.

Surpluses

Figure 3.8 shows the same demand and supply curves we have just examined, but this time the initial price is $8 per pound of coffee. Because we no longer have a balance between quantity demanded and quantity supplied, this price is not the equilibrium price. At a price of $8, we read over to the demand curve to determine the quantity of coffee consumers will be willing to buy—15 million pounds per month. The supply curve tells us what sellers will offer for sale—35 million pounds per month. The difference, 20 million pounds of coffee per month, is called a surplus. More

> **surplus**
>
> The amount by which the quantity supplied exceeds the quantity demanded at the current price.

generally, a **surplus** is the amount by which the quantity supplied exceeds the quantity demanded at the current price. There is, of course, no surplus at the equilibrium price; a surplus occurs only if the current price exceeds the equilibrium price.

FIGURE 3.8 A Surplus in the Market for Coffee
At a price of $8, the quantity supplied is 35 million pounds of coffee per month and the quantity demanded is 15 million pounds per month; there is a surplus of 20 million pounds of coffee per month. Given a surplus, the price will fall quickly toward the equilibrium level of $6.

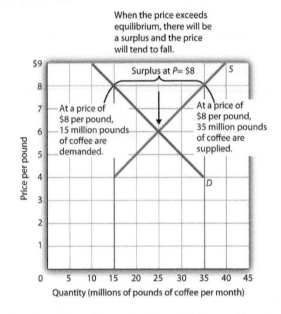

A surplus in the market for coffee will not last long. With unsold coffee on the market, sellers will begin to reduce their prices to clear out unsold coffee. As the price of coffee begins to fall, the quantity of coffee supplied begins to decline. At the same time, the quantity of coffee demanded begins to rise. Remember that the reduction in quantity supplied is a movement *along* the supply curve—the curve itself does not shift in response to a reduction in price. Similarly, the increase in quantity demanded is a movement *along* the demand curve—the demand curve does not shift in response to a reduction in price. Price will continue to fall until it reaches its equilibrium level, at which the demand and supply curves intersect. At that point, there will be no tendency for price to fall further. In general, surpluses in the marketplace are short-lived. The prices of most goods and services adjust quickly, eliminating the surplus. Later on, we will discuss some markets in which adjustment of price to equilibrium may occur only very slowly or not at all.

Shortages

shortage

The amount by which the quantity demanded exceeds the quantity supplied at the current price.

Just as a price above the equilibrium price will cause a surplus, a price below equilibrium will cause a shortage. A **shortage** is the amount by which the quantity demanded exceeds the quantity supplied at the current price.

Figure 3.9 shows a shortage in the market for coffee. Suppose the price is $4 per pound. At that price, 15 million pounds of coffee would be supplied per month, and 35 million pounds would be demanded per month. When more coffee is demanded than supplied, there is a shortage.

FIGURE 3.9 A Shortage in the Market for Coffee
At a price of $4 per pound, the quantity of coffee demanded is 35 million pounds per month and the quantity supplied is 15 million pounds per month. The result is a shortage of 20 million pounds of coffee per month.

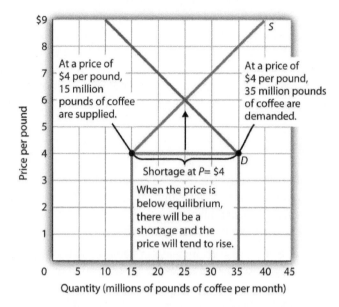

In the face of a shortage, sellers are likely to begin to raise their prices. As the price rises, there will be an increase in the quantity supplied (but not a change in supply) and a reduction in the quantity demanded (but not a change in demand) until the equilibrium price is achieved.

Shifts in Demand and Supply

FIGURE 3.10 Changes in Demand and Supply
A change in demand or in supply changes the equilibrium solution in the model. Panels (a) and (b) show an increase and a decrease in demand, respectively; Panels (c) and (d) show an increase and a decrease in supply, respectively.

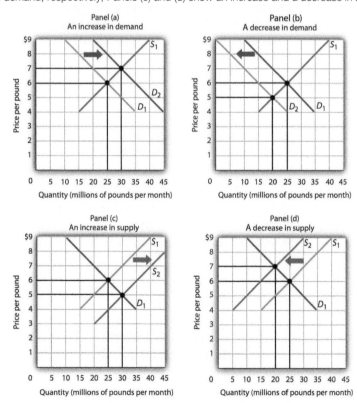

A change in one of the variables (shifters) held constant in any model of demand and supply will create a change in demand or supply. A shift in a demand or supply curve changes the equilibrium price and equilibrium quantity for a good or service. Figure 3.10 combines the information about changes in the demand and supply of coffee presented in Figure 3.2, Figure 3.3, Figure 3.5, and Figure 3.6. In each case, the original equilibrium price is $6 per pound, and the corresponding equilibrium quantity is 25 million pounds of coffee per month. Figure 3.10 shows what happens with an increase in demand, a reduction in demand, an increase in supply, and a reduction in supply. We then look at what happens if both curves shift simultaneously. Each of these possibilities is discussed in turn below.

An Increase in Demand

An increase in demand for coffee shifts the demand curve to the right, as shown in Panel (a) of Figure 3.10. The equilibrium price rises to $7 per pound. As the price rises to the new equilibrium level, the quantity supplied increases to 30 million pounds of coffee per month. Notice that the supply curve does not shift; rather, there is a movement along the supply curve.

Demand shifters that could cause an increase in demand include a shift in preferences that leads to greater coffee consumption; a lower price for a complement to coffee, such as doughnuts; a higher price for a substitute for coffee, such as tea; an increase in income; and an increase in population. A change in buyer expectations, perhaps due to predictions of bad weather lowering expected yields on coffee plants and increasing future coffee prices, could also increase current demand.

A Decrease in Demand

Panel (b) of Figure 3.10 shows that a decrease in demand shifts the demand curve to the left. The equilibrium price falls to $5 per pound. As the price falls to the new equilibrium level, the quantity supplied decreases to 20 million pounds of coffee per month.

Demand shifters that could reduce the demand for coffee include a shift in preferences that makes people want to consume less coffee; an increase in the price of a complement, such as doughnuts; a reduction in the price of a substitute, such as tea; a reduction in income; a reduction in population; and a change in buyer expectations that leads people to expect lower prices for coffee in the future.

An Increase in Supply

An increase in the supply of coffee shifts the supply curve to the right, as shown in Panel (c) of Figure 3.10. The equilibrium price falls to $5 per pound. As the price falls to the new equilibrium level, the quantity of coffee demanded increases to 30 million pounds of coffee per month. Notice that the demand curve does not shift; rather, there is movement along the demand curve.

Possible supply shifters that could increase supply include a reduction in the price of an input such as labor, a decline in the returns available from alternative uses of the inputs that produce coffee, an improvement in the technology of coffee production, good weather, and an increase in the number of coffee-producing firms.

A Decrease in Supply

Panel (d) of Figure 3.10 shows that a decrease in supply shifts the supply curve to the left. The equilibrium price rises to $7 per pound. As the price rises to the new equilibrium level, the quantity demanded decreases to 20 million pounds of coffee per month.

Possible supply shifters that could reduce supply include an increase in the prices of inputs used in the production of coffee, an increase in the returns available from alternative uses of these inputs, a decline in production because of problems in technology (perhaps caused by a restriction on pesticides used to protect coffee beans), a reduction in the number of coffee-producing firms, or a natural event, such as excessive rain.

Heads Up!

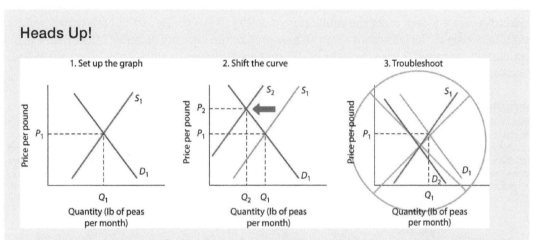

You are likely to be given problems in which you will have to shift a demand or supply curve.

Suppose you are told that an invasion of pod-crunching insects has gobbled up half the crop of fresh peas, and you are asked to use demand and supply analysis to predict what will happen to the price and quantity of peas demanded and supplied. Here are some suggestions.

Put the quantity of the good you are asked to analyze on the horizontal axis and its price on the vertical axis. Draw a downward-sloping line for demand and an upward-sloping line for supply. The initial equilibrium price is determined by the intersection of the two curves. Label the equilibrium solution. You may find it helpful to use a number for the equilibrium price instead of the letter "P." Pick a price that seems plausible, say, 79¢ per pound. Do not worry about the precise positions of the demand and supply curves; you cannot be expected to know what they are.

Step 2 can be the most difficult step; the problem is to decide which curve to shift. The key is to remember the difference between a change in demand or supply and a change in quantity demanded or supplied. At each price, ask yourself whether the given event would change the quantity demanded. Would the fact that a bug has attacked the pea crop change the quantity demanded at a price of, say, 79¢ per pound? Clearly not; none of the demand shifters have changed. The event would, however, reduce the quantity supplied at this price, and the supply curve would shift to the left. There is a change in supply and a reduction in the quantity demanded. There is no change in demand.

Next check to see whether the result you have obtained makes sense. The graph in Step 2 makes sense; it shows price rising and quantity demanded falling.

It is easy to make a mistake such as the one shown in the third figure of this Heads Up! One might, for example, reason that when fewer peas are available, fewer will be demanded, and therefore the demand curve will shift to the left. This suggests the price of peas will fall—but that does not make sense. If only half as many fresh peas were available, their price would surely rise. The error here lies in confusing a change in quantity demanded with a change in demand. Yes, buyers will end up buying fewer peas. But no, they will not demand fewer peas at each price than before; the demand curve does not shift.

Simultaneous Shifts

As we have seen, when *either* the demand or the supply curve shifts, the results are unambiguous; that is, we know what will happen to both equilibrium price and equilibrium quantity, so long as we know whether demand or supply increased or decreased. However, in practice, several events may occur at around the same time that cause *both* the demand and supply curves to shift. To figure out what happens to equilibrium price and equilibrium quantity, we must know not only in which direction the demand and supply curves have shifted but also the relative amount by which each curve shifts. Of course, the demand and supply curves could shift in the same direction or in opposite directions, depending on the specific events causing them to shift.

For example, all three panels of Figure 3.11 show a decrease in demand for coffee (caused perhaps by a decrease in the price of a substitute good, such as tea) and a simultaneous decrease in the supply of coffee (caused perhaps by bad weather). Since reductions in demand and supply, considered separately, each cause the equilibrium quantity to fall, the impact of both curves shifting simultaneously to the left means that the new equilibrium quantity of coffee is less than the old equilibrium quantity. The effect on the equilibrium price, though, is ambiguous. Whether the equilibrium price is higher, lower, or unchanged depends on the extent to which each curve shifts.

FIGURE 3.11 Simultaneous Decreases in Demand and Supply
Both the demand and the supply of coffee decrease. Since decreases in demand and supply, considered separately, each cause equilibrium quantity to fall, the impact of both decreasing simultaneously means that a new equilibrium quantity of coffee must be less than the old equilibrium quantity. In Panel (a), the demand curve shifts farther to the left than does the supply curve, so equilibrium price falls. In Panel (b), the supply curve shifts farther to the left than does the demand curve, so the equilibrium price rises. In Panel (c), both curves shift to the left by the same amount, so equilibrium price stays the same.

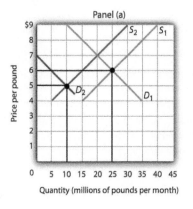

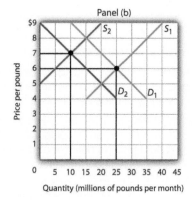

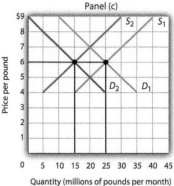

If the demand curve shifts farther to the left than does the supply curve, as shown in Panel (a) of Figure 3.11, then the equilibrium price will be lower than it was before the curves shifted. In this case the new equilibrium price falls from $6 per pound to $5 per pound. If the shift to the left of the supply curve is greater than that of the demand curve, the equilibrium price will be higher than it was before, as shown in Panel (b). In this case, the new equilibrium price rises to $7 per pound. In Panel (c), since both curves shift to the left by the same amount, equilibrium price does not change; it remains $6 per pound.

Regardless of the scenario, changes in equilibrium price and equilibrium quantity resulting from two different events need to be considered separately. If both events cause equilibrium price or quantity to move in the same direction, then clearly price or quantity can be expected to move in that direction. If one event causes price or quantity to rise while the other causes it to fall, the extent by which each curve shifts is critical to figuring out what happens. Figure 3.12 summarizes what may happen to equilibrium price and quantity when demand and supply both shift.

FIGURE 3.12 Simultaneous Shifts in Demand and Supply

If simultaneous shifts in demand and supply cause equilibrium price or quantity to move in the same direction, then equilibrium price or quantity clearly moves in that direction. If the shift in one of the curves causes equilibrium price or quantity to rise while the shift in the other curve causes equilibrium price or quantity to fall, then the relative amount by which each curve shifts is critical to figuring out what happens to that variable.

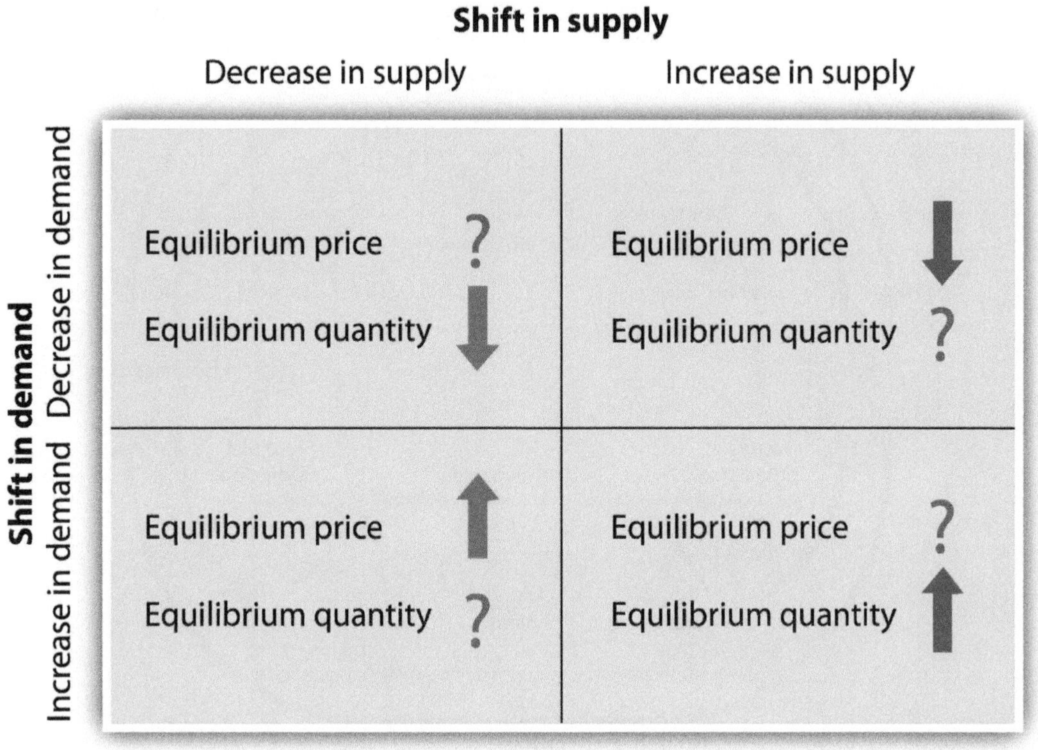

As demand and supply curves shift, prices adjust to maintain a balance between the quantity of a good demanded and the quantity supplied. If prices did not adjust, this balance could not be maintained.

Notice that the demand and supply curves that we have examined in this chapter have all been drawn as linear. This simplification of the real world makes the graphs a bit easier to read without sacrificing the essential point: whether the curves are linear or nonlinear, demand curves are downward sloping and supply curves are generally upward sloping. As circumstances that shift the demand curve or the supply curve change, we can analyze what will happen to price and what will happen to quantity.

An Overview of Demand and Supply: The Circular Flow Model

Implicit in the concepts of demand and supply is a constant interaction and adjustment that economists illustrate with the circular flow model. The **circular flow model** provides a look at how markets work and how they are related to each other. It shows flows of spending and income through the economy.

A great deal of economic activity can be thought of as a process of exchange between households and firms. Firms supply goods and services to households. Households buy these goods and services from firms. Households supply factors of production—labor, capital, and natural resources—that firms require. The payments firms make in exchange for these factors represent the incomes households earn.

The flow of goods and services, factors of production, and the payments they generate is illustrated in Figure 3.13. This circular flow model of the economy shows the interaction of households and firms as they exchange goods and services and factors of production. For simplicity, the model here shows only the private domestic economy; it omits the government and foreign sectors.

circular flow model

Model that provides a look at how markets work and how they are related to each other.

FIGURE 3.13 The Circular Flow of Economic Activity

This simplified circular flow model shows flows of spending between households and firms through product and factor markets. The inner arrows show goods and services flowing from firms to households and factors of production flowing from households to firms. The outer flows show the payments for goods, services, and factors of production. These flows, in turn, represent millions of individual markets for products and factors of production.

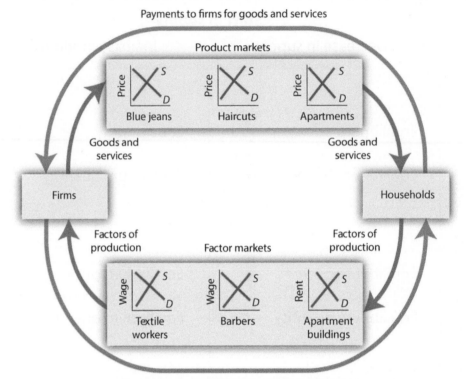

product markets

Markets in which firms supply goods and services demanded by households.

factor markets

Markets in which households supply factors of production—labor, capital, and natural resources—demanded by firms.

The circular flow model shows that goods and services that households demand are supplied by firms in **product markets**. The exchange for goods and services is shown in the top half of Figure 3.13. The bottom half of the exhibit illustrates the exchanges that take place in factor markets. **factor markets** are markets in which households supply factors of production—labor, capital, and natural resources—demanded by firms.

Our model is called a circular flow model because households use the income they receive from their supply of factors of production to buy goods and services from firms. Firms, in turn, use the payments they receive from households to pay for their factors of production.

The demand and supply model developed in this chapter gives us a basic tool for understanding what is happening in each of these product or factor markets and also allows us to see how these markets are interrelated. In Figure 3.13, markets for three goods and services that households want—blue jeans, haircuts, and apartments—create demands by firms for textile workers, barbers, and apartment buildings. The equilibrium of supply and demand in each market determines the price and quantity of that item. Moreover, a change in equilibrium in one market will affect equilibrium in related markets. For example, an increase in the demand for haircuts would lead to an increase in demand for barbers. Equilibrium price and quantity could rise in both markets. For some purposes, it will be adequate to simply look at a single market, whereas at other times we will want to look at what happens in related markets as well.

In either case, the model of demand and supply is one of the most widely used tools of economic analysis. That widespread use is no accident. The model yields results that are, in fact, broadly consistent with what we observe in the marketplace. Your mastery of this model will pay big dividends in your study of economics.

Key Takeaways

- The equilibrium price is the price at which the quantity demanded equals the quantity supplied. It is determined by the intersection of the demand and supply curves.
- A surplus exists if the quantity of a good or service supplied exceeds the quantity demanded at the current price; it causes downward pressure on price. A shortage exists if the quantity of a good or service demanded exceeds the quantity supplied at the current price; it causes upward pressure on price.
- An increase in demand, all other things unchanged, will cause the equilibrium price to rise; quantity supplied will increase. A decrease in demand will cause the equilibrium price to fall; quantity supplied will decrease.
- An increase in supply, all other things unchanged, will cause the equilibrium price to fall; quantity demanded will increase. A decrease in supply will cause the equilibrium price to rise; quantity demanded will decrease.
- To determine what happens to equilibrium price and equilibrium quantity when both the supply and demand curves shift, you must know in which direction each of the curves shifts and the extent to which each curve shifts.
- The circular flow model provides an overview of demand and supply in product and factor markets and suggests how these markets are linked to one another.

Try It!

What happens to the equilibrium price and the equilibrium quantity of DVD rentals if the price of movie theater tickets increases and wages paid to DVD rental store clerks increase, all other things unchanged? Be sure to show all possible scenarios, as was done in Figure 3.11. Again, you do not need actual numbers to arrive at an answer. Just focus on the general position of the curve(s) before and after events occurred.

Case in Point: Demand, Supply, and Obesity

Source: © 2010 Jupiterimages Corporation

Why are so many Americans fat? Put so crudely, the question may seem rude, but, indeed, the number of obese Americans has increased by more than 50% over the last generation, and obesity may now be the nation's number one health problem. According to Sturm Roland in a recent RAND Corporation study, "Obesity appears to have a stronger association with the occurrence of chronic medical conditions, reduced physical health-related quality of life and increased health care and medication expenditures than smoking or problem drinking."

Many explanations of rising obesity suggest higher demand for food. What more apt picture of our sedentary life style is there than spending the afternoon watching a ballgame on TV, while eating chips and salsa, followed by a dinner of a lavishly topped, take-out pizza? Higher income has also undoubtedly contributed to a rightward shift in the demand curve for food. Plus, any additional food intake translates into more weight increase because we spend so few calories preparing it, either directly or in the process of earning the income to buy it. A study by economists Darius Lakdawalla and Tomas Philipson suggests that about 60% of the recent growth in weight may be explained in this way—that is, demand has shifted to the right, leading to an increase in the equilibrium quantity of food consumed and, given our less strenuous life styles, even more weight gain than can be explained simply by the increased amount we are eating.

What accounts for the remaining 40% of the weight gain? Lakdawalla and Philipson further reason that a rightward shift in demand would by itself lead to an increase in the quantity of food as well as an increase in the price of food. The problem they have with this explanation is that over the post-World War II period, the relative price of food has declined by an average of 0.2 percentage points per year. They explain the fall in the price of food by arguing that agricultural innovation has led to a substantial rightward shift in the supply curve of food. As shown, lower food prices and a higher equilibrium quantity of food have resulted from simultaneous rightward shifts in demand and supply and that the rightward shift in the supply of food from S_1 to S_2 has been substantially larger than the rightward shift in the demand curve from D_1 to D_2.

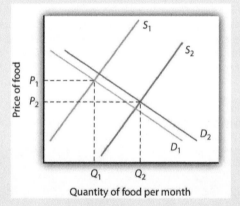

Sources: Based on Roland, Sturm, "The Effects of Obesity, Smoking, and Problem Drinking on Chronic Medical Problems and Health Care Costs," Health Affairs, 2002; 21(2): 245–253. Lakdawalla, Darius and Tomas Philipson, "The Growth of Obesity and Technological Change: A Theoretical and Empirical Examination," National Bureau of Economic Research Working Paper no. w8946, May 2002.

Answer to Try It! Problem

An increase in the price of movie theater tickets (a substitute for DVD rentals) will cause the demand curve for DVD rentals to shift to the right. An increase in the wages paid to DVD rental store clerks (an increase in the cost of a factor of production) shifts the supply curve to the left. Each event taken separately causes equilibrium price to rise. Whether equilibrium quantity will be higher or lower depends on which curve shifted more.

If the demand curve shifted more, then the equilibrium quantity of DVD rentals will rise [Panel (a)].

If the supply curve shifted more, then the equilibrium quantity of DVD rentals will fall [Panel (b)].

If the curves shifted by the same amount, then the equilibrium quantity of DVD rentals would not change [Panel (c)].

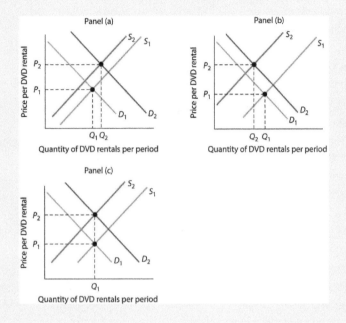

3.5 Review and Practice

Summary

In this chapter we have examined the model of demand and supply. We found that a demand curve shows the quantity demanded at each price, all other things unchanged. The law of demand asserts that an increase in price reduces the quantity demanded and a decrease in price increases the quantity demanded, all other things unchanged. The supply curve shows the quantity of a good or service that sellers will offer at various prices, all other things unchanged. Supply curves are generally upward sloping: an increase in price generally increases the quantity supplied, all other things unchanged.

The equilibrium price occurs where the demand and supply curves intersect. At this price, the quantity demanded equals the quantity supplied. A price higher than the equilibrium price increases the quantity supplied and reduces the quantity demanded, causing a surplus. A price lower than the equilibrium price increases the quantity demanded and reduces the quantity supplied, causing a shortage. Usually, market surpluses and shortages are short-lived. Changes in demand or supply, caused by changes in the determinants of demand and supply otherwise held constant in the analysis, change the equilibrium price and output. The circular flow model allows us to see how demand and supply in various markets are related to one another.

Concept Problems

1. What do you think happens to the demand for pizzas during the Super Bowl? Why?
2. Which of the following goods are likely to be classified as normal goods or services? Inferior? Defend your answer.
   a. Beans

b. Tuxedos

c. Used cars

d. Used clothing

e. Computers

f. Books reviewed in *The New York Times*

g. Macaroni and cheese

h. Calculators

i. Cigarettes

j. Caviar

k. Legal services

3. Which of the following pairs of goods are likely to be classified as substitutes? Complements? Defend your answer.

a. Peanut butter and jelly

b. Eggs and ham

c. Nike brand and Reebok brand sneakers

d. IBM and Apple Macintosh brand computers

e. Dress shirts and ties

f. Airline tickets and hotels

g. Gasoline and tires

h. Beer and wine

i. Faxes and first-class mail

j. Cereal and milk

k. Cereal and eggs

4. A study found that lower airfares led some people to substitute flying for driving to their vacation destinations. This reduced the demand for car travel and led to reduced traffic fatalities, since air travel is safer per passenger mile than car travel. Using the logic suggested by that study, suggest how each of the following events would affect the number of highway fatalities in any one year.

a. An increase in the price of gasoline

b. A large reduction in rental rates for passenger vans

c. An increase in airfares

5. Children under age 2 are now allowed to fly free on U.S. airlines; they usually sit in their parents' laps. Some safety advocates have urged that they be required to be strapped in infant seats, which would mean their parents would have to purchase tickets for them. Some economists have argued that such a measure would actually increase infant fatalities. Can you say why?

6. The graphs below show four possible shifts in demand or in supply that could occur in particular markets. Relate each of the events described below to one of them.

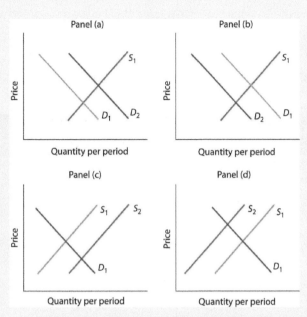

a. How did the heavy rains in South America in 1997 affect the market for coffee?

b. The Surgeon General decides french fries are not bad for your health after all and issues a report endorsing their use. What happens to the market for french fries?

c. How do you think rising incomes affect the market for ski vacations?

d. A new technique is discovered for manufacturing computers that greatly lowers their production cost. What happens to the market for computers?

e. How would a ban on smoking in public affect the market for cigarettes?

7. As low-carb diets increased in popularity, egg prices rose sharply. How might this affect the monks' supply of cookies or private retreats? (See the Case in Point on the Monks of St. Benedict's.)

8. Gasoline prices typically rise during the summer, a time of heavy tourist traffic. A "street talk" feature on a radio station sought tourist reaction to higher gasoline prices. Here was one response: "I don't like 'em [the higher prices] much. I think the gas companies just use any excuse to jack up prices, and they're doing it again now." How does this tourist's perspective differ from that of economists who use the model of demand and supply?

9. The introduction to the chapter argues that preferences for coffee changed in the 1990s and that excessive rain hurt yields from coffee plants. Show and explain the effects of these two circumstances on the coffee market.

10. With preferences for coffee remaining strong in the early part of the century, Vietnam entered the market as a major exporter of coffee. Show and explain the effects of these two circumstances on the coffee market.

11. The study on the economics of obesity discussed in the Case in Point in this chapter on that topic also noted that another factor behind rising obesity is the decline in cigarette smoking as the price of cigarettes has risen. Show and explain the effect of higher cigarette prices on the market for food. What does this finding imply about the relationship between cigarettes and food?

12. In 2004, *The New York Times* reported that India might be losing its outsourcing edge due to rising wages[1] The reporter noted that a recent report "projected that if India continued to produce college graduates at the current rate, demand would exceed supply by 20% in the main outsourcing markets by 2008." Using the terminology you learned in this chapter, explain what he meant to say was happening in the market for Indian workers in outsourcing jobs. In particular, is demand for Indian workers increasing or decreasing? Is the supply of Indian workers increasing or decreasing? Which is shifting faster? How do you know?

13. For more than a century, milk producers have produced skim milk, which contains virtually no fat, along with regular milk, which contains 4% fat. But a century ago, skim milk accounted for only about 1% of total production, and much of it was fed to hogs. Today, skim and other

reduced-fat milks make up the bulk of milk sales. What curve shifted, and what factor shifted it?

14. Suppose firms in the economy were to produce fewer goods and services. How do you think this would affect household spending on goods and services? (*Hint:* Use the circular flow model to analyze this question.)

Numerical Problems

Problems 1–5 are based on the graph below.

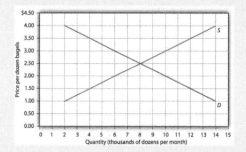

1. At a price of $1.50 per dozen, how many bagels are demanded per month?
2. At a price of $1.50 per dozen, how many bagels are supplied per month?
3. At a price of $3.00 per dozen, how many bagels are demanded per month?
4. At a price of $3.00 per dozen, how many bagels are supplied per month?
5. What is the equilibrium price of bagels? What is the equilibrium quantity per month?

Problems 6–9 are based on the model of demand and supply for coffee as shown in Figure 3.10 You can graph the initial demand and supply curves by using the following values, with all quantities in millions of pounds of coffee per month:

Price	Quantity demanded	Quantity supplied
$3	40	10
4	35	15
5	30	20
6	25	25
7	20	30
8	15	35
9	10	40

6. Suppose the quantity demanded rises by 20 million pounds of coffee per month at each price. Draw the initial demand and supply curves based on the values given in the table above. Then draw the new demand curve given by this change, and show the new equilibrium price and quantity.

7. Suppose the quantity demanded falls, relative to the values given in the above table, by 20 million pounds per month at prices between $4 and $6 per pound; at prices between $7 and $9 per pound, the quantity demanded becomes zero. Draw the new demand curve and show the new equilibrium price and quantity.

8. Suppose the quantity supplied rises by 20 million pounds per month at each price, while the quantities demanded retain the values shown in the table above. Draw the new supply curve and show the new equilibrium price and quantity.

9. Suppose the quantity supplied falls, relative to the values given in the table above, by 20 million pounds per month at prices above $5; at a price of $5 or less per pound, the quantity supplied becomes zero. Draw the new supply curve and show the new equilibrium price and quantity.

Problems 10–15 are based on the demand and supply schedules for gasoline below (all quantities are in thousands of gallons per week):

Price per gallon	Quantity demanded	Quantity supplied
$1	8	0
2	7	1
3	6	2
4	5	3
5	4	4
6	3	5
7	2	6
8	1	7

10. Graph the demand and supply curves and show the equilibrium price and quantity.

11. At a price of $3 per gallon, would there be a surplus or shortage of gasoline? How much would the surplus or shortage be? Indicate the surplus or shortage on the graph.

12. At a price of $6 per gallon, would there be a surplus or shortage of gasoline? How much would the surplus or shortage be? Show the surplus or shortage on the graph.

13. Suppose the quantity demanded increased by 2,000 gallons per month at each price. At a price of $3 per gallon, how much would the surplus or shortage be? Graph the demand and supply curves and show the surplus or shortage.

14. Suppose the quantity supplied decreased by 2,000 gallons per month at each price for prices between $4 and $8 per gallon. At prices less than $4 per gallon the quantity supplied becomes zero, while the quantities demanded retain the values shown in the table. At a price of $4 per gallon, how much would the surplus or shortage be? Graph the demand and supply curves and show the surplus or shortage.

15. If the demand curve shifts as in problem 13 and the supply curve shifts as in problem 14, without drawing a graph or consulting the data, can you predict whether equilibrium price increases or decreases? What about equilibrium quantity? Now draw a graph that shows what the new equilibrium price and quantity are.

Endnotes

1. Noam Scheiber, "As a Center for Outsourcing, India Could Be Losing Its Edge," *New York Times*, May 9, 2004, p. BU3.

CHAPTER 4
Applications of Demand and Supply

4.1 Start Up: A Composer Logs On

"Since the age of seven, I knew that I would be a musician. And from age fourteen, I knew that I would be a composer," says Israeli-born Ofer Ben-Amots. What he did not know was that he would use computers to carry out his work. He is now a professor of music at Colorado College, and Dr. Ben-Amots's compositions and operas have been performed in the United States, Europe, and Japan.

For over 30 years, he has used musical composition software in creating his music. "The output is extremely elegant. Performers enjoy looking at such a clear and clean score. The creation of parts out of a full score is as easy as pressing the <ENTER> key on the keyboard." Changes can easily be inserted into the notation file, which eliminates the need for recopying. In addition, Dr. Ben-Amots uses computers for playback. "I can listen to a relatively accurate 'digital performance' of the score at any given point, with any tempo or instrumentation I choose. The sound quality has improved so much that digital files sound almost identical to real performance." When his use of computers started, he began to produce CDs on his own. Today, he mostly streams his music on online sites such as YouTube, SoundCloud, and Facebook, so that anyone in the world can hear his music. He engages in self-publication of scores and self-marketing. "In my case, I get to keep the copyrights on all of my music. This would have been impossible ten to twelve years ago when composers trans-ferred their rights to publishers. Home pages on the World Wide Web allow me to promote my own work." Professor Ben-Amots also changed the way he teaches music composition. New application software, such as GarageBand, has opened the way for anyone interested to try to compose music. Whereas his music composition classes used to have music theory prerequisites, today his classes are open to all.

Dr. Ben-Amots started out in 1989 with a Macintosh SE30 that had 4 megabytes of random access memory (RAM) and an 80-megabyte hard drive. It cost him about $3,000. Today, he uses a MacBook Pro with several gigabytes of memory (a bit in a computer has a value of 0 or 1, a byte is 8 bits, a megabyte is slightly more than 1 million bytes, and a gigabyte is slightly more than 1,000 megabytes). His new computer cost about $2,200. Put another way, his first computer had a cost per megabyte of RAM of about $750. His present computer costs much less than a thousandth of that amount per megabyte of RAM and is far more powerful. The dramatic rise in the power of personal computers as they fell so steeply in price is just one of the stories about markets we will tell in this chapter, which aims to help you understand how the model of demand and supply applies to the real world.

In the first section of this chapter, we will look at several markets that you are likely to have participated in or be familiar with—the market for personal computers, the markets for crude oil and for gasoline, and the stock market. You probably own or have access to a computer. We have all been affected by the sharp swings in the prices of oil and gasoline in recent years. The performance of the stock market is always a major news item and may affect you personally, if not now then in the future. The concepts of demand and supply go a long way in explaining the behavior of equi-librium prices and quantities in all of these markets. The purpose of this section is to allow you to practice using the model of demand and supply and to get you to start thinking about the myriad ways the model of demand and supply can be applied.

In the second part of the chapter we will look at markets in which the government plays a large role in determining prices. By legislating maximum or minimum prices, the government has kept the prices of certain goods below or above equilibrium. We will look at the arguments for direct government intervention in controlling prices as well as the consequences of such policies. As we shall see, preventing the price of a good from finding its own equilibrium often has consequences that may be at odds with the intentions of the policy makers who put the regulations in place.

In the third section of the chapter we will look at the market for health care. This market is important because how well (or poorly) it works can be a matter of life and death and because it has special characteristics. In particular, markets in which participants do not pay for goods directly but rather have insurers who then pay the suppliers of the goods, operate somewhat differently from those in which participants pay directly for their purchases. This extension of demand and supply analysis, while only scratching the surface on the issues associated with the market for health care, reveals much about how such markets operate. This analysis has become particularly important in the wake of the passage of the Patient Protection and Affordable Care Act in the United States in 2010—sometimes referred to (especially by opponents) as "Obamacare."

4.2 Putting Demand and Supply to Work

Learning Objectives

1. Learn how to apply the model of demand and supply to the behavior of equilibrium prices and output in a variety of markets.
2. Learn basic vocabulary on the organization of firms and explain how the model of demand and supply can be used to understand prices of shares of stock.

A shift in either demand or supply, or in both, leads to a change in equilibrium price and equilibrium quantity. We begin this chapter by examining markets in which prices adjust quickly to changes in demand or supply: the market for personal computers, the markets for crude oil and gasoline, and the stock market. These markets are thus direct applications of the model of demand and supply.

The Personal Computer Market

In the 1960s, to speak of computers was to speak of IBM, the dominant maker of large mainframe computers used by business and government agencies. Then between 1976, when Apple Computer introduced its first desktop computer, and 1981, when IBM produced its first personal computers (PCs), the computer usage expanded dramatically. Only 8.2% of U. S. households owned a personal computer in 1984. By 2003, 62% did. After that, the U.S. Census Bureau began asking only about Internet usage. By 2009, more than two-thirds of households had home Internet access. The tools of demand and supply tell the story from an economic perspective.

Technological change has been breathtakingly swift in the computer industry. Because personal computers have changed so dramatically in performance and in the range of the functions they perform, we shall speak of "quality-adjusted" personal computers. The price per unit of quality-adjusted desktop computers fell by about half every 50 months during the period 1976–1989. In the first half of the 1990s, those prices fell by half every 28 months. In the second half of the 1990s, the "halving time" fell to every 24 months.[1]

There are other indicators of the phenomenal change in computers. Between 1993 and 1998, the Bureau of Labor Statistics estimates that central processing unit (CPU) speed rose 1,263%, system memory increased 1,500%, hard drive capacity soared by 3,700%, and monitor size went up 13%. It seems safe to say that the dizzying pace of change recorded in the 1990s has increased in this century. A "computer" today is not the same good as a "computer" even five years ago. To make them comparable, we must adjust for changes in quality.

Initially, most personal computers were manufactured by Apple or Compaq; both companies were very profitable. The potential for profits attracted IBM and other firms to the industry. Unlike large mainframe computers, personal computer clones turned out to be fairly easy to manufacture. As shown in Table 4.1, the top two personal computer manufacturers, Lenovo and HP, each produced about 20% of the personal computers sold in the world in the third quarter of 2016, with another 35% produced by the next four companies. This is a far cry from the more than 90% of the mainframe computer market that IBM once held. The market has become far more competitive.

TABLE 4.1 Personal Computer Shipments, Market Percentage Shares by Vendors, World and United States, 3rd Quarter 2016

Company	Percentage of World Shipments	Company	Percentage of U.S. Shipments
Lenovo	20.9	HP	29.7
HP	20.4	Dell	24.0
Dell	14.7	Lenovo	14.1
Asus	7.8	Apple	12.9
Apple	7.2	Asus	5.1
Acer Group	6.7	Others	14.2
Others	22.3		

Source: Based on data from Gartner Says Worldwide PC Shipments Declined 5.7 Percent in Third Quarter of 2016, October 11, 2016, http://www.gartner.com/newsroom/id/3474218. Data are preliminary.

Figure 4.1 illustrates changes that have occurred in the computer market. The horizontal axis shows the quantity of quality-adjusted personal computers. Thus, the quantity axis can be thought of as a unit of computing power. Similarly, the price axis shows the price per unit of computing power. The rapid increase in the number of firms, together with dramatic technological improvements, led to an increase in supply, shifting the supply curve in Figure 4.1 to the right from S_1 to S_2.

Demand also shifted to the right from D_1 to D_2, as incomes rose and new uses for computers, from e-mail and social networking to Voice over Internet Protocol (VoIP) and Radio Frequency ID (RFID) tags (which allow wireless tracking of commercial shipments via desktop computers), altered the preferences of consumer and business users. Because we observe a fall in equilibrium price and an increase in equilibrium quantity, we conclude that the rightward shift in supply has outweighed the rightward shift in demand. The power of market forces has profoundly affected the way we live and work. One indication of the increasing importance of computers was that in August 2011, Exxon Mobil, an oil company that had been largest company in the United States in terms of the value of its outstanding stock, was the surpassed by Apple Computer Inc., whose value reached $350 billion.

FIGURE 4.1 The Personal Computer Market

The supply curve for quality-adjusted personal computers shifted markedly to the right, reducing the equilibrium price from P_1 to P_2 and increasing the equilibrium quantity from Q_1 to Q_2 in 2011.

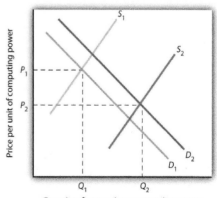

The Markets for Crude Oil and for Gasoline

The market for crude oil took a radical turn in 1973. The price per barrel of crude oil quadrupled between 1973 and 1974. Price remained high until the early 1980s but fell back drastically and remained low for about two decades. In 2004, the price of oil began to move upward and by 2008 had reached $147 per barrel.

What caused the dramatic increase in gasoline and oil prices in 2008? It appeared to be increasing worldwide demand outpacing producers' ability—or willingness—to increase production much. This increase in demand is illustrated in Figure 4.2.

FIGURE 4.2 Increasing Demand for Crude Oil

The price of oil was $35 per barrel at the beginning of 2004, as determined by the intersection of world demand, D_1, and world supply, S_1. Increasing world demand, prompted largely by increasing demand from China as well as from other countries, shifted world demand to D_2, pushing the price as high as $140 per barrel by the middle of 2008.

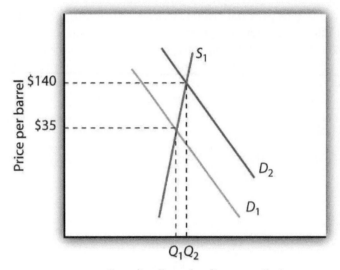

Barrels of crude oil per period

Higher oil prices also increase the cost of producing virtually every good or service since the production of most goods requires transportation. These costs inevitably translate into higher prices for nearly all goods and services. Supply curves of the goods and services thus affected shift to the left, putting downward pressure on output and upward pressure on prices.

Graphically, the impact of higher gasoline prices on businesses that use gasoline is illustrated in Figure 4.3. Because higher gasoline prices increase the cost of doing business, they shift the supply curves for nearly all businesses to the left, putting upward pressure on prices and downward pressure on output. In the case shown here, the supply curve in a typical industry shifts from S_1 to S_2. This increases the equilibrium price from P_1 to P_2 and reduces the equilibrium quantity from Q_1 to Q_2.

FIGURE 4.3 The Impact of Higher Gasoline Prices
Higher gasoline prices increase the cost of producing virtually every good or service. In the case shown here, the supply curve in a typical industry shifts from S_1 to S_2. This increases the equilibrium price from P_1 to P_2 and reduces equilibrium quantity from Q_1 to Q_2.

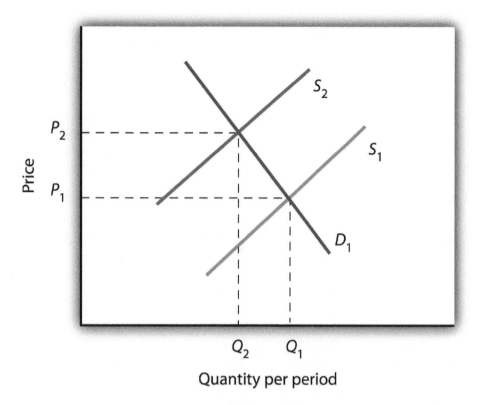

As the world economy slowed dramatically in the second half of 2008, the demand curve for oil shifted to the left. By November 2008, the price per barrel had dropped to below $60 per barrel. As gas prices also subsided, so did the threat of higher prices in other industries.

Oil prices had climbed back to the $100 per barrel range by 2014 and then plunged to about half that by the end of that year. They stayed comparatively low for the next two years. The main reason for the fall in oil prices was increased supply, primarily from Saudi Arabia, as it tried to maintain market share, and from Iran, as it returned to world markets after sanctions were lifted. Increased production in the United States, from a relatively new process often referred to as fracking, also contributed. Analysis of the oil market for this period would focus on a shift in the supply curve to the right, leading to higher output and lower price. Then, the lower gasoline prices would lower the cost of producing other goods and services. In other words, the supply curve in Figure 4.3 would shift to the right of the original supply curve.

The Stock Market

The circular flow model suggests that capital, like other factors of production, is supplied by households to firms. Firms, in turn, pay income to those households for the use of their capital. Generally speaking, however, capital is actually owned by firms themselves. General Motors owns its assembly plants, and Wal-Mart owns its stores; these firms therefore own their capital. But firms, in turn, are owned by people—and those people, of course, live in households. It is through their ownership of firms that households own capital.

sole proprietorship

A firm owned by one individual.

partnership

A firm owned by several individuals.

corporation

A firm owned by shareholders who own stock in the firm.

corporate stock

Shares in the ownership of a corporation.

stock market

The set of institutions in which shares of stock are bought and sold.

A firm may be owned by one individual (a **sole proprietorship**), by several individuals (a **partnership**), or by shareholders who own stock in the firm (a **corporation**). Although most firms in the United States are sole proprietorships or partnerships, the bulk of the nation's total output (about 90%) is produced by corporations. Corporations also own most of the capital (machines, plants, buildings, and the like).

This section describes how the prices of shares of **corporate stock**, shares in the ownership of a corporation, are determined by the interaction of demand and supply. Ultimately, the same forces that determine the value of a firm's stock determine the value of a sole proprietorship or partnership.

When a corporation needs funds to increase its capital or for other reasons, one means at its disposal is to issue new stock in the corporation. (Other means include borrowing funds or using past profits.) Once the new shares have been sold in what is called an initial public offering (IPO), the corporation receives no further funding as shares of its stock are bought and sold on the secondary market. The secondary market is the market for stocks that have been issued in the past, and the daily news reports about stock prices almost always refer to activity in the secondary market. Generally, the corporations whose shares are traded are not involved in these transactions.

The **stock market** is the set of institutions in which shares of stock are bought and sold. The New York Stock Exchange (NYSE) is one such institution. There are many others all over the world, such as the DAX in Germany and the Bolsa in Mexico. To buy or sell a share of stock, one places an order with a stockbroker who relays the order to one of the traders at the NYSE or at some other exchange.

The process through which shares of stock are bought and sold can seem chaotic. At many exchanges, traders with orders from customers who want to buy stock shout out the prices those customers are willing to pay. Traders with orders from customers who want to sell shout out offers of prices at which their customers are willing to sell. Some exchanges use electronic trading, but the principle is the same: if the price someone is willing to pay matches the price at which someone else is willing to sell, the trade is made. The most recent price at which a stock has traded is reported almost instantaneously throughout the world.

FIGURE 4.4 Demand and Supply in the Stock Market

The equilibrium price of stock shares in Intel Corporation is initially $25, determined by the intersection of demand and supply curves D_1 and S_1, at which Q_1 million shares are traded each day.

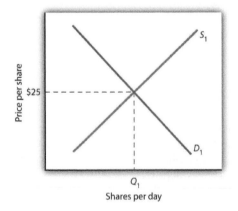

Figure 4.4 applies the model of demand and supply to the determination of stock prices. Suppose the demand curve for shares in Intel Corporation is given by D_1 and the supply by S_1. (Even though the total number of shares outstanding is fixed at any point in time, the supply curve is not vertical. Rather, the supply curve is upward sloping because it represents how many shares current owners are prepared to sell at each price, and that number will be greater at higher prices.) Suppose that these curves intersect at a price of $25, at which Q_1 shares are traded each day. If the price were higher, more shares would be offered for sale than would be demanded, and the price would quickly fall. If the price were lower, more shares would be demanded than would be supplied, and the price would quickly rise. In general, we can expect the prices of shares of stock to move quickly to their equilibrium levels.

The intersection of the demand and supply curves for shares of stock in a particular company determines the equilibrium price for a share of stock. But what determines the demand and supply for shares of a company's stock?

The owner of a share of a company's stock owns a share of the company, and, hence, a share of its profits; typically, a corporation will retain and reinvest some of its profits to increase its future profitability. The profits kept by a company are called **retained earnings**. Profits distributed to shareholders are called **dividends**. Because a share of stock gives its owner a claim on part of a company's future profits, it follows that the expected level of future profits plays a role in determining the value of its stock.

Of course, those future profits cannot be known with certainty; investors can only predict what they might be, based on information about future demand for the company's products, future costs of production, information about the soundness of a company's management, and so on. Stock prices in the real world thus reflect estimates of a company's profits projected into the future.

The downward slope of the demand curve suggests that at lower prices for the stock, more people calculate that the firm's future earnings will justify the stock's purchase. The upward slope of the supply curve tells us that as the price of the stock rises, more people conclude that the firm's future earnings do not justify holding the stock and therefore offer to sell it. At the equilibrium price, the number of shares supplied by people who think holding the stock no longer makes sense just balances the number of shares demanded by people who think it does.

What factors, then, cause the demand or supply curves for shares of stocks to shift? The most important factor is a change in the expectations of a company's future profits. Suppose Intel announces a new generation of computer chips that will lead to faster computers with larger memories. Current owners of Intel stock would adjust upward their estimates of what the value of a share of Intel stock should be. At the old equilibrium price of $25 fewer owners of Intel stock would be willing to sell. Since this would be true at every possible share price, the supply curve for Intel stock would shift to the left, as shown in Figure 4.5. Just as the expectation that a company will be more profitable shifts the supply curve for its stock to the left, that same change in expectations will cause more people to want to purchase the stock, shifting the demand curve to the right. In Figure 4.5, we see the supply curve shifting to the left, from S_1 to S_2, while the demand curve shifts to the right, from D_1 to D_2.

Other factors may alter the price of an individual corporation's share of stock or the level of stock prices in general. For example, demographic change and rising incomes have affected the demand for stocks in recent years. For example, with a large proportion of the U.S. population nearing retirement age and beginning to think about and plan for their lives during retirement, the demand for stocks has risen.

Information on the economy as a whole is also likely to affect stock prices. If the economy overall is doing well and people expect that to continue, they may become more optimistic about how profitable companies will be in general, and thus the prices of stocks will rise. Conversely, expectations of a sluggish economy, as happened in the fall of 2008, could cause stock prices in general to fall.

The stock market is bombarded with new information every minute of every day. Firms announce their profits of the previous quarter. They announce that they plan to move into a new product line or sell their goods in another country. We learn that the price of Company A's good, which is a substitute for one sold by Company B, has risen. We learn that countries sign trade agreements, launch wars, or make peace. All of this information may affect stock prices because any information can affect how buyers and sellers value companies.

retained earnings

Profits kept by a company.

dividends

Profits distributed to shareholders.

FIGURE 4.5 A Change in Expectations Affects the Price of Corporate Stock
If financial investors decide that a company is likely to be more profitable, then the supply of the stock shifts to the left (in this case, from S_1 to S_2), and the demand for the stock shifts to the right (in this case, from D_1 to D_2), resulting in an increase in price from P_1 to P_2.

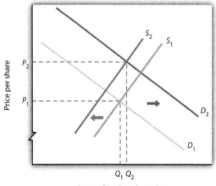

Shares of Intel stock per day

Key Takeaways

- Technological change, which has caused the supply curve for computing power to shift to the right, is the main reason for the rapid increase in equilibrium quantity and decrease in equilibrium price of personal computers.
- The increase in crude oil and gasoline prices in 2008 was driven primarily by increased demand for crude oil, an increase that was created by economic growth throughout the world. Crude oil and gas prices fell markedly as world economic growth subsided later in the year.
- Higher gasoline prices increased the cost of producing virtually every good and service, shifting supply curves for most goods and services to the left. This tended to push prices up and output down.
- Demand and supply determine prices of shares of corporate stock. The equilibrium price of a share of stock strikes a balance between those who think the stock is worth more and those who think it is worth less than the current price.
- If a company's profits are expected to increase, the demand curve for its stock shifts to the right and the supply curve shifts to the left, causing equilibrium price to rise. The opposite would occur if a company's profits were expected to decrease.
- Other factors that influence the price of corporate stock include demographic and income changes and the overall health of the economy.

Try It!

Suppose an airline announces that its earnings this year are lower than expected due to reduced ticket sales. The airline spokesperson gives no information on how the company plans to turn things around. Use the model of demand and supply to show and explain what is likely to happen to the price of the airline's stock.

Case in Point: The Great Recession, the Arab Spring, and the Oil Market

Source: © Thinkstock

Oil markets were on a roller coaster ride between 2007 and 2011. Even after the official start of the recession in the United States in December 2007, oil prices continued to climb, peaking in the summer of 2008 at over $130 per barrel. Although demand in the United States and Europe was already weakening, growth in the rest of the world, particularly in China and India, was still strong. Overall, demand was rising.

Oil prices dropped precipitously following the start of the financial crisis and the deepening of the recession in the fall of 2008. Within a few months, the price of oil had dropped to around $40 and was in the $70 to $80 range for much of the rest of 2009 and the first half of 2010.

The so-called Arab Spring actually began with demonstrations late in 2010 in Tunisia. They quickly spread to Egypt, Bahrain, Syria, Yemen, Algeria, Jordan, Morocco, and Yemen. There were demonstrations in Saudi Arabia, Kuwait, Lebanon, Mauritania, and Sudan. By the fall of 2011, the movement had toppled the regimes of Zine El Abidine Ben Ali in Tunisia, Hosni Mubarak in Egypt, and Muammar al-Gaddafi in Libya.

The movement had a large impact on oil prices as it raised questions about the security of oil supplies. The supply curve of oil shifted to the left, forcing the price upward. Not only were several key suppliers of oil affected, but at times the ability to transport oil through the Suez Canal was affected.

Oil prices rose to well over $100 per barrel by early 2011. They then began to subside again as some of the uprisings were subdued or ending, especially in the oil-rich Gulf countries. By the fall of 2011, oil prices had fallen about 20% as compared to earlier in the year.

Answer to Try It! Problem

The information given in the problem suggests that the airline's profits are likely to fall below expectations. Current owners of the airline's stock and potential buyers of the stock would adjust downward their estimates of what the value of the corporation's stock should be. As a result the supply curve for the stock would increase, shifting it to the right, while the demand curve for the stock would decrease, shifting it to the left. As a result, equilibrium price of the stock falls from P_1 to P_2. What happens to equilibrium quantity depends on the extent to which each curve shifts. In the diagram, equilibrium quantity is shown to decrease from Q_1 to Q_2.

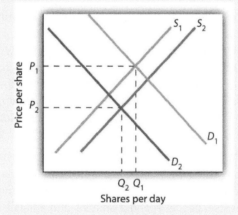

4.3 Government Intervention in Market Prices: Price Floors and Price Ceilings

Learning Objectives

1. Use the model of demand and supply to explain what happens when the government imposes price floors or price ceilings.
2. Discuss the reasons why governments sometimes choose to control prices and the consequences of price control policies.

So far in this chapter and in the previous chapter, we have learned that markets tend to move toward their equilibrium prices and quantities. Surpluses and shortages of goods are short-lived as prices adjust to equate quantity demanded with quantity supplied.

In some markets, however, governments have been called on by groups of citizens to intervene to keep prices of certain items higher or lower than what would result from the market finding its own equilibrium price. In this section we will examine agricultural markets and apartment rental markets—two markets that have often been subject to price controls. Through these examples, we will identify the effects of controlling prices. In each case, we will look at reasons why governments have chosen to control prices in these markets and the consequences of these policies.

Agricultural Price Floors

price floor

A minimum allowable price set above the equilibrium price.

Governments often seek to assist farmers by setting price floors in agricultural markets. A minimum allowable price set above the equilibrium price is a **price floor**. With a price floor, the government forbids a price below the minimum. (Notice that, if the price floor were for whatever reason set below the equilibrium price, it would be irrelevant to the determination of the price in the market since nothing would prohibit the price from rising to equilibrium.) A price floor that is set above the equilibrium price creates a surplus.

Figure 4.6 shows the market for wheat. Suppose the government sets the price of wheat at P_F. Notice that P_F is above the equilibrium price of P_E. At P_F, we read over to the demand curve to find that the quantity of wheat that buyers will be willing and able to purchase is W_1 bushels. Reading over to the supply curve, we find that sellers will offer W_2 bushels of wheat at the price floor of P_F. Because P_F is above the equilibrium price, there is a surplus of wheat equal to $(W_2 - W_1)$ bushels. The surplus persists because the government does not allow the price to fall.

FIGURE 4.6 Price Floors in Wheat Markets

A price floor for wheat creates a surplus of wheat equal to $(W_2 - W_1)$ bushels.

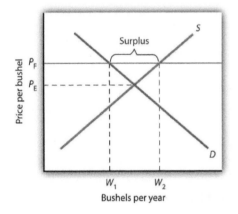

Why have many governments around the world set price floors in agricultural markets? Farming has changed dramatically over the past two centuries. Technological improvements in the form of new equipment, fertilizers, pesticides, and new varieties of crops have led to dramatic increases in crop output per acre. Worldwide production capacity has expanded markedly. As we have learned, technological improvements cause the supply curve to shift to the right, reducing the price of food. While such price reductions have been celebrated in computer markets, farmers have successfully lobbied for government programs aimed at keeping their prices from falling.

While the supply curve for agricultural goods has shifted to the right, the demand has increased with rising population and with rising income. But as incomes rise, people spend a smaller and smaller fraction of their incomes on food. While the demand for food has increased, that increase has not been nearly as great as the increase in supply. Figure 4.7 shows that the supply curve has shifted much farther to the right, from S_1 to S_2, than the demand curve has, from D_1 to D_2. As a result, equilibrium quantity has risen dramatically, from Q_1 to Q_2, and equilibrium price has fallen, from P_1 to P_2.

On top of this long-term historical trend in agriculture, agricultural prices are subject to wide swings over shorter periods. Droughts or freezes can sharply reduce supplies of particular crops, causing sudden increases in prices. Demand for agricultural goods of one country can suddenly dry up if the government of another country imposes trade restrictions against its products, and prices can fall. Such dramatic shifts in prices and quantities make incomes of farmers unstable.

The Great Depression of the 1930s led to a major federal role in agriculture. The Depression affected the entire economy, but it hit farmers particularly hard. Prices received by farmers plunged nearly two-thirds from 1930 to 1933. Many farmers had a tough time keeping up mortgage payments. By 1932, more than half of all farm loans were in default.

Farm legislation passed during the Great Depression has been modified many times, but the federal government has continued its direct involvement in agricultural markets. This has meant a variety of government programs that guarantee a minimum price for some types of agricultural products. These programs have been accompanied by government purchases of any surpluses, by requirements to restrict acreage in order to limit those surpluses, by crop or production restrictions, subsidized crop insurance programs, and the like .

To see how such policies work, look back at Figure 4.6. At P_F, W_2 bushels of wheat will be supplied. With that much wheat on the market, there is market pressure on the price of wheat to fall. To prevent price from falling, the government buys the surplus of (W_2 - W_1) bushels of wheat, so that only W_1 bushels are actually available to private consumers for purchase on the market. The government can store the surpluses or find special uses for them. For example, surpluses generated in the United States have been shipped to developing countries as grants-in-aid or distributed to local school lunch programs. As a variation on this program, the government can require farmers who want to participate in the price support program to reduce acreage in order to limit the size of the surpluses.

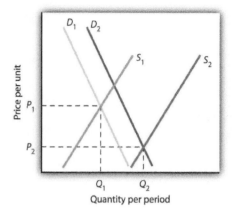

FIGURE 4.7 Supply and Demand Shifts for Agricultural Products
A relatively large increase in the supply of agricultural products, accompanied by a relatively small increase in demand, has reduced the price received by farmers and increased the quantity of agricultural goods.

After 1973, the government stopped buying the surpluses (with some exceptions) and simply guaranteed farmers a "target price." If the average market price for a crop fell below the crop's target price, the government paid the difference. If, for example, a crop had a market price of $3 per unit and a target price of $4 per unit, the government would give farmers a payment of $1 for each unit sold. Farmers would thus receive the market price of $3 plus a government payment of $1 per unit. For farmers to receive these payments, they had to agree to remove acres from production and to comply with certain conservation provisions. These restrictions sought to reduce the size of the surplus generated by the target price, which acted as a kind of price floor. The most recent 2014 farm bill uses the term reference price instead of target price. Payments to farms, or agribusinesses, when crop prices fall below a certain level operate primarily through crop insurance programs, the premiums and deductibles of which are subsidized by the federal government.

What are the effects of such farm support programs? The intention is to boost and stabilize farm incomes. But, with price floors, consumers pay more for food than they would otherwise, and governments spend heavily to finance the programs. With the target or reference price approach, consumers pay less, but government financing of the program continues.

Help to farmers has sometimes been justified on the grounds that it boosts incomes of "small" farmers. However, since farm aid has generally been allotted on the basis of how much farms produce rather than on a per-farm basis, most federal farm support has gone to the largest farms. If the goal is to eliminate poverty among farmers, farm aid could be redesigned to supplement the incomes of small or poor farmers rather than to undermine the functioning of agricultural markets.

In 1996, the U.S. Congress passed the Federal Agriculture Improvement and Reform Act of 1996, or FAIR. The thrust of the new legislation was to do away with the various programs of price support for most crops and hence provide incentives for farmers to respond to market price signals. To protect farmers through a transition period, the act provided for continued payments that were scheduled to decline over a seven-year period. However, with prices for many crops falling in 1998, the U.S. Congress passed an emergency aid package that increased payments to farmers. The farm bills of the 2000s—specifically those of 2002, 2008, and 2014—were passed with bipartisan congressional majorities regardless of which party controlled Congress or the White House. While specifics vary, they revised the notion of target, or reference, pricing and have provided various forms of payments, such as payments when prices on some crops fall below certain levels or in the form of subsidized crop insurance premiums and even payments of deductibles on insurance policies.

Each of these farm bills temporarily replaces the permanent farm support laws from 1938 and 1949. Thus, if there is no modern bill in effect, the farm sector would be governed by these now very outdated laws. Broad legislative support is created by putting the agricultural supports described here with the reauthorization of SNAP, the Supplemental Nutrition Assistance Program more commonly referred to as food stamps, conservation programs, and other programs into a single legislative bill. Thus, the continued passage of similar bills every five or six years seems likely.

Rental Price Ceilings

The purpose of rent control is to make rental units cheaper for tenants than they would otherwise be. Unlike agricultural price controls, rent control in the United States has been largely a local phenomenon, although there were national rent controls in effect during World War II. Currently, about 200 cities and counties have some type of rent control provisions, and about 10% of rental units in the United States are now subject to price controls. New York City's rent control program, which began in 1943, is among the oldest in the country. Many other cities in the United States adopted some form of rent control in the 1970s. Rent controls have been pervasive in Europe since World War I, and many large cities in poorer countries have also adopted rent controls.

Rent controls in different cities differ in terms of their flexibility. Some cities allow rent increases for specified reasons, such as to make improvements in apartments or to allow rents to keep pace with price increases elsewhere in the economy. Often, rental housing constructed after the imposition of the rent control ordinances is exempted. Apartments that are vacated may also be decontrolled. For simplicity, the model presented here assumes that apartment rents are controlled at a price that does not change.

FIGURE 4.8 Effect of a Price Ceiling on the Market for Apartments

A price ceiling on apartment rents that is set below the equilibrium rent creates a shortage of apartments equal to $(A_2 - A_1)$ apartments.

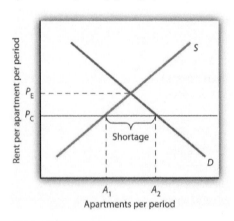

Apartments per period

Figure 4.8 shows the market for rental apartments. Notice that the demand and supply curves are drawn to look like all the other demand and supply curves you have encountered so far in this text: the demand curve is downward-sloping and the supply curve is upward-sloping.

The demand curve shows that a higher price (rent) reduces the quantity of apartments demanded. For example, with higher rents, more young people will choose to live at home with their parents. With lower rents, more will choose to live in apartments. Higher rents may encourage more apartment sharing; lower rents would induce more people to live alone.

The supply curve is drawn to show that as rent increases, property owners will be encouraged to offer more apartments to rent. Even though an aerial photograph of a city would show apartments to be fixed at a point in time, owners of those properties will decide how many to rent depending on the amount of rent they anticipate. Higher rents may also induce some homeowners to rent out apartment space. In addition, renting out apartments implies a certain level of service to renters, so that low rents may lead some property owners to keep some apartments vacant.

price ceiling

A maximum allowable price.

Rent control is an example of a **price ceiling**, a maximum allowable price. With a price ceiling, the government forbids a price above the maximum. A price ceiling that is set below the equilibrium price creates a shortage that will persist.

Suppose the government sets the price of an apartment at P_C in Figure 4.8. Notice that P_C is below the equilibrium price of P_E. At P_C, we read over to the supply curve to find that sellers are willing to offer A_1 apartments. Reading over to the demand curve, we find that consumers would like to rent A_2 apartments at the price ceiling of P_C. Because P_C is below the equilibrium price, there is a shortage of apartments equal to $(A_2 - A_1)$. (Notice that if the price ceiling were set above the equilibrium price it would have no effect on the market since the law would not prohibit the price from settling at an equilibrium price that is lower than the price ceiling.)

If rent control creates a shortage of apartments, why do some citizens nonetheless clamor for rent control and why do governments often give in to the demands? The reason generally given for rent control is to keep apartments affordable for low- and middle-income tenants.

But the reduced quantity of apartments supplied must be rationed in some way, since, at the price ceiling, the quantity demanded would exceed the quantity supplied. Current occupants may be reluctant to leave their dwellings because finding other apartments will be difficult. As apartments do become available, there will be a line of potential renters waiting to fill them, any of whom is willing to pay the controlled price of P_C or more. In fact, reading up to the demand curve in Figure 4.9 from A_1 apartments, the quantity available at P_C, you can see that for A_1 apartments, there are potential renters willing and able to pay P_B. This often leads to various "backdoor" payments to apartment owners, such as large security deposits, payments for things renters may not want (such as furniture), so-called "key" payments ("The monthly rent is $500 and the key price is $3,000"), or simple bribes.

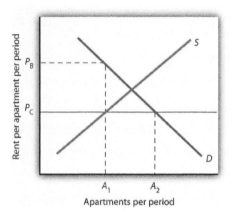

FIGURE 4.9 The Unintended Consequences of Rent Control
Controlling apartment rents at P_C creates a shortage of ($A_2 - A_1$) apartments. For A_1 apartments, consumers are willing and able to pay P_B, which leads to various "backdoor" payments to apartment owners.

In the end, rent controls and other price ceilings often end up hurting some of the people they are intended to help. Many people will have trouble finding apartments to rent. Ironically, some of those who do find apartments may actually end up paying more than they would have paid in the absence of rent control. And many of the people that the rent controls do help (primarily current occupants, regardless of their income, and those lucky enough to find apartments) are not those they are intended to help (the poor). There are also costs in government administration and enforcement.

Because New York City has the longest history of rent controls of any city in the United States, its program has been widely studied. There is general agreement that the rent control program has reduced tenant mobility, led to a substantial gap between rents on controlled and uncontrolled units, and favored long-term residents at the expense of newcomers to the city.[2] These distortions have grown over time, another frequent consequence of price controls.

A more direct means of helping poor tenants, one that would avoid interfering with the functioning of the market, would be to subsidize their incomes. As with price floors, interfering with the market mechanism may solve one problem, but it creates many others at the same time.

Key Takeaways

- Price floors create surpluses by fixing the price above the equilibrium price. At the price set by the floor, the quantity supplied exceeds the quantity demanded.
- In agriculture, price floors have created persistent surpluses of a wide range of agricultural commodities. Governments typically purchase the amount of the surplus or impose production restrictions in an attempt to reduce the surplus.
- Price ceilings create shortages by setting the price below the equilibrium. At the ceiling price, the quantity demanded exceeds the quantity supplied.
- Rent controls are an example of a price ceiling, and thus they create shortages of rental housing.
- It is sometimes the case that rent controls create "backdoor" arrangements, ranging from requirements that tenants rent items that they do not want to outright bribes, that result in rents higher than would exist in the absence of the ceiling.

Try It!

A minimum wage law is another example of a price floor. Draw demand and supply curves for unskilled labor. The horizontal axis will show the quantity of unskilled labor per period and the vertical axis will show the hourly wage rate for unskilled workers, which is the price of unskilled labor. Show and explain the effect of a minimum wage that is above the equilibrium wage.

Case in Point: Corn: It Is Not Just Food Any More

Source: © 2010 Jupiterimages Corporation

Government support for corn dates back to the Agricultural Act of 1938 and, in one form or another, has been part of agricultural legislation ever since. Types of supports have ranged from government purchases of surpluses to target pricing, land set asides, and loan guarantees. According to one estimate, the U.S. government spent nearly $42 billion to support corn between 1995 and 2004.

Then, during the period of rising oil prices of the late 1970s and mounting concerns about dependence on foreign oil from volatile regions in the world, support for corn, not as a food, but rather as an input into the production of ethanol—an alternative to oil-based fuel—began. Ethanol tax credits were part of the Energy Act of 1978. Since 1980, a tariff of 50¢ per gallon against imported ethanol, even higher today, has served to protect domestic corn-based ethanol from imported ethanol, in particular from sugar-cane-based ethanol from Brazil.

The Energy Policy Act of 2005 was another milestone in ethanol legislation. Through loan guarantees, support for research and development, and tax credits, it mandated that 4 billion gallons of ethanol be used by 2006 and 7.5 billion gallons by 2012. Ethanol production had already reached 6.5 billion gallons by 2007, so new legislation in 2007 upped the ante to 15 billion gallons by 2015.

Beyond the increased amount the government is spending to support corn and corn-based ethanol, criticism of the policy has three major prongs:

1. Corn-based ethanol does little to reduce U.S. dependence on foreign oil because the energy required to produce a gallon of corn-based ethanol is quite high. A 2006 National

Academy of Sciences paper estimated that one gallon of ethanol is needed to bring 1.25 gallons of it to market. Other studies show an even less favorable ratio.

2. Biofuels, such as corn-based ethanol, are having detrimental effects on the environment, with increased deforestation, stemming from more land being used to grow fuel inputs, contributing to global warming.

3. The diversion of corn and other crops from food to fuel is contributing to rising food prices and an increase in world hunger. C. Ford Runge and Benjamin Senauer wrote in *Foreign Affairs* that even small increases in prices of food staples have severe consequences on the very poor of the world, and "Filling the 25-gallon tank of an SUV with pure ethanol requires over 450 pounds of corn—which contains enough calories to feed one person for a year."

Some of these criticisms may be contested as exaggerated: Will the ratio of energy-in to energy-out improve as new technologies emerge for producing ethanol? Did not other factors, such as weather and rising food demand worldwide, contribute to higher grain prices? Nonetheless, it is clear that corn-based ethanol is no free lunch. It is also clear that the end of government support for corn is nowhere to be seen.

Sources: Based on Alexei Barrionuevo, "Mountains of Corn and a Sea of Farm Subsidies," New York Times, November 9, 2005, online version; David Freddoso, "Children of the Corn," National Review Online, May 6, 2008; C. Ford Runge and Benjamin Senauer, "How Biofuels Could Starve the Poor," Foreign Affairs, May/June 2007, online version; Michael Grunwald, "The Clean Energy Scam," Time 171:14 (April 7, 2008): 40–45.

Answer to Try It! Problem

A minimum wage (W_{min}) that is set above the equilibrium wage would create a surplus of unskilled labor equal to ($L_2 - L_1$). That is, L_2 units of unskilled labor are offered at the minimum wage, but companies only want to use L_1 units at that wage. Because unskilled workers are a substitute for a skilled workers, forcing the price of unskilled workers higher would increase the demand for skilled labor and thus increase their wages.

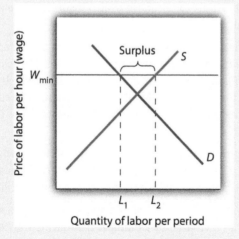

4.4 The Market for Health-Care Services

There has been much discussion over the past three decades about the health-care problem in the United States. Much of this discussion has focused on rising spending for health care. In this section, we will apply the model of demand and supply to health care to see what we can learn about some of the reasons behind rising spending in this important sector of the economy.

Figure 4.10 shows the share of U.S. output devoted to health care since 1960. In 1960, about 5% of total output was devoted to health care; by 2009 this share had risen to 17.3%. It reached 17.8% in 2015. That means that we are devoting more of our spending to health care and less to other goods and services.

The Affordable Care Act (ACA) of 2010, also known as Obamacare, dramatically impacted health care services. A major goal of the legislation was to increase the percentage of the population with health insurance and this certainly happened. The provisions of the Act are extensive. Employer-based coverage was retained, with employers with over 50 employees who choose not to offer health insurance required to pay a fee instead. For those lacking insurance through an employer or through a government program such as Medicare or Medicaid, it encouraged states to create health care exchanges (with a federal exchange for people living in states choosing not to create their own), where people could purchase insurance. Subsidies for the insurance premiums on policies bought through the exchanges are available on a sliding scale basis for people earning up to 400% of the poverty level. Insurance companies are required to offer policies that meet certain standards of coverage and they are not allowed to deny coverage based on pre-existing conditions. Insurance companies are required to provide coverage for children on their parent's policies up to the age of 26. The cut off age prior to the Affordable Care Act had typically been 21. Health insurers were no longer allowed to place life-time limits on coverage or to rescind coverage, except in cases of fraud. The Act also requires individuals to purchase health insurance (the so-called individual mandate) or to pay a financial penalty.

The ACA also provided for the expansion of Medicaid to include adults without dependent children and with incomes up to 138% of the poverty level. Medicaid and the Children's Health Insurance Program (CHIP) had already covered other poor people. In the initial years, the federal government provides all funding for the Medicaid expansion. That support is slated to be reduced to 90% by 2020 and to remain at that level. By 2016, 31 states plus the District of Columbia had chosen to expand Medicaid.

The Act passed Congress with no support from Republicans, who immediately began talking about "repeal and replace." Indeed, changes are likely with the election of Republican Donald Trump in 2016 and with Republican majorities in both the Senate and the House.

In this section, we will use the model of demand and supply to shed light on one reason why spending on health care has increased by looking at the role insurance plays in altering market outcomes. This analysis will not answer all the questions you may have about this important market, but it will hopefully be a start.

FIGURE 4.10 Health-Care Spending as a Percentage of U.S. Output, 1960–2015
Health care's share of total U.S. output rose from about 5% in 1960 to about 17.8% in 2015.

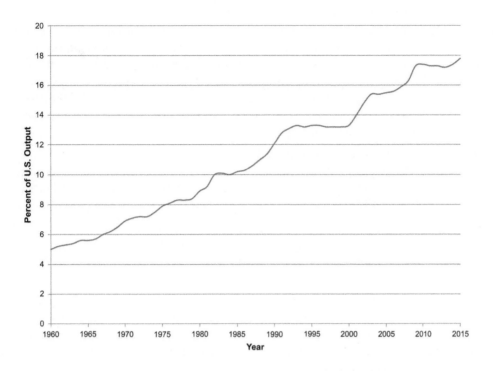

Source: Based on data from Centers for Medicare & Medicaid Services, Office of the Actuary, National Health Statistics Group; U.S. Department of Commerce, Bureau of Economic Analysis; and U.S. Bureau of the Census. available at https://www.cms.gov/Research-Statistics-Data-and-Systems/Statistics-Trends-and-Reports/NationalHealthExpendData/NationalHealthAccountsHistorical.html.

The Demand and Supply for Health Care

When we speak of "health care," we are speaking of the entire health-care industry. This industry produces services ranging from heart transplant operations to therapeutic massages; it produces goods ranging from X-ray machines to aspirin tablets. Clearly each of these goods and services is exchanged in a particular market. To assess the market forces affecting health care, we will focus first on just one of these markets: the market for physician office visits. When you go to the doctor, you are part of the demand for these visits. Your doctor, by seeing you, is part of the supply.

Figure 4.11 shows the market, assuming that it operates in a fashion similar to other markets. The demand curve D_1 and the supply curve S_1 intersect at point E, with an equilibrium price of $30 per office visit. The equilibrium quantity of office visits per week is 1,000,000.

We can use the demand and supply graph to show total spending, which equals the price per unit (in this case, $30 per visit) times the quantity consumed (in this case, 1,000,000 visits per week). Total spending for physician office visits thus equals $30,000,000 per week ($30 times 1,000,000 visits). We show total spending as the area of a rectangle bounded by the price and the quantity. It is the shaded region in Figure 4.11.

The picture in Figure 4.11 misses a crucial feature of the market. Most people in the United States have health insurance, provided either by private firms, by private purchases, or by the government. With health insurance, people agree to pay a fixed amount to the insurer in exchange for the insurer's agreement to pay for most of the health-care expenses they incur. While insurance

FIGURE 4.11 Total Spending for Physician Office Visits
Total spending on physician office visits is $30 per visit multiplied by 1,000,000 visits per week, which equals $30,000,000. It is the shaded area bounded by price and quantity.

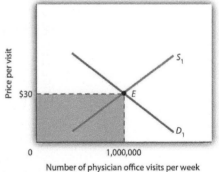

plans differ in their specific provisions, let us suppose that all individuals have plans that require them to pay $10 for an office visit; the insurance company will pay the rest.

How will this insurance affect the market for physician office visits? If it costs only $10 for a visit instead of $30, people will visit their doctors more often. The quantity of office visits demanded will increase. In Figure 4.12, this is shown as a movement along the demand curve. Think about your own choices. When you get a cold, do you go to the doctor? Probably not, if it is a minor cold. But if you feel like you are dying, or wish you were, you probably head for the doctor. Clearly, there are lots of colds in between these two extremes. Whether you drag yourself to the doctor will depend on the severity of your cold and what you will pay for a visit. At a lower price, you are more likely to go to the doctor; at a higher price, you are less likely to go.

In the case shown, the quantity of office visits rises to 1,500,000 per week. But that suggests a potential problem. The quantity of visits supplied at a price of $30 per visit was 1,000,000. According to supply curve S_1, it will take a price of $50 per visit to increase the quantity supplied to 1,500,000 visits (Point F on S_1). But consumers—patients—pay only $10.

third-party payer

An agent other than the seller or the buyer who pays part of the price of a good or service.

Insurers make up the difference between the fees doctors receive and the price patients pay. In our example, insurers pay $40 per visit of insured patients to supplement the $10 that patients pay. When an agent other than the seller or the buyer pays part of the price of a good or service, we say that the agent is a **third-party payer**.

Notice how the presence of a third-party payer affects total spending on office visits. When people paid for their own visits, and the price equaled $30 per visit, total spending equaled $30 million per week. Now doctors receive $50 per visit and provide 1,500,000 visits per week. Total spending has risen to $75 million per week ($50 times 1,500,000 visits, shown by the darkly shaded region plus the lightly shaded region).

FIGURE 4.12 Total Spending for Physician Office Visits Covered by Insurance
With insurance, the quantity of physician office visits demanded rises to 1,500,000. The supply curve shows that it takes a price of $50 per visit to increase the quantity supplied to 1,500,000 visits. Patients pay $10 per visit and insurance pays $40 per visit. Total spending rises to $75,000,000 per week, shown by the darkly shaded region plus the lightly shaded region.

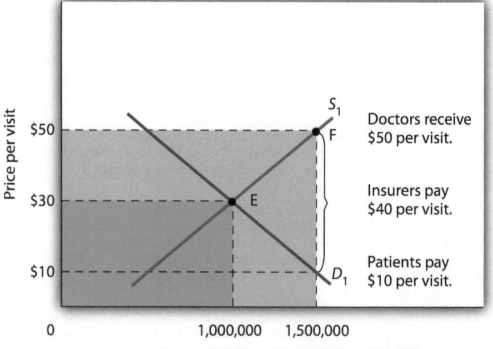

The response described in Figure 4.12 holds for many different types of goods and services covered by insurance or otherwise paid for by third-party payers. For example, the availability of scholarships and subsidized tuition at public and private universities increases the quantity of education demanded and the total expenditures on higher education. In markets with third-party payers, an equilibrium is achieved, but it is not at the intersection of the demand and supply curves. The effect of third-party payers is to decrease the price that consumers directly pay for the goods and services they consume and to increase the price that suppliers receive. Consumers use more than they would in the absence of third-party payers, and providers are encouraged to supply more than they otherwise would. The result is increased total spending.

How might spending in markets characterized by third-party payers be reduced, if that is a goal? In the case of health care insurance, one mechanism would be to require patients to pay a larger share of their own health-care consumption directly, reducing the payments made by third-party payers. One way to do this is with policies that have higher out-of-pocket requirements for such things as co-pays and deductibles. Allowing people to accumulate tax-free private medical savings accounts allows people to more easily cover such expenses. Another option is to use insurance companies as the agents that limit spending. A third option is government regulation.

Since its enactment in 2010, Republicans began talking about the "repeal and replacement" of the Affordable Care Act. With the end of the Obama administration and the election of Donald Trump and Republican majorities in Congress, the country is waiting to see what kinds of changes may occur yet again in the health care market in the United States. Some of the alternative proposals mention expansion of health savings accounts, the use of high-risk insurance pools for covering individuals with pre-existing conditions rather than requiring insurers to cover such people as the ACA does, tax credits rather than subsidies for buying health insurance, and more flexibility in terms of the insurance coverage offered.

Key Takeaways

- The rising share of the output of the United States devoted to health care represents a rising opportunity cost. More spending on health care means less spending on other goods and services, compared to what would have transpired had health-care spending not risen so much.
- The model of demand and supply can be used to show the effect of third-party payers on total spending. With third-party payers (for example, health insurers), the quantity of services consumed rises, as does spending.

Try It!

The provision of university education through taxpayer-supported state universities is another example of a market with a third-party payer. Use the model of demand and supply to discuss the impact this has on the higher education market. Specifically, draw a graph similar to Figure 4.12. How would you label the axes? Show the equilibrium price and quantity in the absence of a third-party payer and indicate total spending on education. Now show the impact of lower tuition As a result of state support for education. How much education do students demand at the lower tuition? How much tuition must educational institutions receive to produce that much education? How much spending on education will occur? Compare total spending before and after a third-party payer enters this market.

Case in Point: Oregon's Experiments in Health Care

Source: © Shutterstock, Inc.

The health-care industry presents us with a dilemma. Clearly, it makes sense for people to have health insurance. Just as clearly, health insurance, like other types of insurances that involve third-party payers, generates a substantial increase in spending for health care. If that spending is to be limited, some mechanism must be chosen to do it. For the past thirty years, Oregon has experimented in various ways to control its spending on Medicaid, the program that focuses on providing health care for its poor residents.

Until 1987 Oregon had a Medicaid plan similar to plans in many other states. Households whose incomes were lower than 50% of the poverty line qualified for Medicaid. Then, it began its first experiment to manage health-care spending by essentially refusing to be a third-party payer for certain services. It decided that it would no longer fund organ transplants and that it would use the money saved to give better care to pregnant women. The decision turned out to be a painful one; the first year, a seven-year-old boy with leukemia, who might have been saved with a bone marrow transplant, died. But state officials argued that the shift of expenditures to pregnant women would ultimately save more lives.

The state gradually expanded its concept of determining what services to fund and what services not to fund. It collapsed a list of 10,000 different diagnoses that had been submitted to its Medicaid program in the past into a list of more than 700 condition-treatment pairs. One such pair, for example, is appendicitis-appendectomy. Health-care officials then ranked these pairs in order of priority. The rankings were based on such factors as the seriousness of a particular condition and the cost and efficacy of treatments. The state announced that it would provide Medicaid to all households below the poverty line, but that it would not fund any procedure ranked below a certain level, initially number 588 on its list. The plan also set a budget limit for any one year; if spending rose above that limit, the legislature must appropriate additional money or drop additional procedures from the list of those covered by the plan. The Oregon Health Plan officially began operation in 1994.

While the Oregon plan was applied only to households below the poverty line that were not covered by other programs, it suggests a means of reducing health-care spending. Clearly, if part of the health-care problem is excessive provision of services, a system designed to cut services must determine what treatments not to fund.

Professors Jonathan Oberlander, Theodore Marmor, and Lawrence Jacobs studied the impact of this plan in practice through the year 2000 and found that, in contrast to initial expectations, excluded procedures were generally ones of marginal medical value, so the "line in the sand" had little practical significance. In addition, they found that patients were often able to receive supposedly excluded services when physicians, for example, treated an uncovered illness in conjunction with a covered one. During the period of the study, the number of people covered by the plan expanded substantially and yet rationing of services essentially did not occur. How do they explain this seeming contradiction? Quite simply: state government increased revenues from various sources to support the plan. Indeed, they argue that, because treatments that might not be included were explicitly stated, political pressure made excluding them even more difficult and may have inadvertently increased the cost of the program.

In the early 2000s, Oregon, like many other states, confronted severe budgetary pressures. To limit spending, it chose the perhaps less visible strategy of reducing the number of people covered through the plan. Once serving more than 100,000 people, budget cuts reduced the number served to about 17,000. Whereas in 1996, 11% of Oregonians lacked health insurance, in 2008 16% did.

Trailblazing again, in 2008 Oregon realized that its budget allowed room for coverage for a few thousand additional people. How to choose among the 130,000 eligibles? Oregon embarked on its second experiment: it held a lottery. More than 90,000 people queued up, hoping to be lucky winners. There were slots for 10,000.

The lottery presented a unique opportunity in social policy research to assess the effects of expanding the public health care program because it allowed for the comparison between those who were randomly selected to receive Medicaid insurance and those who applied for coverage but were not selected. A group of researchers led by Professor Amy N. Finkelstein embarked on a major study to learn the effects on health outcomes, health care usage, finances, and well-being of low-income adults. Results showed that Medicaid coverage increased health care use across a variety of settings, improved financial security (by significantly lowering medical debt and essentially eliminating the likelihood of a catastrophic medical expenditure), improved self-reported estimations of health and happiness, and reduced rates of depression among enrollees. However it led to no detectable changes in several measures of physical health (such as blood pressure or cholesterol levels), employment rates, or earnings. A finding that received a great deal of attention in the media was that the rate of visits to emergency rooms increased. The expectation by many had been that the newly insured would substitute the more expensive emergency room visits with office visits to their primary care doctors. In this study, both types of care increased, suggesting that the two types of health care settings are complements. Their complementarity could be driven by the patients seeking more care of both types and by physicians who, in certain medical situations, may deem the emergency room a better option and encourage patients to go there.

The third experiment began with the introduction of the Medicaid expansion in 2014 as part of the Affordable Care Act. Oregon sought for and received a waiver from the federal government on how it delivered care to its low-income residents. It chose to create 16 coordinated care organizations (CCOs), with patient-centered primary care homes that use teams to coordinate care with the twin goals to improve care and hold down costs. The CCOs are paid on a per-member basis rather than on the number of services provided. When they achieve certain quality metrics, the CCOs receive bonus payments. Enrollment in Medicaid in Oregon has gone from around 600,000 people to well over a million. The most recent study of the current program by the Oregon Health Authority reports declining per capita emergency room visits (in contrast to the study during the period of the lottery), decreased hospital readmissions, and increased screenings for such things as substance abuse. The CCOs are meeting most of their quality metrics. The report also states that Oregon is meeting financial goals set by the federal government to reduce the growth in spending per member by 2 percentage points per year compared to what it was predicted the increase would have been without the reorganization.

Sources: Based on Amy N. Finkelstein, Ph.D., Sarah L. Taubman, Ph.D., Heidi L. Allen, Ph.D., Bill J. Wright, Ph.D., and Katherine Baicker, Ph.D., "Effect of Medicaid Coverage on ED Use — Further Evidence from Oregon's Experiment," New England Journal of Medicine 375:16 (October 20, 2016): 1505-1507; Jonathan Oberlander, Theodore Marmor, and Lawrence Jacobs, "Rationing Medical Care: Rhetoric and Reality in the Oregon Health Plan," Canadian Medical Association Journal 164: 11 (May 29, 2001): 1583–1587; Oregon Health Authority, Oregon Health System Transformation: Annual Update, January 2016 at http://www.oregon.gov/oha/Metrics/Pages/HST-Reports.aspx; William Yardley, "Drawing Lots for Health Care," The New York Times, March 13, 2008: p. A12.

Answer to Try It! Problem

Without a third-party payer for education, the graph shows equilibrium tuition of P_1 and equilibrium quantity of education of Q_1. State support for education lowers tuition that students pay to P_2. As a result, students demand Q_2 courses per year. To provide that amount of education, educational institutions require tuition per course of P_3. Without a third-party payer, spending on education is $0P_1EQ_1$. With a third-party payer, spending rises to $0P_3FQ_2$.

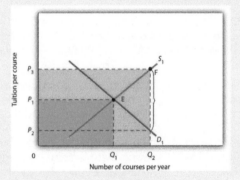

4.5 Review and Practice

Summary

In this chapter we used the tools of demand and supply to understand a wide variety of market outcomes. We learned that technological change and the entry of new sellers has caused the supply curve of personal computers to shift markedly to the right, thereby reducing equilibrium price and increasing equilibrium quantity. Market forces have made personal computers a common item in offices and homes.

Crude oil and gasoline prices soared in 2008 and then fell back, rising again in 2011 as a result of the disruption created by the Arab Spring. We looked at the causes of these increases as well as their impacts. Crude oil prices rose in large part As a result of increased demand, particularly from China. Higher prices for crude oil led to higher prices for gasoline. Those higher prices not only hurt consumers of gasoline, they also put upward pressure on the prices of a wide range of goods and services. Crude oil and gasoline prices then decreased dramatically in the last part of 2008, as world growth declined.

The model of demand and supply also explains the determination of stock prices. The price per share of corporate stock reflects the market's estimate of the expected profitability of the firm. Any information about the firm that causes potential buyers or current owners of corporate stock to reevaluate how profitable they think the firm is, or will be, will cause the equilibrium price of the stock to change.

We then examined markets in which some form of government price control keeps price permanently above or below equilibrium. A price floor leads to persistent surpluses because it is set above the equilibrium price, whereas a price ceiling, because it is set below the equilibrium price, leads to persistent shortages. We saw that interfering with the market mechanism may solve one problem but often creates other problems at the same time. We discussed what some of these unintended consequences might be. For example, agricultural price floors aimed at boosting farm income have also raised prices for consumers and cost taxpayers dearly, and the bulk of government payments have gone to large farms. Rent controls have lowered rents, but they have also reduced the quantity of rental housing supplied, created shortages, and sometimes led to various forms of "backdoor" payments, which sometimes force the price of rental housing above what would exist in the absence of controls.

Finally, we looked at the market for health care and a special feature behind demand and supply in this market that helps to explain why the share of output of the United States that is devoted to health care has risen. Health care is an example of a market in which there are third-party payers (primarily private insurers and the government). With third-party payers the quantity of health-care services consumed rises, as does health-care spending.

Concept Problems

1. Like personal computers, digital cameras have become a common household item. Digital camera prices have plunged in the last 10 years. Use the model of demand and supply to explain the fall in price and increase in quantity.

2. Enron Corp. was one of several corporations convicted of fraud in its accounting practices during the early part of this decade. It had created dummy corporations to hide massive borrowing and to give it the appearance of extraordinary profitability. Use the model of demand and supply to explain the likely impact of such convictions on the stocks of other corporations.

3. During World War II there was a freeze on wages, and corporations found they could evade the freeze by providing other fringe benefits such as retirement funds and health insurance for their employees. The Office of Price Administration, which administered the wage freeze, ruled that the offer of retirement funds and health literature was not a violation of the freeze. The Internal Revenue Service went along with this and ruled that employer-financed retirement and health insurance plans were not taxable income. Was the wage freeze an example of a price floor or a price ceiling? Use the model of demand and supply to explain why employers began to offer such benefits to their employees.

4. The text argues that political instability in potential suppliers of oil such as Iraq and Venezuela accounts for a relatively steep supply curve for crude oil such as the one shown in Figure 4.2 Suppose that this instability eases considerably and that the world supply curve for crude oil becomes much flatter. Draw such a curve, and explain its implications for the world economy and for typical consumers.

5. Suppose that technological change affects the dairy industry in the same way it has affected the computer industry. However, suppose that dairy price supports remain in place. How would this affect government spending on the dairy program? Use the model of demand and supply to support your answer.

6. People often argue that there is a "shortage" of child care. Using the model of demand and supply, evaluate whether this argument is likely to be correct.

7. "During most of the past 50 years the United States has had a surplus of farmers, and this has been the root of the farm problem." Comment.

8. Suppose the Department of Agriculture ordered all farmers to reduce the acreage they plant by 10%. Would you expect a 10% reduction in food production? Why or why not?

9. The text argues that the increase in gasoline prices had a particularly strong impact on low-income people. Name some other goods and services for which a sharp increase in price would have a similar impact on people with low incomes.

10. Suppose that the United States and the European Union impose a price ceiling on crude oil of $25 per barrel. Explain, and illustrate graphically, how this would affect the markets for crude oil and for gasoline in the United States and in the European Union.

11. Given that rent controls can actually hurt low-income people, devise a housing strategy that would provide affordable housing for those whose incomes fall below the poverty line (in 2010, this was about $22,314 for a family of four).

12. Using the model of demand and supply, show and explain how an increase in the share individuals must pay directly for medical care affects the quantity they consume. Explain how this would address the total amount of spending on health care.

13. Given that people pay premiums for their health insurance, how can we say that insurance lowers the prices people pay for health-care services?

14. Suppose that physicians now charge $30 for an office visit and insurance policies require patients to pay 33 1/3% of the amount they pay the physicians, so the out-of-pocket cost to consumers is $10 per visit. In an effort to control costs, the government imposes a price ceiling of $27 per office visit. Using a demand and supply model, show how this policy would affect the market for health care.

15. Do you think the U.S. health-care system requires reform? Why or why not? If you think reform is in order, explain the approach to reform you advocate.

Numerical Problems

Problems 1–4 are based on the following demand and supply schedules for corn (all quantities are in millions of bushels per year).

Price per bushel	Quantity demanded	Quantity supplied
$0	6	0
1	5	1
2	4	2
3	3	3
4	2	4
5	1	5
6	0	6

1. Draw the demand and supply curves for corn. What is the equilibrium price? The equilibrium quantity?

2. Suppose the government now imposes a price floor at $4 per bushel. Show the effect of this program graphically. How large is the surplus of corn?

3. With the price floor, how much do farmers receive for their corn? How much would they have received if there were no price floor?

4. If the government buys all the surplus corn, how much will it spend?

Problems 5–9 are based on the following hypothetical demand and supply curves for apartments

Rent/Month	Number of Apts. Demanded/Month	Number of Apts. Supplied/Month
$0	120,000	0
200	100,000	20,000
400	80,000	40,000
600	60,000	60,000
800	40,000	80,000
1000	20,000	100,000
1200	0	120,000

5. Draw the demand and supply curves for apartments.

6. What is the equilibrium rent per month? At this rent, what is the number of apartments demanded and supplied per month?

7. Suppose a ceiling on rents is set at $400 per month. Characterize the situation that results from this policy.

8. At the rent ceiling, how many apartments are demanded? How many are supplied?

9. How much are people willing to pay for the number of apartments supplied at the ceiling? Describe the arrangements to which this situation might lead.

Endnotes

1. Ilkka Tuomi, "The Lives and Death of Moore's Law." http://www.firstmonday.org/issues/issue7_11/tuomi/index. *First Monday* (http://www.firstmonday.org) is a peer-reviewed journal on the Internet.
2. Richard Arnott, "Time for Revisionism on Rent Control," *Journal of Economic Perspectives* 9(1) (Winter, 1995): 99–120.

CHAPTER 5
Elasticity: A Measure of Response

5.1 Start Up: Raise Fares? Lower Fares? What's a Public Transit Manager To Do?

Imagine that you are the manager of the public transportation system for a large metropolitan area. Operating costs for the system have soared in the last few years, and you are under pressure to boost revenues. What do you do?

An obvious choice would be to raise fares. That will make your customers angry, but at least it will generate the extra revenue you need—or will it? The law of demand says that raising fares will reduce the number of passengers riding on your system. If the number of passengers falls only a little, then the higher fares that your remaining passengers are paying might produce the higher revenues you need. But what if the number of passengers falls by so much that your higher fares actually reduce your revenues? If that happens, you will have made your customers mad and your financial problem worse!

Maybe you should recommend *lower* fares. After all, the law of demand also says that lower fares will increase the number of passengers. Having more people use the public transportation system could more than offset a lower fare you collect from each person. But it might not. What *will* you do?

Your job and the fiscal health of the public transit system are riding on your making the correct decision. To do so, you need to know just how responsive the quantity demanded is to a price change. You need a measure of responsiveness.

Economists use a measure of responsiveness called elasticity. **Elasticity** is the ratio of the percentage change in a dependent variable to a percentage change in an independent variable. If the dependent variable is y, and the independent variable is x, then the elasticity of y with respect to a change in x is given by:

$$e\, y,x\ =\ \%\ \text{change in } y\ \%\ \text{change in } x$$

A variable such as y is said to be more elastic (responsive) if the percentage change in y is large relative to the percentage change in x. It is less elastic if the reverse is true.

As manager of the public transit system, for example, you will want to know how responsive the number of passengers on your system (the dependent variable) will be to a change in fares (the independent variable). The concept of elasticity will help you solve your public transit pricing problem and a great many other issues in economics. We will examine several elasticities in this chapter—all will tell us how responsive one variable is to a change in another.

elasticity

The ratio of the percentage change in a dependent variable to a percentage change in an independent variable.

5.2 The Price Elasticity of Demand

Learning Objectives

1. Explain the concept of price elasticity of demand and its calculation.
2. Explain what it means for demand to be price inelastic, unit price elastic, price elastic, perfectly price inelastic, and perfectly price elastic.
3. Explain how and why the value of the price elasticity of demand changes along a linear demand curve.
4. Understand the relationship between total revenue and price elasticity of demand.
5. Discuss the determinants of price elasticity of demand.

We know from the law of demand how the quantity demanded will respond to a price change: it will change in the opposite direction. But how *much* will it change? It seems reasonable to expect, for example, that a 10% change in the price charged for a visit to the doctor would yield a different percentage change in quantity demanded than a 10% change in the price of a Ford Mustang. But how much is this difference?

price elasticity of demand

The percentage change in quantity demanded of a particular good or service divided by the percentage change in the price of that good or service, all other things unchanged.

To show how responsive quantity demanded is to a change in price, we apply the concept of elasticity. The **price elasticity of demand** for a good or service, e_D, is the percentage change in quantity demanded of a particular good or service divided by the percentage change in the price of that good or service, all other things unchanged. Thus we can write

EQUATION 5.1

$$e_D = \frac{\% \text{ change in quantity demanded}}{\% \text{ change in price}}$$

Because the price elasticity of demand shows the responsiveness of quantity demanded to a price change, assuming that other factors that influence demand are unchanged, it reflects movements *along* a demand curve. With a downward-sloping demand curve, price and quantity demanded move in opposite directions, so the price elasticity of demand is always negative. A positive percentage change in price implies a negative percentage change in quantity demanded, and vice versa. Sometimes you will see the absolute value of the price elasticity measure reported. In essence, the minus sign is ignored because it is expected that there will be a negative (inverse) relationship between quantity demanded and price. In this text, however, we will retain the minus sign in reporting price elasticity of demand and will say "the absolute value of the price elasticity of demand" when that is what we are describing.

Heads Up!

Be careful not to confuse elasticity with slope. The slope of a line is the change in the value of the variable on the vertical axis divided by the change in the value of the variable on the horizontal axis between two points. Elasticity is the ratio of the percentage changes. The slope of a demand curve, for example, is the ratio of the change in price to the change in quantity between two points on the curve. The price elasticity of demand is the ratio of the percentage change in quantity to the percentage change in price. As we will see, when computing elasticity at different points on a linear demand curve, the slope is constant—that is, it does not change—but the value for elasticity will change.

Computing the Price Elasticity of Demand

Finding the price elasticity of demand requires that we first compute percentage changes in price and in quantity demanded. We calculate those changes between two points on a demand curve.

Figure 5.1 shows a particular demand curve, a linear demand curve for public transit rides. Suppose the initial price is $0.80, and the quantity demanded is 40,000 rides per day; we are at point A on the curve. Now suppose the price falls to $0.70, and we want to report the responsiveness of the quantity demanded. We see that at the new price, the quantity demanded rises to 60,000 rides per day (point B). To compute the elasticity, we need to compute the percentage changes in price and in quantity demanded between points A and B.

FIGURE 5.1 Responsiveness and Demand
The demand curve shows how changes in price lead to changes in the quantity demanded. A movement from point A to point B shows that a $0.10 reduction in price increases the number of rides per day by 20,000. A movement from B to A is a $0.10 increase in price, which reduces quantity demanded by 20,000 rides per day.

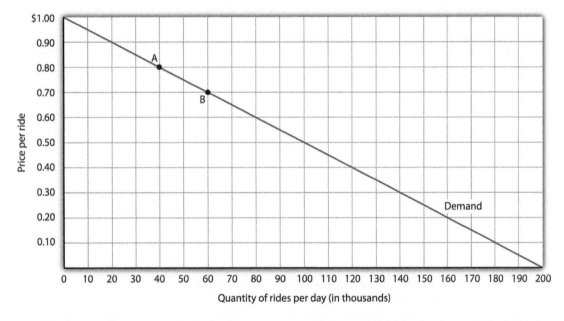

We measure the percentage change between two points as the change in the variable divided by the *average* value of the variable between the two points. Thus, the percentage change in quantity between points A and B in Figure 5.1 is computed relative to the *average* of the quantity values at points A and B: (60,000 + 40,000)/2 = 50,000. The percentage change in quantity, then, is 20,000/50,000, or 40%. Likewise, the percentage change in price between points A and B is based on the *average* of the two prices: ($0.80 + $0.70)/2 = $0.75, and so we have a percentage change of -0.10/0.75, or -13.33%. The price elasticity of demand between points A and B is thus 40%/(-13.33%) = -3.00.

arc elasticity

Measure of elasticity
based on percentage
changes relative to the
average value of each
variable between two
points.

This measure of elasticity, which is based on percentage changes relative to the average value of each variable between two points, is called **arc elasticity**. The arc elasticity method has the advantage that it yields the same elasticity whether we go from point A to point B or from point B to point A. It is the method we shall use to compute elasticity.

For the arc elasticity method, we calculate the price elasticity of demand using the average value of price, $\bar{P}$, and the average value of quantity demanded, $\bar{Q}$. We shall use the Greek letter Δ to mean "change in," so the change in quantity between two points is ΔQ and the change in price is ΔP. Now we can write the formula for the price elasticity of demand as

EQUATION 5.2

$$e_D = \frac{\Delta Q \big/ \bar{Q}}{\Delta P \big/ \bar{P}}$$

The price elasticity of demand between points A and B is thus:

$$e_D = \frac{\dfrac{20{,}000}{(40{,}000 + 60{,}000)/2}}{\dfrac{-\$0.10}{(\$0.80 + \$0.70)/2}} = \frac{40\%}{-13.33\%} = -3.00$$

With the arc elasticity formula, the elasticity is the same whether we move from point A to point B or from point B to point A. If we start at point B and move to point A, we have:

$$e_D = \frac{\dfrac{-20{,}000}{(60{,}000 + 40{,}000)/2}}{\dfrac{0.10}{(\$0.70 + \$0.80)/2}} = \frac{-40\%}{13.33\%} = -3.00$$

The arc elasticity method gives us an estimate of elasticity. It gives the value of elasticity at the midpoint over a range of change, such as the movement between points A and B. For a precise computation of elasticity, we would need to consider the response of a dependent variable to an extremely small change in an independent variable. The fact that arc elasticities are approximate suggests an important practical rule in calculating arc elasticities: we should consider only small changes in independent variables. We cannot apply the concept of arc elasticity to large changes.

Another argument for considering only small changes in computing price elasticities of demand will become evident in the next section. We will investigate what happens to price elasticities as we move from one point to another along a linear demand curve.

Heads Up!

Notice that in the arc elasticity formula, the method for computing a percentage change differs from the standard method with which you may be familiar. That method measures the percentage change in a variable relative to its original value. For example, using the standard method, when we go from point A to point B, we would compute the percentage change in quantity as 20,000/40,000 = 50%. The percentage change in price would be –$0.10/$0.80 = –12.5%. The price elasticity of demand would then be 50%/(–12.5%) = –4.00. Going from point B to point A, however, would yield a different elasticity. The percentage change in quantity would be –20,000/60,000, or –33.33%. The percentage change in price would be $0.10/$0.70 = 14.29%. The price elasticity of demand would thus be –33.33%/14.29% = –2.33. By using the average quantity and average price to calculate percentage changes, the arc elasticity approach avoids the necessity to specify the direction of the change and, thereby, gives us the same answer whether we go from A to B or from B to A.

Price Elasticities Along a Linear Demand Curve

What happens to the price elasticity of demand when we travel along the demand curve? The answer depends on the nature of the demand curve itself. On a linear demand curve, such as the one in Figure 5.2, elasticity becomes smaller (in absolute value) as we travel downward and to the right.

FIGURE 5.2 Price Elasticities of Demand for a Linear Demand Curve
The price elasticity of demand varies between different pairs of points along a linear demand curve. The lower the price and the greater the quantity demanded, the lower the absolute value of the price elasticity of demand.

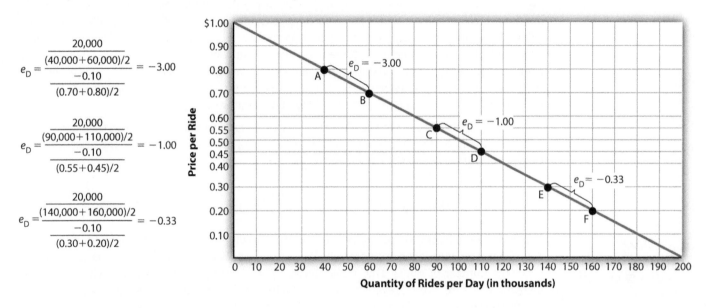

$$e_D = \frac{\dfrac{20{,}000}{(40{,}000+60{,}000)/2}}{\dfrac{-0.10}{(0.70+0.80)/2}} = -3.00$$

$$e_D = \frac{\dfrac{20{,}000}{(90{,}000+110{,}000)/2}}{\dfrac{-0.10}{(0.55+0.45)/2}} = -1.00$$

$$e_D = \frac{\dfrac{20{,}000}{(140{,}000+160{,}000)/2}}{\dfrac{-0.10}{(0.30+0.20)/2}} = -0.33$$

Figure 5.2 shows the same demand curve we saw in Figure 5.1. We have already calculated the price elasticity of demand between points A and B; it equals -3.00. Notice, however, that when we use the same method to compute the price elasticity of demand between other sets of points, our answer varies. For each of the pairs of points shown, the changes in price and quantity demanded are the same (a $0.10 decrease in price and 20,000 additional rides per day, respectively). But at the high prices and low quantities on the upper part of the demand curve, the percentage change in quantity is relatively large, whereas the percentage change in price is relatively small. The absolute value of the price elasticity of demand is thus relatively large. As we move down the demand curve, equal changes in quantity represent smaller and smaller percentage changes, whereas equal changes in price represent larger and larger percentage changes, and the absolute value of the elasticity measure declines. Between points C and D, for example, the price elasticity of demand is -1.00, and between points E and F the price elasticity of demand is -0.33.

On a linear demand curve, the price elasticity of demand varies depending on the interval over which we are measuring it. For any linear demand curve, the absolute value of the price elasticity of demand will fall as we move down and to the right along the curve.

The Price Elasticity of Demand and Changes in Total Revenue

total revenue

A firm's output multiplied by the price at which it sells that output.

Suppose the public transit authority is considering raising fares. Will its total revenues go up or down? **Total revenue** is the price per unit times the number of units sold.[1] In this case, it is the fare times the number of riders. The transit authority will certainly want to know whether a price increase will cause its total revenue to rise or fall. In fact, determining the impact of a price change on total revenue is crucial to the analysis of many problems in economics.

We will do two quick calculations before generalizing the principle involved. Given the demand curve shown in Figure 5.2, we see that at a price of $0.80, the transit authority will sell 40,000 rides per day. Total revenue would be $32,000 per day ($0.80 times 40,000). If the price were lowered by $0.10 to $0.70, quantity demanded would increase to 60,000 rides and total revenue would increase to $42,000 ($0.70 times 60,000). The reduction in fare *increases* total revenue. However, if the initial price had been $0.30 and the transit authority reduced it by $0.10 to $0.20, total revenue would *decrease* from $42,000 ($0.30 times 140,000) to $32,000 ($0.20 times 160,000). So it appears that the impact of a price change on total revenue depends on the initial price and, by implication, the original elasticity. We generalize this point in the remainder of this section.

The problem in assessing the impact of a price change on total revenue of a good or service is that a change in price always changes the quantity demanded in the opposite direction. An increase in price reduces the quantity demanded, and a reduction in price increases the quantity demanded. The question is how much. Because total revenue is found by multiplying the price per unit times the quantity demanded, it is not clear whether a change in price will cause total revenue to rise or fall.

We have already made this point in the context of the transit authority. Consider the following three examples of price increases for gasoline, pizza, and diet cola.

Suppose that 1,000 gallons of gasoline per day are demanded at a price of $4.00 per gallon. Total revenue for gasoline thus equals $4,000 per day (=1,000 gallons per day times $4.00 per gallon). If an increase in the price of gasoline to $4.25 reduces the quantity demanded to 950 gallons per day, total revenue rises to $4,037.50 per day (=950 gallons per day times $4.25 per gallon). Even though people consume less gasoline at $4.25 than at $4.00, total revenue rises because the higher price more than makes up for the drop in consumption.

Next consider pizza. Suppose 1,000 pizzas per week are demanded at a price of $9 per pizza. Total revenue for pizza equals $9,000 per week (=1,000 pizzas per week times $9 per pizza). If an increase in the price of pizza to $10 per pizza reduces quantity demanded to 900 pizzas per week, total revenue will still be $9,000 per week (=900 pizzas per week times $10 per pizza). Again, when price goes up, consumers buy less, but this time there is no change in total revenue.

Now consider diet cola. Suppose 1,000 cans of diet cola per day are demanded at a price of $0.50 per can. Total revenue for diet cola equals $500 per day (=1,000 cans per day times $0.50 per can). If an increase in the price of diet cola to $0.55 per can reduces quantity demanded to 880 cans per month, total revenue for diet cola falls to $484 per day (=880 cans per day times $0.55 per can). As in the case of gasoline, people will buy less diet cola when the price rises from $0.50 to $0.55, but in this example total revenue drops.

In our first example, an increase in price increased total revenue. In the second, a price increase left total revenue unchanged. In the third example, the price rise reduced total revenue. Is there a way to predict how a price change will affect total revenue? There is; the effect depends on the price elasticity of demand.

Elastic, Unit Elastic, and Inelastic Demand

To determine how a price change will affect total revenue, economists place price elasticities of demand in three categories, based on their absolute value. If the absolute value of the price elasticity of demand is greater than 1, demand is termed **price elastic**. If it is equal to 1, demand is **unit price elastic**. And if it is less than 1, demand is **price inelastic**.

Relating Elasticity to Changes in Total Revenue

When the price of a good or service changes, the quantity demanded changes in the opposite direction. Total revenue will move in the direction of the variable that changes by the larger percentage. If the variables move by the same percentage, total revenue stays the same. If quantity demanded changes by a larger percentage than price (i.e., if demand is price elastic), total revenue will change in the direction of the quantity change. If price changes by a larger percentage than quantity demanded (i.e., if demand is price inelastic), total revenue will move in the direction of the price change. If price and quantity demanded change by the same percentage (i.e., if demand is unit price elastic), then total revenue does not change.

When demand is price inelastic, a given percentage change in price results in a smaller percentage change in quantity demanded. That implies that total revenue will move in the direction of the price change: a reduction in price will reduce total revenue, and an increase in price will increase it.

Consider the price elasticity of demand for gasoline. In the example above, 1,000 gallons of gasoline were purchased each day at a price of $4.00 per gallon; an increase in price to $4.25 per gallon reduced the quantity demanded to 950 gallons per day. We thus had an average quantity of 975 gallons per day and an average price of $4.125. We can thus calculate the arc price elasticity of demand for gasoline:

Percentage change in quantity demanded=−50/975=−5.1%
Percentage change in price=0.25/4.125=6.06%
Price elasticity of demand=−5.1%/6.06%=−0.84

The demand for gasoline is price inelastic, and total revenue moves in the direction of the price change. When price rises, total revenue rises. Recall that in our example above, total spending on gasoline (which equals total revenues to sellers) rose from $4,000 per day (=1,000 gallons per day times $4.00) to $4037.50 per day (=950 gallons per day times $4.25 per gallon).

When demand is price inelastic, a given percentage change in price results in a smaller percentage change in quantity demanded. That implies that total revenue will move in the direction of the price change: an increase in price will increase total revenue, and a reduction in price will reduce it.

Consider again the example of pizza that we examined above. At a price of $9 per pizza, 1,000 pizzas per week were demanded. Total revenue was $9,000 per week (=1,000 pizzas per week times $9 per pizza). When the price rose to $10, the quantity demanded fell to 900 pizzas per week. Total revenue remained $9,000 per week (=900 pizzas per week times $10 per pizza). Again, we have an

price elastic

Situation in which the absolute value of the price elasticity of demand is greater than 1.

unit price elastic

Situation in which the absolute value of the price elasticity of demand is equal to 1.

price inelastic

Situation in which the absolute value of the price of elasticity of demand is less than 1.

average quantity of 950 pizzas per week and an average price of $9.50. Using the arc elasticity method, we can compute:

Percentage change in quantity demanded=−100/950=−10.5%
Percentage change in price=$1.00/$9.50=10.5%
Price elasticity of demand=−10.5%/10.5%=−1.0

Demand is unit price elastic, and total revenue remains unchanged. Quantity demanded falls by the same percentage by which price increases.

Consider next the example of diet cola demand. At a price of $0.50 per can, 1,000 cans of diet cola were purchased each day. Total revenue was thus $500 per day (=$0.50 per can times 1,000 cans per day). An increase in price to $0.55 reduced the quantity demanded to 880 cans per day. We thus have an average quantity of 940 cans per day and an average price of $0.525 per can. Computing the price elasticity of demand for diet cola in this example, we have:

Percentage change in quantity demanded=−120/940=−12.8%
Percentage change in price=$0.05/$0.525=9.5%
Price elasticity of demand=−12.8%/9.5%=−1.3

The demand for diet cola is price elastic, so total revenue moves in the direction of the quantity change. It falls from $500 per day before the price increase to $484 per day after the price increase.

A demand curve can also be used to show changes in total revenue. Figure 5.3 shows the demand curve from Figure 5.1 and Figure 5.2. At point A, total revenue from public transit rides is given by the area of a rectangle drawn with point A in the upper right-hand corner and the origin in the lower left-hand corner. The height of the rectangle is price; its width is quantity. We have already seen that total revenue at point A is $32,000 ($0.80 × 40,000). When we reduce the price and move to point B, the rectangle showing total revenue becomes shorter and wider. Notice that the area gained in moving to the rectangle at B is greater than the area lost; total revenue rises to $42,000 ($0.70 × 60,000). Recall from Figure 5.2 that demand is elastic between points A and B. In general, demand is elastic in the upper half of any linear demand curve, so total revenue moves in the direction of the quantity change.

FIGURE 5.3 Changes in Total Revenue and a Linear Demand Curve
Moving from point A to point B implies a reduction in price and an increase in the quantity demanded. Demand is elastic between these two points. Total revenue, shown by the areas of the rectangles drawn from points A and B to the origin, rises. When we move from point E to point F, which is in the inelastic region of the demand curve, total revenue falls.

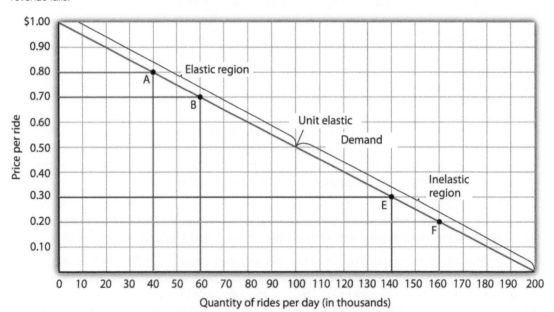

A movement from point E to point F also shows a reduction in price and an increase in quantity demanded. This time, however, we are in an inelastic region of the demand curve. Total revenue now moves in the direction of the price change—it falls. Notice that the rectangle drawn from point F is smaller in area than the rectangle drawn from point E, once again confirming our earlier calculation.

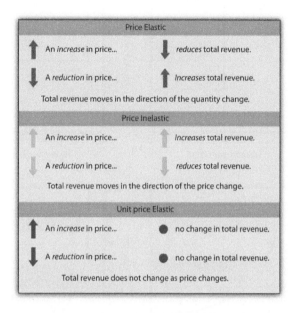

We have noted that a linear demand curve is more elastic where prices are relatively high and quantities relatively low and less elastic where prices are relatively low and quantities relatively high. We can be even more specific. *For any linear demand curve, demand will be price elastic in the upper half of the curve and price inelastic in its lower half. At the midpoint of a linear demand curve, demand is unit price elastic.*

Constant Price Elasticity of Demand Curves

Figure 5.4 shows four demand curves over which price elasticity of demand is the same at all points. The demand curve in Panel (a) is vertical. This means that price changes have no effect on quantity demanded. The numerator of the formula given in Equation 5.1 for the price elasticity of demand (percentage change in quantity demanded) is zero. The price elasticity of demand in this case is therefore zero, and the demand curve is said to be **perfectly inelastic**. This is a theoretically extreme case, and no good that has been studied empirically exactly fits it. A good that comes close, at least over a specific price range, is insulin. A diabetic will not consume more insulin as its price falls but, over some price range, will consume the amount needed to control the disease.

perfectly inelastic

Situation in which the price elasticity of demand is zero.

FIGURE 5.4 Demand Curves with Constant Price Elasticities

The demand curve in Panel (a) is perfectly inelastic. The demand curve in Panel (b) is perfectly elastic. Price elasticity of demand is −1.00 all along the demand curve in Panel (c), whereas it is −0.50 all along the demand curve in Panel (d).

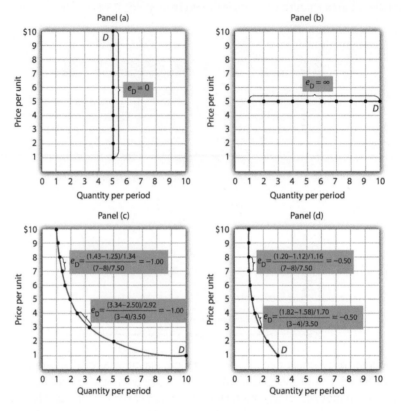

As illustrated in Figure 5.4, several other types of demand curves have the same elasticity at every point on them. The demand curve in Panel (b) is horizontal. This means that even the smallest price changes have enormous effects on quantity demanded. The denominator of the formula given in Equation 5.1 for the price elasticity of demand (percentage change in price) approaches zero. The price elasticity of demand in this case is therefore infinite, and the demand curve is said to be **perfectly elastic**.[2] This is the type of demand curve faced by producers of standardized products such as wheat. If the wheat of other farms is selling at $4 per bushel, a typical farm can sell as much wheat as it wants to at $4 but nothing at a higher price and would have no reason to offer its wheat at a lower price.

The nonlinear demand curves in Panels (c) and (d) have price elasticities of demand that are negative; but, unlike the linear demand curve discussed above, the value of the price elasticity is constant all along each demand curve. The demand curve in Panel (c) has price elasticity of demand equal to −1.00 throughout its range; in Panel (d) the price elasticity of demand is equal to −0.50 throughout its range. Empirical estimates of demand often show curves like those in Panels (c) and (d) that have the same elasticity at every point on the curve.

Heads Up!

Do not confuse price inelastic demand and perfectly inelastic demand. Perfectly inelastic demand means that the change in quantity is zero for any percentage change in price; the demand curve in this case is vertical. Price inelastic demand means only that the percentage change in quantity is less than the percentage change in price, not that the change in quantity is zero. With price inelastic (as opposed to perfectly inelastic) demand, the demand curve itself is still downward sloping.

Determinants of the Price Elasticity of Demand

The greater the absolute value of the price elasticity of demand, the greater the responsiveness of quantity demanded to a price change. What determines whether demand is more or less price elastic? The most important determinants of the price elasticity of demand for a good or service are the availability of substitutes, the importance of the item in household budgets, and time.

Availability of Substitutes

The price elasticity of demand for a good or service will be greater in absolute value if many close substitutes are available for it. If there are lots of substitutes for a particular good or service, then it is easy for consumers to switch to those substitutes when there is a price increase for that good or service. Suppose, for example, that the price of Ford automobiles goes up. There are many close substitutes for Fords—Chevrolets, Chryslers, Toyotas, and so on. The availability of close substitutes tends to make the demand for Fords more price elastic.

If a good has no close substitutes, its demand is likely to be somewhat less price elastic. There are no close substitutes for gasoline, for example. The price elasticity of demand for gasoline in the intermediate term of, say, three–nine months is generally estimated to be about -0.5. Since the absolute value of price elasticity is less than 1, it is price inelastic. We would expect, though, that the demand for a particular brand of gasoline will be much more price elastic than the demand for gasoline in general.

Importance in Household Budgets

One reason price changes affect quantity demanded is that they change how much a consumer can buy; a change in the price of a good or service affects the purchasing power of a consumer's income and thus affects the amount of a good the consumer will buy. This effect is stronger when a good or service is important in a typical household's budget.

A change in the price of jeans, for example, is probably more important in your budget than a change in the price of pencils. Suppose the prices of both were to double. You had planned to buy four pairs of jeans this year, but now you might decide to make do with two new pairs. A change in pencil prices, in contrast, might lead to very little reduction in quantity demanded simply because pencils are not likely to loom large in household budgets. The greater the importance of an item in household budgets, the greater the absolute value of the price elasticity of demand is likely to be.

Time

Suppose the price of electricity rises tomorrow morning. What will happen to the quantity demanded?

The answer depends in large part on how much time we allow for a response. If we are interested in the reduction in quantity demanded by tomorrow afternoon, we can expect that the response will be very small. But if we give consumers a year to respond to the price change, we can expect the response to be much greater. We expect that the absolute value of the price elasticity of demand will be greater when more time is allowed for consumer responses.

Consider the price elasticity of crude oil demand. Economists Afshin Javan and Nahl Zahran estimated short- and long-run price elasticities of demand for crude oil in twenty-five nations for the period 1993 to 2012. They found that for virtually every country, the price elasticities were negative and the long-run price elasticities were greater (in absolute value) than were the short-run price elasticities. Specifically, the short-run price elasticities ranged from -0.05 to -0.20, while the long run price elasticities ranged from -0.11 to -0.36. As you can see, the research was reported in a journal published by OPEC (Organization of Petroleum Exporting Countries), an organization whose members have profited greatly from the inelasticity of demand for their product. When it has chosen to restrict output, OPEC, which produces about 40 percent of the world's crude oil, has been able to put upward pressure on the price of crude. That has increased OPEC's (and all other oil producers') total revenues and reduced total cost.

TABLE 5.1 Short- and Long-Run Price Elasticities of the Demand for Crude Oil
For most countries, price elasticity of demand for crude oil tends to be greater (in absolute value) in the long run than in the short run.

Group	Country	Short-Run Price Elasticity of Demand	Long-Run Price Elasticity of Demand
North America	United States	−0.09	−0.24
	Canada	−0.06	−0.16
	Mexico	−0.08	−0.21
Europe	Germany	-0.11	−0.14
	France	−0.16	−0.22
	Italy	−0.20	−0.27
	Spain	−0.20	−0.28
	United Kingdom	−0.14	−0.19
	Turkey	-0.14	−0.18
Developed Asia	Japan	−0.16	−0.24
	South Korea	−0.14	−0.22
Emerging Asia	Thailand	−0.06	−0.14
	Philippines	−0.16	−0.36
Latin America	Brazil	−0.09	−0.19
	Argentina	−0.05	−0.11

Source: Based on data from Afshin Javan and Nahl Zahran, "Dynamic Panel Data Approaches for Estimating Oil Demand Elasticity," OPEC Energy Review 39:1 (March 2015): 62. The estimates are based on data for the period 1993 to 2012. Only countries for which both short-run and long-run price elasticities of demand were estimated are shown above.

Key Takeaways

- The price elasticity of demand measures the responsiveness of quantity demanded to changes in price; it is calculated by dividing the percentage change in quantity demanded by the percentage change in price.

- Demand is price inelastic if the absolute value of the price elasticity of demand is less than 1; it is unit price elastic if the absolute value is equal to 1; and it is price elastic if the absolute value is greater than 1.

- Demand is price elastic in the upper half of any linear demand curve and price inelastic in the lower half. It is unit price elastic at the midpoint.

- When demand is price inelastic, total revenue moves in the direction of a price change. When demand is unit price elastic, total revenue does not change in response to a price change. When demand is price elastic, total revenue moves in the direction of a quantity change.

- The absolute value of the price elasticity of demand is greater when substitutes are available, when the good is important in household budgets, and when buyers have more time to adjust to changes in the price of the good.

Try It!

You are now ready to play the part of the manager of the public transit system. Your finance officer has just advised you that the system faces a deficit. Your board does not want you to cut service, which means that you cannot cut costs. Your only hope is to increase revenue. Would a fare increase boost revenue?

You consult the economist on your staff who has researched studies on public transportation elasticities. She reports that the estimated price elasticity of demand for the first few months after a price change is about −0.3, but that after several years, it will be about −1.5.

1. Explain why the estimated values for price elasticity of demand differ.
2. Compute what will happen to ridership and revenue over the next few months if you decide to raise fares by 5%.
3. Compute what will happen to ridership and revenue over the next few years if you decide to raise fares by 5%.
4. What happens to total revenue now and after several years if you choose to raise fares?

Case in Point: Price Elasticity of Home Water Demand in Phoenix, Arizona

Source: © Shutterstock

Like many other cities in the U.S. southwest, Phoenix, Arizona grew rapidly in the latter part of the twentieth and first part of the twenty-first century. Located at the edge of a desert, Phoenix receives on average a meager eight inches of rain each year. Average temperature is about 75 degrees Fahrenheit and summer days often see temperatures over 100 degrees. Meeting increased water demand will be a challenge for the city under any circumstance. If the National Resources Defense Council's prediction of higher temperatures and less precipitation pans out, the picture gets even worse. Thus, knowing how water consumption responds to price changes is important for designing policies that will assure sustainable water use over time.

A study by James Yoo, Silvio Simonit, Ann P. Kinzig, and Charles Perrings investigated the price elasticity of residential water demand in Phoenix from 2000 to 2008. Their findings conform closely to expectations regarding factors that typically affect price elasticity of demand. In particular, with few substitutes for water, they were expecting a fairly low price elasticity of demand and that it would be higher in absolute value in the long run compared to the short run. Their estimate of price elasticity between 2000 and 2002 was -0.66. It rose to -1.155 over the interval 2000 to 2008. This suggests that over time consumers can adjust by such changes as buying appliances with higher water efficiency and by redesigning their yards.

They also found that low-income/low-water users exhibited greater price responsiveness than high-income/high-water users. Again, this result is expected since the water bill is more important in the budget of a low-income family than it is in a high-income family's budget. The policy implication of this finding is that, if policy makers want to reduce water usage in the area, increasing price will alter the behavior of the low-income/low-water users more than that of high-income/high-water users. To substantially alter the behavior of high-income/high-waters users they would need to increase price even more for water consumption above a certain level. The authors point out that outdoor irrigation associated with relatively high-income/high-water using households accounts for most residential water use in Phoenix.

Source: Based on James Yoo, Silvio Simonit, Ann P. Kinzig, and Charles Perrings. "Estimating the Price Elasticity of Residential Water Demand: The Case of Phoenix, Arizona," Applied Economic Perspectives and Policy, 36:2 (June 2014): 333-350.

Answers to Try It! Problems

1. The absolute value of price elasticity of demand tends to be greater when more time is allowed for consumers to respond. Over time, riders of the commuter rail system can organize car pools, move, or otherwise adjust to the fare increase.

2. Using the formula for price elasticity of demand and plugging in values for the estimate of price elasticity (–0.5) and the percentage change in price (5%) and then rearranging terms, we can solve for the percentage change in quantity demanded as:
e_D = %Δ in Q/%Δ in P; –0.5 = %Δ in Q/5%; (–0.5)(5%) = %Δ in Q = –2.5%.
Ridership falls by 2.5% in the first few months.

3. Using the formula for price elasticity of demand and plugging in values for the estimate of price elasticity over a few years (–1.5) and the percentage change in price (5%), we can solve for the percentage change in quantity demanded as:
e_D = %Δ in Q/%Δ in P; –1.5 = %Δ in Q/5%; (–1.5)(5%) = %Δ in Q = –7.5%.
Ridership falls by 7.5% over a few years.

4. Total revenue rises immediately after the fare increase, since demand over the immediate period is price inelastic. Total revenue falls after a few years, since demand changes and becomes price elastic.

5.3 Responsiveness of Demand to Other Factors

Learning Objectives

1. Explain the concept of income elasticity of demand and its calculation.
2. Classify goods as normal or inferior depending on their income elasticity of demand.
3. Explain the concept of cross price elasticity of demand and its calculation.
4. Classify goods as substitutes or complements depending on their cross price elasticity of demand.

Although the response of quantity demanded to changes in price is the most widely used measure of elasticity, economists are interested in the response to changes in the demand shifters as well.

Two of the most important measures show how demand responds to changes in income and to changes in the prices of related goods and services.

Income Elasticity of Demand

We saw in the chapter that introduced the model of demand and supply that the demand for a good or service is affected by income. We measure the **income elasticity of demand**, e_Y, as the percentage change in quantity demanded *at a specific price* divided by the percentage change in income that produced the demand change, all other things unchanged:

EQUATION 5.3

$$e_Y = \frac{\% \text{ change in quantity demanded}}{\% \text{ change in income}}$$

The symbol Y is often used in economics to represent income. Because income elasticity of demand reports the responsiveness of quantity demanded to a change in income, all other things unchanged (including the price of the good), it reflects a shift in the demand curve at a given price. Remember that price elasticity of demand reflects movements *along* a demand curve in response to a change in price.

A positive income elasticity of demand means that income and demand move in the same direction—an increase in income increases demand, and a reduction in income reduces demand. As we learned, a good whose demand rises as income rises is called a normal good.

Studies show that most goods and services are normal, and thus their income elasticities are positive. Goods and services for which demand is likely to move in the same direction as income include housing, seafood, rock concerts, and medical services.

If a good or service is inferior, then an increase in income reduces demand for the good. That implies a negative income elasticity of demand. Goods and services for which the income elasticity of demand is likely to be negative include used clothing, beans, and urban public transit. For example, the studies we have already cited concerning the demands for urban public transit in France and in Madrid found the long-run income elasticities of demand to be negative (-0.23 in France and -0.25 in Madrid).[3]

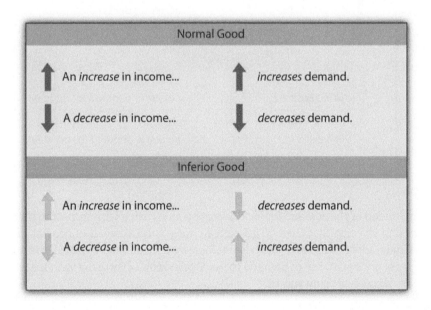

When we compute the income elasticity of demand, we are looking at the change in the quantity demanded at a specific price. We are thus dealing with a change that shifts the demand curve. An increase in income shifts the demand for a normal good to the right; it shifts the demand for an inferior good to the left.

---

income elasticity of demand

The percentage change in quantity demanded at a specific price divided by the percentage change in income that produced the demand change, all other things unchanged.

Cross Price Elasticity of Demand

The demand for a good or service is affected by the prices of related goods or services. A reduction in the price of salsa, for example, would increase the demand for chips, suggesting that salsa is a complement of chips. A reduction in the price of chips, however, would reduce the demand for peanuts, suggesting that chips are a substitute for peanuts.

cross price elasticity of demand

It equals the percentage change in the quantity demanded of one good or service at a specific price divided by the percentage change in the price of a related good or service.

The measure economists use to describe the responsiveness of demand for a good or service to a change in the price of another good or service is called the **cross price elasticity of demand**, $e_{A, B}$. It equals the percentage change in the quantity demanded of one good or service *at a specific price* divided by the percentage change in the price of a related good or service. We are varying the price of a related good when we consider the cross price elasticity of demand, so the response of quantity demanded is shown as a shift in the demand curve.

The cross price elasticity of the demand for good A with respect to the price of good B is given by:

EQUATION 5.4

$$e_{A, B} = \frac{\text{\% change in quantity demanded of good A}}{\text{\% change in price of good B}}$$

Cross price elasticities of demand define whether two goods are substitutes, complements, or unrelated. If two goods are substitutes, an increase in the price of one will lead to an increase in the demand for the other—the cross price elasticity of demand is positive. If two goods are complements, an increase in the price of one will lead to a reduction in the demand for the other—the cross price elasticity of demand is negative. If two goods are unrelated, a change in the price of one will not affect the demand for the other—the cross price elasticity of demand is zero.

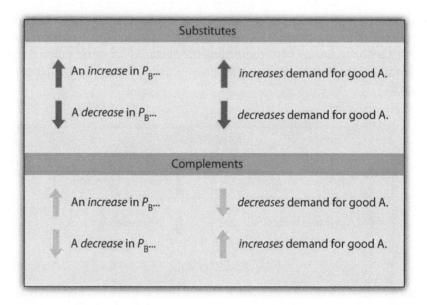

An examination of the demand for local television advertising with respect to the price of local radio advertising revealed that the two goods are clearly substitutes. A 10 percent increase in the price of local radio advertising led to a 10 percent increase in demand for local television advertising, so that the cross price elasticity of demand for local television advertising with respect to changes in the price of radio advertising was 1.0.[4]

Heads Up!

Notice that with income elasticity of demand and cross price elasticity of demand we are primarily concerned with whether the measured value of these elasticities is positive or negative. In the case of income elasticity of demand this tells us whether the good or service is normal or inferior. In the case of cross price elasticity of demand it tells us whether two goods are substitutes or complements. With price elasticity of demand we were concerned with whether the measured absolute value of this elasticity was greater than, less than, or equal to 1, because this gave us information about what happens to total revenue as price changes. The terms elastic and inelastic apply to price elasticity of demand. They are not used to describe income elasticity of demand or cross price elasticity of demand.

Key Takeaways

- The income elasticity of demand reflects the responsiveness of demand to changes in income. It is the percentage change in quantity demanded *at a specific price* divided by the percentage change in income, ceteris paribus.
- Income elasticity is positive for normal goods and negative for inferior goods.
- The cross price elasticity of demand measures the way demand for one good or service responds to changes in the price of another. It is the percentage change in the quantity demanded of one good or service *at a specific price* divided by the percentage change in the price of another good or service, all other things unchanged.
- Cross price elasticity is positive for substitutes, negative for complements, and zero for goods or services whose demands are unrelated.

Try It!

Suppose that when the price of bagels rises by 10%, the demand for cream cheese falls by 3% at the current price, and that when income rises by 10%, the demand for bagels increases by 1% at the current price. Calculate the cross price elasticity of demand for cream cheese with respect to the price of bagels and tell whether bagels and cream cheese are substitutes or complements. Calculate the income elasticity of demand and tell whether bagels are normal or inferior.

Case in Point: Various Demand Elasticities for Conventional and Organic Milk

Source: © Thinkstock

Peruse the milk display at any supermarket and you will see a number of items that you would not have seen a decade ago. Choices include fat content; with or without lactose; animal milks or milk substitutes, such as soy or almond milk; flavors; and organic or conventional milk. Whereas in the 1990s only specialty stores stocked organic milk, today it is readily available in most supermarkets. In fact, the market share for organic milk has grown, as sales of conventional milk have been fairly constant while sales of organic milk have increased.

Professors Pedro Alviola and Oral Capps have estimated various demand elasticities associated with conventional and organic milk, based on a study of 38,000 households. Their results are summarized in the following table.

Elasticity Measure	Organic Milk	Conventional Milk
Own-price elasticity	−2.00	−0.87
Cross-price elasticity	0.70	0.18
Income elasticity	0.27	−0.01

Organic milk is price elastic, while conventional milk is price inelastic. Both cross-price elasticities are positive, indicating that these two kinds of milk are substitutes but their estimated values differ. In particular, a 1% increase in the price of conventional milk leads to a 0.70% increase in the quantity demanded of organic milk, while a 1% increase in the price of organic milk leads to an increase in the quantity demanded of conventional milk of only 0.18%. This asymmetry suggests that organic milk consumers have considerable reluctance in switching back to what they may perceive as a lower-quality product. Finally, the income elasticity estimates suggest that organic milk is a normal good, while conventional milk is an inferior good. As might be expected, in the sample used in the study, purchasers of organic milk are more affluent as a group than are purchasers of conventional milk.

Being a fairly new product, organic milk studies are just becoming available and the authors point out that other researchers using different data sets have calculated different values for these elasticities. Over time, as more data become available and various studies are compared, this type of work is likely to influence milk marketing and pricing.

Source: Based on Pedro A. Alviola IV and Oral Capps Jr., "Household Demand Analysis of Organic and Conventional Fluid Milk in the United States Based on the 2004 Nielsen Homescan Panel," Agribusiness 26:3 (2010): 369–388.

Answer to Try It! Problem

Using the formula for cross price elasticity of demand, we find that $e_{AB} = (−3\%)/(10\%) = −0.3$. Since the e_{AB} is negative, bagels and cream cheese are complements. Using the formula for income elasticity of demand, we find that $e_Y = (+1\%)/(10\%) = +0.1$. Since e_Y is positive, bagels are a normal good.

5.4 Price Elasticity of Supply

Learning Objectives

1. Explain the concept of elasticity of supply and its calculation.
2. Explain what it means for supply to be price inelastic, unit price elastic, price elastic, perfectly price inelastic, and perfectly price elastic.

3. Explain why time is an important determinant of price elasticity of supply.
4. Apply the concept of price elasticity of supply to the labor supply curve.

The elasticity measures encountered so far in this chapter all relate to the demand side of the market. It is also useful to know how responsive quantity supplied is to a change in price.

Suppose the demand for apartments rises. There will be a shortage of apartments at the old level of apartment rents and pressure on rents to rise. All other things unchanged, the more responsive the quantity of apartments supplied is to changes in monthly rents, the lower the increase in rent required to eliminate the shortage and to bring the market back to equilibrium. Conversely, if quantity supplied is less responsive to price changes, price will have to rise more to eliminate a shortage caused by an increase in demand.

This is illustrated in Figure 5.5. Suppose the rent for a typical apartment had been R_0 and the quantity Q_0 when the demand curve was D_1 and the supply curve was either S_1 (a supply curve in which quantity supplied is less responsive to price changes) or S_2 (a supply curve in which quantity supplied is more responsive to price changes). Note that with either supply curve, equilibrium price and quantity are initially the same. Now suppose that demand increases to D_2, perhaps due to population growth. With supply curve S_1, the price (rent in this case) will rise to R_1 and the quantity of apartments will rise to Q_1. If, however, the supply curve had been S_2, the rent would only have to rise to R_2 to bring the market back to equilibrium. In addition, the new equilibrium number of apartments would be higher at Q_2. Supply curve S_2 shows greater responsiveness of quantity supplied to price change than does supply curve S_1.

FIGURE 5.5 Increase in Apartment Rents Depends on How Responsive Supply Is

The more responsive the supply of apartments is to changes in price (rent in this case), the less rents rise when the demand for apartments increases.

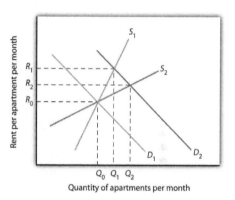

We measure the **price elasticity of supply** (e_S) as the ratio of the percentage change in quantity supplied of a good or service to the percentage change in its price, all other things unchanged:

EQUATION 5.5

$$e_S = \frac{\% \text{ change in quantity supplied}}{\% \text{ change in price}}$$

price elasticity of supply

The ratio of the percentage change in quantity supplied of a good or service to the percentage change in its price, all other things unchanged.

Because price and quantity supplied usually move in the same direction, the price elasticity of supply is usually positive. The larger the price elasticity of supply, the more responsive the firms that supply the good or service are to a price change.

Supply is price elastic if the price elasticity of supply is greater than 1, unit price elastic if it is equal to 1, and price inelastic if it is less than 1. A vertical supply curve, as shown in Panel (a) of Figure 5.6, is perfectly inelastic; its price elasticity of supply is zero. The supply of Beatles' songs is perfectly inelastic because the band no longer exists. A horizontal supply curve, as shown in Panel (b) of Figure 5.6, is perfectly elastic; its price elasticity of supply is infinite. It means that suppliers are willing to supply any amount at a certain price.

FIGURE 5.6 Supply Curves and Their Price Elasticities

The supply curve in Panel (a) is perfectly inelastic. In Panel (b), the supply curve is perfectly elastic.

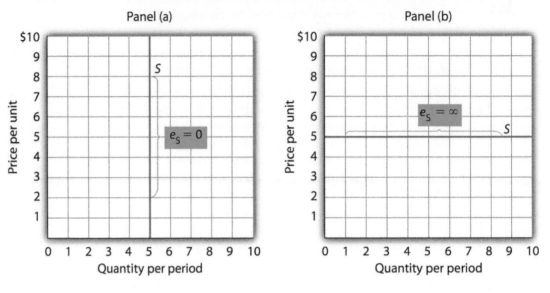

Time: An Important Determinant of the Elasticity of Supply

Time plays a very important role in the determination of the price elasticity of supply. Look again at the effect of rent increases on the supply of apartments. Suppose apartment rents in a city rise. If we are looking at a supply curve of apartments over a period of a few months, the rent increase is likely to induce apartment owners to rent out a relatively small number of additional apartments. With the higher rents, apartment owners may be more vigorous in reducing their vacancy rates, and, indeed, with more people looking for apartments to rent, this should be fairly easy to accomplish. Attics and basements are easy to renovate and rent out as additional units. In a short period of time, however, the supply response is likely to be fairly modest, implying that the price elasticity of supply is fairly low. A supply curve corresponding to a short period of time would look like S_1 in Figure 5.5. It is during such periods that there may be calls for rent controls.

If the period of time under consideration is a few years rather than a few months, the supply curve is likely to be much more price elastic. Over time, buildings can be converted from other uses and new apartment complexes can be built. A supply curve corresponding to a longer period of time would look like S_2 in Figure 5.5.

Elasticity of Labor Supply: A Special Application

The concept of price elasticity of supply can be applied to labor to show how the quantity of labor supplied responds to changes in wages or salaries. What makes this case interesting is that it has sometimes been found that the measured elasticity is negative, that is, that an increase in the wage rate is associated with a reduction in the quantity of labor supplied.

In most cases, labor supply curves have their normal upward slope: higher wages induce people to work more. For them, having the additional income from working more is preferable to having more leisure time. However, wage increases may lead some people in very highly paid jobs to cut back on the number of hours they work because their incomes are already high and they would rather have more time for leisure activities. In this case, the labor supply curve would have a negative slope. The reasons for this phenomenon are explained more fully in a later chapter. The Case in Point in this section gives another example where an increase in the wage may reduce the number of hours of work.

Key Takeaways

- The price elasticity of supply measures the responsiveness of quantity supplied to changes in price. It is the percentage change in quantity supplied divided by the percentage change in price. It is usually positive.

- Supply is price inelastic if the price elasticity of supply is less than 1; it is unit price elastic if the price elasticity of supply is equal to 1; and it is price elastic if the price elasticity of supply is greater than 1. A vertical supply curve is said to be perfectly inelastic. A horizontal supply curve is said to be perfectly elastic.

- The price elasticity of supply is greater when the length of time under consideration is longer because over time producers have more options for adjusting to the change in price.

- When applied to labor supply, the price elasticity of supply is usually positive but can be negative. If higher wages induce people to work more, the labor supply curve is upward sloping and the price elasticity of supply is positive. In some very high-paying professions or other unusual circumstances, the labor supply curve may have a negative slope, which leads to a negative price elasticity of supply.

Try It!

In the late 1990s, it was reported on the news that the high-tech industry was worried about being able to find enough workers with computer-related expertise. Job offers for recent college graduates with degrees in computer science went with high salaries. It was also reported that more undergraduates than ever were majoring in computer science. Compare the price elasticity of supply of computer scientists at that point in time to the price elasticity of supply of computer scientists over a longer period of, say, 1999 to 2009.

Case in Point: Child Labor in Pakistan

Source: © Thinkstock

Professor Sonia Bhalotra investigated the role of household poverty in child labor. Imagine a household with two parents and two children, a boy and a girl. If only the parents work, the family income may be less than an amount required for subsistence. In order to at least raise the income of the family to subsistence, will the labor of both children be added? If only one child will work, will it be the boy or the girl? How do the motivations of parents to send their children to work affect the design of policies to encourage education? Will a program that reduces school fees or improves school quality lead to more education or would a program that provides cash or food to households who send their children to school work better?

Using information on over 3,000 children in an area of rural Pakistan where their labor force participation is high, child wage labor is common, and gender differences in education and work of children prevail, Professor Bhalotra specifically estimated how changes in wages for boys and girls affect the number of hours they work. She focused on wage work outside the home because it usually involves more hours and less flexibility than, say, work on one's own farm, which essentially rules out going to school.

She argues that if the work of a child is geared toward the family hitting a target level of income, then an increase in the wage will lead to fewer hours of work. That is, the labor supply elasticity will be negative and the labor supply curve will have a negative slope. For boys, she finds that the wage elasticity is about −0.5. For girls, she finds that the wage elasticity is about 0, meaning the labor supply curve is vertical. To further her hypothesis that the labor supply decision for boys but not for girls is compelled by household poverty, she notes that separate estimates show that the income of the family from sources other than having their children work reduces the amount that boys work but has no effect on the amount that girls work. Other research she has undertaken on labor supply of children on household-run farms provides further support for these gender differences: Girls from families that own relatively larger farms were both more likely to work and less likely to go to school than girls from households with farms of smaller acreage.

Why the gender differences and how do these findings affect drafting of policies to encourage schooling? For boys, cash or food given to households could induce parents to send their sons to school. For girls, household poverty reduction may not work. Their relatively lower level of participating in schooling may be related to an expected low impact of education on their future wages. Expectations about when they will get married and whether or not they should work as adults, especially if it means moving to other areas, may also play a role. For girls, policies that alter attitudes toward girls' education and in the longer term affect educated female adult earnings may be more instrumental in increasing their educational attainment.

Source: Based on Sonia Bhalotra, "Is Child Work Necessary?" Oxford Bulletin of Economics and Statistics 69:1 (2007): 29–55.

Answer to Try It! Problem

While at a point in time the supply of people with degrees in computer science is very price inelastic, over time the elasticity should rise. That more students were majoring in computer science lends credence to this prediction. As supply becomes more price elastic, salaries in this field should rise more slowly.

5.5 Review and Practice

Summary

This chapter introduced a new tool: the concept of elasticity. Elasticity is a measure of the degree to which a dependent variable responds to a change in an independent variable. It is the percentage change in the dependent variable divided by the percentage change in the independent variable, all other things unchanged.

The most widely used elasticity measure is the price elasticity of demand, which reflects the responsiveness of quantity demanded to changes in price. Demand is said to be price elastic if the absolute value of the price elasticity of demand is greater than 1, unit price elastic if it is equal to 1, and price inelastic if it is less than 1. The price elasticity of demand is useful in forecasting the response of quantity demanded to price changes; it is also useful for predicting the impact a price change will have on total revenue. Total revenue moves in the direction of the quantity change if demand is price elastic, it moves in the direction of the price change if demand is price inelastic, and it does not change if demand is unit price elastic. The most important determinants of the price elasticity of demand are the availability of substitutes, the importance of the item in household budgets, and time.

Two other elasticity measures commonly used in conjunction with demand are income elasticity and cross price elasticity. The signs of these elasticity measures play important roles. A positive income elasticity tells us that a good is normal; a negative income elasticity tells us the good is inferior. A positive cross price elasticity tells us that two goods are substitutes; a negative cross price elasticity tells us they are complements.

Elasticity of supply measures the responsiveness of quantity supplied to changes in price. The value of price elasticity of supply is generally positive. Supply is classified as being price elastic, unit price elastic, or price inelastic if price elasticity is greater than 1, equal to 1, or less than 1, respectively. The length of time over which supply is being considered is an important determinant of the price elasticity of supply.

Concept Problems

1. Explain why the price elasticity of demand is generally a negative number, except in the cases where the demand curve is perfectly elastic or perfectly inelastic. What would be implied by a positive price elasticity of demand?
2. Explain why the sign (positive or negative) of the cross price elasticity of demand is important.
3. Explain why the sign (positive or negative) of the income elasticity of demand is important.
4. Economists Dale Heien and Cathy Roheim Wessells found that the price elasticity of demand for fresh milk is -0.63 and the price elasticity of demand for cottage cheese is -1.1.[5] Why do you think the elasticity estimates differ?
5. The price elasticity of demand for health care has been estimated to be -0.2. Characterize this demand as price elastic, unit price elastic, or price inelastic. The text argues that the greater the importance of an item in consumer budgets, the greater its elasticity. Health-care costs account for a relatively large share of household budgets. How could the price elasticity of demand for health care be such a small number?
6. Suppose you are able to organize an alliance that includes all farmers. They agree to follow the group's instructions with respect to the quantity of agricultural products they produce. What might the group seek to do? Why?
7. Suppose you are the chief executive officer of a firm, and you have been planning to reduce your prices. Your marketing manager reports that the price elasticity of demand for your product is -0.65. How will this news affect your plans?
8. Suppose the income elasticity of the demand for beans is -0.8. Interpret this number.
9. Transportation economists generally agree that the cross price elasticity of demand for automobile use with respect to the price of bus fares is about 0. Explain what this number means.
10. Suppose the price elasticity of supply of tomatoes as measured on a given day in July is 0. Interpret this number.
11. The price elasticity of supply for child-care workers has been estimated to be quite high, about 2. What will happen to the wages of child-care workers as demand for them increases, compared to what would happen if the measured price elasticity of supply were lower?
12. Studies suggest that a higher tax on cigarettes would reduce teen smoking and premature deaths. Should cigarette taxes therefore be raised?

Numerical Problems

1. Economist David Romer found that in introductory economics classes a 10% increase in class attendance is associated with a 4% increase in course grade.[6] What is the elasticity of course grade with respect to class attendance?
2. Refer to Figure 5.2 and
   a. Using the arc elasticity of demand formula, compute the price elasticity of demand between points B and C.
   b. Using the arc elasticity of demand formula, compute the price elasticity of demand between points D and E.
   c. How do the values of price elasticity of demand compare? Why are they the same or different?

    d. Compute the slope of the demand curve between points B and C.

    e. Computer the slope of the demand curve between points D and E.

    f. How do the slopes compare? Why are they the same or different?

3. Suppose a bumper crop of oranges in Florida drove down orange prices. As juice makers costs fell, they cut prices by about 15%. Value oriented customers were tempted to buy more orange juice. In fact, the unit volume of frozen juices rose by about 6%.

    a. Given these numbers, and assuming there were no changes in demand shifters for frozen orange juice, what was the price elasticity of demand for frozen orange juice?

    b. What do you think happened to total spending on frozen orange juice? Why?

4. Suppose you are the manager of a restaurant that serves an average of 400 meals per day at an average price per meal of $20. On the basis of a survey, you have determined that reducing the price of an average meal to $18 would increase the quantity demanded to 450 per day.

    a. Compute the price elasticity of demand between these two points.

    b. Would you expect total revenues to rise or fall? Explain.

    c. Suppose you have reduced the average price of a meal to $18 and are considering a further reduction to $16. Another survey shows that the quantity demanded of meals will increase from 450 to 500 per day. Compute the price elasticity of demand between these two points.

    d. Would you expect total revenue to rise or fall as a result of this second price reduction? Explain.

    e. Compute total revenue at the three meal prices. Do these totals confirm your answers in (b) and (d) above?

5. The text notes that, for any linear demand curve, demand is price elastic in the upper half and price inelastic in the lower half. Consider the following demand curves:

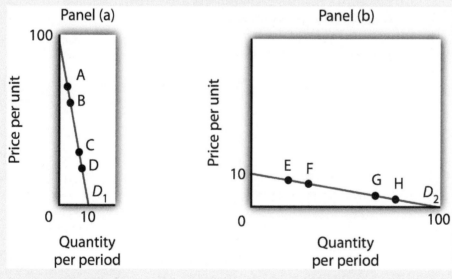

The table gives the prices and quantities corresponding to each of the points shown on the two demand curves.

Demand curve D_1 [Panel (a)]			Demand curve D_2 [Panel (b)]		
	Price	Quantity		Price	Quantity
A	80	2	E	8	20
B	70	3	F	7	30
C	30	7	G	3	70
D	20	8	H	2	80

a. Compute the price elasticity of demand between points A and B and between points C and D on demand curve D_1 in Panel (a). Are your results consistent with the notion that a linear demand curve is price elastic in its upper half and price inelastic in its lower half?

b. Compute the price elasticity of demand between points E and F and between points G and H on demand curve D_2 in Panel (b). Are your results consistent with the notion that a linear demand curve is price elastic in its upper half and price inelastic in its lower half?

c. Compare total spending at points A and B on D_1 in Panel (a). Is your result consistent with your finding about the price elasticity of demand between those two points?

d. Compare total spending at points C and D on D_1 in Panel (a). Is your result consistent with your finding about the price elasticity of demand between those two points?

e. Compare total spending at points E and F on D_2 in Panel (b). Is your result consistent with your finding about the price elasticity of demand between those two points?

f. Compare total spending at points G and H on D_2 in Panel (b). Is your result consistent with your finding about the price elasticity of demand between those two points?

6. Suppose Janice buys the following amounts of various food items depending on her weekly income:

Weekly Income	Hamburgers	Pizza	Ice Cream Sundaes
$500	3	3	2
$750	4	2	2

a. Compute Janice's income elasticity of demand for hamburgers.
b. Compute Janice's income elasticity of demand for pizza.
c. Compute Janice's income elasticity of demand for ice cream sundaes.
d. Classify each good as normal or inferior.

7. Suppose the following table describes Jocelyn's weekly snack purchases, which vary depending on the price of a bag of chips:

Price of bag of chips	Bags of chips	Containers of salsa	Bags of pretzels	Cans of soda
$1.00	2	3	1	4
$1.50	1	2	2	4

a. Compute the cross price elasticity of salsa with respect to the price of a bag of chips.
b. Compute the cross price elasticity of pretzels with respect to the price of a bag of chips.
c. Compute the cross price elasticity of soda with respect to the price of a bag of chips.
d. Are chips and salsa substitutes or complements? How do you know?
e. Are chips and pretzels substitutes or complements? How do you know?
f. Are chips and soda substitutes or complements? How do you know?

8. The table below describes the supply curve for light bulbs:

Price per light bulb	Quantity supplied per day
$1.00	500
1.50	3,000
2.00	4,000
2.50	4,500
3.00	4,500

Compute the price elasticity of supply and determine whether supply is price elastic, price inelastic, perfectly elastic, perfectly inelastic, or unit elastic:

 a. when the price of a light bulb increases from $1.00 to $1.50.

 b. when the price of a light bulb increases from $1.50 to $2.00.

 c. when the price of a light bulb increases from $2.00 to $2.50.

 d. when the price of a light bulb increases from $2.50 to $3.00.

Endnotes

1. Notice that since the number of units sold of a good is the same as the number of units bought, the definition for total revenue could also be used to define total spending. Which term we use depends on the question at hand. If we are trying to determine what happens to revenues of sellers, then we are asking about total revenue. If we are trying to determine how much consumers spend, then we are asking about total spending.

2. Division by zero results in an undefined solution. Saying that the price elasticity of demand is infinite requires that we say the denominator "approaches" zero.

3. See Georges Bresson, Joyce Dargay, Jean-Loup Madre, and Alain Pirotte, "Economic and Structural Determinants of the Demand for French Transport: An Analysis on a Panel of French Urban Areas Using Shrinkage Estimators." *Transportation Research: Part A* 38: 4 (May 2004): 269–285. See also Anna Matas. "Demand and Revenue Implications of an Integrated Transport Policy: The Case of Madrid." *Transport Reviews* 24:2 (March 2004): 195–217.

4. Robert B. Ekelund, S. Ford, and John D. Jackson. "Are Local TV Markets Separate Markets?" *International Journal of the Economics of Business* 7:1 (2000): 79–97.

5. Dale M. Heien and Cathy Roheim Wessels, "The Demand for Dairy Products: Structure, Prediction, and Decomposition," *American Journal of Agricultural Economics* 70:2 (May 1988): 219–228.

6. David Romer, "Do Students Go to Class? Should They?" *Journal of Economic Perspectives* 7:3 (Summer 1993): 167–174.

CHAPTER 6
Markets, Maximizers, and Efficiency

6.1 Start Up: A Drive in the Country

Suppose you decide to take a drive. For purposes of this example, we will assume that you have a car available, that the weather is pleasant, and that there is an area nearby that will be perfect for your drive.

Your decision to take this drive is a choice. Since economics deals with choices, we can put economics to work in thinking about it. Economists assume that people make choices that maximize the value of some objective. You are a consumer; we assume that taking a drive is a choice that maximizes your utility—the satisfaction you obtain from your use of goods and services and from the activities you pursue.

You certainly plan to enjoy the drive; that enjoyment is the benefit you expect from it. But you will give up some things as well. Your drive will take some time, time you could have spent doing something else. It will take some gasoline; what you spend for the gasoline could have been used for something else. The drive will also generate some wear and tear on your car. That will cost you the price of repair and maintenance and reduced resale value of your car. The opportunity cost of your drive will thus include the value of the best other use of your time and the value of the best other use of the funds your drive will require. To maximize utility you will weigh the benefits of the drive against the cost of the drive and maximize the difference between those benefits and costs.

This chapter introduces the method through which maximizing choices can be made. This method applies not just to your decision to take a drive, but also to Wal-Mart's decision to hire extra workers and to USX Corporation's to produce extra steel. The method we will learn can be applied to the analysis of any choice; we will use it throughout our investigation of microeconomics.

We will also see how maximizing choices by individuals and by firms can lead to an allocation of resources that generates the greatest gains possible for the economy as a whole. In this analysis, we will put a new item in our toolkit, the method through which individuals and firms maximize, together with demand and supply analysis, to see how the marketplace can guide resources to their best uses.

We will also examine cases in which maximizing choices do not guide resources to their best uses. That possibility is suggested by another aspect of your choice to take a drive. In addition to the costs you will consider, there will be costs imposed on others. Your drive will pollute the air, so part of the opportunity cost of the drive will be the value of the slightly cleaner air people in your area might have had. Resources such as the air we breathe will almost certainly be misallocated as the result of maximizing choices. We will see just how misallocation of an economy's resources can occur and how this misallocation could be fixed.

6.2 The Logic of Maximizing Behavior

Learning Objectives

1. Explain the maximization assumption that economists make in explaining the behavior of consumers and firms.
2. Explain and illustrate the concepts of marginal benefit and marginal cost and apply them to understanding the marginal decision rule.

economic profit

The difference between total revenue and total cost.

To say that individuals maximize is to say that they pick some objective and then seek to maximize its value. A sprinter might want to maximize his or her speed; a politician might want to maximize the probability that he or she will win the next election. Economists pay special attention to two groups of maximizers: consumers and firms. We assume that consumers seek to maximize utility and that firms seek to maximize **economic profit**, which is the difference between total revenue and total cost. The costs involved in this concept of economic profit are computed in the economic sense—as the opportunity costs, or value of the best opportunity forgone.

The assumption of maximizing behavior lies at the heart of economic analysis. As we explore its implications, however, we must keep in mind the distinction between models and the real world. Our model assumes that individuals make choices in a way that achieves a maximum value for some clearly defined objective. In using such a model, economists do not assume that people actually go through the calculations we will describe. What economists do argue is that people's behavior is broadly consistent with such a model. People may not consciously seek to maximize anything, but they behave as though they do.

The Analysis of Maximizing Behavior

net benefit

The total benefit of an activity minus its opportunity cost.

The activities of consumers and firms have benefits, and they also have opportunity costs. We assume that given these benefits and costs, consumers and firms will make choices that maximize the **net benefit** of each activity—the total benefit of the activity minus its opportunity cost. The specific measures of benefit and cost vary with the kind of choice being made. In the case of a firm's choices in production, for example, the total benefit of production is the revenue a firm receives from selling the product; the total cost is the opportunity cost the firm incurs by producing it. The net benefit is thus total revenue minus total opportunity cost, or economic profit.

Economists maintain that in order to maximize net benefit, consumers and firms evaluate each activity at the margin—they consider the additional benefit and the additional cost of another unit of the activity. Should you "supersize" your order at McDonald's? Will the additional beverage and the additional french fries be worth the extra cost? Should a firm hire one more worker? Will the benefits to the firm of hiring this worker be worth the additional cost of hiring him or her?

marginal benefit

The amount by which an additional unit of an activity increases its total benefit.

marginal cost

The amount by which an additional unit of an activity increases its total cost.

The **marginal benefit** is the amount by which an additional unit of an activity increases its total benefit. It is the amount by which the extra french fries increase your satisfaction, or the extra revenue the firm expects to bring in by hiring another worker. The **marginal cost** is the amount by which an additional unit of an activity increases its total cost. You will pay more to supersize your McDonald's order; the firm's labor costs will rise when it hires another worker.

To determine the quantity of any activity that will maximize its net benefit, we apply the **marginal decision rule**: If the marginal benefit of an additional unit of an activity exceeds the marginal cost, the quantity of the activity should be increased. If the marginal benefit is less than the marginal cost, the quantity should be reduced. Net benefit is maximized at the point at which marginal benefit equals marginal cost. The marginal decision rule is at the heart of the economic way of thinking. The rule basically says this: If the additional benefit of one more unit exceeds the extra cost, do it; if not, do not. This simple logic gives us a powerful tool for the analysis of choice. Perhaps more than any other rule in economic analysis, the marginal decision rule typifies the way in which economists analyze problems. We shall apply it in every chapter that follows in the microeconomics portion of this text.

Maximizing choices must be made within the parameters imposed by some **constraint**, which is a boundary that limits the range of choices that can be made. We assume that a consumer seeks the greatest satisfaction possible within the limits of his or her income or budget. A firm cannot produce beyond the limits of its production capacity at a point in time.

The marginal decision rule forms the foundation for the structure economists use to analyze all choices. At first glance, it may seem that a consumer seeking satisfaction from, say, pizza has little in common with an entrepreneur seeking profit from the production of custom-designed semiconductors. But maximizing choices always follow the marginal decision rule—and that rule holds regardless of what is being maximized or who is doing the maximizing.

To see how the logic of maximizing choices works, we will examine a specific problem. We will then extend that problem to the general analysis of maximizing choices.

A Problem in Maximization

Suppose a college student, Laurie Phan, faces two midterms tomorrow, one in economics and another in accounting. She has already decided to spend 5 hours studying for the two examinations. This decision imposes a constraint on the problem. Suppose that Ms. Phan's goal is to allocate her 5 hours of study so that she increases her total score for the two exams by as much as possible.

Ms. Phan expects the relationship between the time she spends studying for the economics exam and the total gain in her score to be as given by the second row of the table in Panel (a) of Figure 6.1. We interpret the expected total gain in her score as the total benefit of study. She expects that 1 hour of study will raise her score by 18 points; 2 hours will raise it by 32 points, and so on. These values are plotted in Panel (b). Notice that the total benefit curve rises, but by smaller and smaller amounts, as she studies more and more. The slope of the curve, which in this case tells us the rate at which her expected score rises with increased study time, falls as we travel up and to the right along the curve.

---

marginal decision rule

If the marginal benefit of an additional unit of an activity exceeds the marginal cost, the quantity of the activity should be increased. If the marginal benefit is less than the marginal cost, the quantity should be reduced.

constraint

A boundary that limits the range of choices that can be made.

FIGURE 6.1 The Benefits of Studying Economics

The table in Panel (a) shows the total benefit and marginal benefit of the time Laurie Phan spends studying for her economics exam. Panel (b) shows the total benefit curve. Panel (c) shows the marginal benefit curve, which is given by the slope of the total benefit curve in Panel (b).

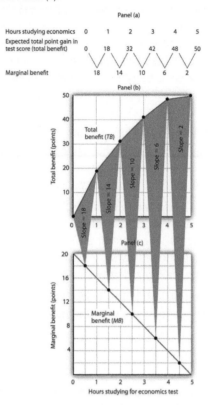

Now look at the third row in the table in Panel (a). It tells us the amount by which each additional hour of study increases her expected score; it gives the marginal benefit of studying for the economics exam. Marginal benefit equals the amount by which total benefit rises with each additional hour of study. Because these marginal benefits are given by the changes in total benefits from additional hours of study, they equal the slope of the total benefit curve. We see this in the relationship between Panels (b) and (c) of Figure 6.1. The decreasing slope of the total benefit curve in Panel (b) gives us the downward-sloping marginal benefit curve in Panel (c).

The marginal benefit curve tells us what happens when we pass from one point to another on the total benefit curve, so we have plotted marginal benefits at the midpoints of the hourly intervals in Panel (c). For example, the total benefit curve in Panel (b) tells us that, when Ms. Phan increases her time studying for the economics exam from 2 hours to 3 hours, her total benefit rises from 32 points to 42 points. The increase of 10 points is the marginal benefit of increasing study time for the economics exam from 2 hours to 3 hours. We mark the point for a marginal benefit of 10 points midway between 2 and 3 hours. Because marginal values tell us what happens as we pass from one quantity to the next, we shall always plot them at the midpoints of intervals of the variable on the horizontal axis.

We can perform the same kind of analysis to obtain the marginal benefit curve for studying for the accounting exam. Figure 6.2 presents this curve. Like the marginal benefit curve for studying economics, it slopes downward. Once again, we have plotted marginal values at the midpoints of the intervals. Increasing study time in accounting from 0 to 1 hour increases Ms. Phan's expected accounting score by 14 points.

Ms. Phan's marginal benefit curves for studying typify a general phenomenon in economics. Marginal benefit curves for virtually all activities, including the activities of consumers and of firms, slope downward. Think about your own experience with studying. On a given day, the first hour spent studying a certain subject probably generates a greater marginal benefit than the second, and the second hour probably generates a greater marginal benefit than the third. You may reach a point at which an extra hour of study is unlikely to yield any benefit at all. Of course, our example of Laurie Phan's expected exam scores is a highly stylized one. One could hardly expect a student to have a precise set of numbers to guide him or her in allocating study time. But it is certainly the case that students have a rough idea of the likely payoff of study time in different subjects. If you were faced with exams in two subjects, it is likely that you would set aside a certain amount of study time, just as Ms. Phan did in our example. And it is likely that your own experience would serve as a guide in determining how to allocate that time. Economists do not assume that people have numerical scales in their heads with which to draw marginal benefit and marginal cost curves. They merely assume that people act as if they did.

The nature of marginal benefits can change with different applications. For a restaurant, the marginal benefit of serving one more meal can be defined as the revenue that meal produces. For a consumer, the marginal benefit of one more slice of pizza can be considered in terms of the additional satisfaction the pizza will create. But whatever the nature of the benefit, marginal benefits generally fall as quantities increase.

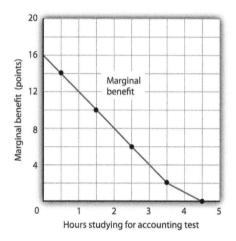

FIGURE 6.2 The Marginal Benefits of Studying Accounting

The marginal benefit Laurie Phan expects from studying for her accounting exam is shown by the marginal benefit curve. The first hour of study increases her expected score by 14 points, the second hour by 10 points, the third by 6 points, and so on.

Ms. Phan's falling marginal benefit from hours spent studying accounting has special significance for our analysis of her choice concerning how many hours to devote to economics. In our problem, she had decided to devote 5 hours to studying the two subjects. That means that the opportunity cost of an hour spent studying economics equals the benefit she would have gotten spending that hour studying accounting.

Suppose, for example, that she were to consider spending all 5 hours studying accounting. The marginal benefit curve for studying for her accounting exam tells us that she expects that the fifth hour will add nothing to her score. Shifting that hour to economics would cost nothing. We can say that the marginal cost of the first hour spent studying economics is zero. We obtained this value from the marginal benefit curve for studying accounting in Figure 6.2.

Similarly, we can find the marginal cost of the second hour studying economics. That requires giving up the fourth hour spent on accounting. Figure 6.2 tells us that the marginal benefit of that hour equals 2—that is the marginal cost of spending the second hour studying economics.

Figure 6.3 shows the marginal cost curve of studying economics. We see that at first, time devoted to studying economics has a low marginal cost. As time spent studying economics increases, however, it requires her to give up study time in accounting that she expects will be more and more productive. The marginal cost curve for studying economics can thus be derived from the marginal benefit curve for studying accounting. Figure 6.3 also shows the marginal benefit curve for studying economics that we derived in Panel (b) of Figure 6.1.

FIGURE 6.3 The Marginal Benefits and Marginal Costs of Studying Economics
The marginal benefit curve from Panel (c) of Figure 6.1 is shown together with the marginal costs of studying economics. The marginal cost curve is derived from the marginal benefit curve for studying accounting shown in Figure 6.2.

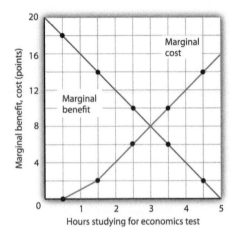

Just as marginal benefit curves generally slope downward, marginal cost curves generally slope upward, as does the one in Figure 6.3. In the case of allocating time, the phenomenon of rising marginal cost results from the simple fact that, the more time a person devotes to one activity, the less time is available for another. And the more one reduces the second activity, the greater the forgone marginal benefits are likely to be. That means the marginal cost curve for that first activity rises.

Because we now have marginal benefit and marginal cost curves for studying economics, we can apply the marginal decision rule. This rule says that, to maximize the net benefit of an activity, a decision maker should increase an activity up to the point at which marginal benefit equals marginal cost. That occurs where the marginal benefit and marginal cost curves intersect, with 3 hours spent studying economics and 2 hours spent studying accounting.

Using Marginal Benefit and Marginal Cost Curves to Find Net Benefits

We can use marginal benefit and marginal cost curves to show the total benefit, the total cost, and the net benefit of an activity. We will see that equating marginal benefit to marginal cost does, indeed, maximize net benefit. We will also develop another tool to use in interpreting marginal benefit and cost curves.

Panel (a) of Figure 6.4 shows the marginal benefit curve we derived in Panel (c) of Figure 6.1. The corresponding point on the marginal benefit curve gives the marginal benefit of the first hour of study for the economics exam, 18 points. This same value equals the area of the rectangle bounded by 0 and 1 hour of study and the marginal benefit of 18. Similarly, the marginal benefit of the second hour, 14 points, is shown by the corresponding point on the marginal benefit curve and by the area of the shaded rectangle bounded by 1 and 2 hours of study. The total benefit of 2 hours of study equals the sum of the areas of the first two rectangles, 32 points. We continue this procedure through the fifth hour of studying economics; the areas for each of the shaded rectangles are shown in the graph.

FIGURE 6.4 The Benefits and Costs of Studying Economics
Panel (a) shows the marginal benefit curve of Figure 6.1. The total benefit of studying economics at any given quantity of study time is given approximately by the shaded area below the marginal benefit curve up to that level of study. Panel (b) shows the marginal cost curve from Figure 6.3. The total cost of studying economics at any given quantity of study is given approximately by the shaded area below the marginal cost curve up to that level of study.

Panel (a)

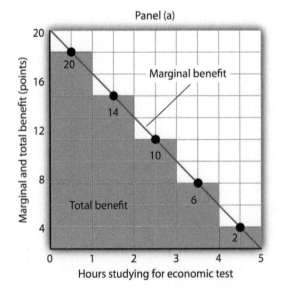

Panel (b)

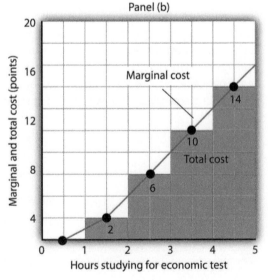

Two features of the curve in Panel (a) of Figure 6.4 are particularly important. First, note that the sum of the areas of the five rectangles, 50 points, equals the total benefit of 5 hours of study given in the table in Panel (a) of Figure 6.1. Second, notice that the shaded areas are approximately equal to the area under the marginal benefit curve between 0 and 5 hours of study. We can pick any quantity of study time, and the total benefit of that quantity equals the sum of the shaded rectangles between zero and that quantity. Thus, the total benefit of 2 hours of study equals 32 points, the sum of the areas of the first two rectangles.

Now consider the marginal cost curve in Panel (b) of Figure 6.4. The areas of the shaded rectangles equal the values of marginal cost. The marginal cost of the first hour of study equals zero; there is thus no rectangle under the curve. The marginal cost of the second hour of study equals 2 points; that is the area of the rectangle bounded by 1 and 2 hours of study and a marginal cost of 2. The marginal cost of the third hour of study is 6 points; this is the area of the shaded rectangle bounded by 2 and 3 hours of study and a marginal cost of 6.

Looking at the rectangles in Panel (b) over the range of 0 to 5 hours of study, we see that the areas of the five rectangles total 32, the total cost of spending all 5 hours studying economics. And looking at the rectangles, we see that their area is approximately equal to the area under the marginal cost curve between 0 and 5 hours of study.

We have seen that the areas of the rectangles drawn with Laurie Phan's marginal benefit and marginal cost curves equal the total benefit and total cost of studying economics. We have also seen that these areas are roughly equal to the areas under the curves themselves. We can make this last statement much stronger. Suppose, instead of thinking in intervals of whole hours, we think in terms of smaller intervals, say, of 12 minutes. Then each rectangle would be only one-fifth as wide as the rectangles we drew in Figure 6.4. Their areas would still equal the total benefit and total cost of study, and the sum of those areas would be closer to the area under the curves. We have done this for Ms. Phan's marginal benefit curve in Figure 6.5; notice that the areas of the rectangles closely approximate the area under the curve. They still "stick out" from either side of the curve as did the rectangles we drew in Figure 6.4, but you almost need a magnifying glass to see that. The smaller the interval we choose, the closer the areas under the marginal benefit and marginal cost curves will be to total benefit and total cost. For purposes of our model, we can imagine that the intervals are as small as we like. Over a particular range of quantity, the area under a marginal benefit curve equals the total benefit of that quantity, and the area under the marginal cost curve equals the total cost of that quantity.

FIGURE 6.5 The Marginal Benefit Curve and Total Benefit

When the increments used to measure time allocated to studying economics are made smaller, in this case 12 minutes instead of whole hours, the area under the marginal benefit curve is closer to the total benefit of studying that amount of time.

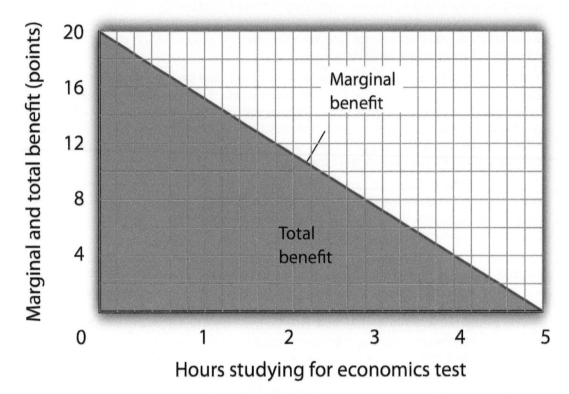

deadweight loss

The loss in net benefits resulting from a failure to carry out an activity at the most efficient level.

Panel (a) of Figure 6.6 shows marginal benefit and marginal cost curves for studying economics, this time without numbers. We have the usual downward-sloping marginal benefit curve and upward-sloping marginal cost curve. The marginal decision rule tells us to choose D hours studying economics, the quantity at which marginal benefit equals marginal cost at point C. We know that the total benefit of study equals the area under the marginal benefit curve over the range from A to D hours of study, the area ABCD. Total cost equals the area under the marginal cost curve over the same range, or ACD. The difference between total benefit and total cost equals the area between marginal benefit and marginal cost between A and D hours of study; it is the green-shaded triangle ABC. This difference is the net benefit of time spent studying economics. Panel (b) of Figure 6.6 introduces another important concept. If an activity is carried out at a level less than the efficient level, then net benefits are forgone. The loss in net benefits resulting from a failure to carry out an activity at the efficient level is called a **deadweight loss**.

FIGURE 6.6 Using Marginal Benefit and Marginal Cost Curves to Determine Net Benefit
In Panel (a) net benefits are given by the difference between total benefits (as measured by the area under the marginal benefit curve up to any given level of activity) and total costs (as measured by the area under the marginal cost curve up to any given level of activity). Maximum net benefits are found where the marginal benefit curve intersects the marginal cost curve at activity level D. Panel (b) shows that if the level of the activity is restricted to activity level E, net benefits are reduced from the light-green shaded triangle ABC in Panel (a) to the smaller area ABGF. The forgone net benefits, or deadweight loss, is given by the purple-shaded area FGC. If the activity level is increased from D to J, as shown in Panel (c), net benefits declined by the deadweight loss measured by the area CHI.

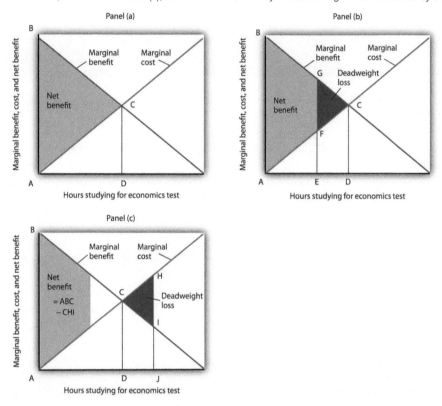

Now suppose a person increases study time from D to J hours as shown in Panel (c). The area under the marginal cost curve between D and J gives the total cost of increasing study time; it is DCHJ. The total benefit of increasing study time equals the area under the marginal benefit curve between D and J; it is DCIJ. The cost of increasing study time in economics from D hours to J hours exceeds the benefit. This gives us a deadweight loss of CHI. The net benefit of spending J hours studying economics equals the net benefit of studying for D hours less the deadweight loss, or ABC *minus* CHI. Only by studying up to the point at which marginal benefit equals marginal cost do we achieve the maximum net benefit shown in Panel (a).

We can apply the marginal decision rule to the problem in Figure 6.6 in another way. In Panel (b), a person studies economics for E hours. Reading up to the marginal benefit curve, we reach point G. Reading up to the marginal cost curve, we reach point F. Marginal benefit at G exceeds marginal cost at F; the marginal decision rule says economics study should be increased, which would take us toward the intersection of the marginal benefit and marginal cost curves. Spending J hours studying economics, as shown in Panel (c), is too much. Reading up to the marginal benefit and marginal cost curves, we see that marginal cost exceeds marginal benefit, suggesting that study time be reduced.

This completes our introduction to the marginal decision rule and the use of marginal benefit and marginal cost curves. We will spend the remainder of the chapter applying the model.

Heads Up!

It is easy to make the mistake of assuming that if an activity is carried out up to the point where marginal benefit equals marginal cost, then net benefits must be zero. Remember that following the marginal decision rule and equating marginal benefits and costs *maximizes* net benefits. It makes the *difference* between total benefits and total cost as large as possible.

Key Takeaways

- Economists assume that decision makers make choices in the way that maximizes the value of some objective.
- Maximization involves determining the change in total benefit and the change in total cost associated with each unit of an activity. These changes are called marginal benefit and marginal cost, respectively.
- If the marginal benefit of an activity exceeds the marginal cost, the decision maker will gain by increasing the activity.
- If the marginal cost of an activity exceeds the marginal benefit, the decision maker will gain by reducing the activity.
- The area under the marginal benefit curve for an activity gives its total benefit; the area under the marginal cost curve gives the activity's total cost. Net benefit equals total benefit less total cost.
- The marginal benefit rule tells us that we can maximize the net benefit of any activity by choosing the quantity at which marginal benefit equals marginal cost. At this quantity, the net benefit of the activity is maximized.

Try It!

Suppose Ms. Phan still faces the exams in economics and in accounting, and she still plans to spend a total of 5 hours studying for the two exams. However, she revises her expectations about the degree to which studying economics and accounting will affect her scores on the two exams. She expects studying economics will add somewhat less to her score, and she expects studying accounting will add more. The result is the table below of expected total benefits and total costs of hours spent studying economics. Notice that several values in the table have been omitted. Fill in the missing values in the table. How many hours of study should Ms. Phan devote to economics to maximize her net benefit?

Hours studying economics	0	1	2	3	4	5
Total benefit	0	14	24	30		32
Total cost	0	2	8		32	50
Net benefit	0	12		12	0	−18

Now compute the marginal benefits and costs of hours devoted to studying economics, completing the table below.

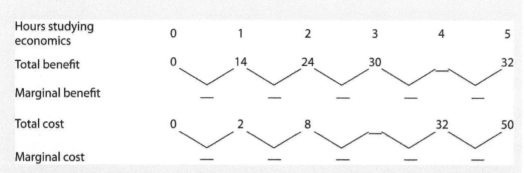

Hours studying economics	0	1	2	3	4	5
Total benefit	0	14	24	30		32
Marginal benefit		—	—	—	—	—
Total cost	0	2	8		32	50
Marginal cost		—	—	—	—	—

Draw the marginal benefit and marginal cost curves for studying economics (remember to plot marginal values at the midpoints of the respective hourly intervals). Do your curves intersect at the "right" number of hours of study—the number that maximizes the net benefit of studying economics?

Case in Point: Preventing Oil Spills

Source: © 2010 Jupiterimages Corporation

Do we spill enough oil in our oceans and waterways? It is a question that perhaps only economists would ask—and, as economists, we should ask it.

There is, of course, no virtue in an oil spill. It destroys wildlife and fouls shorelines. Cleanup costs can be tremendous. However, preventing oil spills has costs as well: greater enforcement expenditures and higher costs to shippers of oil and, therefore, higher costs of goods such as gasoline to customers. The only way to prevent oil spills completely is to stop drilling for and shipping oil. That is a cost few people would accept. But what is the right balance between environmental protection and the satisfaction of consumer demand for oil?

Vanderbilt University economist Mark Cohen examined the U.S. Coast Guard's efforts to reduce oil spills when transporting oil through its enforcement of shipping regulations in coastal waters and on rivers. He focused on the costs and benefits resulting from the Coast Guard's enforcement efforts in 1981. On the basis of the frequency of oil spills before the Coast Guard began its enforcement, Mr. Cohen estimated that the Coast Guard prevented 1,159,352 gallons of oil from being spilled in 1981.

Given that there was a total of 824,921 gallons of oil actually spilled in 1981, should the Coast Guard have attempted to prevent even more spillage? Mr. Cohen estimated that the marginal benefit of preventing one more gallon from being spilled was $7.27 ($3.42 in cleanup costs, $3 less in environmental damage, and $0.85 worth of oil saved). The marginal cost of preventing one more gallon from being spilled was $5.50. Mr. Cohen suggests that because the marginal benefit of more vigorous enforcement exceeded the marginal cost, more vigorous Coast Guard efforts would have been justified.

More vigorous efforts have, indeed, been pursued. In 1989, the Exxon oil tanker Exxon Valdez ran aground, spilling 10.8 million gallons of oil off the coast of Alaska. The spill damaged the shoreline of a national forest, four national wildlife refuges, three national parks, five state parks, four critical habitat areas, and a state game refuge. Exxon was ordered to pay $900 million in damages; a federal jury found Exxon and the captain guilty of criminal negligence and imposed an additional $5 billion in punitive damages. In 2008, The Supreme Court reduced the assessment of punitive damages to $507 million, with the majority arguing that the original figure was too high in comparison to the compensatory damages for a case in which the actions of the defendant, Exxon, were "reprehensible" but not intentional.

Perhaps the most important impact of the Exxon Valdez disaster was the passage of the Oil Pollution Act of 1990. It increased shipper liability from $14 million to $100 million. It also required double-hulled tankers for shipping oil.

The European Union (EU) has also strengthened its standards for oil tankers. The 2002 breakup of the oil tanker Prestige off the coast of Spain resulted in the spillage of 3.2 million gallons of oil. The EU had planned to ban single-hulled tankers, phasing in the ban between 2003 and 2015. The sinking of the Prestige led the EU to move up that deadline.

Tanker spill crises have led both the United States and the European Union to tighten up their regulations of oil tankers. The result has been a reduction in the quantity of oil spilled, which was precisely what economic research had concluded was needed. Whereas the total quantity of oil spilled from tankers in the 1970s was over 3 million tons, for the decade of the 2000s the total was 212,000 tons—a decline of over 90%—even as the amount of oil shipped rose dramatically.

The year 2010 saw another kind of major oil spill resulting from offshore drilling. The explosion of the Deepwater Horizon oil rig in the Gulf of Mexico on April 20, 2010, in which 11 workers were killed and 17 injured, led to a spill of 4.1 million barrels into the Gulf over a 3-month period. This spill was about 40% larger than the second largest offshore drilling spill off the U.S. coast and 19 times bigger than the Exxon Valdez spill. So far, no major legislation affecting oil drilling has passed, though, after a five-month drilling moratorium, the U.S. Department of the Interior has made changes to its enforcement practices.

Whether or not new legislation concerning offshore oil drilling is needed and how it should be constructed is being hotly debated. A preliminary study by Alan Krupnick, Sarah Campbell, Mark A. Cohen, and Ian W. H. Parry for the organization Resources for the Future estimated the annual benefits of preventing a catastrophic spill to be between $16.1 billion and $29.5 billion. The annual costs of a ban they estimate to be about $65 billion, from which they conclude that cost-benefit analysis does not justify a ban. On the other hand, they argue that regulation that would increase the costs of extraction by 10% or $11 billion annually would pass a cost-benefit analysis test and that regulation that raises extraction cost by 20% or $22 billion would pass the test at the upper end of the benefits estimate only. It should be noted that the Oil Pollution Act of 1990 was passed about a year and a half after the Exxon Valdez incident.

Sources: *Based on Mark A. Cohen, "The Costs and Benefits of Oil Spill Prevention and Enforcement," Journal of Environmental Economics and Management 13:2(June 1986): 167–188; International Tanker Owners Pollution Federation Limited, Oil Tanker Spill Statistics 2010, available at http://www.itopf.com;Alan Krupnick, Sarah Campbell, Mark A. Cohen, and Ian W. H. Parry, "Understanding the Costs and Benefits of Deepwater Oil Drilling Regulation,"Discussion Paper Resources for the Future RFF DP 10–62 (January 2011); Rick S. Kurtz, "Coastal Oil Pollution: Spills, Crisis, and Policy Change," Review ofPolicy Research, 21:2 (March 2004): 201–219; David S. Savage, "Justices Slash Exxon Valdez Verdict," Los Angeles Times, June 26, 2008, p. A1; Ger-*

ardShields, "Gulf Oil Disaster: One Year Later," The Advocate (Baton Rouge, Louisiana), April 20, 2011, p. 1; and Edwin Unsworth, "Europe Gets Tougher onAging Oil Tankers," Business Insurance, 36:48 (December 2, 2002): 33–34.

Answer to Try It! Problem

Here are the completed data table and the table showing total and marginal benefit and cost.

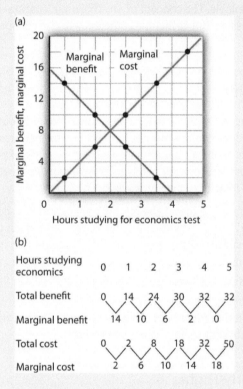

(a)

(b)

Hours studying economics	0	1	2	3	4	5
Total benefit	0	14	24	30	32	32
Marginal benefit		14	10	6	2	0
Total cost	0	2	8	18	32	50
Marginal cost		2	6	10	14	18

Ms. Phan maximizes her net benefit by reducing her time studying economics to 2 hours. The change in her expectations reduced the benefit and increased the cost of studying economics. The completed graph of marginal benefit and marginal cost is at the far left. Notice that answering the question using the marginal decision rule gives the same answer.

6.3 Maximizing in the Marketplace

Learning Objectives

1. Explain what is meant by an efficient allocation of resources in an economy and describe the market conditions that must exist to achieve this goal.
2. Define consumer and producer surplus.
3. Discuss the relationship between efficiency and equity.

In perhaps the most influential book in economics ever written, *An Inquiry into the Nature and Causes of the Wealth of Nations*, published in 1776, Adam Smith argued that the pursuit of self-interest in a marketplace would promote the general interest. He said resources would be guided, as if by an "invisible hand," to their best uses. That invisible hand was the marketplace.

Smith's idea was radical for its time; he saw that the seemingly haphazard workings of the marketplace could promote the common good. In this section, we will use the tools we have developed thus far to see the power of Smith's invisible hand. Efforts by individuals to maximize their own net benefit can maximize net benefit for the economy as a whole.

When the net benefits of all economic activities are maximized, economists say the allocation of resources is **efficient**. This concept of efficiency is broader than the notion of efficient production that we encountered when discussing the production possibilities curve. There, we saw that the economy's factors of production would be efficient *in production* if they were allocated according to the principle of comparative advantage. That meant producing as much as possible with the factors of production available. The concept of an efficient allocation of resources incorporates production, as in that discussion, but it includes efficiency in the consumption of goods and services as well.

efficient

The allocation of resources when the net benefits of all economic activities are maximized.

Achieving Efficiency

Imagine yourself arriving at the store to purchase some food. In your choice, you will weigh your own benefits and costs to maximize your net benefit. The farmers, the distributors, and the grocer have sought to maximize their net benefits as well. How can we expect that all those efforts will maximize net benefits for the economy as a whole? How can we expect the marketplace to achieve an efficient allocation of food, or of anything else?

One condition that must be met if the market's allocation is to be efficient is that the marketplace must be competitive or function as if it were. We will have a great deal more to say about competitive markets versus less competitive ones in subsequent chapters. For now, we can simply note that a competitive market is one with many buyers and sellers in each market and in which entry and exit are fairly easy. No one controls the price; the forces of demand and supply determine price.

The second condition that must hold if the market is to achieve an efficient allocation concerns property rights. We turn to that topic in the next section.

The Role of Property Rights

A smoothly functioning market requires that producers possess property rights to the goods and services they produce and that consumers possess property rights to the goods and services they buy. **Property rights** are a set of rules that specify the ways in which an owner can use a resource.

property rights

A set of rules that specify the ways in which an owner can use a resource.

Consider the tomato market. Farmers who grow tomatoes have clearly defined rights to their land and to the tomatoes they produce and sell. Distributors who purchase tomatoes from farmers and sell them to grocers have clear rights to the tomatoes until they sell them to grocers. The grocers who purchase the tomatoes retain rights to them until they sell them to consumers. When you buy a tomato, you have the exclusive right to its use.

A system of property rights forms the basis for all market exchange. Before exchange can begin, there must be a clear specification of who owns what. The system of property rights must also show what purchasers are acquiring when they buy rights to particular resources. Because property rights must exist if exchange is to occur, and because exchange is the process through which economic efficiency is achieved, a system of property rights is essential to the efficient allocation of resources.

Imagine what would happen in the market for tomatoes if property rights were not clearly defined. Suppose, for example, that grocers could not legally prevent someone from simply grabbing some tomatoes and leaving without paying for them. If that were the case, grocers would not be likely to offer tomatoes for sale. If it were the case for all grocery items, there would not be grocery stores at all.

Although property rights vary for different resources, two characteristics are required if the marketplace is to achieve an efficient allocation of resources:

1. Property rights must be exclusive. An **exclusive property right** is one that allows its owner to prevent others from using the resource. The owner of a house, for example, has the right to exclude others from the use of the house. If this right did not exist, ownership would have little value; it is not likely that the property could be exchanged in a market. And the inability to sell property would limit the incentive of owners to maintain it.

2. Property rights must be transferable. A **transferable property right** is one that allows the owner of a resource to sell or lease it to someone else. In the absence of transferability, no exchange could occur.

Markets and the Efficiency Condition

A competitive market with well-defined and transferable property rights satisfies the **efficiency condition**. If met, we can assume that the market's allocation of resources will be efficient.

Consider again your purchase of tomatoes. Suppose the curves of demand and supply for tomatoes are those given in Figure 6.7; the equilibrium price equals $1.50 per pound. Suppose further that the market satisfies the efficiency condition. With that assumption, we can relate the model of demand and supply to our analysis of marginal benefits and costs.

The demand curve tells us that the last pound of tomatoes was worth $1.50; we can think of that as the marginal benefit of the last pound of tomatoes since that is how much consumers were willing to pay. We can say that about any price on a market demand curve; a demand curve can be considered as a marginal benefit curve. Similarly, the supply curve can be considered the marginal cost curve. In the case of the tomato market, for example, the price tells us that the marginal cost of producing the last pound of tomatoes is $1.50. This marginal cost is considered in the economic sense—other goods and services worth $1.50 were not produced in order to make an additional pound of tomatoes available.

On what basis can we presume that the price of a pound of tomatoes equals its marginal cost? The answer lies in our marginal decision rule. Profit-maximizing tomato producers will produce more tomatoes as long as their marginal benefit exceeds their marginal cost. What is the marginal benefit to a producer of an extra pound of tomatoes? It is the price that the producer will receive. What is the marginal cost? It is the value that must be given up to produce an extra pound of tomatoes.

Producers maximize profit by expanding their production up to the point at which their marginal cost equals their marginal benefit, which is the market price. The price of $1.50 thus reflects the marginal cost to society of making an additional pound of tomatoes available.

At the equilibrium price and output of tomatoes, then, the marginal benefit of tomatoes to consumers, as reflected by the price they are willing to pay, equals the marginal cost of producing tomatoes. Where marginal benefit equals marginal cost, net benefit is maximized. The equilibrium quantity of tomatoes, as determined by demand and supply, is efficient.

exclusive property right

A property right that allows its owner to prevent others from using the resource.

transferable property right

A property right that allows the owner of a resource to sell or lease it to someone else.

efficiency condition

A situation that requires a competitive market with well-defined and transferable property rights.

FIGURE 6.7 Demand and Supply and the Efficiency Condition
In a competitive market with exclusive and transferable property rights, such as the market for tomatoes, the efficiency condition is met. Buyers and sellers are faced with all of the relevant benefits and costs, and the equilibrium price equals the marginal cost to society of producing that good, here $2.50 per pound. We can interpret the market demand and supply curve as marginal benefit and marginal cost curves, respectively.

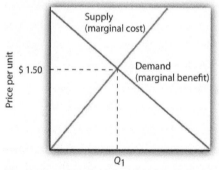

Pounds of tomatoes per period

Producer and Consumer Surplus

Think about the last thing you purchased. You bought it because you expected that its benefits would exceed its opportunity cost; you expected that the purchase would make you better off. The seller sold it to you because he or she expected that the money you paid would be worth more than the value of keeping the item. The seller expected to be better off as a result of the sale. Exchanges in the marketplace have a remarkable property: Both buyers and sellers expect to emerge from the transaction better off.

consumer surplus

The amount by which the total benefits to consumers from consuming a good exceed their total expenditures on the good.

Panel (a) of Figure 6.8 shows a market demand curve for a particular good. Suppose the price equals OB and the quantity equals OE. The area under the demand curve over the range of quantities from the origin at O to the quantity at E equals the total benefit of consuming OE units of the good. It is the area OCDE. Consumers pay for this benefit; their total expenditures equal the rectangle OBDE, which is the dark shaded region in the graph. Because the total benefits exceed total expenditures, there is a consumer surplus given by the triangle BCD. **Consumer surplus** is the amount by which the total benefits to consumers from consuming a good exceed their total expenditures on the good.

FIGURE 6.8 Consumer and Producer Surplus

Consumer surplus [Panel (a)] measures the difference between total benefit of consuming a given quantity of output and the total expenditures consumers pay to obtain that quantity. Here, total benefits are given by the shaded area OCDE; total expenditures are given by the rectangle OBDE. The difference, shown by the triangle BCD, is consumer surplus.

Producer surplus [Panel b)] measures the difference between total revenue received by firms at a given quantity of output and the total cost of producing it. Here, total revenue is given by the rectangle OBDE, and total costs are given by the area OADE. The difference, shown by the triangle ABD is producer surplus.

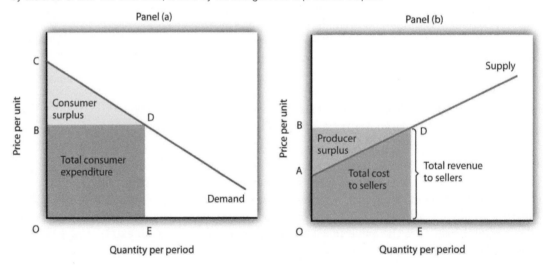

Now consider the sellers' side of transactions. Panel (b) of Figure 6.8 shows a market supply curve; recall that it gives us marginal cost. Suppose the market price equals OB and quantity supplied is OE; those are the same values we had in Panel (a). The price times the quantity equals the total revenue received by sellers. It is shown as the shaded rectangle OBDE. The total revenue received by sellers equals total expenditures by consumers.

producer surplus

The difference between the total revenue received by sellers and their total cost.

The total cost to sellers is the area under the marginal cost curve; it is the area OADE. That cost is less than revenue. The difference between the total revenue received by sellers and their total cost is called **producer surplus**. In Panel (b) it is the light-shaded triangle ABD.

FIGURE 6.9 Net Benefit: The Sum of Consumer and Producer Surplus

The sum of consumer surplus and producer surplus measures the net benefit to society of any level of economic activity. Net benefit is maximized when production and consumption are carried out at the level where the demand and supply curves intersect. Here, the net benefit to society equals the area ACD. It is the sum of consumer surplus, BCD, and producer surplus, ABD.

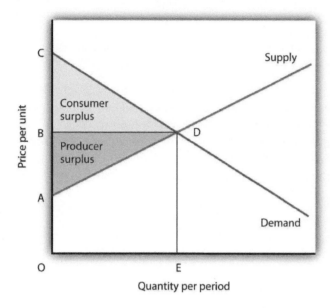

We put the demand and supply curves of Figure 6.8 Panels (a) and (b) together in Figure 6.9. The intersection of the two curves determines the equilibrium price, OB, and the equilibrium quantity, OE. The shaded regions give us consumer and producer surplus. The sum of these two surpluses is net benefit. This net benefit is maximized where the demand and supply curves intersect.

Efficiency and Equity

Consumer demands are affected by incomes. Demand, after all, reflects ability as well as willingness to pay for goods and services. The market will be more responsive to the preferences of people with high incomes than to those of people with low incomes.

In a market that satisfies the efficiency condition, an efficient allocation of resources will emerge from any particular distribution of income. Different income distributions will result in different, but still efficient, outcomes. For example, if 1% of the population controls virtually all the income, then the market will efficiently allocate virtually all its production to those same people.

What is a fair, or equitable, distribution of income? What is an unfair distribution? Should everyone have the same income? Is the current distribution fair? Should the rich have less and the poor have more? Should the middle class have more? Equity is very much in the mind of the observer. What may seem equitable to one person may seem inequitable to another. There is, however, no test we can apply to determine whether the distribution of income is or is not equitable. That question requires a normative judgment.

Determining whether the allocation of resources is or is not efficient is one problem. Determining whether the distribution of income is fair is another. The governments of all nations act in some way to redistribute income. That fact suggests that people generally have concluded that leaving the distribution of income solely to the market would not be fair and that some redistribution is desirable. This may take the form of higher taxes for people with higher incomes than for those with lower incomes. It may take the form of special programs, such as welfare programs, for low-income people.

Whatever distribution society chooses, an efficient allocation of resources is still preferred to an inefficient one. Because an efficient allocation maximizes net benefits, the gain in net benefits could be distributed in a way that leaves all people better off than they would be at any inefficient allocation. If an efficient allocation of resources seems unfair, it must be because the distribution of income is unfair.

Key Takeaways

- In a competitive system in which the interaction of demand and supply determine prices, the corresponding demand and supply curves can be considered marginal benefit and marginal cost curves, respectively.

- An efficient allocation of resources is one that maximizes the net benefit of each activity. We expect it to be achieved in markets that satisfy the efficiency condition, which requires a competitive market and well-defined, transferable property rights.

- Consumer surplus is the amount by which the total benefit to consumers from some activity exceeds their total expenditures for it.

- Producer surplus is the amount by which the total revenues of producers exceed their total costs.

- An inequitable allocation of resources implies that the distribution of income and wealth is inequitable. Judgments about equity are normative judgments.

Try It!

Draw hypothetical demand and supply curves for a typical product, say coffee. Now show the areas of consumer and producer surplus. Under what circumstances is the market likely to be efficient?

Case in Point: Bah Humbug!

Source: © Thinkstock

Professor Joel Waldfogel, in his book *Scroogenomics*, derides Christmas gift giving as only an economist would. Based on repeated surveys from students in his classes (which asked them to compare value and price of gifts they received and of items they bought for themselves) and estimates of annual Christmas spending in the United States of $66 billion in 2007, he concludes that $12 billion, roughly 18% of the total, constituted deadweight loss. And that doesn't count the 2.8 billion hours collectively spent shopping for the stuff.

The crux of his argument is that when you buy something for yourself, the price you pay is at least equal to the value of the satisfaction you get from the item. For some items, the consumer surplus (the difference between the value to you of the item and the price you pay), may be small or even zero, but for other items it may be large. One example he gives where consumer surplus may be huge is the purchase of a $20 antibiotic for your child with an ear infection who has been screaming all night. But what are the chances that consumer surplus will be positive for an item you receive as a gift? "Relative to how much satisfaction their [gift givers] expenditures could have given us, their choices destroy value. Take that, Santa," writes Professor Waldfogel.

Doesn't sentimental value make up for the differences between the price of an item you receive, say a $50 sweater, and the value you attach to it, say $25? If you attach $50 in sentimental value to the sweater, then it is really worth $75 to you, which is more than the $50 price paid by the gift giver. The problem with this line of argument is that if the gift giver had chosen a sweater for you that you actually liked—one that you valued at least at the purchase price of $50—its total value to you would then have been $100. Compared to giving you a sweater you actually liked, giving you the one you did not much care for destroyed value.

The surveys have also questioned the relationship of the gift giver to the gift recipient to see if giver knowledge of the recipient leads to more gift giving efficiency. The results are as one might expect. Gifts from aunts, uncles, and grandparents generated between 75 and 80 cents of satisfaction per dollar spent. Friends generated 91 cents, parents 97 cents, siblings 99 cents, and significant others 102 cents of satisfaction per dollar spent. In general, frequency of contact between giver and receiver increases the yield of a gift.

While acknowledging that there are some situations in which gifts may create value for recipients beyond what they could have purchased for themselves, such as when a recipient receives a CD of a band he or she was unfamiliar with but turns out to love, overall Waldfogel's estimates reveal a great loss for society. What to do about it? Giving cash would work but there seems to be a stigma associated with doing so, especially for certain kinds of relationships between givers and receivers. Gift registries solve the problem for newlyweds and could do so for Christmas gifts if that idea caught on. Since outside of your immediate circle you are unlikely to select a gift that does not destroy value, he suggests giving cash, if that is not too uncomfortable, or gift cards, possibly ones for charitable causes. Of course, people often forget to use their gift cards. When that happens, the benefit is not lost but rather goes to the retailer, which was not likely the intention of the gift giver. He thus suggests that retailers team up with charities so that any amount not redeemed after a certain time period goes to a charity stated on the gift card.

Parodying Karl Marx's *Communist Manifesto*, he concludes, "A specter has been haunting the rich economies of the West, and that specter is wasteful gift giving. Gift givers of the world unite. You have nothing to lose but deadweight loss and a world of satisfaction to gain."

Source: Based on Joel Waldfogel, Scroogenomics: Why You Shouldn't Buy Presents for the Holidays (Princeton: Princeton University Press, 2009).

Answer to Try It! Problem

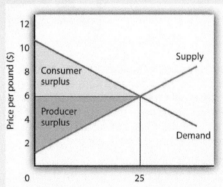

Quantity (millions of pounds of coffee per month)

On the assumption that the coffee market is competitive and that it is characterized by well-defined exclusive and transferable property rights, the coffee market meets the efficiency condition. That means that the allocation of resources shown at the equilibrium will be the one that maximizes the net benefit of all activities. The net benefit is shared by coffee consumers (as measured by consumer surplus) and coffee producers (as measured by producer surplus).

6.4 Market Failure

Private decisions in the marketplace may not be consistent with the maximization of the net benefit of a particular activity. The failure of private decisions in the marketplace to achieve an efficient allocation of scarce resources is called **market failure**. Markets will not generate an efficient allocation of resources if they are not competitive or if property rights are not well defined and fully transferable. Either condition will mean that decision makers are not faced with the marginal benefits and costs of their choices.

Think about the drive that we had you take at the beginning of this chapter. You faced some, but not all, of the opportunity costs involved in that choice. In particular, your choice to go for a drive would increase air pollution and might increase traffic congestion. That means that, in weighing the marginal benefits and marginal costs of going for a drive, not all of the costs would be counted. As a result, the net benefit of the allocation of resources such as the air might not be maximized.

market failure

The failure of private decisions in the marketplace to achieve an efficient allocation of scarce resources.

Noncompetitive Markets

The model of demand and supply assumes that markets are competitive. No one in these markets has any power over the equilibrium price; each consumer and producer takes the market price as given and responds to it. Under such conditions, price is determined by the intersection of demand and supply.

In some markets, however, individual buyers or sellers are powerful enough to influence the market price. In subsequent chapters, we will study cases in which producers or consumers are in a position to affect the prices they charge or must pay, respectively. We shall find that when individual firms or groups of firms have market power, which is the ability to change the market price, the price will be distorted—it will not equal marginal cost.

Public Goods

public good

A good for which the cost of exclusion is prohibitive and for which the marginal cost of an additional user is zero.

private good

A good for which exclusion is possible and for which the marginal cost of another user is positive.

Some goods are unlikely to be produced and exchanged in a market because of special characteristics of the goods themselves. The benefits of these goods are such that exclusion is not feasible. Once they are produced, anyone can enjoy them; there is no practical way to exclude people who have not paid for them from consuming them. Furthermore, the marginal cost of adding one more consumer is zero. A good for which the cost of exclusion is prohibitive and for which the marginal cost of an additional user is zero is a **public good**. A good for which exclusion is possible and for which the marginal cost of another user is positive is a **private good**.

National defense is a public good. Once defense is provided, it is not possible to exclude people who have not paid for it from its consumption. Further, the cost of an additional user is zero—an army does not cost any more if there is one more person to be protected. Other examples of public goods include law enforcement, fire protection, and efforts to preserve species threatened with extinction.

Free Riders

Suppose a private firm, Terror Alert, Inc., develops a completely reliable system to identify and intercept 98% of any would-be terrorists that might attempt to enter the United States from anywhere in the world. This service is a public good. Once it is provided, no one can be excluded from the system's protection on grounds that he or she has not paid for it, and the cost of adding one more person to the group protected is zero. Suppose that the system, by eliminating a potential threat to U.S. security, makes the average person in the United States better off; the benefit to each household from the added security is worth $40 per month (about the same as an earthquake insurance premium). There are roughly 113 million households in the United States, so the total benefit of the system is $4.5 billion per month. Assume that it will cost Terror Alert, Inc., $1 billion per month to operate. The benefits of the system far outweigh the cost.

Suppose that Terror Alert installs its system and sends a bill to each household for $20 for the first month of service—an amount equal to half of each household's benefit. If each household pays its bill, Terror Alert will enjoy a tidy profit; it will receive revenues of more than $2.25 billion per month.

free riders

People or firms that consume a public good without paying for it.

But will each household pay? Once the system is in place, each household would recognize that it will benefit from the security provided by Terror Alert whether it pays its bill or not. Although some households will voluntarily pay their bills, it seems unlikely that very many will. Recognizing the opportunity to consume the good without paying for it, most would be free riders. **Free riders** are people or firms that consume a public good without paying for it. Even though the total benefit of the system is $4.5 billion, Terror Alert will not be faced by the marketplace with a signal that suggests that the system is worthwhile. It is unlikely that it will recover its cost of $1 billion per month. Terror Alert is not likely to get off the ground.

The bill for $20 from Terror Alert sends the wrong signal, too. An efficient market requires a price equal to marginal cost. But the marginal cost of protecting one more household is zero; adding one more household adds nothing to the cost of the system. A household that decides not to pay Terror Alert anything for its service is paying a price equal to its marginal cost. But doing that, being a free rider, is precisely what prevents Terror Alert from operating.

Because no household can be excluded and because the cost of an extra household is zero, the efficiency condition will not be met in a private market. What is true of Terror Alert, Inc., is true of public goods in general: they simply do not lend themselves to private market provision.

Public Goods and the Government

Because many individuals who benefit from public goods will not pay for them, private firms will produce a smaller quantity of public goods than is efficient, if they produce them at all. In such cases, it may be desirable for government agencies to step in. Government can supply a greater quantity of the good by direct provision, by purchasing the public good from a private agency, or by subsidizing consumption. In any case, the cost is financed through taxation and thus avoids the free-rider problem.

Most public goods are provided directly by government agencies. Governments produce national defense and law enforcement, for example. Private firms under contract with government agencies produce some public goods. Park maintenance and fire services are public goods that are sometimes produced by private firms. In other cases, the government promotes the private consumption or production of public goods by subsidizing them. Private charitable contributions often support activities that are public goods; federal and state governments subsidize these by allowing taxpayers to reduce their tax payments by a fraction of the amount they contribute.

While the market will produce some level of public goods in the absence of government intervention, we do not expect that it will produce the quantity that maximizes net benefit. Figure 6.10 illustrates the problem. Suppose that provision of a public good such as national defense is left entirely to private firms. It is likely that some defense services would be produced; suppose that equals Q_1 units per period. This level of national defense might be achieved through individual contributions. But it is very unlikely that contributions would achieve the correct level of defense services. The efficient quantity occurs where the demand, or marginal benefit, curve intersects the marginal cost curve, at Q^*. The deadweight loss is the shaded area ABC; we can think of this as the net benefit of government intervention to increase the production of national defense from Q_1 up to the efficient quantity, Q^*.

FIGURE 6.10 Public Goods and Market Failure
Because free riders will prevent firms from being able to require consumers to pay for the benefits received from consuming a public good, output will be less than the efficient level. In the case shown here, private donations achieved a level of the public good of Q_1 per period. The efficient level is Q^*. The deadweight loss is shown by the triangle ABC.

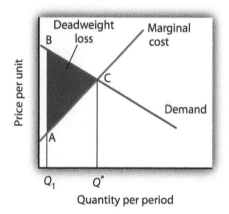

Heads Up!

Note that the definitions of public and private goods are based on characteristics of the goods themselves, not on whether they are provided by the public or the private sector. Postal services are a private good provided by the public sector. The fact that these goods are produced by a government agency does not make them a public good.

External Costs and Benefits

Suppose that in the course of production, the firms in a particular industry generate air pollution. These firms thus impose costs on others, but they do so outside the context of any market exchange—no agreement has been made between the firms and the people affected by the pollution. The firms thus will not be faced with the costs of their action. A cost imposed on others outside of any market exchange is an **external cost**.

external cost

A cost imposed on others outside of any market exchange.

We saw an example of an external cost in our imaginary decision to go for a drive. Here is another: violence on television, in the movies, and in video games. Many critics argue that the violence that pervades these media fosters greater violence in the real world. By the time a child who spends the average amount of time watching television finishes elementary school, he or she will have seen 100,000 acts of violence, including 8,000 murders, according to the American Psychological Association. Thousands of studies of the relationship between violence in the media and behavior have concluded that there is a link between watching violence and violent behaviors. Video games are a major element of the problem, as young children now spend hours each week playing them. Fifty percent of fourth-grade graders say that their favorite video games are the "first person shooter" type.[1]

Any tendency of increased violence resulting from increased violence in the media constitutes an external cost of such media. The American Academy of Pediatrics reported in 2001 that homicides were the fourth leading cause of death among children between the ages of 10 and 14 and the second leading cause of death for people aged 15 to 24 and has recommended a reduction in exposure to media violence.[2] It seems reasonable to assume that at least some of these acts of violence can be considered an external cost of violence in the media.

An action taken by a person or firm can also create benefits for others, again in the absence of any market agreement; such a benefit is called an **external benefit**. A firm that builds a beautiful building generates benefits to everyone who admires it; such benefits are external.

external benefit

An action taken by a person or firm that creates benefits for others in the absence of any market agreement.

External Costs and Efficiency

FIGURE 6.11 External Costs
When firms in an industry generate external costs, the supply curve S_1 reflects only their private marginal costs, MC_P. Forcing firms to pay the external costs they impose shifts the supply curve to S_2, which reflects the full marginal cost of the firms' production, MC_e. Output is reduced and price goes up. The deadweight loss that occurs when firms are not faced with the full costs of their decisions is shown by the shaded area in the graph.

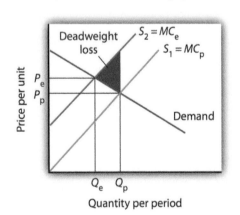

The case of the polluting firms is illustrated in Figure 6.11. The industry supply curve S_1 reflects private marginal costs, MC_p. The market price is P_p for a quantity Q_p. This is the solution that would occur if firms generating external costs were not forced to pay those costs. If the external costs generated by the pollution were added, the new supply curve S_2 would reflect higher marginal costs, MC_e. Faced with those costs, the market would generate a lower equilibrium quantity, Q_e. That quantity would command a higher price, P_e. The failure to confront producers with the cost of their pollution means that consumers do not pay the full cost of the good they are purchasing. The level of output and the level of pollution are therefore higher than would be economically efficient. If a way could be found to confront producers with the full cost of their choices, then consumers would be faced with a higher cost as well. Figure 6.11 shows that consumption would be reduced to the efficient level, Q_e, at which demand and the full marginal cost curve (MC_e) intersect. The deadweight loss generated by allowing the external cost to be generated with an output of Q_p is given as the shaded region in the graph.

External Costs and Government Intervention

If an activity generates external costs, the decision makers generating the activity will not be faced with its full costs. Agents who impose these costs will carry out their activities beyond the efficient level; those who consume them, facing too low a price, will consume too much. As a result, producers and consumers will carry out an excessive quantity of the activity. In such cases, government may try to intervene to reduce the level of the activity toward the efficient quantity. In the case shown in Figure 6.11, for example, firms generating an external cost have a supply curve S_1 that reflects their private marginal costs, MC_p. A per-unit pollution fee imposed on the firms would increase their marginal costs to MC_e, thus shifting the supply curve to S_2, and the efficient level of production would emerge. Taxes or other restrictions may be imposed on the activity that generates the external cost in an effort to confront decision makers with the costs that they are imposing. In many areas, firms and consumers that pollute rivers and lakes are required to pay fees based on the amount they pollute. Firms in many areas are required to purchase permits in order to pollute the air; the requirement that permits be purchased serves to confront the firms with the costs of their choices.

Another approach to dealing with problems of external costs is direct regulation. For example, a firm may be ordered to reduce its pollution. A person who turns his or her front yard into a garbage dump may be ordered to clean it up. Participants at a raucous party may be told to be quiet. Alternative ways of dealing with external costs are discussed later in the text.

Common Property Resources

Common property resources[3] are resources for which no property rights have been defined. The difficulty with common property resources is that individuals may not have adequate incentives to engage in efforts to preserve or protect them. Consider, for example, the relative fates of cattle and buffalo in the United States in the nineteenth century. Cattle populations increased throughout the century, while the buffalo nearly became extinct. The chief difference between the two animals was that exclusive property rights existed for cattle but not for buffalo.

> **common property resource**
>
> Resources for which no property rights have been defined.

Owners of cattle had an incentive to maintain herd sizes. A cattle owner who slaughtered all of his or her cattle without providing for replacement of the herd would not have a source of future income. Cattle owners not only maintained their herds but also engaged in extensive efforts to breed high-quality livestock. They invested time and effort in the efficient management of the resource on which their livelihoods depended.

Buffalo hunters surely had similar concerns about the maintenance of buffalo herds, but they had no individual stake in doing anything about them—the animals were a common property resource. Thousands of individuals hunted buffalo for a living. Anyone who cut back on hunting in order to help to preserve the herd would lose income—and face the likelihood that other hunters would go on hunting at the same rate as before.

Today, exclusive rights to buffalo have been widely established. The demand for buffalo meat, which is lower in fat than beef, has been increasing, but the number of buffalo in the United States is rising rapidly. If buffalo were still a common property resource, that increased demand, in the absence of other restrictions on hunting of the animals, would surely result in the elimination of the animal. Because there are exclusive, transferable property rights in buffalo and because a competitive market brings buyers and sellers of buffalo and buffalo products together, we can be reasonably confident in the efficient management of the animal.

When a species is threatened with extinction, it is likely that no one has exclusive property rights to it. Whales, condors, grizzly bears, elephants in Central Africa—whatever the animal that is threatened—are common property resources. In such cases a government agency may impose limits on the killing of the animal or destruction of its habitat. Such limits can prevent the excessive private use of a common property resource. Alternatively, as was done in the case of the buffalo, private rights can be established, giving resource owners the task of preservation.

Key Takeaways

- Public sector intervention to increase the level of provision of public goods may improve the efficiency of resource allocation by overcoming the problem of free riders.
- Activities that generate external costs are likely to be carried out at levels that exceed those that would be efficient; the public sector may seek to intervene to confront decision makers with the full costs of their choices.
- Some private activities generate external benefits.
- A common property resource is unlikely to be allocated efficiently in the marketplace.

Try It!

The manufacture of memory chips for computers generates pollutants that generally enter rivers and streams. Use the model of demand and supply to show the equilibrium price and output of chips. Assuming chip manufacturers do not have to pay the costs these pollutants impose, what can you say about the efficiency of the quantity of chips produced? Show the area of dead-weight loss imposed by this external cost. Show how a requirement that firms pay these costs as they produce the chips would affect the equilibrium price and output of chips. Would such a requirement help to satisfy the efficiency condition? Explain.

Case in Point: Protecting Wildlife by Establishing Private Property Rights

Source: © Thinkstock

Imagine that you are a rural landowner in Kenya. You grow crops, sell them, and earn a return. You raise livestock, sell them, and earn a return on them as well. Wild animals, from birds to ele-phants, are also found on your property, but you are severely restricted in terms of what you can do with them. In Kenya, wildlife ownership and user rights are largely the property of the state (i.e., wildlife is owned by all the citizens of Kenya). But if wild animals kill some of your cattle, the loss is entirely yours, as the state will not compensate you. And do not seriously think about offering wildlife viewing on your property because that is restricted by the state to about 5% of the rangelands where the wildlife are found. If crops and livestock were treated in the same way as wildlife in Kenya, how much of their production would continue in these areas?

Mike Norton-Griffiths, a long-time resident of Kenya and researcher of conservation and land use policy, argues that the lack of private property rights for wildlife explains why wild animal popula-tions there have been dwindling. Since 1977, when Kenya banned all sport hunting and all other consumptive uses of wildlife, the large animal wildlife population there has fallen by 60 to 70%. Over the same period, human population has grown by more than 3% per year, crop production by more than 8% per year, and livestock population has been stable.

To reverse the decline in wildlife population, Norton-Griffiths argues that property rights for wildlife should be changed so that returns to wildlife become competitive with returns to crops and live-stock. This would mean that rural landowners would be allowed to generate income from wildlife from activities such as sales of wildlife between landowners and to the public sector, ranching for local and overseas and local trade, sales of wildlife products, tanning, making of trophies and curios, and sport hunting.

Private property rights for wildlife (sometimes referred to as private sector conservation) have been established in much of southern Africa (South Africa, Botswana, Namibia, and Zimbabwe). In those countries, there exist over 9,000 private game ranches and 1,100 private nature reserves. These private areas engage in wildlife viewing services, sport hunting, live game sales, and bush meat production.

The bounce back in wildlife population in the southern African countries is remarkable, even though the animals may move from property to property. For example, the wildlife population on private game ranches in Namibia has increased by about 70%. Similarly in Europe, rural landowners have invested in raising game birds, even though the birds can move freely from property to property, because they can sell the rights to game bird hunting on their property.

Peter Kareiva, the chief scientist for the Nature Conservancy, and Michelle Marvier, a professor at Santa Clara University, support a conservation-for-people approach. They argue that it does not make sense to pit people against nature. Rather, human well-being should become a part of biodiversity conservation efforts. If humans can benefit from managing wildlife, the wildlife may benefit as well.

Sources: Based on Peter Kareiva and Michael Marvier, "Conservation for the People," Scientific American 297:4 (October 2007): 50–57; Mike Norton-Griffiths, "How Many Wildebeest Do You Need?" World Economics, 8:2 (April–June 2007): 41–64.

Answer to Try It! Problem

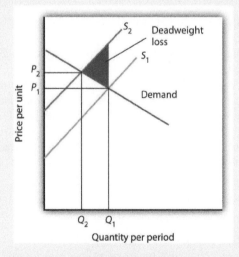

In the absence of any regulation, chip producers are not faced with the costs of the pollution their operations generate. The market price is thus P_1 and the quantity Q_1. The efficiency condition is not met; the price is lower and the quantity greater than would be efficient. If producers were forced to face the cost of their pollution as well as other production costs, the supply curve would shift to S_2, the price would rise to P_2, and the quantity would fall to Q_2. The new solution satisfies the efficiency condition.

6.5 Review And Practice

Summary

Economists insist that individuals do not make choices willy-nilly. Rather, economists assume that individuals make choices in a purposeful way, one that seeks the maximum value for some objective. We assume that consumers seek to maximize utility and that firms seek to maximize profits.

Whatever is being maximized, choices are based on the marginal decision rule. Following this rule results in an allocation that achieves the greatest degree of utility or profit possible.

If utility- and profit-maximizing choices are made in the context of a price system that confronts decision makers with all of the costs and all of the benefits of their choices, the allocation of resources will be efficient. An efficient allocation is one that maximizes the net benefit of every activity. The concepts of consumer and producer surplus show us how this net benefit is shared. Equity is a separate issue, one that calls for a normative evaluation of the fairness of the distribution of income.

The allocation of resources will be inefficient in the absence of competitive markets. It will also be inefficient if property rights are not exclusive and transferable. These two conditions break down when there are public goods, common property resources, or external benefits or costs. In each of these cases, public sector intervention may improve the efficiency of resource allocation. When a market fails to achieve the efficient solution, net benefit falls short of the maximum possible. Deadweight loss is the amount by which net benefit falls below the net benefit possible at the efficient solution.

Concept Problems

1. What is achieved by selecting the quantity of an activity at which marginal benefit equals marginal cost?

2. Suppose the marginal benefit of an activity exceeds the marginal cost. What does the marginal decision rule say a maximizing decision maker will do?

3. Suppose you are a discus hurler and your goal is to maximize the distance you achieve. You "produce" discus hurls by practicing. The total benefit of practice is distance achieved, and the input that achieves this distance is hours of practice. Describe the total benefit curve of practice. What point on the curve would you select?

4. This chapter argues that consumers maximize utility and firms maximize profits. What do you suppose each of the following might be presumed to maximize?

    a. A minister or rabbi

    b. A United States Senator

    c. The manager of a major league baseball team

    d. The owner of a major league baseball team

    e. The director of a charitable organization

5. For each of the following goods, indicate whether exclusive, transferable property rights exist and whether the good poses a problem for public policy. If it does, does the problem relate to a problem of property rights?

    a. Clean air

    b. Tomatoes

    c. Housing

    d. Blue whales

6. The dry-cleaning industry is a major source of air pollution. What can you conclude about the price and output of dry-cleaning services?

7. Economists often recommend that polluters such as dry-cleaning establishments be charged fees for the pollution they emit. Critics of this idea respond that the establishments would simply respond by passing these charges on to their customers, leaving the level of pollution unchanged. Comment on this objection.

8. Government agencies often require that children be inoculated against communicable diseases such as polio and measles. From the standpoint of economic efficiency, is there any justification for such a requirement?

9. Which of the following goods or services are public? Why or why not?

 a. Libraries

 b. Fire protection

 c. Television programs

 d. Health care

 e. Water for household consumption

10. If a village in Botswana is granted several licenses to kill elephants, how does this give it an incentive to preserve elephants and increase the size of the herd? How does the international ban on ivory sales affect the incentive in Botswana to preserve the elephant?

11. The number of fish caught in the ocean has fallen in recent years partly as a result of more intensive fishing efforts and the use of more sophisticated equipment. Fish in the ocean are a common property resource. How might this fact be related to declining fish catches? How do you think this drop in the catch affects the price of seafood?

Numerical Problems

1. Joe Higgins is thinking about how much time to spend studying for a biology exam tomorrow. Using "utility units" he measures the benefits and costs of study; his calculations are shown in the following table.

Hours spent studying	0	1	2	3	4	5	6
Total benefit	0	100	180	240	280	300	300
Total cost	0	50	100	150	200	250	300
Net benefit	—	—	—	—	—	—	

 a. Fill in the fourth row for net benefit in the table. Use the midpoint convention to emphasize that the net benefit is a marginal value showing the gain as hours spent increase by one-hour increments.

 b. Using a graph similar to Panel (a) of Figure 6.1 show the marginal benefit curve and verify that the area under the curve at 3 hours of study corresponds to the total benefit of that much study. (Hint: Remember that marginal values are plotted at the midpoints of the corresponding intervals on the horizontal axis.)

 c. Use a graph similar to Panel (b) of Figure 6.1 to show the marginal cost curve and verify that the area under the curve at 3 hours of study corresponds to the total cost of that much study.

 d. Use a graph similar to Panel (a) of Figure 6.6 to combine the marginal benefit and marginal cost curves you drew in parts (a) and (b).

 e. Based on the marginal decision rule, how many hours should Joe spend studying for his biology exam?

2. Now suppose some friends of Joe's call to say they are having a party tonight. Joe calculates that the party is now his best alternative to study, and he increases his estimate of the cost

of each hour of study. One hour of study now costs 70; two hours cost 140; three hours 210, four hours 280; five hours 350; and six hours 470.

   a. Draw the new marginal benefit and marginal cost curves as in Problem 1, part (d):
   b. Based on the marginal decision rule, identify the new solution that maximizes the net benefit of study time.

3. The local gasoline market in a particular city has demand and supply curves given by the following data. (All quantities are in millions of gallons per month.)

Price per gallon	$1.00	$1.50	$2.00	$2.50	$3.00	$3.50	$4.00
Quantity demanded	6	5	4	3	2	1	0
Quantity supplied	0	1	2	3	4	5	6

   a. Plot the demand and supply curves, and determine the equilibrium price and quantity.
   b. Show the areas of consumer and producer surplus.
   c. Now suppose that the community determines that each gallon of gasoline consumed imposes $0.50 in pollution costs. Accordingly, a $0.50-per-gallon tax is imposed. The tax is imposed on sellers of gasoline, and it has the effect of increasing by $0.50 the price required to induce the quantities supplied in the table. For example, a price of $2.00 is now required for a quantity of 1 million gallons to be supplied each month. Plot the new supply curve.
   d. Approximate the new equilibrium price and output.
   e. Does the price increase by the full amount of the tax? If not, explain why.
   f. Would your answer be different if the demand for gasoline were perfectly inelastic?

4. The flu vaccination market has the demand and supply curves given by the following data. (All quantities are in thousands.)

Price per vaccination	$10	$15	$20	$25	$30
Quantity demanded	90	80	70	60	50
Quantity supplied	50	60	70	80	90

   a. Plot the demand and supply curves, and determine the equilibrium price and quantity.
   b. Show the areas of consumer and producer surplus.
   c. Now suppose that each vaccination given generates an external benefit, as those who do not get vaccinated are less likely to get the flu when others do get vaccinated. As a result, suppliers receive a $10 subsidy from the government for each vaccine. For example, if consumers pay $10 per vaccination, suppliers receive $20, so only $10 from consumers is required to induce suppliers to offer 70,000 vaccinations per month. Plot the new supply curve.
   d. Determine the new equilibrium price and quantity.
   e. Does the price fall by the full amount of the subsidy? If not, explain why.
   f. What is the total amount that consumers now pay for the new equilibrium quantity of vaccinations?
   g. What is the total subsidy that suppliers receive from the government at the new equilibrium quantity of vaccinations?

5. Given the following information about the supply of and demand for apples:

Price per pound	Quantity demanded (pounds per month)	Quantity Supplied (pounds per month
$0.50	12,000	0
0.75	10,000	2,000
1.00	8,000	4,000
1.25	6,000	6,000
1.50	4,000	8,000
1.75	2,000	10,000
2.00	0	12,000

a. Draw a graph similar to Figure 6.9

b. Assuming the market for apples meets the efficiency condition, show the equilibrium price and quantity that maximizes net benefit to society.

c. Identify the area of consumer surplus and the area of producer surplus.

Endnotes

1. See Report of the Committee on Commerce, Science, and Transportation, *Children's Protection From Violent Programming Act*, Senate Report 106–509 (October 26, 2000), Washington, D.C.: U.S. Government Printing Office, 2000, and Michael Rich, "Violent Video Games Testimony," Chicago City Council, October 30, 2000, at http://www.aap.org/advocacy/rich-videogameviolence.pdf.

2. Mark Rosenberg, "Successful State Strategies," Adolescent Health Leadership Forum, December 6, 2003, at http://www.aap.org/advocacy/ahproject/AHLSuccessful StateStrategiesMRosenberg.pps.

3. Common property resources are sometimes referred to as open access resources.

CHAPTER 7
The Analysis of Consumer Choice

7.1 Start Up: A Day at the Grocery Store

You are in the checkout line at the grocery store when your eyes wander over to the ice cream display. It is a hot day and you could use something to cool you down before you get into your hot car. The problem is that you have left your checkbook and credit and debit cards at home—*on purpose*, actually, because you have decided that you only want to spend $20 today at the grocery store. You are uncertain whether or not you have brought enough cash with you to pay for the items that are already in your cart. You put the ice cream bar into your cart and tell the clerk to let you know if you go over $20 because that is all you have. He rings it up and it comes to $22. You have to make a choice. You decide to keep the ice cream and ask the clerk if he would mind returning a box of cookies to the shelf.

We all engage in these kinds of choices every day. We have budgets and must decide how to spend them. The model of utility theory that economists have constructed to explain consumer choice assumes that consumers will try to maximize their utility. For example, when you decided to keep the ice cream bar and return the cookies, you, consciously or not, applied the marginal decision rule to the problem of maximizing your utility: You bought the ice cream because you expect that eating it will give you greater satisfaction than would consuming the box of cookies.

Utility theory provides insights into demand. It lets us look behind demand curves to see how utility-maximizing consumers can be expected to respond to price changes. While the focus of this chapter is on consumers making decisions about what goods and services to buy, the same model can be used to understand how individuals make other types of decisions, such as how much to work and how much of their incomes to spend now or to sock away for the future.

We can approach the analysis of utility maximization in two ways. The first two sections of the chapter cover the marginal utility concept, while the final section examines an alternative approach using indifference curves.

7.2 The Concept of Utility

Learning Objectives

1. Define what economists mean by utility.
2. Distinguish between the concepts of total utility and marginal utility.
3. State the law of diminishing marginal utility and illustrate it graphically.
4. State, explain, and illustrate algebraically the utility-maximizing condition.

Why do you buy the goods and services you do? It must be because they provide you with satisfaction—you feel better off because you have purchased them. Economists call this satisfaction *utility*.

The concept of utility is an elusive one. A person who consumes a good such as peaches gains utility from eating the peaches. But we cannot measure this utility the same way we can measure a peach's weight or calorie content. There is no scale we can use to determine the quantity of utility a peach generates.

Francis Edgeworth, one of the most important contributors to the theory of consumer behavior, imagined a device he called a *hedonimeter* (after hedonism, the pursuit of pleasure):

> *"[L]et there be granted to the science of pleasure what is granted to the science of energy; to imagine an ideally perfect instrument, a psychophysical machine, continually registering the height of pleasure experienced by an individual.... From moment to moment the hedonimeter varies; the delicate index now flickering with the flutter of passions, now steadied by intellectual activity, now sunk whole hours in the neighborhood of zero, or momentarily springing up towards infinity."*[1]

Perhaps some day a hedonimeter will be invented. The utility it measures will not be a characteristic of particular goods, but rather of each consumer's reactions to those goods. The utility of a peach exists not in the peach itself, but in the preferences of the individual consuming the peach. One consumer may wax ecstatic about a peach; another may say it tastes OK.

When we speak of maximizing utility, then, we are speaking of the maximization of something we cannot measure. We assume, however, that each consumer acts as if he or she can measure utility and arranges consumption so that the utility gained is as high as possible.

Total Utility

total utility

The number of units of utility that a consumer gains from consuming a given quantity of a good, service, or activity during a particular time period.

If we could measure utility, **total utility** would be the number of units of utility that a consumer gains from consuming a given quantity of a good, service, or activity during a particular time period. The higher a consumer's total utility, the greater that consumer's level of satisfaction.

Panel (a) of Figure 7.1 shows the total utility Henry Higgins obtains from attending movies. In drawing his total utility curve, we are imagining that he can measure his total utility. The total utility curve shows that when Mr. Higgins attends no movies during a month, his total utility from attending movies is zero. As he increases the number of movies he sees, his total utility rises. When he consumes 1 movie, he obtains 36 units of utility. When he consumes 4 movies, his total utility is 101. He achieves the maximum level of utility possible, 115, by seeing 6 movies per month. Seeing a seventh movie adds nothing to his total utility.

FIGURE 7.1 Total Utility and Marginal Utility Curves

Panel (a) shows Henry Higgins's total utility curve for attending movies. It rises as the number of movies increases, reaching a maximum of 115 units of utility at 6 movies per month. Marginal utility is shown in Panel (b); it is the slope of the total utility curve. Because the slope of the total utility curve declines as the number of movies increases, the marginal utility curve is downward sloping.

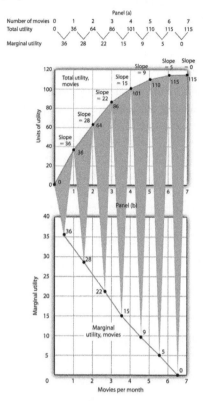

Mr. Higgins's total utility rises at a decreasing rate. The rate of increase is given by the slope of the total utility curve, which is reported in Panel (a) of Figure 7.1 as well. The slope of the curve between 0 movies and 1 movie is 36 because utility rises by this amount when Mr. Higgins sees his first movie in the month. It is 28 between 1 and 2 movies, 22 between 2 and 3, and so on. The slope between 6 and 7 movies is zero; the total utility curve between these two quantities is horizontal.

Marginal Utility

The amount by which total utility rises with consumption of an additional unit of a good, service, or activity, all other things unchanged, is **marginal utility**. The first movie Mr. Higgins sees increases his total utility by 36 units. Hence, the marginal utility of the first movie is 36. The second increases his total utility by 28 units; its marginal utility is 28. The seventh movie does not increase his total utility; its marginal utility is zero. Notice that in the table marginal utility is listed between the columns for total utility because, similar to other marginal concepts, marginal utility is the change in utility as we go from one quantity to the next. Mr. Higgins's marginal utility curve is plotted in Panel (b) of Figure 7.1 The values for marginal utility are plotted midway between the numbers of movies attended. The marginal utility curve is downward sloping; it shows that Mr. Higgins's marginal utility for movies declines as he consumes more of them.

Mr. Higgins's marginal utility from movies is typical of all goods and services. Suppose that you are *really* thirsty and you decide to consume a soft drink. Consuming the drink increases your utility, probably by a lot. Suppose now you have another. That second drink probably increases your utility by less than the first. A third would increase your utility by still less. This tendency of marginal utility to decline beyond some level of consumption during a period is called the **law of diminishing marginal utility**. This law implies that all goods and services eventually will have downward-sloping marginal utility curves. It is the law that lies behind the negatively sloped mar-

marginal utility

The amount by which total utility rises with consumption of an additional unit of a good, service, or activity, all other things unchanged.

law of diminishing marginal utility

This tendency of marginal utility to decline beyond some level of consumption during a period.

ginal benefit curve for consumer choices that we examined in the chapter on markets, maximizers, and efficiency.

One way to think about this effect is to remember the last time you ate at an "all you can eat" cafeteria-style restaurant. Did you eat only one type of food? Did you consume food without limit? No, because of the law of diminishing marginal utility. As you consumed more of one kind of food, its marginal utility fell. You reached a point at which the marginal utility of another dish was greater, and you switched to that. Eventually, there was no food whose marginal utility was great enough to make it worth eating, and you stopped.

What if the law of diminishing marginal utility did not hold? That is, what would life be like in a world of constant or increasing marginal utility? In your mind go back to the cafeteria and imagine that you have rather unusual preferences: Your favorite food is creamed spinach. You start with that because its marginal utility is highest of all the choices before you in the cafeteria. As you eat more, however, its marginal utility does not fall; it remains higher than the marginal utility of any other option. Unless eating more creamed spinach somehow increases your marginal utility for some other food, you will eat only creamed spinach. And until you have reached the limit of your body's capacity (or the restaurant manager's patience), you will not stop. Failure of marginal utility to diminish would thus lead to extraordinary levels of consumption of a single good to the exclusion of all others. Since we do not observe that happening, it seems reasonable to assume that marginal utility falls beyond some level of consumption.

Maximizing Utility

Economists assume that consumers behave in a manner consistent with the maximization of utility. To see how consumers do that, we will put the marginal decision rule to work. First, however, we must reckon with the fact that the ability of consumers to purchase goods and services is limited by their budgets.

The Budget Constraint

The total utility curve in Figure 7.1 shows that Mr. Higgins achieves the maximum total utility possible from movies when he sees six of them each month. It is likely that his total utility curves for other goods and services will have much the same shape, reaching a maximum at some level of consumption. We assume that the goal of each consumer is to maximize total utility. Does that mean a person will consume each good at a level that yields the maximum utility possible?

budget constraint

A restriction that total spending cannot exceed the budget available.

The answer, in general, is no. Our consumption choices are constrained by the income available to us and by the prices we must pay. Suppose, for example, that Mr. Higgins can spend just $25 per month for entertainment and that the price of going to see a movie is $5. To achieve the maximum total utility from movies, Mr. Higgins would have to exceed his entertainment budget. Since we assume that he cannot do that, Mr. Higgins must arrange his consumption so that his total expenditures do not exceed his **budget constraint**: a restriction that total spending cannot exceed the budget available.

Suppose that in addition to movies, Mr. Higgins enjoys concerts, and the average price of a concert ticket is $10. He must select the number of movies he sees and concerts he attends so that his monthly spending on the two goods does not exceed his budget.

Individuals may, of course, choose to save or to borrow. When we allow this possibility, we consider the budget constraint not just for a single period of time but for several periods. For example, economists often examine budget constraints over a consumer's lifetime. A consumer may in some years save for future consumption and in other years borrow on future income for present consumption. Whatever the time period, a consumer's spending will be constrained by his or her budget.

To simplify our analysis, we shall assume that a consumer's spending in any one period is based on the budget available in that period. In this analysis consumers neither save nor borrow. We could extend the analysis to cover several periods and generate the same basic results that we shall establish using a single period. We will also carry out our analysis by looking at the consumer's choices about buying only two goods. Again, the analysis could be extended to cover more goods and the basic results would still hold.

Applying the Marginal Decision Rule

Because consumers can be expected to spend the budget they have, utility maximization is a matter of arranging that spending to achieve the highest total utility possible. If a consumer decides to spend more on one good, he or she must spend less on another in order to satisfy the budget constraint.

The marginal decision rule states that an activity should be expanded if its marginal benefit exceeds its marginal cost. The marginal benefit of this activity is the utility gained by spending an additional $1 on the good. The marginal cost is the utility lost by spending $1 less on another good.

How much utility is gained by spending another $1 on a good? It is the marginal utility of the good divided by its price. The utility gained by spending an additional dollar on good X, for example, is

$$\frac{MU_X}{P_X}$$

This additional utility is the *marginal benefit* of spending another $1 on the good.

Suppose that the marginal utility of good X is 4 and that its price is $2. Then an extra $1 spent on X buys 2 additional units of utility ($MU_X / P_X = 4 / 2 = 2$). If the marginal utility of good X is 1 and its price is $2, then an extra $1 spent on X buys 0.5 additional units of utility ($MU_X / P_X = 1 / 2 = 0.5$).

The loss in utility from spending $1 less on another good or service is calculated the same way: as the marginal utility divided by the price. The *marginal cost* to the consumer of spending $1 less on a good is the loss of the additional utility that could have been gained from spending that $1 on the good.

Suppose a consumer derives more utility by spending an additional $1 on good X rather than on good Y:

EQUATION 7.1

$$\frac{MU_X}{P_X} > \frac{MU_Y}{P_Y}$$

The marginal benefit of shifting $1 from good Y to the consumption of good X exceeds the marginal cost. In terms of utility, the gain from spending an additional $1 on good X exceeds the loss in utility from spending $1 less on good Y. The consumer can increase utility by shifting spending from Y to X.

As the consumer buys more of good X and less of good Y, however, the marginal utilities of the two goods will change. The law of diminishing marginal utility tells us that the marginal utility of good X will fall as the consumer consumes more of it; the marginal utility of good Y will rise as the consumer consumes less of it. The result is that the value of the left-hand side of Equation 7.1 will fall and the value of the right-hand side will rise as the consumer shifts spending from Y to X. When the two sides are equal, total utility will be maximized. In terms of the marginal decision rule, the consumer will have achieved a solution at which the marginal benefit of the activity (spending more on good X) is equal to the marginal cost:

EQUATION 7.2

$$\frac{MU_X}{P_X} = \frac{MU_Y}{P_Y}$$

We can extend this result to all goods and services a consumer uses. Utility maximization requires that the ratio of marginal utility to price be equal for all of them, as suggested in Equation 7.3:

EQUATION 7.3

$$\frac{MU_A}{P_A} = \frac{MU_B}{P_B} = \frac{MU_C}{P_C} = \ldots = \frac{MU_n}{P_n}$$

Equation 7.3 states the **utility-maximizing condition**: Utility is maximized when total outlays equal the budget available and when the ratios of marginal utilities to prices are equal for all goods and services.

Consider, for example, the shopper introduced in the opening of this chapter. In shifting from cookies to ice cream, the shopper must have felt that the marginal utility of spending an additional dollar on ice cream exceeded the marginal utility of spending an additional dollar on cookies. In terms of Equation 7.1, if good X is ice cream and good Y is cookies, the shopper will have lowered the value of the left-hand side of the equation and moved toward the utility-maximizing condition, as expressed by Equation 7.1.

The Problem of Divisibility

If we are to apply the marginal decision rule to utility maximization, goods must be divisible; that is, it must be possible to buy them in any amount. Otherwise we cannot meaningfully speak of spending $1 more or $1 less on them. Strictly speaking, however, few goods are completely divisible.

Even a small purchase, such as an ice cream bar, fails the strict test of being divisible; grocers generally frown on requests to purchase one-half of a $2 ice cream bar if the consumer wants to spend an additional dollar on ice cream. Can a consumer buy a little more movie admission, to say nothing of a little more car?

In the case of a car, we can think of the quantity as depending on characteristics of the car itself. A car with a compact disc player could be regarded as containing "more car" than one that has only a cassette player. Stretching the concept of quantity in this manner does not entirely solve the problem. It is still difficult to imagine that one could purchase "more car" by spending $1 more.

Remember, though, that we are dealing with a model. In the real world, consumers may not be able to satisfy Equation 7.3 precisely. The model predicts, however, that they will come as close to doing so as possible.

utility-maximizing condition

Utility is maximized when total outlays equal the budget available and when the ratios of marginal utilities to prices are equal for all goods and services.

Key Takeaways

- The utility of a good or service is determined by how much satisfaction a particular consumer obtains from it. Utility is not a quality inherent in the good or service itself.
- Total utility is a conceptual measure of the number of units of utility a consumer gains from consuming a good, service, or activity. Marginal utility is the increase in total utility obtained by consuming one more unit of a good, service, or activity.
- As a consumer consumes more and more of a good or service, its marginal utility falls.
- Utility maximization requires seeking the greatest total utility from a given budget.
- Utility is maximized when total outlays equal the budget available and when the ratios of marginal utility to price are equal for all goods and services a consumer consumes; this is the utility-maximizing condition.

Try It!

A college student, Ramón Juárez, often purchases candy bars or bags of potato chips between classes; he tries to limit his spending on these snacks to $8 per week. A bag of chips costs $0.75 and a candy bar costs $0.50 from the vending machines on campus. He has been purchasing an average of 6 bags of chips and 7 candy bars each week. Mr. Juárez is a careful maximizer of utility, and he estimates that the marginal utility of an additional bag of chips during a week is 6. In your answers use B to denote candy bars and C to denote potato chips.

1. How much is he spending on snacks? How does this amount compare to his budget constraint?
2. What is the marginal utility of an additional candy bar during the week?

Case in Point: Changing Lanes and Raising Utility

Source: © 2010 Jupiterimages Corporation

In preparation for sitting in the slow, crowded lanes for single-occupancy-vehicles, T. J. Zane used to stop at his favorite coffee kiosk to buy a $2 cup of coffee as he headed off to work on Interstate 15 in the San Diego area. Since 1996, an experiment in road pricing has caused him and others to change their ways—and to raise their total utility.

Before 1996, only car-poolers could use the specially marked high-occupancy-vehicles lanes. With those lanes nearly empty, traffic authorities decided to allow drivers of single-occupancy-vehicles to use those lanes, so long as they paid a price. Now, electronic signs tell drivers how much it will cost them to drive on the special lanes. The price is recalculated every 6 minutes depending on the traffic. On one morning during rush hour, it varied from $1.25 at 7:10 a.m., to $1.50 at 7:16 a.m., to $2.25 at 7:22 a.m., and to $2.50 at 7:28 a.m. The increasing tolls over those few minutes caused some drivers to opt out and the toll fell back to $1.75 and then increased to $2 a few minutes later. Drivers do not have to stop to pay the toll since radio transmitters read their FasTrak transponders and charge them accordingly.

When first instituted, these lanes were nicknamed the "Lexus lanes," on the assumption that only wealthy drivers would use them. Indeed, while the more affluent do tend to use them heavily, surveys have discovered that they are actually used by drivers of all income levels.

Mr. Zane, a driver of a 1997 Volkswagen Jetta, is one commuter who chooses to use the new option. He explains his decision by asking, "Isn't it worth a couple of dollars to spend an extra half-hour with your family?" He continues, "That's what I used to spend on a cup of coffee at Starbucks. Now I've started bringing my own coffee and using the money for the toll."

We can explain his decision using the model of utility-maximizing behavior; Mr. Zane's out-of-pocket commuting budget constraint is about $2. His comment tells us that he realized that the marginal utility of spending an additional 30 minutes with his family divided by the $2 toll was higher than the marginal utility of the store-bought coffee divided by its $2 price. By reallocating his $2 commuting budget, the gain in utility of having more time at home exceeds the loss in utility from not sipping premium coffee on the way to work.

From this one change in behavior, we do not know whether or not he is actually maximizing his utility, but his decision and explanation are certainly consistent with that goal.

Source: Based on John Tierney, "The Autonomist Manifesto (Or, How I learned to Stop Worrying and Love the Road)," New York Times Magazine, September 26, 2004, 57–65.

Answers to Try It! Problems

1. He is spending $4.50 (= $0.75 × 6) on potato chips and $3.50 (= $0.50 × 7) on candy bars, for a total of $8. His budget constraint is $8.
2. In order for the ratios of marginal utility to price to be equal, the marginal utility of a candy bar must be 4. Let the marginal utility and price of candy bars be MU_B and P_B, respectively, and the marginal utility and price of a bag of potato chips be MU_C and P_C, respectively. Then we want

$$\frac{MU_C}{P_C} = \frac{MU_B}{P_B}$$

We know that P_C is $0.75 and P_B equals $0.50. We are told that MU_C is 6. Thus

$$\frac{6}{0.75} = \frac{MU_B}{0.50}$$

Solving the equation for MU_B, we find that it must equal 4.

7.3 Utility Maximization and Demand

Learning Objectives

1. Derive an individual demand curve from utility-maximizing adjustments to changes in price.
2. Derive the market demand curve from the demand curves of individuals.
3. Explain the substitution and income effects of a price change.
4. Explain the concepts of normal and inferior goods in terms of the income effect.

Choices that maximize utility—that is, choices that follow the marginal decision rule—generally produce downward-sloping demand curves. This section shows how an individual's utility-maximizing choices can lead to a demand curve.

Deriving an Individual's Demand Curve

Suppose, for simplicity, that Mary Andrews consumes only apples, denoted by the letter A, and oranges, denoted by the letter O. Apples cost $2 per pound and oranges cost $1 per pound, and her budget allows her to spend $20 per month on the two goods. We assume that Ms. Andrews will adjust her consumption so that the utility-maximizing condition holds for the two goods: The ratio of marginal utility to price is the same for apples and oranges. That is,

EQUATION 7.4

$$\frac{MU_A}{\$2} = \frac{MU_O}{\$1}$$

Here MU_A and MU_O are the marginal utilities of apples and oranges, respectively. Her spending equals her budget of $20 per month; suppose she buys 5 pounds of apples and 10 of oranges.

Now suppose that an unusually large harvest of apples lowers their price to $1 per pound. The lower price of apples increases the marginal utility of each $1 Ms. Andrews spends on apples, so that at her current level of consumption of apples and oranges

EQUATION 7.5

$$\frac{MU_A}{\$1} > \frac{MU_O}{\$1}$$

Ms. Andrews will respond by purchasing more apples. As she does so, the marginal utility she receives from apples will decline. If she regards apples and oranges as substitutes, she will also buy fewer oranges. That will cause the marginal utility of oranges to rise. She will continue to adjust her spending until the marginal utility per $1 spent is equal for both goods:

EQUATION 7.6

$$\frac{MU_A}{\$1} = \frac{MU_O}{\$1}$$

Suppose that at this new solution, she purchases 12 pounds of apples and 8 pounds of oranges. She is still spending all of her budget of $20 on the two goods [(12 x $1)+(8 x $1)=$20].

FIGURE 7.2 Utility Maximization and an Individual's Demand Curve
Mary Andrews's demand curve for apples, d, can be derived by determining the quantities of apples she will buy at each price. Those quantities are determined by the application of the marginal decision rule to utility maximization. At a price of $2 per pound, Ms. Andrews maximizes utility by purchasing 5 pounds of apples per month. When the price of apples falls to $1 per pound, the quantity of apples at which she maximizes utility increases to 12 pounds per month.

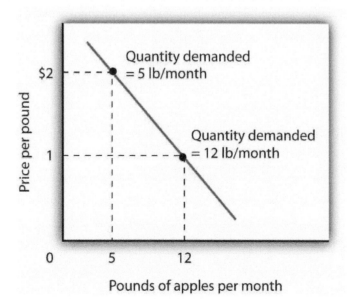

It is through a consumer's reaction to different prices that we trace the consumer's demand curve for a good. When the price of apples was $2 per pound, Ms. Andrews maximized her utility by purchasing 5 pounds of apples, as illustrated in Figure 7.2. When the price of apples fell, she increased the quantity of apples she purchased to 12 pounds.

Heads Up!

Notice that, in this example, Ms. Andrews maximizes utility where not only the ratios of marginal utilities to price are equal, but also the marginal utilities of both goods are equal. But, the equal-marginal-utility outcome is only true here because the prices of the two goods are the same: each good is priced at $1 in this case. If the prices of apples and oranges were different, the marginal utilities at the utility maximizing solution would have been different. The condition for maximizing utility—consume where the ratios of marginal utility to price are equal—holds regardless. The utility-maximizing condition is not that consumers maximize utility by equating marginal utilities.

$$\text{Utility maximizing condition is:} \qquad \frac{MU_X}{P_X} = \frac{MU_Y}{P_Y}$$

$$\text{Utility maximizing condition is } \underline{not}: \qquad MU_X \neq MU_Y$$

From Individual to Market Demand

The market demand curves we studied in previous chapters are derived from individual demand curves such as the one depicted in Figure 7.2. Suppose that in addition to Ms. Andrews, there are two other consumers in the market for apples—Ellen Smith and Koy Keino. The quantities each consumes at various prices are given in Figure 7.3, along with the quantities that Ms. Andrews consumes at each price. The demand curves for each are shown in Panel (a). The market demand curve for all three consumers, shown in Panel (b), is then found by adding the quantities demanded at each price for all three consumers. At a price of $2 per pound, for example, Ms. Andrews demands 5 pounds of apples per month, Ms. Smith demands 3 pounds, and Mr. Keino demands 8 pounds. A total of 16 pounds of apples are demanded per month at this price. Adding the individual quantities demanded at $1 per pound yields market demand of 40 pounds per month. This method of adding amounts along the horizontal axis of a graph is referred to as summing horizontally. The market demand curve is thus the horizontal summation of all the individual demand curves.

FIGURE 7.3 Deriving a Market Demand Curve

The demand schedules for Mary Andrews, Ellen Smith, and Koy Keino are given in the table. Their individual demand curves are plotted in Panel (a). The market demand curve for all three is shown in Panel (b).

		Quantity Demanded		
Price	Andrews	Keino	Smith	Market
$2	5	8	3	16
1	12	10	18	40

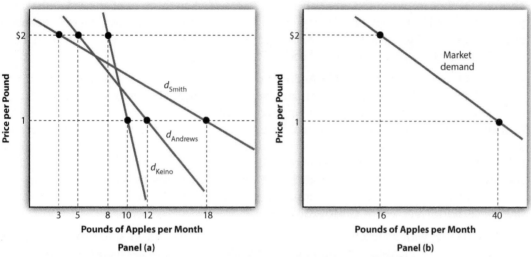

Panel (a)

Panel (b)

Individual demand curves, then, reflect utility-maximizing adjustment by consumers to various market prices. Once again, we see that as the price falls, consumers tend to buy more of a good. Demand curves are downward-sloping as the law of demand asserts.

Substitution and Income Effects

We saw that when the price of apples fell from $2 to $1 per pound, Mary Andrews increased the quantity of apples she demanded. Behind that adjustment, however, lie two distinct effects: the substitution effect and the income effect. It is important to distinguish these effects, because they can have quite different implications for the elasticity of the demand curve.

First, the reduction in the price of apples made them cheaper relative to oranges. Before the price change, it cost the same amount to buy 2 pounds of oranges or 1 pound of apples. After the price change, it cost the same amount to buy 1 pound of either oranges or apples. In effect, 2 pounds of oranges would exchange for 1 pound of apples before the price change, and 1 pound of oranges would exchange for 1 pound of apples after the price change.

Second, the price reduction essentially made consumers of apples richer. Before the price change, Ms. Andrews was purchasing 5 pounds of apples and 10 pounds of oranges at a total cost to her of $20. At the new lower price of apples, she could purchase this same combination for $15. In effect, the price reduction for apples was equivalent to handing her a $5 bill, thereby increasing her purchasing power. Purchasing power refers to the quantity of goods and services that can be purchased with a given budget.

income-compensated price change

An imaginary exercise in which we assume that when the price of a good or service changes, the consumer's income is adjusted so that he or she has just enough to purchase the original combination of goods and services at the new set of prices.

substitution effect

The change in a consumer's consumption of a good in response to an income-compensated price change.

To distinguish between the substitution and income effects, economists consider first the impact of a price change with no change in the consumer's ability to purchase goods and services. An **income-compensated price change** is an imaginary exercise in which we assume that when the price of a good or service changes, the consumer's income is adjusted so that he or she has just enough to purchase the original combination of goods and services at the new set of prices. Ms. Andrews was purchasing 5 pounds of apples and 10 pounds of oranges before the price change. Buying that same combination after the price change would cost $15. The income-compensated price change thus requires us to take $5 from Ms. Andrews when the price of apples falls to $1 per pound. She can still buy 5 pounds of apples and 10 pounds of oranges. If, instead, the price of apples increased, we would give Ms. Andrews more money (i.e., we would "compensate" her) so that she could purchase the same combination of goods.

With $15 and cheaper apples, Ms. Andrews *could* buy 5 pounds of apples and 10 pounds of oranges. But would she? The answer lies in comparing the marginal benefit of spending another $1 on apples to the marginal benefit of spending another $1 on oranges, as expressed in Equation 7.5. It shows that the extra utility per $1 she could obtain from apples now exceeds the extra utility per $1 from oranges. She will thus increase her consumption of apples. If she had only $15, any increase in her consumption of apples would require a reduction in her consumption of oranges. In effect, she responds to the income-compensated price change for apples by substituting apples for oranges. The change in a consumer's consumption of a good in response to an income-compensated price change is called the **substitution effect**.

Suppose that with an income-compensated reduction in the price of apples to $1 per pound, Ms. Andrews would increase her consumption of apples to 9 pounds per month and reduce her consumption of oranges to 6 pounds per month. The substitution effect of the price reduction is an increase in apple consumption of 4 pounds per month.

The substitution effect always involves a change in consumption in a direction opposite that of the price change. When a consumer is maximizing utility, the ratio of marginal utility to price is the same for all goods. An income-compensated price reduction increases the extra utility per dollar available from the good whose price has fallen; a consumer will thus purchase more of it. An income-compensated price increase reduces the extra utility per dollar from the good; the consumer will purchase less of it.

In other words, when the price of a good falls, people react to the lower price by substituting or switching toward that good, buying more of it and less of other goods, *if* we artificially hold the consumer's ability to buy goods constant. When the price of a good goes up, people react to the higher price by substituting or switching away from that good, buying less of it and instead buying more of other goods. By examining the impact of consumer purchases of an income-compensated price change, we are looking at *just* the change in relative prices of goods and eliminating any impact on consumer buying that comes from the effective change in the consumer's ability to purchase goods and services (that is, we hold the consumer's purchasing power constant).

income effect

The change in consumption of a good resulting from the implicit change in income because of a price change.

To complete our analysis of the impact of the price change, we must now consider the $5 that Ms. Andrews effectively gained from it. After the price reduction, it cost her just $15 to buy what cost her $20 before. She has, in effect, $5 more than she did before. Her additional income may also have an effect on the number of apples she consumes. The change in consumption of a good resulting from the implicit change in income because of a price change is called the **income effect** of a price change. When the price of a good rises, there is an implicit reduction in income. When the price of a good falls, there is an implicit increase. When the price of apples fell, Ms. Andrews (who was consuming 5 pounds of apples per month) received an implicit increase in income of $5.

Suppose Ms. Andrews uses her implicit increase in income to purchase 3 more pounds of apples and 2 more pounds of oranges per month. She has already increased her apple consumption to 9 pounds per month because of the substitution effect, so the added 3 pounds brings her consumption level to 12 pounds per month. That is precisely what we observed when we derived her demand curve; it is the change we would observe in the marketplace. We see now, however, that her increase in quantity demanded consists of a substitution effect and an income effect. Figure 7.4 shows the combined effects of the price change.

FIGURE 7.4 The Substitution and Income Effects of a Price Change

This demand curve for Ms. Andrews was presented in Figure 7.3. It shows that a reduction in the price of apples from $2 to $1 per pound increases the quantity Ms. Andrews demands from 5 pounds of apples to 12. This graph shows that this change consists of a substitution effect and an income effect. The substitution effect increases the quantity demanded by 4 pounds, the income effect by 3, for a total increase in quantity demanded of 7 pounds.

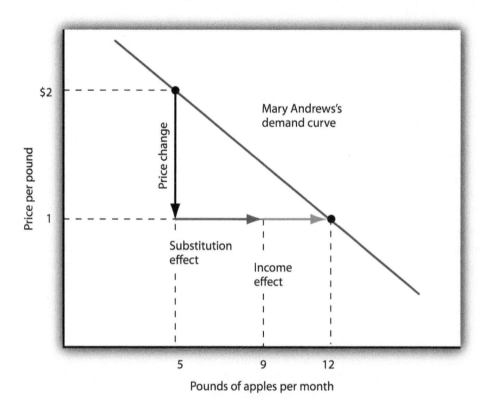

The size of the substitution effect depends on the rate at which the marginal utilities of goods change as the consumer adjusts consumption to a price change. As Ms. Andrews buys more apples and fewer oranges, the marginal utility of apples will fall and the marginal utility of oranges will rise. If relatively small changes in quantities consumed produce large changes in marginal utilities, the substitution effect that is required to restore the equality of marginal-utility-to-price ratios will be small. If much larger changes in quantities consumed are needed to produce equivalent changes in marginal utilities, then the substitution effect will be large.

The magnitude of the income effect of a price change depends on how responsive the demand for a good is to a change in income and on how important the good is in a consumer's budget. When the price changes for a good that makes up a substantial fraction of a consumer's budget, the change in the consumer's ability to buy things is substantial. A change in the price of a good that makes up a trivial fraction of a consumer's budget, however, has little effect on his or her purchasing power; the income effect of such a price change is small.

Because each consumer's response to a price change depends on the sizes of the substitution and income effects, these effects play a role in determining the price elasticity of demand. All other things unchanged, the larger the substitution effect, the greater the absolute value of the price elasticity of demand. When the income effect moves in the same direction as the substitution effect, a greater income effect contributes to a greater price elasticity of demand as well. There are, however, cases in which the substitution and income effects move in opposite directions. We shall explore these ideas in the next section.

Normal and Inferior Goods

The nature of the income effect of a price change depends on whether the good is normal or inferior. The income effect reinforces the substitution effect in the case of normal goods; it works in the opposite direction for inferior goods.

Normal Goods

A normal good is one whose consumption increases with an increase in income. When the price of a normal good falls, there are two identifying effects:

1. The substitution effect contributes to an increase in the quantity demanded because consumers substitute more of the good for other goods.

2. The reduction in price increases the consumer's ability to buy goods. Because the good is normal, this increase in purchasing power further increases the quantity of the good demanded through the income effect.

In the case of a normal good, then, the substitution and income effects reinforce each other. Ms. Andrews's response to a price reduction for apples is a typical response to a lower price for a normal good.

An increase in the price of a normal good works in an equivalent fashion. The higher price causes consumers to substitute more of other goods, whose prices are now relatively lower. The substitution effect thus reduces the quantity demanded. The higher price also reduces purchasing power, causing consumers to reduce consumption of the good via the income effect.

Inferior Goods

In the chapter that introduced the model of demand and supply, we saw that an inferior good is one for which demand falls when income rises. It is likely to be a good that people do not really like very much. When incomes are low, people consume the inferior good because it is what they can afford. As their incomes rise and they can afford something they like better, they consume less of the inferior good. When the price of an inferior good falls, two things happen:

1. Consumers will substitute more of the inferior good for other goods because its price has fallen relative to those goods. The quantity demanded increases as a result of the substitution effect.

2. The lower price effectively makes consumers richer. But, because the good is inferior, this reduces quantity demanded.

The case of inferior goods is thus quite different from that of normal goods. The income effect of a price change works in a direction *opposite* to that of the substitution effect in the case of an inferior good, whereas it reinforces the substitution effect in the case of a normal good.

FIGURE 7.5 Substitution and Income Effects for Inferior Goods
The substitution and income effects work against each other in the case of inferior goods. The consumer begins at point A, consuming q_1 units of the good at a price P_1. When the price falls to P_2, the consumer moves to point B, increasing quantity demanded to q_2. The substitution effect increases quantity demanded to q_s, but the income effect reduces it from q_s to q_2.

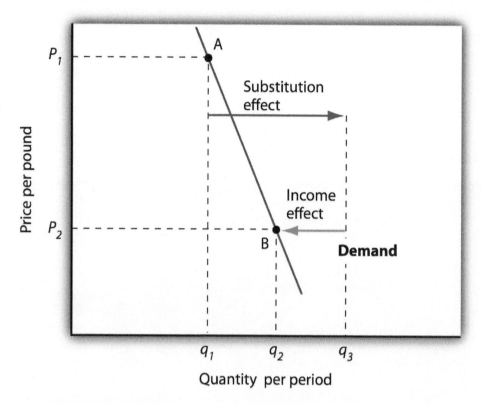

Figure 7.5 illustrates the substitution and income effects of a price reduction for an inferior good. When the price falls from P_1 to P_2, the quantity demanded by a consumer increases from q_1 to q_2. The substitution effect increases quantity demanded from q_1 to q_s. But the income effect reduces quantity demanded from q_s to q_2; the substitution effect is stronger than the income effect. The result is consistent with the law of demand: A reduction in price increases the quantity demanded. The quantity demanded is smaller, however, than it would be if the good were normal. Inferior goods are therefore likely to have less elastic demand than normal goods.

Key Takeaways

- Individual demand curves reflect utility-maximizing adjustment by consumers to changes in price.
- Market demand curves are found by summing horizontally the demand curves of all the consumers in the market.
- The substitution effect of a price change changes consumption in a direction opposite to the price change.
- The income effect of a price change reinforces the substitution effect if the good is normal; it moves consumption in the opposite direction if the good is inferior.

Try It!

Ilana Drakulic has an entertainment budget of $200 per semester, which she divides among purchasing CDs, going to concerts, eating in restaurants, and so forth. When the price of CDs fell from $20 to $10, her purchases rose from 5 per semester to 10 per semester. When asked how many she would have bought if her budget constraint were $150 (since with $150 she could continue to buy 5 CDs and as before still have $100 for spending on other items), she said she would have bought 8 CDs. What is the size of her substitution effect? Her income effect? Are CDs normal or inferior for her? Which exhibit, Figure 7.4 or Figure 7.5, depicts more accurately her demand curve for CDs?

Case in Point: Found! An Upward-Sloping Demand Curve

Source: © 2010 Jupiterimages Corporation

The fact that income and substitution effects move in opposite directions in the case of inferior goods raises a tantalizing possibility: What if the income effect were the *stronger* of the two? Could demand curves be upward sloping?

The answer, from a theoretical point of view, is yes. If the income effect in Figure 7.5 were larger than the substitution effect, the decrease in price would reduce the quantity demanded below q_1. The result would be a reduction in quantity demanded in response to a reduction in price. The demand curve would be upward sloping!

The suggestion that a good could have an upward-sloping demand curve is generally attributed to Robert Giffen, a British journalist who wrote widely on economic matters late in the nineteenth century. Such goods are thus called Giffen goods. To qualify as a Giffen good, a good must be inferior and must have an income effect strong enough to overcome the substitution effect. The example often cited of a possible Giffen good is the potato during the Irish famine of 1845–1849. Empirical analysis by economists using available data, however, has refuted the notion of the upward-sloping demand curve for potatoes at that time. The most convincing parts of the refutation were to point out that (a) given the famine, there were not more potatoes available for purchase then and (b) the price of potatoes may not have even increased during the period!

A recent study by Robert Jensen and Nolan Miller, though, suggests the possible discovery of at least one Giffen good. They began their search by thinking about the type of good that would be likely to exhibit Giffen behavior and argued that, like potatoes for the poor Irish, it would be a main dietary staple of a poor population. In such a situation, purchases of the item are such a large percentage of the diet of the poor that when the item's price rises, the implicit income of the poor falls drastically. In order to subsist, the poor reduce consumption of other goods so they can buy more of the staple. In so doing, they are able to reach a caloric intake that is higher than what can be achieved by buying more of other preferred foods that unfortunately supply fewer calories.

Their empirical work shows that in Hunan province in southern China rice is a Giffen good for poor consumers. Rice provides calories at a relatively low cost and dominates the diet, while meat is considered the tastier but higher cost-per-calorie food. In order to look at individual household decision making, they conducted a field experiment in which randomly selected poor households were given vouchers, redeemable with local merchants, for price reductions of varying sizes on the staple good. Households and merchants were given explicit instructions that selling the vouchers for cash or reselling the staple good would result in dismissal from the program and audits of the program seemed to confirm that participants were conforming to the ground rules. Overall about 1,300 households participated. Households also completed a detailed questionnaire reporting what they ate and drank, as well as other characteristics of the family on income, employment, other expenditures, and the like. They then divided the households into two categories: 1) those who were so poor that, prior to the experiment, almost all of their calories were from the staple good (Households in this category would not be expected to show Giffen behavior because their extreme poverty gives them no choice but to consume less of the staple when its price rises.) and 2) those who were somewhat less poor in the sense that, prior to the experiment, they got at least 20% of their calories from sources other than the staple good. Households in this "poor-but-not-too-poor" group exhibited Giffen behavior. In particular, they estimated that a 1% increase in the price of rice leads to a 0.45% increase in rice consumption.

A similar experiment by the authors on wheat consumption in Gansu province in northern China showed less evidence of its being a Giffen good, probably because there are more substitutes available for the specific form of wheat—wheat flour used to make wheat-based foods in the home—that was the subject of the experiment. In Gansu, people also consume wheat noodles at restaurants or road-side stands or buy wheat-based products from stores in prepared forms. A study by David McKenzie tested whether tortillas were a Giffen good for poor Mexicans. He found that they were an inferior good but not a Giffen good and similarly speculated that the availability of substitutes was the likely reason.

Jensen and Miller argue that despite the fact that their research is the first to uncover a real example of a Giffen good, other examples are likely waiting to be discovered in areas of the world where the population is poor but not-too-poor and where there are few substitutes for the staple good.

Sources: Based on Robert Jensen and Nolan Miller, "Giffen Behavior and Subsistence Consumption," American Economic Review 98:4 (2008): 1553–1577; David McKenzie, "Are Tortillas a Giffen Good in Mexico?" Economics Bulletin 15:1 (2002): 1–7.

Answer to Try It! Problem

One hundred fifty dollars is the income that allows Ms. Drakulic to purchase the same items as before, and thus can be used to measure the substitution effect. Looking only at the income-compensated price change (that is, holding her to the same purchasing power as in the original relative price situation), we find that the substitution effect is 3 more CDs (from 5 to 8). The CDs that she buys beyond 8 constitute her income effect; it is 2 CDs. Because the income effect reinforces the substitution effect, CDs are a normal good for her and her demand curve is similar to that shown in Figure 7.4.

7.4 Indifference Curve Analysis: An Alternative Approach to Understanding Consumer Choice

Learning Objectives

1. Explain utility maximization using the concepts of indifference curves and budget lines.
2. Explain the notion of the marginal rate of substitution and how it relates to the utility-maximizing solution.
3. Derive a demand curve from an indifference map.

Economists typically use a different set of tools than those presented in the chapter up to this point to analyze consumer choices. While somewhat more complex, the tools presented in this section give us a powerful framework for assessing consumer choices.

We will begin our analysis with an algebraic and graphical presentation of the budget constraint. We will then examine a new concept that allows us to draw a map of a consumer's preferences. Then we can draw some conclusions about the choices a utility-maximizing consumer could be expected to make.

The Budget Line

As we have already seen, a consumer's choices are limited by the budget available. Total spending for goods and services can fall short of the budget constraint but may not exceed it.

Algebraically, we can write the budget constraint for two goods X and Y as:

EQUATION 7.7

$$P_X Q_X + P_Y Q_Y \leq B$$

where P_X and P_Y are the prices of goods X and Y and Q_X and Q_Y are the quantities of goods X and Y chosen. The total income available to spend on the two goods is B, the consumer's budget. Equation 7.7 states that total expenditures on goods X and Y (the left-hand side of the equation) cannot exceed B.

Suppose a college student, Janet Bain, enjoys skiing and horseback riding. A day spent pursuing either activity costs $50. Suppose she has $250 available to spend on these two activities each semester. Ms. Bain's budget constraint is illustrated in Figure 7.6.

For a consumer who buys only two goods, the budget constraint can be shown with a budget line. A **budget line** shows graphically the combinations of two goods a consumer can buy with a given budget.

budget line

Graphically shows the combinations of two goods a consumer can buy with a given budget.

The budget line shows all the combinations of skiing and horseback riding Ms. Bain can purchase with her budget of $250. She could also spend less than $250, purchasing combinations that lie below and to the left of the budget line in Figure 7.6. Combinations above and to the right of the budget line are beyond the reach of her budget.

FIGURE 7.6 The Budget Line

The budget line shows combinations of the skiing and horseback riding Janet Bain could consume if the price of each activity is $50 and she has $250 available for them each semester. The slope of this budget line is –1, the negative of the price of horseback riding divided by the price of skiing.

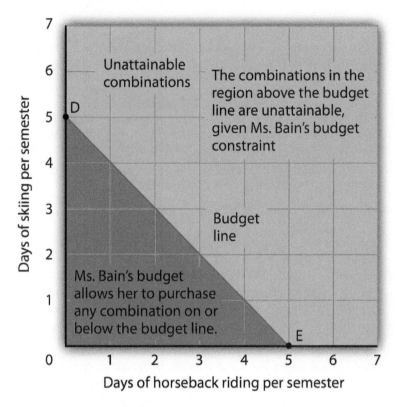

The vertical intercept of the budget line (point D) is given by the number of days of skiing per month that Ms. Bain could enjoy, if she devoted all of her budget to skiing and none to horseback riding. She has $250, and the price of a day of skiing is $50. If she spent the entire amount on skiing, she could ski 5 days per semester. She would be meeting her budget constraint, since:

$$\$50 \times 0 + \$50 \times 5 = \$250$$

The horizontal intercept of the budget line (point E) is the number of days she could spend horseback riding if she devoted her $250 entirely to that sport. She could purchase 5 days of either skiing or horseback riding per semester. Again, this is within her budget constraint, since:

$$\$50 \times 5 + \$50 \times 0 = \$250$$

Because the budget line is linear, we can compute its slope between any two points. Between points D and E the vertical change is –5 days of skiing; the horizontal change is 5 days of horseback riding. The slope is thus $-5/5 = -1$. More generally, we find the slope of the budget line by finding the vertical and horizontal intercepts and then computing the slope between those two points. The vertical intercept of the budget line is found by dividing Ms. Bain's budget, B, by the price of skiing, the good on the vertical axis (P_S). The horizontal intercept is found by dividing B by the price of horseback riding, the good on the horizontal axis (P_H). The slope is thus:

EQUATION 7.8

$$\text{Slope} = -\frac{B/P_S}{B/P_H}$$

Simplifying this equation, we obtain

EQUATION 7.9

$$\text{Slope} = -\frac{B}{P_S} \times \frac{P_H}{B} = -\frac{P_H}{P_S}$$

After canceling, Equation 7.9 shows that the slope of a budget line is the negative of the price of the good on the horizontal axis divided by the price of the good on the vertical axis.

Heads Up!

It is easy to go awry on the issue of the slope of the budget line: It is the negative of the price of the good on the *horizontal* axis divided by the price of the good on the *vertical* axis. But does not slope equal the change in the *vertical* axis divided by the change in the *horizontal* axis? The answer, of course, is that the definition of slope has not changed. Notice that Equation 7.8 gives the vertical change divided by the horizontal change between two points. We then manipulated Equation 7.8 a bit to get to Equation 7.9 and found that slope also equaled the negative of the price of the good on the horizontal axis divided by the price of the good on the vertical axis. Price is not the variable that is shown on the two axes. The axes show the quantities of the two goods.

Indifference Curves

indifference curve

Graph that shows combinations of two goods that yield equal levels of utility.

Suppose Ms. Bain spends 2 days skiing and 3 days horseback riding per semester. She will derive some level of total utility from that combination of the two activities. There are other combinations of the two activities that would yield the same level of total utility. Combinations of two goods that yield equal levels of utility are shown on an **indifference curve**.[2] Because all points along an indifference curve generate the same level of utility, economists say that a consumer is *indifferent* between them.

Figure 7.7 shows an indifference curve for combinations of skiing and horseback riding that yield the same level of total utility. Point X marks Ms. Bain's initial combination of 2 days skiing and 3 days horseback riding per semester. The indifference curve shows that she could obtain the same level of utility by moving to point W, skiing for 7 days and going horseback riding for 1 day. She could also get the same level of utility at point Y, skiing just 1 day and spending 5 days horseback riding. Ms. Bain is indifferent among combinations W, X, and Y. We assume that the two goods are divisible, so she is indifferent between *any* two points along an indifference curve.

FIGURE 7.7 An Indifference Curve

The indifference curve *A* shown here gives combinations of skiing and horseback riding that produce the same level of utility. Janet Bain is thus indifferent to which point on the curve she selects. Any point below and to the left of the indifference curve would produce a lower level of utility; any point above and to the right of the indifference curve would produce a higher level of utility.

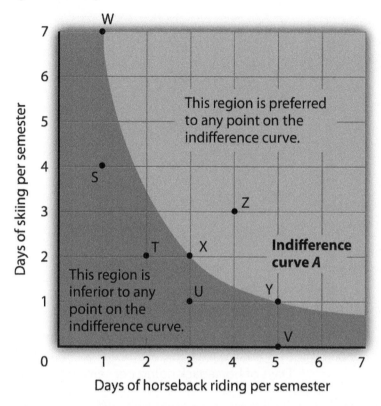

Now look at point T in Figure 7.7. It has the same amount of skiing as point X, but fewer days are spent horseback riding. Ms. Bain would thus prefer point X to point T. Similarly, she prefers X to U. What about a choice between the combinations at point W and point T? Because combinations X and W are equally satisfactory, and because Ms. Bain prefers X to T, she must prefer W to T. In general, any combination of two goods that lies below and to the left of an indifference curve for those goods yields less utility than any combination on the indifference curve. Such combinations are *inferior* to combinations on the indifference curve.

Point Z, with 3 days of skiing and 4 days of horseback riding, provides more of both activities than point X; Z therefore yields a higher level of utility. It is also superior to point W. In general, any combination that lies above and to the right of an indifference curve is preferred to any point on the indifference curve.

We can draw an indifference curve through any combination of two goods. Figure 7.8 shows indifference curves drawn through each of the points we have discussed. Indifference curve *A* from Figure 7.7 is inferior to indifference curve *B*. Ms. Bain prefers all the combinations on indifference curve *B* to those on curve *A*, and she regards each of the combinations on indifference curve *C* as inferior to those on curves *A* and *B*.

Although only three indifference curves are shown in Figure 7.8, in principle an infinite number could be drawn. The collection of indifference curves for a consumer constitutes a kind of map illustrating a consumer's preferences. Different consumers will have different maps. We have good reason to expect the indifference curves for all consumers to have the same basic shape as those shown here: They slope downward, and they become less steep as we travel down and to the right along them.

FIGURE 7.8 Indifference Curves

Each indifference curve suggests combinations among which the consumer is indifferent. Curves that are higher and to the right are preferred to those that are lower and to the left. Here, indifference curve *B* is preferred to curve *A*, which is preferred to curve *C*.

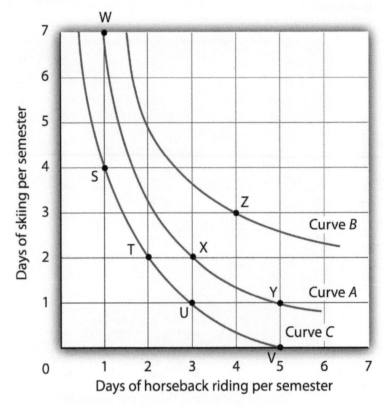

The slope of an indifference curve shows the rate at which two goods can be exchanged without affecting the consumer's utility. Figure 7.9 shows indifference curve *C* from Figure 7.8. Suppose Ms. Bain is at point S, consuming 4 days of skiing and 1 day of horseback riding per semester. Suppose she spends another day horseback riding. This additional day of horseback riding does not affect her utility if she gives up 2 days of skiing, moving to point T. She is thus willing to give up 2 days of skiing for a second day of horseback riding. The curve shows, however, that she would be willing to give up at most 1 day of skiing to obtain a third day of horseback riding (shown by point U).

FIGURE 7.9 The Marginal Rate of Substitution

The marginal rate of substitution is equal to the absolute value of the slope of an indifference curve. It is the maximum amount of one good a consumer is willing to give up to obtain an additional unit of another. Here, it is the number of days of skiing Janet Bain would be willing to give up to obtain an additional day of horseback riding. Notice that the marginal rate of substitution (*MRS*) declines as she consumes more and more days of horseback riding.

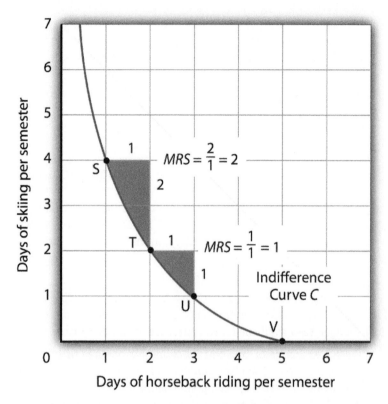

The maximum amount of one good a consumer would be willing to give up in order to obtain an additional unit of another is called the **marginal rate of substitution (*MRS*)**, which is equal to the absolute value of the slope of the indifference curve between two points. Figure 7.9 shows that as Ms. Bain devotes more and more time to horseback riding, the rate at which she is willing to give up days of skiing for additional days of horseback riding—her marginal rate of substitution—diminishes.

marginal rate of substitution

The maximum amount of one good a consumer would be willing to give up in order to obtain an additional unit of another.

The Utility-Maximizing Solution

We assume that each consumer seeks the highest indifference curve possible. The budget line gives the combinations of two goods that the consumer can purchase with a given budget. Utility maximization is therefore a matter of selecting a combination of two goods that satisfies two conditions:

1. The point at which utility is maximized must be within the attainable region defined by the budget line.

2. The point at which utility is maximized must be on the highest indifference curve consistent with condition 1.

Figure 7.10 combines Janet Bain's budget line from Figure 7.6 with her indifference curves from Figure 7.8. Our two conditions for utility maximization are satisfied at point X, where she skis 2 days per semester and spends 3 days horseback riding.

FIGURE 7.10 The Utility-Maximizing Solution
Combining Janet Bain's budget line and indifference curves from Figure 7.6 and Figure 7.8, we find a point that (1) satisfies the budget constraint and (2) is on the highest indifference curve possible. That occurs for Ms. Bain at point X.

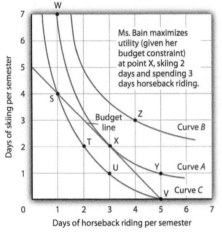

The highest indifference curve possible for a given budget line is tangent to the line; the indifference curve and budget line have the same slope at that point. The absolute value of the slope of the indifference curve shows the *MRS* between two goods. The absolute value of the slope of the budget line gives the price ratio between the two goods; it is the rate at which one good exchanges for another in the market. At the point of utility maximization, then, the rate at which the consumer is willing to exchange one good for another equals the rate at which the goods can be exchanged in the market. For any two goods X and Y, with good X on the horizontal axis and good Y on the vertical axis,

EQUATION 7.10

$$\mathrm{MRS}_{X,Y} = \frac{P_X}{P_Y}$$

Utility Maximization and the Marginal Decision Rule

How does the achievement of The Utility Maximizing Solution in Figure 7.10 correspond to the marginal decision rule? That rule says that additional units of an activity should be pursued, if the marginal benefit of the activity exceeds the marginal cost. The observation of that rule would lead a consumer to the highest indifference curve possible for a given budget.

Suppose Ms. Bain has chosen a combination of skiing and horseback riding at point S in Figure 7.11. She is now on indifference curve C. She is also on her budget line; she is spending all of the budget, $250, available for the purchase of the two goods.

FIGURE 7.11 Applying the Marginal Decision Rule
Suppose Ms. Bain is initially at point S. She is spending all of her budget, but she is not maximizing utility. Because her marginal rate of substitution exceeds the rate at which the market asks her to give up skiing for horseback riding, she can increase her satisfaction by moving to point D. Now she is on a higher indifference curve, E. She will continue exchanging skiing for horseback riding until she reaches point X, at which she is on curve A, the highest indifference curve possible.

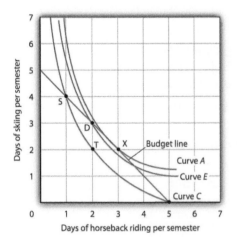

An exchange of two days of skiing for one day of horseback riding would leave her at point T, and she would be as well off as she is at point S. Her marginal rate of substitution between points S and T is 2; her indifference curve is steeper than the budget line at point S. The fact that her indifference curve is steeper than her budget line tells us that the rate at which she is *willing* to exchange the two goods differs from the rate the market asks. She would be willing to give up as many as 2 days of skiing to gain an extra day of horseback riding; the market demands that she give up only one. The marginal decision rule says that if an additional unit of an activity yields greater benefit than its cost, it should be pursued. If the benefit to Ms. Bain of one more day of horseback riding equals the benefit of 2 days of skiing, yet she can get it by giving up only 1 day of skiing, then the benefit of that extra day of horseback riding is clearly greater than the cost.

Because the market asks that she give up less than she is willing to give up for an additional day of horseback riding, she will make the exchange. Beginning at point S, she will exchange a day of skiing for a day of horseback riding. That moves her along her budget line to point D. Recall that we can draw an indifference curve through any point; she is now on indifference curve E. It is above and to the right of indifference curve C, so Ms. Bain is clearly better off. And that should come as no surprise. When she was at point S, she was willing to give up 2 days of skiing to get an extra day of horseback riding. The market asked her to give up only one; she got her extra day of riding at a bargain! Her move along her budget line from point S to point D suggests a very important principle. If a consumer's indifference curve intersects the budget line, then it will always be possible for the consumer to make exchanges along the budget line that move to a higher indifference curve. Ms. Bain's new indifference curve at point D also intersects her budget line; she's still willing to give up more skiing than the market asks for additional riding. She will make another exchange and move along her budget line to point X, at which she attains the highest indifference curve possible with her budget. Point X is on indifference curve A, which is tangent to the budget line.

Having reached point X, Ms. Bain clearly would not give up still more days of skiing for additional days of riding. Beyond point X, her indifference curve is flatter than the budget line—her marginal rate of substitution is less than the absolute value of the slope of the budget line. That means that the rate at which she would be willing to exchange skiing for horseback riding is less than the market asks. She cannot make herself better off than she is at point X by further rearranging her consumption. Point X, where the rate at which she is willing to exchange one good for another equals the rate the market asks, gives her the maximum utility possible.

Utility Maximization and Demand

Figure 7.11 showed Janet Bain's utility-maximizing solution for skiing and horseback riding. She achieved it by selecting a point at which an indifference curve was tangent to her budget line. A change in the price of one of the goods, however, will shift her budget line. By observing what happens to the quantity of the good demanded, we can derive Ms. Bain's demand curve.

Panel (a) of Figure 7.12 shows the original solution at point X, where Ms. Bain has $250 to spend and the price of a day of either skiing or horseback riding is $50. Now suppose the price of horseback riding falls by half, to $25. That changes the horizontal intercept of the budget line; if she spends all of her money on horseback riding, she can now ride 10 days per semester. Another way to think about the new budget line is to remember that its slope is equal to the negative of the price of the good on the horizontal axis divided by the price of the good on the vertical axis. When the price of horseback riding (the good on the horizontal axis) goes down, the budget line becomes flatter. Ms. Bain picks a new utility-maximizing solution at point Z.

FIGURE 7.12 Utility Maximization and Demand

By observing a consumer's response to a change in price, we can derive the consumer's demand curve for a good. Panel (a) shows that at a price for horseback riding of $50 per day, Janet Bain chooses to spend 3 days horseback riding per semester. Panel (b) shows that a reduction in the price to $25 increases her quantity demanded to 4 days per semester. Points X and Z, at which Ms. Bain maximizes utility at horseback riding prices of $50 and $25, respectively, become points X′ and Z′ on her demand curve, d, for horseback riding in Panel (b).

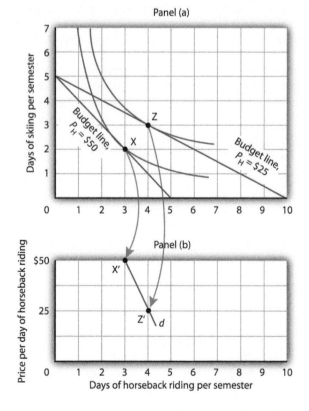

The solution at Z involves an increase in the number of days Ms. Bain spends horseback riding. Notice that only the price of horseback riding has changed; all other features of the utility-maximizing solution remain the same. Ms. Bain's budget and the price of skiing are unchanged; this is reflected in the fact that the vertical intercept of the budget line remains fixed. Ms. Bain's preferences are unchanged; they are reflected by her indifference curves. Because all other factors in the solution are unchanged, we can determine two points on Ms. Bain's demand curve for horseback riding from her indifference curve diagram. At a price of $50, she maximized utility at point X, spending 3 days horseback riding per semester. When the price falls to $25, she maximizes utility at point Z, riding 4 days per semester. Those points are plotted as points X′ and Z′ on her demand curve for horseback riding in Panel (b) of Figure 7.12.

Key Takeaways

- A budget line shows combinations of two goods a consumer is able to consume, given a budget constraint.
- An indifference curve shows combinations of two goods that yield equal satisfaction.
- To maximize utility, a consumer chooses a combination of two goods at which an indifference curve is tangent to the budget line.
- At the utility-maximizing solution, the consumer's marginal rate of substitution (the absolute value of the slope of the indifference curve) is equal to the price ratio of the two goods.
- We can derive a demand curve from an indifference map by observing the quantity of the good consumed at different prices.

Try It!

1. Suppose a consumer has a budget for fast-food items of $20 per week and spends this money on two goods, hamburgers and pizzas. Suppose hamburgers cost $5 each and pizzas cost $10. Put the quantity of hamburgers purchased per week on the horizontal axis and the quantity of pizzas purchased per week on the vertical axis. Draw the budget line. What is its slope?
2. Suppose the consumer in part (a) is indifferent among the combinations of hamburgers and pizzas shown. In the grid you used to draw the budget lines, draw an indifference curve passing through the combinations shown, and label the corresponding points A, B, and C. Label this curve I.

Combination	Hamburgers/week	Pizzas/week
A	5	0
B	3	½
C	0	3

3. The budget line is tangent to indifference curve I at B. Explain the meaning of this tangency.

Case in Point: Preferences Prevail in P.O.W. Camps

Source: © 2010 Jupiterimages Corporation

Economist R. A. Radford spent time in prisoner of war (P.O.W.) camps in Italy and Germany during World War II. He put this unpleasant experience to good use by testing a number of economic theories there. Relevant to this chapter, he consistently observed utility-maximizing behavior.

In the P.O.W. camps where he stayed, prisoners received rations, provided by their captors and the Red Cross, including tinned milk, tinned beef, jam, butter, biscuits, chocolate, tea, coffee, cigarettes, and other items. While all prisoners received approximately equal official rations (though some did manage to receive private care packages as well), their marginal rates of substitution between goods in the ration packages varied. To increase utility, prisoners began to engage in trade.

Prices of goods tended to be quoted in terms of cigarettes. Some camps had better organized markets than others but, in general, even though prisoners of each nationality were housed separately, so long as they could wander from bungalow to bungalow, the "cigarette" prices of goods were equal across bungalows. Trade allowed the prisoners to maximize their utility.

Consider coffee and tea. Panel (a) shows the indifference curves and budget line for typical British prisoners and Panel (b) shows the indifference curves and budget line for typical French prisoners. Suppose the price of an ounce of tea is 2 cigarettes and the price of an ounce of coffee is 1 cigarette. The slopes of the budget lines in each panel are identical; all prisoners faced the same prices. The price ratio is 1/2.

Suppose the ration packages given to all prisoners contained the same amounts of both coffee and tea. But notice that for typical British prisoners, given indifference curves which reflect their general preference for tea, the *MRS* at the initial allocation (point A) is less than the price ratio. For French prisoners, the *MRS* is greater than the price ratio (point B). By trading, both British and French prisoners can move to higher indifference curves. For the British prisoners, the utility-maximizing solution is at point E, with more tea and little coffee. For the French prisoners the utility-maximizing solution is at point E', with more coffee and less tea. In equilibrium, both British and French prisoners consumed tea and coffee so that their *MRS*'s equal 1/2, the price ratio in the market.

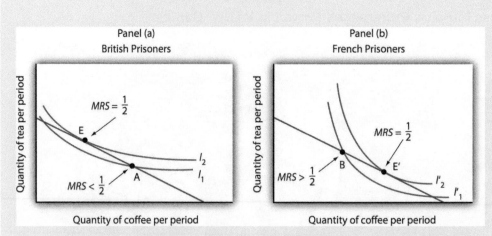

Source: Based on R. A. Radford, "The Economic Organisation of a P.O.W. Camp," Economica 12 (November 1945): 189–201; and Jack Hirshleifer, Price Theory and Applications (Englewood Cliffs, NJ: Prentice Hall, 1976): 85–86.

Answers to Try It! Problems

1. The budget line is shown in Panel (a). Its slope is –$5/$10 = –0.5.
2. Panel (b) shows indifference curve I. The points A, B, and C on I have been labeled.
3. The tangency point at B shows the combinations of hamburgers and pizza that maximize the consumer's utility, given the budget constraint. At the point of tangency, the marginal rate of substitution (MRS) between the two goods is equal to the ratio of prices of the two goods. This means that the rate at which the consumer is willing to exchange one good for another equals the rate at which the goods can be exchanged in the market.

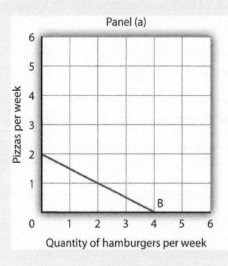
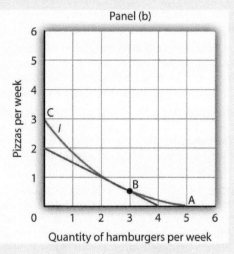

7.5 Review and Practice

Summary

In this chapter we have examined the model of utility-maximizing behavior. Economists assume that consumers make choices consistent with the objective of achieving the maximum total utility possible for a given budget constraint.

Utility is a conceptual measure of satisfaction; it is not actually measurable. The theory of utility maximization allows us to ask how a utility-maximizing consumer would respond to a particular event.

By following the marginal decision rule, consumers will achieve the utility-maximizing condition: Expenditures equal consumers' budgets, and ratios of marginal utility to price are equal for all pairs of goods and services. Thus, consumption is arranged so that the extra utility per dollar spent is equal for all goods and services. The marginal utility from a particular good or service eventually diminishes as consumers consume more of it during a period of time.

Utility maximization underlies consumer demand. The amount by which the quantity demanded changes in response to a change in price consists of a substitution effect and an income effect. The substitution effect always changes quantity demanded in a manner consistent with the law of demand. The income effect of a price change reinforces the substitution effect in the case of normal goods, but it affects consumption in an opposite direction in the case of inferior goods.

An alternative approach to utility maximization uses indifference curves. This approach does not rely on the concept of marginal utility, and it gives us a graphical representation of the utility-maximizing condition.

Concept Problems

1. Suppose you really, *really* like ice cream. You *adore* ice cream. Does the law of diminishing marginal utility apply to your ice cream consumption?

2. If two commodities that you purchase on a regular basis carry the same price, does that mean they both provide the same total utility? Marginal utility?

3. If a person goes to the bowling alley planning to spend $15 but comes away with $5, what, if anything, can you conclude about the marginal utility of the alternatives (for example, bowl another line, have a soda or a sandwich) available to the person at the time he or she leaves?

4. Which do you like more—going to the movies or watching rented DVDs at home? If you engage in both activities during the same period, say a week, explain why.

5. Do you tend to eat more at a fixed-price buffet or when ordering from an a la carte menu? Explain, using the marginal decision rule that guides your behavior.

6. Suppose there is a bill to increase the tax on cigarettes by $1 per pack coupled with an income tax cut of $500. Suppose a person smokes an average of 500 packs of cigarettes per year—and would thus face a tax increase of about $500 per year from the cigarette tax at the person's current level of consumption. The income tax measure would increase the person's after-tax income by $500. Would the combined measures be likely to have any effect on the person's consumption of cigarettes? Why or why not?

7. How does an increase in income affect a consumer's budget line? His or her total utility?

8. Why can Ms. Bain not consume at point Y in Figure 7.10?

9. Suppose Ms. Bain is now consuming at point V in Figure 7.10. Use the marginal decision rule to explain why a shift to X would increase her utility.

10. Suppose that you are a utility maximizer and so is your economics instructor. What can you conclude about your respective marginal rates of substitution for movies and concerts?

Numerical Problems

1. The table shows the total utility Joseph derives from eating pizza in the evening while studying.

Pieces of pizza/evening	Total Utility
0	0
1	30
2	48
3	60
4	70
5	78
6	80
7	76

   a. How much marginal utility does Joseph derive from the third piece of pizza?

   b. After eating how many pieces of pizza does marginal utility start to decline?

   c. If the pizza were free, what is the maximum number of pieces Joseph would eat in an evening?

   d. On separate diagrams, construct Joseph's total utility and marginal utility curves for pizza. Does the law of diminishing marginal utility hold? How do you know?

2. Suppose the marginal utility of good A is 20 and its price is $4, and the marginal utility of good B is 50 and its price is $5. The individual to whom this information applies is spending $20 on each good. Is he or she maximizing satisfaction? If not, what should the individual do to increase total satisfaction? On the basis of this information, can you pick an optimum combination? Why or why not?

3. John and Marie settle down to watch the evening news. Marie is content to watch the entire program, while John continually switches channels in favor of possible alternatives. Draw the likely marginal utility curves for watching the evening news for the two individuals. Whose marginal utility curve is likely to be steeper?

4. Li, a very careful maximizer of utility, consumes two services, going to the movies and bowling. She has arranged her consumption of the two activities so that the marginal utility of going to a movie is 20 and the marginal utility of going bowling is 10. The price of going to a movie is $10, and the price of going bowling is $5. Show that she is satisfying the requirement for utility maximization. Now show what happens when the price of going bowling rises to $10.

5. The table shows the total utility (*TU*) that Jeremy receives from consuming different amounts of two goods, X and Y, per month.

Quantity	TU $_X$	MU $_X$	MU$_X$/P$_X$	TU $_Y$	MU $_Y$	MU$_Y$/P$_Y$
0	0			0		
1	50			75		
2	88			117		
3	121			153		
4	150			181		
5	175			206		
6	196			225		
7	214			243		
8	229			260		
9	241			276		

    a. Fill in the other columns of the table by calculating the marginal utilities for goods X and Y and the ratios of marginal utilities to price for the two goods. Assume that the price of both goods X and Y is $3. Be sure to use the "midpoint convention" when you fill out the table.

    b. If Jeremy allocates $30 to spend on both goods, how many units will he buy of each?

    c. How much will Jeremy spend on each good at the utility maximizing combination?

    d. How much total utility will Jeremy experience by buying the utility-maximizing combination?

    e. Suppose the price of good Y increases to $6. How many units of X and Y will he buy to maximize his utility now?

    f. Draw Jeremy's demand curve for good Y between the prices of $6 and $3.

6. Sid is a commuter-student at his college. During the day, he snacks on cartons of yogurt and the "house special" sandwiches at the Student Center cafeteria. A carton of yogurt costs $1.20; the Student Center often offers specials on the sandwiches, so their price varies a great deal. Sid has a budget of $36 per week for food at the Center. Five of Sid's indifference curves are given by the schedule below; the points listed in the tables correspond to the points shown in the graph.

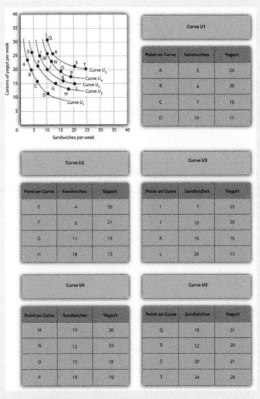

Curve U1

Point on Curve	Sandwiches	Yogurt
A	2	24
B	4	20
C	7	16
D	10	11

Curve U2

Point on Curve	Sandwiches	Yogurt
E	4	26
F	8	21
G	13	15
H	18	13

Curve U3

Point on Curve	Sandwiches	Yogurt
I	7	25
J	10	20
K	16	16
L	20	15

Curve U4

Point on Curve	Sandwiches	Yogurt
M	10	26
N	12	23
O	15	18
P	19	19

Curve U5

Point on Curve	Sandwiches	Yogurt
Q	10	21
R	12	26
S	20	21
T	24	20

a. Use the set of Sid's indifference curves shown as a guide in drawing your own graph grid. Draw Sid's indifference curves and budget line, assuming sandwiches cost $3.60. Identify the point at which he maximizes utility. How many sandwiches will he consume? How many cartons of yogurt? (*Hint:* All of the answers in this exercise occur at one of the combinations given in the tables on this page.)

b. Now suppose the price of sandwiches is cut to $1.20. Draw the new budget line. Identify the point at which Sid maximizes utility. How many sandwiches will he consume? How many cartons of yogurt?

c. Now draw the budget lines implied by a price of yogurt of $1.20 and sandwich prices of $0.90 and $1.80. With the observations you've already made for sandwich prices of $3.60 and $1.20, draw the demand curve. Explain how this demand curve illustrates the law of demand.

7. Consider a consumer who each week purchases two goods, X and Y. The following table shows three different combinations of the two goods that lie on three of her indifference curves—*A*, *B*, and *C*.

Indifference Curve	Quantities of goods X and Y, respectively	Quantitities of goods X and Y, respectively	Quantities of goods X and Y, respectively
A	1 unit of X and 4 of Y	2 units of X and 2 of Y	3 units of X and 1 of Y
B	1 unit of X and 7 of Y	3 units of X and 2 of Y	5 units of X and 1 of Y
C	2 units of X and 5 of Y	4 units of X and 3 of Y	7 units of X and 2 of Y

a. With good X on the horizontal axis and good Y on the vertical axis, draw the implied indifference curves. Be sure to label all curves and axes completely.

b. On Curve *A*, what is the marginal rate of substitution (*MRS*) between the first two combinations of goods X and Y?

c. Suppose this consumer has $500 available to spend on goods X and Y and that each costs $100. Add her budget line to the graph you drew in part (a). What is the slope of the budget line?

d. What is the utility-maximizing combination of goods X and Y for this consumer? (Assume in this exercise that the utility-maximizing combination always occurs at one of the combinations shown in the table.)

e. What is the *MRS* at the utility-maximizing combination?

f. Now suppose the price of good X falls to $50. Draw the new budget line onto your graph and identify the utility-maximizing combination. What is the MRS at the utility-maximizing combination? How much of each good does she consume?

g. Draw the demand curve for good X between prices of $50 and $100, assuming it is linear in this range.

Endnotes

1. Francis Y. Edgeworth, *Mathematical Psychics: An Essay on the Application of Mathematics to the Moral Sciences* (New York: Augustus M. Kelley, 1967), p. 101. First Published 1881.

2. Limiting the situation to two goods allows us to show the problem graphically. By stating the problem of utility maximization with equations, we could extend the analysis to any number of goods and services.

CHAPTER 8
Production and Cost

8.1 Start Up: Street Cleaning Around the World

It is dawn in Shanghai, China. Already thousands of Chinese are out cleaning the city's streets. They are using brooms.

On the other side of the world, night falls in Washington, D.C., where the streets are also being cleaned—by a handful of giant street-sweeping machines driven by a handful of workers.

The difference in method is not the result of a greater knowledge of modern technology in the United States—the Chinese know perfectly well how to build street-sweeping machines. It is a production decision based on costs in the two countries. In China, where wages are relatively low, an army of workers armed with brooms is the least expensive way to produce clean streets. In Washington, where labor costs are high, it makes sense to use more machinery and less labor.

All types of production efforts require choices in the use of factors of production. In this chapter we examine such choices. Should a good or service be produced using relatively more labor and less capital? Or should relatively more capital and less labor be used? What about the use of natural resources?

In this chapter we see why firms make the production choices they do and how their costs affect their choices. We will apply the marginal decision rule to the production process and see how this rule ensures that production is carried out at the lowest cost possible. We examine the nature of production and costs in order to gain a better understanding of supply. We thus shift our focus to **firms**, organizations that produce goods and services. In producing goods and services, firms combine the factors of production—labor, capital, and natural resources—to produce various products.

Economists assume that firms engage in production in order to earn a profit and that they seek to make this profit as large as possible. That is, economists assume that firms apply the marginal decision rule as they seek to maximize their profits. Whether we consider the operator of a shoe-shine stand at an airport or the firm that produces airplanes, we will find there are basic relationships between the use of factors of production and output levels, and between output levels and costs, that apply to all production. The production choices of firms and their associated costs are at the foundation of supply.

firms

Organizations that produce goods and services.

8.2 Production Choices and Costs: The Short Run

Learning Objectives

1. Understand the terms associated with the short-run production function—total product, average product, and marginal product—and explain and illustrate how they are related to each other.
2. Explain the concepts of increasing, diminishing, and negative marginal returns and explain the law of diminishing marginal returns.

3. Understand the terms associated with costs in the short run—total variable cost, total fixed cost, total cost, average variable cost, average fixed cost, average total cost, and marginal cost—and explain and illustrate how they are related to each other.
4. Explain and illustrate how the product and cost curves are related to each other and to determine in what ranges on these curves marginal returns are increasing, diminishing, or negative.

short run

A planning period over which the managers of a firm must consider one or more of their factors of production as fixed in quantity.

Our analysis of production and cost begins with a period economists call the short run. The **short run** in this microeconomic context is a planning period over which the managers of a firm must consider one or more of their factors of production as fixed in quantity. For example, a restaurant may regard its building as a fixed factor over a period of at least the next year. It would take at least that much time to find a new building or to expand or reduce the size of its present facility. Decisions concerning the operation of the restaurant during the next year must assume the building will remain unchanged. Other factors of production could be changed during the year, but the size of the building must be regarded as a constant.

fixed factor of production

A factor of production whose quantity cannot be changed during a particular period.

When the quantity of a factor of production cannot be changed during a particular period, it is called a **fixed factor of production**. For the restaurant, its building is a fixed factor of production for at least a year. A factor of production whose quantity can be changed during a particular period is called a **variable factor of production**; factors such as labor and food are examples.

variable factor of production

A factor of production whose quantity can be changed during a particular period.

While the managers of the restaurant are making choices concerning its operation over the next year, they are also planning for longer periods. Over those periods, managers may contemplate alternatives such as modifying the building, building a new facility, or selling the building and leaving the restaurant business. The planning period over which a firm can consider *all* factors of production as variable is called the **long run**.

long run

The planning period over which a firm can consider all factors of production as variable.

At any one time, a firm will be making both short-run and long-run choices. The managers may be planning what to do for the next few weeks and for the next few years. Their decisions over the next few weeks are likely to be short-run choices. Decisions that will affect operations over the next few years may be long-run choices, in which managers can consider changing every aspect of their operations. Our analysis in this section focuses on the short run. We examine long-run choices later in this chapter.

The Short-Run Production Function

production function

The relationship between factors of production and the output of a firm.

A firm uses factors of production to produce a product. The relationship between factors of production and the output of a firm is called a **production function** Our first task is to explore the nature of the production function.

Consider a hypothetical firm, Acme Clothing, a shop that produces jackets. Suppose that Acme has a lease on its building and equipment. During the period of the lease, Acme's capital is its fixed factor of production. Acme's variable factors of production include things such as labor, cloth, and electricity. In the analysis that follows, we shall simplify by assuming that labor is Acme's *only* variable factor of production.

Total, Marginal, and Average Products

Figure 8.1 shows the number of jackets Acme can obtain with varying amounts of labor (in this case, tailors) and its given level of capital. A **total product curve** shows the quantities of output that can be obtained from different amounts of a variable factor of production, assuming other factors of production are fixed.

Notice what happens to the slope of the total product curve in Figure 8.1. Between 0 and 3 units of labor per day, the curve becomes steeper. Between 3 and 7 workers, the curve continues to slope upward, but its slope diminishes. Beyond the seventh tailor, production begins to decline and the curve slopes downward.

We measure the slope of any curve as the vertical change between two points divided by the horizontal change between the same two points. The slope of the total product curve for labor equals the change in output (ΔQ) divided by the change in units of labor (ΔL):

$$\text{Slope of the total product curve} = \Delta Q / \Delta L$$

The slope of a total product curve for any variable factor is a measure of the change in output associated with a change in the amount of the variable factor, with the quantities of all other factors held constant. The amount by which output rises with an additional unit of a variable factor is the **marginal product** of the variable factor. Mathematically, marginal product is the ratio of the change in output to the change in the amount of a variable factor. The **marginal product of labor** (MP_L), for example, is the amount by which output rises with an additional unit of labor. It is thus the ratio of the change in output to the change in the quantity of labor ($\Delta Q/\Delta L$), all other things unchanged. It is measured as the slope of the total product curve for labor.

EQUATION 8.1

$$MP_L = \Delta Q / \Delta L$$

In addition we can define the **average product** of a variable factor. It is the output per unit of variable factor. The **average product of labor** (AP_L), for example, is the ratio of output to the number of units of labor (Q/L).

EQUATION 8.2

$$AP_L = Q / L$$

The concept of average product is often used for comparing productivity levels over time or in comparing productivity levels among nations. When you read in the newspaper that productivity is rising or falling, or that productivity in the United States is nine times greater than productivity in China, the report is probably referring to some measure of the average product of labor.

The total product curve in Panel (a) of Figure 8.2 is repeated from Figure 8.1. Panel (b) shows the marginal product and average product curves. Notice that marginal product is the slope of the total product curve, and that marginal product rises as the slope of the total product curve increases, falls as the slope of the total product curve declines, reaches zero when the total product curve achieves its maximum value, and becomes negative as the total product curve slopes downward. As in other parts of this text, marginal values are plotted at the midpoint of each interval. The marginal product of the fifth unit of labor, for example, is plotted between 4 and 5 units of labor. Also notice that the marginal product curve intersects the average product curve at the maximum point on the average product curve. When marginal product is above average product, average product is rising. When marginal product is below average product, average product is falling.

total product curve

Graph that shows the quantities of output that can be obtained from different amounts of a variable factor of production, assuming other factors of production are fixed.

FIGURE 8.1 Acme Clothing's Total Product Curve

The table gives output levels per day for Acme Clothing Company at various quantities of labor per day, assuming the firm's capital is fixed. These values are then plotted graphically as a total product curve.

Point on graph	A	B	C	D	E	F	G	H	I
Units of labor per day	0	1	2	3	4	5	6	7	8
Jackets per day	0.0	1.0	3.0	7.0	9.0	10.0	10.7	11.0	10.5

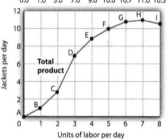

marginal product

The amount by which output rises with an additional unit of a variable factor.

marginal product of labor

The amount by which output rises with an additional unit of labor.

average product

The output per unit of variable factor.

average product of labor

The ratio of output to the number of units of labor (Q/L).

FIGURE 8.2 From Total Product to the Average and Marginal Product of Labor
The first two rows of the table give the values for quantities of labor and total product from Figure 8.1. Marginal product, given in the third row, is the change in output resulting from a one-unit increase in labor. Average product, given in the fourth row, is output per unit of labor. Panel (a) shows the total product curve. The slope of the total product curve is marginal product, which is plotted in Panel (b). Values for marginal product are plotted at the midpoints of the intervals. Average product rises and falls. Where marginal product is above average product, average product rises. Where marginal product is below average product, average product falls. The marginal product curve intersects the average product curve at the maximum point on the average product curve.

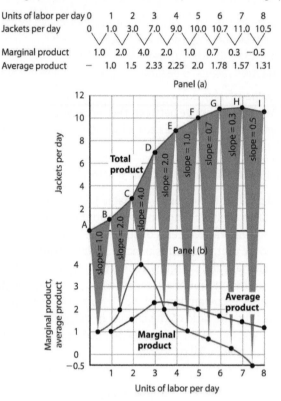

As a student you can use your own experience to understand the relationship between marginal and average values. Your grade point average (GPA) represents the average grade you have earned in all your course work so far. When you take an additional course, your grade in that course represents the marginal grade. What happens to your GPA when you get a grade that is higher than your previous average? It rises. What happens to your GPA when you get a grade that is lower than your previous average? It falls. If your GPA is a 3.0 and you earn one more B, your marginal grade equals your GPA and your GPA remains unchanged.

The relationship between average product and marginal product is similar. However, unlike your course grades, which may go up and down willy-nilly, marginal product always rises and then falls, for reasons we will explore shortly. As soon as marginal product falls below average product, the average product curve slopes downward. While marginal product is above average product, whether marginal product is increasing or decreasing, the average product curve slopes upward.

As we have learned, maximizing behavior requires focusing on making decisions at the margin. For this reason, we turn our attention now toward increasing our understanding of marginal product.

Increasing, Diminishing, and Negative Marginal Returns

Adding the first worker increases Acme's output from 0 to 1 jacket per day. The second tailor adds 2 jackets to total output; the third adds 4. The marginal product goes up because when there are more workers, each one can specialize to a degree. One worker might cut the cloth, another might sew the seams, and another might sew the buttonholes. Their increasing marginal products are reflected by the increasing slope of the total product curve over the first 3 units of labor and by the upward slope of the marginal product curve over the same range. The range over which marginal products are increasing is called the range of **increasing marginal returns**. Increasing marginal returns exist in the context of a total product curve for labor, so we are holding the quantities of other factors constant. Increasing marginal returns may occur for any variable factor.

The fourth worker adds less to total output than the third; the marginal product of the fourth worker is 2 jackets. The data in Figure 8.2 show that marginal product continues to decline after the fourth worker as more and more workers are hired. The additional workers allow even greater opportunities for specialization, but because they are operating with a fixed amount of capital, each new worker adds less to total output. The fifth tailor adds only a single jacket to total output. When each additional unit of a variable factor adds less to total output, the firm is experiencing **diminishing marginal returns**. Over the range of diminishing marginal returns, the marginal product of the variable factor is positive but falling. Once again, we assume that the quantities of all other factors of production are fixed. Diminishing marginal returns may occur for any variable factor. Panel (b) shows that Acme experiences diminishing marginal returns between the third and seventh workers, or between 7 and 11 jackets per day.

After the seventh unit of labor, Acme's fixed plant becomes so crowded that adding another worker actually reduces output. When additional units of a variable factor reduce total output, given constant quantities of all other factors, the company experiences **negative marginal returns**. Now the total product curve is downward sloping, and the marginal product curve falls below zero. Figure 8.3 shows the ranges of increasing, diminishing, and negative marginal returns. Clearly, a firm will never intentionally add so much of a variable factor of production that it enters a range of negative marginal returns.

The idea that the marginal product of a variable factor declines over some range is important enough, and general enough, that economists state it as a law. The **law of diminishing marginal returns** holds that the marginal product of any variable factor of production will eventually decline, assuming the quantities of other factors of production are unchanged.

increasing marginal returns

The range over which each additional unit of a variable factor adds more to total output than the previous unit.

diminishing marginal returns

The range over which each additional unit of a variable factor adds less to total output than the previous unit.

negative marginal returns

The range over which additional units of a variable factor reduce total output, given constant quantities of all other factors.

law of diminishing marginal returns

The marginal product of any variable factor of production will eventually decline, assuming the quantities of other factors of production are unchanged.

FIGURE 8.3 Increasing Marginal Returns, Diminishing Marginal Returns, and Negative Marginal Returns

This graph shows Acme's total product curve from Figure 8.1 with the ranges of increasing marginal returns, diminishing marginal returns, and negative marginal returns marked. Acme experiences increasing marginal returns between 0 and 3 units of labor per day, diminishing marginal returns between 3 and 7 units of labor per day, and negative marginal returns beyond the 7th unit of labor.

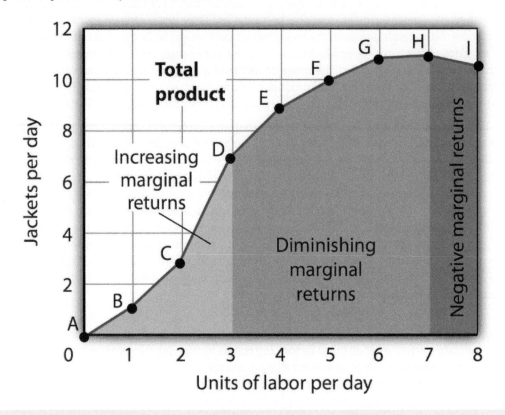

Heads Up!

It is easy to confuse the concept of diminishing marginal returns with the idea of negative marginal returns. To say a firm is experiencing diminishing marginal returns is not to say its output is falling. Diminishing marginal returns mean that the marginal product of a variable factor is declining. Output is still increasing as the variable factor is increased, but it is increasing by smaller and smaller amounts. As we saw in Figure 8.2 and Figure 8.3, the range of diminishing marginal returns was between the third and seventh workers; over this range of workers, output rose from 7 to 11 jackets. Negative marginal returns started after the seventh worker.

To see the logic of the law of diminishing marginal returns, imagine a case in which it does not hold. Say that you have a small plot of land for a vegetable garden, 10 feet by 10 feet in size. The plot itself is a fixed factor in the production of vegetables. Suppose you are able to hold constant all other factors—water, sunshine, temperature, fertilizer, and seed—and vary the amount of labor devoted to the garden. How much food could the garden produce? Suppose the marginal product of labor kept increasing or was constant. Then you could grow an *unlimited* quantity of food on your small plot—enough to feed the entire world! You could add an unlimited number of workers to your plot and still increase output at a constant or increasing rate. If you did not get enough output with, say, 500 workers, you could use 5 million; the five-millionth worker would add at least as much to total output as the first. If diminishing marginal returns to labor did not occur, the total product curve would slope upward at a constant or increasing rate.

The shape of the total product curve and the shape of the resulting marginal product curve drawn in Figure 8.2 are typical of *any* firm for the short run. Given its fixed factors of production, increasing the use of a variable factor will generate increasing marginal returns at first; the total product curve for the variable factor becomes steeper and the marginal product rises. The opportunity to gain from increased specialization in the use of the variable factor accounts for this range of increasing marginal returns. Eventually, though, diminishing returns will set in. The total product curve will become flatter, and the marginal product curve will fall.

Costs in the Short Run

A firm's costs of production depend on the quantities and prices of its factors of production. Because we expect a firm's output to vary with the firm's use of labor in a specific way, we can also expect the firm's costs to vary with its output in a specific way. We shall put our information about Acme's product curves to work to discover how a firm's costs vary with its level of output.

We distinguish between the costs associated with the use of variable factors of production, which are called **variable costs**, and the costs associated with the use of fixed factors of production, which are called **fixed costs**. For most firms, variable costs includes costs for raw materials, salaries of production workers, and utilities. The salaries of top management may be fixed costs; any charges set by contract over a period of time, such as Acme's one-year lease on its building and equipment, are likely to be fixed costs. A term commonly used for fixed costs is *overhead*. Notice that fixed costs exist only in the short run. In the long run, the quantities of all factors of production are variable, so that all long-run costs are variable.

Total variable cost (TVC) is cost that varies with the level of output. **Total fixed cost (TFC)** is cost that does not vary with output. **Total cost (TC)** is the sum of total variable cost and total fixed cost:

EQUATION 8.3

$$TVC + TFC = TC$$

From Total Production to Total Cost

Next we illustrate the relationship between Acme's total product curve and its total costs. Acme can vary the quantity of labor it uses each day, so the cost of this labor is a variable cost. We assume capital is a fixed factor of production in the short run, so its cost is a fixed cost.

Suppose that Acme pays a wage of $100 per worker per day. If labor is the only variable factor, Acme's total variable costs per day amount to $100 times the number of workers it employs. We can use the information given by the total product curve, together with the wage, to compute Acme's total variable costs.

We know from Figure 8.1 that Acme requires 1 worker working 1 day to produce 1 jacket. The total variable cost of a jacket thus equals $100. Three units of labor produce 7 jackets per day; the total variable cost of 7 jackets equals $300. Figure 8.4 shows Acme's total variable costs for producing each of the output levels given in Figure 8.1.

Figure 8.4 gives us costs for several quantities of jackets, but we need a bit more detail. We know, for example, that 7 jackets have a total variable cost of $300. What is the total variable cost of 6 jackets?

variable costs

The costs associated with the use of variable factors of production.

fixed costs

The costs associated with the use of fixed factors of production.

total variable cost

Cost that varies with the level of output.

total fixed cost

Cost that does not vary with output.

total cost

The sum of total variable cost and total fixed cost.

FIGURE 8.4 Computing Variable Costs

The points shown give the variable costs of producing the quantities of jackets given in the total product curve in Figure 8.1 and Figure 8.2. Suppose Acme's workers earn $100 per day. If Acme produces 0 jackets, it will use no labor—its variable cost thus equals $0 (Point A′). Producing 7 jackets requires 3 units of labor; Acme's variable cost equals $300 (Point D′).

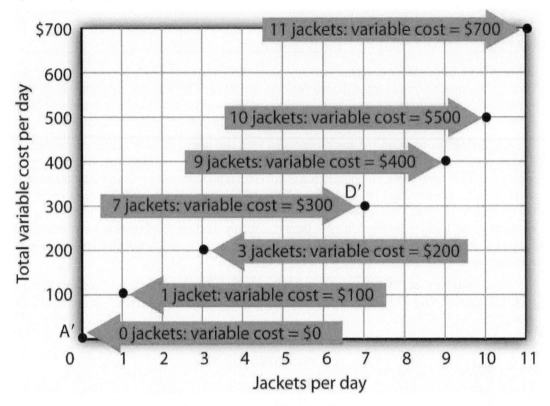

We can estimate total variable costs for other quantities of jackets by inspecting the total product curve in Figure 8.1. Reading over from a quantity of 6 jackets to the total product curve and then down suggests that the Acme needs about 2.8 units of labor to produce 6 jackets per day. Acme needs 2 full-time and 1 part-time tailors to produce 6 jackets. Figure 8.5 gives the precise total variable costs for quantities of jackets ranging from 0 to 11 per day. The numbers in boldface type are taken from Figure 8.4; the other numbers are estimates we have assigned to produce a total variable cost curve that is consistent with our total product curve. You should, however, be certain that you understand how the numbers in boldface type were found.

FIGURE 8.5 The Total Variable Cost Curve

Total variable costs for output levels shown in Acme's total product curve were shown in Figure 8.4. To complete the total variable cost curve, we need to know the variable cost for each level of output from 0 to 11 jackets per day. The variable costs and quantities of labor given in Figure 8.4 are shown in boldface in the table here and with black dots in the graph. The remaining values were estimated from the total product curve in Figure 8.1 and Figure 8.2. For example, producing 6 jackets requires 2.8 workers, for a variable cost of $280.

Quantity/day	0	1.0	2.0	3.0	4.0	5.0	6.0	7.0	8.0	9.0	10.0	11.0
Labor/day	0	**1.00**	1.63	**2.00**	2.33	2.58	2.80	**3.00**	3.38	**4.00**	**5.00**	**7.00**
Total variable cost	**$0**	**$100**	$163	**$200**	$233	$258	$280	**$300**	$338	**$400**	**$500**	**$700**

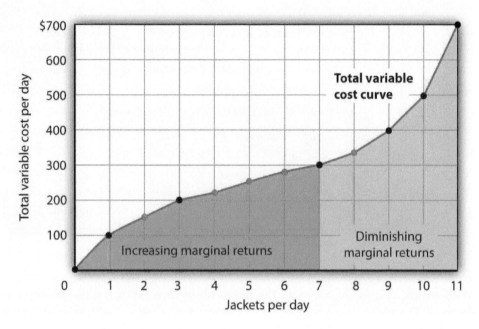

Suppose Acme's present plant, including the building and equipment, is the equivalent of 20 units of capital. Acme has signed a long-term lease for these 20 units of capital at a cost of $200 per day. In the short run, Acme cannot increase or decrease its quantity of capital—it must pay the $200 per day no matter what it does. Even if the firm cuts production to zero, it must still pay $200 per day in the short run.

Acme's total cost is its total fixed cost of $200 plus its total variable cost. We add $200 to the total variable cost curve in Figure 8.5 to get the total cost curve shown in Figure 8.6.

FIGURE 8.6 From Variable Cost to Total Cost
We add total fixed cost to the total variable cost to obtain total cost. In this case, Acme's total fixed cost equals $200 per day.

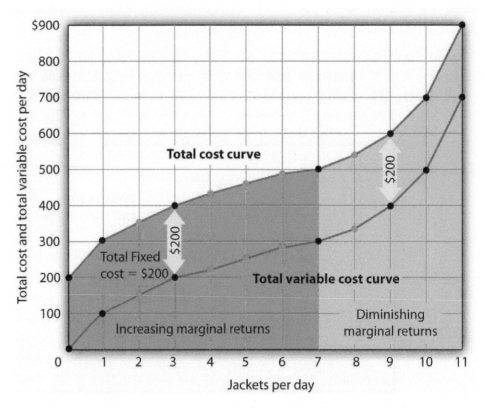

Notice something important about the shapes of the total cost and total variable cost curves in Figure 8.6. The total cost curve, for example, starts at $200 when Acme produces 0 jackets—that is its total fixed cost. The curve rises, but at a decreasing rate, up to the seventh jacket. Beyond the seventh jacket, the curve becomes steeper and steeper. The slope of the total variable cost curve behaves in precisely the same way.

Recall that Acme experienced increasing marginal returns to labor for the first three units of labor—or the first seven jackets. Up to the third worker, each additional worker added more and more to Acme's output. Over the range of increasing marginal returns, each additional jacket requires less and less additional labor. The first jacket required one tailor; the second required the addition of only a part-time tailor; the third required only that Acme boost that part-time tailor's hours to a full day. Up to the seventh jacket, each additional jacket requires less and less additional labor, and thus costs rise at a decreasing rate; the total cost and total variable cost curves become flatter over the range of increasing marginal returns.

Acme experiences diminishing marginal returns beyond the third unit of labor—or the seventh jacket. Notice that the total cost and total variable cost curves become steeper and steeper beyond this level of output. In the range of diminishing marginal returns, each additional unit of a factor adds less and less to total output. That means each additional unit of output requires larger and larger increases in the variable factor, and larger and larger increases in costs.

Marginal and Average Costs

average total cost

Total cost divided by quantity; it is the firm's total cost per unit of output.

Marginal and average cost curves, which will play an important role in the analysis of the firm, can be derived from the total cost curve. *Marginal cost* shows the additional cost of each additional unit of output a firm produces. This is a specific application of the general concept of marginal cost presented earlier. Given the marginal decision rule's focus on evaluating choices at the margin, the marginal cost curve takes on enormous importance in the analysis of a firm's choices. The second curve we shall derive shows the firm's average total cost at each level of output. **Average total cost (ATC)** is total cost divided by quantity; it is the firm's total cost per unit of output:

EQUATION 8.4

$$ATC = TC / Q$$

We shall also discuss **average variable cost**s *(AVC)*, which is the firm's variable cost per unit of output; it is total variable cost divided by quantity:

EQUATION 8.5

$$AVC = TVC / Q$$

We are still assessing the choices facing the firm in the short run, so we assume that at least one factor of production is fixed. Finally, we will discuss **average fixed cost** *(AFC)*, which is total fixed cost divided by quantity:

EQUATION 8.6

$$AFC = TFC / Q$$

Marginal cost *(MC)* is the amount by which total cost rises with an additional unit of output. It is the ratio of the change in total cost to the change in the quantity of output:

EQUATION 8.7

$$MC = \Delta TC / \Delta Q$$

It equals the slope of the total cost curve. Figure 8.7 shows the same total cost curve that was presented in Figure 8.6. This time the slopes of the total cost curve are shown; these slopes equal the marginal cost of each additional unit of output. For example, increasing output from 6 to 7 units ($\Delta Q = 1$) increases total cost from \$480 to \$500 ($\Delta TC = \$20$). The seventh unit thus has a marginal cost of \$20 ($\Delta TC / \Delta Q = \$20 / 1 = \$20$). Marginal cost falls over the range of increasing marginal returns and rises over the range of diminishing marginal returns.

average variable cost

Total variable cost divided by quantity; it is the firm's total variable cost per unit of output.

average fixed cost

Total fixed cost divided by quantity.

Heads Up!

Notice that the various cost curves are drawn with the quantity of output on the horizontal axis. The various product curves are drawn with quantity of a factor of production on the horizontal axis. The reason is that the two sets of curves measure different relationships. Product curves show the relationship between output and the quantity of a factor; they therefore have the factor quantity on the horizontal axis. Cost curves show how costs vary with output and thus have output on the horizontal axis.

FIGURE 8.7 Total Cost and Marginal Cost

Marginal cost in Panel (b) is the slope of the total cost curve in Panel (a).

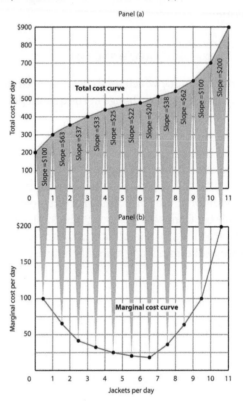

Figure 8.8 shows the computation of Acme's short-run average total cost, average variable cost, and average fixed cost and graphs of these values. Notice that the curves for short-run average total cost and average variable cost fall, then rise. We say that these cost curves are U-shaped. Average fixed cost keeps falling as output increases. This is because the fixed costs are spread out more and more as output expands; by definition, they do not vary as labor is added. Since average total cost (*ATC*) is the sum of average variable cost (*AVC*) and average fixed cost (*AFC*), i.e.,

EQUATION 8.8

$$AVC + AFC = ATC$$

the distance between the *ATC* and *AVC* curves keeps getting smaller and smaller as the firm spreads its overhead costs over more and more output.

FIGURE 8.8 Marginal Cost, Average Fixed Cost, Average Variable Cost, and Average Total Cost in the Short Run

Total cost figures for Acme Clothing are taken from Figure 8.7. The other values are derived from these. Average total cost (ATC) equals total cost divided by quantity produced; it also equals the sum of the average fixed cost (AFC) and average variable cost (AVC) (exceptions in table are due to rounding to the nearest dollar); average variable cost is variable cost divided by quantity produced. The marginal cost (MC) curve (from Figure 8.7) intersects the ATC and AVC curves at the lowest points on both curves. The AFC curve falls as quantity increases.

Quantity/day	0	1	2	3	4	5	6	7	8	9	10	11
Total cost	$200	$300	$363	$400	$433	$458	$480	$500	$538	$600	$700	$900
AFC		$200	$100	$67	$50	$40	$33	$29	$25	$22	$20	$18
AVC		$100	$82	$67	$58	$52	$47	$43	$42	$44	$50	$64
ATC		$300	$182	$133	$108	$92	$80	$71	$67	$67	$70	$82
MC		$100	$63	$37	$33	$25	$22	$20	$38	$62	$100	$200

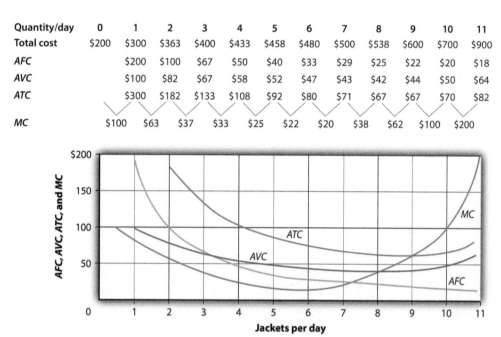

Figure 8.8 includes the marginal cost data and the marginal cost curve from Figure 8.7. The marginal cost curve intersects the average total cost and average variable cost curves at their lowest points. When marginal cost is below average total cost or average variable cost, the average total and average variable cost curves slope downward. When marginal cost is greater than short-run average total cost or average variable cost, these average cost curves slope upward. The logic behind the relationship between marginal cost and average total and variable costs is the same as it is for the relationship between marginal product and average product.

We turn next in this chapter to an examination of production and cost in the long run, a planning period in which the firm can consider changing the quantities of any or all factors.

Key Takeaways

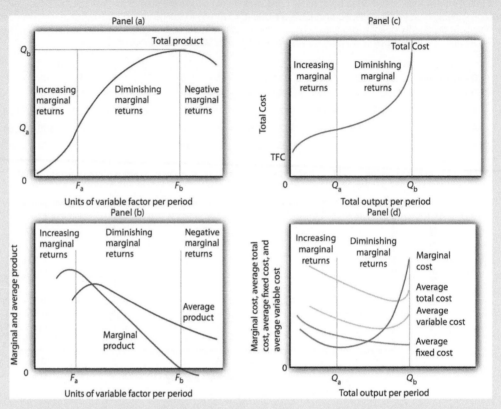

- In Panel (a), the total product curve for a variable factor in the short run shows that the firm experiences increasing marginal returns from zero to F_a units of the variable factor (zero to Q_a units of output), diminishing marginal returns from F_a to F_b (Q_a to Q_b units of output), and negative marginal returns beyond F_b units of the variable factor.

- Panel (b) shows that marginal product rises over the range of increasing marginal returns, falls over the range of diminishing marginal returns, and becomes negative over the range of negative marginal returns. Average product rises when marginal product is above it and falls when marginal product is below it.

- In Panel (c), total cost rises at a decreasing rate over the range of output from zero to Q_a This was the range of output that was shown in Panel (a) to exhibit increasing marginal returns. Beyond Q_a, the range of diminishing marginal returns, total cost rises at an increasing rate. The total cost at zero units of output (shown as the intercept on the vertical axis) is total fixed cost.

- Panel (d) shows that marginal cost falls over the range of increasing marginal returns, then rises over the range of diminishing marginal returns. The marginal cost curve intersects the average total cost and average variable cost curves at their lowest points. Average fixed cost falls as output increases. Note that average total cost equals average variable cost plus average fixed cost.

- Assuming labor is the variable factor of production, the following definitions and relations describe production and cost in the short run:

Try It!

1. Suppose Acme gets some new equipment for producing jackets. The table below gives its new production function. Compute marginal product and average product and fill in the bottom two rows of the table. Referring to Figure 8.2, draw a graph showing Acme's new

total product curve. On a second graph, below the one showing the total product curve you drew, sketch the marginal and average product curves. Remember to plot marginal product at the midpoint between each input level. On both graphs, shade the regions where Acme experiences increasing marginal returns, diminishing marginal returns, and negative marginal returns.

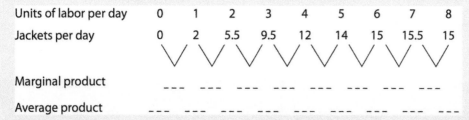

Units of labor per day	0	1	2	3	4	5	6	7	8
Jackets per day	0	2	5.5	9.5	12	14	15	15.5	15
Marginal product									
Average product									

2. Draw the points showing total variable cost at daily outputs of 0, 1, 3, 7, 9, 10, and 11 jackets per day when Acme faced a wage of $100 per day. (Use Figure 8.5 as a model.) Sketch the total variable cost curve as shown in Figure 8.4. Now suppose that the wage rises to $125 per day. On the same graph, show the new points and sketch the new total variable cost curve. Explain what has happened. What will happen to Acme's marginal cost curve? Its average total, average variable, and average fixed cost curves? Explain.

Case in Point: The Production of Fitness

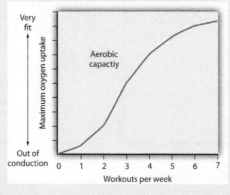

How much should an athlete train?

Sports physiologists often measure the "total product" of training as the increase in an athlete's aerobic capacity—the capacity to absorb oxygen into the bloodstream. An athlete can be thought of as producing aerobic capacity using a fixed factor (his or her natural capacity) and a variable input (exercise). The chart shows how this aerobic capacity varies with the number of workouts per week. The curve has a shape very much like a total product curve—which, after all, is precisely what it is.

The data suggest that an athlete experiences increasing marginal returns from exercise for the first three days of training each week; indeed, over half the total gain in aerobic capacity possible is achieved. A person can become even more fit by exercising more, but the gains become smaller with each added day of training. The law of diminishing marginal returns applies to training.

The increase in fitness that results from the sixth and seventh workouts each week is small. Studies also show that the costs of daily training, in terms of increased likelihood of injury, are high. Many trainers and coaches now recommend that athletes—at all levels of competition—take a day or two off each week.

While in his more recent books Mr. Galloway has not reproduced this graph, he continues to advise runners to take days off. For example, in his 2010 marathon training book, he counsels that every marathoner, including those training for the Olympics, take two days off from running each week.

Sources: Based on Jeff Galloway, Galloway's Book on Running (Bolinas, CA: Shelter Publications, 2002), p. 56; Jeff Galloway, Marathon: You Can Do it (Bolinas, CA: Shelter Publications, 2010), p. 114.

Answers to Try It! Problems

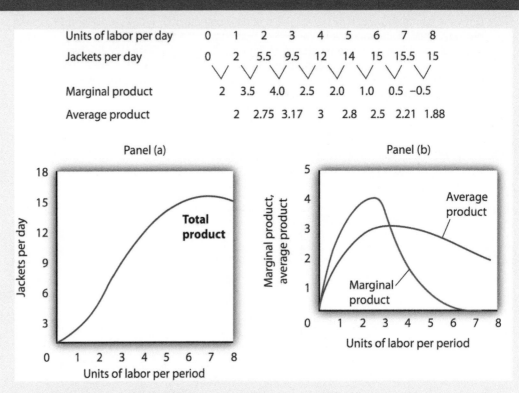

Units of labor per day	0	1	2	3	4	5	6	7	8
Jackets per day	0	2	5.5	9.5	12	14	15	15.5	15
Marginal product		2	3.5	4.0	2.5	2.0	1.0	0.5	–0.5
Average product		2	2.75	3.17	3	2.8	2.5	2.21	1.88

1. The increased wage will shift the total variable cost curve upward; the old and new points and the corresponding curves are shown at the right.

2. The total variable cost curve has shifted upward because the cost of labor, Acme's variable factor, has increased. The marginal cost curve shows the additional cost of each additional unit of output a firm produces. Because an increase in output requires more labor, and because labor now costs more, the marginal cost curve will shift upward. The increase in total variable cost will increase total cost; average total and average variable costs will rise as well. Average fixed cost will not change.

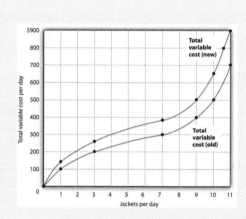

8.3 Production Choices and Costs: The Long Run

Learning Objectives

1. Apply the marginal decision rule to explain how a firm chooses its mix of factors of production in the long run.
2. Define the long-run average cost curve and explain how it relates to economies and diseconomies of scale.

In a long-run planning perspective, a firm can consider changing the quantities of *all* its factors of production. That gives the firm opportunities it does not have in the short run. First, the firm can select the mix of factors it wishes to use. Should it choose a production process with lots of labor and not much capital, like the street sweepers in China? Or should it select a process that uses a great deal of capital and relatively little labor, like street sweepers in the United States? The second thing the firm can select is the scale (or overall size) of its operations. In the short run, a firm can increase output only by increasing its use of a variable factor. But in the long run, all factors are variable, so the firm can expand the use of all of its factors of production. The question facing the firm in the long run is: How much of an expansion or contraction in the scale of its operations should it undertake? Alternatively, it could choose to go out of business.

In its long-run planning, the firm not only regards all factors as variable, but it regards all costs as variable as well. There are no fixed costs in the long run. Because all costs are variable, the structure of costs in the long run differs somewhat from what we saw in the short run.

Choosing the Factor Mix

How shall a firm decide what mix of capital, labor, and other factors to use? We can apply the marginal decision rule to answer this question.

Suppose a firm uses capital and labor to produce a particular good. It must determine how to produce the good and the quantity it should produce. We address the question of how much the firm should produce in subsequent chapters, but certainly the firm will want to produce whatever quantity it chooses at as low a cost as possible. Another way of putting that goal is to say that the firm seeks the maximum output possible at every level of total cost.

At any level of total cost, the firm can vary its factor mix. It could, for example, substitute labor for capital in a way that leaves its total cost unchanged. In terms of the marginal decision rule, we can think of the firm as considering whether to spend an additional \$1 on one factor, hence \$1 less on another. The marginal decision rule says that a firm will shift spending among factors as long as the marginal benefit of such a shift exceeds the marginal cost.

What is the marginal benefit, say, of an additional \$1 spent on capital? An additional unit of capital produces the marginal product of capital. To determine the marginal benefit of \$1 spent on capital, we divide capital's marginal product by its price: MP_K/P_K. The price of capital is the "rent" paid for the use of a unit of capital for a given period. If the firm already owns the capital, then this rent is an opportunity cost; it represents the return the firm could get by renting the capital to another user or by selling it and earning interest on the money thus gained.

If capital and labor are the only factors, then spending an additional \$1 on capital while holding total cost constant means taking \$1 out of labor. The cost of that action will be the output lost from cutting back \$1 worth of labor. That cost equals the ratio of the marginal product of labor to the price of labor, MP_L/P_L, where the price of labor is the wage.

Suppose that a firm's marginal product of labor is 15 and the price of labor is \$5 per unit; the firm gains 3 units of output by spending an additional \$1 on labor. Suppose further that the marginal product of capital is 50 and the price of capital is \$50 per unit, so the firm would lose 1 unit of output by spending \$1 less on capital.

$$\frac{MP_L}{P_L} > \frac{MP_K}{P_K}$$

$$\frac{15}{5} > \frac{50}{50}$$

The firm achieves a net gain of 2 units of output, without any change in cost, by transferring \$1 from capital to labor. It will continue to transfer funds from capital to labor as long as it gains more output from the additional labor than it loses in output by reducing capital. As the firm shifts spending in this fashion, however, the marginal product of labor will fall and the marginal product of capital will rise. At some point, the ratios of marginal product to price will be equal for the two factors. At this point, the firm will obtain the maximum output possible for a given total cost:

EQUATION 8.9

$$\frac{MP_L}{P_L} = \frac{MP_K}{P_K}$$

Suppose that a firm that uses capital and labor is satisfying Equation 8.9 when suddenly the price of labor rises. At the current usage levels of the factors, a higher price of labor (P_L') lowers the ratio of the marginal product of labor to the price of labor:

$$\frac{MP_L}{P_L'} < \frac{MP_K}{P_K}$$

The firm will shift funds out of labor and into capital. It will continue to shift from labor to capital until the ratios of marginal product to price are equal for the two factors. In general, a profit-maximizing firm will seek a combination of factors such that

EQUATION 8.10

$$\frac{MP_1}{P_1} = \frac{MP_2}{P_2} = \ldots = \frac{MP_n}{P_n}$$

When a firm satisfies the condition given in Equation 8.10 for efficient use, it produces the greatest possible output for a given cost. To put it another way, the firm achieves the lowest possible cost for a given level of output.

As the price of labor rises, the firm will shift to a factor mix that uses relatively more capital and relatively less labor. As a firm increases its ratio of capital to labor, we say it is becoming more **capital intensive**. A lower price for labor will lead the firm to use relatively more labor and less capital, reducing its ratio of capital to labor. As a firm reduces its ratio of capital to labor, we say it is becoming more **labor intensive**. The notions of labor-intensive and capital-intensive production are purely relative; they imply only that a firm has a higher or lower ratio of capital to labor.

Sometimes economists speak of labor-intensive versus capital-intensive countries in the same manner. One implication of the marginal decision rule for factor use is that firms in countries where labor is relatively expensive, such as the United States, will use capital-intensive production methods. Less developed countries, where labor is relatively cheap, will use labor-intensive methods.

Now that we understand how to apply the marginal decision rule to the problem of choosing the mix of factors, we can answer the question that began this chapter: Why does the United States employ a capital-intensive production process to clean streets while China chooses a labor-intensive process? Given that the same technology—know-how—is available, both countries could, after all, use the same production process. Suppose for a moment that the relative prices of labor and capital are the same in China and the United States. In that case, China and the United States can be expected to use the same method to clean streets. But the price of labor relative to the price of capital is, in fact, far lower in China than in the United States. A lower relative price for labor increases the ratio of the marginal product of labor to its price, making it efficient to substitute labor for capital. China thus finds it cheaper to clean streets with lots of people using brooms, while the United States finds it efficient to clean streets with large machines and relatively less labor.

Maquiladoras, plants in Mexico where processing is done using low-cost workers and labor-intensive methods, allow some U.S. firms to have it both ways. They complete part of the production process in the United States, using capital-intensive methods. They then ship the unfinished goods to *maquiladoras*. For example, many U.S. clothing manufacturers produce cloth at U.S. plants on large high-speed looms. They then ship the cloth to Mexico, where it is fashioned into clothing by workers using sewing machines. Another example is plastic injection molding, which requires highly skilled labor and is made in the U.S. The parts are molded in Texas border towns and are then shipped to *maquiladoras* and used in cars and computers. The resulting items are shipped back to the United States, labeled "Assembled in Mexico from U.S. materials." Overall maquiladoras import 97% of the components they use, of which 80 to 85% come from the U.S.

The *maquiladoras* have been a boon to workers in Mexico, who enjoy a higher demand for their services and receive higher wages as a result. The system also benefits the U.S. firms that participate and U.S. consumers who obtain less expensive goods than they would otherwise. It works because different factor prices imply different mixes of labor and capital. Companies are able to carry out the capital-intensive side of the production process in the United States and the labor-intensive side in Mexico. [1]

Costs in the Long Run

As in the short run, costs in the long run depend on the firm's level of output, the costs of factors, and the quantities of factors needed for each level of output. The chief difference between long- and short-run costs is there are no fixed factors in the long run. There are thus no fixed costs. All costs are variable, so we do not distinguish between total variable cost and total cost in the long run: total cost *is* total variable cost.

The long-run average cost (*LRAC*) curve shows the firm's lowest cost per unit at each level of output, assuming that all factors of production are variable. The *LRAC* curve assumes that the firm has chosen the optimal factor mix, as described in the previous section, for producing any level of output. The costs it shows are therefore the lowest costs possible for each level of output. It is important to note, however, that this does not mean that the minimum points of each short-run

capital intensive

Situation in which a firm has a high ratio of capital to labor.

labor intensive

Situation in which a firm has a high ratio of labor to capital.

long-run average cost curve

Graph showing the firms lowest cost per unit at each level of output, assuming that all factors of production are variable.

ATC curves lie on the *LRAC* curve. This critical point is explained in the next paragraph and expanded upon even further in the next section.

Figure 8.9 shows how a firm's *LRAC* curve is derived. Suppose Lifetime Disc Co. produces compact discs (CDs) using capital and labor. We have already seen how a firm's average total cost curve can be drawn in the short run for a given quantity of a particular factor of production, such as capital. In the short run, Lifetime Disc might be limited to operating with a given amount of capital; it would face one of the short-run average total cost curves shown in Figure 8.9. If it has 30 units of capital, for example, its average total cost curve is ATC_{30}. In the long run the firm can examine the average total cost curves associated with varying levels of capital. Four possible short-run average total cost curves for Lifetime Disc are shown in Figure 8.9 for quantities of capital of 20, 30, 40, and 50 units. The relevant curves are labeled ATC_{20}, ATC_{30}, ATC_{40}, and ATC_{50} respectively. The *LRAC* curve is derived from this set of short-run curves by finding the lowest average total cost associated with each level of output. Again, notice that the U-shaped *LRAC* curve is an envelope curve that surrounds the various short-run ATC curves. With the exception of ATC_{40}, in this example, the lowest cost per unit for a particular level of output in the long run is not the minimum point of the relevant short-run curve.

FIGURE 8.9 Relationship Between Short-Run and Long-Run Average Total Costs
The *LRAC* curve is found by taking the lowest average total cost curve at each level of output. Here, average total cost curves for quantities of capital of 20, 30, 40, and 50 units are shown for the Lifetime Disc Co. At a production level of 10,000 CDs per week, Lifetime minimizes its cost per CD by producing with 20 units of capital (point A). At 20,000 CDs per week, an expansion to a plant size associated with 30 units of capital minimizes cost per unit (point B). The lowest cost per unit is achieved with production of 30,000 CDs per week using 40 units of capital (point C). If Lifetime chooses to produce 40,000 CDs per week, it will do so most cheaply with 50 units of capital (point D).

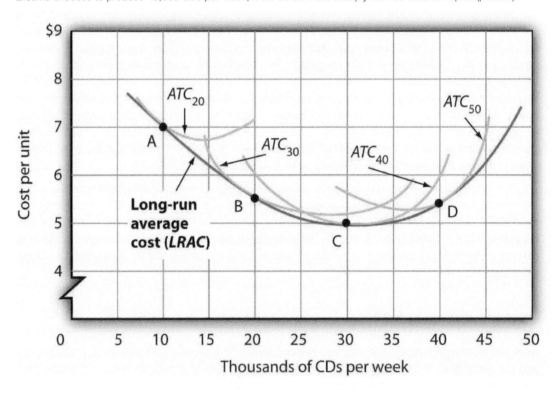

Economies and Diseconomies of Scale

Notice that the long-run average cost curve in Figure 8.9 first slopes downward and then slopes upward. The shape of this curve tells us what is happening to average cost as the firm changes its scale of operations. A firm is said to experience **economies of scale** when long-run average cost declines as the firm expands its output. A firm is said to experience **diseconomies of scale** when long-run average cost increases as the firm expands its output. **Constant returns to scale** occur when long-run average cost stays the same over an output range.

Why would a firm experience economies of scale? One source of economies of scale is gains from specialization. As the scale of a firm's operation expands, it is able to use its factors in more specialized ways, increasing their productivity. Another source of economies of scale lies in the economies that can be gained from mass production methods. As the scale of a firm's operation expands, the company can begin to utilize large-scale machines and production systems that can substantially reduce cost per unit.

Why would a firm experience diseconomies of scale? At first glance, it might seem that the answer lies in the law of diminishing marginal returns, but this is not the case. The law of diminishing marginal returns, after all, tells us how output changes as a single factor is increased, with all other factors of production held constant. In contrast, diseconomies of scale describe a situation of rising average cost even when the firm is free to vary any or all of its factors as it wishes. Diseconomies of scale are generally thought to be caused by management problems. As the scale of a firm's operations expands, it becomes harder and harder for management to coordinate and guide the activities of individual units of the firm. Eventually, the diseconomies of management overwhelm any gains the firm might be achieving by operating with a larger scale of plant, and long-run average costs begin rising. Firms experience constant returns to scale at output levels where there are neither economies nor diseconomies of scale. For the range of output over which the firm experiences constant returns to scale, the long-run average cost curve is horizontal.

Firms are likely to experience all three situations, as shown in Figure 8.10. At very low levels of output, the firm is likely to experience economies of scale as it expands the scale of its operations. There may follow a range of output over which the firm experiences constant returns to scale—empirical studies suggest that the range over which firms experience constant returns to scale is often very large. And certainly there must be some range of output over which diseconomies of scale occur; this phenomenon is one factor that limits the size of firms. A firm operating on the upward-sloping part of its *LRAC* curve is likely to be undercut in the market by smaller firms operating with lower costs per unit of output.

The Size Distribution of Firms

Economies and diseconomies of scale have a powerful effect on the sizes of firms that will operate in any market. Suppose firms in a particular industry experience diseconomies of scale at relatively low levels of output. That industry will be characterized by a large number of fairly small firms. The restaurant market appears to be such an industry. Barbers and beauticians are another example.

If firms in an industry experience economies of scale over a very wide range of output, firms that expand to take advantage of lower cost will force out smaller firms that have higher costs. Such industries are likely to have a few large firms instead of many small ones. In the refrigerator industry, for example, the size of firm necessary to achieve the lowest possible cost per unit is large enough to limit the market to only a few firms. In most cities, economies of scale leave room for only a single newspaper.

One factor that can limit the achievement of economies of scale is the demand facing an individual firm. The scale of output required to achieve the lowest unit costs possible may require sales

economies of scale

Situation in which the long-run average cost declines as the firm expands its output.

diseconomies of scale

Situation in which the long-run average cost increases as the firm expands its output.

constant returns to scale

Situation in which the long-run average cost stays the same over an output range.

FIGURE 8.10 Economies and Diseconomies of Scale and Long-Run Average Cost

The downward-sloping region of the firm's *LRAC* curve is associated with economies of scale. There may be a horizontal range associated with constant returns to scale. The upward-sloping range of the curve implies diseconomies of scale.

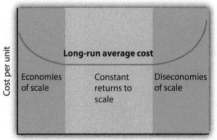

Output per period

that exceed the demand facing a firm. A grocery store, for example, could minimize unit costs with a large store and a large volume of sales. But the demand for groceries in a small, isolated community may not be able to sustain such a volume of sales. The firm is thus limited to a small scale of operation even though this might involve higher unit costs.

Key Takeaways

- A firm chooses its factor mix in the long run on the basis of the marginal decision rule; it seeks to equate the ratio of marginal product to price for all factors of production. By doing so, it minimizes the cost of producing a given level of output.
- The long-run average cost (*LRAC*) curve is derived from the average total cost curves associated with different quantities of the factor that is fixed in the short run. The *LRAC* curve shows the lowest cost per unit at which each quantity can be produced when all factors of production, including capital, are variable.
- A firm may experience economies of scale, constant returns to scale, or diseconomies of scale. Economies of scale imply a downward-sloping long-run average cost (*LRAC*) curve. Constant returns to scale imply a horizontal *LRAC* curve. Diseconomies of scale imply an upward-sloping *LRAC* curve.
- A firm's ability to exploit economies of scale is limited by the extent of market demand for its products.
- The range of output over which firms experience economies of scale, constant return to scale, or diseconomies of scale is an important determinant of how many firms will survive in a particular market.

Try It!

1. Suppose Acme Clothing is operating with 20 units of capital and producing 9 units of output at an average total cost of $67, as shown in Figure 8.8. How much labor is it using?
2. Suppose it finds that, with this combination of capital and labor, $MP_K/P_K > MP_L/P_L$. What adjustment will the firm make in the long run? Why does it not make this same adjustment in the short run?

Case in Point: Telecommunications Equipment, Economies of Scale, and Outage Risk

Source: © 2010 Jupiterimages Corporation

How big should the call switching equipment a major telecommunications company uses be? Having bigger machines results in economies of scale but also raises the risk of larger outages that will affect more customers.

Verizon Laboratories economist Donald E. Smith examined both the economies of scale available from larger equipment and the greater danger of more widespread outages. He concluded that companies should not use the largest machines available because of the outage danger and that they should not use the smallest size because that would mean forgoing the potential gains from economies of scale of larger sizes.

Switching machines, the large computers that handle calls for telecommunications companies, come in four basic "port matrix sizes." These are measured in terms of Digital Cross-Connects (DCS's). The four DCS sizes available are 6,000; 12,000; 24,000; and 36,000 ports. Different machine sizes are made with the same components and thus have essentially the same probability of breaking down. Because larger machines serve more customers, however, a breakdown in a large machine has greater consequences for the company.

The costs of an outage have three elements. The first is lost revenue from calls that would otherwise have been completed. Second, the FCC requires companies to provide a credit of one month of free service after any outage that lasts longer than one minute. Finally, an outage damages a company's reputation and inevitably results in dissatisfied customers—some of whom may switch to other companies.

But, there are advantages to larger machines. A company has a "portfolio" of switching machines. Having larger machines lowers costs in several ways. First, the initial acquisition of the machine generates lower cost per call completed the greater the size of the machine. When the company must make upgrades to the software, having fewer—and larger—machines means fewer upgrades and thus lower costs.

In deciding on matrix size companies should thus compare the cost advantages of a larger matrix with the disadvantages of the higher outage costs associated with those larger matrixes.

Mr. Smith concluded that the economies of scale outweigh the outage risks as a company expands beyond 6,000 ports but that 36,000 ports is "too big" in the sense that the outage costs outweigh the advantage of the economies of scale. The evidence thus suggests that a matrix size in the range of 12,000 to 24,000 ports is optimal.

Source: Based on Donald E. Smith, "How Big Is Too Big? Trading Off the Economies of Scale of Larger Telecommunications Network Elements Against the Risk of Larger Outages," European Journal of Operational Research, 173 (1) (August 2006): 299–312.

Answers to Try It! Problems

1. To produce 9 jackets, Acme uses 4 units of labor.
2. In the long run, Acme will substitute capital for labor. It cannot make this adjustment in the short run, because its capital is fixed in the short run.

8.4 Review and Practice

Summary

In this chapter we have concentrated on the production and cost relationships facing firms in the short run and in the long run.

In the short run, a firm has at least one factor of production that it cannot vary. This fixed factor limits the firm's range of factor choices. As a firm uses more and more of a variable factor (with fixed quantities of other factors of production), it is likely to experience at first increasing, then diminishing, then negative marginal returns. Thus, the short-run total cost curve has a positive value at a zero level of output (the firm's total fixed cost), then slopes upward at a decreasing rate (the range of increasing marginal returns), and then slopes upward at an increasing rate (the range of diminishing marginal returns).

In addition to short-run total product and total cost curves, we derived a firm's marginal product, average product, average total cost, average variable cost, average fixed cost, and marginal cost curves.

If the firm is to maximize profit in the long run, it must select the cost-minimizing combination of factors for its chosen level of output. Thus, the firm must try to use factors of production in accordance with the marginal decision rule. That is, it will use factors so that the ratio of marginal product to factor price is equal for all factors of production.

A firm's long-run average cost (*LRAC*) curve includes a range of economies of scale, over which the curve slopes downward, and a range of diseconomies of scale, over which the curve slopes upward. There may be an intervening range of output over which the firm experiences constant returns to scale; its *LRAC* curve will be horizontal over this range. The size of operations necessary to reach the lowest point on the *LRAC* curve has a great deal to do with determining the relative sizes of firms in an industry.

This chapter has focused on the nature of production processes and the costs associated with them. These ideas will prove useful in understanding the behavior of firms and the decisions they make concerning supply of goods and services.

Concept Problems

1. Which of the following would be considered long-run choices? Which are short-run choices?

    a. A dentist hires a new part-time dental hygienist.

    b. The local oil refinery plans a complete restructuring of its production processes, including relocating the plant.

    c. A farmer increases the quantity of water applied to his or her fields.

    d. A law partnership signs a 3-year lease for an office complex.

    e. The university hires a new football coach on a 3-year contract.

2. "There are no fixed costs in the long run." Explain.

3. Business is booming at the local McDonald's restaurant. It is contemplating adding a new grill and french-fry machine, but the day supervisor suggests simply hiring more workers. How should the manager decide which alternative to pursue?

4. Suppose that the average age of students in your economics class is 23.7 years. If a new 19-year-old student enrolls in the class, will the average age in the class rise or fall? Explain how this relates to the relationship between average and marginal values.

5. Barry Bond's career home run average in his first 15 years in major league baseball (through 1997) was 33 home runs per season. In 2001, he hit 73 home runs. What happened to his career home run average? What effect did his performance in 2001 have on his career home run average? Explain how this relates to the relationship between average and marginal values.

6. Suppose a firm is operating at the minimum point of its short-run average total cost curve, so that marginal cost equals average total cost. Under what circumstances would it choose to alter the size of its plant? Explain.

7. What happens to the difference between average total cost and average variable cost as a firm's output expands? Explain.

8. How would each of the following affect average total cost, average variable cost, and marginal cost?

    a. An increase in the cost of the lease of the firm's building

    b. A reduction in the price of electricity

    c. A reduction in wages

    d. A change in the salary of the president of the company

9. Consider the following types of firms. For each one, the long-run average cost curve eventually exhibits diseconomies of scale. For which firms would you expect diseconomies of scale to set in at relatively low levels of output? Why?

    a. A copy shop

    b. A hardware store

    c. A dairy

    d. A newspaper

    e. An automobile manufacturer

    f. A restaurant

10. As car manufacturers incorporate more sophisticated computer technology in their vehicles, auto-repair shops require more computerized testing equipment, which is quite expensive, in order to repair newer cars. How is this likely to affect the shape of these firms' long-run average total cost curves? How is it likely to affect the number of auto-repair firms in any market?

Numerical Problems

1. The table below shows how the number of university classrooms cleaned in an evening varies with the number of janitors:

Janitors per evening	0	1	2	3	4	5	6	7
Classrooms cleaned per evening	0	3	7	12	16	17	17	16

   a. What is the marginal product of the second janitor?
   b. What is the average product of four janitors?
   c. Is the addition of the third janitor associated with increasing, diminishing, or negative marginal returns? Explain.
   d. Is the addition of the fourth janitor associated with increasing, diminishing, or negative marginal returns? Explain.
   e. Is the addition of the seventh janitor associated with increasing, diminishing, or negative marginal returns? Explain.
   f. Draw the total product, average product, and marginal product curves and shade the regions corresponding to increasing marginal returns, decreasing marginal returns, and negative marginal returns.
   g. Calculate the slope of the total product curve as each janitor is added.
   h. Characterize the nature of marginal returns in the region where

      1. The slope of the total product curve is positive and increasing.
      2. The slope of the total product curve is positive and decreasing.
      3. The slope of the total product curve is negative.

2. Suppose a firm is producing 1,000 units of output. Its average fixed costs are $100. Its average variable costs are $50. What is the total cost of producing 1,000 units of output?

3. The director of a nonprofit foundation that sponsors 8-week summer institutes for graduate students analyzed the costs and expected revenues for the next summer institute and recommended that the session be canceled. In her analysis she included a share of the foundation's overhead—the salaries of the director and staff and costs of maintaining the office—to the program. She estimated costs and revenues as follows:

Projected revenues (from tuition and fees)	$300,000
Projected costs	
Overhead	$ 50,000
Room and board for students	$100,000
Costs for faculty and miscellaneous	$175,000
Total costs	$325,000

What was the error in the director's recommendation?

4. The table below shows the total cost of cleaning classrooms:

Classrooms cleaned per evening	0	3	7	12	16	17
Total cost	$100	$200	$300	$400	$500	$600

   a. What is the average fixed cost of cleaning three classrooms?
   b. What is the average variable cost of cleaning three classrooms?
   c. What is the average fixed cost of cleaning seven classrooms?
   d. What is the average variable cost of cleaning seven classrooms?
   e. What is the marginal cost of cleaning the seventeenth classroom?
   f. What is the average total cost of cleaning twelve classrooms?

5. The average total cost for printing 10,000 copies of an issue of a magazine is $0.45 per copy. For 20,000 copies, the average total cost is $0.35 apiece; for 30,000, the average total cost is $0.30 per copy. The average total cost continues to decline slightly over every level of output that the publishers of the magazine have considered. Sketch the approximate shapes of the average and marginal cost curves. What are some variable costs of publishing magazines? Some fixed costs?

6. The information in the table explains the production of socks. Assume that the price per unit of the variable factor of production (L) is $20 and the price per unit of the fixed factor of production (K) is $5.

Units of Fixed Factor (K)	Units of Variable Factor (L)	Total Product (Q)
10	0	0
10	1	2
10	2	5
10	3	12
10	4	15
10	5	16

a. Add columns to the table and calculate the values for : Marginal Product of Labor (MP_L), Total Variable Cost (TVC), Total Fixed Cost (TFC), Total Cost (TC), Average Variable Cost (AVC), Average Fixed Cost (AFC), Average Total Cost (ATC), and Marginal Cost (MC).

b. On two sets of axes, graph the Total Product and Marginal Product curves. Be sure to label curves and axes and remember to plot marginal product using the midpoint convention. Indicate the point on each graph at which diminishing marginal returns appears to begin.

c. Graph Total Variable Cost, Total Fixed Cost, and Total Cost on another set of axes. Indicate the point on the graph at which diminishing marginal returns appears to begin.

d. Graph the Average Fixed Cost, Average Variable Cost, Average Total Cost, and Marginal Cost curves on another set of axes. Indicate the point at which diminishing marginal returns appears to begin.

7. The table below shows the long-run average cost of producing knives:

Knives per hour	1,000	2,000	3,000	4,000	5,000	6,000
Cost per knife	$2	$1.50	$1.00	$1.00	$1.20	$1.30

a. Draw the long-run average cost curve for knives.

b. Shade the regions corresponding to economies of scale, constant returns to scale, and diseconomies of scale.

c. In the region of the long-run average cost curve that corresponds to economies of scale, what is happening to the cost per knife?

d. In the region of the long-run average cost curve that corresponds to constant returns to scale, what is happening to the cost per knife?

e. In the region of the long-run average cost curve that corresponds to diseconomies of scale, what is happening to the cost per knife?

8. Suppose a firm finds that the marginal product of capital is 60 and the marginal product of labor is 20. If the price of capital is $6 and the price of labor is $2.50, how should the firm adjust its mix of capital and labor? What will be the result?

9. A firm minimizes its costs by using inputs such that the marginal product of labor is 10 and the marginal product of capital is 20. The price of capital is $10 per unit. What must the price of labor be?

10. Suppose that the price of labor is $10 per unit and the price of capital is $20 per unit.

a. Assuming the firm is minimizing its cost, if the marginal product of labor is 50, what must the marginal product of capital be?

b. Suppose the price of capital increases to $25 per unit, while the price of labor stays the same. To minimize the cost of producing the same level of output, would the firm become more capital-intensive or labor-intensive? Explain.

Endnotes

1. Lucinda Vargas, "Maquiladoras: Impact on Texas Border Cities," in *The Border Economy*, Federal Reserve Bank of Dallas (June 2001): 25–29; William C. Gruben, "Have Mexico's Maquiladoras Bottomed Out?", Southwest Economy, Federal Reserve Bank of Dallas (January/February, 2004), pp. 14–15.

CHAPTER 9

Competitive Markets for Goods and Services

9.1 Start Up: Life on the Farm

They produce a commodity that is essential to our daily lives, one for which the demand is virtually assured. And yet many—even as farm prices are reaching record highs—seem to live on the margin of failure. Thousands are driven out of business each year. We provide billions of dollars in aid for them, but still we hear of the hardships many of them face. They are our nation's farmers.

What is it about farmers, and farming, that arouses our concern? Much of the answer probably lies in our sense that farming is fundamental to the American way of life. Our country was built, in large part, by independent men and women who made their living from the soil. Many of us perceive their plight as our plight. But part of the answer lies in the fact that farmers do, in fact, face a difficult economic environment. Most of them operate in highly competitive markets, markets that tolerate few mistakes and generally offer small rewards. Finally, perhaps our concern is stirred by our recognition that the farmers' plight is our blessing. The low prices that make life difficult for farmers are the low prices we enjoy as consumers of food.

What keeps the returns to farming as low as they are? What holds many farmers in a situation in which they always seem to be just getting by? In this chapter we shall see that prices just high enough to induce firms to continue to produce are precisely what we would expect to prevail in a competitive market. We will examine a model of how competitive markets work. Not only does this model help to explain the situation facing farmers, but it will also help us to understand the determination of price and output in a wide range of markets. A farm is a firm, and our analysis of such a firm in a competitive market will give us the tools to analyze the choices of all firms operating in competitive markets.

We will put the concepts of marginal cost, average variable cost, and average total cost to work to see how firms in a competitive market respond to market forces. We will see how firms adjust to changes in demand and supply in the short run and in the long run. In all of this, we will be examining how firms use the marginal decision rule.

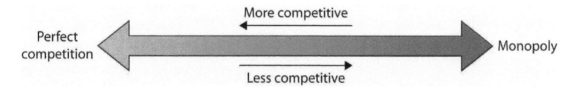

The competitive model introduced in this chapter lies at one end of a spectrum of market models. At the other end is the monopoly model. It assumes a market in which there is no competition, a market in which only a single firm operates. Two models that fall between the extremes of perfect competition and monopoly are monopolistic competition and oligopoly.

9.2 Perfect Competition: A Model

1. Explain what economists mean by perfect competition.
2. Identify the basic assumptions of the model of perfect competition and explain why they imply price-taking behavior.

Virtually all firms in a market economy face competition from other firms. In this chapter, we will be working with a model of a highly idealized form of competition called "perfect" by economists.

perfect competition

Model of the market based on the assumption that a large number of firms produce identical goods consumed by a large number of buyers.

Perfect competition is a model of the market based on the assumption that a large number of firms produce identical goods consumed by a large number of buyers. The model of perfect competition also assumes that it is easy for new firms to enter the market and for existing ones to leave. And finally, it assumes that buyers and sellers have complete information about market conditions.

As we examine these assumptions in greater detail, we will see that they allow us to work with the model more easily. No market fully meets the conditions set out in these assumptions. As is always the case with models, our purpose is to understand the way things work, not to describe them. And the model of perfect competition will prove enormously useful in understanding the world of markets.

Assumptions of the Model

price takers

Individuals or firms who must take the market price as given.

The assumptions of the model of perfect competition, taken together, imply that individual buyers and sellers in a perfectly competitive market accept the market price as given. No one buyer or seller has any influence over that price. Individuals or firms who must take the market price as given are called **price takers**. A consumer or firm that takes the market price as given has no ability to influence that price. A price-taking firm or consumer is like an individual who is buying or selling stocks. He or she looks up the market price and buys or sells at that price. The price is determined by demand and supply in the market—not by individual buyers or sellers. In a perfectly competitive market, each firm and each consumer is a price taker. A price-taking consumer assumes that he or she can purchase any quantity at the market price—without affecting that price. Similarly, a price-taking firm assumes it can sell whatever quantity it wishes at the market price without affecting the price.

You are a price taker when you go into a store. You observe the prices listed and make a choice to buy or not. Your choice will not affect that price. Should you sell a textbook back to your campus bookstore at the end of a course, you are a price-taking seller. You are confronted by a market price and you decide whether to sell or not. Your decision will not affect that price.

To see how the assumptions of the model of perfect competition imply price-taking behavior, let us examine each of them in turn.

Identical Goods

In a perfectly competitive market for a good or service, one unit of the good or service cannot be differentiated from any other on any basis. A bushel of, say, hard winter wheat is an example. A bushel produced by one farmer is identical to that produced by another. There are no brand preferences or consumer loyalties.

The assumption that goods are identical is necessary if firms are to be price takers. If one farmer's wheat were perceived as having special properties that distinguished it from other wheat, then that farmer would have some power over its price. By assuming that all goods and services produced by firms in a perfectly competitive market are identical, we establish a necessary condition for price-taking behavior. Economists sometimes say that the goods or services in a perfectly competitive market are *homogeneous*, meaning that they are all alike. There are no brand differences in a perfectly competitive market.

A Large Number of Buyers and Sellers

How many buyers and sellers are in our market? The answer rests on our presumption of price-taking behavior. There are so many buyers and sellers that none of them has any influence on the market price regardless of how much any of them purchases or sells. A firm in a perfectly competitive market can react to prices, but cannot affect the prices it pays for the factors of production or the prices it receives for its output.

Ease of Entry and Exit

The assumption that it is easy for other firms to enter a perfectly competitive market implies an even greater degree of competition. Firms in a market must deal not only with the large number of competing firms but also with the possibility that still more firms might enter the market.

Later in this chapter, we will see how ease of entry is related to the sustainability of economic profits. If entry is easy, then the promise of high economic profits will quickly attract new firms. If entry is difficult, it won't.

The model of perfect competition assumes easy exit as well as easy entry. The assumption of easy exit strengthens the assumption of easy entry. Suppose a firm is considering entering a particular market. Entry may be easy, but suppose that getting out is difficult. For example, suppliers of factors of production to firms in the industry might be happy to accommodate new firms but might require that they sign long-term contracts. Such contracts could make leaving the market difficult and costly. If that were the case, a firm might be hesitant to enter in the first place. Easy exit helps make entry easier.

Complete Information

We assume that all sellers have complete information about prices, technology, and all other knowledge relevant to the operation of the market. No one seller has any information about production methods that is not available to all other sellers. If one seller had an advantage over other sellers, perhaps special information about a lower-cost production method, then that seller could exert some control over market price—the seller would no longer be a price taker.

We assume also that buyers know the prices offered by every seller. If buyers did not know about prices offered by different firms in the market, then a firm might be able to sell a good or service for a price other than the market price and thus could avoid being a price taker.

The availability of information that is assumed in the model of perfect competition implies that information can be obtained at low cost. If consumers and firms can obtain information at low cost, they are likely to do so. Information about the marketplace may come over the internet, over the airways in a television commercial, or over a cup of coffee with a friend. Whatever its source, we assume that its low cost ensures that consumers and firms have enough of it so that everyone buys or sells goods and services at market prices determined by the intersection of demand and supply curves.

The assumptions of the perfectly competitive model ensure that each buyer or seller is a price taker. The market, not individual consumers or firms, determines price in the model of perfect competition. No individual has enough power in a perfectly competitive market to have any impact on that price.

Perfect Competition and the Real World

The assumptions of identical products, a large number of buyers, easy entry and exit, and perfect information are strong assumptions. The notion that firms must sit back and let the market determine price seems to fly in the face of what we know about most real firms, which is that firms customarily do set prices. Yet this is the basis for the model of demand and supply, the power of which you have already seen.

When we use the model of demand and supply, we assume that market forces determine prices. In this model, buyers and sellers respond to the market price. They are price takers. The assumptions of the model of perfect competition underlie the assumption of price-taking behavior. Thus we are using the model of perfect competition whenever we apply the model of demand and supply.

We can understand most markets by applying the model of demand and supply. Even though those markets do not fulfill all the assumptions of the model of perfect competition, the model allows us to understand some key features of these markets.

Changes within your lifetime have made many markets more competitive. Falling costs of transportation, together with dramatic advances in telecommunications, have opened the possibility of entering markets to firms all over the world. A company in South Korea can compete in the market for steel in the United States. A furniture maker in New Mexico can compete in the market for furniture in Japan. A firm can enter the world market simply by creating a web page to advertise its products and to take orders.

In the remaining sections of this chapter, we will learn more about the response of firms to market prices. We will see how firms respond, in the short run and in the long run, to changes in demand and to changes in production costs. In short, we will be examining the forces that constitute the supply side of the model of demand and supply.

We will also see how competitive markets work to serve consumer interests and how competition acts to push economic profits down, sometimes eliminating them entirely. When we have finished we will have a better understanding of the market conditions facing farmers and of the conditions that prevail in any competitive industry.

Key Takeaways

- The central characteristic of the model of perfect competition is the fact that price is determined by the interaction of demand and supply; buyers and sellers are price takers.
- The model assumes: a large number of firms producing identical (homogeneous) goods or services, a large number of buyers and sellers, easy entry and exit in the industry, and complete information about prices in the market.
- The model of perfect competition underlies the model of demand and supply.

Try It!

Which of the following goods and services are likely produced in a perfectly competitive industry? Relate your answer to the assumptions of the model of perfect competition.

1. International express mail service
2. Corn
3. Athletic shoes

Case in Point: Entering and Exiting the Burkha Industry

Source: © 2010 Jupiterimages Corporation

Muhammed Ibrahim Islamadin was driving a cab in Kabul, Afghanistan, when the Taliban took over the country. He foresaw the repression that would follow and sensed an opportunity.

He sold his taxicab and set up a shop for sewing and selling burkhas, the garments required of all women under the Taliban's rule. Mr. Islamadin had an easy task selling, as women caught outdoors with exposed skin were routinely beaten by the Taliban's religious police. He told *The Wall Street Journal*, "This was very bad for them, but it was good for me."

Of course, Mr. Islamadin was not the only producer to get into the industry. Other Afghani merchants, as well as merchants from Pakistan and China, also jumped at the opportunity.

The entry of new firms exemplifies an important characteristic of perfect competition. Whenever there is an opportunity to earn economic profits—even an unexpected opportunity—new firms will enter, provided that entry is easy.

The model of perfect competition also assumes that exit will be easy if and when a firm experiences economic losses. When the Taliban rulers were ousted by the United States and its allies in 2001, Mr. Islamadin expected that the demand for burkhas would begin to fall. It did. The sales fell 50% almost immediately. Prices fell as well, generally by about 20%.

It was simple for Mr. Islamadin to leave the industry. He gave his remaining stock of burkhas to a brother who was producing them in the countryside where women continued to wear them. As for Mr. Islamadin, he has made plans to go into the glassware business. He expects the demand for glass teacups to be strong whatever happens in Afghanistan's critical future.

Source: Based on Andrew Higgins, "With Islamic Dress, Out Goes the Guy Who Sold Burkhas," The Wall Street Journal, December 19, 2001, p. A1.

Answers to Try It! Problems

1. Not perfectly competitive—There are few sellers in this market (Fedex, UPS, and the United States Postal Services are the main ones in the United States) probably because of the difficulty of entry and exit. To provide these services requires many outlets and a large transportation fleet, for example.
2. Perfectly competitive—There are many firms producing a largely homogeneous product and there is good information about prices. Entry and exit is also fairly easy as firms can switch among a variety of crops.
3. Not perfectly competitive—The main reason is that goods are not identical.

9.3 Output Determination in the Short Run

Learning Objectives

1. Show graphically how an individual firm in a perfectly competitive market can use total revenue and total cost curves or marginal revenue and marginal cost curves to determine the level of output that will maximize its economic profit.
2. Explain when a firm will shut down in the short run and when it will operate even if it is incurring economic losses.
3. Derive the firm's supply curve from the firm's marginal cost curve and the industry supply curve from the supply curves of individual firms.

Our goal in this section is to see how a firm in a perfectly competitive market determines its output level in the short run—a planning period in which at least one factor of production is fixed in quantity. We shall see that the firm can maximize economic profit by applying the marginal decision rule and increasing output up to the point at which the marginal benefit of an additional unit of output is just equal to the marginal cost. This fact has an important implication: over a wide range of output, the firm's marginal cost curve is its supply curve.

Price and Revenue

Each firm in a perfectly competitive market is a price taker; the equilibrium price and industry output are determined by demand and supply. Figure 9.1 shows how demand and supply in the market for radishes, which we shall assume are produced under conditions of perfect competition, determine total output and price. The equilibrium price is $0.40 per pound; the equilibrium quantity is 10 million pounds per month.

Because it is a price taker, each firm in the radish industry assumes it can sell all the radishes it wants at a price of $0.40 per pound. No matter how many or how few radishes it produces, the firm expects to sell them all at the market price.

The assumption that the firm expects to sell all the radishes it wants at the market price is crucial. If a firm did not expect to sell all of its radishes at the market price—if it had to lower the price to sell some quantities—the firm would not be a price taker. And price-taking behavior is central to the model of perfect competition.

Radish growers—and perfectly competitive firms in general—have no reason to charge a price lower than the market price. Because buyers have complete information and because we assume each firm's product is identical to that of its rivals, firms are unable to charge a price higher than the market price. For perfectly competitive firms, the price is very much like the weather: they may complain about it, but in perfect competition there is nothing any of them can do about it.

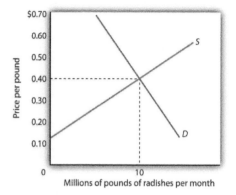

FIGURE 9.1 The Market for Radishes
Price and output in a competitive market are determined by demand and supply. In the market for radishes, the equilibrium price is $0.40 per pound; 10 million pounds per month are produced and purchased at this price.

Total Revenue

While a firm in a perfectly competitive market has no influence over its price, it does determine the output it will produce. In selecting the quantity of that output, one important consideration is the revenue the firm will gain by producing it.

A firm's **total revenue** is found by multiplying its output by the price at which it sells that output. For a perfectly competitive firm, total revenue (*TR*) is the market price (*P*) times the quantity the firm produces (*Q*), or

total revenue

A firm's output multiplied by the price at which it sells that output.

EQUATION 9.1

$$TR = P \times Q$$

The relationship between market price and the firm's total revenue curve is a crucial one. Panel (a) of Figure 9.2 shows total revenue curves for a radish grower at three possible market prices: $0.20, $0.40, and $0.60 per pound. Each total revenue curve is a linear, upward-sloping curve. At any price, the greater the quantity a perfectly competitive firm sells, the greater its total revenue. Notice that the greater the price, the steeper the total revenue curve is.

FIGURE 9.2 Total Revenue, Marginal Revenue, and Average Revenue

Panel (a) shows different total revenue curves for three possible market prices in perfect competition. A total revenue curve is a straight line coming out of the origin. The slope of a total revenue curve is *MR*; it equals the market price (*P*) and *AR* in perfect competition. Marginal revenue and average revenue are thus a single horizontal line at the market price, as shown in Panel (b). There is a different marginal revenue curve for each price.

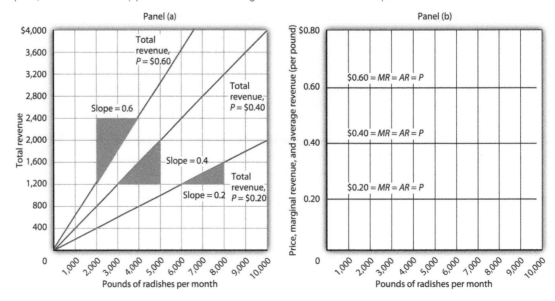

Price, Marginal Revenue, and Average Revenue

marginal revenue

The increase in total revenue from a one-unit increase in quantity.

The slope of a total revenue curve is particularly important. It equals the change in the vertical axis (total revenue) divided by the change in the horizontal axis (quantity) between any two points. The slope measures the rate at which total revenue increases as output increases. We can think of it as the increase in total revenue associated with a 1-unit increase in output. The increase in total revenue from a 1-unit increase in quantity is **marginal revenue**. Thus marginal revenue (*MR*) equals the slope of the total revenue curve.

How much additional revenue does a radish producer gain from selling one more pound of radishes? The answer, of course, is the market price for 1 pound. Marginal revenue equals the market price. Because the market price is not affected by the output choice of a single firm, the marginal revenue the firm gains by producing one more unit is always the market price. The marginal revenue curve shows the relationship between marginal revenue and the quantity a firm produces. For a perfectly competitive firm, the marginal revenue curve is a horizontal line at the market price. If the market price of a pound of radishes is $0.40, then the marginal revenue is $0.40. Marginal revenue curves for prices of $0.20, $0.40, and $0.60 are given in Panel (b) of Figure 9.2. In perfect competition, a firm's marginal revenue curve is a horizontal line at the market price.

average revenue

Total revenue divided by quantity.

Price also equals **average revenue**, which is total revenue divided by quantity. Equation 9.1 gives total revenue, *TR*. To obtain average revenue (*AR*), we divide total revenue by quantity, *Q*. Because total revenue equals price (*P*) times quantity (*Q*), dividing by quantity leaves us with price.

EQUATION 9.2

$$AR = \frac{TR}{Q} = \frac{P \times Q}{Q} = P$$

The marginal revenue curve is a horizontal line at the market price, and average revenue equals the market price. The average and marginal revenue curves are given by the same horizontal line. This is consistent with what we have learned about the relationship between marginal and average values. When the marginal value exceeds the average value, the average value will be rising. When the marginal value is less than the average value, the average value will be falling. What happens when the average and marginal values do not change, as in the horizontal curves of Panel (b) of Figure 9.2? The marginal value must equal the average value; the two curves coincide.

Marginal Revenue, Price, and Demand for the Perfectly Competitive Firm

We have seen that a perfectly competitive firm's marginal revenue curve is simply a horizontal line at the market price and that this same line is also the firm's average revenue curve. For the perfectly competitive firm, $MR = P = AR$. The marginal revenue curve has another meaning as well. It is the demand curve facing a perfectly competitive firm.

Consider the case of a single radish producer, Tony Gortari. We assume that the radish market is perfectly competitive; Mr. Gortari runs a perfectly competitive firm. Suppose the market price of radishes is $0.40 per pound. How many pounds of radishes can Mr. Gortari sell at this price? The answer comes from our assumption that he is a price taker: He can sell *any* quantity he wishes at this price. How many pounds of radishes will he sell if he charges a price that exceeds the market price? None. His radishes are identical to those of every other firm in the market, and everyone in the market has complete information. That means the demand curve facing Mr. Gortari is a horizontal line at the market price as illustrated in Figure 9.3. Notice that the curve is labeled *d* to distinguish it from the market demand curve, *D*, in Figure 9.1. The horizontal line in Figure 9.3 is also Mr. Gortari's marginal revenue curve, *MR*, and his average revenue curve, *AR*. It is also the market price, *P*.

Of course, Mr. Gortari could charge a price below the market price, but why would he? We assume he can sell all the radishes he wants at the market price; there would be no reason to charge a lower price. Mr. Gortari faces a demand curve that is a horizontal line at the market price. In our subsequent analysis, we shall refer to the horizontal line at the market price simply as marginal revenue. We should remember, however, that this same line gives us the market price, average revenue, and the demand curve facing the firm.

More generally, we can say that *any* perfectly competitive firm faces a horizontal demand curve at the market price. We saw an example of a horizontal demand curve in the chapter on elasticity. Such a curve is perfectly elastic, meaning that any quantity is demanded at a given price.

FIGURE 9.3 Price, Marginal Revenue, and Demand

A perfectly competitive firm faces a horizontal demand curve at the market price. Here, radish grower Tony Gortari faces demand curve *d* at the market price of $0.40 per pound. He could sell q_1 or q_2—or any other quantity—at a price of $0.40 per pound.

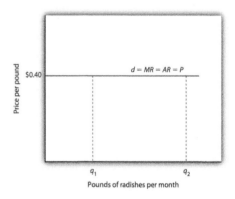

Economic Profit in the Short Run

A firm's economic profit is the difference between total revenue and total cost. Recall that total cost is the opportunity cost of producing a certain good or service. When we speak of economic profit we are speaking of a firm's total revenue less the total opportunity cost of its operations.

As we learned, a firm's total cost curve in the short run intersects the vertical axis at some positive value equal to the firm's total fixed costs. Total cost then rises at a decreasing rate over the range of increasing marginal returns to the firm's variable factors. It rises at an increasing rate over the range of diminishing marginal returns. Figure 9.4 shows the total cost curve for Mr. Gortari, as well as the total revenue curve for a price of $0.40 per pound. Suppose that his total fixed cost is $400 per month. For any given level of output, Mr. Gortari's economic profit is the vertical distance between the total revenue curve and the total cost curve at that level.

FIGURE 9.4 Total Revenue, Total Cost, and Economic Profit

Economic profit is the vertical distance between the total revenue and total cost curves (revenue minus costs). Here, the maximum profit attainable by Tony Gortari for his radish production is $938 per month at an output of 6,700 pounds.

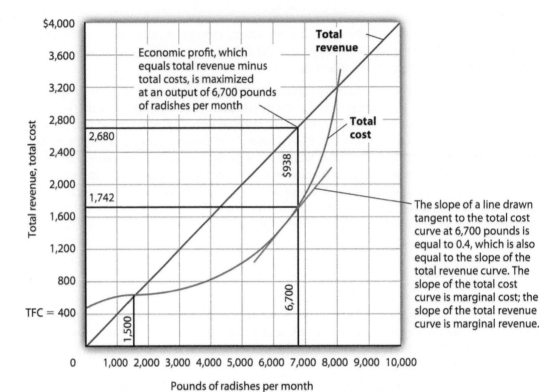

Let us examine the total revenue and total cost curves in Figure 9.4 more carefully. At zero units of output, Mr. Gortari's total cost is $400 (his total fixed cost); total revenue is zero. Total cost continues to exceed total revenue up to an output of 1,500 pounds per month, at which point the two curves intersect. At this point, economic profit equals zero. As Mr. Gortari expands output above 1,500 pounds per month, total revenue becomes greater than total cost. We see that at a quantity of 1,500 pounds per month, the total revenue curve is steeper than the total cost curve. Because revenues are rising faster than costs, profits rise with increased output. As long as the total revenue curve is steeper than the total cost curve, profit increases as the firm increases its output.

The total revenue curve's slope does not change as the firm increases its output. But the total cost curve becomes steeper and steeper as diminishing marginal returns set in. Eventually, the total cost and total revenue curves will have the same slope. That happens in Figure 9.4 at an output of 6,700 pounds of radishes per month. Notice that a line drawn tangent to the total cost curve at that quantity has the same slope as the total revenue curve.

As output increases beyond 6,700 pounds, the total cost curve continues to become steeper. It becomes steeper than the total revenue curve, and profits fall as costs rise faster than revenues. At an output slightly above 8,000 pounds per month, the total revenue and cost curves intersect again, and economic profit equals zero. Mr. Gortari achieves the greatest profit possible by producing 6,700 pounds of radishes per month, the quantity at which the total cost and total revenue curves have the same slope. More generally, we can conclude that a perfectly competitive firm maximizes economic profit at the output level at which the total revenue curve and the total cost curve have the same slope.

Applying the Marginal Decision Rule

The slope of the total revenue curve is marginal revenue; the slope of the total cost curve is marginal cost. Economic profit, the difference between total revenue and total cost, is maximized where marginal revenue equals marginal cost. This is consistent with the marginal decision rule, which holds that a profit-maximizing firm should increase output until the marginal benefit of an additional unit equals the marginal cost. The marginal benefit of selling an additional unit is measured as marginal revenue. Finding the output at which marginal revenue equals marginal cost is thus an application of our marginal decision rule.

Figure 9.5 shows how a firm can use the marginal decision rule to determine its profit-maximizing output. Panel (a) shows the market for radishes; the market demand curve (D), and supply curve (S) that we had in Figure 9.1; the market price is $0.40 per pound. In Panel (b), the MR curve is given by a horizontal line at the market price. The firm's marginal cost curve (MC) intersects the marginal revenue curve at the point where profit is maximized. Mr. Gortari maximizes profits by producing 6,700 pounds of radishes per month. That is, of course, the result we obtained in Figure 9.4, where we saw that the firm's total revenue and total cost curves differ by the greatest amount at the point at which the slopes of the curves, which equal marginal revenue and marginal cost, respectively, are equal.

FIGURE 9.5 Applying the Marginal Decision Rule
The market price is determined by the intersection of demand and supply. As always, the firm maximizes profit by applying the marginal decision rule. It takes the market price, $0.40 per pound, as given and selects an output at which MR equals MC. Economic profit per unit is the difference between ATC and price (here, $0.14 per pound); economic profit is profit per unit times the quantity produced ($0.14 × 6,700 = $938).

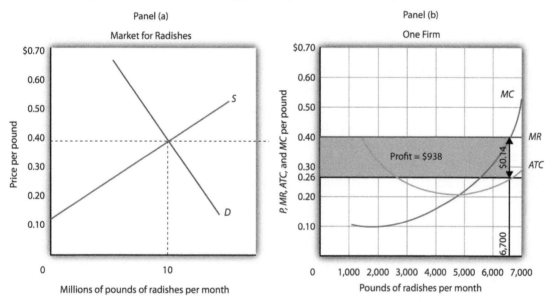

We can use the graph in Figure 9.5 to compute Mr. Gortari's economic profit. **Economic profit per unit** is the difference between price and average total cost. At the profit-maximizing output of 6,700 pounds of radishes per month, average total cost (ATC) is $0.26 per pound, as shown in Panel (b). Price is $0.40 per pound, so economic profit per unit is $0.14. Economic profit is found by multiplying economic profit per unit by the number of units produced; the firm's economic profit is thus $938 ($0.14 × 6,700). It is shown graphically by the area of the shaded rectangle in Panel (b); this area equals the vertical distance between marginal revenue (MR) and average total cost (ATC) at an output of 6,700 pounds of radishes times the number of pounds of radishes produced, 6,700, in Figure 9.5.

economic profit per unit

The difference between price and average total cost.

Heads Up!

Look carefully at the rectangle that shows economic profit in Panel (b) of Figure 9.5. It is found by taking the profit-maximizing quantity, 6,700 pounds, then reading up to the ATC curve and the firm's demand curve at the market price. Economic profit per unit equals price minus average total cost ($P - ATC$).

The firm's economic profit equals economic profit per unit times the quantity produced. It is found by extending horizontal lines from the ATC and MR curve to the vertical axis and taking the area of the rectangle formed.

There is no reason for the profit-maximizing quantity to correspond to the lowest point on the ATC curve; it does not in this case. Students sometimes make the mistake of calculating economic profit as the difference between the price and the lowest point on the ATC curve. That gives us the maximum economic profit per unit, but we assume that firms maximize economic profit, not economic profit per unit. The firm's economic profit equals economic profit per unit times quantity. The quantity that maximizes economic profit is determined by the intersection of ATC and MR.

Economic Losses in the Short Run

economic loss

The amount by which a firm's total cost exceeds its total revenue.

In the short run, a firm has one or more inputs whose quantities are fixed. That means that in the short run the firm cannot leave its industry. Even if it cannot cover *all* of its costs, including both its variable and fixed costs, going entirely out of business is not an option in the short run. The firm may close its doors, but it must continue to pay its fixed costs. It is forced to accept an **economic loss**, the amount by which its total cost exceeds its total revenue.

Suppose, for example, that a manufacturer has signed a 1-year lease on some equipment. It must make payments for this equipment during the term of its lease, whether it produces anything or not. During the period of the lease, the payments represent a fixed cost for the firm.

A firm that is experiencing economic losses—whose economic profits have become negative—in the short run may either continue to produce or shut down its operations, reducing its output to zero. It will choose the option that minimizes its losses. The crucial test of whether to operate or shut down lies in the relationship between price and average variable cost.

Producing to Minimize Economic Loss

Suppose the demand for radishes falls to D_2, as shown in Panel (a) of Figure 9.6. The market price for radishes plunges to $0.18 per pound, which is below average total cost. Consequently Mr. Gortari experiences negative economic profits—a loss. Although the new market price falls short of average total cost, it still exceeds average variable cost, shown in Panel (b) as AVC. Therefore, Mr. Gortari should continue to produce an output at which marginal cost equals marginal revenue. These curves (labeled MC and MR_2) intersect in Panel (b) at an output of 4,444 pounds of radishes per month.

FIGURE 9.6 Suffering Economic Losses in the Short Run

Tony Gortari experiences a loss when price drops below *ATC*, as it does in Panel (b) as a result of a reduction in demand. If price is above *AVC*, however, he can minimize his losses by producing where *MC* equals MR_2. Here, that occurs at an output of 4,444 pounds of radishes per month. The price is $0.18 per pound, and average total cost is $0.23 per pound. He loses $0.05 per pound, or $222.20 per month.

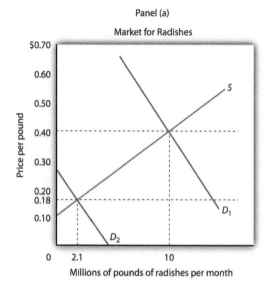

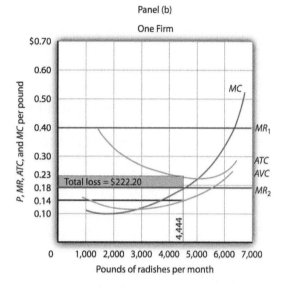

When producing 4,444 pounds of radishes per month, Mr. Gortari faces an average total cost of $0.23 per pound. At a price of $0.18 per pound, he loses a nickel on each pound produced. Total economic losses at an output of 4,444 pounds per month are thus $222.20 per month (=4,444×$0.05).

No producer likes a loss (that is, negative economic profit), but the loss solution shown in Figure 9.6 is the best Mr. Gortari can attain. Any level of production other than the one at which marginal cost equals marginal revenue would produce even greater losses.

Suppose Mr. Gortari were to shut down and produce no radishes. Ceasing production would reduce variable costs to zero, but he would still face fixed costs of $400 per month (recall that $400 was the vertical intercept of the total cost curve in Figure 9.4). By shutting down, Mr. Gortari would lose $400 per month. By continuing to produce, he loses only $222.20.

Mr. Gortari is better off producing where marginal cost equals marginal revenue because at that output price exceeds average variable cost. Average variable cost is $0.14 per pound, so by continuing to produce he covers his variable costs, with $0.04 per pound left over to apply to fixed costs. Whenever price is greater than average variable cost, the firm maximizes economic profit (or minimizes economic loss) by producing the output level at which marginal revenue and marginal cost curves intersect.

Shutting Down to Minimize Economic Loss

Suppose price drops below a firm's average variable cost. Now the best strategy for the firm is to shut down, reducing its output to zero. The minimum level of average variable cost, which occurs at the intersection of the marginal cost curve and the average variable cost curve, is called the **shutdown point**. Any price below the minimum value of average variable cost will cause the firm to shut down. If the firm were to continue producing, not only would it lose its fixed costs, but it would also face an additional loss by not covering its variable costs.

Figure 9.7 shows a case where the price of radishes drops to $0.10 per pound. Price is less than average variable cost, so Mr. Gortari not only would lose his fixed cost but would also incur additional losses by producing. Suppose, for example, he decided to operate where marginal cost equals marginal revenue, producing 1,700 pounds of radishes per month. Average variable cost equals $0.14 per pound, so he would lose $0.04 on each pound he produces ($68) plus his fixed cost of $400 per

shutdown point

The minimum level of average variable cost, which occurs at the intersection of the marginal cost curve and the average variable cost curve.

month. He would lose $468 per month. If he shut down, he would lose only his fixed cost. Because the price of $0.10 falls below his average variable cost, his best course would be to shut down.

FIGURE 9.7 Shutting Down
The market price of radishes drops to $0.10 per pound, so MR_3 is below Mr. Gortari's AVC. Thus he would suffer a greater loss by continuing to operate than by shutting down. Whenever price falls below average variable cost, the firm will shut down, reducing its production to zero.

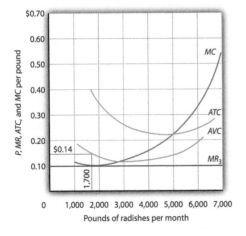

Shutting down is not the same thing as going out of business. A firm shuts down by closing its doors; it can reopen them whenever it expects to cover its variable costs. We can even think of a firm's decision to close at the end of the day as a kind of shutdown point; the firm makes this choice because it does not anticipate that it will be able to cover its variable cost overnight. It expects to cover those costs the next morning when it reopens its doors.

Marginal Cost and Supply

In the model of perfect competition, we assume that a firm determines its output by finding the point where the marginal revenue and marginal cost curves intersect. Provided that price exceeds average variable cost, the firm produces the quantity determined by the intersection of the two curves.

A supply curve tells us the quantity that will be produced at each price, and that is what the firm's marginal cost curve tells us. The firm's supply curve in the short run is its marginal cost curve for prices above the average variable cost. At prices below average variable cost, the firm's output drops to zero.

Panel (a) of Figure 9.8 shows the average variable cost and marginal cost curves for a hypothetical astrologer, Madame LaFarge, who is in the business of providing astrological consultations over the telephone. We shall assume that this industry is perfectly competitive. At any price below $10 per call, Madame LaFarge would shut down. If the price is $10 or greater, however, she produces an output at which price equals marginal cost. The marginal cost curve is thus her supply curve at all prices greater than $10.

FIGURE 9.8 Marginal Cost and Supply
The supply curve for a firm is that portion of its MC curve that lies above the AVC curve, shown in Panel (a). To obtain the short-run supply curve for the industry, we add the outputs of each firm at each price. The industry supply curve is given in Panel (b).

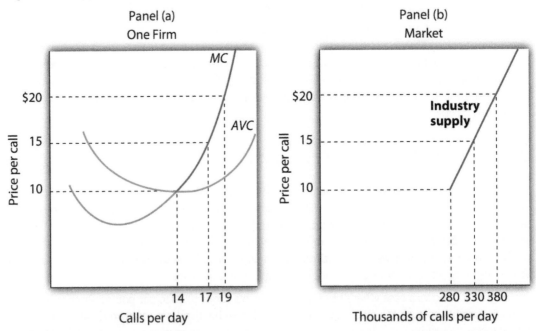

Now suppose that the astrological forecast industry consists of Madame LaFarge and thousands of other firms similar to hers. The market supply curve is found by adding the outputs of each firm at each price, as shown in Panel (b) of Figure 9.8. At a price of $10 per call, for example,

Madame LaFarge supplies 14 calls per day. Adding the quantities supplied by all the other firms in the market, suppose we get a quantity supplied of 280,000. Notice that the market supply curve we have drawn is linear; throughout the book we have made the assumption that market demand and supply curves are linear in order to simplify our analysis.

Looking at Figure 9.8, we see that profit-maximizing choices by firms in a perfectly competitive market will generate a market supply curve that reflects marginal cost. Provided there are no external benefits or costs in producing a good or service, a perfectly competitive market satisfies the efficiency condition.

Key Takeaways

- Price in a perfectly competitive industry is determined by the interaction of demand and supply.
- In a perfectly competitive industry, a firm's total revenue curve is a straight, upward-sloping line whose slope is the market price. Economic profit is maximized at the output level at which the slopes of the total revenue and total cost curves are equal, provided that the firm is covering its variable cost.
- To use the marginal decision rule in profit maximization, the firm produces the output at which marginal cost equals marginal revenue. Economic profit per unit is price minus average total cost; total economic profit equals economic profit per unit times quantity.
- If price falls below average total cost, but remains above average variable cost, the firm will continue to operate in the short run, producing the quantity where $MR = MC$ doing so minimizes its losses.
- If price falls below average variable cost, the firm will shut down in the short run, reducing output to zero. The lowest point on the average variable cost curve is called the shutdown point.
- The firm's supply curve in the short run is its marginal cost curve for prices greater than the minimum average variable cost.

Try It!

Assume that Acme Clothing, the firm introduced in the chapter on production and cost, produces jackets in a perfectly competitive market. Suppose the demand and supply curves for jackets intersect at a price of $81. Now, using the marginal cost and average total cost curves for Acme shown here:

Quantity/day	0	1	2	3	4	5	6	7	8	9	10	11
Total cost	$200	$300	$363	$400	$433	$458	$480	$500	$538	$600	$700	$900
AFC		$200	$100	$67	$50	$40	$33	$29	$25	$22	$20	$18
AVC		$100	$82	$67	$58	$52	$47	$43	$42	$44	$50	$64
ATC		$300	$182	$133	$108	$92	$80	$71	$67	$67	$70	$82
MC		$100	$63	$37	$33	$25	$22	$20	$38	$62	$100	$200

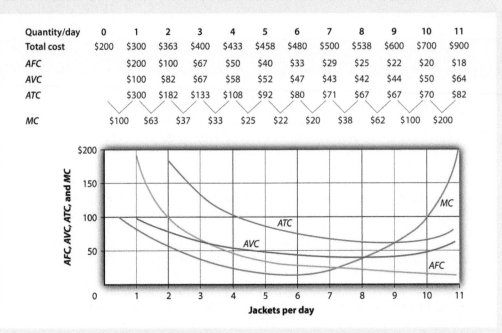

Estimate Acme's profit-maximizing output per day (assume the firm selects a whole number). What are Acme's economic profits per day?

Case in Point: Not Out of Business 'Til They Fall from the Sky

Source: © 2010 Jupiterimages Corporation

The 66 satellites were poised to start falling from the sky. The hope was that the pieces would burn to bits on their way down through the atmosphere, but there was the chance that a building or a person would take a direct hit.

The satellites were the primary communication devices of Iridium's satellite phone system. Begun in 1998 as the first truly global satellite system for mobile phones—providing communications across deserts, in the middle of oceans, and at the poles—Iridium expected five million subscribers to pay $7 a minute to talk on $3,000 handsets. In the climate of the late 1990s, users opted for cheaper, though less secure and less comprehensive, cell phones. By the end of the decade, Iridium had declared bankruptcy, shut down operations, and was just waiting for the satellites to start plunging from their orbits around 2007.

The only offer for Iridium's $5 billion system came from an ex-CEO of a nuclear reactor business, Dan Colussy, and it was for a measly $25 million. "It's like picking up a $150,000 Porsche 911 for $750," wrote *USA Today* reporter, Kevin Maney.

The purchase turned into a bonanza. In the wake of September 11, 2001, and then the wars in Afghanistan and Iraq, demand for secure communications in remote locations skyrocketed. New customers included the U.S. and British militaries, as well as reporters in Iraq, who, when traveling with the military were barred from using less secure systems that were easier to track.

The nonprofit organization Operation Call Home bought time to allow members of the 81st Armor Brigade of the Washington National Guard to communicate with their families at home. Airlines and shipping lines also signed up.

As the new Iridium became unburdened from the debt of the old one and technology improved, the lower fixed and variable costs contributed to Iridium's revival, but clearly a critical element in the turnaround has been increased demand. The launching of an additional seven spare satellites and other tinkering extended the life of the system. The firm was temporarily shut down but, with its new owners and new demand for its services, came roaring back.

Why did Colussy buy Iridium? A top executive in the new firm said that Colussy just found the elimination of the satellites a terrible waste. Perhaps he had some niche uses in mind, as even before September 11, 2001, he had begun to enroll some new customers, such as the Colombian national police, who no doubt found the system useful in fighting drug lords. But it was in the aftermath of 9/11 that its subscriber list really began to grow and its re-opening was deemed a stroke of genius.

Today the majority of Iridium's revenues come from private businesses involved in transportation, mining, forestry, recreation, construction, and emergency services, but government and military agencies remain important customers. It plans to launch its next-generation satellites in 2016 and 2017.

Sources: Based on Kevin Maney, "Remember Those 'Iridium's Going to Fail' Jokes? Prepare to Eat Your Hat," USA Today, April 9, 2003: p. 3B. Michael Mecham, "Handheld Comeback: A Resurrected Iridium Counts Aviation, Antiterrorism Among Its Growth Fields," Aviation Week and Space Technology, 161: 9 (September 6, 2004): p. 58. Press Release, July 28, 2016 at Iridium.com.

Answer to Try It! Problem

At a price of $81, Acme's marginal revenue curve is a horizontal line at $81. The firm produces the output at which marginal cost equals marginal revenue; the curves intersect at a quantity of near 9 jackets per day. Acme's average total cost at this level of output equals $67, for an economic profit per jacket of $14. Acme's economic profit per day equals about $126.

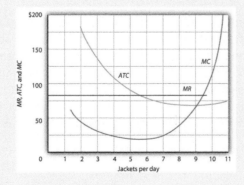

9.4 Perfect Competition in the Long Run

Learning Objectives

1. Distinguish between economic profit and accounting profit.
2. Explain why in long-run equilibrium in a perfectly competitive industry firms will earn zero economic profit.
3. Describe the three possible effects on the costs of the factors of production that expansion or contraction of a perfectly competitive industry may have and illustrate the resulting long-run industry supply curve in each case.
4. Explain why under perfection competition output prices will change by less than the change in production cost in the short run, but by the full amount of the change in production cost in the long run.
5. Explain the effect of a change in fixed cost on price and output in the short run and in the long run under perfect competition.

In the long run, a firm is free to adjust all of its inputs. New firms can enter any market; existing firms can leave their markets. We shall see in this section that the model of perfect competition predicts that, at a long-run equilibrium, production takes place at the lowest possible cost per unit and that all economic profits and losses are eliminated.

Economic Profit and Economic Loss

Economic profits and losses play a crucial role in the model of perfect competition. The existence of economic profits in a particular industry attracts new firms to the industry in the long run. As new firms enter, the supply curve shifts to the right, price falls, and profits fall. Firms continue to enter the industry until economic profits fall to zero. If firms in an industry are experiencing economic losses, some will leave. The supply curve shifts to the left, increasing price and reducing losses. Firms continue to leave until the remaining firms are no longer suffering losses—until economic profits are zero.

Before examining the mechanism through which entry and exit eliminate economic profits and losses, we shall examine an important key to understanding it: the difference between the accounting and economic concepts of profit and loss.

Economic Versus Accounting Concepts of Profit and Loss

Economic profit equals total revenue minus total cost, where cost is measured in the economic sense as opportunity cost. An economic loss (negative economic profit) is incurred if total cost exceeds total revenue.

explicit costs

Charges that must be paid for factors of production such as labor and capital.

accounting profit

Profit computed using only explicit costs.

Accountants include only explicit costs in their computation of total cost. **Explicit costs** include charges that must be paid for factors of production such as labor and capital, together with an estimate of depreciation. Profit computed using only explicit costs is called **accounting profit**. It is the measure of profit firms typically report; firms pay taxes on their accounting profits, and a corporation reporting its profit for a particular period reports its accounting profits. To compute his accounting profits, Mr. Gortari, the radish farmer, would subtract explicit costs, such as charges for labor, equipment, and other supplies, from the revenue he receives.

Economists recognize costs in addition to the explicit costs listed by accountants. If Mr. Gortari were not growing radishes, he could be doing something else with the land and with his own efforts. Suppose the most valuable alternative use of his land would be to produce carrots, from which Mr. Gortari could earn $250 per month in accounting profits. The income he forgoes by not producing carrots is an opportunity cost of producing radishes. This cost is not explicit; the return Mr. Gortari could get from producing carrots will not appear on a conventional accounting statement of his accounting profit. A cost that is included in the economic concept of opportunity cost, but that is not an explicit cost, is called an **implicit cost**.

implicit cost

A cost that is included in the economic concept of opportunity cost but that is not an explicit cost.

The Long Run and Zero Economic Profits

Given our definition of economic profits, we can easily see why, in perfect competition, they must always equal zero in the long run. Suppose there are two industries in the economy, and that firms in Industry A are earning economic profits. By definition, firms in Industry A are earning a return greater than the return available in Industry B. That means that firms in Industry B are earning less than they could in Industry A. Firms in Industry B are experiencing economic losses.

Given easy entry and exit, some firms in Industry B will leave it and enter Industry A to earn the greater profits available there. As they do so, the supply curve in Industry B will shift to the left, increasing prices and profits there. As former Industry B firms enter Industry A, the supply curve in Industry A will shift to the right, lowering profits in A. The process of firms leaving Industry B and entering A will continue until firms in both industries are earning zero economic profit. That suggests an important long-run result: *Economic profits in a system of perfectly competitive markets will, in the long run, be driven to zero in all industries.*

Eliminating Economic Profit: The Role of Entry

The process through which entry will eliminate economic profits in the long run is illustrated in Figure 9.9, which is based on the situation presented in Figure 9.5. The price of radishes is $0.40 per pound. Mr. Gortari's average total cost at an output of 6,700 pounds of radishes per month is $0.26 per pound. Profit per unit is $0.14 ($0.40 - $0.26). Mr. Gortari thus earns a profit of $938 per month (=$0.14 × 6,700).

FIGURE 9.9 Eliminating Economic Profits in the Long Run
If firms in an industry are making an economic profit, entry will occur in the long run. In Panel (b), a single firm's profit is shown by the shaded area. Entry continues until firms in the industry are operating at the lowest point on their respective average total cost curves, and economic profits fall to zero.

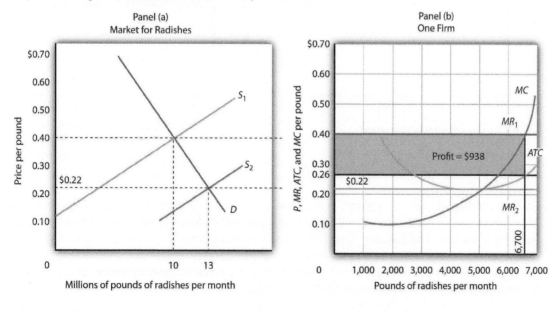

Profits in the radish industry attract entry in the long run. Panel (a) of Figure 9.9 shows that as firms enter, the supply curve shifts to the right and the price of radishes falls. New firms enter as long as there are economic profits to be made—as long as price exceeds *ATC* in Panel (b). As price falls, marginal revenue falls to MR_2 and the firm reduces the quantity it supplies, moving along the marginal cost (*MC*) curve to the lowest point on the *ATC* curve, at $0.22 per pound and an output of 5,000 pounds per month. Although the output of individual firms falls in response to falling prices, there are now more firms, so industry output rises to 13 million pounds per month in Panel (a).

Eliminating Losses: The Role of Exit

Just as entry eliminates economic profits in the long run, exit eliminates economic losses. In Figure 9.10, Panel (a) shows the case of an industry in which the market price P_1 is below *ATC*. In Panel (b), at price P_1 a single firm produces a quantity q_1, assuming it is at least covering its average variable cost. The firm's losses are shown by the shaded rectangle bounded by its average total cost C_1 and price P_1 and by output q_1.

Because firms in the industry are losing money, some will exit. The supply curve in Panel (a) shifts to the left, and it continues shifting as long as firms are suffering losses. Eventually the supply curve shifts all the way to S_2, price rises to P_2, and economic profits return to zero.

FIGURE 9.10 Eliminating Economic Losses in the Long Run
Panel (b) shows that at the initial price P_1, firms in the industry cannot cover average total cost (MR_1 is below *ATC*). That induces some firms to leave the industry, shifting the supply curve in Panel (a) to S_2, reducing industry output to Q_2 and raising price to P_2. At that price (MR_2), firms earn zero economic profit, and exit from the industry ceases. Panel (b) shows that the firm increases output from q_1 to q_2; total output in the market falls in Panel (a) because there are fewer firms. Notice that in Panel (a) quantity is designated by uppercase *Q*, while in Panel (b) quantity is designated by lowercase *q*. This convention is used throughout the text to distinguish between the quantity supplied in the market (*Q*) and the quantity supplied by a typical firm (*q*).

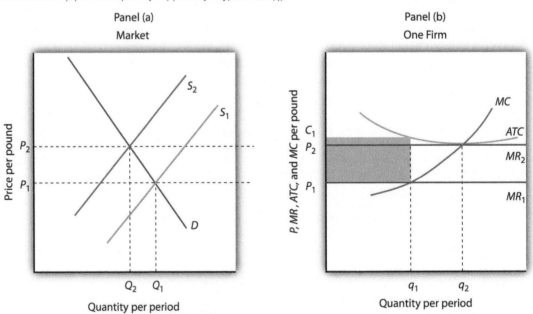

Entry, Exit, and Production Costs

constant-cost industry

Industry in which expansion does not affect the prices of factors of production.

In our examination of entry and exit in response to economic profit or loss in a perfectly competitive industry, we assumed that the *ATC* curve of a single firm does not shift as new firms enter or existing firms leave the industry. That is the case when expansion or contraction does not affect prices for the factors of production used by firms in the industry. When expansion of the industry does not affect the prices of factors of production, it is a **constant-cost industry**. In some cases, however, the entry of new firms may affect input prices.

As new firms enter, they add to the demand for the factors of production used by the industry. If the industry is a significant user of those factors, the increase in demand could push up the market price of factors of production for all firms in the industry. If that occurs, then entry into an industry will boost average costs at the same time as it puts downward pressure on price. Long-run equilibrium will still occur at a zero level of economic profit and with firms operating on the lowest point on the *ATC* curve, but that cost curve will be somewhat higher than before entry occurred. Suppose, for example, that an increase in demand for new houses drives prices higher and induces entry. That will increase the demand for workers in the construction industry and is likely to result in higher wages in the industry, driving up costs.

An industry in which the entry of new firms bids up the prices of factors of production and thus increases production costs is called an **increasing-cost industry**. As such an industry expands in the long run, its price will rise.

Some industries may experience reductions in input prices as they expand with the entry of new firms. That may occur because firms supplying the industry experience economies of scale as they increase production, thus driving input prices down. Expansion may also induce technological changes that lower input costs. That is clearly the case of the computer industry, which has enjoyed falling input costs as it has expanded. An industry in which production costs fall as firms enter in the long run is a **decreasing-cost industry**.

Just as industries may expand with the entry of new firms, they may contract with the exit of existing firms. In a constant-cost industry, exit will not affect the input prices of remaining firms. In an increasing-cost industry, exit will reduce the input prices of remaining firms. And, in a decreasing-cost industry, input prices may rise with the exit of existing firms.

The behavior of production costs as firms in an industry expand or reduce their output has important implications for the **long-run industry supply curve**, a curve that relates the price of a good or service to the quantity produced after all long-run adjustments to a price change have been completed. Every point on a long-run supply curve therefore shows a price and quantity supplied at which firms in the industry are earning zero economic profit. Unlike the short-run market supply curve, the long-run industry supply curve does not hold factor costs and the number of firms unchanged.

Figure 9.11 shows three long-run industry supply curves. In Panel (a), S_{CC} is a long-run supply curve for a constant-cost industry. It is horizontal. Neither expansion nor contraction by itself affects market price. In Panel (b), S_{IC} is a long-run supply curve for an increasing-cost industry. It rises as the industry expands. In Panel (c), S_{DC} is a long-run supply curve for a decreasing-cost industry. Its downward slope suggests a falling price as the industry expands.

increasing-cost industry

Industry in which the entry of new firms bids up the prices of factors of production and thus increases production costs.

decreasing-cost industry

Industry in which production costs fall in the long run as firms enter.

long-run industry supply curve

A curve that relates the price of a good or service to the quantity produced after all long-run adjustments to a price change have been completed.

FIGURE 9.11 Long-Run Supply Curves in Perfect Competition
The long-run supply curve for a constant-cost, perfectly competitive industry is a horizontal line, S_{CC}, shown in Panel (a). The long-run curve for an increasing-cost industry is an upward-sloping curve, S_{IC}, as in Panel (b). The downward-sloping long-run supply curve, S_{DC}, for a decreasing cost industry is given in Panel (c).

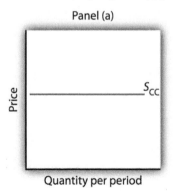
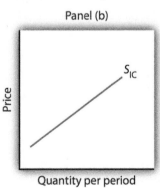
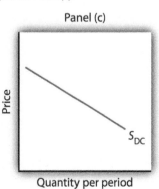

Changes in Demand and in Production Cost

The primary application of the model of perfect competition is in predicting how firms will respond to changes in demand and in production costs. To see how firms respond to a particular change, we determine how the change affects demand or cost conditions and then see how the profit-maximizing solution is affected in the short run and in the long run. Having determined how the profit-maximizing firms of the model would respond, we can then predict firms' responses to similar changes in the real world.

In the examples that follow, we shall assume, for simplicity, that entry or exit do not affect the input prices facing firms in the industry. That is, we assume a constant-cost industry with a horizontal long-run industry supply curve similar to S_{CC} in Figure 9.11. We shall assume that firms are covering their average variable costs, so we can ignore the possibility of shutting down.

Changes in Demand

Changes in demand can occur for a variety of reasons. There may be a change in preferences, incomes, the price of a related good, population, or consumer expectations. A change in demand causes a change in the market price, thus shifting the marginal revenue curves of firms in the industry.

Let us consider the impact of a change in demand for oats. Suppose new evidence suggests that eating oats not only helps to prevent heart disease, but also prevents baldness in males. This will, of course, increase the demand for oats. To assess the impact of this change, we assume that the industry is perfectly competitive and that it is initially in long-run equilibrium at a price of $1.70 per bushel. Economic profits equal zero.

The initial situation is depicted in Figure 9.12. Panel (a) shows that at a price of $1.70, industry output is Q_1 (point A), while Panel (b) shows that the market price constitutes the marginal revenue, MR_1, facing a single firm in the industry. The firm responds to that price by finding the output level at which the MC and MR_1 curves intersect. That implies a level of output q_1 at point A′.

The new medical evidence causes demand to increase to D_2 in Panel (a). That increases the market price to $2.30 (point B), so the marginal revenue curve for a single firm rises to MR_2 in Panel (b). The firm responds by increasing its output to q_2 in the short run (point B′). Notice that the firm's average total cost is slightly higher than its original level of $1.70; that is because of the U shape of the curve. The firm is making an economic profit shown by the shaded rectangle in Panel (b). Other firms in the industry will earn an economic profit as well, which, in the long run, will attract entry by new firms. New entry will shift the supply curve to the right; entry will continue as long as firms are making an economic profit. The supply curve in Panel (a) shifts to S_2, driving the price down in the long run to the original level of $1.70 per bushel and returning economic profits to zero in long-run equilibrium. A single firm will return to its original level of output, q_1 (point A′) in Panel (b), but because there are more firms in the industry, industry output rises to Q_3 (point C) in Panel (a).

FIGURE 9.12 Short-Run and Long-Run Adjustments to an Increase in Demand

The initial equilibrium price and output are determined in the market for oats by the intersection of demand and supply at point A in Panel (a). An increase in the market demand for oats, from D_1 to D_2 in Panel (a), shifts the equilibrium solution to point B. The price increases in the short run from $1.70 per bushel to $2.30. Industry output rises to Q_2. For a single firm, the increase in price raises marginal revenue from MR_1 to MR_2; the firm responds in the short run by increasing its output to q_2. It earns an economic profit given by the shaded rectangle. In the long run, the opportunity for profit attracts new firms. In a constant-cost industry, the short-run supply curve shifts to S_2; market equilibrium now moves to point C in Panel (a). The market price falls back to $1.70. The firm's demand curve returns to MR_1, and its output falls back to the original level, q_1. Industry output has risen to Q_3 because there are more firms.

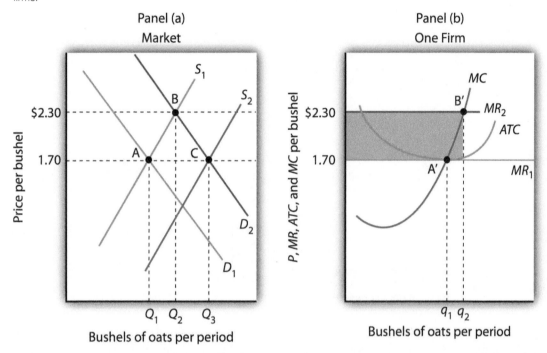

Panel (a)
Market

Panel (b)
One Firm

A reduction in demand would lead to a reduction in price, shifting each firm's marginal revenue curve downward. Firms would experience economic losses, thus causing exit in the long run and shifting the supply curve to the left. Eventually, the price would rise back to its original level, assuming changes in industry output did not lead to changes in input prices. There would be fewer firms in the industry, but each firm would end up producing the same output as before.

Changes in Production Cost

A firm's costs change if the costs of its inputs change. They also change if the firm is able to take advantage of a change in technology. Changes in production cost shift the ATC curve. If a firm's variable costs are affected, its marginal cost curves will shift as well. Any change in marginal cost produces a similar change in industry supply, since it is found by adding up marginal cost curves for individual firms.

Suppose a reduction in the price of oil reduces the cost of producing oil changes for automobiles. We shall assume that the oil-change industry is perfectly competitive and that it is initially in long-run equilibrium at a price of $27 per oil change, as shown in Panel (a) of Figure 9.13. Suppose that the reduction in oil prices reduces the cost of an oil change by $3.

FIGURE 9.13 A Reduction in the Cost of Producing Oil Changes

The initial equilibrium price, $27, and quantity, Q_1, of automobile oil changes are determined by the intersection of market demand, D_1, and market supply, S_1 in Panel (a). The industry is in long-run equilibrium; a typical firm, shown in Panel (b), earns zero economic profit. A reduction in oil prices reduces the marginal and average total costs of producing an oil change by $3. The firm's marginal cost curve shifts to MC_2, and its average total cost curve shifts to ATC_2. The short-run industry supply curve shifts down by $3 to S_2. The market price falls to $26; the firm increases its output to q_2 and earns an economic profit given by the shaded rectangle. In the long run, the opportunity for profit shifts the industry supply curve to S_3. The price falls to $24, and the firm reduces its output to the original level, q_1. It now earns zero economic profit once again. Industry output in Panel (a) rises to Q_3 because there are more firms; price has fallen by the full amount of the reduction in production costs.

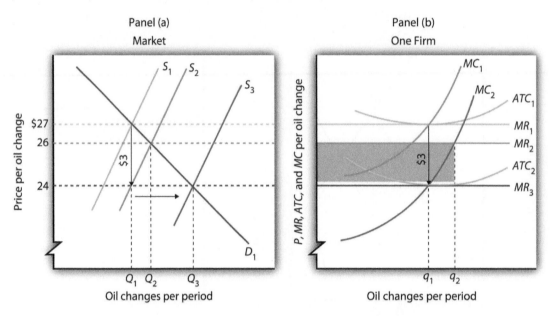

A reduction in production cost shifts the firm's cost curves down. The firm's average total cost and marginal cost curves shift down, as shown in Panel (b). In Panel (a) the supply curve shifts from S_1 to S_2. The industry supply curve is made up of the marginal cost curves of individual firms; because each of them has shifted downward by $3, the industry supply curve shifts downward by $3.

Notice that price in the short run falls to $26; it does not fall by the $3 reduction in cost. That is because the supply and demand curves are sloped. While the supply curve shifts downward by $3, its intersection with the demand curve falls by less than $3. The firm in Panel (b) responds to the lower price and lower cost by increasing output to q_2, where MC_2 and MR_2 intersect. That leaves firms in the industry with an economic profit; the economic profit for the firm is shown by the shaded rectangle in Panel (b). Profits attract entry in the long run, shifting the supply curve to the right to S_3 in Panel (a) Entry will continue as long as firms are making an economic profit—it will thus continue until the price falls by the full amount of the $3 reduction in cost. The price falls to $24, industry output rises to Q_3, and the firm's output returns to its original level, q_1.

An increase in variable costs would shift the average total, average variable, and marginal cost curves upward. It would shift the industry supply curve upward by the same amount. The result in the short run would be an increase in price, but by less than the increase in cost per unit. Firms would experience economic losses, causing exit in the long run. Eventually, price would increase by the full amount of the increase in production cost.

Some cost increases will not affect marginal cost. Suppose, for example, that an annual license fee of $5,000 is imposed on firms in a particular industry. The fee is a fixed cost; it does not affect marginal cost. Imposing such a fee shifts the average total cost curve upward but causes no change in marginal cost. There is no change in price or output in the short run. Because firms are suffering economic losses, there will be exit in the long run. Prices ultimately rise by enough to cover the cost of the fee, leaving the remaining firms in the industry with zero economic profit.

Price will change to reflect whatever change we observe in production cost. A change in variable cost causes price to change in the short run. In the long run, any change in average total cost changes price by an equal amount.

The message of long-run equilibrium in a competitive market is a profound one. The ultimate beneficiaries of the innovative efforts of firms are consumers. Firms in a perfectly competitive world earn zero profit in the long-run. While firms can earn accounting profits in the long-run, they cannot earn economic profits.

Key Takeaways

- The economic concept of profit differs from accounting profit. The accounting concept deals only with explicit costs, while the economic concept of profit incorporates explicit and implicit costs.

- The existence of economic profits attracts entry, economic losses lead to exit, and in long-run equilibrium, firms in a perfectly competitive industry will earn zero economic profit.

- The long-run supply curve in an industry in which expansion does not change input prices (a constant-cost industry) is a horizontal line. The long-run supply curve for an industry in which production costs increase as output rises (an increasing-cost industry) is upward sloping. The long-run supply curve for an industry in which production costs decrease as output rises (a decreasing-cost industry) is downward sloping.

- In a perfectly competitive market in long-run equilibrium, an increase in demand creates economic profit in the short run and induces entry in the long run; a reduction in demand creates economic losses (negative economic profits) in the short run and forces some firms to exit the industry in the long run.

- When production costs change, price will change by less than the change in production cost in the short run. Price will adjust to reflect fully the change in production cost in the long run.

- A change in fixed cost will have no effect on price or output in the short run. It will induce entry or exit in the long run so that price will change by enough to leave firms earning zero economic profit.

Try It!

Consider Acme Clothing's situation in "Try It!". Suppose this situation is typical of firms in the jacket market. Explain what will happen in the market for jackets in the long run, assuming nothing happens to the prices of factors of production used by firms in the industry. What will happen to the equilibrium price? What is the equilibrium level of economic profits?

Case in Point: Competition in the Market for Generic Prescription Drugs

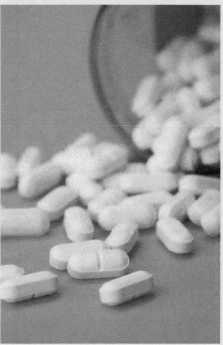

Source: © 2010 Jupiterimages Corporation

Generic prescription drugs are essentially identical substitutes for more expensive brand-name prescription drugs. Since the passage of the Drug Competition and Patent Term Restoration Act of 1984 (commonly referred to as the Hatch-Waxman Act) made it easier for manufacturers to enter the market for generic drugs, the generic drug industry has taken off. Generic drugs represented 19 percent of the prescription drug industry in 1984 and today represent nearly 90 percent of prescriptions but only 28 percent of drug spending. U.S. generic sales were $29 billion in 1995 and soared to $176 billion in 2009. Health care cost savings from generics amounted to $87 billion dollars in 2005 and $254 billion in 2014.

The Federal Drug Administration reports that, roughly speaking, the greater the number of generic competitors the lower the price of the generic drugs. As shown in the figure below, while the entry of a single generic drug manufacturer only results in the price falling by 6 percent compared to the pre-expiry branded drug price, two competitors results in a price decrease of a whopping 48 percent. Six to thirteen manufacturers leads to the ratio of the average generic drug price to the branded drug price falling between 20 percent and 26 percent. That ratio falls to single digits when the number of competitors rises to 17 or more.

FIGURE 9.14 Generic Competition and Drug Prices

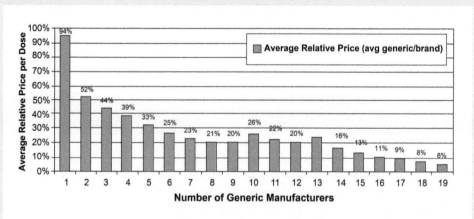

The generic drug industry is largely characterized by the attributes of a perfectly competitive market. Competitors have good information about the product and sell identical products. The 1984 legislation eased entry into this market. And as the model of perfect competition predicts, entry has driven prices down, benefiting consumers to the tune of now hundreds of billions of dollars each year.

Sources: Based on U.S. Food and Drug Administration, "Generic Competition and Drug Prices," available at http://bit.ly/2fldH9h and Generic Pharmaceutical Association, "Generic Drug Savings in the U.S., 7th Annual Edition:2015," available at http://www.gphaonline.org/media/wysiwyg/PDF/GPhA_Savings_Report_2015.pdf.

Answer to Try It! Problem

The availability of economic profits will attract new firms to the jacket industry in the long run, shifting the market supply curve to the right. Entry will continue until economic profits are eliminated. The price will fall; Acme's marginal revenue curve shifts down. The equilibrium level of economic profits in the long run is zero.

9.5 Review and Practice

Summary

The assumptions of the model of perfect competition ensure that every decision maker is a price taker—the interaction of demand and supply in the market determines price. Although most firms in real markets have some control over their prices, the model of perfect competition suggests how changes in demand or in production cost will affect price and output in a wide range of real-world cases.

A firm in perfect competition maximizes profit in the short run by producing an output level at which marginal revenue equals marginal cost, provided marginal revenue is at least as great as the minimum value of average variable cost. For a perfectly competitive firm, marginal revenue equals price and average revenue. This implies that the firm's marginal cost curve is its short-run supply curve for values greater than average variable cost. If price drops below average variable cost, the firm shuts down.

If firms in an industry are earning economic profit, entry by new firms will drive price down until economic profit achieves its long-run equilibrium value of zero. If firms are suffering economic losses, exit by existing firms will continue until price rises to eliminate the losses and economic profits are zero. A long-run equilibrium may be changed by a change in demand or in production cost, which would affect supply. The adjustment to the change in the short run is likely to result in economic profits or losses; these will be eliminated in the long run by entry or by exit.

Concept Problems

1. Explain how each of the assumptions of perfect competition contributes to the fact that all decision makers in perfect competition are price takers.

2. If the assumptions of perfect competition are not likely to be met in the real world, how can the model be of any use?

3. Explain the difference between marginal revenue, average revenue, and price in perfect competition.

4. Suppose the only way a firm can increase its sales is to lower its price. Is this a perfectly competitive firm? Why or why not?

5. Consider the following goods and services. Which are the most likely to be produced in a perfectly competitive industry? Which are not? Explain why you made the choices you did, relating your answer to the assumptions of the model of perfect competition.

    a. Coca-Cola and Pepsi

    b. Potatoes

    c. Private physicians in your local community

    d. Government bonds and corporate stocks

    e. Taxicabs in Lima, Peru—a city that does not restrict entry or the prices drivers can charge

    f. Oats

6. Explain why an economic profit of zero is acceptable to a firm.

7. Explain why a perfectly competitive firm whose average total cost exceeds the market price may continue to operate in the short run. What about the long run?

8. You have decided to major in biology rather than computer science. A news report suggests that the salaries of computer science majors are increasing. How does this affect the opportunity cost of your choice?

9. Explain how each of the following events would affect the marginal cost curves of firms and thus the supply curve in a perfectly competitive market in the short run.

    a. An increase in wages

    b. A tax of $1 per unit of output imposed on the seller

    c. The introduction of cost-cutting technology

    d. The imposition of an annual license fee of $1,000

10. In a perfectly competitive market, who benefits from an event that lowers production costs for firms?

11. Dry-cleaning establishments generate a considerable amount of air pollution in producing cleaning services. Suppose these firms are allowed to pollute without restriction and that reducing their pollution would add significantly to their production costs. Who benefits from the fact that they pollute the air? Now suppose the government requires them to reduce their pollution. Who will pay for the cleanup? (Assume dry cleaning is a perfectly competitive industry, and answer these questions from a long-run perspective.)

12. The late columnist William F. Buckley, commenting on a strike by the Teamsters Union against UPS in 1997, offered this bit of economic analysis to explain how UPS had succeeded in reducing its average total cost: "UPS had done this by economies of scale. Up to a point (where the marginal cost equals the price of the marginal unit), the larger the busi-

ness, the less the per-unit cost." Use the concept of economies of scale, together with the information presented in this chapter, to explain the error in Mr. Buckley's statement. [1]

13. Suppose that a perfectly competitive industry is in long-run equilibrium and experiences an increase in production cost. Who will bear the burden of the increase? Is this fair?

14. Economists argue that the ultimate beneficiaries of the efforts of perfectly competitive firms are consumers. In what sense is this the case? Do the owners of perfectly competitive firms derive any long-run benefit from their efforts?

15. Explain carefully why a fixed license fee does not shift a firm's marginal cost curve in the short run. What about the long run?

Numerical Problems

1. The graph below provides revenue and cost information for a perfectly competitive firm producing paper clips.

Output	Total Revenue	Total Variable Cost	Total Fixed Cost
1	$1,000	$1,500	$500
2	$2,000	$2,000	$500
3	$3,000	$2,600	$500
4	$4,000	$3,900	$500
5	$5,000	$5,000	$500

a. How much are total fixed costs?

b. About how much are total variable costs if 5,000 paper clips are produced?

c. What is the price of a paper clip?

d. What is the average revenue from producing paper clips?

e. What is the marginal revenue of producing paper clips?

f. Over what output range will this firm earn economic profits?

g. Over what output range will this firm incur economic losses?

h. What is the slope of the total revenue curve?

i. What is the slope of the total cost curve at the profit-maximizing number of paper clips per hour?

j. At about how many paper clips per hour do economic profits seem to be at a maximum?

2. Suppose rocking-chair manufacturing is a perfectly competitive industry in which there are 1,000 identical firms. Each firm's total cost is related to output per day as follows:

Quantity	Total cost	Quantity	Total cost
0	$500	5	$2,200
1	$1,000	6	$2,700
2	$1,300	7	$3,300
3	$1,500	8	$4,400
4	$1,800		

a. Prepare a table that shows total variable cost, average total cost, and marginal cost at each level of output.

b. Plot the average total cost, average variable cost, and marginal cost curves for a single firm (remember that values for marginal cost are plotted at the midpoint of the respective intervals).

c. What is the firm's supply curve? How many chairs would the firm produce at prices of $350, $450, $550, and $650? (In computing quantities, assume that a firm produces a certain number of completed chairs each day; it does not produce fractions of a chair on any one day.)

d. Suppose the demand curve in the market for rocking chairs is given by the following table:

Price	Quantity of chairs Demanded/day	Price	Quantity of chairs Demanded/day
$650	5,000	$450	7,000
$550	6,000	$350	8,000

Plot the market demand curve for chairs. Compute and plot the market supply curve, using the information you obtained for a single firm in part (c). What is the equilibrium price? The equilibrium quantity?

e. Given your solution in part (d), plot the total revenue and total cost curves for a single firm. Does your graph correspond to your solution in part (c)? Explain.

3. The following table shows the total output, total revenue, total variable cost, and total fixed cost of a firm. What level of output should the firm produce? Should it shut down? Should it exit the industry? Explain.

Output	Total revenue	Total variable cost	Total fixed cost
1	$1,000	$1,500	$500
2	$2,000	$2,000	$500
3	$3,000	$2,600	$500
4	$4,000	$3,900	$500
5	$5,000	$5,000	$500

4. Suppose a rise in fuel costs increases the cost of producing oats by $0.50 per bushel. Illustrate graphically how this change will affect the oat market and a single firm in the market in the short run and in the long run.

5. Suppose the demand for car washes in Collegetown falls as a result of a cutback in college enrollment. Show graphically how the price and output for the market and for a single firm will be affected in the short run and in the long run. Assume the market is perfectly competitive and that it is initially in long-run equilibrium at a price of $12 per car wash. Assume also that input prices don't change as the market responds to the change in demand.

6. Suppose that the market for dry-erase pens is perfectly competitive and that the pens cost $1 each. The industry is in long-run equilibrium. Now suppose that an increase in the cost of ink raises the production cost of the pens by $.25 per pen.

a. Using a graph that shows the market as a whole and a typical firm in this market, illustrate the short run effects of the change.

b. Is the price likely to rise by $.25? Why or why not?

c. If it doesn't, are firms likely to continue to operate in the short run? Why or why not?

d. What is likely to happen in the long run? Illustrate your results with a large, clearly labeled graph.

Endnotes

1. William F. Buckley, "The Teamsters' Package Deal," Corlandt Forum, Vol. 10, Issue 10, 25 October 1997, p. 285.

CHAPTER 10

Monopoly

10.1 Start Up: Surrounded by Monopolies

If your college or university is like most, you spend a lot of time, and money, dealing with firms that face very little competition. Your campus bookstore is likely to be the only local firm selling the texts that professors require you to read. Your school may have granted an exclusive franchise to a single firm for food service and to another firm for vending machines. A single firm may provide your utilities—electricity, natural gas, and water.

Unlike the individual firms we have previously studied that operate in a competitive market, taking the price, which is determined by demand and supply, as given, in this chapter we investigate the behavior of firms that have their markets all to themselves. As the only suppliers of particular goods or services, they face the downward-sloping market demand curve alone.

We will find that firms that have their markets all to themselves behave in a manner that is in many respects quite different from the behavior of firms in perfect competition. Such firms continue to use the marginal decision rule in maximizing profits, but their freedom to select from the price and quantity combinations given by the market demand curve affects the way in which they apply this rule.

We will show that a monopoly firm is likely to produce less and charge more for what it produces than firms in a competitive industry. As a result, a monopoly solution is likely to be inefficient from society's perspective. We will explore the policy alternatives available to government agencies in dealing with monopoly firms. First, though, we will look at characteristics of monopoly and at conditions that give rise to monopolies in the first place.

10.2 The Nature of Monopoly

Learning Objectives

1. Define monopoly and the relationship between price setting and monopoly power.
2. List and explain the sources of monopoly power and how they can change over time.
3. Define what is meant by a natural monopoly.

Monopoly is at the opposite end of the spectrum of market models from perfect competition. A **monopoly** firm has no rivals. It is the only firm in its industry. There are no close substitutes for the good or service a monopoly produces. Not only does a monopoly firm have the market to itself, but it also need not worry about other firms entering. In the case of monopoly, entry by potential rivals is prohibitively difficult.

A monopoly does not take the market price as given; it determines its own price. It selects from its demand curve the price that corresponds to the quantity the firm has chosen to produce in order to earn the maximum profit possible. The entry of new firms, which eliminates profit in the long run in a competitive market, cannot occur in the monopoly model.

monopoly

A firm that is the only producer of a good or service for which there are no close substitutes and for which entry by potential rivals is prohibitively difficult.

price setter

A firm that sets or picks price based on its output decision.

monopoly power

The ability to act as a price setter.

A firm that sets or picks price based on its output decision is called a **price setter**. A firm that acts as a price setter possesses **monopoly power**. We shall see in the next chapter that monopolies are not the only firms that have this power; however, the absence of rivals in monopoly gives it much more price-setting power.

As was the case when we discussed perfect competition in the previous chapter, the assumptions of the monopoly model are rather strong. In assuming there is one firm in a market, we assume there are no other firms producing goods or services that could be considered part of the same market as that of the monopoly firm. In assuming blocked entry, we assume, for reasons we will discuss below, that no other firm can enter that market. Such conditions are rare in the real world. As always with models, we make the assumptions that define monopoly in order to simplify our analysis, not to describe the real world. The result is a model that gives us important insights into the nature of the choices of firms and their impact on the economy.

Sources of Monopoly Power

Why are some markets dominated by single firms? What are the sources of monopoly power? Economists have identified a number of conditions that, individually or in combination, can lead to domination of a market by a single firm and create barriers that prevent the entry of new firms.

barriers to entry

Characteristic of a particular market that block the entry of new firms in a monopoly market.

Barriers to entry are characteristics of a particular market that block new firms from entering it. They include economies of scale, special advantages of location, high sunk costs, a dominant position in the ownership of some of the inputs required to produce the good, and government restrictions. These barriers may be interrelated, making entry that much more formidable. Although these barriers might allow one firm to gain and hold monopoly control over a market, there are often forces at work that can erode this control.

Economies of Scale

Scale economies and diseconomies define the shape of a firm's long-run average cost (*LRAC*) curve as it increases its output. If long-run average cost declines as the level of production increases, a firm is said to experience *economies of scale*.

natural monopoly

A firm that confronts economies of scale over the entire range of outputs demanded in its industry.

A firm that confronts economies of scale over the entire range of outputs demanded in its industry is a **natural monopoly**. Utilities that distribute electricity, water, and natural gas to some markets are examples. In a natural monopoly, the *LRAC* of any one firm intersects the market demand curve where long-run average costs are falling or are at a minimum. If this is the case, one firm in the industry will expand to exploit the economies of scale available to it. Because this firm will have lower unit costs than its rivals, it can drive them out of the market and gain monopoly control over the industry.

Suppose there are 12 firms, each operating at the scale shown by ATC_1 (average total cost) in Figure 10.1. A firm that expanded its scale of operation to achieve an average total cost curve such as ATC_2 could produce 240 units of output at a lower cost than could the smaller firms producing 20 units each. By cutting its price below the minimum average total cost of the smaller plants, the larger firm could drive the smaller ones out of business. In this situation, the industry demand is not large enough to support more than one firm. If another firm attempted to enter the industry, the natural monopolist would always be able to undersell it.

FIGURE 10.1 Economies of Scale Lead to Natural Monopoly
A firm with falling *LRAC* throughout the range of outputs relevant to existing demand (*D*) will monopolize the industry. Here, one firm operating with a large plant (*ATC*$_2$) produces 240 units of output at a lower cost than the $7 cost per unit of the 12 firms operating at a smaller scale (*ATC*$_1$), and producing 20 units of output each.

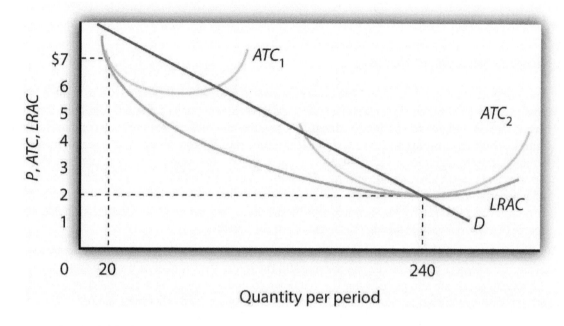

Location

Sometimes monopoly power is the result of location. For example, sellers in markets isolated by distance from their nearest rivals have a degree of monopoly power. The local movie theater in a small town has a monopoly in showing first-run movies. Doctors, dentists, and mechanics in isolated towns may also be monopolists.

Sunk Costs

The greater the cost of establishing a new business in an industry, the more difficult it is to enter that industry. That cost will, in turn, be greater if the outlays required to start a business are unlikely to be recovered if the business should fail.

Suppose, for example, that entry into a particular industry requires extensive advertising to make consumers aware of the new brand. Should the effort fail, there is no way to recover the expenditures for such advertising. An expenditure that has already been made and that cannot be recovered is called a **sunk cost**.

sunk cost

An expenditure that has already been made and that cannot be recovered.

If a substantial fraction of a firm's initial outlays will be lost upon exit from the industry, exit will be costly. Difficulty of exit can make for difficulty of entry. The more firms have to lose from an unsuccessful effort to penetrate a particular market, the less likely they are to try. The potential for high sunk costs could thus contribute to the monopoly power of an established firm by making entry by other firms more difficult.

Restricted Ownership of Raw Materials and Inputs

In very few cases the source of monopoly power is the ownership of strategic inputs. If a particular firm owns all of an input required for the production of a particular good or service, then it could emerge as the only producer of that good or service.

The Aluminum Company of America (ALCOA) gained monopoly power through its ownership of virtually all the bauxite mines in the world (bauxite is the source of aluminum). The International Nickel Company of Canada at one time owned virtually all the world's nickel. De Beers acquired rights to nearly all the world's diamond production, giving it enormous power in the market for diamonds. With new diamond supplies in Canada, Australia, and Russia being developed and sold independently of DeBeers, however, this power has declined, and today DeBeers controls a substantially smaller percentage of the world's supply.

Government Restrictions

Another important basis for monopoly power consists of special privileges granted to some business firms by government agencies. State and local governments have commonly assigned exclusive franchises—rights to conduct business in a specific market—to taxi and bus companies, to cable television companies, and to providers of telephone services, electricity, natural gas, and water, although the trend in recent years has been to encourage competition for many of these services. Governments might also regulate entry into an industry or a profession through licensing and certification requirements. Governments also provide patent protection to inventors of new products or production methods in order to encourage innovation; these patents may afford their holders a degree of monopoly power during the 17-year life of the patent.

network effects

Situations where products become more useful the larger the number of users of the product.

Patents can take on extra importance when network effects are present. **Network effects** arise in situations where products become more useful the larger the number of users of the product. For example, one advantage of using the Windows computer operating system is that so many other people use it. That has advantages in terms of sharing files and other information.

Key Takeaways

- An industry with a single firm, in which entry is blocked, is called a monopoly.
- A firm that sets or picks price depending on its output decision is called a price setter. A price setter possesses monopoly power.
- The sources of monopoly power include economies of scale, locational advantages, high sunk costs associated with entry, restricted ownership of key inputs, and government restrictions, such as exclusive franchises, licensing and certification requirements, and patents.
- A firm that confronts economies of scale over the entire range of output demanded in an industry is a natural monopoly.

Try It!

What is the source of monopoly power—if any—in each of the following situations?

1. The U.S. Food and Drug Administration granted Burroughs Wellcome exclusive rights until 2005 to manufacture and distribute AZT, a drug used in the treatment of AIDS.
2. John and Mary Doe run the only shoe repair shop in town.
3. One utility company distributes residential electricity in your town.
4. The widespread use of automatic teller machines (ATMs) has proven a boon to Diebold, the principal manufacturer of the machines.

Case in Point: The Ambassador Bridge Fights to Maintain Its Monopoly

Source: © 2010 Jupiterimages Corporation

Matty Moroun has been enjoying his monopoly power. His company owns the nearly ninety-year-old Ambassador Bridge, a suspension bridge that is the only connection for all vehicle types between Detroit, Michigan, and Windsor, Ontario. He purchased the bridge from Warren Buffet in 1974 for $30 million. It's likely worth many multiples of that now. Mr. Maroun once suggested $3 billion. One quarter of U.S. merchandise trade with Canada, almost $200 billion a year, makes its way between the two countries via this bridge. *Forbes* writers Stephane Fitch and Joann Muller dubbed the bridge "the best monopoly you never heard of."

Despite complaints of high and rising tolls—he has more than doubled fares for cars and tripled fares for trucks—Mr. Moroun has held on for a long time. Kenneth Davies, a lawyer who often battles Mr. Moroun in court, is a grudging admirer. "He's very intelligent and very aggressive. His avarice and greed are just American capitalism at work," he told *Forbes*.

What are the sources of his monopoly power? With the closest alternative bridge across the Detroit River two hours away, location is a big plus, and the cost of creating any new transportation link is high. Moreover, he has a status not shared by most other monopolists. The Michigan Supreme Court ruled in 2008 that the city of Detroit cannot regulate his business because of the bridge's international nature. Canadian courts have barred any effort by Canadian authorities to regulate him. The company will not even allow inspectors from the government of the United States to set foot on his bridge.

Increased security since 9/11 caused delays, but Mr. Moroun has eased these by increasing his own spending on security to $50,000 a week and by building additional inspection stations and gifting them to the U.S. inspection agency. Even a monopolist understands the importance of keeping his customers content! Mr. Maroun has also proposed building a new span just next to the existing span.

Currently, though, the Canadian government has committed to building the Gordie Howe International Bridge, named for the former Canadian hockey star, close by. Successive Canadian governments have deemed this $4 to $5 billion project so important that the current plan has Canada footing the entire bill, with costs to be recouped over time through toll collections. The Moroun company has fought the project fiercely through the court system for more than a decade, and Mr. Maroun even spent a night in jail before finally obeying a court order. "There has been litigation and fights that have hampered considerable efforts by three Canadian governments and two U.S. presidents to modernize the most significant border crossing in North America," said Dwight Duncan, interim chair of the Windsor-Detroit Bridge Authority. In a surprise move in February 2016, the son of Matty Moroun sent an email to the *Toronto Star* suggesting the Morouns might be willing to sell the bridge. Duncan has recommended that the Canadian government enter into discussions to purchase the bridge.

Will this bring an end to this monopoly? Estimates vary on when the construction of the Gordie Howe International Bridge could be completed. Some say 2020, others 2022. Will the saga end with two government-owned bridges or with one government owned and the other privately owned? Only time will tell.

Sources: Based on Linda Diebel, "Olive Branch Could End Detroit-Windsor Bridge Wars," The Star, February 13, 2016; Stephane Fitch and Joann Muller, "The Troll Under the Bridge," Forbes 174:10 (November 15, 2004): 134–139; Anne Jarvis, "Will Canada Buy the Ambassador Bridge," The Windsor Star, July 28, 2016; John Gallagher, "Plan Uses Parkway to Ease Ambassador Bridge Traffic," Detroit Free Press, May 1, 2008; "State Supreme Court Sides With Ambassador Bridge in Dispute," Detroit News, May 7, 2008; and "A Floating Detroit River Bridge?" The Toronto Star, July 30, 2010.

Answers to Try It! Problems

1. The government's grant of an exclusive franchise to the drug gave the firm monopoly power.
2. While John and Mary have the only shop in town, this is an easy entry business. Further, there may be competitors in the nearby town. John and Mary probably have monopoly power, but they do not have a monopoly.
3. Natural monopoly.
4. Patent with strong network effects.

10.3 The Monopoly Model

Learning Objectives

1. Explain the relationship between price and marginal revenue when a firm faces a downward-sloping demand curve.
2. Explain the relationship between marginal revenue and elasticity along a linear demand curve.
3. Apply the marginal decision rule to explain how a monopoly maximizes profit.

Analyzing choices is a more complex challenge for a monopoly firm than for a perfectly competitive firm. After all, a competitive firm takes the market price as given and determines its profit-maximizing output. Because a monopoly has its market all to itself, it can determine not only its output but its price as well. What kinds of price and output choices will such a firm make?

We will answer that question in the context of the marginal decision rule: a firm will produce additional units of a good until marginal revenue equals marginal cost. To apply that rule to a monopoly firm, we must first investigate the special relationship between demand and marginal revenue for a monopoly.

Monopoly and Market Demand

Because a monopoly firm has its market all to itself, it faces the market demand curve. Figure 10.2 compares the demand situations faced by a monopoly and a perfectly competitive firm. In Panel (a), the equilibrium price for a perfectly competitive firm is determined by the intersection of the demand and supply curves. The market supply curve is found simply by summing the supply curves of individual firms. Those, in turn, consist of the portions of marginal cost curves that lie above the average variable cost curves. The marginal cost curve, MC, for a single firm is illustrated. Notice the break in the horizontal axis indicating that the quantity produced by a single firm is a trivially small fraction of the whole. In the perfectly competitive model, one firm has *nothing* to do with the determination of the market price. Each firm in a perfectly competitive industry faces a horizontal demand curve defined by the market price.

FIGURE 10.2 Perfect Competition Versus Monopoly
Panel (a) shows the determination of equilibrium price and output in a perfectly competitive market. A typical firm with marginal cost curve MC is a price taker, choosing to produce quantity q at the equilibrium price P. In Panel (b) a monopoly faces a downward-sloping market demand curve. As a profit maximizer, it determines its profit-maximizing output. Once it determines that quantity, however, the price at which it can sell that output is found from the demand curve. The monopoly firm can sell additional units only by lowering price. The perfectly competitive firm, by contrast, can sell any quantity it wants at the market price.

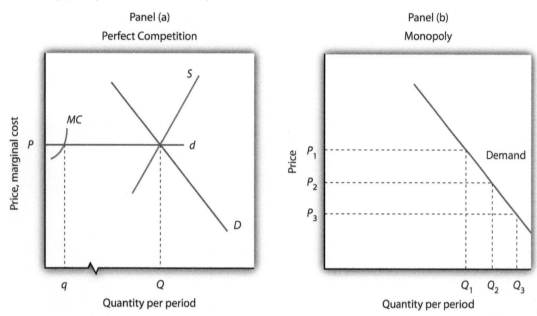

Contrast the situation shown in Panel (a) with the one faced by the monopoly firm in Panel (b). Because it is the only supplier in the industry, the monopolist faces the downward-sloping market demand curve alone. It may choose to produce any quantity. But, unlike the perfectly competitive firm, which can sell all it wants at the going market price, a monopolist can sell a greater quantity only by cutting its price.

Suppose, for example, that a monopoly firm can sell quantity Q_1 units at a price P_1 in Panel (b). If it wants to increase its output to Q_2 units—and sell that quantity—it must reduce its price to P_2. To sell quantity Q_3 it would have to reduce the price to P_3. The monopoly firm may choose its price and output, but it is restricted to a combination of price and output that lies on the demand curve. It could not, for example, charge price P_1 and sell quantity Q_3. To be a price setter, a firm must face a downward-sloping demand curve.

Total Revenue and Price Elasticity

A firm's elasticity of demand with respect to price has important implications for assessing the impact of a price change on total revenue. Also, the price elasticity of demand can be different at different points on a firm's demand curve. In this section, we shall see why a monopoly firm will always select a price in the elastic region of its demand curve.

Suppose the demand curve facing a monopoly firm is given by Equation 10.1, where Q is the quantity demanded per unit of time and P is the price per unit:

EQUATION 10.1

$$Q = 10 - P$$

This demand equation implies the demand schedule shown in Figure 10.3. Total revenue for each quantity equals the quantity times the price at which that quantity is demanded. The monopoly firm's total revenue curve is given in Panel (b). Because a monopolist must cut the price of every unit in order to increase sales, total revenue does not always increase as output rises. In this case, total revenue reaches a maximum of $25 when 5 units are sold. Beyond 5 units, total revenue begins to decline.

FIGURE 10.3 Demand, Elasticity, and Total Revenue

Suppose a monopolist faces the downward-sloping demand curve shown in Panel (a). In order to increase the quantity sold, it must cut the price. Total revenue is found by multiplying the price and quantity sold at each price. Total revenue, plotted in Panel (b), is maximized at $25, when the quantity sold is 5 units and the price is $5. At that point on the demand curve, the price elasticity of demand equals −1.

Price	$10	9	8	7	6	5	4	3	2	1	0
Quantity	0	1	2	3	4	5	6	7	8	9	10
Total revenue	$ 0	9	16	21	24	25	24	21	16	9	0

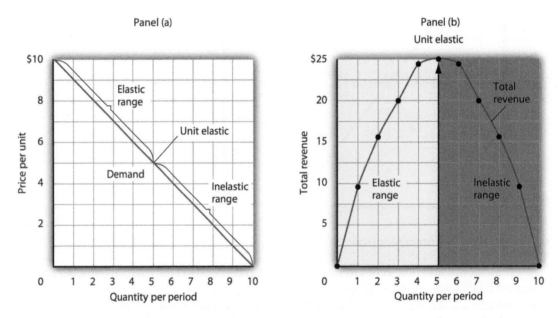

The demand curve in Panel (a) of Figure 10.3 shows ranges of values of the price elasticity of demand. We have learned that price elasticity varies along a linear demand curve in a special way: Demand is price elastic at points in the upper half of the demand curve and price inelastic in the lower half of the demand curve. If demand is price elastic, a price reduction increases total revenue. To sell an additional unit, a monopoly firm must lower its price. The sale of one more unit will increase revenue because the percentage increase in the quantity demanded exceeds the percentage decrease in the price. The elastic range of the demand curve corresponds to the range over which the total revenue curve is rising in Panel (b) of Figure 10.3.

If demand is price inelastic, a price reduction reduces total revenue because the percentage increase in the quantity demanded is less than the percentage decrease in the price. Total revenue falls as the firm sells additional units over the inelastic range of the demand curve. The downward-sloping portion of the total revenue curve in Panel (b) corresponds to the inelastic range of the demand curve.

Finally, recall that the midpoint of a linear demand curve is the point at which demand becomes unit price elastic. That point on the total revenue curve in Panel (b) corresponds to the point at which total revenue reaches a maximum.

The relationship among price elasticity, demand, and total revenue has an important implication for the selection of the profit-maximizing price and output: A monopoly firm will never choose a price and output in the inelastic range of the demand curve. Suppose, for example, that the monopoly firm represented in Figure 10.3 is charging $3 and selling 7 units. Its total revenue is thus $21. Because this combination is in the inelastic portion of the demand curve, the firm could increase its total revenue by raising its price. It could, at the same time, reduce its total cost. Raising price means reducing output; a reduction in output would reduce total cost. If the firm is operating in the inelastic range of its demand curve, then it is not maximizing profits. The firm could earn a higher profit by raising price and reducing output. It will continue to raise its price until it is in the elastic portion of its demand curve. A profit-maximizing monopoly firm will therefore select a price and output combination in the elastic range of its demand curve.

Of course, the firm could choose a point at which demand is unit price elastic. At that point, total revenue is maximized. But the firm seeks to maximize profit, not total revenue. A solution that maximizes total revenue will not maximize profit unless marginal cost is zero.

Demand and Marginal Revenue

In the perfectly competitive case, the additional revenue a firm gains from selling an additional unit—its marginal revenue—is equal to the market price. The firm's demand curve, which is a horizontal line at the market price, is also its marginal revenue curve. But a monopoly firm can sell an additional unit only by lowering the price. That fact complicates the relationship between the monopoly's demand curve and its marginal revenue.

Suppose the firm in Figure 10.3 sells 2 units at a price of $8 per unit. Its total revenue is $16. Now it wants to sell a third unit and wants to know the marginal revenue of that unit. To sell 3 units rather than 2, the firm must lower its price to $7 per unit. Total revenue rises to $21. The marginal revenue of the third unit is thus $5. But the *price* at which the firm sells 3 units is $7. Marginal revenue is less than price.

To see why the marginal revenue of the third unit is less than its price, we need to examine more carefully how the sale of that unit affects the firm's revenues. The firm brings in $7 from the sale of the third unit. But selling the third unit required the firm to charge a price of $7 instead of the $8 the firm was charging for 2 units. Now the firm receives less for the first 2 units. The marginal revenue of the third unit is the $7 the firm receives for that unit *minus* the $1 reduction in revenue for each of the first two units. The marginal revenue of the third unit is thus $5. (In this chapter we assume that the monopoly firm sells all units of output at the same price. In the next chapter, we will look at cases in which firms charge different prices to different customers.)

Marginal revenue is less than price for the monopoly firm. Figure 10.4 shows the relationship between demand and marginal revenue, based on the demand curve introduced in Figure 10.3. As always, we follow the convention of plotting marginal values at the midpoints of the intervals.

FIGURE 10.4 Demand and Marginal Revenue

The marginal revenue curve for the monopoly firm lies below its demand curve. It shows the additional revenue gained from selling an additional unit. Notice that, as always, marginal values are plotted at the midpoints of the respective intervals.

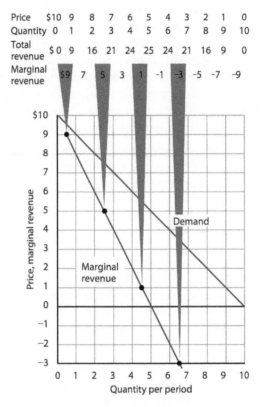

Price	$10	9	8	7	6	5	4	3	2	1	0
Quantity	0	1	2	3	4	5	6	7	8	9	10
Total revenue	$0	9	16	21	24	25	24	21	16	9	0
Marginal revenue		$9	7	5	3	1	-1	-3	-5	-7	-9

When the demand curve is linear, as in Figure 10.4, the marginal revenue curve can be placed according to the following rules: the marginal revenue curve is always below the demand curve and the marginal revenue curve will bisect any horizontal line drawn between the vertical axis and the demand curve. To put it another way, the marginal revenue curve will be twice as steep as the demand curve. The demand curve in Figure 10.4 is given by the equation $Q = 10 - P$, which can be written $P = 10 - Q$. The marginal revenue curve is given by $P = 10 - 2Q$, which is twice as steep as the demand curve.

The marginal revenue and demand curves in Figure 10.4 follow these rules. The marginal revenue curve lies below the demand curve, and it bisects any horizontal line drawn from the vertical axis to the demand curve. At a price of $6, for example, the quantity demanded is 4. The marginal revenue curve passes through 2 units at this price. At a price of 0, the quantity demanded is 10; the marginal revenue curve passes through 5 units at this point.

Just as there is a relationship between the firm's demand curve and the price elasticity of demand, there is a relationship between its marginal revenue curve and elasticity. Where marginal revenue is positive, demand is price elastic. Where marginal revenue is negative, demand is price inelastic. Where marginal revenue is zero, demand is unit price elastic.

When marginal revenue is …	then demand is …
positive,	price elastic.
negative,	price inelastic.
zero,	unit price elastic.

A firm would not produce an additional unit of output with negative marginal revenue. And, assuming that the production of an additional unit has some cost, a firm would not produce the extra unit if it has zero marginal revenue. Because a monopoly firm will generally operate where marginal revenue is positive, we see once again that it will operate in the elastic range of its demand curve.

Monopoly Equilibrium: Applying the Marginal Decision Rule

Profit-maximizing behavior is always based on the marginal decision rule: Additional units of a good should be produced as long as the marginal revenue of an additional unit exceeds the marginal cost. The maximizing solution occurs where marginal revenue equals marginal cost. As always, firms seek to maximize economic profit, and costs are measured in the economic sense of opportunity cost.

Figure 10.5 shows a demand curve and an associated marginal revenue curve facing a monopoly firm. The marginal cost curve is like those we derived earlier; it falls over the range of output in which the firm experiences increasing marginal returns, then rises as the firm experiences diminishing marginal returns.

FIGURE 10.5 The Monopoly Solution
The monopoly firm maximizes profit by producing an output Q_m at point G, where the marginal revenue and marginal cost curves intersect. It sells this output at price P_m.

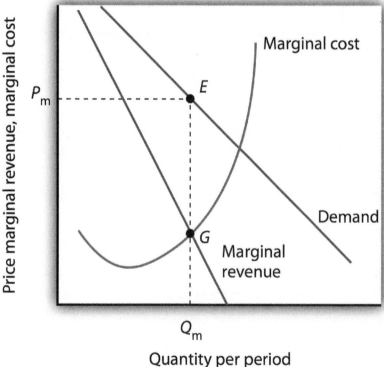

FIGURE 10.6 Computing Monopoly Profit

A monopoly firm's profit per unit is the difference between price and average total cost. Total profit equals profit per unit times the quantity produced. Total profit is given by the area of the shaded rectangle ATC_mP_mEF.

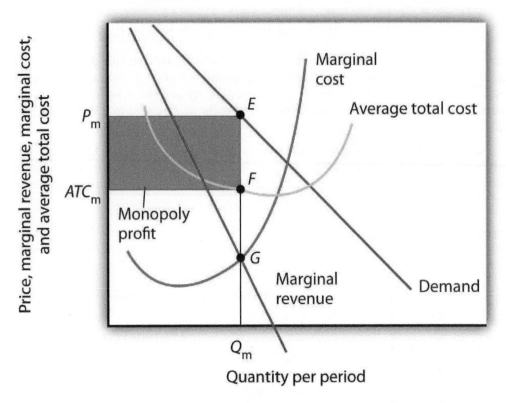

To determine the profit-maximizing output, we note the quantity at which the firm's marginal revenue and marginal cost curves intersect (Q_m in Figure 10.5). We read up from Q_m to the demand curve to find the price P_m at which the firm can sell Q_m units per period. The profit-maximizing price and output are given by point E on the demand curve.

Thus we can determine a monopoly firm's profit-maximizing price and output by following three steps:

1. Determine the demand, marginal revenue, and marginal cost curves.
2. Select the output level at which the marginal revenue and marginal cost curves intersect.
3. Determine from the demand curve the price at which that output can be sold.

Once we have determined the monopoly firm's price and output, we can determine its economic profit by adding the firm's average total cost curve to the graph showing demand, marginal revenue, and marginal cost, as shown in Figure 10.6. The average total cost (ATC) at an output of Q_m units is ATC_m. The firm's profit per unit is thus $P_m - ATC_m$. Total profit is found by multiplying the firm's output, Q_m, by profit per unit, so total profit equals $Q_m(P_m - ATC_m)$—the area of the shaded rectangle in Figure 10.6.

Heads Up!

Dispelling Myths About Monopoly

Three common misconceptions about monopoly are:

1. Because there are no rivals selling the products of monopoly firms, they can charge whatever they want.

2. Monopolists will charge whatever the market will bear.
3. Because monopoly firms have the market to themselves, they are guaranteed huge profits.

As Figure 10.5 shows, once the monopoly firm decides on the number of units of output that will maximize profit, the price at which it can sell that many units is found by "reading off" the demand curve the price associated with that many units. If it tries to sell Q_m units of output for more than P_m, some of its output will go unsold. The monopoly firm can set its price, but is restricted to price and output combinations that lie on its demand curve. It cannot just "charge whatever it wants." And if it charges "all the market will bear," it will sell either 0 or, at most, 1 unit of output.

Neither is the monopoly firm guaranteed a profit. Consider Figure 10.6. Suppose the average total cost curve, instead of lying below the demand curve for some output levels as shown, were instead everywhere above the demand curve. In that case, the monopoly will incur losses no matter what price it chooses, since average total cost will always be greater than any price it might charge. As is the case for perfect competition, the monopoly firm can keep producing in the short run so long as price exceeds average variable cost. In the long run, it will stay in business only if it can cover all of its costs.

Key Takeaways

- If a firm faces a downward-sloping demand curve, marginal revenue is less than price.
- Marginal revenue is positive in the elastic range of a demand curve, negative in the inelastic range, and zero where demand is unit price elastic.
- If a monopoly firm faces a linear demand curve, its marginal revenue curve is also linear, lies below the demand curve, and bisects any horizontal line drawn from the vertical axis to the demand curve.
- To maximize profit or minimize losses, a monopoly firm produces the quantity at which marginal cost equals marginal revenue. Its price is given by the point on the demand curve that corresponds to this quantity.

Try It!

The Troll Road Company is considering building a toll road. It estimates that its linear demand curve is as shown below. Assume that the fixed cost of the road is $0.5 million per year. Maintenance costs, which are the only other costs of the road, are also given in the table.

Tolls per trip	$1.00	0.90	0.80	0.70	0.60	0.50
Number of trips per year (in millions)	1	2	3	4	5	6
Maintenance cost per year (in millions)	$0.7	1.2	1.8	2.9	4.2	6.0

1. Using the midpoint convention, compute the profit-maximizing level of output.
2. Using the midpoint convention, what price will the company charge?
3. What is marginal revenue at the profit-maximizing output level? How does marginal revenue compare to price?

Case in Point: Profit-Maximizing Sports Teams

Source: © 2010 Jupiterimages Corporation

Love of the game? Love of the city? Are those the factors that influence owners of professional sports teams in setting admissions prices? Four economists at the University of Vancouver have what they think is the answer for one group of teams: professional hockey teams set admission prices at levels that maximize their profits. They regard hockey teams as monopoly firms and use the monopoly model to examine the team's behavior.

The economists, Donald G. Ferguson, Kenneth G. Stewart, John Colin H. Jones, and Andre Le Dressay, used data from three seasons to estimate demand and marginal revenue curves facing each team in the National Hockey League. They found that demand for a team's tickets is affected by population and income in the team's home city, the team's standing in the National Hockey League, and the number of superstars on the team.

Because a sports team's costs do not vary significantly with the number of fans who attend a given game, the economists assumed that marginal cost is zero. The profit-maximizing number of seats sold per game is thus the quantity at which marginal revenue is zero, provided a team's stadium is large enough to hold that quantity of fans. This unconstrained quantity is labeled Q_u, with a corresponding price P_u in the graph.

Stadium size and the demand curve facing a team might prevent the team from selling the profit-maximizing quantity of tickets. If its stadium holds only Q_c fans, for example, the team will sell that many tickets at price P_c; its marginal revenue is positive at that quantity. Economic theory thus predicts that the marginal revenue for teams that consistently sell out their games will be positive, and the marginal revenue for other teams will be zero.

The economists' statistical results were consistent with the theory. They found that teams that do not typically sell out their games operate at a quantity at which marginal revenue is about zero and that teams with sellouts have positive marginal revenue. These results suggest that these teams are very sophisticated in their use of pricing to maximize profits.

Not all studies of sporting event pricing have confirmed this conclusion. While a study of major league baseball ticket pricing by Leo Kahane and Stephen Shmanske and one of baseball spring training game tickets by Michael Donihue, David Findlay, and Peter Newberry suggested that tickets are priced where demand is unit elastic, some other studies of ticket pricing of sporting events have found that tickets are priced in the inelastic region of the demand curve. On its face, this would mean that team owners were not maximizing profits. Why would team owners do this? Are they really charging too little? To fans, it certainly may not seem so!

While some have argued that owners want to please fans by selling tickets for less than the profit-maximizing price, others argue they do so for possible political considerations, for example, keeping prices below the profit-maximizing level could help when they are asking for subsidies for building new stadiums. In line with the notion that team owners do behave like other profit-maximizing firms, another line of research, for example, that proposed by Anthony Krautmann and David Berri, has been to recognize that owners also get revenue from selling concessions so that getting more fans at the game may boost revenue from other sources.

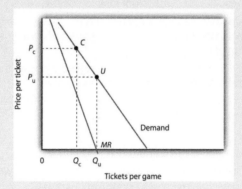

Sources: Based on Michael R. Donihue, David W. Findlay, and Peter W. Newberry, "An Analysis of Attendance at Major League Baseball Spring Games," Journal of Sports Economics 8:1 (February 2007): 39–61; Donald G. Ferguson et al., "The Pricing of Sports Events: Do Teams Maximize Profit?" Journal of Industrial Economics 39:3 (March 1991): 297–310 and personal interview; Leo Kahane and Stephen Shmanske, "Team Roster Turnover and Attendance in Major League Baseball," Applied Economics 29 (1997): 425–431; and Anthony C. Krautmann and David J. Berri, "Can We Find It at the Concessions?" Journal of Sports Economics 8:2 (April 2007): 183–191.

Answers to Try It! Problems

Maintenance costs constitute the variable costs associated with building the road. In order to answer the first four parts of the question, you will need to compute total revenue, marginal revenue, and marginal cost, as shown at right:

1. Using the "midpoint" convention, the profit-maximizing level of output is 2.5 million trips per year. With that number of trips, marginal revenue ($0.60) equals marginal cost ($0.60).
2. Again, we use the "midpoint" convention. The company will charge a toll of $0.85.
3. The marginal revenue is $0.60, which is less than the $0.85 toll (price).

Price per trip	$1.00	0.90	0.80	0.70	0.60	0.50
Number of trips per year (in millions)	1	2	3	4	5	6
Total variable costs per year (in millions)	$0.7	1.2	1.8	2.9	4.2	6.0
Total revenue (in millions)	$1.00	1.80	2.40	2.80	3.00	3.00
Marginal revenue		$0.80	0.60	0.40	0.20	0.00
Marginal cost		$0.50	0.60	1.10	1.30	1.80

10.4 Assessing Monopoly

Learning Objectives

1. Explain and illustrate that a monopoly firm produces an output that is less than the efficient level and why this results in a deadweight loss to society.
2. Explain and illustrate how the higher price that a monopoly charges, compared to an otherwise identical perfectly competitive firm, transfers part of consumer surplus to the monopolist and raises questions of equity.
3. Considering both advantages and disadvantages, discuss the potential effects that a monopoly may have on consumer choices, price, quality of products, and technological innovations.
4. Discuss the public policy responses to monopoly.

We have seen that for monopolies pursuing profit maximization, the outcome differs from the case of perfect competition. Does this matter to society? In this section, we will focus on the differences that stem from market structure and assess their implications.

Efficiency, Equity, and Concentration of Power

A monopoly firm determines its output by setting marginal cost equal to marginal revenue. It then charges the price at which it can sell that output, a price determined by the demand curve. That price exceeds marginal revenue; it therefore exceeds marginal cost as well. That contrasts with the case in perfect competition, in which price and marginal cost are equal. The higher price charged by a monopoly firm may allow it a profit—in large part at the expense of consumers, whose reduced options may give them little say in the matter. The monopoly solution thus raises problems of efficiency, equity, and the concentration of power.

Monopoly and Efficiency

The fact that price in monopoly exceeds marginal cost suggests that the monopoly solution violates the basic condition for economic efficiency, that the price system must confront decision makers with all of the costs and all of the benefits of their choices. Efficiency requires that consumers confront prices that equal marginal costs. Because a monopoly firm charges a price greater than marginal cost, consumers will consume less of the monopoly's good or service than is economically efficient.

To contrast the efficiency of the perfectly competitive outcome with the inefficiency of the monopoly outcome, imagine a perfectly competitive industry whose solution is depicted in Figure 10.7. The short-run industry supply curve is the summation of individual marginal cost curves; it may be regarded as the marginal cost curve for the industry. A perfectly competitive industry achieves equilibrium at point C, at price P_c and quantity Q_c.

FIGURE 10.7 Perfect Competition, Monopoly, and Efficiency

Given market demand and marginal revenue, we can compare the behavior of a monopoly to that of a perfectly competitive industry. The marginal cost curve may be thought of as the supply curve of a perfectly competitive industry. The perfectly competitive industry produces quantity Q_c and sells the output at price P_c. The monopolist restricts output to Q_m and raises the price to P_m.

Reorganizing a perfectly competitive industry as a monopoly results in a deadweight loss to society given by the shaded area GRC. It also transfers a portion of the consumer surplus earned in the competitive case to the monopoly firm.

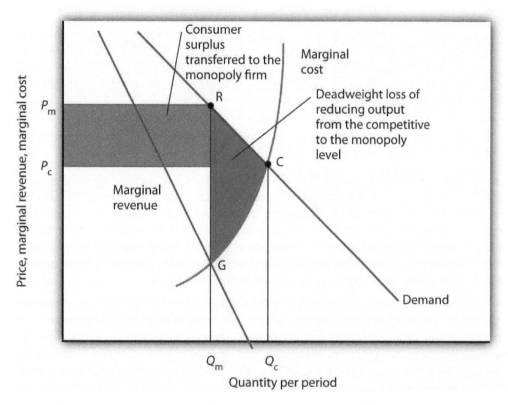

Now, suppose that all the firms in the industry merge and a government restriction prohibits entry by any new firms. Our perfectly competitive industry is now a monopoly. Assume the monopoly continues to have the same marginal cost and demand curves that the competitive industry did. The monopoly firm faces the same market demand curve, from which it derives its marginal revenue curve. It maximizes profit at output Q_m and charges price P_m. Output is lower and price higher than in the competitive solution.

Society would gain by moving from the monopoly solution at Q_m to the competitive solution at Q_c. The benefit to consumers would be given by the area under the demand curve between Q_m and Q_c; it is the area $Q_m RCQ_c$. An increase in output, of course, has a cost. Because the marginal cost curve measures the cost of each additional unit, we can think of the area under the marginal cost curve over some range of output as measuring the total cost of that output. Thus, the total cost of increasing output from Q_m to Q_c is the area under the marginal cost curve over that range—the area $Q_m GCQ_c$. Subtracting this cost from the benefit gives us the net gain of moving from the monopoly to the competitive solution; it is the shaded area GRC. That is the potential gain from moving to the efficient solution. The area GRC is a deadweight loss.

Monopoly and Equity

The monopoly solution raises issues not just of efficiency but also of equity. Figure 10.7 shows that the monopolist charges price P_m rather than the competitive price P_c; the higher price charged by the monopoly firm reduces consumer surplus. Consumer surplus is the difference between what consumers are willing to pay for a good and what they actually pay. It is measured by the area under the demand curve and above the price of the good over the range of output produced.

If the industry were competitive, consumer surplus would be the area below the demand curve and above P_cC. With monopoly, consumer surplus would be the area below the demand curve and above P_mR. Part of the reduction in consumer surplus is the area under the demand curve between Q_c and Q_m; it is contained in the deadweight loss area GRC. But consumers also lose the area of the rectangle bounded by the competitive and monopoly prices and by the monopoly output; this lost consumer surplus is transferred to the monopolist.

The fact that society suffers a deadweight loss due to monopoly is an efficiency problem. But the transfer of a portion of consumer surplus to the monopolist is an equity issue. Is such a transfer legitimate? After all, the monopoly firm enjoys a privileged position, protected by barriers to entry from competition. Should it be allowed to extract these gains from consumers? We will see that public policy suggests that the answer is no. Regulatory efforts imposed in monopoly cases often seek to reduce the degree to which monopoly firms extract consumer surplus from consumers by reducing the prices these firms charge.

Monopoly and the Concentration of Power

The objections to monopoly run much deeper than worries over economic efficiency and high prices. Because it enjoys barriers that block potential rivals, a monopoly firm wields considerable market power. For many people, that concentration of power is objectionable. A decentralized, competitive market constantly tests the ability of firms to satisfy consumers, pushes them to find new products and new and better production methods, and whittles away economic profits. Firms that operate in the shelter of monopoly may be largely immune to such pressures. Consumers are likely to be left with fewer choices, higher costs, and lower quality.

Perhaps more important in the view of many economists is the fact that the existence of economic profits provides both an incentive and the means for monopolists to aggressively protect their position and extend it if possible. These economists point out that monopolists may be willing to spend their economic profits in attempts to influence political leaders and public authorities (including regulatory authorities) who can help them maintain or enhance their monopoly position. Graft and corruption may be the result, claim these critics. Indeed, Microsoft has been accused by its rivals of bullying computer manufacturers into installing its web browser, Internet Explorer, exclusively on their computers.

Attitudes about Microsoft reflect these concerns. Even among people who feel that its products are good and fairly priced, there is uneasiness about our seeming dependence on them. And once it has secured its dominant position, will it charge more for its products? Will it continue to innovate?

Public Policy Toward Monopoly

Pulling together what we have learned in this chapter on monopoly and previously on perfect competition, Table 10.1 summarizes the differences between the models of perfect competition and monopoly. Most importantly we note that whereas the perfectly competitive firm is a price taker, the monopoly firm is a price setter. Because of this difference, we can object to monopoly on grounds of economic efficiency; monopolies produce too little and charge too much. Also, the high price and persistent profits strike many as inequitable. Others may simply see monopoly as an unacceptable concentration of power.

TABLE 10.1 Characteristics of Perfect Competition and Monopoly

Characteristic or Event	Perfect Competition	Monopoly
Market	Large number of sellers and buyers producing a homogeneous good or service, easy entry.	Large number of buyers, one seller. Entry is blocked.
Demand and marginal revenue curves	The firm's demand and marginal revenue curve is a horizontal line at the market price.	The firm faces the market demand curve; marginal revenue is below market demand.
Price	Determined by demand and supply; each firm is a price taker. Price equals marginal cost.	The monopoly firm determines price; it is a price setter. Price is greater than marginal cost.
Profit maximization	Firms produce where marginal cost equals marginal revenue.	Firms produce where marginal cost equals marginal revenue and charge the corresponding price on the demand curve.
Profit	Entry forces economic profit to zero in the long run.	Because entry is blocked, a monopoly firm can sustain an economic profit in the long run.
Efficiency	The equilibrium solution is efficient because price equals marginal cost.	The equilibrium solution is inefficient because price is greater than marginal cost.

Public policy toward monopoly generally recognizes two important dimensions of the monopoly problem. On the one hand, the combining of competing firms into a monopoly creates an inefficient and, to many, inequitable solution. On the other hand, some industries are characterized as natural monopolies; production by a single firm allows economies of scale that result in lower costs.

The combining of competing firms into a monopoly firm or unfairly driving competitors out of business is generally forbidden in the United States. Regulatory efforts to prevent monopoly fall under the purview of the nation's antitrust laws, discussed in more detail in a later chapter.

At the same time, we must be careful to avoid the mistake of simply assuming that competition is the alternative to monopoly, that every monopoly can and should be replaced by a competitive market. One key source of monopoly power, after all, is economies of scale. In the case of natural monopoly, the alternative to a single firm is many small, high-cost producers. We may not like having only one local provider of water, but we might like even less having dozens of providers whose costs—and prices—are higher. Where monopolies exist because economies of scale prevail over the entire range of market demand, they may serve a useful economic role. We might want to regulate their production and pricing choices, but we may not want to give up their cost advantages.

Where a natural monopoly exists, the price charged by the firm and other aspects of its behavior may be subject to regulation. Water or natural gas, for example, are often distributed by a public utility—a monopoly firm—at prices regulated by a state or local government agency. Typically, such agencies seek to force the firm to charge lower prices, and to make less profit, than it would otherwise seek.

Although economists are hesitant to levy blanket condemnations of monopoly, they are generally sharply critical of monopoly power where no rationale for it exists. When firms have substantial monopoly power only as the result of government policies that block entry, there may be little defense for their monopoly positions.

Public policy toward monopoly aims generally to strike the balance implied by economic analysis. Where rationales exist, as in the case of natural monopoly, monopolies are permitted—and their prices are regulated. In other cases, monopoly is prohibited outright. Societies are likely to at least consider taking action of some kind against monopolies unless they appear to offer cost or other technological advantages.

The Fragility of Monopoly Power

An important factor in thinking about public policy toward monopoly is to recognize that monopoly power can be a fleeting thing. Firms constantly seek out the market power that monopoly offers. When conditions are right to achieve this power, firms that succeed in carving out monopoly positions enjoy substantial profits. But the potential for high profits invites continuing attempts to break down the barriers to entry that insulate monopolies from competition.

Technological change and the pursuit of profits chip away constantly at the entrenched power of monopolies. Breathtaking technological change has occurred in the telecommunications industry. Catalog companies are challenging the monopoly positions of some retailers; internet booksellers and online textbook companies such as Flatworldknowledge.com are challenging the monopoly power of your university's bookstore; and Federal Express, UPS, and other companies are taking on the U.S. Postal Service. The assaults on monopoly power are continuous. Thus, even the monopoly firm must be on the lookout for potential competitors.

Potential rivals are always beating at the door and thereby making the monopoly's fragile market contestable—that is, open to entry, at least in the sense of rival firms producing "close enough," if not perfect, substitutes—close enough that they might eliminate the firm's monopoly power.

Key Takeaways

- A monopoly firm produces an output that is less than the efficient level. The result is a deadweight loss to society, given by the area between the demand and marginal cost curves over the range of output between the output chosen by the monopoly firm and the efficient output.
- The higher price charged by the monopoly firm compared to the perfectly competitive firm reduces consumer surplus, part of which is transferred to the monopolist. This transfer generates an equity issue.
- The monopoly firm's market power reduces consumers' choices and may result in higher prices, but there may be advantages to monopoly as well, such as economies of scale and technological innovations encouraged by the patent system.
- Public policy toward monopoly consists of antitrust laws and regulation of natural monopolies.
- Forces that limit the power of monopoly firms are the constant effort by other firms to capture some of the monopoly firm's profits and technological change that erodes monopoly power.

Try It!

Does the statement below better describe a firm operating in a perfectly competitive market or a firm that is a monopoly?

1. The demand curve faced by the firm is downward-sloping.
2. The demand curve and the marginal revenue curves are the same.
3. Entry and exit are relatively difficult.
4. The firm is likely to be concerned about antitrust laws.
5. Consumer surplus would be increased if the firm produced more output.

Case in Point: Technological Change, Public Policy, and Competition in Telecommunications

Source: © 2010 Jupiterimages Corporation

Back in the olden days—before 1984—to use a telephone in the United States almost certainly meant being a customer of AT&T. Ma Bell, as the company was known, provided local and long-distance service to virtually every U.S. household. AT&T was clearly a monopoly.

The Justice Department began its battle with AT&T in the 1970s, charging it with monopolizing the industry. The case culminated in a landmark 1984 ruling that broke the company up into seven so-called "Baby Bells" that would provide local telephone service. AT&T would continue to provide long-distance service.

In effect, the ruling replaced a single national monopoly with seven regional monopolies in local telephone service. AT&T maintained its monopoly position in long-distance service—for a while. The turmoil that has followed illustrates the fragility of monopoly power.

Technological developments in the industry have brought dramatic changes. Companies found ways to challenge AT&T's monopoly position in long-distance telephone service. Cable operators sprang up, typically developing monopoly power over the provision of cable television in their regional markets, but also offering phone service. Mobile phone service, provided by AT&T, and others such as Verizon and Sprint, has led many consumers to do without land-line phone service entirely. Companies that had traditionally been telephone companies have begun providing cable services as well as Internet access. The ready availability of video services on the Internet threatens to make cable providers outmoded middlemen.

What is the status of AT&T today? While no longer a monopoly, it is a major player in all of the areas related to telecommunications and larger than all of its competitors in the United States. In 2011, it began the process of buying T-Mobile USA, a mobile service provider focused on the youth market. By the end of that year, however, in the face of strong opposition from the Department of Justice and the Federal Communications Commission on the grounds that the merger would stifle competition in the industry, AT&T announced that it was dropping the deal. Does AT&T have market power today? Undoubtedly. Is it a monopoly? Not anymore.

Source: Based on Company Monitor, USA Telecommunication Report, Q2 2011: 69–79.

Answers to Try It! Problems

1. monopoly
2. perfect competition
3. monopoly
4. monopoly
5. monopoly

10.5 Review and Practice

Summary

This chapter has examined the profit-maximizing behavior of monopoly firms. Monopoly occurs if an industry consists of a single firm and entry into that industry is blocked.

Potential sources of monopoly power include the existence of economies of scale over the range of market demand, locational advantages, high sunk costs associated with entry, restricted ownership of raw materials and inputs, and government restrictions such as licenses or patents. Network effects for certain products further increase the market power that patents afford.

Because the demand curve faced by the monopolist is downward-sloping, the firm is a price setter. It will maximize profits by producing the quantity of output at which marginal cost equals marginal revenue. The profit-maximizing price is then found on the demand curve for that quantity.

Because a typical monopolist holds market price above marginal cost, the major impact of monopoly is a reduction in efficiency. Compared to a competitive market, the monopoly is characterized by more centralized power, potential higher profits, and less pressure to be responsive to consumer preferences. Public policy toward monopoly includes antitrust laws and, in the case of natural monopolies, regulation of price and other aspects of the firm's behavior.

Concept Problems

1. Consider the following firms. Would you regard any of them as a monopoly? Why or why not? Could you use the monopoly model in analyzing the choices of any of them? Explain.
   a. the best restaurant in town
   b. your barber or beautician
   c. your local telephone company
   d. your campus bookstore
   e. Microsoft
   f. Amtrak
   g. the United States Postal Service
2. Explain the difference between the demand curve facing a monopoly firm and the demand curve facing a perfectly competitive firm.
3. What are the necessary conditions for a monopoly position in the market to be established?
4. A monopoly firm is free to charge any price it wishes. What constrains its choice of a price?
5. Suppose the government were to impose an annual license fee on a monopolist that just happened to be equal to its economic profits for a particular year. How would such a fee

affect price and output? Do you think that such a fee would be appropriate? Why or why not?

6. Name one monopoly firm you deal with. What is the source of its monopoly power? Do you think it seeks to maximize its profits?

7. "A monopolist will never produce so much output as to operate in the inelastic portion of the demand curve." Explain.

8. "A monopoly is not efficient, and its pricing behavior leads to losses to society." What does this statement mean? Should society ban monopolies?

9. A small town located 30 miles from the nearest town has only one service station. Is the service station a monopoly? Why or why not?

10. Explain why under monopoly price is greater than marginal revenue, while under perfect competition price is equal to marginal revenue.

11. In what sense can the monopoly equilibrium be considered inequitable?

12. What is a natural monopoly? Should a natural monopoly be allowed to exist?

13. Give some examples of industries in which you think natural monopoly conditions are likely to prevail. Why do you think so?

14. People often blame the high prices for events such as professional football and basketball and baseball games on the high salaries of professional athletes. Assuming one of these teams is a monopoly, use the model to refute this argument.

15. How do the following events affect a monopoly firm's price and output? How will it affect the firm's profits? Illustrate your answers graphically.

   a. an increase in labor costs in the market in which the firm operates

   b. a reduction in the price of gasoline

   c. the firm's Chief Executive Officer persuades the Board to increase his or her annual salary

   d. demand for the firm's product falls

   e. demand for the firm's product rises

   f. the price of a substitute for the firm's product rises

Numerical Problems

1. A university football team estimates that it faces the demand schedule shown for tickets for each home game it plays. The team plays in a stadium that holds 60,000 fans. It estimates that its marginal cost of attendance, and thus for tickets sold, is zero.

Price per ticket	Tickets per game
$100	0
80	20,000
60	40,000
40	60,000
20	80,000
0	100,000

   a. Draw the demand and marginal revenue curves. Compute the team's profit-maximizing price and the number of tickets it will sell at that price.

   b. Determine the price elasticity of demand at the price you determined in part (a).

   c. How much total revenue will the team earn?

   d. Now suppose the city in which the university is located imposes a $10,000 annual license fee on all suppliers of sporting events, including the University. How does this affect the price of tickets?

  e. Suppose the team increases its spending for scholarships for its athletes. How will this affect ticket prices, assuming that it continues to maximize profit?

  f. Now suppose that the city imposes a tax of $10 per ticket sold. How would this affect the price charged by the team?

2. A monopoly firm faces a demand curve given by the following equation: $P = \$500 - 10Q$, where Q equals quantity sold per day. Its marginal cost curve is $MC = \$100$ per day. Assume that the firm faces no fixed cost.

  a. How much will the firm produce?

  b. How much will it charge?

  c. Can you determine its profit per day? (Hint: you can; state how much it is.)

  d. Suppose a tax of $1,000 per day is imposed on the firm. How will this affect its price?

  e. How would the $1,000 per day tax its output per day?

  f. How would the $1,000 per day tax affect its profit per day?

  g. Now suppose a tax of $100 per unit is imposed. How will this affect the firm's price?

  h. How would a $100 per unit tax affect the firm's profit maximizing output per day?

  i. How would the $100 per unit tax affect the firms profit per day?

The World of Imperfect Competition

11.1 Start Up: The Excitement of Groupon: What Rivals Will It Face?

Groupon, the online coupon company offering time-limited deals requiring a minimum number of buyers, seemed to come out of nowhere. It was founded in 2008. In 2009, it operated in 30 cities in the United States and had 120 employees, 2 million subscribers, and revenues of $33 million. By the end of 2010, it operated in 565 cities around the world, had 4,000 employees, 51 million subscribers, and revenue of $760 million. Its first quarter 2011 revenue of $645 million was almost as much as the total revenue for 2010. By mid-2011, it had 8,000 employees and 83 million subscribers. On June 2, it announced plans for an initial sale of its stock. On November 4, 2011 it raised $700 million, which made it the largest initial public offering of a U.S. internet company since 2004 when Google raised $1.7 billion.

Despite the hoopla surrounding what some referred to at the time as the fastest growing company ever, its founding CEO Andrew Mason once remarked, "By this time next year, we will either be on our way to becoming one of the great technology brands or a cool idea by people who were out-executed and out-innovated by others." With such a meteoric rise, why such a tempered comment? The company held a market share in 2011 of over 60 percent in the United States. One of its main competitors was LivingSocial, which received funding from Amazon. Would it be easy or hard for other firms to enter this industry? The Dealmap was letting consumers know about all the daily deals in a city, and Facebook was beginning to talk about offering local discounts as well. Network effects also seemed weak, as businesses and consumers could easily work with or check out other sites.

In other words, in what type of market structure would Groupon continue to exist? Neither perfect competition nor monopoly seemed likely. In 2011 Groupon was charging businesses half of the discounted price of a voucher. Could it hold onto this price-setting power? Would it be able to find strategies to maintain its dominance? Could it create brand loyalty? Would "Groupon anxiety," a term defined by the Urban Dictionary to mean "the preoccupation and feeling of anxiousness and not being able to sleep knowing that a new Groupon will be released after 1am" give way to "Groupon fatigue," asked the *Economist*?

Its beginnings hardly suggest the aloof world of perfect competition where consumers are indifferent about which firm has produced a particular product, where each firm knows it can sell all it wants at the going market price, and where firms must settle for zero economic profit in the long run. Nor is it the world of monopoly, where a single firm maximizes its profits, believing that barriers to entry will keep out would-be competitors, at least for a while. This is the world of imperfect competition, one that lies between the idealized extremes of perfect competition and monopoly. It is a world in which firms battle over market shares, in which economic profits may persist, in which rivals try to outguess each other with pricing, advertising, and product-development strategies.

imperfect condition

A market structure with
more than one firm in an
industry in which at least
one firm is a price setter.

The spectrum of business enterprise ranges from perfectly competitive firms to monopoly. Between these extremes lies the business landscape in which the vast majority of firms—those in the world of imperfect competition—actually operate. **Imperfect competition** is a market structure with more than one firm in an industry in which at least one firm is a price setter. An imperfectly competitive firm has a degree of monopoly power, either based on product differentiation that leads to a downward-sloping demand curve or resulting from the interaction of rival firms in an industry with only a few firms.

There are two broad categories of imperfectly competitive markets. The first is one in which many firms compete, each offering a slightly different product. The second is one in which the industry is dominated by a few firms. Important features of both kinds of markets are advertising and price discrimination, which we examine later in this chapter.

Unlike the chapters on perfect competition and monopoly, this chapter does not provide a single model to explain firms' behavior. There are too many variations on an uncertain theme for one model to explain the complexities of imperfect competition. Rather, the chapter provides an overview of some of the many different models and explanations advanced by economists for the behavior of firms in the imperfectly competitive markets. The analytical tools you have acquired in the course of studying the models of competitive and monopoly markets will be very much in evidence in this discussion.

In Groupon's case, the going got much tougher over the ensuing years. Its founder, Mr. Mason, was fired in 2013 and he subsequently remarked that Groupon was a "stupid, boring idea that just happened to resonate." Its revenue from daily deals has remained flat since 2011, but it has branched out into other areas of e-commerce, such as selling goods at a discount at "Groupon Goods" and food delivery at "Groupon to Go." *Fortune* writer Erin Griffith has put the blame for lackluster performance on low barriers to entry into Groupon's markets. There is even a company called Groupon Clone that builds the software that competitors need to offer their own daily deals and they have done just that. Groupon not only spent to acquire dozens of those competitors but also has had to fight harder to get new customers. The company has not been able to consolidate its market power and indeed continues to inhabit the world of imperfect competition.[1]

11.2 Monopolistic Competition: Competition Among Many

Learning Objectives

1. Explain the main characteristics of a monopolistically competitive industry, describing both its similarities and differences from the models of perfect competition and monopoly.
2. Explain and illustrate both short-run equilibrium and long-run equilibrium for a monopolistically competitive firm.
3. Explain what it means to say that a firm operating under monopolistic competition has excess capacity in the long run and discuss the implications of this conclusion.

monopolistic competition

A model characterized by
many firms producing
similar but differentiated
products in a market with
easy entry and exit.

The first model of an imperfectly competitive industry that we shall investigate has conditions quite similar to those of perfect competition. The model of monopolistic competition assumes a large number of firms. It also assumes easy entry and exit. This model differs from the model of perfect competition in one key respect: it assumes that the goods and services produced by firms are differentiated. This differentiation may occur by virtue of advertising, convenience of location, product quality, reputation of the seller, or other factors. Product differentiation gives firms producing a particular product some degree of price-setting or monopoly power. However, because of the availability of close substitutes, the price-setting power of monopolistically competitive firms is quite limited. **Monopolistic competition** is a model characterized by many firms producing similar but differentiated products in a market with easy entry and exit.

Restaurants are a monopolistically competitive sector; in most areas there are many firms, each is different, and entry and exit are very easy. Each restaurant has many close substitutes—these may include other restaurants, fast-food outlets, and the deli and frozen-food sections at local supermarkets. Other industries that engage in monopolistic competition include retail stores, barber and beauty shops, auto-repair shops, service stations, banks, and law and accounting firms.

Profit Maximization

Suppose a restaurant raises its prices slightly above those of similar restaurants with which it competes. Will it have any customers? Probably. Because the restaurant is different from other restaurants, some people will continue to patronize it. Within limits, then, the restaurant can set its own prices; it does not take the market prices as given. In fact, differentiated markets imply that the notion of a single "market price" is meaningless.

Because products in a monopolistically competitive industry are differentiated, firms face downward-sloping demand curves. Whenever a firm faces a downward-sloping demand curve, the graphical framework for monopoly can be used. In the short run, the model of monopolistic competition looks exactly like the model of monopoly. An important distinction between monopoly and monopolistic competition, however, emerges from the assumption of easy entry and exit. In monopolistic competition, entry will eliminate any economic profits in the long run. We begin with an analysis of the short run.

The Short Run

Because a monopolistically competitive firm faces a downward-sloping demand curve, its marginal revenue curve is a downward-sloping line that lies below the demand curve, as in the monopoly model. We can thus use the model of monopoly that we have already developed to analyze the choices of a monopsony in the short run.

Figure 11.1 shows the demand, marginal revenue, marginal cost, and average total cost curves facing a monopolistically competitive firm, Mama's Pizza. Mama's competes with several other similar firms in a market in which entry and exit are relatively easy. Mama's demand curve D_1 is downward-sloping; even if Mama's raises its prices above those of its competitors, it will still have some customers. Given the downward-sloping demand curve, Mama's marginal revenue curve MR_1 lies below demand. To sell more pizzas, Mama's must lower its price, and that means its marginal revenue from additional pizzas will be less than price.

FIGURE 11.1 Short-Run Equilibrium in Monopolistic Competition

Looking at the intersection of the marginal revenue curve MR_1 and the marginal cost curve MC, we see that the profit-maximizing quantity is 2,150 units per week. Reading up to the average total cost curve ATC, we see that the cost per unit equals $9.20. Price, given on the demand curve D_1, is $10.40, so the profit per unit is $1.20. Total profit per week equals $1.20 times 2,150, or $2,580; it is shown by the shaded rectangle.

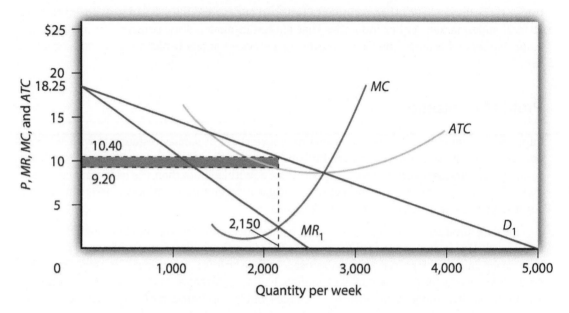

Given the marginal revenue curve MR and marginal cost curve MC, Mama's will maximize profits by selling 2,150 pizzas per week. Mama's demand curve tells us that it can sell that quantity at a price of $10.40. Looking at the average total cost curve ATC, we see that the firm's cost per unit is $9.20. Its economic profit per unit is thus $1.20. Total economic profit, shown by the shaded rectangle, is $2,580 per week.

The Long Run

We see in Figure 11.1 that Mama's Pizza is earning an economic profit. If Mama's experience is typical, then other firms in the market are also earning returns that exceed what their owners could be earning in some related activity. Positive economic profits will encourage new firms to enter Mama's market.

As new firms enter, the availability of substitutes for Mama's pizzas will increase, which will reduce the demand facing Mama's Pizza and make the demand curve for Mama's Pizza more elastic. Its demand curve will shift to the left. Any shift in a demand curve shifts the marginal revenue curve as well. New firms will continue to enter, shifting the demand curves for existing firms to the left, until pizza firms such as Mama's no longer make an economic profit. The zero-profit solution occurs where Mama's demand curve is tangent to its average total cost curve—at point A in Figure 11.2. Mama's price will fall to $10 per pizza and its output will fall to 2,000 pizzas per week. Mama's will just cover its opportunity costs, and thus earn zero economic profit. At any other price, the firm's cost per unit would be greater than the price at which a pizza could be sold, and the firm would sustain an economic loss. Thus, the firm and the industry are in long-run equilibrium. There is no incentive for firms to either enter or leave the industry.

FIGURE 11.2 Monopolistic Competition in the Long Run

The existence of economic profits in a monopolistically competitive industry will induce entry in the long run. As new firms enter, the demand curve D_1 and marginal revenue curve MR_1 facing a typical firm will shift to the left, to D_2 and MR_2. Eventually, this shift produces a profit-maximizing solution at zero economic profit, where D_2 is tangent to the average total cost curve ATC (point A). The long-run equilibrium solution here is an output of 2,000 units per week at a price of $10 per unit.

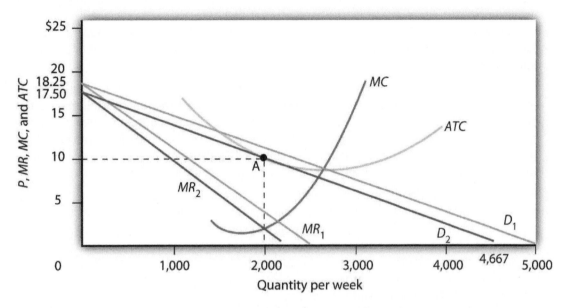

Had Mama's Pizza and other similar restaurants been incurring economic losses, the process of moving to long-run equilibrium would work in reverse. Some firms would exit. With fewer substitutes available, the demand curve faced by each remaining firm would shift to the right. Price and output at each restaurant would rise. Exit would continue until the industry was in long-run equilibrium, with the typical firm earning zero economic profit.

Such comings and goings are typical of monopolistic competition. Because entry and exit are easy, favorable economic conditions in the industry encourage start-ups. New firms hope that they can differentiate their products enough to make a go of it. Some will; others will not. Competitors to Mama's may try to improve the ambience, play different music, offer pizzas of different sizes and types. It might take a while for other restaurants to come up with just the right product to pull customers and profits away from Mama's. But as long as Mama's continues to earn economic profits, there will be incentives for other firms to try.

Heads Up!

The term "monopolistic competition" is easy to confuse with the term "monopoly." Remember, however, that the two models are characterized by quite different market conditions. A monopoly is a single firm with high barriers to entry. Monopolistic competition implies an industry with many firms, differentiated products, and easy entry and exit.

Why is the term monopolistic competition used to describe this type of market structure? The reason is that it bears some similarities to both perfect competition and to monopoly. Monopolistic competition is similar to perfect competition in that in both of these market structures many firms make up the industry and entry and exit are fairly easy. Monopolistic competition is similar to monopoly in that, like monopoly firms, monopolistically competitive firms have at least some discretion when it comes to setting prices. However, because monopolistically competitive firms produce goods that are close substitutes for those of rival firms, the degree of monopoly power that monopolistically competitive firms possess is very low.

Excess Capacity: The Price of Variety

The long-run equilibrium solution in monopolistic competition always produces zero economic profit at a point to the left of the minimum of the average total cost curve. That is because the zero profit solution occurs at the point where the downward-sloping demand curve is tangent to the average total cost curve, and thus the average total cost curve is itself downward-sloping. By expanding output, the firm could lower average total cost. The firm thus produces less than the output at which it would minimize average total cost. A firm that operates to the left of the lowest point on its average total cost curve has **excess capacity**.

Because monopolistically competitive firms charge prices that exceed marginal cost, monopolistic competition is inefficient. The marginal benefit consumers receive from an additional unit of the good is given by its price. Since the benefit of an additional unit of output is greater than the marginal cost, consumers would be better off if output were expanded. Furthermore, an expansion of output would reduce average total cost. But monopolistically competitive firms will not voluntarily increase output, since for them, the marginal revenue would be less than the marginal cost.

One can thus criticize a monopolistically competitive industry for falling short of the efficiency standards of perfect competition. But monopolistic competition is inefficient because of product differentiation. Think about a monopolistically competitive activity in your area. Would consumers be better off if all the firms in this industry produced identical products so that they could match the assumptions of perfect competition? If identical products were impossible, would consumers be better off if some of the firms were ordered to shut down on grounds the model predicts there will be "too many" firms? The inefficiency of monopolistic competition may be a small price to pay for a wide range of product choices. Furthermore, remember that perfect competition is merely a model. It is not a goal toward which an economy might strive as an alternative to monopolistic competition.

Key Takeaways

- A monopolistically competitive industry features some of the same characteristics as perfect competition: a large number of firms and easy entry and exit.
- The characteristic that distinguishes monopolistic competition from perfect competition is differentiated products; each firm is a price setter and thus faces a downward-sloping demand curve.
- Short-run equilibrium for a monopolistically competitive firm is identical to that of a monopoly firm. The firm produces an output at which marginal revenue equals marginal cost and sets its price according to its demand curve.
- In the long run in monopolistic competition any economic profits or losses will be eliminated by entry or by exit, leaving firms with zero economic profit.
- A monopolistically competitive industry will have some excess capacity; this may be viewed as the cost of the product diversity that this market structure produces.

Try It!

Suppose the monopolistically competitive restaurant industry in your town is in long-run equilibrium, when difficulties in hiring cause restaurants to offer higher wages to cooks, servers, and dishwashers. Using graphs similar to Figure 11.1 and Figure 11.2, explain the effect of the wage increase on the industry in the short run and in the long run. Be sure to include in your answer an explanation of what happens to price, output, and economic profit.

Case in Point: Craft Brewers: The Rebirth of a Monopolistically Competitive Industry

Source: © 2010 Jupiterimages Corporation

In the early 1900s, there were about 2,000 local beer breweries across America. Prohibition in the 1920s squashed the industry; after the repeal of Prohibition, economies of scale eliminated smaller breweries. By the early 1980s only about 40 remained in existence.

But the American desire for more variety has led to the rebirth of the nearly defunct industry. To be sure, large, national beer companies dominated the overall ale market in 1980 and they still do today. But their emphasis on similarly tasting, light lagers (at least, until they felt threatened enough by the new craft brewers to come up with their own specialty brands) left many niches to be filled. One niche has been filled by imports, while another niche has been filled by domestic specialty or "craft" breweries. In 2015, about 72 percent of beer sales were from large breweries, 16 percent from imports, and about 12 percent from craft breweries. The new craft brewers, which include contract brewers, regional specialty brewers, microbreweries, and brewpubs, offer choice.

Aided by the recent legalization in most states of brewpubs, establishments where beers are manufactured and retailed on the same premises, the number of microbreweries grew substantially over the last 30 years. Colorado Springs, a medium-sized city and hometown to the authors of your textbook, had twenty-eight local breweries in mid-2016, with several new ones slated to open over the next few months.

To what extent does this industry conform to the model of monopolistic competition? Clearly, the microbreweries sell differentiated products, giving them some degree of price-setting power. If you were to sample a few brewpubs in your area you would surely find a range of prices for house beers.

Entry into the industry seems fairly easy, judging from the phenomenal growth of the industry. In 1985 there were about 100 breweries. Fifteen years later, there were about 1,500. In 2015, there were more than 4,000. The start-up cost ranges from $100,000 to $400,000, according to Kevin Head, the owner of the Rhino Bar, also in Missoula.

The monopolistically competitive model also predicts that while firms can earn positive economic profits in the short run, entry of new firms will shift the demand curve facing each firm to the left and economic profits will fall toward zero. Some firms will exit as competitors win customers away from them. In the combined microbrewery and brewpub subsectors of the craft beer industry in 2015, for example, there were 617 openings and 67 closings.

Sources: Based on Stephanie Earls, "An Ever-Evolving Local Beer Scene," The Gazette, September 29, 2016, p. Go 8; Jim Ludwick, "The Art of Zymurgy—It's the Latest Thing: Microbrewers Are Tapping into the New Specialty Beer Market," Missoulian (November 29, 1996): p. A1; Brewers Association, "2015 Craft Brewing Statistics,"; Brewers Association, "2015 Craft Brewing Statistics," https://www.brewersassociation.org/statistics/number-of-breweries/.

Answer to Try It! Problem

As shown in Panel (a), higher wages would cause both MC and ATC to increase. The upward shift in MC from MC_1 to MC_2 would cause the profit-maximizing level of output (number of meals served per week, in this case) to fall from q_1 to q_2 and price to increase from P_1 to P_2. The increase in ATC from ATC_1 to ATC_2 would mean that some restaurants would be earning negative economic profits, as shown by the shaded area.

As shown in Panel (b), in the long run, as some restaurants close down, the demand curve faced by the typical remaining restaurant would shift to the right from D_1 to D_2. The demand curve shift leads to a corresponding shift in marginal revenue from MR_1 to MR_2. Price would increase further from P_2 to P_3, and output would increase to q_3, above q_2. In the new long-run equilibrium, restaurants would again be earning zero economic profit.

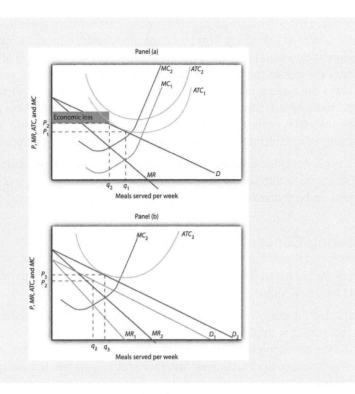

11.3 Oligopoly: Competition Among the Few

Learning Objectives

1. Explain the main characteristics of an oligopoly, differentiating it from other types of market structures.
2. Explain the measures that are used to determine the degree of concentration in an industry.
3. Explain and illustrate the collusion model of oligopoly.
4. Discuss how game theory can be used to understand the behavior of firms in an oligopoly.

In July, 2005, General Motors Corporation (GMC) offered "employee discount pricing" to virtually all GMC customers, not just employees and their relatives. This new marketing strategy introduced by GMC obviously affected Ford, Chrysler, Toyota and other automobile and truck manufacturers; Ford matched GMC's employee-discount plan by offering up to $1,000 to its own employees who convinced friends to purchase its cars and trucks. Ford also offered its customers the same prices paid by its employees. By mid-July, Chrysler indicated that it was looking at many alternatives, but was waiting for GMC to make its next move. Ultimately, Chrysler also offered employee discount pricing.

Toyota had to respond. It quickly developed a new marketing strategy of its own, which included lowering the prices of its cars and offering new financing terms. The responses of Ford, Chrysler, and Toyota to GMC's pricing strategy obviously affected the outcome of that strategy. Similarly, a decision by Procter & Gamble to lower the price of Crest toothpaste may elicit a response from Colgate-Palmolive, and that response will affect the sales of Crest. In an **oligopoly**, the fourth and final market structure that we will study, the market is dominated by a few firms, each of which recognizes that its own actions will produce a response from its rivals and that those responses will affect it.

oligopoly

Situation in which a market is dominated by a few firms, each of which recognizes that its own actions will produce a response from its rivals and that those responses will affect it.

The firms that dominate an oligopoly recognize that they are interdependent: What one firm does affects each of the others. This interdependence stands in sharp contrast to the models of perfect competition and monopolistic competition, where we assume that each firm is so small that it assumes the rest of the market will, in effect, ignore what it does. A perfectly competitive firm responds to the market, not to the actions of any other firm. A monopolistically competitive firm responds to its own demand, not to the actions of specific rivals. These presumptions greatly simplify the analysis of perfect competition and monopolistic competition. We do not have that luxury in oligopoly, where the interdependence of firms is the defining characteristic of the market.

Some oligopoly industries make standardized products: steel, aluminum, wire, and industrial tools. Others make differentiated products: cigarettes, automobiles, computers, ready-to-eat breakfast cereal, and soft drinks.

Measuring Concentration in Oligopoly

Oligopoly means that a few firms dominate an industry. But how many is "a few," and how large a share of industry output does it take to "dominate" the industry?

Compare, for example, the ready-to-eat breakfast cereal industry and the ice cream industry. The cereal market is dominated by two firms, Kellogg's and General Mills, which together hold more than half the cereal market. This oligopoly operates in a highly concentrated market. The market for ice cream, where the four largest firms account for just less than a third of output, is much less concentrated.

concentration ratio

The percentage of output accounted for by the largest firms in an industry.

One way to measure the degree to which output in an industry is concentrated among a few firms is to use a **concentration ratio**, which reports the percentage of output accounted for by the largest firms in an industry. The higher the concentration ratio, the more the firms in the industry take account of their rivals' behavior. The lower the concentration ratio, the more the industry reflects the characteristics of monopolistic competition or perfect competition.

The U.S. Census Bureau, based on surveys it conducts of manufacturing firms every five years, reports concentration ratios. These surveys show concentration ratios for the largest 4, 8, 20, and 50 firms in each industry category. Some concentration ratios from the 2012 survey, the latest available, are reported in Table 11.1. Notice that the four-firm concentration ratio for breakfast cereals is 79 percent; for ice cream it is 46 percent.

TABLE 11.1 Concentration Ratios and Herfindahl–Hirschman Indexes
Two measures of industry concentration are reported by the Census Bureau: concentration ratios and the Herfindahl–Hirschman Index (HHI).

Industry	Largest 4 firms	Largest 8 firms	Largest 20 firms	Largest 50 firms	HHI
Ice cream	45.9	64.6	82.6	94.0	666
Breakfast cereals	79.2	93.7	99.8	100	2333
Tobacco manufacturing	87.8	93.6	97.8	99.9	2897
Men's and boys' cut and sew apparel	23.9	35.4	55.5	78.2	236
Women's and girls' cut and sew apparel	21.9	30.3	45.6	62.8	236
Automobiles	60.2	88.7	99.1	99.7	1178
Sporting and athletic goods	32.3	46.7	58.8	72.5	373
Dental laboratories	21.1	28.3	36.3	43.4	136

Source: Based on data from Share of Value of Shipments Accounting for by the 4, 8, 20, and 50 Largest Companies for industry codes: 311520, 311230, 312230, 315220, 315240, 336111, 339920, 339116, 2012. U.S. Economic Census at factfinder.census.gov/faces/nav/jsf/pages/searchresults.xhtml?refresh=t

An alternative measure of concentration is found by squaring the percentage share (stated as a whole number) of each firm in an industry, then summing these squared market shares to derive a **Herfindahl-Hirschman Index (HHI)**. The largest HHI possible is the case of monopoly, where one firm has 100% of the market; the index is 100^2, or 10,000. An industry with two firms, each with 50% of total output, has an HHI of 5,000 ($50^2 + 50^2$). In an industry with 10,000 firms that have 0.01% of the market each, the HHI is 1. Herfindahl–Hirschman Indexes reported by the Census Bureau are also given in Table 11.1. Notice that the HHI is 2,333 for breakfast cereals and only 666 for ice cream, suggesting that the ice cream industry is more competitive than the breakfast cereal industry.

In some cases, the census data understate the degree to which a few firms dominate the market. One problem is that industry categories may be too broad to capture significant cases of industry dominance. The sporting goods industry, for example, appears to be highly competitive if we look just at measures of concentration, but markets for individual goods, such as golf clubs, running shoes, and tennis rackets, tend to be dominated by a few firms. Further, the data reflect shares of the national market. A tendency for regional domination does not show up. For example, the concrete industry appears to be highly competitive. But concrete is produced in local markets—it is too expensive to ship it very far—and many of these local markets are dominated by a handful of firms.

The census data can also overstate the degree of actual concentration. The "automobiles" category, for example, has a four-firm concentration ratio that suggests the industry is strongly dominated by four large firms (in fact, U.S. production is dominated by three: General Motors, Ford, and Chrysler). Those firms hardly account for all car sales in the United States, however, as other foreign producers have captured a large portion of the domestic market. Including those foreign competitors suggests a far less concentrated industry than the census data imply.

The Collusion Model

There is no single model of profit-maximizing oligopoly behavior that corresponds to economists' models of perfect competition, monopoly, and monopolistic competition. Uncertainty about the interaction of rival firms makes specification of a single model of oligopoly impossible. Instead, economists have devised a variety of models that deal with the uncertain nature of rivals' responses in different ways. In this section we review one type of oligopoly model, the collusion model. After examining this traditional approach to the analysis of oligopoly behavior, we shall turn to another method of examining oligopolistic interaction: game theory.

Firms in any industry could achieve the maximum profit attainable if they all agreed to select the monopoly price and output and to share the profits. One approach to the analysis of oligopoly is to assume that firms in the industry collude, selecting the monopoly solution.

Suppose an industry is a **duopoly**, an industry with two firms. Figure 11.3 shows a case in which the two firms are identical. They sell identical products and face identical demand and cost conditions. To simplify the analysis, we will assume that each has a horizontal marginal cost curve, MC. The demand and marginal revenue curves are the same for both firms. We find the combined demand curve for the two firms, $D_{combined}$, by adding the individual demand curves together. Because one firm's demand curve, D_{firm}, represents one-half of market demand, it is the same as the combined marginal revenue curve for the two firms. If these two firms act as a monopoly, together they produce Q_m and charge a price P_m. This result is achieved if each firm selects its profit-maximizing output, which equals $1/2\ Q_m$. This solution is inefficient; the efficient solution is price P_c and output Q_c, found where the combined market demand curve $D_{combined}$ and the marginal cost curve MC intersect.

Herfindahl-Hirschman Index (HHI)

An alternative measure of concentration found by squaring the percentage share (stated as a whole number) of each firm in an industry, then summing these squared market shares.

duopoly

An industry that has only two firms.

FIGURE 11.3 Monopoly Through Collusion

Two identical firms have the same horizontal marginal cost curve *MC*. Their demand curves D_{firm} and marginal revenue curves MR_{firm} are also identical. The combined demand curve is $D_{combined}$; the combined marginal revenue curve is $MR_{combined}$. The profits of the two firms are maximized if each produces 1/2 Q_m at point A. Industry output at point B is thus Q_m and the price is P_m. At point C, the efficient solution output would be Q_c, and the price would equal *MC*.

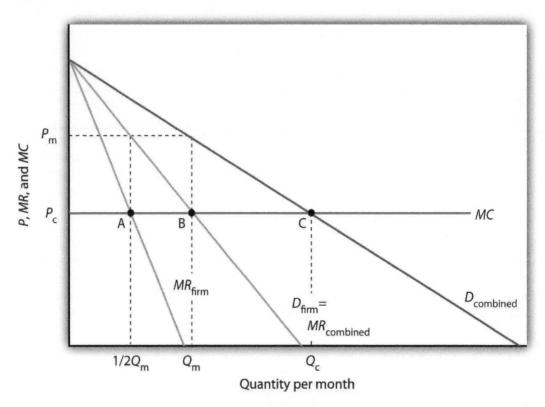

overt collusion

When firms openly agree on price, output, and other decisions aimed at achieving monopoly profits.

In the simplest form of collusion, **overt collusion**, firms openly agree on price, output, and other decisions aimed at achieving monopoly profits. Firms that coordinate their activities through overt collusion and by forming collusive coordinating mechanisms make up a **cartel**.

Firms form a cartel to gain monopoly power. A successful cartel can earn large profits, but there are several problems with forming and maintaining one. First, in many countries, including the United States, cartels are generally illegal.[2] They are banned, because their purpose is to raise prices and restrict output. Second, the cartel may not succeed in inducing all firms in the industry to join. Firms that remain outside the cartel can compete by lowering price, and thus they prevent the cartel from achieving the monopoly solution. Third, there is always an incentive for individual members to cheat on cartel agreements. Suppose the members of a cartel have agreed to impose the monopoly price in their market and to limit their output accordingly. Any one firm might calculate that it could charge slightly less than the cartel price and thus capture a larger share of the market for itself. Cheating firms expand output and drive prices down below the level originally chosen.

The Organization of Petroleum Exporting Countries (OPEC), perhaps the best-known cartel, is made up of 13 oil-producing countries. In the 1970s, OPEC successfully acted like a monopoly by restricting output and raising prices. By the mid-1980s, however, the monopoly power of the cartel had been weakened by expansion of output by nonmember producers such as Mexico and Norway and by cheating among the cartel members.

cartel

Firms that coordinate their activities through overt collusion and by forming collusive coordinating mechanisms.

tacit collusion

An unwritten, unspoken understanding through which firms agree to limit their competition.

An alternative to overt collusion is **tacit collusion**, an unwritten, unspoken understanding through which firms agree to limit their competition. Firms may, for example, begin following the price leadership of a particular firm, raising or lowering their prices when the leader makes such a change. The price leader may be the largest firm in the industry, or it may be a firm that has been particularly good at assessing changes in demand or cost. At various times, tacit collusion has been alleged to occur in a wide range of industries, including steel, cars, and breakfast cereals.

It is difficult to know how common tacit collusion is. The fact that one firm changes its price shortly after another one does cannot prove that a tacit conspiracy exists. After all, we expect to see the prices of all firms in a perfectly competitive industry moving together in response to changes in demand or production costs.

Game Theory and Oligopoly Behavior

Oligopoly presents a problem in which decision makers must select strategies by taking into account the responses of their rivals, which they cannot know for sure in advance. The Start Up feature at the beginning of this chapter suggested the uncertainty eBay faces as it considers the possibility of competition from Google. A choice based on the recognition that the actions of others will affect the outcome of the choice and that takes these possible actions into account is called a **strategic choice**. **Game theory** is an analytical approach through which strategic choices can be assessed.

Among the strategic choices available to an oligopoly firm are pricing choices, marketing strategies, and product-development efforts. An airline's decision to raise or lower its fares—or to leave them unchanged—is a strategic choice. The other airlines' decision to match or ignore their rival's price decision is also a strategic choice. IBM boosted its share in the highly competitive personal computer market in large part because a strategic product-development strategy accelerated the firm's introduction of new products.

Once a firm implements a strategic decision, there will be an outcome. The outcome of a strategic decision is called a **payoff**. In general, the payoff in an oligopoly game is the change in economic profit to each firm. The firm's payoff depends partly on the strategic choice it makes and partly on the strategic choices of its rivals. Some firms in the airline industry, for example, raised their fares in 2005, expecting to enjoy increased profits as a result. They changed their strategic choices when other airlines chose to slash their fares, and all firms ended up with a payoff of lower profits—many went into bankruptcy.

We shall use two applications to examine the basic concepts of game theory. The first examines a classic game theory problem called the prisoners' dilemma. The second deals with strategic choices by two firms in a duopoly.

The Prisoners' Dilemma

Suppose a local district attorney (DA) is certain that two individuals, Frankie and Johnny, have committed a burglary, but she has no evidence that would be admissible in court.

The DA arrests the two. On being searched, each is discovered to have a small amount of cocaine. The DA now has a sure conviction on a possession of cocaine charge, but she will get a conviction on the burglary charge only if at least one of the prisoners confesses and implicates the other.

The DA decides on a strategy designed to elicit confessions. She separates the two prisoners and then offers each the following deal: "If you confess and your partner doesn't, you will get the minimum sentence of one year in jail on the possession and burglary charges. If you both confess, your sentence will be three years in jail. If your partner confesses and you do not, the plea bargain is off and you will get six years in prison. If neither of you confesses, you will each get two years in prison on the drug charge."

The two prisoners each face a dilemma; they can choose to confess or not confess. Because the prisoners are separated, they cannot plot a joint strategy. Each must make a strategic choice in isolation.

strategic choice

A choice based on the recognition that the actions of others will affect the outcome of the choice and that takes these possible actions into account.

game theory

An analytical approach through which strategic choices can be assessed.

payoff

The outcome of a strategic decision.

The outcomes of these strategic choices, as outlined by the DA, depend on the strategic choice made by the other prisoner. The payoff matrix for this game is given in Figure 11.4. The two rows represent Frankie's strategic choices; she may confess or not confess. The two columns represent Johnny's strategic choices; he may confess or not confess. There are four possible outcomes: Frankie and Johnny both confess (cell A), Frankie confesses but Johnny does not (cell B), Frankie does not confess but Johnny does (cell C), and neither Frankie nor Johnny confesses (cell D). The portion at the lower left in each cell shows Frankie's payoff; the shaded portion at the upper right shows Johnny's payoff.

If Johnny confesses, Frankie's best choice is to confess—she will get a three-year sentence rather than the six-year sentence she would get if she did not confess. If Johnny does not confess, Frankie's best strategy is still to confess—she will get a one-year rather than a two-year sentence. In this game, Frankie's best strategy is to confess, regardless of what Johnny does. When a player's best strategy is the same regardless of the action of the other player, that strategy is said to be a **dominant strategy**. Frankie's dominant strategy is to confess to the burglary.

For Johnny, the best strategy to follow, if Frankie confesses, is to confess. The best strategy to follow if Frankie does not confess is also to confess. Confessing is a dominant strategy for Johnny as well. A game in which there is a dominant strategy for each player is called a **dominant strategy equilibrium**. Here, the dominant strategy equilibrium is for both prisoners to confess; the payoff will be given by cell A in the payoff matrix.

From the point of view of the two prisoners together, a payoff in cell D would have been preferable. Had they both denied participation in the robbery, their combined sentence would have been four years in prison—two years each. Indeed, cell D offers the lowest combined prison time of any of the outcomes in the payoff matrix. But because the prisoners cannot communicate, each is likely to make a strategic choice that results in a more costly outcome. Of course, the outcome of the game depends on the way the payoff matrix is structured.

FIGURE 11.4 Payoff Matrix for the Prisoners' Dilemma
The four cells represent each of the possible outcomes of the prisoners' game.

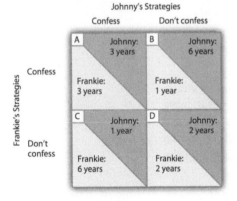

dominant strategy

When a player's best strategy is the same regardless of the action of the other player.

dominant strategy equilibrium

A game in which there is a dominant strategy for each player.

Repeated Oligopoly Games

The prisoners' dilemma was played once, by two players. The players were given a payoff matrix; each could make one choice, and the game ended after the first round of choices.

The real world of oligopoly has as many players as there are firms in the industry. They play round after round: a firm raises its price, another firm introduces a new product, the first firm cuts its price, a third firm introduces a new marketing strategy, and so on. An oligopoly game is a bit like a baseball game with an unlimited number of innings—one firm may come out ahead after one round, but another will emerge on top another day. In the computer industry game, the introduction of personal computers changed the rules. IBM, which had won the mainframe game quite handily, struggles to keep up in a world in which rivals continue to slash prices and improve quality.

Oligopoly games may have more than two players, so the games are more complex, but this does not change their basic structure. The fact that the games are repeated introduces new strategic considerations. A player must consider not just the ways in which its choices will affect its rivals now, but how its choices will affect them in the future as well.

We will keep the game simple, however, and consider a duopoly game. The two firms have colluded, either tacitly or overtly, to create a monopoly solution. As long as each player upholds the agreement, the two firms will earn the maximum economic profit possible in the enterprise.

There will, however, be a powerful incentive for each firm to cheat. The monopoly solution may generate the maximum economic profit possible for the two firms combined, but what if one firm captures some of the other firm's profit? Suppose, for example, that two equipment rental firms, Quick Rent and Speedy Rent, operate in a community. Given the economies of scale in the business and the size of the community, it is not likely that another firm will enter. Each firm has about half the market, and they have agreed to charge the prices that would be chosen if the two combined as a single firm. Each earns economic profits of $20,000 per month.

Quick and Speedy could cheat on their arrangement in several ways. One of the firms could slash prices, introduce a new line of rental products, or launch an advertising blitz. This approach would not be likely to increase the total profitability of the two firms, but if one firm could take the other by surprise, it might profit at the expense of its rival, at least for a while.

We will focus on the strategy of cutting prices, which we will call a strategy of cheating on the duopoly agreement. The alternative is not to cheat on the agreement. Cheating increases a firm's profits *if* its rival does not respond. Figure 11.5 shows the payoff matrix facing the two firms at a particular time. As in the prisoners' dilemma matrix, the four cells list the payoffs for the two firms. If neither firm cheats (cell D), profits remain unchanged.

This game has a dominant strategy equilibrium. Quick's preferred strategy, regardless of what Speedy does, is to cheat. Speedy's best strategy, regardless of what Quick does, is to cheat. The result is that the two firms will select a strategy that lowers their combined profits!

Quick Rent and Speedy Rent face an unpleasant dilemma. They want to maximize profit, yet each is likely to choose a strategy inconsistent with that goal. If they continue the game as it now exists, each will continue to cut prices, eventually driving prices down to the point where price equals average total cost (presumably, the price-cutting will stop there). But that would leave the two firms with zero economic profits.

Both firms have an interest in maintaining the status quo of their collusive agreement. Overt collusion is one device through which the monopoly outcome may be maintained, but that is illegal. One way for the firms to encourage each other not to cheat is to use a tit-for-tat strategy. In a **tit-for-tat strategy** a firm responds to cheating by cheating, and it responds to cooperative behavior by cooperating. As each firm learns that its rival will respond to cheating by cheating, and to cooperation by cooperating, cheating on agreements becomes less and less likely.

Still another way firms may seek to force rivals to behave cooperatively rather than competitively is to use a **trigger strategy**, in which a firm makes clear that it is willing and able to respond to cheating by permanently revoking an agreement. A firm might, for example, make a credible threat to cut prices down to the level of average total cost—and leave them there—in response to any price-cutting by a rival. A trigger strategy is calculated to impose huge costs on any firm that cheats—and on the firm that threatens to invoke the trigger. A firm might threaten to invoke a trigger in hopes that the threat will forestall any cheating by its rivals.

Game theory has proved to be an enormously fruitful approach to the analysis of a wide range of problems. Corporations use it to map out strategies and to anticipate rivals' responses. Governments use it in developing foreign-policy strategies. Military leaders play war games on computers using the basic ideas of game theory. Any situation in which rivals make strategic choices to which competitors will respond can be assessed using game theory analysis.

One rather chilly application of game theory analysis can be found in the period of the Cold War when the United States and the former Soviet Union maintained a nuclear weapons policy that was described by the acronym MAD, which stood for *mutually assured destruction*. Both countries had enough nuclear weapons to destroy the other several times over, and each threatened to launch sufficient nuclear weapons to destroy the other country if the other country launched a nuclear attack against it or any of its allies. On its face, the MAD doctrine seems, well, mad. It was, after all, a commitment by each nation to respond to any nuclear attack with a counterattack that many scientists expected would end human life on earth. As crazy as it seemed, however, it worked. For 40 years, the two nations did not go to war. While the collapse of the Soviet Union in 1991 ended

FIGURE 11.5 To Cheat or Not to Cheat: Game Theory in Oligopoly

Two rental firms, Quick Rent and Speedy Rent, operate in a duopoly market. They have colluded in the past, achieving a monopoly solution. Cutting prices means cheating on the arrangement; not cheating means maintaining current prices. The payoffs are changes in monthly profits, in thousands of dollars. If neither firm cheats, then neither firm's profits will change. In this game, cheating is a dominant strategy equilibrium.

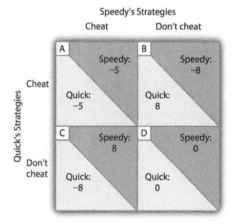

tit-for-tat strategy

Situation in which a firm responds to cheating by cheating, and responds to cooperative behavior by cooperating.

trigger strategy

Situation in which a firm makes clear that it is willing and able to respond to cheating by permanently revoking an agreement.

the need for a MAD doctrine, during the time that the two countries were rivals, MAD was a very effective trigger indeed.

Of course, the ending of the Cold War has not produced the ending of a nuclear threat. Several nations now have nuclear weapons. The threat that Iran will introduce nuclear weapons, given its stated commitment to destroy the state of Israel, suggests that the possibility of nuclear war still haunts the world community.

Key Takeaways

- The key characteristics of oligopoly are a recognition that the actions of one firm will produce a response from rivals and that these responses will affect it. Each firm is uncertain what its rivals' responses might be.
- The degree to which a few firms dominate an industry can be measured using a concentration ratio or a Herfindahl–Hirschman Index.
- One way to avoid the uncertainty firms face in oligopoly is through collusion. Collusion may be overt, as in the case of a cartel, or tacit, as in the case of price leadership.
- Game theory is a tool that can be used to understand strategic choices by firms.
- Firms can use tit-for-tat and trigger strategies to encourage cooperative behavior by rivals.

Try It!

Which model of oligopoly would seem to be most appropriate for analyzing firms' behavior in each of the situations given below?

1. When South Airlines lowers its fare between Miami and New York City, North Airlines lowers its fare between the two cities. When South Airlines raises its fare, North Airlines does too.
2. Whenever Bank A raises interest rates on car loans, other banks in the area do too.
3. In 1986, Saudi Arabia intentionally flooded the market with oil in order to punish fellow OPEC members for cheating on their production quotas.
4. In July 1998, Saudi Arabia floated a proposal in which a group of eight or nine major oil-exporting countries (including OPEC members and some nonmembers, such as Mexico) would manage world oil prices by adjusting their production.

Case in Point: Car Parts Makers Caught in Global Price-Fixing Scheme

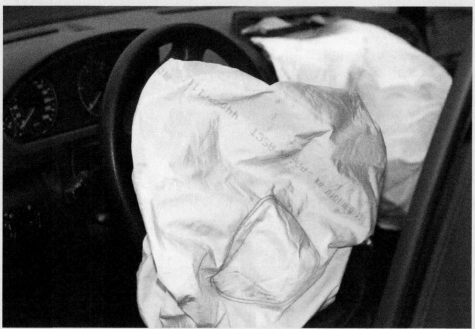

Source: © Shutterstock, Inc.

The price-fixing case against companies that supply automobile parts came to light in February 2010 on a Tuesday evening when the U.S. Department of Justice raided the U.S. offices in Michigan, Ohio, and Kentucky of three parts suppliers—Denso Corporation, Yazaki North America, and Tokai Rika. As reported by Dan Strumpf and Peter Yost in the *San Diego Union Tribune*, Justice Department spokesperson Gina Talamona stated at the time, "The antitrust division is investigating the possibility of anticompetitive cartel conduct…We are coordinating with the European Commission and other foreign competition authorities." A spokesperson for Tokai Rika said at the time," We haven't done anything wrong. We'll supply them with all the information."

By 2012, all three companies had agreed to pay criminal fines as part of plea bargain agreements and some executives had agreed to service prison time. In some cases, the companies exacerbated their predicaments when their executives told employees to delete emails and destroy paper documents before the raids.

By the middle of 2016, a total of 64 individuals and 44 companies that supply parts ranging from seat belts and ignition coils to air bags and windshield wipers to all the major car manufacturers had been charged and had agreed to pay more than $2.7 billion in fines. And the charges, indictments, plea bargaining, and prison sentences continue to roll along. In some cases, the behaviors had transpired for a decade or more.

"It's a very, very safe assumption that U.S. consumers paid more and sometimes significantly more, for their automobiles as a result of the conspiracy," said Brent Snyder, a deputy assistant attorney general at the Department of Justice in an interview with a *USA Today* reporter.

Industry analysts argue that the car parts industry is a likely one for collusion. There are only so many companies that supply each of the parts and their products are mostly standardized and homogeneous. Reducing competition by collectively setting prices and adopting bid-rigging schemes was too tempting. It's also illegal.

Sources: Based on Eric Tucker, "Auto parts price-fixing probe rattles industry," Associated Press, May 25, 2014 at http://bigstory.ap.org/article/auto-parts-price-fixing-probe-rattles-industry; Dan Strumpf and Peter Yost, Associated press writers, "FBI Raids Toyota Supplier Denso in Antitrust Probe," San Diego Union Tribune, February 24, 2010; U.S. Department of Justice, "Nishikawa Agrees to Plead Guilty and Pay $130 Million Criminal Fine for Fixing Prices of Automotive Parts," press release, July 20, 2016.

Answers to Try It! Problems

1. North Airlines seems to be practicing a price strategy known in game theory as tit-for-tat.
2. The banks could be engaged in tacit collusion, with Bank A as the price leader.
3. Saudi Arabia appears to have used a trigger strategy, another aspect of game theory. In general, of course, participants hope they will never have to "pull" the trigger, because doing so harms all participants. After years of cheating by other OPEC members, Saudi Arabia did undertake a policy that hurt all members of OPEC, including itself; OPEC has never since regained the prominent role it played in oil markets.
4. Saudi Arabia seems to be trying to create another oil cartel, a form of overt collusion.

11.4 Extensions of Imperfect Competition: Advertising and Price Discrimination

Learning Objectives

1. Discuss the possible effects of advertising on competition, price, and output.
2. Define price discrimination, list the conditions that make it possible, and explain the relationship between the price charged and price elasticity of demand.

The models of monopoly and of imperfectly competitive markets allow us to explain two commonly observed features of many markets: advertising and price discrimination. Firms in markets that are not perfectly competitive try to influence the positions of the demand curves they face, and hence profits, through advertising. Profits may also be enhanced by charging different customers different prices. In this section we will discuss these aspects of the behavior of firms in markets that are not perfectly competitive.

Advertising

Firms in monopoly, monopolistic competition, and oligopoly use advertising when they expect it to increase their profits. We see the results of these expenditures in a daily barrage of advertising on television, radio, newspapers, magazines, billboards, passing buses, park benches, the mail, home telephones, and the ubiquitous pop-up advertisements on our computers—in virtually every medium imaginable. Is all this advertising good for the economy?

We have already seen that a perfectly competitive economy with fully defined and easily transferable property rights will achieve an efficient allocation of resources. There is no role for advertising in such an economy, because everyone knows that firms in each industry produce identical products. Furthermore, buyers already have complete information about the alternatives available to them in the market.

But perfect competition contrasts sharply with imperfect competition. Imperfect competition can lead to a price greater than marginal cost and thus generate an inefficient allocation of resources. Firms in an imperfectly competitive market may advertise heavily. Does advertising cause inefficiency, or is it part of the solution? Does advertising insulate imperfectly competitive firms from competition and allow them to raise their prices even higher, or does it encourage greater competition and push prices down?

There are two ways in which advertising could lead to higher prices for consumers. First, the advertising itself is costly; it amounts to hundreds of billions of dollars annually in the United

States. By pushing up production costs, advertising may push up prices. If the advertising serves no socially useful purpose, these costs represent a waste of resources in the economy. Second, firms may be able to use advertising to manipulate demand and create barriers to entry. If a few firms in a particular market have developed intense brand loyalty, it may be difficult for new firms to enter—the advertising creates a kind of barrier to entry. By maintaining barriers to entry, firms may be able to sustain high prices.

But advertising has its defenders. They argue that advertising provides consumers with useful information and encourages price competition. Without advertising, these defenders argue, it would be impossible for new firms to enter an industry. Advertising, they say, promotes competition, lowers prices, and encourages a greater range of choice for consumers.

Advertising, like all other economic phenomena, has benefits as well as costs. To assess those benefits and costs, let us examine the impact of advertising on the economy.

Advertising and Information

Advertising does inform us about products and their prices. Even critics of advertising generally agree that when advertising advises consumers about the availability of new products, or when it provides price information, it serves a useful function. But much of the information provided by advertising appears to be of limited value. Hearing that "Pepsi is the right one, baby" or "Tide gets your clothes whiter than white" may not be among the most edifying lessons consumers could learn.

Some economists argue, however, that even advertising that seems to tell us nothing may provide useful information. They note that a consumer is unlikely to make a repeat purchase of a product that turns out to be a dud. Advertising an inferior product is likely to have little payoff; people who do try it are not likely to try it again. It is not likely a firm could profit by going to great expense to launch a product that produced only unhappy consumers. Thus, if a product is heavily advertised, its producer is likely to be confident that many consumers will be satisfied with it and make repeat purchases. If this is the case, then the fact that the product is advertised, regardless of the content of that advertising, signals consumers that at least its producer is confident that the product will satisfy them.

Advertising and Competition

If advertising creates consumer loyalty to a particular brand, then that loyalty may serve as a barrier to entry to other firms. Some brands of household products, such as laundry detergents, are so well established they may make it difficult for other firms to enter the market.

In general, there is a positive relationship between the degree of concentration of market power and the fraction of total costs devoted to advertising. This relationship, critics argue, is a causal one; the high expenditures on advertising are the cause of the concentration. To the extent that advertising increases industry concentration, it is likely to result in higher prices to consumers and lower levels of output. The higher prices associated with advertising are not simply the result of passing on the cost of the advertising itself to consumers; higher prices also derive from the monopoly power the advertising creates.

But advertising may encourage competition as well. By providing information to consumers about prices, for example, it may encourage price competition. Suppose a firm in a world of no advertising wants to increase its sales. One way to do that is to lower price. But without advertising, it is extremely difficult to inform potential customers of this new policy. The likely result is that there would be little response, and the price experiment would probably fail. Price competition would thus be discouraged in a world without advertising.

Empirical studies of markets in which advertising is not allowed have confirmed that advertising encourages price competition. One of the most famous studies of the effects of advertising looked at pricing for prescription eyeglasses. In the early 1970s, about half the states in the United States banned advertising by firms making prescription eyeglasses; the other half allowed it. A comparison of prices in the two groups of states by economist Lee Benham showed that the cost of prescription eyeglasses was far lower in states that allowed advertising than in states that banned it.[3] Mr. Benham's research proved quite influential—virtually all states have since revoked their bans on such advertising. Similarly, a study of the cigarette industry revealed that before the 1970 ban on radio and television advertising market shares of the leading cigarette manufacturers had been declining, while after the ban market shares and profit margins increased.[4]

Advertising may also allow more entry by new firms. When Kia, a South Korean automobile manufacturer, entered the U.S. low-cost compact car market in 1994, it flooded the airwaves with advertising. Suppose such advertising had not been possible. Could Kia have entered the market in the United States? It seems highly unlikely that any new product could be launched without advertising. The absence of advertising would thus be a barrier to entry that would increase the degree of monopoly power in the economy. A greater degree of monopoly power would, over time, translate into higher prices and reduced output.

Advertising is thus a two-edged sword. On the one hand, the existence of established and heavily advertised rivals may make it difficult for a new firm to enter a market. On the other hand, entry into most industries would be virtually impossible without advertising.

Economists do not agree on whether advertising helps or hurts competition in particular markets, but one general observation can safely be made—a world with advertising is more competitive than a world without advertising would be. The important policy question is more limited—and more difficult to answer: Would a world with *less* advertising be more competitive than a world with more?

Price Discrimination

Throughout the text up to this point, we have assumed that firms sold all units of output at the same price. In some cases, however, firms can charge different prices to different consumers. If such an opportunity exists, the firm can increase profits further.

price discrimination

Situation in which a firm charges different prices for the same good or service to different consumers, even though there is no difference in the cost to the firm of supplying these consumers.

When a firm charges different prices for the same good or service to different consumers, even though there is no difference in the cost to the firm of supplying these consumers, the firm is engaging in **price discrimination**. Except for a few situations of price discrimination that have been declared illegal, such as manufacturers selling their goods to distributors at different prices when there are no differences in cost, price discrimination is generally legal.

The potential for price discrimination exists in all market structures except perfect competition. As long as a firm faces a downward-sloping demand curve and thus has some degree of monopoly power, it may be able to engage in price discrimination. But monopoly power alone is not enough to allow a firm to price discriminate. Monopoly power is one of three conditions that must be met:

1. **A Price-Setting Firm** The firm must have some degree of monopoly power—it must be a price setter. A price-taking firm can only take the market price as given—it is not in a position to make price choices of any kind. Thus, firms in perfectly competitive markets will not engage in price discrimination. Firms in monopoly, monopolistically competitive, or oligopolistic markets may engage in price discrimination.

2. **Distinguishable Customers** The market must be capable of being fairly easily segmented—separated so that customers with different elasticities of demand can be identified and treated differently.

3. **Prevention of Resale** The various market segments must be isolated in some way from one another to prevent customers who are offered a lower price from selling to customers who are charged a higher price. If consumers can easily resell a product, then discrimination is unlikely

to be successful. Resale may be particularly difficult for certain services, such as dental check-ups.

Examples of price discrimination abound. Senior citizens and students are often offered discount fares on city buses. Children receive discount prices for movie theater tickets and entrance fees at zoos and theme parks. Faculty and staff at colleges and universities might receive discounts at the campus bookstore. Airlines give discount prices to customers who are willing to stay over a Saturday night. Physicians might charge wealthy patients more than poor ones. People who save coupons are able to get discounts on many items. In all these cases a firm charges different prices to different customers for what is essentially the same product.

Not every instance of firms charging different prices to different customers constitutes price discrimination. Differences in prices may reflect different costs associated with providing the product. One buyer might require special billing practices, another might require delivery on a particular day of the week, and yet another might require special packaging. Price differentials based on differences in production costs are not examples of price discrimination.

Why would a firm charge different prices to different consumers? The answer can be found in the marginal decision rule and in the relationship between marginal revenue and elasticity.

Suppose an airline has found that its long-run profit-maximizing solution for a round-trip flight between Minneapolis and Cleveland, when it charges the same price to all passengers, is to carry 300 passengers at $200 per ticket. The airline has a degree of monopoly power, so it faces a downward-sloping demand curve. The airline has noticed that there are essentially two groups of customers on each flight: people who are traveling for business reasons and people who are traveling for personal reasons (visiting family or friends or taking a vacation). We will call this latter group "tourists." Of the 300 passengers, 200 are business travelers and 100 are tourists. The airline's revenue from business travelers is therefore currently $40,000 ($200 times 200 business travelers) and from tourists is currently $20,000 ($200 times 100 tourists).

It seems likely that the price elasticities of demand of these two groups for a particular flight will differ. Tourists may have a wide range of substitutes: They could take their trips at a different time, they could vacation in a different area, or they could easily choose not to go at all. Business travelers, however, might be attending meetings or conferences at a particular time and in a particular city. They have options, of course, but the range of options is likely to be more limited than the range of options facing tourists. Given all this, tourists are likely to have relatively more price elastic demand than business travelers for a particular flight.

The difference in price elasticities suggests the airline could increase its profit by adjusting its pricing. To simplify, suppose that at a price of about $200 per ticket, demand by tourists is relatively price elastic and by business travelers is relatively less price elastic. It is plausible that the marginal cost of additional passengers is likely to be quite low, since the number of crewmembers will not vary and no food is served on short flights. Thus, if the airline can increase its revenue, its profits will increase. Suppose the airline lowers the price for tourists to $190. Suppose that the lower price encourages 10 more tourists to take the flight. Of course, the airline cannot charge different prices to different tourists; rather it charges $190 to all, now 110, tourists. Still, the airline's revenue from tourist passengers increases from $20,000 to $20,900 ($190 times 110 tourists). Suppose it charges $250 to its business travelers. As a result, only 195 business travelers take the flight. The airline's revenue from business travelers still rises from $40,000 to $48,750 ($250 times 195 business travelers). The airline will continue to change the mix of passengers, and increase the number of passengers, so long as doing so increases its profit. Because tourist demand is relatively price elastic, relatively small reductions in price will attract relatively large numbers of additional tourists. Because business demand is relatively less elastic, relatively large increases in price will discourage relatively small numbers of business travelers from making the trip. The airline will continue to reduce its price to tourists and raise its price to business travelers as long as it gains profit from doing so.

Of course, the airline can impose a discriminatory fare structure only if it can distinguish tourists from business travelers. Airlines typically do this by looking at the travel plans of their customers. Trips that involve a stay over a weekend, for example, are more likely to be tourist related, whereas trips that begin and end during the workweek are likely to be business trips. Thus, airlines charge much lower fares for trips that extend through a weekend than for trips that begin and end on weekdays.

In general, price-discrimination strategies are based on differences in price elasticity of demand among groups of customers and the differences in marginal revenue that result. A firm will seek a price structure that offers customers with more elastic demand a lower price and offers customers with relatively less elastic demand a higher price.

It is always in the interest of a firm to discriminate. Yet most of the goods and services that we buy are not offered on a discriminatory basis. A grocery store does not charge a higher price for vegetables to vegetarians, whose demand is likely to be less elastic than that of its omnivorous customers. An audio store does not charge a different price for Pearl Jam's compact disks to collectors seeking a complete collection than it charges to casual fans who could easily substitute a disk from another performer. In these cases, firms lack a mechanism for knowing the different demands of their customers and for preventing resale.

Key Takeaways

- If advertising reduces competition, it tends to raise prices and reduce quantities produced. If it enhances competition, it tends to lower prices and increase quantities produced.
- In order to engage in price discrimination, a firm must be a price setter, must be able to identify consumers whose elasticities differ, and must be able to prevent resale of the good or service among consumers.
- The price-discriminating firm will adjust its prices so that customers with more elastic demand pay lower prices than customers with less elastic demand.

Try It!

Explain why price discrimination is often found in each of the following settings. Does it make sense in terms of price elasticity of demand?

1. Senior citizen discounts for travel
2. Food sold cheaper if the customer has a coupon for the item
3. College scholarships to students with the best academic records or to students with special athletic, musical, or other skills

Case in Point: Pricing Costa Rica's National Parks

Source: © 2010 Jupiterimages Corporation

Costa Rica boasts some of the most beautiful national parks in the world. An analysis by Francisco Alpizar, an economist who currently serves as director and senior research fellow of the Environment and Development Initiative Center for Central America, suggests that Costa Rica should increase the degree to which it engages in price discrimination in pricing its national parks.

The country has experimented with a wide range of prices for its national parks, with the price varying between $.80 and $15 for a daily visit. With data on the resultant number of visitors at each price, Professor Alpizar was able to estimate the demand curve, compute the price elasticity of demand, and develop a recommendation for pricing the country's national parks.

Presumably, foreign visitors have a relatively less elastic demand for visiting the parks than do local citizens. Local citizens have better knowledge of substitutes for the parks—namely other areas in Costa Rica. And, of course, once foreign travelers are in the country, they have already committed the expense of getting there, and are less likely to be willing to pass up a visit to national parks based on pricing considerations.

Costa Rica already discriminates to a large degree. At the time of the study, foreigners were charged $7 per day to visit the parks; locals were charged $2. Professor Alpizar proposed increasing the degree of discrimination.

He estimated that the price elasticity of foreign demand for visits to Costa Rica's national parks is –0.68. That, of course, suggests inelastic demand. Costa Rica could increase its revenue from foreign visitors by increasing the fee. Professor Alpizar proposed increasing the fee for foreigners to $10. He proposed that the price charged to Costa Ricans remain at $2—a price that he calculated equals the marginal cost of an additional visit.

Professor Alpizar calculated a fee of $10 per visit by a foreigner would more than pay the country's fixed cost of maintaining its extensive park system, which utilizes 24 percent of the country's land. The higher price would thus allow the government to meet the major costs of operating the national parks. Charging a $2 fee to locals would satisfy the efficiency requirement that price equal marginal cost for local visitors; the $10 fee to foreigners would permit the country to exploit its monopoly power in permitting people to visit the parks. The Costa Rican government asked Professor Alpizar to design three pilot projects aimed at incorporating his proposal to raise park fees to foreign visitors.

In 2014, national park entry fees were raised for foreign tourists and now average about $13 with a price range from $5 to $50. The entry fees for the vast majority of the twenty-eight national parks are between $10 and $15. For Costa Ricans, many parks still cost $2 per day, although entrance to some can be as high as $7.50. Local tourists are offered free entry on the second Wednesday of each month. There are no free days for foreign tourists.

Source: Based on Francisco Alpizar, "The Pricing of Protected Areas in Nature-Based Tourism: A Local Prospective," Ecological Economics, 56(2) (February 2006): 294–307 and personal correspondence with Professor Alpizar; " Costa Rica sets higher park entrance fees in bid for more revenue for protected areas," Tico Times, May 14, 2014 at http://www.ticotimes.net/2014/05/14/ in-a-bid-for-more-revenue-for-protected-areas-costa-rica-sets-higher-park-entrance-fees; and Costa Rica Travel Blog at https://costaricatravelblog.com/2014/07/26/costa-rica-national-park- wildlife-refuge-and-biological-reserve-entrance-fees-set-to-increase-heres-how-much-a-visit-to- each-will-cost/.

Answers to Try It! Problems

1. Senior citizens are (usually!) easy to identify, and for travel, preventing resale is usually quite easy as well. For example, a picture ID is required to board an airplane. Airlines might be expected to oppose implementing the rule since it is costly for them. The fact that they support the rule can be explained by how it aids them in practicing price discrimination, by preventing the resale of discount tickets, which now can easily be matched to the purchasing customers. The demand for air travel by senior citizens is likely to be more elastic than it is for other passengers, especially business travelers, since the purpose of their travel is largely discretionary (often touristic in nature) and since their time is likely to be less costly, making them more willing to seek out information on travel alternatives than the rest of the population.

2. Since the customer must present the coupon at the point of sale, identification is easy. Willingness to search for and cut out coupons suggests a high degree of price consciousness and thus a greater price elasticity of demand.

3. Such students are likely to have more choices of where to attend college. As we learned in an earlier chapter on elasticity, demand is likely to be more elastic when substitutes are available for it. Enrollment procedures make identification and prevention of resale very easy.

11.5 Review and Practice

Summary

This chapter examined the world of imperfect competition that exists between the idealized extremes of perfect competition and monopoly. Imperfectly competitive markets exist whenever there is more than one seller in a market and at least one seller has some degree of control over price.

We discussed two general types of imperfectly competitive markets: monopolistic competition and oligopoly. Monopolistic competition is characterized by many firms producing similar but differentiated goods and services in a market with easy entry and exit. Oligopoly is characterized by relatively few firms producing either standardized or differentiated products. There may be substantial barriers to entry and exit.

In the short run, a monopolistically competitive firm's pricing and output decisions are the same as those of a monopoly. In the long run, economic profits will be whittled away by the entry of new firms and new products that increase the number of close substitutes. An industry dominated by a few firms is an oligopoly. Each oligopolist is aware of its interdependence with other firms in the industry and is constantly aware of the behavior of its rivals. Oligopolists engage in strategic decision making in order to determine their best output and pricing strategies as well as the best forms of nonprice competition.

Advertising in imperfectly competitive markets can increase the degree of competitiveness by encouraging price competition and promoting entry. It can also decrease competition by establishing brand loyalty and thus creating barriers to entry.

Where conditions permit, a firm can increase its profits by price discrimination, charging different prices to customers with different elasticities of demand. To practice price discrimination, a price-setting firm must be able to segment customers that have different elasticities of demand and must be able to prevent resale among its customers.

Concept Problems

1. What are the major distinctions between a monopolistically competitive industry and an oligopolistic industry?

2. What is the difference between a price taker and a price setter? Which do you think a firm would prefer to be? Why?

3. In the model of monopolistic competition, we say that there is product differentiation. What does this mean, and how does it differ from the assumption of homogeneous goods in perfect competition?

4. In the following list of goods and services, determine whether the item is produced under conditions of monopolistic competition or of oligopoly.

    a. soft drinks

    b. exercise drinks

    c. office supply stores

    d. massage therapists

    e. accountants

    f. colleges and universities

    g. astrologists

5. Suppose a city experiences substantial population growth. What is likely to happen to profits in the short run and in the long run in the market for haircuts, a monopolistically competitive market?

6. Some professors grade students on the basis of an absolute percentage of the highest score earned on each test given during the semester. All students who get within a certain percentage of the highest score earned get an A. Why do these professors not worry that the students will get together and collude in such a way as to keep the high score in the class equal to a very low total?

7. Your parents probably told you to avoid tit-for-tat behavior. Why does it make sense for firms to do it?

8. What model of oligopoly behavior did the car parts makers that were discussed in the Case in Point follow? How might they have achieved their goal and still stayed within the law?

9. Explain why a price increase for foreigners would increase Costa Rica's total revenue and profits from operating its national park system.

10. Restaurants typically charge much higher prices for dinner than for lunch, despite the fact that the cost of serving these meals is about the same. Why do you think this is the case? (*Hint:* Think about the primary consumers of these meals and their respective elasticities.)

11. What effect do you think advertising to discourage cigarette smoking will have on teens? On adults? What changes might occur in the cigarette market as a result?

12. Many manufacturers of clothing and other consumer goods open stores in outlet malls where they charge much lower prices than they charge in their own stores located within cities. Outlet malls are typically located a considerable distance from major metropolitan areas, and

stores in them typically charge much lower prices than do stores located within cities. Given that both sets of stores are often owned by the same firm, explain this price discrimination based on likely differences in the price elasticity of demand between consumers in the two types of stores.

13. Suppose a particular state were to ban the advertising of prices charged by firms that provide laser eye surgery. What effect do you think that would have on the price of this service?

14. The Case in Point on microbreweries noted that a large number of such breweries open every year. Yet, the model of monopolistic competition predicts that the long run equilibrium solution in such markets is one of zero economic profits. Why do firms enter such industries?

15. Many lawyers advertise their services. Do you think this raises or lowers the price of legal services? Explain your answer carefully.

Numerical Problems

1. Suppose the monopolistically competitive barber shop industry in a community is in long-run equilibrium, and that the typical price is $20 per haircut. Moreover, the population is rising.

   a. Illustrate the short-run effects of a change on the price and output of a typical firm in the market.

   b. Show what happens in the long run. Will the final price be higher than $20? Equal $20? Be less than $20? Assume that nothing happens to the cost of producing haircuts.

   c. Suppose that, initially, the price of a typical children's haircut is $10. Do you think this represents price discrimination? Why or why not?

2. Consider the same industry as in Problem 1. Suppose the market is in long-run equilibrium and that an annual license fee is imposed on barber shops.

   a. Illustrate the short-run effects of the change on the price and output of haircuts for a typical firm in the community.

   b. Now show what happens to price and output for a typical firm in the long run.

   c. Who pays the fee in the long run? How does this compare to the conclusions of the model of perfect competition?

3. Industry A consists of four firms, each of which has an equal share of the market.

   a. Compute the Herfindahl-Hirschman index for the industry.

   b. Industry B consists of 10 firms, each of which has an equal share of the market. Compare the Herfindahl–Hirschman Indexes for the two industries.

   c. Now suppose that there are 100 firms in the industry, each with equal shares. What is the Herfindahl-Hirschman index for this industry?

   d. State the general relationship between the competitiveness of an industry and its Herfindahl-Hirschman index.

4. Given the payoff matrix (shown below) for a duopoly, consisting of Firm A and Firm B, in which each firm is considering an expanded advertising campaign, answer the following questions (all figures in the payoff matrix give changes in annual profits in millions of dollars):

   a. Does Firm A have a dominant strategy?

   b. Does Firm B have a dominant strategy?

   c. Is there a dominant strategy equilibrium? Explain.

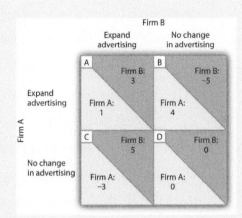

5. Suppose that two industries each have a four-firm concentration ratio of 75%.

    a. Explain what this means.

    b. Suppose that the HHI of the first industry is 425, and that the HHI of the second is 260. Which would you say is the more competitive? Why?

6. Suppose that a typical firm in a monopolistically competitive industry faces a demand curve given by:

    $q = 60 - (1/2)p$, where q is quantity sold per week.

    The firm's marginal cost curve is given by: $MC = 60$.

    a. How much will the firm produce in the short run?

    b. What price will it charge?

    c. Draw the firm's demand, marginal revenue, and marginal cost curves. Does this solution represent a long-run equilibrium? Why or why not?

Endnotes

1. "Groupon Anxiety: The Online-Coupon Firm Will Have to Move Fast to Retain Its Impressive Lead," Economist, March 17, 2011, p. 70–71; Julianne Pepitone, "Groupon Files to Raise $750 million in IPO," CNNMoney.com; Erin Griffith, "Counterpoint: Groupon is Not a Success," Fortune, March 20, 2015, http://fortune.com/2015/03/20/groupon-success/.

2. One legal cartel is the NCAA, which many economists regard as a successful device through which member firms (colleges and universities) collude on a wide range of rules through which they produce sports.

3. Lee Benham, "The Effect of Advertising on the Price of Eyeglasses," *Journal of Law and Economics* 15(2) (1972): 337–352.

4. Woodrow Eckard, "Competition and the Cigarette TV Advertising Ban," *Economic Inquiry* 29(1) (January 1991), 119–133.

CHAPTER 12
Wages and Employment in Perfect Competition

12.1 Start Up: College Pays

On NBC's 2005 television series, *The Apprentice: Street Smarts vs. Book Smarts*, the contestants without college degrees who were chosen for the program were earning three times as much as those with college degrees. The two sides fought valiantly against each other, and the final episode pitted 37 year old, "street smart" Tana, a top-selling sales woman for Mary Kay, against 26 year old, "book smart" Kendra, a real estate agent. At the end of the Apprentice series, it was Kendra, the college graduate, to whom then *Apprentice* host, now President Donald Trump, shouted, "You're hired!" As the array of contestants in the series demonstrates, not every college graduate earns more than every high school graduate, but on average, that is certainly the case.

One way of measuring the payoff from college is to compare the extent to which the wages of college-trained workers exceed the wages of high school–trained workers. In the United States the payoff from college has soared over the last 30 years.

In 1979, male college graduates 25 years of age and older earned 30% more than male high school graduates in the same age bracket. By 2009 the gap had increased more than two and a half times—male college graduates earned a stunning 79% more than male high school graduates. Female college graduates gained as well. Female college graduates 25 years of age and older earned 56% more than their high school–educated counterparts in 1979; that gap increased to a whopping 96% by 2009.

The dramatic widening of the wage gap between workers with different levels of education reflects the operation of demand and supply in the market for labor. For reasons we will explore in this chapter, the demand for college graduates was increasing while the demand for high school graduates—particularly male high school graduates—was slumping.

Why would the demand curves for different kinds of labor shift? What determines the demand for labor? What about the supply? How do changes in demand and supply affect wages and employment? In this chapter we will apply what we have learned so far about production, profit maximization, and utility maximization to answer those questions in the context of a perfectly competitive market for labor.

This is the first of three chapters focusing on factor markets, that is, on markets in which households supply factors of production—labor, capital, and natural resources—demanded by firms. Look back at the circular flow model introduced in the initial chapter on demand and supply. The bottom half of the circular flow model shows that households earn income from firms by supplying factors of production to them. The total income earned by households thus equals the total income earned by the labor, capital, and natural resources supplied to firms. Our focus in this chapter is on labor markets that operate in a competitive environment in which the individual buyers and sellers of labor are assumed to be price takers. Other chapters on factor markets will discuss competitive markets for capital and for natural resources and imperfectly competitive markets for labor and for other factors of production.

We can view the labor market as a single market, as suggested in Panel (a) of Figure 12.1. Here we assume that all workers are identical, that there is a single market for them, and that they all earn the same wage, W; the level of employment is L. Although the assumption of a single labor market flies wildly in the face of reality, economists often use it to highlight broad trends in the market. For example, if we want to show the impact of an increase in the demand for labor throughout the economy, we can show labor as a single market in which the increase in demand raises wages and employment.

FIGURE 12.1 Alternative Views of the Labor Market

One way to analyze the labor market is to assume that it is a single market with identical workers, as in Panel (a). Alternatively, we could examine specific pieces of the market, focusing on particular job categories or even on job categories in particular regions, as the graphs in Panel (b) suggest.

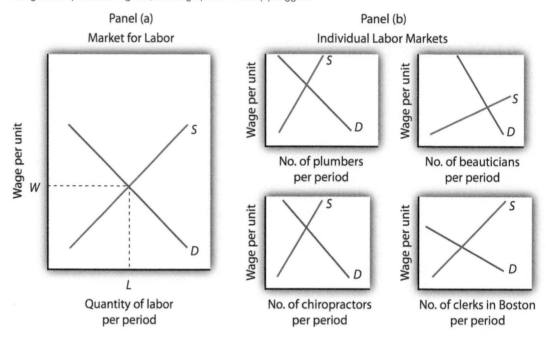

But we can also use demand and supply analysis to focus on the market for a particular group of workers. We might examine the market for plumbers, beauticians, or chiropractors. We might even want to focus on the market for, say, clerical workers in the Boston area. In such cases, we would examine the demand for and the supply of a particular segment of workers, as suggested by the graphs in Panel (b) of Figure 12.1.

Macroeconomic analysis typically makes use of the highly aggregated approach to labor-market analysis illustrated in Panel (a), where labor is viewed as a single market. Microeconomic analysis typically assesses particular markets for labor, as suggested in Panel (b).

When we use the model of demand and supply to analyze the determination of wages and employment, we are assuming that market forces, not individuals, determine wages in the economy. The model says that equilibrium wages are determined by the intersection of the demand and supply curves for labor in a particular market. Workers and firms in the market are thus price takers; they take the market-determined wage as given and respond to it. We are, in this instance, assuming that perfect competition prevails in the labor market. Just as there are some situations in the analysis of markets for goods and services for which such an assumption is inappropriate, so there are some cases in which the assumption is inappropriate for labor markets. We examine such cases in a later chapter. In this chapter, however, we will find that the assumption of perfect competition can give us important insights into the forces that determine wages and employment levels for workers.

We will begin our analysis of labor markets in the next section by looking at the forces that influence the demand for labor. In the following section we will turn to supply. In the final section, we will use what we have learned to look at labor markets at work.

12.2 The Demand for Labor

Learning Objectives

1. Apply the marginal decision rule to determine the quantity of labor that a firm in a perfectly competitive market will demand and illustrate this quantity graphically using the marginal revenue product and marginal factor cost curves.
2. Describe how to find the market demand curve for labor and discuss the factors that can cause the market demand curve for labor to shift.

A firm must have labor to produce goods and services. But how much labor will the firm employ? A profit-maximizing firm will base its decision to hire additional units of labor on the marginal decision rule: If the extra output that is produced by hiring one more unit of labor adds more to total revenue than it adds to total cost, the firm will increase profit by increasing its use of labor. It will continue to hire more and more labor up to the point that the extra revenue generated by the additional labor no longer exceeds the extra cost of the labor.

For example, if a computer software company could increase its annual total revenue by $50,000 by hiring a programmer at a cost of $49,000 per year, the marginal decision rule says that it should do so. Since the programmer will add $49,000 to total cost and $50,000 to total revenue, hiring the programmer will increase the company's profit by $1,000. If still another programmer would increase annual total revenue by $48,000 but would also add $49,000 to the firm's total cost, that programmer should not be hired because he or she would add less to total revenue than to total cost and would reduce profit.

Marginal Revenue Product and Marginal Factor Cost

The amount that an additional unit of a factor adds to a firm's total revenue during a period is called the **marginal revenue product (MRP)** of the factor. An additional unit of a factor of production adds to a firm's revenue in a two-step process: first, it increases the firm's output. Second, the increased output increases the firm's total revenue. We find marginal revenue product by multiplying the marginal product *(MP)* of the factor by the marginal revenue *(MR)*.

marginal revenue product

The amount that an additional unit of a factor adds to a firm's total revenue during a period.

EQUATION 12.1

$$MRP = MP \times MR$$

In a perfectly competitive market the marginal revenue a firm receives equals the market-determined price *P*. Therefore, for firms in perfect competition, we can express marginal revenue product as follows:

EQUATION 12.2

$$\text{In perfect competition, } MRP = MP \times P$$

The marginal revenue product of labor (MRP_L) is the marginal product of labor (MP_L) times the marginal revenue (which is the same as price under perfect competition) the firm obtains from additional units of output that result from hiring the additional unit of labor. If an additional worker adds 4 units of output per day to a firm's production, and if each of those 4 units sells for $20, then the worker's marginal revenue product is $80 per day. With perfect competition, the marginal revenue product for labor, MRP_L, equals the marginal product of labor, MP_L, times the price, *P*, of the good or service the labor produces:

EQUATION 12.3

$$\text{In perfect competition, } MRP_L = MP_L \times P$$

The law of diminishing marginal returns tells us that if the quantity of a factor is increased while other inputs are held constant, its marginal product will eventually decline. If marginal product is falling, marginal revenue product must be falling as well.

Suppose that an accountant, Stephanie Lancaster, has started an evening call-in tax advisory service. Between the hours of 7 p.m. and 10 p.m., customers can call and get advice on their income taxes. Ms. Lancaster's firm, TeleTax, is one of several firms offering similar advice; the going market price is $10 per call. Ms. Lancaster's business has expanded, so she hires other accountants to handle the calls. She must determine how many accountants to hire.

As Ms. Lancaster adds accountants, her service can take more calls. The table in Figure 12.2 gives the relationship between the number of accountants available to answer calls each evening and the number of calls TeleTax handles. Panel (a) shows the increase in the number of calls handled by each additional accountant—that accountant's marginal product. The first accountant can handle 13 calls per evening. Adding a second accountant increases the number of calls handled by 20. With two accountants, a degree of specialization is possible if each accountant takes calls dealing with questions about which he or she has particular expertise. Hiring the third accountant increases TeleTax's output per evening by 23 calls.

Suppose the accountants share a fixed facility for screening and routing calls. They also share a stock of reference materials to use in answering calls. As more accountants are added, the firm will begin to experience diminishing marginal returns. The fourth accountant increases output by 20 calls. The marginal product of additional accountants continues to decline after that. The marginal product curve shown in Panel (a) of Figure 12.2 thus rises and then falls.

Each call TeleTax handles increases the firm's revenues by $10. To obtain marginal revenue product, we multiply the marginal product of each accountant by $10; the marginal revenue product curve is shown in Panel (b) of Figure 12.2.

FIGURE 12.2 Marginal Product and Marginal Revenue Product

The table gives the relationship between the number of accountants employed by TeleTax each evening and the total number of calls handled. From these values we derive the marginal product and marginal revenue product curves.

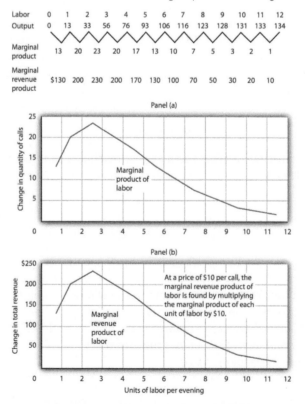

We can use Ms. Lancaster's marginal revenue product curve to determine the quantity of labor she will hire. Suppose accountants in her area are available to offer tax advice for a nightly fee of $150. Each additional accountant Ms. Lancaster hires thus adds $150 per night to her total cost. The amount a factor adds to a firm's total cost per period is called its **marginal factor cost (MFC)**. Marginal factor cost *(MFC)* is the change in total cost *(ΔTC)* divided by the change in the quantity of the factor *(Δf)*:

> **marginal factor cost**
>
> The amount that an additional unit of a factor adds to a firm's total cost per period.

EQUATION 12.4

$$\text{MFC} = \frac{\Delta \text{TC}}{\Delta f}$$

The marginal factor cost to TeleTax of additional accountants ($150 per night) is shown as a horizontal line in Figure 12.3. It is simply the market wage (i.e., the price per unit of labor).

FIGURE 12.3 Marginal Revenue Product and Demand
The downward-sloping portion of a firm's marginal revenue product curve is its demand curve for a variable factor. At a marginal factor cost of $150, TeleTax hires the services of five accountants.

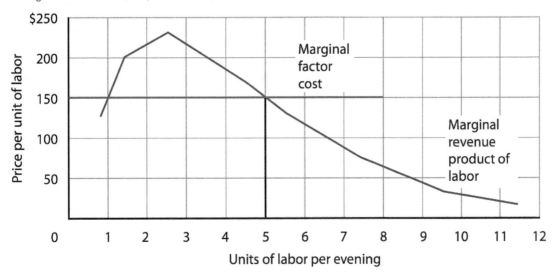

TeleTax will maximize profit by hiring additional units of labor up to the point where the downward-sloping portion of the marginal revenue product curve intersects the marginal factor cost curve; we see in Figure 12.3 that it will hire five accountants. Based on the information given in the table in Figure 12.2, we know that the five accountants will handle a total of 93 calls per evening; TeleTax will earn total revenue of $930 per evening. The firm pays $750 for the services of the five accountants—that leaves $180 to apply to the fixed cost associated with the tax advice service and the implicit cost of Stephanie Lancaster's effort in organizing the service. Recall that these implicit costs include the income forgone (that is, opportunity cost) by not shifting her resources, including her own labor, to her next best alternative.

If TeleTax had to pay a higher price for accountants, it would face a higher marginal factor cost curve and would hire fewer accountants. If the price were lower, TeleTax would hire more accountants. The downward-sloping portion of TeleTax's marginal revenue product curve shows the number of accountants it will hire at each price for accountants; it is thus the firm's demand curve for accountants. It is the portion of the curve that exhibits diminishing returns, and a firm will always seek to operate in the range of diminishing returns to the factors it uses.

It may seem counterintuitive that firms do not operate in the range of increasing returns, which would correspond to the upward-sloping portion of the marginal revenue product curve. However, to do so would forgo profit-enhancing opportunities. For example, in Figure 12.3, adding the second accountant adds $200 to revenue but only $150 to cost, so hiring that accountant clearly adds to profit. But why stop there? What about hiring a third accountant? That additional hire adds even more to revenue ($230) than to cost. In the region of increasing returns, marginal revenue product rises. With marginal factor cost constant, not to continue onto the downward-sloping part of the marginal revenue curve would be to miss out on profit-enhancing opportunities. The firm continues adding accountants until doing so no longer adds more to revenue than to cost, and that necessarily occurs where the marginal revenue product curve slopes downward.

In general, then, we can interpret the downward-sloping portion of a firm's marginal revenue product curve for a factor as its demand curve for that factor.[1] We find the market demand for labor by adding the demand curves for individual firms.

Heads Up!

The Two Rules Lead to the Same Outcome
In the chapter on competitive output markets we learned that profit-maximizing firms will increase output so long as doing so adds more to revenue than to cost, or up to the point where marginal revenue, which in perfect competition is the same as the market-determined price, equals marginal cost. In this chapter we have learned that profit-maximizing firms will hire labor up to the point where marginal revenue product equals marginal factor cost. Is it possible that a firm that follows the marginal decision rule for hiring labor would end up producing a different quantity of output compared to the quantity of output it would choose if it followed the marginal decision rule for deciding directly how much output to produce? Is there a conflict between these two marginal decision rules?

The answer is no. These two marginal decision rules are really just two ways of saying the same thing: one rule is in terms of quantity of output and the other in terms of the quantity of factors required to produce that quantity of output. Hiring an additional unit of a factor means producing a certain amount of additional output.

Using the example of TeleTax, at \$150 per accountant per night, we found that Ms. Lancaster maximizes profit by hiring five accountants. The MP_L of the fifth accountant is ΔQ; it is 17. At five accountants, the marginal cost of a call is $\Delta TC/\Delta Q$ = \$150/17 = \$8.82, which is less than the price of \$10 per call, so hiring that accountant adds to her profit. At six accountants, the marginal cost of a call would be \$150/13 = \$11.54, which is greater than the \$10 price, so hiring a sixth accountant would lower profit. The profit-maximizing output of 93 calls, found by comparing marginal cost and price, is thus consistent with the profit-maximizing quantity of labor of five accountants, found by comparing marginal revenue product and marginal factor cost.

Shifts in Labor Demand

The fact that a firm's demand curve for labor is given by the downward-sloping portion of its marginal revenue product of labor curve provides a guide to the factors that will shift the curve. In perfect competition, marginal revenue product equals the marginal product of labor times the price of the good that the labor is involved in producing; anything that changes either of those two variables will shift the curve. The marginal revenue product of labor will change when there is a change in the quantities of other factors employed. It will also change as a result of a change in technology, a change in the price of the good being produced, or a change in the number of firms hiring the labor.

Changes in the Use of Other Factors of Production

complementary factors of production

Factors of production for which an increase in the use of one increases the demand for the other.

As a firm changes the quantities of different factors of production it uses, the marginal product of labor may change. Having more reference manuals, for example, is likely to make additional accountants more productive—it will increase their marginal product. That increase in their marginal product would increase the demand for accountants. When an increase in the use of one factor of production increases the demand for another, the two factors are **complementary factors of production**.

One important complement of labor is human capital, the set of skills and abilities workers bring to the production of goods and services. When workers gain additional human capital, their marginal product rises. The demand for them by firms thus increases. This is perhaps one reason why you have decided to pursue a college education.

Other inputs may be regarded as substitutes for each other. A robot, for example, may substitute for some kinds of assembly-line labor. Two factors are **substitute factors of production** if the increased use of one lowers the demand for the other.

> **substitute factors of production**
>
> Factors of production for which an increase in the use of one decreases the demand for the other.

Changes in Technology

Technological changes can increase the demand for some workers and reduce the demand for others. The production of a more powerful computer chip, for example, may increase the demand for software engineers. It may also allow other production processes to be computerized and thus reduce the demand for workers who had been employed in those processes.

Technological changes have significantly increased the economy's output over the past century. The application of sophisticated technologies to production processes has boosted the marginal products of workers who have the skills these technologies require. That has increased the demand for skilled workers. The same technologies have been a substitute for less-skilled workers, and the demand for those workers has fallen. As the Case in Point on the impact of computer technology implies, envisioning the impact of technological change on demand for different kinds of labor may be something to keep in mind as you consider educational options. As you consider your major, for example, you should keep in mind that some occupations may benefit from technological changes; others may not.

Changes in Product Demand

A change in demand for a final product changes its price, at least in the short run. An increase in the demand for a product increases its price and increases the demand for factors that produce the product. A reduction in demand for a product reduces its price and reduces the demand for the factors used in producing it. Because the demand for factors that produce a product depends on the demand for the product itself, factor demand is said to be **derived demand**. That is, factor demand is derived from the demand for the product that uses the factor in its production.

> **derived demand**
>
> Refers to the idea that demand for factors of production depends on the demand for the products that use the factors of production.

Suppose, for example, that the demand for airplanes increases. The price and quantity of airplanes available will go up. A higher price for airplanes increases the marginal revenue product of labor of airplane-assembly workers and thus increases the demand for these workers.

Just as increases in the demand for particular goods or services increase the demand for the workers that produce them, so reductions in demand for particular goods or services will reduce the demand for the workers that produce them. An example is the relationship between the demand for train travel and the demand for conductors. Over the years, the fall in demand for train travel has reduced the demand for railroad conductors.

Changes in the Number of Firms

We can determine the demand curve for any factor by adding the demand for that factor by each of the firms using it. If more firms employ the factor, the demand curve shifts to the right. A reduction in the number of firms shifts the demand curve to the left. For example, if the number of restaurants in an area increases, the demand for waiters and waitresses in the area goes up. We expect to see local wages for these workers rise as a result.

Key Takeaways

- In using the model of demand and supply to examine labor markets, we assume in this chapter that perfect competition exists—that all workers and employers are price takers.
- A firm's demand curve for a factor is the downward-sloping portion of the marginal revenue product curve of the factor.
- The market demand for labor is found by adding the demand curves for labor of individual firms.
- The market demand for labor will change as a result of a change in the use of a complementary input or a substitute input, a change in technology, a change in the price of the good produced by labor, or a change in the number of firms that employ the labor.

Try It!

How would each of the following affect the demand for labor by the accounting advice service, TeleTax, described in this chapter?

1. A reduction in the market price for a tax advice call
2. An increase in the market fee for the accountants that TeleTax hires
3. An increase in the marginal product of each accountant due to an expansion of the facility for screening and routing calls and an increase in the number of reference materials available to the accountants

Case in Point: Computer Technology Increases the Demand for Some Workers and Reduces the Demand for Others

Source: © 2010 Jupiterimages Corporation

". . . [M]oving an object, performing a calculation, communicating a piece of information or resolving a discrepancy . . . [W]hich of these tasks can be performed by a computer?" ask economists David H. Autor, Frank Levy, and Richard J. Murname.

In general, computers are good at performing routine tasks (with routine tasks in this context not referring to tasks which are ordinary or mundane but rather tasks which are explicit and codifiable) and substitute for labor that had performed such tasks in the past. Conversely, computers are complements for workers performing nonroutine tasks, i.e., tasks that require such attributes as creativity, flexibility, and problem-solving. As the price of computers has fallen in recent decades, the demand for labor performing nonroutine tasks, usually college-educated workers, has grown, while the demand for labor performing routine tasks has fallen. The chart below illustrates how computerization likely affects demand for different kinds of labor.

	Routine Tasks	Nonroutine Tasks
Analytic and Interactive Tasks		
Examples:	• Record-keeping • Calculation • Repetitive customer service (e.g., bank teller)	• Forming/testing hypotheses • Medical diagnosis • Legal writing • Persuading/selling • Managing others
Computer Impact:	• Substantial substitution	• Strong complementarities
Manual Tasks		
Examples:	• Picking or sorting • Repetitive assembly	• Janitorial services • Truck driving
Computer Impact:	• Substantial substitution	• Limited opportunities for substitution or complementary

In studying the impact of computerization on labor demand, the authors have also noted the changes in tasks (task-shifting) that different occupations have come to encompass. For example, the Department of Labor's *Occupation Outlook Handbook* in 1976 described the tasks of a secretary to include typing, taking shorthand, and dealing with callers. By 2000, the *Handbook* recognized that with office automation the job of secretary has morphed to include such new responsibilities as providing training and orientation to new staff and conducting internet research.

This line of research seems to suggest a continuing polarization of employment, with the incorporation of more and more technology in the workplace expanding opportunities for the highly skilled and for the least skilled. But in a recent study by Dr. Autor, he argues that while some of the tasks in middle-skills job will be automated, there are aspects of those jobs that will not easily be replaced by machines. These jobs range from medical support occupations (such as radiology or nurse technicians) to repair occupations (such as plumbers and electricians). At the minimum these jobs require some personal interaction but also some problem-solving and flexibility.

Finally, addressing the question of whether machines will put most of us out of work, Dr. Autor emphasizes that, while the headlines tend to focus on machines substituting for workers, the research shows that there are many examples of machines and workers being complements to each other. Does he foresee a future where human labor becomes superfluous? On this, Dr. Autor quotes 1966 Economics Nobel Prize winner Herbert Simon, who was responding to the 1960s' automation scare by saying, "Insofar as they are economic problems at all, the world's problems in this generation and the next are problems of scarcity, not of intolerable abundance. The bogeyman of automation consumes worrying capacity that should be saved for real problems. . . ."

Sources: Based on David H. Autor, Frank Levy, and Richard J. Murname, "The Skill Content of Recent Technological Change: An Empirical Exploration," Quarterly Journal of Economics, 118: 4 (November 2003): 1279–1333; David H. Autor, "Why Are There Still So Many Jobs? The History and Future of Workplace Automation," Journal of Economic Perspectives 29:3 (Summer 2015): 3-30.

Answers to Try It! Problems

1. A reduction in market price would decrease the marginal revenue product of labor. Since the demand for labor is the downward-sloping portion of the marginal revenue product curve, the demand for labor by TeleTax would shift to the left.

2. An increase in the market fee that TeleTax pays the accountants it hires corresponds to an increase in marginal factor cost. TeleTax's demand curve would not shift; rather TeleTax would move up along its same demand curve for accountants. As a result, TeleTax would hire fewer accountants.

3. An increase in the marginal product of each accountant corresponds to a rightward shift in the marginal revenue product curve and hence a rightward shift in TeleTax's demand curve for accountants.

12.3 The Supply of Labor

Learning Objectives

1. Explain the income and substitution effects of a wage change and how they affect the shape of the labor supply curve.
2. Discuss the factors that can cause the supply curve for labor to shift.

The demand for labor is one determinant of the equilibrium wage and equilibrium quantity of labor in a perfectly competitive market. The supply of labor, of course, is the other.

Economists think of the supply of labor as a problem in which individuals weigh the opportunity cost of various activities that can fill an available amount of time and choose how to allocate it. Everyone has 24 hours in a day. There are lots of uses to which we can put our time: we can raise children, work, sleep, play, or participate in volunteer efforts. To simplify our analysis, let us assume that there are two ways in which an individual can spend his or her time: in work or in leisure. Leisure is a type of consumption good; individuals gain utility directly from it. Work provides income that, in turn, can be used to purchase goods and services that generate utility.

The more work a person does, the greater his or her income, but the smaller the amount of leisure time available. An individual who chooses more leisure time will earn less income than would otherwise be possible. There is thus a tradeoff between leisure and the income that can be earned from work. We can think of the supply of labor as the flip side of the demand for leisure. The more leisure people demand, the less labor they supply.

Two aspects of the demand for leisure play a key role in understanding the supply of labor. First, leisure is a normal good. All other things unchanged, an increase in income will increase the demand for leisure. Second, the opportunity cost or "price" of leisure is the wage an individual can earn. A worker who can earn $10 per hour gives up $10 in income by consuming an extra hour of leisure. The $10 wage is thus the price of an hour of leisure. A worker who can earn $20 an hour faces a higher price of leisure.

Income and Substitution Effects

Suppose wages rise. The higher wage increases the price of leisure. We saw in the chapter on consumer choice that consumers substitute more of other goods for a good whose price has risen. The substitution effect of a higher wage causes the consumer to substitute labor for leisure. To put it another way, the higher wage induces the individual to supply a greater quantity of labor.

We can see the logic of this substitution effect in terms of the marginal decision rule. Suppose an individual is considering a choice between extra leisure and the additional income from more work. Let MU_{Le} denote the marginal utility of an extra hour of leisure. What is the price of an extra hour of leisure? It is the wage W that the individual forgoes by not working for an hour. The extra utility of $1 worth of leisure is thus given by MU_{Le}/W.

Suppose, for example, that the marginal utility of an extra hour of leisure is 20 and the wage is $10 per hour. Then MU_{Le}/W equals 20/10, or 2. That means that the individual gains 2 units of utility by spending an additional $1 worth of time on leisure. For a person facing a wage of $10 per hour, $1 worth of leisure would be the equivalent of 6 minutes of leisure time.

Let MU_Y be the marginal utility of an additional $1 of income ($Y$ is the abbreviation economists generally assign to income). The price of $1 of income is just $1, so the price of income P_Y is always $1. Utility is maximized by allocating time between work and leisure so that:

EQUATION 12.5

$$\frac{MU_Y}{P_Y} = \frac{MU_{Le}}{W}$$

Now suppose the wage rises from W to W'. That reduces the marginal utility of $1 worth of leisure, MU_{Le}/W, so that the extra utility of earning $1 will now be greater than the extra utility of $1 worth of leisure:

EQUATION 12.6

$$\frac{MU_Y}{P_Y} > \frac{MU_{Le}}{W'}$$

Faced with the inequality in Equation 12.6, an individual will give up some leisure time and spend more time working. As the individual does so, however, the marginal utility of the remaining leisure time rises and the marginal utility of the income earned will fall. The individual will continue to make the substitution until the two sides of the equation are again equal. For a worker, the substitution effect of a wage increase always reduces the amount of leisure time consumed and increases the amount of time spent working. A higher wage thus produces a positive substitution effect on labor supply.

But the higher wage also has an income effect. An increased wage means a higher income, and since leisure is a normal good, the quantity of leisure demanded will go up. And that means a *reduction* in the quantity of labor supplied.

For labor supply problems, then, the substitution effect is always positive; a higher wage induces a greater quantity of labor supplied. But the income effect is always negative; a higher wage implies a higher income, and a higher income implies a greater demand for leisure, and more leisure means a lower quantity of labor supplied. With the substitution and income effects working in opposite directions, it is not clear whether a wage increase will increase or decrease the quantity of labor supplied—or leave it unchanged.

Figure 12.4 illustrates the opposite pull of the substitution and income effects of a wage change facing an individual worker. A janitor, Meredith Wilson, earns $10 per hour. She now works 42 hours per week, on average, earning $420.

FIGURE 12.4 The Substitution and Income Effects of a Wage Change

The substitution and income effects influence Meredith Wilson's supply of labor when she gets a pay raise. At a wage of $10 per hour, she supplies 42 hours of work per week (point A). At $15 per hour, the substitution effect pulls in the direction of an increased quantity of labor supplied, and the income effect pulls in the opposite direction.

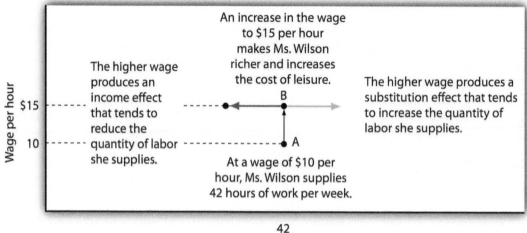

Now suppose Ms. Wilson receives a $5 raise to $15 per hour. As shown in Figure 12.4, the substitution effect of the wage change induces her to increase the quantity of labor she supplies; she substitutes some of her leisure time for additional hours of work. But she is richer now; she can afford more leisure. At a wage of $10 per hour, she was earning $420 per week. She could earn that same amount at the higher wage in just 28 hours. With her higher income, she can certainly afford more leisure time. The income effect of the wage change is thus negative; the quantity of labor supplied falls. The effect of the wage increase on the quantity of labor Ms. Wilson actually supplies depends on the relative strength of the substitution and income effects of the wage change. We will see what Ms. Wilson decides to do in the next section.

Wage Changes and the Slope of the Supply Curve

What would any one individual's supply curve for labor look like? One possibility is that over some range of labor hours supplied, the substitution effect will dominate. Because the marginal utility of leisure is relatively low when little labor is supplied (that is, when most time is devoted to leisure), it takes only a small increase in wages to induce the individual to substitute more labor for less leisure. Further, because few hours are worked, the income effect of those wage changes will be small.

Figure 12.5 shows Meredith Wilson's supply curve for labor. At a wage of $10 per hour, she supplies 42 hours of work per week (point A). An increase in her wage to $15 per hour boosts her quantity supplied to 48 hours per week (point B). The substitution effect thus dominates the income effect of a higher wage.

FIGURE 12.5 A Backward-Bending Supply Curve for Labor
As the wage rate increases from $10 to $15 per hour, the quantity of labor Meredith Wilson supplies increases from 42 to 48 hours per week. Between points A and B, the positive substitution effect of the wage increase outweighs the negative income effect. As the wage rises above $15, the negative income effect just offsets the substitution effect, and Ms. Wilson's supply curve becomes a vertical line between points B and C. As the wage rises above $20, the income effect becomes stronger than the substitution effect, and the supply curve bends backward between points C and D.

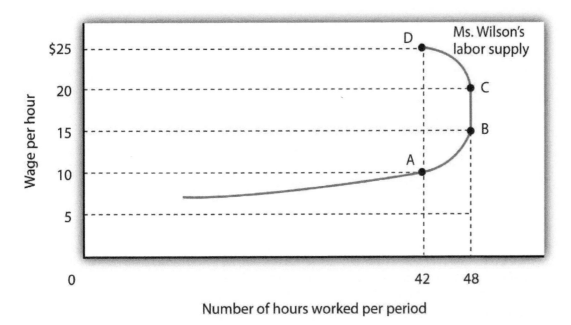

It is possible that beyond some wage rate, the negative income effect of a wage increase could just offset the positive substitution effect; over that range, a higher wage would have no effect on the quantity of labor supplied. That possibility is illustrated between points B and C on the supply curve in Figure 12.5; Ms. Wilson's supply curve is vertical. As wages continue to rise, the income effect becomes even stronger, and additional increases in the wage reduce the quantity of labor she supplies. The supply curve illustrated here bends backward beyond point C and thus assumes a negative slope. The supply curve for labor can thus slope upward over part of its range, become vertical, and then bend backward as the income effect of higher wages begins to dominate the substitution effect.

It is quite likely that some individuals have backward-bending supply curves for labor—beyond some point, a higher wage induces those individuals to work less, not more. However, supply curves for labor in specific labor markets are generally upward sloping. As wages in one industry rise relative to wages in other industries, workers shift their labor to the relatively high-wage one. An increased quantity of labor is supplied in that industry. While some exceptions have been found, the mobility of labor between competitive labor markets is likely to prevent the total number of hours worked from falling as the wage rate increases. Thus we shall assume that supply curves for labor in particular markets are upward sloping.

Shifts in Labor Supply

What events shift the supply curve for labor? People supply labor in order to increase their utility—just as they demand goods and services in order to increase their utility. The supply curve for labor will shift in response to changes in the same set of factors that shift demand curves for goods and services.

Changes in Preferences

A change in attitudes toward work and leisure can shift the supply curve for labor. If people decide they value leisure more highly, they will work fewer hours at each wage, and the supply curve for labor will shift to the left. If they decide they want more goods and services, the supply curve is likely to shift to the right.

Changes in Income

An increase in income will increase the demand for leisure, reducing the supply of labor. We must be careful here to distinguish movements along the supply curve from shifts of the supply curve itself. An income change resulting from a change in wages is shown by a movement along the curve; it produces the income and substitution effects we already discussed. But suppose income is from some other source: a person marries and has access to a spouse's income, or receives an inheritance, or wins a lottery. Those nonlabor increases in income are likely to reduce the supply of labor, thereby shifting the supply curve for labor of the recipients to the left.

Changes in the Prices of Related Goods and Services

Several goods and services are complements of labor. If the cost of child care (a complement to work effort) falls, for example, it becomes cheaper for workers to go to work, and the supply of labor tends to increase. If recreational activities (which are a substitute for work effort) become much cheaper, individuals might choose to consume more leisure time and supply less labor.

Changes in Population

An increase in population increases the supply of labor; a reduction lowers it. Labor organizations have generally opposed increases in immigration because their leaders fear that the increased number of workers will shift the supply curve for labor to the right and put downward pressure on wages.

Changes in Expectations

One change in expectations that could have an effect on labor supply is life expectancy. Another is confidence in the availability of Social Security. Suppose, for example, that people expect to live longer yet become less optimistic about their likely benefits from Social Security. That could induce an increase in labor supply.

Labor Supply in Specific Markets

The supply of labor in particular markets could be affected by changes in any of the variables we have already examined—changes in preferences, incomes, prices of related goods and services, population, and expectations. In addition to these variables that affect the supply of labor in general, there are changes that could affect supply in specific labor markets.

A change in wages in related occupations could affect supply in another. A sharp reduction in the wages of surgeons, for example, could induce more physicians to specialize in, say, family practice, increasing the supply of doctors in that field. Improved job opportunities for women in other fields appear to have decreased the supply of nurses, shifting the supply curve for nurses to the left.

The supply of labor in a particular market could also shift because of a change in entry requirements. Most states, for example, require barbers and beauticians to obtain training before entering the profession. Elimination of such requirements would increase the supply of these workers. Financial planners have, in recent years, sought the introduction of tougher licensing requirements, which would reduce the supply of financial planners.

Worker preferences regarding specific occupations can also affect labor supply. A reduction in willingness to take risks could lower the supply of labor available for risky occupations such as farm work (the most dangerous work in the United States), law enforcement, and fire fighting. An increased desire to work with children could raise the supply of child-care workers, elementary school teachers, and pediatricians.

Key Takeaways

- A higher wage increases the opportunity cost or price of leisure and increases worker incomes. The effects of these two changes pull the quantity of labor supplied in opposite directions.

- A wage increase raises the quantity of labor supplied through the substitution effect, but it reduces the quantity supplied through the income effect. Thus an individual's supply curve of labor may be positively or negatively sloped, or have sections that are positively sloped, sections that are negatively sloped, and vertical sections. While some exceptions have been found, the labor supply curves for specific labor markets are generally upward sloping.

- The supply curve for labor will shift as a result of a change in worker preferences, a change in nonlabor income, a change in the prices of related goods and services, a change in population, or a change in expectations.

- In addition to the effects on labor supply of the variables just cited, other factors that can change the supply of labor in particular markets are changes in wages in related markets or changes in entry requirements.

Try It!

Economists Laura Duberstein and Karen Oppenheim Mason analyzed the labor-supply decisions of 1,383 mothers with preschool-aged children in the Detroit Metropolitan area.[2]

They found that respondents were more likely to work the higher the wage, less likely to work if they preferred a traditional family structure with a husband as the primary breadwinner, less likely to work if they felt that care provided by others was strongly inferior to a mother's care, and less likely to work if child-care costs were higher. Given these findings, explain how each of the following would affect the labor supply of mothers with preschool-aged children.

1. An increase in the wage
2. An increase in the preference for a traditional family structure
3. An increased sense that child care is inferior to a mother's care
4. An increase in the cost of child care

(Remember to distinguish between movements along the curve and shifts of the curve.) Is the labor supply curve positively or negatively sloped? Does the substitution effect or income effect dominate?

Case in Point: An Airline Pilot's Lament

Source: © 2010 Jupiterimages Corporation

Arguably, no single sector of the U.S. economy was hit harder by the events of 9/11 than the airline industry. By the time passengers did start returning, though, more than just the routine of getting through airport security had changed. Rather, the structure of the industry had begun to shift from domination by large national carriers—such as Delta, American, and United—operating according to the hub-and-spoke model, to increased competition from lower-cost regional carriers offering point-to-point service. Efforts by the large carriers in the early 2000s to reign in their costs and restore their financial health led to agreements with their labor unions that resulted in lower wages for most categories of airline workers.

How have airline employees responded to lower wages? Some categories of workers, such as mechanics, have little flexibility in deciding how many hours to work, but others, such as pilots, do. Below is an explanation by a female pilot who works for a major airline of the impact of wages cuts on her labor supply:

"We were normally scheduled for anywhere from 15 to 18 days a month, which translated into 80 to 95 hours of flying and around 280 hours of duty time. Duty time includes flight planning, preflighting, crew briefing, boarding, pre-flight checks of the airplane, etc. We bid for a monthly schedule that would fall somewhere in that range. After we were assigned our schedule for a month, we usually had the flexibility to drop or trade trips within certain constraints. Without going into the vast complexities of our contract, I can tell you that, in general, we were allowed to drop down to 10 days a month, provided the company could cover the trips we wanted to drop, and still be considered a full-time employee. Generally, at that time, my goal was to work a minimum of 10 to 12 days a month and a maximum of 15 days a month.

After the first round of pay cuts, the typical month became 16 to 20 days of flying. With that round of pay cuts, my general goal became to work a minimum of 15 days a month and a maximum of 17 days a month. I imagine that with another round of cuts my goal would be to keep my pay as high as I possibly can.

Basically, I have a target income in mind. Anything above that was great, but I chose to have more days at home rather than more pay. As my target income became more difficult to achieve, I chose to work more days and hours to keep close to my target income...When total compensation drops by more than 50% it is difficult to keep your financial head above water no matter how well you have budgeted."

Source: Based on a personal interview.

Answer to Try It! Problem

The first question is about willingness to work as the wage rate changes. It thus refers to movement along the labor supply curve. That mothers of preschool-age children are more willing to work the higher the wage implies an upward-sloping labor supply curve. When the labor supply curve is upward sloping, the substitution effect dominates the income effect. The other three questions refer to factors that cause the labor supply curve to shift. In all three cases, the circumstances imply that the labor supply curve would shift to the left.

12.4 Labor Markets at Work

Learning Objectives

1. Explain and illustrate how wage and employment levels are determined in a perfectly competitive market and for an individual firm within that market.
2. Describe the forces that can raise or lower the equilibrium wage in a competitive market and illustrate these processes.
3. Describe the ways that government can increase wages and incomes.

We have seen that a firm's demand for labor depends on the marginal product of labor and the price of the good the firm produces. We add the demand curves of individual firms to obtain the market demand curve for labor. The supply curve for labor depends on variables such as population and worker preferences. Supply in a particular market depends on variables such as worker preferences, the skills and training a job requires, and wages available in alternative occupations. Wages are determined by the intersection of demand and supply.

Once the wage in a particular market has been established, individual firms in perfect competition take it as given. Because each firm is a price taker, it faces a horizontal supply curve for labor at the market wage. For one firm, changing the quantity of labor it hires does not change the wage. In the context of the model of perfect competition, buyers and sellers are price takers. That means that a firm's choices in hiring labor do not affect the wage.

The operation of labor markets in perfect competition is illustrated in Figure 12.6. The wage W_1 is determined by the intersection of demand and supply in Panel (a). Employment equals L_1 units of labor per period. An individual firm takes that wage as given; it is the supply curve s_1 facing the firm. This wage also equals the firm's marginal factor cost. The firm hires l_1 units of labor, a quantity determined by the intersection of its marginal revenue product curve for labor MRP_1 and the supply curve s_1. We use lowercase letters to show quantity for a single firm and uppercase letters to show quantity in the market.

FIGURE 12.6 Wage Determination and Employment in Perfect Competition
Wages in perfect competition are determined by the intersection of demand and supply in Panel (a). An individual firm takes the wage W_1 as given. It faces a horizontal supply curve for labor at the market wage, as shown in Panel (b). This supply curve s_1 is also the marginal factor cost curve for labor. The firm responds to the wage by employing l_1 units of labor, a quantity determined by the intersection of its marginal revenue product curve MRP_1 and its supply curve s_1.

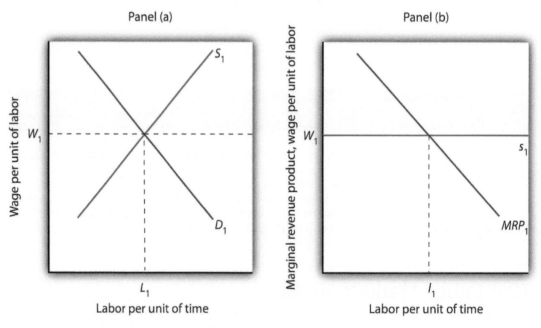

Changes in Demand and Supply

If wages are determined by demand and supply, then changes in demand and supply should affect wages. An increase in demand or a reduction in supply will raise wages; an increase in supply or a reduction in demand will lower them.

Panel (a) of Figure 12.7 shows how an increase in the demand for labor affects wages and employment. The shift in demand to D_2 pushes the wage to W_2 and boosts employment to L_2. Such an increase implies that the marginal product of labor has increased, that the number of firms has risen, or that the price of the good the labor produces has gone up. As we have seen, the marginal product of labor could rise because of an increase in the use of other factors of production, an improvement in technology, or an increase in human capital.

FIGURE 12.7 Changes in the Demand for and Supply of Labor

Panel (a) shows an increase in demand for labor; the wage rises to W_2 and employment rises to L_2. A reduction in labor demand, shown in Panel (b), reduces employment and the wage level. An increase in the supply of labor, shown in Panel (c), reduces the wage to W_2 and increases employment to L_2. Panel (d) shows the effect of a reduction in the supply of labor; wages rise and employment falls.

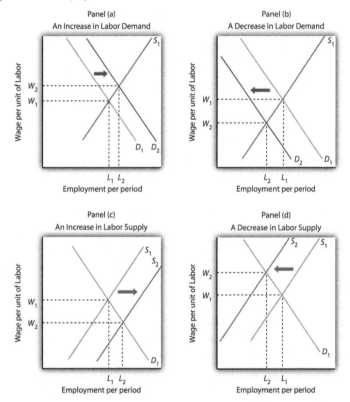

Clearly, a rising demand for labor has been the dominant trend in the market for U.S. labor through most of the nation's history. Wages and employment have generally risen as the availability of capital and other factors of production have increased, as technology has advanced, and as human capital has increased. All have increased the productivity of labor, and all have acted to increase wages.

Panel (b) of Figure 12.7 shows a reduction in the demand for labor to D_2. Wages and employment both fall. Given that the demand for labor in the aggregate is generally increasing, reduced labor demand is most often found in specific labor markets. For example, a slump in construction activity in a particular community can lower the demand for construction workers. Technological changes can reduce as well as increase demand. The Case in Point on wages and technology suggests that technological changes since the late 1970s have tended to reduce the demand for workers with only a high school education while increasing the demand for those with college degrees.

Panel (c) of Figure 12.7 shows the impact of an increase in the supply of labor. The supply curve shifts to S_2, pushing employment to L_2 and cutting the wage to W_2. For labor markets as a whole, such a supply increase could occur because of an increase in population or an increase in the amount of work people are willing to do. For individual labor markets, supply will increase as people move into a particular market.

Just as the demand for labor has increased throughout much of the history of the United States, so has the supply of labor. Population has risen both through immigration and through natural increases. Such increases tend, all other determinants of wages unchanged, to reduce wages. The fact that wages have tended to rise suggests that demand has, in general, increased more rapidly than supply. Still, the more supply rises, the smaller the increase in wages will be, even if demand is rising.

Finally, Panel (d) of Figure 12.7 shows the impact of a reduction in labor supply. One dramatic example of a drop in the labor supply was caused by a reduction in population after the outbreak of bubonic plague in Europe in 1348—the so-called Black Death. The plague killed about one-third of the people of Europe within a few years, shifting the supply curve for labor sharply to the left. Wages doubled during the period.[3]

The fact that a reduction in the supply of labor tends to increase wages explains efforts by some employee groups to reduce labor supply. Members of certain professions have successfully promoted strict licensing requirements to limit the number of people who can enter the profession—U.S. physicians have been particularly successful in this effort. Unions often seek restrictions in immigration in an effort to reduce the supply of labor and thereby boost wages.

Competitive Labor Markets and the Minimum Wage

The Case in Point on technology and the wage gap points to an important social problem. Changes in technology boost the demand for highly educated workers. In turn, the resulting wage premium for more highly educated workers is a signal that encourages people to acquire more education. The market is an extremely powerful mechanism for moving resources to the areas of highest demand. At the same time, however, changes in technology seem to be leaving less educated workers behind. What will happen to people who lack the opportunity to develop the skills that the market values highly or who are unable to do so?

In order to raise wages of workers whose wages are relatively low, governments around the world have imposed minimum wages. A minimum wage works like other price floors. The impact of a minimum wage is shown in Panel (a) of Figure 12.8. Suppose the current equilibrium wage of unskilled workers is W_1, determined by the intersection of the demand and supply curves of these workers. The government determines that this wage is too low and orders that it be increased to W_m, a minimum wage. This strategy reduces employment from L_1 to L_2, but it raises the incomes of those who continue to work. The higher wage also increases the quantity of labor supplied to L_3. The gap between the quantity of labor supplied and the quantity demanded, $L_3 - L_2$, is a surplus—a surplus that increases unemployment.

FIGURE 12.8 Alternative Responses to Low Wages

Government can respond to a low wage by imposing a minimum wage of W_m in Panel (a). This increases the quantity of labor supplied and reduces the quantity demanded. It does, however, increase the income of those who keep their jobs. Another way the government can boost wages is by raising the demand for labor in Panel (b). Both wages and employment rise.

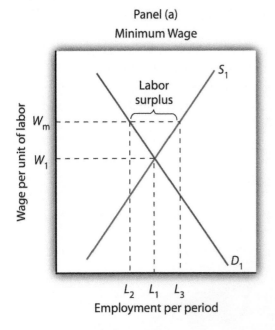

Panel (a)
Minimum Wage

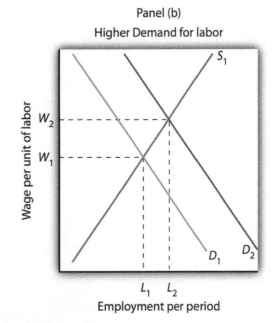

Panel (b)
Higher Demand for labor

Some economists oppose increases in the minimum wage on grounds that such increases boost unemployment. Other economists argue that the demand for unskilled labor is relatively inelastic, so a higher minimum wage boosts the incomes of unskilled workers as a group. That gain, they say, justifies the policy, even if it increases unemployment.

An alternative approach to imposing a legal minimum is to try to boost the demand for labor. Such an approach is illustrated in Panel (b). An increase in demand to D_2 pushes the wage to W_2 and at the same time increases employment to L_2. Public sector training programs that seek to increase human capital are examples of this policy.

Still another alternative is to subsidize the wages of workers whose incomes fall below a certain level. Providing government subsidies—either to employers who agree to hire unskilled workers or to workers themselves in the form of transfer payments—enables people who lack the skills—and the ability to acquire the skills—needed to earn a higher wage to earn more without the loss of jobs implied by a higher minimum wage. Such programs can be costly. They also reduce the incentive for low-skilled workers to develop the skills that are in greater demand in the marketplace.

Key Takeaways

- Wages in a competitive market are determined by demand and supply.
- An increase in demand or a reduction in supply will increase the equilibrium wage. A reduction in demand or an increase in supply will reduce the equilibrium wage.
- The government may respond to low wages for some workers by imposing the minimum wage, by attempting to increase the demand for those workers, or by subsidizing the wages of workers whose incomes fall below a certain level.

Try It!

Assuming that the market for construction workers is perfectly competitive, illustrate graphically how each of the following would affect the demand or supply for construction workers. What would be the impact on wages and on the number of construction workers employed?

1. The demand for new housing increases as more people move into the community.
2. Changes in societal attitudes lead to more women wanting to work in construction.
3. Improved training makes construction workers more productive.
4. New technology allows much of the framing used in housing construction to be built by robots at a factory and then shipped to construction sites.

Case in Point: Technology and the Wage Gap

Source: © 2010 Jupiterimages Corporation

Why has the gap in wages between more educated and less educated workers been growing in the United States since the early 1980s? According to Harvard economists Claudia Goldin and Lawrence Katz, the answer to this question rests on comparing changes in demand to changes in supply. In a nutshell, their argument is that for the last century or so, technological change has increased the relative demand for skilled, educated workers. (Technological change does not necessarily favor skill and education but it has on average in this period.) Before around 1980, the relative supply of skilled, educated workers was increasing fast enough to cause first a reduction in the wage gap until about 1950 and then a stable gap for about 30 years. Since then, the increase in supply of skilled, educated workers has not kept pace. Voila! The wage gap has grown.

Yes, they argue, other candidate explanations such as immigration, outsourcing, and the strengthening and then weakening of labor unions may have played a role, but these forces were not dominant. The real story is the race between technology and education, which they lay out in their book of the same name.

They dub the twentieth century the Human Capital Century in America. For the first 75 years or so of the century, the U.S. led the world in investing in mass education—expanding free compulsory high school education and encouraging college education. By the late 1970s, high school graduation rates had plateaued and increases in college graduation rates began to slow down. Specifically, from 1915 to 1960, the relative supply of college graduates increased 3% annually and rose to almost 4% annually from 1960 to 1980. Over this period, education was winning the race over technology. From 1980 onward, the increase has been only 2% annually and technology began to win. The story for high school graduation rate changes is similar.

What happened? Why is the U.S. no longer a leader in education attainment? Well, other countries saw the benefits of expanding education, made the investments, and are reaping the rewards. Goldin and Katz note that in those countries where education is winning the race, there has been little change in educational wage inequality and more modest change in overall wage inequality.

Seeing the high returns to more schooling, why are American youth not jumping in and consuming more? The authors identify two factors: 1) lack of college readiness both of youth who drop out of high school and of many high school graduates and 2) financial access to college for many who are ready for college. To address these, they advocate: 1) more access to quality pre-school education for children from disadvantaged families 2) improvement in K-12 education so that more youth become college ready, and 3) more generosity, especially for low-income youth, and transparency in financial aid for college.

Source: Based on Claudia Goldin and Lawrence F. Katz, The Race Between Education and Technology (Cambridge: The Belknap Press of Harvard University, 2008).

Answers to Try It! Problems

1. An increase in the demand for new housing would shift the demand curve for construction workers to the right, as shown in Figure 12.7, Panel (a). Both the wage rate and the employment in construction rise.

2. A larger number of women wanting to work in construction means an increase in labor supply, as shown in Figure 12.7, Panel (c). An increase in the supply of labor reduces the wage rate and increases employment.

3. Improved training would increase the marginal revenue product of construction workers and hence increase demand for them. Wages and employment would rise, as shown in Figure 12.7, Panel (a).

4. The robots are likely to serve as a substitute for labor. That will reduce demand, wages, and employment of construction workers, as shown in Panel (b).

12.5 Review and Practice

Summary

In this chapter we have extended our understanding of the operation of perfectly competitive markets by looking at the market for labor. We found that the common sense embodied in the marginal decision rule is alive and well. A firm should hire additional labor up to the point at which the marginal benefit of doing so equals the marginal cost.

The demand curve for labor is given by the downward-sloping portion of the marginal revenue product (MRP) curve of labor. A profit-maximizing firm will hire labor up to the point at which its marginal revenue product equals its marginal factor cost. The demand for labor shifts whenever there is a change in (1) related factors of production, including investment in human capital; (2) technology; (3) product demand; and (4) the number of firms.

The quantity of labor supplied is closely linked to the demand for leisure. As more hours are worked, income goes up, but the marginal cost of work, measured in terms of forgone leisure, also increases. We saw that the substitution effect of a wage increase always increases the quantity of labor supplied. But the income effect of a wage increase reduces the quantity of labor supplied. It is possible that, above some wage, the income effect more than offsets the substitution effect. At or above that wage, an individual's supply curve for labor is backward bending. Supply curves for labor in individual markets, however, are likely to be upward sloping.

Because competitive labor markets generate wages equal to marginal revenue product, workers who add little to the value of a firm's output will receive low wages. The public sector can institute a minimum wage, seek to improve these workers' human capital, or subsidize their wages.

Conceptual Problems

1. Explain the difference between the marginal product of a factor and the marginal revenue product of a factor. What factors would change a factor's marginal product? Its marginal revenue product?

2. In perfectly competitive input markets, the factor price and the marginal factor cost are the same. True or false? Explain.

3. Many high school vocational education programs are beginning to shift from an emphasis on training students to perform specific tasks to training students to learn new tasks. Students are taught, for example, how to read computer manuals so that they can more easily learn new systems. Why has this change occurred? Do you think the change is desirable?

4. How would an increase in the prices of crops of fresh produce that must be brought immediately to market—so-called truck crops—affect the wages of workers who harvest those crops? How do you think it would affect the quantity of labor supplied?

5. If individual labor supply curves of all individuals are backward bending, does this mean that a market supply curve for labor in a particular industry will also be backward bending? Why or why not?

6. There was an unprecedented wave of immigration to the United States during the latter third of the nineteenth century. Wages, however, rose at a rapid rate throughout the period. Why was the increase in wages surprising in light of rising immigration, and what probably caused it?

7. Suppose you were the economic adviser to the president of a small underdeveloped country. What advice would you give him or her with respect to how the country could raise the productivity of its labor force? (*Hint:* What factors increase labor productivity?)

8. The text argues that the effect of a minimum wage on the incomes of workers depends on whether the demand for their services is elastic or inelastic. Explain why.

9. How would a successful effort to increase the human capital of unskilled workers affect their wage? Why?

10. Do you think that bank tellers and automatic tellers are substitutes or complements? Explain.

11. What does the airline pilot's supply curve in the Case in Point on how she has dealt with wage cutbacks look like? Does the substitution effect or the income effect dominate? How do you know?

12. Given the evidence cited in the Case in Point on the increasing wage gap between workers with college degrees and those who have only completed high school, how has the greater use by firms of high-tech capital affected the marginal products of workers with college degrees? How has it affected their marginal revenue product?

13. Explain how each of the following events would affect wages in a particular labor market:

    a. an increase in labor productivity in the market.

    b. an increase in the supply of labor in the market.

    c. an increase in wages in another labor market that can be easily entered by workers in the first labor market.

    d. a reduction in wages in another market whose workers can easily enter the first market.

    e. an increase in the price of the good labor in the market produces.

14. How can a supply curve for labor be backward bending? Suppose the equilibrium wage occurs in the downward-sloping portion of the curve. How would an increase in the demand for labor in the market affect the wage? How would this affect the quantity of labor supplied?

15. How do you think a wage increase would affect the quantity of labor supplied by each of the following speakers?

    a. "I want to earn as much money as possible."

    b. "I am happy with my current level of income and want to maintain it."

    c. "I love my work; the wage I'm paid has nothing to do with the amount of work I want to do."

    d. "I would work the same number of hours regardless of the wage I am paid."

Numerical Problems

1. Felicia Álvarez, a bakery manager, faces the total product curve shown, which gives the relationship between the number of bakers she hires each day and the number of loaves of bread she produces, assuming all other factors of production are given.

Number of bakers per day	Loaves of bread per day
0	0
1	400
2	700
3	900
4	1,025
5	1,100
6	1,150

Assume that bakers in the area receive a wage of $100 per day and that the price of bread is $1.00 per loaf.

   a. Plot the bakery's marginal revenue product curve (remember that marginal values are plotted at the mid-points of the respective intervals).

   b. Plot the bakery's marginal factor cost curve on the same graph.

   c. How many bakers will Ms. Álvarez employ per day?

d. Suppose that the price of bread falls to $.80 per loaf. How will this affect the marginal revenue product curve for bakers at the firm? Plot the new curve.

e. How will the change in (d) above affect the number of bakers Ms. Álvarez hires?

f. Suppose the price of bread rises to $1.20 per loaf. How will this affect the marginal revenue product curve for bakers? Plot the new curve.

g. How will the development in (f) above affect the number of bakers that Ms. Álvarez employs?

2. Suppose that wooden boxes are produced under conditions of perfect competition and that the price of a box is $10. The demand and supply curves for the workers who make these boxes are given in the table.

Wage per day	Workers demanded	Workers supplied
$100	6,000	12,000
80	7,000	10,000
60	8,000	8,000
40	9,000	6,000
20	10,000	4,000

Plot the demand and supply curves for labor, and determine the equilibrium wage for box makers.

3. Assume that the market for nurses is perfectly competitive, and that the initial equilibrium wage for registered nurses is $30 per hour. Illustrate graphically how each of the following events will affect the demand or supply for nurses. State the impact on wages and on the number of nurses employed (in terms of the direction of the changes that will occur).

a. New hospital instruments reduce the amount of time physicians must spend with patients in intensive care and increase the care that nurses can provide.

b. The number of doctors increases.

c. Changes in the labor market lead to greater demand for the services of women in a wide range of occupations. The demand for nurses, however, does not change.

d. New legislation establishes primary-care facilities in which nurses care for patients with minor medical problems. No supervision by physicians is required in the facilities.

e. The wage for nurses rises.

4. Plot the supply curves for labor implied by each of the following statements. In this problem, actual numbers are not important; rather you should think about the shape of the curve.

a. "I'm sorry, kids, but now that I'm earning more, I just can't afford to come home early in the afternoon, so I won't be there when you get home from school."

b. "They can pay me a lot or they can pay me a little. I'll still put in my 8 hours a day."

c. "Wow! With the raise the boss just gave me, I can afford to knock off early each day."

5. At an hourly wage of $10 per hour, Marcia Fanning is willing to work 36 hours per week. Between $30 and $40 per hour, she is willing to work 40 hours per week. At $50 per hour, she is willing to work 35 hours per week.

a. Assuming her labor supply curve is linear between the data points mentioned, draw Ms. Fanning's labor supply curve.

b. Given her labor supply curve, how much could she earn per week at the wage of $10 per hour? $30 per hour? $40 per hour? $50 per hour?

c. Does the substitution or income effect dominate wages between $10 and $30 per hour? Between $30 and $40 per hour? Between $40 and $50 per hour?

d. How much would she earn at each hypothetical wage rate?

6. Jake Goldstone is working 30 hours per week. His marginal utility of income is 2, his marginal utility of leisure is 60, and his hourly wage is $20. Assume throughout this problem that the income effect is zero.

a. Is Mr. Goldstone maximizing his utility?

   b. Would working more or less increase his utility?

   c. If his wage rose to $30 per hour, would he be maximizing his utility by working 30 hours per week? If not, should he work more or fewer hours?

   d. At a wage of $40 per hour, would he be maximizing his utility? If not, would working more or less than 30 hours per week increase his utility?

7. The table below describes the perfectly competitive market for dishwashers.

Wage per day	Quantity demanded per day (in thousands)	Quantity supplied per day (in thousands)
$50	4.0	1.0
100	3.5	2.0
150	3.0	3.0
200	2.5	4.0
250	2.0	5.0

   a. Draw the demand and supply curves for dishwashers.

   b. What is the equilibrium daily wage rate and quantity of dishwashers?

   c. What is the total (i.e., cumulative) daily income of dishwashers at the equilibrium daily wage?

   d. At a minimum daily wage of $200 per day, how many dishwashers will be employed? How many will be unemployed? What will be the total daily income of dishwashers?

   e. At a minimum wage of $250 per day, how many dishwashers will be employed? How many will be unemployed? What will be the total daily income of dishwashers?

Endnotes

---

1. Strictly speaking, it is only that part of the downward-sloping portion over which variable costs are at least covered. This is the flip-side of what you learned about a firm's supply curve in the chapter on competitive output markets: Only the portion of the rising marginal cost curve that lies above the minimum point of the average variable cost curve constitutes the supply curve of a perfectly competitive firm.

2. Laura Duberstein and Karen Oppenheim Mason, "Do Child Care Costs Influence Women's Work Plans? Analysis for a Metropolitan Area," Research Report, Population Studies Center, University of Michigan, Ann Arbor, July 1991.

3. Carlo M. Cipolla, *Before the Industrial Revolution: European Society and Economy, 1000–1700*, 2nd ed. (New York: Norton, 1980), pp. 200–202. The doubling in wages was a doubling in real terms, meaning that the purchasing power of an average worker's wage doubled.

CHAPTER 13
Interest Rates and the Markets for Capital and Natural Resources

13.1 Start Up: Mars—Here We Come!

Visit the website of Space X. You will be greeted by the announcement that the purpose of the company is nothing less than "to revolutionize space technology, with the ultimate goal of enabling people to live on other planets." You will be regaled with accomplishments to date: in 2010, the only private company ever to return a spacecraft, named Dragon and launched by Falcon 9, from low-Earth orbit; in 2012, the first private company to send a spacecraft, Dragon, to attach to the International Space Station, exchange cargo, and return safely to earth; in 2015, after delivering 11 satellites to orbit, making the first successful orbital class, pinpoint landing of a rocket. And SpaceX currently has billions of dollars of contracts with private companies and with NASA.

Founded in 2002 by Elon Musk, the company had had 27 successful launches of its Falcon 9 rockets as of August 2016. On September 4, 2016, its rocket exploded on the launchpad at Cape Canaveral. It was carrying satellites worth millions. Though the company has a good safety record overall, this setback raised questions about its goals of maintaining a steady satellite launch schedule while keeping costs below that of competitors, such as the French multinational company Arianespace and the American-Russian joint venture International Launch Services.

And then there's the issue of moving forward with manned space flights. In a 2016 interview with the Guardian, Mr. Musk said that SpaceX expects to get people to Mars in 2025, which would mean beginning to get cargo flights there by 2018.

Where does the financial capital for these projects come from? Mr. Musk reportedly put in $100 million and has gotten venture capital from others, including $1 billion from Alphabet, Inc., the parent company of Google.

This capital project, although perhaps bigger and more ambitious, shares basic characteristics with others. The production of capital—the goods used in producing other goods and services—requires sacrificing consumption. The returns to capital will be spread over the period in which the capital is used. The choice to acquire capital is thus a choice to give up consumption today in hopes of returns in the future. Because those returns are far from certain, the choice to acquire capital is inevitably a risky one.[1]

For all its special characteristics, however, capital is a factor of production. As we investigate the market for capital, the concepts of marginal revenue product, marginal factor cost, and the marginal decision rule that we have developed will continue to serve us. The big difference is that the benefits and costs of holding capital are distributed over time.

We will also examine markets for natural resources in this chapter. Like decisions involving capital, choices in the allocation of natural resources have lasting effects. For potentially exhaustible natural resources such as oil, the effects of those choices last forever.

For the analysis of capital and natural resources, we shift from the examination of outcomes in the current period to the analysis of outcomes distributed over many periods. Interest rates, which link the values of payments that occur at different times, will be central to our analysis.

13.2 Time and Interest Rates

Learning Objectives

1. Define interest and the interest rate.
2. Describe and show algebraically how to compute present value.
3. List and explain the factors that affect what the present value of some future payment will be.

Time, the saying goes, is nature's way of keeping everything from happening all at once. And the fact that everything does not happen at once introduces an important complication in economic analysis.

When a company decides to use funds to install capital that will not begin to produce income for several years, it needs a way to compare the significance of funds spent now to income earned later. It must find a way to compensate financial investors who give up the use of their funds for several years, until the project begins to pay off. How can payments that are distributed across time be linked to one another? Interest rates are the linkage mechanism; we shall investigate how they achieve that linkage in this section.

The Nature of Interest Rates

Consider a delightful problem of choice. Your Aunt Carmen offers to give you $10,000 now or $10,000 in one year. Which would you pick?

Most people would choose to take the payment now. One reason for that choice is that the average level of prices is likely to rise over the next year. The purchasing power of $10,000 today is thus greater than the purchasing power of $10,000 a year hence. There is also a question of whether you can count on receiving the payment. If you take it now, you have it. It is risky to wait a year; who knows what will happen?

Let us eliminate both of these problems. Suppose that you are confident that the average level of prices will not change during the year, and you are absolutely certain that if you choose to wait for the payment, you and it will both be available. Will you take the payment now or wait?

Chances are you would *still* want to take the payment now. Perhaps there are some things you would like to purchase with it, and you would like them sooner rather than later. Moreover, if you wait a year to get the payment, you will not be able to use it while you are waiting. If you take it now, you can choose to spend it now or wait.

Now suppose Aunt Carmen wants to induce you to wait and changes the terms of her gift. She offers you $10,000 now or $11,000 in one year. In effect, she is offering you a $1,000 bonus if you will wait a year. If you agree to wait a year to receive Aunt Carmen's payment, you will be accepting her *promise* to provide funds instead of the funds themselves. Either will increase your **wealth**, which is the sum of all your assets less all your liabilities. **Assets** are anything you have that is of value; **liabilities** are obligations to make future payments. Both a $10,000 payment from Aunt Carmen now and her promise of $11,000 in a year are examples of assets. The alternative to holding wealth is to consume it. You could, for example, take Aunt Carmen's $10,000 and spend it for a trip to Europe, thus reducing your wealth. By making a better offer—$11,000 instead of $10,000—Aunt Carmen is trying to induce you to accept an asset you will not be able to consume during the year.

The $1,000 bonus Aunt Carmen is offering if you will wait a year for her payment is interest. In general, **interest** is a payment made to people who agree to postpone their use of wealth. The **interest rate** represents the opportunity cost of using wealth today, expressed as a percentage of the amount of wealth whose use is postponed. Aunt Carmen is offering you $1,000 if you will pass up the $10,000 today. She is thus offering you an interest rate of 10% ($1,000 / $10,000 = 0.1 = 10%).

Suppose you tell Aunt Carmen that, given the two options, you would still rather have the $10,000 today. She now offers you $11,500 if you will wait a year for the payment—an interest rate of 15% ($1,500 / $10,000 = 0.15 = 15%). The more she pays for waiting, the higher the interest rate.

You are probably familiar with the role of interest rates in loans. In a loan, the borrower obtains a payment now in exchange for promising to repay the loan in the future. The lender thus must postpone his or her use of wealth until the time of repayment. To induce lenders to postpone their use of their wealth, borrowers offer interest. Borrowers are willing to pay interest because it allows them to acquire the sum now rather than having to wait for it. And lenders require interest payments to compensate them for postponing their own use of their wealth.

Interest Rates and Present Value

We saw in the previous section that people generally prefer to receive a payment of some amount today rather than wait to receive that same amount later. We may conclude that the value today of a payment in the future is less than the dollar value of the future payment. An important application of interest rates is to show the relationship between the current and future values of a particular payment.

To see how we can calculate the current value of a future payment, let us consider an example similar to Aunt Carmen's offer. This time you have $1,000 and you deposit it in a bank, where it earns interest at the rate of 10% per year.

How much will you have in your bank account at the end of one year? You will have the original $1,000 plus 10% of $1,000, or $1,100:

$$\$1,000 + (0.10)(\$1,000) = \$1,100$$

More generally, if we let P_0 equal the amount you deposit today, r the percentage rate of interest, and P_1 the balance of your deposit at the end of 1 year, then we can write:

EQUATION 13.1

$$P_0 + rP_0 = P_1$$

Factoring out the P_0 term on the left-hand side of Equation 13.1, we have:

EQUATION 13.2

$$P_0(1 + r) = P_1$$

Equation 13.2 shows how to determine the future value of a payment or deposit made today. Now let us turn the question around. We can ask what P_1, an amount that will be available 1 year from now, is worth today. We solve for this by dividing both sides of Equation 13.2 by $(1 + r)$ to obtain:

wealth

The sum of assets less liabilities.

assets

Anything of value.

liabilities

Obligations to make future payments.

interest

A payment made to people who agree to postpone their use of wealth.

interest rate

The opportunity cost of using wealth today, expressed as a percentage of the amount of wealth whose use is postponed.

EQUATION 13.3

$$P_0 = \frac{P_1}{(1+r)}$$

present value

An amount that would equal a particular future value if deposited today at a specific interest rate.

Equation 13.3 suggests how we can compute the value today, P_0, of an amount P_1 that will be paid a year hence. An amount that would equal a particular future value if deposited today at a specific interest rate is called the **present value** of that future value.

More generally, the present value of any payment to be received n periods from now =

EQUATION 13.4

$$P_0 = \frac{P_n}{(1+r)^n}$$

Suppose, for example, that your Aunt Carmen offers you the option of $1,000 now or $15,000 in 30 years. We can use Equation 13.4 to help you decide which sum to take. The present value of $15,000 to be received in 30 years, assuming an interest rate of 10%, is:

$$P_0 = \frac{P_{30}}{(1+r)^{30}} = \frac{\$15,000}{(1+0.10)^{30}} = \$859.63$$

Assuming that you could earn that 10% return with certainty, you would be better off taking Aunt Carmen's $1,000 now; it is greater than the present value, at an interest rate of 10%, of the $15,000 she would give you in 30 years. The $1,000 she gives you now, assuming an interest rate of 10%, in 30 years will grow to:

$$\$1,000(1 + 0.10)^{30} = \$17,449.40$$

The present value of some future payment depends on three things.

1. **The Size of the Payment Itself.** The bigger the future payment, the greater its present value.

2. **The Length of the Period Until Payment.** The present value depends on how long a period will elapse before the payment is made. The present value of $15,000 in 30 years, at an interest rate of 10%, is $859.63. But that same sum, if paid in 20 years, has a present value of $2,229.65. And if paid in 10 years, its present value is more than twice as great: $5,783.15. The longer the time period before a payment is to be made, the lower its present value.

3. **The Rate of Interest.** The present value of a payment of $15,000 to be made in 20 years is $2,229.65 if the interest rate is 10%; it rises to $5,653.34 at an interest rate of 5%. The lower the interest rate, the higher the present value of a future payment. Table 13.1 gives present values of a payment of $15,000 at various interest rates and for various time periods.

TABLE 13.1 Time, Interest Rates, and Present Value
The higher the interest rate and the longer the time until payment is made, the lower the present value of a future payment. The table below shows the present value of a future payment of $15,000 under different conditions. The present value of $15,000 to be paid in five years is $11,752.89 if the interest rate is 5%. Its present value is just $391.26 if it is to be paid in 20 years and the interest rate is 20%.

Present Value of $15,000				
	Time until payment			
Interest rate (%)	5 years	10 years	15 years	20 years
5	$11,752.89	$9,208.70	$7,215.26	$5,653.34
10	9,313.82	5,783.15	3,590.88	2,229.65
15	7,457.65	3,707.77	1,843.42	916.50
20	6,028.16	2,422.58	973.58	391.26

The concept of present value can also be applied to a series of future payments. Suppose you have been promised $1,000 at the end of each of the next 5 years. Because each payment will occur at a different time, we calculate the present value of the series of payments by taking the value of each payment separately and adding them together. At an interest rate of 10%, the present value P_0 is:

$$P_0 = \frac{\$1,000}{1.10} + \frac{\$1,000}{(1.10)^2} + \frac{\$1,000}{(1.10)^3} + \frac{\$1,000}{(1.10)^4} + \frac{\$1,000}{(1.10)^5} = \$3,790.78$$

Interest rates can thus be used to compare the values of payments that will occur at different times. Choices concerning capital and natural resources require such comparisons, so you will find applications of the concept of present value throughout this chapter, but the concept of present value applies whenever costs and benefits do not all take place in the current period.

State lottery winners often have a choice between a single large payment now or smaller payments paid out over a 25- or 30-year period. Comparing the single payment now to the present value of the future payments allows winners to make informed decisions. For example, in June 2005 Brad Duke, of Boise, Idaho, became the winner of one of the largest lottery prizes ever. Given the alternative of claiming the $220.3 million jackpot in 30 annual payments of $7.4 million or taking $125.3 million in a lump sum, he chose the latter. Holding unchanged all other considerations that must have been going through his mind, he must have thought his best rate of return would be greater than 4.17%. Why 4.17%? Using an interest rate of 4.17%, $125.3 million is equal to slightly less than the present value of the 30-year stream of payments. At all interest rates greater than 4.17%, the present value of the stream of benefits would be less than $125.3 million. At all interest rates less than 4.17%, the present value of the stream of payments would be more than $125.3 million. Our present value analysis suggests that if he thought the interest rate he could earn was more than 4.17%, he should take the lump sum payment, which he did.

Key Takeaways

- People generally prefer to receive a specific payment now rather than to wait and receive it later.
- Interest is a payment made to people who agree to postpone their use of wealth.
- We compute the present value, P_0, of a sum to be received in n years, P_n, as:

$$P_0 = \frac{P_n}{(1+r)^n}$$

- The present value of a future payment will be greater the larger the payment, the sooner it is due, and the lower the rate of interest.

Try It!

Suppose your friend Sara asks you to lend her $5,000 so she can buy a used car. She tells you she can pay you back $5,200 in a year. Reliable Sara always keeps her word. Suppose the interest rate you could earn by putting the $5,000 in a savings account is 5%. What is the present value of her offer? Is it a good deal for you or not? What if the interest rate on your savings account is only 3%?

Case in Point: Waiting for Death and Life Insurance

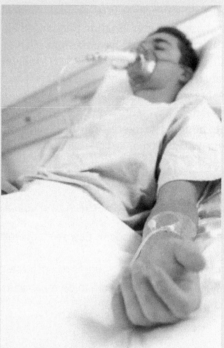

Source: © 2010 Jupiterimages Corporation

It is a tale that has become all too familiar.

Call him Roger Johnson. He has just learned that his cancer is not treatable and that he has only a year or two to live. Mr. Johnson is unable to work, and his financial burdens compound his tragic medical situation. He has mortgaged his house and sold his other assets in a desperate effort to get his hands on the cash he needs for care, for food, and for shelter. He has a life insurance policy, but it will pay off only when he dies. If only he could get some of that money sooner…

The problem facing Mr. Johnson has spawned a market solution—companies and individuals that buy the life insurance policies of the terminally ill. Mr. Johnson could sell his policy to one of these companies or individuals and collect the purchase price. The buyer takes over his premium payments. When he dies, the company will collect the proceeds of the policy.

The industry is called the viatical industry (the term *viatical* comes from *viaticum*, a Christian sacrament given to a dying person). It provides the terminally ill with access to money while they are alive; it provides financial investors a healthy interest premium on their funds.

It is a chilling business. Potential buyers pore over patient's medical histories, studying T-cell counts and other indicators of a patient's health. From the buyer's point of view, a speedy death is desirable, because it means the investor will collect quickly on the purchase of a patient's policy.

A patient with a life expectancy of less than six months might be able to sell his or her life insurance policy for 80% of the face value. A $200,000 policy would thus sell for $160,000. A person with a better prognosis will collect less. Patients expected to live two years, for example, might get only 60% of the face value of their policies.

Are investors profiting from the misery of others? Of course they are. But, suppose that investors refused to take advantage of the misfortune of the terminally ill. That would deny dying people the chance to acquire funds that they desperately need. As is the case with all voluntary exchange, the viatical market creates win-win situations. Investors "win" by earning high rates of return on their investment. And the dying patient? He or she is in a terrible situation, but the opportunity to obtain funds makes that person a "winner" as well.

In recent years, this industry has been renamed the life settlements industry, with policy transfers being offered to healthier, often elderly, policyholders. These healthier individuals are sometimes turning over their policies for a payment to third parties who pay the premiums and then collect the benefit when the policyholders die. Expansion of this practice has begun to raise costs for life insurers, who assumed that individuals would sometimes let their policies lapse, with the result that the insurance company does not have to pay claims on them. Businesses buying life insurance policies are not likely to let them lapse.

Sources: Based on personal Interview and Liam Pleven and Rachel Emma Silverman, "Investors Seek Profit in Strangers' Deaths," The Wall Street Journal Online, 2 May 2006, p. C1.

Answer to Try It! Problem

The present value of $5,200 payable in a year with an interest rate of 5% is:

$$P_0 = \frac{\$5,200}{(1+0.05)^1} = \$4,952.38$$

Since the present value of $5,200 is less than the $5,000 Sara has asked you to lend her, you would be better off refusing to make the loan. Another way of evaluating the loan is that Sara is offering a return on your $5,000 of 200/5,000 = 4%, while the bank is offering you a 5% return. On the other hand, if the interest rate that your bank is paying is 3%, then the present value of what Sara will pay you in a year is:

$$P_0 = \frac{\$5,200}{(1+0.03)^1} = \$5,048.54$$

With your bank only paying a 3% return, Sara's offer looks like a good deal.

13.3 Interest Rates and Capital

Learning Objectives

1. Define investment, explain how to determine the net present value of an investment project, and explain how the net present value calculation aids the decision maker in determining whether or not to pursue an investment project.
2. Explain the demand curve for capital and the factors that can cause it to shift.
3. Explain and illustrate the loanable funds market and explain how changes in the demand for capital affect that market and vice versa.

The quantity of capital that firms employ in their production of goods and services has enormously important implications for economic activity and for the standard of living people in the economy enjoy. Increases in capital increase the marginal product of labor and boost wages at the same time they boost total output. An increase in the stock of capital therefore tends to raise incomes and improve the standard of living in the economy.

Capital is often a fixed factor of production in the short run. A firm cannot quickly retool an assembly line or add a new office building. Determining the quantity of capital a firm will use is likely to involve long-run choices.

The Demand for Capital

A firm uses additional units of a factor until marginal revenue product equals marginal factor cost. Capital is no different from other factors of production, save for the fact that the revenues and costs it generates are distributed over time. As the first step in assessing a firm's demand for capital, we determine the present value of marginal revenue products and marginal factor costs.

Capital and Net Present Value

Suppose Carol Stein is considering the purchase of a new $95,000 tractor for her farm. Ms. Stein expects to use the tractor for five years and then sell it; she expects that it will sell for $22,000 at the end of the five-year period. She has the $95,000 on hand now; her alternative to purchasing the tractor could be to put $95,000 in a bond account earning 7% annual interest.

Ms. Stein expects that the tractor will bring in additional annual revenue of $50,000 but will cost $30,000 per year to operate, for net revenue of $20,000 annually. For simplicity, we shall suppose that this net revenue accrues at the end of each year.

net present value (NPV)

The value equal to the present value of all the revenues expected from an asset minus the present value of all the costs associated with it.

Should she buy the tractor? We can answer this question by computing the tractor's **net present value (NPV)**, which is equal to the present value of all the revenues expected from an asset minus the present value of all the costs associated with it. We thus measure the difference between the present value of marginal revenue products and the present value of marginal factor costs. If NPV is greater than zero, purchase of the asset will increase the profitability of the firm. A negative NPV implies that the funds for the asset would yield a higher return if used to purchase an interest-bearing asset. A firm will maximize profits by acquiring additional capital up to the point that the present value of capital's marginal revenue product equals the present value of marginal factor cost.

If the revenues generated by an asset in period n equal R_n and the costs in period n equal C_n, then the net present value NPV_0 of an asset expected to last for n years is:

EQUATION 13.5

$$NPV_0 = R_0 - C_0 + \frac{R_1 - C_1}{1 + r} + ... + \frac{R_n - C_n}{(1 + r)^n}$$

To purchase the tractor, Ms. Stein pays $95,000. She will receive additional revenues of $50,000 per year from increased planting and more efficient harvesting, less the operating cost per year of $30,000, plus the $22,000 she expects to get by selling the tractor at the end of five years. The net present value of the tractor, NPV_0 is thus given by:

$$NPV_0 = -\$95,000 + \frac{\$20,000}{1.07} + \frac{\$20,000}{1.07^2} + \frac{\$20,000}{1.07^3} + \frac{\$20,000}{1.07^4} + \frac{\$42,000}{1.07^5} = \$2,690$$

Given the cost of the tractor, the net returns Ms. Stein projects, and an interest rate of 7%, Ms. Stein will increase her profits by purchasing the tractor. The tractor will yield a return whose present value is $2,690 greater than the return that could be obtained by the alternative of putting the $95,000 in a bond account yielding 7%.

Ms. Stein's acquisition of the tractor is called investment. Economists define **investment** as an addition to capital stock. Any acquisition of new capital goods therefore qualifies as investment.

investment

An addition to capital stock.

The Demand Curve for Capital

Our analysis of Carol Stein's decision regarding the purchase of a new tractor suggests the forces at work in determining the economy's demand for capital. In deciding to purchase the tractor, Ms. Stein considered the price she would have to pay to obtain the tractor, the costs of operating it, the marginal revenue product she would receive by owning it, and the price she could get by selling the tractor when she expects to be done with it. Notice that with the exception of the purchase price of the tractor, *all* those figures were projections. Her decision to purchase the tractor depends almost entirely on the costs and benefits she *expects* will be associated with its use.

Finally, Ms. Stein converted all those figures to a net present value based on the interest rate prevailing at the time she made her choice. A positive *NPV* means that her profits will be increased by purchasing the tractor. That result, of course, depends on the prevailing interest rate. At an interest rate of 7%, the *NPV* is positive. At an interest rate of 8%, the *NPV* would be negative. At that interest rate, Ms. Stein would do better to put her funds elsewhere.

At any one time, millions of choices like that of Ms. Stein concerning the acquisition of capital will be under consideration. Each decision will hinge on the price of a particular piece of capital, the expected cost of its use, its expected marginal revenue product, its expected scrap value, and the interest rate. Not only will firms be considering the acquisition of new capital, they will be considering retaining existing capital as well. Ms. Stein, for example, may have other tractors. Should she continue to use them, or should she sell them? If she keeps them, she will experience a stream of revenues and costs over the next several periods; if she sells them, she will have funds now that she could use for something else. To decide whether a firm should keep the capital it already has, we need an estimate of the *NPV* of each unit of capital. Such decisions are always affected by the interest rate. At higher rates of interest, it makes sense to sell some capital rather than hold it. At lower rates of interest, the *NPV* of holding capital will rise.

Because firms' choices to acquire new capital and to hold existing capital depend on the interest rate, the **demand curve for capital** in Figure 13.1, which shows the quantity of capital firms intend to hold at each interest rate, is downward-sloping. At point A, we see that at an interest rate of 10%, $8 trillion worth of capital is demanded in the economy. At point B, a reduction in the interest rate to 7% increases the quantity of capital demanded to $9 trillion. At point C, at an interest rate of 4%, the quantity of capital demanded is $10 trillion. A reduction in the interest rate increases the quantity of capital demanded.

demand curve for capital

Shows the quantity of capital firms intend to hold at each interest rate.

The demand curve for capital for the economy is found by summing the demand curves of all holders of capital. Ms. Stein's demand curve, for example, might show that at an interest rate of 8%, she will demand the capital she already has—suppose it is $600,000 worth of equipment. If the interest rate drops to 7%, she will add the tractor; the quantity of capital she demands rises to $695,000. At interest rates greater than 8%, she might decide to reduce her maintenance efforts for some of the capital she already has; the quantity of capital she demands would fall below $600,000. As with the demand for capital in the economy, we can expect individual firms to demand a smaller quantity of capital when the interest rate is higher.

FIGURE 13.1 The Demand Curve for Capital

The quantity of capital firms will want to hold depends on the interest rate. The higher the interest rate, the less capital firms will want to hold.

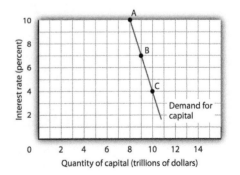

Shifts in the Demand for Capital

Why might the demand for capital change? Because the demand for capital reflects the marginal revenue product of capital, anything that changes the marginal revenue product of capital will shift the demand for capital. Our search for demand shifters must thus focus on factors that change the marginal product of capital, the prices of the goods capital produces, and the costs of acquiring and holding capital. Let us discuss some factors that could affect these variables and thus shift the demand for capital.

Changes in Expectations

Choices concerning capital are always based on expectations. Net present value is computed from the expected revenues and costs over the expected life of an asset. If firms' expectations change, their demand for capital will change. If something causes firms to revise their sales expectations upward (such as stronger than expected sales in the recent past), it is likely to increase their demand for capital. Similarly, an event that dampens firms' expectations (such as recent weak sales) is likely to reduce their demand for capital.

Technological Change

Technological changes can increase the marginal product of capital and thus boost the demand for capital. The discovery of new ways to integrate computers into production processes, for example, has dramatically increased the demand for capital in the last few years. Many universities are adding new classroom buildings or renovating old ones so they can better use computers in instruction, and businesses use computers in nearly every facet of operations.

Changing Demand for Goods and Services

Ultimately, the source of demand for factors of production is the demand for the goods and services produced by those factors. Economists say that the demand for a factor is a "derived" demand—derived, that is, from the demand for what the factor produces. As population and incomes expand, we can expect greater demand for goods and services, a change that will increase the demand for capital.

Changes in Relative Factor Prices

Firms achieve the greatest possible output for a given total cost by operating where the ratios of marginal product to factor price are equal for all factors of production. For a firm that uses labor (L) and capital (K), for example, this requires that $MP_L/P_L = MP_K/P_K$, where MP_L and MP_K are the marginal products of labor and capital, respectively, P_L and P_K are the prices of labor and capital, respectively. Suppose these equalities hold and the price of labor rises. The ratio of the marginal product of labor to its price goes down, and the firm substitutes capital for labor. Similarly, an increase in the price of capital, all other things unchanged, would cause firms to substitute other factors of production for capital. The demand for capital, therefore, would fall.

Changes in Tax Policy

Government can indirectly affect the price of capital through changes in tax policy. For example, suppose the government enacts an investment tax credit for businesses, that is, a deduction of a certain percentage of their spending on capital from their profits before paying taxes. Such a policy would effectively lower the price of capital, causing firms to substitute capital for other factors of production and increasing the demand for capital. The repeal of an investment tax credit would lead to a decrease in the demand for capital.

The Market for Loanable Funds

When a firm decides to expand its capital stock, it can finance its purchase of capital in several ways. It might already have the funds on hand. It can also raise funds by selling shares of stock, as we discussed in a previous chapter. When a firm sells stock, it is selling shares of ownership of the firm. It can borrow the funds for the capital from a bank. Another option is to issue and sell its own bonds. A **bond** is a promise to pay back a certain amount at a certain time. When a firm borrows from a bank or sells bonds, of course, it accepts a liability—it must make interest payments to the bank or the owners of its bonds as they come due.

Regardless of the method of financing chosen, a critical factor in the firm's decision on whether to acquire and hold capital and on how to finance the capital is the interest rate. The role of the interest rate is obvious when the firm issues its own bonds or borrows from a bank. But even when the firm uses its own funds to purchase the capital, it is forgoing the option of lending those funds directly to other firms by buying their bonds or indirectly by putting the funds in bank accounts, thereby allowing the banks to lend the funds. The interest rate gives the opportunity cost of using funds to acquire capital rather than putting the funds to the best alternative use available to the firm.

The interest rate is determined in a market in the same way that the price of potatoes is determined in a market: by the forces of demand and supply. The market in which borrowers (demanders of funds) and lenders (suppliers of funds) meet is the **loanable funds market**.

We will simplify our model of the role that the interest rate plays in the demand for capital by ignoring differences in actual interest rates that specific consumers and firms face in the economy. For example, the interest rate on credit cards is higher than the mortgage rate of interest, and large, established companies can borrow funds or issue bonds at lower interest rates than new, start-up companies can. Interest rates that firms face depend on a variety of factors, such as riskiness of the loan, the duration of the loan, and the costs of administering the loan. However, since we will focus on general tendencies that cause interest rates to rise or fall and since the various interest rates in the economy tend to move up and down together, the conclusions we reach about the market for loanable funds and how firms and consumers respond to interest rate changes will still be valid.

The Demand for Loanable Funds

In the previous section we learned that a firm's decision to acquire and keep capital depends on the net present value of the capital in question, which in turn depends on the interest rate. The lower the interest rate, the greater the amount of capital that firms will want to acquire and hold, since lower interest rates translate into more capital with positive net present values. The desire for more capital means, in turn, a desire for more loanable funds. Similarly, at higher interest rates, less capital will be demanded, because more of the capital in question will have negative net present values. Higher interest rates therefore mean less funding demanded.

bond

A promise to pay back a certain amount at a certain time.

loanable funds market

The market in which borrowers (demanders of funds) and lenders (suppliers of funds) meet.

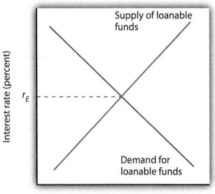

saving

Income not spent on
consumption.

dissaving

Consumption that exceeds
income during a given
period.

Thus the demand for loanable funds is downward-sloping, like the demand
for virtually everything else, as shown in Figure 13.2. The lower the interest rate,
the more capital firms will demand. The more capital that firms demand, the
greater the funding that is required to finance it.

The Supply of Loanable Funds

Lenders are consumers or firms that decide that they are willing to forgo some
current use of their funds in order to have more available in the future. Lenders
supply funds to the loanable funds market. In general, higher interest rates make
the lending option more attractive.

For consumers, however, the decision is a bit more complicated than it is for
firms. In examining consumption choices across time, economists think of consumers as having an expected stream of income over their lifetimes. It is that
expected income that defines their consumption possibilities. The problem for
consumers is to determine when to consume this income. They can spend less of
their projected income now and thus have more available in the future. Alternatively, they can boost their current spending by borrowing against their future
income.

Saving is income not spent on consumption. (We shall ignore taxes in this
analysis.) **Dissaving** occurs when consumption exceeds income during a period.
Dissaving means that the individual's saving is negative. Dissaving can be
financed either by borrowing or by using past savings. Many people, for example, save in preparation for retirement and then dissave during their retirement years.

Saving adds to a household's wealth. Dissaving reduces it. Indeed, a household's wealth is the
sum of the value of all past saving less all past dissaving.

We can think of saving as a choice to postpone consumption. Because interest rates are a payment paid to people who postpone their use of wealth, interest rates are a kind of reward paid to
savers. Will higher interest rates encourage the behavior they reward? The answer is a resounding
"maybe." Just as higher wages might not increase the quantity of labor supplied, higher interest
rates might not increase the quantity of saving. The problem, once again, lies in the fact that the
income and substitution effects of a change in interest rates will pull in opposite directions.

Consider a hypothetical consumer, Tom Smith. Let us simplify the analysis of Mr. Smith's
choices concerning the timing of consumption by assuming that there are only two periods: the
present period is period 0, and the next is period 1. Suppose the interest rate is 8% and his income
in both periods is expected to be $30,000.

Mr. Smith could, of course, spend $30,000 in period 0 and $30,000 in period 1. In that case, his
saving equals zero in both periods. But he has alternatives. He could, for example, spend more than
$30,000 in period 0 by borrowing against his income for period 1. Alternatively, he could spend less
than $30,000 in period 0 and use his saving—and the interest he earns on that saving—to boost his
consumption in period 1. If, for example, he spends $20,000 in period 0, his saving in period 0 equals
$10,000. He will earn $800 interest on that saving, so he will have $40,800 to spend in the next period.

Suppose the interest rate rises to 10%. The increase in the interest rate has boosted the price of
current consumption. Now for every $1 he spends in period 0 he gives up $1.10 in consumption in
period 1, instead of $1.08, which was the amount that would have been given up in consumption in
period 1 when the interest rate was 8%. A higher price produces a substitution effect that reduces
an activity—Mr. Smith will spend less in the current period due to the substitution effect. The substitution effect of a higher interest rate thus boosts saving. But the higher interest rate also means
that he earns more income on his saving. Consumption in the current period is a normal good, so
an increase in income can be expected to increase current consumption. But an increase in current
consumption implies a reduction in saving. The income effect of a higher interest rate thus tends

to reduce saving. Whether Mr. Smith's saving will rise or fall in response to a higher interest rate depends on the relative strengths of the substitution and income effects.

To see how an increase in interest rates might reduce saving, imagine that Mr. Smith has decided that his goal is to have $40,800 to spend in period 1. At an interest rate of 10%, he can reduce his saving below $10,000 and still achieve his goal of having $40,800 to spend in the next period. The income effect of the increase in the interest rate has reduced his saving, and consequently his desire to supply funds to the loanable funds market.

Because changes in interest rates produce substitution and income effects that pull saving in opposite directions, we cannot be sure what will happen to saving if interest rates change. The combined effect of all consumers' and firms' decisions, however, generally leads to an upward-sloping supply curve for loanable funds, as shown in Figure 13.2. That is, the substitution effect usually dominates the income effect.

The equilibrium interest rate is determined by the intersection of the demand and supply curves in the market for loanable funds.

Capital and the Loanable Funds Market

If the quantity of capital demanded varies inversely with the interest rate, and if the interest rate is determined in the loanable funds market, then it follows that the demand for capital and the loanable funds market are interrelated. Because the acquisition of new capital is generally financed in the loanable funds market, a change in the demand for capital leads to a change in the demand for loanable funds—and that affects the interest rate. A change in the interest rate, in turn, affects the quantity of capital demanded on any demand curve.

The relationship between the demand for capital and the loanable funds market thus goes both ways. Changes in the demand for capital affect the loanable funds market, and changes in the loanable funds market can affect the quantity of capital demanded.

Changes in the Demand for Capital and the Loanable Funds Market

Figure 13.3 suggests how an increased demand for capital by firms will affect the loanable funds market, and thus the quantity of capital firms will demand. In Panel (a) the initial interest rate is r_1. At r_1 in Panel (b) K_1 units of capital are demanded (on curve D_1). Now suppose an improvement in technology increases the marginal product of capital, shifting the demand curve for capital in Panel (b) to the right to D_2. Firms can be expected to finance the increased acquisition of capital by demanding more loanable funds, shifting the demand curve for loanable funds to D_2 in Panel (a). The interest rate thus rises to r_2. Consequently, in the market for capital the demand for capital is greater and the interest rate is higher. The new quantity of capital demanded is K_2 on demand curve D_2.

FIGURE 13.3 Loanable Funds and the Demand for Capital

The interest rate is determined in the loanable funds market, and the quantity of capital demanded varies with the interest rate. Thus, events in the loanable funds market and the demand for capital are interrelated. If the demand for capital increases to D_2 in Panel (b), the demand for loanable funds is likely to increase as well. Panel (a) shows the result in the loanable funds market—a shift in the demand curve for loanable funds from D_1 to D_2 and an increase in the interest rate from r_1 to r_2. At r_2, the quantity of capital demanded will be K_2, as shown in Panel (b).

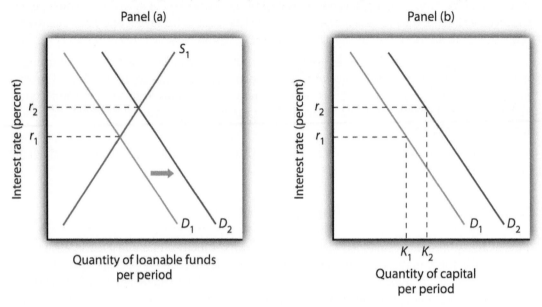

Changes in the Loanable Funds Market and the Demand for Capital

Events in the loanable funds market can also affect the quantity of capital firms will hold. Suppose, for example, that consumers decide to increase current consumption and thus to supply fewer funds to the loanable funds market at any interest rate. This change in consumer preferences shifts the supply curve for loanable funds in Panel (a) of Figure 13.4 from S_1 to S_2 and raises the interest rate to r_2. If there is no change in the demand for capital D_1, the quantity of capital firms demand falls to K_2 in Panel (b).

FIGURE 13.4 A Change in the Loanable Funds Market and the Quantity of Capital Demanded

A change that begins in the loanable funds market can affect the quantity of capital firms demand. Here, a decrease in consumer saving causes a shift in the supply of loanable funds from S_1 to S_2 in Panel (a). Assuming there is no change in the demand for capital, the quantity of capital demanded falls from K_1 to K_2 in Panel (b).

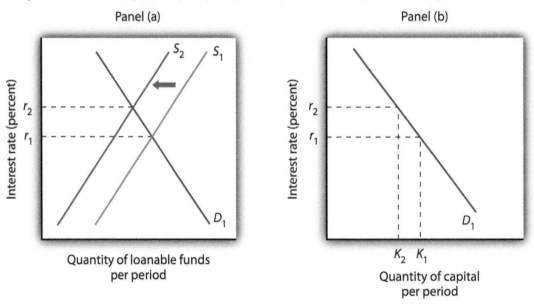

Our model of the relationship between the demand for capital and the loanable funds market thus assumes that the interest rate is determined in the market for loanable funds. Given the demand curve for capital, that interest rate then determines the quantity of capital firms demand.

Table 13.2 shows that a change in the quantity of capital that firms demand can begin with a change in the demand for capital or with a change in the demand for or supply of loanable funds. A change in the demand for capital affects the demand for loanable funds and hence the interest rate in the loanable funds market. The change in the interest rate leads to a change in the quantity of capital demanded. Alternatively, a change in the loanable funds market, which leads to a change in the interest rate, causes a change in quantity of capital demanded.

TABLE 13.2 Two Routes to Changes in the Quantity of Capital Demanded
A change in the quantity of capital that firms demand can begin with a change in the demand for capital or with a change in the demand or supply of loanable funds.

A change originating in the capital market	A change originating in the loanable funds market
1. A change in the demand for capital leads to…	1. A change in the demand for or supply of loanable funds leads to …
2.…a change in the demand for loanable funds, which leads to…	2.…a change in the interest rate, which leads to…
3.…a change in the interest rate, which leads to…	3.…a change in the quantity of capital demanded.
4.…a change in the quantity of captial demanded.	

Key Takeaways

- The net present value (*NPV*) of an investment project is equal to the present value of its expected revenues minus the present value of its expected costs. Firms will want to undertake those investments for which the *NPV* is greater than or equal to zero.
- The demand curve for capital shows that firms demand a greater quantity of capital at lower interest rates. Among the forces that can shift the demand curve for capital are changes in expectations, changes in technology, changes in the demands for goods and services, changes in relative factor prices, and changes in tax policy.
- The interest rate is determined in the market for loanable funds. The demand curve for loanable funds has a negative slope; the supply curve has a positive slope.
- Changes in the demand for capital affect the loanable funds market, and changes in the loanable funds market affect the quantity of capital demanded.

Try It!

Suppose that baby boomers become increasingly concerned about whether or not the government will really have the funds to make Social Security payments to them over their retirement years. As a result, they boost saving now. How would their decisions affect the market for loanable funds and the demand curve for capital?

Case in Point: "A Social Program From Which Everybody Wins"

Source: © Thinkstock

In the 1960s in Michigan an experiment was conducted on a sample of 123 at-risk children. Through a random selection process, 58 children were selected to receive the intensive High/Scope Perry Preschool Program, while 65 children were placed in the control group. The program lasted for one or two short academic years and consisted of 2.5 hours per day in a center, home visits of 1.5 hours per day, and group meetings with parents. These 123 people have been surveyed periodically up to age 40.

The program was funded by government and total taxpayer cost per participant was about $15,000 in 2000 dollars. What were the program benefits? For the individuals, the main potential monetary benefit is increased earnings. For the public, potential benefits include higher tax receipts due to higher earnings, reductions in crime, and lower welfare payments to the recipients who participated in the program.

The following table shows the net present value (*NPV*), assuming an interest rate of 3%, for the individuals and for the public, as calculated by Clive Belfield et al. Notice that the specific benefits and costs are quite different depending on whether one is looking from the perspective of the individuals or of the public. For example, the participants' families had lower childcare costs during the program; this is irrelevant to the public. The public incurred the cost of the program, while the participants did not. The benefits to the public of education for the average participant came in the form of lower grade retention and lower placement in special education classes, outweighing the public subsidy to more years of schooling by participants on average. The main benefit to the public stems from lower crime costs.

Assuming an interest rate of 3%, the lifetime net *NPV* to the average participant is just under $50,000 and it is about $180,000 to the public. To check how sensitive these results are to the choice of the interest rate, the researchers also calculated the *NPV* assuming a 7% interest rate. In that case, the *NPV* to the average participant was about $17,000 and about $67,000 to the public. Even pairing more conservative assumptions about the additional tax revenues, savings from reduced crime, and such with the higher interest rate did not alter the main finding of a positive *NPV* for males. For females, some of their very conservative estimates yielded a small negative *NPV* (about –$5,000), primarily due to lower female crime rates in general. They conclude that this analysis, along with other research on the costs and benefits of early education, provides compelling evidence that investment in early education pays off.

To the Average Participant:	*NPV*[*] for Participants Only	*NPV*[*] for General Public
Program benefits		
Childcare	$906	$0
Education	–$160	$7,303
Earnings	$50,448	$14,078
Crime	$0	$171,473
Welfare	–$2,005	$2,768
Total benefits	$49,190	$195,622
Program costs	$0	$15,166
Net present value	$49,190	$180,455
[*]**Assuming a 3% interest rate**		

Sources: Based on Clive R. Belfield, Milagros Nores, Steve Barnett, and Lawrence Schweinhart, "The High/Scope Perry Preschool Program: Cost-Benefit Analysis Using Data From the Age-40 Followup," Journal of Human Resources 41:1 (2006): 162–186.

Answer to Try It! Problem

An increase in saving at each interest rate implies a rightward shift in the supply curve of loanable funds. As a result, the equilibrium interest rate falls. With the lower interest rate, there is movement downward to the right along the demand-for-capital curve, as shown.

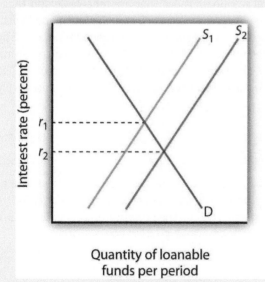

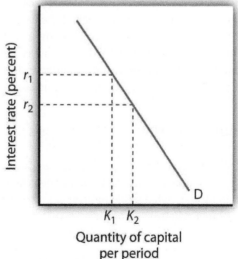

13.4 Natural Resources and Conservation

Learning Objectives

1. Distinguish between exhaustible and renewable natural resources.
2. Discuss the market for exhaustible natural resources in terms of factors that influence both demand and supply.
3. Discuss the market for renewable natural resources and relate the market outcome to carrying capacity.
4. Explain and illustrate the concept of economic rent.

Natural resources are the gifts of nature. They include everything from oil to fish in the sea to magnificent scenic vistas. The stock of a natural resource is the quantity of the resource with which the earth is endowed. For example, a certain amount of oil lies in the earth, a certain population of fish live in the sea, and a certain number of acres make up an area such as Yellowstone National Park or Manhattan. These stocks of natural resources, in turn, can be used to produce a flow of goods and services. Each year, we can extract a certain quantity of oil, harvest a certain quantity of fish, and enjoy a certain number of visits to Yellowstone.

As with capital, we examine the allocation of natural resources among alternative uses across time. By definition, natural resources cannot be produced. Our consumption of the services of natural resources in one period can affect their availability in future periods. We must thus consider the extent to which the expected demands of future generations should be taken into account when we allocate natural resources.

Natural resources often present problems of property rights in their allocation. A resource for which exclusive property rights have not been defined will be allocated as a common property resource. In such a case, we expect that the marketplace will not generate incentives to use the resource efficiently. In the absence of government intervention, natural resources that are common property may be destroyed. In this section, we shall consider natural resources for which exclusive property rights have been defined. The public sector's role in the allocation of common property resources is investigated in the chapter on the environment.

renewable natural resource

A resource whose services can be used in one period without necessarily reducing the stock of the resource that will be available in subsequent periods.

exhaustible natural resource

A resource whose services cannot be used in one period without reducing the stock of the resource that will be available in subsequent periods.

We can distinguish two categories of natural resources, those that are renewable and those that are not. A **renewable natural resource** is one whose services can be used in one period without necessarily reducing the stock of the resource that will be available in subsequent periods. The fact that they *can* be used in such a manner does not mean that they *will* be; renewable natural resources can be depleted. Wilderness areas, land, and water are renewable natural resources. The consumption of the services of an **exhaustible natural resource**, on the other hand, necessarily reduces the stock of the resource. Oil and coal are exhaustible natural resources.

Exhaustible Natural Resources

Owners of exhaustible natural resources can be expected to take the interests of future as well as current consumers into account in their extraction decisions. The greater the expected future demand for an exhaustible natural resource, the greater will be the quantity preserved for future use.

Expectations and Resource Extraction

Suppose you are the exclusive owner of a deposit of oil in Wyoming. You know that any oil you pump from this deposit and sell cannot be replaced. You are aware that this is true of all the world's oil; the consumption of oil inevitably reduces the stock of this resource.

If the quantity of oil in the earth is declining and the demand for this oil is increasing, then it is likely that the price of oil will rise in the future. Suppose you expect the price of oil to increase at an annual rate of 15%.

Given your expectation, should you pump some of your oil out of the ground and sell it? To answer that question, you need to know the interest rate. If the interest rate is 10%, then your best alternative is to leave your oil in the ground. With oil prices expected to rise 15% per year, the dollar value of your oil will increase faster if you leave it in the ground than if you pump it out, sell it, and purchase an interest-earning asset. If the market interest rate were greater than 15%, however, it would make sense to pump the oil and sell it now and use the revenue to purchase an interest-bearing asset. The return from the interest-earning asset, say 16%, would exceed the 15% rate at which you expect the value of your oil to increase. Higher interest rates thus reduce the willingness of resource owners to preserve these resources for future use.

The supply of an exhaustible resource such as oil is thus governed by its current price, its expected future price, and the interest rate. An increase in the expected future price—or a reduction in the interest rate—reduces the supply of oil today, preserving more for future use. If owners of oil expect lower prices in the future, or if the interest rate rises, they will supply more oil today and conserve less for future use. This relationship is illustrated in Figure 13.5. The current demand D for these services is given by their marginal revenue product (MRP). Suppose S_1 reflects the current marginal cost of extracting the resource, the prevailing interest rate, and expectations of future demand for the resource. If the interest rate increases, owners will be willing to supply more of the natural resource at each price, thereby shifting the supply curve to the right to S_2. The current price of the resource will fall. If the interest rate falls, the supply curve for the resource will shift to the left to S_3 as more owners of the resource decide to leave more of the resource in the earth. As a result, the current price rises.

Resource Prices Over Time

Since using nonrenewable resources would seem to mean exhausting a fixed supply, then one would expect the prices of exhaustible natural resources to rise over time as the resources become more and more scarce. Over time, however, the prices of most exhaustible natural resources have fluctuated considerably relative to the prices of all other goods and services. Figure 13.6 shows the prices of four major exhaustible natural resources 1980 to 2015. Prices have been adjusted for inflation to reflect the prices of these resources relative to other prices.

During the final two decades of the twentieth century, exhaustible natural resource prices were generally falling. With the start of the current century, their prices first rose, then fell, then rose, and then fell back again. In short, why do prices of natural resources fluctuate as they do? Should the process of continuing to "exhaust" them just drive their prices up over time?

FIGURE 13.5 Future Generations and Exhaustible Natural Resources
The current demand D for services of an exhaustible resource is given by the marginal revenue product (MRP). S_1 reflects the current marginal cost of extracting the resource, the prevailing interest rate, and expectations of future demand for the resource. The level of current consumption is thus at Q_1. If the interest rate rises, the supply curve shifts to S_2, causing the price of the resource to fall to P_2 and the quantity consumed to rise to Q_2. A drop in the interest rate shifts the supply curve to S_3, leading to an increase in price to P_3 and a decrease in consumption to Q_3.

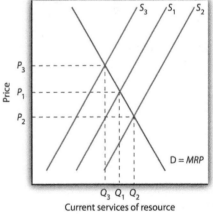

FIGURE 13.6 Natural Resource Prices, 1980–2015

The chart shows changes in the prices of four exhaustible resources—copper, zinc, oil, and coal from 1980–2015.

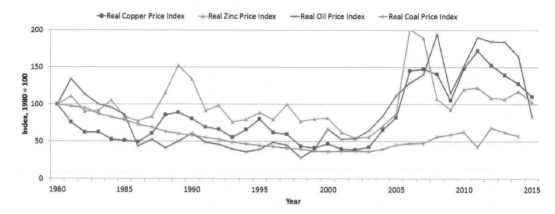

Sources: Based on data from Implicit Price Deflator, GDP: Economic Report of the President 2011, Table B-3; Copper and Zinc Prices: Statistical Abstract of the United States, 2011 and U.S. Geological Survey Minerals Yearbook; Copper and Zinc: U.S. Geological Survey Mineral Commodity Summaries, various editions; Oil: U.S. Energy Information Administration / Annual Energy Review 2011, Table 5.18, data from U.S. EIA website; Oil: U.S. Energy Information Administration / Annual Energy Review 2011, Table 5.18, data from U.S. EIA website.

In setting their expectations, people in the marketplace must anticipate not only future demand but also future supply as well. Demand in future periods could fall short of expectations if new technologies produce goods and services using less of a natural resource. That has clearly happened. The quantity of energy—which is generally produced using exhaustible fossil fuels—used to produce a unit of output has fallen by more than half in the last three decades. At the same time, rising income levels around the world, particularly in China and India over the last two decades, have led to increased demand for energy. Supply increases when previously unknown deposits of natural resources are discovered and when technologies are developed to extract and refine resources more cheaply. Figure 13.7 shows that discoveries that reduce the demand below expectations and increase the supply of natural resources can push prices down in a way that people in previous periods might not have anticipated. This scenario explains the fall in some prices of natural resources in the latter part of the twentieth century and in the most recent period. To explain the periods of increase in exhaustible natural resources prices, we can say that the factors contributing to increased demand for energy and some other exhaustible natural resources were outweighing the factors contributing to increased supply, resulting in higher prices.

Will we ever run out of exhaustible natural resources? Past experience suggests that we will not. If no new technologies or discoveries that reduce demand or increase supply occur, then resource prices will rise. As they rise, consumers of these resources will demand lower quantities of these resources. Eventually, the price of a particular resource could rise so high that the quantity demanded would fall to zero. At that point, no more of the resource would be used. There would still be some of the resource in the earth—it simply would not be practical to use more of it. The market simply will not allow us to "run out" of exhaustible natural resources.

Renewable Natural Resources

As is the case with exhaustible natural resources, our consumption of the services of renewable natural resources can affect future generations. Unlike exhaustible resources, however, renewable resources can be consumed in a way that does not diminish their stocks.

Carrying Capacity and Future Generations

The quantity of a renewable natural resource that can be consumed in any period without reducing the stock of the resource available in the next period is its **carrying capacity**. Suppose, for example, that a school of 10 million fish increases by 1 million fish each year. The carrying capacity of the school is therefore 1 million fish per year—the harvest of 1 million fish each year will leave the size of the population unchanged. Harvests that exceed a resource's carrying capacity reduce the stock of the resource; harvests that fall short of it increase that stock.

As is the case with exhaustible natural resources, future generations have a stake in current consumption of a renewable resource. Figure 13.8 shows the efficient level of consumption of such a resource. Suppose Q_{cap} is the carrying capacity of a particular resource and S_1 is the supply curve that reflects the current marginal cost of utilizing the resource, including costs for the labor and capital required to make its services available, given the interest rate and expected future demand. The efficient level of consumption in the current period is found at point E, at the intersection of the current period's demand and supply curves. Notice that in the case shown, current consumption at Q_1 is less than the carrying capacity of the resource. A larger stock of this resource will be available in subsequent periods than is available now.

FIGURE 13.7 An Explanation for Falling Resource Prices

Demand for resources has increased over time from D_1 to D_2, but this shift in demand is less than it would have been (D_3) if technologies for producing goods and services using less resource per unit of output had not been developed. Supply of resources has increased from S_1 to S_2 as a result of the discovery of deposits of natural resources and/or development of new technologies for extracting and refining resources. As a result, the prices of many natural resources have fallen.

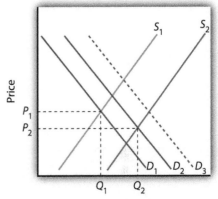

carrying capacity

The quantity of a renewable natural resource that can be consumed in any period without reducing the stock of the resource available in the next period.

FIGURE 13.8 Future Generations and
Renewable Resources
The efficient quantity of services to consume is
determined by the intersection S_1 and the
demand curve D. This intersection occurs at
point E at a quantity of Q_1. This lies below the
carrying capacity Q_{cap}. An increase in interest
rates, however, shifts the supply curve to S_2.
The efficient level of current consumption rises
to Q_2, which now exceeds the carrying capacity
of the resource.

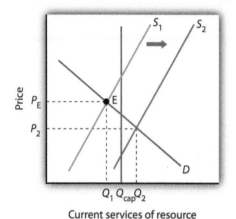

Current services of resource

Now suppose interest rates increase. As with nonrenewable resources,
higher interest rates shift the supply curve to the right, as shown by S_2. The result
is an increase in current consumption to Q_2. Now consumption exceeds the carrying capacity, and the stock of the resource available to future generations will
be reduced. While this solution may be efficient, the resource will not be sustained over time at current levels.

If society is concerned about a reduction in the amount of the resource available in the future, further steps may be required to preserve it. For example, if
trees are being cut down faster than they are being replenished in a particular
location, such as the Amazon in Brazil, a desire to maintain biological diversity
might lead to conservation efforts.

Economic Rent and The Market for Land

We turn finally to the case of land that is used solely for the space it affords for
other activities—parks, buildings, golf courses, and so forth. We shall assume that
the carrying capacity of such land equals its quantity.

FIGURE 13.9 The Market for Land
The price of a one-acre parcel of land is determined by the intersection of a vertical supply curve
and the demand curve for the parcel. The sum paid for the parcel, shown by the shaded area, is
economic rent.

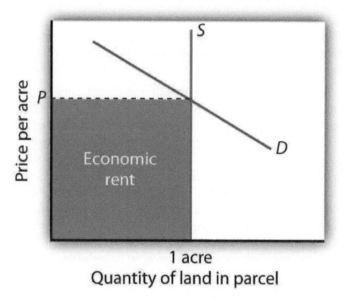

1 acre
Quantity of land in parcel

economic rent

The amount by which any
price exceeds the
minimum price necessary
to make a resource
available.

The supply of land is a vertical line. The quantity of land in a particular location is fixed. Suppose, for example, that the price of a one-acre parcel of land is zero. At a price of zero, there is still
one acre of land; quantity is unaffected by price. If the price were to rise, there would still be only
one acre in the parcel. That means that the price of the parcel exceeds the minimum
price—zero—at which the land would be available. The amount by which any price exceeds the
minimum price necessary to make a resource available is called **economic rent**.

The concept of economic rent can be applied to any factor of production that is in fixed supply
above a certain price. In this sense, much of the salary received by Judge Judy constitutes economic
rent. At a low enough salary, she might choose to leave the television industry. How low would
depend on what she could earn in a best alternative occupation. If she earns $45 million per year
now but could earn $200,000 in a best alternative occupation, then $44.8 million of her salary is
economic rent. Most of her current earnings are in the form of economic rent, because her salary

substantially exceeds the minimum price necessary to keep her supplying her resources to current purposes.

Key Takeaways

- Natural resources are either exhaustible or renewable.
- The demand for the services of a natural resource in any period is given by the marginal revenue product of those services.
- Owners of natural resources have an incentive to take into account the current price, the expected future demand for them, and the interest rate when making choices about resource supply.
- The services of a renewable natural resource may be consumed at levels that are below or greater than the carrying capacity of the resource.
- The payment for a resource above the minimum price necessary to make the resource available is economic rent.

Try It!

You have just been given an oil well in Texas by Aunt Carmen. The current price of oil is $45 per barrel, and it is estimated that your oil deposit contains about 10,000 barrels of oil. For simplicity, assume that it does not cost anything to extract the oil and get it to market and that you must decide whether to empty the well now or wait until next year. Suppose the interest rate is 10% and that you expect that the price of oil next year will rise to $54 per barrel. What should you do? Would your decision change if the choice were to empty the well now or in two years?

Case in Point: Betting on Natural Resource Prices

Source: © Thinkstock

Back in 1981, Julian Simon, an economist at the Cato Institute, issued a challenge to those who argued that rising prices signaled that the earth was likely to run out of natural resources. He and many other economists argued that rising prices would lead firms to make substitutions and to seek new discoveries and new technologies that would bring prices back down. He told doubters to pick any five exhaustible natural resources. If their average price, adjusted for inflation, rose over the next decade, Simon would pay $1,000. If their price fell, however, he would get the $1,000. Paul Ehrlich, an ecologist, took Mr. Simon up on his offer. Mr. Ehrlich is the author of the 1968 book, *The Population Bomb*, that argued resource scarcity would lead to the starvation of hundreds of millions of people by 1990. Mr. Ehrlich picked chromium, copper, nickel, tin, and tungsten. Since their prices fell over the decade, Mr. Ehrlich paid Mr. Simon $1,000.

In 1990, Mr. Simon offered a "double-or-quits" rematch for any future date. Mr. Simon died in 1998 and Mr. Ehrlich did not agree to take him on again. If the original bet had been recalculated in 2011, Mr. Ehrlich would have won. The index of the average price of the five resources went from 100 in 1980 down between 40 and 60 for much of the 1990s and by 2011 had returned to about 100.

What has happened to the prices of these resources since? As of 2015, the prices of four of them had fallen, each from between 32% to 45%. Only the price of tungsten rose and it did so by 29%. So over the recent period, Mr. Simon again would have won.

Those in the Simon camp, who have been dubbed the Cornucopians, tend to respond to periods when resource prices are rising by saying that the rises are due to increased demand and that new supplies, technologies, or substitutes will be found over time that will bring prices back down. Those in the Ehrlich camp, who have been dubbed the Malthusians, after Thomas Malthus, the late eighteenth-century economist who argued that population grown would exceed the growth of food supplies, tend to respond to price declines by saying they reflect temporary demand reductions and to price increases by saying that scarcity is finally taking over.

Which way would you bet for 2015 to 2025?

Sources: Based on "The Revenge of Malthus: A Famous Bet Recalculated," Economist, August 6, 2011, online at http://www.economist.com/node/21525472; U.S. Geological Survey, Mineral Commodity Summaries 2016 online at http://minerals.usgs.gov/minerals/pubs/mcs/.

Answer to Try It! Problem

Since you expect oil prices to rise ($54 − 45)/$45 = 20% and the interest rate is only 10%, you would be better off waiting a year before emptying the well. Another way of seeing this is to compute the present value of the oil a year from now:

$$P_O = (\$54 * 10,000)/(1 + 0.10)^1 = \$490,909.09$$

Since $490,909 is greater than the $45*10,000 = $450,000 you could earn by emptying the well now, the present value calculation shows the rewards of waiting a year.

If the choice is to empty the well now or in 2 years, however, you would be better off emptying it now, since the present value is only $446,280.99:

$$P_O = (\$54 * 10,000)/(1 + 0.10)^2 = \$446,280.99$$

13.5 Review and Practice

Summary

Time is the complicating factor when we analyze capital and natural resources. Because current choices affect the future stocks of both resources, we must take those future consequences into account. And because a payment in the future is worth less than an equal payment today, we need to convert the dollar value of future consequences to present value. We determine the present value of a future payment by dividing the amount of that payment by $(1 + r)^n$, where r is the interest rate and n is the number of years until the payment will occur. The present value of a given future value is smaller at higher values of n and at higher interest rates.

Interest rates are determined in the market for loanable funds. The demand for loanable funds is derived from the demand for capital. At lower interest rates, the quantity of capital demanded increases. This, in turn, leads to an increase in the demand for loanable funds. In the aggregate, the supply curve of loanable funds is likely to be upward-sloping.

We assume that firms determine whether to acquire an additional unit of capital by (NPV) of the asset. When NPV equals zero, the present value of capital's marginal revenue product equals the present value of its marginal factor cost. The demand curve for capital shows the quantity of capital demanded at each interest rate. Among the factors that shift the demand curve for capital are changes in expectations, new technology, change in demands for goods and services, and change in relative factor prices.

Markets for natural resources are distinguished according to whether the resources are exhaustible or renewable. Owners of natural resources have an incentive to consider future as well as present demands for these resources. Land, when it has a vertical supply curve, generates a return that consists entirely of rent. In general, economic rent is return to a resource in excess of the minimum price necessary to make that resource available.

Concept Problems

1. The charging of interest rates is often viewed with contempt. Do interest rates serve any useful purpose?

2. How does an increase in interest rates affect the present value of a future payment?

3. How does an increase in the size of a future payment affect the present value of the future payment?

4. Two payments of $1,000 are to be made. One of them will be paid one year from today and the other will be paid two years from today. Which has the greater present value? Why?

5. The essay on the viatical settlements industry suggests that investors pay only 80% of the face value of a life insurance policy that is expected to be paid off in six months. Why? Would it not be fairer if investors paid the full value?

6. How would each of the following events affect the demand curve for capital?

    a. A prospective cut in taxes imposed on business firms

    b. A reduction in the price of labor

    c. An improvement in technology that increases capital's marginal product

    d. An increase in interest rates

7. If developed and made practical, fusion technology would allow the production of virtually unlimited quantities of cheap, pollution-free energy. Some scientists predict that the technology for fusion will be developed within the next few decades. How does an expectation that fusion will be developed affect the market for oil today?

8. Is the rent paid for an apartment economic rent? Explain.

9. Film director Brett Ratner (Rush Hour, After the Sunset, and others) commented to a *New York Times* (November 13, 2004, p. A19) reporter that, "If he weren't a director, Mr. Ratner said he would surely be taking orders at McDonald's." How much economic rent is Mr. Ratner likely earning?

10. Suppose you own a ranch, and that commercial and residential development start to take place around your ranch. How will this affect the value of your property? What will happen to the quantity of land? What kind of return will you earn?

11. Explain why higher interest rates tend to increase the current use of natural resources.

Numerical Problems

Use the tables below to answer Problems 1–5. The first table gives the present value of $1 at the end of different time periods, given different interest rates. For example, at an interest rate of 10%, the present value of $1 to be paid in 20 years is $0.149. At 10% interest, the present value of $1,000 to be paid in 20 years equals $1,000 times 0.149, or $149. The second table gives the present value of a stream of payments of $1 to be made at the end of each period for a given number of periods. For example, at 10% interest, the present value of a series of $1 payments, made at the end of each year for the next 10 years, is $6.145. Using that same interest rate, the present value of a series of 10 payments of $1,000 each is $1,000 times 6.145, or $6,145.

TABLE 13.3 Present Value of $1 to Be Received at the End of a Given Number of Periods

	Percent Interest									
Period	2	4	6	8	10	12	14	16	18	20
1	0.980	0.962	0.943	0.926	0.909	0.893	0.877	0.862	0.847	0.833
2	0.961	0.925	0.890	0.857	0.826	0.797	0.769	0.743	0.718	0.694
3	0.942	0.889	0.840	0.794	0.751	0.712	0.675	0.641	0.609	0.579
4	0.924	0.855	0.792	0.735	0.683	0.636	0.592	0.552	0.515	0.442
5	0.906	0.822	0.747	0.681	0.621	0.567	0.519	0.476	0.437	0.402
10	0.820	0.676	0.558	0.463	0.386	0.322	0.270	0.227	0.191	0.162
15	0.743	0.555	0.417	0.315	0.239	0.183	0.140	0.180	0.084	0.065
20	0.673	0.456	0.312	0.215	0.149	0.104	0.073	0.051	0.037	0.026
25	0.610	0.375	0.233	0.146	0.092	0.059	0.038	0.024	0.016	0.010
40	0.453	0.208	0.097	0.046	0.022	0.011	0.005	0.003	0.001	0.001
50	0.372	0.141	0.054	0.021	0.009	0.003	0.001	0.001	0	0

TABLE 13.4 Present Value of $1 to Be Received at the End of Each Period for a Given Number of Periods

	Percent Interest									
Period	2	4	6	8	10	12	14	16	18	20
1	0.980	0.962	0.943	0.926	0.909	0.893	0.877	0.862	0.847	0.833
2	1.942	1.886	1.833	1.783	1.736	1.690	1.647	1.605	1.566	1.528
3	2.884	2.775	2.673	2.577	2.487	2.402	2.322	2.246	2.174	2.106
4	3.808	3.630	3.465	3.312	3.170	3.037	2.910	2.798	2.690	2.589
5	4.713	4.452	4.212	3.993	3.791	3.605	3.433	3.274	3.127	2.991
10	8.983	8.111	7.360	6.710	6.145	5.650	5.216	4.833	4.494	4.192
15	12.849	11.718	9.712	8.559	7.606	6.811	6.142	5.575	5.092	4.675
20	16.351	13.590	11.470	9.818	8.514	7.469	6.623	5.929	5.353	4.870
25	19.523	15.622	12.783	10.675	9.077	7.843	6.873	6.097	5.467	4.948
30	22.396	17.292	13.765	11.258	9.427	8.055	7.003	6.177	5.517	4.979
40	27.355	19.793	15.046	11.925	9.779	8.244	7.105	6.233	5.548	4.997
50	31.424	21.482	15.762	12.233	9.915	8.304	7.133	6.246	5.554	4.999

1. Your Uncle Arthur, not to be outdone by Aunt Carmen, offers you a choice. You can have $10,000 now or $30,000 in 15 years. If you took the payment now, you could put it in a bond

fund or bank account earning 8% interest. Use present value analysis to determine which alternative is better.

2. Remember Carol Stein's tractor? We saw that at an interest rate of 7%, a decision to purchase the tractor would pay off; its net present value is positive. Suppose the tractor is still expected to yield $20,000 in net revenue per year for each of the next 5 years and to sell at the end of 5 years for $22,000; and the purchase price of the tractor still equals $95,000. Use Tables (a) and (b) to compute the net present value of the tractor at an interest rate of 8%.

3. Mark Jones is thinking about going to college. If he goes, he will earn nothing for the next four years and, in addition, will have to pay tuition and fees totaling $10,000 per year. He also would not earn the $25,000 per year he could make by working full time during the next four years. After his four years of college, he expects that his income, both while working and in retirement, will be $20,000 per year more, over the next 50 years, than it would have been had he not attended college. Should he go to college? Assume that each payment for college and dollar of income earned occur at the end of the years in which they occur. Ignore possible income taxes in making your calculations. Decide whether you should attend college, assuming each of the following interest rates:

    a. 2%

    b. 4%

    c. 6%

    d. 8%

4. A new health club has just opened up in your town. Struggling to bring in money now, the club is offering 10-year memberships for a one-time payment now of $800. You cannot be sure that you will still be in town for the next 10 years, but you expect that you will be. You anticipate that your benefit of belonging to the club will be $10 per month (think of this as an annual benefit of $120). Decide whether you should join at each of the following interest rates:

    a. 2%

    b. 4%

    c. 6%

    d. 8%

5. You have just purchased a new home. No money was required as a down payment; you will be making payments of $2,000 per month (think of these as annual payments of $24,000) for the next 30 years. Determine the present value of your future payments at each of the following interest rates:

    a. 2%

    b. 4%

    c. 6%

    d. 8%

6. You own several barrels of wine; over the years, the value of this wine has risen at an average rate of 10% per year. It is expected to continue to rise in value, but at a slower and slower rate. Assuming your goal is to maximize your revenue from the wine, at what point will you sell it?

7. You have been given a coin collection. You have no personal interest in coins; your only interest is to make money from it. You estimate that the current value of the collection is $10,000. You are told the coins are likely to rise in value over time by 5% per year. What should you do with the collection? On what factors does your answer depend?

8. The Case in Point on the increasing scarcity of oil suggested that the Khurais complex is expected to add 1.2 million barrels to world oil production by 2009. Suppose that world production that year what otherwise be 87 million barrels per day. Assume that the price elasticity of demand for oil is –0.5. By how much would you expect the addition of oil from the Khurais complex to reduce the world oil price?

Endnotes

1. Tara Clarke, "Will There Finally Be a Chance to Invest in SpaceX Stock in 2016?", Money, Morning, April 28, 2016 at http://moneymorning.com/2015/12/22/will-there-finally-be-a-chance-to-invest-in-spacex-stock-in-2016/; Steve Lohr, "SpaceX's Explosion Reverberates Across Space, Satellite and Telecom Industries," The New York Times, September 4, 2016 at http://www.nytimes.com/2016/09/05/business/spacexs-explosion-reverberates-across-space-satellite-and-telecom-industries.html?mwrsm=Email&_r=0; "Elon Musk: 'Chances are we're all living in a simulation,'" The Guardian, June 2, 2016 at https://www.theguardian.com/technology/2016/jun/02/elon-musk-tesla-space-x-paypal-hyperloop-simulation

CHAPTER 14

Imperfectly Competitive Markets for Factors of Production

14.1 Start Up: Hockey Players Frozen Out

On October 30, 2004, Columbus Blue Jackets' center Todd Marchant would ordinarily have been getting ready to open the 2004–2005 National Hockey League (NHL) season before a packed house in a game against the Dallas Stars in Dallas. Instead, he was home and devoting his season to coaching his six-year-old daughter's hockey team.

Mr. Marchant was home because the Commissioner of the NHL, Gary Bettman, had ordered players locked out on September 15, when training camp was scheduled to begin and when the contract between the NHL and the Players Association expired. Mr. Bettman had warned for five years that he would take the drastic action of shutting down the hockey season unless owners and players could agree on a system to limit player salaries. In the NHL, player salaries amounted to 75% of team revenues. By contrast, player salaries represented 64% of team revenues in the National Football League and 59% of revenues in the American Basketball Association. Mr. Bettman contended that the league's 30 franchises had lost a combined $500 million in the previous two years.

Players and owners alike had a great deal of money at stake. The NHL was selling 90% of its seats available during the regular season and generating $2.1 billion per year in revenues. "No one likes losing money, but this year everyone involved in hockey may be losing something," Mr. Marchant told *Business Week*. Mr. Marchant lost $2.9 million as a result of the lockout.

Mr. Bettman and the owners were holding out for a "salary cap" that would limit player salaries to 53% of team revenues. According to Mark Hyman of *Business Week*, that would reduce average salaries in hockey from $1.8 million to $1.3 million. "We're not going to play under a salary cap; we're dead set against it," Brad Lucovich, defenseman for Dallas, told *Business Week*. But the owners were similarly adamant. They were perfectly willing to forego revenues from the season—and to avoid paying player salaries—to establish a salary cap.

Were the owners being greedy? Or were the players at fault? For economists, the notions of "greed" or "blame" were not the issue. Economists assume that all individuals act in their own self-interest. In the case of the hockey lockout, which eliminated the 2004–05 season, players and owners were in a face-off in which a great deal of money was at stake. Owners had tried to establish a cap in 1994; the resulting labor dispute shut down half the season. Ultimately, the players prevailed and no caps were imposed. The 2005 lockout ended in nearly the opposite way. In the new contract, player salaries are capped and may not exceed 54% of league revenues.[1] To most observers, it seemed that the team owners had won this battle.

The National Football League lockout of 2011 lasted more than four months. The issues were similar—players' share of league revenues, salary caps, and free agency. Both sides could point to victories in the settlement that was reached. Fortunately for the fans, the dispute took placing during the off-season.

Revolutionary changes in the rules that govern relations between the owners of sports teams and the players they hire have produced textbook examples of the economic forces at work in the determination of wages in imperfectly competitive markets. Markets for labor and other factors of production can diverge from the conditions of perfect competition in several ways, all of which involve price-setting behavior. Firms that purchase inputs may be price setters. Suppliers of inputs may have market power as well: a firm may have monopoly control over some key input or input suppliers may band together to achieve market power. Workers may organize unions. Suppliers of services, such as physicians and hairdressers, have formed associations that exert power in the marketplace.

This chapter applies the marginal decision rule to the analysis of imperfectly competitive markets for labor and other factors of production. Imperfect competition in these markets generally results in a reduction in the quantity of an input used, relative to the competitive equilibrium. The price of the input, however, could be higher or lower than in perfect competition, depending on the nature of the market structure involved.

14.2 Price-Setting Buyers: The Case of Monopsony

Learning Objectives

1. Define monopsony and differentiate it from monopoly.
2. Apply the marginal decision rule to the profit-maximizing solution of a monopsony buyer.
3. Discuss situations of monopsony in the real world.

We have seen that market power in product markets exists when firms have the ability to set the prices they charge, within the limits of the demand curve for their products. Depending on the factor supply curve, firms may also have some power to set prices they pay in factor markets.

A firm can set price in a factor market if, instead of a market-determined price, it faces an upward-sloping supply curve for the factor. This creates a fundamental difference between price-taking and price-setting firms in factor markets. A price-taking firm can hire any amount of the factor at the market price; it faces a horizontal supply curve for the factor at the market-determined price, as shown in Panel (a) of Figure 14.1. A price-setting firm faces an upward-sloping supply curve such as S in Panel (b). It obtains Q_1 units of the factor when it sets the price P_1. To obtain a larger quantity, such as Q_2, it must offer a higher price, P_2.

FIGURE 14.1 Factor Market Price Takers and Price Setters
A price-taking firm faces the market-determined price P for the factor in Panel (a) and can purchase any quantity it wants at that price. A price-setting firm faces an upward-sloping supply curve S in Panel (b). The price-setting firm sets the price consistent with the quantity of the factor it wants to obtain. Here, the firm can obtain Q_1 units at a price P_1, but it must pay a higher price per unit, P_2, to obtain Q_2 units.

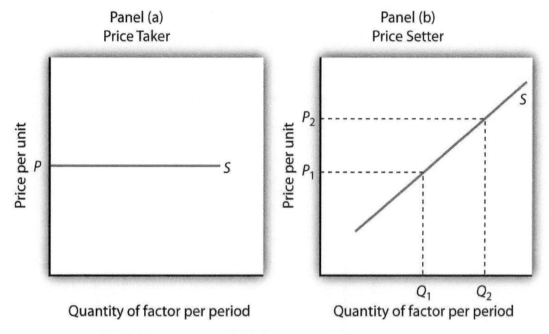

Consider a situation in which one firm is the only buyer of a particular factor. An example might be an isolated mining town where the mine is the single employer. A market in which there is only one buyer of a good, service, or factor of production is called a **monopsony**. Monopsony is the buyer's counterpart of monopoly. Monopoly means a single seller; monopsony means a single buyer.

Assume that the suppliers of a factor in a monopsony market are price takers; there is perfect competition in factor supply. But a single firm constitutes the entire market for the factor. That means that the monopsony firm faces the upward-sloping market supply curve for the factor. Such a case is illustrated in Figure 14.2, where the price and quantity combinations on the supply curve for the factor are given in the table.

monopsony

A market in which there is only one buyer of a good, service, or factor of production.

FIGURE 14.2 Supply and Marginal Factor Cost

The table gives prices and quantities for the factor supply curve plotted in the graph. Notice that the marginal factor cost curve lies above the supply curve.

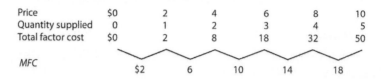

Price	$0	2	4	6	8	10
Quantity supplied	0	1	2	3	4	5
Total factor cost	$0	2	8	18	32	50
MFC		$2	6	10	14	18

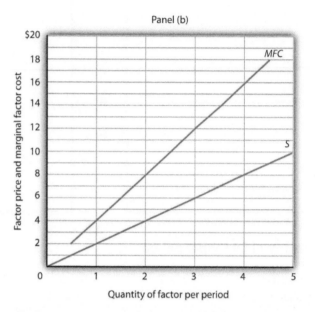

Suppose the monopsony firm is now using three units of the factor at a price of $6 per unit. Its total factor cost is $18. Suppose the firm is considering adding one more unit of the factor. Given the supply curve, the only way the firm can obtain four units of the factor rather than three is to offer a higher price of $8 for all four units of the factor. That would increase the firm's total factor cost from $18 to $32. The marginal factor cost of the fourth unit of the factor is thus $14. It includes the $8 the firm pays for the fourth unit plus an additional $2 for each of the three units the firm was already using, since it has increased the prices for the factor to $8 from $6. The marginal factor cost (MFC) exceeds the price of the factor. We can plot the MFC for each increase in the quantity of the factor the firm uses; notice in Figure 14.2 that the MFC curve lies above the supply curve. As always in plotting in marginal values, we plot the $14 midway between units three and four because it is the increase in factor cost as the firm goes from three to four units.

Monopsony Equilibrium and the Marginal Decision Rule

The marginal decision rule, as it applies to a firm's use of factors, calls for the firm to add more units of a factor up to the point that the factor's MRP is equal to its MFC. Figure 14.3 illustrates this solution for a firm that is the only buyer of labor in a particular market.

The firm faces the supply curve for labor, S, and the marginal factor cost curve for labor, MFC. The profit-maximizing quantity is determined by the intersection of the MRP and MFC curves—the firm will hire L_m units of labor. The wage at which the firm can obtain L_m units of labor is given by the supply curve for labor; it is W_m. Labor receives a wage that is less than its MRP.

If the monopsony firm was broken up into a large number of small firms and all other conditions in the market remained unchanged, then the sum of the MRP curves for individual firms would be the market demand for labor. The equilibrium wage would be W_c, and the quantity of labor demanded would be L_c. Thus, compared to a competitive market, a monopsony solution generates a lower factor price and a smaller quantity of the factor demanded.

Monopoly and Monopsony: A Comparison

There is a close relationship between the models of monopoly and monopsony. A clear understanding of this relationship will help to clarify both models.

Figure 14.4 compares the monopoly and monopsony equilibrium solutions. Both types of firms are price setters: The monopoly is a price setter in its product market; the monopsony is a price setter in its factor market. Both firms must change price to change quantity: The monopoly must lower its product price to sell an additional unit of output, and the monopsony must pay more to hire an additional unit of the factor. Because both types of firms must adjust prices to change quantities, the marginal consequences of their choices are not given by the prices they charge (for products) or pay (for factors). For a monopoly, marginal revenue is less than price; for a monopsony, marginal factor cost is greater than price.

FIGURE 14.3 Monopsony Equilibrium

Given the supply curve for labor, S, and the marginal factor cost curve, MFC, the monopsony firm will select the quantity of labor at which the MRP of labor equals its MFC. It thus uses L_m units of labor (determined by at the intersection of MRP and MFC) and pays a wage of W_m per unit (the wage is taken from the supply curve at which L_m units of labor are available). The quantity of labor used by the monopsony firm is less than would be used in a competitive market (L_c); the wage paid, W_m, is lower than would be paid in a competitive labor market.

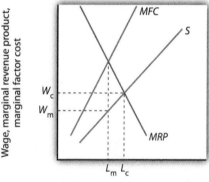

Quantity of labor per period

FIGURE 14.4 Monopoly and Monopsony

The graphs and the table provide a comparison of monopoly and monopsony.

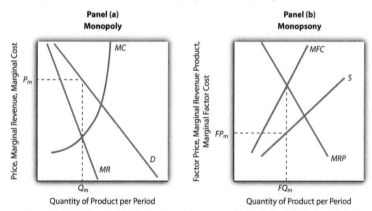

Market Choice	Monopoly	Monopsony
Nature of pricing choice	Price setter in product market.	Price setter in factor market.
Marginal consequences of choices	Selling an additional unit generates marginal revenue *MR*, which is less than *product price*.	Using an additional unit generates marginal *factor cost MFC*, which is greater than *factor price*.
Profit-maximizing solution	Produce where *MR* equals marginal cost *MC*—Q_m in Panel (a).	Use the factor at the quantity where *MRP* equals *MFC*—FQ_m in Panel (b).
Price	Determined by the point on the demand curve *D* that corresponds to the profit-maximizing quantity of product—P_m in Panel (a).	Determined by the point on the supply curve that corresponds to the profit-maximizing quantity of the factor—FP_m in Panel (b).

Both types of firms follow the marginal decision rule: A monopoly produces a quantity of the product at which marginal revenue equals marginal cost; a monopsony employs a quantity of the factor at which marginal revenue product equals marginal factor cost. Both firms set prices at which they can sell or purchase the profit-maximizing quantity. The monopoly sets its product price based on the demand curve it faces; the monopsony sets its factor price based on the factor supply curve it faces.

Monopsony in the Real World

monopsony power

Situation in which a buyer faces an upward-sloping supply curve for a good, service, or factor of production.

Although cases of pure monopsony are rare, there are many situations in which buyers have a degree of monopsony power. A buyer has **monopsony power** if it faces an upward-sloping supply curve for a good, service, or factor of production.

For example, a firm that accounts for a large share of employment in a small community may be large enough relative to the labor market that it is not a price taker. Instead, it must raise wages to attract more workers. It thus faces an upward-sloping supply curve and has monopsony power. Because buyers are more likely to have monopsony power in factor markets than in product markets, we shall focus on those.

The next section examines monopsony power in professional sports.

Monopsonies in Sports

Professional sports provide a setting in which economists can test theories of wage determination in competitive versus monopsony labor markets. In their analyses, economists assume professional teams are profit-maximizing firms that hire labor (athletes and other workers) to produce a product: entertainment bought by the fans who watch their games and by other firms that sponsor the games. Fans influence revenues directly by purchasing tickets and indirectly by generating the ratings that determine television and radio advertising revenues from broadcasts of games.

In a competitive system, a player should receive a wage equal to his or her *MRP*—the increase in team revenues the player is able to produce. As New York Yankees owner George Steinbrenner once put it, "You measure the value of a ballplayer by how many fannies he puts in the seats."

The monopsony model, however, predicts that players facing monopsony employers will receive wages that are less than their *MRP*s. A test of monopsony theory, then, would be to determine whether players in competitive markets receive wages equal to their *MRP*s and whether players in monopsony markets receive less.

Since the late 1970s, there has been a major shift in the rules that govern relations between professional athletes and owners of sports teams. The shift has turned the once monopsonistic market for professional athletes into a competitive one. Before 1977, for example, professional baseball players in the United States played under the terms of the "reserve clause," which specified that a player was "owned" by his team. Once a team had acquired a player's contract, the team could sell, trade, retain, or dismiss the player. Unless the team dismissed him, the player was unable to offer his services for competitive bidding by other teams. Moreover, players entered major league baseball through a draft that was structured so that only one team had the right to bid for any one player. Throughout a player's career, then, there was always only one team that could bid on him—each player faced a monopsony purchaser for his services to major league baseball.

Conditions were similar in other professional sports. Many studies have shown that the salaries of professional athletes in various team sports fell far short of their *MRP*s while monopsony prevailed.

When the reserve clauses were abandoned, players' salaries shot up—just as economic theory predicts. Because players could offer their services to other teams, owners began to bid for their services. Profit-maximizing owners were willing to pay athletes their *MRP*s. Average annual salaries for baseball players rose from about $50,000 in 1975 to nearly $1.4 million in 1997. Average annual player salaries in men's basketball rose from $109,000 in 1976 to $2.24 million in 1998. Football players worked under an almost pure form of monopsony until 1989, when a few players were allowed free agency status each year. In 1993, when 484 players were released to the market as free agents, those players received pay increases averaging more than 100%. Under the NFL collective bargaining agreement in effect in 1998, players could become unrestricted free agents if they had been playing for four years. There were 305 unrestricted free agents (out of a total player pool of approximately 1,700) that year. About half signed new contracts with their old teams while the other half signed with new teams. Table 14.1 illustrates the impact of free agency in four professional sports.

TABLE 14.1 The Impact of Free Agency

Free agency has increased player share of total revenues in each of the major men's team sports. Table 14.1 gives player salaries as a percentage of team revenues for major league baseball (MLB), the National Basketball Association (NBA), the National Football League (NFL) and the National Hockey League (NHL) during the 1970–1973 period that players in each league worked under monopsony conditions and in 1998, when players in each league had gained the right of free agency.

Player Salaries As Percentage of Team Revenues				
	MLB	NBA	NFL	NHL
1970–73	15.9	46.1	34.4	21.3
1998	48.4	54.2	55.4	58.4

Source: Based on data from Gerald W. Scully, "Player Salary Share and the Distribution of Player Earnings," *Managerial and Decision Economics*, 25 (2004): 77–86.

Given the dramatic impact on player salaries of more competitive markets for athletes, events such as the 2004–2005 lockout in hockey came as no surprise. The agreement between the owners of hockey teams and the players in 2005 to limit the total payroll of each team reinstates some of the old monopsony power of the owners. Players had a huge financial stake in resisting such attempts.

Monopsony in Other Labor Markets

A firm that has a dominant position in a local labor market may have monopsony power in that market. Even if a firm does not dominate the total labor market, it may have monopsony power over certain types of labor. For example, a hospital may be the only large employer of nurses in a local market, and it may have monopsony power in employing them.

Colleges and universities generally pay part-time instructors considerably less for teaching a particular course than they pay full-time instructors. In part, the difference reflects the fact that full-time faculty members are expected to have more training and are expected to contribute far more in other areas. But the monopsony model suggests an additional explanation.

Part-time instructors are likely to have other regular employment. A university hiring a local accountant to teach a section of accounting does not have to worry that that person will go to another state to find a better offer as a part-time instructor. For part-time teaching, then, the university may be the only employer in town—and thus able to exert monopsony power to drive the part-time instructor's wage below the instructor's *MRP*.

Monopsony in Other Factor Markets

Monopsony power may also exist in markets for factors other than labor. The military in different countries, for example, has considerable monopsony power in the market for sophisticated military goods. Major retailers often have some monopsony power with respect to some of their suppliers. Sears, for example, is the only wholesale buyer of Craftsman brand tools. One major development in medical care in recent years has been the emergence of managed care organizations that contract with a large number of employers to purchase medical services on behalf of employees.

These organizations often have sufficient monopsony power to force down the prices charged by providers such as drug companies, physicians, and hospitals. Countries in which health care is provided by the government, such as Canada and the United Kingdom, are able to exert monopsony power in their purchase of health care services.

Whatever the source of monopsony power, the expected result is the same. Buyers with monopsony power are likely to pay a lower price and to buy a smaller quantity of a particular factor than buyers who operate in a more competitive environment.

Key Takeaways

- In the monopsony model there is one buyer for a good, service, or factor of production. A monopsony firm is a price setter in the market in which it has monopsony power.
- The monopsony buyer selects a profit-maximizing solution by employing the quantity of factor at which marginal factor cost (*MFC*) equals marginal revenue product (*MRP*) and paying the price on the factor's supply curve corresponding to that quantity.
- A degree of monopsony power exists whenever a firm faces an upward-sloping supply curve for a factor.

Try It!

Suppose a firm is the only employer of labor in an isolated area and faces the supply curve for labor suggested by the following table. Plot the supply curve. To compute the marginal factor cost curve, compute total factor cost and then the values for the marginal factor cost curve (remember to plot marginal values at the midpoints of the respective intervals). (Hint: follow the example of Figure 14.2.) Compute *MRP* and plot the *MRP* curve on the same graph on which you have plotted supply and *MFC*.

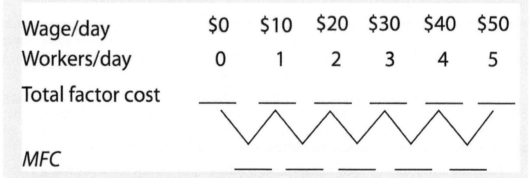

Wage/day	$0	$10	$20	$30	$40	$50
Workers/day	0	1	2	3	4	5
Total factor cost	___	___	___	___	___	___
MFC		___	___	___	___	___

Now suppose you are given the following data for the firm's total product at each quantity of labor. Compute marginal product. Assume the firm sells its product for $10 per unit in a perfectly competitive market. Compute *MRP* and plot the *MRP* curve on the same graph on which you have plotted supply and *MFC*. Remember to plot marginal values at the midpoints of the respective axes.

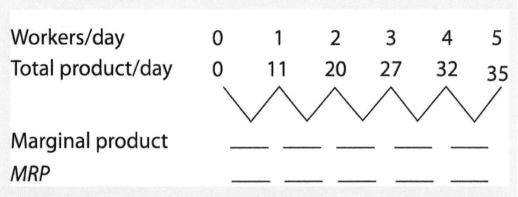

Workers/day	0	1	2	3	4	5
Total product/day	0	11	20	27	32	35
Marginal product		___	___	___	___	___
MRP		___	___	___	___	___

How much labor will the firm employ? What wage will it pay?

Case in Point: Major League Baseball Player Salaries and Monopsony

Source: © 2010 Jupiterimages Corporation

As discussed in the text, professional Major League Baseball (MLB) players, as well as players in other professional sports, historically faced complete monopsony power for their entire careers in the sport. They were drafted to play for a specific team and could be traded to another team, but could only market their services freely if they were released by the team that "owned" them at the time.

The monopsony power of MLB teams over players began to weaken in 1968 when the players' union, The Major League Baseball Players Association (MLBPA), signed its first collective bargaining agreement with MLB. These agreements have over time weakened monopsony power by addressing such issues as minimum salaries, pension benefits, processes for salary arbitration, and, most importantly in 1977 for baseball, allowing for free agency for some players. Free agency essentially lets players see what salary they can garner on the open market.

Economist Gerald Scully, whose work we introduced in Table 14.1, also pioneered statistical methods for estimating the MRP of baseball players using a two-step process. First, he studied the determinants of team attendance. He found that in addition to factors such as population and income in a team's home city, the team's win-loss record had a strong effect on attendance. Second, he examined the player characteristics that determined win-loss records. He found that for hitters, the batting average was the variable most closely associated with a team's winning percentage. For pitchers, it was the earned-run average—the number of earned runs allowed by a pitcher per nine innings pitched. With equations that predicted a team's attendance and its win-loss record, he was able to take a particular player, describe him by his statistics, and compute his *MRP*. He then subtracted costs associated with each player for such things as transportation, lodging, meals, and uniforms to obtain a player's net *MRP*. He then compared net *MRP*s to salaries. Over the years, many other economists have applied this basic method to other time periods and other sports where monopsony power has been affected by players' unions and especially by free agency.

A recent study by economists Brad R. Humphreys and Hyunwoong Pyun at West Virginia University, using a modified version of Scully's technique, reported on how monopsony power has evolved in MLB in the 2000s. They divide players by MLB experience into rookies, those with two to six years experience who are eligible for salary arbitration, and those with seven years of experience or more who are eligible for free agency. They calculated the degree of monopsony power, measured as players' salaries as a percent of *MRP*, for each group, and an average degree of monopsony power during each of the collective bargaining agreements (CBAs) in effect between 2000 and 2011. The closer the salary as a percent of net *MRP* is to zero, the lower the degree of monopsony power (since zero would mean players were receiving salaries equal to their net *MRP*s.

The table shows that free agents' salaries on average deviated from the *MRP*s by about 20%. For arbitration eligible players the deviation is about 75% and for rookies it is nearly 90%. The table also shows that each of the successive collective bargaining agreements reduced somewhat the degree of monopsony power. In looking at how players with different experience levels fared under the different agreements, they found that the benefits went mainly to the free agents. Hence they concluded that the MLBPA in the 2000s has concentrated mainly on improving conditions for that group and not for rookies or for the arbitration eligible group.

Of course, players with less experience have the chance to become free agents. In the sample the researchers analyzed, less than 50% of them did.

Types of Players		Salary as % of net MRP
All Players		0.504
Experience Group	Rookies	0.877
	Arbitration Eligible	0.753
	Free Agents	0.209
CBA period	2000-2002	0.556
	2003-2006	0.526
	2007-2011	0.456

Sources: Based on Brad R. Humphreys and Hyunwoong Pyun, "Monopsony Exploitation in Professional Sport: Evidence from Major League Baseball Position Players, 2000-2011," unpublished paper, November 30, 2015.

Answer to Try It! Problem

The completed tables are shown in Panel (a). Drawing the supply (*S*), *MFC*, and *MRP* curves, we have Panel (b). The monopsony firm will employ three units of labor per day (the quantity at which *MRP* = *MFC*) and will pay a wage taken from the supply curve: $30 per day.

Panel (a)

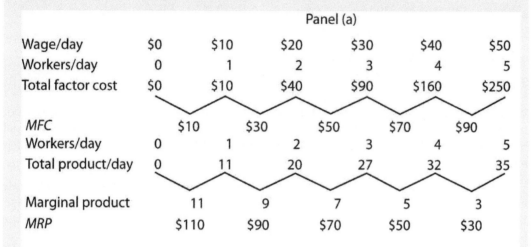

Wage/day	$0	$10	$20	$30	$40	$50
Workers/day	0	1	2	3	4	5
Total factor cost	$0	$10	$40	$90	$160	$250

MFC		$10	$30	$50	$70	$90	
Workers/day	0	1	2	3	4	5
Total product/day	0	11	20	27	32	35

Marginal product		11	9	7	5	3	
MRP		$110	$90	$70	$50	$30	

Panel (b)

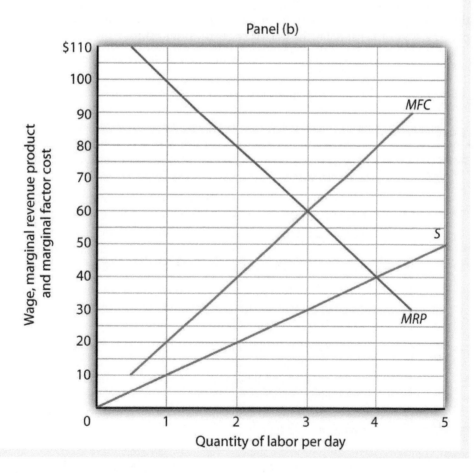

14.3 Monopsony and the Minimum Wage

Learning Objectives

1. Compare the impact of a minimum wage on employment in the case where the labor market is perfectly competitive to the case of a monopsony labor market.
2. Discuss the debate among economists concerning the impact of raising the minimum wage.

We have seen that wages will be lower in monopsony than in otherwise similar competitive labor markets. In a competitive market, workers receive wages equal to their *MRP*s. Workers employed by monopsony firms receive wages that are less than their *MRP*s. This fact suggests sharply different conclusions for the analysis of minimum wages in competitive versus monopsony conditions.

In a competitive market, the imposition of a minimum wage above the equilibrium wage necessarily reduces employment, as we learned in the chapter on perfectly competitive labor markets. In a monopsony market, however, a minimum wage above the equilibrium wage could *increase* employment at the same time as it boosts wages!

Figure 14.5 shows a monopsony employer that faces a supply curve, *S*, from which we derive the marginal factor cost curve, *MFC*. The firm maximizes profit by employing L_m units of labor and paying a wage of $4 per hour. The wage is below the firm's *MRP*.

FIGURE 14.5 Minimum Wage and Monopsony

A monopsony employer faces a supply curve *S*, a marginal factor cost curve *MFC*, and a marginal revenue product curve *MRP*. It maximizes profit by employing L_m units of labor and paying a wage of $4 per hour. The imposition of a minimum wage of $5 per hour makes the dashed sections of the supply and *MFC* curves irrelevant. The marginal factor cost curve is thus a horizontal line at $5 up to L_1 units of labor. *MRP* and *MFC* now intersect at L_2 so that employment increases.

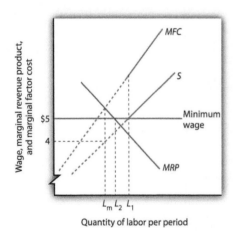

Quantity of labor per period

Now suppose the government imposes a minimum wage of $5 per hour; it is illegal for firms to pay less. At this minimum wage, L_1 units of labor are supplied. To obtain any smaller quantity of labor, the firm must pay the minimum wage. That means that the section of the supply curve showing quantities of labor supplied at wages below $5 is irrelevant; the firm cannot pay those wages. Notice that the section of the supply curve below $5 is shown as a dashed line. If the firm wants to hire more than L_1 units of labor, however, it must pay wages given by the supply curve.

Marginal factor cost is affected by the minimum wage. To hire additional units of labor up to L_1, the firm pays the minimum wage. The additional cost of labor beyond L_1 continues to be given by the original *MFC* curve. The *MFC* curve thus has two segments: a horizontal segment at the minimum wage for quantities up to L_1 and the solid portion of the *MFC* curve for quantities beyond that.

The firm will still employ labor up to the point that *MFC* equals *MRP*. In the case shown in Figure 14.5, that occurs at L_2. The firm thus increases its employment of labor in response to the minimum wage.

How the labor market for unskilled workers operates has become an arena for debate among economists, especially over the last 20 years. Is this labor market better described by assuming a perfectly competitive one, in which case a higher minimum wage would increase unemployment, or an imperfectly competitive one, in which case a higher minimum wage could increase employment or have little or no effect on it? Or are there other influences on this market, which go beyond these models? The Case in Point provides an introduction to the debate. Surveys of economists over the last two decades show some shifting of opinion on this issue. In response to the statement in a 1990 survey, "A minimum wage increases unemployment among young and unskilled workers," only 17.5% of economists surveyed disagreed, while 19.5% agreed with provisos, and 62.4% agreed. In response to the same survey question in 2011, 25.2% disagreed, 24% agreed with proviso, and 39.4% agreed.[2]

Key Takeaways

- In a competitive labor market, an increase in the minimum wage reduces employment and increases unemployment.
- A minimum wage could increase employment in a monopsony labor market at the same time it increases wages.
- Some economists argue that the monopsony model characterizes all labor markets and that this justifies a national increase in the minimum wage but others are less convinced, though sentiment among economists has shifted over time. For example, a survey that has been tracking this question showed there is no longer a majority of economists who agree completely that minimum wage increases lead to more unemployment for young and unskilled workers.

Try It!

Using the data in the "Try It!" from Section 2, suppose a minimum wage of $40 per day is imposed. How will this affect the firm's use of labor?

Case in Point: The Minimum Wage Debate

Source: © 2010 Jupiterimages Corporation

The study that sparked the controversy was an analysis by David Card and Alan Krueger of employment in the fast food industry in Pennsylvania and New Jersey. New Jersey increased its minimum wage to $5.05 per hour in 1992, when the national minimum wage was $4.25 per hour. The two economists surveyed 410 fast food restaurants in the Burger King, KFC, Roy Rogers, and Wendy's chains just before New Jersey increased its minimum and again 10 months after the increase.

There was no statistically significant change in employment in the New Jersey franchises, but employment fell in the Pennsylvania franchises. Thus, employment in the New Jersey franchises "rose" relative to employment in the Pennsylvania franchises. Card and Krueger's results were widely interpreted as showing an increase in employment in New Jersey as a result of the increase in the minimum wage there.

So, do minimum wages reduce employment or not? Some economists interpreted the Card and Krueger results as suggesting monopsony power in the labor market. Economist Alan Manning has noted that the frictionless world of perfect competition, in which even small cuts in wages below the going competitive rate would cause all the workers to change jobs, does not reflect the real world in which changing jobs is costly, information on other jobs may be hard to get, and non-wage characteristics, such as commuting convenience, may affect preferences for different jobs. These market imperfections give employers some discretion over pay and hence some monopsony power. While he cautions that this line of argument does not mean that all labor market interventions, such as increasing the minimum wage, will be desirable, it does suggest the desirability of open-mindedness towards particular policy proposals.

The Card and Krueger research led to a proliferation of empirical work over the recent decade, which included hundreds of individual studies that vary in time, place, populations studied (such as teens or restaurant workers), and statistical techniques used, as well as metastudies, or "studies of studies." Economist John Schmitt evaluated many of these pertaining to the United States and concluded that "…what is striking…is how often the weight of the empirical evidence is either inconclusive (statistically insignificant or positive in some cases and negative in others) or suggestive of only small economic effects."

Dr. Schmitt also reviewed the many channels through which companies may adjust to a higher minimum wage besides cutting employment: cuts in hours, lower raises for more highly paid workers, price increases, profit reductions, reductions in costly turnovers, and designing new work processes to engender great work effort, to name a few. Any firm may use a combination of these, and some of the adjustment mechanisms may favor low-wage workers (lower turnover), others may hurt them (cuts in benefits), while others may have a neutral effect (lower profits). With so much "noise," it may not be possible to fully understand the "why" of the small employment effect.

In 2015 and 2016, many cities and states passed laws raising their minimum wage and the level of the minimum wage increase at the federal level became a part of the 2016 presidential campaign. It will be interesting to see how the new wage of minimum wage increases—some of which are substantial—affect employment.

Sources: Based on David Card and Alan B. Krueger, "Minimum Wages and Employment: A Case Study of the Fast-Food Industry in New Jersey and Pennsylvania," American Economic Review, 84 (1994): 772–93; Alan Manning, "Monopsony and the Efficiency of Labour Market Interventions," Labour Economics, 11(2) (April 2004): 145–63; John Schmitt," Explaining the Small Employment Effects of the Minimum Wage in the United States," Industrial Relations 54:4 (October 2015): 547-81.

Answer to Try It! Problem

The imposition of a minimum wage of $40 per day makes the *MFC* curve a horizontal line at $40, up to the *S* curve. In this case, the firm adds a fourth worker and pays the required wage, $40.

14.4 Price Setters on the Supply Side

Buyers are not the only agents capable of exercising market power in factor-pricing choices. Suppliers of factor services can exercise market power and act as price setters themselves in two ways. First, a supplier may be a monopoly or have a degree of monopoly power in the supply of a factor. In that case, economists analyze the firm's choices as they would analyze those of any other imperfectly competitive firm. Second, individual suppliers of a factor of production may band together in an association to gain clout in the marketplace. Farmers, for example, often join forces to offset what they perceive as unfair market power on the part of buyers of their products. Workers may join together in a union in order to enhance their bargaining power with their employers. Each case is discussed below.

Monopoly Suppliers

A firm with monopoly power over a particular factor can be expected to behave like any other monopoly. It will choose its output where the marginal revenue and marginal cost curves intersect and charge a price taken from its demand curve.

FIGURE 14.6 Monopoly Factor Supply

A monopoly supplier of a factor of production acts just as any other monopoly firm. Here, the monopoly faces the demand curve D and the marginal revenue curve MR. Given the marginal cost curve MC, it maximizes profit by supplying Q_m and charging a price P_m.

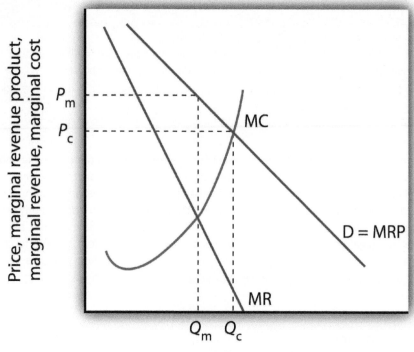

A monopoly supplier of a factor faces a demand curve that represents the MRP of the factor. This situation is illustrated in Figure 14.6. The firm will charge a price P_m equal to the MRP of the factor and sell Q_m units of the factor.

Unions

labor union

An association of workers that seeks to raise wages and to improve working conditions.

collective bargaining

A process of negotiation of worker contracts between unions and employers.

strike

A refusal by union members to work.

craft unions

Organizations uniting skilled workers in the same trade.

Workers in a competitive market receive a wage equal to their MRP. If they face monopsony power, they get less. Regardless of the market structure, workers are likely to seek higher wages and better working conditions. One way they can try to improve their economic status is to organize into a **labor union**, an association of workers that seeks to raise wages and to improve working conditions. Unions represent their members in **collective bargaining**, a process of negotiation of worker contracts between unions and employers. To strengthen its position, a union may threaten a **strike**—a refusal by union members to work—unless its demands are met.

A Brief History of Unions

Workers have united to try to better their lot at least since the Middle Ages, when the first professional guilds were formed in Europe. In the United States, "workingmen's societies" sprang up in the late eighteenth century. These organizations were **craft unions** uniting skilled workers in the same trade in an attempt to increase wages, shorten working hours, and regulate working conditions for their members.

One goal unions consistently sought was a **closed shop**, where only union members can be hired—an arrangement that gives unions monopoly power in the supply of labor. A second objective was to gain greater political and economic strength by joining together associations of different crafts. Union goals went largely unfulfilled until the twentieth century, when the courts began to favor collective bargaining between workers and employers in disputes over wages and working conditions. Closed-shop arrangements are illegal in the United States today, but many states permit **union shop** arrangements, in which a firm is allowed to hire nonunion workers who are required to join the union within a specified period. About 20 states have **right-to-work laws** which prohibit union shop rules.

The development of the **industrial union**, a form of union that represents the employees of a particular industry, regardless of their craft, also aided the growth of the labor movement. The largest industrial union in the United States, the AFL-CIO, was formed in 1955, when unions accounted for just over 35% of the labor force. The AFL-CIO remains an important economic and political force, but union strength has fallen since its peak in the 1950s; today, less than 10% of workers in the private sector belong to unions. Quite dramatically, in 2005, three unions, representing about a third of the total membership, withdrew from the AFL-CIO. The break-away unions argued that they would be more successful working on their own to recruit new members. The impact of this break-up will not be known for several years.

Part of the reason for the failure of unions to represent a larger share of workers lies in the market forces that govern wages. As the marginal revenue product of workers has risen throughout the economy, their wages have increased as well—whether they belonged to a union or not. Impressive economy-wide wage gains over the last two centuries may be one reason why the attraction of unions has remained weak.

Higher Wages and Other Union Goals

Higher wages once dominated the list of union objectives, but more recent agreements have also focused on nonwage issues involving job security, health insurance, provision of child care, and job safety. Unions such as the United Auto Workers have negotiated contracts under which members who are laid off will continue to receive payments nearly equal to the wages they earned while on the job. They have also pushed hard for retirement pensions and for greater worker involvement in management decisions.

Union efforts to obtain higher wages have different effects on workers depending on the nature of the labor market. When unions confront an employer with monopsony power, their task is clear: they seek a wage closer to *MRP* than the employer is paying. If the labor market is a competitive one in which wages are determined by demand and supply, the union's task is more difficult. Increasing the wage requires either increasing the demand for labor or reducing the supply. If the union merely achieves a higher wage in the absence of an increase in demand or a reduction in supply, then the higher wage will create a surplus of labor, or unemployment.

Increasing Demand

The demand for labor in a competitive market is found by summing the *MRP* curves of individual firms. Increasing demand thus requires increasing the marginal product of labor or raising the price of the good produced by labor.

One way that unions can increase the marginal product of their members is by encouraging investment in their human capital. Consequently, unions may pressure firms to implement training programs. Some unions conduct training efforts themselves.

Another way to increase the *MRP* of a factor is to reduce the use by firms of substitute factors. Unions generally represent skilled workers, and they are vigorous proponents of minimum wage laws that make unskilled workers more expensive. A higher minimum wage induces firms to sub-

closed shop

A firm in which only union members can be hired.

union shop

A firm that is allowed to hire nonunion workers who are required to join the union within a specified period.

right-to-work laws

Laws that prohibit union shop rules.

industrial union

A form of union that represents the employees of a particular industry, regardless of their craft.

stitute skilled for unskilled labor and thus increases the demand for the skilled workers unions represent.

Still another way to increase the *MRP* of labor is to increase the demand for the products labor produces. The form this union activity generally takes is in the promotion of "Made in the U.S.A." goods. Unions have also promoted restrictive trade legislation aimed at reducing the supply of foreign goods and thus increasing the demand for domestic ones.

Reducing Labor Supply

Unions can restrict the supply of labor in two ways. First, they can seek to slow the growth of the labor force; unions from the earliest times have aggressively opposed immigration. Union support for Social Security also cut the labor supply by encouraging workers to retire early. Second, unions can promote policies that make it difficult for workers to enter a particular craft. Unions representing plumbers and electrical workers, for example, have restricted the number of people who can enter these crafts in some areas by requiring that workers belong to a union and then limiting the union's membership.

Bilateral Monopoly

bilateral monopoly

Situation in which a monopsony buyer faces a monopoly seller.

Suppose a union has negotiated a closed-shop arrangement (in a country where such arrangements are legal) with an employer that possesses monopsony power in its labor market. The union has a kind of monopoly in the supply of labor. A situation in which a monopsony buyer faces a monopoly seller is called **bilateral monopoly**. Wages in this model are indeterminate, with the actual wage falling somewhere between the pure monopoly and pure monopsony outcomes.

Figure 14.7 shows the same monopsony situation in a labor market that was shown in Figure 14.3 The employer will seek to pay a wage W_m for a quantity of labor L_m. The union will seek W_u, the highest wage the employer would be willing to pay for that quantity of labor. This wage is found on the *MRP* curve. The model of bilateral monopoly does not tell us the wage that will emerge. Whether the final wage will be closer to what the union seeks or closer to what the employer seeks will depend on the bargaining strength of the union and of the employer.

FIGURE 14.7 Bilateral Monopoly

If the union has monopoly power over the supply of labor and faces a monopsony purchaser of the labor the union represents, the wage negotiated between the two will be indeterminate. The employer will hire L_m units of the labor per period. The employer wants a wage W_m on the supply curve S. The union will seek a wage close to the maximum the employer would be willing to pay for this quantity, W_u, at the intersection of the marginal revenue product (*MRP*) and the marginal factor cost (*MFC*) curves. The actual wage will be somewhere between these two amounts.

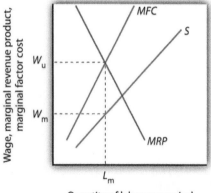

Quantity of labor per period

Unions and the Economy: An Assessment

Where unions operate effectively in otherwise competitive markets, they may reduce economic efficiency. Efforts to increase demand for American workers through restricting imports or to increase demand for skilled workers by restricting opportunities for unskilled workers almost certainly reduce economic efficiency. Artificial restrictions on the supply of labor reduce efficiency as well. In each case, the wage gain will increase the cost of producing a good or service and thus shift its supply curve to the left. Such efforts, if successful, increase the earnings of union members by creating higher prices and smaller quantities for consumers. They may also reduce the profitability of their employers.

Other attempts by unions to raise wages by increasing the demand for their members are not likely to create inefficiency. For example, union efforts to increase worker productivity or to encourage consumers to buy products made by union members do not reduce economic efficiency.

In the case of bilateral monopoly, the amount of labor employed is restricted by the monopsony firm to a quantity that falls short of the efficient level. In effect, the efficiency damage has already been done. The labor union seeks merely to offset the monopsony firm's ability to restrict the wage.

Are unions successful in their primary goal of increasing wages? An examination of the impact on wages paid by firms that faced organizing drives by unions between 1984 and 1999 found virtually no change in wages attributable to union organizing efforts. The study examined firms in which unions had either barely won or had barely lost the election. It found that unions that had eked out victories had gone on to organize workers but had had no significant impact on wages or on productivity. [3] Other evidence, however, suggests that unions do tend to raise wages for their members. Controlling for other factors that affect wages, over the period 1973 to 2002, unions appear to have increased wages by about 17% on average. [4] Part of the explanation of this finding is that unions have had the most success in organizing in the public sector, where union pressure for higher wages is most likely to be successful.

Other Suppliers and Monopoly Power

Just as workers can unionize to gain a degree of monopoly power in the marketplace, so other suppliers can organize with a similar goal. Two of the most important types of organizations aimed at garnering market power are professional associations and producers' cooperatives.

Professional Associations

Professional people generally belong to organizations that represent their interests. For example, physicians in the United States belong to the American Medical Association (AMA), and lawyers belong to the American Bar Association (ABA). Both organizations work vigorously to advance the economic interests of their members.

Professional organizations often lobby for legislation that protects their members. They may seek to restrict competition by limiting the number of individuals who can be licensed to practice a particular profession. The AMA has been very successful in limiting the number of physicians, thus maintaining higher salaries than would otherwise exist. The ABA has fought legal reforms aimed at limiting awards to plaintiffs who win damage suits; such reforms would be likely to reduce the incomes of lawyers.

Producers' Cooperatives

Independent producers sometimes band together into a cooperative for the purpose of selling their products. The cooperative sets the price and assigns production quotas to individual firms. In effect, a cooperative acts as a legal cartel.

Because they violate the provisions of laws that outlaw such arrangements in most industries, producers' cooperatives must be authorized by Congress. Farmers have sometimes been given such rights when they are confronted by monopsony buyers. For example, Congress granted dairy farmers the right to form cooperatives in the 1920s because they faced monopsony buyers. High transportation costs for fresh milk, together with economies of scale in processing milk, generally left only one dairy processor to buy raw milk from dairy farmers in a particular area. By forming a cooperative, farmers could counter the monopsony power of a processor with monopoly power of their own, creating a bilateral monopoly.

Today, with much lower transportation costs, dairy farmers can deal with a national market so that processors no longer have monopsony power. But dairy farmers continue to have the right to form cooperatives. As we have seen in an earlier chapter, dairy farmers also enjoy protection from federal programs that are designed to keep dairy prices high.

Key Takeaways

- A firm that has monopoly power in the supply of a factor makes choices in the same manner as any monopoly firm; it maximizes profit by selecting a level of output at which marginal revenue equals marginal cost and selling that output at a price determined by the demand curve.
- Unions have traditionally sought to raise wages and to improve working conditions by exerting market power over the supply of labor.
- In bilateral monopoly, a monopsony buyer faces a monopoly seller. Prices in the model are indeterminate.
- Professional associations often seek market power through their influence on government policy.
- Producers' cooperatives, a form of legal cartel, have been organized in some agricultural markets in an effort to offset the perceived monopsony power of some buyers of agricultural products.

Try It!

Consider the case of bilateral monopoly illustrated in Figure 14.7. Over what range of wages will employment be higher than it would have been if there was a monopsony buyer of labor but no monopoly in the supply of labor?

Case in Point: Boeing vs. Its Union and the National Labor Relations Board

Source: © Altair78, http://commons.wikimedia.org/wiki/File:Boeing_787_Dreamliner_arrival_Airventure_2011.jpg

A high-profile case erupted in April 2011 when the National Labor Relations Board (NLRB), an independent government agency created in 1935 to guarantee the rights of employees to bargain collectively and to investigate charges of unfair labor practices, accused Boeing of illegally setting up a plant for assembling 787 Dreamliners in North Charleston, South Carolina, in order to retaliate against its Seattle-based union, the International Association of Machinists and Aerospace Workers, who brought the case to the Board.

The $750 million factory represents the largest single investment ever made in the state of South Carolina, a right-to-work state. The *New York Times* reported that South Carolina governor Nikki Haley said, "Boeing was a dream come true for South Carolina. They came in and brought the hope of the American dream to this state to create real-good-quality jobs." The board requested that a judge order Boeing to move its Dreamliner production back to Washington state.

At issue was whether Boeing made its decision to locate in South Carolina in order to punish its unionized workers in Seattle, Washington, for past strikes. A Boeing executive had stated to the *Seattle Times* that an "overriding factor" in the location decision was that "we can't afford to have a work stoppage every three years."

Republicans blamed President Obama, whose NLRB appointees took on the case. The *New York Times* reported that President Obama said he did not want to discuss a case brought on by an independent agency but that "as a general proposition, companies need to have freedom to relocate."

Then, in December 2011, Boeing and the Machinists union reached an agreement whereby Boeing agreed to produce a new version of the 737 jet in the Seattle area and the union agreed to ask the NLRB to drop its case, which it did. Still, the issues raised by this case had become a major topic of discussion during the 2012 U.S. presidential election season. According to Steven Greenhouse in the *New York Times*, it is no less than a case that had "grown into a political conflagration, fanned by deep resentments between North and South, Democrats and Republicans, union and nonunion workers, and fans and foes of Big Government."

Sources: Based on Steven Greenhouse, "Boeing Labor Dispute Is Making New Factory a Political Football," New York Times, p. A1, June 30, 2011; Steven Greenhouse, "Labor Board Drops Case Against Boeing After Union Reaches Accord," New York Times, December 10, 2011, p. 3.

Answer to Try It! Problem

Any wage negotiated between the monopsony (the firm hiring the labor) and the monopoly (the union representing the labor) that falls between W_m and W_u will lead to a quantity of labor employed that is greater than L_m. The portion of the supply curve below the negotiated wage becomes irrelevant since the firm cannot hire workers for those wages. The supply curve thus becomes a horizontal line at the negotiated wage until the negotiated wage intersects the supply curve; at wages higher than the negotiated wage, the existing supply curve is operative. Up to the quantity of labor at the intersection of the negotiated wage and the supply curve, the wage and *MFC* are the same. At any wage between W_m and W_u, the firm will maximize profit by employing labor where *MRP* and *MFC* are equal, and this will occur at a quantity of labor that is greater than L_m.

14.5 Review and Practice

Summary

Factor markets diverge from perfect competition whenever buyers and/or sellers are price setters rather than price takers. A firm that is the sole purchaser of a factor is a monopsony. The distinguishing feature of the application of the marginal decision rule to monopsony is that the *MFC* of the factor exceeds its price. Less of the factor is used than would be the case if the factor were demanded by many firms. The price paid by the monopsony firm is determined from the factor supply curve; it is less than the competitive price would be. The lower quantity and lower price that occur in a monopsony factor market arise from features of the market that are directly analogous to the higher product price and lower product quantity chosen in monopoly markets. A price floor (e.g., a minimum wage) can induce a monopsony to increase its use of a factor.

Sellers can also exercise power to set price. A factor can be sold by a monopoly firm, which is likely to behave in a way that corresponds to the monopoly model.

When there are a large number of sellers, they may band together in an organization that seeks to exert a degree of market power on their behalf. Workers (sellers of labor), for example, have organized unions to seek better wages and working conditions. This goal can be accomplished by restricting the available supply or by increasing the demand for labor. When a union represents all of a monopsony firm's workers, a bilateral monopoly exists. A bilateral monopoly results in a kind of price-setters' standoff, in which the firm seeks a low wage and the union a high one.

Professional associations may seek to improve the economic position of their members by supporting legislation that reduces supply or raises demand. Some agricultural producers join producers' cooperatives to exert some power over price and output. Agricultural cooperatives must be authorized by Congress; otherwise, they would violate laws against collusion in the marketplace.

Concept Problems

1. Unions have generally advocated restrictions on goods and services imported from other countries. Why?

2. There is a growing tendency in the United States for hospitals to merge, reducing competition in local markets. How are such mergers likely to affect the market for nurses?

3. When a town has a single university, the university may have monopsony power in the hiring of part-time faculty. But what about the hiring of full-time faculty? (*Hint:* The market for full-time faculty is a national one.)

4. Former television host David Letterman earned more than $10 million per year from CBS. Why do you suppose he earned so much? Is there any reason to believe he was underpaid?

5. Suppose a union obtains a union shop agreement with firms in a particular industry. Is there any limit to the wages the union can achieve for its workers?

6. It is illegal for firms in most industries to join together in a producers' cooperative. Yet such arrangements are common in agriculture. Why?

7. In proposing an increase in the minimum wage in 2005, the Democratic Party argued that in some markets, a higher minimum wage could actually increase employment for unskilled workers. How could this happen?

8. In 2005–06 the maximum salary of professional basketball players with up to three years of experience in the Women's National Basketball Association (WNBA) stood at $42,000, while the maximum salary for a WNBA player in 2005 was $90,000 (the average was somewhere between $46,000 and $60,000 (depending on whether one's source was the Players Union or the WNBA league itself). The minimum salary of a (male) rookie professional NBA basketball player in 2005–06 was $398,762 (WNBA rookies earned only slightly more than $30,000 that year). The average NBA salary in 2005–06 was $4,037,899. Why was there such a large discrepancy?

9. The Case in Point on professional sports suggests that most professional athletes now receive salaries equal to their marginal revenue products. These are typically quite high. Are such high salaries fair? Why or why not?

10. Large retail firms often advertise that their "buying power" allows them to obtain goods at lower prices and hence offer lower prices to their consumers. Explain the economic logic of this claim.

Numerical Problems

Suppose a firm faces the following supply schedule for labor by unskilled workers:

Wage per day	Number of workers
$0	0
8	1
16	2
24	3
32	4
40	5
48	6
56	7
64	8
72	9
80	10

1. In terms of its supply of labor, what sort of firm is this? Explain. Add columns for total factor cost and marginal factor cost and fill them in.
2. Plot the supply and marginal factor cost curves for this firm. Remember to plot marginal values at the midpoints of the intervals.
3. Suppose the firm faces the following total product schedule for labor:

Number of workers	Output per day
0	0
1	92
2	176
3	252
4	320
5	380
6	432
7	476
8	512
9	540
10	560

Compute the schedules for the firm's marginal product and marginal revenue product curves, assuming the price of the good the firm produces is $1 and that the firm operates in a perfectly competitive product market.

4. Add the marginal revenue product curve from Problem 3 to your graph in Problem 2, and determine the number of workers the firm will employ and the wage it will pay.
5. Now suppose the firm is required to pay a minimum wage of $48 per day. Show what will happen to the quantity of labor the firm will hire and the wage it will pay.
6. Suppose that the market for cranberries is perfectly competitive and that the price is $4 per pound. Suppose that an increase in demand for cranberries raises the price to $6 per pound in a matter of a few weeks.

    a. Illustrate the increase in demand in the market and in the case of a typical firm in the short run.

    b. Illustrate what happens in the long run in this industry. Assuming that the cost per unit of production remains unchanged throughout, what will the new price be?

    c. Now suppose that the industry is permitted to organize all firms into a producers' cooperative that maximizes profits. Starting with the solution that you had in (b), illustrate the impact of this change on industry price and output.

7. Again, consider the market for cranberries. The industry is perfectly competitive and the price of cranberries is $4 per pound. Suppose a reduction in the cost of obtaining water reduces the variable and average total cost by $1 per pound at all output levels.

    a. Illustrate graphically the impact of the change in the short run. Will the price fall by $1? Why or why not?

    b. Now show the impact of the $1 reduction in cost in the long run. Who benefits from the reduction in cost?

    c. Assume again that the producers in the industry are permitted to band together in a cooperative that maximizes profits. Now show the short run impact of the cost reduction on the price and output of cranberries.

    d. Now show the long run impact of the change. Who benefits from the reduction in cost?

    e. Compare your responses to parts (b) and (d), and explain the difference, if any.

8. A single firm is the sole purchaser of labor in its market. It faces a supply curve given by $q = (1/4)w + 1,000$, where q is hours of work supplied per day, and w is the hourly wage.

    a. Draw a graph of the firm's supply curve.

    b. Show the firm's marginal factor cost curve on the same graph you used in (a).

Endnotes

1. Mark Hyman, "An Entire Season in the Penalty Box?" *Business Week*, 3906 (November 1, 2004): 94–95; David Fay, "Game On: NHL Lockout Finally Over," *The Washington Times*, July 14, 2005, p. C1.

2. Dan Fuller and Doris Geide-Stevenson, "Consensus Among Economists—an Update," Journal of Economic Education 45:2 (April-June, 2014): 131-46.

3. John Dinardo and David S. Lee, "Economic Impacts of New Unionization on Private Sector Employers: 1984–2001," *The Quarterly Journal of Economics* 119(4) (November 2004): 1383–1441.

4. David G. Blanchflower and Alex Bryson, "What Effect Do Unions Have on Wages Now and Would Freeman and Medoff be Surprised?" *Journal of Labor Research* 25:3 (Summer 2004): 383–414.

Public Finance and Public Choice

15.1 Start Up: Where Your Tax Dollars Go

You pay sales taxes on most of the goods you purchase. If you smoke or drink or drive a car, you pay taxes on cigarettes, alcohol, and gasoline. If you work, you may pay income and payroll taxes.

What does the government do with the taxes it collects? If you go to a public school, you are a consumer of public sector services. You also consume the services of the public sector when you drive on a public street or go to a public park. You consume public sector services since you are protected by law enforcement agencies and by the armed forces. And the production of everything else you consume is affected by regulations imposed by local, state, or federal agencies.

The public sector is a crucially important segment of the economy, due in part to its size. The nearly 90,000 government jurisdictions in the United States, from local fire protection districts to the federal government, either produce or purchase about one-fifth of all domestic goods and services. The U.S. government is the largest single purchaser of goods and services in the world.

This chapter examines the role of government in a market economy and the ways in which the taxes that support government affect economic behavior. The study of government expenditure and tax policy and of their impact on the economy is called **public finance**.

We will also explore the economics of public sector choices. Economists put the notions of self-interest and the marginal decision rule to work in the analysis of choices made by people in the public sector—voters, government employees, interest groups, and politicians.

public finance

The study of government expenditure and tax policy and of their impact on the economy.

15.2 The Role of Government in a Market Economy

Learning Objectives

1. Discuss and illustrate government responses to the market failures of public goods, external costs and benefits, and imperfect competition and how these responses have the potential to reduce deadweight loss.
2. Define behavioral economics and explain how findings in this area of economics may be used to design government policy.
3. Discuss ways in which governments redistribute income.

What do we want from our government? One answer is that we want a great deal more than we did several decades ago. The role of government has expanded dramatically in the last 80+ years. In 1929 (the year the Commerce Department began keeping annual data on macroeconomic performance in the United States), government expenditures at all levels (state, local, and federal) were less than 10% of the nation's total output, which is called gross domestic product (GDP). In the current century, that share has more than tripled.

Government expenditures

All spending by government agencies.

Government revenues

All funds received by government agencies.

Figure 15.1 shows total government expenditures and revenues as a percentage of GDP from 1929 to 2015. All levels of government are included. **Government expenditures** include all spending by government agencies. **Government revenues** include all funds received by government agencies. The primary component of government revenues is taxes; revenue also includes miscellaneous receipts from fees, fines, and other sources. We will look at types of government revenues and expenditures later in this chapter.

FIGURE 15.1 Government Expenditures and Revenues as a Percentage of GDP
The figure shows government expenditures and revenues as a percentage of GDP, the most widely used measure of economic activity, since 1929. It also shows government purchases, shown here as government consumption plus gross investment, both as a percentage of GDP. The gap between government expenditures and government purchases represents transfer payments.

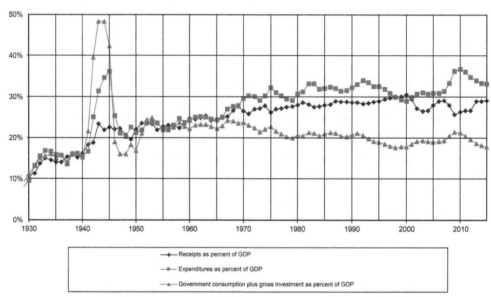

Source: Based on data from U.S. Department of Commerce, Bureau of Economic Analysis, NIPA Tables 1.1.5 and 3.1, September 29, 2016.

government purchases

Goods or services purchased by a government agency.

transfer payments

Payments made by government agencies to individuals in the form of grants rather than in return for labor or other services.

Figure 15.1 also shows government purchases as a percentage of GDP. **Government purchases** happen when a government agency purchases or produces a good or a service. We measure government purchases to suggest the opportunity cost of government. Whether a government agency purchases a good or service or produces it, factors of production are being used for public sector, rather than private sector, activities. A city police department's purchase of new cars is an example of a government purchase. Spending for public education is another example.

Government expenditures and purchases are not equal because much government spending is not for the purchase of goods and services. The primary source of the gap is **transfer payments**, payments made by government agencies to individuals in the form of grants rather than in return for labor or other services. Transfer payments represent government expenditures but not government purchases. Governments engage in transfer payments in order to redistribute income from one group to another. The various welfare programs for low-income people are examples of transfer payments. Social Security is the largest transfer payment program in the United States. This program transfers income from people who are working (by taxing their pay) to people who have retired. Interest payments on government debt, which are also a form of expenditure, are another example of an expenditure that is not counted as a government purchase.

Several points about Figure 15.1 bear special attention. Note first the path of government purchases. Government purchases relative to GDP rose dramatically during World War II, then dropped back to about their prewar level almost immediately afterward. Government purchases rose again, though less sharply, during the Korean War. This time, however, they did not drop back very far after the war. It was during this period that military spending rose to meet the challenge posed by the former Soviet Union and other communist states—the "Cold War." Government purchases have ranged between 17 and 23% of GDP ever since. The Vietnam War, the Persian Gulf War, and the wars in Afghanistan and Iraq did not have the impact on purchases that characterized World War II or even the Korean War. A second development, the widening gap between expenditures and purchases, has occurred since the 1960s. This reflects the growth of federal transfer programs, principally Social Security, programs to help people pay for health-care costs, and aid to low-income people. We will discuss these programs later in this chapter.

Finally, note the relationship between expenditures and receipts. When a government's revenues equal its expenditures for a particular period, it has a **balanced budget**. A **budget surplus** occurs if a government's revenues exceed its expenditures, while a **budget deficit** exists if government expenditures exceed revenues.

Prior to 1980, revenues roughly matched expenditures for the public sector as a whole, except during World War II. But expenditures remained consistently higher than revenues between 1980 and 1996. The federal government generated very large deficits during this period, deficits that exceeded surpluses that typically occur at the state and local levels of government. The largest increases in spending came from Social Security and increased health-care spending at the federal level. Efforts by the federal government to reduce and ultimately eliminate its deficit, together with surpluses among state and local governments, put the combined budget for the public sector in surplus beginning in 1997. As of 1999, the Congressional Budget Office was predicting that increased federal revenues produced by a growing economy would continue to produce budget surpluses well into the twenty-first century.

That rather rosy forecast was set aside after September 11, 2001. Terrorist attacks on the United States and later on several other countries led to sharp and sustained increases in federal spending for wars in Afghanistan and Iraq, as well as expenditures for Homeland Security. The administration of George W. Bush proposed, and Congress approved, a tax cut. The combination of increased spending on the aforementioned items and others, as well as tax cuts, produced substantial deficits. The deficit grew markedly wider following the recession that began in December 2007. As incomes fell, tax receipts fell. Expenditures grew due to increased spending associated with the American Recovery and Reinvestment Act of 2009 designed to stimulate the economy. It included such things as extended unemployment co8mpensation, increased assistance for the poor, and increased infrastructure spending.

The evidence presented in Figure 15.1 does not fully capture the rise in demand for public sector services. In addition to governments that spend more, people in the United States have clearly chosen governments that do more. The scope of regulatory activity conducted by governments at all levels, for example, has risen sharply in the last several decades. Regulations designed to prevent discrimination, to protect consumers, and to protect the environment are all part of the response to a rising demand for public services, as are federal programs in health care and education.

Figure 15.2 summarizes the main revenue sources and types of expenditures for the U.S. federal government and for the European Union. In the United States, most revenues came from personal income taxes and from payroll taxes. Most expenditures were for transfer payments to individuals. Federal purchases were primarily for national defense; the "other purchases" category includes things such as spending for transportation projects and for the space program. Interest payments on the national debt and grants by the federal government to state and local governments were the other major expenditures. The situation in the European Union differs primarily by the fact that substantially less is spent on defense.

balanced budget

Situation that occurs when a government's revenues equal its expenditures for a particular period.

budget surplus

Situation that occurs when a government's revenues exceed its expenditures.

budget deficit

Situation that occurs when government expenditures exceed revenues.

FIGURE 15.2 Government Revenue Sources and Expenditures: 2015

The four panels show the sources of government revenues and the shares of expenditures on various activities for the federal government in the United States and the European Union in 2015.

USA: Where It Comes From

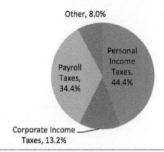

USA: Where It Goes

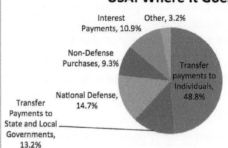

EU: Where It Comes From

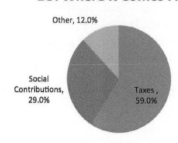

EU: Where It Goes

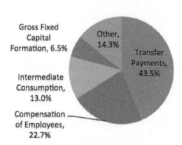

Sources: Based on data from U.S. Department of Commerce, Bureau of Economic Analysis, NIPA Table 3.2, September 29, 2016 and Eurostat Statistics Explained, online March 2016 available at http://ec.europa.eu/eurostat/statistics-explained/index.php/Main_Page

To understand the role of government, it will be useful to distinguish four broad types of government involvement in the economy. First, the government attempts to respond to market failures to allocate resources efficiently. In a particular market, efficiency means that the quantity produced is determined by the intersection of a demand curve that reflects all the benefits of consuming a particular good or service and a supply curve that reflects the opportunity costs of producing it. Second, government agencies act to encourage or discourage the consumption of certain goods and services. The prohibition of drugs such as heroin and cocaine is an example of government seeking to discourage consumption of these drugs. Third, the government redistributes income through programs such as welfare and Social Security. Fourth, the government can use its spending and tax policies to influence the level of economic activity and the price level.

We will examine the first three of these aspects of government involvement in the economy in this chapter. The fourth, efforts to influence the level of economic activity and the price level, fall within the province of macroeconomics.

Responding to Market Failure

In an earlier chapter on markets and efficiency, we learned that a market maximizes net benefit by achieving a level of output at which marginal benefit equals marginal cost. That is the efficient solution. In most cases, we expect that markets will come close to achieving this result—that is the important lesson of Adam Smith's idea of the market as an invisible hand, guiding the economy's scarce factors of production to their best uses. That is not always the case, however.

We have studied several situations in which markets are unlikely to achieve efficient solutions. In an earlier chapter, we saw that private markets are likely to produce less than the efficient quantities of public goods such as national defense. They may produce too much of goods that generate external costs and too little of goods that generate external benefits. In cases of imperfect competition, we have seen that the market's output of goods and services is likely to fall short of the efficient level. In all these cases, it is possible that government intervention will move production levels closer to their efficient quantities. In the next three sections, we shall review how a government could improve efficiency in the cases of public goods, external costs and benefits, and imperfect competition.

Public Goods

A public good is a good or service for which exclusion is prohibitively costly and for which the marginal cost of adding another consumer is zero. National defense, law enforcement, and generally available knowledge are examples of public goods.

The difficulty posed by a public good is that, once it is produced, it is freely available to everyone. No consumer can be excluded from consumption of the good on grounds that he or she has not paid for it. Consequently, each consumer has an incentive to be a free rider in consuming the good, and the firms providing a public good do not get a signal from consumers that reflects their benefit of consuming the good.

Certainly we can expect some benefits of a public good to be revealed in the market. If the government did not provide national defense, for example, we would expect some defense to be produced, and some people would contribute to its production. But because free-riding behavior will be common, the market's production of public goods will fall short of the efficient level.

The theory of public goods is an important argument for government involvement in the economy. Government agencies may either produce public goods themselves, as do local police departments, or pay private firms to produce them, as is the case with many government-sponsored research efforts. An important debate in the provision of public education revolves around the question of whether education should be produced by the government, as is the case with traditional public schools, or purchased by the government, as is done in charter schools.

External Costs and Benefits

External costs are imposed when an action by one person or firm harms another, outside of any market exchange. The **social cost** of producing a good or service equals the private cost plus the external cost of producing it. In the case of external costs, private costs are less than social costs.

Similarly, external benefits are created when an action by one person or firm benefits another, outside of any market exchange. The **social benefit** of an activity equals the private benefit revealed in the market plus external benefits. When an activity creates external benefits, its social benefit will be greater than its private benefit.

The lack of a market transaction means that the person or firm responsible for the external cost or benefit does not face the full cost or benefit of the choice involved. We expect markets to produce more than the efficient quantity of goods or services that generate external costs and less than the efficient quantity of goods or services that generate external benefits.

Consider the case of firms that produce memory chips for computers. The production of these chips generates water pollution. The cost of this pollution is an external cost; the firms that generate it do not face it. These firms thus face some, but not all, of the costs of their production choices. We can expect the market price of chips to be lower, and the quantity produced greater, than the efficient level.

Inoculations against infectious diseases create external benefits. A person getting a flu shot, for example, receives private benefits; he or she is less likely to get the flu. But there will be external benefits as well: Other people will also be less likely to get the flu because the person getting the shot is less likely to have the flu. Because this latter benefit is external, the social benefit of flu shots exceeds the private benefit, and the market is likely to produce less than the efficient quantity of flu shots. Public, private, and charter schools often require such inoculations in an effort to get around the problem of external benefits.

Imperfect Competition

In a perfectly competitive market, price equals marginal cost. If competition is imperfect, however, individual firms face downward-sloping demand curves and will charge prices greater than marginal cost. Consumers in such markets will be faced by prices that exceed marginal cost, and the allocation of resources will be inefficient.

An imperfectly competitive private market will produce less of a good than is efficient. As we saw in the chapter on monopoly, government agencies seek to prohibit monopoly in most markets and to regulate the prices charged by those monopolies that are permitted. Government policy toward monopoly is discussed more fully in a later chapter.

Assessing Government Responses to Market Failure

In each of the models of market failure we have reviewed here—public goods, external costs and benefits, and imperfect competition—the market may fail to achieve the efficient result. There is a potential for government intervention to move inefficient markets closer to the efficient solution.

Figure 15.3 reviews the potential gain from government intervention in cases of market failure. In each case, the potential gain is the deadweight loss resulting from market failure; government intervention may prevent or limit this deadweight loss. In each panel, the deadweight loss resulting from market failure is shown as a shaded triangle.

FIGURE 15.3 Correcting Market Failure

In each panel, the potential gain from government intervention to correct market failure is shown by the deadweight loss avoided, as given by the shaded triangle. In Panel (a), we assume that a private market produces Q_m units of a public good. The efficient level, Q_e, is defined by the intersection of the demand curve D_1 for the public good and the supply curve S_1. Panel (b) shows that if the production of a good generates an external cost, the supply curve S_1 reflects only the private cost of the good. The market will produce Q_m units of the good at price P_1. If the public sector finds a way to confront producers with the social cost of their production, then the supply curve shifts to S_2, and production falls to the efficient level Q_e. Notice that this intervention results in a higher price, P_2, which confronts consumers with the real cost of producing the good. Panel (c) shows the case of a good that generates external benefits. Purchasers of the good base their choices on the private benefit, and the market demand curve is D_1. The market quantity is Q_m. This is less than the efficient quantity, Q_e, which can be achieved if the activity that generates external benefits is subsidized. That would shift the market demand curve to D_2, which intersects the market supply curve at the efficient quantity. Finally, Panel (d) shows the case of a monopoly firm that produces Q_m units and charges a price P_1. The efficient level of output, Q_e, could be achieved by imposing a price ceiling at P_2. As is the case in each of the other panels, the potential gain from such a policy is the elimination of the deadweight loss shown as the shaded area in the exhibit.

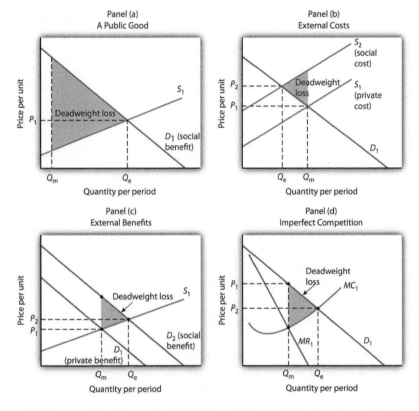

Panel (a) of Figure 15.3 illustrates the case of a public good. The market will produce some of the public good; suppose it produces the quantity Q_m. But the demand curve that reflects the social benefits of the public good, D_1, intersects the supply curve at Q_e; that is the efficient quantity of the good. Public sector provision of a public good may move the quantity closer to the efficient level.

Panel (b) shows a good that generates external costs. Absent government intervention, these costs will not be reflected in the market solution. The supply curve, S_1, will be based only on the private costs associated with the good. The market will produce Q_m units of the good at a price P_1. If the government were to confront producers with the external cost of the good, perhaps with a tax on the activity that creates the cost, the supply curve would shift to S_2 and reflect the social cost of the good. The quantity would fall to the efficient level, Q_e, and the price would rise to P_2.

Panel (c) gives the case of a good that generates external benefits. The demand curve revealed in the market, D_1, reflects only the private benefits of the good. Incorporating the external benefits of the good gives us the demand curve D_2 that reflects the social benefit of the good. The market's output of Q_m units of the good falls short of the efficient level Q_e. The government may seek to move the market solution toward the efficient level through subsidies or other measures to encourage the activity that creates the external benefit.

Finally, Panel (d) shows the case of imperfect competition. A firm facing a downward-sloping demand curve such as D_1 will select the output Q_m at which the marginal cost curve MC_1 intersects the marginal revenue curve MR_1. The government may seek to move the solution closer to the efficient level, defined by the intersection of the marginal cost and demand curves.

While it is important to recognize the potential gains from government intervention to correct market failure, we must recognize the difficulties inherent in such efforts. Government officials may lack the information they need to select the efficient solution. Even if they have the information, they may have goals other than the efficient allocation of resources. Each instance of government intervention involves an interaction with utility-maximizing consumers and profit-maximizing firms, none of whom can be assumed to be passive participants in the process. So, while the potential exists for improved resource allocation in cases of market failure, government intervention may not always achieve it.

The late George Stigler, winner of the Nobel Prize for economics in 1982, once remarked that people who advocate government intervention to correct every case of market failure reminded him of the judge at an amateur singing contest who, upon hearing the first contestant, awarded first prize to the second. Stigler's point was that even though the market is often an inefficient allocator of resources, so is the government likely to be. Government may improve on what the market does; it can also make it worse. The choice between the market's allocation and an allocation with government intervention is always a choice between imperfect alternatives. We will examine the nature of public sector choices later in this chapter and explore an economic explanation of why government intervention may fail to move market solutions closer to their efficient levels.

Irrational Behavior

behavioral
economics

An area of economics that
draws on psychology and
neuroscience to
understand how and why
individuals make
decisions.

The growing field of **behavioral economics**—an area of economics that draws on psychology and neuroscience to understand how and why individuals make decisions—has led to consideration of new areas for government policy. Using experiments and surveys, behavioral economists have found that people's decisions are subject to cognitive limitations and biases, as well as to emotions, resulting in seemingly irrational choices.[1]

For example, 1955 Nobel Prize–winning economist Herbert Simon noted that people possess neither unlimited abilities nor unlimited time for processing information and hence may not solve all problems optimally. Instead they may resort to rules of thumb. They are being rational but their rationality is "bounded." For example, a rule of thumb such as "you get what you pay for" may lead people to pay more for something when the cheaper version is just as good or better.

Behavioral economics has also found that people have bounded willpower (i.e., that they lack complete self-control and have a bias toward the present). Surprising? Hardly. Some people may eat, drink, or spend too much or exercise, save, or work too little. They may even be aware of their self-control problems and try to counter them. For example, they may choose to buy cigarettes by the pack instead of by the carton, which is cheaper; they may make New Year's resolutions; they may have more of their salaries withheld than necessary in order to be sure they will get a tax refund so they can purchase goods they do not have the willpower to save for on their own.

Other findings suggest overconfidence (surveys show that 90% of people think they are among the top 50% in such areas as driving ability and health); loss aversion (getting extreme utility loss from negative outcomes that fall below a reference point and only mild utility increases from gains above the reference point); and over-reaction or under-reaction to information. Moreover, their errors persist—always thinking of themselves as above average in various areas despite evidence to the contrary and always putting off changes in behavior that they know would make them better off.

How might government policy be changed to help people make better decisions? One concrete proposal is for government to mandate that when employees become eligible for joining retirement plans, the default option would be signing them up instead of the more common approach of inviting them to do so. Though they could still opt out, studies have shown that a switch in the default option greatly increases participation in retirement plans. The change appears to reduce procrastination. The policy could be improved further by taking into account the notion of loss aversion. Building on studies that have shown that people are overly reluctant to sell stocks that have gone down in price because they do not want to have to admit the loss to themselves, Richard Thaler has suggested that employers not only switch the retirement plan default but additionally sign employees up for a plan that automatically increases their contribution rates, timed to coincide with any increases in salary they may be receiving. Never seeing a reduction in take-home pay, the employee avoids facing loss aversion.

But are people really being irrational? Perhaps an excess of optimism is good for mental health even if it leads one to make mistakes. Focusing on the present may beat out worrying about the future. Even if people are at times irrational, to what extent should government get involved? Most countries seem to have accepted that imposing speed limits and seat belt use is appropriate. Should sugary soft drinks be banned or at least taxed? Should government simply alert citizens to sign up for retirement plans or mandate companies to make signing up the default option?

To what extent should the model of *homo economicus* be altered to better understand economic outcomes? Will the extra dose of reality in looking at the way people make decisions contribute to or detract from the ability of economists to understand or explain economic outcomes? With the advent of new methods of testing, such as brain studies, these questions are likely to take center stage in coming years, both within and outside of the economics profession.

Income Redistribution

The proposition that a private market will allocate resources efficiently if the efficiency condition is met always comes with a qualification: the allocation of resources will be efficient *given the initial distribution of income*. If 5% of the people receive 95% of the income, it might be efficient to allocate roughly 95% of the goods and services produced to them. But many people (at least 95% of them!) might argue that such a distribution of income is undesirable and that the allocation of resources that emerges from it is undesirable as well.

There are several reasons to believe that the distribution of income generated by a private economy might not be satisfactory. For example, the incomes people earn are in part due to luck. Much income results from inherited wealth and thus depends on the family into which one happens to have been born. Likewise, talent is distributed in unequal measure. Many people suffer handicaps that limit their earning potential. Changes in demand and supply can produce huge changes in the values—and the incomes—the market assigns to particular skills. Given all this, many people argue that incomes should not be determined solely by the marketplace.

A more fundamental reason for concern about income distribution is that people care about the welfare of others. People with higher incomes often have a desire to help people with lower incomes. This preference is demonstrated in voluntary contributions to charity and in support of government programs to redistribute income.

A public goods argument can be made for government programs that redistribute income. Suppose that people of all income levels feel better off knowing that financial assistance is being provided to the poor and that they experience this sense of well-being whether or not they are the ones who provide the assistance. In this case, helping the poor is a public good. When the poor are better off, other people feel better off; this benefit is nonexclusive. One could thus argue that leaving private charity to the marketplace is inefficient and that the government should participate in income redistribution. Whatever the underlying basis for redistribution, it certainly occurs. The governments of every country in the world make some effort to redistribute income.

Experiments conducted by behavioral economists also provide insights into notions of fairness. In various versions of the "ultimatum game," experimenters tell one player in the game to propose to give a share of an amount of money (say $10) to the other player. If the other player accepts the offer, both players keep their shares of the total. If the other player refuses the offer, both walk away with nothing.

If the responding player were selfish, he or she would accept any positive offer, and a selfish proposer would offer only a small amount, perhaps a penny or a nickel. In actual experiments, though, proposing players tend to offer about 40% of the total ($4 in this example) and responding players tend to reject offers of less than 20% ($2 in this example). The conclusion seems to hold even when substantial sums of money are used to play the game. Rejecting any offer that leaves both players better off seems irrational and suggests a concern for fairness.

means-tested transfer payments

Transfer payment for which the recipient qualifies on the basis of income.

non-means-tested transfer payments

Transfer payment for which income is not a qualifying factor.

Programs to redistribute income can be divided into two categories. One transfers income to poor people; the other transfers income based on some other criterion. A **means-tested transfer payment** is one for which the recipient qualifies on the basis of income; means-tested programs transfer income from people who have more to people who have less. The largest means-tested program in the United States is Medicaid, which provides health care to the poor. Other means-tested programs include Temporary Assistance to Needy Families (TANF) and food stamps. A **non-means-tested transfer payment** is one for which income is not a qualifying factor. Social Security, a program that taxes workers and their employers and transfers this money to retired workers, is the largest non-means-tested transfer program. Indeed, it is the largest transfer program in the United States. It transfers income from working families to retired families. Given that retired families are, on average, wealthier than working families, Social Security is a somewhat regressive program. Other non-means tested transfer programs include Medicare, unemployment compensation, and programs that aid farmers.

Figure 15.4 shows federal spending on means-tested and non-means-tested programs as a percentage of GDP, the total value of output, since 1962. As the chart suggests, the bulk of income redistribution efforts in the United States are non-means-tested programs.

FIGURE 15.4 Federal Transfer Payment Spending
The chart shows federal means-tested and non-means-tested transfer payment spending as a percentage of GDP from 1962–2015.

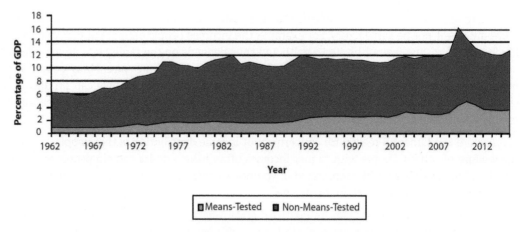

Source: Based on data from Congressional Budget Office, The Budget and Economic Outlook: Fiscal Years 2000-2009 , Table F-13 for 1962-1998; The Budget and Economic Outlook: Fiscal Years 2011 to 2021 for years 1999-2010, Table E-10 with means-tested as Medicaid plus income security and non-means tested everything else; The Budget and Economic Outlook: 2016 to 2026, Table F-5 for years 2011 to 2015 with means-tested as Medicaid plus income security and non-means tested everything else.

The fact that most transfer payments in the United States are not means-tested leads to something of a paradox: some transfer payments involve taxing people whose incomes are relatively low to give to people whose incomes are relatively high. Social Security, for example, transfers income from people who are working to people who have retired. But many retired people enjoy higher incomes than working people in the United States. Aid to farmers, another form of non-means-tested payments, transfers income to farmers, who on average are wealthier than the rest of the population. These situations have come about because of policy decisions, which we discuss later in the chapter.

Key Takeaways

- One role of government is to correct problems of market failure associated with public goods, external costs and benefits, and imperfect competition.

- Government intervention to correct market failure always has the potential to move markets closer to efficient solutions and thus reduce deadweight losses. There is, however, no guarantee that these gains will be achieved.

- Experiments and surveys undertaken by behavioral economists suggest that consumers may not always make rational decisions. Thus, governments may seek to alter the provision of certain goods and services or the amounts consumed based on the notion that consumers will otherwise consume too much or too little of the goods.

- Governments redistribute income through transfer payments. Such redistribution often goes from people with higher incomes to people with lower incomes, but other transfer payments go to people who are relatively better off.

Try It!

Here is a list of actual and proposed government programs. Each is a response to one of the justifications for government activity described in the text: correction of market failure (due to public goods, external costs, external benefits, or imperfect competition); encouragement or discouragement of consumption due to consumers not making rational choices; and redistribution of income. In each case, identify the source of demand for the activity described.

1. The Justice Department sought to prevent Microsoft Corporation from releasing Windows '98, arguing that the system's built-in Internet browser represented an attempt by Microsoft to monopolize the market for browsers.

2. In 2004, Congress considered a measure that would extend taxation of cigarettes to vendors that sell cigarettes over the Internet.

3. The federal government engages in research to locate asteroids that might hit the earth, and studies how impacts from asteroids could be prevented.

4. The federal government increases spending for food stamps for people whose incomes fall below a certain level.

5. The federal government increases benefits for recipients of Social Security.

6. The Environmental Protection Agency sets new standards for limiting the emission of pollutants into the air.

7. A state utilities commission regulates the prices charged by utilities that provide natural gas to homes and businesses.

Case in Point: Externalities, Irrationalities, and Smoking

Source: © 2010 Jupiterimages Corporation

Smokers impose tremendous costs on themselves. Based solely on the degree to which smoking shortens their life expectancy, the cost per pack of cigarettes is estimated to be $35.64. That cost, of course, is a private cost. In addition to that private cost, smokers impose costs on others. Those external costs come in three ways. First, they increase health care costs and thus increase health insurance premiums. Second, smoking causes fires that destroy property. Third, other people die each year as a result of secondhand smoke. Various estimates of these external costs put them at about $.40 per pack. If a tax were to be based solely on external effects, one would also need to recognize that smokers also generate external benefits. They contribute to retirement programs and to Social Security and then die sooner than nonsmokers. They thus subsidize the retirement programs of the rest of the population. So from the perspective of externalities, the optimal tax would be less than $.40 per pack.

Cigarette taxes, though, are much higher than that. Should they be? Is that fair? One rationale is simply that "sin" taxes are a source of government revenue. Economists Jonathan Gruber and Botond Koszegi suggest something else—that an excise tax on cigarettes of as much as $4.76 per pack may actually improve the welfare of smokers. Smokers, they argue, are "time-inconsistent." Lacking self-control or willpower, they seek the immediate gratification of a cigarette and then regret their decisions later. Higher taxes would serve to reduce the quantity of cigarettes demanded and thus reduce behavior smokers would otherwise regret. Their argument is that smokers impose "internalities" on themselves and that higher taxes would reduce this.

Where does this lead us? If smokers are "rationally addicted" to smoking (i.e., they have weighed the benefits and costs of smoking and have chosen to smoke), then the only program for public policy is to design a tax that takes into account the net external costs of smoking. Current excise taxes on cigarettes seem to more than accomplish that. But if the decision to smoke is an irrational one, welfare may be improved by higher excise taxes on smoking.

In a study titled, "Do Cigarette Taxes Make Smokers Happier," Gruber and Sendhil Mullainathan used self-reported happiness measures and variations in cigarette excise taxes across states to see the effect of excise taxes on happiness of people who have a propensity to smoke. They found that people with a propensity to smoke were significantly happier with higher cigarette excise taxes. This finding, they argue, is more consistent with a model based on bounded willpower and time inconsistency than one based on rational addiction.

Sources: Based on Jonathan Gruber and Botond Koszegi, "Tax Incidence When Individuals Are Time-Inconsistent: The Case of Cigarette Excise Taxes," Journal of Public Economics 88 (2004);

1959–1987; Jonathan H. Gruber and Sendhil Mullainathan, "Do Cigarette Taxes Make Smokers Happier?" Journal of Economic Analysis and Policy: Advances in Economic Policy 5:1 (2005): 1–45.

Answers to Try It! Problems

1. This is an attempt to deal with monopoly, so it is a response to imperfect competition.
2. Cigarette consumption may result from an irrational decision.
3. Protecting the earth from such a calamity is an example of a public good.
4. Food Stamps are a means-tested program to redistribute income.
5. Social Security is an example of a non-means-tested income redistribution program.
6. This is a response to external costs.
7. This is a response to monopoly, so it falls under the imperfect competition heading.

15.3 Financing Government

Learning Objectives

1. Explain the ability-to-pay and the benefits-received principles of taxation.
2. Distinguish among regressive, proportional, and progressive taxes.
3. Define tax incidence analysis and explain and illustrate the conditions under which the burden of an excise tax falls mainly on buyers or sellers.

If government services are to be provided, people must pay for them. The primary source of government revenue is taxes. In this section we examine the principles of taxation, compare alternative types of taxes, and consider the question of who actually bears the burden of taxes.

In addition to imposing taxes, governments obtain revenue by charging **user fees**, which are fees levied on consumers of government-provided services. The tuition and other fees charged by public universities and colleges are user fees, as are entrance fees at national parks. Finally, government agencies might obtain revenue by selling assets or by holding bonds on which they earn interest.

user fees

Fees levied on consumers of government-provided services.

Principles of Taxation

Virtually anything can be taxed, but what should be taxed? Are there principles to guide us in choosing a system of taxes?

Jean-Baptiste Colbert, a minister of finance in seventeenth-century France, is generally credited with one of the most famous principles of taxation:

"The art of taxation consists in so plucking the goose as to obtain the largest possible amount of feathers with the smallest possible amount of hissing."

Economists, who do not typically deal with geese, cite two criteria for designing a tax system. The first is based on the ability of people to pay taxes and the second focuses on the benefits they receive from particular government services.

Ability to Pay

ability-to-pay principle

Principle that holds that people with more income should pay more taxes.

The **ability-to-pay principle** holds that people with more income should pay more taxes. As income rises, the doctrine asserts, people are able to pay more for public services; a tax system should therefore be constructed so that taxes rise too. Wealth, the total of assets less liabilities, is sometimes used as well as income as a measure of ability to pay.

The ability-to-pay doctrine lies at the heart of tax systems that link taxes paid to income received. The relationship between taxes and income may take one of three forms: taxes can be regressive, proportional, or progressive.

Regressive Tax

regressive tax

A tax that takes a higher percentage of income as income falls.

A **regressive tax** is one that takes a higher percentage of income as income falls. Taxes on cigarettes, for example, are regressive. Cigarettes are an inferior good—their consumption falls as incomes rise. Thus, people with lower incomes spend more on cigarettes than do people with higher incomes. The cigarette taxes paid by low-income people represent a larger share of their income than do the cigarette taxes paid by high-income people and are thus regressive.

Proportional Tax

proportional tax

Tax that takes a fixed percentage of income, no matter what the level of income.

A **proportional tax** is one that takes a fixed percentage of income. Total taxes rise as income rises, but taxes are equal to the same percentage no matter what the level of income. Some people argue that the U.S. income tax system should be changed into a flat tax system, a tax that would take the same percentage of income from all taxpayers. Such a tax would be a proportional tax.

Progressive Tax

progressive tax

A tax that takes a higher percentage of income as income rises.

A **progressive tax** is one that takes a higher percentage of income as income rises. The federal income tax is an example of a progressive tax. Table 15.1 shows federal income tax rates for various brackets of income for a married couple in 2016. As shown in the table, at higher income levels, couples faced a higher percentage tax rate. Any income over $466,950, for example, was taxed at a rate of 39.6%.

TABLE 15.1 Federal Income Tax Brackets, 2016
The federal income tax is progressive. The percentage tax rate rises as adjusted gross income rises.

2016 adjusted gross income (married couple)	Personal income tax rate applied to bracket
Less than $18,550	10%
$18,550–$75,300	15%
$75,300–$151,900	25%
$151,900–$231,450	28%
$231,450–$413,350	33%
$413,450–$466,950	35%
Greater than $466,950	39.6%

While a pure flat tax would be proportional, most proposals for such a tax would exempt some income from taxation. Suppose, for example, that households paid a "flat" tax of 20% on all income over $40,000 per year. This tax would be progressive. A household with an income of $25,000 per year would pay no tax. One with an income of $50,000 per year would pay a tax of $2,000 (.2 times $10,000), or 4% of its income. A household with an income of $100,000 per year would pay a tax of $12,000 (.2 times $60,000) per year, or 12% of its income. A flat tax with an income exemption would thus be a progressive tax.

Benefits Received

An alternative criterion for establishing a tax structure is the **benefits-received principle**, which holds that a tax should be based on the benefits received from the government services funded by the tax.

Local governments rely heavily on taxes on property, in large part because the benefits of many local services, including schools, streets, and the provision of drainage for wastewater, are reflected in higher property values. Suppose, for example, that public schools in a particular area are especially good. People are willing to pay more for houses served by those schools, so property values are higher; property owners benefit from better schools. The greater their benefit, the greater the property tax they pay. The property tax can thus be viewed as a tax on benefits received from some local services.

User fees for government services apply the benefits-received principle directly. A student paying tuition, a visitor paying an entrance fee at a national park, and a motorist paying a highway toll are all paying to consume a publicly provided service; they are thus paying directly for something from which they expect to benefit. Such fees can be used only for goods for which exclusion is possible; a user fee could not be applied to a service such as national defense.

Income taxes to finance public goods may satisfy both the ability-to-pay and benefits-received principles. The demand for public goods generally rises with income. Thus, people with higher incomes benefit more from public goods. The benefits-received principle thus suggests that taxes should rise with income, just as the ability-to-pay principle does. Consider, for example, an effort financed through income taxes by the federal government to clean up the environment. People with higher incomes will pay more for the cleanup than people with lower incomes, consistent with the ability-to-pay principle. Studies by economists consistently show that people with higher incomes have a greater demand for environmental improvement than do people with lower incomes—a clean environment is a normal good. Requiring people with higher incomes to pay more for the cleanup can thus be justified on the benefits-received principle as well.

Certainly taxes cannot respond precisely to benefits received. Neither the ability-to-pay nor the benefits-received doctrine gives us a recipe for determining just what each person "should" pay in taxes, but these doctrines give us a framework for thinking about the justification for particular taxes.

benefits-received principle

Principle that holds that a tax should be based on the benefits received from the government services funded by the tax.

Types of Taxes

FIGURE 15.5 Sources of Government Revenue
The chart shows sources of revenue for federal, state, and local governments in the United States. The data omit revenues from government-owned utilities and liquor stores. All figures are in billions of dollars. Data are for 2015.

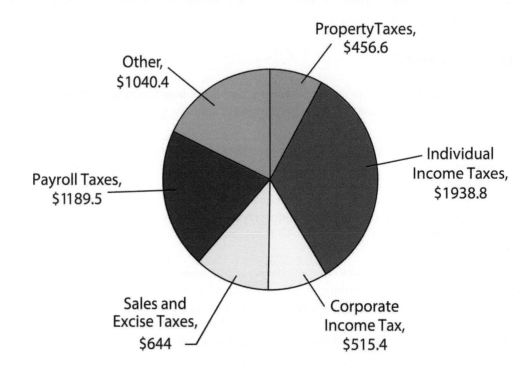

Source: Based on data from U.S. Department of Commerce, Bureau of Economic Analysis, NIPA Table 3.2 and 3.2, September 29, 2016.

It is hard to imagine anything that has not been taxed at one time or another. Windows, closets, buttons, junk food, salt, death—all have been singled out for special taxes. In general, taxes fall into one of four primary categories. **Income taxes** are imposed on the income earned by a person or firm; **property taxes** are imposed on assets; **sales taxes** are imposed on the value of goods sold; and **excise taxes** are imposed on specific goods or services. Figure 15.5 shows the major types of taxes financing all levels of government in the United States.

Personal Income Taxes

The federal personal income tax is the largest single source of tax revenue in the United States; most states and many cities tax income as well. All income tax systems apply a variety of exclusions to a taxpayer's total income before arriving at **taxable income**, the amount of income that is actually subject to the tax. In the U.S. federal income tax system, for example, a family deducted several thousand dollars for each member of the family as part of its computation of taxable income.

Income taxes can be structured to be regressive, proportional, or progressive. Income tax systems in use today are progressive.

In analyzing the impact of a progressive tax system on taxpayer choice, economists focus on the **marginal tax rate**. This is the tax rate that would apply to an additional $1 of taxable income earned. Suppose an individual was earning taxable income of $8,000 and paid federal income taxes of $800, or 10% of taxable income (ignoring exemptions that would eliminate taxes for such an individual). Suppose the next tax bracket of 15% starts at $8,001 and the taxpayer were to receive $100

Sidebar definitions

income tax

Taxes imposed on the income earned by a person or firm.

property tax

Taxes imposed on assets.

sales tax

Taxes imposed on the value of goods sold.

excise tax

Taxes imposed on specific goods or services.

taxable income

The amount of income that is actually subject to any tax.

marginal tax rate

The tax rate that would apply to an additional $1 of taxable income earned.

more of taxable income. That $100 would be taxed at a rate of 15%. That person thus faces a marginal tax rate of 15%.

Economists argue that choices are made at the margin; it is thus the marginal tax rate that is most likely to affect decisions. Say that the individual in our example is considering taking on additional work that would increase his or her income to $15,000 per year. With a marginal tax rate of 15%, the individual would keep $5,950 of the additional $7,000 earned. It is that $5,950 that the individual will weigh against the opportunity cost in forgone leisure in deciding whether to do the extra work.

Property Taxes

Property taxes are taxes imposed on assets. Local governments, for example, generally impose a property tax on business and personal property. A government official (typically a local assessor) determines the property's value, and a proportional tax rate is then applied to that value.

Property ownership tends to be concentrated among higher income groups; economists generally view property taxes as progressive. That conclusion, however, rests on assumptions about who actually pays the tax, an issue examined later in this chapter.

Sales Taxes

Sales taxes are taxes imposed as a percentage of firms' sales and are generally imposed on retail sales. Some items, such as food and medicine, are often exempted from sales taxation.

People with lower incomes generally devote a larger share of their incomes to consumption of goods covered by sales taxes than do people with higher incomes. Sales taxes are thus likely to be regressive.

Excise Taxes

An excise tax is imposed on specific items. In some cases, excise taxes are justified as a way of discouraging the consumption of demerit goods, such as cigarettes and alcoholic beverages. In other cases, an excise tax is a kind of benefits-received tax. Excise taxes on gasoline, for example, are typically earmarked for use in building and maintaining highways, so that those who pay the tax are the ones who benefit from the service provided.

The most important excise tax in the United States is the payroll tax imposed on workers' earnings. The proceeds of this excise on payrolls finance Social Security and Medicare benefits. Most U.S. households pay more in payroll taxes than in any other taxes.

Tax Incidence Analysis

Next time you purchase an item at a store, notice the sales tax imposed by your state, county, and city. The clerk rings up the total, then adds up the tax. The store is the entity that "pays" the sales tax, in the sense that it sends the money to the government agencies that imposed it, but you are the one who actually foots the bill—or are you? Is it possible that the sales tax affects the price of the item itself?

These questions relate to **tax incidence analysis**, a type of economic analysis that seeks to determine where the actual burden of a tax rests. Does the burden fall on consumers, workers, owners of capital, owners of natural resources, or owners of other assets in the economy? When a tax imposed on a good or service increases the price by the amount of the tax, the burden of the tax falls on consumers. If instead it lowers wages or lowers prices for some of the other factors of production used in the production of the good or service taxed, the burden of the tax falls on owners

tax incidence analysis

A type of economic analysis that seeks to determine where the actual burden of a tax rests.

of these factors. If the tax does not change the product's price or factor prices, the burden falls on the owner of the firm—the owner of capital. If prices adjust by a fraction of the tax, the burden is shared.

Figure 15.6 gives an example of tax incidence analysis. Suppose D_1 and S_1 are the demand and supply curves for beef. The equilibrium price is $3 per pound; the equilibrium quantity is 3 million pounds of beef per day. Now suppose an excise tax of $2 per pound of beef is imposed. It does not matter whether the tax is levied on buyers or on sellers of beef; the important thing to see is that the tax drives a $2 per pound "wedge" between the price buyers pay and the price sellers receive. This tax is shown as the vertical green line in the exhibit; its height is $2.

FIGURE 15.6 Tax Incidence in the Model of Demand and Supply
Suppose the market price of beef is $3 per pound; the equilibrium quantity is 3 million pounds per day. Now suppose an excise tax of $2 per pound is imposed, shown by the vertical green line. We insert this tax wedge between the demand and supply curves. It raises the market price to $4 per pound, suggesting that buyers pay half the tax in the form of a higher price. Sellers receive a price of $2 per pound; they pay half the tax by receiving a lower price. The equilibrium quantity falls to 2 million pounds per day.

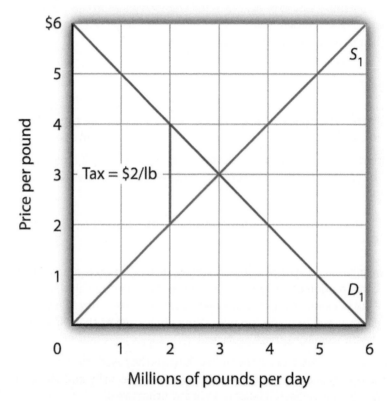

We insert our tax "wedge" between the demand and supply curves. In our example, the price paid by buyers rises to $4 per pound. The price received by sellers falls to $2 per pound; the other $2 goes to the government. The quantity of beef demanded and supplied falls to 2 million pounds per day. In this case, we conclude that buyers bear half the burden of the tax (the price they pay rises by $1 per pound), and sellers bear the other half (the price they receive falls by $1 per pound). In addition to the change in price, a further burden of the tax results from the reduction in consumer and in producer surplus. We have not shown this reduction in the graph.

Figure 15.7 shows how tax incidence varies with the relative elasticities of demand and supply. All four panels show markets with the same initial price, P_1, determined by the intersection of demand D_1 and supply S_1. We impose an excise tax, given by the vertical green line. As before, we insert this tax wedge between the demand and supply curves. We assume the amount of the tax per unit is the same in each of the four markets.

FIGURE 15.7 Tax Incidence and the Elasticity of Demand and of Supply

We show the effect of an excise tax, given by the vertical green line, in the same way that we did in Figure 15.6. We see that buyers bear most of the burden of such a tax in cases of relatively elastic supply (Panel (a)) and of relatively inelastic demand (Panel (d)). Sellers bear most of the burden in cases of relatively inelastic supply (Panel (b)) and of relatively elastic demand (Panel (c)).

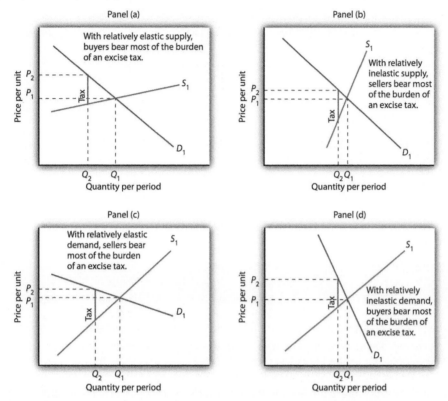

In Panel (a), we have a market with a relatively elastic supply curve S_1. When we insert our tax wedge, the price rises to P_2; the price increase is nearly as great as the amount of the tax. In Panel (b), we have the same demand curve as in Panel (a), but with a relatively inelastic supply curve S_2. This time the price paid by buyers barely rises; sellers bear most of the burden of the tax. When the supply curve is relatively elastic, the bulk of the tax burden is borne by buyers. When supply is relatively inelastic, the bulk of the burden is borne by sellers.

Panels (c) and (d) of the exhibit show the same tax imposed in markets with identical supply curves S_1. With a relatively elastic demand curve D_1 in Panel (c) (notice that we are in the upper half, that is, the elastic portion of the curve), most of the tax burden is borne by sellers. With a relatively inelastic demand curve D_1 in Panel (d) (notice that we are in the lower half, that is, the inelastic portion of the curve), most of the burden is borne by buyers. If demand is relatively elastic, then sellers bear more of the burden of the tax. If demand is relatively inelastic, then buyers bear more of the burden.

Table 15.2 provides an estimate of the federal tax burden for different quintiles (groups containing 20% of the population) of the U.S. population and for different taxes, based on estimates of who bears the burden of a tax, not on who pays the tax. For example, studies argue that, even though businesses pay half of the payroll taxes, the burden of payroll taxes actually falls on households. The reason is that the supply curve of labor is relatively inelastic, as shown in Panel (b) of Figure 15.7. Taking these adjustments into account, the table shows progressivity in federal taxes overall but that the payroll and excise taxes are regressive while the other types of taxes are progressive.

TABLE 15.2 Federal Tax Burdens in the United States (All Numbers in %)
In a regressive tax system, people in the lowest quintiles face the highest tax rates. A proportional system imposes the same rates on everyone; a progressive system imposes higher rates on people in higher deciles. The table gives estimates of the burden on each quintile of federal taxes for all tax units by expanded cash income adjusted for family size in 2016. As you can see, the tax structure in the United States is progressive.

Cash Income Percentile	Individual Income Tax	Payroll Tax	Corporate Income Tax	Estate Tax	Excise Tax	Effective Federal Tax Rate, 2016
Lowest quintile	−10.2	8.0	0.9	*	1.8	0.5
Second quintile	−3.1	7.5	1.0	*	1.3	6.8
Middle quintile	2.1	7.9	1.5	*	1.0	12.5
Fourth quintile	5.8	8.4	1.9	*	0.8	16.9
Highest quintile	15.4	5.9	3.8	0.2	0.6	26.0
Top 1%	24.8	2.3	5.8	0.5	0.4	33.9
All quintiles	9.7	6.9	2.9	0.1	0.8	20.4
*Less than 0.05						

Source: Based on data from Urban and Brookings Institution, Tax Policy Center at http://www.taxpolicycenter.org/briefing-book/are-federal-taxes-progressive.

Key Takeaways

- The primary principles of taxation are the ability-to-pay and benefits-received principles.
- The percentage of income taken by a regressive tax rises as income falls. A proportional tax takes a constant percentage of income regardless of income level. A progressive tax takes a higher percentage of income as taxes as incomes rise.
- The marginal tax rate is the tax rate that applies to an additional dollar of income earned.
- Tax incidence analysis seeks to determine who ultimately bears the burden of a tax.
- The major types of taxes are income taxes, sales taxes, property taxes, and excise taxes.
- Buyers bear most of the burden of an excise tax when supply is relatively elastic and when demand is relatively inelastic; sellers bear most of the burden when supply is relatively inelastic and when demand is relatively elastic.
- The federal tax system in the United States is progressive.

Try It!

Consider three goods, A, B, and C. The prices of all three goods are determined by demand and supply (that is, the three industries are perfectly competitive) and equal $100. The supply curve for good A is perfectly elastic; the supply curve for good B is a typical, upward-sloping curve; and the supply curve for good C is perfectly inelastic. Suppose the federal government imposes a tax of $20 per unit on suppliers of each good. Explain and illustrate graphically how the tax will affect the price of each good in the short run. Show whether the equilibrium quantity will rise, fall, or remain unchanged. Who bears the burden of the tax on each good in the short run? (Hint: Review the chapter on the elasticity for a discussion of perfectly elastic and perfectly inelastic supply curves; remember that the tax increases variable cost by $20 per unit.)

Case in Point: What Are Marginal Tax Rates?

Source: © 2010 Jupiterimages Corporation

We speak often of the importance of tax rates at the margin—of how much of an extra dollar earned through labor or interest on saving will be kept by the decision-maker. It turns out, however, that figuring out just what that marginal tax rate is is not an easy task.

Consider the difficulty of untangling just what those marginal tax rates are. First, Americans face a bewildering complex of taxes. They all face the federal income tax. Each state—and many cities—levy additional taxes on income. Then there is the FICA payroll tax, federal and state corporate income taxes, and excise taxes, as well as federal, state, and local sales taxes. A person trying to figure out his or her marginal tax rate cannot stop there. Gaining an additional dollar of income will affect not only taxes but eligibility for various transfer payment programs in the level of payments the individual or household can expect to receive. Given the enormous complexity involved, it is safe to say that no one really knows what his or her marginal rate is.

Economists Laurence J. Kotlikoff and David Rapson of Boston University have taken on the task of sorting out marginal tax rates for the United States. They used a commercial tax analysis program, Economic Security Planner™, and added their own computer programs to incorporate the effect of additional income on various transfer payment programs. Their analysis assumed the taxpayer lived in Massachusetts, but the general tenor of their results applies to people throughout the United States.

Consider a 60-year-old couple earning $10,000 per year. That couple is eligible for a variety of welfare programs. With food stamps, there is a dollar-for-dollar reduction in aid for each additional dollar of income earned. In effect, the couple faces an effective marginal tax rate of 100%. Considering all other taxes and welfare programs, the economists concluded that the couple faced a marginal tax rate of about 50% on labor income. Overall, they found that a pattern of marginal rates for various ages and income levels could be described in a single word: "bizarre."

The tables below give the economists' estimates of marginal rates for current year labor supply for a single individual and for couples with children at various incomes and ages. While the overall structure of taxes in the United States is progressive, the special treatment of welfare programs can add a strong element of regressivity.

Marginal Net Tax Rates on Current-Year Labor Supply (Couples, percentages)					
	Total Annual Household Earnings (000s)				
Age	10	20	30	50	75
30	−14.2	42.5	42.3	24.4	36.9
45	−11.4	41.7	41.8	35.8	36.1
60	50.9	32.0	36.3	36.3	45.5
Age	100	150	200	300	500
30	37.0	45.9	36.8	43.9	44.0
45	36.1	45.1	35.9	40.0	43.2
60	45.5	47.7	43.2	45.8	45.0

Source: Based on data from Laurence J. Kotlikoff and David Rapson, "Does It Pay, At the Margin, to Work and Save?" NBER Tax Policy & the Economy, 2007, 21(1): 83–143. The tables shown here are Tables 4.2 and 4.3 in the article.

Marginal Net Tax Rates on Current-Year Labor Supply (Individuals, percentages)					
	Total Annual Household Earnings (000s)				
Age	10	20	30	50	75
30	72.3	42.9	42.9	37.0	37.0
45	−9.8	42.9	42.6	37.0	36.1
60	39.5	37.3	37.7	46.4	45.5
Age	125	150	200	250	
30	36.2	36.9	42.0	41.5	
45	36.1	36.5	42.0	41.5	
60	38.8	44.0	45.0	44.0	

Look again at our 60-year-old couple. It faces a very high marginal tax rate. A younger couple with the same income actually faces a negative marginal tax rate—increasing its labor income by a dollar actually increases its after-tax income by more than a dollar. Why the difference? The economists assumed that the younger couple would have children and thus qualify for a variety of programs, including the Earned Income Tax Credit. The couple at age 60 still faces the dollar-for-dollar reduction in payments in the Food Stamp program. No one designed these marginal incentives. They simply emerge from the bewildering mix of welfare and tax programs households face.

Answer to Try It! Problem

The tax adds a $20 wedge between the price paid by buyers and received by sellers. In Panel (a), the price rises to $120; the entire burden is borne by buyers. In Panel (c), the price remains $100; sellers receive just $80. Therefore, sellers bear the burden of the tax. In Panel (b), the price rises by less than $20, and the burden is shared by buyers and sellers. The relative elasticities of demand and supply determine whether the tax is borne primarily by buyers or sellers, or shared equally by both groups.

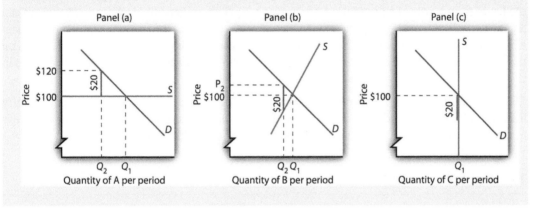

15.4 Choices in the Public Sector

Learning Objectives

1. Compare public interest theory and public choice theory.
2. Use public choice theory to explain rational abstention and why legislative choices may serve special interests.

How are choices made in the public sector? This section examines two perspectives on public sector choice. The first is driven by our examination of market failure. Choices in the public sector are a matter of locating problems of market failure, determining the efficient solution, and finding ways to achieve it. This approach, called the **public interest theory** of government, assumes that the goal of government is to seek an efficient allocation of resources.

An alternative approach treats public sector choices like private sector choices. The body of economic thought based on the assumption that individuals involved in public sector choices make those choices to maximize their own utility is called **public choice theory**. Public choice theory argues that individuals in the public sector make choices that maximize their utility—whether as voters, politicians, or bureaucrats, people seek solutions consistent with their self-interest. People who operate business firms may try to influence public sector choices to increase the profits of their firms. The effort to influence public choices to advance one's own self-interest is called **rent-seeking behavior**.

Public Interest Theory

In the approach to the analysis of public sector choices known as **public interest theory**, decision making is a technical matter. The task of government officials is to locate the efficient solution and find a way to move the economy to that point.

public interest theory

Theory that assumes that the goal of government is to seek an efficient allocation of resources.

public choice theory

Body of economic thought based on the assumption that individuals involved in public sector choices make those choices to maximize their own utility.

rent-seeking behavior

The effort to influence public choices to advance one's own self-interest.

Principles of Economics

cost-benefit analysis

A type of economic analysis that seeks to quantify the costs and benefits of an activity.

For a public good, the efficient solution occurs where the demand curve that reflects social benefits intersects the supply curve for producing the good; that is, the solution at quantity Q_e and price P_1 given in Panel (a) of Figure 15.3 Because this demand curve for a public good is not revealed in the market, the task for government officials is to find a way to estimate these curves and then to arrange for the production of the optimum quantity. For this purpose, economists have developed an approach called **cost-benefit analysis**, which seeks to quantify the costs and benefits of an activity. Public officials can use cost-benefit analysis to try to locate the efficient solution. In general, the efficient solution occurs where the net benefit of the activity is maximized.

Public sector intervention to correct market failure presumes that market prices do not reflect the benefits and costs of a particular activity. If those prices are generated by a market that we can regard as perfectly competitive, then the failure of prices to convey information about costs or benefits suggests that there is a free-rider problem on the demand side or an external cost problem on the supply side. In either case, it is necessary to estimate costs or benefits that are not revealed in the marketplace.

The public interest perspective suggests an approach in which policy makers identify instances of potential market failure and then look for ways to correct them. Public choice theory instead looks at what motivates the people making those policy choices.

The Public Choice Perspective

Public choice theory discards the notion that people in the public sector seek to maximize net benefits to society as a whole. Rather, it assumes that each participant in the public sector seeks to maximize his or her own utility. This section introduces the flavor of the public choice approach by examining two of its more important conclusions: that many people will abstain from voting, and that legislative choices are likely to serve special interests.

Economics and Voting: The Rational Abstention Problem

Public choice theory argues that individuals do not leave their self-interests behind when they enter the voting booth—or even when they are thinking about whether to go to the voting booth. The assumption of utility maximization by voters helps us to understand why most people do not vote in most elections.

Suppose your state is about to hold a referendum on expanded support for state recreation areas, to be financed by an increase in the state sales tax. Given your own likely use of these areas and the way in which you expect to be affected by the tax, you estimate that you will be better off if the program passes. In fact, you have calculated that the present value of your net benefits from the program is $1,000. Will you vote?

As a utility maximizer, you will vote if the marginal benefits to you of voting exceed the marginal costs. One benefit of voting is the possibility that your vote will cause the measure to be passed. That would be worth $1,000 to you. But $1,000 is a benefit to you of voting only if it is your vote that determines the outcome.

The probability that any statewide election will be decided by a single vote is, effectively, zero. State elections that are decided by as many as a few hundred votes are likely to be subject to several recounts, each of which is likely to produce a different result. The outcomes of extremely close elections are ordinarily decided in the courts or in legislative bodies; there is no chance that one vote would, in fact, determine the outcome. Thus, the $1,000 benefit that you expect to receive will not be a factor in your decision about whether to vote. The other likely benefit of voting is the satisfaction you receive from performing your duty as a citizen in a free society. There may be additional personal benefits as well from the chance to visit with other people in your precinct. The opportunity cost of voting would be the value of the best alternative use of your time, together with possible transportation costs.

The fact that no one vote is likely to determine the outcome means that a decision about whether to vote is likely to rest on individual assessments of the satisfactions versus the costs of voting. Most people making such decisions find the costs are greater. In most elections, most people who are eligible to vote do not vote. Public choice analysis suggests that such a choice is rational; a decision not to vote because the marginal costs outweigh the marginal benefits is called **rational abstention**.

rational abstention

A decision not to vote because the marginal costs outweigh the marginal benefits.

Rational abstention suggests there is a public sector problem of external benefits. Elections are a way of assessing voter preferences regarding alternative outcomes. An election is likely to do a better job of reflecting voter preferences when more people vote. But the benefits of an outcome that reflects the preferences of the electorate do not accrue directly to any one voter; a voter faces only some of the benefits of voting and essentially all of the costs. Voter turnouts are thus likely to be lower than is economically efficient.

In the 2000 presidential election, for example, just 50.7% of the voting-age population actually cast votes. President Bush received 47.9% of the vote, which means he was elected with the support of just 24% of the electorate. Mr. Bush actually received fewer votes than his opponent, Albert Gore, Jr. Mr. Bush, however, won a majority in the Electoral College. The Case in Point essay describes the 2000 election in more detail. Voter turnout was higher in the 2004 and 2008 presidential elections.

Legislative Choice and Special Interests

One alternative to having the general public vote on issues is to elect representatives who will make choices on their behalf. Public choice theory suggests that there are some difficulties with this option as well.

Suppose legislators seek to maximize the probability that they will be reelected. That requires that a legislator appeal to a majority of voters in his or her district. Suppose that each legislator can, at zero cost, learn the preferences of every voter in his or her district. Further, suppose that every voter knows, at zero cost, precisely how every government program will affect him or her.

In this imaginary world of costless information and ambitious legislators, each representative would support programs designed to appeal to a majority of voters. Organized groups would play no special role. Each legislator would already know how every voter feels about every issue, and every voter would already know how every program will affect him or her. A world of costless information would have no lobbyists, no pressure groups seeking a particular legislative agenda. No voter would be more important than any other.

Now let us drop the assumption that information is costless but retain the assumption that each legislator's goal is to be reelected. Legislators no longer know how people in the district feel about each issue. Furthermore, voters may not be sure how particular programs will affect them. People can obtain this information, but it is costly.

In this more realistic world of costly information, special-interest groups suddenly play an important role. A legislator who does not know how elderly voters in his or her district feel about a certain issue may find a conversation with a representative of the American Association of Retired Persons (AARP) to be a useful source of information. A chat with a lobbyist for the Teamster's Union may reveal something about the views of union members in the district. These groups also may be able to influence voter preferences through speeches and through public information and political action efforts.

A legislator in a world of costly information thus relies on special-interest groups for information and for support. To ensure his or her reelection, the legislator might try to fashion a program that appeals not to a majority of individuals but to a coalition of special-interest groups capable of delivering the support of a majority of voters. These groups are likely to demand something in exchange for their support of a particular candidate; they are likely to seek special programs to benefit their members. The role of special-interest groups is thus inevitable, given the cost of information and the desire of politicians to win elections. In the real world, it is not individual voters who count but well-organized groups that can deliver the support of voters to a candidate.

Public choice theorists argue that the inevitable importance of special-interest groups explains many choices the public sector makes. Consider, for example, the fact noted earlier in this chapter that a great many U.S. transfer payments go to groups, many of whose members are richer than the population as a whole. In the public choice perspective, the creation of a federal transfer program, even one that is intended to help poor people, will lead to competition among interest groups to be at the receiving end of the transfers. To win at this competition, a group needs money and organization—things poor people are not likely to have. In the competition for federal transfers, then, it is the nonpoor who often win.

The perception of growing power of special-interest groups in the United States has led to proposals for reform. One is the imposition of term limits, which restrict the number of terms a legislator can serve. Term limits were first established in Colorado in 1990; California and Oklahoma established term limits the same year. Subsequently, 18 other states adopted them. They have been found unconstitutional in four State Supreme Courts (Massachusetts, Oregon, Washington, and Wyoming). They have been repealed by the state legislatures of Idaho and Utah. Thus, term limits now apply in 15 states.[2]

One argument for term limits from the public choice perspective is that over time, incumbent legislators establish such close relationships with interest groups that they are virtually assured reelection; limiting terms may weaken these relationships and weaken special interests. The Supreme Court ruled in 1995 that individual states could not impose term limits on members of Congress. If such limits are to prevail at the federal level, a constitutional amendment will be required.

Arguments against the term limits approach include the fact that term limits automatically remove experienced legislators who could be very effective. They also restrict voter choice.

A second type of reform effort is a proposal that campaigns for seats in Congress be federally funded. If candidates did not need to seek funding from special interests, the influence of these groups would wane.

Key Takeaways

- Public interest theory examines government as an institution that seeks to maximize public well-being or net social benefit. It assumes government will seek the efficient solution to market failure problems.
- Public choice theory assumes that individuals engage in rent-seeking behavior by pursuing their self-interest in their dealings with the public sector; they continue to try to maximize utility or profit.
- It may be rational for eligible voters to abstain from voting, according to the public choice theory.
- Public choice theory suggests that politicians seeking reelection will try to appeal to coalitions of special-interest groups.

Try It!

Here is a list of possible explanations for government programs and policies. In each case, identify whether the explanation reflects the public interest theory or the public choice theory of government action.

1. "It is possible to explain much government activity by investigating the public's demand for government services, but one should not ignore the incentives for increased supply of government services."

2. "Through careful application of cost-benefit analysis, we can identify the amount of a public good that should be provided by the government."

3. "The determination of what are merit or demerit goods is inherently political rather than scientific and more often than not can be traced to the efforts of groups with an ax to grind or some private motive to pursue."

4. "While it is possible that policy makers follow some well-reasoned-out application of ability-to-pay or benefit-received principles, it is more credible to recognize that many of the taxes in this country reflect the fact that groups find it in their interest to organize to get tax burdens shifted to others."

5. "It is in the public interest to correct the market failure caused by monopoly firms. Therefore, it behooves us to do so."

Case in Point: The Presidential Election of 2000

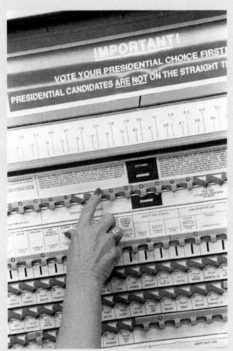

Source: © 2010 Jupiterimages Corporation

Public opinion polls on the eve of the election between George W. Bush and Al Gore showed the race to be a toss-up. Ordinarily, one might expect this to produce a large turnout. But barely more than half—50.7%—of registered voters went to the polls.

The 2000 election provides an illustration of the concept of rational abstention. It also illustrates another point made in the text. If an election is close, the outcome is likely to be determined in the courts.

Florida, with its 25 electoral votes, proved to be the decisive state. The winner of that state's electoral votes would win the presidency. The outcome in that state was not determined until late November, when Florida's Secretary of State, Republican Katherine Harris, declared George Bush the winner by a few hundred votes. Mr. Gore took the case to court. The Florida State Supreme Court ordered a recount.

The recounting process proved to be one of the most bizarre chapters in American political history. Thousands of lawyers descended on the state. Each ballot in key counties was scrutinized in an effort to determine which candidate each voter "intended" to choose. Chads, the small pieces of paper that are removed from a punch-card ballot, turned out to be of crucial importance. "Hanging chads," which occurred when the ballot was not thoroughly punched and which literally remained hanging from the ballot, prevented a ballot from being counted by the state's electric counting machines. The Florida's Supreme Court ruled that the roughly 170,000 ballots that had been discarded by the machines because they were not properly punched had to be re-examined.

As the recounting went on, other controversies arose. Pursuant to Florida law, Ms. Harris had ordered County Clerks to remove ex-felons from their registered voter lists. One clerk, seeing her own name on the list, refused to remove the names. Ms. Harris had come up with a list of 57,700 ex-felons for her "scrub list." The precise number of voters removed is not known. *Harper's Magazine* columnist Greg Palast charges that 90% of the voters on the scrub list were not, in fact, ex-felons. He notes that they were, however, black—and likely to vote Democratic—90% of ex-felons who are allowed to vote vote Democratic.

In the end, the case went to the United States Supreme Court. The Court decided, by a single vote, that Ms. Harris's certification of the outcome would stand, and George Bush became the president-elect of the United States.

All elections have stories of irregularities. The 2000 election was certainly no exception. What made it different was that the outcome came down to the votes in a single state. The official tally in Florida had Mr. Bush with 2,912,790 and Mr. Gore with 2,912,253. What was the "real" outcome? No one will ever know.

Sources: Based on Florida Secretary of State, John Fund, "Vote Early and..." The Wall Street Journal, December 12, 2001; Greg Palast, "The Great Florida Ex-Con Game," Harper's Magazine, March 1, 2002; and U. S. Supreme Court, George W. Bush et al. vs. Albert Gore, Jr. et al., December 12, 2000.

Answer to Try It! Problem

Statements (2) and (5) reflect a public interest perspective. Statements (1), (3), and (4) reflect a public choice perspective.

15.5 Review and Practice

Summary

In this chapter we examined the role of the public sector in the market economy. Since 1929, both the size and scope of government activities in the market have expanded considerably in the United States.

People demand government participation in three areas of economic activity. First, people may want correction of market failure involving public goods, external costs and benefits, and inefficient allocation created by imperfect competition. In each case of market failure, the shift from an inefficient allocation to an efficient one has the potential to eliminate or reduce deadweight losses.

Second, people may seek government intervention to counteract irrational behaviors. Third, people often want government to participate in the transfer of income. Programs to transfer income have grown dramatically in the United States within the past few decades. The bulk of transfer payment spending is not means-tested.

Government activity is financed primarily by taxes. Two principles of taxation are the ability-to-pay principle, which holds that tax payments should rise with income, and the benefits-received principle, which holds that tax payments should be based on the benefits each taxpayer receives. Taxes may be regressive, proportional, or progressive. The major types of taxes in the United States are income taxes, sales and excise taxes, and property taxes. Economists seek to determine who bears the burden of a tax by examining its incidence. Taxes may be borne by buyers or sellers, depending on the relative elasticities of demand and supply.

Two broad perspectives are used to examine choices in the public sector. One is the public interest approach, which uses cost-benefit analysis to find the efficient solution to resource allocation problems. It assumes that the goal of the public sector is to maximize net social benefits. Cost-benefit analysis requires the estimation of benefits and costs that are not revealed in the marketplace. The second approach to the analysis of the public sector is public choice theory, which assumes utility-maximizing and rent-seeking behavior on the part of participants in the public sector and those trying to influence it. We examined two insights stemming from public choice theory: the problem of rational abstention from voting and the role of special interests.

Concept Problems

1. Identify each of the following government programs as efforts to correct market failure, to promote or discourage the consumption of goods subject to irrational decisions, or to transfer income.

    a. Head Start, a preschool program for low-income children

    b. Sports leagues for children sponsored by local governments

    c. A program to limit air pollution generated by power plants

    d. Species preservation efforts by the government

2. Public Broadcasting System (PBS) stations regularly solicit contributions from viewers. Yet only about 11% of these viewers, who on average have much higher incomes than the rest of the population, ever contribute. Why?

3. Do you expect to benefit from the research efforts sponsored by the American Cancer Society? Do you contribute? If you answered "Yes," then "No," does this make you a free rider?

4. Suppose the population of the United States increases. What will happen to the demand for national defense? What will happen to the efficient quantity of defense?

5. How could a program that redistributes income from rich to poor be considered a public good?

6. Local governments typically supply tennis courts but not bowling alleys. Can you give a public choice explanation for this phenomenon? How about a public interest explanation?

7. Find out the turnout at the most recent election for student body president at your school. Does the turnout indicate student apathy?

8. Some welfare programs reduce benefits by $1 for every $1 that recipients earn; in effect, this is a tax of 100% on recipient earnings. Who pays the tax?

9. Suppose the quality of elementary education is a public good. How might we infer the demand for elementary school quality from residential property values?

10. V.I. Lenin, founder of the former Soviet Union, wrote that "the State is a machine for the oppression of one class by another." Explain whether Lenin's view typifies the public interest or the public choice school of public sector choice.

11. Sugar prices in the United States are several times higher than the world price of sugar. This disparity results from a federal government program that keeps enough foreign-produced sugar out of the United States to hold U.S. sugar prices at a high level. The program raises the price of all sweetened foods produced in the United States; it boosts food costs for the

average household by more than a hundred dollars per year. Who benefits from the program? Why do you suppose it exists?

12. What would your prediction be as to how a reduction in marginal tax rates would affect the quantity of labor supplied?

13. Given that we cannot have a perfectly accurate count of the votes in any election, is there any point in having elections at all?

Numerical Problems

1. In an effort to beautify their neighborhood, four households are considering leasing a small section of vacant land for a park. For a monthly leasing fee, the owner of the vacant land is willing to arrange for some of the maintenance and to make the park available only to the four households. The demand curves for the four households (A, B, C, and D) wanting parkland are as follows (all demand curves are linear):

	Acres of Parkland Demanded per Month			
Price per month	A	B	C	D
$100	0	0	0	0
$75	1	0	0	0
$50	2	1⅓	0	0
$25	3	2⅔	2	0
$0	4	4	4	1

Draw the demand curves for the four neighbors, and show the neighborhood demand curve for parkland.

2. Suppose the owner of the vacant land will provide for and maintain a neighborhood park at a fee of $125 per acre; the neighbors may lease up to 5 acres of land per month. Add this information to the graph you drew in Problem 1, and show the efficient solution. Are the neighbors likely to achieve this solution? Explain the problems involved in achieving it.

3. The perfectly competitive blank compact disc industry is in long-run equilibrium, selling blank discs for $5 apiece. Now the government imposes an excise tax of $2 per disc produced.

   a. Show what happens to the price and output of discs in the short run.

   b. Now show the impact in the long run.

   c. Who pays the tax? (Note: Show quantities as Q_1, Q_2, etc.)

4. A monopoly firm has just taken over the blank compact-disc industry. There have been technological advances that have lowered production cost, but the monopoly firm charges a price greater than average total cost, even in the long run. As it turns out, the firm is still selling compact discs for $5. The government imposes an excise tax of $2 per disc produced.

   a. What happens to price?

   b. What happens to output?

   c. Compare your results to your answer in Problem 3 and explain.

5. The following hypothetical data give annual spending on various goods and services for households at different income levels. Assume that an excise tax on any of these would, in the long run, be shifted fully to consumers.

Income range	Average income	Food	Clothing	Entertainment
$0–$25,000	$20,000	$5,000	$1,000	$500
$25,000–$50,000	$40,000	$8,000	$2,000	$2,000
$50,000–$75,000	$65,000	$9,750	$3,250	$5,200
$75,000–$100,000	$80,000	$10,000	$4,000	$8,000
> $100,000	$200,000	$16,000	$10,000	$30,000

Determine whether a tax on any of the following goods would be progressive, proportional, or regressive.

a. Food.

b. Clothing.

c. Entertainment.

Endnotes

1. The information in this section is based largely on Richard H. Thaler and Sendhil Mullainathan, "Behavioral Economics" *Concise Encyclopedia of Economics 2011* at http://www.econlib.org and Ian M. McDonald, "For the Student: Behavioral Economics," *Australian Economic Review* 41(2) (2008): 222–228.

2. "Legislative Term Limits: An Overview," National Conference of State Legislatures, April 22, 2005.

CHAPTER 16
Antitrust Policy and Business Regulation

16.1 Start Up: The Plastic War

The $2.5 trillion market for credit and debit cards received a major jolt in 2004 when the U.S. Supreme Court let stand a lower court ruling that Visa and MasterCard had violated the nation's antitrust laws by prohibiting banks who issued Visa and/or MasterCard from issuing Discover or American Express cards. The court found that, rather than competing with each other, Visa and MasterCard had cooperated with each other by increasing their "intercharge fees," the fees credit card companies charge to merchants who accept credit cards for payment, in lock-step. And, by locking Discover and American Express out of many markets, Visa and MasterCard were guilty of anti-competitive behavior.

The court's ruling spelled major trouble for Visa and MasterCard. Under U.S. law, a competitor that has been damaged by the anticompetitive practices of dominant firms can recover triple the damages that actually occurred. Rivals Discover and American Express filed suits against Visa and MasterCard. In 2008, American Express reached an agreement with MasterCard and Visa for a settlement of $4 billion and Discover settled for $2.8 billion. Together, the two agreements represented the largest judgments up to that time in America's antitrust history. This is but one example of the credit card industry's 40 years of skirmishes with the nation's antitrust laws. In the example just discussed, the government brought the case against the credit card companies. In other situations, retailers have brought cases against them over such things as how debit cards could be treated or the right to impose surcharges on purchases, where legal in states. All of these situations involve one major theme of this chapter. [1]

In this chapter we will also examine some of the limits government imposes on the actions of private firms. The first part of the chapter considers the effort by the U.S. government to limit firms' monopoly power and to encourage competition in the marketplace. The second part looks at those policies in the context of the global economy. We will also examine efforts to modify antitrust policy to make the U.S. economy more competitive internationally. In the third part of the chapter we will consider other types of business regulation, including those that seek to enhance worker and consumer safety, as well as deregulation efforts over the last 30 years.

16.2 Antitrust Laws and Their Interpretation

Learning Objectives

1. Define antitrust policies and tell when and why they were introduced in the United States.
2. Discuss highlights in the history of antitrust policies in the United States, focusing on major issues.
3. Explain the guidelines the Justice Department uses in dealing with mergers.

antitrust policy

Policy by which government attempts to prevent the acquisition and exercise of monopoly power and to encourage competition in the marketplace.

In the decades after the Civil War, giant corporations and cartels began to dominate railroads, oil, banking, meat packing, and a dozen other industries. These businesses were led by entrepreneurs who, rightly or wrongly, have come to be thought of as "robber barons" out to crush their competitors, monopolize their markets, and gouge their customers. The term "robber baron" was associated with such names as J.P. Morgan and Andrew Carnegie in the steel industry, Philip Armour and Gustavas and Edwin Swift in meat packing, James P. Duke in tobacco, and John D. Rockefeller in the oil industry. They gained their market power through cartels and other business agreements aimed at restricting competition. Some formed *trusts*, a combination of corporations designed to consolidate, coordinate, and control the operations and policies of several companies. It was in response to the rise of these cartels and giant firms that antitrust policy was created in the United States. **Antitrust policy** refers to government attempts to prevent the acquisition and exercise of monopoly power and to encourage competition in the marketplace.

A Brief History of Antitrust Policy

The final third of the nineteenth century saw two major economic transitions. The first was industrialization—a period in which U.S. firms became far more capital intensive. The second was the emergence of huge firms able to dominate whole industries. In the oil industry, for example, Standard Oil of Ohio (after 1899, the Standard Oil Company of New Jersey) began acquiring smaller firms, eventually controlling 90% of U.S. oil-refining capacity. American Tobacco gained control of up to 90% of the market for most tobacco products, excluding cigars.

Public concern about the monopoly power of these giants led to a major shift in U.S. policy. What had been an economic environment in which the government rarely intervened in the affairs of private firms was gradually transformed into an environment in which government agencies took on a much more vigorous role. The first arena of intervention was antitrust policy, which authorized the federal government to challenge the monopoly power of firms head-on. The application of this policy, however, has followed a wandering and rocky road.

The Sherman Antitrust Act

The Sherman Antitrust Act of 1890 remains the cornerstone of U.S. antitrust policy. The Sherman Act outlawed contracts, combinations, and conspiracies in restraint of trade.

illegal per se

Actions taken by firms that are illegal in and of themselves without regard to the circumstances under which they occur.

An important issue in the interpretation of the Sherman Act concerns which actions by firms are **illegal per se**, meaning illegal in and of itself without regard to the circumstances under which it occurs. Shoplifting, for example, is illegal per se; courts do not inquire whether shoplifters have a good reason for stealing something in determining whether their acts are illegal. One key question of interpretation is whether it is illegal per se to control a large share of a market. Another is whether a merger that is likely to produce substantial monopoly power is illegal per se.

rule of reason

Rule stating that whether or not a particular business practice is illegal depends on the circumstances surrounding the action.

Two landmark Supreme Court cases in 1911 in which the Sherman Act was effectively used to break up Standard Oil and American Tobacco enunciated the **rule of reason**, which holds that whether or not a particular business practice is illegal depends on the circumstances surrounding the action. In both cases, the companies held dominant market positions, but the Court made it clear that it was their specific "unreasonable" behaviors that the breakups were intended to punish. In determining what was illegal and what was not, emphasis was placed on the conduct, not the structure or size, of the firms.

In the next 10 years, the Court threw out antitrust suits brought by government prosecutors against Eastman Kodak, International Harvester, United Shoe Machinery, and United States Steel. The Court determined that none of them had used unreasonable means to achieve their dominant positions in the industry. Rather, they had successfully exploited economies of scale to reduce costs below competitors' costs and had used reasonable means of competition to reap the rewards of efficiency.

The rule of reason suggests that "bigness" is no offense if it has been achieved through legitimate business practices. This precedent, however, was challenged in 1945 when the U.S. Court of Appeals ruled against the Aluminum Company of America (Alcoa). The court acknowledged that Alcoa had been able to capture over 90% of the aluminum industry through reasonable business practices. Nevertheless, the court held that by sheer size alone, Alcoa was in violation of the prohibition against monopoly.

In a landmark 1962 court case involving a proposed merger between United Shoe Machinery and the Brown Shoe Company, one of United's competitors, the Supreme Court blocked the merger because the resulting firm would have been so efficient that it could have undersold all of its competitors. The Court recognized that lower shoe prices would have benefited consumers, but chose to protect competitors instead.

The Alcoa case and the Brown Shoe case, along with many other antitrust cases in the 1950s and 1960s, added confusion and uncertainty to the antitrust environment by appearing to reinvoke the doctrine of per se illegality. In the government's case against Visa and MasterCard, the government argued successfully that the behavior of the two firms was a per se violation of the Sherman Act.

The Sherman Act also aimed, in part, to prevent **price-fixing**, in which two or more firms agree to set prices or to coordinate their pricing policies. For example, in the 1950s General Electric, Westinghouse, and several other manufacturers colluded to fix prices. They agreed to assign market segments in which one firm would sell at a lower price than the others. In 1961, the General Electric–Westinghouse agreement was declared illegal. The companies paid a multimillion-dollar fine, and their officers served brief jail sentences. In 2008, three manufactures of liquid crystal display panels—the flat screens used in televisions, cell phones, personal computers, and such—agreed to pay $585 million in fines for price fixing, with LG Display paying $400 million, Sharp Corporation paying $120 million, and Chunghwa Picture Tubes paying $65 million. The $400 million fine to LG is still less than the record single fine of $500 million paid in 1999 by F. Hoffman-LaRoche, the Swiss pharmaceutical company, in a case involving fixing prices of vitamin supplements.

price-fixing

Situation in which two or more firms agree to set prices or to coordinate their pricing policies.

Other Antitrust Legislation

Concerned about the continued growth of monopoly power, in 1914 Congress created the Federal Trade Commission (FTC), a five-member commission that, along with the antitrust division of the Justice Department, has the power to investigate firms that use illegal business practices.

In addition to establishing the FTC, Congress enacted new antitrust laws intended to strengthen the Sherman Act. The Clayton Act (1914) clarifies the illegal per se provision of the Sherman Act by prohibiting the purchase of a rival firm if the purchase would substantially decrease competition, and outlawing interlocking directorates, in which there are the same people sitting on the boards of directors of competing firms. More significantly, the act prohibits price discrimination that is designed to lessen competition or that tends to create a monopoly and exempts labor unions from antitrust laws.

The Sherman and Clayton acts, like other early antitrust legislation, were aimed at preventing mergers that reduce the number of firms in a single industry. The consolidation of two or more producers of the same good or service is called a **horizontal merger**. Such mergers increase concentration and, therefore, the likelihood of collusion among the remaining firms.

horizontal merger

The consolidation of two or more producers of the same good or service.

The Celler–Kefauver Act of 1950 extended the antitrust provisions of earlier legislation by blocking **vertical mergers**, which are mergers between firms at different stages in the production and distribution of a product if a reduction in competition will result. For example, the acquisition by Ford Motor Company of a firm that supplies it with steel would be a vertical merger.

vertical merger

Mergers between firms at different stages in the production and distribution of a product.

U.S. Antitrust Policy Today

The "bigness is badness" doctrine dominated antitrust policy from 1945 to the 1970s. But the doctrine always had its critics. If a firm is more efficient than its competitors, why should it be punished? Critics of the antitrust laws point to the fact that of the 500 largest companies in the United States in 1950, over 100 no longer exist. New firms, including such giants as Walmart, Microsoft, and Federal Express, have taken their place. The critics argue that the emergence of these new firms is evidence of the dynamism and competitive nature of the modern corporate scene.

contestable

Open to entry by potential rivals.

There is no evidence to suggest, for example, that the degree of concentration across all industries has increased over the past 25 years. Global competition and the use of the internet as a marketing tool have increased the competitiveness of a wide range of industries. Moreover, critics of antitrust policy argue that it is not necessary that an industry be perfectly competitive to achieve the benefits of competition. It need merely be **contestable**—open to entry by potential rivals. A large firm may be able to prevent small firms from competing, but other equally large firms may enter the industry in pursuit of the high profits earned by the initial large firm. For example, Time Warner, primarily a competitor in the publishing and entertainment industries, has in recent years become a main competitor in the cable television market.

Currently, the Justice Department follows guidelines based on the Herfindahl–Hirschman Index (HHI). The HHI, introduced in an earlier chapter, is calculated by summing the squared percentage market shares of all firms in an industry, where the percentages are expressed as whole numbers (for example 30% would be expressed as 30). The higher the value of the index, the greater the degree of concentration. Possible values of the index range from 0 in the case of perfect competition to 10,000 ($= 100^2$) in the case of a monopoly.

Current guidelines stipulate that any industry with an HHI under 1,000 is unconcentrated. Except in unusual circumstances, mergers of firms with a postmerger index under 1,000 will not be challenged. The Justice Department has said it would challenge proposed mergers with a postmerger HHI between 1,500 and 2,500 if the index increased by more than 100 points. Industries with an index greater than 2,500 are deemed highly concentrated, and the Justice Department has said it would challenge mergers in these industries if the postmerger index would increase by 100 points or more and presume likely that the merger would enhance market power if the HHI rises by more than 200 points. Table 16.1 summarizes these guidelines, which are used in conjunction with other considerations.

TABLE 16.1 The Herfindahl-Hirschman Index and Antitrust Policy

The Department of Justice (DOJ) and the Federal Trade Commission (FTC) have adopted the following guidelines for merger policy based on the Herfindahl-Hirschman Index.

If the postmerger Herfindahl-Hirschman Index is found to be...	Then the Justice Department will likely take the following action:
Unconcentrated (<1,500)	No challenge
Moderately concentrated (1,500–2,500)	Challenge if postmerger index changes by more than 100 points
Highly concentrated (>2,500)	Challenge if postmerger index changes by more than 100 points, with presumption of enhanced market power if change is more than 200 points

Source: Based on data from U.S. Department of Justice and Federal Trade Commission, Horizontal Merger Guidelines, issued August 19, 2010.

The Justice Department used the change in the HHI in 2011 when it sued to prevent the merger of AT&T with T-Mobile USA. In the complaint it filed, it noted that the merger would result in a national HHI of 3,100 and an increase of 700 points. In 96 of 100 regional markets, the postmerger

HHI would exceed 2,500, would rise by more than 200 points in 91 of them, and would rise by more than 100 points in six of them.[2]

One difficulty with the use of the HHI is that its value depends on the definition of the market. With a sufficiently narrow definition of the market, even a highly competitive market could have an HHI close to the value for a monopoly. The late George Stigler commented on the difficulty in a fanciful discussion of the definition of the relevant market for cameras:

> *Consider the problem of defining a market within which the existence of competition or some form of monopoly is to be determined. The typical antitrust case is an almost impudent exercise in economic gerrymandering. The plaintiff sets the market, at a maximum, as one state in area and including only aperture-priority SLR cameras selling between $200 and $250. This might be called J-Shermanizing the market, after Senator John Sherman. The defendant will in turn insist that the market be world-wide, and include not only all cameras, but all portrait artists and all transportation media, since a visit is a substitute for a picture. This might also be called T-Shermanizing the market, after the Senator's brother, General William Tecumseh Sherman. Depending on who convinces the judge, the concentration ratio will be awesome or trivial, with a large influence on the verdict.[3]*

Of course, the definition of the relevant market is not a matter of arbitrarily defining the market as absurdly narrow or broad. There are economic tests to determine the range of goods or services that should be included in a particular market. Consider, for example, the market for refrigerators. Given the relatively low cost of shipping refrigerators, the relevant area might encompass all of North America, given the existence of the North American Free Trade Agreement (NAFTA), which establishes a tariff-free trade zone including Canada, the United States, and Mexico. What sorts of goods should be included? Presumably, any device that is powered by electricity or by natural gas and that keeps things cold would qualify. Certainly, a cool chest that requires ice that people take on picnics would not be included. The usual test is the cross price elasticity of demand. If it is high between any two goods, then those goods are candidates for inclusion in the market.

Should the entire world be the geographic region for the market for refrigerators? That is an empirical question. If the cross price elasticities for refrigerator brands worldwide are high, then one would conclude that the world is the relevant geographical definition of the market.

In the 1980s both the courts and the Justice Department held that bigness did not necessarily translate into badness, and corporate mergers proliferated. Merger activity waxed and waned (particularly during recessions) over the ensuing years. It has been substantial in most years.

Key Takeaways

- The government uses antitrust policies to maintain competitive markets in the economy.
- The Sherman Antitrust Act of 1890 and subsequent legislation defined illegal business practices, but these acts are subject to widely varying interpretations by government agencies and by the courts.
- Although price-fixing is illegal per se, most business practices that may lessen competition are interpreted under the rule of reason.
- The Justice Department and Federal Trade Commission use the Herfindahl-Hirschman Index to determine whether mergers should be challenged in particular industries.

Try It!

According to what basic principle did the U.S. Supreme Court find Eastman Kodak not guilty of violating antitrust laws? According to what basic principle did the Court block the merger of Brown Shoe Company and one of its competitors, United Shoe Machinery? Do you agree or disagree with the Court's choices?

Case in Point: Does Antitrust Policy Help Consumers?

Source: © 2010 Jupiterimages Corporation

The Department of Justice and the Federal Trade Commission spend a great deal of money enforcing U.S. antitrust laws. Firms defending themselves may spend even more.

The government's first successful use of the Sherman Act came in its action against Standard Oil in 1911. The final decree broke Standard into 38 independent companies. Did the breakup make consumers better off?

In 1899, Standard controlled 88% of the market for refined oil products. But, by 1911, its share of the market had fallen to 64%. New discoveries of oil had sent gasoline prices down in the years before the ruling. After the ruling, gasoline prices began rising. It does not appear that the government's first major victory in an antitrust case had a positive impact on consumers.

In general, antitrust cases charging monopolization take so long to be resolved that, by the time a decree is issued, market conditions are likely to have changed in a way that makes the entire effort seem somewhat frivolous. For example, the government charged IBM with monopolization in 1966. That case was finally dropped in 1982 when the market had changed so much that the original premise of the case was no longer valid. In 1998 the Department of Justice began a case against against Microsoft, accusing it of monopolizing the market for Internet browsers by bundling the browser with its operating system, Windows. A trial in 2000 ended with a judgment that Microsoft be split in two with one company having the operating system and another having applications. An appeals court overturned that decision a year later.

Actions against large firms such as Microsoft are politically popular. However, neither policy makers nor economists have been able to establish that they serve consumer interests.

We have seen that the Department of Justice and the Federal Trade Commission have a policy of preventing mergers in industries that are highly concentrated. But, mergers often benefit consumers by achieving reductions in cost. Perhaps the most surprising court ruling involving such a merger came in 1962 when the Supreme Court ruled that a merger in shoe manufacturing would achieve lower costs to consumers. The Court prevented the merger on grounds the new company would be able to charge a lower price than its rivals! Clearly, the Court chose to protect firms rather than to enhance consumer welfare.

What about actions against price-fixing? The Department of Justice investigates roughly 100 price-fixing cases each year. In many cases, these investigations result in indictments. Those cases would, if justified, result in lower prices for consumers. But, economist Michael F. Sproul, in an examination of 25 price-fixing cases for which adequate data were available, found that prices actually *rose* in the four years following most indictments.

Economists Robert W. Crandall and Clifford Winston have asked a very important question: Has all of this effort enhanced consumer welfare? They conclude that the Department of Justice and the Federal Trade Commission would best serve the economy by following a policy of benign neglect in cases of monopolization, proposed mergers, and efforts by firms to exploit technological gains by lowering price. The economists conclude that antitrust actions should be limited to the most blatant cases of price-fixing or mergers that would result in monopolies. In contrast, law professor Jonathan Baker argued in the same journal that such a minimalist approach could be harmful to consumer welfare. One argument he makes is that antitrust laws and their enforcement create a deterrence effect.

A recent paper by Orley Ashenfelter and Daniel Hosken analyzed the impact of five mergers in the consumer products industry that seemed to be most problematic for antitrust enforcement agencies. In four of the five cases prices rose following the mergers and in the fifth case the merger had little effect on price. While they do not conclude that this small study should be used to determine the appropriate level of government enforcement of antitrust policy, they state that those who advocate less intervention should note that the price effects were not negative, as they would have been if these mergers were producing cost decreases and passing them on to consumers. Those advocating more intervention should note that the price increases they observed after these mergers were not very large.

Sources: Based on Orley Ashenfelter and Daniel Hosken, "The Effect of Mergers on Consumer Prices: Evidence from Five Selected Cases," National Bureau of Economic Research Working Paper 13859, March 2008; James B. Baker, "The Case for Antitrust Enforcement," Journal of Economic Perspectives, 17:4 (Fall 2003): 27–50; Robert W. Crandall and Clifford Winston, "Does Antitrust Policy Improve Consumer Welfare? Assessing the Evidence," Journal of Economic Perspectives, 17:4 (Fall 2003): 3–26; Michael F. Sproul, "Antitrust and Prices," Journal of Political Economy, 101 (August 1993): 741–54.

Answer to Try It! Problem

In the case of Eastman Kodak, the Supreme Court argued that the rule of reason be applied. Even though the company held a dominant position in the film industry, its conduct was deemed reasonable. In the proposed merger between United Shoe Machinery and Brown Shoe, the court clearly chose to protect the welfare of firms in the industry rather than the welfare of consumers.

16.3 Antitrust and Competitiveness in a Global Economy

Learning Objectives

1. Define joint ventures and explain the evolution of U.S. antitrust policy towards them.
2. Discuss other antitrust policy changes that relate to U.S. firms competing with foreign firms.

In the early 1980s, U.S. imports from foreign firms rose faster than U.S. exports. In 1986 the trade deficit reached a record level at that time. Antitrust laws played a relatively minor role in increasing the deficit, but business interests and politicians pressed for the relaxation of antitrust policy in order to make U.S. firms more competitive against multinational companies headquartered in other countries.

joint ventures

Cooperative arrangements between two or more firms that otherwise would violate antitrust laws.

Antitrust enforcement was altered in the late 1980s so that horizontally competitive U.S. firms could cooperate in research and development (R&D) ventures aimed at innovation, cost-cutting technological advances, and new product development. In an antitrust context, **joint ventures** refer to cooperative arrangements between two or more firms that otherwise would violate antitrust laws. Proponents of the change argued that foreign multinational firms were not subject to stringent antitrust restrictions and therefore had a competitive advantage over U.S. firms. The International Competition Policy Advisory Committee (ICPAC) was formed in the Department of Justice in 1997 in recognition of the dramatic increases in both international commerce and international anticompetitive activity. Composed of a panel of business, industrial relations, academic, economic, and legal experts, ICPAC is to provide advice and information to the department on international antitrust issues such as transnational cartels and international anticompetitive business practices.

Cooperative Ventures Abroad

Policymakers who revised U.S. antitrust restrictions on joint ventures pointed out that Japanese and European firms are encouraged to cooperate and to collude not only in basic R&D projects, but in production and marketing as well.

The evidence is difficult to interpret, but in Japan, for example, a substantial percentage of research projects are sponsored jointly by firms in the same market. Moreover, the evidence is fairly clear that Japan allows horizontal consolidations and mergers in moderately concentrated markets where antitrust policy would be applied in the United States. Mergers that create substantial monopoly power in Japan are not typically prosecuted by the government.

In Europe, the potential competitive threat to U.S. firms is twofold. First, as the European Union (EU) moved toward economic unification in 1992, it relaxed antitrust enforcement for mergers between firms in different nations, even though they would become a single transnational firm in the near future. In 1984, for example, the European Community (EC), the forerunner of the EU, adopted a regulation that provided blanket exemptions from antitrust provisions against collusion in R&D for firms whose total market share did not exceed 20%. This exemption included horizontal R&D and extended to production and distribution to the point of final sale. Moreover, firms that had a market share greater than 20% could apply for an exemption based on a case-by-case examination.

The U.S. government has relaxed antitrust restrictions in some cases in an effort to make domestic firms more competitive in global competition. For example, producers of semiconductors were allowed to form a research consortium, Sematech, in order to promote the U.S. semiconductor industry. This type of joint venture was formerly prohibited. Sematech has since created the International Sematech Manufacturing Initiative (ISMI), a wholly owned subsidiary dedicated to improve the productivity and cost performance of equipment and manufacturing operations well beyond a narrowly defined semiconductor industry. Its membership includes both domestic and foreign firms, and they collectively represent half of the world's integrated circuit (semiconductor and microchip) production. In this case, we see the U.S. government is supporting cooperation among multinational and international firms ostensibly for product improvement. One suspects, however, that member firms gain a competitive advantage over non-member firms wherever in the world they are located.

Antitrust Policy and U.S. Competitiveness

In the 1980s Congress passed several laws that relaxed the antitrust prohibition against cooperation among U.S. firms, including the National Cooperative Research Act of 1984 (NCRA) and the Omnibus Trade and Competitiveness Act (OTCA).

The NCRA provided a simple registration procedure for joint ventures in R&D. The NCRA protects members of registered joint ventures from punitive antitrust penalties if the venture is later found to illegally reduce competition or otherwise act in restraint of trade. Between 1984 and 1990 over 200 research joint ventures were registered, substantially more than were formed over the same period within the EC.

Congress passed the OTCA in 1988. The OTCA made unfair methods of competition by foreign firms and importers punishable under the U.S. antitrust laws. It also changed the wording of existing laws concerning "dumping" (selling below cost) by foreign firms. In the past, a domestic firm that claimed injury from a foreign competitor had to prove that the foreign firm was "undercutting" the U.S. market prices. The OTCA changed this provision to the much less restrictive term "underselling" and specifically stated that the domestic firm did not have to prove predatory intent. This legislation opened the door for U.S. competitors to use antitrust laws to *prevent* competition from foreigners, quite the opposite of the laws' original purpose. Dumping is discussed further in a later chapter.

In another policy shift, the Justice Department announced in 1988 that the rule of reason would replace per se illegality in analysis of joint ventures that would increase U.S. competitiveness. The Justice Department uses the domestic guidelines and the Herfindahl–Hirschman Index to determine whether a proposed joint venture would increase concentration and thereby lessen competition. In making that assessment, the Justice Department also looks at (1) whether the firms directly compete in other markets, (2) the possible impact on vertical markets, and (3) whether any offsetting efficiency benefits outweigh the anticompetitiveness of the joint venture. Although mergers between two firms in a moderately or highly concentrated industry are prohibited, joint ventures between them may be allowed.

The major antitrust issues to be resolved in the first decade of the twenty-first century go beyond joint R&D ventures. The World Trade Organization, the international organization created in 1995 to supervise world trade, has established a group to study issues relating to the interaction between trade and competition policy, including anticompetitive practices. Nations currently have quite different antitrust laws, as the Case in Point in this section illustrates. The United States has argued against any internationalization of antitrust issues that would reduce its ability to apply U.S. laws. On the other hand, the United States, via the 1994 International Antitrust Enforcement Assistance Act, is negotiating bilateral agreements that allow antitrust agencies in different countries to exchange information for use in antitrust enforcement. The issue of how to deal with anticompetitive practices on a worldwide basis remains unresolved, and this area of antitrust practice and policy will be closely watched and studied by economists.

Key Takeaways

- Increased imports in the last 25 years have led to a rethinking of American antitrust policy.
- One response by the U.S. to international competition is the encouragement of joint ventures.
- U.S. firms that have been "undersold" by foreign firms can charge those firms with "dumping."
- The World Trade Organization is studying the interactions of trade, competition, and antitrust issues.

Try It!

Suppose that long-distance companies in the United States form a joint venture to explore alternative technologies in telephone services. Would such an effort suggest any danger of collusion? Would it be likely to be permitted?

Case in Point: The United States and the European Union—Worlds Apart

Source: © 2010 Jupiterimages Corporation

The European Union's initial reaction to the proposed merger of Boeing and McDonnell Douglas in 1997 was to threaten to impose tariffs on Boeing planes entering the continent if the deal went through. The issue brought the United States and its European partners to the brink of a trade war.

The *Brookings Review* reported that President Bill Clinton then responded to the EU's threat saying, "I'm concerned about what appears to be the reasons for the objection to the Boeing-McDonnell Douglas merger by the European Union, and we have some options ourselves when actions are taken in this regard." The president seemed to be suggesting retaliatory trade sanctions, such as U.S. tariffs on European-made planes.

At the last minute, the EU allowed the merger on two conditions: that Boeing give up its exclusive supply deals and agreed to license to its competitors (meaning Airbus) McDonnell technology that had been developed with U.S. government support.

In the press, the incident was reported as an incipient trade war. Europe was trying to protect its own airline industry; the United States its own. According to New York University economist Eleanor Fox, though, the dispute stemmed not from countries trying to protect their own companies but from differing antitrust laws.

Ms. Fox argues that U.S. antitrust law is consumer oriented. The question for the Federal Trade Commission was whether the merger made consumers worse off by raising the price of jets to airlines. The FTC reasoned that McDonnell Douglas had no reasonable chance of making and selling new fleets on its own and thus did not constitute a competitive force in the marketplace. With McDonnell Douglas deemed competitively insignificant, the merger was permissible.

However, European Union antitrust laws consider not only consumers but also unfair competitive advantages of dominant firms. Because Boeing held 20-year exclusive contracts with three airlines that represent more than 10% of the market for airline manufacture, the merger magnified Boeing's competitive advantage over other firms (primarily Airbus) that sell aircraft. The conditions that the EU impose thus made the merger subject to its antitrust laws.

The policy difference is fundamental. Americans argue that they seek to protect competition, while the EU protects competitors—even if consumers suffer as a result. The *Economist*, a British newsmagazine, reports American antitrust policy makers tend to rely on market forces to dampen monopoly power and argue that relying on regulation may tend to diminish innovation and, in the long run, competition. Europeans argue that regulation is necessary in order to ensure that all firms have a reasonable chance to compete.

The difference in the two approaches to antitrust is vividly illustrated in the treatment of Microsoft by the United States and by the European Union. While the United States initially attempted to prosecute Microsoft for violating the Sherman Act by bundling Internet Explorer with its Windows software, it has since permitted it. The European Union has come down very hard on Microsoft, fining it €1.4 billion ($2.2 billion) and ordering the firm to supply firms using Windows the complete documentation of the system. U.S. authorities argue that such restrictions make Microsoft a less innovative company and argue that the computer market is a highly competitive one as it is and that the imposition of a regulatory burden risks stifling the competition that exists.

Sources: Based on Eleanor M. Fox, "Antitrust Regulation Across International Borders," The Brookings Review, 16(1) (Winter 1998): 30–32; "Oceans Apart," Economist, May 1, 2008, 387(8578): 78–79.

Answer to Try It! Problem

A joint venture between competing long-distance companies carries the danger that they may end up colluding. It is also possible that only some long-distance firms would be involved to the exclusion of other rival firms, as happened in the joint venture between General Motors and Toyota. On the other hand, the venture might be allowed in the U.S. under the notion that the firms might need to cooperate to face global competition. Another consideration is that technological change in this industry is occurring so rapidly that competitors can emerge from anywhere. Cable companies, internet providers, and cellular-phone companies all compete with regular telephone companies.

16.4 Regulation: Protecting People from the Market

Learning Objectives

1. Compare the public interest and public choice theories of regulation.
2. Discuss the costs and benefits of consumer protection laws.
3. Discuss the pros and cons of the trend toward deregulation over the last quarter century.

regulation

Government power to control the choices of private firms or individuals.

Antitrust policies are primarily concerned with limiting the accumulation and use of market power. Government **regulation** is used to control the choices of private firms or individuals. Regulation may constrain the freedom of firms to enter or exit markets, to establish prices, to determine product design and safety, and to make other business decisions. It may also limit the choices made by individuals.

In general terms, there are two types of regulatory agencies. One group attempts to protect consumers by limiting the possible abuse of market power by firms. The other attempts to influence business decisions that affect consumer and worker safety. Regulation is carried out by more than 50 federal agencies that interpret the applicable laws and apply them in the specific situations they find in real-world markets. Table 16.2 lists some of the major federal regulatory agencies, many of which are duplicated at the state level.

TABLE 16.2 Selected Federal Regulatory Agencies and Their Missions

Financial Markets	
Federal Reserve Board	Regulates banks and other financial institutions
Federal Deposit Insurance Corporation	Regulates and insures banks and other financial institutions
Securities and Exchange Commission	Regulates and requires full disclosure in the securities (stock) markets
Commodity Futures Trading Commission	Regulates trading in futures markets
Consumer Financial Protection Bureau	Enforces federal consumer financial laws and protects consumers in the financial marketplace
Product Markets	
Department of Justice, Antitrust Division	Enforces antitrust laws
Federal Communications Commission	Regulates broadcasting and telephone industries
Federal Trade Commission	Focuses efforts on consumer protection, false advertising, and unfair trade practices
Federal Maritime Commission	Regulates international shipping
Surface Transportation Board	Regulates railroads, trucking, and noncontiguous domestic water transportation
Federal Energy Regulatory Commission	Regulates pipelines
Health and Safety	
Occupational Health and Safety Administration	Regulates health and safety in the workplace
National Highway Traffic Safety Administration	Regulates and sets standards for motor vehicles
Federal Aviation Administration	Regulates air and traffic aviation safety
Food and Drug Administration	Regulates food and drug producers; emphasis on purity, labeling, and product safety
Consumer Product Safety Commission	Regulates product design and labeling to reduce risk of consumer injury
Energy and the Environment	
Environmental Protection Agency	Sets standards for air, water, toxic waste, and noise pollution
Department of Energy	Sets national energy policy
Nuclear Regulatory Commission	Regulates nuclear power plants
Corps of Engineers	Sets policies on construction near rivers, harbors, and waterways
Labor Markets	
Equal Employment Opportunity Commission	Enforces antidiscrimination laws in the workplace
National Labor Relations Board	Enforces rules and regulations governing contract bargaining and labor relations between companies and unions

Theories of Regulation

Competing explanations for why there is so much regulation range from theories that suggest regulation protects the public interest to those that argue regulation protects the producers or serves the interests of the regulators. The distinction corresponds to our discussion in the last chapter of the public interest versus the public choice understanding of government policy in general.

The Public Interest Theory of Regulation

The public interest theory of regulation holds that regulators seek to find market solutions that are economically efficient. It argues that the market power of firms in imperfectly competitive markets must be controlled. In the case of natural monopolies (discussed in an earlier chapter), regulation is viewed as necessary to lower prices and increase output. In the case of oligopolistic industries, regulation is often advocated to prevent cutthroat competition.

The public interest theory of regulation also holds that firms may have to be regulated in order to guarantee the availability of certain goods and services—such as electricity, medical facilities, and telephone service—that otherwise would not be profitable enough to induce unregulated firms to provide them in a given community. Firms providing such goods and services are often granted licenses and franchises that prevent competition. The regulatory authority allows the firm to set prices above average cost in the protected market in order to cover losses in the target community. In this way, the firms are allowed to earn, indeed are guaranteed, a reasonable rate of return overall.

Proponents of the public interest theory also justify regulation of firms by pointing to externalities, such as pollution, that are not taken into consideration when unregulated firms make their decisions. As we have seen, in the absence of property rights that force the firms to consider all of the costs and benefits of their decisions, the market may fail to allocate resources efficiently.

The Public Choice Theory of Regulation

capture theory of regulation

Theory stating that government regulations often end up serving the regulated firms rather than their customers.

The public interest theory of regulation assumes that regulations serve the interests of consumers by restricting the harmful actions of business firms. That assumption, however, is now widely challenged by advocates of the public choice theory of regulation, which rests on the premise that all individuals, including public servants, are driven by self-interest. They prefer the **capture theory of regulation**, which holds that government regulations often end up serving the regulated firms rather than their customers.

Competing firms always have an incentive to collude or operate as a cartel. The public is protected from such collusion by a pervasive incentive for firms to cheat. Capture theory asserts that firms seek licensing and other regulatory provisions to prevent other firms from entering the market. Firms seek price regulation to prevent price competition. In this view, the regulators take over the role of policing cartel pricing schemes; individual firms in a cartel would be incapable of doing so themselves.

Because it is practically impossible for the regulatory authorities to have as much information as the firms they are regulating, and because these authorities often rely on information provided by those firms, the firms find ways to get the regulators to enforce regulations that protect profits. The regulators get "captured" by the very firms they are supposed to be regulating.

In addition to its use of the capture theory, the public choice theory of regulation argues that employees of regulatory agencies are not an exception to the rule that people are driven by self-interest. They maximize their own satisfaction, not the public interest. This insight suggests that regulatory agencies seek to expand their bureaucratic structure in order to serve the interests of the bureaucrats. As the people in control of providing government protection from the rigors of the market, bureaucrats respond favorably to lobbyists and special interests.

Public choice theory views the regulatory process as one in which various groups jockey to pursue their respective interests. Firms might exploit regulation to limit competition. Consumers might seek lower prices or changes in products. Regulators themselves might pursue their own interests in expanding their prestige or incomes. The abstract goal of economic efficiency is unlikely to serve the interest of any one group; public choice theory does not predict that efficiency will be a goal of the regulatory process. Regulation might improve on inefficient outcomes, but it might not.

Consumer Protection

Every day we come into contact with regulations designed to protect consumers from unsafe products, unscrupulous sellers, or our own carelessness. Seat belts are mandated in cars and airplanes; drivers must provide proof of liability insurance; deceptive advertising is illegal; firms cannot run "going out of business" sales forever; electrical and plumbing systems in new construction must be inspected and approved; packaged and prepared foods must carry certain information on their labels; cigarette packages must warn users of the dangers involved in smoking; gasoline stations must prevent gas spillage; used-car odometers must be certified as accurate. The list of regulations is seemingly endless.

There are often very good reasons behind consumer protection regulation, and many economists accept such regulation as a legitimate role and function of government agencies. But there are costs as well as benefits to consumer protection.

The Benefits of Consumer Protection

Consumer protection laws are generally based on one of two conceptual arguments. The first holds that consumers do not always know what is best for them. This is the view underlying government efforts to encourage the use of merit goods and discourage the use of demerit goods. The second suggests that consumers simply do not have sufficient information to make appropriate choices.

Laws prohibiting the use of certain products are generally based on the presumption that not all consumers make appropriate choices. Drugs such as cocaine and heroin are illegal for this reason. Children are barred from using products such as cigarettes and alcohol on grounds they are incapable of making choices in their own best interest.

Other regulations presume that consumers are rational but may not have adequate information to make choices. Rather than expect consumers to determine whether a particular prescription drug is safe and effective, for example, federal regulations require the Food and Drug Administration to make that determination for them.

The benefit of consumer protection occurs when consumers are prevented from making choices they would regret if they had more information. A consumer who purchases a drug that proves ineffective or possibly even dangerous will presumably stop using it. By preventing the purchase in the first place, the government may save the consumer the cost of learning that lesson.

One problem in assessing the benefits of consumer protection is that the laws themselves may induce behavioral changes that work for or against the intent of the legislation. For example, requirements for childproof medicine containers appear to have made people more careless with medicines. Requirements that mattresses be flame-resistant may make people more careless about smoking in bed. In some cases, then, the behavioral changes attributed to consumer protection laws may actually worsen the problem the laws seek to correct.

An early study on the impact of seat belts on driving behavior indicated that drivers drove more recklessly when using seat belts, presumably because the seat belts made them feel more secure.[4] A recent study, however, found that this was not the case and suggests that use of seat belts may make drivers more safety-conscious.[5]

In any event, these "unintended" behavioral changes can certainly affect the results achieved by these laws.

The Cost of Consumer Protection

Regulation aimed at protecting consumers can benefit them, but it can also impose costs. It adds to the cost of producing goods and services and thus boosts prices. It also restricts the freedom of choice of individuals, some of whom are willing to take more risks than others.

Those who demand, and are willing to pay the price for, high-quality, safe, warranted products can do so. But some argue that people who demand and prefer to pay (presumably) lower prices for lower-quality products that may have risks associated with their use should also be allowed to exercise this preference. By increasing the costs of goods, consumer protection laws may adversely affect the poor, who are forced to purchase higher-quality products; the rich would presumably buy higher-quality products in the first place.

To assess whether a particular piece of consumer protection is desirable requires a careful look at how it stacks up against the marginal decision rule. The approach of economists is to attempt to determine how the costs of a particular regulation compare to its benefits.

Economists W. Mark Crain and Thomas D. Hopkins estimated the cost of consumer protection regulation in 2001 and found that the total cost was $843 billion, or $7,700 per household in the United States.[6]

Deregulating the Economy

Concern that regulation might sometimes fail to serve the public interest prompted a push to deregulate some industries, beginning in the late 1970s. In 1978, for example, Congress passed the Airline Deregulation Act, which removed many of the regulations that had prevented competition in the airline industry. Safety regulations were not affected. The results of deregulation included a substantial reduction in airfares, the merger and consolidation of airlines, and the emergence of frequent flier plans and other marketing schemes designed to increase passenger miles. Not all the consequences of deregulation were applauded, however. Many airlines, unused to the demands of a competitive, unprotected, and unregulated environment, went bankrupt or were taken over by other airlines. Large airlines abandoned service to small and midsized cities, and although most of these routes were picked up by smaller regional airlines, some consumers complained about inadequate service. Nevertheless, the more competitive airline system today is probably an improvement over the highly regulated industry that existed in the 1970s. It is certainly cheaper. An extensive study by economist Clifford Winston in the late 1990s examined several major industries, from airlines to banking and natural gas, and found that deregulation had substantially improved consumer welfare. Benefits included lower prices and better service.[7]

But there are forces working in the opposite direction as well. Many businesses continue to turn to the government for protection from competition. Public choice theory suggests that more, not less, regulation is often demanded by firms threatened with competition at home and abroad. More and more people seem to demand environmental protection, including clear air, clean water, and regulation of hazardous waste and toxic waste. Indeed, as incomes rise over time, there is evidence that the demand for safety rises. This market phenomenon began before the birth of regulatory agencies and can be seen in the decline in unintentional injury deaths over the course of the last hundred years.[8] And there is little reason to expect less demand for regulations in the areas of civil rights, handicapped rights, gay rights, medical care, and elderly care.

The basic test of rationality—that marginal benefits exceed marginal costs—should guide the formulation of regulations. While economists often disagree about which, if any, consumer protection regulations are warranted, they do tend to agree that market incentives ought to be used when appropriate and that the most cost-effective policies should be pursued.

Key Takeaways

- Federal, state, and local governments regulate the activities of firms and consumers.
- The public interest theory of regulation asserts that regulatory efforts act to move markets closer to their efficient solutions.
- The public choice theory of regulation argues that regulatory efforts serve private interests, not the public interest.
- Consumer protection efforts may sometimes be useful, but they tend to produce behavioral responses that often negate the effort at protection.
- Deregulation efforts through the 1990s generally produced large gains in consumer welfare, though demand for more regulation is rising in certain areas, especially finance.

Try It!

The deregulation of the airline industry has generally led to lower fares and increased quantities produced. Use the model of demand and supply to show this change. What has happened to consumer surplus in the market? (*Hint:* You may want to refer back to the earlier discussion of consumer surplus.)

Case in Point: Do Consumer Protection Laws Protect Consumers?

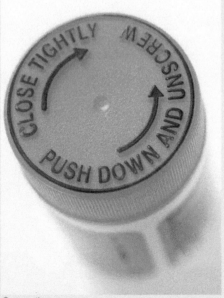

Source: © 2010 Jupiterimages Corporation

Economist W. Kip Viscusi of the Harvard Law School has long advocated economic approaches to health and safety regulations. Economic approaches recognize 1) behavioral responses to technological regulations; 2) performance-oriented standards as opposed to command-and-control regulations; and 3) the opportunity cost of regulations. Below are some examples of how these economic approaches would improve health and safety policy.

Behavioral responses: Consider the requirement, imposed in 1972, that aspirin containers have childproof caps. That technological change seemed straightforward enough. But, according to Mr. Viscusi, the result has not been what regulators expected. Mr. Viscusi points out that childproof caps are more difficult to open. They thus increase the cost of closing the containers properly. An increase in the cost of any activity reduces the quantity demanded. So, childproof caps result in fewer properly closed aspirin containers.

Mr. Viscusi calls the response to childproof caps a "lulling effect." Parents apparently think of containers as safer and are, as a result, less careful with them. Aspirin containers, as well as other drugs with childproof caps, tend to be left open. Mr. Viscusi says that the tragic result is a dramatic increase in the number of children poisoned each year. Hence, he urges government regulators to take behavioral responses into account when promulgating technological solutions. He also advocates well-articulated hazard warnings that give consumers information on which to make their own choices.

Performance-oriented standards: Once a health and safety problem has been identified, the economic approach would be to allow individuals or firms discretion in how to address the problem as opposed to mandating a precise solution. Flexibility allows a standard to be met in a less costly way and can have greater impact than command-and-control approaches. Mr. Viscusi cites empirical evidence that worker fatality rates would be about one-third higher were it not for the financial incentives firms derive from creating a safer workplace and thereby reducing the workers' compensation premiums they pay. In contrast, empirical estimates of the impact of OSHA regulations, most of which are of the command-and-control type, range from nil to a five to six percent reduction in worker accidents that involve days lost from work.

Opportunity cost of regulations: Mr. Viscusi has estimated the cost per life saved on scores of regulations. Some health and safety standards have fairly low cost per life saved. For example, car seat belts and airplane cabin fire protection cost about $100,000 per life saved. Automobile side impact standards and the children's sleepwear flammability ban, at about $1 million per life saved, are also fairly inexpensive. In contrast, the asbestos ban costs $131 million per life saved, regulations concerning municipal solid waste landfills cost about $23 billion per life saved, and regulations on Atrazine/alachlor in drinking water cost a whopping $100 billion per life saved. "A regulatory system based on sound economic principles would reallocate resources from the high-cost to the low-cost regulations. That would result in more lives saved at the same cost to society."

Sources: Based on W. Kip Viscusi, "Safety at Any Price?" Regulation, Fall 2002: 54–63; W. Kip Viscusi, "The Lulling Effect: The Impact of Protective Bottlecaps on Aspirin and Analgesic Poisonings," American Economic Review 74(2) (1984): 324–27.

Answer to Try It! Problem

Deregulation of the airline industry led to sharply reduced fares and expanded output, suggesting that supply increased. That should significantly increase consumer surplus. Specifically, the supply curve shifted from S_1 to S_2. Consumer surplus is the difference between the total benefit received by consumers and total expenditures by consumers. Before deregulation, when the price was B and the quantity was Q_1, the consumer surplus was BCD. The lower rates following deregulation reduced the price to consumers to, say, F, and increased the quantity to Q_2 on the graph, thereby increasing consumer surplus to FCG.

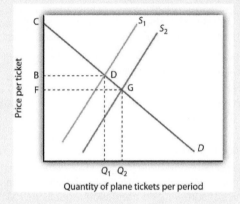

Quantity of plane tickets per period

16.5 Review and Practice

Summary

This chapter has shown that government intervention in markets takes the form of antitrust action to prevent the abuse of market power and regulations aimed at achieving socially desired objectives that are not or cannot be provided by an unregulated market system.

We saw that antitrust policy has evolved from a view that big business was bad business to an attempt to assess how the behavior of firms and the structure of markets affect social welfare and the public interest. The rule of reason rather than per se illegality guides most antitrust policy today, but because there is considerable debate concerning the appropriate role of government antitrust policy and regulation, application of the rule of reason in specific cases is uneven. Prosecution and enforcement of the nation's antitrust laws has varied over time.

The rising role of a global economy in the last half of the twentieth century reduced the degree of market power held by domestic firms. Policymakers have reconsidered antitrust policy and what types of joint ventures and cooperation among competing firms should be allowed. U.S. antitrust policy has not been abandoned, but since the early 1980s it has been applied with greater consideration of its implications for the competitiveness of U.S. businesses against Asian, European, and other firms. Whether or not antitrust laws among nations will be made more compatible with each other is an issue for the future.

We saw that there are many different schools of thought concerning regulation. One group believes that regulation serves the public interest. Another believes that much current regulation protects regulated firms from competitive market forces and that the regulators are captured by the firms they are supposed to regulate. Yet another group points out that the regulators may do little more than serve their own interests, which include increasing the bureaucratic reach of their agencies.

Finally, the chapter looked at the complex issues surrounding consumer protection regulations. Consumer protection legislation has costs, borne by consumers and taxpayers. Economists are not in agreement concerning which, if any, consumer protection regulations are warranted. They do agree, however, that market incentives ought to be used when appropriate and that the most cost-effective policies should be pursued.

Concept Problems

1. Apex Manufacturing charges Zenith Manufacturing with predatory pricing (that is, selling below cost). What do you think the antitrust authorities will want to consider before they determine whether to prosecute Zenith for unfair practices in restraint of trade?

2. Some states require firms to close on Sunday. What types of firms support these laws? Why? What types of firms do not support these laws? Why?

3. Individual taxis in New York, Chicago, and many other cities must have permits, but there are only a fixed number of permits. The permits are typically sold in the marketplace. Who benefits from such a regulation?

4. What do you predict is the impact on workers' wages of safety regulations in the workplace if the labor market is competitive?

5. Many states require barbers and beauticians to be licensed. Using the public interest theory of regulation as a base, what, if any, arguments could you make to support such a regulation? Do you think consumers gain from such regulations? Why not just allow anyone to open up a barber shop or beauty salon?

6. Suppose a landowner is required to refrain from developing his or her land in order to preserve the habitat of an endangered species. The restriction reduces the value of the land by 50%, to $1 million. Under present law, the landowner does not have to be compensated. Several proposals considered by Congress would require that this landowner be compensated. How does this affect the cost of the regulation?

7. A study by the Federal Trade Commission compared the prices of legal services in cities that allowed advertising by lawyers to prices of those same services in cities that did not. It found that the prices of simple wills with trust provisions were 11% higher in cities that did not allow advertising than they were in cities that did.[9] This, presumably, suggests the cost of such regulation. What might be the benefits? Do you think that such advertising should be restricted?

8. Economist W. Kip Viscusi, whose work was cited in the Case in Point, and Gerald Cavallo studied the effects of federal regulations requiring cigarette lighter safety mechanisms.[10] Explain how this technological improvement might improve safety and how it might reduce safety.

9. Explain how licensing requirements for providers of particular services result in higher prices for such services. Are such requirements justified? Why or why not?

10. What is so bad about price-fixing? Why does the government prohibit it?

11. In a 1956 antitrust case against DuPont, the Justice Department argued that the firm held a near monopoly in the cellophane market. DuPont argued that the definition of the market should be changed to include all wrapping paper. Why is this issue of market definition important? (DuPont's position prevailed.)

12. The Case in Point on the efficacy of antitrust enforcement painted a rather negative view of antitrust enforcement. Do you agree with this assessment? Why or why not?

13. The Case in Point on Boeing and the European Union discussed a situation in which a foreign government, the European Union, attempted to exert authority over a relationship between two U.S. firms. How is this possible?

Numerical Problems

In 1986, Pepsi announced its intention to buy 7-Up, and Coca-Cola proposed buying Dr Pepper. The table below shows the market shares held by the soft-drink firms in 1986. Assume that the remaining 15% of the market is composed of 15 firms, each with a market share of 1%.

Company	Market share (percent)
Coca-Cola	39
PepsiCo	28
Dr Pepper	7
7-Up	6

1. Calculate the Herfindahl–Hirschman Index (HHI) for the industry as it was structured in 1986.
2. Calculate the postmerger HHI if only PepsiCo had bought 7-Up.
3. Calculate the postmerger HHI if only Coca-Cola had bought Dr Pepper.
4. How would you expect the Justice Department to respond to each merger considered separately? To both?

(By the way, the proposed mergers *were* challenged, and neither was completed.)

Endnotes

1. Eric Dash, "MasterCard Will Pay $1.8 Billion to a Rival," *New York Times*, June 26, 2008, p. C4; and United States vs. Visa U.S.A., Inc., 344 F.3d 229 (2d. Circuit 2003); "The 40 Year War: Credit Cards and Antitrust Law," The American Banker, September 15, 2016 at http://www.americanbanker.com/gallery/the-40-year-war-credit-cards-and-antitrust-law-1068689-1.html

2. Complaint, United States of America, Department of Justice, Antitrust Division v. AT&T Inc, T-Mobile USA, Inc., and Deutsche Telekom AG, Case: 1:11-cv-01560, August 31, 2011.

3. G. J. Stigler, "The Economists and the Problem of Monopoly," *American Economic Review Papers and Proceedings* 72(2) (May 1982): 8–9.

4. Sam Peltzman, "The Effects of Automobile Safety Regulations," *Journal of Political Economy* 83 (August 1975): 677–725.

5. Alma Cohen and Liran Einan, "The Effects of Mandatory Seat Belt Laws on Driving Behaviour and Traffic Fatalities," *Review of Economics and Statistics* 85(4) (November 2003): 828–43.

6. W. Mark Crain and Thomas D. Hopkins, "The Impact of Regulatory Costs on Small Firms," Report for the Office of Advocacy, U.S. Small Business Administration, Washington, D.C., RFP No. SBAHQ-00-R-0027, October 2001, p. 1.

7. Clifford Winston, "U.S. Industry Adjustment to Economic Deregulation," *Journal of Economic Perspectives* 12(3) (Summer 1998): 89–110.

8. W. Kip Viscusi, "Safety at Any Price?" *Regulation*, Fall 2002: 54–63.

9. See Carolyn Cox and Susan Foster, "The Costs and Benefits of Occupational Regulation," Federal Trade Commission, October 1990, p. 31.

10. W. Kip Viscusi, "The Lulling Effect: The Impact of Protective Bottlecaps on Aspirin and Analgesic Poisonings," *American Economic Review* 74(2) (1984): 324–27.

CHAPTER 17

International Trade

17.1 Start Up: Trade Winds

Rapid increases in the flow of goods and services between vastly different nations and cultures have changed what people eat, how they dress, and even how they communicate with one another. For you, increased trade has meant greater choice of what to buy and often lower prices.

Look through your room. Chances are it is full of items from all around the world. The relatively free trade that exists today provides you with expanded choices. No one forced you to buy that shirt from India or that e-book reader whose components are manufactured in various countries in Asia. Presumably you bought them because you preferred them to other shirts and e-book readers you might have bought, perhaps because they had certain characteristics—style, color, perceived quality, or price—that you favored.

Your gains are being experienced worldwide because the winds of international trade have blown generally freer in the past few decades. Nations all over the world have dramatically lowered the barriers they impose on the products of other countries.

One region that was once closed to virtually all trade but is now open is Eastern Europe and the countries that made up the former Soviet Union. A key part of these countries' attempts to create market capitalist economic systems has been the opening of their borders to international trade.

In Western Europe, the members of the European Union (EU) have eliminated virtually every restriction on the free flow of goods and services among them. A truckload of electronic equipment from Italy now passes through France on its way to Spain with no more restrictions than would be encountered by a truck delivering goods from Michigan to Illinois. The purchase of the equipment can even be arranged using a new currency, the euro, which has been adopted by most EU nations.

Canada, Mexico, and the United States, while not adopting a common currency, have created a similar free trade area, the North American Free Trade Area (NAFTA). NAFTA has resulted in a dramatic increase in trade between Canada, the United States, and Mexico.

President Bush proposed and Congress passed in 2005 the creation of a Central American Free Trade Association (CAFTA) that would create a free trade area south of Mexico and linked to the United States. It abolished most tariff restrictions between the United States and six countries of Central America—Costa Rica, the Dominican Republic, El Salvador, Guatemala, Honduras, and Nicaragua. President Bush also proposed free trade agreements with Peru, Colombia, Panama, and South Korea. The agreement with Peru passed at the end of 2007. Free trade agreements with the other three countries finally passed under the administration of President Obama in late 2011.

While many other bilateral and regional free trade agreements have gone into effect in countries around the world, a major worldwide proposal has faltered. In 1995, the World Trade Organization (WTO) was established to "help trade flow smoothly, freely, fairly and predictably" among member nations. Since 2008, it has had 153 member countries. Since World War II, the General Agreement on Tariffs and Trade (GATT)—WTO's predecessor—and WTO have generated a series of agreements that slashed trade restraints among members. These agreements have helped propel international trade, but the negotiations leading to these agreements have always been protracted and tumultuous and issues of nationalism and patriotism are often not far from the surface. The current and ninth round of trade talks are referred to as the Doha Round, because they were officially launched in Doha, Qatar, in 2001. Fifteen years later, talks were still mired in controversy over the removal of agricultural export subsidies and lowering of trade barriers of various kinds.

Another proposal that seems to have faltered is the Trans-Pacific Partnership. This proposed agreement among 12 countries in the Pacific, including the United States and excluding China, was to lower various forms of trade barriers and included provisions related to such things as environmental and labor standards, protection of intellectual property, and mechanisms for settling disputes. For the United States, it was negotiated by the Obama administration. During the 2016 U.S. presidential election campaign, both major party candidates announced their opposition to the agreement, and in January 2017, President Trump signed an executive order withdrawing the United States. Whether other countries involved will go ahead or whether another agreement, perhaps including China, will come into play is still unknown.

Still trade is more extensive and much freer than it was fifty or one hundred years ago. The 2008 financial crisis severely tested the attitudes of many countries toward working toward and implementing agreements that lead to freer trade. Some countries did take protectionist measures, but by and large they held to their trading system commitments and did not adopt import restrictions. A 2010 study by Hiau Looi Kee, Cristina Neagu, and Alessandro Nicita for the World Bank found that while many countries did adjust their tariffs upward or impose other restrictions on selective products, most changes were on products that did not have a significant effect on trade flows. They estimated that these protectionist policies explain less than 2% of the decline in world trade that occurred during the crisis period.[1]

Why have so many countries moved to make trade freer? What are the effects of free trade? Why do efforts to eliminate trade restrictions meet with resistance? Why do many nations continue to impose barriers against some foreign goods and services? How do such barriers affect the economy? How do such barriers affect *you*? Why has there been a call by some in the United States and in some other countries in recent years to dial back trade agreements?

This chapter will answer these questions by developing a model of international trade based on the idea of comparative advantage, introduced in an earlier chapter. The model predicts that free international trade will benefit the countries that participate in it. Free trade does not benefit every individual, however. Most people benefit from free trade, but some are hurt. We will then look at the phenomenon of two-way trade, in which countries both import and export the same goods. The last part of the chapter examines the effects of trade restrictions and evaluates the arguments made for such restrictions. Economists tend to be skeptical of their validity.

17.2 The Gains from Trade

Learning Objectives

1. Differentiate between an absolute advantage in producing some good and a comparative advantage.
2. Explain and illustrate the conditions under which two countries can mutually benefit from trading with each other.
3. Explain and illustrate how the terms of trade determine the extent to which each country specializes.
4. Explain and illustrate the mutual benefits of trade.

To model the effects of trade, we begin by looking at a hypothetical country that does not engage in trade and then see how its production and consumption change when it does engage in trade.

Production and Consumption Without International Trade

Suppose the hypothetical country of Roadway is completely isolated from the rest of the world. It neither exports nor imports goods and services. We shall use the production possibilities model to analyze Roadway's ability to produce goods and services.

A production possibilities curve illustrates the production choices available to an economy. Recall that the production possibilities curve for a particular country is determined by the factors of production and the technology available to it.

Figure 17.1 shows a production possibilities curve for Roadway. We assume that it produces only two goods—trucks and boats. Roadway must be operating somewhere on its production possibilities curve or it will be wasting resources or engaging in inefficient production. If it were operating inside the curve at a point such as D, then a combination on the curve, such as B, would provide more of both goods (Roadway produces 3,000 more trucks and 3,000 more boats per year at B than at D). At any point inside the curve, Roadway's production would not be efficient. Point E suggests an even higher level of output than points A, B, or C, but because point E lies outside Roadway's production possibilities curve, it cannot be attained.

We have learned that the absolute value of the slope of a production possibilities curve at any point gives the quantity of the good on the vertical axis that must be given up to produce an additional unit of the good on the horizontal axis. It thus gives the opportunity cost of producing another unit of the good on the horizontal axis.

FIGURE 17.1 Roadway's Production Possibilities Curve

The production possibilities curve for Roadway shows the combinations of trucks and boats that it can produce, given the factors of production and technology available to it. To maximize the value of total production, Roadway must be operating somewhere along this curve. Production at point D implies that Roadway is failing to use its resources fully and efficiently; production at point E is unobtainable.

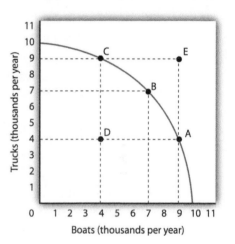

FIGURE 17.2 Measuring Opportunity Cost in Roadway

The slope of the production possibilities curve at any point is equal to the slope of a line tangent to the curve at that point. The absolute value of the slope equals the opportunity cost of increased boat production. Moving down and to the right along its production possibilities curve, the opportunity cost of boat production increases; this is an application of the law of increasing opportunity cost.

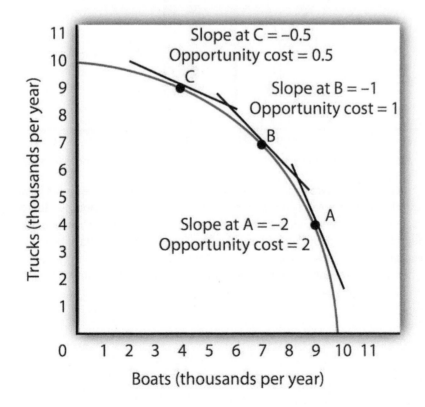

462   **Principles of Economics**

Figure 17.2 shows the opportunity cost of producing boats at points A, B, and C. Recall that the slope of a curve at any point is equal to the slope of a line drawn tangent to the curve at that point. The slope of a line tangent to the production possibilities curve at point B, for example, is -1. The opportunity cost of producing one more boat is thus one truck. As the law of increasing opportunity costs predicts, in order to produce more boats, Roadway must give up more and more trucks for each additional boat. Roadway's opportunity cost of producing boats increases as we travel down and to the right on its production possibilities curve.

Comparative Advantage

People participate in international trade because they make themselves better off by doing so. In this section we will find that countries that participate in international trade are able to consume more of all goods and services than they could consume while producing in isolation from the rest of the world.

Suppose the world consists of two countries, Roadway and Seaside. Their production possibilities curves are given in Figure 17.3. Roadway's production possibilities curve in Panel (a) is the same as the one in Figure 17.1 and Figure 17.2. Seaside's curve is given in Panel (b).

FIGURE 17.3 Comparative Advantage in Roadway and Seaside
Roadway's production possibilities curve is given in Panel (a); it is the same one we saw in Figure 17.1 and Figure 17.2. The production possibilities curve for a second hypothetical country, Seaside, is given in Panel (b). If no trade occurs between the two countries, suppose that Roadway is at Point A and that Seaside is at Point A′. Notice that the opportunity cost of an additional boat in Roadway is two trucks, while the opportunity cost of an additional boat in Seaside is 0.2 trucks. Clearly, Seaside has a comparative advantage in the production of boats.

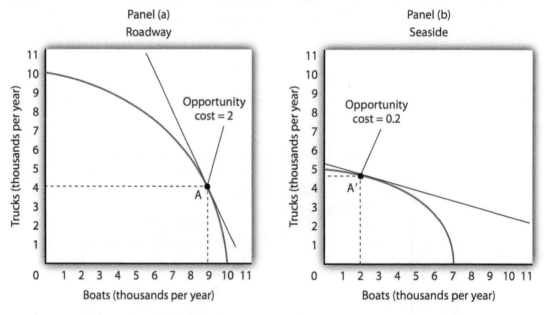

Each country produces two goods, boats and trucks. Suppose no trade occurs between the two countries and that they are each currently operating on their production possibilities curves at points A and A′ in Figure 17.3. We will assume that the two countries have chosen to operate at these points through the workings of demand and supply. That is, resources have been guided to their current uses as producers have responded to the demands of consumers in the two countries. In turn, consumers have responded to the prices charged by sellers of boats and trucks.

The two countries differ in their respective abilities to produce trucks and boats. As we can see by looking at the intersection of the production possibilities curves with the vertical axes in Figure 17.3, Roadway is able to produce more trucks than Seaside. If Roadway concentrated all of its resources on the production of trucks, it could produce 10,000 trucks per year. Seaside could produce only 5,000. Now look at the intersection of the production possibilities curves with the horizontal axes. If Roadway concentrated all of its resources on the production of boats, it could produce 10,000 boats. Seaside could produce only 7,000 boats. Because Roadway is capable of producing more of both goods, we can infer that it has more resources or is able to use its labor and capital resources more productively than Seaside. When an economy or individual can produce more of any good per unit of labor than another country or individual, that country or person is said to have an **absolute advantage.**

Despite the fact that Roadway can produce more of both goods, it can still gain from trade with Seaside—and Seaside can gain from trade with Roadway. The key lies in the opportunity costs of the two goods in the two countries. The country with a lower opportunity cost for a particular good or service has a comparative advantage in producing it and will export it to the other country.

We can determine opportunity costs in the two countries by comparing the slopes of their respective production possibilities curves at the points where they are producing. At point A in Panel (a) of Figure 17.3, one additional boat costs two trucks in Roadway; that is its opportunity cost. At point A′ in Panel (b), 1 additional boat in Seaside costs only 0.2 truck. Alternatively, we can ask about the opportunity cost of an additional truck. In Roadway, an additional truck costs 0.5 boats. In Seaside, it costs five boats. Roadway thus has a comparative advantage in producing trucks; Seaside has a comparative advantage in producing boats. This situation is suggested pictorially in Figure 17.4.

FIGURE 17.4 A Picture of Comparative Advantage in Roadway and Seaside
The exhibit gives a picture of Roadway's comparative advantage in trucks and Seaside's comparative advantage in boats.

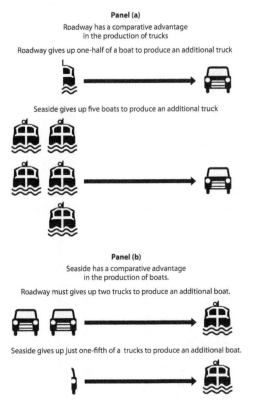

Panel (a)
Roadway has a comparative advantage in the production of trucks

Roadway gives up one-half of a boat to produce an additional truck

Seaside gives up five boats to produce an additional truck

Panel (b)
Seaside has a comparative advantage in the production of boats.

Roadway must gives up two trucks to produce an additional boat.

Seaside gives up just one-fifth of a trucks to produce an additional boat.

Specialization and the Gains from Trade

We have so far assumed that no trade occurs between Roadway and Seaside. Now let us assume that trade opens up. The fact that the opportunity costs differ between the two countries suggests the possibility for mutually advantageous trade. The opportunities created by trade will induce a greater degree of specialization in both countries, specialization that reflects comparative advantage.

Trade and Specialization

Before trade, truck producers in Roadway could exchange a truck for half a boat. In Seaside, however, a truck could be exchanged for five boats. Once trade opens between the two countries, truck producers in Roadway will rush to export trucks to Seaside.

Boat producers in Seaside enjoy a similar bonanza. Before trade, one of their boats could be exchanged for one-fifth of a truck. By shipping their boats to Roadway, they can get two trucks for each boat. Boat producers in Seaside will rush to export boats to Roadway.

terms of trade

The rate at which a country can trade domestic products for imported products.

Once trade between Roadway and Seaside begins, the **terms of trade**, the rate at which a country can trade domestic products for imported products, will seek market equilibrium. The final terms of trade will be somewhere between one-half boats for one truck found in Roadway and five boats for one truck in Seaside. Suppose the terms of trade are one boat for one truck. (How the specific terms of trade are actually determined is not important for this discussion. It is enough to know that the final terms of trade will lie somewhere between Seaside's and Roadway's opportunity costs for boat and truck production.) Roadway's truck producers will now get one boat per truck—a far better exchange than was available to them before trade.

Roadway's manufacturers will move to produce more trucks and fewer boats until they reach the point on their production possibilities curve at which the terms of trade equals the opportunity cost of producing trucks. That occurs at point B in Panel (a) of Figure 17.5; Roadway now produces 7,000 trucks and 7,000 boats per year.

FIGURE 17.5 International Trade Induces Greater Specialization

Before trade, Roadway is producing at point A in Panel (a) and Seaside is producing at point A′ in Panel (b). The terms of trade are one, meaning that one boat exchanges for one truck. Roadside moves along its production possibilities curve to point B, at which the curve has a slope of −1. Roadside will produce more trucks (and fewer boats). Seaside moves along its production possibilities curve to point B′, at which the slope equals −1. Seaside will produce more boats (and fewer trucks). Trade leads each country in the direction of producing more of the good in which it has a comparative advantage.

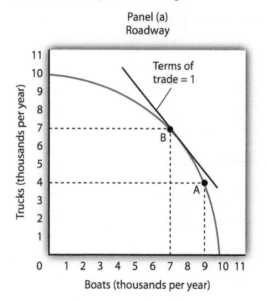

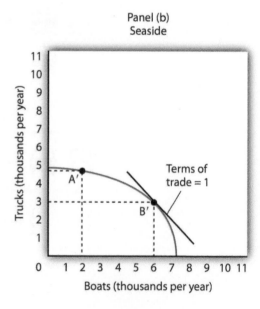

Similarly, Seaside will specialize more in boat production. As shown in Panel (b) of Figure 17.5, producers will shift resources out of truck production and into boat production until they reach the point on their production possibilities curve at which the terms of trade equal the opportunity cost of producing boats. This occurs at point B'; Seaside produces 3,000 trucks and 6,000 boats per year.

We see that trade between the two countries causes each country to specialize in the good in which it has a comparative advantage. Roadway produces more trucks, and Seaside produces more boats. The specialization is not, however, complete. The law of increasing opportunity cost means that, as an economy moves along its production possibilities curve, the cost of additional units rises. An economy with a comparative advantage in a particular good will expand its production of that good only up to the point where its opportunity cost equals the terms of trade.

As a result of trade, Roadway now produces more trucks and fewer boats. Seaside produces more boats and fewer trucks. Through exchange, however, both countries are likely to end up consuming more of *both* goods.

Figure 17.6 shows one such possibility. Suppose Roadway ships 2,500 trucks per year to Seaside in exchange for 2,500 boats, as shown in the table in Figure 17.6. Roadway thus emerges with 4,500 trucks (the 7,000 it produces at B minus the 2,500 it ships) and 9,500 boats. It has 500 more of each good than it did before trade. The precise amounts of each good shipped will depend on demand an supply. The essential point is that Roadway will produce more of the good—trucks—in which it has a comparative advantage. It will export that good to a country, or countries, that has a comparative advantage in something else.

FIGURE 17.6 The Mutual Benefits of Trade

Roadway and Seaside each consume more of both goods when there is trade between them. The table shows values of production before trade (BT) and after trade (AT). Here, the terms of trade are one truck in exchange for one boat. As shown in Panel (a) and in the exhibit's table, Roadway exports 2,500 trucks to Seaside in exchange for 2,500 boats and ends up consuming at point C, which is outside its production possibilities curve. Similarly, in Panel (b), Seaside ends up consuming at point C', which is outside its production possibilities curve. Trade allows both countries to consume more than they are capable of producing.

Production and Consumption of Trucks and Boats							
	Roadway				Seaside		
	Production		Consumption		Production		Consumption	
	BT	AT	BT	AT	BT	AT	BT	AT
Trucks	4,000	7,000	4,000	4,500	4,750	3,000	4,750	5,500
Boats	9,000	7,000	9,000	9,500	2,000	6,000	2,000	3,500

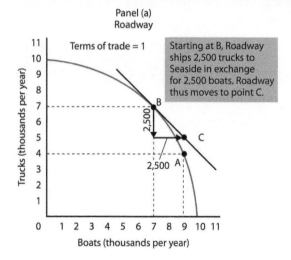

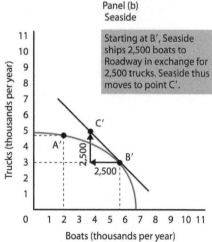

How does Seaside fare? When trade began, factors of production shifted into boat production, in which Seaside had a comparative advantage. Seaside tripled its production of boats—from 2,000 per year to 6,000 per year. It sends 2,500 of those boats to Roadway, so it ends up with 3,500 boats per year. It reduces its production of trucks to 3,000 per year, but receives 2,500 more from Roadway. That leaves it with 5,500. Seaside emerges from the opening of trade with 1,500 more boats and 750 more trucks than it had before trade.

As Roadway trades trucks for boats, its production remains at point B. But it now consumes combination C; it has more of both goods than it had at A, the solution before trade. Seaside's production remains at point B′, but it now consumes at point C′, where it has more trucks and more boats than it had before trade.

Although all countries can increase their consumption through trade, not everyone in those countries will be happy with the result. In the case of Roadway and Seaside, for example, some boat producers in Roadway will be displaced as cheaper boats arrive from Seaside. Some truck producers in Seaside will be displaced as cheaper trucks arrive from Roadway. The production possibilities model suggests that the resources displaced will ultimately find more productive uses. They will produce trucks in Roadway and boats in Seaside. *But* there will be a period of painful transition as workers and owners of capital and natural resources move from one activity to another. That transition will be completed when the two countries are back on their respective production possibilities curves. Full employment will be restored, which means both countries will be back at the same level of employment they had before trade.

Finally, note the fact that the two countries end up at C (Panel (a)) and C′ (Panel (b)). These points lie *outside* the production possibilities curves of both countries. Notice that each country *produces* on its production possibilities curve, but international trade allows both countries to *consume* a combination of goods they would be incapable of producing!

We see this same phenomenon in individual households. Each household specializes in an activity in which it has a comparative advantage. For one household, that may be landscaping, for another, it may be the practice of medicine, for another it may be the provision of childcare. Whatever the activity, specialization allows the household to earn income that can be used to purchase housing, food, clothing, and so on. Imagine for a moment how your household would fare if it had to produce every good or service it consumed. The members of such a household would work very hard, but it is inconceivable that the household could survive if it relied on itself for everything it consumed. By specializing in the activity in which each individual has a comparative advantage, people are able to consume far more than they could produce themselves.

Despite the transitional problems affecting some factors of production, the potential benefits from free trade are large. For this reason, most economists are strongly in favor of opening markets and extending international trade throughout the world. The economic case has been a powerful force in moving the world toward freer trade.

Key Takeaways

- In order to maximize the value of its output, a country must be producing a combination of goods and services that lies on its production possibilities curve.
- Suppose two countries each produce two goods and their opportunity costs differ. If this is the case, there is an opportunity for trade between the two countries that will leave both better off.
- International trade leads countries to specialize in goods and services in which they have a comparative advantage.
- The terms of trade determine the extent to which each country will specialize. Each will increase production of the good or service in which it has a comparative advantage up to the point where the opportunity cost of producing it equals the terms of trade.

- Free international trade can increase the availability of all goods and services in all the countries that participate in it. Trade allows countries to consume combinations of goods and services they would be unable to produce.
- While free trade increases the total quantity of goods and services available to each country, there are both winners and losers in the short run.

Try It!

Suppose the world consists of two countries, Alpha and Beta. Both produce only two goods, computers and washing machines. Suppose that Beta is much more populous than Alpha, but because workers in Alpha have more physical and human capital, Alpha is able to produce more of both goods than Beta.

Specifically, suppose that if Alpha devotes all its factors of production to computers, it is able to produce 10,000 per month, and if it devotes all its factors of production to washing machines, it is able to produce 10,000 per month. Suppose the equivalent amounts for Beta are 8,000 computers and 8,000 washing machines per month. Sketch typical, bowed-out production possibilities curves for the two countries. (You only have numbers for the end points of the production possibilities curves. Use them to sketch curves of a typical shape. Place washing machines on the vertical axis and computers on the horizontal axis.)

Assume the computers and washing machines produced in the two countries are identical. Assume that no trade occurs between the two countries. In Alpha, at the point on its production possibilities curve at which it is operating, the opportunity cost of an additional washing machine is 0.5 computers. At the point on its production possibilities curve at which it is operating, the opportunity cost of an additional washing machine in Beta is 3.5 computers. How many computers exchange for a washing machine in Alpha? Beta?

Now suppose trade occurs, and the terms of trade are two washing machines for one computer. How will the production of the two goods be affected in each economy? Show your results graphically and explain them.

Case in Point: Where Does U.S. Comparative Advantage Lie?

Source: © 2010 Jupiterimages Corporation

A flight across the United States almost gives a birds-eye view of an apparent comparative advantage for the United States. One sees vast expanses of farmland. Surely agricultural goods represent an important comparative advantage for the United States.

Indeed, agricultural goods did once dominate American exports but those days are long gone. As the pie charts below show, agricultural goods were 15% of U.S. exports in 1980 but were only 6% in 2014. In contrast, manufactured goods' share has held steady at about 60% over the 34-year period, while exports of services have increased from 18% to 30%.

FIGURE 17.7 Composition of U.S. Exports, 1980 and 2014

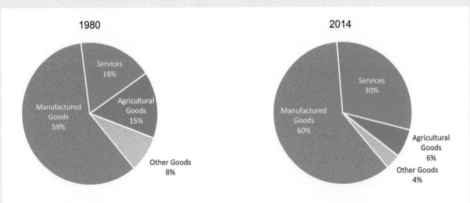

Source: Based on data from U.S. Census Bureau, Foreign Trade Statistics; Bureau of Economic Analysis, International Services; U.S. Department of Agriculture, Foreign Agricultural Trade of the United States; CEA Calculations. The Economic Benefits of Trade, May 2015, Executive Office of the President of the United States

In terms of size, the time-series graph shows that over the same period, agricultural exports have grown about 50%, manufactured goods exports about four-fold, and service exports about six-fold.

FIGURE 17.8 U.S. Exports of Goods and Services, 1980-2014
Note: All values in real 2009 dollars, deflated using the U.S. GDP deflator.

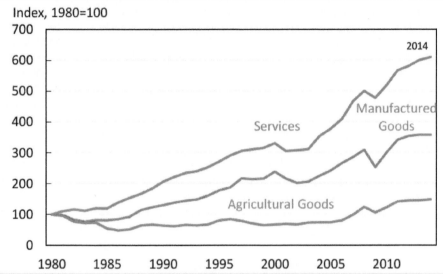

Source: Based on data from U.S. Census Bureau, Foreign Trade Statistics; Bureau of Economic Analysis,
International Services; U.S. Department of Agriculture, Foreign Agricultural Trade of the United States. The
Economics Benefits of U.S. Trade, May 2015, Executive Office of the President of the United States.

What types of goods in each category are exported? In colonial times, tobacco and cotton were the primary agricultural exports. Today, the top three categories of agricultural exports are oilseeds and pulses (such as soybeans and oil), horticultural products (such as vegetables and nuts), and grains and feeds (such as wheat, rice and corn). Remarkably, in 2014, about half of U.S.-produced wheat, rice, and soybeans were exported. Interestingly, trade has offered agricultural producers a better market for some products in low demand (and hence low- priced) domestically. For example, the U.S. exports chicken paws to China.

The U.S. Bureau of Economic Analysis has developed nine broad categories of services that are tradable: insurance; government; financial; travel; maintenance and repair; telecom, computers, and information; transport; intellectual property; and other business services. All of these categories have been growing, but the categories that have experienced the fastest growth are insurance and financial services.

Contrary to popular lore, exports of manufactured goods have also increased—by 40% between 2009 and 2014. While the U.S. still has a trade deficit in this category, it has shrunk 20% since its peak in 2006. The categories of exported manufactured goods that dominate are machines, electronic equipment, aircraft, and vehicles.

However, due to the increased use of global supply chains, the gross dollar amounts of manufactured goods do not really tell the full story of where U.S. comparative advantage in manufactured goods lies. Apple products illustrate the point. While, for example, the iPhone is *assembled* in China, it is designed in the U.S. and its components are produced by factories located in many other countries. In an award-winning thesis for her undergraduate degree at Harvard, Lauren Dai used a fairly new database, the World Input-Output Database, to look at global value chains. She concluded that richer countries, like Japan and the U.S., dominate early stages of production or "upstream of global supply chains." She found that while the gross trade statistics suggest that the U.S. may be losing its comparative advantage in electronics, in fact the U.S. edge in this industry, as well as in high-technology manufacturing industries, remains strong.

Sources: Based on U.S. Council of Economic Advisers, The Economic Benefits of U.S. Trade, May 2015, at https://www.whitehouse.gov/administration/eop/cea/factsheets-reports; Lauren Dai, "The Comparative Advantage of Nations: How Global Supply Chains Change Our Understanding of Comparative Advantage," Harvard Political Review, features, June 25, 2013, at http://harvardpolitics.com/features/senior-theses-collection/the-comparative-advantage-of-nations-how-global-supply-chains-change-our-understanding-of-comparative-advantage/.

Answer to Try It! Problem

Here are sketches of possible production possibilities curves. Alpha is operating at a point such as R_1, while Beta is operating at a point such as S_1. In Alpha, 1 computer trades for 2 washing machines; in Beta, 3.5 computers trade for one washing machine. If trade opens between the two economies and the terms of trade are 1.5, then Alpha will produce more washing machines and fewer computers (moving to a point such as R_2), while Beta will produce more computers and fewer washing machines (moving to a point such as S_2). Though you were not asked to do this, the graphs demonstrate that it is possible that trade will result in both countries having more of both goods. If, for example, Alpha ships 2,000 washing machines to Beta in exchange for 3,000 computers, then the two economies will move to points R_3 and S_3, respectively, consuming more of both goods than they had before trade. There are many points along the tangent lines drawn at points R_2 and S_2 that are up to the right and therefore contain more of both goods. We have chosen points R_3 and S_3 at specific points, but any point along the tangent line that is up to the right from R_1 and S_1 would suffice to illustrate the fact that both countries can end up consuming more of both goods.

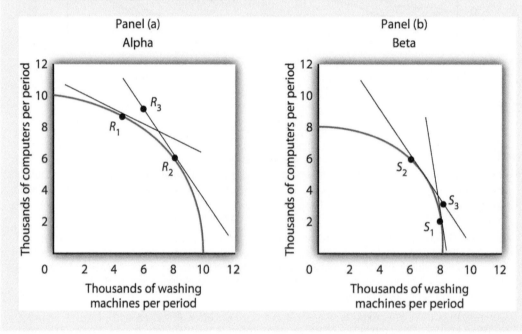

17.3 Two-Way Trade

Learning Objectives

1. Distinguish between one-way trade and two-way trade.
2. Explain why two-way trade may occur.

The model of trade presented thus far assumed that countries specialize in producing the good in which they have a comparative advantage and, therefore, engage in one-way trade. **One-way (or interindustry) trade** occurs when countries specialize in producing the goods in which they have a comparative advantage and then export those goods so they can import the goods in which they do not have a comparative advantage.

However, when we look at world trade, we also see countries exchanging the same goods or goods in the same industry category. For example, the United States may both export construction materials to Canada and import them from Canada. American car buyers can choose Chevrolets, Fords, and Chryslers. They can also choose imported cars such as Toyotas. Japanese car buyers may choose to purchase Toyotas—or imported cars such as Chevrolets, Fords, and Chryslers. The United States imports cars from Japan and exports cars to it. Conversely, Japan imports cars from the United States and exports cars to it. International trade in which countries both import and export the same or similar goods is called **two-way (or intraindustry) trade.**

Two reasons countries import and export the same goods are variations in transportation costs and seasonal effects. In the example of the United States and Canada both importing and exporting construction materials, transportation costs are the likely explanation. It may be cheaper for a contractor in northern Maine to import construction materials from the eastern part of Canada than to buy them in the United States. For a contractor in Vancouver, British Columbia, it may be cheaper to import construction materials from somewhere in the western part of the United States than to buy them in Canada. By engaging in trade, both the American and Canadian contractors save on transportation costs. Seasonal factors explain why the United States both imports fruit from and exports fruit to Chile.

Another explanation of two-way trade in similar goods lies in recognizing that not all goods are produced under conditions of perfect competition. Once this assumption is relaxed, we can explain two-way trade in terms of a key feature of monopolistic competition and some cases of oligopoly: product differentiation. Suppose two countries have similar endowments of factors of production and technologies available to them, but their products are differentiated—clocks produced by different manufacturers, for example, are different. Consumers in the United States buy some clocks produced in Switzerland, just as consumers in Switzerland purchase some clocks produced in the United States. Indeed, if two countries are similar in their relative endowments of factors of production and in the technologies available to them, two-way trade based on product differentiation is likely to be more significant than one-way trade based on comparative advantage.

In comparison to the expansion of one-way trade based on comparative advantage, expansion of two-way trade may entail lower adjustment costs. In the case of two-way trade, there is specialization within industries rather than movement of factors of production out of industries that compete with newly imported goods and into export industries. Such adjustments are likely to be faster and less painful for labor and for the owners of the capital and natural resources involved.

Because two-way trade often occurs in the context of imperfect competition, we cannot expect it to meet the efficiency standards of one-way trade based on comparative advantage and the underlying assumption of perfectly competitive markets. But, as we discussed in the chapter on imperfect competition, the inefficiency must be weighed against the benefits derived from product differentiation. People in the United States are not limited to buying only the kinds of cars produced in the United States, just as people in Japan are not limited to buying only cars produced in Japan.

one-way (or interindustry) trade

Situation in which countries specialize in producing the goods in which they have a comparative advantage and then export those goods so they can import the goods in which they do not have a comparative advantage.

two-way (or intraindustry) trade

International trade in which countries both import and export the same or similar goods.

Key Takeaways

- Specialization and trade according to comparative advantage leads to one-way trade.
- A large percentage of trade among countries with similar factor endowments is two-way trade, in which countries import and export the same or similar goods and services.

- Two-way trade is often explained by variations in transportation costs and seasonal factors; in similar goods it often occurs in the context of models of imperfect competition.
- Adjustment costs associated with expansion of two-way trade may be lower than for expansion of one-way trade.

Try It!

The text argues that two-way trade must be a result of transportation cost, climate, or imperfect competition. Explain why.

Case in Point: Two- Way Trade in Water: A Growth Industry

Source: © 2010 Jupiterimages Corporation

In the 1930s, the successful introduction into the United States of French-made Perrier showed that U.S. consumers were open to a "new" bottled beverage. Since then, the U.S. bottled water business has taken off and bottled water is now the second largest commercial beverage category by volume, after carbonated soft drinks.

Seeing the increased popularity of bottled water, both PepsiCo and Coca-Cola launched their own bottled water brands, Aquafina and Dasani, respectively. Both of these brands are made from purified tap water. Dasani has minerals added back into it; Aquafina does not. Other brands of water come from springs or artesian wells. While domestic brands of water have multiplied, Americans still drink some imported brands, though imported brands represent only about 1.5% of U.S. consumption.

U.S. bottled water companies are also eyeing markets in other countries. As *New York Times* columnist and book author Thomas Friedman noted as he was being shown around a customer call center in Bangalore, India, the water on the desktops of the telemarketers was none other than Coke's Dasani. One of the authors of this textbook spent an evening in a small town in Turkey about halfway between Istanbul and Ankara called Kizilcahamam (meaning "reddish baths") and learned from a local municipal publication in the hotel room that mineral water from the town is exported to Iran, Iraq, Syria, Afghanistan, and Azerbaijan.

Whether the differences in brands of water are perceived or real, it may not be too long before restaurants develop water lists next to their beer and wine lists. In the United Stages and in other countries around the world, there is likely to be a domestic section and an imported section on those lists. Two-way trade in water seems destined to be a growth industry for some time to come.

Sources: Based on Thomas L. Friedman, "What Goes Around..." The New York Times, February 26, 2004, p. A27; Tom McGrath and Kate Dailey, "Liquid Assets," Men's Health 19:2 (March 2004): 142–49; Statistics from Beverage Marketing Corporation, press release "Bottled Water Recovers Somewhat From Recessionary Years, New Report From Beverage Marketing Corporation Shows," September 2011, http://www.beveragemarketing.com/?section=pressreleases.

Answer to Try It! Problem

In the absence of one of these factors, there would only be one-way, or interindustry, trade, which would take place according to comparative advantage, as described in the first section of this chapter, with a country specializing in and exporting the goods in which it has a comparative advantage and importing goods in which it does not. Efficiency differences would be the only basis for trade.

17.4 Restrictions on International Trade

Learning Objectives

1. Define the term protectionist policy and illustrate the general impact in a market subject to protectionist policy.
2. Describe the various forms of protectionist policy.
3. Discuss and assess the arguments used to justify trade restrictions.

In spite of the strong theoretical case that can be made for free international trade, every country in the world has erected at least some barriers to trade. Trade restrictions are typically undertaken in an effort to protect companies and workers in the home economy from competition by foreign firms. A **protectionist policy** is one in which a country restricts the importation of goods and services produced in foreign countries. The slowdown in the U.S. economy late in 2007 and in 2008 produced a new round of protectionist sentiment—one that became a factor in the 2008 U.S. presidential campaign.

protectionist policy

Policy that restricts the importation of goods and services produced in foreign countries.

The United States, for example, uses protectionist policies to limit the quantity of foreign-produced sugar coming into the United States. The effect of this policy is to reduce the supply of sugar in the U.S. market and increase the price of sugar in the United States. The 2008 U.S. Farm Bill sweetened things for sugar growers even more. It raised the price they are guaranteed to receive and limited imports of foreign sugar so that American growers will always have at least 85% of the domestic market. The bill for the first time set an income limit—only growers whose incomes fall below $1.5 million per year (for couples) or $750,000 for individuals will receive direct subsidies.[2]

The U.S. price of sugar is almost triple the world price of sugar, thus reducing the quantity consumed in the United States. The program benefits growers of sugar beets and sugar cane at the expense of consumers.

Calls for more protectionism were also part of the 2016 U.S. presidential campaign. The candidates from both major parties came out against the proposed Trans-Pacific Partnership agreement. In addition, the platforms of both parties suggested employing protectionist measures when trade seemed unfair, for one reason or another.

In general, protectionist policies imposed for a particular good always reduce its supply, raise its price, and reduce the equilibrium quantity, as shown in Figure 17.9. Protection often takes the form of an import tax or a limit on the amount that can be imported, but it can also come in the form of voluntary export restrictions and other barriers.

FIGURE 17.9 The Impact of Protectionist Policies

Protectionist policies reduce the quantities of foreign goods and services supplied to the country that imposes the restriction. As a result, such policies shift the supply curve to the left for the good or service whose imports are restricted. In the case shown, the supply curve shifts to S_2, the equilibrium price rises to P_2, and the equilibrium quantity falls to Q_2.

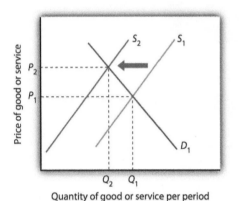

Tariffs

A **tariff** is a tax on imported goods and services. The average tariff on dutiable imports in the United States (that is, those imports on which a tariff is imposed) is about 4%. Some imports have much higher tariffs. For example, the U.S. tariff on imported frozen orange juice is 35 cents per gallon (which amounts to about 40% of value). The tariff on imported canned tuna is 35%, and the tariff on imported shoes ranges between 2% and 48%.

A tariff raises the cost of selling imported goods. It thus shifts the supply curve for goods to the left, as in Figure 17.9. The price of the protected good rises and the quantity available to consumers falls.

Antidumping Proceedings

tariff

A tax on imported goods and services.

dumping

The practice of a foreign firm charging a price in other countries that is below the price it charges in its home country.

One of the most common protectionist measures now in use is the antidumping proceeding. A domestic firm, faced with competition by a foreign competitor, files charges with its government that the foreign firm is **dumping**, or charging an "unfair" price. Under rules spelled out in international negotiations that preceded approval of the World Trade Organization, an unfair price was defined as a price below production cost or below the price the foreign firm charges for the same good in its own country. While these definitions may seem straightforward enough, they have proven to be quite troublesome. The definition of "production cost" is a thoroughly arbitrary procedure. In defining cost, the government agency invariably includes a specification of a "normal" profit. That normal profit can be absurdly high. The United States Department of Justice, which is the U.S. agency in charge of determining whether a foreign firm has charged an unfair price, has sometimes defined normal profit rates as exceeding production cost by well over 50%, a rate far higher than exists in most U.S. industry.

The practice of a foreign firm charging a price in the United States that is below the price it charges in its home country is common. The U.S. market may be more competitive, or the foreign firm may simply be trying to make its product attractive to U.S. buyers that are not yet accustomed to its product. In any event, such price discrimination behavior is not unusual and is not necessarily "unfair."

In the United States, once the Department of Justice has determined that a foreign firm is guilty of charging an unfair price, the U.S. International Trade Commission must determine that the foreign firm has done material harm to the U.S. firm. If a U.S. firm has suffered a reduction in sales and thus in employment it will typically be found to have suffered material harm, and punitive duties will be imposed.

Quotas

A **quota** is a direct restriction on the total quantity of a good or service that may be imported during a specified period. Quotas restrict total supply and therefore increase the domestic price of the good or service on which they are imposed. Quotas generally specify that an exporting country's share of a domestic market may not exceed a certain limit.

In some cases, quotas are set to raise the domestic price to a particular level. Congress requires the Department of Agriculture, for example, to impose quotas on imported sugar to keep the wholesale price in the United States above 22 cents per pound. The world price is typically less than 10 cents per pound.

A quota restricting the quantity of a particular good imported into an economy shifts the supply curve to the left, as in Figure 17.9. It raises price and reduces quantity.

An important distinction between quotas and tariffs is that quotas do not increase costs to foreign producers; tariffs do. In the short run, a tariff will reduce the profits of foreign exporters of a good or service. A quota, however, raises price but not costs of production and thus may increase profits. Because the quota imposes a limit on quantity, any profits it creates in other countries will not induce the entry of new firms that ordinarily eliminates profits in perfect competition. By definition, entry of new foreign firms to earn the profits available in the United States is blocked by the quota.

> **quota**
>
> A direct restriction on the total quantity of a good or service that may be imported during a specified period.

Voluntary Export Restrictions

Voluntary export restrictions are a form of trade barrier by which foreign firms agree to limit the quantity of goods exported to a particular country. They became prominent in the United States in the 1980s, when the U.S. government persuaded foreign exporters of automobiles and steel to agree to limit their exports to the United States.

Although such restrictions are called voluntary, they typically are agreed to only after pressure is applied by the country whose industries they protect. The United States, for example, has succeeded in pressuring many other countries to accept quotas limiting their exports of goods ranging from sweaters to steel.

A voluntary export restriction works precisely like an ordinary quota. It raises prices for the domestic product and reduces the quantity consumed of the good or service affected by the quota. It can also increase the profits of the firms that agree to the quota because it raises the price they receive for their products.

> **voluntary export restrictions**
>
> A form of trade barrier by which foreign firms agree to limit the quantity of goods exported to a particular country.

Other Barriers

In addition to tariffs and quotas, measures such as safety standards, labeling requirements, pollution controls, and quality restrictions all may have the effect of restricting imports.

Many restrictions aimed at protecting consumers in the domestic market create barriers as a purely unintended, and probably desirable, side effect. For example, limitations on insecticide levels in foods are often more stringent in the United States than in other countries. These standards tend to discourage the import of foreign goods, but their primary purpose appears to be to protect consumers from harmful chemicals, not to restrict trade. But other nontariff barriers seem to serve no purpose other than to keep foreign goods out. Tomatoes produced in Mexico, for example, compete with those produced in the United States. But Mexican tomatoes tend to be smaller than U.S. tomatoes. The United States once imposed size restrictions to "protect" U.S. *consumers* from small tomatoes. The result was a highly effective trade barrier that protected U.S. producers and raised U.S. tomato prices. Those restrictions were abolished under terms of the North American Free Trade Agreement, which has led to a large increase in U.S. imports of Mexican tomatoes and a reduction in U.S. tomato production.[3]

Justifications for Trade Restriction: An Evaluation

The conceptual justification for free trade is one of the oldest arguments in economics; there is no disputing the logic of the argument that free trade increases global production, worldwide consumption, and international efficiency. But critics stress that the argument is a theoretical one. In the real world, they say, there are several arguments that can be made to justify protectionist measures.

Infant Industries

infant industry

A new domestic industry with potential economies of scale.

One argument for trade barriers is that they serve as a kind of buffer to protect fledgling domestic industries. Initially, firms in a new industry may be too small to achieve significant economies of scale and could be clobbered by established firms in other countries. A new domestic industry with potential economies of scale is called an **infant industry.**

Consider the situation in which firms in a country are attempting to enter a new industry in which many large firms already exist in the international arena. The foreign firms have taken advantage of economies of scale and have therefore achieved relatively low levels of production costs. New firms, facing low levels of output and higher average costs, may find it difficult to compete. The infant industry argument suggests that by offering protection during an industry's formative years, a tariff or quota may allow the new industry to develop and prosper.

The infant industry argument played a major role in tariff policy in the early years of U.S. development. The high tariffs of the early nineteenth century were typically justified as being necessary to allow U.S. firms to gain a competitive foothold in the world economy. As domestic industries became established, tariff rates fell. Subsequent increases in tariffs were a response in part to internal crises: the Civil War and the Great Depression. Tariff rates have fallen dramatically since 1930.

Critics of the infant industry argument say that once protection is in place, it may be very difficult to remove. Inefficient firms, they contend, may be able to survive for long periods under the umbrella of infant industry protection.

Strategic Trade Policy

A new version of the infant industry argument has been used in the past few years as technological developments have spawned whole new industries and transformed existing ones. The new version of the infant industry argument assumes an imperfectly competitive market.

Suppose technological change has given rise to a new industry. Given the economies of scale in this industry, only a few firms are likely to dominate it worldwide—it will likely emerge as an oligopoly. The firms that dominate the industry are likely to earn economic profits that will persist. Furthermore, because there will be only a few firms, they will be located in only a few countries. Their governments could conceivably impose taxes on these firms' profits that would enhance economic well-being within the country. The potential for such gains may justify government efforts to assist firms seeking to acquire a dominant position in the new industry.

Government aid could take the form of protectionist trade policies aimed at allowing these firms to expand in the face of foreign competition, assistance with research and development efforts, programs to provide workers with special skills needed by the industry, or subsidies in the form of direct payments or special tax treatment. Any such policy aimed at promoting the development of key industries that may increase a country's domestic well-being through trade with the rest of the world is known as a **strategic trade policy.**

Although strategic trade policy suggests a conceptually positive role for government in international trade, proponents of the approach note that it has dangers. Firms might use the strategic trade argument even if their development were unlikely to offer the gains specified in the theory. The successful application of the approach requires that the government correctly identify industries in which a country can, in fact, gain dominance—something that may not be possible. Various European governments provided subsidies to firms that were involved in the production of Airbus, which is now a major competitor in the airplane industry. On the other hand, Britain and France subsidized the development of the supersonic plane called the Concorde. After only a few Concordes had been produced, it became obvious that the aircraft was a financially losing proposition and production was halted. The airline has now gone out of business.

Finally, those firms whose success strategic trade policy promotes might have sufficient political clout to block the taxes that would redistribute the gains of the policies to the population in general. Thus, the promise of strategic trade policy is unlikely to be fulfilled.

National Security

It is sometimes argued that the security of the United States would be threatened if this country depended on foreign powers as the primary source of strategic materials. In time of war, the United States might be cut off from sources of foreign supply and lose some of the materials upon which U.S. industry depends.

One area where the national security argument is applied is the oil industry. Given the volatility of the political situation in the Middle East, some people say, the United States should protect the domestic oil industry in order to ensure adequate production capability in the event Middle Eastern supplies are cut off.

An alternative to tariff protection of strategic commodities is to stockpile those commodities for use in time of crisis. For example, the United States maintains a strategic petroleum reserve for use in case of a cutoff in foreign supplies or domestic crises. For example, strategic oil reserves were tapped in the wake of pipeline and refinery disruptions following Hurricane Katrina in 2005.

Job Protection

The desire to maintain existing jobs threatened by foreign competition is probably the single most important source of today's protectionist policies. Some industries that at one time had a comparative advantage are no longer among the world's lowest-cost producers; they struggle to stay afloat. Cost cutting leads to layoffs, and layoffs lead to demands for protection.

The model of international trade in perfect competition suggests that trade will threaten some industries. As countries specialize in activities in which they have a comparative advantage, sectors in which they do not have this advantage will shrink. Maintaining those sectors through trade barriers blocks a nation from enjoying the gains possible from free trade.

A further difficulty with the use of trade barriers to shore up employment in a particular sector is that it can be an enormously expensive strategy. Suppose enough of a foreign good is kept out of the United States to save one U.S. job. That shifts the supply curve slightly to the left, raising prices for U.S. consumers and reducing their consumer surplus. The loss to consumers is the cost per job saved. Estimates of the cost of saving *one* job in the steel industry through restrictions on steel imports, for example, go as high as $800,000 per year.

strategic trade policy

A policy aimed at promoting the development of key industries that may increase a countrys domestic well-being through trade with the rest of the world.

Cheap Foreign Labor and Outsourcing

One reason often given for the perceived need to protect American workers against free international trade is that workers must be protected against cheap foreign labor. This is an extension of the job protection argument in the previous section. From a theoretical point of view, of course, if foreign countries can produce a good at lower cost than we can, it is in our collective interest to obtain it from them. But workers counter by saying that the low wages of foreign workers means that foreign workers are exploited. To compete with foreign workers, American workers would have to submit themselves to similar exploitation. This objection, however, fails to recognize that differences in wage rates generally reflect differences in worker productivity.

Consider the following example: Suppose U.S. workers in the tool industry earn $20 per hour while Indonesian workers in the tool industry earn only $2 per hour. If we assume that the tool industry is competitive, then the wages in both countries are based on the marginal revenue product of the workers. The higher wage of U.S. workers must mean that they have a higher marginal product—they are more productive. The higher wage of U.S. workers need not mean that labor costs are higher in the United States than in Indonesia.

Further, we have seen that what matters for trade is comparative advantage, not comparative labor costs. When each nation specializes in goods and services in which it has a comparative advantage—measured in the amounts of other goods and services given up to produce them—then world production, and therefore world consumption, rises. By definition, each nation will have a comparative advantage in *something*.

outsourcing

Situation in which firms in a developed country transfer some of their activities abroad in order to take advantage of lower labor costs in other countries.

A particularly controversial issue in industrialized economies is **outsourcing**, in which firms in a developed country transfer some of their activities abroad in order to take advantage of lower labor costs in other countries. Generally speaking, the practice of outsourcing tends to reduce costs for the firms that do it. These firms often expand production and increase domestic employment, as is discussed in the accompanying Case in Point essay.

Differences in Environmental Standards

Another justification for protectionist measures is that free trade is unfair if it pits domestic firms against foreign rivals who do not have to adhere to the same regulatory standards. In the debate over NAFTA, for example, critics warned that Mexican firms, facing relatively lax pollution control standards, would have an unfair advantage over U.S. firms if restraints on trade between the two countries were removed.

Economic theory suggests, however, that differences in pollution-control policies can be an important source of comparative advantage. In general, the demand for environmental quality is positively related to income. People in higher-income countries demand higher environmental quality than do people in lower-income countries. That means that pollution has a lower cost in poorer than in richer countries. If an industry generates a great deal of pollution, it may be more efficient to locate it in a poor country than in a rich country. In effect, a poor country's lower demand for environmental quality gives it a comparative advantage in production of goods that generate a great deal of pollution.

Provided the benefits of pollution exceed the costs in the poor country, with the costs computed based on the preferences and incomes of people in that country, it makes sense for more of the good to be produced in the poor country and less in the rich country. Such an allocation leaves people in both countries better off than they would be otherwise. Then, as freer trade leads to higher incomes in the poorer countries, people there will also demand improvements in environmental quality.

Do economists support *any* restriction on free international trade? Nearly all economists would say no. The gains from trade are so large, and the cost of restraining it so high, that it is hard to find any satisfactory reason to limit trade.

Key Takeaways

- Protectionist measures seek to limit the quantities of goods and services imported from foreign countries. They shift the supply curve for each of the goods or services protected to the left.
- The primary means of protection are tariffs and quotas.
- Antidumping proceedings have emerged as a common means of protection.
- Voluntary export restrictions are another means of protection; they are rarely voluntary.
- Other protectionist measures can include safety standards, restrictions on environmental quality, labeling requirements, and quality standards.
- Protectionist measures are sometimes justified using the infant industry argument, strategic trade policy, job protection, "cheap" foreign labor and outsourcing, national security, and differences in environmental standards.

Try It!

Suppose the United States imposes a quota reducing its imports of shoes by one-half (roughly 85–90% of the shoes now sold in the United States are imported). Assume that shoes are produced under conditions of perfect competition and that the equilibrium price of shoes is now $50 per pair. Illustrate and explain how this quota will affect the price and output of shoes in the United States.

Case in Point: Outsourcing, Insourcing, and Employment

Source: © 2010 Jupiterimages Corporation

The phenomenon of outsourcing has become common as the Internet and other innovations in communication have made it easier for firms to transfer aspects of their production overseas. At the same time, countries such as India and China have invested heavily in education and have produced a sizable workforce of professional people capable of filling relatively high level positions for firms in more developed countries.

The very idea of outsourcing rankles politicians on the left and on the right. In the United States, there have been numerous congressional hearings on outsourcing and proposals to block firms that engage in the practice from getting government contracts.

By outsourcing, firms are able to reduce their production costs. As we have seen, a reduction in production costs translates into increased output and falling prices. From a consumer's point of view, then, outsourcing should be a very good thing. The worry many commentators express, however, is that outsourcing will decimate employment in the United States, particularly among high-level professionals. Matthew J. Slaughter, an economist at Dartmouth University, examined employment trends from 1991 to 2001 among multinational U.S. firms that had outsourced jobs. Those firms outsourced 2.8 million jobs during the period.

Were the 2.8 million jobs simply lost? Mr. Slaughter points out that there are three reasons to expect that the firms that reduced production costs by outsourcing would actually increase their domestic employment. First, by lowering cost, firms are likely to expand the quantity they produce. The foreign workers who were hired, who Mr. Slaughter refers to as "affiliate workers," appeared to be complements to American workers rather than substitutes. If they are complements rather than substitutes, then outsourcing could lead to increased employment in the country that does the outsourcing.

A second reason outsourcing could increase employment is that by lowering production cost, firms that increase the *scale* of their operations through outsourcing need more domestic workers to sell the increased output, to coordinate its distribution, and to develop the infrastructure to handle all those goods.

Finally, firms that engage in outsourcing are also likely to increase the *scope* of their operations. They will need to hire additional people to explore other product development, to engage in research, and to seek out new markets for the firm's output.

Thus, Mr. Slaughter argues that outsourcing may lead to increased employment because domestic workers are complements to foreign workers, because outsourcing expands the scale of a firm's operations, and because it expands the scope of operations. What did the evidence show? Remember the 2.8 million jobs that multinational firms based in the United States outsourced between 1991 and 2001? Employment at those same U.S. firms *increased* by 5.5 million jobs during the period. Thus, with the phenomena of complementarity, increases in scale, and increases of scope, each job outsourced led to almost two *additional* jobs in the United States.

The experience of two quite dissimilar firms illustrates the phenomenon. Walmart began expanding its operations internationally in about 1990. Today, it manages its global operations from its headquarters in Bentonville, Arkansas where it employs 15,000 people. Roughly 1,500 of these people coordinate the flow of goods among Walmart's stores throughout the world. Those 1,500 jobs would not exist were it not for globalization. Xilinx, the high technology research and development firm, generates sales of about $1.5 billion per year. Sixty-five percent of its sales are generated outside the United States. But 80% of its employees are in the United States.

Outsourcing, then, generates jobs. It does not destroy them. Mr. Slaughter concluded that, in terms of the impact on jobs in the United States, the expansion of U.S. multinationals into other countries is actually a phenomenon to encourage rather than one to fret about.

Mr. Slaughter and coresearcher Robert Kimmitt make a similar case for insourcing, production, and jobs generated by multinationals based outside the United States that build plants inside the United States. In 2007, these companies employed almost 2 million Americans with average compensation of nearly $80,000. Contrary to popular belief, the unionization rates of the United States affiliates of these companies were about 50% higher than for the rest of the U.S. private sector.

Source: Based on Matthew J. Slaughter, "Globalization and Employment by U.S. Multinationals: A Framework and Facts," Daily Tax Report (March 26, 2004): 1–12; Robert M. Kimmitt and Matthew J. Slaughter, "How to Jump-Start American Manufacturing," The Washington Post, A17, August 13, 2010.

Answer to Try It! Problem

The quota shifts the supply curve to the left, increasing the price of shoes in the United States and reducing the equilibrium quantity. In the case shown, the price rises to $68. Because you are not given the precise positions of the demand and supply curves, you can only conclude that price rises; your graph may suggest a different price. The important thing is that the new price is greater than $50.

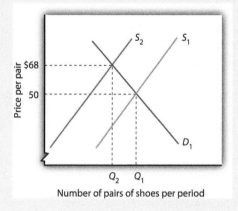

Number of pairs of shoes per period

17.5 Review and Practice

Summary

In this chapter we have seen how international trade makes it possible for countries to improve on their domestic production possibilities.

A country that is operating on its production possibilities curve can obtain more of all goods by opening its markets to free international trade. Free trade allows nations to consume goods beyond their domestic production possibilities curves. If nations specialize in the production of goods and services in which they have a comparative advantage, total output increases. Free trade enhances production possibilities on a worldwide scale. It does not benefit everyone, however. Some workers and owners of other factors of production will be hurt by free trade, at least in the short run.

Contrary to the implication of the model of specialization based on comparative advantage, not all trade is one-way trade. Two-way trade in the *same* goods may arise from variations in transportation costs and seasonal influences. Two-way trade in *similar* goods is often the result of imperfect competition. Much trade among high-income countries is two-way trade.

The imposition of trade barriers such as tariffs, antidumping proceedings, quotas, or voluntary export restrictions raises the equilibrium price and reduces the equilibrium quantity of the restricted good. Although there are many arguments in favor of such restrictions on free trade, economists generally are against protectionist measures and supportive of free trade.

Concept Problems

1. Explain how through trade a country can consume at levels beyond the reach of its production possibilities.
2. Why do countries place restrictions on international trade?

3. What is the difference between a tariff and a quota?

4. The Case in Point on America's shifting comparative advantage suggests that the United States may have a comparative advantage over other countries in the production of high-tech capital goods. What do you think might be the sources of this advantage?

5. "I know a lawyer who can type 100 words per minute but pays a secretary $10 per hour to type court briefs. But the secretary can only type 50 words per minute. I have told my lawyer friend a hundred times she would be better off doing the typing herself, but she just will not listen." Who has the better part of this disagreement, the lawyer or the friend? Explain.

6. Which individuals in the United States might benefit from a tariff placed on the importation of shoes? Who might lose?

7. Explain why economists argue that protectionist policies lead to the misallocation of resources in the domestic economy.

8. Tomatoes grow well in Kansas. Why do the people of Kansas buy most of their tomatoes from Florida, Mexico, and California?

9. Under what circumstances will a country both export and import the products of the same industry?

10. Suppose the United States imposes a quota on copper imports. Who might be helped? Who might be hurt?

11. Some people argue that international trade is fine, but that firms in different countries should play on a "level playing field." They argue that if a good can be produced more cheaply abroad than at home, tariffs should be imposed on the good so that the costs of producing it are the same everywhere. What do you think of this argument?

12. Suppose wages in the Philippines are one-tenth of wages in the United States. Why do all U.S. firms not just move production to the Philippines?

Numerical Problems

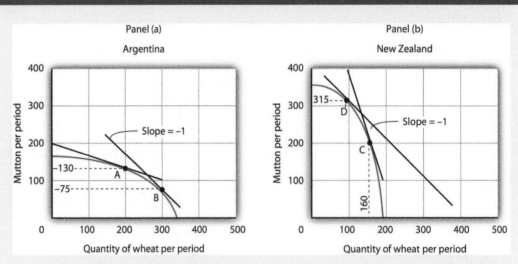

1. Argentina and New Zealand each produce wheat and mutton under conditions of perfect competition, as shown on the accompanying production possibilities curves. Assume that there is no trade between the two countries and that Argentina is now producing at point A and New Zealand at point C.

   a. What is the opportunity cost of producing each good in Argentina?

   b. What is the opportunity cost of producing each good in New Zealand?

   c. Which country has a comparative advantage in which good? Explain.

   d. Explain how international trade would affect wheat production in Argentina.

   e. How would international trade affect mutton production?

f. Explain how international trade would affect wheat production in New Zealand. How would it affect mutton production?

g. How would trade between the two countries affect consumption of wheat and mutton in each country?

2. Assume that trade opens between Argentina and New Zealand and that, with trade, a pound of mutton exchanges for a bushel of wheat. Before trade, Argentina produced at point A and New Zealand produced at point C. Argentina moves to point B, while New Zealand moves to point D. Calculate and illustrate graphically an exchange between Argentina and New Zealand that would leave both countries with more of both goods than they had before trade.

3. Assume that the world market for producing radios is monopolistically competitive. Suppose that the price of a typical radio is $25.

a. Why is this market likely to be characterized by two-way trade?

b. Suppose that Country A levies a tax of $5 on each radio produced within its borders. Will radios continue to be produced in Country A? If they are, what will happen to their price? If they are not, who will produce them?

c. If you concluded that radios will continue to be produced in Country A, explain what will happen to their price in the short run. Illustrate your answer graphically.

d. What will happen to their price in the long run?

4. Suppose radio producers in Country A file a successful anti-dumping complaint against their competitors, and that the result is the imposition of a $10 per radio tariff on imported radios.

a. Illustrate and explain how the $10 tariff will affect radio producers in Country A in the *short* run.

b. Illustrate and explain how the $10 tariff will affect radio producers in Country A in the *long* run.

c. How will the level of employment be affected in Country A?

d. Explain how the tariff will affect consumers in Country A. Who will benefit from the anti-dumping action? Who will bear the burden of the action?

Endnotes

1. Hiau Looi Kee, Cristina Neagu, and Alessandro Nicita, "Is Protectionism On the Rise? Assessing National Trade Policies During the Crisis of 2008," World Bank Policy Research Working Paper Series, no. 5274, April 2010.
2. "Who Wants to Be a Millionaire?" *The Wall Street Journal*, May 14, 2008, p. A20.
3. Ramon G. Guajardo and Homero A. Elizondo, "North American Tomato Market: A Spatial Equilibrium Perspective," *Applied Economics*, 35(3) (February 2003): 315–22.

CHAPTER 18

The Economics of the Environment

18.1 Start Up: Environmental Headwinds

Industrialization of the last few centuries has increased standards of living but has also generated concerns about the environment in which we live. To address such issues as air and water quality, countries have developed laws to reduce pollution. In the United States, the Clean Air Act of 1970, as well as later amendments to it, and the establishment of the Environmental Protection Agency (EPA) became the main governmental vehicles for improving the environment. As the EPA reminds us in its *Plain English Guide to the Clean Air Act*[1], motivation for cleaning up the environment came from some very visible events (such as the five days in 1948 when a thick cloud of air pollution enveloped the industrial town of Donora, Pennsylvania and led to 20 deaths and 6,000 of the town's 14,000 inhabitants sickened or the 1952 "killer fog" in London that led to over 3,000 deaths and required workers with lanterns to guide buses through the thick smog) and from the more general negative health effects (such as respiratory problems from tiny airborne particles or cancer and birth defects from toxic chemicals such as benzene and vinyl chloride).

Since pollution does not respect national borders, international efforts became part of the strategy for dealing with environmental issues. For example, by the 1970s scientists had determined that chlorofluorocarbons (CFCs), widely used as propellants in hairsprays and deodorants and as coolants in refrigerators and air conditioners, were destroying stratospheric ozone. In 1987, over 190 countries, including the United States, signed the Montreal Protocol which called for the elimination of the use of these chemicals. Indeed, the United States had essentially banned their use as propellants in 1978. Still, it is estimated that under current policies it will take about 60 years for the so-called "ozone hole" to begin to heal, as substitutes for some uses of CFCs have been more difficult to find.

Another major international effort, launched in Rio De Janeiro in 1992, is the United Nations Framework Convention on Climate Change (UNFCCC) which seeks to address the issue of global warming. Its goal is to stabilize greenhouse gas emissions from human-made sources in order to keep the earth's temperature from rising to dangerous levels. The 1997 Kyoto Protocol required industrialized countries to set binding emissions targets. President Bill Clinton signed the Kyoto agreement, but it was not ratified by the United States Congress. President George W. Bush withdrew the United States from the agreement citing the damage to the economy that implementation would cause, the fact that rapidly industrializing economies, such as China and India, were excluded, and questions about the underlying science of global warming. Some other countries failed to comply. The most recent attempt to reduce global warming, also under the UNFCCC, is the Paris Agreement which was negotiated in December 2015 and went into force in November 2016, once at least 55 countries representing at least 55 percent of greenhouse gas emissions had ratified it. The goal is to limit global warming to 2 degrees Celsius compared to pre-Industrial Revolution levels, with all countries submitting plans for how much they expect to cut emissions. These plans are then to be updated every few years. Richer countries agreed to provide financial assistance to poor countries to help them in achieving their goals. The negotiations took place while Barack Obama was president. Recognizing that ratification by Congress was not possible, his administration planned to meet the U.S. obligations through a regulation known as the Clean Power Plan. How the administration of Donald Trump will proceed is unknown at the time of this writing. During the 2016 presidential campaign, President Trump mentioned scrapping U.S. participation but has since said that he has not decided. The Trump administration could work towards rescinding certain regulations, leave existing policies in place, or come up with alternative policies for meeting the goals of the agreement.

Even when there is a consensus on desired environmental outcomes, there is still the question of how to bring those outcomes about. In this chapter, we shall put the analytical tools we have developed to work on the problems of the environment. We will begin by developing a model based on marginal benefits and marginal costs of pollution and explore how ill-defined property rights make environmental problems especially challenging to address. We will then look at alternative means for addressing environmental problems. Direct controls, in which government agencies tell polluters what they must do to reduce pollution, remain an important means of government regulation. Two alternatives that economists often advocate are taxes on pollutants and marketable pollutions rights. These market-based systems have gained in importance. Multinational units (such as the European Union), a number of individual countries (such as India, Japan, New Zealand, and Kazakhstan), as well as a number of states or provinces within countries (such as Quebec and California), have implemented or are currently working on various forms of cap-and-trade, market-based systems designed to lower greenhouse gas emissions.[2]

Related issues include those of common property resources, those scarce resources for which no property rights are defined, and exhaustible natural resources, those resources whose stocks decline as they are used. These topics were discussed in the chapters on efficiency and natural resources, respectively.

18.2 Maximizing the Net Benefits of Pollution

Learning Objectives

1. Explain why pollution can be said to have benefits as well as costs and describe the nature of these benefits and costs.
2. Using marginal benefit and marginal cost curves, apply the marginal decision rule to show and explain what is meant by the efficient level of emissions and abatement.
3. Explain the Coase theorem and what it implies about the conditions under which the private market is likely to achieve an efficient outcome.

We all pollute the environment. We do so not because we get some perverse satisfaction from polluting, but because activities that give us utility inevitably pollute. We do not drive our cars in order to dump carbon monoxide into the air but because we gain utility from the transportation and convenience cars provide. Firms pollute the environment if doing so allows them to produce goods and services at lower cost.

The benefits we derive from pollution are indirect. We obtain them from other activities that generate pollution. But that is not unusual—there are many things we do because of the other benefits they produce. Firms benefit from hiring labor not because their owners enjoy hiring workers but because those workers produce greater profits. We purchase electricity not because we enjoy the feeling of having the stuff racing through wires in the house but because the electricity produces light, heat, and other services more cheaply than would alternatives such as candles or fires. In purchasing this electricity, of course, we are demanding a good whose production inevitably degrades the environment. We pollute in the process of obtaining more of other goods and services we enjoy. We thus benefit from our pollution.

Of course, we suffer from the pollution we all generate as well. Smog-choked air damages our health and robs us of scenic views. We may not be able to fish or swim in polluted rivers. Just as the generation of pollution makes many of the activities we pursue less expensive, the fact that we have pollution increases many costs. Polluted rivers increase the cost of producing drinking water. Polluted air requires us to spend more on health care and to paint our buildings more often. Polluted soils produce less food.

Like any other activity, then, pollution has benefits as well as costs. The difficulty with pollution problems is that decision makers experience the benefits of their own choices to pollute the environment, but the costs spill over to everyone who breathes the air or consumes the water. These costs are examples of external costs. Recall that external costs produce one type of market failure and that market failures lead to inefficiency in the allocation of resources. The environment presents us with an allocation problem in which decision makers are not faced with all the benefits and costs of their choices. Environmental resources will not, in such cases, be allocated efficiently. Economists who examine and analyze environmental problems try to determine what an efficient allocation of the environment would most likely be—one that maximizes the difference between the total benefits and total costs of our pollution.

A second task of environmental economics is to find ways to get from where we are, typically with more pollution than is efficient, to the efficient solution. We have learned that private markets often fail to achieve efficient solutions to environmental problems because property rights are difficult to define and to exchange. We will see, however, that environmental economists have devised innovative ways to introduce property rights to environmental policy and to harness market forces to improve rather than degrade environmental quality.

Pollution and Scarcity

Pollution exists whenever human activity generates a sufficient concentration of a substance in the environment to cause harm to people or to resources valued by people. Many potentially harmful substances are natural features of the environment, but they are not generally regarded as pollutants. Pollution is the product of people, not nature.

Pollution implies scarcity. If an activity emits harmful by-products into the environment, then the emission of the by-products is an alternative to some other activity. A scarcity problem exists at the point where harm occurs. A fire burning in a fireplace at a cabin in the forest whose smoke goes unnoticed does not suggest a scarcity problem. But when there are other people who will be harmed by the smoke, then one person's enjoyment of the fire becomes an alternative to another person's enjoyment of fresh air. Fresh air has become scarce, and pollution has become an economic problem.

Economists generally argue that pollution that harms plants or animals imposes a cost if the plants or animals are valued by people. When a farmer uses a pesticide that damages another farmer's crop, for example, a pollution problem occurs. If an oil spill in the ocean damages sea animals that people care about, there is a pollution problem. It is, after all, people who make the choices that lead to pollution. It is people who can choose to limit their pollution. Economists therefore examine pollution problems from the perspective of the preferences of people.

The Efficient Level of Pollution

The efficient level of pollution is the quantity at which its total benefits exceed its total costs by the greatest possible amount. This occurs where the marginal benefit of an additional unit of pollution equals its marginal cost.

Figure 18.1 shows how we can determine an efficient quantity of pollution. Suppose two neighbors in a remote mountain area, Mary and Jane, burn fires in their cabins that generate air pollution that harms two other individuals, Sam and Richard, who live downwind. We shall assume that Mary and Jane are the only polluters and that Sam and Richard are the only people harmed by the pollution. We shall ignore, for example, the effect of Mary and Jane's emissions on the possible problem of global warming.

pollution
Situation that exists when human activity produces a sufficient concentration of a substance in the environment to cause harm to people or to resources valued by people.

FIGURE 18.1 Determining the Efficient Level of Pollution

Mary and Jane each benefit from polluting the environment by emitting smoke from their fires. In Panel (a), we see that Mary's demand curve for emitting smoke is given by D_M and that Jane's demand curve is given by D_J. To determine the total demand curve, D_T, we determine the amount that each person will emit at various prices. At a price of $13 per day, for example, Mary will emit 20 pounds per day. Jane will emit 14 pounds per day, for a total of 34 pounds per day on demand curve D_T. Notice that if the price were $0 per unit, Mary would emit 40 pounds per day, Jane would emit 20, and emissions would total 60 pounds per day on curve D_T. The marginal cost curve for pollution is determined in Panel (b) by taking the marginal cost curves for each person affected by the pollution. In this case, the only people affected are Sam and Richard. Sam's marginal cost curve is MC_S, and Richard's marginal cost curve is MC_R. Because Sam and Richard are each affected by the same pollution, we add their marginal cost curves vertically. For example, if the total quantity of the emissions is 34 pounds per day, the marginal cost of the 34th pound to Richard is $4, it is $9 to Sam, for a total marginal cost of the 34th unit of $13. In Panel (c), we put D_T and MC_T together to find the efficient solution. The two curves intersect at a level of emissions of 34 pounds per day, which occurs at a price of $13 per pound.

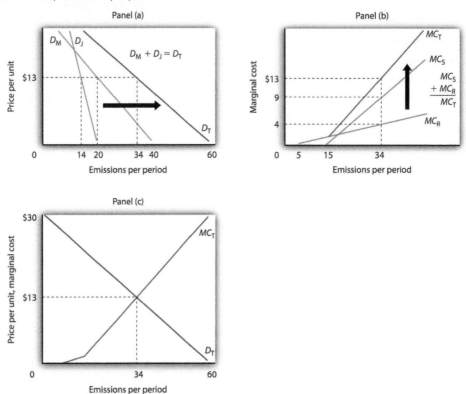

Suppose, as is often the case, that no mechanism exists to charge Mary and Jane for their emissions; they can pollute all they want and never have to compensate society (that is, pay Sam and Richard) for the damage they do. Alternatively, suppose there is no mechanism for Sam and Richard to pay Mary and Jane to get them to reduce their pollution. In either situation, the pollution generated by Mary and Jane imposes an external cost on Sam and Richard. Mary and Jane will pollute up to the point that the marginal benefit of additional pollution to them has reached zero—that is, up to the point where the marginal benefit matches their marginal cost. They ignore the external costs they impose on "society"—Sam and Richard.

Mary's and Jane's demand curves for pollution are shown in Panel (a). These demand curves, D_M and D_J, show the quantities of emissions each generates at each possible price, assuming such a fee were assessed. At a price of $13 per unit, for example, Mary will emit 20 units of pollutant per period and Jane will emit 14. Total emissions at a price of $13 would be 34 units per period. If the price of emissions were zero, total emissions would be 60 units per period. Whatever the price they face, Mary and Jane will emit additional units of the pollutant up to the point that their marginal benefit equals that price. We can therefore interpret their demand curves as their marginal benefit curves for emissions. Their combined demand curve D_T gives the marginal benefit to society (that is, to Mary and Jane) of pollution. Each person in our problem, Mary, Jane, Sam, and Richard, follows the marginal decision rule and thus attempts to maximize utility.

In Panel (b) we see how much Sam and Richard are harmed; the marginal cost curves, MC_S and MC_R, show their respective valuations of the harm imposed on them by each additional unit of emissions. Notice that over a limited range, some emissions generate no harm. At very low levels, neither Sam nor Richard is even aware of the emissions. Richard begins to experience harm as the quantity of emissions goes above 5 pounds per day; it is here that pollution begins to occur. As emissions increase, the additional harm each unit creates becomes larger and larger—the marginal cost curves are upward sloping. The first traces of pollution may be only a minor inconvenience, but as pollution goes up, the problems it creates become more serious—and its marginal cost rises.

Because the same emissions affect both Sam and Richard, we add their marginal cost curves vertically to obtain their combined marginal cost curve MC_T. The 34th unit of emissions, for example, imposes an additional cost of $9 on Sam and $4 on Richard. It thus imposes a total marginal cost of $13.

The efficient quantity of emissions is found at the intersection of the demand (D_T) and marginal cost (MC_T) curves in Panel (c) of Figure 18.1, with 34 units of the pollutant emitted. The marginal benefit of the 34th unit of emissions, as measured by the demand curve D_T, equals its marginal cost, MC_T, at that level. The quantity at which the marginal benefit curve intersects the marginal cost curve maximizes the net benefit of an activity.

We have already seen that in the absence of a mechanism to charge Mary and Jane for their emissions, they face a price of zero and would emit 60 units of pollutant per period. But that level of pollution is inefficient. Indeed, as long as the marginal cost of an additional unit of pollution exceeds its marginal benefit, as measured by the demand curve, there is too much pollution; the net benefit of emissions would be greater with a lower level of the activity.

Just as too much pollution is inefficient, so is too little. Suppose Mary and Jane are not allowed to pollute; emissions equal zero. We see in Panel (c) that the marginal benefit of dumping the first unit of pollution is quite high; the marginal cost it imposes on Sam and Richard is zero. Because the marginal benefit of additional pollution exceeds its marginal cost, the net benefit to society would be increased by increasing the level of pollution. That is true at any level of pollution below 34 units, the efficient solution.

The notion that too little pollution could be inefficient may strike you as strange. To see the logic of this idea, imagine that the pollutant involved is carbon monoxide, a pollutant emitted whenever combustion occurs, and it is deadly. It is, for example, emitted when you drive a car. Now suppose that no emissions of carbon monoxide are allowed. Among other things, this would require a ban on all driving. Surely the benefits of some driving would exceed the cost of the pollution created. The problem in pollution policy from an economic perspective is to find the quantity of pollution at which total benefits exceed total costs by the greatest possible amount—the solution at which marginal benefit equals marginal cost.

Property Rights and the Coase Theorem

The problem of getting the efficient amount of pollution arises because no one owns the right to the air. If someone did, then that owner could decide how to use it. If a nonowner did not like the way the owner was using it, then he or she could try to pay the owner to change the way the air was being used.

In our earlier example, if Mary and Jane own the right to the air, but Sam and Richard do not like how much Mary and Jane are polluting it, Sam and Richard can offer to pay Mary and Jane to cut back on the amount they are polluting. Alternatively, if Sam and Richard own the air, then in order to pollute it, Mary and Jane would have to compensate the owners. Bargaining among the affected parties, if costless, would lead to the efficient amount of pollution. Costless bargaining requires that all parties know the source of the pollution and are able to measure the quantity emitted by each agent.

Specifically, suppose Mary and Jane own the right to dump pollutants into the air and had been emitting 60 units of the pollution per day. If Sam and Richard offer to pay them $13 for each unit of pollutant they cut back, Mary and Jane will reduce their pollution to 34 units, since the marginal benefit to them of the 35th to 60th unit is less than $13. Sam and Richard are better off since the marginal cost of those last 26 units of pollution is greater than $13 per unit. The efficient outcome of 34 units of pollution is thus achieved. Mary and Jane could reduce their emissions by burning their fires for less time, by selecting more efficient fireplaces, or by other measures. Many people, for example, have reduced their emissions by changing to gas-burning fireplaces rather than burning wood.

Coase theorem

The proposition that if property rights are well defined and if bargaining is costless, then the private market can achieve an efficient outcome regardless of which of the affected parties holds the property rights.

While the well-being of the affected parties is not independent of who owns the property right (each would be better off owning rather than not owning the right), the establishment of who owns the air leads to a solution that solves the externality problem and leads to an efficient market outcome. The proposition that if property rights are well defined and if bargaining is costless, the private market can achieve an efficient outcome regardless of which of the affected parties holds the property rights is known as the **Coase theorem**, named for the Nobel-Prize-winning economist Ronald Coase who generally is credited with this idea.

Suppose instead that Sam and Richard own the right to the air. They could charge Mary and Jane $13 per unit of pollution emitted. Mary and Jane would willingly pay for the right to emit 34 units of pollution, but not for any more, since beyond that amount the marginal benefit of each unit of pollution emitted is less than $13. Sam and Richard would willingly accept payments for 34 units of pollution at $13 each since the marginal cost to them for each of those units is less than $13.

In most cases, however, Coase stressed that the conditions for private parties to achieve an efficient outcome on their own are not present. Property rights may not be defined. Even if one party owns a right, enforcement may be difficult. Suppose Sam and Richard own the right to clean air but many people, not just two as in our example, contribute to polluting it. Would each producer that pollutes have to strike a deal with Sam and Richard? Could the government enforce all those deals? And what if there are many owners as well? Enforcement becomes increasingly difficult and striking deals becomes more and more costly. Finally, monitoring is extremely difficult in most environmental problems. While it is generally possible to detect the presence of pollutants, determining their source is virtually impossible. And determining who is harmed and by how much is a monumental undertaking in most pollution problems.

Nonetheless, it is the insight that the Coase theorem provides that has led economists to consider solutions to environmental problems that attempt to use the establishment of property rights and market mechanisms in various ways to bring about the efficient market outcome. Before considering alternative ways of controlling pollution, we look first at how the benefits and costs might be measured so that we have a better sense of what the efficient solution is.

Another insight that comes from Coase's analysis is that the notion of "harm" is a reciprocal one. In our first example, it is tempting to conclude that Mary and Jane, by burning fires in their fireplaces, are "harming" Sam and Richard. But if Sam and Richard were not located downwind of the smoke, there would be no harm. In effect, Mr. Coase insists that the harm cannot be attributed to one party or another. Sam and Richard "cause" the harm by locating downwind of the fireplaces. While there is clearly harm in this situation, we could as easily attribute it to either the generators of the smoke or the recipients of the smoke. Before Coase wrote his article, "The Problem of Social Cost" in 1960, the general presumption was that decision makers such as Mary and Jane "cause" the harm and that they should be taxed for the costs they impose. Mr. Coase pointed out the alternative that Sam and Richard could avoid the harm by moving. Indeed, all sorts of alternative solutions come to mind even in this simple example. Mary and Jane could select types of wood that emit less smoke. They could use fireplaces that emit less smoke. They could make arrangements to time their burning to minimize the total amount of smoke that affects Sam and Richard. The goal, Coase said, is to select the most efficient from the alternatives available.[3]

Consider a different problem. Suppose that an airport has been built several miles outside the developed portion of a small city. No one lives close enough to the airport to be "harmed" by the noise inevitably generated by the operation of the airport. As time passes, people are likely to build houses near the airport to take advantage of jobs at the airport or to gain easy access to it. Those people will now be "harmed" by noise from the airport. But what is the cause of this harm? By definition, there was no "harm" before people started living close to the airport. True, it is the airport that generates the noise. But the noise causes harm *only* because people now live near it. Just as Mary and Jane's campfires only generate "harm" if someone is downwind of the smoke, the noise from the airport causes damage only if someone lives near the airport. The problem of the noise could be mitigated in several ways. First, people could have chosen not to live near the airport. Once they have chosen to live near the airport, they could reduce the noise with better insulation or with better windows. Alternatively, the airport management could choose different flight patterns to reduce noise that affects neighboring homeowners. It is always the case that there are several potential ways of mitigating the effects of airport operations; the economic problem is to select the most efficient from among those alternatives.

The Measurement of Benefits and Costs

Saying that the efficient level of pollution occurs at a certain rate of emissions, as we have done so far, is one thing. Determining the actual positions of the demand and marginal cost curves that define that efficient solution is quite another. Economists have devised a variety of methods for measuring these curves.

Benefits: The Demand for Emissions

A demand curve for emitting pollutants shows the quantity of emissions demanded per unit of time at each price. It can, as we have seen, be taken as a marginal benefit curve for emitting pollutants.

The general approach to estimating demand curves involves observing quantities demanded at various prices, together with the values of other determinants of demand. In most pollution problems, however, the price charged for emitting pollutants has always been zero—we simply do not know how the quantity of emissions demanded will vary with price.

One approach to estimating the demand curve for pollution utilizes the fact that this demand occurs because pollution makes other activities cheaper. If we know how much the emission of one more unit of a pollutant saves, then we can infer how much consumers or firms would pay to dump it.

Suppose, for example, that there is no program to control automobile emissions—motorists face a price of zero for each unit of pollution their cars emit. Suppose that a particular motorist's car emits an average of 10 pounds of carbon monoxide per week. Its owner could reduce emissions to 9 pounds per week at a cost of $1 per week. This $1 is the marginal cost of reducing emissions from 10 to 9 pounds per week. It is also the maximum price the motorist would pay to increase emissions from 9 to 10 pounds per week—it is the marginal benefit of the 10th pound of pollution. We say that it is the maximum price because if asked to pay more, the motorist would choose to reduce emissions at a cost of $1 instead.

Now suppose that emissions have been reduced to 9 pounds per week and that the motorist could reduce them to 8 at an additional cost of $2 per week. The marginal cost of reducing emissions from 9 to 8 pounds per week is $2. Alternatively, this is the maximum price the motorist would be willing to pay to increase emissions to 9 from 8 pounds; it is the marginal benefit of the 9th pound of pollution. Again, if asked to pay more than $2, the motorist would choose to reduce emissions to 8 pounds per week instead.

FIGURE 18.2 Abatement Costs and
Demand

A car emits an average of 10 pounds of CO per
week when no restrictions are imposed—when
the price of emissions is zero. The marginal
cost of abatement (MC_A) is the cost of
eliminating a unit of emissions; this is the
interpretation of the curve when read from right
to left. The same curve can be read from left to
right as the marginal benefit of emissions (MB_E).

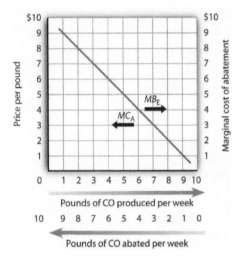

We can thus think of the marginal benefit of an additional unit of pollution as the added cost of not emitting it. It is the saving a polluter enjoys by dumping additional pollution rather than paying the cost of preventing its emission. Figure 18.2 shows this dual interpretation of cost and benefit. Initially, our motorist emits 10 pounds of carbon monoxide per week. Reading from right to left, the curve measures the marginal costs of pollution abatement (MC_A). We see that the marginal cost of abatement rises as emissions are reduced. That makes sense; the first reductions in emissions will be achieved through relatively simple measures such as modifying one's driving technique to minimize emissions (such as accelerating more slowly), or getting tune-ups more often. Further reductions, however, might require burning more expensive fuels or installing more expensive pollution-control equipment.

Read from left to right, the curve in Figure 18.2 shows the marginal benefit of additional emissions (MB_E). Its negative slope suggests that the first units of pollution emitted have very high marginal benefits, because the cost of not emitting them would be very high. As more of a pollutant is emitted, however, its marginal benefit falls—the cost of preventing these units of pollution becomes quite low.

Economists have also measured demand curves for emissions by using surveys in which polluters are asked to report the costs to them of reducing their emissions. In cases in which polluters are charged for the emissions they create, the marginal benefit curve can be observed directly.

As we saw in Figure 18.1, the marginal benefit curves of individual polluters are added horizontally to obtain a market demand curve for pollution. This curve measures the additional benefit to society of each additional unit of pollution.

The Marginal Cost of Emissions

Pollutants harm people and the resources they value. The marginal cost curve for a pollutant shows the additional cost imposed by each unit of the pollutant. As we saw in Figure 18.1, the marginal cost curves for all the individuals harmed by a particular pollutant are added vertically to obtain the marginal cost curve for the pollutant.

Like the marginal benefit curve for emissions, the marginal cost curve can be interpreted in two ways, as suggested in Figure 18.3. When read from left to right, the curve measures the marginal cost of additional units of emissions (MC_E). If increasing the motorists' emissions from four pounds of carbon monoxide per week to five pounds of carbon monoxide per week imposes an external cost of $2, though, the marginal benefit of not being exposed to that unit of pollutant must be $2. The marginal cost curve can thus be read from right to left as a marginal benefit curve for abating emissions (MB_A). This marginal benefit curve is, in effect, the demand curve for cleaner air.

Economists estimate the marginal cost curve of pollution in several ways. One is to infer it from the demand for goods for which environmental quality is a complement. Another is to survey people, asking them what pollution costs—or what they would pay to reduce it. Still another is to determine the costs of damages created by pollution directly.

For example, environmental quality is a complement of housing. The demand for houses in areas with cleaner air is greater than the demand for houses in areas that are more polluted. By observing the relationship between house prices and air quality, economists can learn the value people place on cleaner air—and thus the cost of dirtier air. Studies have been conducted in cities all over the world to determine the relationship between air quality and house prices so that a measure of the demand for cleaner air can be made. They show that increased pollution levels result in lower house values.[4]

Surveys are also used to assess the marginal cost of emissions. The fact that the marginal cost of an additional unit of emissions is the marginal benefit of avoiding the emissions suggests that surveys can be designed in two ways. Respondents can be asked how much they would be harmed by an increase in emissions, or they can be asked what they would pay for a reduction in emissions. Economists often use both kinds of questions in surveys designed to determine marginal costs.

A third kind of cost estimate is based on objects damaged by pollution. Increases in pollution, for example, require buildings to be painted more often; the increased cost of painting is one measure of the cost of added pollution.

While all of the attempts to measure cost are imperfect, the alternative is to not try to quantify cost at all. To economists, such an ostrich-like approach of sticking one's head in the sand would be unacceptable.

FIGURE 18.3 The Marginal Cost of Emissions and the Marginal Benefit of Abatement

The marginal cost of the first few units of emissions is zero and then rises once emissions begin to harm people. That is the point at which the air becomes a scarce resource. Read from left to right the curve gives the marginal cost of emissions (MC_E). Read from right to left, the curve gives the marginal benefit of abatement (MB_A).

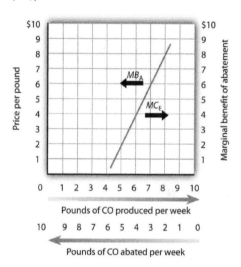

The Efficient Level of Emissions and Abatement

Whether economists measure the marginal benefits and marginal costs of emissions or, alternatively, the marginal benefits and marginal costs of abatement, the policy implications are the same from an economic perspective. As shown in Panel (a) of Figure 18.4, applying the marginal decision rule in the case of emissions suggests that the efficient level of pollution occurs at six pounds of CO emitted per week. At any lower level, the marginal benefits of the pollution would outweigh the marginal costs. At a higher level, the marginal costs of the pollution would outweigh the marginal benefits.

FIGURE 18.4 The Efficient Level of Emissions and Pollution Abatement

In Panel (a) we combine the marginal benefit of emissions (MB_E) with the marginal cost of emissions (MC_E). The efficient solution occurs at the intersection of the two curves. Here, the efficient quantity of emissions is six pounds of CO per week. In Panel (b), we have the same curves read from right to left. The marginal cost curve for emissions becomes the marginal benefit of abatement (MB_A). The marginal benefit curve for emissions becomes the marginal cost of abatement (MC_A). With no abatement program, emissions total ten pounds of CO per week. The efficient degree of abatement is to reduce emissions by four pounds of CO per week to six pounds per week.

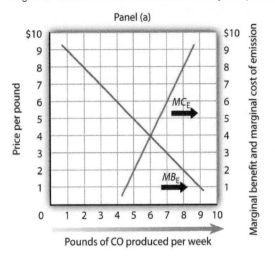

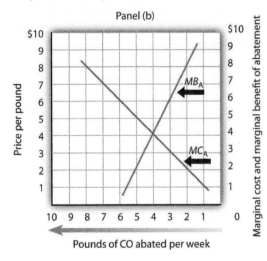

As shown in Panel (b) of Figure 18.4, application of the marginal decision rule suggests that the efficient level of *abatement* effort is to reduce pollution by 4 pounds of CO produced per week. That is, reduce the level of pollution from the 10 pounds per week that would occur at a zero price to 6 pounds per week. For any greater effort at abating the pollution, the marginal cost of the abatement efforts would exceed the marginal benefit.

Key Takeaways

- Pollution is related to the concept of scarcity. The existence of pollution implies that an environmental resource has alternative uses and is thus scarce.
- Pollution has benefits as well as costs; the emission of pollutants benefits people by allowing other activities to be pursued at lower costs. The efficient rate of emissions occurs where the marginal benefit of emissions equals the marginal cost they impose.
- The marginal benefit curve for emitting pollutants can also be read from right to left as the marginal cost of abating emissions. The marginal cost curve for increased emission levels can also be read from right to left as the demand curve for improved environmental quality.
- The Coase theorem suggests that if property rights are well-defined and if transactions are costless, then the private market will reach an efficient solution. These conditions, however, are not likely to be present in typical environmental situations. Even if such conditions do not exist, Coase's arguments still yield useful insights to the mitigation of environmental problems.
- Surveys are sometimes used to measure the marginal benefit curves for emissions and the marginal cost curves for increased pollution levels. Marginal cost curves may also be inferred from other relationships. Two that are commonly used are the demand for housing and the relationship between pollution and production.

Try It!

The table shows the marginal benefit to a paper mill of polluting a river and the marginal cost to residents who live downstream. In this problem assume that the marginal benefits and marginal costs are measured at (not between) the specific quantities shown.

Plot the marginal benefit and marginal cost curves. What is the efficient quantity of pollution? Explain why neither one ton nor five tons is an efficient quantity of pollution. In the absence of pollution fees or taxes, how many units of pollution do you expect the paper mill will choose to produce? Why?

Quantity of pollution (tons per week)	Marginal benefit	Marginal cost
0	$110	$0
1	100	8
2	90	20
3	80	35
4	70	70
5	60	150
6	0	300

Case in Point: Estimating a Demand Curve for Environmental Quality

Source: © 2010 Jupiterimages Corporation

How do economists estimate demand curves for environmental quality? One recent example comes from work by Louisiana State University economist David M. Brasington and Auburn University economist Diane Hite. Using data from Ohio's six major metropolitan areas (Akron, Cincinnati, Cleveland, Columbus, Dayton, and Toledo), the economists studied the relationship between house prices and the distance between individual houses and hazardous waste sites. From this, they were able to estimate the demand curve for environmental quality—at least in terms of the demand for locations farther from environmental hazards.

The economists used actual real estate transactions in 1991 to get data on house prices. In that year, there were 1,192 hazardous sites in the six metropolitan areas. The study was based on 44,255 houses. The median distance between a house and a hazardous site was 1.08 miles. The two economists found, as one would expect, that house prices were higher the greater the distance between the house and a hazardous site. All other variables unchanged, increasing the distance from a house to a hazardous site by 10% increased house value by 0.3%.

Other characteristics of the demand curve shed light on the relationship between environmental quality and other goods. For example, the study showed that people substitute house size for environmental quality. A house closer to a hazardous waste site is cheaper; people take advantage of the lower price of such sites to purchase larger houses.

While house size and environmental quality were substitutes, school quality, measured by student scores on achievement tests, was a complement. If the price of school quality were to fall by 10%, household would buy 8% more environmental quality. The cross-price elasticity between environmental quality and school quality was thus estimated to be −0.80.

There is no marketplace for environmental quality. Estimating the demand curve for such quality requires economists to examine other data to try to infer what the demand curve is. The study by Professors Brasington and Hite illustrates the use of an examination of an actual market, the market for houses, to determine characteristics of the demand curve for environmental quality.

Source: Based on David M. Brasington and Diane Hite, "Demand for Environmental Quality: A Spatial Hedonic Analysis," Regional Science & Urban Economics, 35(1) (January 2005): 57–82.

Answer to Try It! Problem

The efficient quantity of pollution is four tons per week. At one ton of pollution, the marginal benefit exceeds the marginal cost. If the paper mill expands production, the additional pollution generated leads to additional benefits for it that are greater than the additional cost to the residents nearby. At five tons, the marginal cost of polluting exceeds the marginal benefit. Reducing production, and hence pollution, brings the marginal costs and benefits closer.

In the absence of any fees, taxes, or other charges for its pollution, the paper mill will likely choose to generate six tons per week, where the marginal benefit has fallen to zero.

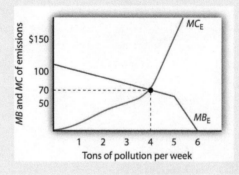

18.3 Alternatives in Pollution Control

Learning Objectives

1. Explain why command-and-control approaches to reducing pollution are inefficient.
2. Explain what is meant by incentive approaches to pollution reduction and discuss examples of them, explaining their advantages and disadvantages.

Suppose that the goal of public policy is to reduce the level of emissions. Three types of policy alternatives could be applied. The first is persuasion—people can be exhorted to reduce their emissions. The second relies on direct controls, and the third uses incentives to induce reductions in emissions.

Moral Suasion

Back in the days when preventing forest fires was a goal of public policy, a cartoon character called Smokey the Bear once asked us to be careful with fire. Signs everywhere remind us not to litter. Some communities have mounted campaigns that admonish us to "Give a hoot—don't pollute."

These efforts to influence our choices are examples of **moral suasion**, an effort to change people's behavior by appealing to their sense of moral values. Moral suasion is widely used as a tactic in attempting to reduce pollution. It has, for example, been fairly successful in campaigns against littering, which can be considered a kind of pollution. Efforts at moral suasion are not generally successful in reducing activities that pollute the air and water. Pleas that people refrain from driving on certain days when pollution is very great, for example, achieve virtually no compliance.

Moral suasion appears to be most effective in altering behaviors that are not already widespread and for which the cost of compliance is low. It is easy to be careful with one's fires or to avoid littering.

Moral suasion does not, however, appear to lead to significant changes in behavior when compliance costs are high or when the activity is already widely practiced. It is therefore not likely to be an effective tool for reducing most forms of pollution.

> **moral suasion**
>
> An effort to change people's behavior by appealing to their sense of moral values.

Command and Control

In the most widely used regulatory approach to environmental pollution, a government agency tells a polluting agent how much pollution it can emit or requires the agent to use a particular production method aimed at reducing emissions. This method, in which the government agency tells a firm or individual how much or by what method emissions must be adjusted, is called the **command-and-control-approach**.

Economists are generally critical of the command-and-control approach for two reasons. First, it achieves a given level of emissions reduction at a higher cost than what would be required to achieve that amount of reduction if market incentives (discussed below) were implemented. Second, it gives polluters no incentive to explore technological and other changes that might reduce the demand for emissions.

Suppose two firms, A and B, each dump 500 tons of a certain pollutant per month and that there is no fee imposed (that is, the price for their emissions equals zero). Total emissions for the two firms thus equal 1,000 tons per month. The pollution control authority decides to cut this in half and orders each firm to reduce its emissions to 250 tons per month, for a total reduction of 500 tons. This is a command-and-control regulation because it specifies the amount of reduction

> **command-and-control approach**
>
> Approach in which a government agency specifies how much or by what method a polluting agent must adjust its emissions.

each firm must make. Although it may seem fair to require equal reductions by the two firms, this approach is likely to generate excessive costs.

Suppose that Firm A is quite old and that the reduction in emissions to 250 tons per period would be extremely costly. Suppose that removing the 251st ton costs this firm $1,000 per month. Put another way, the marginal benefit to Firm A of emitting the 251st ton would be $1,000.

Suppose Firm B, a much newer firm, already has some pollution-control equipment in place. Reducing its emissions to 250 tons imposes a cost, but a much lower cost than to Firm A. Indeed, suppose Firm B could reduce its emissions to 249 tons at an additional cost of $100; the marginal benefit to Firm B of emitting the 249th ton is $100.

If two firms have different marginal benefits of emissions, the allocation of resources is inefficient. The same level of emissions could be achieved at a lower cost. Suppose, for example, Firm A is permitted to increase its emissions to 251 tons while Firm B reduces emissions to 249. Firm A saves $1,000, while the cost to Firm B is just $100. Society achieves a net gain of $900, and the level of emissions remains at 500 tons per month.

As long as Firm A's marginal benefit of emissions exceeds Firm B's, a saving is realized by shifting emissions from B to A. At the point at which their marginal benefits are equal, no further reduction in the cost of achieving a given level of emissions is possible, and the allocation of emissions is efficient. When a given reduction in emissions is achieved so that the marginal benefit of an additional unit of emissions is the same for all polluters, it is a **least-cost reduction in emissions**. A command-and-control approach is unlikely to achieve a least-cost reduction in emissions.

The inefficiency of command-and-control regulation is important for two reasons. First, of course, it wastes scarce resources. If the same level of air or water quality could be achieved at a far lower cost, then surely it makes sense to use the cheaper method. Perhaps even more significant, reliance on command-and-control regulation makes environmental quality far more expensive than it needs to be—and that is likely to result in an unwillingness to achieve the improvements that would be economically efficient.

There is a further difficulty with the command-and-control approach. Once firms A and B have been told to reduce their emissions to 250 tons per period, neither firm has an incentive to try to do better. Neither firm will engage in research seeking to reduce its emissions below 250 tons.

Another way to see the difficulty with command-and-control approaches to pollution control is to imagine that a similar method were in use for other resource allocation problems. Suppose, for example, that labor were allocated according to a command-and-control mechanism. Rather than leaving labor allocation to the marketplace, suppose that firms were simply told how much labor to use. Such a system would clearly be unworkable.

Incentive Approaches

least-cost reduction in emissions

Situation in which emissions are reduced so that the marginal benefit of an additional unit of pollution is the same for all polluters.

incentive approaches

Approaches to pollution regulation that create market-like incentives to encourage reductions in pollution but allow individual decision makers to decide how much to pollute.

Markets allocate resources efficiently when the price system confronts decision makers with the costs and benefits of their decisions. Prices create incentives—they give producers an incentive to produce more and consumers an incentive to economize. Regulatory efforts that seek to create market-like incentives to encourage reductions in pollution, but that allow individual decision makers to determine how much to pollute, are called **incentive approaches**.

Emissions Taxes

One incentive approach to pollution control relies on taxes. If a tax is imposed on each unit of emissions, polluters will reduce their emissions until the marginal benefit of emissions equals the tax, and a least-cost reduction in emissions is achieved.

Emissions taxes are widely used in Europe. France, for example, has enacted taxes on the sulfur dioxide and nitrous oxide emissions of power plants and other industrial firms. Spain has imposed taxes on the dumping of pollutants into the country's waterways. Emissions taxes have long been imposed on firms that dump pollutants into some river systems in Europe.

Emissions taxes are also being used in economies making the transition from socialism to a market system. In China, taxes are used to limit the emission by firms of water pollutants. By law, 80% of the money collected from these taxes goes back to the firms themselves for emissions control projects. The tax in China is a rudimentary one. The level of a firm's emissions is determined by visual inspection of the water just downstream from the point at which the firm emits pollutants. Taxes are imposed based on a guess as to how much the firm has emitted. A similar approach is used in China to limit emissions of particulate matter, an important air pollutant. While the method appears primitive, it is nevertheless successful. During the 1990s, China had the fastest growing economy in the world. Total economic activity increased in China at an annual rate of about 10% per year. Despite this phenomenal increase in economic activity, international estimates of China's emissions of particulates suggest that they were down 50% during the decade. China's emissions of effluents were unchanged during this period of phenomenal growth.

Taxes are also used to limit pollution in the countries of the former Soviet Union. Rather than basing taxes on an estimate of marginal cost, taxes are set according to complicated engineering formulae. In Lithuania, for example, the tax on sulfide emissions in the water has been set at several million dollars per ton. Needless to say, that tax is not even collected.

The important role of pollution taxes in improving environmental quality is often misunderstood. For example, an intriguing battle in the courts followed Argentina's attempt to use taxes to control air pollution. Environmental groups went to federal court, charging that the taxes constituted a "license to pollute." The unfortunate result was that the Argentine government withdrew its effort to control pollution through taxation without finding an adequate substitute policy.[5]

An emissions tax requires, of course, that a polluter's emissions be monitored. The polluter is then charged a tax equal to the tax per unit times the quantity of emissions. The tax clearly gives the polluter an incentive to reduce emissions. It also ensures that reductions will be accomplished by those polluters that can achieve them at the lowest cost. Polluters for whom reductions are most costly will generally find it cheaper to pay the emissions tax.

In cases where it is difficult to monitor emissions, a tax could be imposed indirectly. Consider, for example, farmers' use of fertilizers and pesticides. Rain may wash some of these materials into local rivers, polluting the water. Clearly, it would be virtually impossible to monitor this runoff and assess responsible farmers a charge for their emissions. But it would be possible to levy a tax on these materials when they are sold, confronting farmers with a rough measure of the cost of the pollution their use of these materials imposes.

Marketable Pollution Permits

An alternative to emissions taxes is marketable pollution permits, which allow their owners to emit a certain quantity of pollution during a particular period. The introduction to this chapter dealt with an example of marketable pollution permits; each of the permits to dump a metric ton of greenhouse gases that is purchased results in a reduction in the cost of meeting the goal of reducing the emissions of these gases.

To see how this works, suppose that Firms A and B are again told that they must reduce their emissions to 250 tons of a pollutant per month. This time, however, they are given 250 permits each—one permit allows the emission of one ton per month. They can trade their permits; a firm that emits less than its allotted 250 tons can sell some of its permits to another firm that wants to emit more.

We saw that Firm B can reduce its emissions below 250 tons for a much lower cost than Firm A. For example, it could reduce its emissions to 249 tons for $100. Firm A would be willing to pay $1,000 for the right to emit the 251st ton of emissions. Clearly, a mutually profitable exchange is possible. In fact, as long as their marginal benefits of pollution differ, the firms can profit from exchange. Equilibrium will be achieved at the least-cost solution at which the marginal benefits for both firms are equal.

One virtue of using marketable permits is that this approach represents only a modest departure from traditional command-and-control regulation. Once a polluter has been told to reduce its emissions to a certain quantity, it has a right to emit that quantity. Polluters will exchange rights only if doing so increases their utility or profits—allowing rights to be exchanged can only make them better off. Another benefit, of course, is that such exchanges allow a shift from the inefficient allocation created by command-and-control regulation to an efficient allocation in which pollution is reduced at the lowest possible cost. Finally, each firm will have an incentive to explore ways to reduce its emissions further, either to be able to sell more rights or to require purchasing fewer permits.

Merits of Incentive Approaches

Incentive systems, either emissions taxes or tradable permits, can achieve reductions in emissions at a far lower cost than command-and-control regulation. Even more important, however, are the long-run incentives they create for technological change. A firm that is ordered to reduce its emissions to a certain level has no incentive to do better, whereas a firm facing an emissions tax has a constant incentive to seek out new ways to lower its emissions and thus lower its taxes. Similarly, a firm faces a cost for using an emissions permit—the price that could be obtained from selling the permit—so it will seek ways to reduce emissions. As firms discover new ways to lower their costs of reducing emissions, the demand for emissions permits will fall, lowering the efficient quantity of emissions—and improving environmental quality even further.

Public Policy and Pollution: The Record

Federal efforts to control air and water pollution in the United States have produced mixed results. Air quality has generally improved; water quality has improved in some respects but deteriorated in others.

Figure 18.5 shows how annual average concentrations of airborne pollutants in major U.S. cities have declined since 1980. Lead concentrations have dropped most dramatically, largely because of the increased use of unleaded gasoline.

FIGURE 18.5 U.S. Air Pollution Levels, 1990-2015
The average concentration of major air pollutants in U.S. cities has declined over the past few decades.

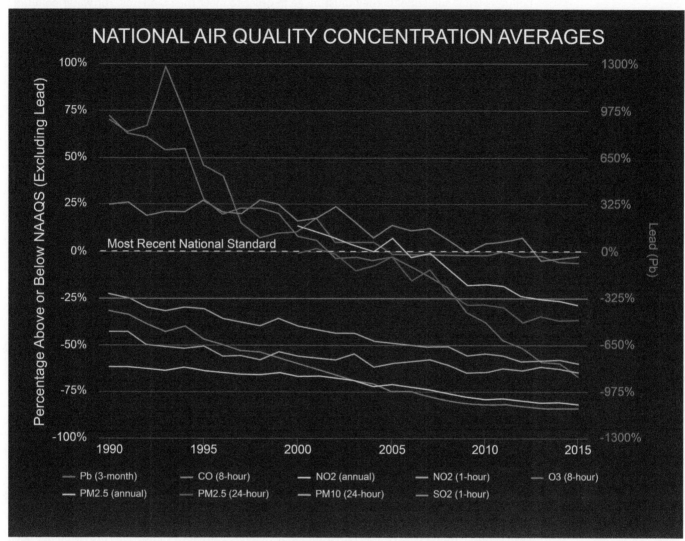

Source: Based on data from U.S. Environmental Protection Agency, Our Nation's Air: Status and Trends Through 2015 available at https://gispub.epa.gov/air/trendsreport/2016/

Public policy has generally stressed command-and-control approaches to air and water pollution. To reduce air pollution, the EPA sets air quality standards that regions must achieve, then tells polluters what adjustments they must make in order to meet the standards. For water pollution, the Environmental Protection Agency (EPA) has set emissions limits based on the technologies it considers reasonable to require of polluters. If the implementation of a particular technology will reduce a polluter's emissions by 20%, for example, the EPA will require a 20% reduction in emissions. National standards have been imposed; no effort has been made to consider the benefits and costs of pollution in individual streams. Further, the EPA's technology-based approach pays little attention to actual water quality—and has produced few gains.

Moreover, environmental problems go beyond national borders. For example, sulfur dioxide emitted from plants in the United States can result in acid rain in Canada and elsewhere. Another possible pollution problem that extends across national borders is suggested by the global warming hypothesis.

Many scientists have argued that increasing emissions of greenhouse gases, caused partly by the burning of fossil fuels, trap ever more of the sun's energy and make the planet warmer. Global warming, they argue, could lead to flooding of coastal areas, losses in agricultural production, and the elimination of many species. If this global warming hypothesis is correct, then carbon dioxide is a pollutant with global implications, one that calls for a global solution.

At the 1997 United Nations conference in Kyoto, Japan, the industrialized countries agreed to cuts in carbon dioxide emissions of 5.2% below the 1990 level by 2010. At the 1998 conference in Buenos Aires, Argentina, 170 countries agreed on a two-year action plan for designing mechanisms to reduce emissions and procedures to encourage transfers of new energy technologies to developing countries.

While the delegates to the conferences sign the various protocols, countries are not bound by them until ratified by appropriate governmental bodies. By 2005, the vast majority of the world's nations had ratified the agreement. The United States had neither signed nor ratified the agreement.

Debates at these conferences have been over the extent to which developing countries should be required to reduce their emissions and over the role that market mechanisms should play. Developing countries argue that their share in total emissions is fairly small and that it is unfair to ask them to give up economic growth, given their lower income levels. As for how emissions reductions will be achieved, the United States has been the strongest advocate for emissions trading in which each country would receive a certain number of tradable emissions rights. This provision has been incorporated in the agreement.

That market approaches have entered the national and international debates on dealing with environmental issues, and to a large extent have even been used, demonstrates the power of economic analysis. Economists have long argued that as pollution-control authorities replace command-and-control strategies with incentive approaches, society will reap huge savings. The economic argument has rested on acknowledging the opportunity costs of addressing environmental concerns and thus has advocated policies that achieve improvements in the environment in the least costly ways.

Key Takeaways

- Public sector intervention is generally needed to move the economy toward the efficient solution in pollution problems.
- Command-and-control approaches are the most widely used methods of public sector intervention, but they are inefficient.

- The exchange of pollution rights can achieve a given reduction in emissions at the lowest cost possible. It also creates incentives to reduce pollution demand through technological change.
- Tax policy can also achieve a least-cost reduction in emissions.

Try It!

Based on your answer to the previous Try It! problem, a tax of what amount would result in the efficient quantity of pollution?

Case in Point: "No" Vote on Revenue-Neutral Carbon Tax for Washington State

Source: © Shutterstock

Among the many issues that confronted voters in Washington state in the elections of November 2016 was Initiative 732, a proposal in that state to tax carbon emissions, starting at $15 per ton of carbon dioxide in the first year, $25 in the second, and then rising each year by the inflation rate plus 3.5% annually until it reached $100 per ton at the 2016 price level. The formula translated into a 25 cents additional tax on a gallon of gas and an additional $8 per month to the average electric bill. The plan was expected to generate about $2 billion a year in revenue, which was to be returned to taxpayers through a one-percentage point reduction in the state sales tax, the elimination of a business tax, and a rebate of up to $1,500 per year to the state's roughly 460,000 low-income workers. The initiative was modeled on a similar scheme which began in British Columbia, Canada in 2008 that is credited with inducing a 7% reduction in fuel consumption per person and a 4% increase in an average car's fuel efficiency. As Wall Street Journal writer Greg Ip argued, "By embedding the cost of carbon dioxide emissions in the prices consumers and business pay for energy, such a tax automatically encourages conservation and makes renewable energy more appealing, without regulations and subsidies that distort investment or undercut growth. Because the revenue is used to cut other taxes, it doesn't crimp incomes or undermine business competitiveness." In other words, it is an example of an incentive approach to environmental improvement. And then by lowering taxes elsewhere, the proposal was designed to have little or no effect on overall income and thus to not harm the economy as a whole.

The proposal met opposition from across the political spectrum. Some people opposed to the measure were probably putting little importance on the reduction in the use of fossil fuels, perhaps because they are not worried about pollution or the possible effects of human-induced climate change. Some opposition voters might be enjoying the lower gasoline or electricity prices and simultaneously were feeling skeptical that the tax reductions would compensate them personally for the higher fuel prices. The somewhat surprising resistance from those who do think reducing pollution and climate change are important stemmed from how the revenue raised from the tax was to be spent. Some environmentalists preferred revenues be used for clean energy developments and to assist workers and communities most impacted by climate change, for example.

On November 8, the initiative was resoundingly defeated, with about 40% of the votes for and 60% against. It is too early to say whether or not similar initiatives will be tried in other states. In a post-election statement from the co-chair of the organization that spearheaded Initiative 732, economist Yoram Bauman said, "While we did not pass the nation's first carbon tax, many states around the country are looking at I-732 as a model and we expect a nationwide movement to take root in the years ahead. We will look back at this as a lost opportunity to create history in Washington State, but also as a catalyst for much needed U.S. leadership on climate action." Time will tell.

Source: Based on Greg Ip, "A Carbon Tax That Won't Hurt Growth," The Wall Street Journal, September 29, 2016: A2; http://carbonwa.org/5910-2/.

Answer to Try It! Problem

The paper mill will reduce its pollution until the marginal benefit of polluting equals the tax. In this case a tax of $70 would cause the paper mill to reduce its pollution to 4 tons, the efficient level. At pollution levels below that amount, the marginal benefit of polluting exceeds the tax, and so the paper mill is better off polluting and paying the tax. At pollution levels greater than that amount, the marginal benefit of polluting is less than the tax.

18.4 Review and Practice

Summary

Pollution is a by-product of human activity. It occurs when the environment becomes scarce—when dumping garbage imposes a cost. There are benefits as well as costs to pollution; the efficient quantity of pollution occurs where the difference between total benefits and total costs is maximized. This solution is achieved where the marginal benefit of additional pollution equals the marginal cost. We have seen that an alternative approach shows that efficiency is also achieved where the marginal benefit of pollution abatement equals the marginal cost of abatement.

Economists measure the benefits of pollution in terms of the costs of not dumping the pollution. The same curve can be read from left to right as the marginal benefit curve for emissions and from right to left as the marginal cost curve for abatement.

The costs of pollution are measured in two ways. One is through direct surveys. Respondents can be asked how much compensation they would be willing to accept in exchange for a reduction in environmental pollution; alternatively, they can be asked how much they would pay for an improvement in environmental quality. A second approach infers the marginal cost of increased pollution from other relationships. The effects of pollution on house prices or rental values, for example, allow economists to estimate the value people place on environmental quality. Pollution costs can also be estimated on the basis of the costs they impose on firms in production.

Three types of policies are available to reduce pollution. Moral suasion is sometimes used, but it is effective only under limited conditions. Command-and-control regulation is used most commonly, but it is likely to be inefficient. It also fails to provide incentives for technological change in the long run. The most promising policies are the incentive approaches, which include emissions taxes and marketable pollution permits. Both can be designed to reduce emissions at the lowest cost possible, and both create an incentive for firms to search out new and cheaper ways to reduce emissions.

Although public policy has stressed command-and-control methods in the past, pollution rights exchanges are now being introduced. Past policies may have been inefficient, but they have succeeded in improving air quality, at least in the nation's cities.

Concept Problems

1. We have noted that economists consider the benefits and costs of pollution from the perspective of people's preferences. Some critics argue, however, that the interests of plants and animals should be considered: for example, if pollution is harming trees, the trees have a right to protection. Do you think that is a good idea? How would it be implemented?

2. List five choices you make that result in pollution. What price do you pay to pollute the environment? Does that price affect your choices?

3. In any urban area, what group is likely to be exposed to a greater level of pollution—rich people or poor people? (*Hint:* Utilize the findings of economists concerning the relationship between house prices and pollution levels.)

4. Suppose the accompanying graph shows the demand and marginal cost curves, *D* and *MC*, for a pollutant in a particular area. How do you think future economic and population growth will affect the efficient rate of emissions per period, *Q*, and thus the level of pollution?

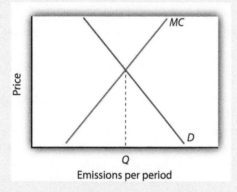

5. "Environmental quality is not just a matter of technical efficiency; it's about how people relate to nature. Economists are completely off base in their analysis of the benefits and costs of pollution." What is your opinion of this quote?

6. Campaigns that exhort us to "Give a hoot—don't pollute" imply that anyone who pollutes the environment is uncaring—that people who are concerned about environmental quality would not be dumping garbage into the environment. Is that true?

7. We have seen that a system of marketable pollution permits achieves the same solution as a system of emissions taxes. Which do you think would be fairer? Why?

8. Many environmentalists are horrified by the notion of marketable pollution permits advocated by economists. These environmentalists insist that pollution is wrong, and that no one should be able to buy the right to pollute the environment. What do you think?

9. Some people object that charging firms for their emissions will do no good—firms will simply raise their prices and go on doing what they were doing before. Comment on this objection to emissions taxes.

10. Suppose firms in a perfectly competitive industry generate water pollution as a by-product of their production, and they are not charged for this. Who benefits from their use of the environment as a dumping ground? If an emissions tax is imposed, costs to these firms increase and emissions drop. Who will bear the burden of this tax? Is that fair?

11. The Case in Point on measurement suggested that the demand curve for locating a house farther from a hazardous waste site could be inferred from property value studies. Explain how this could be the case.

12. Does the road pricing system in Singapore strike you as fair? Would you like to see such a system in your own area? Why or why not?

Numerical Problems

1. Suppose the dry-cleaning industry is perfectly competitive. The process of dry cleaning generates emissions that pollute the air, and firms now emit this pollution at no cost. Suppose that the long run equilibrium price for dry cleaning a typical item is $5, and a pollution-control program increases the marginal cost by $1 per item.

   a. How will the pollution-control program affect the price of dry-cleaning services in the short run? Explain and illustrate graphically.

   b. Explain and illustrate graphically how the program will affect the output of dry-cleaning services in the short run.

   c. Explain and illustrate graphically how the $1 increase in cost will affect the price of dry-cleaning services in the long run.

   d. Explain and illustrate graphically how the cost increase will affect the quantity of dry-cleaning services produced in the long run.

   e. Who pays for pollution control in the industry? Explain, relating your answer to the basic conclusion about long-run equilibrium in a perfectly competitive industry.

2. Now suppose the dry-cleaning industry in the community is monopolistically competitive. Suppose the initial price per unit of dry-cleaning is $6. Suppose that a charge levied on dry-cleaning firms for the pollution they generate increases the cost of a unit of dry-cleaning by $1.

   a. Explain and illustrate graphically how the $1 charge will affect the price charged by typical firm in the short run.

   b. Explain and illustrate graphically how the $1 charge will affect the typical firm's output in the short run.

   c. Now explain and illustrate graphically how the $1 charge will affect price and output of a typical firm in the long run. Through what mechanism does this occur?

   d. Compare your answers for a world of monopolistically competitive firms to a world of perfectly competitive firms. Is there any significant difference between the conclusions of the two models?

3. Suppose local government regulations allow only a single firm to provide dry-cleaning services to a local community, and this firm generates pollution as in Problem 1. The firm initially charges a price of $4 per item. Now a pollution-control program is imposed, increasing the firm's marginal and average total costs by $1 per item.

   a. Explain and illustrate graphically how the program will affect the firm's price and output.

   b. Who pays for the pollution-control program?

4. Suppose the marginal benefit (*MB*) and marginal cost (*MC*) curves for emitting particulate matter are given by the following schedules, where *E* is the quantity of emissions per period. The marginal benefits and costs are measured at the quantities of emissions shown.

E/period	MB	MC
0	$230	$0
200	190	10
400	150	30
600	110	50
800	70	70
1,000	30	90

  a. Plot the marginal benefit and marginal cost curves and state the efficient quantity of emissions per period.

  b. What quantity of emissions will occur when the price of emissions is zero?

  c. What tax rate would achieve the efficient rate of emissions?

5. Now suppose that rising incomes increase marginal cost as follows:

E/period	New MC
0	$0
200	30
400	70
600	110
800	150
1,000	190

  a. Plot the new marginal cost curve in the graph you drew in Problem 4. What is the new efficient quantity of emissions per period?

  b. What quantity of emissions will occur when the price of emissions is zero?

  c. What tax rate would achieve the efficient rate of emissions?

6. The text contains the following statement: "All other variables unchanged, increasing the distance from a house to a hazardous site by 10% increased house value by 0.3%." What is the price elasticity of house prices with respect to proximity to a hazardous waste site?

Endnotes

1. Environmental Protection Agency, The Plain English Guide to the Environmental Protection Act, Publication No. EPA-456/K-07-001, April 2007 available at https://www.epa.gov/clean-air-act-overview/plain-english-guide-clean-air-act.

2. The Environmental Defense Fund, The Institute for Climate Economics, and International Emissions Trading Association, The World's Carbon Markets: A Case Study Guide to Emissions Trading, available at https://www.edf.org/climate/worlds-carbon-markets.

3. R. H. Coase, "The Problem of Social Cost," Journal of Law and Economics 3 (October 1960): 1–44.

4. See, for example, Nir Becker and Doron Lavee, "The Benefits and Costs of Noise Reduction," Journal of Environmental Planning and Management, 46:1 (January 2003): 97–111, which shows the negative relationship between apartment prices and noise levels (a form of pollution) in Israel.

5. The observations on pollution taxes in China, Argentina, and Lithuania are from Randall A. Bluffstone, "Environmental Taxes in Developing and Transition Economies," Public Finance & Management 3:1 (Spring, 2003): 143–75.

CHAPTER 19
Inequality, Poverty, and Discrimination

19.1 Start Up: Occupy Wall Street and the World

It all began September 17, 2011, with a march by thousands of demonstrators unhappy with all sorts of things about the United States—the distribution of income, with rallying cries on behalf of the 99%; "greed" on Wall Street; the bailout of many banks; capitalism in general; and a variety of other perceived ills, from hostility to certain nonfinancial companies such as Walmart and Starbucks to calls for the United States to pull out of military operations around the world and to abolish the Federal Reserve Bank. The symbol of the movement became the occupation of a small park in the neighborhood of Wall Street—Zuccotti Park. Two months later, the park continued to be jammed with demonstrators using it as a campground, after which New York City Mayor Michael Bloomberg shut it down as a place for overnight lodging.

Well before then, the "Occupy Wall Street" movement had become a national phenomenon and then an international phenomenon. The *Economist* in mid-October reported demonstrations in more than 900 cities and in more than 80 countries. The demonstrators generally rejected the entire concept of making specific demands, preferring instead to protest in support of an ill-defined, but clearly compelling, message—whatever that message might have been.

Who were the demonstrators? Douglas Schoen, who once worked as a pollster for President Bill Clinton, had his survey firm interview about 200 protesters occupying Zuccotti Park in mid-October of 2011 about their views. According to Schoen's survey, the Zuccotti Park demonstrators were committed to a radical redistribution of income and sharp increases in government regulation of the economy, with 98% of them supporting civil disobedience to further their aims and 31% advocating violent measures to achieve their goals. A Pew survey at about the same time found Americans divided in their opinion about the "Occupy Wall Street" movement, with nearly 40% in support and about 35% opposed. At the same time, support and opposition for the Tea Party were running 32% in favor and 44% opposed.[1]

Whatever the makeup of the groups demonstrating throughout the world, they clearly brought the issues examined in this chapter—poverty, discrimination, and the distribution of income—to the forefront of public attention. It was not obvious why inequality and related complaints had suddenly become an important issue. As we will see in this chapter, inequality in the U.S. distribution of income had begun increasing in 1967; it has continued to rise ever since.

At about the same time as the movement was in the news, the poverty rate in the United States reached its highest level since 1993. The number of people below the U.S. poverty line in 2010—an annual income of $22,314 for a family of four—rose to 15.1% of the population. The number of people considered to be below the poverty level rose to 46.2 million, the highest number ever recorded in the history of the United States. That number has since fallen somewhat to 43.2 million people. Those statistics came more than four decades after President Lyndon B. Johnson stood before the Congress of the United States to make his first State of the Union address in 1964 to declare a new kind of war, a War on Poverty. "This administration today here and now declares unconditional war on poverty in America," the President said. "Our aim is not only to relieve the symptoms of poverty but to cure it; and, above all, to prevent it." In the United States that year, 35.1 million people, about

22% of the population, were, by the official definition, poor. Today, while the number of people in poverty is higher, the percentage in poverty is much lower.

The President's plan included stepped-up federal aid to low-income people, an expanded health-care program for the poor, new housing subsidies, expanded federal aid to education, and job training programs. The proposal became law later that same year. More than four decades and trillions of dollars in federal antipoverty spending later, the nation seems to have made little progress toward the President's goal.

In this chapter, we shall also explore the problem of discrimination. Being at the lower end of the income distribution and being poor are more prevalent among racial minorities and among women than among white males. To a degree, this situation may reflect discrimination. We shall investigate the economics of discrimination and its consequences for the victims and for the economy. We shall also assess efforts by the public sector to eliminate discrimination.

Questions of fairness often accompany discussions of income inequality, poverty, and discrimination. Answering them ultimately involves value judgments; they are normative questions, not positive ones. You must decide for yourself if a particular distribution of income is fair or if society has made adequate progress toward reducing poverty or discrimination. The material in this chapter will not answer those questions for you; rather, in order for you to have a more informed basis for making your own value judgments, it will shed light on what economists have learned about these issues through study and testing of hypotheses.

19.2 Income Inequality

Learning Objectives

1. Explain how the Lorenz curve and the Gini coefficient provide information on a country's distribution of income.
2. Discuss and evaluate the factors that have been looked at to explain changes in the distribution of income in the United States.

Income inequality in the United States has soared in the last half century. According to the Congressional Budget Office, between 1979 and 2007, real average household income—taking into account government transfers and federal taxes—rose 62%. For the top 1% of the population, it grew 275%. For others in the top 20% of the population, it grew 65%. For the 60% of the population in the middle, it grew a bit under 40% and for the 20% of the population at the lowest end of the income distribution, it grew about 18%.[2]

Increasingly, education is the key to a better material life. The gap between the average annual incomes of high school graduates and those with a bachelor's degree increased substantially over the last half century. A recent study undertaken at the Georgetown University Center on Education and the Workforce concluded that people with a bachelor's degree earn 84% more over a lifetime than do people who are high school graduates only. That college premium is up from 75% in 1999.[3] Moreover, education is not an equal opportunity employer. A student from a family in the upper end of the income distribution is much more likely to get a college degree than a student whose family is in the lower end of the income distribution.

That inequality perpetuates itself. College graduates marry other college graduates and earn higher incomes. Those who do not go to college earn lower incomes. Some may have children out of wedlock—an almost sure route to poverty. That does not, of course, mean that young people who go to college are assured high incomes while those who do not are certain to experience poverty, but the odds certainly push in that direction.

We shall learn in this section how the degree of inequality can be measured. We shall examine the sources of rising inequality and consider what policy measures, if any, are suggested. In this section on inequality we are essentially focusing the way the economic pie is shared, while setting aside the important fact that the size of the economic pie has certainly grown over time.

A Changing Distribution of Income

We have seen that the income distribution has become more unequal. This section describes a graphical approach to measuring the equality, or inequality, of the distribution of income.

Measuring Inequality

The primary evidence of growing inequality is provided by census data. Households are asked to report their income, and they are ranked from the household with the lowest income to the household with the highest income. The Census Bureau then reports the percentage of total income earned by those households ranked among the bottom 20%, the next 20%, and so on, up to the top 20%. Each 20% of households is called a quintile. The bureau also reports the share of income going to the top 5% of households.

Income distribution data can be presented graphically using a **Lorenz curve**, a curve that shows cumulative shares of income received by individuals or groups. It was developed by economist Max O. Lorenz in 1905. To plot the curve, we begin with the lowest quintile and mark a point to show the percentage of total income those households received. We then add the next quintile and its share and mark a point to show the share of the lowest 40% of households. Then, we add the third quintile, and then the fourth. Since the share of income received by all the quintiles will be 100%, the last point on the curve always shows that 100% of households receive 100% of the income.

Lorenz curve
A curve that shows cumulative shares of income received by individuals or groups.

If every household in the United States received the same income, the Lorenz curve would coincide with the 45-degree line drawn in Figure 19.1. The bottom 20% of households would receive 20% of income; the bottom 40% would receive 40%, and so on. If the distribution of income were completely unequal, with one household receiving all the income and the rest zero, then the Lorenz curve would be shaped like a backward L, with a horizontal line across the bottom of the graph at 0% income and a vertical line up the right-hand side. The vertical line would show, as always, that 100% of families still receive 100% of income. Actual Lorenz curves lie between these extremes. The closer a Lorenz curve lies to the 45-degree line, the more equal the distribution. The more bowed out the curve, the less equal the distribution. We see in Figure 19.1 that the Lorenz curve for the United States became more bowed out between 1967 and 2015.

FIGURE 19.1 The Distribution of U.S. Income, 1967 and 2015

The distribution of income among households in the United States became more unequal from 1967 to 2015. The shares of income received by each of the first four quintiles fell, while the share received by the top 20% rose sharply. The Lorenz curve for 2015 was more bowed out than was the curve for 1967. (Mean income adjusted for inflation and reported in 2015 dollars; percentages do not sum to 100% due to rounding.)

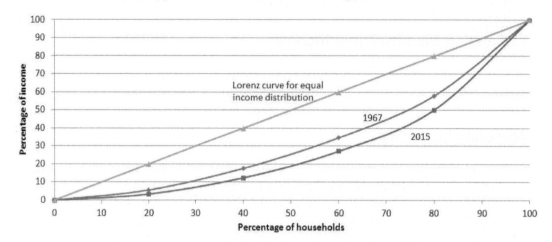

Source: Based on data from Bernadette D. Proctor, Jessica L. Semega, and Melissa A. Kollar, U.S. Census Bureau, Current Population Reports P60-256(RV), Income and Poverty in the United States: 2015, U.S. Government printing Office, Washington, DC, 2016,Table A-3; U.S. Census Bureau, Current Population Survey, 2016 Annual Social and Economic Supplement, Table HINC-05.

Gini coefficient

A measure of inequality expressed as the ratio of the area between the Lorenz curve and a 45° line and the total area under the 45° line.

The degree of inequality is often measured with a **Gini coefficient**, the ratio between the Lorenz curve and the 45° line and the total area under the 45° line. The smaller the Gini coefficient, the more equal the income distribution. Larger Gini coefficients mean more unequal distributions. The Census Bureau reported that the Gini coefficient was 0.359 in 1967 and 0.457 in 2010.[4]

Mobility and Income Distribution

When we speak of the bottom 20% or the middle 20% of families, we are not speaking of a static group. Some families who are in the bottom quintile one year move up to higher quintiles in subsequent years; some families move down. Because people move up and down the distribution, we get a quite different picture of income change when we look at the incomes of a fixed set of persons over time rather than comparing average incomes for a particular quintile at a particular point in time, as was done in Figure 19.1.

Addressing the question of mobility requires that researchers follow a specific group of families over a long period of time. Since 1968, the Panel Survey of Income Dynamics (PSID) at the University of Michigan has followed more than 5,000 families and their descendents. The effort has produced a much deeper understanding of changes in income inequality than it is possible to obtain from census data, which simply take a snapshot of incomes at a particular time.

Based on the University of Michigan's data, Federal Reserve Bank of Boston economist Katharine Bradbury compared mobility over the decades through 2005. She concluded that on most mobility measures, family income mobility was significantly lower in the 1990s and early 2000s than in earlier periods. Moreover, when families move out of a quintile, they move less. Finally, she notes that for the recent decades moving across quintiles has become harder to achieve precisely because of the increased income inequality.[5]

Explaining Inequality

Everyone agrees that the distribution of income in the United States generally became more equal during the first two decades after World War II and that it has become more unequal since 1968. While some people conclude that this increase in inequality suggests the latter period was unfair, others want to know why the distribution changed. We shall examine some of the explanations.

Family Structure

Clearly, an important source of rising inequality since 1968 has been the sharp increase in the number of families headed by women. In 2010, the median income of families headed by married couples was 2.5 times that of families headed by women without a spouse. The percentage of families headed by women with no spouse present has nearly doubled since 1968 and is thus contributing to increased inequality across households.

Technological and Managerial Change

Technological change has affected the demand for labor. One of the most dramatic changes since the late 1970s has been an increase in the demand for skilled labor and a reduction in the demand for unskilled labor.

The result has been an increase in the gap between the wages of skilled and unskilled workers. That has produced a widening gap between college- and high-school-trained workers.

Technological change has meant the integration of computers into virtually every aspect of production. And that has increased the demand for workers with the knowledge to put new methods to work—and to adapt to the even more dramatic changes in production likely to come. At the same time, the demand for workers who do not have that knowledge has fallen.

Along with new technologies that require greater technical expertise, firms are adopting new management styles that require stronger communication skills. The use of production teams, for example, shifts decision-making authority to small groups of assembly-line workers. That means those workers need more than the manual dexterity that was required of them in the past. They need strong communication skills. They must write effectively, speak effectively, and interact effectively with other workers. Workers who cannot do so simply are not in demand to the degree they once were.

The "intellectual wage gap" seems likely to widen as we move even further into the twenty-first century. That is likely to lead to an even higher degree of inequality and to pose a challenge to public policy for decades to come. Increasing education and training could lead to reductions in inequality. Indeed, individuals seem to have already begun to respond to this changing market situation, since the percentage who graduate from high school and college is rising.

Tax Policy

Did tax policy contribute to rising inequality over the past four decades? The tax changes most often cited in the fairness debate are the Reagan tax cuts introduced in 1981 and the Bush tax cuts introduced in 2001, 2002, and 2003.

An analysis of the Bush tax cuts by the Tax Foundation combines the three Bush tax cuts and assumes they occurred in 2003. Table 19.1 gives the share of total income tax liability for each quintile before and after the Bush tax cuts. It also gives the share of the Bush tax cuts received by each quintile.

TABLE 19.1 Income Tax Liability Before and After the Bush Tax Cuts
The share of total tax relief received by the first four quintiles was modest, while those in the top quintile received more than two-thirds of the total benefits of the three tax cuts. However, the share of income taxes paid by each of the first four quintiles fell as a result of the tax cuts, while the share paid by the top quintile rose.

Quintile	Share of income tax liability before tax cuts	Share of income tax liability after tax cuts	Share of total tax relief
First quintile	0.5%	0.3%	1.2%
Second quintile	2.3%	1.9%	4.2%
Third quintile	5.9%	5.2%	9.4%
Fourth quintile	12.6%	11.6%	17.5%
Top quintile	78.7%	81.0%	67.7%

Source: Based on data from William Ahern, "Comparing the Kennedy, Reagan, and Bush Tax Cuts," Tax Foundation Fiscal Facts, August 24, 2004.

Tax cuts under George W. Bush were widely criticized as being tilted unfairly toward the rich. And certainly, Table 19.1 shows that the share of total tax relief received by the first four quintiles was modest, while those in the top quintile garnered more than two-thirds of the total benefits of the three tax cuts. Looking at the second and third columns of the table, however, gives a different perspective. The share of income taxes paid by each of the first four quintiles fell as a result of the tax cuts, while the share paid by the top quintile rose. Further, we see that each of the first four quintiles paid a very small share of income taxes before and after the tax cuts, while those in the top quintile ended up shouldering more than 80% of the total income tax burden. We saw in Figure 19.1 that those in the top quintile received just over half of total income. After the Bush tax cuts, they paid 81% of income taxes. Others are quick to point out that those same tax cuts were accompanied by reductions in expenditures for some social service programs designed to help lower income families. Still others point out that the tax cuts contributed to an increase in the federal deficit and, therefore, are likely to have distributional effects over many years and across several generations. Whether these changes increased or decreased fairness in the society is ultimately a normative question.

Methodology

The method by which the Census Bureau computes income shares has been challenged by some observers. For example, quintiles of households do not contain the same number of people. Rea Hederman of the Heritage Foundation, a conservative think tank, notes that the top 20% of households contains about 25% of the population. Starting in 2006, the Census Bureau report began calculating a measure called "equivalence-adjusted income" to take into account family size. The Gini coefficient for 2010 using this adjustment fell slightly from 0.469 to 0.457. The trend over time in the two Gini coefficients is similar. Two other flaws pointed out by Mr. Hederman are that taxes and benefits from noncash programs that help the poor are not included. While some Census studies attempt to take these into account and report lower inequality, other studies do not receive as much attention as the main Census annual report.[6]

Even studies that look at incomes over a decade may not capture lifetime income. For example, people in retirement may have a low income but their consumption may be bolstered by drawing on their savings. Younger people may be borrowing to go to school, buy a house, or for other things. The annual income approach of the Census data does not capture this and even the ten-year look in the mobility study mentioned above is too short a period.

This suggests that more precise measurements may provide more insight into explaining inequality.

Key Takeaways

- The distribution of income can be illustrated with a Lorenz curve. If all households had the same income, the Lorenz curve would be a 45° line. In general, the more equal the distribution of income, the closer the Lorenz curve will be to the 45° line. A more bowed out curves shows a less equal distribution. The Gini coefficient is another method for describing the distribution of income.

- The distribution of income has, according to the Census Bureau, become somewhat more unequal in the United States during the past 40 years.

- The degree of mobility up and down the distribution of income appears to have declined in recent years.

- Among the factors explaining increased inequality have been changes in family structure and changes in the demand for labor that have rewarded those with college degrees and have penalized unskilled workers.

- Assessing the fairness of tax policy changes is a normative issue that could include looking at how a new policy affects the share of taxes paid by different quintiles as well as its impact on other variables such as government deficits and social programs.

Try It!

The accompanying Lorenz curves show the distribution of income in a country before taxes and welfare benefits are taken into account (curve *A*) and after taxes and welfare benefits are taken into account (curve *B*). Do taxes and benefits serve to make the distribution of income in the country more equal or more unequal?

Case in Point: Attitudes and Inequality

Source: © 2010 Jupiterimages Corporation

In a fascinating examination of attitudes in the United States and in continental Western Europe, economists Alberto Alesina of Harvard University and George-Marios Angeletos of the Massachusetts Institute of Technology suggest that attitudes about the nature of income earning can lead to quite different economic systems and outcomes concerning the distribution of income.

The economists cite survey evidence from the World Values Survey, which concludes that 71% of Americans, and only 40% of Europeans, agree with the proposition: *"The poor could become rich if they just tried hard enough."* Further, Americans are much more likely to attribute material success to hard work, while Europeans tend to attribute success to factors such as luck, connections, and even corruption. The result, according to Professors Alesina and Angeletos, is that Americans select a government that is smaller and engages in less redistributive activity than is selected by Europeans. Government in continental Western Europe is 50% larger than in the United States, the tax system in Europe is much more progressive than in the United States, regulation of labor and product markets is more extensive in Europe, and redistributive programs are more extensive in Europe than in the United States. As a result, the income distribution in Europe is much more equal than in the United States.

People get what they expect. The economists derive two sets of equilibria. Equilibrium in a society in which people think incomes are a result of luck, connections, and corruption turns out to be precisely that. And, in a society in which people believe incomes are chiefly the result of effort and skill, they are. In the latter society, people work harder and invest more. In the United States, the average worker works 1,600 hours per year. In Europe, the average worker works 1,200 hours per year.

So, who is right—Americans with their "you get what you deserve" or Europeans with their "you get what luck, connections, and corruption bring you" attitude? The two economists show that people get, in effect, what they expect. European values and beliefs produce societies that are more egalitarian. American values and beliefs produce the American result: a society in which the distribution of income is more unequal, the government smaller, and redistribution relatively minor. Professors Alesina and Angeletos conclude that Europeans tend to underestimate the degree to which people can improve their material well-being through hard work, while Americans tend to overestimate that same phenomenon.

Source: Based on Alberto Alesina and George-Marios Angeletos, "Fairness and Redistribution," American Economic Review 95:4 (September, 2005) 960–80.

Answer to Try It! Problem

The Lorenz curve showing the distribution of income after taxes and benefits are taken into account is less bowed out than the Lorenz curve showing the distribution of income before taxes and benefits are taken into account. Thus, income is more equally distributed after taking them into account.

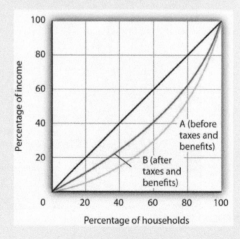

19.3 The Economics of Poverty

Learning Objectives

1. Distinguish between relative and absolute measures of poverty and discuss the uses and merits of each.
2. Describe the demographics of poverty in the United States.
3. Describe the forms of welfare programs in the United States and the reform of welfare in the mid-1990s.
4. Discuss the factors that have been looked at to explain the persistence of poverty in the United States.

Poverty in the United States is something of a paradox. Per capita incomes in this country are among the highest on earth. Yet, the United States has a greater percentage of its population below the official poverty line than in the other industrialized nations. How can a nation that is so rich have so many people who are poor?

There is no single answer to the question of why so many people are poor. But we shall see that there are economic factors at work that help to explain poverty. We shall also examine the nature of the government's response to poverty and the impact that response has. First, however, we shall examine the definition of poverty and look at some characteristics of the poor in the United States.

Defining Poverty

Suppose you were asked to determine whether a particular family was poor or not poor. How would you do it?

You might begin by listing the goods and services that would be needed to provide a minimum standard of living and then finding out if the family's income was enough to purchase those items. If it were not, you might conclude that the family was poor. Alternatively, you might examine the family's income relative to the incomes of other families in the community or in the nation. If the family was on the low end of the income scale, you might classify it as poor.

These two approaches represent two bases on which poverty is defined. The first is an **absolute income test**, which sets a specific income level and defines a person as poor if his or her income falls below that level. The second is a **relative income test**, in which people whose incomes fall at the bottom of the income distribution are considered poor. For example, we could rank households according to income as we did in the previous section on income inequality and define the lowest one-fifth of households as poor. In 2015, any U.S. household with an annual income below $23,000 fell in this category.

In contrast, to determine who is poor according to the absolute income test, we define a specific level of income, independent of how many households fall above or below it. The federal government defines a household as poor if the household's annual income falls below a dollar figure called the **poverty line**. In 2015 the poverty line for a family of four was an income of $24,257. Table 19.2 shows the poverty line for various family sizes.

absolute income test

Income test that sets a specific income level and defines a person as poor if his or her income falls below that level.

relative income test

Income test in which people whose incomes fall at the bottom of the income distribution are considered poor.

poverty line

Amount of annual income below which the federal government defines a household as poor.

TABLE 19.2 Weighted Average Poverty Thresholds in 2015, by Size of Family

The Census Bureau uses a set of 48 money income thresholds that vary by family size and composition to determine who is in poverty. The "Weighted Average Poverty Thresholds" in the accompanying table is a summary of the 48 thresholds used by the census bureau. It provides a general sense of the "poverty line" based on the relative number of families by size and composition.

Number of People in Household	Poverty Line
One person	$12,082
Two people	15,391
Three people	18,871
Four people	24,257
Five people	28,741
Six people	32,542
Seven people	36,998
Eight people	41,029
Nine people or more	49,177

Source: Based on data from Bernadette D. Proctor, Jessica L. Semega, and Melissa A. Kollar, U.S. Census Bureau, Current Population Reports P60-256(RV), Income and Poverty in the United States: 2015, U.S. Government printing Office, Washington, DC, 2016, p. 43.

The concept of a poverty line grew out of a Department of Agriculture study in 1955 that found families spending one-third of their incomes on food. With the one-third figure as a guide, the Department then selected food plans that met the minimum daily nutritional requirements established by the federal government. The cost of the least expensive plan for each household size was multiplied by three to determine the income below which a household would be considered poor. The government used this method to count the number of poor people from 1959 to 1969. The poverty line was adjusted each year as food prices changed. Beginning in 1969, the poverty line was adjusted annually by the average percentage price change for all consumer goods, not just changes in the price of food.

There is little to be said for this methodology for defining poverty. No attempt is made to establish an income at which a household could purchase basic necessities. Indeed, no attempt is made in the definition to establish what such necessities might be. The day has long passed when the average household devoted one-third of its income to food purchases; today such purchases account for less than one-seventh of household income. Still, it is useful to have some threshold that is consistent from one year to the next so that progress—or the lack thereof—in the fight against poverty can be assessed. In addition, the U.S. Census Bureau and the Bureau of Labor Statistics have begun working on more broad-based alternative measures of poverty. The new Supplemental Poverty Measure is based on expenses for food, clothing, shelter, and utilities; adjusts for geographic differences; adds in various in-kind benefits such as school lunches, housing subsidies, and energy assistance; includes tax credits; and then subtracts out taxes, work expenses, and out-of-pocket medical expenses.[7]

poverty rate

The percentage of the population that falls below the poverty line.

The percentage of the population that falls below the poverty line is called the **poverty rate**. Figure 19.2 shows both the number of people and the percentage of the population that fell below the poverty line each year since 1959.

FIGURE 19.2 The Poverty Rate in the United States, 1959–2015
The curve shows the percentage of people who lived in households that fell below the poverty line in each year from 1959 to 2015. The poverty rate fell through the 1960s and since has been hovering between about 12% and 15%. It tends to rise during recessions.

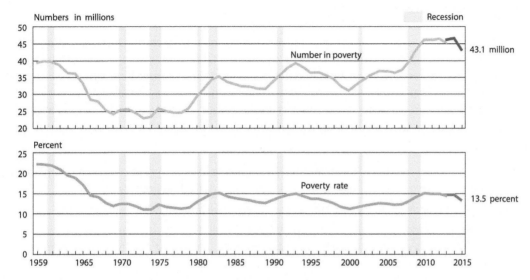

Source: Bernadette D. Proctor, Jessica L. Semega, and Melissa A. Kollar, U.S. Census Bureau, Current Population Reports P60-256(RV), Income and Poverty in the United States: 2015, U.S. Government printing Office, Washington, DC, 2016, Figure 4, p. 12.

Despite its shortcomings, measuring poverty using an absolute measure allows for the possibility of progress in reducing it; using a relative measure of poverty does not, since there will always be a lowest 1/5, or 1/10 of the population. But relative measures do make an important point: Poverty is in large measure a relative concept. In the United States, people defined as poor have much higher incomes than most of the world's people or even than average Americans did as recently as the early 1970s. By international and historical standards, the average poor person in the United States is rich! The material possessions of America's poor would be considered lavish in another time and in another place. For example, based on data from 2005 to 2009, 42% of poor households in the United States owned their own homes, nearly 75% owned a car, and 64% have cable or satellite TV. Over 80% of poor households had air conditioning. Forty years ago, only 36% of the entire population in the United States had air conditioning. The average poor person in the United States has more living space than the average *person* in London, Paris, Vienna, or Athens.[8]

We often think of poverty as meaning that poor people are unable to purchase adequate food. Yet, according to Department of Agriculture surveys, 83% of poor people report that they have adequate food and 96% of poor parents report that their children are never hungry because they cannot afford food. In short, poor people in the United States enjoy a standard of living that would be considered quite comfortable in many parts of the developed world—and lavish in the less developed world.[9]

But people judge their incomes relative to incomes of people around them, not relative to people everywhere on the planet or to people in years past. You may feel poor when you compare yourself to some of your classmates who may have fancier cars or better clothes. And a family of four in a Los Angeles slum with an annual income of $13,000 surely does not feel rich because its income is many times higher than the average family income in Ethiopia or of Americans of several decades ago. While the material possessions of poor Americans are vast by Ethiopian standards, they are low in comparison to how the average American lives. What we think of as poverty clearly depends more on what people around us are earning than on some absolute measure of income.

Both the absolute and relative income approaches are used in discussions of the poverty problem. When we speak of the number of poor people, we are typically using an absolute income test of poverty. When we speak of the problems of those at the bottom of the income distribution, we are speaking in terms of a relative income test. In the European Union, for example, the poverty line is set at 60% of the median income of each member nation in a particular year. That is an example of a relative measure of poverty. In the rest of this section, we focus on the absolute income test of poverty used in the United States.

The Demographics of Poverty

There is no iron law of poverty that dictates that a household with certain characteristics will be poor. Nonetheless, poverty is much more highly concentrated among some groups than among others. The six characteristics of families that are important for describing who in the United States constitute the poor are whether or not the family is headed by a female, age, the level of education, whether or not the head of the family is working, the race of the household, and geography.

Figure 19.3 shows poverty rates for various groups and for the population as a whole in 2015. What does it tell us?

1. A family headed by a female is more than five times as likely to live in poverty as compared to a family with two parents present. This fact contributes to child poverty.

2. Children under 18 are about two times more likely to be poor than older (65 and over) persons.

3. The less education the adults in the family have, the more likely the family is to be poor. A college education is an almost sure ticket out of poverty; the poverty rate for college graduates is just 4.5%.

4. The poverty rate is higher among those who do not work than among those who do. The poverty rate for people who did not work was about seven times the poverty rate of those who worked full time.

5. The prevalence of poverty varies by race and ethnicity. Specifically, the poverty rate in 2015 for whites (non-Hispanic origin) was less than half that for Hispanics or of blacks.

6. The poverty rate in cities is higher than in other areas of residence.

The incidence of poverty soars when several of these demographic factors associated with poverty are combined. For example, the poverty rate for families with children that are headed by women who lack a high school education is higher than 50%.

The new, more broad-based Supplemental Poverty Measure shows an increase of only 0.1 compared to the official poverty rate measure, but bigger differences for different segments of the population. For example, a smaller percentage of people under the age of 18 are poor according to the supplemental poverty measure (18.2% versus 22.5%), while a larger percentage of those over 64 years of age are considered poor (15.9% versus 9.0%). The new measure also shows lower poverty rates among blacks, renters, people living outside metropolitan areas, and those covered by only public health insurance. Other groups show the same or higher poverty rates.[10]

FIGURE 19.3 The Demographics of Poverty in the United States, 2015

Poverty rates in the United States vary significantly according to a variety of demographic factors. Panels (a) through (f) compare poverty rates among different groups of the U.S. population. The data are for 2015.

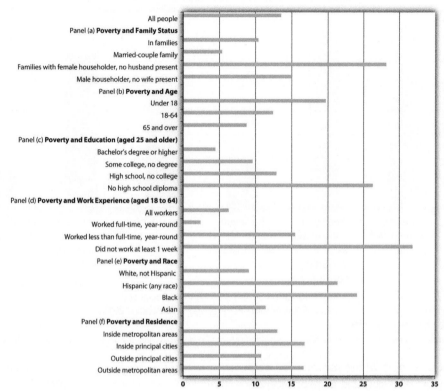

Source: Based on data from Bernadette D. Proctor, Jessica L. Semega, and Melissa A. Kollar, U.S. Census Bureau, Current Population Reports, P60-256(RV), Income and Poverty in the United States: 2015, U.S. Government Printing Office, Washington, DC, 2016: Tables 3 and 4.

Government Policy and Poverty

Consider a young single parent with three small children. The parent is not employed and has no support from other relatives. What does the government provide for the family?

The primary form of cash assistance is likely to come from a program called Temporary Assistance for Needy Families (TANF). This program began with the passage of the Personal Responsibility and Work Opportunity Reconciliation Act of 1996. It replaced Aid to Families with Dependent Children (AFDC). TANF is funded by the federal government but administered through the states. Eligibility is limited to two years of continuous payments and to five years in a person's lifetime, although 20% of a state's caseload may be exempted from this requirement.

In addition to this assistance, the family is likely to qualify for food stamps, which are vouchers that can be exchanged for food at the grocery store. The family may also receive rent vouchers, which can be used as payment for private housing. The family may qualify for Medicaid, a program that pays for physician and hospital care as well as for prescription drugs.

A host of other programs provide help ranging from counseling in nutrition to job placement services. The parent may qualify for federal assistance in attending college. The children may participate in the Head Start program, a program of preschool education designed primarily for low-income children. If the poverty rate in the area is unusually high, local public schools the children attend may receive extra federal aid. **Welfare programs** are the array of programs that government provides to alleviate poverty.

In addition to public sector support, a wide range of help is available from private sector charities. These may provide scholarships for education, employment assistance, and other aid.

Figure 19.4 shows participation rates in the major federal programs to help the poor.

welfare programs

The array of programs that government provides to alleviate poverty.

FIGURE 19.4 Welfare Programs and the Poor
Many people who fall below the poverty line have not received aid from particular programs.

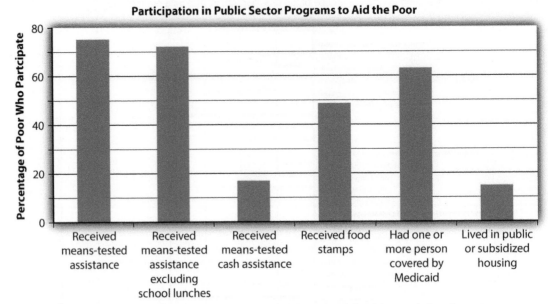

Source: U.S. Census Bureau, Current Population Survey, 2015 Annual Social and Economic Supplement.
POV26: Program Participation Status of Household - Poverty Status of People: 2015
All Races -- Below poverty level

Source: Based on data from U.S. Census Bureau, Current Population Survey, 2015 Annual Social and Economic Supplement, POV 26.

Not all people whose incomes fall below the poverty line received aid. In 2015, a substantial majority of those counted as poor received some form of aid. However, as shown in Figure 19.4, the percentages who were helped by individual programs were much lower. Less than 20% of people below the poverty line received some form of cash assistance in 2015. About 49% received food stamps and over 60% lived in a household in which one or more people received medical services through Medicaid. Only about one-seventh of the people living in poverty received some form of housing aid.

Although for the most part poverty programs are federally funded, individual states set eligibility standards and administer the programs. Allowing states to establish their own programs was a hallmark feature of the 1996 welfare reform. As state budgets have come under greater pressure, many states have tightened standards.

Cash Versus Noncash Assistance

cash assistance

A money payment that an aid recipient can spend as he or she wishes.

noncash assistance

The provision of specific goods and services, such as food or medical services, job training, or subsidized child care rather than cash.

Aid provided to people falls into two broad categories: cash and noncash assistance. **Cash assistance** is a money payment that a recipient can spend as he or she wishes. **Noncash assistance** is the provision of specific goods and services, such as food or medical services, job training, or subsidized child care rather than cash.

Noncash assistance is the most important form of aid to the poor. The large share of noncash relative to cash assistance raises two issues. First, since the poor would be better off (that is, reach a higher level of satisfaction) with cash rather than noncash assistance, why is noncash aid such a large percentage of total aid to the poor? Second, the importance of noncash assistance raises an important issue concerning the methodology by which the poverty rate is measured in the United States. We examine these issues in turn.

1. Why Noncash Aid?

   Suppose you had a choice between receiving $515 or a television set worth $515. Neither gift is taxable. Which would you take?

Given a choice between cash and an equivalent value in merchandise, you would probably take the cash. Unless the television set happened to be exactly what you would purchase with the $515, you could find some other set of goods and services that you would prefer to the TV set. The same is true of funds that you can spend on anything versus funds whose spending is restricted. Given a choice of $515 that you could spend on anything and $515 that you could spend only on food, which would you choose? A given pool of funds allows consumers a greater degree of satisfaction than does a specific set of goods and services.

We can conclude that poor people who receive government aid would be better off from their own perspectives with cash grants than with noncash aid. Why, then, is most government aid given as noncash benefits?

Economists have suggested two explanations. The first is based on the preferences of donors. Recipients might prefer cash, but the preferences of donors matter also. The donors, in this case, are taxpayers. Suppose they want poor people to have specific things—perhaps food, housing, and medical care.

Given such donor preferences, it is not surprising to find aid targeted at providing these basic goods and services. A second explanation has to do with the political clout of the poor. The poor are not likely to be successful competitors in the contest to be at the receiving end of public sector income redistribution efforts; most redistribution goes to people who are not poor. But firms that provide services such as housing or medical care might be highly effective lobbyists for programs that increase the demand for their products. They could be expected to seek more help for the poor in the form of noncash aid that increases their own demand and profits.[11]

2. Poverty Management and Noncash Aid

Only cash income is counted in determining the official poverty rate. The value of food, medical care, or housing provided through various noncash assistance programs is not included in household income. That is an important omission, because most government aid is noncash aid. Data for the official poverty rate thus do not reflect the full extent to which government programs act to reduce poverty.

The Census Bureau estimates the impact of noncash assistance on poverty. If a typical household would prefer, say, $515 in cash to $515 in food stamps, then $515 worth of food stamps is not valued at $515 in cash. Economists at the Census Bureau adjust the value of noncash aid downward to reflect an estimate of its lesser value to households. Suppose, for example, that given the choice between $515 in food stamps and $475 in cash, a household reports that it is indifferent between the two—either would be equally satisfactory. That implies that $515 in food stamps generates satisfaction equal to $475 in cash; the food stamps are thus "worth" $475 to the household.

Welfare Reform

The welfare system in the United States came under increasing attack in the 1980s and early 1990s. It was perceived to be expensive, and it had clearly failed to eliminate poverty. Many observers worried that welfare was becoming a way of life for people who had withdrawn from the labor force, and that existing welfare programs did not provide an incentive for people to work. President Clinton made welfare reform one of the key issues in the 1992 presidential campaign.

The Personal Responsibility and Work Opportunity Reconciliation Act of 1996 was designed to move people from welfare to work. It eliminated the entitlement aspect of welfare by defining a maximum period of eligibility. It gave states considerable scope in designing their own programs. In the first years following welfare reform, the number of people on welfare dropped by several million. Much research on the impact of reform showed that caseloads declined and employment increased and that the law did not have an adverse effect on poverty or the well-being of children. This positive outcome seemed to have resulted from an expansion of the earned income tax credit that also occurred, the overall low unemployment rate until the most recent few years, and larger behavioral responses than had been expected.[12]

Advocates of welfare reform proclaimed victory, while critics pointed to the booming economy, the tight labor market, and the general increase in the number of jobs over the same period. The recession that began at the end of 2007 and the ensuing slow recovery in the unemployment rate provided a real-time test of the effects of the reform. Economists Marianne Bitler and Hilary Hoynes analyzed the impact of welfare reform during the Great Recession on nonelderly families with children. They found that participation in cash assistance programs seemed less responsive to the downturn but that participation in noncash safety net programs, particularly the food stamp program, had become more responsive. They did find some evidence that the increase in poverty or near-poverty status might have been greater than it would have been without the reform.[13]

Explaining Poverty

Just as the increase in income inequality begs for explanation, so does the question of why poverty seems so persistent. Should not the long periods of economic growth in the 1980s and 1990s and from 2003 to late 2007 have substantially reduced poverty? Have the various government programs been ineffective?

Clearly, some of the same factors that have contributed to rising income inequality have also contributed to the persistence of poverty. In particular, the increases in households headed by females and the growing gaps in wages between skilled and unskilled workers have been major contributors.

Tax policy changes have reduced the extent of poverty. In addition to general reductions in tax rates, the Earned Income Tax Credit, which began in 1975 and was expanded in the 1990s, provides people below a certain income level with a supplement for each dollar of income earned. This supplement, roughly 30 cents for every dollar earned, is received as a tax refund at the end of the year.

FIGURE 19.5 Share of Individuals Living in Households with Income Below Half of Household-Size-Adjusted Median Income, Various Countries

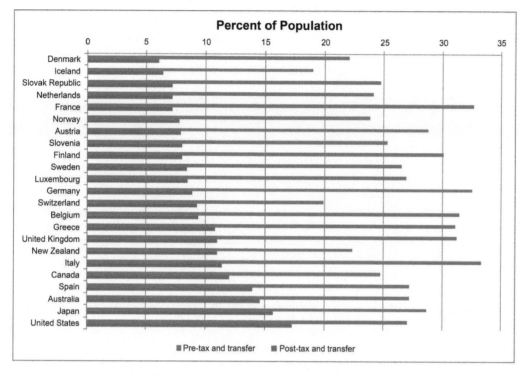

Source: Based on data from Economic Policy Institute. 2012. "Relative poverty rate in the United States and selected OECD countries, late 2000s" [chart] and "Extent to which taxes and transfer programs reduce the relative poverty rate, selected OECD countries, late 2000s ". The State of Working America. Washington, D.C.: Economic Policy Institute. October 16, 2016. http://stateofworkingamerica. org/chart/swa-poverty-figure-7w-relative-poverty-rate/ and http://stateofworkingamerica.org/chart/swa-poverty-figure-7z-effect-taxes-transfer/.

Taken together, though, transfer payment and tax programs in the United States are less effective in reducing poverty than are the programs of other developed countries. Figure 19.5 shows the share of households, after adjusting for size, with incomes below half the national median. The figure shows this share before and after tax and transfer payment programs are considered. Clearly, the United States is the least aggressive in seeking to eliminate poverty among the various countries shown.

Poverty and Work

How does poverty relate to work? Look back at Figure 19.3. Many of the poor are children or adults over age 65 and some are already working full time. Taken together, these three groups represent more than half of those in poverty. Also included amongst the poor are people who are ill or disabled, people who do not work due to family or home reasons, and people who are in school. The Census Bureau found in 2010 that of the nation's 46.2 million poor people, nearly 3 million reported they were not working or worked only part of the year or part time because they could not find full-time work.[14] So, while more employment opportunities would partly alleviate poverty, reducing unemployment is clearly only part of the answer.

Poverty and Welfare Programs

How effective have government programs been in alleviating poverty? The Census Bureau's supplemental poverty measure begins to answer that question. For example, those calculations show a reduction of two percentage points in the poverty rate, from 18% to 16%, when the earned income tax credit is included, ceteris paribus. Inclusion of the Supplemental Nutritional Assistance Program reduced the poverty rate by 1.7%, and housing subsidies reduced it by 0.9%. Other programs each had smaller effects on poverty reduction. But it is also important to distinguish between the poverty rate and the degree of poverty. Cash programs might reduce the degree of poverty but might not affect a family's income enough to actually move that family above the poverty line. Thus, even though the gap between the family's income and the poverty line is lessened, the family is still classified as poor and would thus still be included in the poverty-rate figures.

Key Takeaways

- Poverty may be defined according to a relative or an absolute definition.
- Official estimates of the number of people who are "poor" are typically based on an absolute definition of poverty, one that many view as inadequate and dated.
- Several demographic factors appear to be associated with poverty. Families headed by single women are three times as likely to be poor as are other families. Poverty is also associated with low levels of education and with minority status.
- There is a wide range of welfare programs; the majority of welfare spending is for noncash assistance. Those receiving this aid do not have it counted as income in the official calculations of poverty.
- Welfare reform has focused on requiring recipients to enter the labor force. Many poor people, however, are not candidates for the labor force.

Try It!

The Smiths, a family of four, have an income of $20,500 in 2006. Using the absolute income test approach and the data given in the chapter, determine if this family is poor. Use the relative income test to determine if this family is poor.

Case in Point: Welfare Reform in Britain and in the United States

Source: © 2010 Jupiterimages Corporation

The governments of the United States and of Great Britain have taken sharply different courses in their welfare reform efforts. In the United States, the primary reform effort was undertaken in 1996, with the declaration to eliminate welfare as an entitlement and the beginning of programs that required recipients to enter the labor force within two years. President Clinton promised to "end welfare as we know it."

In Britain, the government of Tony Blair took a radically different approach. Prime Minister Blair promised to "make welfare popular again." His government undertook to establish what he called a "third way" to welfare reform, one that emphasized returning recipients to the workforce but that also sought explicitly to end child poverty.

The British program required recipients to get counseling aimed at encouraging them to return to the labor force. It did not, however, require that they obtain jobs. It also included a program of "making work pay," the primary feature of which was the creation of a National Minimum Wage, one that was set higher than the minimum wage in the United States. In the United States, the minimum wage equaled 34% of median private sector wages in 2002; the British minimum wage was set at 45% of the median private sector wage in 2002.

The British program, which was called the New Deal, featured tax benefits for poor families with children, whether they worked or not. It also included a Sure Start program of child care for poor people with children under three years old. In short, the Blair program was a more extensive social welfare program than the 1996 act in the United States.

The table below compares results of the two programs in terms of their impact on child poverty, using an "absolute" poverty line and also using a relative poverty line.

Child Poverty Rates, Pre- and Post- Reform		
United Kingdom	Absolute (percent)	Relative (percent)
1997–1998	24	25
2002–2003	12	21
Change	–12	–4
United States	Absolute (percent)	Relative (percent)
1992	19	38
2001	13	35
Change	–6	–3

Child Poverty Rates in Single-Mother Families, Pre- and Post- Reform		
United Kingdom	Absolute (percent)	Relative (percent)
1997–1998	40	41
2002–2003	15	33
Change	–25	–8
United States	Absolute (percent)	Relative (percent)
1992	44	67
2001	28	59
Change	–16	–8

The relative measure of child poverty is the method of measuring poverty adopted by the European Union. It draws the poverty line at 60% of median income. The poverty line is thus a moving target against which it is more difficult to make progress.

Hills and Waldfogel compared the British results to those in the United States in terms of the relative impact on welfare caseloads, employment of women having families, and reduction in child poverty. They note that reduction in welfare caseloads was much greater in the United States, with caseloads falling from 5.5 million to 2.3 million. In Britain, the reduction in caseloads was much smaller. In terms of impact on employment among women, the United States again experienced a much more significant increase. In terms of reduction of child poverty, however, the British approach clearly achieved a greater reduction. The British approach also increased incomes of families in the bottom 10% of the income distribution (i.e., the bottom decile) by more than that achieved in the United States. In Britain, incomes of families in the bottom decile rose 22%, and for families with children they rose 24%. In the United States, those in the bottom decile had more modest gains.

Would the United States ever adopt a New Deal program such as the Blair program in Great Britain? That, according to Hills and Waldfogel, would require a change in attitudes in the United States that they regard as unlikely.

Source: Based on John Hills and Jane Waldfogel, "A 'Third Way' in Welfare Reform? Evidence from the United Kingdom," Journal of Policy Analysis and Management, 23(4) (2004): 765–88.

Answer to Try It! Problem

According to the absolute income test, the Smiths are poor because their income of $20,500 falls below the 2006 poverty threshold of $20,614. According to the relative income test, they are not poor because their $20,500 income is above the upper limit of the lowest quintile, $20,035.

19.4 The Economics of Discrimination

Learning Objectives

1. Define discrimination, identify some sources of it, and illustrate Becker's model of discrimination using demand and supply in a hypothetical labor market.
2. Assess the effectiveness of government efforts to reduce discrimination in the United States.

We have seen that being a female head of household or being a member of a racial minority increases the likelihood of being at the low end of the income distribution and of being poor. In the real world, we know that on average women and members of racial minorities receive different wages from white male workers, even though they may have similar qualifications and backgrounds. They might be charged different prices or denied employment opportunities. This section examines the economic forces that create such discrimination, as well as the measures that can be used to address it.

Discrimination in the Marketplace: A Model

Discrimination occurs when people with similar economic characteristics experience different economic outcomes because of their race, sex, or other noneconomic characteristics. A black worker whose skills and experience are identical to those of a white worker but who receives a lower wage is a victim of discrimination. A woman denied a job opportunity solely on the basis of her gender is the victim of discrimination. To the extent that discrimination exists, a country will not be allocating resources efficiently; the economy will be operating inside its production possibilities curve.

Pioneering work on the economics of discrimination was done by Gary S. Becker, an economist at the University of Chicago, who won the Nobel Prize in economics in 1992. He suggested that discrimination occurs because of people's preferences or attitudes. If enough people have prejudices against certain racial groups, or against women, or against people with any particular characteristic, the market will respond to those preferences.

In Becker's model, discriminatory preferences drive a wedge between the outcomes experienced by different groups. Discriminatory preferences can make salespeople less willing to sell to one group than to another or make consumers less willing to buy from the members of one group than from another or to make workers of one race or sex or ethnic group less willing to work with those of another race, sex, or ethnic group.

Let us explore Becker's model by examining labor-market discrimination against black workers. We begin by assuming that no discriminatory preferences or attitudes exist. For simplicity, suppose that the supply curves of black and white workers are identical; they are shown as a single curve in Figure 19.6. Suppose further that all workers have identical marginal products; they are equally productive. In the absence of racial preferences, the demand for workers of both races would be D. Black and white workers would each receive a wage W per unit of labor. A total of L black workers and L white workers would be employed.

> **discrimination**
>
> When people with similar economic characteristics experience different economic outcomes because of their race, sex, or other noneconomic characteristics.

Now suppose that employers have discriminatory attitudes that cause them to assume that a black worker is less productive than an otherwise similar white worker. Now employers have a lower demand, D_B, for black than for white workers. Employers pay black workers a lower wage, W_B, and employ fewer of them, L_B instead of L, than they would in the absence of discrimination.

Sources of Discrimination

As illustrated in Figure 19.6, racial prejudices on the part of employers produce discrimination against black workers, who receive lower wages and have fewer employment opportunities than white workers. Discrimination can result from prejudices among other groups in the economy as well.

One source of discriminatory prejudices is other workers. Suppose, for example, that white workers prefer not to work with black workers and require a wage premium for doing so. Such preferences would, in effect, raise the cost to the firm of hiring black workers. Firms would respond by demanding fewer of them, and wages for black workers would fall.

Another source of discrimination against black workers could come from customers. If the buyers of a firm's product prefer not to deal with black employees, the firm might respond by demanding fewer of them. In effect, prejudice on the part of consumers would lower the revenue that firms can generate from the output of black workers.

Whether discriminatory preferences exist among employers, employees, or consumers, the impact on the group discriminated against will be the same. Fewer members of that group will be employed, and their wages will be lower than the wages of other workers whose skills and experience are otherwise similar.

Race and sex are not the only characteristics that affect hiring and wages. Some studies have found that people who are short, overweight, or physically unattractive also suffer from discrimination, and charges of discrimination have been voiced by disabled people and by homosexuals. Whenever discrimination occurs, it implies that employers, workers, or customers have discriminatory preferences. For the effects of such preferences to be felt in the marketplace, they must be widely shared.

There are, however, market pressures that can serve to lessen discrimination. For example, if some employers hold discriminatory preferences but others do not, it will be profit enhancing for those who do not to hire workers from the group being discriminated against. Because workers from this group are less expensive to hire, costs for non-discriminating firms will be lower. If the market is at least somewhat competitive, firms who continue to discriminate may be driven out of business.

Discrimination in the United States Today

Reacting to demands for social change brought on most notably by the civil rights and women's movements, the federal government took action against discrimination. In 1954, the U.S. Supreme Court rendered its decision that so-called separate but equal schools for black and white children were inherently unequal, and the Court ordered that racially segregated schools be integrated. The Equal Pay Act of 1963 requires employers to pay the same wages to men and women who do substantially the same work. Federal legislation was passed in 1965 to ensure that minorities were not denied the right to vote.

Congress passed the most important federal legislation against discrimination in 1964. The Civil Rights Act barred discrimination on the basis of race, sex, or ethnicity in pay, promotion, hiring, firing, and training. An Executive Order issued by President Lyndon Johnson in 1967 required

FIGURE 19.6 Prejudice and Discrimination

If employers, customers, or employees have discriminatory preferences, and those preferences are widespread, then the marketplace will result in discrimination. Here, black workers receive a lower wage and fewer of them are employed than would be the case in the absence of discriminatory preferences.

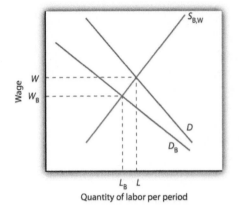

federal contractors to implement affirmative action programs to ensure that members of minority groups and women were given equal opportunities in employment. The practical effect of the order was to require that these employers increase the percentage of women and minorities in their work forces. Affirmative action programs for minorities followed at most colleges and universities.

What has been the outcome of these efforts to reduce discrimination? A starting point is to look at wage differences among different groups. Gaps in wages between males and females and between blacks and whites have fallen over time. In 1955, the wages of black men were about 60% of those of white men; in 2015, they were 74% of those of white men. For black men, the reduction in the wage gap occurred primarily between 1965 and 1973. In contrast, the gap between the wages of black women and white men closed more substantially, and progress in closing the gap continued after 1973, albeit at a slower rate. Specifically, the wages of black women were about 35% of those of white men in 1955, 58% in 1975, and 67% in 2015, a slightly lower fraction than a few years earlier. For white women, the pattern of gain is still different. The wages of white women were about 65% of those of white men in 1955 and fell to about 60% from the mid-1960s to the late 1970s. The wages of white females relative to white males have improved, however, over the last 40 years. In 2015, white female wages were 81% of white male wages. While there has been improvement in wage gaps between black men, black women, and white women vis-à-vis white men, a substantial gap still remains. Figure 19.7 shows the wage differences for the period 1970–2015.

FIGURE 19.7 The Wage Gap

The exhibit shows the wages of white women, black women, and black men as a percentage of the wages of white men from 1970–2015. As you can see, the gap has closed considerably, but there remains a substantial gap between the wages of white men and those of other groups in the economy. Part of the difference is a result of discrimination.

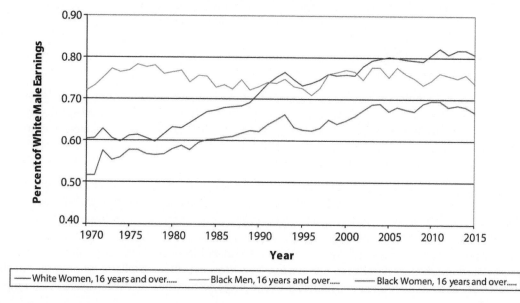

Source: Based on data from Current Population Survey, Table 37. Median weekly earnings of full-time wage and salary workers, by selected characteristics, Bureau of Labor Statistics, Available at http://www.bls.gov/cps/tables.htm.

One question that economists try to answer is the extent to which the gaps are due to discrimination per se and the extent to which they reflect other factors, such as differences in education, job experience, or choices that individuals in particular groups make about labor-force participation. Once these factors are accounted for, the amount of the remaining wage differential due to discrimination is less than the raw differentials presented in Figure 19.7 would seem to indicate.

There is evidence as well that the wage differential due to discrimination against women and blacks, as measured by empirical studies, has declined over time. For example, a number of studies have concluded that black men in the 1980s and 1990s experienced a 12 to 15% loss in earnings due to labor-market discrimination.[15] University of Chicago economist James Heckman denies that the entire 12% to 15% differential is due to racial discrimination, pointing to problems inherent in measuring and comparing human capital among individuals. Nevertheless, he reports that the earnings loss due to discrimination similarly measured would have been between 30 and 40% in 1940 and still over 20% in 1970.[16]

Can civil rights legislation take credit for the reductions in labor-market discrimination over time? To some extent, yes. A study by Heckman and John J. Donohue III, a law professor at Northwestern University, concluded that the landmark 1964 Civil Rights Act, as well as other civil rights activity leading up to the act, had the greatest positive impact on blacks in the South during the decade following its passage. Evidence of wage gains by black men in other regions of the country was, however, minimal. Most federal activity was directed toward the South, and the civil rights effort shattered an entire way of life that had subjugated black Americans and had separated them from mainstream life.[17]

In recent years, affirmative action programs have been under attack. Proposition 209, passed in California in 1996, and Initiative 200, passed in Washington State in 1998, bar preferential treatment due to race in admission to public colleges and universities in those states. The 1996 Hopwood case against the University of Texas, decided by the United States Court of Appeals for the Fifth Circuit, eliminated the use of race in university admissions, both public and private, in Texas, Louisiana, and Mississippi. Then Supreme Court decisions in 2003 concerning the use of affirmative action at the University of Michigan upheld race conscious admissions, so long as applicants are still considered individually and decisions are based of multiple criteria.

Controversial research by two former Ivy League university presidents, political scientist Derek Bok of Harvard University and economist William G. Bowen of Princeton University, concluded that affirmative action policies have created the backbone of the black middle class and taught white students the value of integration. The study focused on affirmative action at 28 elite colleges and universities. It found that while blacks enter those institutions with lower test scores and grades than those of whites, receive lower grades, and graduate at a lower rate, after graduation blacks earn advanced degrees at rates identical to those of their former white classmates and are more active in civic affairs.[18]

While stricter enforcement of civil rights laws or new programs designed to reduce labor-market discrimination may serve to further improve earnings of groups that have been historically discriminated against, wage gaps between groups also reflect differences in choices and in "premarket" conditions, such as family environment and early education. Some of these premarket conditions may themselves be the result of discrimination.

The narrowing in wage differentials may reflect the dynamics of the Becker model at work. As people's preferences change, or are forced to change due to competitive forces and changes in the legal environment, discrimination against various groups will decrease. However, it may be a long time before discrimination disappears from the labor market, not only due to remaining discriminatory preferences but also because the human capital and work characteristics that people bring to the labor market are decades in the making. The election of Barack Obama as president of the United States in 2008 is certainly a hallmark in the long and continued struggle against discrimination.

Key Takeaways

- Discrimination means that people of similar economic characteristics experience unequal economic outcomes as a result of noneconomic factors such as race or sex.
- Discrimination occurs in the marketplace only if employers, employees, or customers have discriminatory preferences and if such preferences are widely shared.

- Competitive markets will tend to reduce discrimination if enough individuals lack such prejudices and take advantage of discrimination practiced by others.

- Government intervention in the form of antidiscrimination laws may have reduced the degree of discrimination in the economy. There is considerable disagreement on this question but wage gaps have declined over time in the United States.

Try It!

Use a production possibilities curve to illustrate the impact of discrimination on the production of goods and services in the economy. Label the horizontal axis as consumer goods per year. Label the vertical axis as capital goods per year. Label a point A that shows an illustrative bundle of the two which can be produced given the existence of discrimination. Label another point B that lies on the production possibilities curve above and to the right of point A. Use these two points to describe the outcome that might be expected if discrimination were eliminated.

Case in Point: Early Intervention Programs

Source: © 2010 Jupiterimages Corporation

Many authors have pointed out that differences in "pre-market" conditions may drive observed differences in market outcomes for people in different groups. Significant inroads to the reduction of poverty may lie in improving the educational opportunities available to minority children and others living in poverty-level households, but at what point in their lives is the pay-off to intervention the largest? Professor James Heckman, in an op-ed essay in *The Wall Street Journal*, argues that the key to improving student performance and adult competency lies in early intervention in education.

Professor Heckman notes that spending on children after they are already in school has little impact on their later success. Reducing class sizes, for example, does not appear to promote gains in factors such as attending college or earning higher incomes. What does seem to matter is earlier intervention. By the age of eight , differences in learning abilities are essentially fixed. But, early intervention to improve cognitive and especially non-cognitive abilities (the latter include qualities such as perseverance, motivation, and self-restraint) has been shown to produce significant benefits. In an experiment begun several decades ago known as the Perry intervention, four-year-old children from disadvantaged homes were given programs designed to improve their chances for success in school. Evaluations of the program 40 years later found that it had a 15 to 17% rate of return in terms of the higher wages earned by men and women who had participated in the program compared to those from similar backgrounds who did not—the program's benefit-cost ratio was 8 to 1. Professor Heckman argues that even earlier intervention among disadvantaged groups would be desirable—perhaps as early as six months of age.

Economists Rob Grunewald and Art Rolnick of the Federal Reserve Bank of Minneapolis have gone so far as to argue that, because of the high returns to early childhood development programs, which they estimate at 12% per year to the public, state and local governments, can promote more economic development in their areas by supporting early childhood programs than they currently do by offering public subsidies to attract new businesses to their locales or to build new sports stadiums, none of which offers the prospects of such a high rate of return.

Sources: Based on James Heckman, "Catch 'em Young," The Wall Street Journal, January 10, 2006, p. A-14; Rob Grunewald and Art Rolnick, "Early Childhood Development on a Large Scale," Federal Reserve Bank of Minneapolis The Region, June 2005.

Answer to Try It! Problem

Discrimination leads to an inefficient allocation of resources and results in production levels that lie inside the production possibilities curve (*PPC*) (point A). If discrimination were eliminated, the economy could increase production to a point on the *PPC*, such as B.

19.5 Review and Practice

Summary

In this chapter, we looked at three issues related to the question of fairness: income inequality, poverty, and discrimination.

The distribution of income in the United States has become more unequal in the last four decades. Among the factors contributing to increased inequality have been changes in family structure, technological change, and tax policy. While rising inequality can be a concern, there is a good deal of movement of families up and down the distribution of income, though recently mobility may have decreased somewhat.

Poverty can be measured using an absolute or a relative income standard. The official measure of poverty in the United States relies on an absolute standard. This measure tends to overstate the poverty rate because it does not count noncash welfare aid as income. The new supplemental poverty measures have begun to take these programs into account. Poverty is concentrated among female-headed households, minorities, people with relatively little education, and people who are not in the labor force. Children have a particularly high poverty rate.

Welfare reform in 1996 focused on moving people off welfare and into work. It limits the number of years that individuals can receive welfare payments and allows states to design the specific parameters of their own welfare programs. Following the reform, the number of people on welfare fell dramatically. The long-term impact on poverty is still under investigation.

Federal legislation bans discrimination. Affirmative action programs, though controversial, are designed to enhance opportunities for minorities and women. Wage gaps between women and white males and between blacks and white males have declined since the 1950s. For black males, however, most of the reduction occurred between 1965 and 1973. Much of the decrease in wage gaps is due to acquisition of human capital by women and blacks, but some of the decrease also reflects a reduction in discrimination.

Concept Problems

1. Explain how rising demand for college-educated workers and falling demand for high-school-educated workers contributes to increased inequality of the distribution of income.

2. Discuss the advantages and disadvantages of the following three alternatives for dealing with the rising inequality of wages.

    a. Increase the minimum wage each year so that wages for unskilled workers rise as fast as wages for skilled workers.

    b. Subsidize the wages of unskilled workers.

    c. Do nothing.

3. How would you define poverty? How would you determine whether a particular family is poor? Is the test you have proposed an absolute or a relative test?

4. Why does the failure to adjust the poverty line for regional differences in living costs lead to an understatement of poverty in some states and an overstatement of poverty in others?

5. The text argues that welfare recipients could achieve higher levels of satisfaction if they received cash rather than in-kind aid. Use the same argument to make a case that gifts given at Christmas should be in cash rather than specific items. Why do you suppose they usually are not?

6. Suppose a welfare program provides a basic grant of $10,000 per year to poor families but reduces the grant by $1 for every $1 of income earned. How would such a program affect a household's incentive to work?

7. Welfare reform calls for a two-year limit on welfare payments, after which recipients must go to work. Suppose a recipient with children declines work offers. Should aid be cut? What about the children?

8. How would you tackle the welfare problem? State the goals you would seek, and explain how the measures you propose would work to meet those goals.

9. Suppose a common but unfounded belief held that people with blue eyes were not as smart as people with brown eyes. What would we expect to happen to the relative wages of the two groups? Suppose you were an entrepreneur who knew that the common belief was wrong. What could you do to enhance your profits? Suppose other entrepreneurs acted in the same way. How would the wages of people with blue eyes be affected?

10. The Case in Point on Income Inequality in the United States versus continental Western Europe argues that people get, in effect, what they expect. People in the United States attribute success to hard work and skill, while people in Continental Western Europe attribute success to connections, luck, and corruption. With what set of views do you agree? Explain.

11. The Case in Point on welfare reform in Britain versus that in the United States argues that the British system, before it could be adopted in the United States, would require a change in attitudes in the United States. What sort of change would it require? Do you prefer the British approach? Why or why not?

12. James Heckman of the University of Chicago advocates a program of early intervention targeted at low income families. What are the advantages of such an approach? The disadvantages?

13. Give five reasons that the income distribution in the United States has become more unequal in the last several decades. Do you regard this as a problem for society? Why or why not?

14. Suppose that all welfare aid were converted to programs of cash assistance. Total spending on welfare would remain unchanged. How would this affect the poverty rate? Why?

Numerical Problems

1. Here are income distribution data for three countries, from the *Human Development Report 2005*, table 15. Note that here we report only four data points rather than the five associated with each quintile. These emphasize the distribution at the extremes of the distribution.

	Poorest 10%	Poorest 20%	Richest 20%	Richest 10%
Panama	0.7	2.4	60.3	43.3
Sweden	3.6	9.1	36.6	22.2
Singapore	1.9	5.0	49.0	32.8

   a. Plot the Lorenz curves for each in a single graph.

   b. Compare the degree of inequality for the three countries. (Do not forget to convert the data to cumulative shares; e.g., the lowest 80% of the population in Panama receives 39.7% of total income.)

   c. Compare your results to the Lorenz curve given in the text for the United States. Which country in your chart appears closest to the United States in terms of its income distribution?

2. Looking at Figure 19.6 suppose the wage that black workers are receiving in a discriminatory environment, W_B, is $25 per hour, while the wage that white workers receive, W, is $30 per hour. Now suppose a regulation is imposed that requires that black workers be paid $30 per hour also.

   a. How does this affect the employment of black workers?

   b. How does this affect the wages of black workers?

   c. How does this affect their total income? Explain.

3. Suppose the poverty line in the United States was set according to the test required in the European Union: a household is poor if its income is less than 60% of the median household income. Here are annual data for median household income in the United States for the

period 1994–2004. The data also give the percentage of the households that fall below 60% of the median household income.

	Median Household Income in the U.S.	Percent of households with income below 60% of median
1994	40,677	30.1
1995	41,943	30.4
1996	42,544	29.9
1997	43,430	29.1
1998	45,003	27.8
1999	46,129	27.1
2000	46,058	26.4
2001	45,062	27.4
2002	44,546	27.8
2003	44,482	28.3
2004	44,389	28.3

Source: U.S Census Bureau, Current Population Reports, P60-229; Income in 2004 CPI-U-RS adjusted dollars; column 3 estimated by authors using Table A-1, p. 31.

   a. Plot the data on a graph.

   b. Is this a relative or an absolute definition of poverty?

   c. Why do you think the percent of households with incomes below 60% of the median fell from 1994 to 2000 and has risen since?

   d. Discuss the measurement issues involved in the data you have presented.

   e. Discuss the elements of the system of counting the incomes of low income people in the United States and explain how it relates to your answer in (d).

4. Consider the following model of the labor market in the United States. Suppose that the labor market consists of two parts, a market for skilled workers and the market for unskilled workers, with different demand and supply curves for each as given below. The initial wage for skilled workers is $20 per hour; the initial wage for unskilled workers is $7 per hour.

   a. Draw the demand and supply curves for the two markets so that they intersect at the wages given above.

   b. How does increased demand for skilled workers and a reduced demand for unskilled workers affect the initial solution?

   c. How is the Lorenz curve for the United States economy affected by this development? Illustrate the old and the new Lorenz curves.

   d. Suppose there is an increase in immigration from Mexico. How will this affect the two markets for labor?

   e. Suppose Professor Heckman's recommendation for early intervention for low income children is followed and that it has the impact he predicts. How will this affect the two markets today? In 20 years? Illustrate and explain how the demand and/or supply curves in each market will be affected.

   f. What would the impact of the change in (d) be on the Lorenz curve for the United States 20 years from now?

Endnotes

1. "Not Quite Together," *Economist*, October 22, 2011; Douglas Schoen, "Polling the Occupy Wall Street Crowd," *Wall Street Journal Online*, October 18, 2011; "Public Divided Over Occupy Wall Street Movement," Pew Charitable Trust Pew Research Center for the People & the Press, http://www.people-press.org/2011/10/24/public-divided-over-occupy-wall-street-movement/.

2. Congressional Budget Office, "Trends in the Distribution of Household Income Between 1979 and 2007," October 2011, http://www.cbo.gov/ftpdocs/124xx/doc12485/10-25-HouseholdIncome.pdf.

3. Anthony P. Carnevale, Stephen J. Rose, and Ban Cheah, *The College Payoff: Education, Occupation, and Lifetime Earnings*, Georgetown University Center on Education and the Workforce: 2011, http://cew.georgetown.edu/collegepayoff.

4. Carmen DeNavas-Walt, Bernadette D. Proctor, and Jessica C. Smith, U.S. Census Bureau, Current Population Reports, P60-239, *Income, Poverty, and Health Insurance Coverage in the United States: 2010*, U.S. Government Printing Office, Washington, DC, 2011.

5. Katharine Bradbury, "Trends in U.S. Family Income Mobility, 1969–2006," Federal Reserve Bank of Boston Working Paper no. 11-10, October 20, 2011.

6. Rea S. Hederman, Jr., "Census Report Adds New Twist to Income Inequality Data," Heritage Foundation, Policy Research and Analysis, No. 1592, August 29, 2007.

7. Kathleen Short, U.S. Census Bureau, Current Population Reports P60-241, *Supplemental Poverty Measure: 2010*, U.S. Government Printing Office, Washington, DC, November 2011.

8. Robert Rector and Rachel Sheffield, "Understanding Poverty in the United States: Surprising Facts about America's Poor," Heritage Foundation, Policy Research & Analysis, No. 2607, September 13, 2011.

9. Ibid.

10. Kathleen Short, U.S. Census Bureau, Current Population Reports P60-241, *Supplemental Poverty Measure: 2010*, U.S. Government Printing Office, Washington, DC, November 2011.

11. Students who have studied rent seeking behavior will recognize this argument. It falls within the public choice perspective of public finance theory.

12. Marianne P. Bitler and Hilary W. Hoynes, "The State of the Social Safety Net in the Post-Welfare Reform Era," *Brookings Papers on Economic Activity* (Fall 2010): 71–127.

13. Marianne P. Bitler and Hilary W. Hoynes, "The State of the Social Safety Net in the Post-Welfare Reform Era," *Brookings Papers on Economic Activity* (Fall 2010): 71–127.

14. Current Population Survey, Annual Social and Economic Supplement 2010, Table POV24.

15. William A. Darity and Patrick L. Mason, "Evidence on Discrimination in Employment," *Journal of Economic Perspectives* 12:2 (Spring 1998): 63–90.

16. James J. Heckman, "Detecting Discrimination," *Journal of Economic Perspectives* 12:2 (Spring 1998): 101–16.

17. John J. Donohue III and James Heckman, "Continuous Versus Episodic Change: The Impact of Civil Rights Policy on the Economic Status of Blacks," *Journal of Economic Literature* 29 (December 1991): 1603–43.

18. Derek Bok and William G. Bowen, *The Shape of the River: Long-Term Consequences of Considering Race in College and University Admissions* (Princeton, N. J.: Princeton University Press, 1998).

CHAPTER 20

Macroeconomics: The Big Picture

20.1 Start Up: Economy Limps Along

The U.S. economy seemed to be doing well overall after the recession of 2001. Growth had been normal, unemployment had stayed low, and inflation seemed to be under control. The economy began to unravel at the end of 2007—total output fell in the fourth quarter and again in the first quarter of 2008. It recovered—barely—in the second quarter. Then things went sour..very sour. The economies of the United States and those of much of the world were rocked by the worst financial crisis in nearly 80 years.

A good deal of the U.S. economy's momentum when things were going well had been fueled by rising house prices. Between 1995 and 2007, housing prices in the United States more than doubled. As house prices rose, consumers who owned houses felt wealthier and increased their consumption purchases. That helped fuel economic growth. The boom in housing prices had been encouraged by policies of the nation's monetary authority, the Federal Reserve, which had shifted to an expansionary monetary policy that held short-term interest rates below the inflation rate. Another development, subprime mortgages—mortgage loans to buyers whose credit or income would not ordinarily qualify for mortgage loans—helped bring on the ultimate collapse. When they were first developed, subprime mortgage loans seemed a hugely profitable investment for banks and a good deal for home buyers. Financial institutions developed a wide range of instruments based on "mortgage-backed securities." As long as house prices kept rising, the system worked and was profitable for virtually all players in the mortgage market. Many firms undertook investments in mortgage-backed securities that assumed house prices would keep rising. Large investment banks bet heavily that house prices would continue rising. Powerful members of Congress pressured two government-sponsored enterprises, Fannie Mae (the Federal National Mortgage Association) and Freddie Mac (the Federal Home Loan Mortgage Corporation), to be even more aggressive in encouraging banks to make mortgage loans to low-income families. The pressure came from the executive branch of government as well—under both Democratic and Republican administrations. In 1996, the Department of Housing and Urban Development (under Bill Clinton, a Democrat) required that 12% of mortgages purchased by Fannie Mae and Freddie Mac be for households with incomes less than 60% of the median income in their region. That target was increased to 20% in 2000, 22% in 2005 (then under George W. Bush, a Republican), and was to have increased to 28% in 2008.[1] But that final target would not be reached, as both Fannie Mae and Freddie Mac were seized by the government in 2008. To top things off, a loosening in bank and investment bank regulations gave financial institutions greater leeway in going overboard with purchases of mortgage-backed securities. As house prices began falling in 2007, a system based on the assumption they would continue rising began to unravel very fast. The investment bank Bear Stearns and insurance company American International Group (AIG) required massive infusions of federal money to keep them afloat. In September of 2008, firm after firm with assets tied to mortgage-backed securities began to fail. In some cases, the government rescued them; in other cases, such as Lehman Brothers, they were allowed to fail.

The financial crisis had dramatic and immediate effects on the economy. The economy's total output fell at an annual rate of 3.7% in the third quarter of 2008 and 8.9% in the fourth quarter of 2008. Consumers, having weathered higher gasoline prices and higher food prices for most of the year, reduced their consumption expenditures as the value of their houses and the stocks they held plunged—consumption fell at an annual rate of 3.8% in the third quarter and 5.1% in the fourth quarter. As cold fear gripped financial markets and expectations of further slowdown ensued, firms cut down on investment spending, which includes spending on plant and equipment used in production. While this nonresidential investment component of output fell at an annual rate of 0.8%, the residential component fell even faster as housing investment sank at an annual rate of 23.9%. Government purchases and net exports rose, but not enough to offset reductions in consumption and private investment. As output shrank, unemployment rose sharply. Through the first nine months of 2008 there was concern that price levels in the United States and in most of the world economies were rising rapidly, but toward the end of the year the concern shifted to whether or not the price level might fall.

This recession, which officially began in December 2007 and ended in June 2009, was brutal: At 18 months in length, it was the longest U.S. recession since World War II. The nation's output fell by more than 5%, making it the deepest recession since World War II. The unemployment rate rose dramatically, hitting 10% in October 2009 and remaining above 9% throughout 2010. To many people in 2010 and 2011, it certainly did not feel as if the "Great Recession," as many had begun to refer to it, had really ended. The unemployment rate had come down some but still remained elevated. Housing prices still seemed to be falling or, at best, crawling along a floor.

What did the continuation of the recovery look like? The increase in the nation's output averaged just over 2%, but that was less than increases from previous recoveries. The unemployment rate fell markedly and was below 5% at the beginning of 2017. The number of jobs had recovered completely and then millions more were added. However, the labor force participation rate also seemed low. Wage growth stagnated for much of the decade of the 2010s, only beginning to rise in 2016. And woe to those without at last some post-secondary education: Of the more than 11 million jobs added from the bottom of the Great Recession until 2016, 99% of them went to workers with at least some education beyond high school.[2] House prices did recover on average but not in every location. Consumer confidence rose dramatically but productivity languished.

An important question, of course, is why the recovery was so slow. Several factors have contributed to the slow pace of expansion.

First, the financial crisis that developed in 2008, as mentioned, was particularly severe. Financial crises shake confidence and limit investment. Uncertainty was also created by increased government regulation of economic activity and by the possibility of increased taxes.

Furthermore, the impact of massive government debts—propelled by government deficits going into the recession, the fall in revenue due to the recession, and massive government stimulus programs in response to the recession—added to a general uncertainty about what future policies might be required. Domestic political battles may have contributed to this uncertainty as well. External factors, such as economic crises in Europe, also threatened the economy.

Output, employment, and the price level are the key variables in the study of macroeconomics, which is the analysis of aggregate values of economic variables. What determines a country's output, and why does output in some economies expand while in others it contracts? Why do some economies grow faster than others? What causes prices throughout an economy to fluctuate, and how do such fluctuations affect people? What causes employment and unemployment? Why does a country's unemployment rate fluctuate? Why do different countries have different unemployment rates?

We would pronounce an economy "healthy" if its annual output of goods and services were growing at a rate it can sustain, its price level stable, and its unemployment rate low. What would constitute "good" numbers for each of these variables depends on time and place, but those are the outcomes that most people would agree are desirable for the aggregate economy. When the economy deviates from what is considered good performance, there are often calls for the government to "do something" to improve performance. How government policies affect economic performance is a major topic of macroeconomics. When the financial and economic crises struck throughout the world in 2008, there was massive intervention from world central banks and from governments throughout the world in an effort to stimulate their economies.

This chapter provides a preliminary sketch of the most important macroeconomic issues: growth of total output and the business cycle, changes in the price level, and unemployment. Grappling with these issues will be important to you not only in your exploration of macroeconomics but throughout your life.

20.2 Growth of Real GDP and Business Cycles

Learning Objectives

1. Define real gross domestic product and explain how its calculation avoids both double-counting and the effects of changes in the price level.
2. Identify the phases of a business cycle.
3. Relate business cycles to the overall long-run trend in real GDP in the United States.

To determine whether the economy of a nation is growing or shrinking in size, economists use a measure of total output called real GDP. **Real GDP**, short for real gross domestic product, is the total value of all final goods and services produced during a particular year or period, adjusted to eliminate the effects of changes in prices. Let us break that definition up into parts.

Notice that only "final" goods and services are included in GDP. Many goods and services are purchased for use as inputs in producing something else. For example, a pizza parlor buys flour to make pizzas. If we counted the value of the flour and the value of the pizza, we would end up counting the flour twice and thus overstating the value of total production. Including only final goods avoids double-counting. If the flour is produced during a particular period but has not been sold, then it is a "final good" for that period and is counted.

We want to determine whether the economy's output is growing or shrinking. If each final good or service produced, from hammers to haircuts, were valued at its current market price, and then we were to add the values of all such items produced, we would not know if the total had changed because output changed or because prices changed or both. The market value of all final goods and services produced can rise even if total output falls. To isolate the behavior of total output only, we must hold prices constant at some level. For example, if we measure the value of basketball output over time using a fixed price for valuing the basketballs, then only an increase in the number of basketballs produced could increase the value of the contribution made by basketballs to total output. By making such an adjustment for basketballs and all other goods and services, we obtain a value for real GDP. In contrast, **nominal GDP**, usually just referred to as gross domestic product (GDP), is the total value of final goods and services for a particular period valued in terms of prices for that period. For example, real GDP fell in the third quarter of 2008. But, because the price level in the United States was rising, nominal GDP rose 3.6%.

We will save a detailed discussion of the computation of GDP for another chapter. In this section, our goal is to use the concept of real GDP to look at the **business cycle**—the economy's pattern of expansion, then contraction, then expansion again—and at growth of real GDP.

real GDP

The total value of all final goods and services produced during a particular year or period, adjusted to eliminate the effects of changes in prices.

nominal GDP

The total value of final goods and services for a particular period valued in terms of prices for that period.

business cycle

The economy's pattern of expansion, then contraction, then expansion again.

Phases of the Business Cycle

Figure 20.1 shows a stylized picture of a typical business cycle. It shows that economies go through periods of increasing and decreasing real GDP, but that over time they generally move in the direction of increasing levels of real GDP. A sustained period in which real GDP is rising is an **expansion**; a sustained period in which real GDP is falling is a **recession**. Typically, an economy is said to be in a recession when real GDP drops for two consecutive quarters, but in the United States, the responsibility of defining precisely when the economy is in recession is left to the Business Cycle Dating Committee of the National Bureau of Economic Research (NBER). The committee defines a recession as a "significant decline in economic activity spread across the economy, lasting more than a few months, normally visible in real GDP, real income, employment, industrial production, and wholesale-retail sales."[3]

At time t_1 in Figure 20.1, an expansion ends and real GDP turns downward. The point at which an expansion ends and a recession begins is called the **peak** of the business cycle. Real GDP then falls during a period of recession. Eventually it starts upward again (at time t_2). The point at which a recession ends and an expansion begins is called the **trough** of the business cycle. The expansion continues until another peak is reached at time t_3.[4] A complete business cycle is defined by the passage from one peak to the next.

Because the Business Cycle Dating Committee dates peaks and troughs by specific months, and because real GDP is estimated only on a quarterly basis by the Bureau of Economic Analysis, the committee relies on a variety of other indicators that are published monthly, including real personal income, employment, industrial production, and real wholesale and retail sales. The committee typically determines that a recession has happened long after it has actually begun and sometimes ended! In large part, that avoids problems when data released about the economy are revised, and the committee avoids having to reverse itself on its determination of when a recession begins or ends, something it has never done. In December 2008, the committee announced that a recession in the United States had begun in December 2007. In September 2010, the committee announced that this recession had ended in June 2009.

FIGURE 20.1 Phases of the Business Cycle

The business cycle is a series of expansions and contractions in real GDP. The cycle begins at a peak and continues through a recession, a trough, and an expansion. A new cycle begins at the next peak. Here, the first peak occurs at time t_1, the trough at time t_2, and the next peak at time t_3. Notice that there is a tendency for real GDP to rise over time.

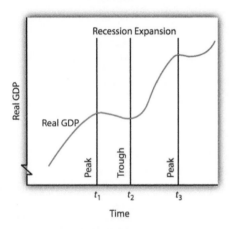

Business Cycles and the Growth of Real GDP in the United States

Figure 20.2 shows movements in real GDP in the United States from 1960 to 2016. Over those years, the economy experienced eight recessions, shown by the shaded areas in the chart. Although periods of expansion have been more prolonged than periods of recession, we see the cycle of economic activity that characterizes economic life.

FIGURE 20.2 Expansions and Recessions, 1960–2016

The chart shows movements in real GDP since 1960. Recessions—periods of falling real GDP—are shown as shaded areas. On average, the annual rate of growth of real GDP over the period was 3.1% per year.

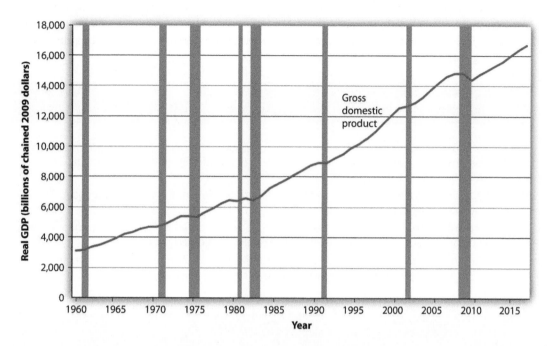

Source: Based on data from Bureau of Economic Analysis, NIPA Table 1.1.6 (revised November 29, 2016). Real Gross Domestic Product, Chained Dollars [Billions of chained (2009) dollars]. Seasonally adjusted at annual rates. Data are through 3rd quarter 2016.

Real GDP clearly grew between 1960 and 2016. While the economy experienced expansions and recessions, its general trend during the period was one of rising real GDP. The average annual rate of growth of real GDP was about 3.1%.

During the post–World War II period, the average expansion has lasted 58 months, and the average recession has lasted about 11 months. The 2001 recession, which lasted eight months, was thus slightly shorter than the average. The 2007–2009 recession lasted 18 months; it was the longest of the post–World War II period.

Economists have sought for centuries to explain the forces at work in a business cycle. Not only are the currents that move the economy up or down intellectually fascinating but also an understanding of them is of tremendous practical importance. A business cycle is not just a movement along a curve in a textbook. It is new jobs for people, or the loss of them. It is new income, or the loss of it. It is the funds to build new schools or to provide better health care—or the lack of funds to do all those things. The story of the business cycle is the story of progress and plenty, of failure and sacrifice.

During the most recent recession, the job outlook for college graduates deteriorated. According to a National Association of Colleges and Employers study, 20% of college graduates seeking jobs were able to obtain one after graduation in 2009. In 2010, that percentage rose to 24%, but the average salary had slipped 1.7% from the previous year. The unemployment rate for college graduates under age 25 rose from 3.7% in April 2007 to 8% in April 2010. Over the same two-year period, the unemployment rate for high school graduates who had never enrolled in college rose from 11.4% to 24.5%.[5]

The effects of recessions extend beyond the purely economic realm and influence the social fabric of society as well. Suicide rates and property crimes—burglary, larceny, and motor vehicle theft tend to rise during recessions. Even popular music appears to be affected. Terry F. Pettijohn II, a psychologist at Coastal Carolina University, has studied Billboard No. 1 songs from 1955 to 2003. He finds that during recessions, popular songs tend to be longer and slower, and to have more serious lyrics. "It's 'Bridge over Troubled Water' or 'That's What Friends Are For'," he says. During expansions, songs tend to be faster, shorter, and somewhat sillier, such as "At the Hop" or "My Sharona."[6]

In our study of macroeconomics, we will gain an understanding of the forces at work in the business cycle. We will also explore policies through which the public sector might act to make recessions less severe and, perhaps, to prolong expansions. We turn next to an examination of price-level changes and unemployment.

Key Takeaways

- Real gross domestic product (real GDP) is a measure of the value of all final goods and services produced during a particular year or period, adjusted to eliminate the effects of price changes.
- The economy follows a path of expansion, then contraction, then expansion again. These fluctuations make up the business cycle.
- The point at which an expansion becomes a recession is called the peak of a business cycle; the point at which a recession becomes an expansion is called the trough.
- Over time, the general trend for most economies is one of rising real GDP. On average, real GDP in the United States has grown at a rate of over 3% per year since 1960.

Try It!

The data below show the behavior of real GDP in Turkey from the first quarter of 2001 through the third quarter of 2002. Use the data to plot real GDP in Turkey and indicate the phases of the business cycle.

Period	Real GDP (billions of New Turkish lira, 1987 prices)
First quarter, 2001	24.1
Second quarter, 2001	26.0
Third quarter, 2001	33.1
Fourth quarter, 2001	27.1
First quarter, 2002	24.6
Second quarter, 2002	28.3
Third quarter, 2002	35.7

Case in Point: The Art of Predicting Recessions

Source: © Shutterstock, Inc.

People who make a living tracking the economy and trying to predict its future do not do a very good job at predicting turning points in economic activity. The 52 economists surveyed by the *Wall Street Journal* each month did predict that the economy would slip into a recession in the third quarter of 2008. They made that prediction, however, in October—after the third quarter had ended. In September, the last month of the third quarter, the average forecast among the 52 economists had the economy continuing to grow through the third and fourth quarters of 2008. That September survey was taken before the financial crisis hit, a crisis that took virtually everyone by surprise. Of course, as we have already noted, the third-quarter downturn had not been identified as a recession by the NBER's Business Cycle Dating Committee as of November of 2008.

Predicting business cycle turning points has always been a tricky business. The experience of the recession of 2001 illustrates this. As the accompanying table shows, even as late as September 10, 2001, only 13 out of the 100 Blue Chip forecasters had answered in the affirmative to the question, "Has the United States slipped into a recession?" even though we now know the recession had begun the previous March. Comparing the data that were originally released by the U.S. Bureau of Economic Analysis shortly after the end of each quarter with the revised data that were released after July 2002 provides an important insight into explaining why the forecasters seem to have done so badly. As the graph on pre-revision and post-revision estimates of real GDP growth shows, the data released shortly after the end of each quarter showed an economy expanding through the second quarter of 2001, whereas the revised data show the economy contracting modestly in the first quarter of 2001 and then more forcefully in the second quarter. Only after the attacks on the World Trade Center in New York City and the Pentagon in Washington, D.C., on September 11, 2001, did most of the Blue Chip forecasters realize the economy was in recession.

The National Bureau of Economic Research (NBER) Business Cycle Dating Committee in November 2001 released a press announcement dating the onset of the recession as March 2001. The committee argued that "before the attacks of September 11, it is possible that the decline in the economy would have been too mild to qualify as a recession. The attacks clearly deepened the contraction and may have been an important factor in turning the episode into a recession." While surprising at the time, the revised data suggest that the committee made a good call.

This episode in economic history also points out the difference between the common definition of a recession as two consecutive quarters of declining real GDP and the NBER Dating Committee's continued insistence that it does not define a recession in this way. Rather the committee looks not only at real GDP but also at employment, income, and other factors. The behavior of employment during 2001 seems to have been an important factor in the November 2001 decision to proclaim March 2001 as the peak despite the misleading information on real GDP coming out of the Bureau of Economic Analysis at the time. The slow pickup in employment may also, though, have made it hesitate to call November 2001 the trough until July 2003.

Question posed: "Has the United States slipped into a recession?"		
Date	Percent of Blue Chip responders answering "Yes"	Percent of Blue Chip responders answering "No"
February 2001	5	95
June 2001	7	93
July 2001	13	87
August 2001	5	85
September 10, 2001	13	87
September 19, 2001	82	18

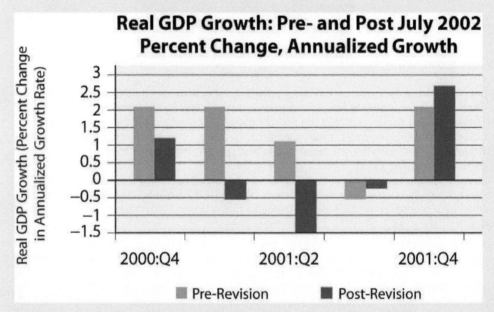

Sources: *Based on Phil Izzo, "Economists Expect Crisis to Deepen," Wall Street Journal Online, October 10, 2008; Kevin L. Kliesen, "The 2001 Recession: How Was It Different and What Developments May Have Caused It?" Federal Reserve Bank of St. Louis Review, September/October 2003: 23–37; http://www.nber.org/cycles/; "Press Release," Business Cycle Dating Committee, National Bureau of Economic Research, press release, Cambridge, Massachusetts, July 17, 2002.*

Answer to Try It! Problem

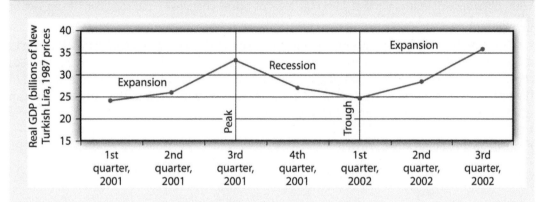

20.3 Price-Level Changes

Learning Objectives

1. Define inflation and deflation, explain how their rates are determined, and articulate why price-level changes matter.
2. Explain what a price index is and outline the general steps in computing a price index.
3. Describe and compare different price indexes.
4. Explain how to convert nominal values to real values and explain why it is useful to make this calculation.
5. Discuss the biases that may arise from price indexes that employ fixed market baskets of goods and services.

Concern about changes in the price level has always dominated economic discussion. With inflation in the United States generally averaging only between 2% and 3% each year since 1990, it may seem surprising how much attention the behavior of the price level still commands. Yet inflation was a concern in 2004 when there was fear that the rising price of oil could trigger higher prices in other areas. Just the year before, when inflation fell below 2%, there was talk about the risk of deflation. That did not happen; prices continued rising. Inflation rose substantially in the first half of 2008, renewing fears about subsequent further increases. And 2010 brought renewed concern of possible deflation. Just what are inflation and deflation? How are they measured? And most important, why do we care? These are some of the questions we will explore in this section.

Inflation is an increase in the average level of prices, and **deflation** is a decrease in the average level of prices. In an economy experiencing inflation, most prices are likely to be rising, whereas in an economy experiencing deflation, most prices are likely to be falling.

There are two key points in these definitions:

1. Inflation and deflation refer to changes in the average level of prices, not to changes in particular prices. An increase in medical costs is not inflation. A decrease in gasoline prices is not deflation. Inflation means the average level of prices is rising, and deflation means the average level of prices is falling.
2. Inflation and deflation refer to *rising* prices and *falling* prices, respectively; therefore, they do not have anything to do with the *level* of prices at any one time. "High" prices do not imply the presence of inflation, nor do "low" prices imply deflation. Inflation means a positive *rate of change* in average prices, and deflation means a negative *rate of change* in average prices.

inflation

An increase in the average level of prices.

deflation

A decrease in the average level of prices.

Why Do We Care?

What difference does it make if the average level of prices changes? First, consider the impact of inflation.

Inflation is measured as the annual rate of increase in the average level of prices. Figure 20.3 shows how volatile inflation has been in the United States over the past four decades. In the 1960s the inflation rate rose, and it became dramatically worse in the 1970s. The inflation rate plunged in the 1980s and continued to ease downward in the 1990s. It remained low in the early 2000s, began to accelerate in 2007, and has remained low since then.

FIGURE 20.3 Inflation, 1960–2016
The U.S. inflation rate, measured as the annual rate of change in the average level of prices paid by consumers, varied considerably over the 1960–2016 period.

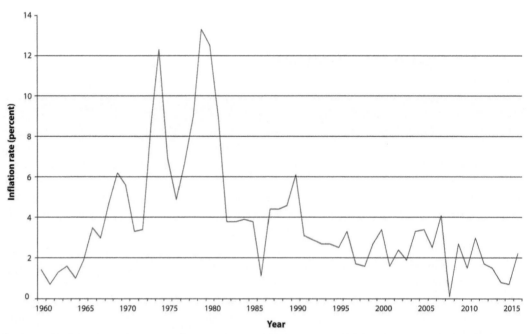

Source: Based on data from Bureau of Labor Statistics, All Urban Consumers CPI-U, 1982–84 = 100, Dec.–Dec. inflation rate. Data are through October 2016.

Whether one regards inflation as a "good" thing or a "bad" thing depends very much on one's economic situation. If you are a borrower, unexpected inflation is a good thing—it reduces the value of money that you must repay. If you are a lender, it is a bad thing because it reduces the value of future payments you will receive. Whatever any particular person's situation may be, inflation always produces the following effects on the economy: it reduces the value of money and it reduces the value of future monetary obligations. It can also create uncertainty about the future.

Suppose that you have just found a $10 bill you stashed away in 1990. Prices have increased by about 50% since then; your money will buy less than what it would have purchased when you put it away. Your money has thus lost value.

Money loses value when its purchasing power falls. Since inflation is a rise in the level of prices, the amount of goods and services a given amount of money can buy falls with inflation.

Just as inflation reduces the value of money, it reduces the value of future claims on money. Suppose you have borrowed $100 from a friend and have agreed to pay it back in one year. During the year, however, prices double. That means that when you pay the money back, it will buy only half as much as it could have bought when you borrowed it. That is good for you but tough on the person who lent you the money. Of course, if you and your friend had anticipated such rapid inflation, you might have agreed to pay back a larger sum to adjust for it. When people anticipate inflation, they can adjust for its consequences in determining future obligations. But *unanticipated* inflation helps borrowers and hurts lenders.

Inflation's impact on future claims can be particularly hard on people who must live on a fixed income, that is, on an income that is predetermined through some contractual arrangement and does not change with economic conditions. An annuity, for example, typically provides a fixed stream of money payments. Retirement pensions sometimes generate fixed income. Inflation erodes the value of such payments.

Given the danger posed by inflation for people on fixed incomes, many retirement plans provide for indexed payments. An indexed payment is one whose dollar amount changes with the rate of change in the price level. If a payment changes at the same rate as the rate of change in the price level, the purchasing power of the payment remains constant. Social Security payments, for example, are indexed to maintain their purchasing power.

Because inflation reduces the purchasing power of money, the threat of future inflation can make people reluctant to lend for long periods. From a lender's point of view, the danger of a long-term commitment of funds is that future inflation will wipe out the value of the amount that will eventually be paid back. Lenders are reluctant to make such commitments.

Uncertainty can be particularly pronounced in countries where extremely high inflation is a threat. **Hyperinflation** is generally defined as an inflation rate in excess of 200% per year. It is always caused by the rapid printing of money. Several countries have endured episodes of hyperinflation. The worst case was in Hungary immediately after World War II, when Hungary's price level was tripling *every day*. The second-worst case of hyperinflation belongs to Zimbabwe, which is the first country to have experienced hyperinflation in the 21st century. Zimbabwe's price index was doubling daily: a loaf of bread that cost 200,000 Zimbabwe dollars in February 2008 cost 1.6 trillion Zimbabwe dollars by August.[7] The annual inflation rate reached 89.7 sextillion percent in November of that year.[8] (On the off chance you haven't been counting in the sextillions a lot lately, 89.7 sextillion equates to 897 followed by 20 zeroes.) Two months later, Zimbabwe finally gave up on printing money and took the Zimbabwe dollar out of circulation. Exchange is now carried out using U.S. dollars or South African rand—and Zimbabwe's period of hyperinflation has come to an end.

> **hyperinflation**
> An inflation rate in excess of 200% per year.

Do the problems associated with inflation imply that deflation would be a good thing? The answer is simple: no. Like inflation, deflation changes the value of money and the value of future obligations. It also creates uncertainty about the future.

If there is deflation, the real value of a given amount of money rises. In other words, if there had been deflation since 2000, a $10 bill you had stashed away in 2000 would buy more goods and services today. That sounds good, but should you buy $10 worth of goods and services now when you would be able to buy even more for your $10 in the future if the deflation continues? When Japan experienced deflation in the late 1990s and early 2000s, Japanese consumers seemed to be doing just that—waiting to see if prices would fall further. They were spending less per person and, as we will see throughout our study of macroeconomics, less consumption often meant less output, fewer jobs, and the prospect of a recurring recession.

And, if you had to use the $10 to pay back a debt you owed, the purchasing power of your money would be higher than when you borrowed the money. The lender would feel good about being able to buy more with the $10 than you were able to, but you would feel like you had gotten a raw deal.

Unanticipated deflation hurts borrowers and helps lenders. If the parties anticipate the deflation, a loan agreement can be written to reflect expected changes in the price level.

The threat of deflation can make people reluctant to borrow for long periods. Borrowers become reluctant to enter into long-term contracts because they fear that deflation will raise the value of the money they must pay back in the future. In such an environment, firms may be reluctant to borrow to build new factories, for example. This is because they fear that the prices at which they can sell their output will drop, making it difficult for them to repay their loans.

Deflation was common in the United States in the latter third of the 19th century. In the 20th century, there was a period of deflation after World War I and again during the Great Depression in the 1930s.

Price Indexes

How do we actually measure inflation and deflation (that is, changes in the price level)? Price-level change is measured as the percentage rate of change in the level of prices. But how do we find a price level?

Economists measure the price level with a price index. A **price index** is a number whose movement reflects movement in the average level of prices. If a price index rises 10%, it means the average level of prices has risen 10%.

There are four steps one must take in computing a price index:

1. Select the kinds and quantities of goods and services to be included in the index. A list of these goods and services, and the quantities of each, is the "market basket" for the index.

2. Determine what it would cost to buy the goods and services in the market basket in some period that is the base period for the index. A **base period** is a time period against which costs of the market basket in other periods will be compared in computing a price index. Most often, the base period for an index is a single year. If, for example, a price index had a base period of 1990, costs of the basket in other periods would be compared to the cost of the basket in 1990. We will encounter one index, however, whose base period stretches over three years.

3. Compute the cost of the market basket in the current period.

4. Compute the price index. It equals the current cost divided by the base-period cost of the market basket.

EQUATION 20.1

$$\text{Price index} = \text{current cost of basket} / \text{base-period cost of basket}$$

(While published price indexes are typically reported with this number multiplied by 100, our work with indexes will be simplified by omitting this step.)

Suppose that we want to compute a price index for movie fans, and a survey of movie watchers tells us that a typical fan rents 4 movies on DVD and sees 3 movies in theaters each month. At the theater, this viewer consumes a medium-sized soft drink and a medium-sized box of popcorn. Our market basket thus might include 4 DVD rentals, 3 movie admissions, 3 medium soft drinks, and 3 medium servings of popcorn.

Our next step in computing the movie price index is to determine the cost of the market basket. Suppose we surveyed movie theaters and DVD-rental stores in 2015 to determine the average prices of these items, finding the values given in Table 20.1. At those prices, the total monthly cost of our movie market basket in 2015 was $48. Now suppose that in 2016 the prices of movie admissions and DVD rentals rise, soft-drink prices at movies fall, and popcorn prices remain unchanged. The combined effect of these changes pushes the 2016 cost of the basket to $50.88.

price index

A number whose movement reflects movement in the average level of prices.

base period

A time period against which costs of the market basket in other periods will be compared in computing a price index.

TABLE 20.1 Pricing a Market Basket
To compute a price index, we need to define a market basket and determine its price. The table gives the composition of the movie market basket and prices for 2011 and 2012. The cost of the entire basket rises from $48 in 2011 to $50.88 in 2012.

Item	Quantity in Basket	2015 Price	Cost in 2015 Basket	2016 Price	Cost in 2016 Basket
DVD rental	4	$2.25	$9.00	$2.97	$11.88
Movie admission	3	7.75	23.25	8.00	24.00
Popcorn	3	2.25	6.75	2.25	6.75
Soft drink	3	3.00	9.00	2.75	8.25
Total cost of basket		**2015**	$48.00	**2016**	$50.88

Using the data in Table 20.1, we could compute price indexes for each year. Recall that a price index is the ratio of the current cost of the basket to the base-period cost. We can select any year we wish as the base year; take 2015. The 2016 movie price index (MPI) is thus

EQUATION 20.2

$$\text{MPI}_{2016} = \$50.88/\$48 = 1.06$$

The value of any price index in the base period is always 1. In the case of our movie price index, the 2015 index would be the current (2015) cost of the basket, $48, divided by the base-period cost, which is the same thing: $48/$48 = 1.

The Consumer Price Index (CPI)

One widely used price index in the United States is the **consumer price index (CPI)**, a price index whose movement reflects changes in the prices of goods and services typically purchased by consumers. When the media report the U.S. inflation rate, the number cited is usually a rate computed using the CPI. The CPI is also used to determine whether people's incomes are keeping up with the costs of the things they buy. The CPI is often used to measure changes in the cost of living, though as we shall see, there are problems in using it for this purpose.

consumer price index (CPI)

A price index whose movement reflects changes in the prices of goods and services typically purchased by consumers.

The market basket for the CPI contains thousands of goods and services. The composition of the basket is determined by the Bureau of Labor Statistics (BLS), an agency of the Department of Labor, based on Census Bureau surveys of household buying behavior. Surveyors tally the prices of the goods and services in the basket each month in cities all over the United States to determine the current cost of the basket. The major categories of items in the CPI are food and beverages, housing, apparel, transportation, medical care, recreation, education and communication, and other goods and services.

The current cost of the basket of consumer goods and services is then compared to the base-period cost of that same basket. The base period for the CPI is 1982–1984; the base-period cost of the basket is its average cost over this period. Each month's CPI thus reflects the ratio of the current cost of the basket divided by its base-period cost.

EQUATION 20.3

$$\text{CPI} = \text{current cost of basket} / 1982–1984 \text{ cost of basket}$$

Like many other price indexes, the CPI is computed with a fixed market basket. The composition of the basket generally remains unchanged from one period to the next. Because buying patterns change, however, the basket is revised accordingly on a periodic basis. The base period, though, was still 1982–1984.

The Implicit Price Deflator

Values for nominal and real GDP, described earlier in this chapter, provide us with the information to calculate the most broad-based price index available. The **implicit price deflator**, a price index for all final goods and services produced, is the ratio of nominal GDP to real GDP.

In computing the implicit price deflator for a particular period, economists define the market basket quite simply: it includes all the final goods and services produced during that period. The nominal GDP gives the current cost of that basket; the real GDP adjusts the nominal GDP for changes in prices. The implicit price deflator is thus given by

EQUATION 20.4

$$\text{Implicit price deflator} = \text{nominal GDP} / \text{real GDP}$$

For example, in 2015, nominal GDP in the United States was $18,036.6 billion, and real GDP was $16,397.2 billion. Thus, the implicit price deflator was 1.100. Following the convention of multiplying price indexes by 100, the published number for the implicit price deflator was 110.

In our analysis of the determination of output and the price level in subsequent chapters, we will use the implicit price deflator as the measure of the price level in the economy.

The PCE Price Index

The Bureau of Economic Analysis also produces price index information for each of the components of GDP (that is, a separate price index for consumer prices, prices for different components of gross private domestic investment, and government spending). The **personal consumption expenditures price index**, or PCE price index, includes durable goods, nondurable goods, and services and is provided along with estimates for prices of each component of consumption spending. Because prices for food and energy can be volatile, the price measure that excludes food and energy is often used as a measure of underlying, or "core," inflation. Note that the PCE price index differs substantially from the consumer price index, primarily because it is not a "fixed basket" index.[9] The PCE price index has become a politically important measure of inflation since the Federal Reserve (discussed in detail in later chapters) uses it as its primary measure of price levels in the United States.

Computing the Rate of Inflation or Deflation

The rate of inflation or deflation is the percentage rate of change in a price index between two periods. Given price-index values for two periods, we can calculate the rate of inflation or deflation as the change in the index divided by the initial value of the index, stated as a percentage:

EQUATION 20.5

$$\text{Rate of inflation or deflation} = \text{change in index} / \text{initial value of index} \times 100 = \text{percent change in index}$$

To calculate inflation in movie prices over the 2015–2016 period, for example, we could apply Equation 20.5 to the price indexes we computed for those two years as follows:

EQUATION 20.6

$$\text{Movie inflation rate in 2016} = (1.06 - 1.00) / 1.00 \times 100 = 0.06 \times 100 = 6\%$$

The CPI is often used for calculating price-level change for the economy. For example, the rate of inflation in 2015 can be computed from the December 2014 price level (2.348) and the December 2015 level (2.365):

EQUATION 20.7

$$\text{Inflation rate} = (2.365 - 2.348) / 2.348 \times 100 = 0.007 \times 100 = 0.7\%$$

Computing Real Values Using Price Indexes

Suppose your uncle started college in 2001 and had a job busing dishes that paid $5 per hour. In 2015 you had the same job; it paid $6 per hour. Which job paid more?

At first glance, the answer is straightforward: $6 is a higher wage than $5. But $1 had greater purchasing power in 2001 than in 2015 because prices were lower in 2001 than in 2015. To obtain a valid comparison of the two wages, we must use dollars of equivalent purchasing power. A value expressed in units of constant purchasing power is a **real value**. A value expressed in dollars of the current period is called a **nominal value**. The $5 wage in 2001 and the $6 wage in 2015 are nominal wages.

real value

A value expressed in units of constant purchasing power.

nominal value

A value expressed in dollars of the current period.

To convert nominal values to real values, we divide by a price index. The real value for a given period is the nominal value for that period divided by the price index for that period. This procedure gives us a value in dollars that have the purchasing power of the base period for the price index used. Using the CPI, for example, yields values expressed in dollars of 1982–1984 purchasing power, the base period for the CPI. The real value of a nominal amount X at time t, X_t, is found using the price index for time t:

EQUATION 20.8

$$\text{Real value of } X_t = X_t / \text{price index at time } t$$

Let us compute the real value of the $6 wage for busing dishes in 2015 versus the $5 wage paid to your uncle in 2001. The CPI in 2001 was 176.7; in 2015 it was 236.5. Real wages for the two years were thus

$$\text{Real wage in 2001} = \$5/1.767 = \$2.83$$

$$\text{Real wage in 2015} = \$6/2.365 = \$2.54$$

Given the nominal wages in our example, you earned about 10% less in real terms in 2015 than your uncle did in 2001.

Price indexes are useful. They allow us to see how the general level of prices has changed. They allow us to estimate the rate of change in prices, which we report as the rate of inflation or deflation. And they give us a tool for converting nominal values to real values so we can make better comparisons of economic performance across time.

Are Price Indexes Accurate Measures of Price-Level Changes?

Price indexes that employ fixed market baskets are likely to overstate inflation (and understate deflation) for four reasons:

1. Because the components of the market basket are fixed, the index does not incorporate consumer responses to changing relative prices.
2. A fixed basket excludes new goods and services.
3. Quality changes may not be completely accounted for in computing price-level changes.
4. The type of store in which consumers choose to shop can affect the prices they pay, and the price indexes do not reflect changes consumers have made in where they shop.

To see how these factors can lead to inaccurate measures of price-level changes, suppose the price of chicken rises and the price of beef falls. The law of demand tells us that people will respond by consuming less chicken and more beef. But if we use a fixed market basket of goods and services in computing a price index, we will not be able to make these adjustments. The market basket holds constant the quantities of chicken and beef consumed. The importance in consumer budgets of the higher chicken price is thus overstated, while the importance of the lower beef price is understated. More generally, a fixed market basket will overstate the importance of items that rise in price and understate the importance of items that fall in price. This source of bias is referred to as the substitution bias.

The new-product bias, a second source of bias in price indexes, occurs because it takes time for new products to be incorporated into the market basket that makes up the CPI. A good introduced to the market after the basket has been defined will not, of course, be included in it. But a new good, once successfully introduced, is likely to fall in price. When VCRs were first introduced, for example, they generally cost more than $1,000. Within a few years, an equivalent machine cost less than $200. But when VCRs were introduced, the CPI was based on a market basket that had been defined in the early 1970s. There was no VCR in the basket, so the impact of this falling price was not reflected in the index. The DVD player was introduced into the CPI within a year of its availability.

A third price index bias, the quality-change bias, comes from improvements in the quality of goods and services. Suppose, for example, that Ford introduces a new car with better safety features and a smoother ride than its previous model. Suppose the old model cost $20,000 and the new model costs $24,000, a 20% increase in price. Should economists at the Bureau of Labor Statistics (BLS) simply record the new model as being 20% more expensive than the old one? Clearly, the new model is not the same product as the old model. BLS economists faced with such changes try to adjust for quality. To the extent that such adjustments understate quality change, they overstate any increase in the price level.

The fourth source of bias is called the outlet bias. Households can reduce some of the impact of rising prices by shopping at superstores or outlet stores (such as T.J. Maxx, Wal-Mart, or factory outlet stores), though this often means they get less customer service than at traditional department stores or at smaller retail stores. However, since such shopping has increased in recent years, it must be that for their customers, the reduction in prices has been more valuable to them than loss of service. Prior to 1998, the CPI did not account for a change in the number of households shopping at these newer kinds of stores in a timely manner, but the BLS now does quarterly surveys and updates its sample of stores much more frequently. Another form of this bias arises because the government data collectors do not collect price data on weekends and holidays, when many stores run sales.

Economists differ on the degree to which these biases result in inaccuracies in recording price-level changes. In late 1996, Michael Boskin, an economist at Stanford University, chaired a panel of economists appointed by the Senate Finance Committee to determine the magnitude of the problem in the United States. The panel reported that the CPI was overstating inflation in the United States by 0.8 to 1.6 percentage points per year. Their best estimate was 1.1 percentage points, as shown in Table 20.2. Since then, the Bureau of Labor Statistics has made a number of changes to correct for these sources of bias and since August 2002 has reported a new consumer price index called the Chained Consumer Price Index for all Urban Consumers (C-CPU-U) that attempts to provide a closer approximation to a "cost-of-living" index by utilizing expenditure data that reflect the substitutions that consumers make across item categories in response to changes in relative prices.[10] However, a 2006 study by Robert Gordon, a professor at Northwestern University and a member of the original 1996 Boskin Commission, estimates that the total bias then to still be about 0.8 percentage points per year, as also shown in Table 20.2. The Bureau of Labor Statistics has continued to work on this issue.

TABLE 20.2 Estimates of Bias in the Consumer Price Index

The Boskin Commission reported that the CPI overstates the rate of inflation by 0.8 to 1.6 percentage points due to the biases shown, with a best-guess estimate of 1.1. A 2006 study by Robert Gordon estimates that the bias fell but is still about 0.8 percentage points.

Sources of Bias	1997 Estimate	2006 Estimate
Substitution	0.4	0.4
New products and quality change	0.6	0.3
Switching to new outlets	0.1	0.1
Total	1.1	0.8
Plausible range	0.8–1.6	—

Source: Based on data from Robert J. Gordon, "The Boskin Commission Report: A Retrospective One Decade Later" (National Bureau of Economic Research Working Paper 12311, June 2006), available at http://www.nber.org/papers/w12311.

These findings of upward bias have enormous practical significance. With annual inflation running below 2% in three out of the last 10 years and averaging 2.7% over the 10 years, it means that the United States has come close to achieving price stability for almost a decade.

To the extent that the computation of price indexes overstates the rate of inflation, then the use of price indexes to correct nominal values results in an understatement of gains in real incomes. For example, average nominal hourly earnings of U.S. production workers were $13.01 in 1998 and $17.42 in 2007. Adjusting for CPI-measured inflation, the average real hourly earnings was $7.98 in 1998 and $8.40 in 2007, suggesting that real wages rose about 5.3% over the period. If inflation was overstated by 0.8% per year over that entire period, as suggested by Gordon's updating of the Boskin Commission's best estimate, then, adjusting for this overstatement, real wages should have been reported as $7.98 for 1998 and $9.01 for 2007, a gain of nearly 13%.

Also, because the CPI is used as the basis for calculating U.S. government payments for programs such as Social Security and for adjusting tax brackets, this price index affects the government's budget balance, the difference between government revenues and government expenditures. The Congressional Budget Office has estimated that correcting the biases in the index would have increased revenue by $2 billion and reduced outlays by $4 billion in 1997. By 2007, the U.S. government's budget would have had an additional $140 billion if the bias were removed.

Key Takeaways

- Inflation is an increase in the average level of prices, and deflation is a decrease in the average level of prices. The rate of inflation or deflation is the percentage rate of change in a price index.
- The consumer price index (CPI) is the most widely used price index in the United States.
- Nominal values can be converted to real values by dividing by a price index.
- Inflation and deflation affect the real value of money, of future obligations measured in money, and of fixed incomes. Unanticipated inflation and deflation create uncertainty about the future.
- Economists generally agree that the CPI and other price indexes that employ fixed market baskets of goods and services do not accurately measure price-level changes. Biases include the substitution bias, the new-product bias, the quality-change bias, and the outlet bias.

Try It!

Suppose that nominal GDP is $10 trillion in 2013 and $11 trillion in 2004, and that the implicit price deflator has gone from 1.063 in 2003 to 1.091 in 2044. Compute real GDP in 2013 and 2014. Using the percentage change in the implicit price deflator as the gauge, what was the inflation rate over the period?

Case in Point: Take Me Out to the Ball Game ...

Source: © Shutterstock, Inc.

The cost of a trip to the old ball game rose 3.7% in 2016, according to *Team Marketing Report*, a Chicago-based newsletter. The report bases its estimate on its fan price index, whose market basket includes four adult average-priced tickets, two small draft beers, four small soft drinks, four regular-sized hot dogs, parking for one car, two game programs, and two least expensive, adult-sized adjustable baseball caps. The average price of the market basket was $219.53 in 2016.

Team Marketing compiles the cost of the basket for each of major league baseball's 30 teams. According to this compilation, the Boston Red Sox was the most expensive team to watch in 2016; the Arizona Diamondbacks was the cheapest. The table shows the cost of the fan price index market basket for 2016.

Team	Basket Cost	Team	Basket Cost
Boston Red Sox	$360.66	Seattle Mariners	$209.00
New York Yankees	$337.20	Texas Rangers	$204.56
Chicago Cubs	$312.32	Kansas City Royals	$202.52
Philadelphia Phillies	$258.50	Oakland Athletics	$198.84
San Francisco Giants	$255.04	Pittsburgh Pirates	$195.84
St. Louis Cardinals	$243.96	Colorado Rockies	$193.96
Houston Astros	$242.00	Milwaukee Brewers	$190.82
Washington Nationals	$234.36	Baltimore Orioles	$183.34
Los Angeles Dodgers	$234.10	San Diego Padres	$182.82
Toronto Blue Jays	$231.76	Cleveland Indians	$179.44
Chicago White Sox	$229.50	Atlanta Braves	$178.02
New York Mets	$223.56	Cincinnati Reds	$166.54
Detroit Tigers	$214.52	Tampa Bay Rays	$154.16
Miami Marlins	$214.22	Arizona Diamondbacks	$132.10
Minnesota Twins	$212.12		
Los Angeles Angels	$210.80	**MLB Average**	**$219.53**

Source: Based on data from Team Marketing Report, "TMR's Fan Cost Index Major League Baseball 2016," available at http://www.teammarketing.com.

Answer to Try It! Problem

Rearranging Equation 20.4, real GDP = nominal GDP/implicit price deflator. Therefore,

Real GDP in 2013 = $10 trillion/1.063 = $9.4 trillion.

Real GDP in 2014 = $11 trillion/1.091 = $10.1 trillion.

Thus, in this economy in real terms, GDP has grown by $0.7 trillion.

To find the rate of inflation, we refer to Equation 20.5, and we calculate:

Inflation rate in 2014 = $(1.091 - 1.063)/1.063 \times 100 = 0.026 \times 100 = 2.6\%$

Thus, the price level rose 2.6% between 2013 and 2014.

20.4 Unemployment

Learning Objectives

1. Explain how unemployment is measured in the United States.
2. Define three different types of unemployment.
3. Define and illustrate graphically what is meant by the natural level of employment. Relate the natural level of employment to the natural rate of unemployment.

For an economy to produce all it can and achieve a solution on its production possibilities curve, the factors of production in the economy must be fully employed. Failure to fully employ these factors leads to a solution inside the production possibilities curve in which society is not achieving the output it is capable of producing.

In thinking about the employment of society's factors of production, we place special emphasis on labor. The loss of a job can wipe out a household's entire income; it is a more compelling human problem than, say, unemployed capital, such as a vacant apartment. In measuring unemployment, we thus focus on labor rather than on capital and natural resources.

Measuring Unemployment

labor force

The total number of people working or unemployed.

unemployment rate

The percentage of the labor force that is unemployed.

The Bureau of Labor Statistics defines a person as unemployed if he or she is not working but is looking for and available for work. The **labor force** is the total number of people working or unemployed. The **unemployment rate** is the percentage of the labor force that is unemployed.

To estimate the unemployment rate, government surveyors fan out across the country each month to visit roughly 60,000 households. At each of these randomly selected households, the surveyor asks about the employment status of each adult (everyone age 16 or over) who lives there. Many households include more than one adult; the survey gathers information on about roughly 100,000 adults. The surveyor asks if each adult is working. If the answer is yes, the person is counted as employed. If the answer is no, the surveyor asks if that person has looked for work at some time during the previous four weeks and is available for work at the time of the survey. If the answer to that question is yes, the person is counted as unemployed. If the answer is no, that person is not counted as a member of the labor force. Figure 20.4 shows the survey's results for the civilian (non-military) population for October 2016. The unemployment rate is then computed as the number of people unemployed divided by the labor force—the sum of the number of people not working but available and looking for work plus the number of people working. In October 2016, the unemployment rate was 4.6%.

FIGURE 20.4 Computing the Unemployment Rate

A monthly survey of households divides the civilian adult population into three groups. Those who have jobs are counted as employed; those who do not have jobs but are looking for them and are available for work are counted as unemployed; and those who are not working and are not looking for work are not counted as members of the labor force. The unemployment rate equals the number of people looking for work divided by the sum of the number of people looking for work and the number of people employed. Values are for October 2016. All numbers are in thousands.

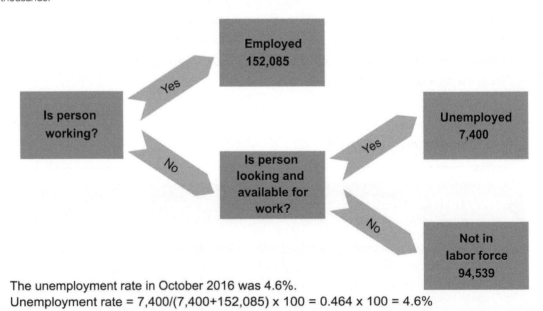

The unemployment rate in October 2016 was 4.6%.
Unemployment rate = 7,400/(7,400+152,085) x 100 = 0.464 x 100 = 4.6%

There are several difficulties with the survey. The old survey, designed during the 1930s, put the "Are you working?" question differently depending on whether the respondent was a man or woman. A man was asked, "Last week, did you do any work for pay or profit?" A woman was asked, "What were you doing for work last week, keeping house or something else?" Consequently, many women who were looking for paid work stated that they were "keeping house"; those women were not counted as unemployed. The BLS did not get around to fixing the survey—asking women the same question it asked men—until 1994. The first time the new survey question was used, the unemployment rate among women rose by 0.5 percentage point. More than 50 million women are in the labor force; the change added more than a quarter of a million workers to the official count of the unemployed.[11]

The problem of understating unemployment among women has been fixed, but others remain. A worker who has been cut back to part-time work still counts as employed, even if that worker would prefer to work full time. A person who is out of work, would like to work, has looked for work in the past year, and is available for work, but who has given up looking, is considered a discouraged worker. Discouraged workers are not counted as unemployed, but a tally is kept each month of the number of discouraged workers.

The official measures of employment and unemployment can yield unexpected results. For example, when firms expand output, they may be reluctant to hire additional workers until they can be sure the demand for increased output will be sustained. They may respond first by extending the hours of employees previously reduced to part-time work or by asking full-time personnel to work overtime. None of that will increase employment, because people are simply counted as "employed" if they are working, regardless of how much or how little they are working. In addition, an economic expansion may make discouraged workers more optimistic about job prospects, and they may resume their job searches. Engaging in a search makes them unemployed again—and increases unemployment. Thus, an economic expansion may have little effect initially on employment and may even increase unemployment.

Types of Unemployment

Workers may find themselves unemployed for different reasons. Each source of unemployment has quite different implications, not only for the workers it affects but also for public policy.

Figure 20.5 applies the demand and supply model to the labor market. The price of labor is taken as the real wage, which is the nominal wage divided by the price level; the symbol used to represent the real wage is the Greek letter omega, ω. The supply curve is drawn as upward sloping, though steep, to reflect studies showing that the quantity of labor supplied at any one time is nearly fixed. Thus, an increase in the real wage induces a relatively small increase in the quantity of labor supplied. The demand curve shows the quantity of labor demanded at each real wage. The lower the real wage, the greater the quantity of labor firms will demand. In the case shown here, the real wage, ω_e, equals the equilibrium solution defined by the intersection of the demand curve D_1 and the supply curve S_1. The quantity of labor demanded, L_e, equals the quantity supplied. The employment level at which the quantity of labor demanded equals the quantity supplied is called the **natural level of employment**. It is sometimes referred to as full employment.

natural level of employment

The employment level at which the quantity of labor demanded equals the quantity supplied.

FIGURE 20.5 The Natural Level of Employment

The employment level at which the quantity of labor demanded equals the quantity supplied is called the natural level of employment. Here, the natural level of employment is L_e, which is achieved at a real wage ω_e.

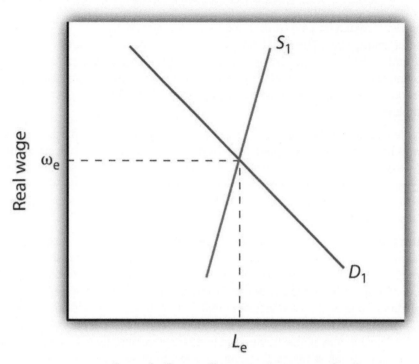

Level of employment per period

Even if the economy is operating at its natural level of employment, there will still be some unemployment. The rate of unemployment consistent with the natural level of employment is called the **natural rate of unemployment**. Business cycles may generate additional unemployment. We discuss these various sources of unemployment below.

Frictional Unemployment

Even when the quantity of labor demanded equals the quantity of labor supplied, not all employers and potential workers have found each other. Some workers are looking for jobs, and some employers are looking for workers. During the time it takes to match them up, the workers are unemployed. Unemployment that occurs because it takes time for employers and workers to find each other is called **frictional unemployment**.

The case of college graduates engaged in job searches is a good example of frictional unemployment. Those who did not land a job while still in school will seek work. Most of them will find jobs, but it will take time. During that time, these new graduates will be unemployed. If information about the labor market were costless, firms and potential workers would instantly know everything they needed to know about each other and there would be no need for searches on the part of workers and firms. There would be no frictional unemployment. But information is costly. Job searches are needed to produce this information, and frictional unemployment exists while the searches continue.

The government may attempt to reduce frictional unemployment by focusing on its source: information costs. Many state agencies, for example, serve as clearinghouses for job market information. They encourage firms seeking workers and workers seeking jobs to register with them. To the extent that such efforts make labor-market information more readily available, they reduce frictional unemployment.

Structural Unemployment

Another reason there can be unemployment even if employment equals its natural level stems from potential mismatches between the skills employers seek and the skills potential workers offer. Every worker is different; every job has its special characteristics and requirements. The qualifications of job seekers may not match those that firms require. Even if the number of employees firms demand equals the number of workers available, people whose qualifications do not satisfy what firms are seeking will find themselves without work. Unemployment that results from a mismatch between worker qualifications and the characteristics employers require is called **structural unemployment**.

Structural unemployment emerges for several reasons. Technological change may make some skills obsolete or require new ones. The widespread introduction of personal computers since the 1980s, for example, has lowered demand for typists who lacked computer skills.

Structural unemployment can occur if too many or too few workers seek training or education that matches job requirements. Students cannot predict precisely how many jobs there will be in a particular category when they graduate, and they are not likely to know how many of their fellow students are training for these jobs. Structural unemployment can easily occur if students guess wrong about how many workers will be needed or how many will be supplied.

Structural unemployment can also result from geographical mismatches. Economic activity may be booming in one region and slumping in another. It will take time for unemployed workers to relocate and find new jobs. And poor or costly transportation may block some urban residents from obtaining jobs only a few miles away.

Public policy responses to structural unemployment generally focus on job training and education to equip workers with the skills firms demand. The government publishes regional labor-market information, helping to inform unemployed workers of where jobs can be found. The North American Free Trade Agreement (NAFTA), which created a free trade region encompassing Mexico, the United States, and Canada, has created some structural unemployment in the three countries. In the United States, the legislation authorizing the pact also provided for job training programs for displaced U.S. workers.

Although government programs may reduce frictional and structural unemployment, they cannot eliminate it. Information in the labor market will always have a cost, and that cost creates frictional unemployment. An economy with changing demands for goods and services, changing technology, and changing production costs will always have some sectors expanding and others contracting—structural unemployment is inevitable. An economy at its natural level of employment will therefore have frictional and structural unemployment.

Cyclical Unemployment

Of course, the economy may not be operating at its natural level of employment, so unemployment may be above or below its natural level. In a later chapter we will explore what happens when the economy generates employment greater or less than the natural level. **Cyclical unemployment** is unemployment in excess of the unemployment that exists at the natural level of employment.

Figure 20.6 shows the unemployment rate in the United States for the period from 1960 through 2016. We see that it has fluctuated considerably. How much of it corresponds to the natural rate of unemployment varies over time with changing circumstances. For example, in a country with a demographic "bulge" of new entrants into the labor force, frictional unemployment is likely to be high, because it takes the new entrants some time to find their first jobs. This factor alone would raise the natural rate of unemployment. A demographic shift toward more mature workers would lower the natural rate. During recessions, highlighted in Figure 20.6, the part of unemployment that is cyclical unemployment grows. The analysis of fluctuations in the unemployment rate,

structural unemployment

Unemployment that results from a mismatch between worker qualifications and the characteristics employers require.

cyclical unemployment

Unemployment in excess of the unemployment that exists at the natural level of employment.

and the government's responses to them, will occupy center stage in much of the remainder of this book.

FIGURE 20.6 Unemployment Rate, 1960–2016

The chart shows the unemployment rate for each year from 1960 to 2016. Recessions are shown as shaded areas.

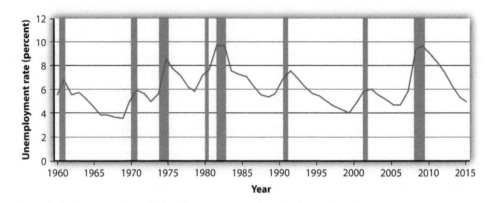

Source: Based on data from Table B-12 through 2015; Bureau of Labor Statistics, Unemployment rate, average through October 2016.

Key Takeaways

- People who are not working but are looking and available for work at any one time are considered unemployed. The unemployment rate is the percentage of the labor force that is unemployed.
- When the labor market is in equilibrium, employment is at the natural level and the unemployment rate equals the natural rate of unemployment.
- Even if employment is at the natural level, the economy will experience frictional and structural unemployment. Cyclical unemployment is unemployment in excess of that associated with the natural level of employment.

Try It!

Given the data in the table, compute the unemployment rate in Year 1 and in Year 2. Explain why, in this example, both the number of people employed and the unemployment rate increased.

Year	Number employed (in millions)	Number unemployed (in millions)
1	20	2
2	21	2.4

Case in Point: Might Increased Structural Unemployment Explain the "Jobless Recovery" Following the 2001 Recession?

Source: © Shutterstock, Inc.

The U.S. 2001 recession was mild by historical standards, but recovery in terms of increased employment seemed painfully slow in coming. Economists Erica Goshen and Simon Potter at the Federal Reserve Bank of New York think the reason for the slow recovery in jobs may have actually reflected structural changes in the U.S. economy. They argue that during the recession permanent rather than temporary layoffs predominated and that it takes longer for firms to hire workers into new positions than to hire them back into former jobs.

What is their evidence? When the layoff is temporary, the employer "suspends" the job, due to slack demand, and the employee expects to be recalled once demand picks up. With a permanent layoff, the employer eliminates the job. So, they looked at the contribution of temporary layoffs to the unemployment rate during the recent recession compared to the situation in the four recessions before 1990. In the earlier recessions, unemployment from temporary layoffs rose when the economy was shrinking and fell after the economy began to recover. In both the 1991 and 2001 recessions, temporary layoffs were minor. Then, the authors examined job flows in 70 industries. They classified layoffs in an industry as being cyclical in nature if the job losses during the recession were reversed during the recovery but structural if job losses for the industry continued during the recovery. Their analysis revealed that during the recession of the early 1980s, job losses were about evenly split between cyclical and structural changes. In the 1991 recession and then more strongly in the 2001 recession, structural changes dominated. "Most of the industries that lost jobs during the [2001] recession—for example, communications, electronic equipment, and securities and commodities brokers—[were] still losing jobs" in 2003. "The trend revealed . . . is one in which jobs are relocated from some industries to others, not reclaimed by the same industries that lost them earlier."

The authors suggest three possible reasons for the recent increased role of structural change: (1) The structural decline in some industries could be the result of overexpansion in those industries during the 1990s. The high tech and telecommunications industries in particular could be examples of industries that were overbuilt before the 2001 recession. (2) Improved government policies may have reduced cyclical unemployment. Examination of macroeconomic policy in future chapters will return to this issue. (3) New management strategies to reduce costs may be promoting leaner staffing. For firms adopting such strategies, a recession may provide an opportunity to reorganize the production process permanently and reduce payrolls in the process.

Goshen and Potter point out that, for workers, finding new jobs is harder than simply returning to old ones. For firms, making decisions about the nature of new jobs is time consuming at best. The uncertainty created by the war in Iraq and the imposition of new accounting standards following the "Enron"-like scandals may have further prolonged the creation of new jobs.

Source: *Based on Erica L. Goshen and Simon Potter, "Has Structural Change Contributed to a Jobless Recovery?" Federal Reserve Bank of New York Current Issues in Economics and Finance 9, no. 8 (August 2003): 1–7.*

Answer to Try It! Problem

In Year 1 the total labor force includes 22 million workers, and so the unemployment rate is 2/22 × 100 = 9.1%. In Year 2 the total labor force numbers 23.4 million workers; therefore the unemployment rate is 2.4/23.4 × 100 = 10.3%. In this example, both the number of people employed and the unemployment rate rose, because more people (23.4 − 22 = 1.4 million) entered the labor force, of whom 1 million found jobs and 0.4 million were still looking for jobs.

20.5 Review and Practice

Summary

In this chapter we examined growth in real GDP and business cycles, price-level changes, and unemployment. We saw how these phenomena are defined and looked at their consequences.

Examining real GDP, rather than nominal GDP, over time tells us whether the economy is expanding or contracting. Real GDP in the United States shows a long upward trend, but with the economy going through phases of expansion and recession around that trend. These phases make up the business cycle. An expansion reaches a peak, and the economy falls into a recession. The recession reaches a trough and begins an expansion again.

Inflation is an increase in the price level and deflation is a decrease in the price level. The rate of inflation or deflation is the percentage rate of change in a price index. We looked at the calculation of the consumer price index (CPI) and the implicit price deflator. The CPI is widely used in the calculation of price-level changes. There are, however, biases in its calculation: the substitution bias, the new-product bias, the quality-change bias, and the outlet bias.

Inflation and deflation affect economic activity in several ways. They change the value of money and of claims on money. Unexpected inflation benefits borrowers and hurts lenders. Unexpected deflation benefits lenders and hurts borrowers. Both inflation and deflation create uncertainty and make it difficult for individuals and firms to enter into long-term financial commitments.

The unemployment rate is measured as the percentage of the labor force not working but seeking work. Frictional unemployment occurs because information about the labor market is costly; it takes time for firms seeking workers and workers seeking firms to find each other. Structural unemployment occurs when there is a mismatch between the skills offered by potential workers and the skills sought by firms. Both frictional and structural unemployment occur even if employment and the unemployment rate are at their natural levels. Cyclical unemployment is unemployment that is in excess of that associated with the natural level of employment.

Concept Problems

1. Describe the phases of a business cycle.

2. On the basis of recent news reports, what phase of the business cycle do you think the economy is in now? What is the inflation or deflation rate? The unemployment rate?

3. Suppose you compare your income this year and last year and find that your nominal income fell but your real income rose. How could this have happened?

4. Suppose you calculate a grocery price inflation rate. Using the arguments presented in the chapter, explain possible sources of upward bias in the rate you calculate, relative to the actual trend of food prices.

5. Name three items you have purchased during the past year that have increased in quality during the year. What kind of adjustment would you make in assessing their prices for the CPI?

6. Why do some people gain and other people lose from inflation and deflation?

7. Suppose unemployed people leave a state to obtain jobs in other states. What do you predict will happen to the unemployment rate in the state experiencing the out-migration? What might happen to the unemployment rates in the states experiencing in-migration?

8. Minority teenagers have the highest unemployment rates of any group. One reason for this phenomenon is high transportation costs for many minority teens. What form of unemployment (cyclical, frictional, or structural) do high transportation costs suggest?

9. Welfare reforms enacted in 1996 put more pressure on welfare recipients to look for work. The new law mandated cutting off benefits after a certain length of time. How do you think this provision might affect the unemployment rate?

10. American workers work more hours than their European counterparts. Should Congress legislate a shorter workweek?

Numerical Problems

1. Plot the quarterly data for real GDP for the last two years. (You can find the data online at http://bit.ly/2pnLBBD. Relate recent changes in real GDP to the concept of the phases of the business cycle.)

2. Suppose that in 2013, the items in the market basket for our movie price index cost $53.40. Use the information in the chapter to compute the price index for that year. How does the rate of movie price inflation from 2012 to 2013 compare with the rate from 2011 to 2012?

3. Recompute the movie price indexes for 2011 and 2012 using 2012 as the base year. Now compute the rate of inflation for the 2011–2012 period. Compare your result to the inflation rate calculated for that same period using 2011 as the base year.

4. Here are some statistics for August 2006. Compute the unemployment rate for that month (all figures are in thousands).

Population (Civilian, noninstitutional)	229,167
Civilian Labor Force	151,698
Participation Rate	66.2%
Not in Labor Force	77,469
Employed	144,579
Unemployed	7,119

5. Suppose an economy has 10,000 people who are not working but looking and available for work and 90,000 people who are working. What is its unemployment rate? Now suppose 4,000 of the people looking for work get discouraged and give up their searches. What hap-

pens to the unemployment rate? Would you interpret this as good news for the economy or bad news? Explain.

6. The average price of going to a baseball game in 2016, based on the observations in the Case in Point, was $219.53. Using this average as the equivalent of a base year, compute fan price indexes for:

   a. The New York Yankees.
   b. The Chicago Cubs.
   c. The Boston Red Sox.
   d. The Tampa Bay Rays.
   e. The team of your choice.

7. Suppose you are given the following data for a small economy:

   Number of unemployed workers: 1,000,000.

   Labor force: 10,000,000.

   Based on this data, answer the following:

   a. What is the unemployment rate?
   b. Can you determine whether the economy is operating at its full employment level?
   c. Now suppose people who had been seeking jobs become discouraged, and give up their job searches. The labor force shrinks to 900,500 workers, and unemployment falls to 500,000 workers. What is the unemployment rate now? Has the economy improved?

8. Nominal GDP for an economy is $10 trillion. Real GDP is $9 trillion. What is the value of the implicit price deflator?

9. Suppose you are given the following data for an economy:

Month	Real GDP	Employment
1	$10.0 trillion	100 million
2	$10.4 trillion	104 million
3	$10.5 trillion	105 million
4	$10.3 trillion	103 million
5	$10.2 trillion	102 million
6	$10.3 trillion	103 million
7	$10.6 trillion	106 million
8	$10.7 trillion	107 million
9	$10.6 trillion	106 million

   a. Plot the data for real GDP, with the time period on the horizontal axis and real GDP on the vertical axis.
   b. There are two peaks. When do they occur?
   c. When does the trough occur?

10. The Consumer Price Index in Period 1 is 107.5. It is 103.8 in Period 2. Is this a situation of inflation or deflation? What is the rate?

Endnotes

1. Russell Roberts, "How Government Stoked the Mania," *Wall Street Journal*, October 3, 2008, p. A21.
2. Anthony P. Carnevele, Tamara Jayasundera, and Artem Gulish, "Divided Recovery: College Haves and Have-Nots," Georgetown University Center on Education and Workforce, 2016, available at https://cew.georgetown.edu/cew-reports/americas-divided-recovery/
3. "The NBER's Recession Dating Procedure," National Bureau of Economic Research, January 7, 2008.

4. Some economists prefer to break the expansion phase into two parts. The recovery phase is said to be the period between the previous trough and the time when the economy achieves its previous peak level of real GDP. The "expansion" phase is from that point until the following peak.

5. Steven Greenhouse, "Job Market Gets Better for U.S. Graduates, but Only Slightly: Offers Will Increase 5% Over Last Year; Average Starting Salaries Are Down," *The International Herald Tribune*, May 26, 2010, Finance 16.

6. Tamar Lewin, "A Hemline Index, Updated," *New York Times*, October 19, 2008, Section WK, 1.

7. "Zimbabwe Inflation Hits 11,200,000%," CNN.com, August 19, 2008, available at http://edition.cnn.com/2008/BUSINESS/08/19/zimbabwe.inflation/index.html.

8. Steve H. Hanke, "R.I.P. Zimbabwe Dollar," Cato Institute, May 3, 2010, available at http://www.cato.org/zimbabwe.

9. For a comparison of price measures, including a comparison of the PCE price index and the Consumer Price Index, see Brian C. Moyer, "Comparing Price Measures—The CPI and PCE Price Index" (lecture, National Association for Business Economics, 2006 Washington Economic Policy Conference, March 13–14, 2006), available at http://www.bea.gov/papers/pdf/Moyer_NABE.pdf.

10. Robert Cage, John Greenlees, and Patrick Jackman, "Introducing the Chained Consumer Price Index" (paper, Seventh Meeting of the International Working Group on Price Indices, Paris, France, May 2003), available at http://stats.bls.gov/cpi/superlink.htm.

11. For a description of the new survey and other changes introduced in the method of counting unemployment, see Janet L. Norwood and Judith M. Tanur, "Unemployment Measures for the Nineties," *Public Opinion Quarterly* 58, no. 2 (Summer 1994): 277–94.

CHAPTER 21
Measuring Total Output and Income

21.1 Start Up: The Lockup

It is early morning when a half-dozen senior officials enter the room at the Commerce Department in Washington. Once inside, they will have no communication with the outside world until they have completed their work later that day. They will have no telephone, no computer links. They will be able to slip out to an adjoining restroom, but only in pairs. It is no wonder the room is called "the Lockup." The Lockup produces one of the most important indicators of economic activity we have: the official estimate of the value of the economy's total output, known as its gross domestic product (GDP).

When the team has finished its computations, the results will be placed in a sealed envelope. A government messenger will hand carry the envelope to the Executive Office Building and deliver it to a senior adviser to the president of the United States. The adviser will examine its contents, then carry it across the street to the White House and give it to the president.

The senior officials who meet in secret to compute GDP are not spies; they are economists. The adviser who delivers the estimate to the president is the chairman of the Council of Economic Advisers.

The elaborate precautions for secrecy do not end there. At 7:30 the next morning, journalists from all over the world will gather in an electronically sealed auditorium at the Commerce Department. There they will be given the GDP figure and related economic indicators, along with an explanation. The reporters will have an hour to prepare their reports, but they will not be able to communicate with anyone else until an official throws the switch at 8:30. At that instant their computers will connect to their news services, and they will be able to file their reports. These will be major stories on the Internet and in the next editions of the nation's newspapers; the estimate of the previous quarter's GDP will be one of the lead items on television and radio news broadcasts that day.

The clandestine preparations for the release of quarterly GDP figures reflect the importance of this indicator. The estimate of GDP provides the best available reading of macroeconomic performance. It will affect government policy, and it will influence millions of decisions in the private sector. Prior knowledge of the GDP estimate could be used to anticipate the response in the stock and bond markets, so great care is taken that only a handful of trusted officials have access to the information until it is officially released.

The GDP estimate took on huge significance in the fall of 2008 as the United States and much of the rest of the world went through the wrenching experience of the worst financial crisis since the Great Depression of the 1930s. The expectation that the financial crisis would lead to an economic collapse was widespread, and the quarterly announcements of GDP figures were more anxiously awaited than ever.

The primary measure of the ups and downs of economic activity—the business cycle—is real GDP. When an economy's output is rising, the economy creates more jobs, more income, and more opportunities for people. In the long run, an economy's output and income, relative to its population, determine the material standard of living of its people.

Clearly GDP is an important indicator of macroeconomic performance. It is the topic we will consider in this chapter. We will learn that GDP can be measured either in terms of the total value of output produced or as the total value of income generated in producing that output. We will begin with an examination of measures of GDP in terms of output. Our initial focus will be on nominal GDP: the value of total output measured in current prices. We will turn to real GDP—a measure of output that has been adjusted for price level changes—later in the chapter. We will refer to nominal GDP simply as GDP. When we discuss the real value of the measure, we will call it real GDP.

21.2 Measuring Total Output

Learning Objectives

1. Define gross domestic product and its four major spending components and illustrate the various flows using the circular flow model.
2. Distinguish between measuring GDP as the sum of the values of final goods and services and as the sum of values added at each stage of production.
3. Distinguish between gross domestic product and gross national product.

An economy produces a mind-boggling array of goods and services every year. For example, Domino's Pizza produces hundreds of millions of pizzas. The United States Steel Corporation, the nation's largest steel company, produces tens of millions of tons of steel. A small logging company in Colorado produces a couple million board feet of lumber. A university football team draws more than half a million fans to its home games. A pediatric nurse in Los Angeles delivers hundreds of babies and takes care of several hundred additional patients. A list of all the goods and services an economy produces in any year would be virtually endless.

So—what kind of year is the year we are looking at? We would not get very far trying to wade through a list of all the goods and services produced that year. It is helpful to have instead a single number that measures total output in the economy; that number is GDP.

The Components of GDP

We can divide the goods and services produced during any period into four broad components, based on who buys them. These components of GDP are personal consumption (C), gross private domestic investment (I), government purchases (G), and net exports (X_n). Thus

EQUATION 21.1

$$\text{GDP} = \text{consumption (C)} + \text{private investment (I)} + \text{government purchases (G)} + \text{net exports (X}_n\text{)}$$

or

$$\text{GDP} = C + I + G + X_n$$

flow variable

A variable that is measured over a specific period of time.

stock variable

A variable that is independent of time.

We will examine each of these components, and we will see how each fits into the pattern of macroeconomic activity. Before we begin, it will be helpful to distinguish between two types of variables: stocks and flows. A **flow variable** is a variable that is measured over a specific period of time. A **stock variable** is a variable that is independent of time. Income is an example of a flow variable. To say one's income is, for example, $1,000 is meaningless without a time dimension. Is it $1,000 per hour? Per day? Per week? Per month? Until we know the time period, we have no idea what the income figure means. The balance in a checking account is an example of a stock variable. When we learn that the balance in a checking account is $1,000, we know precisely what that means; we do not need a time dimension. We will see that stock and flow variables play very different roles in macroeconomic analysis.

Personal Consumption

Personal consumption is a flow variable that measures the value of goods and services purchased by households during a time period. Purchases by households of groceries, health-care services, clothing, and automobiles—all are counted as consumption.

The production of consumer goods and services accounts for about 70% of total output. Because consumption is such a large part of GDP, economists seeking to understand the determinants of GDP must pay special attention to the determinants of consumption. In a later chapter we will explore these determinants and the impact of consumption on economic activity.

Personal consumption represents a demand for goods and services placed on firms by households. In the chapter on demand and supply, we saw how this demand could be presented in a circular flow model of the economy. Figure 21.1 presents a circular flow model for an economy that produces only personal consumption goods and services. (We will add the other components of GDP to the circular flow as we discuss them.) Spending for these goods flows from households to firms; it is the arrow labeled "Personal consumption." Firms produce these goods and services using factors of production: labor, capital, and natural resources. These factors are ultimately owned by households. The production of goods and services thus generates income to households; we see this income as the flow from firms to households labeled "Factor incomes" in the exhibit.

In exchange for payments that flow from households to firms, there is a flow of consumer goods and services from firms to households. This flow is shown in Figure 21.1 as an arrow going from firms to households. When you buy a soda, for example, your payment to the store is part of the flow of personal consumption; the soda is part of the flow of consumer goods and services that goes from the store to a household—yours.

Similarly, the lower arrow in Figure 21.1 shows the flow of factors of production—labor, capital, and natural resources—from households to firms. If you work for a firm, your labor is part of this flow. The wages you receive are part of the factor incomes that flow from firms to households.

There is a key difference in our interpretation of the circular flow picture in Figure 21.1 from our analysis of the same model in the demand and supply chapter. There, our focus was microeconomics, which examines individual units of the economy. In thinking about the flow of consumption spending from households to firms, we emphasized demand and supply in particular markets—markets for such things as blue jeans, haircuts, and apartments. In thinking about the flow of income payments from firms to households, we focused on the demand and supply for particular factors of production, such as textile workers, barbers, and apartment buildings. Because our focus now is macroeconomics, the study of aggregates of economic activity, we will think in terms of the *total* of personal consumption and the *total* of payments to households.

Private Investment

Gross private domestic investment is the value of all goods produced during a period for use in the production of other goods and services. Like personal consumption, gross private domestic investment is a flow variable. It is often simply referred to as "private investment." A hammer produced for a carpenter is private investment. A printing press produced for a magazine publisher is private investment, as is a conveyor-belt system produced for a manufacturing firm. Capital

personal consumption

A flow variable that measures the value of goods and services purchased by households during a time period.

FIGURE 21.1 Personal Consumption in the Circular Flow
Personal consumption spending flows from households to firms. In return, consumer goods and services flow from firms to households. To produce the goods and services households demand, firms employ factors of production owned by households. There is thus a flow of factor services from households to firms, and a flow of payments of factor incomes from firms to households.

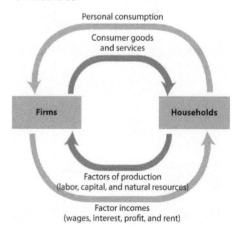

gross private domestic investment

The value of all goods produced during a period for use in the production of other goods and services.

includes all the goods that have been produced for use in producing other goods; it is a stock variable. Private investment is a flow variable that adds to the stock of capital during a period.

Heads Up!

The term "*investment*" can generate confusion. In everyday conversation, we use the term "*investment*" to refer to uses of money to earn income. We say we have invested in a stock or invested in a bond. Economists, however, restrict "*investment*" to activities that increase the economy's stock of capital. The purchase of a share of stock does not add to the capital stock; it is not investment in the economic meaning of the word. We refer to the exchange of financial assets, such as stocks or bonds, as financial investment to distinguish it from the creation of capital that occurs as the result of investment. Only when new capital is produced does investment occur. Confusing the economic concept of private investment with the concept of financial investment can cause misunderstanding of the way in which key components of the economy relate to one another.

Gross private domestic investment includes three flows that add to or maintain the nation's capital stock: expenditures by business firms on new buildings, plants, tools, equipment, and software that will be used in the production of goods and services; expenditures on new residential housing; and changes in business inventories. Any addition to a firm's inventories represents an addition to investment; a reduction subtracts from investment. For example, if a clothing store stocks 1,000 pairs of jeans, the jeans represent an addition to inventory and are part of gross private domestic investment. As the jeans are sold, they are subtracted from inventory and thus subtracted from investment.

By recording additions to inventories as investment and reductions from inventories as subtractions from investment, the accounting for GDP records production in the period in which it occurs. Suppose, for example, that Levi Strauss manufactures 1 million pairs of jeans late in 2015 and distributes them to stores at the end of December. The jeans will be added to inventory; they thus count as investment in 2015 and enter GDP for that year. Suppose they are sold in January 2016. They will be counted as consumption in GDP for 2016 but subtracted from inventory, and from investment. Thus, the production of the jeans will add to GDP in 2015, when they were produced. They will not count in 2016, save for any increase in the value of the jeans resulting from the services provided by the retail stores that sold them.

FIGURE 21.2 Private Investment in the Circular Flow

Private investment constitutes a demand placed on firms by other firms. It also generates factor incomes for households. To simplify the diagram, only the spending flows are shown—the corresponding flows of goods and services have been omitted.

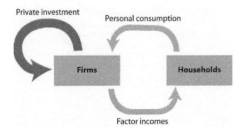

Private investment accounts for about 15% of GDP—but, at times, even less. Despite its relatively small share of total economic activity, private investment plays a crucial role in the macroeconomy for two reasons:

1. Private investment represents a choice to forgo current consumption in order to add to the capital stock of the economy. Private investment therefore adds to the economy's capacity to produce and shifts its production possibilities curve outward. Investment is thus one determinant of economic growth, which is explored in another chapter.

2. Private investment is a relatively volatile component of GDP; it can change dramatically from one year to the next. Fluctuations in GDP are often driven by fluctuations in private investment. We will examine the determinants of private investment in a chapter devoted to the study of investment.

Private investment represents a demand placed on firms for the production of capital goods. While it is a demand placed on firms, it flows from firms. In the circular flow model in Figure 21.2, we see a flow of investment going from firms to firms. The production of goods and services for consumption generates factor incomes to households; the production of capital goods for investment generates income to households as well.

Figure 21.2 shows only spending flows and omits the physical flows represented by the arrows in Figure 21.1. This simplification will make our analysis of the circular flow model easier. It will also focus our attention on spending flows, which are the flows we will be studying.

Government Purchases

Government agencies at all levels purchase goods and services from firms. They purchase office equipment, vehicles, buildings, janitorial services, and so on. Many government agencies also produce goods and services. Police departments produce police protection. Public schools produce education. The National Aeronautics and Space Administration (NASA) produces space exploration.

Government purchases are the sum of purchases of goods and services from firms by government agencies plus the total value of output produced by government agencies themselves during a time period. Government purchases make up about 20% of GDP.

Government purchases are not the same thing as government spending. Much government spending takes the form of **transfer payments**, which are payments that do not require the recipient to produce a good or service in order to receive them. Transfer payments include Social Security and other types of assistance to retired people, welfare payments to poor people, and unemployment compensation to people who have lost their jobs. Transfer payments are certainly significant—they account for roughly half of all federal government spending in the United States. They do not count in a nation's GDP, because they do not reflect the production of a good or service.

Government purchases represent a demand placed on firms, represented by the flow shown in Figure 21.3. Like all the components of GDP, the production of goods and services for government agencies creates factor incomes for households.

government purchases

The sum of purchases of goods and services from firms by government agencies plus the total value of output produced by government agencies themselves during a time period.

transfer payments

Payments that do not require the recipient to produce a good or service in order to receive them.

FIGURE 21.3 Government Purchases in the Circular Flow

Purchases of goods and services by government agencies create demands on firms. As firms produce these goods and services, they create factor incomes for households.

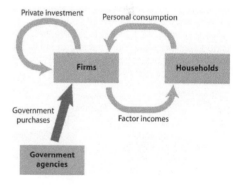

Net Exports

Sales of a country's goods and services to buyers in the rest of the world during a particular time period represent its **exports**. A purchase by a Japanese buyer of a Ford Taurus produced in the United States is a U.S. export. Exports also include such transactions as the purchase of accounting services from a New York accounting firm by a shipping line based in Hong Kong or the purchase of a ticket to Disney World by a tourist from Argentina. **Imports** are purchases of foreign-produced goods and services by a country's residents during a period. United States imports include such transactions as the purchase by Americans of cars produced in Japan or tomatoes grown in Mexico or a stay in a French hotel by a tourist from the United States. Subtracting imports from exports yields **net exports**.

EQUATION 21.2

$$\text{Exports } (X) - \text{imports } (M) = \text{net exports } (X_n)$$

In 2015, foreign buyers purchased $2,264.3 billion worth of goods and services from the United States. In the same year, U.S. residents, firms, and government agencies purchased $ 2,786.3 billion worth of goods and services from foreign countries. The difference between these two figures, −$522.0 billion, represented the net exports of the U.S. economy in 2015. Net exports were negative because imports exceeded exports. Negative net exports constitute a **trade deficit**. The amount of the deficit is the amount by which imports exceed exports. When exports exceed imports there is a **trade surplus**. The magnitude of the surplus is the amount by which exports exceed imports.

The United States has recorded more deficits than surpluses since World War II, but the amounts have typically been relatively small, only a few billion dollars. The trade deficit began to soar, however, in the 1980s and again in the 2000s. We will examine the reasons for persistent trade deficits in another chapter. The rest of the world plays a key role in the domestic economy and, as we will see later in the book, there is nothing particularly good or bad about trade surpluses or deficits. Goods and services produced for export represent roughly 13% of GDP, and the goods and services the United States imports add significantly to our standard of living.

In the circular flow diagram in Figure 21.4, net exports are shown with an arrow connecting firms to the rest of the world. The balance between the flows of exports and imports is net exports. When there is a trade surplus, net exports are positive and add spending to the circular flow. A trade deficit implies negative net exports; spending flows from firms to the rest of the world.

FIGURE 21.4 Net Exports in the Circular Flow

Net exports represent the balance between exports and imports. Net exports can be positive or negative. If they are positive, net export spending flows from the rest of the world to firms. If they are negative, spending flows from firms to the rest of the world.

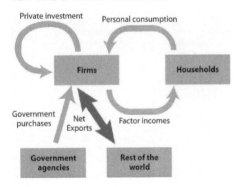

The production of goods and services for personal consumption, private investment, government purchases, and net exports makes up a nation's GDP. Firms produce these goods and services in response to demands from households (personal consumption), from other firms (private investment), from government agencies (government purchases), and from the rest of the world (net exports). All of this production creates factor income for households. Figure 21.5 shows the circular flow model for all the spending flows we have discussed. Each flow is numbered for use in the exercise at the end of this section.

The circular flow model identifies some of the forces at work in the economy, forces that we will be studying in later chapters. For example, an increase in any of the flows that place demands on firms (personal consumption, private investment, government purchases, and exports) will induce firms to expand their production. This effect is characteristic of the expansion phase of the business cycle. An increase in production will require firms to employ more factors of production, which will create more income for households. Households are likely to respond with more consumption, which will induce still more production, more income, and still more consumption. Similarly, a reduction in any of the demands placed on firms will lead to a reduction in output, a reduction in firms' use of factors of production, a reduction in household incomes, a reduction in income, and so on. This sequence of events is characteristic of the contraction phase of the business cycle. Much of our work in macroeconomics will involve an analysis of the forces that prompt such changes in demand and an examination of the economy's response to them.

Figure 21.6 shows the size of the components of GDP in 2015. We see that the production of goods and services for personal consumption accounted for nearly 70% of GDP. Imports exceeded exports, so net exports were negative.

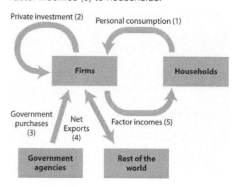

FIGURE 21.5 Spending in the Circular Flow Model

GDP equals the sum of production by firms of goods and services for personal consumption (1), private investment (2), government purchases (3), and net exports (4). The circular flow model shows these flows and shows that the production of goods and services generates factor incomes (5) to households.

FIGURE 21.6 Components of GDP, 2015 in Billions of Dollars

Consumption makes up the largest share of GDP. Net exports were negative in 2015. Total GDP—the sum of personal consumption, private investment, government purchases, and net exports—equaled $18,036.6 billion in 2015.

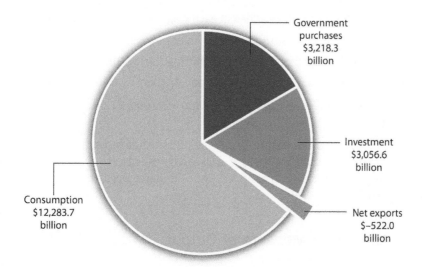

Source: Based on data from Bureau of Economic Analysis, National Income and Product Accounts, Table 1.1.5 (revised January 27, 2017).

Final Goods and Value Added

GDP is the total value of all *final* goods and services produced during a particular period valued at prices in that period. That is not the same as the total value of all goods and services produced during a period. This distinction gives us another method of estimating GDP in terms of output.

Suppose, for example, that a logger cuts some trees and sells the logs to a sawmill. The mill makes lumber and sells it to a construction firm, which builds a house. The market price for the lumber includes the value of the logs; the price of the house includes the value of the lumber. If we try to estimate GDP by adding the value of the logs, the lumber, and the house, we would be counting the lumber twice and the logs three times. This problem is called "double counting," and the economists who compute GDP seek to avoid it.

In the case of logs used for lumber and lumber produced for a house, GDP would include the value of the house. The lumber and the logs would not be counted as additional production because they are intermediate goods that were produced for use in building the house.

value added

The amount by which the value of a firm's output exceeds the value of the goods and services the firm purchases from other firms.

Another approach to estimating the value of final production is to estimate for each stage of production the **value added**, the amount by which the value of a firm's output exceeds the value of the goods and services the firm purchases from other firms. Table 21.1 illustrates the use of value added in the production of a house.

TABLE 21.1 Final Value and Value Added
If we sum the value added at each stage of the production of a good or service, we get the final value of the item. The example shown here involves the construction of a house, which is produced from lumber that is, in turn, produced from logs.

Good	Produced by	Purchased by	Price	Value Added
Logs	Logger	Sawmill	$12,000	$12,000
Lumber	Sawmill	Construction firm	$25,000	$13,000
House	Construction firm	Household	$125,000	$100,000
		Final Value	**$125,000**	
		Sum of Values Added		**$125,000**

Suppose the logs produced by the logger are sold for $12,000 to a mill, and that the mill sells the lumber it produces from these logs for $25,000 to a construction firm. The construction firm uses the lumber to build a house, which it sells to a household for $125,000. (To simplify the example, we will ignore inputs other than lumber that are used to build the house.) The value of the final product, the house, is $125,000. The value added at each stage of production is estimated as follows:

a. The logger adds $12,000 by cutting the logs.
b. The mill adds $13,000 ($25,000 − $12,000) by cutting the logs into lumber.
c. The construction firm adds $100,000 ($125,000 − $25,000) by using the lumber to build a house.

The sum of values added at each stage ($12,000 + $13,000 + $100,000) equals the final value of the house, $125,000.

The value of an economy's output in any period can thus be estimated in either of two ways. The values of final goods and services produced can be added directly, or the values added at each stage in the production process can be added. The Commerce Department uses both approaches in its estimate of the nation's GDP.

GNP: An Alternative Measure of Output

gross national product (GNP)

The total value of final goods and services produced during a particular period with factors of production owned by the residents of a particular country.

While GDP represents the most commonly used measure of an economy's output, economists sometimes use an alternative measure. **Gross national product (GNP)** is the total value of final goods and services produced during a particular period with factors of production owned by the residents of a particular country.

The difference between GDP and GNP is a subtle one. The GDP of a country equals the value of final output produced within the borders of that country; the GNP of a country equals the value of final output produced using factors owned by residents of the country. Most production in a country employs factors of production owned by residents of that country, so the two measures overlap. Differences between the two measures emerge when production in one country employs factors of production *owned* by residents of other countries.

Suppose, for example, that a resident of Bellingham, Washington, owns and operates a watch repair shop across the Canadian–U.S. border in Victoria, British Columbia. The value of watch repair services produced at the shop would be counted as part of Canada's GDP because they are produced in Canada. That value would not, however, be part of U.S. GDP. But, because the watch repair services were produced using capital and labor provided by a resident of the United States, they would be counted as part of GNP in the United States and not as part of GNP in Canada.

Because most production fits in both a country's GDP as well as its GNP, there is seldom much difference between the two measures. The relationship between GDP and GNP is given by

EQUATION 21.3

GDP+net income received from abroad by residents of a nation = GNP

In the third quarter of 2016, for example, GDP equaled $18,675.3 billion. We add income receipts of $848.9 billion earned by residents of the United States from the rest of the world and then subtract income payments of $644.9 billion that went from the United States to the rest of the world to get GNP of $18,879.3 billion for the third quarter of 2016. GNP is often used in international comparisons of income; we shall examine those later in this chapter.

Key Takeaways

- GDP is the sum of final goods and services produced for consumption (*C*), private investment (*I*), government purchases (*G*), and net exports (*X*$_n$). Thus GDP = *C* + *I* + *G* + *X*$_n$.
- GDP can be viewed in the context of the circular flow model. Consumption goods and services are produced in response to demands from households; investment goods are produced in response to demands for new capital by firms; government purchases include goods and services purchased by government agencies; and net exports equal exports less imports.
- Total output can be measured two ways: as the sum of the values of final goods and services produced and as the sum of values added at each stage of production.
- GDP plus net income received from other countries equals GNP. GNP is the measure of output typically used to compare incomes generated by different economies.

Try It!

Here is a two-part exercise.

1. Suppose you are given the following data for an economy:

Personal consumption	$1,000
Home construction	100
Increase in inventories	40
Equipment purchases by firms	60
Government purchases	100
Social Security payments to households	40
Government welfare payments	100
Exports	50
Imports	150

Identify the number of the flow in Figure 21.5 to which each of these items corresponds. What is the economy's GDP?

2. Suppose a dairy farm produces raw milk, which it sells for $1,000 to a dairy. The dairy produces cream, which it sells for $3,000 to an ice cream manufacturer. The ice cream manufacturer uses the cream to make ice cream, which it sells for $7,000 to a grocery store. The grocery store sells the ice cream to consumers for $10,000. Compute the value added at each stage of production, and compare this figure to the final value of the product produced. Report your results in a table similar to that given in Table 21.1.

Case in Point: The Spread of the Value Added Tax

Source: © Shutterstock, Inc.

Outside the United States, the value added tax (VAT) has become commonplace. Governments of more than 120 countries use it as their primary means of raising revenue. While the concept of the VAT originated in France in the 1920s, no country adopted it until after World War II. In 1948, France became the first country in the world to use the VAT. In 1967, Brazil became the first country in the Western Hemisphere to do so. The VAT spread to other western European and Latin American countries in the 1970s and 1980s and then to countries in the Asia/Pacific region, central European and former Soviet Union area, and Africa in the 1990s and early 2000s.

What is the VAT? It is equivalent to a sales tax on final goods and services but is collected at each stage of production.

Take the example given in Table 21.1, which is a simplified illustration of a house built in three stages. If there were a sales tax of 10% on the house, the household buying it would pay $137,500, of which the construction firm would keep $125,000 of the total and turn $12,500 over to the government.

With a 10% VAT, the sawmill would pay the logger $13,200, of which the logger would keep $12,000 and turn $1,200 over to the government. The sawmill would sell the lumber to the construction firm for $27,500—keeping $26,200, which is the $25,000 for the lumber itself and $1,200 it already paid in tax. The government at this stage would get $1,300, the difference between the $2,500 the construction firm collected as tax and the $1,200 the sawmill already paid in tax to the logger at the previous stage. The household would pay the construction firm $137,500. Of that total, the construction firm would turn over to the government $10,000, which is the difference between the $12,500 it collected for the government in tax from the household and the $2,500 in tax that it already paid when it bought the lumber from the sawmill. The table below shows that in the end, the tax revenue generated by a 10% VAT is the same as that generated by a 10% tax on final sales.

Why bother to tax in stages instead of just on final sales? One reason is simply record keeping, since it may be difficult to determine in practice if any particular sale is the final one. In the example, the construction firm does not need to know if it is selling the house to a household or to some intermediary business.

Also, the VAT may lead to higher revenue collected. For example, even if somehow the household buying the house avoided paying the tax, the government would still have collected some tax revenue at earlier stages of production. With a tax on retail sales, it would have collected nothing. The VAT has another advantage from the point of view of government agencies. It has the appearance at each stage of taking a smaller share. The individual amounts collected are not as obvious to taxpayers as a sales tax might be.

Good	Price	Value Added	Tax Collected	– Tax Already Paid	= Value Added Tax
Logs	$12,000	$12,000	$1,200	– $0	= $1,200
Lumber	$25,000	$13,000	$2,500	– $1,200	= $1,300
House	$125,000	$100,000	$12,500	– $2,500	= $10,000
Total			$16,200	–$3,700	= $12,500

Answer to Try It! Problems

1. GDP equals $1,200 and is computed as follows (the numbers in parentheses correspond to the flows in Figure 21.5):

Personal consumption (1)	$1,000
Private investment (2)	200
Housing	100
Equipment and software	60
Inventory change	40
Government purchases (3)	100
Net exports (4)	–100
GDP	$1,200

Notice that neither welfare payments nor Social Security payments to households are included. These are transfer payments, which are not part of the government purchases component of GDP.

2. Here is the table of value added.

Good	Produced by	Purchased by	Price	Value Added
Raw milk	Dairy farm	Dairy	$1,000	$1,000
Cream	Dairy	Ice cream maker	3,000	2,000
Ice cream	Ice cream manufacturer	Grocery store	7,000	4,000
Retail ice cream	Grocery store	Consumer	10,000	3,000
		Final Value	$10,000	
		Sum of Values Added		$10,000

21.3 Measuring Total Income

Learning Objectives

1. Define gross domestic income and explain its relationship to gross domestic product.
2. Discuss the components of gross domestic income.
3. Define disposable personal income and explain how to calculate it from GDP.

gross domestic income (GDI)

The total income generated in an economy by the production of final goods and services during a particular period.

We saw in the last section that the production of goods and services generates factor incomes to households. The production of a given value of goods and services generates an equal value of total income. **Gross domestic income (GDI)** equals the total income generated in an economy by the production of final goods and services during a particular period. It is a flow variable. Because an economy's total output equals the total income generated in producing that output, GDP = GDI. We can estimate GDP either by measuring total output or by measuring total income.

Consider a $4 box of Cheerios. It is part of total output and thus is part of GDP. Who gets the $4? Part of the answer to that question can be found by looking at the cereal box. Cheerios are made from oat flour, wheat starch, sugar, salt, and a variety of vitamins and minerals. Therefore, part of the $4 goes to the farmers who grew the oats, the wheat, and the beets or cane from which the sugar was extracted. Workers and machines at General Mills combined the ingredients, crafted all those little O's, toasted them, and put them in a box. The workers were paid part of the $4 as wages. The owners of General Mills and the capital it used received part of the $4 as profit. The box containing the Cheerios was made from a tree, so a lumber company somewhere received part of the $4. The truck driver who brought the box of cereal to the grocery store got part of the $4, as did the owner of the truck itself and the owner of the oil that fueled the truck. The clerk who rang up the sale at the grocery store was paid part of the $4. And so on.

How much of the $4 was income generated in the production of the Cheerios? The answer is simple: all of it. Some of the money went to workers as wages. Some went to owners of the capital and natural resources used to produce it. Profits generated along the way went to the owners of the firms involved. All these items represent costs of producing the Cheerios and also represent income to households.

Part of the $4 cost of the Cheerios, while it makes up a portion of GDI, does not represent ordinary income actually earned by households. That part results from two other production costs: depreciation and taxes related to the production of the Cheerios. Nevertheless, they are treated as a kind of income; we will examine their role in GDI below.

As it is with Cheerios, so it is with everything else. The value of output equals the income generated as the output is produced.

The Components of GDI

Employee compensation is the largest among the components of factor income. Factor income also includes profit, rent, and interest. In addition, GDI includes charges for depreciation and taxes associated with production. Depreciation and production-related taxes, such as sales taxes, make up part of the cost of producing goods and services and must be accounted for in estimating GDI. We will discuss each of these components of GDI next.

Employee Compensation

Compensation of employees in the form of wages, salaries, and benefits makes up the largest single component of income generated in the production of GDP. In 2015, employee compensation represented over 50% of GDI.

The structure of employee compensation has changed dramatically in the last several decades. In 1950, virtually all employee compensation—95% of it—came in the form of wages and salaries. The remainder, about 5%, came in the form of additional benefits such as employer contributions to retirement programs and health insurance. In 2015, the share of benefits was about 30% of total employee compensation.

Profits

The profit component of income earned by households equals total revenues of firms less costs as measured by conventional accounting. Profits amounted to about 17% of GDI in 2015, down sharply from five decades earlier, when profits represented about 25% of the income generated in GDI.[1]

Profits are the reward the owners of firms receive for being in business. The opportunity to earn profits is the driving force behind production in a market economy.

Rental Income

Rental income, such as the income earned by owners of rental housing or payments for the rent of natural resources, is the smallest component of GDI (about 3.5%); it is the smallest of the income flows to households. The meaning of rent in the computation of GDI is the same as its meaning in conventional usage; it is a charge for the temporary use of some capital asset or natural resource.[2]

Net Interest

Businesses both receive and pay interest. GDI includes net interest, which equals interest paid less interest received by domestic businesses, plus interest received from foreigners less interest paid to foreigners. Interest payments on mortgage and home improvement loans are counted as interest paid by businesses, because homeowners are treated as businesses in the income accounts. In 2015, net interest accounted for nearly 4% of GDI.

Depreciation

Over time the machinery and buildings that are used to produce goods and services wear out or become obsolete. A farmer's tractor, for example, wears out as it is used. A technological change may make some equipment obsolete. The introduction of personal computers, for example, made the electric typewriters used by many firms obsolete. **Depreciation** is a measure of the amount of capital that wears out or becomes obsolete during a period. Depreciation is referred to in official reports as the consumption of fixed capital.

Depreciation is a cost of production, so it represents part of the price charged for goods and services. It is therefore counted as part of the income generated in the production of those goods and services. Depreciation represented about 15.5% of GDI in 2015.

depreciation

A measure of the amount of capital that wears out or becomes obsolete during a period.

Indirect Taxes

The final component of the income measure of GDI is indirect business taxes.[3] **Indirect taxes** are taxes imposed on the production or sale of goods and services or on other business activity. (By contrast, a **direct tax** is a tax imposed directly on income; the personal income and corporate income taxes are direct taxes.) Indirect taxes, which include sales and excise taxes and property taxes, make up part of the cost to firms of producing goods and services. Like depreciation, they are part of the price of those goods and services and are therefore treated as part of the income generated in their production. Indirect business taxes amounted to nearly 7% of GDI in 2015.

Table 21.2 shows the components of GDI in 2015. Employee compensation represented the largest share of GDI. The exhibit also shows the components of GDP for the same year.

In principle, GDP and GDI should be equal, but their estimated values never are, because the data come from different sources. Output data from a sample of firms are used to estimate GDP, while income data from a sample of households are used to estimate GDI. The difference is the statistical discrepancy shown in the right-hand column of Table 21.2. Some of the difficulties with these data are examined in the Case in Point feature on discrepancies between GDP and GDI.

TABLE 21.2 GDP and GDI, 2015
The table shows the composition of GDP and GDI in the third quarter of 2013 (in billions of dollars at an annual rate). Notice the rough equality of the two measures. (They are not quite equal because of measurement errors; the difference is due to a statistical discrepancy and is reduced significantly over time as the data are revised.)

Gross domestic product	$18,036.6	Gross domestic income	$18,290.3
Personal consumption expenditures	$12,283.7	Compensation of employees	9704.1
Gross private domestic investment	$3,056.6	Profits[4]	3079.1
Government consumption expenditures and gross investment	$3,218.3	Rental income of persons	659.6
Net exports of goods and services	−$522.0	Net interest	693.2
		Taxes on production and imports[5]	1,323.6
		Consumption of fixed capital (depreciation)	2,830.8
		Statistical discrepancy	−253.7

Source: Based on data from Bureau of Economic Analysis, National Income and Product Accounts, Tables 1.10 and 1.1.5 (revised January 27, 2017).

Tracing Income from the Economy to Households

We have seen that the production of goods and services generates income for households. Thus, the value of total output equals the value of total income in an economy. But we have also seen that our measure of total income, GDI, includes such things as depreciation and indirect business taxes that are not actually received by households. Households also receive some income, such as transfer payments, that does not count as part of GDP or GDI. Because the income households actually receive plays an important role in determining their consumption, it is useful to examine the relationship between a nation's total output and the income households actually receive.

Table 21.3 traces the path we take in going from GDP to **disposable personal income**, which equals the income households have available to spend on goods and services. We first convert GDP to GNP and then subtract elements of GNP that do not represent income received by households and add payments such as transfer payments that households receive but do not earn in the production of GNP. Disposable personal income is either spent for personal consumption or saved by households.

Specifically, to get from GDP to disposable personal income, we first convert GDP to GNP. Then, we subtract depreciation to obtain net national product and subtract the statistical discrepancy to arrive at national income (i.e., gross national income [GNI] net of depreciation and the statistical discrepancy). Next, we subtract components of GNP and GNI that do not represent income actually received by households, such as taxes on production and imports, corporate profit and payroll taxes (contributions to social insurance), and corporate retained earnings. We add items such as transfer payments that are income to households but are not part of GNP and GNI. The adjustments shown are the most important adjustments in going from GNP and GNI to disposable personal income; several smaller adjustments (e.g., subsidies, business current transfer payments [net], and current surplus of government enterprises) have been omitted.

TABLE 21.3 From GDP to Disposable Personal Income

GDP, a measure of total output, equals GDI, the total income generated in the production of goods and services in an economy. The chart traces the path from GDP to disposable personal income, which equals the income households actually receive.

GDP + net factor earnings from abroad	=	gross national product (GNP)
GNP – depreciation (consumption of fixed capital)	=	net national product (NNP)
NNP – statistical discrepancy	=	national income (NI)
NI – income earned but not received [e.g., taxes on production and imports, social security payroll taxes, corporate profit taxes, and retained earnings] + transfer payments and other income received but not earned in the production of GNP	=	personal income (PI)
PI – personal income taxes	=	disposable personal income (DPI)

Key Takeaways

- Gross domestic product, GDP, equals gross domestic income, GDI, which includes compensation, profits, rental income, indirect taxes, and depreciation.
- We can use GDP, a measure of total output, to compute disposable personal income, a measure of income received by households and available for them to spend.

Try It!

The following income data refer to the same economy for which you had output data in the first part of the previous Try It! Compute GDI from the data below and confirm that your result equals the GDP figure you computed in the previous Try It! Assume that GDP = GNP for this problem (that is, assume all factor incomes are earned and paid in the domestic economy).

Employee compensation	$700
Social Security payments to households	40
Welfare payments	100
Profits	200
Rental income	50
Net interest	25
Depreciation	50
Indirect taxes	175

Case in Point: The GDP–GDI Gap

Source: © Shutterstock, Inc.

GDP equals GDI; at least, that is the way it is supposed to work. But in an enormously complex economy, the measurement of these two variables inevitably goes awry. Estimates of the two are never quite equal. In recent years, the absolute value of the gap has been quite sizable, while in other years, it has been quite small. For example, for the years 2011 through 2015, GDI has differed from GDP by −38.8, −203.3, −137.9, -257.9, and -253.7 billion per year, respectively.

Although the gap seems large at times, it represents a remarkably small fraction of measured activity—around 1.5% or less. Of course, 1.5% of a big number is still a big number. But it is important to remember that, relative to the size of the economy, the gap between GDI and GDP is not large. The gap is listed as a "statistical discrepancy" in the Department of Commerce reporting of the two numbers.

Why does the gap exist? From an accounting point of view, it should not. The total value of final goods and services produced must be equal to the total value of income generated in that production. But output is measured from sales and inventory figures collected from just 10% of commercial establishments. Preliminary income figures are obtained from household surveys, but these represent a tiny fraction of households. More complete income data are provided by income tax returns, but these are available to the economists who estimate GDI only after a two-to four-year delay.

The Department of Commerce issues revisions of its GDP and GDI estimates as more complete data become available. With each revision, the gap between GDP and GDI estimates is significantly reduced.

While GDP and GDI figures cannot provide precise measures of economic activity, they come remarkably close. Indeed, given that the numbers come from entirely different sources, the fact that they come as close as they do provides an impressive check of the accuracy of the department's estimates of GDP and GDI.

Answer to Try It! Problem

GDI equals $1,200. Note that this value equals the value for GDP obtained from the estimate of output in the first part of the previous Try It! Here is the computation:

Employee compensation	$700
Profits	200
Rental income	50
Net interest	25
Depreciation	50
Indirect taxes	175
GDI	$1,200

Once again, note that Social Security and welfare payments to households are transfer payments. They do not represent payments to household factors of production for current output of goods and services, and therefore are not included in GDI.

21.4 GDP and Economic Well-Being

Learning Objectives

1. Discuss and give examples of measurement and conceptual problems in using real GDP as a measure of economic performance and of economic well-being.
2. Explain the use of per capita real GNP or GDP to compare economic performance across countries and discuss its limitations.

GDP is the measure most often used to assess the economic well-being of a country. Besides measuring the pulse of a country, it is the figure used to compare living standards in different countries.

Of course, to use GDP as an indicator of overall economic performance, we must convert nominal GDP to real GDP, since nominal values can rise or fall simply as a result of changes in the price level. For example, the movie *Avatar*, released in 2009, brought in $761 million—the highest amount to date in gross box office receipts, while *Gone with the Wind*, released in 1939, earned only $199 million and ranks 117th in terms of nominal receipts. But does that mean that *Avatar* actually did better than *Gone with the Wind*? After all, the average price of a movie ticket in 1939 was about 25 cents. At the time of *Avatar*, the average ticket price was about $7.50. A better way to compare these two movies in terms of popularity is to control for the price of movie tickets—the same strategy that economists use with real GDP in order to determine whether output is rising or falling. Adjusting the nominal box-office receipts using 2012 movie prices to obtain real revenue reveals that in real terms *Gone with the Wind* continues to be the top real grosser of all time with real box-office receipts of about $1.6 billion. *Avatar*'s real box-office receipts amounted to a mere $776 million.[6] As illustrated by this example on revenues from popular movies, we might draw erroneous conclusions about performance if we base them on nominal values instead of on real values. In contrast, real GDP, despite the problems with price indexes that were explained in another chapter, provides a reasonable measure of the total output of an economy, and changes in real GDP provide an indication of the direction of movement in total output.

We begin this section by noting some of the drawbacks of using real GDP as a measure of the economic welfare of a country. Despite these shortcomings, we will see that it probably remains our best single indicator of macroeconomic performance.

Measurement Problems in Real GDP

There are two measurement problems, other than those associated with adjusting for price level changes, in using real GDP to assess domestic economic performance.

Revisions

The first estimate of real GDP for a calendar quarter is called the advance estimate. It is issued about a month after the quarter ends. To produce a measure so quickly, officials at the Department of Commerce must rely on information from relatively few firms and households. One month later, it issues a revised estimate, and a month after that it issues its final estimate. Often the advance estimate of GDP and the final estimate do not correspond. The recession of 2001, for example, began in March of that year. But the first estimates of real GDP for the second and third quarters of 2001 showed output continuing to rise. It was not until later revisions that it became clear that a recession had been under way.

But the revision story does not end there. Every summer, the Commerce Department issues revised figures for the previous two or three years. Once every five years, the department conducts an extensive analysis that traces flows of inputs and outputs throughout the economy. It focuses on the outputs of some firms that are inputs to other firms. In the process of conducting this analysis, the department revises real GDP estimates for the previous five years. Sometimes the revisions can paint a picture of economic activity that is quite different from the one given even by the revised estimates of GDP. For example, revisions of the data for the 1990–1991 recession issued several years later showed that the recession had been much more serious than had previously been apparent, and the recovery was more pronounced. Concerning the most recent recession, the first estimates of fourth quarter 2008 GDP showed that the U.S. economy shrank by 3.8%. The first revision, however, showed a drop of 6.8%, and the second revision showed a drop of 8.9%!

The Service Sector

Another problem lies in estimating production in the service sector. The output of goods in an economy is relatively easy to compute. There are so many bushels of corn, so many pounds of beef. But what is the output of a bank? Of a hospital? It is easy to record the dollar value of output to enter in nominal GDP, but estimating the quantity of output to use in real GDP is quite another matter. In some cases, the Department of Commerce estimates service sector output based on the quantity of labor used. For example, if this technique were used in the banking industry and banking used 10% more labor, the department would report that production has risen 10%. If the number of employees remains unchanged, reported output remains unchanged. In effect, this approach assumes that output per worker—productivity—in those sectors remains constant when studies have indicated that productivity has increased greatly in the service sector. Since 1990 progress has been made in measurement in this area, which allows in particular for better estimation of productivity changes and price indexes for different service sector industries, but more remains to be done in this large sector of the U.S. economy.[7]

Conceptual Problems with Real GDP

A second set of limitations of real GDP stems from problems inherent in the indicator itself. Real GDP measures market activity. Goods and services that are produced and exchanged in a market are counted; goods and services that are produced but that are not exchanged in markets are not.[8]

Household Production

Suppose you are considering whether to eat at home for dinner tonight or to eat out. You could cook dinner for yourself at a cost of $5 for the ingredients plus an hour or so of your time. Alternatively, you could buy an equivalent meal at a restaurant for perhaps $15. Your decision to eat out rather than cook would add $10 to the GDP.

But that $10 addition would be misleading. After all, if you had stayed home you might have produced an equivalent meal. The only difference is that the value of your time would not have been counted. But surely your time is not worthless; it is just not counted. Similarly, GDP does not count the value of your efforts to clean your own house, to wash your own car, or to grow your own vegetables. In general, GDP omits the entire value added by members of a household who do household work themselves.

There is reason to believe this omission is serious. Economists J. Steven Landefeld and Stephanie H. McCulla of the U.S. Bureau of Economic Analysis estimated in a 2000 paper the value of household output from 1946 to 1997. Their estimate of household output in 1946 was 50% of reported GDP. Since then, that percentage has fallen, because more women have entered the workforce, so that more production that once took place in households now occurs in the market. Households now eat out more, purchase more prepared foods at the grocery store, hire out child-care services they once performed themselves, and so on. Their estimate for 1997, for example, suggests that household production amounted to 36% of reported GDP.[9]

This problem is especially significant when GDP is used to make comparisons across countries. In low-income countries, a much greater share of goods and services is not exchanged in a market. Estimates of GDP in such countries are adjusted to reflect nonmarket production, but these adjustments are inevitably imprecise.

Underground and Illegal Production

Some production goes unreported in order to evade taxes or the law. It is not likely to be counted in GDP. Legal production for which income is unreported in order to evade taxes generally takes place in what is known as the "underground economy." For example, a carpenter might build a small addition to a dentist's house in exchange for orthodontic work for the carpenter's children. Although income has been earned and output generated in this example of bartering, the transaction is unlikely to be reported for income tax or other purposes and thus is not counted in GDP. Illegal activities are not reported for income taxes for obvious reasons and are thus difficult to include in GDP.

Leisure

Leisure is an economic good. All other things being equal, more leisure is better than less leisure.

But all other things are not likely to be equal when it comes to consuming leisure. Consuming more leisure means supplying less work effort. And that means producing less GDP. If everyone decided to work 10% fewer hours, GDP would fall. But that would not mean that people were worse off. In fact, their choice of more leisure would suggest they prefer the extra leisure to the goods and services they give up by consuming it. Consequently, a reduction in GDP would be accompanied by an increase in satisfaction, not a reduction.

The GDP Accounts Ignore "Bads"

Suppose a wave of burglaries were to break out across the United States. One would expect people to respond by buying more and louder burglar alarms, better locks, fiercer German shepherds, and more guard services than they had before. To the extent that they pay for these by dipping into savings rather than replacing other consumption, GDP increases. An epidemic might have much the same effect on GDP by driving up health-care spending. But that does not mean that crime and disease are good things; it means only that crime and disease may force an increase in the production of goods and services counted in the GDP.

Similarly, the GDP accounts ignore the impact of pollution on the environment. We might produce an additional $200 billion in goods and services but create pollution that makes us feel worse off by, say, $300 billion. The GDP accounts simply report the $200 billion in increased production. Indeed, some of the environmental degradation might itself boost GDP. Dirtier air may force us to wash clothes more often, to paint buildings more often, and to see the doctor more often, all of which will tend to increase GDP!

Conclusion: GDP and Human Happiness

More GDP cannot necessarily be equated with more human happiness. But more GDP does mean more of the goods and services we measure. It means more jobs. It means more income. And most people seem to place a high value on these things. For all its faults, GDP does measure the production of most goods and services. And goods and services get produced, for the most part, because we want them. We might thus be safe in giving two cheers for GDP—and holding back the third in recognition of the conceptual difficulties that are inherent in using a single number to summarize the output of an entire economy.

International Comparisons of Real GDP and GNP

Real GDP or GNP estimates are often used in comparing economic performance among countries. In making such comparisons, it is important to keep in mind the general limitations to these measures of economic performance that we noted earlier. Further, countries use different methodologies for collecting and compiling data.

Three other issues are important in comparing real GDP or GNP for different countries: the adjustment of these figures for population, adjusting to a common currency, and the incorporation of nonmarket production.

per capita real GNP or GDP

A country's real GNP or GDP divided by its population.

In international comparisons of real GNP or real GDP, economists generally make comparisons not of real GNP or GDP but of **per capita real GNP or GDP**, which equals a country's real GNP or GDP divided by its population. For example, suppose Country A has a real GDP of about $4,000 billion and Country B has a real GDP of about $40 billion. We can conclude that Country A produced 100 times more goods and services than did Country B. But if Country A has 200 times as many people as Country B (for example, 200 million people in Country A and 1 million in Country B), then Country A's per capita output will be half that of Country B ($20,000 versus $40,000 in this example).

Figure 21.7 compares per capita real GDP for 11 countries in 2015. It is based on data that uses a measure called "international dollars" in order to correct for differences in the purchasing power of $1 across countries. The data also attempt to adjust for nonmarket production (such as that of rural families that grow their own food, make their own clothing, and produce other household goods and services themselves).

FIGURE 21.7 Comparing Per Capita GDP, 2015

There is a huge gap between per capita income in one of the poorest countries in the world, the Central African Republic, and wealthier nations such as the United States and Luxembourg.

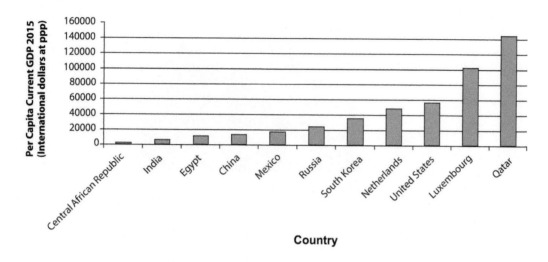

Source: Based on data from World Bank, World Development Indicators Online

The disparities in income are striking; Luxembourg, for example, had an income level nearly 200 times greater than the Central African Republic.

What can we conclude about international comparisons in levels of GDP and GNP? Certainly we must be cautious. There are enormous difficulties in estimating any country's total output. Comparing one country's output to another presents additional challenges. But the fact that a task is difficult does not mean it is impossible. When the data suggest huge disparities in levels of GNP per capita, for example, we observe real differences in living standards.

Key Takeaways

- Real GDP or real GNP is often used as an indicator of the economic well-being of a country.
- Problems in the measurement of real GDP, in addition to problems encountered in converting from nominal to real GDP, stem from revisions in the data and the difficulty of measuring output in some sectors, particularly the service sector.
- Conceptual problems in the use of real GDP as a measure of economic well-being include the facts that it does not include nonmarket production and that it does not properly adjust for "bads" produced in the economy.
- Per capita real GDP or GNP can be used to compare economic performance in different countries.

Try It!

What impact would each of the following have on real GDP? Would economic well-being increase or decrease as a result?

1. On average, people in a country decide to increase the number of hours they work by 5%.
2. Spending on homeland security increases in response to a terrorist attack.
3. The price level and nominal GDP increase by 10%.

Case in Point: Per Capita Real GDP and Olympic Medal Counts

Source: © Shutterstock, Inc.

In the popular lore, the Olympics provide an opportunity for the finest athletes in the world to compete with each other head-to-head on the basis of raw talent and hard work. And yet there are many countries, mostly poor, that have never won any Olympic medals. Are the people who live in those countries lacking in athletic prowess or grit? Hardly. Before each Olympics, we often hear stories about the amazing efforts of athletes from poor countries who overcome obstacles to qualify and then to compete in various sports. For example, a reporter who looked at athletes from Laos who competed in the 2004 Athens Olympics noted that a swimmer, Vilayphone Vong-phachanh, had never practiced in an Olympic-size pool, and a runner, Sirivanh Ketavong, had worn the same running shoes for four years.

Economists Andrew B. Bernard and Meghan R. Busse and their colleagues have been able to predict with astonishing accuracy the number of medals different counties will win on the basis of a handful of factors, none of which rely on a knowledge of sports or of specific athletes. Rather, their analyses are based on four factors: population, per capita income, past performance, and a host effect. This rather simple model has very accurately predicted medal counts by country since it was developed in 2000 based on Olympics performance from 1960 to 1996. For example, the model predicted the 2012 London total medal by country with 98% accuracy. (The 2016 predictions for Brazil, developed by Professor Bernard's colleague, Camila F. Gonzales, were not as accurate, perhaps due to the Russian doping scandal that eliminated Russian athletes from competing in a number of sports.) The importance of population seems obvious, since more populous countries potentially have a larger number of athletes from which to draw. Bernard and Busse explain the importance of the economic variable, country income, by stating that, "…developing Olympic caliber athletes requires considerable expenditure on facilities and personnel. Wealthier countries are more likely to have individuals, organizations, or governments willing to make such an investment. Wealthier countries are also more likely to have athletics as a part of schooling and to have leisure time to devote to sports."

The good news is that as the per capita real GDP in some relatively poor countries has risen, the improved living standards have led to increased Olympic medal counts for them. China's much improved performance provides an example: China won 28 medals in 1988, 100 in 2008 when it served as Olympics host, and still 70 at the 2016 games in Brazil.

While not a perfect measure of the well-being of people in a country, per capita real GDP does tell us about the opportunities available to the average citizen in a country. Americans would surely find it hard to imagine living at the level of consumption of the average Laotian. In *The Progress Paradox: How Life Gets Better While People Feel Worse*, essayist Gregg Easterbrook notes that a higher material standard of living is not associated with higher reported happiness. But, he concludes, the problems of prosperity seem less serious than those of poverty, and prosperity gives people and nations the means to address problems. The Olympic medal count for each nation strongly reflects its average standard of living and hence the opportunities available to its citizens.[10]

Sources: *Based on Andrew B Bernard and Meghan R. Busse, "Who Wins the Olympic Games: Economic Resources and Medal Totals, Review of Economics and Statistics 86:1 (February 2004): 413 – 417; Gregg Easterbrook, The Progress Paradox: How Life Gets Better While People Feel Worse (New York: Random House, 2003); Camila F. Gonzales, "Going for the Gold in the*

Cidade Maravilhosa: Who Will Win the 2016 Olympic Games in Rio de Janeiro?" Tuck School of Business at Dartmouth, July 2016, unpublished; David Wallechinsky, "While I'll Cheer for Laos, Parade Magazine, August 8, 2004, p. 8. Gregg Easterbrook, The Progress Paradox: How Life Gets Better While People Feel Worse (New York: Random House, 2003); Daniel K. N. Johnson and Ayfer Ali, "A Tale of Two Seasons: Participation and Medal Counts at the Summer and Winter Olympic Games," Social Science Quarterly 84, no. 4 (December 2004): 974–93; David Wallechinsky, "Why I'll Cheer for Laos," Parade Magazine, August 8, 2004, p. 8.

Answer to Try It! Problems

1. Real GDP would increase. Assuming the people chose to increase their work effort and forgo the extra leisure, economic well-being would increase as well.

2. Real GDP would increase, but the extra expenditure in the economy was due to an increase in something "bad," so economic well-being would likely be lower.

3. No change in real GDP. For some people, economic well-being might increase and for others it might decrease, since inflation does not affect each person in the same way.

21.5 Review and Practice

Summary

This chapter focused on the measurement of GDP. The total value of output (GDP) equals the total value of income generated in producing that output (GDI). We can illustrate the flows of spending and income through the economy with the circular flow model. Firms produce goods and services in response to demands from households (personal consumption), other firms (private investment), government agencies (government purchases), and the rest of the world (net exports). This production, in turn, creates a flow of factor incomes to households. Thus, GDP can be estimated using two types of data: (1) data that show the total value of output and (2) data that show the total value of income generated by that output.

In looking at GDP as a measure of output, we divide it into four components: consumption, investment, government purchases, and net exports. GDP equals the sum of final values produced in each of these areas. It can also be measured as the sum of values added at each stage of production. The components of GDP measured in terms of income (GDI) are employee compensation, profits, rental income, net interest, depreciation, and indirect taxes.

We also explained other measures of income such as GNP and disposable personal income. Disposable personal income is an important economic indicator, because it is closely related to personal consumption, the largest component of GDP.

GDP is often used as an indicator of how well off a country is. Of course, to use it for this purpose, we must be careful to use real GDP rather than nominal GDP. Still, there are problems with our estimate of real GDP. Problems encountered in converting nominal GDP to real GDP were discussed in the previous chapter. In this chapter we looked at additional measurement problems and conceptual problems.

Frequent revisions in the data sometimes change our picture of the economy considerably. Accounting for the service sector is quite difficult. Conceptual problems include the omission of nonmarket production and of underground and illegal production. GDP ignores the value of leisure and includes certain "bads."

We cannot assert with confidence that more GDP is a good thing and that less is bad. However, real GDP remains our best single indicator of economic performance. It is used not only to indicate how any one economy is performing over time but also to compare the economic performance of different countries.

Concept Problems

1. GDP is used as a measure of macroeconomic performance. What, precisely, does it measure?

2. Many economists have attempted to create a set of social accounts that would come closer to measuring the economic well-being of the society than does GDP. What modifications of the current approach would you recommend to them?

3. Every good produced creates income for the owners of the factors of production that created the product or service. For a recent purchase you made, try to list all the types of factors of production involved in making the product available, and try to determine who received income as a result of your purchase.

4. Explain how the sale of used textbooks in your campus bookstore affects the GDP calculation.

5. Look again at the circular flow diagram in Figure 21.5 and assume it is drawn for the United States. State the flows in which each of the following transactions would be entered.

    a. A consumer purchases fresh fish at a local fish market.

    b. A grocery store acquires 1,000 rolls of paper towels for later resale.

    c. NASA purchases a new Saturn rocket.

    d. People in France flock to see the latest Brad Pitt movie.

    e. A construction firm builds a new house.

    f. A couple from Seattle visits Guadalajara and stays in a hotel there.

    g. The city of Dallas purchases computer paper from a local firm.

6. Suggest an argument for and an argument against counting in GDP all household-produced goods and services that are not sold, such as the value of child care or home-cooked meals.

7. Suppose a nation's firms make heavy use of factors of production owned by residents of foreign countries, while foreign firms make relatively little use of factors owned by residents of that nation. How does the nation's GDP compare to its GNP?

8. Suppose Country A has the same GDP as Country B, and that neither nation's residents own factors of production used by foreign firms, nor do either nation's firms use factors of production owned by foreign residents. Suppose that, relative to Country B, depreciation, indirect business taxes, and personal income taxes in Country A are high, while welfare and Social Security payments to households in Country A are relatively low. Which country has the higher disposable personal income? Why?

9. Suppose that virtually everyone in the United States decides to take life a little easier, and the length of the average workweek falls by 25%. How will that affect GDP? Per capita GDP? How will it affect economic welfare?

10. Comment on the following statement: "It does not matter that the value of the labor people devote to producing things for themselves is not counted in GDP; because we make the same 'mistake' every year, relative values are unaffected."

11. Name some of the services, if any, you produced at home that do get counted in GDP. Are there any goods you produce that are not counted?

12. Some countries, for example the United Kingdom and Italy, have recently decided to include some illegal activities, such as drugs and prostitution, in their calculations of GDP.[11] Other countries do not do this. Should such activities be included?

Numerical Problems

1. Given the following nominal data, compute GDP. Assume net factor incomes from abroad = 0 (that is, GDP = GNP).

Nominal Data for GDP and NNP	$ Billions
Consumption	2,799.8
Depreciation	481.6
Exports	376.2
Gross private domestic investment	671.0
Indirect taxes	331.4
Government purchases	869.7
Government transfer payments	947.8
Imports	481.7

2. Find data for each of the following countries on real GDP and population. Use the data to calculate the GDP per capita for each of the following countries:

   a. Mozambique

   b. India

   c. Pakistan

   d. United States

   e. Canada

   f. Russia

   g. Brazil

   h. Iran

   i. Colombia

3. Now construct a bar graph showing your results in the previous problem, organizing the countries from the highest to the lowest GNP per capita, with countries on the horizontal axis and GNP per capita on the vertical axis.

4. Suppose Country A has a GDP of $4 trillion. Residents of this country earn $500 million from assets they own in foreign countries. Residents of foreign countries earn $300 million from assets they own in Country A. Compute:

   a. Country A's net foreign income.

   b. Country A's GNP.

5. Suppose a country's GDP equals $500 billion for a particular year. Economists in the country estimate that household production equals 40% of GDP.

   a. What is the value of the country's household production for that year?

   b. Counting both GDP and household production, what is the country's total output for the year?

6. A miner extracts iron from the earth. A steel mill converts the iron to steel beams for use in construction. A construction company uses the steel beams to make a building. Assume that the total product of these firms represents the only components of the building and that they will have no other uses. Complete the following table:

Company	Product	Total Sales	Value Added
Acme Mining	iron ore	$100,000	?
Fuller Mill	steel beams	$175,000	?
Crane Construction	building	$1,100,000	?
Total Value Added			?

7. You are given the data below for 2008 for the imaginary country of Amagre, whose currency is the G.

Consumption	350 billion G
Transfer payments	100 billion G
Investment	100 billion G
Government purchases	200 billion G
Exports	50 billion G
Imports	150 billion G
Bond purchases	200 billion G
Earnings on foreign investments	75 billion G
Foreign earnings on Amagre investment	25 billion G

a. Compute net foreign investment.

b. Compute net exports.

c. Compute GDP.

d. Compute GNP.

Endnotes

1. Although reported separately by the Department of Commerce, we have combined proprietors' income (typically independent business owners and farmers) with corporate profits to simplify the discussion.

2. If you have studied microeconomics, you know that the term "*rent*" in economics has a quite different meaning. The national income and product accounts use the accounting, not the economic, meaning of "*rent*."

3. The adjustment for indirect business taxes includes two other minor elements: transfer payments made by business firms and surpluses or deficits of government enterprises.

4. Profit is corporate profit ($1,706.8) plus proprietors' income ($1,360.7), both with inventory valuation and capital consumption adjustment.

5. Indirect taxes include taxes on production and imports of $1,237.6 plus business transfer payments ($161.4) less subsidies ($56.6) and current surplus of government enterprise (–$18.8). Prior to the 2003 National Income and Product Accounts (NIPA) revisions, the category "taxes on production and imports" was, with some technical and other minor adjustments, referred to as "indirect business taxes." See Brent R. Moulton and Eugene P. Seskin, "Preview of the 2003 Comprehensive Revision of the National Income and Product Accounts," Bureau of Economic Analysis, *Survey of Current Business*, June 2003, pp. 17–34.

6. Based on estimates at "Domestic Grosses Adjusted for Ticket Price Inflation," Box Office Mojo, accessed April 10, 2012, http://boxofficemojo.com/alltime/adjusted.htm.

7. Jack E. Triplett and Barry P. Bosworth, "The State of Data for Services Productivity Measurement in the United States," *International Productivity Monitor* 16 (Spring 2008): 53–70.

8. There are two exceptions to this rule. The value of food produced and consumed by farm households is counted in GDP. More important, an estimate of the rental values of owner-occupied homes is included. If a family rents a house, the rental payments are included in GDP. If a family lives in a house it owns, the Department of Commerce estimates what the house would rent for and then includes that rent in the GDP estimate, even though the house's services were not exchanged in the marketplace.

9. J. Steven Landefeld and Stephanie H. McCulla, "Accounting for Nonmarket Household Production within a National Accounts Framework," *Review of Income & Wealth* 46, no. 3 (September 2000): 289–307.

10. Andrew B Bernard and Meghan R. Busse, "Who Wins the Olympic Games: Economic Resources and Medal Totals, Review of Economics and Statistics 86:1 (February 2004): 413 – 417; Gregg Easterbrook, The Progress Paradox: How Life Gets Better While People Feel Worse ; (New York: Random House, 2003); Camila F. Gonzales, "Going for the Gold in the Cidade Maravilhosa: Who Will Win the 2016 Olympic Games in Rio de Janeiro?" Tuck School of Business at Dartmouth, July 2016, unpublished; David Wallechinsky, "While I'll Cheer for Laos, Parade Magazine, August 8, 2004, p. 8. (New York: Random House, 2003); Camila F. Gonzales, "Going for the Gold in the Cidade Maravilhosa: Who Will Win the 2016 Olympic Games in Rio de Janeiro?" Tuck School of Business at Dartmouth, July 2016, unpublished; David Wallechinsky, "While I'll Cheer for Laos, Parade Magazine, August 8, 2004, p. 8.

11. Melvin Backman, "Britain, Italy include drugs and sex in GDP," CNN Money, May 30, 2014, http://money.cnn.com/2014/05/29/news/economy/uk-italy-prostitution-gdp/index.html.

CHAPTER 22
Aggregate Demand and Aggregate Supply

22.1 Start Up: The Great Warning

The first warning came from the Harvard Economic Society, an association of Harvard economics professors, early in 1929. The society predicted in its weekly newsletter that the seven-year-old expansion was coming to an end. Recession was ahead. Almost no one took the warning seriously. The economy, fueled by soaring investment, had experienced stunning growth. The 1920s had seen the emergence of many entirely new industries—automobiles, public power, home appliances, synthetic fabrics, radio, and motion pictures. The decade seemed to have acquired a momentum all its own. Prosperity was not about to end, no matter what a few economists might say.

Summer came, and no recession was apparent. The Harvard economists withdrew their forecast. As it turned out, they lost their nerve too soon. Indeed, industrial production had already begun to fall. The worst downturn in our history, the Great Depression, had begun.

The collapse was swift. The stock market crashed in October 1929. Real GDP plunged nearly 10% by 1930. By the time the economy hit bottom in 1933, real GDP had fallen 30%, unemployment had increased from 3.2% in 1929 to 25% in 1933, and prices, measured by the implicit price deflator, had plunged 23% from their 1929 level. The depression held the economy in its cruel grip for more than a decade; it was not until World War II that full employment was restored.

In this chapter we go beyond explanations of the main macroeconomic variables to introduce a model of macroeconomic activity that we can use to analyze problems such as fluctuations in gross domestic product (real GDP), the price level, and employment: the model of aggregate demand and aggregate supply. We will use this model throughout our exploration of macroeconomics. In this chapter we will present the broad outlines of the model; greater detail, more examples, and more thorough explanations will follow in subsequent chapters.

We will examine the concepts of the aggregate demand curve and the short- and long-run aggregate supply curves. We will identify conditions under which an economy achieves an equilibrium level of real GDP that is consistent with full employment of labor. **Potential output** is the level of output an economy can achieve when labor is employed at its natural level. Potential output is also called the natural level of real GDP. When an economy fails to produce at its potential, there may be actions that the government or the central bank can take to push the economy toward it, and in this chapter we will begin to consider the pros and cons of doing so.

> **potential output**
>
> The level of output an economy can achieve when labor is employed at its natural level.

22.2 Aggregate Demand

Learning Objectives

1. Define potential output, also called the natural level of GDP.

2. Define aggregate demand, represent it using a hypothetical aggregate demand curve, and identify and explain the three effects that cause this curve to slope downward.

3. Distinguish between a change in the aggregate quantity of goods and services demanded and a change in aggregate demand.

4. Use examples to explain how each component of aggregate demand can be a possible aggregate demand shifter.

5. Explain what a multiplier is and tell how to calculate it.

aggregate demand

The relationship between the total quantity of goods and services demanded (from all the four sources of demand) and the price level, all other determinants of spending unchanged.

aggregate demand curve

A graphical representation of aggregate demand.

Firms face four sources of demand: households (personal consumption), other firms (investment), government agencies (government purchases), and foreign markets (net exports). **Aggregate demand** is the relationship between the total quantity of goods and services demanded (from all the four sources of demand) and the price level, all other determinants of spending unchanged. The **aggregate demand curve** is a graphical representation of aggregate demand.

The Slope of the Aggregate Demand Curve

We will use the implicit price deflator as our measure of the price level; the aggregate quantity of goods and services demanded is measured as real GDP. The table in Figure 22.1 gives values for each component of aggregate demand at each price level for a hypothetical economy. Various points on the aggregate demand curve are found by adding the values of these components at different price levels. The aggregate demand curve for the data given in the table is plotted on the graph in Figure 22.1. At point A, at a price level of 1.18, $11,800 billion worth of goods and services will be demanded; at point C, a reduction in the price level to 1.14 increases the quantity of goods and services demanded to $12,000 billion; and at point E, at a price level of 1.10, $12,200 billion will be demanded.

FIGURE 22.1 Aggregate Demand

An aggregate demand curve (*AD*) shows the relationship between the total quantity of output demanded (measured as real GDP) and the price level (measured as the implicit price deflator). At each price level, the total quantity of goods and services demanded is the sum of the components of real GDP, as shown in the table. There is a negative relationship between the price level and the total quantity of goods and services demanded, all other things unchanged.

Point on aggregate demand curve	Price level	$C+$	$I+$	$G+$	$X_n=$	Aggregate demand
A	1.18	8,400	1,820	2,150	−570	11,800
B	1.16	8,450	1,860	2,150	−560	11,900
C	1.14	8,500	1,900	2,150	−550	12,000
D	1.12	8,550	1,940	2,150	−540	12,100
E	1.10	8,600	1,980	2,150	−530	12,200

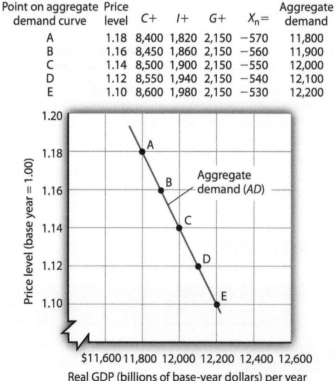

The negative slope of the aggregate demand curve suggests that it behaves in the same manner as an ordinary demand curve. But we *cannot* apply the reasoning we use to explain downward-sloping demand curves in individual markets to explain the downward-sloping aggregate demand curve. There are two reasons for a negative relationship between price and quantity demanded in individual markets. First, a lower price induces people to substitute more of the good whose price has fallen for other goods, increasing the quantity demanded. Second, the lower price creates a higher real income. This normally increases quantity demanded further.

Neither of these effects is relevant to a change in prices in the aggregate. When we are dealing with the average of all prices—the price level—we can no longer say that a fall in prices will induce a change in relative prices that will lead consumers to buy more of the goods and services whose prices have fallen and less of the goods and services whose prices have not fallen. The price of corn may have fallen, but the prices of wheat, sugar, tractors, steel, and most other goods or services produced in the economy are likely to have fallen as well.

Furthermore, a reduction in the price level means that it is not just the prices consumers pay that are falling. It means the prices people receive—their wages, the rents they may charge as landlords, the interest rates they earn—are likely to be falling as well. A falling price level means that goods and services are cheaper, but incomes are lower, too. There is no reason to expect that a change in real income will boost the quantity of goods and services demanded—indeed, no change in real income would occur. If nominal incomes and prices all fall by 10%, for example, real incomes do not change.

Why, then, does the aggregate demand curve slope downward? One reason for the downward slope of the aggregate demand curve lies in the relationship between real wealth (the stocks, bonds, and other assets that people have accumulated) and consumption (one of the four components of aggregate demand). When the price level falls, the real value of wealth increases—it packs more purchasing power. For example, if the price level falls by 25%, then $10,000 of wealth could purchase more goods and services than it would have if the price level had not fallen. An increase in wealth will induce people to increase their consumption. The consumption component of aggregate demand will thus be greater at lower price levels than at higher price levels. The tendency for a change in the price level to affect real wealth and thus alter consumption is called the **wealth effect**; it suggests a negative relationship between the price level and the real value of consumption spending.

wealth effect

The tendency for a change in the price level to affect real wealth and thus alter consumption.

A second reason the aggregate demand curve slopes downward lies in the relationship between interest rates and investment. A lower price level lowers the demand for money, because less money is required to buy a given quantity of goods. What economists mean by money demand will be explained in more detail in a later chapter. But, as we learned in studying demand and supply, a reduction in the demand for something, all other things unchanged, lowers its price. In this case, the "something" is money and its price is the interest rate. A lower price level thus reduces interest rates. Lower interest rates make borrowing by firms to build factories or buy equipment and other capital more attractive. A lower interest rate means lower mortgage payments, which tends to increase investment in residential houses. Investment thus rises when the price level falls. The tendency for a change in the price level to affect the interest rate and thus to affect the quantity of investment demanded is called the **interest rate effect**. John Maynard Keynes, a British economist whose analysis of the Great Depression and what to do about it led to the birth of modern macro-economics, emphasized this effect. For this reason, the interest rate effect is sometimes called the Keynes effect.

interest rate effect

The tendency for a change in the price level to affect the interest rate and thus to affect the quantity of investment demanded.

A third reason for the rise in the total quantity of goods and services demanded as the price level falls can be found in changes in the net export component of aggregate demand. All other things unchanged, a lower price level in an economy reduces the prices of its goods and services relative to foreign-produced goods and services. A lower price level makes that economy's goods more attractive to foreign buyers, increasing exports. It will also make foreign-produced goods and services less attractive to the economy's buyers, reducing imports. The result is an increase in net exports. The **international trade effect** is the tendency for a change in the price level to affect net exports.

international trade effect

The tendency for a change in the price level to affect net exports.

Taken together, then, a fall in the price level means that the quantities of consumption, investment, and net export components of aggregate demand may all rise. Since government purchases are determined through a political process, we assume there is no causal link between the price level and the real volume of government purchases. Therefore, this component of GDP does not contribute to the downward slope of the curve.

In general, a change in the price level, with all other determinants of aggregate demand unchanged, causes a movement along the aggregate demand curve. A movement along an aggregate demand curve is a **change in the aggregate quantity of goods and services demanded**. A movement from point A to point B on the aggregate demand curve in Figure 22.1 is an example. Such a change is a response to a change in the price level.

Notice that the axes of the aggregate demand curve graph are drawn with a break near the origin to remind us that the plotted values reflect a relatively narrow range of changes in real GDP and the price level. We do not know what might happen if the price level or output for an entire economy approached zero. Such a phenomenon has never been observed.

Changes in Aggregate Demand

Aggregate demand changes in response to a change in any of its components. An increase in the total quantity of consumer goods and services demanded at every price level, for example, would shift the aggregate demand curve to the right. A change in the aggregate quantity of goods and services demanded at every price level is a **change in aggregate demand**, which shifts the aggregate demand curve. Increases and decreases in aggregate demand are shown in Figure 22.2.

FIGURE 22.2 Changes in Aggregate Demand

An increase in consumption, investment, government purchases, or net exports shifts the aggregate demand curve AD_1 to the right as shown in Panel (a). A reduction in one of the components of aggregate demand shifts the curve to the left, as shown in Panel (b).

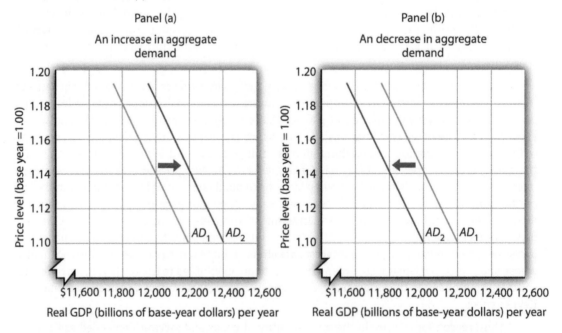

What factors might cause the aggregate demand curve to shift? Each of the components of aggregate demand is a possible aggregate demand shifter. We shall look at some of the events that can trigger changes in the components of aggregate demand and thus shift the aggregate demand curve.

change in the aggregate quantity of goods and services demanded

Movement along an aggregate demand curve.

change in aggregate demand

Change in the aggregate quantity of goods and services demanded at every price level.

Changes in Consumption

Several events could change the quantity of consumption at each price level and thus shift aggregate demand. One determinant of consumption is consumer confidence. If consumers expect good economic conditions and are optimistic about their economic prospects, they are more likely to buy major items such as cars or furniture. The result would be an increase in the real value of consumption at each price level and an increase in aggregate demand. In the second half of the 1990s, sustained economic growth and low unemployment fueled high expectations and consumer optimism. Surveys revealed consumer confidence to be very high. That consumer confidence translated into increased consumption and increased aggregate demand. In contrast, a decrease in consumption would accompany diminished consumer expectations and a decrease in consumer confidence, as happened after the stock market crash of 1929. The same problem has plagued the economies of most Western nations in 2008 as declining consumer confidence has tended to reduce consumption. A survey by the Conference Board in September of 2008 showed that just 13.5% of consumers surveyed expected economic conditions in the United States to improve in the next six months. Similarly pessimistic views prevailed in the previous two months. That contributed to the decline in consumption that occurred in the third quarter of the year.

Another factor that can change consumption and shift aggregate demand is tax policy. A cut in personal income taxes leaves people with more after-tax income, which may induce them to increase their consumption. The federal government in the United States cut taxes in 1964, 1981, 1986, 1997, and 2003; each of those tax cuts tended to increase consumption and aggregate demand at each price level.

In the United States, another government policy aimed at increasing consumption and thus aggregate demand has been the use of rebates in which taxpayers are simply sent checks in hopes that those checks will be used for consumption. Rebates have been used in 1975, 2001, and 2008. In each case the rebate was a one-time payment. Careful studies by economists of the 1975 and 2001 rebates showed little impact on consumption. Final evidence on the impact of the 2008 rebates is not yet in, but early results suggest a similar outcome. In a subsequent chapter, we will investigate arguments about whether temporary increases in income produced by rebates are likely to have a significant impact on consumption.

Transfer payments such as welfare and Social Security also affect the income people have available to spend. At any given price level, an increase in transfer payments raises consumption and aggregate demand, and a reduction lowers consumption and aggregate demand.

Changes in Investment

Investment is the production of new capital that will be used for future production of goods and services. Firms make investment choices based on what they think they will be producing in the future. The expectations of firms thus play a critical role in determining investment. If firms expect their sales to go up, they are likely to increase their investment so that they can increase production and meet consumer demand. Such an increase in investment raises the aggregate quantity of goods and services demanded at each price level; it increases aggregate demand.

Changes in interest rates also affect investment and thus affect aggregate demand. We must be careful to distinguish such changes from the interest rate effect, which causes a movement along the aggregate demand curve. A change in interest rates that results from a change in the price level affects investment in a way that is already captured in the downward slope of the aggregate demand curve; it causes a movement along the curve. A change in interest rates for some other reason shifts the curve. We examine reasons interest rates might change in another chapter.

Investment can also be affected by tax policy. One provision of the Job and Growth Tax Relief Reconciliation Act of 2003 was a reduction in the tax rate on certain capital gains. Capital gains result when the owner of an asset, such as a house or a factory, sells the asset for more than its purchase price (less any depreciation claimed in earlier years). The lower capital gains tax could stimulate investment, because the owners of such assets know that they will lose less to taxes when they sell those assets, thus making assets subject to the tax more attractive.

Changes in Government Purchases

Any change in government purchases, all other things unchanged, will affect aggregate demand. An increase in government purchases increases aggregate demand; a decrease in government purchases decreases aggregate demand.

Many economists argued that reductions in defense spending in the wake of the collapse of the Soviet Union in 1991 tended to reduce aggregate demand. Similarly, increased defense spending for the wars in Afghanistan and Iraq increased aggregate demand. Dramatic increases in defense spending to fight World War II accounted in large part for the rapid recovery from the Great Depression.

Changes in Net Exports

A change in the value of net exports at each price level shifts the aggregate demand curve. A major determinant of net exports is foreign demand for a country's goods and services; that demand will vary with foreign incomes. An increase in foreign incomes increases a country's net exports and aggregate demand; a slump in foreign incomes reduces net exports and aggregate demand. For example, several major U.S. trading partners in Asia suffered recessions in 1997 and 1998. Lower real incomes in those countries reduced U.S. exports and tended to reduce aggregate demand.

exchange rate

The price of a currency in terms of another currency or currencies.

Exchange rates also influence net exports, all other things unchanged. A country's **exchange rate** is the price of its currency in terms of another currency or currencies. A rise in the U.S. exchange rate means that it takes more Japanese yen, for example, to purchase one dollar. That also means that U.S. traders get more yen per dollar. Since prices of goods produced in Japan are given in yen and prices of goods produced in the United States are given in dollars, a rise in the U.S. exchange rate increases the price to foreigners for goods and services produced in the United States, thus reducing U.S. exports; it reduces the price of foreign-produced goods and services for U.S. consumers, thus increasing imports to the United States. A higher exchange rate tends to reduce net exports, reducing aggregate demand. A lower exchange rate tends to increase net exports, increasing aggregate demand.

Foreign price levels can affect aggregate demand in the same way as exchange rates. For example, when foreign price levels fall relative to the price level in the United States, U.S. goods and services become relatively more expensive, reducing exports and boosting imports in the United States. Such a reduction in net exports reduces aggregate demand. An increase in foreign prices relative to U.S. prices has the opposite effect.

The trade policies of various countries can also affect net exports. A policy by Japan to increase its imports of goods and services from India, for example, would increase net exports in India.

The Multiplier

A change in any component of aggregate demand shifts the aggregate demand curve. Generally, the aggregate demand curve shifts by more than the amount by which the component initially causing it to shift changes.

Suppose that net exports increase due to an increase in foreign incomes. As foreign demand for domestically made products rises, a country's firms will hire additional workers or perhaps increase the average number of hours that their employees work. In either case, incomes will rise, and higher incomes will lead to an increase in consumption. Taking into account these other increases in the components of aggregate demand, the aggregate demand curve will shift by more than the initial shift caused by the initial increase in net exports.

The **multiplier** is the ratio of the change in the quantity of real GDP demanded at each price level to the initial change in one or more components of aggregate demand that produced it:

EQUATION 22.1

$$\text{Multiplier} = \frac{\Delta \text{ (real GDP demanded at each price level)}}{\text{initial } \Delta \text{ (component of AD)}}$$

We use the capital Greek letter delta (Δ) to mean "change in." In the aggregate demand–aggregate supply model presented in this chapter, it is the number by which we multiply an initial change in aggregate demand to obtain the amount by which the aggregate demand curve shifts as a result of the initial change. In other words, we can use Equation 22.1 to solve for the change in real GDP demanded at each price level:

EQUATION 22.2

$$\Delta \text{ (real GDP demanded at each price level)} = \text{multiplier} \times \text{initial } \Delta \text{ (component of AD)}$$

Suppose that the initial increase in net exports is $100 billion and that the initial $100-billion increase generates additional consumption of $100 billion at each price level. In Panel (a) of Figure 22.3, the aggregate demand curve shifts to the right by $200 billion—the amount of the initial increase in net exports times the multiplier of 2. We obtained the value for the multiplier in this example by plugging $200 billion (the initial $100-billion increase in net exports plus the $100-billion increase that it generated in consumption) into the numerator of Equation 22.1 and $100 billion into the denominator. Similarly, a decrease in net exports of $100 billion leads to a decrease in aggregate demand of $200 billion at each price level, as shown in Panel (b).

FIGURE 22.3 The Multiplier

A change in one component of aggregate demand shifts the aggregate demand curve by more than the initial change. In Panel (a), an initial increase of $100 billion of net exports shifts the aggregate demand curve to the right by $200 billion at each price level. In Panel (b), a decrease of net exports of $100 billion shifts the aggregate demand curve to the left by $200 billion. In this example, the multiplier is 2.

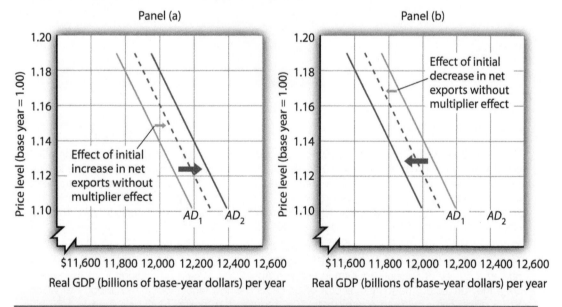

> **multiplier**
>
> The ratio of the change in the quantity of real GDP demanded at each price level to the initial change in one or more components of aggregate demand that produced it.

Key Takeaways

- Potential output is the level of output an economy can achieve when labor is employed at its natural level. When an economy fails to produce at its potential, the government or the central bank may try to push the economy toward its potential.

- The aggregate demand curve represents the total of consumption, investment, government purchases, and net exports at each price level in any period. It slopes downward because of the wealth effect on consumption, the interest rate effect on investment, and the international trade effect on net exports.

- The aggregate demand curve shifts when the quantity of real GDP demanded at each price level changes.
- The multiplier is the number by which we multiply an initial change in aggregate demand to obtain the amount by which the aggregate demand curve shifts at each price level as a result of the initial change.

Try It!

Explain the effect of each of the following on the aggregate demand curve for the United States:

1. A decrease in consumer optimism
2. An increase in real GDP in the countries that buy U.S. exports
3. An increase in the price level
4. An increase in government spending on highways

Case in Point: The Multiplied Economic Impact of SARS on China's Economy

Source: © Shutterstock, Inc.

Severe Acute Respiratory Syndrome (SARS), an atypical pneumonia-like disease, broke onto the world scene in late 2002. In March 2003, the World Health Organization (WHO) issued its first worldwide alert and a month later its first travel advisory, which recommended that travelers avoid Hong Kong and the southern province of China, Guangdong. Over the next few months, additional travel advisories were issued for other parts of China, Taiwan, and briefly for Toronto, Canada. By the end of June, all WHO travel advisories had been removed.

To estimate the overall impact of SARS on the Chinese economy in 2003, economists Wen Hai, Zhong Zhao, and Jian Want of Peking University's China Center for Economic Research conducted a survey of Beijing's tourism industry in April 2003. Based on findings from the Beijing area, they projected the tourism sector of China as a whole would lose $16.8 billion—of which $10.8 billion came from an approximate 50% reduction in foreign tourist revenue and $6 billion from curtailed domestic tourism, as holiday celebrations were cancelled and domestic travel restrictions imposed.

To figure out the total impact of SARS on China's economy, they argued that the multiplier for tourism revenue in China is between 2 and 3. Since the SARS outbreak only began to have a major economic impact after March, they assumed a smaller multiplier of 1.5 for all of 2003. They thus predicted that the Chinese economy would be $25.3 billion smaller in 2003 as a result of SARS.

Source: *Based on Wen Hai, Zhong Zhao, and Jian Wan, "The Short-Term Impact of SARS on the Chinese Economy," Asian Economic Papers 3, no. 1 (Winter 2004): 57–61.*

Answer to Try It! Problems

1. A decline in consumer optimism would cause the aggregate demand curve to shift to the left. If consumers are more pessimistic about the future, they are likely to cut purchases, especially of major items.

2. An increase in the real GDP of other countries would increase the demand for U.S. exports and cause the aggregate demand curve to shift to the right. Higher incomes in other countries will make consumers in those countries more willing and able to buy U.S. goods.

3. An increase in the price level corresponds to a movement up along the unchanged aggregate demand curve. At the higher price level, the consumption, investment, and net export components of aggregate demand will all fall; that is, there will be a reduction in the total quantity of goods and services demanded, but not a shift of the aggregate demand curve itself.

4. An increase in government spending on highways means an increase in government purchases. The aggregate demand curve would shift to the right.

22.3 Aggregate Demand and Aggregate Supply: The Long Run and the Short Run

Learning Objectives

1. Distinguish between the short run and the long run, as these terms are used in macroeconomics.

2. Draw a hypothetical long-run aggregate supply curve and explain what it shows about the natural levels of employment and output at various price levels, given changes in aggregate demand.

3. Draw a hypothetical short-run aggregate supply curve, explain why it slopes upward, and explain why it may shift; that is, distinguish between a change in the aggregate quantity of goods and services supplied and a change in short-run aggregate supply.

4. Discuss various explanations for wage and price stickiness.

5. Explain and illustrate what is meant by equilibrium in the short run and relate the equilibrium to potential output.

short run

In macroeconomic
analysis, a period in which
wages and some other
prices are sticky and do
not respond to changes in
economic conditions.

sticky price

A price that is slow to
adjust to its equilibrium
level, creating sustained
periods of shortage or
surplus.

long run

In macroeconomic
analysis, a period in which
wages and prices are
flexible.

In macroeconomics, we seek to understand two types of equilibria, one corresponding to the short run and the other corresponding to the long run. The **short run** in macroeconomic analysis is a period in which wages and some other prices do not respond to changes in economic conditions. In certain markets, as economic conditions change, prices (including wages) may not adjust quickly enough to maintain equilibrium in these markets. A **sticky price** is a price that is slow to adjust to its equilibrium level, creating sustained periods of shortage or surplus. Wage and price stickiness prevent the economy from achieving its natural level of employment and its potential output. In contrast, the **long run** in macroeconomic analysis is a period in which wages and prices are flexible. In the long run, employment will move to its natural level and real GDP to potential.

We begin with a discussion of long-run macroeconomic equilibrium, because this type of equilibrium allows us to see the macroeconomy after full market adjustment has been achieved. In contrast, in the short run, price or wage stickiness is an obstacle to full adjustment. Why these deviations from the potential level of output occur and what the implications are for the macroeconomy will be discussed in the section on short-run macroeconomic equilibrium.

The Long Run

As we saw in a previous chapter, the natural level of employment occurs where the real wage adjusts so that the quantity of labor demanded equals the quantity of labor supplied. When the economy achieves its natural level of employment, it achieves its potential level of output. We will see that real GDP eventually moves to potential, because all wages and prices are assumed to be flexible in the long run.

Long-Run Aggregate Supply

**long-run aggregate
supply (LRAS) curve**

A graphical representation
that relates the level of
output produced by firms
to the price level in the
long run.

The **long-run aggregate supply (LRAS) curve** relates the level of output produced by firms to the price level in the long run. In Panel (b) of Figure 22.4, the long-run aggregate supply curve is a vertical line at the economy's potential level of output. There is a single real wage at which employment reaches its natural level. In Panel (a) of Figure 22.4, only a real wage of ω_e generates natural employment L_e. The economy could, however, achieve this real wage with any of an infinitely large set of nominal wage and price-level combinations. Suppose, for example, that the equilibrium real wage (the ratio of wages to the price level) is 1.5. We could have that with a nominal wage level of 1.5 and a price level of 1.0, a nominal wage level of 1.65 and a price level of 1.1, a nominal wage level of 3.0 and a price level of 2.0, and so on.

FIGURE 22.4 Natural Employment and Long-Run Aggregate Supply

When the economy achieves its natural level of employment, as shown in Panel (a) at the intersection of the demand and supply curves for labor, it achieves its potential output, as shown in Panel (b) by the vertical long-run aggregate supply curve *LRAS* at Y_P.

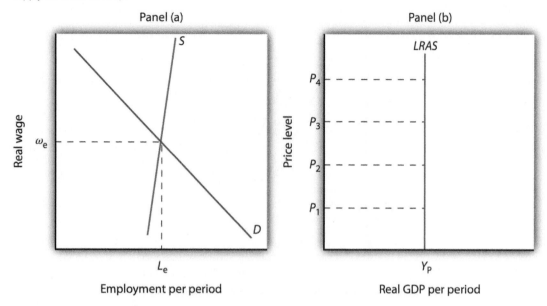

In Panel (b) we see price levels ranging from P_1 to P_4. Higher price levels would require higher nominal wages to create a real wage of ω_e, and flexible nominal wages would achieve that in the long run.

In the long run, then, the economy can achieve its natural level of employment and potential output at any price level. This conclusion gives us our long-run aggregate supply curve. With only one level of output at any price level, the long-run aggregate supply curve is a vertical line at the economy's potential level of output of Y_P.

Equilibrium Levels of Price and Output in the Long Run

The intersection of the economy's aggregate demand curve and the long-run aggregate supply curve determines its equilibrium real GDP and price level in the long run. Figure 22.5 depicts an economy in long-run equilibrium. With aggregate demand at AD_1 and the long-run aggregate supply curve as shown, real GDP is $12,000 billion per year and the price level is 1.14. If aggregate demand increases to AD_2, long-run equilibrium will be reestablished at real GDP of $12,000 billion per year, but at a higher price level of 1.18. If aggregate demand decreases to AD_3, long-run equilibrium will still be at real GDP of $12,000 billion per year, but with the now lower price level of 1.10.

FIGURE 22.5 Long-Run Equilibrium

Long-run equilibrium occurs at the intersection of the aggregate demand curve and the long-run aggregate supply curve. For the three aggregate demand curves shown, long-run equilibrium occurs at three different price levels, but always at an output level of $12,000 billion per year, which corresponds to potential output.

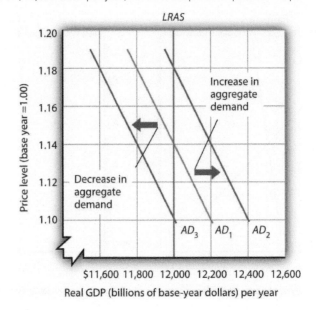

The Short Run

Analysis of the macroeconomy in the short run—a period in which stickiness of wages and prices may prevent the economy from operating at potential output—helps explain how deviations of real GDP from potential output can and do occur. We will explore the effects of changes in aggregate demand and in short-run aggregate supply in this section.

Short-Run Aggregate Supply

FIGURE 22.6 Deriving the Short-Run Aggregate Supply Curve

The economy shown here is in long-run equilibrium at the intersection of AD_1 with the long-run aggregate supply curve. If aggregate demand increases to AD_2, in the short run, both real GDP and the price level rise. If aggregate demand decreases to AD_3, in the short run, both real GDP and the price level fall. A line drawn through points A, B, and C traces out the short-run aggregate supply curve $SRAS$.

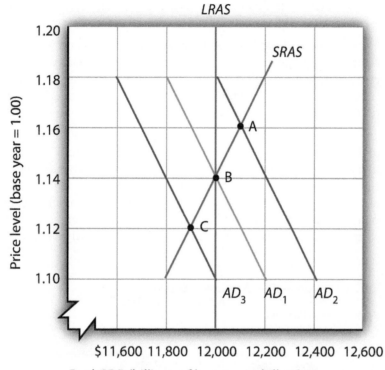

The model of aggregate demand and long-run aggregate supply predicts that the economy will eventually move toward its potential output. To see how nominal wage and price stickiness can cause real GDP to be either above or below potential in the short run, consider the response of the economy to a change in aggregate demand. Figure 22.6 shows an economy that has been operating at potential output of $12,000 billion and a price level of 1.14. This occurs at the intersection of AD_1 with the long-run aggregate supply curve at point B. Now suppose that the aggregate demand curve shifts to the right (to AD_2). This could occur as a result of an increase in exports. (The shift from AD_1 to AD_2 includes the multiplied effect of the increase in exports.) At the price level of 1.14, there is now excess demand and pressure on prices to rise. If all prices in the economy adjusted quickly, the economy would quickly settle at potential output of $12,000 billion, but at a higher price level (1.18 in this case).

Is it possible to expand output above potential? Yes. It may be the case, for example, that some people who were in the labor force but were frictionally or structurally unemployed find work because of the ease of getting jobs at the going nominal wage in such an environment. The result is an economy operating at point A in Figure 22.6 at a higher price level and with output temporarily above potential.

Consider next the effect of a reduction in aggregate demand (to AD_3), possibly due to a reduction in investment. As the price level starts to fall, output also falls. The economy finds itself at a price level–output combination at which real GDP is below potential, at point C. Again, price stickiness is to blame. The prices firms receive are falling with the reduction in demand. Without corresponding reductions in nominal wages, there will be an increase in the real wage. Firms will employ less labor and produce less output.

short-run aggregate supply (SRAS) curve

A graphical representation of the relationship between production and the price level in the short run.

change in the aggregate quantity of goods and services supplied

Movement along the short-run aggregate supply curve.

change in short-run aggregate supply

A change in the aggregate quantity of goods and services supplied at every price level in the short run.

By examining what happens as aggregate demand shifts over a period when price adjustment is incomplete, we can trace out the short-run aggregate supply curve by drawing a line through points A, B, and C. The **short-run aggregate supply (SRAS) curve** is a graphical representation of the relationship between production and the price level in the short run. Among the factors held constant in drawing a short-run aggregate supply curve are the capital stock, the stock of natural resources, the level of technology, and the prices of factors of production.

A change in the price level produces a **change in the aggregate quantity of goods and services supplied** and is illustrated by the movement along the short-run aggregate supply curve. This occurs between points A, B, and C in Figure 22.6.

A change in the quantity of goods and services supplied at every price level in the short run is a **change in short-run aggregate supply**. Changes in the factors held constant in drawing the short-run aggregate supply curve shift the curve. (These factors may also shift the long-run aggregate supply curve; we will discuss them along with other determinants of long-run aggregate supply in the next chapter.)

One type of event that would shift the short-run aggregate supply curve is an increase in the price of a natural resource such as oil. An increase in the price of natural resources or any other factor of production, all other things unchanged, raises the cost of production and leads to a reduction in short-run aggregate supply. In Panel (a) of Figure 22.7, $SRAS_1$ shifts leftward to $SRAS_2$. A decrease in the price of a natural resource would lower the cost of production and, other things unchanged, would allow greater production from the economy's stock of resources and would shift the short-run aggregate supply curve to the right; such a shift is shown in Panel (b) by a shift from $SRAS_1$ to $SRAS_3$.

FIGURE 22.7 Changes in Short-Run Aggregate Supply

A reduction in short-run aggregate supply shifts the curve from $SRAS_1$ to $SRAS_2$ in Panel (a). An increase shifts it to the right to $SRAS_3$, as shown in Panel (b).

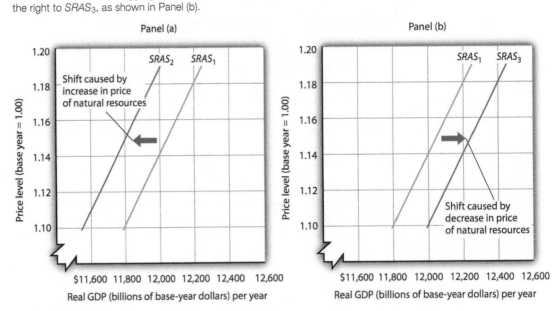

Reasons for Wage and Price Stickiness

Wage or price stickiness means that the economy may not always be operating at potential. Rather, the economy may operate either above or below potential output in the short run. Correspondingly, the overall unemployment rate will be below or above the natural level.

Many prices observed throughout the economy do adjust quickly to changes in market conditions so that equilibrium, once lost, is quickly regained. Prices for fresh food and shares of common stock are two such examples.

Other prices, though, adjust more slowly. Nominal wages, the price of labor, adjust very slowly. We will first look at why nominal wages are sticky, due to their association with the unemployment rate, a variable of great interest in macroeconomics, and then at other prices that may be sticky.

Wage Stickiness

Wage contracts fix nominal wages for the life of the contract. The length of wage contracts varies from one week or one month for temporary employees, to one year (teachers and professors often have such contracts), to three years (for most union workers employed under major collective bargaining agreements). The existence of such explicit contracts means that both workers and firms accept some wage at the time of negotiating, even though economic conditions could change while the agreement is still in force.

Think about your own job or a job you once had. Chances are you go to work each day knowing what your wage will be. Your wage does not fluctuate from one day to the next with changes in demand or supply. You may have a formal contract with your employer that specifies what your wage will be over some period. Or you may have an informal understanding that sets your wage. Whatever the nature of your agreement, your wage is "stuck" over the period of the agreement. Your wage is an example of a sticky price.

One reason workers and firms may be willing to accept long-term nominal wage contracts is that negotiating a contract is a costly process. Both parties must keep themselves adequately informed about market conditions. Where unions are involved, wage negotiations raise the possibility of a labor strike, an eventuality that firms may prepare for by accumulating additional inventories, also a costly process. Even when unions are not involved, time and energy spent discussing wages takes away from time and energy spent producing goods and services. In addition, workers may simply prefer knowing that their nominal wage will be fixed for some period of time.

Some contracts do attempt to take into account changing economic conditions, such as inflation, through cost-of-living adjustments, but even these relatively simple contingencies are not as widespread as one might think. One reason might be that a firm is concerned that while the aggregate price level is rising, the prices for the goods and services it sells might not be moving at the same rate. Also, cost-of-living or other contingencies add complexity to contracts that both sides may want to avoid.

Even markets where workers are not employed under explicit contracts seem to behave as if such contracts existed. In these cases, wage stickiness may stem from a desire to avoid the same uncertainty and adjustment costs that explicit contracts avert.

Finally, minimum wage laws prevent wages from falling below a legal minimum, even if unemployment is rising. Unskilled workers are particularly vulnerable to shifts in aggregate demand.

Price Stickiness

Rigidity of other prices becomes easier to explain in light of the arguments about nominal wage stickiness. Since wages are a major component of the overall cost of doing business, wage stickiness may lead to output price stickiness. With nominal wages stable, at least some firms can adopt a "wait and see" attitude before adjusting their prices. During this time, they can evaluate information about why sales are rising or falling (Is the change in demand temporary or permanent?) and try to assess likely reactions by consumers or competing firms in the industry to any price changes they might make (Will consumers be angered by a price increase, for example? Will competing firms match price changes?).

In the meantime, firms may prefer to adjust output and employment in response to changing market conditions, leaving product price alone. Quantity adjustments have costs, but firms may assume that the associated risks are smaller than those associated with price adjustments.

Another possible explanation for price stickiness is the notion that there are adjustment costs associated with changing prices. In some cases, firms must print new price lists and catalogs, and notify customers of price changes. Doing this too often could jeopardize customer relations.

Yet another explanation of price stickiness is that firms may have explicit long-term contracts to sell their products to other firms at specified prices. For example, electric utilities often buy their inputs of coal or oil under long-term contracts.

Taken together, these reasons for wage and price stickiness explain why aggregate price adjustment may be incomplete in the sense that the change in the price level is insufficient to maintain real GDP at its potential level. These reasons do not lead to the conclusion that no price adjustments occur. But the adjustments require some time. During this time, the economy may remain above or below its potential level of output.

Equilibrium Levels of Price and Output in the Short Run

To illustrate how we will use the model of aggregate demand and aggregate supply, let us examine the impact of two events: an increase in the cost of health care and an increase in government purchases. The first reduces short-run aggregate supply; the second increases aggregate demand. Both events change equilibrium real GDP and the price level in the short run.

A Change in the Cost of Health Care

In the United States, most people receive health insurance for themselves and their families through their employers. In fact, it is quite common for employers to pay a large percentage of employees' health insurance premiums, and this benefit is often written into labor contracts. As the cost of health care has gone up over time, firms have had to pay higher and higher health insurance premiums. With nominal wages fixed in the short run, an increase in health insurance premiums paid by firms raises the cost of employing each worker. It affects the cost of production in the same way that higher wages would. The result of higher health insurance premiums is that firms will choose to employ fewer workers.

Suppose the economy is operating initially at the short-run equilibrium at the intersection of AD_1 and $SRAS_1$, with a real GDP of Y_1 and a price level of P_1, as shown in Figure 22.8. This is the initial equilibrium price and output in the short run. The increase in labor cost shifts the short-run aggregate supply curve to $SRAS_2$. The price level rises to P_2 and real GDP falls to Y_2.

FIGURE 22.8 An Increase in Health Insurance Premiums Paid by Firms
An increase in health insurance premiums paid by firms increases labor costs, reducing short-run aggregate supply from $SRAS_1$ to $SRAS_2$. The price level rises from P_1 to P_2 and output falls from Y_1 to Y_2.

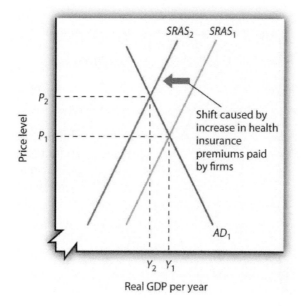

Real GDP per year

A reduction in health insurance premiums would have the opposite effect. There would be a shift to the right in the short-run aggregate supply curve with pressure on the price level to fall and real GDP to rise.

A Change in Government Purchases

Suppose the federal government increases its spending for highway construction. This circumstance leads to an increase in U.S. government purchases and an increase in aggregate demand.

Assuming no other changes affect aggregate demand, the increase in government purchases shifts the aggregate demand curve by a multiplied amount of the initial increase in government purchases to AD_2 in Figure 22.9. Real GDP rises from Y_1 to Y_2, while the price level rises from P_1 to P_2. Notice that the increase in real GDP is less than it would have been if the price level had not risen.

FIGURE 22.9 An Increase in Government Purchases

An increase in government purchases boosts aggregate demand from AD_1 to AD_2. Short-run equilibrium is at the intersection of AD_2 and the short-run aggregate supply curve $SRAS_1$. The price level rises to P_2 and real GDP rises to Y_2.

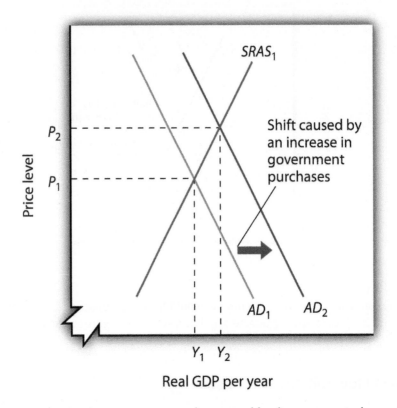

In contrast, a reduction in government purchases would reduce aggregate demand. The aggregate demand curve shifts to the left, putting pressure on both the price level and real GDP to fall.

In the short run, real GDP and the price level are determined by the intersection of the aggregate demand and short-run aggregate supply curves. Recall, however, that the short run is a period in which sticky prices may prevent the economy from reaching its natural level of employment and potential output. In the next section, we will see how the model adjusts to move the economy to long-run equilibrium and what, if anything, can be done to steer the economy toward the natural level of employment and potential output.

Key Takeaways

- The short run in macroeconomics is a period in which wages and some other prices are sticky. The long run is a period in which full wage and price flexibility, and market adjustment, has been achieved, so that the economy is at the natural level of employment and potential output.
- The long-run aggregate supply curve is a vertical line at the potential level of output. The intersection of the economy's aggregate demand and long-run aggregate supply curves determines its equilibrium real GDP and price level in the long run.
- The short-run aggregate supply curve is an upward-sloping curve that shows the quantity of total output that will be produced at each price level in the short run. Wage and price stickiness account for the short-run aggregate supply curve's upward slope.

- Changes in prices of factors of production shift the short-run aggregate supply curve. In addition, changes in the capital stock, the stock of natural resources, and the level of technology can also cause the short-run aggregate supply curve to shift.

- In the short run, the equilibrium price level and the equilibrium level of total output are determined by the intersection of the aggregate demand and the short-run aggregate supply curves. In the short run, output can be either below or above potential output.

Try It!

The tools we have covered in this section can be used to understand the Great Depression of the 1930s. We know that investment and consumption began falling in late 1929. The reductions were reinforced by plunges in net exports and government purchases over the next four years. In addition, nominal wages plunged 26% between 1929 and 1933. We also know that real GDP in 1933 was 30% below real GDP in 1929. Use the tools of aggregate demand and short-run aggregate supply to graph and explain what happened to the economy between 1929 and 1933.

Case in Point: The U.S. Recession of 2001

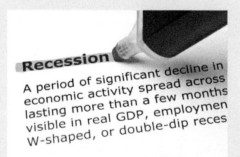

Source: © Shutterstock, Inc.

What were the causes of the U.S. recession of 2001? Economist Kevin Kliesen of the Federal Reserve Bank of St. Louis points to four factors that, taken together, shifted the aggregate demand curve to the left and kept it there for a long enough period to keep real GDP falling for about nine months. They were the fall in stock market prices, the decrease in business investment both for computers and software and in structures, the decline in the real value of exports, and the aftermath of 9/11. Notable exceptions to this list of culprits were the behavior of consumer spending during the period and new residential housing, which falls into the investment category.

During the expansion in the late 1990s, a surging stock market probably made it easier for firms to raise funding for investment in both structures and information technology. Even though the stock market bubble burst well before the actual recession, the continuation of projects already underway delayed the decline in the investment component of GDP. Also, spending for information technology was probably prolonged as firms dealt with Y2K computing issues, that is, computer problems associated with the change in the date from 1999 to 2000. Most computers used only two digits to indicate the year, and when the year changed from '99 to '00, computers did not know how to interpret the change, and extensive reprogramming of computers was required.

Real exports fell during the recession because (1) the dollar was strong during the period and (2) real GDP growth in the rest of the world fell almost 5% from 2000 to 2001.

Then, the terrorist attacks of 9/11, which literally shut down transportation and financial markets for several days, may have prolonged these negative tendencies just long enough to turn what might otherwise have been a mild decline into enough of a downtown to qualify the period as a recession.

During this period the measured price level was essentially stable—with the implicit price deflator rising by less than 1%. Thus, while the aggregate demand curve shifted left as a result of all the reasons given above, there was also a leftward shift in the short-run aggregate supply curve.

Source: *Based on Kevin L. Kliesen, "The 2001 Recession: How Was It Different and What Developments May Have Caused It?," The Federal Reserve Bank of St. Louis Review, September/ October 2003, 23–37.*

Answer to Try It! Problem

All components of aggregate demand (consumption, investment, government purchases, and net exports) declined between 1929 and 1933. Thus the aggregate demand curve shifted markedly to the left, moving from AD_{1929} to AD_{1933}. The reduction in nominal wages corresponds to an increase in short-run aggregate supply from $SRAS_{1929}$ to $SRAS_{1933}$. Since real GDP in 1933 was less than real GDP in 1929, we know that the movement in the aggregate demand curve was greater than that of the short-run aggregate supply curve.

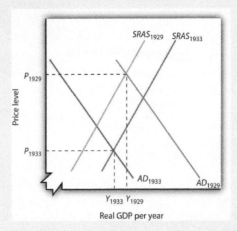

22.4 Recessionary and Inflationary Gaps and Long-Run Macroeconomic Equilibrium

Learning Objectives

1. Explain and illustrate graphically recessionary and inflationary gaps and relate these gaps to what is happening in the labor market.
2. Identify the various policy choices available when an economy experiences an inflationary or recessionary gap and discuss some of the pros and cons that make these choices controversial.

The intersection of the economy's aggregate demand and short-run aggregate supply curves determines equilibrium real GDP and price level in the short run. The intersection of aggregate demand and long-run aggregate supply determines its long-run equilibrium. In this section we will examine the process through which an economy moves from equilibrium in the short run to equilibrium in the long run.

The long run puts a nation's macroeconomic house in order: only frictional and structural unemployment remain, and the price level is stabilized. In the short run, stickiness of nominal wages and other prices can prevent the economy from achieving its potential output. Actual output may exceed or fall short of potential output. In such a situation the economy operates with a gap. When output is above potential, employment is above the natural level of employment. When output is below potential, employment is below the natural level.

Recessionary and Inflationary Gaps

At any time, real GDP and the price level are determined by the intersection of the aggregate demand and short-run aggregate supply curves. If employment is below the natural level of employment, real GDP will be below potential. The aggregate demand and short-run aggregate supply curves will intersect to the left of the long-run aggregate supply curve.

Suppose an economy's natural level of employment is L_e, shown in Panel (a) of Figure 22.10. This level of employment is achieved at a real wage of ω_e. Suppose, however, that the initial real wage ω_1 exceeds this equilibrium value. Employment at L_1 falls short of the natural level. A lower level of employment produces a lower level of output; the aggregate demand and short-run aggregate supply curves, AD and SRAS, intersect to the left of the long-run aggregate supply curve LRAS in Panel (b). The gap between the level of real GDP and potential output, when real GDP is less than potential, is called a **recessionary gap**.

recessionary gap

The gap between the level of real GDP and potential output, when real GDP is less than potential.

FIGURE 22.10 A Recessionary Gap

If employment is below the natural level, as shown in Panel (a), then output must be below potential. Panel (b) shows the recessionary gap $Y_P - Y_1$, which occurs when the aggregate demand curve AD and the short-run aggregate supply curve SRAS intersect to the left of the long-run aggregate supply curve LRAS.

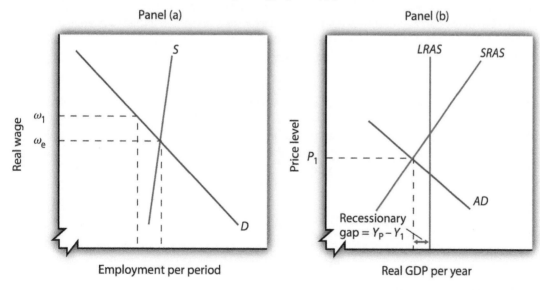

Just as employment can fall short of its natural level, it can also exceed it. If employment is greater than its natural level, real GDP will also be greater than its potential level. Figure 22.11 shows an economy with a natural level of employment of L_e in Panel (a) and potential output of Y_P in Panel (b). If the real wage ω_1 is less than the equilibrium real wage ω_e, then employment L_1 will exceed the natural level. As a result, real GDP, Y_1, exceeds potential. The gap between the level of

inflationary gap

The gap between the level of real GDP and potential output, when real GDP is greater than potential.

real GDP and potential output, when real GDP is greater than potential, is called an **inflationary gap**. In Panel (b), the inflationary gap equals $Y_1 - Y_P$.

FIGURE 22.11 An Inflationary Gap

Panel (a) shows that if employment is above the natural level, then output must be above potential. The inflationary gap, shown in Panel (b), equals $Y_1 - Y_P$. The aggregate demand curve *AD* and the short-run aggregate supply curve *SRAS* intersect to the right of the long-run aggregate supply curve *LRAS*.

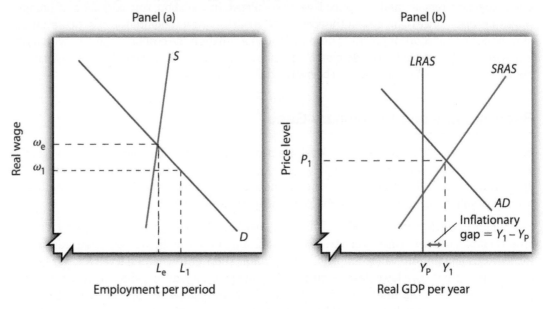

Restoring Long-Run Macroeconomic Equilibrium

We have already seen that the aggregate demand curve shifts in response to a change in consumption, investment, government purchases, or net exports. The short-run aggregate supply curve shifts in response to changes in the prices of factors of production, the quantities of factors of production available, or technology. Now we will see how the economy responds to a shift in aggregate demand or short-run aggregate supply using two examples presented earlier: a change in government purchases and a change in health-care costs. By returning to these examples, we will be able to distinguish the long-run response from the short-run response.

A Shift in Aggregate Demand: An Increase in Government Purchases

Suppose an economy is initially in equilibrium at potential output YP as in Figure 22.12. Because the economy is operating at its potential, the labor market must be in equilibrium; the quantities of labor demanded and supplied are equal.

FIGURE 22.12 Long-Run Adjustment to an Inflationary Gap
An increase in aggregate demand to AD_2 boosts real GDP to Y_2 and the price level to P_2, creating an inflationary gap of $Y_2 - Y_P$. In the long run, as price and nominal wages increase, the short-run aggregate supply curve moves to $SRAS_2$. Real GDP returns to potential.

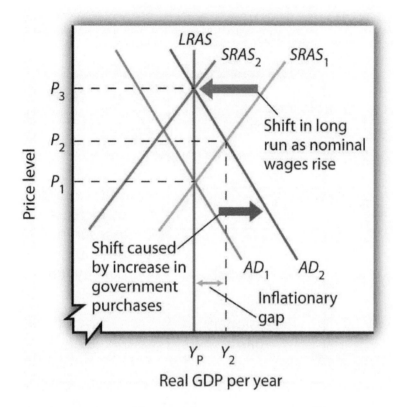

Now suppose aggregate demand increases because one or more of its components (consumption, investment, government purchases, and net exports) has increased at each price level. For example, suppose government purchases increase. The aggregate demand curve shifts from AD_1 to AD_2 in Figure 22.12. That will increase real GDP to Y_2 and force the price level up to P_2 in the short run. The higher price level, combined with a fixed nominal wage, results in a lower real wage. Firms employ more workers to supply the increased output.

The economy's new production level Y_2 exceeds potential output. Employment exceeds its natural level. The economy with output of Y_2 and price level of P_2 is only in short-run equilibrium; there is an inflationary gap equal to the difference between Y_2 and Y_P. Because real GDP is above potential, there will be pressure on prices to rise further.

Ultimately, the nominal wage will rise as workers seek to restore their lost purchasing power. As the nominal wage rises, the short-run aggregate supply curve will begin shifting to the left. It will continue to shift as long as the nominal wage rises, and the nominal wage will rise as long as there is an inflationary gap. These shifts in short-run aggregate supply, however, will reduce real GDP and thus begin to close this gap. When the short-run aggregate supply curve reaches $SRAS_2$, the economy will have returned to its potential output, and employment will have returned to its natural level. These adjustments will close the inflationary gap.

A Shift in Short-Run Aggregate Supply: An Increase in the Cost of Health Care

Again suppose, with an aggregate demand curve at AD_1 and a short-run aggregate supply at $SRAS_1$, an economy is initially in equilibrium at its potential output Y_P, at a price level of P_1, as shown in Figure 22.13. Now suppose that the short-run aggregate supply curve shifts owing to a rise in the cost of health care. As we explained earlier, because health insurance premiums are paid primarily by firms for their workers, an increase in premiums raises the cost of production and causes a reduction in the short-run aggregate supply curve from $SRAS_1$ to $SRAS_2$.

FIGURE 22.13 Long-Run Adjustment to a Recessionary Gap
A decrease in aggregate supply from $SRAS_1$ to $SRAS_2$ reduces real GDP to Y_2 and raises the price level to P_2, creating a recessionary gap of $Y_P - Y_2$. In the long run, as prices and nominal wages decrease, the short-run aggregate supply curve moves back to $SRAS_1$ and real GDP returns to potential.

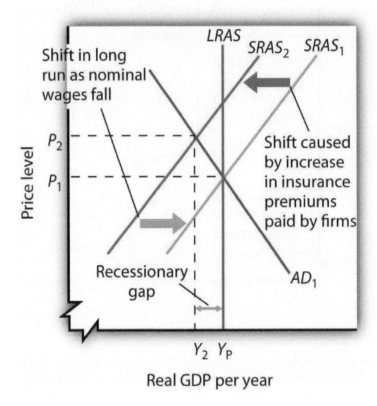

As a result, the price level rises to P_2 and real GDP falls to Y_2. The economy now has a recessionary gap equal to the difference between Y_P and Y_2. Notice that this situation is particularly disagreeable, because both unemployment and the price level rose.

With real GDP below potential, though, there will eventually be pressure on the price level to fall. Increased unemployment also puts pressure on nominal wages to fall. In the long run, the short-run aggregate supply curve shifts back to $SRAS_1$. In this case, real GDP returns to potential at Y_P, the price level falls back to P_1, and employment returns to its natural level. These adjustments will close the recessionary gap.

How sticky prices and nominal wages are will determine the time it takes for the economy to return to potential. People often expect the government or the central bank to respond in some way to try to close gaps. This issue is addressed next.

Gaps and Public Policy

If the economy faces a gap, how do we get from that situation to potential output?

Gaps present us with two alternatives. First, we can do nothing. In the long run, real wages will adjust to the equilibrium level, employment will move to its natural level, and real GDP will move to its potential. Second, we can do something. Faced with a recessionary or an inflationary gap, policy makers can undertake policies aimed at shifting the aggregate demand or short-run aggregate supply curves in a way that moves the economy to its potential. A policy choice to take no action to try to close a recessionary or an inflationary gap, but to allow the economy to adjust on its own to its potential output, is a **nonintervention policy**. A policy in which the government or central bank acts to move the economy to its potential output is called a **stabilization policy**.

Nonintervention or Expansionary Policy?

Figure 22.14 illustrates the alternatives for closing a recessionary gap. In both panels, the economy starts with a real GDP of Y_1 and a price level of P_1. There is a recessionary gap equal to $Y_P - Y_1$. In Panel (a), the economy closes the gap through a process of self-correction. Real and nominal wages will fall as long as employment remains below the natural level. Lower nominal wages shift the short-run aggregate supply curve. The process is a gradual one, however, given the stickiness of nominal wages, but after a series of shifts in the short-run aggregate supply curve, the economy moves toward equilibrium at a price level of P_2 and its potential output of Y_P.

FIGURE 22.14 Alternatives in Closing a Recessionary Gap

Panel (a) illustrates a gradual closing of a recessionary gap. Under a nonintervention policy, short-run aggregate supply shifts from $SRAS_1$ to $SRAS_2$. Panel (b) shows the effects of expansionary policy acting on aggregate demand to close the gap.

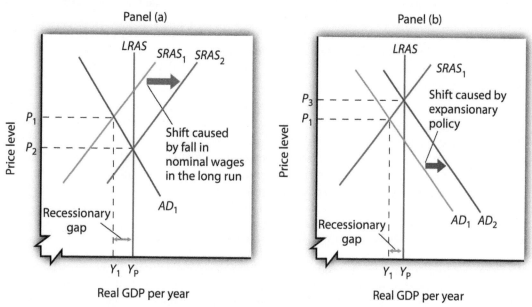

Panel (b) illustrates the stabilization alternative. Faced with an economy operating below its potential, public officials act to stimulate aggregate demand. For example, the government can increase government purchases of goods and services or cut taxes. Tax cuts leave people with more after-tax income to spend, boost their consumption, and increase aggregate demand. As AD_1 shifts to AD_2 in Panel (b) of Figure 22.14, the economy achieves output of Y_P, but at a higher price level, P_3. A stabilization policy designed to increase real GDP is known as an **expansionary policy**.

Nonintervention or Contractionary Policy?

Figure 22.15 illustrates the alternatives for closing an inflationary gap. Employment in an economy with an inflationary gap exceeds its natural level—the quantity of labor demanded exceeds the long-run supply of labor. A nonintervention policy would rely on nominal wages to rise in response

nonintervention policy

A policy choice to take no action to try to close a recessionary or an inflationary gap, but to allow the economy to adjust on its own to its potential output.

stabilization policy

A policy in which the government or central bank acts to move the economy to its potential output.

expansionary policy

A stabilization policy designed to increase real GDP.

to the shortage of labor. As nominal wages rise, the short-run aggregate supply curve begins to shift, as shown in Panel (a), bringing the economy to its potential output when it reaches $SRAS_2$ and P_2.

FIGURE 22.15 Alternatives in Closing an Inflationary Gap

Panel (a) illustrates a gradual closing of an inflationary gap. Under a nonintervention policy, short-run aggregate supply shifts from $SRAS_1$ to $SRAS_2$. Panel (b) shows the effects of contractionary policy to reduce aggregate demand from AD_1 to AD_2 in order to close the gap.

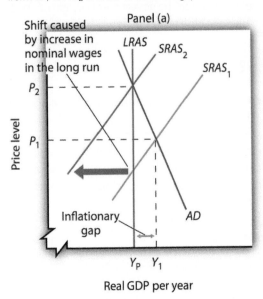
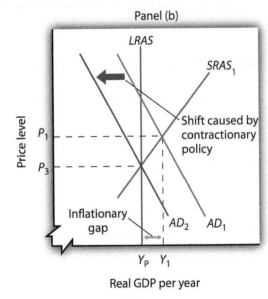

contractionary policy

A stabilization policy designed to reduce real GDP.

fiscal policy

The use of government purchases, transfer payments, and taxes to influence the level of economic activity.

monetary policy

The use of central bank policies to influence the level of economic activity.

A stabilization policy that reduces the level of GDP is a **contractionary policy**. Such a policy would aim at shifting the aggregate demand curve from AD_1 to AD_2 to close the gap, as shown in Panel (b). A policy to shift the aggregate demand curve to the left would return real GDP to its potential at a price level of P_3.

For both kinds of gaps, a combination of letting market forces in the economy close part of the gap and of using stabilization policy to close the rest of the gap is also an option. Later chapters will explain stabilization policies in more detail, but there are essentially two types of stabilization policy: fiscal policy and monetary policy. **Fiscal policy** is the use of government purchases, transfer payments, and taxes to influence the level of economic activity. **Monetary policy** is the use of central bank policies to influence the level of economic activity.

To Intervene or Not to Intervene: An Introduction to the Controversy

How large are inflationary and recessionary gaps? Panel (a) of Figure 22.16 shows potential output versus the actual level of real GDP in the United States since 1960. Real GDP appears to follow potential output quite closely, although you see some periods where there have been inflationary or recessionary gaps. Panel (b) shows the sizes of these gaps expressed as percentages of potential output. The percentage gap is positive during periods of inflationary gaps and negative during periods of recessionary gaps. Over the last 50 years, the economy has seldom departed by more than 5% from its potential output. So the size and duration of the recessionary gap from 2009 to 2011 certainly stand out.

FIGURE 22.16 Real GDP and Potential Output

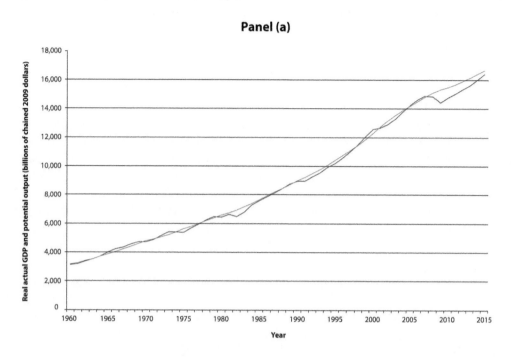

Panel (a) shows potential output (the blue line) and actual real GDP (the purple line) since 1960. Panel (b) shows the gap between potential and actual real GDP expressed as a percentage of potential output. Inflationary gaps are shown in green and recessionary gaps are shown in yellow.

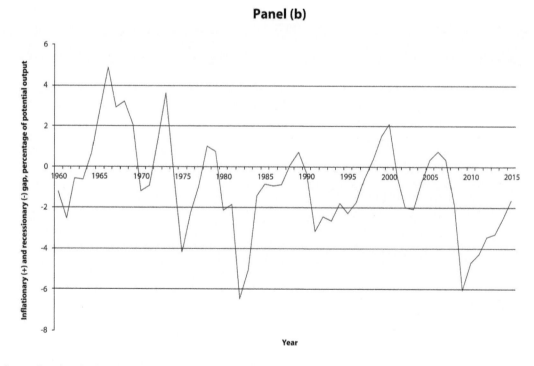

Source: Based on data from Bureau of Economic Analysis, NIPA Table 1.1.6 (revised November 26, 2014). Real Gross Domestic Product, Chained Dollars [Billions of chained (2009) dollars]. Seasonally adjusted at annual rates; Congressional Budget Office, The Budget and Economic Outlook: An Update, August 2016.

Panel (a) gives a long-run perspective on the economy. It suggests that the economy generally operates at about potential output. In Panel (a), the gaps seem minor. Panel (b) gives a short-run perspective; the view it gives emphasizes the gaps. Both of these perspectives are important. While it is reassuring to see that the economy is often close to potential, the years in which there are substantial gaps have real effects: Inflation or unemployment can harm people.

Some economists argue that stabilization policy can and should be used when recessionary or inflationary gaps exist. Others urge reliance on the economy's own ability to correct itself. They sometimes argue that the tools available to the public sector to influence aggregate demand are not likely to shift the curve, or they argue that the tools would shift the curve in a way that could do more harm than good.

Economists who advocate stabilization policies argue that prices are sufficiently sticky that the economy's own adjustment to its potential will be a slow process—and a painful one. For an economy with a recessionary gap, unacceptably high levels of unemployment will persist for too long a time. For an economy with an inflationary gap, the increased prices that occur as the short-run aggregate supply curve shifts upward impose too high an inflation rate in the short run. These economists believe it is far preferable to use stabilization policy to shift the aggregate demand curve in an effort to shorten the time the economy is subject to a gap.

Economists who favor a nonintervention approach accept the notion that stabilization policy can shift the aggregate demand curve. They argue, however, that such efforts are not nearly as simple in the real world as they may appear on paper. For example, policies to change real GDP may not affect the economy for months or even years. By the time the impact of the stabilization policy occurs, the state of the economy might have changed. Policy makers might choose an expansionary policy when a contractionary one is needed or vice versa. Other economists who favor nonintervention also question how sticky prices really are and if gaps even exist.

The debate over how policy makers should respond to recessionary and inflationary gaps is an ongoing one. These issues of nonintervention versus stabilization policies lie at the heart of the macroeconomic policy debate. We will return to them as we continue our analysis of the determination of output and the price level.

Key Takeaways

- When the aggregate demand and short-run aggregate supply curves intersect below potential output, the economy has a recessionary gap. When they intersect above potential output, the economy has an inflationary gap.
- Inflationary and recessionary gaps are closed as the real wage returns to equilibrium, where the quantity of labor demanded equals the quantity supplied. Because of nominal wage and price stickiness, however, such an adjustment takes time.
- When the economy has a gap, policy makers can choose to do nothing and let the economy return to potential output and the natural level of employment on its own. A policy to take no action to try to close a gap is a nonintervention policy.
- Alternatively, policy makers can choose to try to close a gap by using stabilization policy. Stabilization policy designed to increase real GDP is called expansionary policy. Stabilization policy designed to decrease real GDP is called contractionary policy.

Try It!

Using the scenario of the Great Depression of the 1930s, as analyzed in the previous Try It!, tell what kind of gap the U.S. economy faced in 1933, assuming the economy had been at potential output in 1929. Do you think the unemployment rate was above or below the natural rate of unemployment? How could the economy have been brought back to its potential output?

Case in Point: *This Time Is Different, Or Is It?*

Source: © Shutterstock, Inc.

In an analysis that spans 66 countries over nearly eight centuries, economists Carmen Reinhart and Kenneth Rogoff investigate hundreds of financial crises and the economic busts each leaves in its wake. With a database that includes crisis episodes that go back as far as 12th-century China and medieval Europe and continue until the financial crisis of 2007–2008, the authors look at the patterns of economic behavior that characterize the periods leading up to financial crises and the patterns that characterize the recoveries.

They argue that looking over a long period of history is necessary because financial crises are "rare" events. Financial crises occur at varying intervals, and researchers studying a period of 25 years or so may not encounter the equivalent of a 100-year, category 5 hurricane that hits a major, low-lying city with a faulty levee system.

In general, such crises follow periods of relative economic calm. For example, the period in the United States from the mid-1980s until 2007 was often referred to as the Great Moderation. During such periods, inflationary and recessionary gaps may occur, but they are relatively small and short-lived. Societies begin to feel that they have tamed the business cycle, that policy makers have gotten smarter, and that moderation will continue.

But then it happens. The accumulation of too much debt by governments, businesses, or consumers leads to a financial meltdown. As housing prices are run up, for example, people tend to find ways to justify their heavy borrowing and to rationalize the ascent in prices: Demographics have changed; mortgage terms have improved; the regulation we have put in place is better this time; it's better to buy now, before prices go up even more; housing prices won't fall. Memories of the last crisis fade. "This time is different," they argue.

But Reinhart and Rogoff provide convincing evidence that "this time" is usually not different. Large-scale debt buildups lead to crises of confidence, and a financial crisis ensues. The aftermath is typically a severe and prolonged recessionary gap. On average, they find the following to be true:

1. The collapse in asset market prices is large and long-lasting. Housing prices decline an average of 35% over 6 years, and stock prices decline an average of 56% over 3.5 years.

2. Peak-to-trough GDP falls 9% on average, and the recession averages 2 years in length.

3. The unemployment rate rises 7 percentage points over a 4-year period.

4. Government debt swells due to bailout costs and, more importantly, because tax revenues fall off due to lower GDP.

5. V-shaped recoveries in stock prices are more common than V-shaped recoveries in housing prices or employment.

To what extent is the financial crisis of the late 2000s likely to follow this typical pattern? The authors argue that experience with expansionary fiscal policy in such circumstances is actually quite limited. Most often, governments are shut out of borrowing markets when crises hit. Japan's government explicitly tried to implement fiscal stimulus, but the authors warn against drawing conclusions from one such example. The authors caution that governments should weigh any potential benefit of fiscal stimulus against the problem of higher public debt. They also note that central banks in 2007–2008 acted quickly and aggressively with expansionary monetary policies. But, they caution against "push[ing] too far the conceit that we are smarter than our predecessors" (p. 238). The global nature of the current situation only adds to the difficulty of recovering fully.

There was a company failure around 15 years ago that looked like a big deal at the time, but now seems like little more than a blip. The authors quote a trader who, during this event, presciently remarked, "More money has been lost because of four words than at the point of a gun. Those words are 'This time is different.'"

Source: Based on Carmen M. Reinhart and Kenneth S. Rogoff, This Time Is Different: Eight Centuries of Financial Folly (Princeton: Princeton University Press, 2009).

Answer to Try It! Problem

To the graph in the previous Try It! problem we add the long-run aggregate supply curve to show that, with output below potential, the U.S. economy in 1933 was in a recessionary gap. The unemployment rate was above the natural rate of unemployment. Indeed, real GDP in 1933 was about 30% below what it had been in 1929, and the unemployment rate had increased from 3% to 25%. Note that during the period of the Great Depression, wages did fall. The notion of nominal wage and other price stickiness discussed in this section should not be construed to mean complete wage and price inflexibility. Rather, during this period, nominal wages and other prices were not flexible enough to restore the economy to the potential level of output. There are two basic choices on how to close recessionary gaps. Nonintervention would mean waiting for wages to fall further. As wages fall, the short-run aggregate supply curve would continue to shift to the right. The alternative would be to use some type of expansionary policy. This would shift the aggregate demand curve to the right. These two options were illustrated in Figure 22.15.

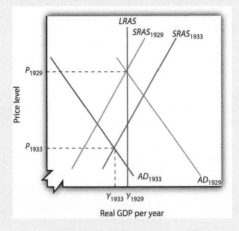

22.5 Review and Practice

Summary

In this chapter, we outlined the model of aggregate demand and aggregate supply. We saw that the aggregate demand curve slopes downward, reflecting the tendency for the aggregate quantity of goods and services demanded to rise as the price level falls and to fall as the price level rises. The negative relationship between the price level and the quantity of goods and services demanded results from the wealth effect for consumption, the interest rate effect for investment, and the international trade effect for net exports. We examined the factors that can shift the aggregate demand curve as well. Generally, the aggregate demand curve shifts by a multiple of the initial amount by which the component causing it to shift changes.

We distinguished between two types of equilibria in macroeconomics—one corresponding to the short run, a period of analysis in which nominal wages and some prices are sticky, and the other corresponding to the long run, a period in which full wage and price flexibility, and hence market adjustment, have been achieved. Long-run equilibrium occurs at the intersection of the aggregate demand curve with the long-run aggregate supply curve. The long-run aggregate supply curve is a vertical line at the economy's potential level of output. Short-run equilibrium occurs at the intersection of the aggregate demand curve with the short-run aggregate supply curve. The short-run aggregate supply curve relates the quantity of total output produced to the price level in the short run. It is upward sloping because of wage and price stickiness. In short-run equilibrium, output can be below or above potential.

If an economy is initially operating at its potential output, then a change in aggregate demand or short-run aggregate supply will induce a recessionary or inflationary gap. Such a gap will be closed in the long run by changes in the nominal wage, which will shift the short-run aggregate supply curve to the left (to close an inflationary gap) or to the right (to close a recessionary gap). Policy makers might respond to a recessionary or inflationary gap with a nonintervention policy, or they could use stabilization policy.

Concept Problems

1. Explain how the following changes in aggregate demand or short-run aggregate supply, other things held unchanged, are likely to affect the level of total output and the price level in the short run.

   a. An increase in aggregate demand

   b. A decrease in aggregate demand

   c. An increase in short-run aggregate supply

   d. A reduction in short-run aggregate supply

2. Explain why a change in one component of aggregate demand will cause the aggregate demand curve to shift by a multiple of the initial change.

3. Use the model of aggregate demand and short-run aggregate supply to explain how each of the following would affect real GDP and the price level in the short run.

   a. An increase in government purchases

   b. A reduction in nominal wages

   c. A major improvement in technology

   d. A reduction in net exports

4. How would an increase in the supply of labor affect the natural level of employment and potential output? How would it affect the real wage, the level of real GDP, and the price level in the short run? How would it affect long-run aggregate supply? What kind of gaps would be created?

5. Give three reasons for the downward slope of the aggregate demand curve.

6. "When the price level falls, people's wealth increases. When wealth increases, the real volume of consumption increases. Therefore, a decrease in the price level will cause the aggregate demand curve to shift to the right." Do you agree? Explain.

7. Suppose the economy has a recessionary gap. We know that if we do nothing, the economy will close the gap on its own. Alternatively, we could arrange for an increase in aggregate demand (say, by increasing government spending) to close the gap. How would your views about the degree of price stickiness in the economy influence your views on whether such a policy would be desirable?

8. The cost of hiring workers includes not only payments made directly to workers, that is, wages, but payments made on behalf of workers as well, such as contributions by employers to pension plans and to health-care insurance for employees. How would a decrease in the cost of employer-provided health insurance affect the economy? Using Figure 22.8 as a guide, draw a graph to illustrate your answer.

9. Suppose nominal wages never changed. What would be the significance of such a characteristic?

10. Suppose the minimum wage were increased sharply. How would this affect the equilibrium price level and output level in the model of aggregate demand and aggregate supply in the short run? In the long run?

11. Explain the short-run impact of each of the following.

    a. A discovery that makes cold fusion a reality, greatly reducing the cost of producing energy

    b. An increase in the payroll tax

Numerical Problems

1. Suppose the aggregate demand and short-run aggregate supply schedules for an economy whose potential output equals $2,700 are given by the table.

	Aggregate Quantity of Goods and Services	
Price Level	Demanded	Supplied
0.50	$3,500	$1,000
0.75	3,000	2,000
1.00	2,500	2,500
1.25	2,000	2,700
1.50	1,500	2,800

   a. Draw the aggregate demand, short-run aggregate supply, and long-run aggregate supply curves.

   b. State the short-run equilibrium level of real GDP and the price level.

   c. Characterize the current economic situation. Is there an inflationary or a recessionary gap? If so, how large is it?

   d. Now suppose aggregate demand increases by $700 at each price level; for example, the aggregate quantity of goods and services demanded at a price level of 0.50 now equals $4,200. Show the new aggregate demand curve, state the new short-run equilibrium price level and real GDP, and state whether there is an inflationary or a recessionary gap and give its size.

2. An economy is characterized by the values in the table for aggregate demand and short-run aggregate supply. Its potential output is $1,500.

	Aggregate Quantity of Goods and Services	
Price Level	Demanded	Supplied
0.50	$2,500	$1,500
0.75	2,000	2,000
1.00	1,500	2,300
1.25	1,000	2,500
1.50	500	2,600

a. Draw the aggregate demand, short-run aggregate supply, and long-run aggregate supply curves.

b. State the equilibrium level of real GDP and the price level.

c. Characterize the current economic situation. Is there an inflationary or a recessionary gap? If so, how large is it?

d. Now suppose that nominal wages rise and that the price level required to induce a particular level of total output rises by 0.50. For example, a price level of 1.00 is now required to induce producers to produce a real GDP of $1,500. Show the new short-run aggregate supply curve, state the new equilibrium price level and real GDP, and state whether there is an inflationary or a recessionary gap and give its size. Why might such a change occur?

3. Suppose the price level in a particular economy equals 1.3 and that the quantity of real GDP demanded at that price level is $1,200. An increase of 0.1 point in the price level reduces the quantity of real GDP demanded by $220, and a reduction of 0.1 point would produce an increase in the quantity of real GDP demanded of $220. Draw the aggregate demand curve and show the price level and quantity of real GDP demanded at three points.

4. Suppose an economy is described by the following aggregate demand and short-run aggregate supply curves. The potential level of output is $10 trillion.

	Aggregate Quantity of Goods and Services	
Price Level	Demanded	Supplied
3.0	$11.0 trillion	$9.0 trillion
3.4	$10.8 trillion	$9.2 trillion
3.8	$10.6 trillion	$9.4 trillion
4.2	$10.4 trillion	$9.6 trillion
4.6	$10.2 trillion	$9.8 trillion
5.0	$10.0 trillion	$10.0 trillion
5.4	$9.8 trillion	$10.2 trillion
5.8	$9.6 trillion	$10.4 trillion
6.2	$9.4 trillion	$10.6 trillion
6.6	$9.2 trillion	$10.8 trillion
7.0	$9.0 trillion	$11.0 trillion

a. Draw the aggregate demand and short-run aggregate supply curves.

b. What is the initial real GDP?

c. What is the initial price level?

d. What kind of gap, if any, exists?

e. After the increase in health-care costs, each level of real GDP requires an increase in the price level of 0.8. For example, producing $9.0 trillion worth of goods and services now requires a price level of 3.8. What is the short-run equilibrium level of real GDP?

f. After the health-care cost increase, what is the new equilibrium price level in the short run?

g. What sort of gap, if any, now exists?

5. According to Alaskan state economist Mark Edwards, the multiplier effect of Alaska's trade with Japan is such that for every $1 billion exported from Alaska to Japan another $600 million is added to the state's economy.[1] Calculate the size of the export multiplier.

6. The Nottinghamshire Research Observatory in England calculated that students who attend Nottingham Technical University spend about £2,760 each in the local economy for a total of £50.45 million. In total, the impact of their spending on the local economy is £63 million.[2] Calculate the size of the student spending multiplier.

7. In Goa, India, the multiplier effect of iron ore exports is calculated to be 1.62.[3] Calculate the impact of an additional 1,000 rupees of iron ore exports on the economy of Goa.

Endnotes

1. Matt Volz, "Trade Officials Hopeful for Japanese Recovery," *Associated Press and Local Wire*, June 22, 2004, BC cycle.

2. "University Brings in £250m to Economy," *Nottingham Evening Post*, November 4, 2004, p. 37.

3. Vidyut Kumar Ta, "Iron Ore Mining Gives Impetus to Goa's Economy," *Times of India*, April 30, 2003.

CHAPTER 23
Economic Growth

23.1 Start Up: How Important Is Economic Growth?

How important is economic growth? The best way to answer that question is to imagine life without growth—to imagine that we did not have the gains growth brings.

For starters, divide your family's current income by six and imagine what your life would be like. Think about the kind of housing your family could afford, the size of your entertainment budget, whether you could still attend school. That will give you an idea of life a century ago in the United States, when average household incomes, adjusted for inflation, were about one-sixth what they are today. People had far smaller homes, they rarely had electricity in their homes, and only a tiny percentage of the population could even consider a college education.

To get a more recent perspective, consider how growth has changed living standards over the past half century or so. In 1950, the United States was the world's richest nation. But if households were rich then, subsequent economic growth has made them far richer. Average per capita real income has more than tripled since then. Indeed, the average household income in 1950, which must have seemed lofty then, was below what we now define as the poverty line for a household of four, even after adjusting for inflation. Economic growth during the last 60-plus years has dramatically boosted our standard of living—and our standard of what it takes to get by.

One gauge of rising living standards is housing. A half century ago, most families did not own homes. Today, almost two-thirds do. Those homes have gotten a lot bigger: new homes built today are more than twice the size of new homes built 50 years ago. Some household appliances, such as telephones or washing machines, that we now consider basic, were luxuries a half century ago. In 1950, less than two-thirds of housing units had complete plumbing facilities. Today, over 99% do.

Economic growth has brought gains in other areas as well. For one thing, we are able to afford more schooling. In 1950, the median number of years of school completed by adults age 25 or over was 6.8. Today, about 88% have completed 12 years of schooling and about a third have completed 4 years of college. We also live longer. A baby born in 1950 had a life expectancy of 68 years. A baby born in 2008 had an expected life of nearly 10 years longer.

Of course, while economic growth can improve our material well-being, it is no panacea. Americans today worry about the level of violence in society, environmental degradation, and what seems to be a loss of basic values. But while it is easy to be dismayed about many challenges of modern life, we can surely be grateful for our material wealth. Our affluence gives us the opportunity to grapple with some of our most difficult problems and to enjoy a range of choices that people only a few decades ago could not have imagined.

We learned a great deal about economic growth in the context of the production possibilities curve. Our purpose in this chapter is to relate the concept of economic growth to the model of aggregate demand and aggregate supply that we developed in the previous chapter and will use throughout our exploration of macroeconomics. We will review the forces that determine a nation's economic growth rate and examine the prospects for growth in the future. We begin by looking at the significance of growth to the overall well-being of society.

23.2 The Significance of Economic Growth

Learning Objectives

1. Define economic growth and explain it using the production possibilities model and the concept of potential output.
2. State the rule of 72 and use it to show how even small differences in growth rates can have major effects on a country's potential output over time.
3. Calculate the percentage rate of growth of output per capita.

To demonstrate the impact of economic growth on living standards of a nation, we must start with a clear definition of economic growth and then study its impact over time. We will also see how population growth affects the relationship between economic growth and the standard of living an economy is able to achieve.

Defining Economic Growth

Economic growth is a long-run process that occurs as an economy's potential output increases. Changes in real GDP from quarter to quarter or even from year to year are short-run fluctuations that occur as aggregate demand and short-run aggregate supply change. Regardless of media reports stating that the economy grew at a certain rate in the last quarter or that it is expected to grow at a particular rate during the next year, short-run changes in real GDP say little about economic growth. In the long run, economic activity moves toward its level of potential output. Increases in potential constitute economic growth.

Earlier we defined economic growth as the process through which an economy achieves an outward shift in its production possibilities curve. How does a shift in the production possibilities curve relate to a change in potential output? To produce its potential level of output, an economy must operate on its production possibilities curve. An increase in potential output thus implies an outward shift in the production possibilities curve. In the framework of the macroeconomic model of aggregate demand and aggregate supply, we show economic growth as a shift to the right in the long-run aggregate supply curve.

There are three key points about economic growth to keep in mind:

1. Growth is a process. It is not a single event; rather, it is an unfolding series of events.
2. We define growth in terms of the economy's ability to produce goods and services, as indicated by its level of potential output.
3. Growth suggests that the economy's ability to produce goods and services is rising. A discussion of economic growth is thus a discussion of the series of events that increase the economy's ability to produce goods and services.

Figure 23.1 shows the record of economic growth for the U.S. economy over the past century. The graph shows annual levels of actual real GDP and of potential output. We see that the economy has experienced dramatic growth over the past century; potential output has soared nearly 20-fold. The figure also reminds us of a central theme of our analysis of macroeconomics: real GDP fluctuates about potential output. Real GDP sagged well below its potential (initially more than 40% below and then remaining at about 20% below for most of the decade) during the Great Depression of the 1930s and rose well above its potential (about 30% above) as the nation mobilized its resources to fight World War II. With the exception of these two periods, real GDP has remained fairly close to the economy's potential output. In the recession of 1981, real GDP was almost 7% below its potential, and during the recession that began at the end of 2007, real GDP fell more than

7% below its potential. In 2015, the economy was about 1.5% below its potential. Nonetheless, since 1950, the actual level of real GDP has deviated from potential output by an average of less than 1%.

FIGURE 23.1 A Century of Economic Growth
At the start of the 21st century, the level of potential output reached a level nearly 20 times its level a century earlier. Over the years, actual real GDP fluctuated about a rising level of potential output.

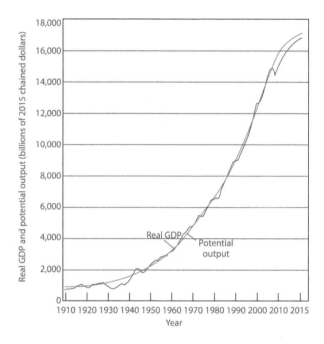

Sources: Based on data from 1910–1949 data from Christina D. Romer, "World War I and the Postwar Depression: A Reinterpretation Based on Alternative Estimates of GNP," Journal of Monetary Economics 22 (1988): 91–115; data for 1950-2015 from Congressional Budget Office, The Budget and Economic Outlook: An Update, August 2016.

We urge you to take some time with Figure 23.1. Over the course of the last century, it is economic growth that has taken center stage. Certainly, the fluctuations about potential output have been important. The recessionary gaps—periods when real GDP slipped below its potential—were often wrenching experiences in which millions of people endured great hardship. The inflationary gaps—periods when real GDP rose above its potential level—often produced dramatic increases in price levels. Those fluctuations mattered. It was the unemployment and/or the inflation that came with them that made headlines. But it was the quiet process of economic growth that pushed living standards ever higher. We must understand growth if we are to understand how we got where we are, and where we are likely to be going during the 21st century.

Figure 23.2 tells us why we use changes in potential output, rather than actual real GDP, as our measure of economic growth. Actual values of real GDP are affected not just by changes in the potential level of output, but also by the cyclical fluctuations about that level of output.

Given our definition of economic growth, we would say that the hypothetical economy depicted in Figure 23.2 grew at a 2.5% annual rate throughout the period. If we used actual values of real GDP, however, we would obtain quite different interpretations. Consider, for example, the first decade of this period: it began with a real GDP of $900 billion and a recessionary gap, and it ended in year 10 with a real GDP of $1,408 billion and an inflationary gap. If we record growth as the annual rate of change between these levels, we find an annual rate of growth of 4.6%—a rather impressive performance.

FIGURE 23.2 Cyclical Change Versus Growth

The use of actual values of real GDP to measure growth can give misleading results. Here, an economy's potential output (shown in green) grows at a steady rate of 2.5% per year, with actual values of real GDP fluctuating about that trend. If we measure growth in the first 10 years as the annual rate of change between beginning and ending values of real GDP, we get a growth rate of 4.6%. The rate for the second decade is 0.5%. Growth estimates based on changes in real GDP are affected by cyclical changes that do not represent economic growth.

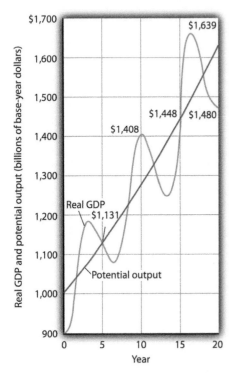

Now consider the second decade shown in Figure 23.2. It began in year 10, and it ended in year 20 with a recessionary gap. If we measure the growth rate over that period by looking at beginning and ending values of actual real GDP, we compute an annual growth rate of 0.5%. Viewed in this way, performance in the first decade is spectacular while performance in the second is rather lackluster. But these figures depend on the starting and ending points we select; the growth rate of potential output was 2.5% throughout the period.

By measuring economic growth as the rate of increase in potential output, we avoid such problems. One way to do this is to select years in which the economy was operating at the natural level of employment and then to compute the annual rate of change between those years. The result is an estimate of the rate at which potential output increased over the period in question. For the economy shown in Figure 23.2, for example, we see that real GDP equaled its potential in years 5 and 15. Real GDP in year 5 was $1,131, and real GDP in year 15 was $1,448. The annual rate of change between these two years was 2.5%. If we have estimates of potential output, of course, we can simply compute annual rates of change between any two years.

The Rule of 72 and Differences in Growth Rates

The Case in Point on presidents and growth at the end of this section suggests a startling fact: the U.S. growth rate began slowing in the 1970s, did not recover until the mid-1990s, only to slow down again in the 2000s. The question we address here is: does it matter? Does a percentage point drop in the growth rate make much difference? It does. To see why, let us investigate what happens when a variable grows at a particular percentage rate.

Suppose two economies with equal populations start out at the same level of real GDP but grow at different rates. Economy A grows at a rate of 3.5%, and Economy B grows at a rate of 2.4%. After a year, the difference in real GDP will hardly be noticeable. After a decade, however, real GDP in Economy A will be 11% greater than in Economy B. Over longer periods, the difference will be more dramatic. After 100 years, for example, income in Economy A will be nearly three times as great as in Economy B. If population growth in the two countries has been the same, the people of Economy A will have a far higher standard of living than those in Economy B. The difference in real GDP per person will be roughly equivalent to the difference that exists today between Great Britain and Mexico.

exponential growth

When a quantity grows at a given percentage rate.

Over time, small differences in growth rates create large differences in incomes. An economy growing at a 3.5% rate increases by 3.5% of its initial value in the first year. In the second year, the economy increases by 3.5% of that new, higher value. In the third year, it increases by 3.5% of a still higher value. When a quantity grows at a given percentage rate, it experiences **exponential growth**. A variable that grows exponentially follows a path such as those shown for potential output in Figure 23.1 and Figure 23.2. These curves become steeper over time because the growth rate is applied to an ever-larger base.

rule of 72

A variable's approximate doubling time equals 72 divided by the growth rate, stated as a whole number.

A variable growing at some exponential rate doubles over fixed intervals of time. The doubling time is given by the **rule of 72**, which states that a variable's approximate doubling time equals 72 divided by the growth rate, stated as a whole number. If the level of income were increasing at a 9% rate, for example, its doubling time would be roughly 72/9, or 8 years.[1]

Let us apply this concept of a doubling time to the reduction in the U.S. growth rate. Had the U.S. economy continued to grow at a 3.5% rate after 1970, then its potential output would have doubled roughly every 20 years (72/3.5 = 20). That means potential output would have doubled by 1990, would double again by 2010, and would double again by 2030. Real GDP in 2030 would thus be eight times as great as its 1970 level. Growing at a 2.4% rate, however, potential output doubles only every

30 years (72/2.4 = 30). It would take until 2000 to double once from its 1970 level, and it would double once more by 2030. Potential output in 2030 would thus be four times its 1970 level if the economy grew at a 2.4% rate (versus eight times its 1970 level if it grew at a 3.5% rate). The 1.1% difference in growth rates produces a 100% difference in potential output by 2030. The different growth paths implied by these growth rates are illustrated in Figure 23.3.

FIGURE 23.3 Differences in Growth Rates

The chart suggests the significance in the long run of a small difference in the growth rate of real GDP. We begin in 1970, when real GDP equaled $2,873.9 billion. If real GDP grew at an annual rate of 3.5% from that year, it would double roughly every 20 years: in 1990, 2010, and 2030. Growth at a 2.4% rate, however, implies doubling every 30 years: in 2000 and 2030. By 2030, the 3.5% growth rate leaves real GDP at twice the level that would be achieved by 2.4% growth.

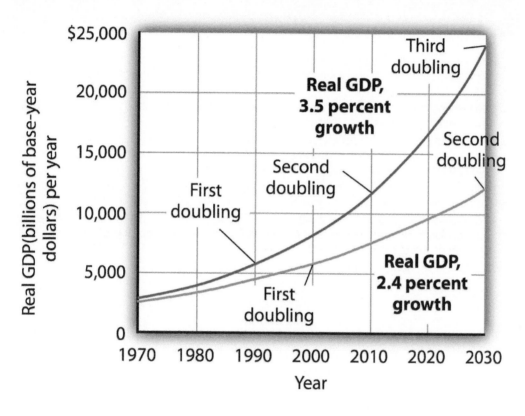

Growth in Output per Capita

Of course, it is not just how fast potential output grows that determines how fast the average person's material standard of living rises. For that purpose, we examine economic growth on a per capita basis. An economy's **output per capita** equals real GDP per person. If we let N equal population, then

output per capita
Real GDP per person.

EQUATION 23.1

$$\text{Output per capita} = \frac{\text{real GDP}}{N}$$

In the United States in 2013, for example, real GDP was $15,759 billion (annual rate). The U.S. population was 315 million. Real U.S. output per capita thus was about $50,000.

We use output per capita as a gauge of an economy's material standard of living. If the economy's population is growing, then output must rise as rapidly as the population if output per capita is to remain unchanged. If, for example, population increases by 2%, then real GDP would have to rise by 2% to maintain the current level of output per capita. If real GDP rises by less than 2%, output per capita will fall. If real GDP rises by more than 2%, output per capita will rise. More generally, we can write:

EQUATION 23.2

% rate of growth of output per capita $\cong$ % rate of growth of output $-$ % rate of growth of population

For economic growth to translate into a higher standard of living on average, economic growth must exceed population growth. From 1970 to 2004, for example, Sierra Leone's population grew at an annual rate of 2.1% per year, while its real GDP grew at an annual rate of 1.4%; its output per capita thus fell at a rate of 0.7% per year. Over the same period, Singapore's population grew at an annual rate of 2.1% per year, while its real GDP grew 7.4% per year. The resultant 5.3% annual growth in output per capita transformed Singapore from a relatively poor country to a country with the one of the highest per capita incomes in the world.

Key Takeaways

- Economic growth is the process through which an economy's production possibilities curve shifts outward. We measure it as the rate at which the economy's potential level of output increases.
- Measuring economic growth as the rate of increase of the actual level of real GDP can lead to misleading results due to the business cycle.
- Growth of a quantity at a particular percentage rate implies exponential growth. When something grows exponentially, it doubles over fixed intervals of time; these intervals may be computed using the rule of 72.
- Small differences in rates of economic growth can lead to large differences in levels of potential output over long periods of time.
- To assess changes in average standards of living, we subtract the percentage rate of growth of population from the percentage rate of growth of output to get the percentage rate of growth of output per capita.

Try It!

Suppose an economy's potential output and real GDP is $5 million in 2000 and its rate of economic growth is 3% per year. Also suppose that its population is 5,000 in 2000, and that its population grows at a rate of 1% per year. Compute GDP per capita in 2000. Now estimate GDP and GDP per capita in 2072, using the rule of 72. At what rate does GDP per capita grow? What is its doubling time? Is this result consistent with your findings for GDP per capita in 2000 and in 2072?

Case in Point: Presidents and Economic Growth

Sources: By Frank Gatteri, United States Army Signal Corps [Public domain], via Wikimedia Commons; By Frank Gatteri, United States Army Signal Corps [Public domain], via Wikimedia Commons; By The White House from Washington, DC (P120612PS-0463 Uploaded by ComputerHotline) [Public domain], via Wikimedia Commons

President	Average Annual Increase in Real GDP (%)	Average Growth Rate (%)
Truman 1949–1952	5.1	5.4
Eisenhower 1953–1960	3.0	3.4
Kennedy-Johnson 1961–1968	5.0	4.4
Nixon-Ford 1969–1976	2.8	3.4
Carter 1977–1980	3.3	3.2
Reagan 1981–1988	3.5	3.3
G. H. W. Bush 1989–1992	2.3	2.8
Clinton 1993–2000	3.9	3.4
G. W. Bush 2001–2008	2.1	2.5
Obama 2009–2016	1.5	1.4

Source: Based on data from Bureau of Economic Analysis, NIPA Table 1.1.6 (revised November 26, 2014). Real Gross Domestic Product, Chained Dollars [Billions of chained (2009) dollars]. Seasonally adjusted at annual rates; Congressional Budget Office, The Budget and Economic Outlook: An Update, August 2016.

Presidents are often judged by the rate at which the economy grew while they were in office. This test is unfair on two counts. First, a president has little to do with the forces that determine growth. And second, such tests simply compute the annual rate of growth in real GDP over the course of a presidential term, which we know can be affected by cyclical factors. A president who takes office when the economy is down and goes out with the economy up will look like an economic star; a president with the bad luck to have reverse circumstances will seem like a dud. Here are annual rates of change in real GDP for each of the postwar presidents, together with rates of economic growth, measured as the annual rate of change in potential output.

The presidents' economic records are clearly affected by luck. Presidents Kennedy, Reagan, Clinton, and Obama for example, began their terms when the economy had a recessionary gap and ended them with an inflationary gap or at about potential output. Real GDP thus rose faster than potential output during their presidencies. The Eisenhower, Nixon-Ford, G. H. W. Bush, and G. W. Bush administrations each started with an inflationary gap or at about potential and ended with a recessionary gap, thus recording rates of real GDP increase below the rate of gain in potential. Jimmy Carter, who came to office and left it with recessionary gaps, presided over a relatively equivalent rate of increase in actual GDP versus potential output.

The data do not fit the pattern for the Truman administration, which started during a recession and ended near potential. Also, notice how low the growth rate was during the Obama administration. So, while the data during his administration just barely registered a higher average increase in real GDP than in the growth rate, it makes sense that the public would feel GDP was just creeping along.

Answer to Try It! Problem

GDP per capita in 2000 equals $1,000 ($5,000,000/5,000). If GDP rises 3% per year, it doubles every 24 years (= 72/3). Thus, GDP will be $10,000,000 in 2024, $20,000,000 in 2048, and $40,000,000 in 2072. Growing at a rate of 1% per year, population will have doubled once by 2072 to 10,000. GDP per capita will thus be $4,000 (= $40,000,000/10,000). Notice that GDP rises by eight times its original level, while the increase in GDP per capita is fourfold. The latter value represents a growth rate in output per capita of 2% per year, which implies a doubling time of 36 years. That gives two doublings in GDP per capita between 2000 and 2072 and confirms a fourfold increase.

23.3 Growth and the Long-Run Aggregate Supply Curve

Learning Objectives

1. Explain and illustrate graphically the concept of the aggregate production function. Explain how its shape relates to the concept of diminishing marginal returns.
2. Derive the long-run aggregate supply curve from the model of the labor market and the aggregate production function.
3. Explain how the long-run aggregate supply curve shifts in responses to shifts in the aggregate production function or to shifts in the demand for or supply of labor.

Economic growth means the economy's potential output is rising. Because the long-run aggregate supply curve is a vertical line at the economy's potential, we can depict the process of economic growth as one in which the long-run aggregate supply curve shifts to the right.

Figure 23.4 illustrates the process of economic growth. If the economy begins at potential output of Y_1, growth increases this potential. The figure shows a succession of increases in potential to Y_2, then Y_3, and Y_4. If the economy is growing at a particular percentage rate, and if the levels shown represent successive years, then the size of the increases will become larger and larger, as indicated in the figure.

Because economic growth can be considered as a process in which the long-run aggregate supply curve shifts to the right, and because output tends to remain close to this curve, it is important to gain a deeper understanding of what determines long-run aggregate supply (*LRAS*). We shall examine the derivation of *LRAS* and then see what factors shift the curve. We shall begin our work by defining an aggregate production function.

The Aggregate Production Function

An **aggregate production function** relates the total output of an economy to the total amount of labor employed in the economy, all other determinants of production (that is, capital, natural resources, and technology) being unchanged. An economy operating on its aggregate production function is producing its potential level of output.

Figure 23.5 shows an aggregate production function (*PF*). It shows output levels for a range of employment between 120 million and 140 million workers. When the level of employment is 120 million, the economy produces a real GDP of $11,500 billion (point A). A level of employment of 130 million produces a real GDP of $12,000 billion (point B), and when 140 million workers are employed, a real GDP of $12,300 billion is produced (point C). In drawing the aggregate production function, the amount of labor varies, but everything else that could affect output, specifically the quantities of other factors of production and technology, is fixed.

The shape of the aggregate production function shows that as employment increases, output increases, but at a decreasing rate. Increasing employment from 120 million to 130 million, for example, increases output by $500 billion to $12,000 billion at point B. The next 10 million workers increase production by $300 billion to $12,300 billion at point C. This example illustrates diminishing marginal returns. **Diminishing marginal returns** occur when additional units of a variable factor add less and less to total output, given constant quantities of other factors.

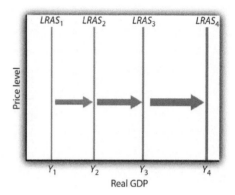

FIGURE 23.4 Economic Growth and the Long-Run Aggregate Supply Curve
Because economic growth is the process through which the economy's potential output is increased, we can depict it as a series of rightward shifts in the long-run aggregate supply curve. Notice that with exponential growth, each successive shift in *LRAS* is larger and larger.

aggregate production function

Function that relates the total output of an economy to the total amount of labor employed in the economy, all other determinants of production (capital, natural resources, and technology) being unchanged.

diminishing marginal returns

Situation that occurs when additional units of a variable factor add less and less to total output, given constant quantities of other factors.

FIGURE 23.5 The Aggregate Production Function

An aggregate production function (*PF*) relates total output to total employment, assuming all other factors of production and technology are fixed. It shows that increases in employment lead to increases in output but at a decreasing rate.

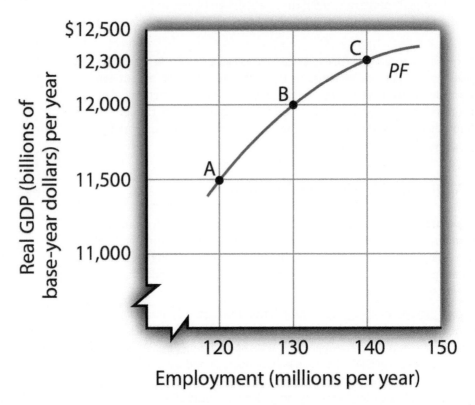

It is easy to picture the problem of diminishing marginal returns in the context of a single firm. The firm is able to increase output by adding workers. But because the firm's plant size and stock of equipment are fixed, the firm's capital per worker falls as it takes on more workers. Each additional worker adds less to output than the worker before. The firm, like the economy, experiences diminishing marginal returns.

The Aggregate Production Function, the Market for Labor, and Long-Run Aggregate Supply

To derive the long-run aggregate supply curve, we bring together the model of the labor market, introduced in the first macro chapter and the aggregate production function.

As we learned, the labor market is in equilibrium at the natural level of employment. The demand and supply curves for labor intersect at the real wage at which the economy achieves its natural level of employment. We see in Panel (a) of Figure 23.6 that the equilibrium real wage is ω_1 and the natural level of employment is L_1. Panel (b) shows that with employment of L_1, the economy can produce a real GDP of Y_P. That output equals the economy's potential output. It is that level of potential output that determines the position of the long-run aggregate supply curve in Panel (c).

FIGURE 23.6 Deriving the Long-Run Aggregate Supply Curve

Panel (a) shows that the equilibrium real wage is ω_1, and the natural level of employment is L_1. Panel (b) shows that with employment of L_1, the economy can produce a real GDP of Y_P. That output equals the economy's potential output. It is at that level of potential output that we draw the long-run aggregate supply curve in Panel (c).

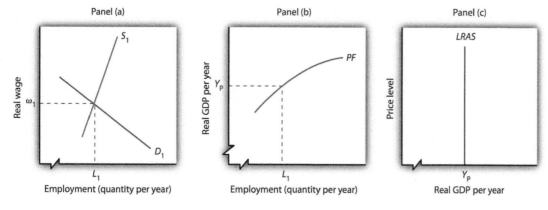

Changes in Long-Run Aggregate Supply

The position of the long-run aggregate supply curve is determined by the aggregate production function and the demand and supply curves for labor. A change in any of these will shift the long-run aggregate supply curve.

Figure 23.7 shows one possible shifter of long-run aggregate supply: a change in the production function. Suppose, for example, that an improvement in technology shifts the aggregate production function in Panel (b) from PF_1 to PF_2. Other developments that could produce an upward shift in the curve include an increase in the capital stock or in the availability of natural resources.

FIGURE 23.7 Shift in the Aggregate Production Function and the Long-Run Aggregate Supply Curve

An improvement in technology shifts the aggregate production function upward in Panel (b). Because labor is more productive, the demand for labor shifts to the right in Panel (a), and the natural level of employment increases to L_2. In Panel (c) the long-run aggregate supply curve shifts to the right to Y_2.

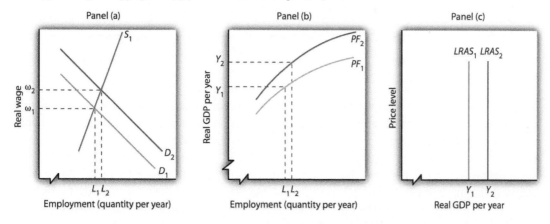

The shift in the production function to PF_2 means that labor is now more productive than before. This will affect the demand for labor in Panel (a). Before the technological change, firms employed L_1 workers at a real wage ω_1. If workers are more productive, firms will find it profitable to hire more of them at ω_1. The demand curve for labor thus shifts to D_2 in Panel (a). The real wage rises to ω_2, and the natural level of employment rises to L_2. The increase in the real wage reflects labor's enhanced **productivity**, the amount of output per worker. To see how potential output changes, we see in Panel (b) how much output can be produced given the new natural level of employment and the new aggregate production function. The real GDP that the economy is capable of producing rises from Y_1 to Y_2. The higher output is a reflection of a higher natural level of employment, along with the fact that labor has become more productive as a result of the techno-

productivity

The amount of output per worker.

logical advance. In Panel (c) the long-run aggregate supply curve shifts to the right to the vertical line at Y_2.

This analysis dispels a common misconception about the impact of improvements in technology or increases in the capital stock on employment. Some people believe that technological gains or increases in the stock of capital reduce the demand for labor, reduce employment, and reduce real wages. Certainly the experience of the United States and most other countries belies that notion. Between 1990 and 2007, for example, the U.S. capital stock and the level of technology increased dramatically. During the same period, employment and real wages rose, suggesting that the demand for labor increased by more than the supply of labor. As some firms add capital or incorporate new technologies, some workers at those firms may lose their jobs. But for the economy as a whole, new jobs become available *and* they generally offer higher wages. The demand for labor rises.

Another event that can shift the long-run aggregate supply curve is an increase in the supply of labor, as shown in Figure 23.8. An increased supply of labor could result from immigration, an increase in the population, or increased participation in the labor force by the adult population. Increased participation by women in the labor force, for example, has tended to increase the supply curve for labor during the past several decades.

FIGURE 23.8 Increase in the Supply of Labor and the Long-Run Aggregate Supply Curve
An increase in the supply of labor shifts the supply curve in Panel (a) to S_2, and the natural level of employment rises to L_2. The real wage falls to ω_2. With increased labor, the aggregate production function in Panel (b) shows that the economy is now capable of producing real GDP at Y_2. The long-run aggregate supply curve in Panel (c) shifts to $LRAS_2$.

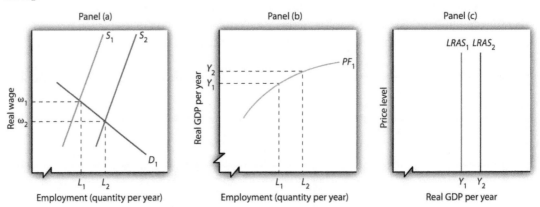

In Panel (a), an increase in the labor supply shifts the supply curve to S_2. The increase in the supply of labor does not change the stock of capital or natural resources, nor does it change technology—it therefore does not shift the aggregate production function. Because there is no change in the production function, there is no shift in the demand for labor. The real wage falls from ω_1 to ω_2 in Panel (a), and the natural level of employment rises from L_1 to L_2. To see the impact on potential output, Panel (b) shows that employment of L_2 can produce real GDP of Y_2. The long-run aggregate supply curve in Panel (c) thus shifts to $LRAS_2$. Notice, however, that this shift in the long-run aggregate supply curve to the right is associated with a reduction in the real wage to ω_2.

Of course, the aggregate production function and the supply curve of labor can shift together, producing higher real wages at the same time population rises. That has been the experience of most industrialized nations. The increase in real wages in the United States between 1990 and 2007, for example, came during a period in which an increasing population increased the supply of labor. The demand for labor increased by more than the supply, pushing the real wage up. The accompanying Case in Point looks at gains in real wages in the face of technological change, an increase in the stock of capital, and rapid population growth in the United States during the 19th century.

Our model of long-run aggregate supply tells us that in the long run, real GDP, the natural level of employment, and the real wage are determined by the economy's production function and by the demand and supply curves for labor. Unless an event shifts the aggregate production function, the demand curve for labor, or the supply curve for labor, it affects neither the natural level of employment nor potential output. Economic growth occurs only if an event shifts the economy's production function or if there is an increase in the demand for or the supply of labor.

Key Takeaways

- The aggregate production function relates the level of employment to the level of real GDP produced per period.
- The real wage and the natural level of employment are determined by the intersection of the demand and supply curves for labor. Potential output is given by the point on the aggregate production function corresponding to the natural level of employment. This output level is the same as that shown by the long-run aggregate supply curve.
- Economic growth can be shown as a series of shifts to the right in *LRAS*. Such shifts require either upward shifts in the production function or increases in demand for or supply of labor.

Try It!

Suppose that the quantity of labor supplied is 50 million workers when the real wage is $20,000 per year and that potential output is $2,000 billion per year. Draw a three-panel graph similar to the one presented in Figure 23.8 to show the economy's long-run equilibrium. Panel (a) of your graph should show the demand and supply curves for labor, Panel (b) should show the aggregate production function, and Panel (c) should show the long-run aggregate supply curve. Now suppose a technological change increases the economy's output with the same quantity of labor as before to $2,200 billion, and the real wage rises to $21,500. In response, the quantity of labor supplied increases to 51 million workers. In the same three panels you have already drawn, sketch the new curves that result from this change. Explain what happens to the level of employment, the level of potential output, and the long-run aggregate supply curve. (Hint: you have information for only one point on each of the curves you draw—two for the supply of labor; simply draw curves of the appropriate shape. Do not worry about getting the scale correct.)

Case in Point: Technological Change, Employment, and Real Wages During the Industrial Revolution

Source: © Shutterstock, Inc.

Technological change and the capital investment that typically comes with it are often criticized because they replace labor with machines, reducing employment. Such changes, critics argue, hurt workers. Using the model of aggregate demand and aggregate supply, however, we arrive at a quite different conclusion. The model predicts that improved technology will increase the demand for labor and boost real wages.

The period of industrialization, generally taken to be the time between the Civil War and World War I, was a good test of these competing ideas. Technological changes were dramatic as firms shifted toward mass production and automation. Capital investment soared. Immigration increased the supply of labor. What happened to workers?

Employment more than doubled during this period, consistent with the prediction of our model. It is harder to predict, from a theoretical point of view, the consequences for real wages. The latter third of the 19th century was a period of massive immigration to the United States. Between 1865 and 1880, more than 5 million people came to the United States from abroad; most were of working age. The pace accelerated between 1880 and 1923, when more than 23 million people moved to the United States from other countries. Immigration increased the supply of labor, which should reduce the real wage. There were thus two competing forces at work: Technological change and capital investment tended to increase real wages, while immigration tended to reduce them by increasing the supply of labor.

The evidence suggests that the forces of technological change and capital investment proved far more powerful than increases in labor supply. Real wages soared 60% between 1860 and 1890. They continued to increase after that. Real wages in manufacturing, for example, rose 37% from 1890 to 1914.

Technological change and capital investment displace workers in some industries. But for the economy as a whole, they increase worker productivity, increase the demand for labor, and increase real wages.

Sources: *Based on wage data taken from Clarence D. Long, Wages and Earnings in the United States, 1860–1990 (Princeton, NJ: Princeton University Press, 1960), p. 109, and from Albert Rees, Wages in Manufacturing, 1890–1914 (Princeton, NJ: Princeton University Press, 1961), pp. 3–5. Immigration figures taken from Gary M. Walton and Hugh Rockoff, History of the American Economy, 6th ed. (New York: Harcourt Brace Jovanovich, 1990), p. 371.*

Answer to Try It! Problem

The production function in Panel (b) shifts up to PF_2. Because it reflects greater productivity of labor, firms will increase their demand for labor, and the demand curve for labor shifts to D_2 in Panel (a). $LRAS_1$ shifts to $LRAS_2$ in Panel (c). Employment and potential output rise. Potential output will be greater than $2,200 billion.

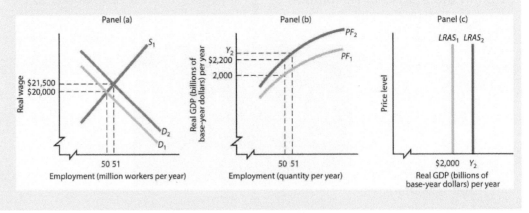

23.4 Determinants of Economic Growth

Learning Objectives

1. Discuss the sources of economic growth.
2. Discuss possible reasons why countries grow at different rates.

In this section, we review the main determinants of economic growth. We also examine the reasons for the widening disparities in economic growth rates among countries in recent years.

The Sources of Economic Growth

As we have learned, there are two ways to model economic growth: (1) as an outward shift in an economy's production possibilities curve, and (2) as a shift to the right in its long-run aggregate supply curve. In drawing either one at a point in time, we assume that the economy's factors of production and its technology are unchanged. Changing these will shift both curves. Therefore, anything that increases the quantity or quality of factors of production or that improves the technology available to the economy contributes to economic growth.

The sources of growth for the U.S. economy in the 20th century were presented in the chapter on choices in production. There we learned that the main sources of growth for the United States from 1960 to 2007 were divided between increases in the quantities of labor and of physical capital (about 65%) and in improvements in the qualities of the factors of production and technology (about 35%). Since 2000, however, the contributions from improvements in factor quality and technology have accounted for about half the economic growth in the United States.

In order to devote resources to increasing physical and human capital and to improving technology—activities that will enhance future production—society must forgo using them now to produce consumer goods. Even though the people in the economy would enjoy a higher standard of living today without this sacrifice, they are willing to reduce present consumption in order to have more goods and services available for the future.

As a college student, you personally made such a choice. You decided to devote time to study that you could have spent earning income. With the higher income, you could enjoy greater consumption today. You made this choice because you expect to earn higher income in the future and thus to enjoy greater consumption in the future. Because many other people in the society also choose to acquire more education, society allocates resources to produce education. The education produced today will enhance the society's human capital and thus its economic growth.

All other things equal, higher saving allows more resources to be devoted to increases in physical and human capital and technological improvement. In other words, saving, which is income not spent on consumption, promotes economic growth by making available resources that can be channeled into growth-enhancing uses.

Explaining Recent Disparities in Growth Rates

Toward the end of the 20th century, it appeared that some of the world's more affluent countries were growing robustly while others were growing more slowly or even stagnating. This observation was confirmed in a major study by the Organisation for Economic Co-operation and Development (OECD),[2] whose members at that time are listed in Table 23.1. The table shows that for the OECD countries as a whole, economic growth per capita fell from an average of 2.2% per year in the 1980s to an average of 1.9% per year in the 1990s. The higher standard deviation in the latter period confirms an increased disparity of growth rates in the more recent period. Moreover, the data on individual countries show that per capita growth in some countries (specifically, the United States, Canada, Ireland, Netherlands, Norway, and Spain) picked up, especially in the latter half of the 1990s, while it decelerated in most of the countries of continental Europe and Japan.

TABLE 23.1 Growing Disparities in Rates of Economic Growth
Variation in the growth in real GDP per capita has widened among the world's leading industrialized economies.

Trend Growth of GDP per Capita					
Country	1980–1990	1990–2000	1996–2000	2000–2007	2008–2013
United States	2.1	2.3	2.8	1.7	1.1
Japan	3.3	1.4	0.9	0.5	0.5
Germany	1.9	1.2	1.7	1.2	1.4
France	1.6	1.5	1.9	1.1	0.7
Italy	2.3	1.5	1.7	0.7	-0.6
United Kingdom	2.2	2.1	2.3	2.1	0.3
Canada	1.4	1.7	2.6	1.6	0.7
Austria	2.1	1.9	2.3	1.7	1.4
Belgium	2.0	1.9	2.3	1.4	0.4
Denmark	1.9	1.9	2.3	1.2	0.2
Finland	2.2	2.1	3.9	2.5	0.3
Greece	0.5	1.8	2.7	2.6	-1.2
Iceland	1.7	1.5	2.6	2.5	0.1
Ireland	3.0	6.4	7.9	3.5	0.8
Luxembourg	4.0	4.5	4.6	2.6	0.6
Netherlands	1.6	2.4	2.7	1.5	0.6
Portugal	3.1	2.8	2.7	1.2	0.2
Spain	2.3	2.7	3.2	1.8	-0.2
Sweden	1.7	1.5	2.6	2.2	1.3
Switzerland	1.4	0.4	1.1	1.2	0.7
Turkey	2.1	2.1	1.9	2.5	3.6
Australia	1.6	2.4	2.8	1.8	1.5
New Zealand	1.4	1.2	1.8	1.9	0.7
Mexico	0.0	1.6	2.7	1.2	1.2
Korea	7.2	5.1	4.2	4.1	3.1
Hungary	—	2.3	3.5	3.1	0.5
Poland	—	4.2	4.8	1.2	0.2
Czech Republic	—	1.7	1.4	3.5	1.3
OECD24*	2.2	1.9	2.2	1.5	1.1
Standard Deviation of OECD24	0.74	1.17	1.37		
*Excludes Czech Republic, Hungary, Korea, Mexico, Poland, and Slovak Republic					

Source: Based on data from Table 1.1 Organisation for Economic Co-operation and Development, Sources of Economic Growth in OECD Countries, 2003: p. 32–33; Economic Co-operation and Development, OECD Economic Outlook 2014:1, OECD Publishing, Paris at http: //dx.doi.org/10.1787/eco_outlook-v2014-1-en.

The study went on to try to explain the reasons for the divergent growth trends. The main findings were:

- In general, countries with accelerating per capita growth rates also experienced significant increases in employment, while those with stagnant or declining employment generally experienced reductions in per capita growth rates.

- Enhancements in human capital contributed to labor productivity and economic growth, but in slower growing countries such improvements were not enough to offset the impact of reduced or stagnant labor utilization.

- Information and communication technology has contributed to economic growth both through rapid technological progress within the information and communication technology industry itself as well as, more recently, through the use of information and communication technology equipment in other industries. This has made an important contribution to growth in several of the faster growing countries.

- Other factors associated with more growth include: investments in physical and human capital, sound macroeconomic policies (especially low inflation), private sector research and development, trade exposure, and better developed financial markets. Results concerning the impact of the size of the government and of public sector research and development on growth were more difficult to interpret.

- With qualifications, the study found that strict regulation of product markets (for example, regulations that reduce competition) and strict employment protection legislation (for example, laws that make hiring and firing of workers more difficult) had negative effects on growth.

- All countries show a large number of firms entering and exiting markets. But, a key difference between the United States and Europe is that new firms in the United States start out smaller and less productive than those of Europe but grow faster when they are successful. The report hypothesizes that lower start-up costs and less strict labor market regulations may encourage U.S. entrepreneurs to enter a market and then to expand, if warranted. European entrepreneurs may be less willing to experiment in a market in the first place.

The disparities in growth rates among countries led to a search for the reasons. The OECD study mentioned above gave some possible explanations. The findings of that study practically begged countries to closely examine their economic policies at a variety of levels and to consider changes that might add flexibility to their economies.

To spur this process, in 2005, the OECD started a new annual publication called *Going for Growth*. The inaugural edition identified five priority structural policy areas specific to each OECD country. The policies were categorized as either improving labor utilization or improving productivity. Suggestions for improved labor utilization ranged from changing tax policies to improving incentives for females to enter, and for older people to remain in, the workforce. Suggestions for improved productivity ranged from education reform to privatization of state-owned industries. As an example, the priorities proposed for the United States in 2005 included (1) limiting increases in labor costs by reforming Medicare to restrain health care costs, (2) encouraging private saving by shifting the burden of taxation toward consumption, (3) improving primary and secondary education, (4) reducing trade-distorting agricultural price supports, and (5) promoting transparency and accountability of corporate governance.[3]

The 2015 edition of *Going for Growth* took stock of the progress made over the ten-year period leading up to 2015. Reform activity has been stronger in some areas (product market regulation, the design of pension systems and unemployment income support programs) than in others. For most countries, the reform efforts have not been substantial enough to eliminate priority areas completely, as shown in Figure 23.9. Panel (b) of that figure gives a sense of how much variation there has been in overall reform responsiveness across countries.

How did the recession in 2008 affect economic growth in the ensuing years? Look back at the last two columns of Table 23.1. They show estimates of potential output per capita from 2000 to 2007 and then from 2008 to 2013. Notice that for almost all of the countries listed, the growth rate of potential output per capita was lower in the early 2000s than it was in the 1996-2000 period. Moreover, it was lower still in the years after the recession. These trends are worrisome and suggest that pushing ahead with the Going for Growth agenda may be even more important ten years on.

FIGURE 23.9 *Going for Growth* Recommendations across Countries, 2007 - 2015

Panel (a) shows that most priorities have been kept over the period. Panel (b) shows that progress on growth-enhancing policies reforms has varied across countries over the period.

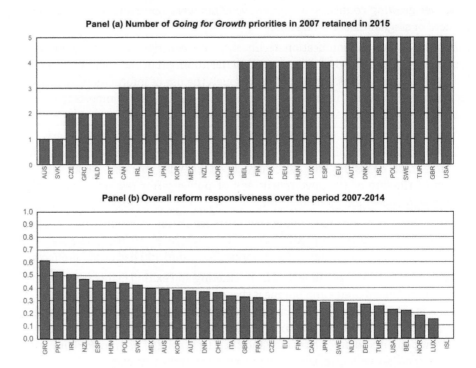

Source: OECD (2015), Economic Policy Reforms 2015: Going for Growth, OECD Publishing, Paris. http://dx.doi.org/10.1787/growth-2015-en.

In closing, it is worth reiterating that economic freedom and higher incomes tend to go together. Countries could not have attained high levels of income if they had not maintained the economic freedom that contributed to high incomes in the first place. Thus, it is also likely that rates of economic growth in the future will be related to the amount of economic freedom countries choose. We shall see in later chapters that monetary and fiscal policies that are used to stabilize the economy in the short run can also have an impact on long-run economic growth.

Key Takeaways

- The main sources of growth for the United States from 1948 to 2007 were divided between increases in the quantities of labor and of physical capital (about 65%) and in improvements in the qualities of the factors of production and technology (about 35%). Since 2000, however, improvements in factor quality and technology have contributed to about half the economic growth in the United States.

- There has been a growing disparity in the rates of economic growth in industrialized countries in recent decades, which may reflect various differences in economic structures and policies.

Try It!

All other things unchanged, compare the position of a country's expected production possibility curve and the expected position of its long-run aggregate supply curve if:

1. Its labor force increases in size by 3% per year compared to 2% per year.
2. Its saving rate falls from 15% to 10%.
3. It passes a law making it more difficult to fire workers.
4. Its level of education rises more quickly than it has in the past.

Case in Point: The Effect of Zombie Firms on the Growth Rate of Potential Output

Source: © Shutterstock, Inc.

Table 23.1 shows that the rates of economic growth over the last decades slowed in many countries and alarmingly so in the most recent period. A recent working paper by OECD economists Müge Adalet McGowan, Dan Andrews and Valentine Millot considers as a possible explanation the role of so-called zombie firms on the growth rate of potential output.

What is a zombie firm? They define zombie firms as firms that persistently have problems meeting their interest rate payments. Zombie firms have previously been studied as an explanation for why Japan has had several decades of stagnant economic performance. The current authors apply this idea to a group of OECD countries over the period 2003 to 2013 and are thus looking at how such firms affected growth both before and after the Great Recession.

Why do zombie firms not just go out of business? In some countries they do so fairly efficiently and recessions even tend to spur the process of getting rid of weak firms. In other countries, however, the process happens more slowly. Reasons for this include poorly constructed bankruptcy processes, banking systems that are overly lenient, and government policy support to shore up such firms. Indeed, some governments propped up such firms even more during the Great Recession in order to try to keep the number of unemployed down.

The authors identify several channels through which zombie firms may hurt economic growth. Firstly, the zombie firms themselves are not strong contributors to growth. Secondly, they may reduce the amount of financial resources available to non-zombie firms. Thus extant more productive firms may not gain as much market share as they would have and new firms that might possibly use more new technologies and be more innovative may be crowded out.

Due to the very detailed firms-level data the authors needed, they are able to include nine countries for the analysis that deals with the ten-year period from 2003 to 2013: Belgium, Finland, France, Italy, Korea, Slovenia, Spain, Sweden and the United Kingdom. When analyzing firms in 2013, they were able to add four countries: Austria, Germany, Luxembourg and Portugal.

The authors found that zombie firms became more prevalent over the 2000s and that the amount of financial resources sunk into them grew. They also found that zombie firms tend to invest and hire less than non-zombie firms and that their presence constrains the growth of more healthy firms as well as of the formation of new and potentially more productive firms. They refer to this as zombie congestion. In terms of the zombie firm impact on potential output, their analysis shows that in some countries, their existence has prevented output from returning to potential following the recession. Moreover, zombie firms tend to suppress potential output growth as fewer resources end up getting allocated to more productive firms. An example of one of their specific findings is estimation of the contribution of technology to growth had the share of zombie firms been held to the level observed in each country in 2004. In Italy growth would have been 0.7% higher and in Spain 1% higher. These numbers may seem small, but think back to the previous discussion in this chapter on how the rule of 72 operates.

In terms of policy, the authors suggest further research on how legal systems, and in particular bankruptcy regimes, might be changed and how financial regulation may be impacting the share of zombie firms in an economy. They also suggest looking at how labor market policies might be changed to facilitate movement of workers from zombie to non-zombie firms.

Source: Based on Müge Adalet McGowan, Dan Andrews and Valentine Millot, "The Walking Dead? Zombie Firms and Productivity Performance in OECD Countries," OECD Economics Department Working Paper No. 1372, January 10, 2017, available at www.oecd.org/eco/workingpapers.

Answer to Try It! Problem

Situations 1 and 4 should lead to a shift further outward in the country's production possibility curve and further to the right in its long-run aggregate supply curve. Situations 2 and 3 should lead to smaller outward shifts in the country's production possibility curve and smaller rightward shifts in its long-run aggregate supply curve.

23.5 Review and Practice

Summary

We saw that economic growth can be measured by the rate of increase in potential output. Measuring the rate of increase in actual real GDP can confuse growth statistics by introducing elements of cyclical variation.

Growth is an exponential process. A variable increasing at a fixed percentage rate doubles over fixed intervals. The doubling time is approximated by the rule of 72. The exponential nature of growth means that small differences in growth rates have large effects over long periods of time. Per capita rates of increase in real GDP are found by subtracting the growth rate of the population from the growth rate of GDP.

Growth can be shown in the model of aggregate demand and aggregate supply as a series of rightward shifts in the long-run aggregate supply curve. The position of the *LRAS* is determined by the aggregate production function and by the demand and supply curves for labor. A rightward shift in *LRAS* results either from an upward shift in the production function, due to increases in factors of production other than labor or to improvements in technology, or from an increase in the demand for or the supply of labor.

Saving plays an important role in economic growth, because it allows for more capital to be available for future production, so the rate of economic growth can rise. Saving thus promotes growth.

In recent years, rates of growth among the world's industrialized countries have grown more disparate. Recent research suggests this may be related to differing labor and product market conditions, differences in the diffusion of information and communications technologies, as well as differences in macroeconomic and trade policies. Evidence on the role that government plays in economic growth was less conclusive.

Concept Problems

1. Suppose the people in a certain economy decide to stop saving and instead use all their income for consumption. They do nothing to add to their stock of human or physical capital. Discuss the prospects for growth of such an economy.

2. Singapore has a saving rate that is roughly three times greater than that of the United States. Its greater saving rate has been one reason why the Singapore economy has grown faster than the U.S. economy. Suppose that if the United States increased its saving rate to, say, twice the Singapore level, U.S. growth would surpass the Singapore rate. Would that be a good idea?

3. Suppose an increase in air pollution causes capital to wear out more rapidly, doubling the rate of depreciation. How would this affect economic growth?

4. Some people worry that increases in the capital stock will bring about an economy in which everything is done by machines, with no jobs left for people. What does the model of economic growth presented in this chapter predict?

5. China's annual rate of population growth was 1.2% from 1975 to 2003 and is expected to be 0.6% from 2003 through 2015. How do you think this will affect the rate of increase in real GDP? How will this affect the rate of increase in per capita real GDP?

6. Suppose technology stops changing. Explain the impact on economic growth.

7. Suppose a series of terrorist attacks destroys half the capital in the United States but does not affect the population. What will happen to potential output and to the real wage?

8. "Given the rate at which scientists are making new discoveries, we will soon reach the point that no further discoveries can be made. Economic growth will come to a stop." Discuss.

9. Suppose real GDP increases during President Obama's term in office at a 5% rate. Would that imply that his policies were successful in "growing the economy"?

10. Suppose that for some country it was found that its economic growth was based almost entirely on increases in quantities of factors of production. Why might such growth be difficult to sustain?

Numerical Problems

1. The population of the world in 2003 was 6.314 billion. It grew between 1975 and 2003 at an annual rate of 1.6%. Assume that it continues to grow at this rate.

    a. Compute the doubling time.

    b. Estimate the world population in 2048 and 2093 (assuming all other things remain unchanged).

2. With a world population in 2003 of 6.314 billion and a projected population growth rate of 1.1% instead (which is the United Nations' projection for the period 2003 to 2015).

    a. Compute the doubling time.

    b. State the year in which the world's population would be 12.628 billion.

3. Suppose a country's population grows at the rate of 2% per year and its output grows at the rate of 3% per year.

    a. Calculate its rate of growth of per capita output.

    b. If instead its population grows at 3% per year and its output grows at 2% per year, calculate its rate of growth of per capita output.

4. The rate of economic growth per capita in France from 1996 to 2000 was 1.9% per year, while in Korea over the same period it was 4.2%. Per capita real GDP was $28,900 in France in 2003, and $12,700 in Korea. Assume the growth rates for each country remain the same.

    a. Compute the doubling time for France's per capita real GDP.

    b. Compute the doubling time for Korea's per capita real GDP.

    c. What will France's per capita real GDP be in 2045?

    d. What will Korea's per capita real GDP be in 2045?

5. Suppose real GDPs in country A and country B are identical at $10 trillion dollars in 2005. Suppose country A's economic growth rate is 2% and country B's is 4% and both growth rates remain constant over time.

    a. On a graph, show country A's potential output until 2025.

    b. On the same graph, show country B's potential output.

    c. Calculate the percentage difference in their levels of potential output in 2025.

Suppose country A's population grows 1% per year and country B's population grows 3% per year.

    d. On a graph, show country A's potential output per capita in 2025.

    e. On the same graph, show country B's potential output per capita in 2025.

    f. Calculate the percentage difference in their levels of potential output per capita in 2025.

6. Two countries, A and B, have identical levels of real GDP per capita. In Country A, an increase in the capital stock increases the potential output by 10%. Country B also experiences a 10% increase in its potential output, but this increase is the result of an increase in its labor force. Using aggregate production functions and labor-market analyses for the two countries, illustrate and explain how these events are likely to affect living standards in the two economies.

7. Suppose the information below characterizes an economy:

Employment (in millions)	Real GDP (in billions)
1	200
2	700
3	1,100
4	1,400
5	1,650
6	1,850
7	2,000
8	2,100
9	2,170
10	2,200

    a. Construct the aggregate production function for this economy.

    b. What kind of returns does this economy experience? How do you know?

    c. Assuming that total available employment is 7 million, draw the economy's long-run aggregate supply curve.

Suppose that improvement in technology means that real GDP at each level of employment rises by $200 billion.

    d. Construct the new aggregate production function for this economy.

    e. Construct the new long-run aggregate supply curve for the economy.

8. In Table 23.1, we can see that Japan's growth rate of per capita real GDP fell from 3.3% per year in the 1980s to 1.4% per year in the 1990s.

    a. Compare the percent increase in its per capita real GDP over the 20-year period to what it would have been if it had maintained the 3.3% per capita growth rate of the 1980s.

    b. Japan's per capita GDP in 1980 was about $24,000 (in U.S. 2000 dollars) in 1980. Calculate what it would have been if the growth rate of the 1980s had been maintained Calculate about how much it is, given the actual growth rates over the two decades.

    c. In Table 23.1, we can see that Ireland's growth rate of per capita real GDP grew from 3.0% per year in the 1980s to 6.4% per year in the 1990s.

    d. Compare the percent increase in its per capita real GDP over the 20-year period to what it would have been if it had maintained the 3.0% per capita growth rate of the 1980s.

    e. Ireland's per capita GDP in 1980 was about $10,000 (in U.S. 2000 dollars). Calculate what it would have been if the growth rate of the 1980s had been maintained. Calculate about how much it is, given the actual growth rates over the two decades.

Endnotes

---

1. Notice the use of the words *roughly* and *approximately*. The actual value of an income of $1,000 growing at rate r for a period of n years is $1,000 \times (1 + r)^n$. After 8 years of growth at a 9% rate, income would thus be $1,000 (1 + 0.09)^8 = $1,992.56. The rule of 72 predicts that its value will be $2,000. The rule of 72 gives an approximation, not an exact measure, of the impact of exponential growth.

2. The material in this section is based on Organisation for Economic Co-operation and Development, *The Sources of Economic Growth in OECD Countries*, 2003.

3. Organisation for Economic Co-operation and Development, *Economic Policy Reforms: Going for Growth 2005*, available at http://www.OECD.org/economics/goingforgrowth.

CHAPTER 24

The Nature and Creation of Money

24.1 Start Up: How Many Macks Does It Cost?

Larry Levine helped a client prepare divorce papers a few years ago. He was paid in mackerel.

"It's the coin of the realm," his client, Mark Bailey told the *Wall Street Journal*. The two men were prisoners at the time at the federal penitentiary at Lompoc, California.

By the time his work on the case was completed, he had accumulated "a stack of macks," Mr. Levine said. He used his fishy hoard to buy items such as haircuts at the prison barber shop, to have his laundry pressed, or to have his cell cleaned.

The somewhat unpleasant fish emerged as the currency of choice in many federal prisons in 1994 when cigarettes, the previous commodity used as currency, were banned. Plastic bags of mackerel sold for about $1 in prison commissaries. Almost no one likes them, so the prison money supply did not get eaten. Prisoners knew other prisoners would readily accept macks, so they were accepted in exchange for goods and services. Their $1 price made them convenient as a unit of account. And, as Mr. Levine's experience suggests, they acted as a store of value. As we shall see, macks served all three functions of money—they were a medium of exchange, a unit of account, and a store of value.[1]

In this chapter and the next we examine money and the way it affects the level of real GDP and the price level. In this chapter, we will focus on the nature of money and the process through which it is created.

As the experience of the prisoners in Lompoc suggests, virtually anything can serve as money. Historically, salt, horses, tobacco, cigarettes, gold, and silver have all served as money. We shall examine the characteristics that define a good as money.

We will also introduce the largest financial institution in the world, the Federal Reserve System of the United States. The Fed, as it is commonly called, plays a key role in determining the quantity of money in the United States. We will see how the Fed operates and how it attempts to control the supply of money.

24.2 What Is Money?

Learning Objectives

1. Define money and discuss its three basic functions.
2. Distinguish between commodity money and fiat money, giving examples of each.
3. Define what is meant by the money supply and tell what is included in the Federal Reserve System's two definitions of it (M1 and M2).

money

Anything that serves as a medium of exchange.

medium of exchange

Anything that is widely accepted as a means of payment.

If cigarettes and mackerel can be used as money, then just what is money? **Money** is anything that serves as a medium of exchange. A **medium of exchange** is anything that is widely accepted as a means of payment. In Romania under Communist Party rule in the 1980s, for example, Kent cigarettes served as a medium of exchange; the fact that they could be exchanged for other goods and services made them money.

Money, ultimately, is defined by people and what they do. When people use something as a medium of exchange, it becomes money. If people were to begin accepting basketballs as payment for most goods and services, basketballs would be money. We will learn in this chapter that changes in the way people use money have created new types of money and changed the way money is measured in recent decades.

The Functions of Money

Money serves three basic functions. By definition, it is a medium of exchange. It also serves as a unit of account and as a store of value—as the "mack" did in Lompoc.

A Medium of Exchange

The exchange of goods and services in markets is among the most universal activities of human life. To facilitate these exchanges, people settle on something that will serve as a medium of exchange—they select something to be money.

barter

When goods are exchanged directly for other goods.

We can understand the significance of a medium of exchange by considering its absence. **Barter** occurs when goods are exchanged directly for other goods. Because no one item serves as a medium of exchange in a barter economy, potential buyers must find things that individual sellers will accept. A buyer might find a seller who will trade a pair of shoes for two chickens. Another seller might be willing to provide a haircut in exchange for a garden hose. Suppose you were visiting a grocery store in a barter economy. You would need to load up a truckful of items the grocer might accept in exchange for groceries. That would be an uncertain affair; you could not know when you headed for the store which items the grocer might agree to trade. Indeed, the complexity—and cost—of a visit to a grocery store in a barter economy would be so great that there probably would not be any grocery stores! A moment's contemplation of the difficulty of life in a barter economy will demonstrate why human societies invariably select something—sometimes more than one thing—to serve as a medium of exchange, just as prisoners in federal penitentiaries accepted mackerel.

A Unit of Account

Ask someone in the United States what he or she paid for something, and that person will respond by quoting a price stated in dollars: "I paid $75 for this radio," or "I paid $15 for this pizza." People do not say, "I paid five pizzas for this radio." That statement might, of course, be literally true in the sense of the opportunity cost of the transaction, but we do not report prices that way for two reasons. One is that people do not arrive at places like Radio Shack with five pizzas and expect to purchase a radio. The other is that the information would not be very useful. Other people may not think of values in pizza terms, so they might not know what we meant. Instead, we report the value of things in terms of money.

unit of account

A consistent means of measuring the value of things.

Money serves as a **unit of account**, which is a consistent means of measuring the value of things. We use money in this fashion because it is also a medium of exchange. When we report the value of a good or service in units of money, we are reporting what another person is likely to have to pay to obtain that good or service.

A Store of Value

The third function of money is to serve as a **store of value**, that is, an item that holds value over time. Consider a $20 bill that you accidentally left in a coat pocket a year ago. When you find it, you will be pleased. That is because you know the bill still has value. Value has, in effect, been "stored" in that little piece of paper.

store of value

An item that holds value over time.

Money, of course, is not the only thing that stores value. Houses, office buildings, land, works of art, and many other commodities serve as a means of storing wealth and value. Money differs from these other stores of value by being readily exchangeable for other commodities. Its role as a medium of exchange makes it a convenient store of value.

Because money acts as a store of value, it can be used as a standard for future payments. When you borrow money, for example, you typically sign a contract pledging to make a series of future payments to settle the debt. These payments will be made using money, because money acts as a store of value.

Money is not a risk-free store of value, however. We saw in the chapter that introduced the concept of inflation that inflation reduces the value of money. In periods of rapid inflation, people may not want to rely on money as a store of value, and they may turn to commodities such as land or gold instead.

Types of Money

Although money can take an extraordinary variety of forms, there are really only two types of money: money that has intrinsic value and money that does not have intrinsic value.

Commodity money is money that has value apart from its use as money. Mackerel in federal prisons is an example of commodity money. Mackerel could be used to buy services from other prisoners; they could also be eaten.

commodity money

Money that has value apart from its use as money.

Gold and silver are the most widely used forms of commodity money. Gold and silver can be used as jewelry and for some industrial and medicinal purposes, so they have value apart from their use as money. The first known use of gold and silver coins was in the Greek city-state of Lydia in the beginning of the seventh century B.C. The coins were fashioned from electrum, a natural mixture of gold and silver.

One disadvantage of commodity money is that its quantity can fluctuate erratically. Gold, for example, was one form of money in the United States in the 19th century. Gold discoveries in California and later in Alaska sent the quantity of money soaring. Some of this nation's worst bouts of inflation were set off by increases in the quantity of gold in circulation during the 19th century. A much greater problem exists with commodity money that can be produced. In the southern part of colonial America, for example, tobacco served as money. There was a continuing problem of farmers increasing the quantity of money by growing more tobacco. The problem was sufficiently serious that vigilante squads were organized. They roamed the countryside burning tobacco fields in an effort to keep the quantity of tobacco, hence money, under control. (Remarkably, these squads sought to control the money supply by burning tobacco grown by other farmers.)

Another problem is that commodity money may vary in quality. Given that variability, there is a tendency for lower-quality commodities to drive higher-quality commodities out of circulation. Horses, for example, served as money in colonial New England. It was common for loan obligations to be stated in terms of a quantity of horses to be paid back. Given such obligations, there was a tendency to use lower-quality horses to pay back debts; higher-quality horses were kept out of circulation for other uses. Laws were passed forbidding the use of lame horses in the payment of debts. This is an example of Gresham's law: the tendency for a lower-quality commodity (bad money) to drive a higher-quality commodity (good money) out of circulation. Unless a means can be found to control the quality of commodity money, the tendency for that quality to decline can threaten its acceptability as a medium of exchange.

fiat money

Money that some authority, generally a government, has ordered to be accepted as a medium of exchange.

currency

Paper money and coins.

checkable deposits

Balances in checking accounts.

check

A written order to a bank to transfer ownership of a checkable deposit.

But something need not have intrinsic value to serve as money. **Fiat money** is money that some authority, generally a government, has ordered to be accepted as a medium of exchange. The **currency**—paper money and coins—used in the United States today is fiat money; it has no value other than its use as money. You will notice that statement printed on each bill: "This note is legal tender for all debts, public and private."

Checkable deposits, which are balances in checking accounts, and traveler's checks are other forms of money that have no intrinsic value. They can be converted to currency, but generally they are not; they simply serve as a medium of exchange. If you want to buy something, you can often pay with a check or a debit card. A **check** is a written order to a bank to transfer ownership of a checkable deposit. A debit card is the electronic equivalent of a check. Suppose, for example, that you have $100 in your checking account and you write a check to your campus bookstore for $30 or instruct the clerk to swipe your debit card and "charge" it $30. In either case, $30 will be transferred from your checking account to the bookstore's checking account. *Notice that it is the checkable deposit, not the check or debit card, that is money*. The check or debit card just tells a bank to transfer money, in this case checkable deposits, from one account to another.

What makes something money is really found in its acceptability, not in whether or not it has intrinsic value or whether or not a government has declared it as such. For example, fiat money tends to be accepted so long as too much of it is not printed too quickly. When that happens, as it did in Russia in the 1990s, people tend to look for other items to serve as money. In the case of Russia, the U.S. dollar became a popular form of money, even though the Russian government still declared the ruble to be its fiat money.

Heads Up!

The term *money*, as used by economists and throughout this book, has the very specific definition given in the text. People can hold assets in a variety of forms, from works of art to stock certificates to currency or checking account balances. Even though individuals may be very wealthy, only when they are holding their assets in a form that serves as a medium of exchange do they, according to the precise meaning of the term, have "money." To qualify as "money," something must be widely accepted as a medium of exchange.

Measuring Money

money supply

The total quantity of money in the economy at any one time.

The total quantity of money in the economy at any one time is called the **money supply**. Economists measure the money supply because it affects economic activity. What should be included in the money supply? We want to include as part of the money supply those things that serve as media of exchange. However, the items that provide this function have varied over time.

Before 1980, the basic money supply was measured as the sum of currency in circulation, traveler's checks, and checkable deposits. Currency serves the medium-of-exchange function very nicely but denies people any interest earnings. (Checking accounts did not earn interest before 1980.)

Over the last few decades, especially as a result of high interest rates and high inflation in the late 1970s, people sought and found ways of holding their financial assets in ways that earn interest and that can easily be converted to money. For example, it is now possible to transfer money from your savings account to your checking account using an automated teller machine (ATM), and then to withdraw cash from your checking account. Thus, many types of savings accounts are easily converted into currency.

liquidity

The ease with which an asset can be converted into currency.

Economists refer to the ease with which an asset can be converted into currency as the asset's **liquidity**. Currency itself is perfectly liquid; you can always change two $5 bills for a $10 bill. Checkable deposits are almost perfectly liquid; you can easily cash a check or visit an ATM. An office building, however, is highly illiquid. It can be converted to money only by selling it, a time-consuming and costly process.

As financial assets other than checkable deposits have become more liquid, economists have had to develop broader measures of money that would correspond to economic activity. In the United States, the final arbiter of what is and what is not measured as money is the Federal Reserve System. Because it is difficult to determine what (and what not) to measure as money, the Fed reports several different measures of money, including M1 and M2.

M1 is the narrowest of the Fed's money supply definitions. It includes currency in circulation, checkable deposits, and traveler's checks. **M2** is a broader measure of the money supply than M1. It includes M1 and other deposits such as small savings accounts (less than $100,000), as well as accounts such as money market mutual funds (MMMFs) that place limits on the number or the amounts of the checks that can be written in a certain period.

M2 is sometimes called the broadly defined money supply, while M1 is the narrowly defined money supply. The assets in M1 may be regarded as perfectly liquid; the assets in M2 are highly liquid, but somewhat less liquid than the assets in M1. Even broader measures of the money supply include large time-deposits, money market mutual funds held by institutions, and other assets that are somewhat less liquid than those in M2. Figure 24.1 shows the composition of M1 and M2 in October 2016.

M1

The narrowest of the Fed's money supply definitions that includes currency in circulation, checkable deposits, and traveler's checks.

M2

A broader measure of the money supply than M1 that includes M1 and other deposits.

FIGURE 24.1 The Two Ms: October 2016

M1, the narrowest definition of the money supply, includes assets that are perfectly liquid. M2 provides a broader measure of the money supply and includes somewhat less liquid assets. Amounts represent money supply data in billions of dollars for October 2016, seasonally adjusted.

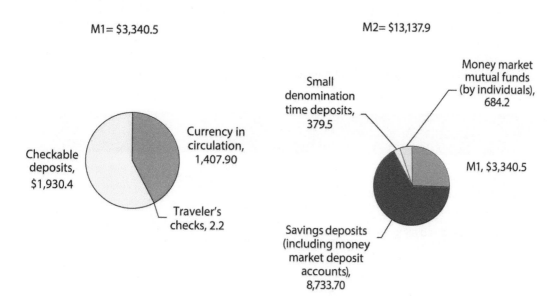

Source: Based on data from Federal Reserve Statistical Release H.6, Tables 3 and 4 (December 1, 2016). Amounts are in billions of dollars for December 2013, seasonally adjusted.

Heads Up!

Credit cards are not money. A credit card identifies you as a person who has a special arrangement with the card issuer in which the issuer will lend you money and transfer the proceeds to another party whenever you want. Thus, if you present a MasterCard to a jeweler as payment for a $500 ring, the firm that issued you the card will lend you the $500 and send that money, less a service charge, to the jeweler. You, of course, will be required to repay the loan later. But a card that says you have such a relationship is not money, just as your debit card is not money.

With all the operational definitions of money available, which one should we use? Economists generally answer that question by asking another: Which measure of money is most closely related to real GDP and the price level? As that changes, so must the definition of money.

In 1980, the Fed decided that changes in the ways people were managing their money made M1 useless for policy choices. Indeed, the Fed now pays little attention to M2 either. It has largely given up tracking a particular measure of the money supply. The choice of what to measure as money remains the subject of continuing research and considerable debate.

Key Takeaways

- Money is anything that serves as a medium of exchange. Other functions of money are to serve as a unit of account and as a store of value.
- Money may or may not have intrinsic value. Commodity money has intrinsic value because it has other uses besides being a medium of exchange. Fiat money serves only as a medium of exchange, because its use as such is authorized by the government; it has no intrinsic value.
- The Fed reports several different measures of money, including M1 and M2.

Try It!

Which of the following are money in the United States today and which are not? Explain your reasoning in terms of the functions of money.

1. Gold
2. A Van Gogh painting
3. A dime

Case in Point: Fiat-less Money

Source: © Georgios Kollidas / Shutterstock.com

"We don't have a currency of our own," proclaimed Nerchivan Barzani, the Kurdish regional government's prime minister in a news interview in 2003. But, even without official recognition by the government, the so-called "Swiss" dinar certainly seemed to function as a fiat money. Here is how the Kurdish area of northern Iraq, during the period between the Gulf War in 1991 and the fall of Saddam Hussein in 2003, came to have its own currency, despite the pronouncement of its prime minister to the contrary.

After the Gulf War, the northern, mostly Kurdish area of Iraq was separated from the rest of Iraq though the enforcement of the no-fly-zone. Because of United Nations sanctions that barred the Saddam Hussein regime in the south from continuing to import currency from Switzerland, the central bank of Iraq announced it would replace the "Swiss" dinars, so named because they had been printed in Switzerland, with locally printed currency, which became known as "Saddam" dinars. Iraqi citizens in southern Iraq were given three weeks to exchange their old dinars for the new ones. In the northern part of Iraq, citizens could not exchange their notes and so they simply continued to use the old ones.

And so it was that the "Swiss" dinar for a period of about 10 years, even without government backing or any law establishing it as legal tender, served as northern Iraq's fiat money. Economists use the word "*fiat*," which in Latin means "let it be done," to describe money that has no intrinsic value. Such forms of money *usually* get their value because a government or authority has declared them to be legal tender, but, as this story shows, it does not really require much "fiat" for a convenient, in-and-of-itself worthless, medium of exchange to evolve.

What happened to both the "Swiss" and "Saddam" dinars? After the Coalition Provisional Authority (CPA) assumed control of all of Iraq, Paul Bremer, then head of the CPA, announced that a new Iraqi dinar would be exchanged for both of the existing currencies over a three-month period ending in January 2004 at a rate that implied that one "Swiss" dinar was valued at 150 "Saddam" dinars. Because Saddam Hussein's regime had printed many more "Saddam" dinars over the 10-year period, while no "Swiss" dinars had been printed, and because the cheap printing of the "Saddam" dinars made them easy to counterfeit, over the decade the "Swiss" dinars became relatively more valuable and the exchange rate that Bremer offered about equalized the purchasing power of the two currencies. For example, it took about 133 times as many "Saddam" dinars as "Swiss" dinars to buy a man's suit in Iraq at the time. The new notes, sometimes called "Bremer" dinars, were printed in Britain and elsewhere and flown into Iraq on 22 flights using Boeing 747s and other large aircraft. In both the northern and southern parts of Iraq, citizens turned in their old dinars for the new ones, suggesting at least more confidence at that moment in the "Bremer" dinar than in either the "Saddam" or "Swiss" dinars.

Sources: *Based on Mervyn A. King, "The Institutions of Monetary Policy" (lecture, American Economics Association Annual Meeting, San Diego, January 4, 2004), available at http://www.bis. org/review/r040202b.pdf; Hal R. Varian, "Paper Currency Can Have Value without Government Backing, but Such Backing Adds Substantially to Its Value," New York Times, January 15, 2004, p. C2.*

Answer to Try It! Problems

1. Gold is not money because it is not used as a medium of exchange. In addition, it does not serve as a unit of account. It may, however, serve as a store of value.
2. A Van Gogh painting is not money. It serves as a store of value. It is highly illiquid but could eventually be converted to money. It is neither a medium of exchange nor a unit of account.
3. A dime is money and serves all three functions of money. It is, of course, perfectly liquid.

24.3 The Banking System and Money Creation

Learning Objectives

1. Explain what banks are, what their balance sheets look like, and what is meant by a fractional reserve banking system.
2. Describe the process of money creation (destruction), using the concept of the deposit multiplier.
3. Describe how and why banks are regulated and insured.

Where does money come from? How is its quantity increased or decreased? The answer to these questions suggests that money has an almost magical quality: *money is created by banks when they issue loans*. In effect, money is created by the stroke of a pen or the click of a computer key.

We will begin by examining the operation of banks and the banking system. We will find that, like money itself, the nature of banking is experiencing rapid change.

Banks and Other Financial Intermediaries

financial intermediary

An institution that amasses funds from one group and makes them available to another.

An institution that amasses funds from one group and makes them available to another is called a **financial intermediary**. A pension fund is an example of a financial intermediary. Workers and firms place earnings in the fund for their retirement; the fund earns income by lending money to firms or by purchasing their stock. The fund thus makes retirement saving available for other spending. Insurance companies are also financial intermediaries, because they lend some of the premiums paid by their customers to firms for investment. Mutual funds make money available to firms and other institutions by purchasing their initial offerings of stocks or bonds.

bank

A financial intermediary that accepts deposits, makes loans, and offers checking accounts.

Banks play a particularly important role as financial intermediaries. Banks accept depositors' money and lend it to borrowers. With the interest they earn on their loans, banks are able to pay interest to their depositors, cover their own operating costs, and earn a profit, all the while maintaining the ability of the original depositors to spend the funds when they desire to do so. One key characteristic of banks is that they offer their customers the opportunity to open checking accounts, thus creating checkable deposits. These functions define a **bank**, which is a financial intermediary that accepts deposits, makes loans, and offers checking accounts.

Over time, some nonbank financial intermediaries have become more and more like banks. For example, brokerage firms usually offer customers interest-earning accounts and make loans. They now allow their customers to write checks on their accounts.

The fact that banks account for a declining share of U.S. financial assets alarms some observers. We will see that banks are more tightly regulated than are other financial institutions; one reason for that regulation is to maintain control over the money supply. Other financial intermediaries do not face the same regulatory restrictions as banks. Indeed, their relative freedom from regulation is one reason they have grown so rapidly. As other financial intermediaries become more important, central authorities begin to lose control over the money supply.

The declining share of financial assets controlled by "banks" began to change in 2008. Many of the nation's largest investment banks—financial institutions that provided services to firms but were not regulated as commercial banks—began having serious financial difficulties as a result of their investments tied to home mortgage loans. As home prices in the United States began falling, many of those mortgage loans went into default. Investment banks that had made substantial purchases of securities whose value was ultimately based on those mortgage loans themselves began failing. Bear Stearns, one of the largest investment banks in the United States, required federal funds to remain solvent. Another large investment bank, Lehman Brothers, failed. In an effort to avoid a similar fate, several other investment banks applied for status as ordinary commercial banks subject to the stringent regulation those institutions face. One result of the terrible financial crisis that crippled the U.S. and other economies in 2008 may be greater control of the money supply by the Fed.

Bank Finance and a Fractional Reserve System

Bank finance lies at the heart of the process through which money is created. To understand money creation, we need to understand some of the basics of bank finance.

Banks accept deposits and issue checks to the owners of those deposits. Banks use the money collected from depositors to make loans. The bank's financial picture at a given time can be depicted using a simplified **balance sheet**, which is a financial statement showing assets, liabilities, and net worth. **Assets** are anything of value. **Liabilities** are obligations to other parties. **Net worth** equals assets less liabilities. All these are given dollar values in a firm's balance sheet. The sum of liabilities plus net worth therefore must equal the sum of all assets. On a balance sheet, assets are listed on the left, liabilities and net worth on the right.

The main way that banks earn profits is through issuing loans. Because their depositors do not typically all ask for the entire amount of their deposits back at the same time, banks lend out most of the deposits they have collected—to companies seeking to expand their operations, to people buying cars or homes, and so on. Banks keep only a fraction of their deposits as cash in their vaults and in deposits with the Fed. These assets are called **reserves**. Banks lend out the rest of their deposits. A system in which banks hold reserves whose value is less than the sum of claims outstanding on those reserves is called a **fractional reserve banking system**.

Table 24.1 shows a consolidated balance sheet for commercial banks in the United States for October 2016. Banks hold reserves against the liabilities represented by their checkable deposits. Notice that these reserves were a small fraction of total deposit liabilities of that month. Most bank assets are in the form of loans.

balance sheet

A financial statement showing assets, liabilities, and net worth.

assets

Anything of value.

liabilities

Obligations to other parties.

net worth

Assets less liabilities.

reserves

Bank assets held as cash in vaults and in deposits with the Federal Reserve.

fractional reserve banking system

System in which banks hold reserves whose value is less than the sum of claims outstanding on those reserves.

TABLE 24.1 The Consolidated Balance Sheet for U.S. Commercial Banks, October 2016
The balance sheet for all commercial banks in the United States shows their financial situation in billions of dollars, seasonally adjusted, in October 2016.

Assets		Liabilities and Net Worth	
Reserves	$2,196.9	Checkable deposits	$11,350.8
Other assets	$1,360.5	Borrowings	$1,968.7
Loans	$9,057.2	Other liabilities	$880.8
Securities	$3,334.9		
Total assets	$15,949.5	Total liabilities	$14,200.3
		Net worth	$1,749.2

Source: Based on data from Federal Reserve Statistical Release H.8 (December 2, 2016).

In the next section, we will learn that money is created when banks issue loans.

Money Creation

required reserves

The quantity of reserves banks are required to hold.

required reserve ratio

The ratio of reserves to checkable deposits a bank must maintain.

excess reserves

Reserves in excess of the required level.

loaned up

When a bank's excess reserves equal zero.

To understand the process of money creation today, let us create a hypothetical system of banks. We will focus on three banks in this system: Acme Bank, Bellville Bank, and Clarkston Bank. Assume that all banks are required to hold reserves equal to 10% of their checkable deposits. The quantity of reserves banks are required to hold is called **required reserves**. The reserve requirement is expressed as a **required reserve ratio**; it specifies the ratio of reserves to checkable deposits a bank must maintain. Banks may hold reserves in excess of the required level; such reserves are called **excess reserves**. Excess reserves plus required reserves equal total reserves.

Because banks earn relatively little interest on their reserves held on deposit with the Federal Reserve, we shall assume that they seek to hold no excess reserves. When a bank's excess reserves equal zero, it is **loaned up**. Finally, we shall ignore assets other than reserves and loans and deposits other than checkable deposits. To simplify the analysis further, we shall suppose that banks have no net worth; their assets are equal to their liabilities.

Let us suppose that every bank in our imaginary system begins with $1,000 in reserves, $9,000 in loans outstanding, and $10,000 in checkable deposit balances held by customers. The balance sheet for one of these banks, Acme Bank, is shown in Table 24.2. The required reserve ratio is 0.1: Each bank must have reserves equal to 10% of its checkable deposits. Because reserves equal required reserves, excess reserves equal zero. Each bank is loaned up.

TABLE 24.2 A Balance Sheet for Acme Bank
We assume that all banks in a hypothetical system of banks have $1,000 in reserves, $10,000 in checkable deposits, and $9,000 in loans. With a 10% reserve requirement, each bank is loaned up; it has zero excess reserves.

Acme Bank			
Assets		**Liabilities**	
Reserves	$1,000	Deposits	$10,000
Loans	$9,000		

Acme Bank, like every other bank in our hypothetical system, initially holds reserves equal to the level of required reserves. Now suppose one of Acme Bank's customers deposits $1,000 in cash in a checking account. The money goes into the bank's vault and thus adds to reserves. The customer now has an additional $1,000 in his or her account. Two versions of Acme's balance sheet are given here. The first shows the changes brought by the customer's deposit: reserves and checkable deposits rise by $1,000. The second shows how these changes affect Acme's balances. Reserves now equal $2,000 and checkable deposits equal $11,000. With checkable deposits of $11,000 and a 10% reserve requirement, Acme is required to hold reserves of $1,100. With reserves equaling $2,000, Acme has $900 in excess reserves.

At this stage, there has been no change in the money supply. When the customer brought in the $1,000 and Acme put the money in the vault, currency in circulation fell by $1,000. At the same time, the $1,000 was added to the customer's checking account balance, so the money supply did not change.

FIGURE 24.2

Acme Bank, Changes in Balance Sheet		Acme Bank, Balance Sheet	
Assets	Liabilities	Assets	Liabilities
Reserves +$1,000	Deposits +$1,000	Reserves $2,000 Loans $9,000	Deposits $11,000
		(Excess reserves = $900)	

Because Acme earns only a low interest rate on its excess reserves, we assume it will try to loan them out. Suppose Acme lends the $900 to one of its customers. It will make the loan by crediting the customer's checking account with $900. Acme's outstanding loans and checkable deposits rise by $900. The $900 in checkable deposits is new money; Acme created it when it issued the $900 loan. Now you know where money comes from—it is created when a bank issues a loan.

FIGURE 24.3

Acme Bank, Changes in Balance Sheet		Acme Bank, Balance Sheet	
Assets	Liabilities	Assets	Liabilities
Loans +$900	Deposits +$900	Reserves $2,000 Loans $9,900	Deposits $11,900

Presumably, the customer who borrowed the $900 did so in order to spend it. That customer will write a check to someone else, who is likely to bank at some other bank. Suppose that Acme's borrower writes a check to a firm with an account at Bellville Bank. In this set of transactions, Acme's checkable deposits fall by $900. The firm that receives the check deposits it in its account at Bellville Bank, increasing that bank's checkable deposits by $900. Bellville Bank now has a check written on an Acme account. Bellville will submit the check to the Fed, which will reduce Acme's deposits with the Fed—its reserves—by $900 and increase Bellville's reserves by $900.

FIGURE 24.4

Acme Bank, Changes in Balance Sheet		Acme Bank, Balance Sheet	
Assets	Liabilities	Assets	Liabilities
Reserves −$900	Deposits −$900	Reserves $1,100 Loans $9,900	Deposits $11,000

Bellville Bank, Changes in Balance Sheet		Bellville Bank, Balance Sheet	
Assets	Liabilities	Assets	Liabilities
Reserves +$900	Deposits +$900	Reserves $1,900 Loans $9,000	Deposits $10,900
		(Excess reserves = $810)	

Notice that Acme Bank emerges from this round of transactions with $11,000 in checkable deposits and $1,100 in reserves. It has eliminated its excess reserves by issuing the loan for $900; Acme is now loaned up. Notice also that from Acme's point of view, it has not created any money! It merely took in a $1,000 deposit and emerged from the process with $1,000 in additional checkable deposits.

The $900 in new money Acme created when it issued a loan has not vanished—it is now in an account in Bellville Bank. Like the magician who shows the audience that the hat from which the rabbit appeared was empty, Acme can report that it has not created any money. There is a wonderful irony in the magic of money creation: banks create money when they issue loans, but no one bank ever seems to keep the money it creates. That is because money is created within the banking system, not by a single bank.

The process of money creation will not end there. Let us go back to Bellville Bank. Its deposits and reserves rose by $900 when the Acme check was deposited in a Bellville account. The $900 deposit required an increase in required reserves of $90. Because Bellville's reserves rose by $900, it now has $810 in excess reserves. Just as Acme lent the amount of its excess reserves, we can expect Bellville to lend this $810. The next set of balance sheets shows this transaction. Bellville's loans and checkable deposits rise by $810.

FIGURE 24.5

Bellville Bank, Changes in Balance Sheet		Bellville Bank, Balance Sheet	
Assets	Liabilities	Assets	Liabilities
Loans +$810	Deposits +$810	Reserves $1,900 Loans $9,810	Deposits $11,710

The $810 that Bellville lent will be spent. Let us suppose it ends up with a customer who banks at Clarkston Bank. Bellville's checkable deposits fall by $810; Clarkston's rise by the same amount. Clarkston submits the check to the Fed, which transfers the money from Bellville's reserve account to Clarkston's. Notice that Clarkston's deposits rise by $810; Clarkston must increase its reserves by $81. But its reserves have risen by $810, so it has excess reserves of $729.

FIGURE 24.6

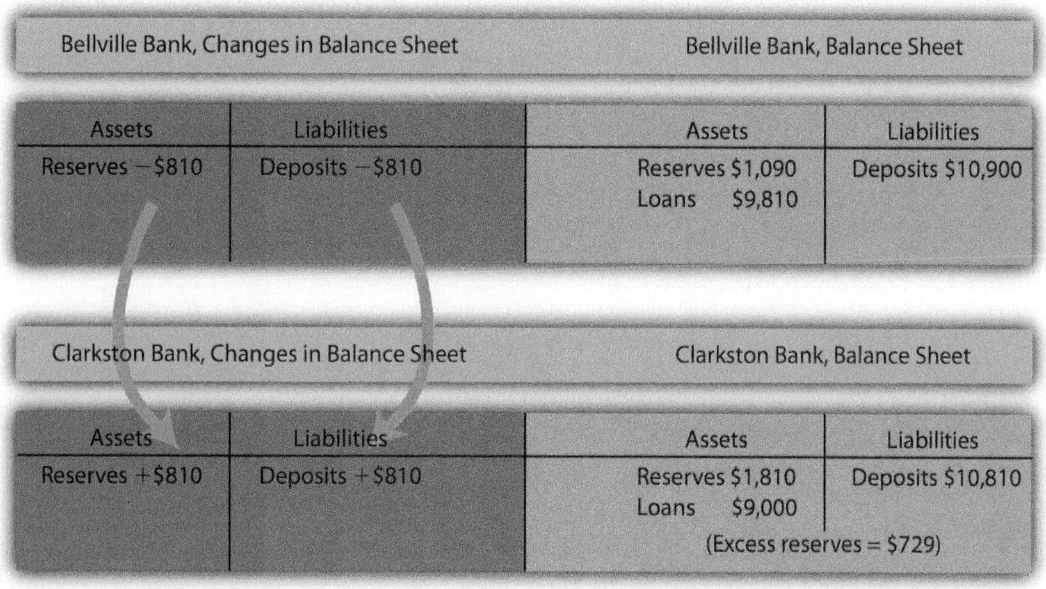

Bellville Bank, Changes in Balance Sheet		Bellville Bank, Balance Sheet	
Assets	Liabilities	Assets	Liabilities
Reserves −$810	Deposits −$810	Reserves $1,090 Loans $9,810	Deposits $10,900

Clarkston Bank, Changes in Balance Sheet		Clarkston Bank, Balance Sheet	
Assets	Liabilities	Assets	Liabilities
Reserves +$810	Deposits +$810	Reserves $1,810 Loans $9,000 (Excess reserves = $729)	Deposits $10,810

Notice that Bellville is now loaned up. And notice that it can report that it has not created any money either! It took in a $900 deposit, and its checkable deposits have risen by that same $900. The $810 it created when it issued a loan is now at Clarkston Bank.

The process will not end there. Clarkston will lend the $729 it now has in excess reserves, and the money that has been created will end up at some other bank, which will then have excess reserves—and create still more money. And that process will just keep going as long as there are excess reserves to pass through the banking system in the form of loans. How much will ultimately be created by the system as a whole? With a 10% reserve requirement, each dollar in reserves backs up $10 in checkable deposits. The $1,000 in cash that Acme's customer brought in adds $1,000 in reserves to the banking system. It can therefore back up an additional $10,000! In just the three banks we have shown, checkable deposits have risen by $2,710 ($1,000 at Acme, $900 at Bellville, and $810 at Clarkston). Additional banks in the system will continue to create money, up to a maximum of $7,290 among them. Subtracting the original $1,000 that had been a part of currency in circulation, we see that the money supply could rise by as much as $9,000.

Heads Up!

Notice that when the banks received new deposits, they could make new loans only up to the amount of their excess reserves, not up to the amount of their deposits and total reserve increases. For example, with the new deposit of $1,000, Acme Bank was able to make additional loans of $900. If instead it made new loans equal to its increase in total reserves, then after the customers who received new loans wrote checks to others, its reserves would be less than the required amount. In the case of Acme, had it lent out an additional $1,000, after checks were written against the new loans, it would have been left with only $1,000 in reserves against $11,000 in deposits, for a reserve ratio of only 0.09, which is less than the required reserve ratio of 0.1 in the example.

The Deposit Multiplier

deposit multiplier

The ratio of the maximum possible change in checkable deposits (ΔD) to the change in reserves (ΔR).

We can relate the potential increase in the money supply to the change in reserves that created it using the **deposit multiplier** (m_d), which equals the ratio of the maximum possible change in checkable deposits (ΔD) to the change in reserves (ΔR). In our example, the deposit multiplier was 10:

EQUATION 24.1

$$m_d = \frac{\Delta D}{\Delta R} = \frac{\$10,000}{\$1,000} = 10$$

To see how the deposit multiplier m_d is related to the required reserve ratio, we use the fact that if banks in the economy are loaned up, then reserves, R, equal the required reserve ratio (rrr) times checkable deposits, D:

EQUATION 24.2

$$R = rrrD$$

A change in reserves produces a change in loans and a change in checkable deposits. Once banks are fully loaned up, the change in reserves, ΔR, will equal the required reserve ratio times the change in deposits, ΔD:

EQUATION 24.3

$$\Delta R = rrr\Delta D$$

Solving for ΔD, we have

EQUATION 24.4

$$\frac{1}{rrr}\Delta R = \Delta D$$

Dividing both sides by ΔR, we see that the deposit multiplier, m_d, is $1/rrr$:

EQUATION 24.5

$$\frac{1}{rrr} = \frac{\Delta D}{\Delta R} = m_d$$

The deposit multiplier is thus given by the reciprocal of the required reserve ratio. With a required reserve ratio of 0.1, the deposit multiplier is 10. A required reserve ratio of 0.2 would produce a deposit multiplier of 5. The higher the required reserve ratio, the lower the deposit multiplier.

Actual increases in checkable deposits will not be nearly as great as suggested by the deposit multiplier. That is because the artificial conditions of our example are not met in the real world. Some banks hold excess reserves, customers withdraw cash, and some loan proceeds are not spent. Each of these factors reduces the degree to which checkable deposits are affected by an increase in reserves. The basic mechanism, however, is the one described in our example, and it remains the case that checkable deposits increase by a multiple of an increase in reserves.

The entire process of money creation can work in reverse. When you withdraw cash from your bank, you reduce the bank's reserves. Just as a deposit at Acme Bank increases the money supply by a multiple of the original deposit, your withdrawal reduces the money supply by a multiple of the amount you withdraw. And just as money is created when banks issue loans, it is destroyed as the loans are repaid. A loan payment reduces checkable deposits; it thus reduces the money supply.

Suppose, for example, that the Acme Bank customer who borrowed the $900 makes a $100 payment on the loan. Only part of the payment will reduce the loan balance; part will be interest. Suppose $30 of the payment is for interest, while the remaining $70 reduces the loan balance. The effect of the payment on Acme's balance sheet is shown below. Checkable deposits fall by $100, loans fall by $70, and net worth rises by the amount of the interest payment, $30.

Similar to the process of money creation, the money reduction process decreases checkable deposits by, at most, the amount of the reduction in deposits times the deposit multiplier.

The Regulation of Banks

FIGURE 24.7

Banks are among the most heavily regulated of financial institutions. They are regulated in part to protect individual depositors against corrupt business practices. Banks are also susceptible to crises of confidence. Because their reserves equal only a fraction of their deposit liabilities, an effort by customers to get all their cash out of a bank could force it to fail. A few poorly managed banks could create such a crisis, leading people to try to withdraw their funds from well-managed banks. Another reason for the high degree of regulation is that variations in the quantity of money have important effects on the economy as a whole, and banks are the institutions through which money is created.

FIGURE 24.7

Changes in Acme Bank's Balance Sheet	
Assets	**Liabilities and net worth**
Loans − $70	Deposits − $100
	Net worth + $30

Deposit Insurance

From a customer's point of view, the most important form of regulation comes in the form of deposit insurance. For commercial banks, this insurance is provided by the Federal Deposit Insurance Corporation (FDIC). Insurance funds are maintained through a premium assessed on banks for every $100 of bank deposits.

If a commercial bank fails, the FDIC guarantees to reimburse depositors up to $250,000 (raised from $100,000 during the financial crisis of 2008) per insured bank, for each account ownership category. From a depositor's point of view, therefore, it is not necessary to worry about a bank's safety.

One difficulty this insurance creates, however, is that it may induce the officers of a bank to take more risks. With a federal agency on hand to bail them out if they fail, the costs of failure are reduced. Bank officers can thus be expected to take more risks than they would otherwise, which, in turn, makes failure more likely. In addition, depositors, knowing that their deposits are insured, may not scrutinize the banks' lending activities as carefully as they would if they felt that unwise loans could result in the loss of their deposits.

Thus, banks present us with a fundamental dilemma. A fractional reserve system means that banks can operate only if their customers maintain their confidence in them. If bank customers lose confidence, they are likely to try to withdraw their funds. But with a fractional reserve system, a bank actually holds funds in reserve equal to only a small fraction of its deposit liabilities. If its customers think a bank will fail and try to withdraw their cash, the bank is likely to fail. Bank panics, in which frightened customers rush to withdraw their deposits, contributed to the failure of one-third of the nation's banks between 1929 and 1933. Deposit insurance was introduced in large part to give people confidence in their banks and to prevent failure. But the deposit insurance that seeks to prevent bank failures may lead to less careful management—and thus encourage bank failure.

Regulation to Prevent Bank Failure

To reduce the number of bank failures, banks are limited in what they can do. Banks are required to maintain a minimum level of net worth as a fraction of total assets. Regulators from the FDIC regularly perform audits and other checks of individual banks to ensure they are operating safely.

The FDIC has the power to close a bank whose net worth has fallen below the required level. In practice, it typically acts to close a bank when it becomes insolvent, that is, when its net worth becomes negative. Negative net worth implies that the bank's liabilities exceed its assets.

When the FDIC closes a bank, it arranges for depositors to receive their funds. When the bank's funds are insufficient to return customers' deposits, the FDIC uses money from the insurance fund for this purpose. Alternatively, the FDIC may arrange for another bank to purchase the failed bank. The FDIC, however, continues to guarantee that depositors will not lose any money.

Regulation in Response to Financial Crises

In the aftermath of the Great Depression and the banking crisis that accompanied it, laws were passed to try to make the banking system safer. The Glass-Steagall Act of that period created the FDIC and the separation between commercial banks and investment banks. Over time, the financial system in the United States and in other countries began to change, and in 1999, a law was passed in the United States that essentially repealed the part of the Glass-Steagall Act that had created the separation between commercial and investment banking. Proponents of eliminating the separation between the two types of banks argued that banks could better diversify their portfolios if allowed to participate in other parts of the financial markets and that banks in other countries operated without such a separation.

Similar to the reaction to the banking crisis of the 1930s, the financial crisis of 2008 and the Great Recession led to calls for financial market reform. The result was the Dodd-Frank Wall Street Reform and Consumer Protection Act, usually referred to as the Dodd-Frank Act, which was passed in July 2010. More than 2,000 pages in length, the regulations to implement most provisions of this act were set to take place over a nearly two-year period, with implementation of some provisions taking even longer. This act created the Consumer Financial Protection Agency to oversee and regulate various aspects of consumer credit markets, such as credit card and bank fees and mortgage contracts. It also created the Financial Stability Oversight Council (FSOC) to assess risks for the entire financial industry. The FSOC can recommend that a nonbank financial firm, such as a hedge fund that is perhaps threatening the stability of the financial system (i.e., getting "too big to fail"), become regulated by the Federal Reserve. If such firms do become insolvent, a process of liquidation similar to what occurs when the FDIC takes over a bank can be applied. The Dodd-Frank Act also calls for implementation of the Volcker rule, which was named after the former chair of the Fed who argued the case. The Volcker rule is meant to ban banks from using depositors' funds to engage in certain types of speculative investments to try to enhance the profits of the bank, at least partly reinstating the separation between commercial and investment banking that the Glass-Steagall Act had created. There are many other provisions in this wide-sweeping legislation that are designed to improve oversight of nonbank financial institutions, increase transparency in the operation of various forms of financial instruments, regulate credit rating agencies such as Moody's and Standard & Poor's, and so on.

The Dodd-Frank act received considerable attention during the 2016 U.S. presidential campaign, with then candidate Donald Trump stating that he would dismantle much of the legislation, which he said made it harder for banks to make loans and for smaller, community banks to function. He also argued that the law had not made the banking system safer and was hampering growth and job creation. With Republicans in Congress also pressing for major adjustments, the next few years may bring either a wholesale re-writing of the law or major changes.

Key Takeaways

- Banks are financial intermediaries that accept deposits, make loans, and provide checking accounts for their customers.
- Money is created within the banking system when banks issue loans; it is destroyed when the loans are repaid.
- An increase (decrease) in reserves in the banking system can increase (decrease) the money supply. The maximum amount of the increase (decrease) is equal to the deposit multiplier times the change in reserves; the deposit multiplier equals the reciprocal of the required reserve ratio.

- Bank deposits are insured and banks are heavily regulated.
- Similar to the passage of the Glass-Steagall Act during the Great Depression, the Dodd-Frank Act was the comprehensive financial reform legislation that responded to the financial crisis in 2008 and the Great Recession.

Try It!

1. Suppose Acme Bank initially has $10,000 in deposits, reserves of $2,000, and loans of $8,000. At a required reserve ratio of 0.2, is Acme loaned up? Show the balance sheet of Acme Bank at present.

2. Now suppose that an Acme Bank customer, planning to take cash on an extended college graduation trip to India, withdraws $1,000 from her account. Show the changes to Acme Bank's balance sheet and Acme's balance sheet after the withdrawal. By how much are its reserves now deficient?

3. Acme would probably replenish its reserves by reducing loans. This action would cause a multiplied contraction of checkable deposits as other banks lose deposits because their customers would be paying off loans to Acme. How large would the contraction be?

Case in Point: A Big Bank Goes Under

It was the darling of Wall Street—it showed rapid growth and made big profits. Washington Mutual, a savings and loan based in the state of Washington, was a relatively small institution whose CEO, Kerry K. Killinger, had big plans. He wanted to transform his little Seattle S&L into the Wal-Mart of banks.

Mr. Killinger began pursuing a relatively straightforward strategy. He acquired banks in large cities such as Chicago and Los Angeles. He acquired banks up and down the east and west coasts. He aggressively extended credit to low-income individuals and families—credit cards, car loans, and mortgages. In making mortgage loans to low-income families, WaMu, as the bank was known, quickly became very profitable. But it was exposing itself to greater and greater risk, according to the *New York Times*.

Housing prices in the United States more than doubled between 1997 and 2007. During that time, loans to even low-income households were profitable. But, as housing prices began falling in 2007, banks such as WaMu began to experience losses as homeowners began to walk away from houses whose values suddenly fell below their outstanding mortgages. WaMu began losing money in 2007 as housing prices began falling. The company had earned $3.6 billion in 2006, and swung to a loss of $67 million in 2007, according to the *Puget Sound Business Journal*. Mr. Killinger was ousted by the board early in September of 2008. The bank failed later that month. It was the biggest bank failure in the history of the United States.

The Federal Deposit Insurance Corporation (FDIC) had just rescued another bank, IndyMac, which was only a tenth the size of WaMu, and would have done the same for WaMu if it had not been able to find a company to purchase it. But in this case, JPMorgan Chase agreed to take it over—its deposits, bank branches, and its troubled asset portfolio. The government and the Fed even negotiated the deal behind WaMu's back! The then chief executive officer of the company, Alan H. Fishman, was reportedly flying from New York to Seattle when the deal was finalized.

The government was anxious to broker a deal that did not require use of the FDIC's depleted funds following IndyMac's collapse. But it would have done so if a buyer had not been found. As the FDIC reports on its Web site: "Since the FDIC's creation in 1933, no depositor has ever lost even one penny of FDIC-insured funds."

An interesting side note: Current Secretary of the Treasury, Steven Mnuchin, led a group of investors who bought the failed IndyMac at auction in 2009.

Sources: *Based on Eric Dash and Andrew Ross Sorkin, "Government Seizes WaMu and Sells Some Assets," New York Times, September 25, 2008, p. A1; Kirsten Grind, "Insiders Detail Reasons for WaMu's Failure," Puget Sound Business Journal, January 23, 2009; and FDIC Web site at https://www.fdic.gov/edie/fdic_info.html.*

Answer to Try It! Problems

1. Acme Bank is loaned up, since $2,000/$10,000 = 0.2, which is the required reserve ratio. Acme's balance sheet is:

Assets	Liabilities plus net worth
Reserves $2,000	Deposits $10,000
Loans $8,000	

2. Acme Bank's balance sheet after losing $1,000 in deposits:

Acme Bank, Changes in Balance Sheet		Acme Bank, Balance Sheet	
Assets	Liabilities	Assets	Liabilities
Reserves −$1,000	Deposits −$1,000	Reserves $1,000	Deposits $9,000
		Loans $8,000	

Required reserves are deficient by $800. Acme must hold 20% of its deposits, in this case $1,800 (0.2 × $9,000 = $1,800), as reserves, but it has only $1,000 in reserves at the moment.

3. The contraction in checkable deposits would be

$$\Delta D = (1/0.2) \times (-\$1,000) = -\$5,000$$

24.4 The Federal Reserve System

Learning Objectives

1. Explain the primary functions of central banks.
2. Describe how the Federal Reserve System is structured and governed.
3. Identify and explain the tools of monetary policy.
4. Describe how the Fed creates and destroys money when it buys and sells federal government bonds.

The Federal Reserve System of the United States, or Fed, is the U.S. central bank. Japan's central bank is the Bank of Japan; the European Union has established the European Central Bank. Most countries have a central bank. A **central bank** performs five primary functions: (1) it acts as a banker to the central government, (2) it acts as a banker to banks, (3) it acts as a regulator of banks, (4) it conducts monetary policy, and (5) it supports the stability of the financial system.

For the first 137 years of its history, the United States did not have a true central bank. While a central bank was often proposed, there was resistance to creating an institution with such enormous power. A series of bank panics slowly increased support for the creation of a central bank. The bank panic of 1907 proved to be the final straw. Bank failures were so widespread, and depositor losses so heavy, that concerns about centralization of power gave way to a desire for an institution that would provide a stabilizing force in the banking industry. Congress passed the Federal Reserve Act in 1913, creating the Fed and giving it all the powers of a central bank.

central bank

A bank that acts as a banker to the central government, acts as a banker to banks, acts as a regulator of banks, conducts monetary policy, and supports the stability of the financial system.

Structure of the Fed

In creating the Fed, Congress determined that a central bank should be as independent of the government as possible. It also sought to avoid too much centralization of power in a single institution. These potentially contradictory goals of independence and decentralized power are evident in the Fed's structure and in the continuing struggles between Congress and the Fed over possible changes in that structure.

In an effort to decentralize power, Congress designed the Fed as a system of 12 regional banks, as shown in Figure 24.8. Each of these banks operates as a kind of bankers' cooperative; the regional banks are owned by the commercial banks in their districts that have chosen to be members of the

Fed. The owners of each Federal Reserve bank select the board of directors of that bank; the board selects the bank's president.

FIGURE 24.8 The 12 Federal Reserve Districts and the Cities Where Each Bank Is Located

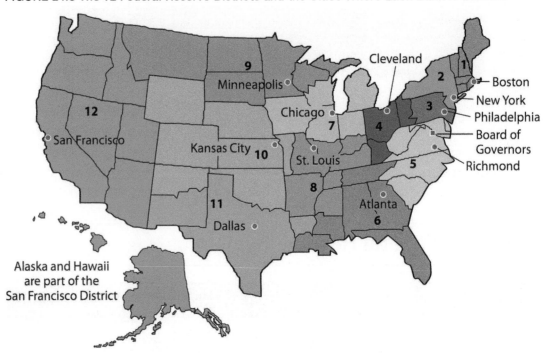

Several provisions of the Federal Reserve Act seek to maintain the Fed's independence. The board of directors for the entire Federal Reserve System is called the Board of Governors. The seven members of the board are appointed by the president of the United States and confirmed by the Senate. To ensure a large measure of independence from any one president, the members of the Board of Governors have 14-year terms. One member of the board is selected by the president of the United States to serve as chairman for a four-year term.

As a further means of ensuring the independence of the Fed, Congress authorized it to buy and sell federal government bonds. This activity is a profitable one that allows the Fed to pay its own bills. The Fed is thus not dependent on a Congress that might otherwise be tempted to force a particular set of policies on it. The Fed is limited in the profits it is allowed to earn; its "excess" profits are returned to the Treasury.

It is important to recognize that the Fed is technically not part of the federal government. Members of the Board of Governors do not legally have to answer to Congress, the president, or anyone else. The president and members of Congress can certainly try to influence the Fed, but they cannot order it to do anything. Congress, however, created the Fed. It could, by passing another law, abolish the Fed's independence. The Fed can maintain its independence only by keeping the support of Congress—and that sometimes requires being responsive to the wishes of Congress.

In recent years, Congress has sought to increase its oversight of the Fed. The chairman of the Federal Reserve Board is required to report to Congress twice each year on its monetary policy, the set of policies that the central bank can use to influence economic activity.

Powers of the Fed

The Fed's principal powers stem from its authority to conduct monetary policy. It has three main policy tools: setting reserve requirements, operating the discount window and other credit facilities, and conducting open-market operations.

Reserve Requirements

The Fed sets the required ratio of reserves that banks must hold relative to their deposit liabilities. In theory, the Fed could use this power as an instrument of monetary policy. It could lower reserve requirements when it wanted to increase the money supply and raise them when it wanted to reduce the money supply. In practice, however, the Fed does not use its power to set reserve requirements in this way. The reason is that frequent manipulation of reserve requirements would make life difficult for bankers, who would have to adjust their lending policies to changing requirements.

The Fed's power to set reserve requirements was expanded by the Monetary Control Act of 1980. Before that, the Fed set reserve requirements only for commercial banks that were members of the Federal Reserve System. Most banks are not members of the Fed; the Fed's control of reserve requirements thus extended to only a minority of banks. The 1980 act required virtually all banks to satisfy the Fed's reserve requirements.

The Discount Window and Other Credit Facilities

A major responsibility of the Fed is to act as a lender of last resort to banks. When banks fall short on reserves, they can borrow reserves from the Fed through its discount window. The **discount rate** is the interest rate charged by the Fed when it lends reserves to banks. The Board of Governors sets the discount rate.

Lowering the discount rate makes funds cheaper to banks. A lower discount rate could place downward pressure on interest rates in the economy. However, when financial markets are operating normally, banks rarely borrow from the Fed, reserving use of the discount window for emergencies. A typical bank borrows from the Fed only about once or twice per year.

Instead of borrowing from the Fed when they need reserves, banks typically rely on the federal funds market to obtain reserves. The **federal funds market** is a market in which banks lend reserves to one another. The **federal funds rate** is the interest rate charged for such loans; it is determined by banks' demand for and supply of these reserves. The ability to set the discount rate is no longer an important tool of Federal Reserve policy.

To deal with the recent financial and economic conditions, the Fed greatly expanded its lending beyond its traditional discount window lending. As falling house prices led to foreclosures, private investment banks and other financial institutions came under increasing pressure. The Fed made credit available to a wide range of institutions in an effort to stem the crisis. In 2008, the Fed bailed out two major housing finance firms that had been established by the government to prop up the housing industry—Fannie Mae (the Federal National Mortgage Association) and Freddie Mac (the Federal Home Mortgage Corporation). Together, the two institutions backed the mortgages of half of the nation's mortgage loans.[2] It also agreed to provide $85 billion to AIG, the huge insurance firm. AIG had a subsidiary that was heavily exposed to mortgage loan losses, and that crippled the firm. The Fed determined that AIG was simply too big to be allowed to fail. Many banks had ties to the giant institution, and its failure would have been a blow to those banks. As the United States faced the worst financial crisis since the Great Depression, the Fed took center stage. Whatever its role in the financial crisis of 2007–2008, the Fed remains an important backstop for banks and other financial institutions needing liquidity. And for that, it uses the traditional discount window, supplemented with a wide range of other credit facilities. The Case in Point in this section discusses these new credit facilities.

discount rate

The interest rate charged by the Fed when it lends reserves to banks.

federal funds market

A market in which banks lend reserves to one another.

federal funds rate

The interest rate charged when one bank lends reserves to another.

Open-Market Operations

The Fed's ability to buy and sell federal government bonds has proved to be its most potent policy tool. A **bond** is a promise by the issuer of the bond (in this case the federal government) to pay the owner of the bond a payment or a series of payments on a specific date or dates. The buying and selling of federal government bonds by the Fed are called **open-market operations**. When the Fed buys or sells government bonds, it adds or subtracts reserves from the banking system. Such changes affect the money supply.

Suppose the Fed buys a government bond in the open market. It writes a check on its own account to the seller of the bond. When the seller deposits the check at a bank, the bank submits the check to the Fed for payment. The Fed "pays" the check by crediting the bank's account at the Fed, so the bank has more reserves.

The Fed's purchase of a bond can be illustrated using a balance sheet. Suppose the Fed buys a bond for $1,000 from one of Acme Bank's customers. When that customer deposits the check at Acme, checkable deposits will rise by $1,000. The check is written on the Federal Reserve System; the Fed will credit Acme's account. Acme's reserves thus rise by $1,000. With a 10% reserve requirement, that will create $900 in excess reserves and set off the same process of money expansion as did the cash deposit we have already examined. The difference is that the Fed's purchase of a bond created new reserves with the stroke of a pen, where the cash deposit created them by removing $1,000 from currency in circulation. The purchase of the $1,000 bond by the Fed could thus increase the money supply by as much as $10,000, the maximum expansion suggested by the deposit multiplier.

FIGURE 24.9

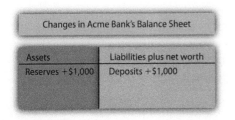

Changes in Acme Bank's Balance Sheet

Assets	Liabilities plus net worth
Reserves +$1,000	Deposits +$1,000

Where does the Fed get $1,000 to purchase the bond? It simply creates the money when it writes the check to purchase the bond. On the Fed's balance sheet, assets increase by $1,000 because the Fed now has the bond; bank deposits with the Fed, which represent a liability to the Fed, rise by $1,000 as well.

When the Fed sells a bond, it gives the buyer a federal government bond that it had previously purchased and accepts a check in exchange. The bank on which the check was written will find its deposit with the Fed reduced by the amount of the check. That bank's reserves and checkable deposits will fall by equal amounts; the reserves, in effect, disappear. The result is a reduction in the money supply. The Fed thus increases the money supply by buying bonds; it reduces the money supply by selling them.

Figure 24.10 shows how the Fed influences the flow of money in the economy. Funds flow from the public—individuals and firms—to banks as deposits. Banks use those funds to make loans to the public—to individuals and firms. The Fed can influence the volume of bank lending by buying bonds and thus injecting reserves into the system. With new reserves, banks will increase their lending, which creates still more deposits and still more lending as the deposit multiplier goes to work. Alternatively, the Fed can sell bonds. When it does, reserves flow out of the system, reducing bank lending and reducing deposits.

The Fed's purchase or sale of bonds is conducted by the Open Market Desk at the Federal Reserve Bank of New York, one of the 12 district banks. Traders at the Open Market Desk are guided by policy directives issued by the Federal Open Market Committee (FOMC). The FOMC consists of the seven members of the Board of Governors plus five regional bank presidents. The president of the New York Federal Reserve Bank serves as a member of the FOMC; the other 11 bank presidents take turns filling the remaining four seats.

The FOMC meets eight times per year to chart the Fed's monetary policies. In the past, FOMC meetings were closed, with no report of the committee's action until the release of the minutes six weeks after the meeting. Faced with pressure to open its proceedings, the Fed began in 1994 issuing a report of the decisions of the FOMC immediately after each meeting.

In practice, the Fed sets targets for the federal funds rate. To achieve a lower federal funds rate, the Fed goes into the open market buying securities and thus increasing the money supply. When the Fed raises its target rate for the federal funds rate, it sells securities and thus reduces the money supply.

Traditionally, the Fed has bought and sold short-term government securities; however, in dealing with the condition of the economy in 2009, wherein the Fed has already set the target for the federal funds rate at near zero, the Fed has announced that it will also be buying longer term government securities. In so doing, it hopes to influence longer term interest rates, such as those related to mortgages.

FIGURE 24.10 The Fed and the Flow of Money in the Economy

Individuals and firms (the public) make deposits in banks; banks make loans to individuals and firms. The Fed can buy bonds to inject new reserves into the system, thus increasing bank lending, which creates new deposits, creating still more lending as the deposit multiplier goes to work. Alternatively, the Fed can sell bonds, withdrawing reserves from the system, thus reducing bank lending and reducing total deposits.

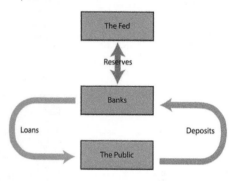

Key Takeaways

- The Fed, the central bank of the United States, acts as a bank for other banks and for the federal government. It also regulates banks, sets monetary policy, and maintains the stability of the financial system.
- The Fed sets reserve requirements and the discount rate and conducts open-market operations. Of these tools of monetary policy, open-market operations are the most important.
- Starting in 2007, the Fed began creating additional credit facilities to help stabilize the financial system.
- The Fed creates new reserves and new money when it purchases bonds. It destroys reserves and thus reduces the money supply when it sells bonds.

Try It!

Suppose the Fed sells $8 million worth of bonds.

1. How do bank reserves change?
2. Will the money supply increase or decrease?
3. What is the maximum possible change in the money supply if the required reserve ratio is 0.2?

Case in Point: Fed Supports the Financial System by Creating New Credit Facilities

Source: © Shutterstock, Inc.

Well before most of the public became aware of the precarious state of the U.S. financial system, the Fed began to see signs of growing financial strains and to act on reducing them. In particular, the Fed saw that short-term interest rates that are often quite close to the federal funds rate began to rise markedly above it. The widening spread was alarming, because it suggested that lender confidence was declining, even for what are generally considered low-risk loans. Commercial paper, in which large companies borrow funds for a period of about a month to manage their cash flow, is an example. Even companies with high credit ratings were having to pay unusually high interest rate premiums in order to get funding, or in some cases could not get funding at all.

To deal with the drying up of credit markets, in late 2007 the Fed began to create an alphabet soup of new credit facilities. Some of these were offered in conjunction with the Department of the Treasury, which had more latitude in terms of accepting some credit risk. The facilities differed in terms of collateral used, the duration of the loan, which institutions were eligible to borrow, and the cost to the borrower. For example, the Primary Dealer Credit Facility (PDCF) allowed primary dealers (i.e., those financial institutions that normally handle the Fed's open market operations) to obtain overnight loans. The Term Asset-Backed Securities Loan Facility (TALF) allowed a wide range of companies to borrow, using the primary dealers as conduits, based on qualified asset-backed securities related to student, auto, credit card, and small business debt, for a three-year period. Most of these new facilities were designed to be temporary. Starting in 2009 and 2010, the Fed began closing a number of them or at least preventing them from issuing new loans.

The common goal of all of these various credit facilities was to increase liquidity in order to stimulate private spending. For example, these credit facilities encouraged banks to pare down their excess reserves (which grew enormously as the financial crisis unfolded and the economy deteriorated) and to make more loans. In the words of then Fed Chairman Ben Bernanke:

> *"Liquidity provision by the central bank reduces systemic risk by assuring market participants that, should short-term investors begin to lose confidence, financial institutions will be able to meet the resulting demands for cash without resorting to potentially destabilizing fire sales of assets. Moreover, backstopping the liquidity needs of financial institutions reduces funding stresses and, all else equal, should increase the willingness of those institutions to lend and make markets."*

The legal authority for most of these new credit facilities came from a particular section of the Federal Reserve Act that allows the Board of Governors "in unusual and exigent circumstances" to extend credit to a wide range of market players.

Sources: *Based on Ben S. Bernanke, "The Crisis and the Policy Response" (Stemp Lecture, London School of Economics, London, England, January 13, 2009)https://www.federalreserve.gov/ newsevents/speech/bernanke20090113a.htm; Richard DiCecio and Charles S. Gascon, "New Monetary Policy Tools?" Federal Reserve Bank of St. Louis Monetary Trends, May 2008; Federal Reserve Board of Governors Web site at http://www.federalreserve.gov/monetarypolicy/default. htm.*

Answer to Try It! Problems

1. Bank reserves fall by $8 million.
2. The money supply decreases.
3. The maximum possible decrease is $40 million, since $\Delta D = (1/0.2) \times (-\$8 \text{ million}) = -\$40$ million.

24.5 Review and Practice

Summary

In this chapter we investigated the money supply and looked at how it is determined. Money is anything that serves as a medium of exchange. Whatever serves as money also functions as a unit of account and as a store of value. Money may or may not have intrinsic value. In the United States, the total of currency in circulation, traveler's checks, and checkable deposits equals M1. A broader measure of the money supply is M2, which includes M1 plus assets that are highly liquid, but less liquid than those in M1.

Banks create money when they issue loans. The ability of banks to issue loans is controlled by their reserves. Reserves consist of cash in bank vaults and bank deposits with the Fed. Banks operate in a fractional reserve system; that is, they maintain reserves equal to only a small fraction of their deposit liabilities. Banks are heavily regulated to protect individual depositors and to prevent crises of confidence. Deposit insurance protects individual depositors. Financial reform legislation was enacted in response to the banking crisis during the Great Depression and again in response to the financial crisis in 2008 and the Great Recession.

A central bank serves as a bank for banks, a regulator of banks, a manager of the money supply, a bank for a nation's government, and a supporter of financial markets generally. In the financial crisis that rocked the United States and much of the world in 2008, the Fed played a central role in keeping bank and nonbank institutions afloat and in keeping credit available. The Federal Reserve System (Fed) is the central bank for the United States. The Fed is governed by a Board of Governors whose members are appointed by the president of the United States, subject to confirmation by the Senate.

The Fed can lend to banks and other institutions through the discount window and other credit facilities, change reserve requirements, and engage in purchases and sales of federal government bonds in the open market. Decisions to buy or sell bonds are made by the Federal Open Market Committee (FOMC); the Fed's open-market operations represent its primary tool for influencing the money supply. Purchases of bonds by the Fed initially increase the reserves of banks. With excess reserves on hand, banks will attempt to increase their loans, and in the process the money supply will change by an amount less than or equal to the deposit multiplier times the change in reserves. Similarly, the Fed can reduce the money supply by selling bonds.

Concept Problems

1. Airlines have "frequent flier" clubs in which customers accumulate miles according to the number of miles they have flown with the airline. Frequent flier miles can then be used to purchase other flights, to rent cars, or to stay in some hotels. Are frequent flier miles money?

2. Debit cards allow an individual to transfer funds directly in a checkable account to a merchant without writing a check. How is this different from the way credit cards work? Are either credit cards or debit cards money? Explain.

3. Many colleges sell special cards that students can use to purchase everything from textbooks or meals in the cafeteria to use of washing machines in the dorm. Students deposit money in their cards; as they use their cards for purchases, electronic scanners remove money from the cards. To replenish a card's money, a student makes a cash deposit that is credited to the card. Would these cards count as part of the money supply?

4. A smart card, also known as an electronic purse, is a plastic card that can be loaded with a monetary value. Its developers argue that, once widely accepted, it could replace the use of currency in vending machines, parking meters, and elsewhere. Suppose smart cards came into widespread use. Present your views on the following issues:

    a. Would you count balances in the purses as part of the money supply? If so, would they be part of M1? M2?

    b. Should any institution be permitted to issue them, or should they be restricted to banks?

    c. Should the issuers be subject to reserve requirements?

    d. Suppose they were issued by banks. How do you think the use of such purses would affect the money supply? Explain your answer carefully.

5. Which of the following items is part of M1? M2?

    a. $0.27 cents that has accumulated under a couch cushion.

    b. Your $2,000 line of credit with your Visa account.

    c. The $210 balance in your checking account.

    d. $417 in your savings account.

    e. 10 shares of stock your uncle gave you on your 18th birthday, which are now worth $520.

    f. $200 in traveler's checks you have purchased for your spring-break trip.

6. In the Middle Ages, goldsmiths took in customers' deposits (gold coins) and issued receipts that functioned much like checks do today. People used the receipts as a medium of exchange. Goldsmiths also issued loans by writing additional receipts against which they were holding no gold to borrowers. Were goldsmiths engaging in fractional reserve banking? Why do you think that customers turned their gold over to goldsmiths? Who benefited from

the goldsmiths' action? Why did such a system generally work? When would it have been likely to fail?

7. A $1,000 deposit in Acme Bank has increased reserves by $1,000. A loan officer at Acme reasons as follows: "The reserve requirement is 10%. That means that the $1,000 in new reserves can back $10,000 in checkable deposits. Therefore I'll loan an additional $10,000." Is there any problem with the loan officer's reasoning? Explain.

8. When the Fed buys and sells bonds through open-market operations, the money supply changes, but there is no effect on the money supply when individuals buy and sell bonds. Explain.

Numerical Problems

1. Consider the following example of bartering:

   1 10-ounce T-bone steak can be traded for 5 soft drinks.
   1 soft drink can be traded for 10 apples.
   100 apples can be traded for a T-shirt.
   5 T-shirts can be exchanged for 1 textbook.
   It takes 4 textbooks to get 1 VCR.

   a. How many 10-ounce T-bone steaks could you exchange for 1 textbook? How many soft drinks? How many apples?

   b. State the price of T-shirts in terms of apples, textbooks, and soft drinks.

   c. Why do you think we use money as a unit of account?

2. Assume that the banking system is loaned up and that any open-market purchase by the Fed directly increases reserves in the banks. If the required reserve ratio is 0.2, by how much could the money supply expand if the Fed purchased $2 billion worth of bonds?

3. Suppose the Fed sells $5 million worth of bonds to Econobank.

   a. What happens to the reserves of the bank?

   b. What happens to the money supply in the economy as a whole if the reserve requirement is 10%, all payments are made by check, and there is no net drain into currency?

   c. How would your answer in part b be affected if you knew that some people involved in the money creation process kept some of their funds as cash?

4. If half the banks in the nation borrow additional reserves totaling $10 million at the Fed discount window, and at the same time the other half of the banks reduce their excess reserves by a total of $10 million, what is likely to happen to the money supply? Explain.

5. Suppose a bank with a 10% reserve requirement has $10 million in reserves and $100 million in checkable deposits, and a major corporation makes a deposit of $1 million.

   a. Explain how the deposit affects the bank's reserves and checkable deposits.

   b. By how much can the bank increase its lending?

6. Suppose a bank with a 25% reserve requirement has $50 million in reserves and $200 million in checkable deposits, and one of the bank's depositors, a major corporation, writes a check to another corporation for $5 million. The check is deposited in another bank.

   a. Explain how the withdrawal affects the bank's reserves and checkable deposits.

   b. By how much will the bank have to reduce its lending?

7. Suppose the bank in problem 6 faces a 20% reserve requirement. The customer writes the same check. How will this affect your answers?

8. Now consider an economy in which the central bank has just purchased $8 billion worth of government bonds from banks in the economy. What would be the effect of this purchase on the money supply in the country, assuming reserve requirements of:

   a. 10%.

      b. 15%.

      c. 20%.

      d. 25%.

9. Now consider the same economy, and the central bank sells $8 billion worth of government bonds to local banks. State the likely effects on the money supply under reserve requirements of:

      a. 10%.

      b. 15%.

      c. 20%.

      d. 25%.

10. How would the purchase of $8 billion of bonds by the central bank from local banks be likely to affect interest rates? How about the effect on interest rates of the sale of $8 billion worth of bonds? Explain your answers carefully.

Endnotes

1. Justin Scheck, "Mackerel Economics in Prison Leads to Appreciation for Oily Fish," *Wall Street Journal*, October 2, 2008, p. A1.
2. Sam Zuckerman, "Feds Take Control of Fannie Mae, Freddie Mac," *The San Francisco Chronicle*, September 8, 2008, p. A-1.

CHAPTER 25
Financial Markets and the Economy

25.1 Start Up: Clamping Down on Money Growth

For nearly three decades, Americans have come to expect very low inflation, on the order of 2% to 3% a year. How did this expectation come to be? Was it always so? Absolutely not.

In July 1979, with inflation approaching 14% and interest rates on three-month Treasury bills soaring past 10%, a desperate President Jimmy Carter took action. He appointed Paul Volcker, the president of the New York Federal Reserve Bank, as chairman of the Fed's Board of Governors. Mr. Volcker made clear that his objective as chairman was to bring down the inflation rate—no matter what the consequences for the economy. Mr. Carter gave this effort his full support.

Mr. Volcker wasted no time in putting his policies to work. He slowed the rate of money growth immediately. The economy's response was swift; the United States slipped into a brief recession in 1980, followed by a crushing recession in 1981–1982. In terms of the goal of reducing inflation, Mr. Volcker's monetary policies were a dazzling success. Inflation plunged below a 4% rate within three years; by 1986 the inflation rate had fallen to 1.1%. The tall, bald, cigar-smoking Mr. Volcker emerged as a folk hero in the fight against inflation. Indeed he has returned 20 years later as part of President Obama's economic team to perhaps once again rescue the U.S. economy.

The Fed's seven-year fight against inflation from 1979 to 1986 made the job for Alan Greenspan, Mr. Volcker's successor, that much easier. To see how the decisions of the Federal Reserve affect key macroeconomic variables—real GDP, the price level, and unemployment—in this chapter we will explore how **financial markets**, markets in which funds accumulated by one group are made available to another group, are linked to the economy.

> **financial markets**
> Markets in which funds accumulated by one group are made available to another group.

This chapter provides the building blocks for understanding financial markets. Beginning with an overview of bond and foreign exchange markets, we will examine how they are related to the level of real GDP and the price level. The second section completes the model of the money market. We have learned that the Fed can change the amount of reserves in the banking system, and that when it does the money supply changes. Here we explain money demand—the quantity of money people and firms want to hold—which, together with money supply, leads to an equilibrium rate of interest.

The model of aggregate demand and supply shows how changes in the components of aggregate demand affect GDP and the price level. In this chapter, we will learn that changes in the financial markets can affect aggregate demand—and in turn can lead to changes in real GDP and the price level. Showing how the financial markets fit into the model of aggregate demand and aggregate supply we developed earlier provides a more complete picture of how the macroeconomy works.

25.2 The Bond and Foreign Exchange Markets

Learning Objectives

1. Explain and illustrate how the bond market works and discuss the relationship between the price of a bond and that bond's interest rate.
2. Explain and illustrate the relationship between a change in demand for or supply of bonds and macroeconomic activity.
3. Explain and illustrate how the foreign exchange market works and how a change in demand for a country's currency or a change in its supply affects macroeconomic activity.

In this section, we will look at the bond market and at the market for foreign exchange. Events in these markets can affect the price level and output for the entire economy.

The Bond Market

In their daily operations and in pursuit of new projects, institutions such as firms and governments often borrow. They may seek funds from a bank. Many institutions, however, obtain credit by selling bonds. The federal government is one institution that issues bonds. A local school district might sell bonds to finance the construction of a new school. Your college or university has probably sold bonds to finance new buildings on campus. Firms often sell bonds to finance expansion. The market for bonds is an enormously important one.

When an institution sells a bond, it obtains the price paid for the bond as a kind of loan. The institution that issues the bond is obligated to make payments on the bond in the future. The interest rate is determined by the price of the bond. To understand these relationships, let us look more closely at bond prices and interest rates.

Bond Prices and Interest Rates

Suppose the manager of a manufacturing company needs to borrow some money to expand the factory. The manager could do so in the following way: he or she prints, say, 500 pieces of paper, each bearing the company's promise to pay the bearer $1,000 in a year. These pieces of paper are bonds, and the company, as the issuer, promises to make a single payment. The manager then offers these bonds for sale, announcing that they will be sold to the buyers who offer the highest prices. Suppose the highest price offered is $950, and all the bonds are sold at that price. Each bond is, in effect, an obligation to repay buyers $1,000. The buyers of the bonds are being paid $50 for the service of lending $950 for a year.

face value of a bond

The amount the issuer of a bond will have to pay on the maturity date.

maturity date

The date when a bond matures, or comes due.

The $1,000 printed on each bond is the **face value of the bond**; it is the amount the issuer will have to pay on the **maturity date** of the bond—the date when the loan matures, or comes due. The $950 at which they were sold is their price. The difference between the face value and the price is the amount paid for the use of the money obtained from selling the bond.

An **interest rate** is the payment made for the use of money, expressed as a percentage of the amount borrowed. Bonds you sold command an interest rate equal to the difference between the face value and the bond price, divided by the bond price, and then multiplied by 100 to form a percentage:

EQUATION 25.1

$$\frac{\text{Face value} - \text{bond price}}{\text{Bond price}} \times 100 = \text{interest rate}$$

At a price of $950, the interest rate is 5.3%

$$\frac{\$1{,}000 - \$950}{\$950} \times 100 = 5.3\ \%$$

The interest rate on any bond is determined by its price. As the price falls, the interest rate rises. Suppose, for example, that the best price the manager can get for the bonds is $900. Now the interest rate is 11.1%. A price of $800 would mean an interest rate of 25%; $750 would mean an interest rate of 33.3%; a price of $500 translates into an interest rate of 100%. The lower the price of a bond relative to its face value, the higher the interest rate.

Bonds in the real world are more complicated than the piece of paper in our example, but their structure is basically the same. They have a face value (usually an amount between $1,000 and $100,000) and a maturity date. The maturity date might be three months from the date of issue; it might be 30 years.

Whatever the period until it matures, and whatever the face value of the bond may be, its issuer will attempt to sell the bond at the highest possible price. Buyers of bonds will seek the lowest prices they can obtain. Newly issued bonds are generally sold in auctions. Potential buyers bid for the bonds, which are sold to the highest bidders. The lower the price of the bond relative to its face value, the higher the interest rate.

Both private firms and government entities issue bonds as a way of raising funds. The original buyer need not hold the bond until maturity. Bonds can be resold at any time, but the price the bond will fetch at the time of resale will vary depending on conditions in the economy and the financial markets.

Figure 25.1 illustrates the market for bonds. Their price is determined by demand and supply. Buyers of newly issued bonds are, in effect, lenders. Sellers of newly issued bonds are borrowers—recall that corporations, the federal government, and other institutions sell bonds when they want to borrow money. Once a newly issued bond has been sold, its owner can resell it; a bond may change hands several times before it matures.

interest rate

Payment made for the use of money, expressed as a percentage of the amount borrowed.

FIGURE 25.1 The Bond Market
The equilibrium price for bonds is determined where the demand and supply curves intersect. The initial solution here is a price of $950, implying an interest rate of 5.3%. An increase in borrowing, all other things equal, increases the supply of bonds to S_2 and forces the price of bonds down to $900. The interest rate rises to 11.1%.

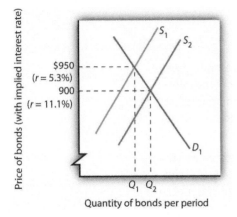

Bonds are not exactly the same sort of product as, say, broccoli or some other good or service. Can we expect bonds to have the same kind of downward-sloping demand curves and upward-sloping supply curves we encounter for ordinary goods and services? Yes. Consider demand. At lower prices, bonds pay higher interest. That makes them more attractive to buyers of bonds and thus increases the quantity demanded. On the other hand, lower prices mean higher costs to borrowers—suppliers of bonds—and should reduce the quantity supplied. Thus, the negative relationship between price and quantity demanded and the positive relationship between price and quantity supplied suggested by conventional demand and supply curves holds true in the market for bonds.

If the quantity of bonds demanded is not equal to the quantity of bonds supplied, the price will adjust almost instantaneously to balance the two. Bond prices are perfectly flexible in that they change immediately to balance demand and supply. Suppose, for example, that the initial price of bonds is $950, as shown by the intersection of the demand and supply curves in Figure 25.1. We will assume that all bonds have equal risk and a face value of $1,000 and that they mature in one year. Now suppose that borrowers increase their borrowing by offering to sell more bonds at every interest rate. This increases the supply of bonds: the supply curve shifts to the right from S_1 to S_2. That, in turn, lowers the equilibrium price of bonds—to $900 in Figure 25.1. The lower price for bonds means a higher interest rate.

The Bond Market and Macroeconomic Performance

The connection between the bond market and the economy derives from the way interest rates affect aggregate demand. For example, investment is one component of aggregate demand, and interest rates affect investment. Firms are less likely to acquire new capital (that is, plant and equipment) if interest rates are high; they're more likely to add capital if interest rates are low.[1]

If bond prices fall, interest rates go up. Higher interest rates tend to discourage investment, so aggregate demand will fall. A fall in aggregate demand, other things unchanged, will mean fewer jobs and less total output than would have been the case with lower rates of interest. In contrast, an increase in the price of bonds lowers interest rates and makes investment in new capital more attractive. That change may boost investment and thus boost aggregate demand.

Figure 25.2 shows how an event in the bond market can stimulate changes in the economy's output and price level. In Panel (a), an increase in demand for bonds raises bond prices. Interest rates thus fall. Lower interest rates increase the quantity of investment demanded, shifting the aggregate demand curve to the right, from AD_1 to AD_2 in Panel (b). Real GDP rises from Y_1 to Y_2; the price level rises from P_1 to P_2. In Panel (c), an increase in the supply of bonds pushes bond prices down. Interest rates rise. The quantity of investment is likely to fall, shifting aggregate demand to the left, from AD_1 to AD_2 in Panel (d). Output and the price level fall from Y_1 to Y_2 and from P_1 to P_2, respectively. Assuming other determinants of aggregate demand remain unchanged, higher interest rates will tend to reduce aggregate demand and lower interest rates will tend to increase aggregate demand.

FIGURE 25.2 Bond Prices and Macroeconomic Activity

An increase in the demand for bonds to D_2 in Panel (a) raises the price of bonds to P^b_2, which lowers interest rates and boosts investment. That increases aggregate demand to AD_2 in Panel (b); real GDP rises to Y_2 and the price level rises to P_2.

An increase in the supply of bonds to S_2 lowers bond prices to P^b_2 in Panel (c) and raises interest rates. The higher interest rate, taken by itself, is likely to cause a reduction in investment and aggregate demand. AD_1 falls to AD_2, real GDP falls to Y_2, and the price level falls to P_2 in Panel (d).

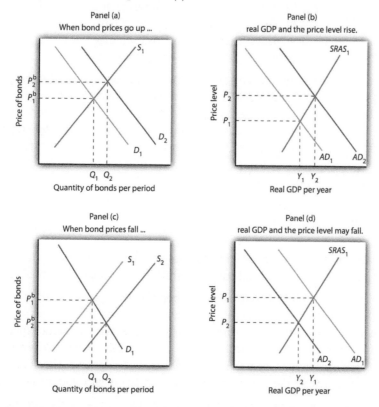

In thinking about the impact of changes in interest rates on aggregate demand, we must remember that some events that change aggregate demand can affect interest rates. We will examine those events in subsequent chapters. Our focus in this chapter is on the way in which events that originate in financial markets affect aggregate demand.

Foreign Exchange Markets

Another financial market that influences macroeconomic variables is the **foreign exchange market**, a market in which currencies of different countries are traded for one another. Since changes in exports and imports affect aggregate demand and thus real GDP and the price level, the market in which currencies are traded has tremendous importance in the economy.

Foreigners who want to purchase goods and services or assets in the United States must typically pay for them with dollars. United States purchasers of foreign goods must generally make the purchase in a foreign currency. An Egyptian family, for example, exchanges Egyptian pounds for dollars in order to pay for admission to Disney World. A German financial investor purchases dollars to buy U.S. government bonds. A family from the United States visiting India, on the other hand, needs to obtain Indian rupees in order to make purchases there. A U.S. bank wanting to purchase assets in Mexico City first purchases pesos. These transactions are accomplished in the foreign exchange market.

The foreign exchange market is not a single location in which currencies are traded. The term refers instead to the entire array of institutions through which people buy and sell currencies. It includes a hotel desk clerk who provides currency exchange as a service to hotel guests, brokers who arrange currency exchanges worth billions of dollars, and governments and central banks that

foreign exchange market

A market in which currencies of different countries are traded for one another.

exchange currencies. Major currency dealers are linked by computers so that they can track currency exchanges all over the world.

The Exchange Rate

A country's exchange rate is the price of its currency in terms of another currency or currencies. On December 12, 2008, for example, the dollar traded for 91.13 Japanese yen, 0.75 euros, 10.11 South African rands, and 13.51 Mexican pesos. There are as many exchange rates for the dollar as there are countries whose currencies exchange for the dollar—roughly 200 of them.

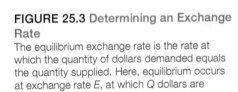

trade-weighted exchange rate

An index of exchange rates.

Economists summarize the movement of exchange rates with a **trade-weighted exchange rate**, which is an index of exchange rates. To calculate a trade-weighted exchange rate index for the U.S. dollar, we select a group of countries, weight the price of the dollar in each country's currency by the amount of trade between that country and the United States, and then report the price of the dollar based on that trade-weighted average. Because trade-weighted exchange rates are so widely used in reporting currency values, they are often referred to as exchange rates themselves. We will follow that convention in this text.

Determining Exchange Rates

The rates at which most currencies exchange for one another are determined by demand and supply. How does the model of demand and supply operate in the foreign exchange market?

The demand curve for dollars relates the number of dollars buyers want to buy in any period to the exchange rate. An increase in the exchange rate means it takes more foreign currency to buy a dollar. A higher exchange rate, in turn, makes U.S. goods and services more expensive for foreign buyers and reduces the quantity they will demand. That is likely to reduce the quantity of dollars they demand. Foreigners thus will demand fewer dollars as the price of the dollar—the exchange rate—rises. Consequently, the demand curve for dollars is downward sloping, as in Figure 25.3.

FIGURE 25.3 Determining an Exchange Rate

The equilibrium exchange rate is the rate at which the quantity of dollars demanded equals the quantity supplied. Here, equilibrium occurs at exchange rate *E*, at which *Q* dollars are exchanged per period.

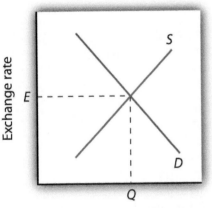

Quantity of dollars per period

The supply curve for dollars emerges from a similar process. When people and firms in the United States purchase goods, services, or assets in foreign countries, they must purchase the currency of those countries first. They supply dollars in exchange for foreign currency. The supply of dollars on the foreign exchange market thus reflects the degree to which people in the United States are buying foreign money at various exchange rates. A higher exchange rate means that a dollar trades for more foreign currency. In effect, the higher rate makes foreign goods and services cheaper to U.S. buyers, so U.S. consumers will purchase more foreign goods and services. People will thus supply more dollars at a higher exchange rate; we expect the supply curve for dollars to be upward sloping, as suggested in Figure 25.3.

In addition to private individuals and firms that participate in the foreign exchange market, most governments participate as well. A government might seek to lower its exchange rate by selling its currency; it might seek to raise the rate by buying its currency. Although governments often participate in foreign exchange markets, they generally represent a very small share of these markets. The most important traders are private buyers and sellers of currencies.

Exchange Rates and Macroeconomic Performance

People purchase a country's currency for two quite different reasons: to purchase goods or services in that country, or to purchase the assets of that country—its money, its capital, its stocks, its bonds, or its real estate. Both of these motives must be considered to understand why demand and supply in the foreign exchange market may change.

One thing that can cause the price of the dollar to rise, for example, is a reduction in bond prices in American markets. Figure 25.4 illustrates the effect of this change. Suppose the supply of bonds in the U.S. bond market increases from S_1 to S_2 in Panel (a). Bond prices will drop. Lower bond prices mean higher interest rates. Foreign financial investors, attracted by the opportunity to earn higher returns in the United States, will increase their demand for dollars on the foreign exchange market in order to purchase U.S. bonds. Panel (b) shows that the demand curve for dollars shifts from D_1 to D_2. Simultaneously, U.S. financial investors, attracted by the higher interest rates at home, become less likely to make financial investments abroad and thus supply fewer dollars to exchange markets. The fall in the price of U.S. bonds shifts the supply curve for dollars on the foreign exchange market from S_1 to S_2, and the exchange rate rises from E_1 to E_2.

FIGURE 25.4 Shifts in Demand and Supply for Dollars on the Foreign Exchange Market
In Panel (a), an increase in the supply of bonds lowers bond prices to P^b_2 (and thus raises interest rates). Higher interest rates boost the demand and reduce the supply for dollars, increasing the exchange rate in Panel (b) to E_2. These developments in the bond and foreign exchange markets are likely to lead to a reduction in net exports and in investment, reducing aggregate demand from AD_1 to AD_2 in Panel (c). The price level in the economy falls to P_2, and real GDP falls from Y_1 to Y_2.

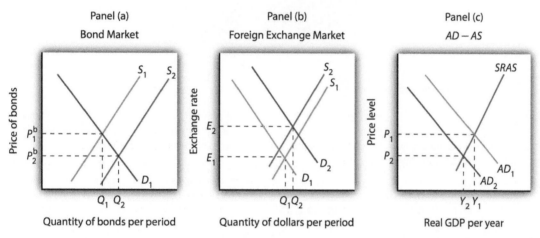

The higher exchange rate makes U.S. goods and services more expensive to foreigners, so it reduces exports. It makes foreign goods cheaper for U.S. buyers, so it increases imports. Net exports thus fall, reducing aggregate demand. Panel (c) shows that output falls from Y_1 to Y_2; the price level falls from P_1 to P_2. This development in the foreign exchange market reinforces the impact of higher interest rates we observed in Figure 25.2, Panels (c) and (d). They not only reduce investment—they reduce net exports as well.

Key Takeaways

- A bond represents a borrower's debt; bond prices are determined by demand and supply.
- The interest rate on a bond is negatively related to the price of the bond. As the price of a bond increases, the interest rate falls.
- An increase in the interest rate tends to decrease the quantity of investment demanded and, hence, to decrease aggregate demand. A decrease in the interest rate increases the quantity of investment demanded and aggregate demand.
- The demand for dollars on foreign exchange markets represents foreign demand for U.S. goods, services, and assets. The supply of dollars on foreign exchange markets represents U.S. demand for foreign goods, services, and assets. The demand for and the supply of dollars determine the exchange rate.
- A rise in U.S. interest rates will increase the demand for dollars and decrease the supply of dollars on foreign exchange markets. As a result, the exchange rate will increase and aggregate demand will decrease. A fall in U.S. interest rates will have the opposite effect.

Try It!

Suppose the supply of bonds in the U.S. market decreases. Show and explain the effects on the bond and foreign exchange markets. Use the aggregate demand/aggregate supply framework to show and explain the effects on investment, net exports, real GDP, and the price level.

Case in Point: Bill Gross's *Mea Culpa*

Source: © Shutterstock, Inc.

In October 2011, bond fund manager Bill Gross sent out an extraordinary open letter titled "Mea Culpa." He was taking the blame for the poor performance of Pimco Total Return Bond Fund, the huge fund he manages. After years of stellar performance, what had gone wrong?

Earlier in 2011, Mr. Gross announced that he would avoid U.S. Treasury bonds. He assumed that as the U.S. and other countries' economies recovered, interest rates would begin to rise and, hence, U.S. bond prices would fall. When Mr. Gross pulled out of U.S. Treasuries, he used some of the cash to buy other types of debt, such as that of emerging markets. He also held onto some cash. He warned others to shun Treasuries as well.

However, as the financial situation in Europe weakened over worries about government debt in various European countries—starting with Greece and then spilling over to Portugal, Spain, Italy, and others—investors around the world flocked toward Treasuries, pushing Treasury bond prices up. It was a rally that Mr. Gross's customers missed.

From where did the financial investors get the funds to buy Treasuries? In part, these funds were obtained from some of the same types of bonds that were then in the Pimco fund portfolio. As a result, the prices of bonds in the Pimco fund fell.

In the letter, Mr. Gross wrote, "The simple fact is that the portfolio at midyear was positioned for what we call a 'New Normal' developed world economy—2% real growth and 2% inflation. When growth estimates quickly changed it was obvious that I had misjudged the fly ball: E-CF or for nonbaseball aficionados—error centerfield." In the fall of 2011, he shifted gears and began buying U.S. Treasuries, assuming that a weak global economy would keep interest rates low. He was foiled again, as interest rates started to rise a bit.

In the end, 2011 turned out to be a bad year for the fund, ranking poorly compared to its peers. But after many successful years, it retained its five-star rating by Morningstar in 2012. We must wait to see whether Mr. Gross will get his groove back. In the letter, he concluded, "There is no 'quit' in me or anyone else on the Pimco premises. The early morning and even midnight hours have gone up, not down, to match the increasing complexity of the global financial markets. The competitive fire burns even hotter. I/we respect our competition but we want to squash them each and every day…"

Source: Based on "Bill Gross Apologizes to Pimco Fund Owners for 'Bad Year,'" Los Angeles Times, October 14, 2011, online version.

Answer to Try It! Problem

If the supply of bonds decreases from S_1 to S_2, bond prices will rise from P^b_1 to P^b_2, as shown in Panel (a). Higher bond prices mean lower interest rates. Lower interest rates in the United States will make financial investments in the United States less attractive to foreigners. As a result, their demand for dollars will decrease from D_1 to D_2, as shown in Panel (b). Similarly, U.S. financial investors will look abroad for higher returns and thus supply more dollars to foreign exchange markets, shifting the supply curve from S_1 to S_2. Thus, the exchange rate will decrease. The quantity of investment rises due to the lower interest rates. Net exports rise because the lower exchange rate makes U.S. goods and services more attractive to foreigners, thus increasing exports, and makes foreign goods less attractive to U.S. buyers, thus reducing imports. Increases in investment and net exports imply a rightward shift in the aggregate demand curve from AD_1 to AD_2. Real GDP and the price level increase.

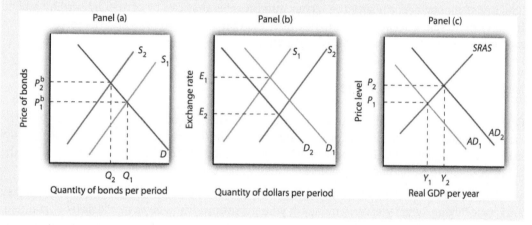

25.3 Demand, Supply, and Equilibrium in the Money Market

Learning Objectives

1. Explain the motives for holding money and relate them to the interest rate that could be earned from holding alternative assets, such as bonds.
2. Draw a money demand curve and explain how changes in other variables may lead to shifts in the money demand curve.
3. Illustrate and explain the notion of equilibrium in the money market.
4. Use graphs to explain how changes in money demand or money supply are related to changes in the bond market, in interest rates, in aggregate demand, and in real GDP and the price level.

In this section we will explore the link between money markets, bond markets, and interest rates. We first look at the demand for money. The demand curve for money is derived like any other demand curve, by examining the relationship between the "price" of money (which, we will see, is the interest rate) and the quantity demanded, holding all other determinants unchanged. We then link the demand for money to the concept of money supply developed in the last chapter, to determine the equilibrium rate of interest. In turn, we show how changes in interest rates affect the macroeconomy.

The Demand for Money

In deciding how much money to hold, people make a choice about how to hold their wealth. How much wealth shall be held as money and how much as other assets? For a given amount of wealth, the answer to this question will depend on the relative costs and benefits of holding money versus other assets. The **demand for money** is the relationship between the quantity of money people want to hold and the factors that determine that quantity.

To simplify our analysis, we will assume there are only two ways to hold wealth: as money in a checking account, or as funds in a bond market mutual fund that purchases long-term bonds on behalf of its subscribers. A bond fund is not money. Some money deposits earn interest, but the return on these accounts is generally lower than what could be obtained in a bond fund. The advantage of checking accounts is that they are highly liquid and can thus be spent easily. We will think of the demand for money as a curve that represents the outcomes of choices between the greater liquidity of money deposits and the higher interest rates that can be earned by holding a bond fund. The difference between the interest rates paid on money deposits and the interest return available from bonds is the cost of holding money.

Motives for Holding Money

One reason people hold their assets as money is so that they can purchase goods and services. The money held for the purchase of goods and services may be for everyday transactions such as buying groceries or paying the rent, or it may be kept on hand for contingencies such as having the funds available to pay to have the car fixed or to pay for a trip to the doctor.

The **transactions demand for money** is money people hold to pay for goods and services they anticipate buying. When you carry money in your purse or wallet to buy a movie ticket or maintain a checking account balance so you can purchase groceries later in the month, you are holding the money as part of your transactions demand for money.

The money people hold for contingencies represents their **precautionary demand for money**. Money held for precautionary purposes may include checking account balances kept for possible home repairs or health-care needs. People do not know precisely when the need for such expenditures will occur, but they can prepare for them by holding money so that they'll have it available when the need arises.

People also hold money for speculative purposes. Bond prices fluctuate constantly. As a result, holders of bonds not only earn interest but experience gains or losses in the value of their assets. Bondholders enjoy gains when bond prices rise and suffer losses when bond prices fall. Because of this, expectations play an important role as a determinant of the demand for bonds. Holding bonds is one alternative to holding money, so these same expectations can affect the demand for money.

John Maynard Keynes, who was an enormously successful speculator in bond markets himself, suggested that bondholders who anticipate a drop in bond prices will try to sell their bonds ahead of the price drop in order to avoid this loss in asset value. Selling a bond means converting it to money. Keynes referred to the **speculative demand for money** as the money held in response to concern that bond prices and the prices of other financial assets might change.

Of course, money is money. One cannot sort through someone's checking account and locate which funds are held for transactions and which funds are there because the owner of the account is worried about a drop in bond prices or is taking a precaution. We distinguish money held for different motives in order to understand how the quantity of money demanded will be affected by a key determinant of the demand for money: the interest rate.

Interest Rates and the Demand for Money

The quantity of money people hold to pay for transactions and to satisfy precautionary and speculative demand is likely to vary with the interest rates they can earn from alternative assets such as bonds. When interest rates rise relative to the rates that can be earned on money deposits, people hold less money. When interest rates fall, people hold more money. The logic of these conclusions about the money people hold and interest rates depends on the people's motives for holding money.

The quantity of money households want to hold varies according to their income and the interest rate; different average quantities of money held can satisfy their transactions and precautionary demands for money. To see why, suppose a household earns and spends $3,000 per month. It spends an equal amount of money each day. For a month with 30 days, that is $100 per day. One way the household could manage this spending would be to leave the money in a checking account, which we will assume pays zero interest. The household would thus have $3,000 in the checking account when the month begins, $2,900 at the end of the first day, $1,500 halfway through the month, and zero at the end of the last day of the month. Averaging the daily balances, we find that the quantity of money the household demands equals $1,500. This approach to money management, which we will call the "cash approach," has the virtue of simplicity, but the household will earn no interest on its funds.

Consider an alternative money management approach that permits the same pattern of spending. At the beginning of the month, the household deposits $1,000 in its checking account and the other $2,000 in a bond fund. Assume the bond fund pays 1% interest per month, or an annual interest rate of 12.7%. After 10 days, the money in the checking account is exhausted, and the household withdraws another $1,000 from the bond fund for the next 10 days. On the 20th day, the final $1,000 from the bond fund goes into the checking account. With this strategy, the household has an average daily balance of $500, which is the quantity of money it demands. Let us call this money management strategy the "bond fund approach."

Remember that both approaches allow the household to spend $3,000 per month, $100 per day. The cash approach requires a quantity of money demanded of $1,500, while the bond fund approach lowers this quantity to $500.

The bond fund approach generates some interest income. The household has $1,000 in the fund for 10 days (1/3 of a month) and $1,000 for 20 days (2/3 of a month). With an interest rate of 1% per month, the household earns $10 in interest each month ([$1,000 × 0.01 × 1/3] + [$1,000 × 0.01 × 2/3]). The disadvantage of the bond fund, of course, is that it requires more attention—$1,000 must be transferred from the fund twice each month. There may also be fees associated with the transfers.

Of course, the bond fund strategy we have examined here is just one of many. The household could begin each month with $1,500 in the checking account and $1,500 in the bond fund, transferring $1,500 to the checking account midway through the month. This strategy requires one less transfer, but it also generates less interest—$7.50 (= $1,500 × 0.01 × 1/2). With this strategy, the household demands a quantity of money of $750. The household could also maintain a much smaller average quantity of money in its checking account and keep more in its bond fund. For simplicity, we can think of any strategy that involves transferring money in and out of a bond fund or another interest-earning asset as a bond fund strategy.

Which approach should the household use? That is a choice each household must make—it is a question of weighing the interest a bond fund strategy creates against the hassle and possible fees associated with the transfers it requires. Our example does not yield a clear-cut choice for any one household, but we can make some generalizations about its implications.

First, a household is more likely to adopt a bond fund strategy when the interest rate is higher. At low interest rates, a household does not sacrifice much income by pursuing the simpler cash strategy. As the interest rate rises, a bond fund strategy becomes more attractive. That means that the higher the interest rate, the lower the quantity of money demanded.

Second, people are more likely to use a bond fund strategy when the cost of transferring funds is lower. The creation of savings plans, which began in the 1970s and 1980s, that allowed easy transfer of funds between interest-earning assets and checkable deposits tended to reduce the demand for money.

Some money deposits, such as savings accounts and money market deposit accounts, pay interest. In evaluating the choice between holding assets as some form of money or in other forms such as bonds, households will look at the differential between what those funds pay and what they could earn in the bond market. A higher interest rate in the bond market is likely to increase this differential; a lower interest rate will reduce it. An increase in the spread between rates on money deposits and the interest rate in the bond market reduces the quantity of money demanded; a reduction in the spread increases the quantity of money demanded.

Firms, too, must determine how to manage their earnings and expenditures. However, instead of worrying about $3,000 per month, even a relatively small firm may be concerned about $3,000,000 per month. Rather than facing the difference of $10 versus $7.50 in interest earnings used in our household example, this small firm would face a difference of $2,500 per month ($10,000 versus $7,500). For very large firms such as Toyota or AT&T, interest rate differentials among various forms of holding their financial assets translate into millions of dollars per day.

How is the speculative demand for money related to interest rates? When financial investors believe that the prices of bonds and other assets will fall, their speculative demand for money goes up. The speculative demand for money thus depends on expectations about future changes in asset prices. Will this demand also be affected by present interest rates?

If interest rates are low, bond prices are high. It seems likely that if bond prices are high, financial investors will become concerned that bond prices might fall. That suggests that high bond prices—low interest rates—would increase the quantity of money held for speculative purposes. Conversely, if bond prices are already relatively low, it is likely that fewer financial investors will expect them to fall still further. They will hold smaller speculative balances. Economists thus expect that the quantity of money demanded for speculative reasons will vary negatively with the interest rate.

The Demand Curve for Money

demand curve for money

Curve that shows the quantity of money demanded at each interest rate, all other things unchanged.

We have seen that the transactions, precautionary, and speculative demands for money vary negatively with the interest rate. Putting those three sources of demand together, we can draw a demand curve for money to show how the interest rate affects the total quantity of money people hold. The **demand curve for money** shows the quantity of money demanded at each interest rate, all other things unchanged. Such a curve is shown in Figure 25.5. An increase in the interest rate reduces the quantity of money demanded. A reduction in the interest rate increases the quantity of money demanded.

The relationship between interest rates and the quantity of money demanded is an application of the law of demand. If we think of the alternative to holding money as holding bonds, then the interest rate—or the differential between the interest rate in the bond market and the interest paid on money deposits—represents the price of holding money. As is the case with all goods and services, an increase in price reduces the quantity demanded.

Other Determinants of the Demand for Money

We draw the demand curve for money to show the quantity of money people will hold at each interest rate, all other determinants of money demand unchanged. A change in those "other determinants" will shift the demand for money. Among the most important variables that can shift the demand for money are the level of income and real GDP, the price level, expectations, transfer costs, and preferences.

Real GDP

A household with an income of $10,000 per month is likely to demand a larger quantity of money than a household with an income of $1,000 per month. That relationship suggests that money is a normal good: as income increases, people demand more money at each interest rate, and as income falls, they demand less.

An increase in real GDP increases incomes throughout the economy. The demand for money in the economy is therefore likely to be greater when real GDP is greater.

The Price Level

The higher the price level, the more money is required to purchase a given quantity of goods and services. All other things unchanged, the higher the price level, the greater the demand for money.

Expectations

The speculative demand for money is based on expectations about bond prices. All other things unchanged, if people expect bond prices to fall, they will increase their demand for money. If they expect bond prices to rise, they will reduce their demand for money.

The expectation that bond prices are about to change actually causes bond prices to change. If people expect bond prices to fall, for example, they will sell their bonds, exchanging them for money. That will shift the supply curve for bonds to the right, thus lowering their price. The importance of expectations in moving markets can lead to a self-fulfilling prophecy.

Expectations about future price levels also affect the demand for money. The expectation of a higher price level means that people expect the money they are holding to fall in value. Given that expectation, they are likely to hold less of it in anticipation of a jump in prices.

Expectations about future price levels play a particularly important role during periods of hyperinflation. If prices rise very rapidly and people expect them to continue rising, people are likely to try to reduce the amount of money they hold, knowing that it will fall in value as it sits in their wallets or their bank accounts. Toward the end of the great German hyperinflation of the early 1920s, prices were doubling as often as three times a day. Under those circumstances, people tried not to hold money even for a few minutes—within the space of eight hours money would lose half its value!

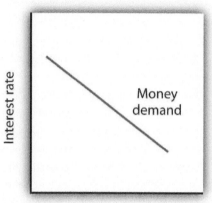

FIGURE 25.5 The Demand Curve for Money
The demand curve for money shows the quantity of money demanded at each interest rate. Its downward slope expresses the negative relationship between the quantity of money demanded and the interest rate.

Quantity of money per period

Transfer Costs

For a given level of expenditures, reducing the quantity of money demanded requires more frequent transfers between nonmoney and money deposits. As the cost of such transfers rises, some consumers will choose to make fewer of them. They will therefore increase the quantity of money they demand. In general, the demand for money will increase as it becomes more expensive to transfer between money and nonmoney accounts. The demand for money will fall if transfer costs decline. In recent years, transfer costs have fallen, leading to a decrease in money demand.

Preferences

Preferences also play a role in determining the demand for money. Some people place a high value on having a considerable amount of money on hand. For others, this may not be important.

Household attitudes toward risk are another aspect of preferences that affect money demand. As we have seen, bonds pay higher interest rates than money deposits, but holding bonds entails a risk that bond prices might fall. There is also a chance that the issuer of a bond will default, that is, will not pay the amount specified on the bond to bondholders; indeed, bond issuers may end up paying nothing at all. A money deposit, such as a savings deposit, might earn a lower yield, but it is a safe yield. People's attitudes about the trade-off between risk and yields affect the degree to which they hold their wealth as money. Heightened concerns about risk in the last half of 2008 led many households to increase their demand for money.

Figure 25.6 shows an increase in the demand for money. Such an increase could result from a higher real GDP, a higher price level, a change in expectations, an increase in transfer costs, or a change in preferences.

FIGURE 25.6 An Increase in Money Demand

An increase in real GDP, the price level, or transfer costs, for example, will increase the quantity of money demanded at any interest rate r, increasing the demand for money from D_1 to D_2. The quantity of money demanded at interest rate r rises from M to M'. The reverse of any such events would reduce the quantity of money demanded at every interest rate, shifting the demand curve to the left.

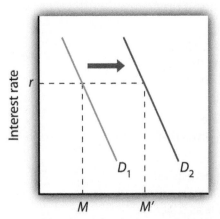

Quantity of money per period

The Supply of Money

The **supply curve of money** shows the relationship between the quantity of money supplied and the market interest rate, all other determinants of supply unchanged. We have learned that the Fed, through its open-market operations, determines the total quantity of reserves in the banking system. We shall assume that banks increase the money supply in fixed proportion to their reserves. Because the quantity of reserves is determined by Federal Reserve policy, we draw the supply curve of money in Figure 25.7 as a vertical line, determined by the Fed's monetary policies. In drawing the supply curve of money as a vertical line, we are assuming the money supply does not depend on the interest rate. Changing the quantity of reserves and hence the money supply is an example of monetary policy.

supply curve of money

Curve that shows the relationship between the quantity of money supplied and the market interest rate, all other determinants of supply unchanged.

FIGURE 25.7 The Supply Curve of Money

We assume that the quantity of money supplied in the economy is determined as a fixed multiple of the quantity of bank reserves, which is determined by the Fed. The supply curve of money is a vertical line at that quantity.

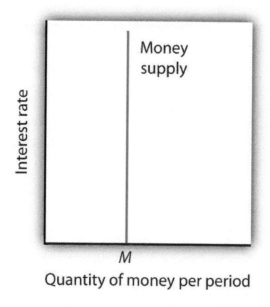

Equilibrium in the Market for Money

The **money market** is the interaction among institutions through which money is supplied to individuals, firms, and other institutions that demand money. **Money market equilibrium** occurs at the interest rate at which the quantity of money demanded is equal to the quantity of money supplied. Figure 25.8 combines demand and supply curves for money to illustrate equilibrium in the market for money. With a stock of money (M), the equilibrium interest rate is r.

money market

The interaction among institutions through which money is supplied to individuals, firms, and other institutions that demand money.

money market equilibrium

The interest rate at which the quantity of money demanded is equal to the quantity of money supplied.

The market for money is in equilibrium if the quantity of money demanded is equal to the quantity of money supplied. Here, equilibrium occurs at interest rate *r*.

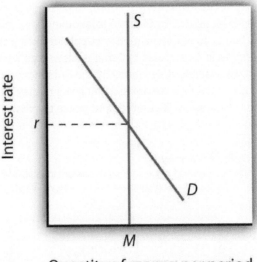

Effects of Changes in the Money Market

A shift in money demand or supply will lead to a change in the equilibrium interest rate. Let's look at the effects of such changes on the economy.

Changes in Money Demand

Suppose that the money market is initially in equilibrium at r_1 with supply curve S and a demand curve D_1 as shown in Panel (a) of Figure 25.9. Now suppose that there is a decrease in money demand, all other things unchanged. A decrease in money demand could result from a decrease in the cost of transferring between money and nonmoney deposits, from a change in expectations, or from a change in preferences.[2] Panel (a) shows that the money demand curve shifts to the left to D_2. We can see that the interest rate will fall to r_2. To see why the interest rate falls, we recall that if people want to hold less money, then they will want to hold more bonds. Thus, Panel (b) shows that the demand for bonds increases. The higher price of bonds means lower interest rates; lower interest rates restore equilibrium in the money market.

FIGURE 25.9 A Decrease in the Demand for Money

A decrease in the demand for money due to a change in transactions costs, preferences, or expectations, as shown in Panel (a), will be accompanied by an increase in the demand for bonds as shown in Panel (b), and a fall in the interest rate. The fall in the interest rate will cause a rightward shift in the aggregate demand curve from AD_1 to AD_2, as shown in Panel (c). As a result, real GDP and the price level rise.

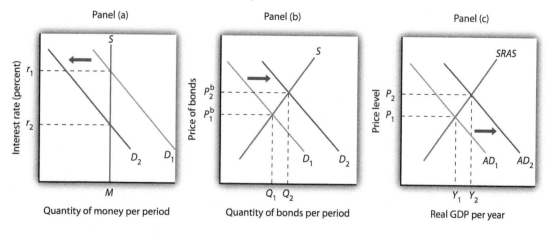

Lower interest rates in turn increase the quantity of investment. They also stimulate net exports, as lower interest rates lead to a lower exchange rate. The aggregate demand curve shifts to the right as shown in Panel (c) from AD_1 to AD_2. Given the short-run aggregate supply curve $SRAS$, the economy moves to a higher real GDP and a higher price level.

An increase in money demand due to a change in expectations, preferences, or transactions costs that make people want to hold more money at each interest rate will have the opposite effect. The money demand curve will shift to the right and the demand for bonds will shift to the left. The resulting higher interest rate will lead to a lower quantity of investment. Also, higher interest rates will lead to a higher exchange rate and depress net exports. Thus, the aggregate demand curve will shift to the left. All other things unchanged, real GDP and the price level will fall.

Changes in the Money Supply

Now suppose the market for money is in equilibrium and the Fed changes the money supply. All other things unchanged, how will this change in the money supply affect the equilibrium interest rate and aggregate demand, real GDP, and the price level?

Suppose the Fed conducts open-market operations in which it buys bonds. This is an example of expansionary monetary policy. The impact of Fed bond purchases is illustrated in Panel (a) of Figure 25.10. The Fed's purchase of bonds shifts the demand curve for bonds to the right, raising bond prices to P^b_2. As we learned, when the Fed buys bonds, the supply of money increases. Panel (b) of Figure 25.10 shows an economy with a money supply of M, which is in equilibrium at an interest rate of r_1. Now suppose the bond purchases by the Fed as shown in Panel (a) result in an increase in the money supply to M'; that policy change shifts the supply curve for money to the right to S_2. At the original interest rate r_1, people do not wish to hold the newly supplied money; they would prefer to hold nonmoney assets. To reestablish equilibrium in the money market, the interest rate must fall to increase the quantity of money demanded. In the economy shown, the interest rate must fall to r_2 to increase the quantity of money demanded to M'.

FIGURE 25.10 An Increase in the Money Supply

The Fed increases the money supply by buying bonds, increasing the demand for bonds in Panel (a) from D_1 to D_2 and the price of bonds to P^b_2. This corresponds to an increase in the money supply to M' in Panel (b). The interest rate must fall to r_2 to achieve equilibrium. The lower interest rate leads to an increase in investment and net exports, which shifts the aggregate demand curve from AD_1 to AD_2 in Panel (c). Real GDP and the price level rise.

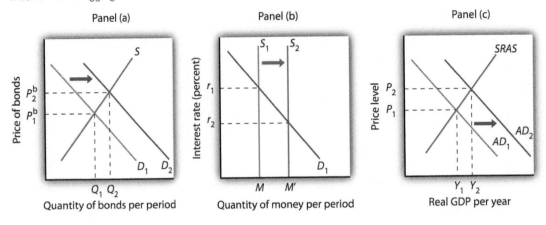

The reduction in interest rates required to restore equilibrium to the market for money after an increase in the money supply is achieved in the bond market. The increase in bond prices lowers interest rates, which will increase the quantity of money people demand. Lower interest rates will stimulate investment and net exports, via changes in the foreign exchange market, and cause the aggregate demand curve to shift to the right, as shown in Panel (c), from AD_1 to AD_2. Given the short-run aggregate supply curve $SRAS$, the economy moves to a higher real GDP and a higher price level.

Open-market operations in which the Fed sells bonds—that is, a contractionary monetary policy—will have the opposite effect. When the Fed sells bonds, the supply curve of bonds shifts to the right and the price of bonds falls. The bond sales lead to a reduction in the money supply, causing the money supply curve to shift to the left and raising the equilibrium interest rate. Higher interest rates lead to a shift in the aggregate demand curve to the left.

As we have seen in looking at both changes in demand for and in supply of money, the process of achieving equilibrium in the money market works in tandem with the achievement of equilibrium in the bond market. The interest rate determined by money market equilibrium is consistent with the interest rate achieved in the bond market.

Key Takeaways

- People hold money in order to buy goods and services (transactions demand), to have it available for contingencies (precautionary demand), and in order to avoid possible drops in the value of other assets such as bonds (speculative demand).
- The higher the interest rate, the lower the quantities of money demanded for transactions, for precautionary, and for speculative purposes. The lower the interest rate, the higher the quantities of money demanded for these purposes.
- The demand for money will change as a result of a change in real GDP, the price level, transfer costs, expectations, or preferences.
- We assume that the supply of money is determined by the Fed. The supply curve for money is thus a vertical line. Money market equilibrium occurs at the interest rate at which the quantity of money demanded equals the quantity of money supplied.
- All other things unchanged, a shift in money demand or supply will lead to a change in the equilibrium interest rate and therefore to changes in the level of real GDP and the price level.

Try It!

In 2005 the Fed was concerned about the possibility that the United States was moving into an inflationary gap, and it adopted a contractionary monetary policy as a result. Draw a four-panel graph showing this policy and its expected results. In Panel (a), use the model of aggregate demand and aggregate supply to illustrate an economy with an inflationary gap. In Panel (b), show how the Fed's policy will affect the market for bonds. In Panel (c), show how it will affect the demand for and supply of money. In Panel (d), show how it will affect the exchange rate. Finally, return to Panel (a) and incorporate these developments into your analysis of aggregate demand and aggregate supply, and show how the Fed's policy will affect real GDP and the price level in the short run.

Case in Point: Money in Today's World

Source: © Shutterstock, Inc.

The models of the money and bond markets presented in this chapter suggest that the Fed can control the interest rate by deciding on a money supply that would lead to the desired equilibrium interest rate in the money market. Yet, Fed policy announcements typically focus on what it wants the federal funds rate to be with scant attention to the money supply. Whereas throughout the 1990s, the Fed would announce a target federal funds rate and also indicate an expected change in the money supply, in 2000, when legislation requiring it to do so expired, it abandoned the practice of setting money supply targets.

Why the shift? The factors that have made focusing on the money supply as a policy target difficult for the past 25 years are first banking deregulation in the 1980s followed by financial innovations associated with technological changes—in particular the maturation of electronic payment and transfer mechanisms—thereafter.

Before the 1980s, M1 was a fairly reliable measure of the money people held, primarily for transactions. To buy things, one used cash, checks written on demand deposits, or traveler's checks. The Fed could thus use reliable estimates of the money demand curve to predict what the money supply would need to be in order to bring about a certain interest rate in the money market.

Legislation in the early 1980s allowed for money market deposit accounts (MMDAs), which are essentially interest-bearing savings accounts on which checks can be written. MMDAs are part of M2. Shortly after, other forms of payments for transactions developed or became more common. For example, credit and debit card use has mushroomed (from $10.8 billion in 1990 to $30 billion in 2000), and people can pay their credit card bills, electronically or with paper checks, from accounts that are part of either M1 or M2. Another innovation of the last 20 years is the automatic transfer service (ATS) that allows consumers to move money between checking and savings accounts at an ATM machine, or online, or through prearranged agreements with their financial institutions. While we take these methods of payment for granted today, they did not exist before 1980 because of restrictive banking legislation and the lack of technological know-how. Indeed, before 1980, being able to pay bills from accounts that earned interest was unheard of.

Further blurring the lines between M1 and M2 has been the development and growing popularity of what are called retail sweep programs. Since 1994, banks have been using retail-sweeping software to dynamically reclassify balances as either checking account balances (part of M1) or MMDAs (part of M2). They do this to avoid reserve requirements on checking accounts. The software not only moves the funds but also ensures that the bank does not exceed the legal limit of six reclassifications in any month. In the last 10 years these retail sweeps rose from zero to nearly the size of M1 itself!

Such changes in the ways people pay for transactions and banks do their business have led economists to think about new definitions of money that would better track what is actually used for the purposes behind the money demand curve. One notion is called MZM, which stands for "money zero maturity." The idea behind MZM is that people can easily use any deposits that do not have specified maturity terms to pay for transactions, as these accounts are quite liquid, regardless of what classification of money they fall into. Some research shows that using MZM allows for a stable picture of the money market. Until more agreement has been reached, though, we should expect the Fed to continue to downplay the role of the money supply in its policy deliberations and to continue to announce its intentions in terms of the federal funds rate.

Source: *Based on Pedre Teles and Ruilin Zhou, "A Stable Money Demand: Looking for the Right Monetary Aggregate," Federal Reserve Bank of Chicago Economic Perspectives 29 (First Quarter, 2005): 50–59, https://www.chicagofed.org/publications/economic-perspectives/2005/1qtr2005-part4-teles-zhou.*

Answer to Try It! Problem

In Panel (a), with the aggregate demand curve AD_1, short-run aggregate supply curve $SRAS$, and long-run aggregate supply curve $LRAS$, the economy has an inflationary gap of $Y_1 - Y_P$. The contractionary monetary policy means that the Fed sells bonds—a rightward shift of the bond supply curve in Panel (b), which decreases the money supply—as shown by a leftward shift in the money supply curve in Panel (c). In Panel (b), we see that the price of bonds falls, and in Panel (c) that the interest rate rises. A higher interest rate will reduce the quantity of investment demanded. The higher interest rate also leads to a higher exchange rate, as shown in Panel (d), as the demand for dollars increases and the supply decreases. The higher exchange rate will lead to a decrease in net exports. As a result of these changes in financial markets, the aggregate demand curve shifts to the left to AD_2 in Panel (a). If all goes according to plan (and we will learn in the next chapter that it may not!), the new aggregate demand curve will intersect $SRAS$ and $LRAS$ at Y_P.

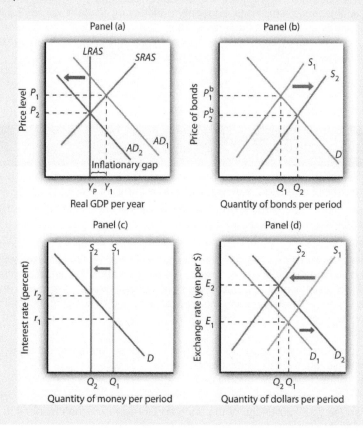

25.4 Review and Practice

Summary

We began this chapter by looking at bond and foreign exchange markets and showing how each is related to the level of real GDP and the price level. Bonds represent the obligation of the seller to repay the buyer the face value by the maturity date; their interest rate is determined by the demand and supply for bonds. An increase in bond prices means a drop in interest rates. A reduction in bond prices means interest rates have risen. The price of the dollar is determined in foreign exchange markets by the demand and supply for dollars.

We then saw how the money market works. The quantity of money demanded varies negatively with the interest rate. Factors that cause the demand curve for money to shift include changes in real GDP, the price level, expectations, the cost of transferring funds between money and nonmoney accounts, and preferences, especially preferences concerning risk. Equilibrium in the market for money is achieved at the interest rate at which the quantity of money demanded equals the quantity of money supplied. We assumed that the supply of money is determined by the Fed. An increase in money demand raises the equilibrium interest rate, and a decrease in money demand lowers the equilibrium interest rate. An increase in the money supply lowers the equilibrium interest rate; a reduction in the money supply raises the equilibrium interest rate.

Concept Problems

1. What factors might increase the demand for bonds? The supply?

2. What would happen to the market for bonds if a law were passed that set a minimum price on bonds that was above the equilibrium price?

3. When the price of bonds decreases, the interest rate rises. Explain.

4. One journalist writing about the complex interactions between various markets in the economy stated: "When the government spends more than it takes in taxes it must sell bonds to finance its excess expenditures. But selling bonds drives interest rates down and thus stimulates the economy by encouraging more investment and decreasing the foreign exchange rate, which helps our export industries." Carefully analyze the statement. Do you agree? Why or why not?

5. What do you predict will happen to the foreign exchange rate if interest rates in the United States increase dramatically over the next year? Explain, using a graph of the foreign exchange market. How would such a change affect real GDP and the price level?

6. Suppose the government were to increase its purchases, issuing bonds to finance these purchases. Use your knowledge of the bond and foreign exchange markets to explain how this would affect investment and net exports.

7. How would each of the following affect the demand for money?

   a. A tax on bonds held by individuals

   b. A forecast by the Fed that interest rates will rise sharply in the next quarter

   c. A wave of muggings

   d. An announcement of an agreement between Congress and the president that, beginning in the next fiscal year, government spending will be reduced by an amount sufficient to eliminate all future borrowing

8. Some low-income countries do not have a bond market. In such countries, what substitutes for money do you think people would hold?

9. Explain what is meant by the statement that people are holding more money than they want to hold.

10. Explain how the Fed's sale of government bonds shifts the supply curve for money.

11. Trace the impact of a sale of government bonds by the Fed on bond prices, interest rates, investment, net exports, aggregate demand, real GDP, and the price level.

Numerical Problems

1. Compute the rate of interest associated with each of these bonds that matures in one year:

Face Value	Selling Price
a. $100	$80
b. $100	$90
c. $100	$95
d. $200	$180
e. $200	$190
f. $200	$195

g. Describe the relationship between the selling price of a bond and the interest rate.

2. Suppose that the demand and supply schedules for bonds that have a face value of $100 and a maturity date one year hence are as follows:

Price ($)	Quantity Demanded	Quantity Supplied
100	0	600
95	100	500
90	200	400
85	300	300
80	400	200
75	500	100
70	600	0

a. Draw the demand and supply curves for these bonds, find the equilibrium price, and determine the interest rate.

b. Now suppose the quantity demanded increases by 200 bonds at each price. Draw the new demand curve and find the new equilibrium price. What has happened to the interest rate?

3. Compute the dollar price of a German car that sells for 40,000 euros at each of the following exchange rates:

a. $1 = 1 euro

b. $1 = 0.8 euro

c. $1 = 0.75 euro

4. Consider the euro-zone of the European Union and Japan. The demand and supply curves for euros are given by the following table (prices for the euro are given in Japanese yen; quantities of euros are in millions):

Price (in Euros)	Euros Demanded	Euros Supplied
75	0	600
70	100	500
65	200	400
60	300	300
55	400	200
50	500	100
45	600	0

a. Draw the demand and supply curves for euros and state the equilibrium exchange rate (in yen) for the euro. How many euros are required to purchase one yen?

b. Suppose an increase in interest rates in the European Union increases the demand for euros by 100 million at each price. At the same time, it reduces the supply by 100 million at each price. Draw the new demand and supply curves and state the new equilibrium exchange rate for the euro. How many euros are now required to purchase one yen?

c. How will the event in (b) affect net exports in the European Union?

d. How will the event in (b) affect aggregate demand in the European Union?

e. How will the event in (b) affect net exports in Japan?

f. How will the event in (b) affect aggregate demand in Japan?

5. Suppose you earn $6,000 per month and spend $200 in each of the month's 30 days. Compute your average quantity of money demanded if:

a. You deposit your entire earnings in your checking account at the beginning of the month.

b. You deposit $2,000 into your checking account on the 1st, 11th, and 21st days of the month.

c. You deposit $1,000 into your checking account on the 1st, 6th, 11th, 16th, 21st, and 26th days of the month.

d. How would you expect the interest rate to affect your decision to opt for strategy (a), (b), or (c)?

6. Suppose the quantity demanded of money at an interest rate of 5% is $2 billion per day, at an interest rate of 3% is $3 billion per day, and at an interest rate of 1% is $4 billion per day. Suppose the money supply is $3 billion per day.

a. Draw a graph of the money market and find the equilibrium interest rate.

b. Suppose the quantity of money demanded decreases by $1 billion per day at each interest rate. Graph this situation and find the new equilibrium interest rate. Explain the process of achieving the new equilibrium in the money market.

c. Suppose instead that the money supply decreases by $1 billion per day. Explain the process of achieving the new equilibrium in the money market.

7. We know that the U.S. economy faced a recessionary gap in 2008 and that the Fed responded with an expansionary monetary policy. Present the results of the Fed's action in a four-panel graph. In Panel (a), show the initial situation, using the model of aggregate demand and aggregate supply. In Panel (b), show how the Fed's policy affects the bond market and bond prices. In Panel (c), show how the market for U.S. dollars and the exchange rate will be affected. In Panel (d), incorporate these developments into your analysis of aggregate demand and aggregate supply, and show how the Fed's policy will affect real GDP and the price level in the short run.

Endnotes

1. Consumption may also be affected by changes in interest rates. For example, if interest rates fall, consumers can more easily obtain credit and thus are more likely to purchase cars and other durable goods. To simplify, we ignore this effect.

2. In this chapter we are looking only at changes that originate in financial markets to see their impact on aggregate demand and aggregate supply. Changes in the price level and in real GDP also shift the money demand curve, but these changes are the result of changes in aggregate demand or aggregate supply and are considered in more advanced courses in macroeconomics.

CHAPTER 26
Monetary Policy and the Fed

26.1 Start Up: The Fed's Extraordinary Challenges in 2008

"The Federal Reserve will employ all available tools to promote the resumption of sustainable economic growth and to preserve price stability. In particular, the Committee anticipates that weak economic conditions are likely to warrant exceptionally low levels of the federal funds rate for some time." So went the statement issued by the Federal Open Market Committee on December 16, 2008, that went on to say that the new target range for the federal funds rate would be between 0% and 0.25%. For the first time in its history, the Fed was targeting a rate below 1%. It was also acknowledging the difficulty of hitting a specific rate target when the target is so low. And, finally, it was experimenting with extraordinary measures based on a section of the Federal Reserve Act that allows it to take such measures when conditions in financial markets are deemed "unusual and exigent."

The Fed was responding to the broad-based weakness of the U.S. economy, the strains in financial markets, and the tightness of credit. Unlike some other moments in U.S. economic history, it did not have to worry about inflation, at least not in the short term. On the same day, consumer prices were reported to have fallen by 1.7% for the month of November. Indeed, commentators were beginning to fret over the possibility of deflation and how the Fed could continue to support the economy when it had already used all of its federal funds rate ammunition.

Anticipating this concern, the Fed's statement went on to discuss other ways it was planning to support the economy over the months to come. These included buying mortgage-backed securities to support the mortgage and housing markets, buying long-term Treasury bills, and creating other new credit facilities to make credit more easily available to households and small businesses. These options recalled a speech that Ben Bernanke had made six years earlier, when he was a member of the Federal Reserve Board of Governors but still nearly four years away from being named its chair, titled "Deflation: Making Sure 'It' Doesn't Happen Here." In the 2002 speech he laid out how these tools, along with tax cuts, were the equivalent of what Nobel prize winning economist Milton Friedman meant by a "helicopter drop" of money. The speech earned Bernanke the nickname of Helicopter Ben.

The Fed's decisions of mid-December put it in uncharted territory. Japan had tried a similar strategy, though somewhat less comprehensively and more belatedly, in the 1990s when faced with a situation similar to that of the United States in 2008 with only limited success. In his 2002 speech, Bernanke suggested that Japanese authorities had not gone far enough. Only history will tell us whether the Fed will be more successful and how well these new strategies will work.

This chapter examines in greater detail monetary policy and the roles of central banks in carrying out that policy. Our primary focus will be on the U.S. Federal Reserve System. The basic tools used by central banks in many countries are similar, but their institutional structure and their roles in their respective countries can differ.

26.2 Monetary Policy in the United States

Learning Objectives

1. Discuss the Fed's primary and secondary goals and relate these goals to the legislation that created the Fed as well as to subsequent legislation that affects the Fed.
2. State and show graphically how expansionary and contractionary monetary policy can be used to close gaps.

In many respects, the Fed is the most powerful maker of economic policy in the United States. Congress can pass laws, but the president must execute them; the president can propose laws, but only Congress can pass them. The Fed, however, both sets and carries out monetary policy. Deliberations about fiscal policy can drag on for months, even years, but the Federal Open Market Committee (FOMC) can, behind closed doors, set monetary policy in a day—and see that policy implemented within hours. The Board of Governors can change the discount rate or reserve requirements at any time. The impact of the Fed's policies on the economy can be quite dramatic. The Fed can push interest rates up or down. It can promote a recession or an expansion. It can cause the inflation rate to rise or fall. The Fed wields enormous power.

But to what ends should all this power be directed? With what tools are the Fed's policies carried out? And what problems exist in trying to achieve the Fed's goals? This section reviews the goals of monetary policy, the tools available to the Fed in pursuing those goals, and the way in which monetary policy affects macroeconomic variables.

Goals of Monetary Policy

When we think of the goals of monetary policy, we naturally think of standards of macroeconomic performance that seem desirable—a low unemployment rate, a stable price level, and economic growth. It thus seems reasonable to conclude that the goals of monetary policy should include the maintenance of full employment, the avoidance of inflation or deflation, and the promotion of economic growth.

But these goals, each of which is desirable in itself, may conflict with one another. A monetary policy that helps to close a recessionary gap and thus promotes full employment may accelerate inflation. A monetary policy that seeks to reduce inflation may increase unemployment and weaken economic growth. You might expect that in such cases, monetary authorities would receive guidance from legislation spelling out goals for the Fed to pursue and specifying what to do when achieving one goal means not achieving another. But as we shall see, that kind of guidance does not exist.

The Federal Reserve Act

When Congress established the Federal Reserve System in 1913, it said little about the policy goals the Fed should seek. The closest it came to spelling out the goals of monetary policy was in the first paragraph of the Federal Reserve Act, the legislation that created the Fed:

"An Act to provide for the establishment of Federal reserve banks, to furnish an elastic currency, [to make loans to banks], to establish a more effective supervision of banking in the United States, and for other purposes."[1]

In short, nothing in the legislation creating the Fed anticipates that the institution will act to close recessionary or inflationary gaps, that it will seek to spur economic growth, or that it will strive to keep the price level steady. There is no guidance as to what the Fed should do when these goals conflict with one another.

The Employment Act of 1946

The first U.S. effort to specify macroeconomic goals came after World War II. The Great Depression of the 1930s had instilled in people a deep desire to prevent similar calamities in the future. That desire, coupled with the 1936 publication of John Maynard Keynes's prescription for avoiding such problems through government policy (*The General Theory of Employment, Interest and Money*), led to the passage of the Employment Act of 1946, which declared that the federal government should "use all practical means . . . to promote maximum employment, production and purchasing power." The act also created the Council of Economic Advisers (CEA) to advise the president on economic matters.

The Fed might be expected to be influenced by this specification of federal goals, but because it is an independent agency, it is not required to follow any particular path. Furthermore, the legislation does not suggest what should be done if the goals of achieving full employment and maximum purchasing power conflict.

The Full Employment and Balanced Growth Act of 1978

The clearest, and most specific, statement of federal economic goals came in the Full Employment and Balanced Growth Act of 1978. This act, generally known as the Humphrey–Hawkins Act, specified that by 1983 the federal government should achieve an unemployment rate among adults of 3% or less, a civilian unemployment rate of 4% or less, and an inflation rate of 3% or less. Although these goals have the virtue of specificity, they offer little in terms of practical policy guidance. The last time the civilian unemployment rate in the United States fell below 4% was 1969, and the inflation rate that year was 6.2%. In 2000, the unemployment rate touched 4%, and the inflation rate that year was 3.4%, so the goals were close to being met. Except for 2007 when inflation hit 4.1%, inflation has hovered between 1.6% and 3.4% in all the other years between 1991 and 2011, so the inflation goal was met or nearly met, but unemployment fluctuated between 4.0% and 9.6% during those years.

The Humphrey-Hawkins Act requires that the chairman of the Fed's Board of Governors report twice each year to Congress about the Fed's monetary policy. These sessions provide an opportunity for members of the House and Senate to express their views on monetary policy.

Federal Reserve Policy and Goals

Perhaps the clearest way to see the Fed's goals is to observe the policy choices it makes. Since 1979, following a bout of double-digit inflation, its actions have suggested that the Fed's primary goal is to keep inflation under control. Provided that the inflation rate falls within acceptable limits, however, the Fed will also use stimulative measures to attempt to close recessionary gaps.

In 1979, the Fed, then led by Paul Volcker, launched a deliberate program of reducing the inflation rate. It stuck to that effort through the early 1980s, even in the face of a major recession. That effort achieved its goal: the annual inflation rate fell from 13.3% in 1979 to 3.8% in 1982. The cost, however, was great. Unemployment soared past 9% during the recession. With the inflation rate below 4%, the Fed shifted to a stimulative policy early in 1983.

In 1990, when the economy slipped into a recession, the Fed, with Alan Greenspan at the helm, engaged in aggressive open-market operations to stimulate the economy, despite the fact that the inflation rate had jumped to 6.1%. Much of that increase in the inflation rate, however, resulted from an oil-price boost that came in the wake of Iraq's invasion of Kuwait that year. A jump in prices that occurs at the same time as real GDP is slumping suggests a leftward shift in short-run aggregate supply, a shift that creates a recessionary gap. Fed officials concluded that the upturn in inflation in 1990 was a temporary phenomenon and that an expansionary policy was an appropriate response to a weak economy. Once the recovery was clearly under way, the Fed shifted to a neutral policy, seeking neither to boost nor to reduce aggregate demand. Early in 1994, the Fed shifted to a contractionary policy, selling bonds to reduce the money supply and raise interest rates. Then Fed Chairman Greenspan indicated that the move was intended to head off any possible increase in inflation from its 1993 rate of 2.7%. Although the economy was still in a recessionary gap when the Fed acted, Greenspan indicated that any acceleration of the inflation rate would be unacceptable.

By March 1997 the inflation rate had fallen to 2.4%. The Fed became concerned that inflationary pressures were increasing and tightened monetary policy, raising the goal for the federal funds interest rate to 5.5%. Inflation remained well below 2.0% throughout the rest of 1997 and 1998. In the fall of 1998, with inflation low, the Fed was concerned that the economic recession in much of Asia and slow growth in Europe would reduce growth in the United States. In quarter-point steps it reduced the goal for the federal funds rate to 4.75%. With real GDP growing briskly in the first half of 1999, the Fed became concerned that inflation would increase, even though the inflation rate at the time was about 2%, and in June 1999, it raised its goal for the federal funds rate to 5% and continued raising the rate until it reached 6.5% in May 2000.

With inflation under control, it then began lowering the federal funds rate to stimulate the economy. It continued lowering through the brief recession of 2001 and beyond. There were 11 rate cuts in 2001, with the rate at the end of that year at 1.75%; in late 2002 the rate was cut to 1.25%, and in mid-2003 it was cut to 1.0%.

Then, with growth picking up and inflation again a concern, the Fed began again in the middle of 2004 to increase rates. By the end of 2006, the rate stood at 5.25% as a result of 17 quarter-point rate increases.

Starting in September 2007, the Fed, since 2006 led by Ben Bernanke, shifted gears and began lowering the federal funds rate, mostly in larger steps or 0.5 to 0.75 percentage points. Though initially somewhat concerned with inflation, it sensed that the economy was beginning to slow down. It moved aggressively to lower rates over the course of the next 15 months, and by the end of 2008, the rate was targeted at between 0% and 0.25%. In late 2008 and through 2013, beginning with the threat of deflation and then progressing into a period during which inflation ran fairly low, the Fed seemed quite willing to use all of its options to try to keep financial markets running smoothly. The Fed attempted, in the initial period, to moderate the recession, and then it tried to support the rather lackluster growth that followed. In January 2014 the Fed went on record to say that it intended to keep the federal funds rate at extremely low levels so long as the unemployment rate stayed above 6.5% and possibly even if it went below that, assuming that inflation remained in check.

In February 2014, Janet Yellen became Fed chair. Over the next couple of years, the economy continued to recover. With the inflation rate still very low and the unemployment rate at about 5%, the Fed finally raised the federal funds rate by a quarter point to the 0.25 to 0.50 range in December 2015. This ended a rather extraordinary, nearly decade-long period of no change in the federal funds target rate. But, due to a rocky economic start in 2016, as it appeared the Chinese economy might be headed for a major slowdown and the improvements in the U.S. economy might also be slowing down, it would be another year before the Fed raised the rate by another quarter point. By then, the unemployment rate had fallen to 4.6% and inflation had picked up a little but was still below 2%.

What can we infer from these episodes in the 1980s, 1990s, and the first part of this century? It seems clear that the Fed is determined not to allow the high inflation rates of the 1970s to occur again. When the inflation rate is within acceptable limits, the Fed will undertake stimulative measures in response to a recessionary gap or even in response to the possibility of a growth slowdown. Those limits seem to have tightened over time. In the late 1990s and early 2000s, it appeared that an inflation rate above 3%—or any indication that inflation might rise above 3%—would lead the Fed to adopt a contractionary policy. Yellen made clear in a speech in January 2017 that the Fed now sees 2% as the appropriate desired rate of inflation. Thus, the inflation goal appears to have fallen over time. If inflation were expected to remain below 2%, however, the Fed would undertake stimulative measures to close a recessionary gap. Noting in the same speech that the Fed believes the unemployment rate to be close to the natural rate of unemployment, Yellen at the start of 2017 is expecting gradual hikes in the federal funds rate over the year. [2]

Monetary Policy and Macroeconomic Variables

We saw in an earlier chapter that the Fed has three tools at its command to try to change aggregate demand and thus to influence the level of economic activity. It can buy or sell federal government bonds through open-market operations, it can change the discount rate, or it can change reserve requirements. It can also use these tools in combination. In the next section of this chapter, where we discuss the notion of a liquidity trap, we will also introduce more extraordinary measures that the Fed has at its disposal.

Most economists agree that these tools of monetary policy affect the economy, but they sometimes disagree on the precise mechanisms through which this occurs, on the strength of those mechanisms, and on the ways in which monetary policy should be used. Before we address some of these issues, we shall review the ways in which monetary policy affects the economy in the context of the model of aggregate demand and aggregate supply. Our focus will be on open-market operations, the purchase or sale by the Fed of federal bonds.

Expansionary Monetary Policy

The Fed might pursue an expansionary monetary policy in response to the initial situation shown in Panel (a) of Figure 26.1. An economy with a potential output of Y_P is operating at Y_1; there is a recessionary gap. One possible policy response is to allow the economy to correct this gap on its own, waiting for reductions in nominal wages and other prices to shift the short-run aggregate supply curve $SRAS_1$ to the right until it intersects the aggregate demand curve AD_1 at Y_P. An alternative is a stabilization policy that seeks to increase aggregate demand to AD_2 to close the gap. An expansionary monetary policy is one way to achieve such a shift.

To carry out an expansionary monetary policy, the Fed will buy bonds, thereby increasing the money supply. That shifts the demand curve for bonds to D_2, as illustrated in Panel (b). Bond prices rise to $P^b{}_2$. The higher price for bonds reduces the interest rate. These changes in the bond market are consistent with the changes in the money market, shown in Panel (c), in which the greater money supply leads to a fall in the interest rate to r_2. The lower interest rate stimulates investment. In addition, the lower interest rate reduces the demand for and increases the supply of dollars in the currency market, reducing the exchange rate to E_2 in Panel (d). The lower exchange rate will stimulate net exports. The combined impact of greater investment and net exports will shift the aggregate demand curve to the right. The curve shifts by an amount equal to the multiplier times the sum of the initial changes in investment and net exports. In Panel (a), this is shown as a shift to AD_2, and the recessionary gap is closed.

FIGURE 26.1 Expansionary Monetary Policy to Close a Recessionary Gap

In Panel (a), the economy has a recessionary gap $Y_P - Y_1$. An expansionary monetary policy could seek to close this gap by shifting the aggregate demand curve to AD_2. In Panel (b), the Fed buys bonds, shifting the demand curve for bonds to D_2 and increasing the price of bonds to P^b_2. By buying bonds, the Fed increases the money supply to M' in Panel (c). The Fed's action lowers interest rates to r_2. The lower interest rate also reduces the demand for and increases the supply of dollars, reducing the exchange rate to E_2 in Panel (d). The resulting increases in investment and net exports shift the aggregate demand curve in Panel (a).

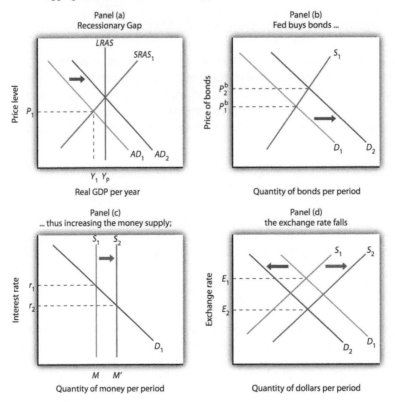

Contractionary Monetary Policy

The Fed will generally pursue a contractionary monetary policy when it considers inflation a threat. Suppose, for example, that the economy faces an inflationary gap; the aggregate demand and short-run aggregate supply curves intersect to the right of the long-run aggregate supply curve, as shown in Panel (a) of Figure 26.2.

FIGURE 26.2 A Contractionary Monetary Policy to Close an Inflationary Gap

In Panel (a), the economy has an inflationary gap $Y_1 - Y_P$. A contractionary monetary policy could seek to close this gap by shifting the aggregate demand curve to AD_2. In Panel (b), the Fed sells bonds, shifting the supply curve for bonds to S_2 and lowering the price of bonds to $P^b{}_2$. The lower price of bonds means a higher interest rate, r_2, as shown in Panel (c). The higher interest rate also increases the demand for and decreases the supply of dollars, raising the exchange rate to E_2 in Panel (d), which will increase net exports. The decreases in investment and net exports are responsible for decreasing aggregate demand in Panel (a).

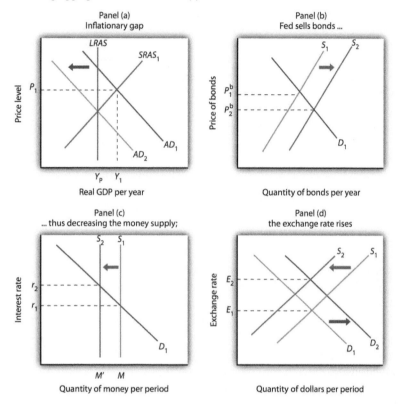

To carry out a contractionary policy, the Fed sells bonds. In the bond market, shown in Panel (b) of Figure 26.2, the supply curve shifts to the right, lowering the price of bonds and increasing the interest rate. In the money market, shown in Panel (c), the Fed's bond sales reduce the money supply and raise the interest rate. The higher interest rate reduces investment. The higher interest rate also induces a greater demand for dollars as foreigners seek to take advantage of higher interest rates in the United States. The supply of dollars falls; people in the United States are less likely to purchase foreign interest-earning assets now that U.S. assets are paying a higher rate. These changes boost the exchange rate, as shown in Panel (d), which reduces exports and increases imports and thus causes net exports to fall. The contractionary monetary policy thus shifts aggregate demand to the left, by an amount equal to the multiplier times the combined initial changes in investment and net exports, as shown in Panel (a).

Key Takeaways

- The Federal Reserve Board and the Federal Open Market Committee are among the most powerful institutions in the United States.
- The Fed's primary goal appears to be the control of inflation. Providing that inflation is under control, the Fed will act to close recessionary gaps.
- Expansionary policy, such as a purchase of government securities by the Fed, tends to push bond prices up and interest rates down, increasing investment and aggregate demand. Contractionary policy, such as a sale of government securities by the Fed, pushes bond prices down, interest rates up, investment down, and aggregate demand shifts to the left.

Try It!

The figure shows an economy operating at a real GDP of Y_1 and a price level of P_1, at the intersection of AD_1 and $SRAS_1$.

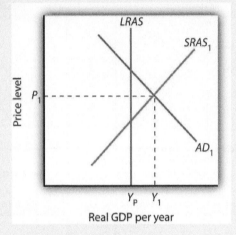

1. What kind of gap is the economy experiencing?
2. What type of monetary policy (expansionary or contractionary) would be appropriate for closing the gap?
3. If the Fed decided to pursue this policy, what type of open-market operations would it conduct?
4. How would bond prices, interest rates, and the exchange rate change?
5. How would investment and net exports change?
6. How would the aggregate demand curve shift?

Case in Point: A Brief History of the Greenspan Fed

Source: Wikimedia Commons

With the passage of time and the fact that the fallout on the economy turned out to be relatively minor, it is hard in retrospect to realize how scary a situation Alan Greenspan and the Fed faced just two months after his appointment as Chairman of the Federal Reserve Board. On October 12, 1987, the stock market had its worst day ever. The Dow Jones Industrial Average plunged

508 points, wiping out more than $500 billion in a few hours of feverish trading on Wall Street. That drop represented a loss in value of over 22%. In comparison, the largest daily drop in 2008 of 778 points on September 29, 2008, represented a loss in value of about 7%.

When the Fed faced another huge plunge in stock prices in 1929—also in October—members of the Board of Governors met and decided that no action was necessary. Determined not to repeat the terrible mistake of 1929, one that helped to usher in the Great Depression, Alan Greenspan immediately reassured the country, saying that the Fed would provide adequate liquidity, by buying federal securities, to assure that economic activity would not fall. As it turned out, the damage to the economy was minor and the stock market quickly regained value.

In the fall of 1990, the economy began to slip into recession. The Fed responded with expansionary monetary policy—cutting reserve requirements, lowering the discount rate, and buying Treasury bonds.

Interest rates fell quite quickly in response to the Fed's actions, but, as is often the case, changes to the components of aggregate demand were slower in coming. Consumption and investment began to rise in 1991, but their growth was weak, and unemployment continued to rise because growth in output was too slow to keep up with growth in the labor force. It was not until the fall of 1992 that the economy started to pick up steam. This episode demonstrates an important difficulty with stabilization policy: attempts to manipulate aggregate demand achieve shifts in the curve, but with a lag.

Throughout the rest of the 1990s, with some tightening when the economy seemed to be moving into an inflationary gap and some loosening when the economy seemed to be possibly moving toward a recessionary gap—especially in 1998 and 1999 when parts of Asia experienced financial turmoil and recession and European growth had slowed down—the Fed helped steer what is now referred to as the Goldilocks (not too hot, not too cold, just right) economy.

The U.S. economy again experienced a mild recession in 2001 under Greenspan. At that time, the Fed systematically conducted expansionary policy. Similar to its response to the 1987 stock market crash, the Fed has been credited with maintaining liquidity following the dot-com stock market crash in early 2001 and the attacks on the World Trade Center and the Pentagon in September 2001.

When Greenspan retired in January 2006, many hailed him as the greatest central banker ever. As the economy faltered in 2008 and as the financial crisis unfolded throughout the year, however, the question of how the policies of Greenspan's Fed played into the current difficulties took center stage. Testifying before Congress in October 2008, he said that the country faces a "once-in-a-century credit tsunami," and he admitted, "I made a mistake in presuming that the self-interests of organizations, specifically banks and others, were such as that they were best capable of protecting their own shareholders and their equity in their firms." The criticisms he has faced are twofold: that the very low interest rates used to fight the 2001 recession and maintained for too long fueled the real estate bubble and that he did not promote appropriate regulations to deal with the new financial instruments that were created in the early 2000s. While supporting some additional regulations when he testified before Congress, he also warned that overreacting could be dangerous: "We have to recognize that this is almost surely a once-in-a-century phenomenon, and, in that regard, to realize the types of regulation that would prevent this from happening in the future are so onerous as to basically suppress the growth rate in the economy and . . . the standards of living of the American people."

Answers to Try It! Problems

1. Inflationary gap
2. Contractionary
3. Open-market sales of bonds
4. The price of bonds would fall. The interest rate and the exchange rate would rise.
5. Investment and net exports would fall.
6. The aggregate demand curve would shift to the left.

26.3 Problems and Controversies of Monetary Policy

Learning Objectives

1. Explain the three kinds of lags that can influence the effectiveness of monetary policy.
2. Identify the macroeconomic targets at which the Fed can aim in managing the economy, and discuss the difficulties inherent in using each of them as a target.
3. Discuss how each of the following influences a central bank's ability to achieve its desired macroeconomic outcomes: political pressures, the degree of impact on the economy (including the situation of a liquidity trap), and the rational expectations hypothesis.

The Fed has some obvious advantages in its conduct of monetary policy. The two policy-making bodies, the Board of Governors and the Federal Open Market Committee (FOMC), are small and largely independent from other political institutions. These bodies can thus reach decisions quickly and implement them immediately. Their relative independence from the political process, together with the fact that they meet in secret, allows them to operate outside the glare of publicity that might otherwise be focused on bodies that wield such enormous power.

Despite the apparent ease with which the Fed can conduct monetary policy, it still faces difficulties in its efforts to stabilize the economy. We examine some of the problems and uncertainties associated with monetary policy in this section.

Lags

Perhaps the greatest obstacle facing the Fed, or any other central bank, is the problem of lags. It is easy enough to show a recessionary gap on a graph and then to show how monetary policy can shift aggregate demand and close the gap. In the real world, however, it may take several months before anyone even realizes that a particular macroeconomic problem is occurring. When monetary authorities become aware of a problem, they can act quickly to inject reserves into the system or to withdraw reserves from it. Once that is done, however, it may be a year or more before the action affects aggregate demand.

recognition lag

The delay between the time a macroeconomic problem arises and the time at which policy makers become aware of it.

The delay between the time a macroeconomic problem arises and the time at which policy makers become aware of it is called a **recognition lag**. The 1990–1991 recession, for example, began in July 1990. It was not until late October that members of the FOMC noticed a slowing in economic activity, which prompted a stimulative monetary policy. In contrast, the most recent recession began in December 2007, and Fed easing began in September 2007.

Recognition lags stem largely from problems in collecting economic data. First, data are available only after the conclusion of a particular period. Preliminary estimates of real GDP, for example, are released about a month after the end of a quarter. Thus, a change that occurs early in a quarter will not be reflected in the data until several months later. Second, estimates of economic indicators are subject to revision. The first estimates of real GDP in the third quarter of 1990, for example, showed it increasing. Not until several months had passed did revised estimates show that a recession had begun. And finally, different indicators can lead to different interpretations. Data on employment and retail sales might be pointing in one direction while data on housing starts and industrial production might be pointing in another. It is one thing to look back after a few years have elapsed and determine whether the economy was expanding or contracting. It is quite another to decipher changes in real GDP when one is right in the middle of events. Even in a world brimming with computer-generated data on the economy, recognition lags can be substantial.

Only after policy makers recognize there is a problem can they take action to deal with it. The delay between the time at which a problem is recognized and the time at which a policy to deal with it is enacted is called the **implementation lag**. For monetary policy changes, the implementation lag is quite short. The FOMC meets eight times per year, and its members may confer between meetings through conference calls. Once the FOMC determines that a policy change is in order, the required open-market operations to buy or sell federal bonds can be put into effect immediately.

Policy makers at the Fed still have to contend with the **impact lag**, the delay between the time a policy is enacted and the time that policy has its impact on the economy.

The impact lag for monetary policy occurs for several reasons. First, it takes some time for the deposit multiplier process to work itself out. The Fed can inject new reserves into the economy immediately, but the deposit expansion process of bank lending will need time to have its full effect on the money supply. Interest rates are affected immediately, but the money supply grows more slowly. Second, firms need some time to respond to the monetary policy with new investment spending—if they respond at all. Third, a monetary change is likely to affect the exchange rate, but that translates into a change in net exports only after some delay. Thus, the shift in the aggregate demand curve due to initial changes in investment and in net exports occurs after some delay. Finally, the multiplier process of an expenditure change takes time to unfold. It is only as incomes start to rise that consumption spending picks up.

The problem of lags suggests that monetary policy should respond not to statistical reports of economic conditions in the recent past but to conditions *expected* to exist in the future. In justifying the imposition of a contractionary monetary policy early in 1994, when the economy still had a recessionary gap, Greenspan indicated that the Fed expected a one-year impact lag. The policy initiated in 1994 was a response not to the economic conditions thought to exist at the time but to conditions expected to exist in 1995. When the Fed used contractionary policy in the middle of 1999, it argued that it was doing so to forestall a possible increase in inflation. When the Fed began easing in September 2007, it argued that it was doing so to forestall adverse effects to the economy of falling housing prices. In these examples, the Fed appeared to be looking forward. It must do so with information and forecasts that are far from perfect.

Estimates of the length of time required for the impact lag to work itself out range from six months to two years. Worse, the length of the lag can vary—when they take action, policy makers cannot know whether their choices will affect the economy within a few months or within a few years. Because of the uncertain length of the impact lag, efforts to stabilize the economy through monetary policy could be destabilizing. Suppose, for example, that the Fed responds to a recessionary gap with an expansionary policy but that by the time the policy begins to affect aggregate demand, the economy has already returned to potential GDP. The policy designed to correct a recessionary gap could create an inflationary gap. Similarly, a shift to a contractionary policy in response to an inflationary gap might not affect aggregate demand until after a self-correction process had already closed the gap. In that case, the policy could plunge the economy into a recession.

Choosing Targets

In attempting to manage the economy, on what macroeconomic variables should the Fed base its policies? It must have some target, or set of targets, that it wants to achieve. The failure of the economy to achieve one of the Fed's targets would then trigger a shift in monetary policy. The choice of a target, or set of targets, is a crucial one for monetary policy. Possible targets include interest rates, money growth rates, and the price level or expected changes in the price level.

Interest Rates

Interest rates, particularly the federal funds rate, played a key role in recent Fed policy. The FOMC does not decide to increase or decrease the money supply. Rather, it engages in operations to nudge the federal funds rate up or down.

implementation lag

The delay between the time at which a problem is recognized and the time at which a policy to deal with it is enacted.

impact lag

The delay between the time a policy is enacted and the time that policy has its impact on the economy.

Up until August 1997, it had instructed the trading desk at the New York Federal Reserve Bank to conduct open-market operations in a way that would either maintain, increase, or ease the current "degree of pressure" on the reserve positions of banks. That degree of pressure was reflected by the federal funds rate; if existing reserves were less than the amount banks wanted to hold, then the bidding for the available supply would send the federal funds rate up. If reserves were plentiful, then the federal funds rate would tend to decline. When the Fed increased the degree of pressure on reserves, it sold bonds, thus reducing the supply of reserves and increasing the federal funds rate. The Fed decreased the degree of pressure on reserves by buying bonds, thus injecting new reserves into the system and reducing the federal funds rate.

The current operating procedures of the Fed focus explicitly on interest rates. At each of its eight meetings during the year, the FOMC sets a specific target or target range for the federal funds rate. When the Fed lowers the target for the federal funds rate, it buys bonds. When it raises the target for the federal funds rate, it sells bonds.

Money Growth Rates

Until 2000, the Fed was required to announce to Congress at the beginning of each year its target for money growth that year and each report dutifully did so. At the same time, the Fed report would mention that its money growth targets were benchmarks based on historical relationships rather than guides for policy. As soon as the legal requirement to report targets for money growth ended, the Fed stopped doing so. Since in recent years the Fed has placed more importance on the federal funds rate, it must adjust the money supply in order to move the federal funds rate to the level it desires. As a result, the money growth targets tended to fall by the wayside, even over the last decade in which they were being reported. Instead, as data on economic conditions unfolded, the Fed made, and continues to make, adjustments in order to affect the federal funds interest rate.

Price Level or Expected Changes in the Price Level

Some economists argue that the Fed's primary goal should be price stability. If so, an obvious possible target is the price level itself. The Fed could target a particular price level or a particular rate of change in the price level and adjust its policies accordingly. If, for example, the Fed sought an inflation rate of 2%, then it could shift to a contractionary policy whenever the rate rose above 2%. One difficulty with such a policy, of course, is that the Fed would be responding to past economic conditions with policies that are not likely to affect the economy for a year or more. Another difficulty is that inflation could be rising when the economy is experiencing a recessionary gap. An example of this, mentioned earlier, occurred in 1990 when inflation increased due to the seemingly temporary increase in oil prices following Iraq's invasion of Kuwait. The Fed faced a similar situation in the first half of 2008 when oil prices were again rising. If the Fed undertakes contractionary monetary policy at such times, then its efforts to reduce the inflation rate could worsen the recessionary gap.

One solution to this problem is to focus not on the past rate of inflation or even the current rate of inflation, but on the expected rate of inflation, as revealed by various indicators, over a period of say six months or a year.

By 2010, the central banks of about 30 developed or developing countries had adopted specific inflation targeting. Inflation targeters include Australia, Brazil, Canada, Great Britain, New Zealand, South Korea, and, most recently, Turkey and Indonesia. A study by economist Carl Walsh found that inflationary experiences among developed countries have been similar, regardless of whether their central banks had explicit or more flexible inflation targets. For developing countries, however, he found that inflation targeting enhanced macroeconomic performance, in terms of both lower inflation and greater overall stability.[3]

Political Pressures

The institutional relationship between the leaders of the Fed and the executive and legislative branches of the federal government is structured to provide for the Fed's independence. Members of the Board of Governors are appointed by the president, with confirmation by the Senate, but the 14-year terms of office provide a considerable degree of insulation from political pressure. A president exercises greater influence in the choice of the chairman of the Board of Governors; that appointment carries a four-year term. Neither the president nor Congress has any direct say over the selection of the presidents of Federal Reserve district banks. They are chosen by their individual boards of directors with the approval of the Board of Governors.

The degree of independence that central banks around the world have varies. A central bank is considered to be more independent if it is insulated from the government by such factors as longer term appointments of its governors and fewer requirements to finance government budget deficits. Studies in the 1980s and early 1990s showed that, in general, greater central bank independence was associated with lower average inflation and that there was no systematic relationship between central bank independence and other indicators of economic performance, such as real GDP growth or unemployment.[4] By the rankings used in those studies, the Fed was considered quite independent, second only to Switzerland and the German *Bundesbank* at the time. Perhaps as a result of such findings, a number of countries have granted greater independence to their central banks in the last decade. The charter for the European Central Bank, which began operations in 1998, was modeled on that of the German *Bundesbank*. Its charter states explicitly that its primary objective is to maintain price stability. Also, since 1998, central bank independence has increased in the United Kingdom, Canada, Japan, and New Zealand.

While the Fed is formally insulated from the political process, the men and women who serve on the Board of Governors and the FOMC are human beings. They are not immune to the pressures that can be placed on them by members of Congress and by the president. The chairman of the Board of Governors meets regularly with the president and the executive staff and also reports to and meets with congressional committees that deal with economic matters.

The Fed was created by the Congress; its charter could be altered—or even revoked—by that same body. The Fed is in the somewhat paradoxical situation of having to cooperate with the legislative and executive branches in order to preserve its independence.

The Degree of Impact on the Economy

The problem of lags suggests that the Fed does not know with certainty *when* its policies will work their way through the financial system to have an impact on macroeconomic performance. The Fed also does not know with certainty *to what extent* its policy decisions will affect the macroeconomy.

For example, investment can be particularly volatile. An effort by the Fed to reduce aggregate demand in the face of an inflationary gap could be partially offset by rising investment demand. But, generally, contractionary policies do tend to slow down the economy as if the Fed were "pulling on a rope." That may not be the case with expansionary policies. Since investment depends crucially on expectations about the future, business leaders must be optimistic about economic conditions in order to expand production facilities and buy new equipment. That optimism might not exist in a recession. Instead, the pessimism that might prevail during an economic slump could prevent lower interest rates from stimulating investment. An effort to stimulate the economy through monetary policy could be like "pushing on a string." The central bank could push with great force by buying bonds and engaging in quantitative easing, but little might happen to the economy at the other end of the string.

What if the Fed cannot bring about a change in interest rates? A **liquidity trap** is said to exist when a change in monetary policy has no effect on interest rates. This would be the case if the money demand curve were horizontal at some interest rate, as shown in Figure 26.3. If a change in the money supply from M to M' cannot change interest rates, then, unless there is some other change in the economy, there is no reason for investment or any other component of aggregate demand to change. Hence, traditional monetary policy is rendered totally ineffective; its degree of impact on the economy is nil. At an interest rate of zero, since bonds cease to be an attractive alternative to money, which is at least useful for transactions purposes, there would be a liquidity trap.

FIGURE 26.3 A Liquidity Trap
When a change in the money supply has no effect on the interest rate, the economy is said to be in a liquidity trap.

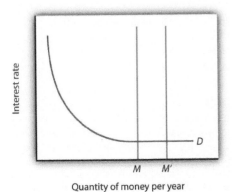

Quantity of money per year

With the federal funds rate in the United States close to zero at the end of 2008, the possibility that the country was in or nearly in a liquidity trap could not be dismissed. As discussed in the introduction to the chapter, at the same time the Fed lowered the federal funds rate to close to zero, it mentioned that it intended to pursue additional, nontraditional measures. What the Fed seeks to do is to make firms and consumers want to spend now by using a tool not aimed at reducing the interest rate, since it cannot reduce the interest rate below zero. It thus shifts its focus to the price level and to avoiding expected deflation. For example, if the public expects the price level to fall by 2% and the interest rate is zero, by holding money, the money is actually earning a positive *real* interest rate of 2%—the difference between the *nominal* interest rate and the expected deflation rate. Since the nominal rate of interest cannot fall below zero (Who would, for example, want to lend at an interest rate below zero when lending is risky whereas cash is not? In short, it does not make sense to lend $10 and get less than $10 back.), expected deflation makes holding cash very attractive and discourages spending since people will put off purchases because goods and services are expected to get cheaper.

To combat this "wait-and-see" mentality, the Fed or another central bank, using a strategy referred to as **quantitative easing**, must convince the public that it will keep interest rates very low by providing substantial reserves for as long as is necessary to avoid deflation. In other words, it is aimed at creating expected inflation. For example, at the Fed's October 2003 meeting, it announced that it would keep the federal funds rate at 1% for "a considerable period." When the Fed lowered the rate to between 0% and 0.25% in December 2008, it added that "the committee anticipates that weak economic conditions are likely to warrant exceptionally low levels of the federal funds rate for some time." After working so hard to convince economic players that it will not tolerate inflation above 2%, the Fed, when in such a situation, must convince the public that it will tolerate inflation, but of course not too much! If it is successful, this extraordinary form of expansionary monetary policy will lead to increased purchases of goods and services, compared to what they would have been with expected deflation. Also, by providing banks with lots of liquidity, the Fed is hoping to encourage them to lend.

The Japanese economy provides an interesting modern example of a country that attempted quantitative easing. With a recessionary gap starting in the early 1990s and deflation in most years from 1995 on, Japan's central bank, the Bank of Japan, began to lower the call money rate (equivalent to the federal funds rate in the United States), reaching near zero by the late 1990s. With growth still languishing, Japan appeared to be in a traditional liquidity trap. In late 1999, the Bank of Japan announced that it would maintain a zero interest rate policy for the foreseeable future, and in March 2001 it officially began a policy of quantitative easing. In 2006, with the price level rising modestly, Japan ended quantitative easing and began increasing the call rate again. It should be noted that the government simultaneously engaged in expansionary fiscal policy.

How well did these policies work in Japan? The economy began to grow modestly in 2003, though deflation between 1% and 2% remained. Some researchers feel that the Bank of Japan ended quantitative easing too early. Also, delays in implementing the policy, as well as delays in restructuring the banking sector, exacerbated Japan's problems.[5]

During the recession of 2008 and 2009 and the recovery period that followed, the Fed argued that it also engaged in credit easing.[6] **Credit easing** is a strategy that involves the extension of central bank lending to influence more broadly the proper functioning of credit markets and to improve liquidity. The specific new credit facilities that the Fed created were discussed in the Case in Point in the chapter on the nature and creation of money. In general, the Fed is hoping that these new credit facilities will improve liquidity in a variety of credit markets, ranging from those used by money market mutual funds to those involved in student and car loans.

> **credit easing**
>
> A strategy that involves the extension of central bank lending to influence more broadly the proper functioning of credit markets and to improve liquidity.

Rational Expectations

One hypothesis suggests that monetary policy may affect the price level but not real GDP. The **rational expectations hypothesis** states that people use all available information to make forecasts about future economic activity and the price level, and they adjust their behavior to these forecasts.

> **rational expectations hypothesis**
>
> Individuals form expectations about the future based on the information available to them, and they act on those expectations.

Figure 26.4 uses the model of aggregate demand and aggregate supply to show the implications of the rational expectations argument for monetary policy. Suppose the economy is operating at Y_P, as illustrated by point A. An increase in the money supply boosts aggregate demand to AD_2. In the analysis we have explored thus far, the shift in aggregate demand would move the economy to a higher level of real GDP and create an inflationary gap. That, in turn, would put upward pressure on wages and other prices, shifting the short-run aggregate supply curve to $SRAS_2$ and moving the economy to point B, closing the inflationary gap in the long run. The rational expectations hypothesis, however, suggests a quite different interpretation.

Suppose people observe the initial monetary policy change undertaken when the economy is at point A and calculate that the increase in the money supply will ultimately drive the price level up to point B. Anticipating this change in prices, people adjust their behavior. For example, if the increase in the price level from P_1 to P_2 is a 10% change, workers will anticipate that the prices they pay will rise 10%, and they will demand 10% higher wages. Their employers, anticipating that the prices they will receive will also rise, will agree to pay those higher wages. As nominal wages increase, the short-run aggregate supply curve *immediately* shifts to $SRAS_2$. The result is an upward movement along the long-run aggregate supply curve, *LRAS*. There is no change in real GDP. The monetary policy has no effect, other than its impact on the price level. This rational expectations argument relies on wages and prices being sufficiently flexible—not sticky, as described in an earlier chapter—so that the change in expectations will allow the short-run aggregate supply curve to shift quickly to $SRAS_2$.

One important implication of the rational expectations argument is that a contractionary monetary policy could be painless. Suppose the economy is at point B in Figure 26.4, and the Fed reduces the money supply in order to shift the aggregate demand curve back to AD_1. In the model of aggregate demand and aggregate supply, the result would be a recession. But in a rational expectations world, people's expectations change, the short-run aggregate supply immediately shifts to the right, and the economy moves painlessly down its long-run aggregate supply curve *LRAS* to point A. Those who support the rational expectations hypothesis, however, also tend to argue that monetary policy should not be used as a tool of stabilization policy.

FIGURE 26.4 Monetary Policy and Rational Expectations

Suppose the economy is operating at point A and that individuals have rational expectations. They calculate that an expansionary monetary policy undertaken at price level P_1 will raise prices to P_2. They adjust their expectations—and wage demands—accordingly, quickly shifting the short-run aggregate supply curve to $SRAS_2$. The result is a movement along the long-run aggregate supply curve *LRAS* to point B, with no change in real GDP.

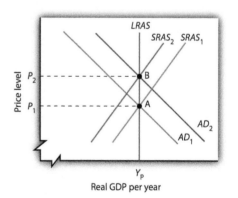

For some, the events of the early 1980s weakened support for the rational expectations hypothesis; for others, those same events strengthened support for this hypothesis. As we saw in the introduction to an earlier chapter, in 1979 President Jimmy Carter appointed Paul Volcker as Chairman of the Federal Reserve and pledged his full support for whatever the Fed might do to contain inflation. Mr. Volcker made it clear that the Fed was going to slow money growth and boost interest rates. He acknowledged that this policy would have costs but said that the Fed would stick to it as long as necessary to control inflation. Here was a monetary policy that was clearly announced and carried out as advertised. But the policy brought on the most severe recession since the Great Depression—a result that seems inconsistent with the rational expectations argument that changing expectations would prevent such a policy from having a substantial effect on real GDP.

Others, however, argue that people were aware of the Fed's pronouncements but were skeptical about whether the anti-inflation effort would persist, since the Fed had not vigorously fought inflation in the late 1960s and the 1970s. Against this history, people adjusted their estimates of inflation downward slowly. In essence, the recession occurred because people were surprised that the Fed was serious about fighting inflation.

Regardless of where one stands on this debate, one message does seem clear: once the Fed has proved it is serious about maintaining price stability, doing so in the future gets easier. To put this in concrete terms, Volcker's fight made Greenspan's work easier, and Greenspan's legacy of low inflation made Bernanke's and, starting in February 2014, Janet Yellen's easier.

Key Takeaways

- Macroeconomic policy makers must contend with recognition, implementation, and impact lags.
- Potential targets for macroeconomic policy include interest rates, money growth rates, and the price level or expected rates of change in the price level.
- Even if a central bank is structured to be independent of political pressure, its officers are likely to be affected by such pressure.
- To counteract liquidity traps or the possibility thereof, central banks have used quantitative-easing and credit-easing strategies.
- No central bank can know in advance how its policies will affect the economy; the rational expectations hypothesis predicts that central bank actions will affect the money supply and the price level but not the real level of economic activity.

Try It!

The scenarios below describe the U.S. recession and recovery in the early 1990s. Identify the lag that may have contributed to the difficulty in using monetary policy as a tool of economic stabilization.

1. The U.S. economy entered into a recession in July 1990. The Fed countered with expansionary monetary policy in October 1990, ultimately lowering the federal funds rate from 8% to 3% in 1992.
2. Investment began to increase, although slowly, in early 1992, and surged in 1993.

Case in Point: The Fed and the ECB: A Tale of Divergent Monetary Policies

Source: © khwi / Shutterstock.com; Rob Crandall / Shutterstock.com

In the spring of 2011, the European Central Bank (ECB) began to raise interest rates, while the Federal Reserve Bank held fast to its low rate policy. With the economies of both Europe and the United States weak, why the split in direction?

For one thing, at the time, the U.S. economy looked weaker than did Europe's economy as a whole. Moreover, the recession in the United States had been deeper. For example, the unemployment rate in the United States more than doubled during the Great Recession and its aftermath, while in the eurozone, it had risen only 40%.

But the divergence also reflected the different legal environments in which the two central banks operate. The ECB has a clear mandate to fight inflation, while the Fed has more leeway in pursuing both price stability and full employment. The ECB has a specific inflation target, and the inflation measure it uses covers all prices. The Fed, with its more flexible inflation target, has tended to focus on "core" inflation, which excludes gasoline and food prices, both of which are apt to be volatile. Using each central bank's preferred inflation measure, European inflation was, at the time of the ECB rate hike, running at 2.6%, while in the United States, it was at 1.6%.

Europe also differs from the United States in its degree of unionization. Because of Europe's higher level of unionization and collective bargaining, there is a sense that any price increases in Europe will translate into sustained inflation more rapidly there than they will in the United States.

Recall, however, that the eurozone is made up of 17 diverse countries. As made evident by the headline news from most of 2011 and into 2012, a number of countries in the eurozone were experiencing sovereign debt crises (meaning that there was fear that their governments could not meet their debt obligations) as well as more severe economic conditions. Higher interest rates make their circumstances that much more difficult. While it is true that various states in the United States can experience very different economic circumstances when the Fed sets what is essentially a "national" monetary policy, having a single monetary policy for different countries presents additional problems. One reason for this this difference is that labor mobility is higher in the United States than it is across the countries of Europe. Also, the United States can use its "national" fiscal policy to help weaker states.

In the fall of 2011, the ECB reversed course. At its first meeting under its new president, Mario Draghi, in November 2011, it lowered rates, citing slower growth and growing concerns about the sovereign debt crisis. A further rate cut followed in December. Interestingly, the inflation rate at the time of the cuts was running at about 3%, which was above the ECB's stated goal of 2%. The ECB argued that it was forecasting lower inflation for the future. So even the ECB has some flexibility and room for discretion.

Sources: *Based on Emily Kaiser and Mark Felsenthal, "Seven Reasons Why the Fed Won't Follow the ECB," Reuters Business and Financial News, April 7, 2011, available* http://www.reuters.

com/article/2011/04/07/us-usa-fed-ecb-idUSTRE73663420110407; David Mchugh, "ECB Cuts Key Rate a Quarter Point to Help Economy," USA Today, December 8, 2011, available http://www.usatoday.com/money/economy/story/2011-12-08/ecb-rate-cut/51733442/1; Fernanda Nechio, "Monetary Policy When One Size Does Not Fit All," Federal Reserve Bank of San Francisco Economic Letter, June 13, 2011.

Answers to Try It! Problems

1. The recognition lag: the Fed did not seem to "recognize" that the economy was in a recession until several months after the recession began.
2. The impact lag: investment did not pick up quickly after interest rates were reduced. Alternatively, it could be attributed to the expansionary monetary policy's not having its desired effect, at least initially, on investment.

26.4 Monetary Policy and the Equation of Exchange

Learning Objectives

1. Explain the meaning of the equation of exchange, $MV = PY$, and tell why it must hold true.
2. Discuss the usefulness of the quantity theory of money in explaining the behavior of nominal GDP and inflation in the long run.
3. Discuss why the quantity theory of money is less useful in analyzing the short run.

So far we have focused on how monetary policy affects real GDP and the price level in the short run. That is, we have examined how it can be used—however imprecisely—to close recessionary or inflationary gaps and to stabilize the price level. In this section, we will explore the relationship between money and the economy in the context of an equation that relates the money supply directly to nominal GDP. As we shall see, it also identifies circumstances in which changes in the price level are directly related to changes in the money supply.

The Equation of Exchange

We can relate the money supply to the aggregate economy by using the equation of exchange:

EQUATION 26.1

$$MV = \text{nominal GDP}$$

The **equation of exchange** shows that the money supply M times its velocity V equals nominal GDP. **Velocity** is the number of times the money supply is spent to obtain the goods and services that make up GDP during a particular time period.

To see that nominal GDP is the price level multiplied by real GDP, recall from an earlier chapter that the implicit price deflator P equals nominal GDP divided by real GDP:

EQUATION 26.2

$$P = \frac{\text{Nominal GDP}}{\text{Real GDP}}$$

Multiplying both sides by real GDP, we have

EQUATION 26.3

$$\text{Nominal GDP} = P \times \text{real GDP}$$

Letting Y equal real GDP, we can rewrite the equation of exchange as

EQUATION 26.4

$$MV = PY$$

We shall use the equation of exchange to see how it represents spending in a hypothetical economy that consists of 50 people, each of whom has a car. Each person has $10 in cash and no other money. The money supply of this economy is thus $500. Now suppose that the sole economic activity in this economy is car washing. Each person in the economy washes one other person's car once a month, and the price of a car wash is $10. In one month, then, a total of 50 car washes are produced at a price of $10 each. During that month, the money supply is spent once.

Applying the equation of exchange to this economy, we have a money supply M of $500 and a velocity V of 1. Because the only good or service produced is car washing, we can measure real GDP as the number of car washes. Thus Y equals 50 car washes. The price level P is the price of a car wash: $10. The equation of exchange for a period of 1 month is

$$\$500 \times 1 = \$10 \times 50$$

Now suppose that in the second month everyone washes someone else's car again. Over the full two-month period, the money supply has been spent twice—the velocity over a period of two months is 2. The total output in the economy is $1,000—100 car washes have been produced over a two-month period at a price of $10 each. Inserting these values into the equation of exchange, we have

$$\$500 \times 2 = \$10 \times 100$$

Suppose this process continues for one more month. For the three-month period, the money supply of $500 has been spent three times, for a velocity of 3. We have

$$\$500 \times 3 = \$10 \times 150$$

The essential thing to note about the equation of exchange is that it always holds. That should come as no surprise. The left side, MV, gives the money supply times the number of times that money is spent on goods and services during a period. It thus measures total spending. The right side is nominal GDP. But that is a measure of total spending on goods and services as well. Nominal GDP is the value of all final goods and services produced during a particular period. Those goods and services are either sold or added to inventory. If they are sold, then they must be part of total spending. If they are added to inventory, then some firm must have either purchased them or paid for their production; they thus represent a portion of total spending. In effect, the equation of exchange says simply that total spending on goods and services, measured as MV, equals total spending on goods and services, measured as PY (or nominal GDP). The equation of exchange is thus an identity, a mathematical expression that is true by definition.

To apply the equation of exchange to a real economy, we need measures of each of the variables in it. Three of these variables are readily available. The Department of Commerce reports the price level (that is, the implicit price deflator) and real GDP. The Federal Reserve Board reports M2, a measure of the money supply. For the second quarter of 2008, the values of these variables at an annual rate were

M = $7,635.4 billion

P = 1.22

Y = 11,727.4 billion

To solve for the velocity of money, V, we divide both sides of Equation 26.4 by M:

EQUATION 26.5

$$V = \frac{PY}{M}$$

Using the data for the second quarter of 2008 to compute velocity, we find that V then was equal to 1.87. A velocity of 1.87 means that the money supply was spent 1.87 times in the purchase of goods and services in the second quarter of 2008.

Money, Nominal GDP, and Price-Level Changes

Assume for the moment that velocity is constant, expressed as $\bar{V}$. Our equation of exchange is now written as

EQUATION 26.6

$$M\bar{V} = PY$$

A constant value for velocity would have two important implications:

1. Nominal GDP could change *only* if there were a change in the money supply. Other kinds of changes, such as a change in government purchases or a change in investment, could have no effect on nominal GDP.

2. A change in the money supply would always change nominal GDP, and by an equal percentage.

In short, if velocity were constant, a course in macroeconomics would be quite simple. The quantity of money would determine nominal GDP; nothing else would matter.

Indeed, when we look at the behavior of economies over long periods of time, the prediction that the quantity of money determines nominal output holds rather well. Figure 26.5 compares long-term averages in the growth rates of M2 and nominal GNP for 11 countries (Canada, Denmark, France, Italy, Japan, the Netherlands, Norway, Sweden, Switzerland, the United Kingdom, and the United States) for more than a century. These are the only countries that have consistent data for such a long period. The lines representing inflation, M2 growth, and nominal GDP growth do seem to move together most of the time, suggesting that velocity is constant when viewed over the long run.

FIGURE 26.5 Inflation, M2 Growth, and GDP Growth

The chart shows the behavior of price-level changes, the growth of M2, and the growth of nominal GDP for 11 countries using the average value of each variable. Viewed in this light, the relationship between money growth and nominal GDP seems quite strong.

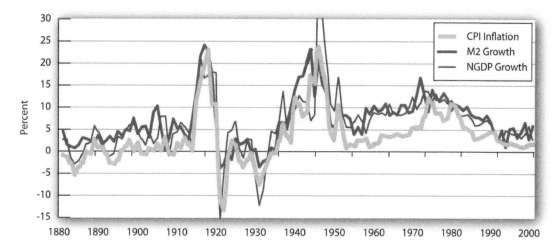

Source: Based on data from Alfred A. Haug and William G. Dewald, "Longer-Term Effects of Monetary Growth on Real and Nominal Variables, Major Industrial Countries, 1880–2001" (European Central Bank Working Paper Series No. 382, August 2004).

Moreover, price-level changes also follow the same pattern that changes in M2 and nominal GNP do. Why is this?

We can rewrite the equation of exchange, $M\bar{V} = PY$, in terms of percentage rates of change. When two products, such as $M\bar{V}$ and PY, are equal, and the variables themselves are changing, then the sums of the percentage rates of change are approximately equal:

EQUATION 26.7

$$\%\Delta M + \%\Delta V \cong \%\Delta P + \%\Delta Y$$

The Greek letter Δ (delta) means "change in." Assume that velocity is constant in the long run, so that $\%\Delta V = 0$. We also assume that real GDP moves to its potential level, Y_P, in the long run. With these assumptions, we can rewrite Equation 26.7 as follows:

EQUATION 26.8

$$\%\Delta M \cong \%\Delta P + \%\Delta Y_P$$

Subtracting $\%\Delta Y_P$ from both sides of Equation 26.8, we have the following:

EQUATION 26.9

$$\%\Delta M - \%\Delta Y_P \cong \%\Delta P$$

Equation 26.9 has enormously important implications for monetary policy. It tells us that, in the long run, the rate of inflation, $\%\Delta P$, equals the difference between the rate of money growth and the rate of increase in potential output, $\%\Delta Y_P$, given our assumption of constant velocity. Because potential output is likely to rise by at most a few percentage points per year, the rate of money growth will be close to the rate of inflation in the long run.

Several recent studies that looked at all the countries on which they could get data on inflation and money growth over long periods found a very high correlation between growth rates of the money supply and of the price level for countries with high inflation rates, but the relationship was much weaker for countries with inflation rates of less than 10%.[7] These findings support the **quantity theory of money**, which holds that in the long run the price level moves in proportion with changes in the money supply, at least for high-inflation countries.

quantity theory of money

In the long run, the price level moves in proportion with changes in the money supply, at least for high-inflation countries.

Why the Quantity Theory of Money Is Less Useful in Analyzing the Short Run

The stability of velocity in the long run underlies the close relationship we have seen between changes in the money supply and changes in the price level. But velocity is not stable in the short run; it varies significantly from one period to the next. Figure 26.6 shows annual values of the velocity of M2 from 1960 to 2013. Velocity is quite variable, so other factors must affect economic activity. Any change in velocity implies a change in the demand for money. For analyzing the effects of monetary policy from one period to the next, we apply the framework that emphasizes the impact of changes in the money market on aggregate demand.

FIGURE 26.6 The Velocity of M2, 1970–2015
The annual velocity of M2 varied about an average of 1.81 between 1970 and 2015.

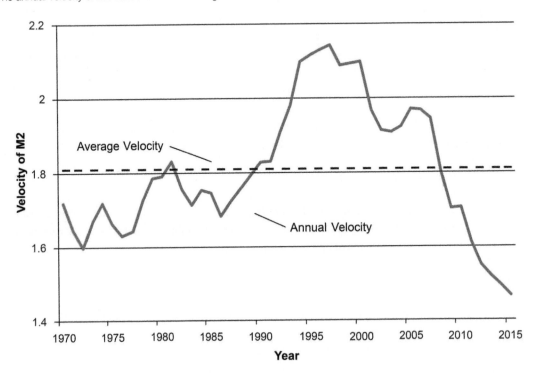

Source: Economic Report of the President, 2017, Tables B-2 and B-26.

The factors that cause velocity to fluctuate are those that influence the demand for money, such as the interest rate and expectations about bond prices and future price levels. We can gain some insight about the demand for money and its significance by rearranging terms in the equation of exchange so that we turn the equation of exchange into an equation for the demand for money. If we multiply both sides of Equation 26.1 by the reciprocal of velocity, 1/V, we have this equation for money demand:

EQUATION 26.10

$$M = \tfrac{1}{V}PY$$

The equation of exchange can thus be rewritten as an equation that expresses the demand for money as a percentage, given by 1/V, of nominal GDP. With a velocity of 1.87, for example, people wish to hold a quantity of money equal to 53.4% (1/1.87) of nominal GDP. Other things unchanged, an increase in money demand reduces velocity, and a decrease in money demand increases velocity.

If people wanted to hold a quantity of money equal to a larger percentage of nominal GDP, perhaps because interest rates were low, velocity would be a smaller number. Suppose, for example, that people held a quantity of money equal to 80% of nominal GDP. That would imply a velocity of

1.25. If people held a quantity of money equal to a smaller fraction of nominal GDP, perhaps owing to high interest rates, velocity would be a larger number. If people held a quantity of money equal to 25% of nominal GDP, for example, the velocity would be 4.

As another example, in the chapter on financial markets and the economy, we learned that money demand falls when people expect inflation to increase. In essence, they do not want to hold money that they believe will only lose value, so they turn it over faster, that is, velocity rises. Expectations of deflation lower the velocity of money, as people hold onto money because they expect it will rise in value.

In our first look at the equation of exchange, we noted some remarkable conclusions that would hold if velocity were constant: a given percentage change in the money supply M would produce an equal percentage change in nominal GDP, and no change in nominal GDP could occur without an equal percentage change in M. We have learned, however, that velocity varies in the short run. Thus, the conclusions that would apply if velocity were constant must be changed.

First, we do not expect a given percentage change in the money supply to produce an equal percentage change in nominal GDP. Suppose, for example, that the money supply increases by 10%. Interest rates drop, and the quantity of money demanded goes up. Velocity is likely to decline, though not by as large a percentage as the money supply increases. The result will be a reduction in the degree to which a given percentage increase in the money supply boosts nominal GDP.

Second, nominal GDP could change even when there is no change in the money supply. Suppose government purchases increase. Such an increase shifts the aggregate demand curve to the right, increasing real GDP and the price level. That effect would be impossible if velocity were constant. The fact that velocity varies, and varies positively with the interest rate, suggests that an increase in government purchases could boost aggregate demand and nominal GDP. To finance increased spending, the government borrows money by selling bonds. An increased supply of bonds lowers their price, and that means higher interest rates. The higher interest rates produce the increase in velocity that must occur if increased government purchases are to boost the price level and real GDP.

Just as we cannot assume that velocity is constant when we look at macroeconomic behavior period to period, neither can we assume that output is at potential. With both V and Y in the equation of exchange variable, in the short run, the impact of a change in the money supply on the price level depends on the degree to which velocity and real GDP change.

In the short run, it is not reasonable to assume that velocity and output are constants. Using the model in which interest rates and other factors affect the quantity of money demanded seems more fruitful for understanding the impact of monetary policy on economic activity in that period. However, the empirical evidence on the long-run relationship between changes in money supply and changes in the price level that we presented earlier gives us reason to pause. As Federal Reserve Governor from 1996 to 2002 Laurence H. Meyer put it: "I believe monitoring money growth has value, even for central banks that follow a disciplined strategy of adjusting their policy rate to ongoing economic developments. The value may be particularly important at the extremes: during periods of very high inflation, as in the late 1970s and early 1980s in the United States ... and in deflationary episodes."[8]

It would be a mistake to allow short-term fluctuations in velocity and output to lead policy makers to completely ignore the relationship between money and price level changes in the long run.

Key Takeaways

- The equation of exchange can be written $MV = PY$.
- When M, V, P, and Y are changing, then $\%\Delta M + \%\Delta V = \%\Delta P + \%\Delta Y$, where Δ means "change in."

- In the long run, V is constant, so $\%\Delta V = 0$. Furthermore, in the long run Y tends toward Y_P, so $\%\Delta M = \%\Delta P$.

- In the short run, V is not constant, so changes in the money supply can affect the level of income.

Try It!

The Case in Point on velocity in the Confederacy during the Civil War shows that, assuming real GDP in the South was constant, velocity rose. What happened to money demand? Why did it change?

Case in Point: Velocity and the Confederacy

Source: © Shutterstock, Inc.

The Union and the Confederacy financed their respective efforts during the Civil War largely through the issue of paper money. The Union roughly doubled its money supply through this process, and the Confederacy printed enough "Confederates" to increase the money supply in the South 20-fold from 1861 to 1865. That huge increase in the money supply boosted the price level in the Confederacy dramatically. It rose from an index of 100 in 1861 to 9,200 in 1865.

Estimates of real GDP in the South during the Civil War are unavailable, but it could hardly have increased very much. Although production undoubtedly rose early in the period, the South lost considerable capital and an appalling number of men killed in battle. Let us suppose that real GDP over the entire period remained constant. For the price level to rise 92-fold with a 20-fold increase in the money supply, there must have been a 4.6-fold increase in velocity. People in the South must have reduced their demand for Confederates.

An account of an exchange for eggs in 1864 from the diary of Mary Chestnut illustrates how eager people in the South were to part with their Confederate money. It also suggests that other commodities had assumed much greater relative value:

> *"She asked me 20 dollars for five dozen eggs and then said she would take it in 'Confederate.' Then I would have given her 100 dollars as easily. But if she had taken my offer of yarn! I haggle in yarn for the millionth part of a thread! … When they ask for Confederate money, I never stop to chafer [bargain or argue]. I give them 20 or 50 dollars cheerfully for anything."*

Sources: *Based on C. Vann Woodward, ed., Mary Chestnut's Civil War (New Haven, CT: Yale University Press, 1981), 749. Money and price data from E. M. Lerner, "Money, Prices, and Wages in the Confederacy, 1861–1865," Journal of Political Economy 63 (February 1955): 20–40.*

Answer to Try It! Problem

People in the South must have reduced their demand for money. The fall in money demand was probably due to the expectation that the price level would continue to rise. In periods of high inflation, people try to get rid of money quickly because it loses value rapidly.

26.5 Review and Practice

Summary

Part of the Fed's power stems from the fact that it has no legislative mandate to seek particular goals. That leaves the Fed free to set its own goals. In recent years, its primary goal has seemed to be the maintenance of an inflation rate below 2% to 3%. Given success in meeting that goal, the Fed has used its tools to stimulate the economy to close recessionary gaps. Once the Fed has made a choice to undertake an expansionary or contractionary policy, we can trace the impact of that policy on the economy.

There are a number of problems in the use of monetary policy. These include various types of lags, the issue of the choice of targets in conducting monetary policy, political pressures placed on the process of policy setting, and uncertainty as to how great an impact the Fed's policy decisions have on macroeconomic variables. We highlighted the difficulties for monetary policy if the economy is in or near a liquidity trap and discussed the use of quantitative easing and credit easing in such situations. If people have rational expectations and respond to those expectations in their wage and price choices, then changes in monetary policy may have no effect on real GDP.

We saw in this chapter that the money supply is related to the level of nominal GDP by the equation of exchange. A crucial issue in that relationship is the stability of the velocity of money and of real GDP. If the velocity of money were constant, nominal GDP could change only if the money supply changed, and a change in the money supply would produce an equal percentage change in nominal GDP. If velocity were constant and real GDP were at its potential level, then the price level would change by about the same percentage as the money supply. While these predictions seem to hold up in the long run, there is less support for them when we look at macroeconomic behavior in the short run. Nonetheless, policy makers must be mindful of these long-run relationships as they formulate policies for the short run.

Concept Problems

1. Suppose the Fed were required to conduct monetary policy so as to hold the unemployment rate below 4%, the goal specified in the Humphrey–Hawkins Act. What implications would this have for the economy?

2. The statutes of the recently established European Central Bank (ECB) state that its primary objective is to maintain price stability. How does this charter differ from that of the Fed? What significance does it have for monetary policy?

3. Do you think the Fed should be given a clearer legislative mandate concerning macroeconomic goals? If so, what should it be?

4. Referring to the Case in Point on targeting, what difference does it make whether the target is the inflation rate of the past year or the expected inflation rate over the next year?

5. In a speech in January 1995,[9] Federal Reserve Chairman Alan Greenspan used a transportation metaphor to describe some of the difficulties of implementing monetary policy. He referred to the criticism levied against the Fed for shifting in 1994 to an anti-inflation, contractionary policy when the inflation rate was still quite low:

> "To successfully navigate a bend in the river, the barge must begin the turn well before the bend is reached. Even so, currents are always changing and even an experienced crew cannot foresee all the events that might occur as the river is being navigated. A year ago, the Fed began its turn (a shift toward an expansionary monetary policy), and it was successful."

Mr. Greenspan was referring, of course, to the problem of lags. What kind of lag do you think he had in mind? What do you suppose the reference to changing currents means?

6. In a speech in August 1999,[10] Mr. Greenspan said,

We no longer have the luxury to look primarily to the flow of goods and services, as conventionally estimated, when evaluating the macroeconomic environment in which monetary policy must function. There are important—but extremely difficult—questions surrounding the behavior of asset prices and the implications of this behavior for the decisions of households and businesses.

The asset price that Mr. Greenspan was referring to was the U.S. stock market, which had been rising sharply in the weeks and months preceding this speech. Inflation and unemployment were both low at that time. What issues concerning the conduct of monetary policy was Mr. Greenspan raising?

7. Suppose we observed an economy in which changes in the money supply produce no changes whatever in nominal GDP. What could we conclude about velocity?

8. Suppose price levels were falling 10% per day. How would this affect the demand for money? How would it affect velocity? What can you conclude about the role of velocity during periods of rapid price change?

9. Suppose investment increases and the money supply does not change. Use the model of aggregate demand and aggregate supply to predict the impact of such an increase on nominal GDP. Now what happens in terms of the variables in the equation of exchange?

10. The text notes that prior to August 1997 (when it began specifying a target value for the federal funds rate), the FOMC adopted directives calling for the trading desk at the New York Federal Reserve Bank to increase, decrease, or maintain the existing degree of pressure on reserve positions. On the meeting dates given in the first column, the FOMC voted to decrease pressure on reserve positions (that is, adopt a more expansionary policy). On the meeting dates given in the second column, it voted to increase reserve pressure:

July 5–6, 1995	February 3–4, 1994
December 19, 1995	January 31–February 1, 1995
January 30–31, 1996	March 25, 1997

Recent minutes of the FOMC can be found at the Federal Reserve Board of Governors website. Pick one of these dates on which a decrease in reserve pressure was ordered and one on which an increase was ordered and find out why that particular policy was chosen.

11. Since August 1997, the Fed has simply set a specific target for the federal funds rate. The four dates below show the first four times after August 1997 that the Fed voted to set a new target for the federal funds rate on the following dates:

September 29, 1998	November 17, 1998
June 29, 1999	August 24, 1999

Pick one of these dates and find out why it chose to change its target for the federal funds rate on that date.

12. Four meetings in 2008 at which the Fed changed the target for the federal funds rate are shown below.

January 30, 2008	March 18, 2008
October 8, 2008	October 29, 2008

Pick one of these dates and find out why it chose to change its target for the federal funds rate on that date.

13. The text notes that a 10% increase in the money supply may not increase the price level by 10% in the short run. Explain why.

14. Trace the impact of an expansionary monetary policy on bond prices, interest rates, investment, the exchange rate, net exports, real GDP, and the price level. Illustrate your analysis graphically.

15. Trace the impact of a contractionary monetary policy on bond prices, interest rates, investment, the exchange rate, net exports, real GDP, and the price level. Illustrate your analysis graphically.

Numerical Problems

1. Here are annual values for M2 and for nominal GDP (all figures are in billions of dollars) for the mid-1990s.

Year	M2	Nominal GDP
1993	3,482.0	$6,657.4
1994	3,498.1	7,072.2
1995	3,642.1	7,397.7
1996	3,820.5	7,816.9
1997	4,034.1	8,304.3

a. Compute the velocity for each year.

b. Compute the fraction of nominal GDP that was being held as money.

c. What is your conclusion about the stability of velocity in this five-year period?

2. Here are annual values for M2 and for nominal GDP (all figures are in billions of dollars) for the mid-2000s.

Year	M2	Nominal GDP
2003	6,055.5	$10,960.8
2004	6,400.7	11,685.9
2005	6,659.7	12,421.9
2006	7,012.3	13,178.4
2007	7,404.3	13,807.5

a. Compute the velocity for each year.

      b. Compute the fraction of nominal GDP that was being held as money.

      c. What is your conclusion about the stability of velocity in this five-year period?

3. The following data show M1 for the years 1993 to 1997, respectively (all figures are in billions of dollars): 1,129.6; 1,150.7; 1,127.4; 1,081.3; 1,072.5.

      a. Compute the M1 velocity for these years. (Nominal GDP for these years is shown in problem 1.)

      b. If you were going to use a money target, would M1 or M2 have been preferable during the 1990s? Explain your reasoning.

4. The following data show M1 for the years 2003 to 2007, respectively (all figures are in billions of dollars): 1,306.1; 1,376.3; 1,374.5; 1,366.5; 1,366.5

      a. Compute the M1 velocity for these years. (Nominal GDP for these years is shown in problem 2.)

      b. If you were going to use a money target, would M1 or M2 have been preferable during the 2000s? Explain your reasoning.

5. Assume a hypothetical economy in which the velocity is constant at 2 and real GDP is always at a constant potential of $4,000. Suppose the money supply is $1,000 in the first year, $1,100 in the second year, $1,200 in the third year, and $1,300 in the fourth year.

      a. Using the equation of exchange, compute the price level in each year.

      b. Compute the inflation rate for each year.

      c. Explain why inflation varies, even though the money supply rises by $100 each year.

      d. If the central bank wanted to keep inflation at zero, what should it have done to the money supply each year?

      e. If the central bank wanted to keep inflation at 10% each year, what money supply should it have targeted in each year?

6. Suppose the velocity of money is constant and potential output grows by 3% per year. By what percentage should the money supply grow in order to achieve the following inflation rate targets?

      a. 0%

      b. 1%

      c. 2%

7. Suppose the velocity of money is constant and potential output grows by 5% per year. For each of the following money supply growth rates, what will the inflation rate be?

      a. 4%

      b. 5%

      c. 6%

8. Suppose that a country whose money supply grew by about 20% a year over the long run had an annual inflation rate of about 20% and that a country whose money supply grew by about 50% a year had an annual inflation rate of about 50%. Explain this finding in terms of the equation of exchange.

Endnotes

1. Federal Reserve Press Release, 12/16/2008. https://www.federalreserve.gov/newsevents/press/monetary/20081216b.htm.
2. Chair Janet L. Yellen, "The Goal of Monetary Policy and How we Pursue Them," speech at the Commonwealth Club, San Francisco on January 18, 2017 available at https://www.federalreserve.gov/newsevents/speech/yellen20170118a.htm.
3. Carl E. Walsh, "Inflation Targeting: What Have We Learned?," *International Finance* 12, no. 2 (2009): 195–233.
4. See, for example, Alberto Alesina and Lawrence H. Summers, "Central Bank Independence and Macroeconomic Performance: Some Comparative Evidence," *Journal of Money, Credit, and Banking* 25, no. 2 (May 1993): 151–62.
5. "Bringing an End to Deflation under the New Monetary Policy Framework," *OECD Economic Surveys: Japan 2008* 4 (April 2008): 49–61 and Mark M. Spiegel, "Did Quantitative Easing by the Bank of Japan Work?" *FRBSF Economic Letter* 2006, no. 28 (October 20, 2006): 1–3.
6. Ben S. Bernanke, "The Crisis and the Policy Response" (Stamp Lecture, London School of Economics, London, England, January 13, 2009) and Janet L. Yellen, "U.S. Monetary Policy Objectives in the Short Run and the Long Run" (speech, Allied Social Sciences Association annual meeting, San Francisco, California, January 4, 2009).

7. For example, one study examined data on 81 countries using inflation rates averaged for the period 1980 to 1993 (John R. Moroney, "Money Growth, Output Growth, and Inflation: Estimation of a Modern Quantity Theory," *Southern Economic Journal* 69, no. 2 [2002]: 398–413) while another examined data on 160 countries over the period 1969–1999 (Paul De Grauwe and Magdalena Polan, "Is Inflation Always and Everywhere a Monetary Phenomenon?" *Scandinavian Journal of Economics* 107, no. 2 [2005]: 239–59).

8. Laurence H. Meyer, "Does Money Matter?" *Federal Reserve Bank of St. Louis Review* 83, no. 5 (September/October 2001): 1–15.

9. Speech by Alan Greenspan before the Board of Directors of the National Association of Home Builders, January 28, 1995.

10. Alan Greenspan, "New challenges for monetary policy," speech delivered before a symposium sponsored by the Federal Reserve Bank of Kansas City in Jackson Hole, Wyoming, on August 27, 1999. Mr. Greenspan was famous for his convoluted speech, which listeners often found difficult to understand. CBS correspondent Andrea Mitchell, to whom Mr. Greenspan is married, once joked that he had proposed to her three times and that she had not understood what he was talking about on his first two efforts.

CHAPTER 27

Government and Fiscal Policy

27.1 Start Up: A Massive Stimulus

Shaken by the severity of both the recession that began in December 2007 and the financial crisis that occurred in the fall of 2008, Congress passed a huge $784 billion stimulus package in February 2009. President Obama described the measure as only "the beginning" of what the federal government ultimately would do to right the economy.

Over a quarter of the American Recovery and Reinvestment Act (ARRA) was for a variety of temporary tax rebates and credits for individuals and firms. For example, each worker making less than $75,000 a year received $400 ($800 for a working couple earning up to $150,000) as a kind of rebate for payroll taxes. That works out to $8 a week. Qualifying college students became eligible for $2,500 tax credits for educational expenses. During a certain period, a first-time homebuyer was eligible for a tax credit. The other roughly three-quarters of the ARRA were for a variety of government spending programs, including temporary transfers to state and local governments, extended unemployment insurance and other transfers to people (such as food stamps), and increased infrastructure spending. The president said that the measure would "ignite spending by businesses and consumers … and make the investment necessary for lasting growth and economic prosperity."[1] Shortly after the passage of the ARRA, Congress passed the Cash for Clunkers program, which for a limited period of time allowed car buyers to trade in less-fuel-efficient cars for rebates of up to $4,500 toward buying new cars that met certain higher fuel-efficiency standards.

The ARRA illustrates an important difficulty of using fiscal policy in an effort to stabilize economic activity. It was passed over a year after the recession began. Only about 20% of the spending called for by the legislation took place in 2009, rising to about two-thirds through the middle of 2010. It was a guess what state the economy would be in then. As it turned out, the recession had officially ended, but there was still a large recessionary gap, and unemployment was still a major concern. There was a great deal of media controversy about how effective the policy had been and whether the resulting increase in national debt was worth it. Concern over the expanded size of the federal government created by the stimulus measures became a rallying cry for the Tea Party movement. A fiscal stimulus package of over $150 billion had already been tried earlier in February 2008 under President George W. Bush. It included $100 billion in temporary tax rebates to households—up to $600 for individuals and $1,200 for couples—and over $50 billion in tax breaks for businesses. The boost to aggregate demand seemed slight—consumers saved much of their rebate money. In November 2008, unemployment insurance benefits were extended for seven additional weeks, in recognition of the growing unemployment problem.

President Obama argued that his proposals for dealing with the economy in the short term would, coincidentally, also promote long-term economic health. Some critics argued for a greater focus on actual tax cuts while others were concerned about whether the spending would focus on getting the greatest employment increase or be driven by political considerations.

How do government tax and expenditure policies affect real GDP and the price level? Why do economists differ so sharply in assessing the likely impact of such policies? Can fiscal policy be used to stabilize the economy in the short run? What are the long-run effects of government spending and taxing?

We begin with a look at the government's budget to see how it spends the tax revenue it collects. Clearly, the government's budget is not always in balance, so we will also look at government deficits and debt. We will then look at how fiscal policy works to stabilize the economy, distinguishing between built-in stabilization methods and discretionary measures. We will end the chapter with a discussion of why fiscal policy is so controversial.

As in the previous chapter on monetary policy, our primary focus will be U.S. policy. However, the tools available to governments around the world are quite similar, as are the issues surrounding the use of fiscal policy.

27.2 Government and the Economy

Learning Objectives

1. Understand the major components of U.S. government spending and sources of government revenues.
2. Define the terms *budget surplus*, *budget deficit*, *balanced budget*, and *national debt*, and discuss their trends over time in the United States.

We begin our analysis of fiscal policy with an examination of government purchases, transfer payments, and taxes in the U.S. economy.

Government Purchases

The government-purchases component of aggregate demand includes all purchases by government agencies of goods and services produced by firms, as well as direct production by government agencies themselves. When the federal government buys staples and staplers, the transaction is part of government purchases. The production of educational and research services by public colleges and universities is also counted in the government-purchases component of GDP.

While government spending has grown over time, government purchases as a share of GDP declined from over 20% until the early 1990s to under 18% in 2001. Since then, though, the percentage of government purchases in GDP began to increase back toward 20% and then beyond. This first occurred as military spending picked up, and then, more recently, it rose even further during the 2007–2009 recession. In the last two years, the percentage has again fallen below 20%.

Figure 27.1 shows federal as well as state and local government purchases as a percentage of GDP from 1960 to 2015. Notice the changes that have occurred over this period. In 1960, the federal government accounted for the majority share of total purchases. Since then, however, federal purchases have fallen by almost half relative to GDP, while state and local purchases relative to GDP have risen.

FIGURE 27.1 Federal, State, and Local Purchases Relative to GDP, 1960–2015

Government purchases were generally above 20% of GDP from 1960 until the early 1990s and then below 20% of GDP except during the 2007-2009 recession.

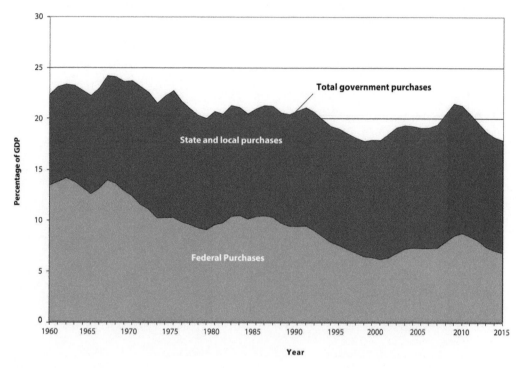

Source: Based on data from Bureau of Economic Analysis, NIPA Table 1.1 and 3.1 (revised November 29, 2016).

Transfer Payments

As explained earlier, transfer payments do not require the recipients to produce a good or service in order to receive the payment. Social Security and welfare benefits are examples of transfer payments. During the 2007-2009 recession, transfers rose.

A number of changes have influenced transfer payments over the past several decades. First, they increased rapidly during the late 1960s and early 1970s. This was the period in which federal programs such as Medicare (health insurance for the elderly) and Medicaid (health insurance for the poor) were created and other programs were expanded.

Figure 27.2 shows that transfer payment spending by the federal government and by state and local governments has risen as a percentage of GDP. In 1960, such spending totaled about 6% of GDP; in recent years, it has been above 16%. The federal government accounts for the bulk of transfer payment spending in the United States.

FIGURE 27.2 Federal, State, and Local Transfer Payments as a Percentage of GDP, 1960–2015

The chart shows transfer payment spending as a percentage of GDP from 1960 through 2015. This spending rose dramatically relative to GDP during the late 1960s and the 1970s as federal programs expanded. More recently, sharp increases in health-care costs have driven upward the spending for transfer payment programs such as Medicare and Medicaid. Transfer payments fluctuate with the business cycle, rising in times of recession and falling during times of expansion. As such, they rose sharply during the deep 2007-2009 recession.

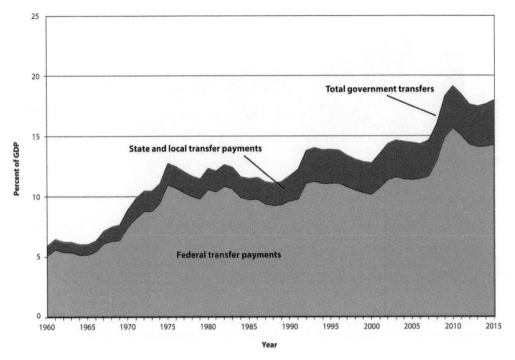

Source: Based on data from Bureau of Economic Analysis, NIPA Table 1.1, 3.2, and 3.3 (revised November 29, 2016).

Transfer payment spending relative to GDP tends to fluctuate with the business cycle. Transfer payments fell during the late 1970s, a period of expansion, then rose as the economy slipped into a recessionary gap during the 1979–1982 period. Transfer payments fell during the expansion that began late in 1982, then began rising in 1989 as the expansion began to slow. Transfer payments continued to rise relative to GDP during the recessions of 1990–1991 and 2001–2002 and then fell as the economy entered expansionary phases after each of those recessions. During the 2007—2009 recession, transfer payments rose again.

When economic activity falls, incomes fall, people lose jobs, and more people qualify for aid. People qualify to receive welfare benefits, such as cash, food stamps, or Medicaid, only if their income falls below a certain level. They qualify for unemployment compensation by losing their jobs. More people qualify for transfer payments during recessions. When the economy expands, incomes and employment rise, and fewer people qualify for welfare or unemployment benefits. Spending for those programs therefore tends to fall during an expansion.

Figure 27.3 summarizes trends in government spending since 1960. It shows three categories of government spending relative to GDP: government purchases, transfer payments, and net interest. Net interest includes payments of interest by governments at all levels on money borrowed, less interest earned on saving.

FIGURE 27.3 Government Spending as a Percentage of GDP, 1960–2015
This chart shows three major categories of government spending as percentages of GDP: government purchases, transfer payments, and net interest.

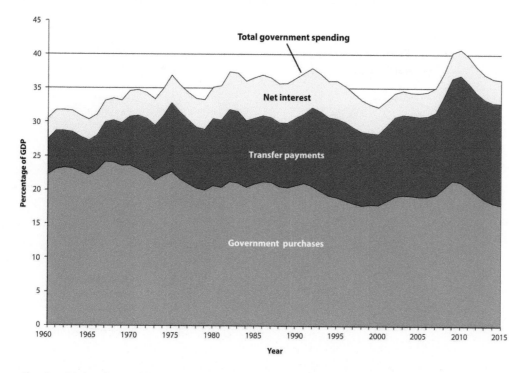

Source: Based on data from Bureau of Economic Analysis, NIPA Table 1.1 and 3.1 (revised November 29, 2016).

Taxes

Taxes affect the relationship between real GDP and personal disposable income; they therefore affect consumption. They also influence investment decisions. Taxes imposed on firms affect the profitability of investment decisions and therefore affect the levels of investment firms will choose. Payroll taxes imposed on firms affect the costs of hiring workers; they therefore have an impact on employment and on the real wages earned by workers.

The bulk of federal receipts come from the personal income tax and from payroll taxes. State and local tax receipts are dominated by property taxes and sales taxes. The federal government, as well as state and local governments, also collects taxes imposed on business firms, such as taxes on corporate profits. Figure 27.4 shows the composition of federal, state, and local receipts in a recent year.

FIGURE 27.4 The Composition of Federal, State, and Local Revenues

Federal receipts come primarily from payroll taxes and from personal taxes such as the personal income tax. State and local tax receipts come from a variety of sources; the most important are property taxes, sales taxes, income taxes, and grants from the federal government. Data are for fourth-quarter 2015, in billions of dollars, seasonally adjusted at annual rates.

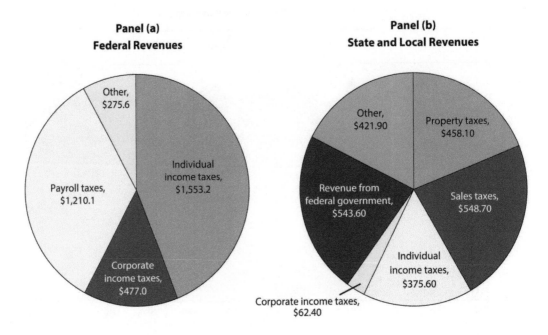

Source: Based on data from Bureau of Economic Analysis, NIPA Table 3.2 and 3.3 (revised November 29, 2016).

The Government Budget Balance

budget surplus

Situation that occurs if government revenues exceed expenditures.

budget deficit

Situation that occurs if government expenditures exceed revenues.

balanced budget

Situation that occurs if the budget surplus equals zero.

The government's budget balance is the difference between the government's revenues and its expenditures. A **budget surplus** occurs if government revenues exceed expenditures. A **budget deficit** occurs if government expenditures exceed revenues. The minus sign is often omitted when reporting a deficit. If the budget surplus equals zero, we say the government has a **balanced budget**.

Figure 27.5 compares federal, state, and local government revenues to expenditures relative to GDP since 1960. The government's budget was generally in deficit since the 1960s, except for a brief period between 1998 and 2001. Bear in mind that these data are for all levels of government.

FIGURE 27.5 Government Revenue and Expenditure as a Percentage of GDP, 1960–2015
The government's budget was generally in deficit since the 1960s, except for a brief period between 1998 and 2001.

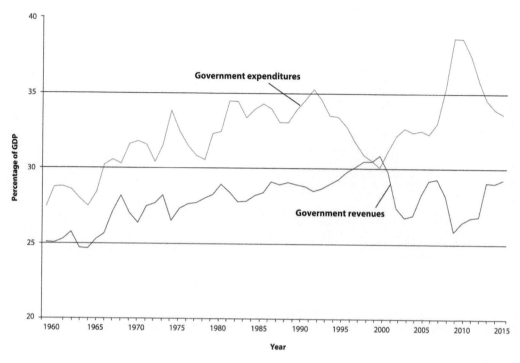

Source: Based on data from Bureau of Economic Analysis, NIPA Table 1.1 and 3.1 (revised November 29, 2016).

The administration of George W. Bush saw a large increase in the federal deficit. In part, this was the result of the government's response to the terrorist attacks in 2001. It also results, however, from large increases in federal spending at all levels together with tax cuts in 2001, 2002, and 2003. The federal deficit grew even larger during the administration of Barack Obama. The increase stemmed from both reduced revenues and increased spending resulting from the recession that began in 2007 and the stimulus.

The National Debt

The **national debt** is the sum of all past federal deficits, minus any surpluses. Figure 27.6 shows the national debt as a percentage of GDP. It suggests that, relative to the level of economic activity, the debt is well below the levels reached during World War II. The ratio of debt to GDP rose from 1981 to 1996 and fell in the last years of the 20th century; it began rising again in 2002 and has risen substantially since the recession that began in 2007.

national debt

The sum of all past federal deficits, minus any surpluses.

FIGURE 27.6 The National Debt and the Economy, 1929–2015
The national debt relative to GDP was at its peak during World War II and then fell dramatically over the next few decades. The ratio of debt to GDP rose from 1981 to 1996 and fell in the last years of the 20th century; it began rising again in 2002, markedly so since 2009.

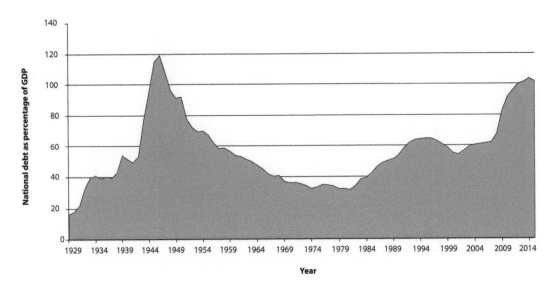

Sources: Data for 1929–1938 from Historical Statistics of the United States, Colonial Times to 1957—not strictly comparable with later data. Data for remaining years from Office of Management and Budget, Budget of the United States Government, Fiscal Year 2016, Historical Tables, Table 7.1.

Judged by international standards, the U.S. national debt relative to its GDP is above average. Figure 27.7 shows national debt as a percentage of GDP for 32 countries in 2013 or 2014. It also shows deficits or surpluses as a percentage of GDP.

In the United States, Congress authorizes the maximum amount of federal government borrowing. In an intense struggle between the Republican-majority U.S. House of Representatives and the Obama administration and the Democratic-majority U.S. Senate in the summer of 2011 that almost resulted in a government shutdown as the then debt ceiling had been reached, the Budget Control Act of 2011 raised the borrowing limit and resulted in a $1 trillion deficit reduction over ten years with additional reductions scheduled to follow. The Act provided for across-the board (with only a few exceptions) spending cuts, called sequestration, if Congress failed to agree on those further deficit-reducing measures. In the fall of 2013 with another debt ceiling breach looming, a 16-day government shutdown did occur when the House of Representatives would only agree to pass a general budget resolution even at the sequestration level if it included provisions to defund the Patient Protection and Affordable Care Act (often referred to as Obamacare), which the Senate refused to go along with. The shutdown ended with legislation, opposed by most Republicans in the House, to raise the debt ceiling and to allow government spending to resume temporarily while an actual spending bill was worked out. In late 2013, Congress finally agreed on a bipartisan two-year budget that reduced sequestration, and in early 2014 it agreed to raise the debt ceiling. Another similar two-year budget deal was reached in November 2015. These deals put these issues aside until after the U.S. presidential election in November 2016.

FIGURE 27.7 Debts and Deficits for 32 Nations, 2013 or 2014

The chart shows national debt as a percentage of GDP and deficits or surpluses as a percentage of GDP in 2013 or 2014. The national debt of the United States relative to its GDP was above average among these nations.

Country	National Dept as percentage of GDP	Deficit (-) or surplus as percentage of GDP
Japan	239.3	-8.5
Greece	179.8	-3.6
Italy	156.2	-3.0
Portugal	149.9	-7.2
Belgium	129.3	-3.1
Ireland	125.4	-3.9
France	119.2	-3.9
Spain	117.7	-5.9
United Kingdom	113.6	-5.7
United States	103.2	-4.9
Austria	102.2	-2.7
Hungary	99.3	-2.5
Slovenia	97.3	-5.0
Canada	94.6	-1.6
Iceland	87.8	-0.1
Germany	82.2	0.3
Netherlands	81.0	-2.4
Israel	77.0	-3.5
Finland	71.0	-3.3
Poland	65.9	-3.3
Denmark	60.6	1.5
Slovak Republic	60.1	-2.8
Czech Republic	57.0	-1.9
Sweden	53.8	-1.7
Mexico	48.7	0.1
Australia	40.7	-2.6
Turkey	39.7	-0.8
Luxembourg	33.7	1.4
Norway	32.4	9.1
Chile	23.1	-0.4
Estonia	13.6	0.7
Average	88.9	-2.3

Source: Based on data from Organisation for Economic Co-operation and Development (OECD). Key Tables from OECD Factbook 2015-2016, p. 183. Data are from 2013 or 2014.

Key Takeaways

- Over the last 50 years, government purchases fell from about 20% of U.S. GDP to below 20%, except for a brief period around the time of the Great Recession.

- Transfer payment spending has risen sharply, both in absolute terms and as a percentage of real GDP since 1960.

- The bulk of federal revenues comes from income and payroll taxes. State and local revenues consist primarily of sales and property taxes.

- The government budget balance is the difference between government revenues and government expenditures.

- The national debt is the sum of all past federal deficits minus any surpluses.

Try It!

What happens to the national debt when there is a budget surplus? What happens to it when there is a budget deficit? What happens to the national debt if there is a decrease in a surplus? What happens to it if the deficit falls?

Case in Point: Options for Reducing the U.S. Federal Budget Deficit

Source: © Leonard Zhukovsky / Shutterstock.com

The Congressional Budget Office (CBO) is a federal agency within the legislative branch of the U.S. government that was created in 1974 to provide nonpartisan and objective information to Congress on budgetary and economic matters. Many of its reports, such as *The Long-Term Budget Outlook* and *The Monthly Budget Review*, come out on a regular schedule. Others are produced as Congress requests or periodically. *Options for Reducing the Deficit* is a periodic publication. These reports typically examine about 100 or so options for raising revenues or reducing expenditures. The reports estimate the budgetary impacts over 10-year time horizons and consider advantages and disadvantages of the options but do not make recommendations.

The December 2016 report provides 115 options divided into 5 categories. The categories in this volume are: mandatory spending other than for health-related programs, discretionary spending other than for health-related programs, revenues other than those related to health, health-related programs and revenues, and the effects of eliminating a Cabinet department.

The report begins by noting the increase in the budget deficit as a percentage of GDP from 2.5% in 2015 to 3.2% in fiscal year 2016, the first such increase since 2009. As a result, federal debt rose as a percent of GDP to 77%, its highest ratio since 1950. The report also notes that under current laws concerning spending and revenues, the deficit rises substantially over the ten-year projection period. Deficits as a percent of GDP are expected to dip in 2017 and 2018 to 3.1% and 2.6% respectively before rising to 4.6% by the end of the projection period. At that point, the debt is projected to be 86% of GDP. The CBO reports that these increases are the results of increases in revenues not keeping pace with increases in spending, primarily for retirement and health care programs due to aging of the population and rising health care costs, as well as rising interest payments on federal debt. It cites the risks of rising debt and deficits as: increased spending as interest payments rise with rising interest rates projected for future years, lower capital stock than otherwise as government borrowing diverts the nation's savings to servicing the debt, less flexibility to respond to national challenges that may arise, and the increased likelihood of a fiscal crisis if lenders to the government become unwilling to lend to the government unless they are compensated with higher and higher interest rates. To return the government to a sustainable budgetary path, they argue, requires increasing revenues, reducing spending, or some combination of the two—not rocket science but the devil of how to do this is in the messy details. As lawmakers and the public consider changes, they might ask: What are acceptable levels for the debt and deficit as percentages of GDP? What types of policy changes might enhance long-term economic growth? Who would bear the burdens of various changes and who would benefit? At what speed should policy changes be implemented?

Just to give a sense of the details in the report, there are 26 options related to mandatory spending. The first one has to do with changing the terms of oil and gas leasing on federal lands, which the report estimates would save about $3 billion over the 10-year period. The last suggests using an alternative measure of inflation for indexing of social security and other mandatory programs. The saving there is estimated to be a whopping $182 billion. The savings from eliminating one of the 15 government departments depends on whether the programs of the department will be cancelled or transferred to another department. If the latter, there might be some savings in administrative costs but in most cases administrative costs are much less than the costs of the programs, which on average are 70% of the total costs of the departments.

As a member of the public, you may want to look at this report to come up with your own assessments of the best, or perhaps the least bad, ways, to reduce the federal deficits and debt.[2]

Source: *Based on Jagadeesh Gokhale, "Generational Accounting," The New Palgrave Dictionary of Economics Online, 2nd ed., 2008.*

Answer to Try It! Problem

A budget surplus leads to a decline in national debt; a budget deficit causes the national debt to grow. If there is a decrease in a budget surplus, national debt still declines but by less than it would have had the surplus not gotten smaller. If there is a decrease in the budget deficit, the national debt still grows, but by less than it would have if the deficit had not gotten smaller.

27.3 The Use of Fiscal Policy to Stabilize the Economy

Learning Objectives

1. Define automatic stabilizers and explain how they work.
2. Explain and illustrate graphically how discretionary fiscal policy works and compare the changes in aggregate demand that result from changes in government purchases, income taxes, and transfer payments.

Fiscal policy—the use of government expenditures and taxes to influence the level of economic activity—is the government counterpart to monetary policy. Like monetary policy, it can be used in an effort to close a recessionary or an inflationary gap.

Some tax and expenditure programs change automatically with the level of economic activity. We will examine these first. Then we will look at how discretionary fiscal policies work. Four examples of discretionary fiscal policy choices were the tax cuts introduced by the Kennedy, Reagan, and George W. Bush administrations and the increase in government purchases proposed by President Clinton in 1993. The 2009 fiscal stimulus bill passed in the first months of the administration of Barack Obama included both tax rebates and spending increases. All were designed to stimulate aggregate demand and close recessionary gaps.

Automatic Stabilizers

Certain government expenditure and taxation policies tend to insulate individuals from the impact of shocks to the economy. Transfer payments have this effect. Because more people become eligible for income supplements when income is falling, transfer payments reduce the effect of a change in real GDP on disposable personal income and thus help to insulate households from the impact of the change. Income taxes also have this effect. As incomes fall, people pay less in income taxes.

Any government program that tends to reduce fluctuations in GDP automatically is called an **automatic stabilizer**. Automatic stabilizers tend to increase GDP when it is falling and reduce GDP when it is rising.

To see how automatic stabilizers work, consider the decline in real GDP that occurred during the recession of 1990–1991. Real GDP fell 1.6% from the peak to the trough of that recession. The reduction in economic activity automatically reduced tax payments, reducing the impact of the downturn on disposable personal income. Furthermore, the reduction in incomes increased transfer payment spending, boosting disposable personal income further. Real disposable personal income thus fell by only 0.9% during the 1990—1991 recession, a much smaller percentage than the reduction in real GDP. Rising transfer payments and falling tax collections helped cushion households from the impact of the recession and kept real GDP from falling as much as it would have otherwise.

Automatic stabilizers have emerged as key elements of fiscal policy. Increases in income tax rates and unemployment benefits have enhanced their importance as automatic stabilizers. The introduction in the 1960s and 1970s of means-tested federal transfer payments, in which individuals qualify depending on their income, added to the nation's arsenal of automatic stabilizers. The advantage of automatic stabilizers is suggested by their name. As soon as income starts to change, they go to work. Because they affect disposable personal income directly, and because changes in disposable personal income are closely linked to changes in consumption, automatic stabilizers act swiftly to reduce the degree of changes in real GDP.

It is important to note that changes in expenditures and taxes that occur through automatic stabilizers do not shift the aggregate demand curve. Because they are automatic, their operation is already incorporated in the curve itself.

Discretionary Fiscal Policy Tools

As we begin to look at deliberate government efforts to stabilize the economy through fiscal policy choices, we note that most of the government's taxing and spending is for purposes other than economic stabilization. For example, the increase in defense spending in the early 1980s under President Ronald Reagan and in the administration of George W. Bush were undertaken primarily to promote national security. That the increased spending affected real GDP and employment was a by-product. The effect of such changes on real GDP and the price level is secondary, but it cannot be ignored. Our focus here, however, is on discretionary fiscal policy that is undertaken with the intention of stabilizing the economy. As we have seen, the tax cuts introduced by the Bush administration were justified as expansionary measures.

Discretionary government spending and tax policies can be used to shift aggregate demand. Expansionary fiscal policy might consist of an increase in government purchases or transfer payments, a reduction in taxes, or a combination of these tools to shift the aggregate demand curve to the right. A contractionary fiscal policy might involve a reduction in government purchases or transfer payments, an increase in taxes, or a mix of all three to shift the aggregate demand curve to the left.

Figure 27.8 illustrates the use of fiscal policy to shift aggregate demand in response to a recessionary gap and an inflationary gap. In Panel (a), the economy produces a real GDP of Y_1, which is below its potential level of Y_p. An expansionary fiscal policy seeks to shift aggregate demand to AD_2 in order to close the gap. In Panel (b), the economy initially has an inflationary gap at Y_1. A contractionary fiscal policy seeks to reduce aggregate demand to AD_2 and close the gap. Now we shall look at how specific fiscal policy options work. In our preliminary analysis of the effects of fiscal policy on the economy, we will assume that at a given price level these policies do not affect interest rates or exchange rates. We will relax that assumption later in the chapter.

FIGURE 27.8 Expansionary and Contractionary Fiscal Policies to Shift Aggregate Demand
In Panel (a), the economy faces a recessionary gap ($Y_P - Y_1$). An expansionary fiscal policy seeks to shift aggregate demand to AD_2 to close the gap. In Panel (b), the economy faces an inflationary gap ($Y_1 - Y_P$). A contractionary fiscal policy seeks to reduce aggregate demand to AD_2 to close the gap.

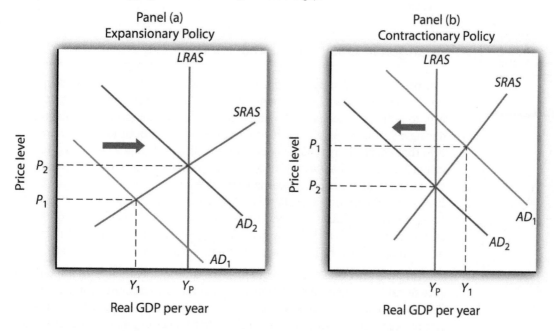

Changes in Government Purchases

One policy through which the government could seek to shift the aggregate demand curve is a change in government purchases. We learned that the aggregate demand curve shifts to the right by an amount equal to the initial change in government purchases times the multiplier. This multiplied effect of a change in government purchases occurs because the increase in government purchases increases income, which in turn increases consumption. Then, part of the impact of the increase in aggregate demand is absorbed by higher prices, preventing the full increase in real GDP that would have occurred if the price level did not rise.

Figure 27.9 shows the effect of an increase in government purchases of $200 billion. The initial price level is P_1 and the initial equilibrium real GDP is $12,000 billion. Suppose the multiplier is 2. The $200 billion increase in government purchases increases the total quantity of goods and services demanded, at a price level of P_1, by $400 billion (the $200 billion increase in government purchases times the multiplier) to $12,400 billion. The aggregate demand thus shifts to the right by that amount to AD_2. The equilibrium level of real GDP rises to $12,300 billion, and the price level rises to P_2.

A reduction in government purchases would have the opposite effect. The aggregate demand curve would shift to the left by an amount equal to the initial change in government purchases times the multiplier. Real GDP and the price level would fall.

Changes in Business Taxes

One of the first fiscal policy measures undertaken by the Kennedy administration in the 1960s was an investment tax credit. An investment tax credit allows a firm to reduce its tax liability by a percentage of the investment it undertakes during a particular period. With an investment tax credit of 10%, for example, a firm that engaged in $1 million worth of investment during a year could reduce its tax liability for that year by $100,000. The investment tax credit introduced by the Kennedy administration was later repealed. It was reintroduced during the Reagan administration in 1981, then abolished by the Tax Reform Act of 1986. President Clinton called for a new investment tax credit in 1993 as part of his job stimulus proposal, but that proposal was rejected by Congress. The Bush administration reinstated the investment tax credit as part of its tax cut package.

An investment tax credit is intended, of course, to stimulate additional private sector investment. A reduction in the tax rate on corporate profits would be likely to have a similar effect. Conversely, an increase in the corporate income tax rate or a reduction in an investment tax credit could be expected to reduce investment.

A change in investment affects the aggregate demand curve in precisely the same manner as a change in government purchases. It shifts the aggregate demand curve by an amount equal to the initial change in investment times the multiplier.

An increase in the investment tax credit, or a reduction in corporate income tax rates, will increase investment and shift the aggregate demand curve to the right. Real GDP and the price level will rise. A reduction in the investment tax credit, or an increase in corporate income tax rates, will reduce investment and shift the aggregate demand curve to the left. Real GDP and the price level will fall.[3]

Changes in Income Taxes

Income taxes affect the consumption component of aggregate demand. An increase in income taxes reduces disposable personal income and thus reduces consumption (but by less than the change in disposable personal income). That shifts the aggregate demand curve leftward by an amount equal to the initial change in consumption that the change in income taxes produces times the multiplier.[4] A reduction in income taxes increases disposable personal income, increases consumption (but by less than the change in disposable personal income), and increases aggregate demand.

Suppose, for example, that income taxes are reduced by $200 billion. Only some of the increase in disposable personal income will be used for consumption and the rest will be saved. Suppose the initial increase in consumption is $180 billion. Then the shift in the aggregate demand curve will be a multiple of $180 billion; if the multiplier is 2, aggregate demand will shift to the right by $360 billion. Thus, as compared to the $200-billion increase in government purchases that we saw in Figure 27.9, the shift in the aggregate demand curve due to an income tax cut is somewhat less, as is the effect on real GDP and the price level.

FIGURE 27.9 An Increase in Government Purchases

The economy shown here is initially in equilibrium at a real GDP of $12,000 billion and a price level of P_1. An increase of $200 billion in the level of government purchases (ΔG) shifts the aggregate demand curve to the right by $400 billion to AD_2. The equilibrium level of real GDP rises to $12,300 billion, while the price level rises to P_2.

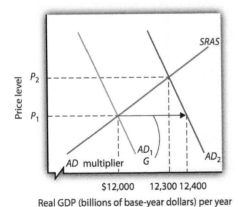

Changes in Transfer Payments

Changes in transfer payments, like changes in income taxes, alter the disposable personal income of households and thus affect their consumption, which is a component of aggregate demand. A change in transfer payments will thus shift the aggregate demand curve because it will affect consumption. Because consumption will change by less than the change in disposable personal income, a change in transfer payments of some amount will result in a smaller change in real GDP than would a change in government purchases of the same amount. As with income taxes, a $200-billion increase in transfer payments will shift the aggregate demand curve to the right by less than the $200-billion increase in government purchases that we saw in Figure 27.9.

Table 27.1 summarizes U.S. fiscal policies undertaken to shift aggregate demand since the 1964 tax cuts. We see that expansionary policies have been chosen in response to recessionary gaps and that contractionary policies have been chosen in response to inflationary gaps. Changes in government purchases and in taxes have been the primary tools of fiscal policy in the United States.

TABLE 27.1 Fiscal Policy in the United States Since 1964

The table lists the major proposed uses of discretionary policy over a period of more than four decades.

Year	Situation	Policy response
1968	Inflationary gap	A temporary tax increase, first recommended by President Johnson's Council of Economic Advisers in 1965, goes into effect. This one-time surcharge of 10% is added to individual income tax liabilities.
1969	Inflationary gap	President Nixon, facing a continued inflationary gap, orders cuts in government purchases.
1975	Recessionary gap	President Ford, facing a recession induced by an OPEC oil-price increase, proposes a temporary 10% tax cut. It is passed almost immediately and goes into effect within two months.
1981	Recessionary gap	President Reagan had campaigned on a platform of increased defense spending and a sharp cut in income taxes. The tax cuts are approved in 1981 and are implemented over a period of three years. The increased defense spending begins in 1981. While the Reagan administration rejects the use of fiscal policy as a stabilization tool, its policies tend to increase aggregate demand early in the 1980s.
1992	Recessionary gap	President Bush had rejected the use of expansionary fiscal policy during the recession of 1990–1991. Indeed, he agreed late in 1990 to a cut in government purchases and a tax increase. In a campaign year, however, he orders a cut in withholding rates designed to increase disposable personal income in 1992 and to boost consumption.
1993	Recessionary gap	President Clinton calls for a $16-billion jobs package consisting of increased government purchases and tax cuts aimed at stimulating investment. The president says the plan will create 500,000 new jobs. The measure is rejected by Congress.
2001	Recessionary gap	President Bush campaigned to reduce taxes in order to reduce the size of government and encourage long-term growth. When he took office in 2001, the economy was weak and the $1.35-billion tax cut was aimed at both long-term tax relief and at stimulating the economy in the short term. It included, for example, a personal income tax rebate of $300 to $600 per household. With unemployment still high a couple of years into the expansion, another tax cut was passed in 2003.
2008	Recessionary gap	Fiscal stimulus package of $150 billion to spur economy. It included $100 billion in tax rebates and $50 billion in tax cuts for businesses.
2009	Recessionary gap	Fiscal stimulus package of $784 billion included tax rebates and increased government spending passed in early days of President Obama's administration.
2010–2012	Recessionary gap	Extensions of the payroll tax reduction and unemployment insurance benefits continued.

Key Takeaways

- Discretionary fiscal policy may be either expansionary or contractionary.
- A change in government purchases shifts the aggregate demand curve at a given price level by an amount equal to the initial change in government purchases times the multiplier. The change in real GDP, however, will be reduced by the fact that the price level will change.
- A change in income taxes or government transfer payments shifts the aggregate demand curve by a multiple of the initial change in consumption (which is less than the change in personal disposable income) that the change in income taxes or transfer payments causes. Then, the change in real GDP will be reduced by the fact that the price level will change.

- A change in government purchases has a larger impact on the aggregate demand curve than does an equal change in income taxes or transfers.
- Changes in business tax rates, including an investment tax credit, can be used to influence the level of investment and thus the level of aggregate demand.

Try It!

Suppose the economy has an inflationary gap. What fiscal policies might be used to close the gap? Using the model of aggregate demand and aggregate supply, illustrate the effect of these policies.

Case in Point: How Large *Is* the Fiscal Multiplier?

Source: © Shutterstock, Inc.

There is a wide range of opinions among economists regarding the size of the fiscal multiplier. In 2011, the American Economic Association's *Journal of Economic Literature* published three papers on this topic in a special section titled "Forum: The Multiplier." The papers provide at least two-and-a-half different answers!

In her paper titled "Can Government Purchases Stimulate the Economy?," Valerie Ramey concludes that the size of the government purchases multiplier depends on many factors but that, when the increase in government purchases is temporary and financed by government borrowing, the multiplier "is probably between 0.8 and 1.5. Reasonable people can argue, however, that the data do not reject 0.5 to 2." This is quite a wide range.

In "An Empirical Analysis of the Revival of Fiscal Activism in the 2000s," John Taylor argues that the various components of the recent fiscal packages (tax cuts, aid to states, and increased government purchases) had little effect on the economy—implying a multiplier of zero or nearly so. Using aggregate quarterly data simulations for the 2000s, he argues that transfers and tax cuts were used by households to increase saving, that the increase in government purchases were too small to have made much of a difference, and that state and local governments used their stimulus dollars for transfers or to reduce their borrowing.

In "On Measuring the Effects of Fiscal Policy in Recessions," Jonathan Parker essentially argues that the statistical models built to date are ultimately inadequate and that we will only be able to get at the answer as better and more refined studies are conducted. Noting that the multiplier effect of fiscal policy is likely to depend on the state of the economy, he concludes that "an important difficulty with further investigation is the limited macroeconomic data available on the effects of policy in recessions (or deep recessions)." Perhaps we need a few more Great Recessions in order to figure this out.

In another American Economic Association publication, the *Journal of Economic Perspectives*, Alan Auerbach, William Gale, and Benjamin Harris provide an extensive review of the variety in multiplier estimates, which they acknowledge is "embarrassingly large" after so many years of trying to measure it. Concerning the 2009 American Recovery and Reinvestment Act, though, they write, "If a fiscal stimulus were ever to be considered appropriate, the beginning of 2009 was such a time....In these circumstances, our judgment is that a fiscal expansion carried much smaller risks than the lack of one would have."

Sources: *Based on Alan J. Auerbach, William G. Gale, and Benjamin H. Harris, "Activist Fiscal Policy," Journal of Economic Perspectives 24, no. 4 (Fall 2010): 141–64; Jonathan A. Parker, "On Measuring the Effects of Fiscal Policy in Recessions," Journal of Economic Literature 49, no. 3 (September 2011): 703–18; Valerie A. Ramey, "Can Government Purchases Stimulate the Economy?," Journal of Economic Literature 49, no. 3 (September 2011): 673–85; John B. Taylor, "An Empirical Analysis of the Revival of Fiscal Activism in the 2000s," Journal of Economic Literature 49, no. 3 (September 2011): 686–702.*

Answer to Try It! Problem

Fiscal policies that could be used to close an inflationary gap include reductions in government purchases and transfer payments and increases in taxes. As shown in Panel (b) of Figure 27.8, the goal would be to shift the aggregate demand curve to the left so that it will intersect the short-run aggregate supply curve at Y_P.

27.4 Issues in Fiscal Policy

Learning Objectives

1. Explain how the various kinds of lags influence the effectiveness of discretionary fiscal policy.
2. Explain and illustrate graphically how crowding out (and its reverse) influences the impact of expansionary or contractionary fiscal policy.
3. Discuss the controversy concerning which types of fiscal policies to use, including the arguments from supply-side economics.

The discussion in the previous section about the use of fiscal policy to close gaps suggests that economies can be easily stabilized by government actions to shift the aggregate demand curve. However, as we discovered with monetary policy in the previous chapter, government attempts at stabilization are fraught with difficulties.

Lags

Discretionary fiscal policy is subject to the same lags that we discussed for monetary policy. It takes some time for policy makers to realize that a recessionary or an inflationary gap exists—the *recognition lag*. Recognition lags stem largely from the difficulty of collecting economic data in a timely and accurate fashion. The current recession was not identified until October 2008, when the Business Cycle Dating Committee of the National Bureau of Economic Research announced that it had begun in December 2007. Then, more time elapses before a fiscal policy, such as a change in government purchases or a change in taxes, is agreed to and put into effect—the *implementation lag*. Finally, still more time goes by before the policy has its full effect on aggregate demand—the *impact lag*.

Changes in fiscal policy are likely to involve a particularly long implementation lag. A tax cut was proposed to presidential candidate John F. Kennedy in 1960 as a means of ending the recession that year. He recommended it to Congress in 1962. It was not passed until 1964, three years after the recession had ended. Some economists have concluded that the long implementation lag for discretionary fiscal policy makes this stabilization tool ineffective. Fortunately, automatic stabilizers respond automatically to changes in the economy. They thus avoid not only the implementation lag but also the recognition lag.

The implementation lag results partly from the nature of bureaucracy itself. The CBO estimate that only a portion of the spending for the stimulus plan passed in 2009 will be spent in the next two years is an example of the implementation lag. Government spending requires bureaucratic approval of that spending. For example, a portion of the stimulus plan must go through the Department of Energy. One division of the department focuses on approving loan guarantees for energy-saving industrial projects. It was created early in 2007 as part of another effort to stimulate economic activity. A Minnesota company, Sage Electrochromics, has developed a process for producing windows that can be darkened or lightened on demand to reduce energy use in buildings. Sage applied two years ago for a guarantee on a loan of $66 million to build a plant that would employ 250 workers. Its application has not been approved. In fact, the loan approval division, which will be crucial for projects in the stimulus plan, has never approved any application made to it in its two years in existence!

Energy Secretary Steven Chu, a Nobel Prize-winning physicist, recognizes the urgency of the problem. In an interview with the *Wall Street Journal*, Dr. Chu said that his agency would have to do better. "Otherwise, it's just going to be a bust," he said.[5]

Crowding Out

Because an expansionary fiscal policy either increases government spending or reduces revenues, it increases the government budget deficit or reduces the surplus. A contractionary policy is likely to reduce a deficit or increase a surplus. In either case, fiscal policy thus affects the bond market. Our analysis of monetary policy showed that developments in the bond market can affect investment and net exports. We shall find in this section that the same is true for fiscal policy.

Figure 27.10 shows the impact of an expansionary fiscal policy: an increase in government purchases. The increase in government purchases increases the deficit or reduces the surplus. In either case, the Treasury will sell more bonds than it would have otherwise, shifting the supply curve for bonds to the right in Panel (a). That reduces the price of bonds, raising the interest rate. The increase in the interest rate reduces the quantity of private investment demanded. The higher interest rate increases the demand for and reduces the supply of dollars in the foreign exchange market, raising the exchange rate in Panel (b). A higher exchange rate reduces net exports. Panel (c) shows the effects of all these changes on the aggregate demand curve. Before the change in government purchases, the economy is in equilibrium at a real GDP of Y_1, determined by the intersection of AD_1 and the short-run aggregate supply curve. The increase in government expenditures would shift the curve outward to AD_2 if there were no adverse impact on investment and net exports. But the reduction in investment and net exports partially offsets this increase. Taking the reduction in investment and net exports into account means that the aggregate demand curve shifts only to AD_3. The tendency for an expansionary fiscal policy to reduce other components of aggregate demand is called **crowding out**. In the short run, this policy leads to an increase in real GDP to Y_2 and a higher price level, P_2.

crowding out

The tendency for an expansionary fiscal policy to reduce other components of aggregate demand.

FIGURE 27.10 An Expansionary Fiscal Policy and Crowding Out

In Panel (a), increased government purchases are financed through the sale of bonds, lowering their price to P^b_2. In Panel (b), the higher interest rate causes the exchange rate to rise, reducing net exports. Increased government purchases would shift the aggregate demand curve to AD_2 in Panel (c) if there were no crowding out. Crowding out of investment and net exports, however, causes the aggregate demand curve to shift only to AD_3. Then a higher price level means that GDP rises only to Y_2.

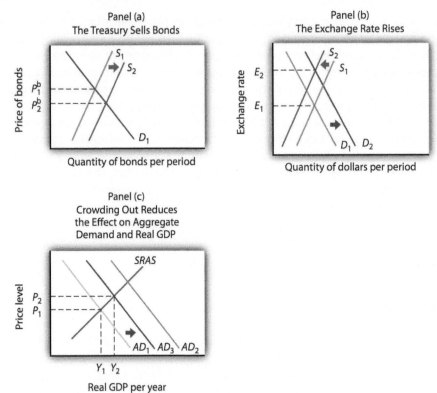

Crowding out reduces the effectiveness of any expansionary fiscal policy, whether it be an increase in government purchases, an increase in transfer payments, or a reduction in income taxes. Each of these policies increases the deficit and thus increases government borrowing. The supply of bonds increases, interest rates rise, investment falls, the exchange rate rises, and net exports fall.

Note, however, that it is private investment that is crowded out. The expansionary fiscal policy could take the form of an increase in the investment component of government purchases. As we have learned, some government purchases are for goods, such as office supplies, and services. But the government can also purchase investment items, such as roads and schools. In that case, government investment may be crowding out private investment.

crowding in

The tendency for a contractionary fiscal policy to increase other components of aggregate demand.

The reverse of crowding out occurs with a contractionary fiscal policy—a cut in government purchases or transfer payments, or an increase in taxes. Such policies reduce the deficit (or increase the surplus) and thus reduce government borrowing, shifting the supply curve for bonds to the left. Interest rates drop, inducing a greater quantity of investment. Lower interest rates also reduce the demand for and increase the supply of dollars, lowering the exchange rate and boosting net exports. This phenomenon is known as "**crowding in**."

Crowding out and crowding in clearly weaken the impact of fiscal policy. An expansionary fiscal policy has less punch; a contractionary policy puts less of a damper on economic activity. Some economists argue that these forces are so powerful that a change in fiscal policy will have no effect on aggregate demand. Because empirical studies have been inconclusive, the extent of crowding out (and its reverse) remains a very controversial area of study.

Also, the fact that government deficits today may reduce the capital stock that would otherwise be available to future generations does not imply that such deficits are wrong. If, for example, the deficits are used to finance public sector investment, then the reduction in private capital provided to the future is offset by the increased provision of public sector capital. Future generations may have fewer office buildings but more schools.

Choice of Policy

Suppose Congress and the president agree that something needs to be done to close a recessionary gap. We have learned that fiscal policies that increase government purchases, reduce taxes, or increase transfer payments—or do a combination of these—all have the potential, theoretically, to raise real GDP. The government must decide which kind of fiscal policy to employ. Because the decision makers who determine fiscal policy are all elected politicians, the choice among the policy options available is an intensely political matter, often reflecting the ideology of the politicians.

For example, those who believe that government is too big would argue for tax cuts to close recessionary gaps and for spending cuts to close inflationary gaps. Those who believe that the private sector has failed to provide adequately a host of services that would benefit society, such as better education or public transportation systems, tend to advocate increases in government purchases to close recessionary gaps and tax increases to close inflationary gaps.

Another area of contention comes from those who believe that fiscal policy should be constructed primarily so as to promote long-term growth. **Supply-side economics** is the school of thought that promotes the use of fiscal policy to stimulate long-run aggregate supply. Supply-side economists advocate reducing tax rates in order to encourage people to work more or more individuals to work and providing investment tax credits to stimulate capital formation.

While there is considerable debate over how strong the supply-side effects are in relation to the demand-side effects, such considerations may affect the choice of policies. Supply-siders tend to favor tax cuts over increases in government purchases or increases in transfer payments. President Reagan advocated tax cuts in 1981 on the basis of their supply-side effects. Coupled with increased defense spending in the early 1980s, fiscal policy under Mr. Reagan clearly stimulated aggregate demand by increasing both consumption and investment. Falling inflation and accelerated growth are signs that supply-side factors may also have been at work during that period. President George W. Bush's chief economic adviser, N. Gregory Mankiw, argued that the Bush tax cuts would encourage economic growth, a supply-side argument. Mr. Bush's next chief economic adviser, Ben Bernanke, who served as chairman of the Federal Reserve Board from 2006 until February 2014, made a similar argument and urged that the Bush tax cuts be made permanent.

Finally, even when there is agreement to stimulate the economy, say through increasing government expenditures on highways, the *how* question remains. How should the expenditures be allocated? Specifically, which states should the highways run through? Each member of Congress has a political stake in the outcome. These types of considerations make the implementation lag particularly long for fiscal policy.

supply-side economics

The school of thought that promotes the use of fiscal policy to stimulate long-run aggregate supply.

Key Takeaways

- Discretionary fiscal policy involves the same kind of lags as monetary policy. However, the implementation lag in fiscal policy is likely to be more pronounced, while the impact lag is likely to be less pronounced.
- Expansionary fiscal policy may result in the crowding out of private investment and net exports, reducing the impact of the policy. Similarly, contractionary policy may "crowd in" additional investment and net exports, reducing the contractionary impact of the policy.
- Supply-side economics stresses the use of fiscal policy to stimulate economic growth. Advocates of supply-side economics generally favor tax cuts to stimulate economic growth.

Try It!

Do the following hypothetical situations tend to enhance or make more difficult the use of fiscal policy as a stabilization tool?

1. Better and more speedily available data on the state of the economy
2. A finding that private sector investment spending is not much affected by interest rate changes
3. A finding that the supply-side effects of a tax cut are substantial

Case in Point: Crowding Out in Canada

Source: © Shutterstock, Inc.

In an intriguing study, economist Baotai Wang examined the degree of crowding out of Canadian private investment as a result of government expenditures from 1961–2000. What made Professor Wang's analysis unusual was that he divided Canadian government expenditures into five categories: expenditures for health and education, expenditures for capital and infrastructure, expenditures for the protection of persons and property (which included defense spending), expenditures for debt services, and expenditures for government and social services.

Mr. Wang found that only government expenditures for capital and infrastructure crowded out private investment. While these expenditures reduced private investment, they represented increased public sector investment for things such as highways and ports.

Expenditures for health and education actually "crowded in" private sector investment. These expenditures, Mr. Wang argued, represented increases in human capital. Such increases complement returns on private sector investment and therefore increase it.

Mr. Wang found that Canadian government expenditures for debt service, the protection of persons and property, and for government and social services had no effect on private sector investment. He argued that expenditures for protection of persons and property may involve some crowding out, but that they also stimulated private investment by firms winning government contracts for defense purchases. The same explanation could be applied to government expenditures for government and social services. These also include an element of investment in human capital.

His results suggest that crowding out depends on the nature of spending done by the government. Some kinds of spending clearly did not crowd out private sector investment in Canada.

Source: *Based on Baotai Wang, "Effects of Government Expenditure on Private Investment: Canadian Empirical Evidence," Empirical Economics 30, no. 2 (September 2005): 493–504.*

Answers to Try It! Problems

1. Data on the economy that are more accurate and more speedily available should enhance the use of fiscal policy by reducing the length of the recognition lag.

2. If private sector investment does not respond much to interest rate changes, then there will be less crowding out when expansionary policies are undertaken. That is, the rising interest rates that accompany expansionary fiscal policy will not reduce investment spending much, making the shift in the aggregate demand curve to the right greater than it would be otherwise. Also, the use of contractionary fiscal policy would be more effective, since the fall in interest rates would "invite in" less investment spending, making the shift in the aggregate demand curve to the left greater than it would otherwise be.

3. Large supply-side effects enhance the impact of tax cuts. For a given expansionary policy, without the supply-side effects, GDP would advance only to the point where the aggregate demand curve intersects the short-run aggregate supply curve. With the supply-side effects, both the short-run and long-run aggregate supply curves shift to the right. The intersection of the *AD* curve with the now increased short-run aggregate supply curve will be farther to the right than it would have been in the absence of the supply-side effects. The potential level of real GDP will also increase.

27.5 Review and Practice

Summary

The government sector plays a major role in the economy. The spending, tax, and transfer policies of local, state, and federal agencies affect aggregate demand and aggregate supply and thus affect the level of real GDP and the price level. An expansionary policy tends to increase real GDP. Such a policy could be used to close a recessionary gap. A contractionary fiscal policy tends to reduce real GDP. A contractionary policy could be used to close an inflationary gap.

Government purchases of goods and services have a direct impact on aggregate demand. An increase in government purchases shifts the aggregate demand curve by the amount of the initial change in government purchases times the multiplier. Changes in personal income taxes or in the level of transfer payments affect disposable personal income. They change consumption, though initially by less than the amount of the change in taxes or transfers. They thus cause somewhat smaller shifts in the aggregate demand curve than do equal changes in government purchases.

There are several issues in the use of fiscal policies for stabilization purposes. They include lags associated with fiscal policy, crowding out, the choice of which fiscal policy tool to use, and the possible burdens of accumulating national debt.

Concept Problems

1. What is the difference between government expenditures and government purchases? How do the two variables differ in terms of their effect on GDP?

2. Federally funded student aid programs generally reduce benefits by $1 for every $1 that recipients earn. Do such programs represent government purchases or transfer payments? Are they automatic stabilizers?

3. Crowding out reduces the degree to which a change in government purchases influences the level of economic activity. Is it a form of automatic stabilizer?

4. Why is it important to try to determine the size of the fiscal policy multiplier?

5. Suppose an economy has an inflationary gap. How does the government's actual budget deficit or surplus compare to the deficit or surplus it would have at potential output?

6. Suppose the president was given the authority to increase or decrease federal spending by as much as $100 billion in order to stabilize economic activity. Do you think this would tend to make the economy more or less stable?

7. Suppose the government increases purchases in an economy with a recessionary gap. How would this policy affect bond prices, interest rates, investment, net exports, real GDP, and the price level? Show your results graphically.

8. Suppose the government cuts transfer payments in an economy with an inflationary gap. How would this policy affect bond prices, interest rates, investment, the exchange rate, net exports, real GDP, and the price level? Show your results graphically.

9. Suppose that at the same time the government undertakes expansionary fiscal policy, such as a cut in taxes, the Fed undertakes contractionary monetary policy. How would this policy affect bond prices, interest rates, investment, net exports, real GDP, and the price level? Show your results graphically.

10. Given the nature of the implementation lag discussed in the text, discuss possible measures that might reduce the lag.

Numerical Problems

1. Look up the table on Federal Receipts and Outlays, by Major Category, in the most recent *Economic Report of the President* available in your library or on the Internet.

    a. Complete the following table:

Category	Total outlays	Percentage of total outlays
National defense		
International affairs		
Health		
Medicare		
Income security		
Social Security		
Net interest		
Other		

    b. Construct a pie chart showing the percentages of spending for each category in the total.

2. Look up the table on ownership of U.S. Treasury securities in the most recent *Economic Report of the President* available on the Internet.

    a. Make a pie chart showing the percentage owned by various groups in the earliest year shown in the table.

    b. Make a pie chart showing the percentage owned by various groups in the most recent year shown in the table.

    c. What are some of the major changes in ownership of U.S. government debt over the period?

3. Suppose a country has a national debt of $5,000 billion, a GDP of $10,000 billion, and a budget deficit of $100 billion.

    a. How much will its new national debt be?

b. Compute its debt-GDP ratio.

c. Suppose its GDP grows by 1% in the next year and the budget deficit is again $100 billion. Compute its new level of national debt and its new debt-GDP ratio.

4. Suppose a country's debt rises by 10% and its GDP rises by 12%.

a. What happens to the debt-GDP ratio?

b. Does the relative level of the initial values affect your answer?

5. The data below show a country's national debt and its prime lending rate.

Year	National debt (billions of $)	Lending rate (%)
1992	4,064	6.0
1993	4,411	6.0
1994	4,692	8.5
1995	4,973	8.7
1996	5,224	8.3
1997	5,413	8.5

a. Plot the relationship between national debt and the lending rate.

b. Based on your graph, does crowding out appear to be a problem?

6. Suppose a country increases government purchases by $100 billion. Suppose the multiplier is 1.5 and the economy's real GDP is $5,000 billion.

a. In which direction will the aggregate demand curve shift and by how much?

b. Explain using a graph why the change in real GDP is likely to be smaller than the shift in the aggregate demand curve.

7. Suppose a country decreases government purchases by $100 billion. Suppose the multiplier is 1.5 and the economy's real GDP is $5,000 billion.

a. In which direction will the aggregate demand curve shift and by how much?

b. Explain using a graph why the change in real GDP is likely to be smaller than the shift in the aggregate demand curve.

8. Suppose a country decreases income taxes by $100 billion, and this leads to an increase in consumption spending of $90 billion. Suppose the multiplier is 1.5 and the economy's real GDP is $5,000 billion.

a. In which direction will the aggregate demand curve shift and by how much?

b. Explain using a graph why the change in real GDP is likely to be smaller than the shift in the aggregate demand curve.

9. Suppose a country increases income taxes by $100 billion, and this leads to a decrease in consumption spending of $90 billion. Suppose the multiplier is 1.5 and the economy's real GDP is $5,000 billion.

a. In which direction will the aggregate demand curve shift and by how much?

b. Explain using a graph why the change in real GDP is likely to be smaller than the shift in the aggregate demand curve.

10. Suppose a country institutes an investment tax credit, and this leads to an increase in investment spending of $100 billion. Suppose the multiplier is 1.5 and the economy's real GDP is $5,000 billion.

a. In which direction will the aggregate demand curve shift and by how much?

b. Explain using a graph why the change in real GDP is likely to be smaller than the shift in the aggregate demand curve.

11. Suppose a country repeals an investment tax credit, and this leads to a decrease in investment spending of $100 billion. Suppose the multiplier is 1.5 and the economy's real GDP is $5,000 billion.

a. In which direction will the aggregate demand curve shift and by how much?

b. Explain using a graph why the change in real GDP is likely to be smaller than the shift in the aggregate demand curve.

12. Explain why the shifts in the aggregate demand curves in questions 7 through 11 above are the same or different in absolute value.

Endnotes

1. Barack Obama, Weekly Address of the President to the Nation, February 14, 2009, available at http://www.whitehouse.gov/blog/09/02/14/A-major-milestone/.

2. Source: Congressional Budget Office, Options for Reducing the Deficit, 2017 to 2026, available at https://www.cbo.gov/publication/52142.

3. Investment also affects the long-run aggregate supply curve, since a change in the capital stock changes the potential level of real GDP. We examined this earlier in the chapter on economic growth.

4. A change in tax rates will change the value of the multiplier. The reason is explained in another chapter.

5. Stephen Power and Neil King, Jr., "Next Challenge on Stimulus: Spending All That Money," Wall Street Journal, February 13, 2009, p. A1.

CHAPTER 28

Consumption and the Aggregate Expenditures Model

28.1 Start Up: A Dismal Year for Retailers

The year the most recent recession in the United States began, 2008, turned out to be the worst holiday shopping season in decades. Why? U.S. consumers were battered from many directions. Housing prices had fallen nearly 20% over the year. The stock market had fallen over 40%. Interest rates were falling, but credit was extremely hard to come by. By December, consumer confidence hit an all-time low amid concerns of rising unemployment. Cutting back seemed like the best defense for weathering this tough environment.

Consumption accounts for the bulk of aggregate demand in the United States and in other countries. In this chapter, we will examine the determinants of consumption and introduce a new model, the aggregate expenditures model, which will give insights into the aggregate demand curve. Any change in aggregate demand causes a change in income, and a change in income causes a change in consumption—which changes aggregate demand and thus income and thus consumption. The aggregate expenditures model will help us to unravel the important relationship between consumption and real GDP.

28.2 Determining the Level of Consumption

Learning Objectives

1. Explain and graph the consumption function and the saving function, explain what the slopes of these curves represent, and explain how the two are related to each other.
2. Compare the current income hypothesis with the permanent income hypothesis, and use each to predict the effect that temporary versus permanent changes in income will have on consumption.
3. Discuss two factors that can cause the consumption function to shift upward or downward.

J. R. McCulloch, an economist of the early nineteenth century, wrote, "Consumption ... is, in fact, the object of industry."[1] Goods and services are produced so that people can use them. The factors that determine consumption thus determine how successful an economy is in fulfilling its ultimate purpose: providing goods and services for people. So, consumption is not just important because it is such a large component of economic activity. It is important because, as McCulloch said, consumption is at the heart of the economy's fundamental purpose.

Consumption and Disposable Personal Income

It seems reasonable to expect that consumption spending by households will be closely related to their disposable personal income, which equals the income households receive less the taxes they pay. Note that disposable personal income and GDP are not the same thing. GDP is a measure of total income; disposable personal income is the income households have available to spend during a specified period.

Real values of disposable personal income and consumption per year from 1960 through 2015 are plotted in Figure 28.1. The data suggest that consumption generally changes in the same direction as does disposable personal income.

consumption function

The relationship between consumption and disposable personal income.

The relationship between consumption and disposable personal income is called the **consumption function**. It can be represented algebraically as an equation, as a schedule in a table, or as a curve on a graph.

FIGURE 28.1 The Relationship between Consumption and Disposable Personal Income, 1960–2015

Plots of consumption and disposable personal income over time suggest that consumption increases as disposable personal income increases.

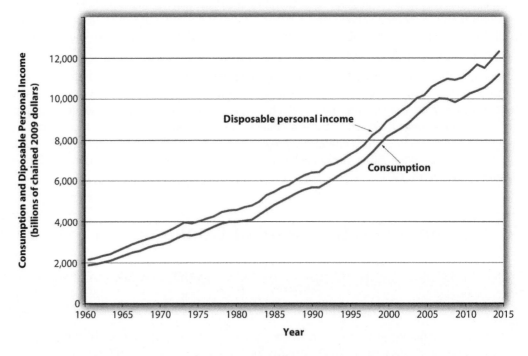

Source: Based on data from U. S. Department of Commerce, Bureau of Economic Analysis, NIPA Tables 1.1.6 and 2.17.6 (revised November 29, 2016).

marginal propensity to consume

The ratio of the change in consumption (ΔC) to the change in disposable personal income (ΔY_d).

Figure 28.2 illustrates the consumption function. The relationship between consumption and disposable personal income that we encountered in Figure 28.1 is evident in the table and in the curve: consumption in any period increases as disposable personal income increases in that period. The slope of the consumption function tells us by how much. Consider points C and D. When disposable personal income (Y_d) rises by $500 billion, consumption rises by $400 billion. More generally, the slope equals the change in consumption divided by the change in disposable personal income. The ratio of the change in consumption (ΔC) to the change in disposable personal income (ΔY_d) is the **marginal propensity to consume** (*MPC*). The Greek letter delta (Δ) is used to denote "change in."

EQUATION 28.1

$$MPC = \frac{\Delta C}{\Delta Y_d}$$

In this case, the marginal propensity to consume equals \$400/\$500 = 0.8. It can be interpreted as the fraction of an extra \$1 of disposable personal income that people spend on consumption. Thus, if a person with an *MPC* of 0.8 received an extra \$1,000 of disposable personal income, that person's consumption would rise by \$0.80 for each extra \$1 of disposable personal income, or \$800.

We can also express the consumption function as an equation

EQUATION 28.2

$$C = \$300 \text{ billion} + 0.8 Y_d$$

FIGURE 28.2 Plotting a Consumption Function

The consumption function relates consumption C to disposable personal income Y_d. The equation for the consumption function shown here in tabular and graphical form is $C = \$300$ billion $+ 0.8Y_d$.

Point on curve	A	B	C	D	E
Y_d (billions)	\$ 0	500	1,000	1,500	2,000
C (billions)	\$300	700	1,100	1,500	1,900

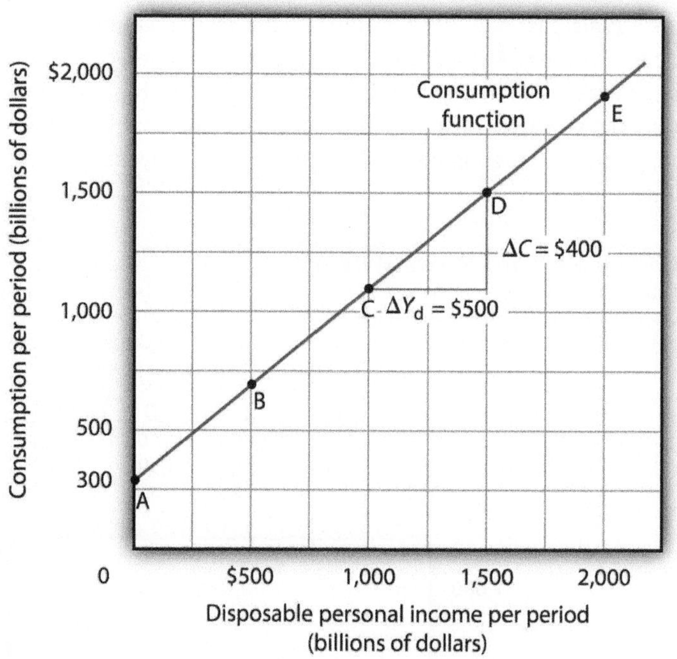

Heads Up!

It is important to note carefully the definition of the marginal propensity to consume. It is the change in consumption divided by the change in disposable personal income. It is not the level of consumption divided by the level of disposable personal income. Using Equation 28.2, at a level of disposable personal income of \$500 billion, for example, the level of consumption will be \$700 billion so that the ratio of consumption to disposable personal income will be 1.4, while the marginal propensity to consume remains 0.8. The marginal propensity to consume is, as its name implies, a marginal concept. It tells us what will happen to an additional dollar of personal disposable income.

Notice from the curve in Figure 28.2 that when disposable personal income equals 0, consumption is \$300 billion. The vertical intercept of the consumption function is thus \$300 billion. Then, for every \$500 billion increase in disposable personal income, consumption rises by \$400 billion. Because the consumption function in our example is linear, its slope is the same between any two points. In this case, the slope of the consumption function, which is the same as the marginal propensity to consume, is 0.8 all along its length.

personal saving

Disposable personal income not spent on consumption during a particular period.

saving function

The relationship between personal saving in any period and disposable personal income in that period.

We can use the consumption function to show the relationship between personal saving and disposable personal income. **Personal saving** is disposable personal income not spent on consumption during a particular period; the value of personal saving for any period is found by subtracting consumption from disposable personal income for that period:

EQUATION 28.3

$$\text{Personal saving} = \text{disposable personal income} - \text{consumption}$$

The **saving function** relates personal saving in any period to disposable personal income in that period. Personal saving is not the only form of saving—firms and government agencies may save as well. In this chapter, however, our focus is on the choice households make between using disposable personal income for consumption or for personal saving.

Figure 28.3 shows how the consumption function and the saving function are related. Personal saving is calculated by subtracting values for consumption from values for disposable personal income, as shown in the table. The values for personal saving are then plotted in the graph. Notice that a 45-degree line has been added to the graph. At every point on the 45-degree line, the value on the vertical axis equals that on the horizontal axis. The consumption function intersects the 45-degree line at an income of $1,500 billion (point D). At this point, consumption equals disposable personal income and personal saving equals 0 (point D′ on the graph of personal saving). Using the graph to find personal saving at other levels of disposable personal income, we subtract the value of consumption, given by the consumption function, from disposable personal income, given by the 45-degree line.

FIGURE 28.3 Consumption and Personal Saving

Personal saving equals disposable personal income minus consumption. The table gives hypothetical values for these variables. The consumption function is plotted in the upper part of the graph. At points along the 45-degree line, the values on the two axes are equal; we can measure personal saving as the distance between the 45-degree line and consumption. The curve of the saving function is in the lower portion of the graph.

Point on curve	A	B	C	D	E
Y_d (billions)	$ 0	500	1,000	1,500	2,000
C (billions)	$300	700	1,100	1,500	1,900
S (billions)	−$300	−200	−100	0	100

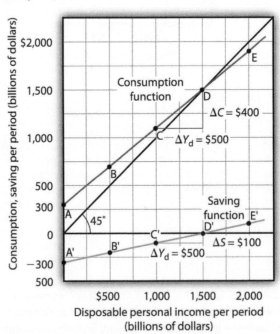

At a disposable personal income of $2,000 billion, for example, consumption is $1,900 billion (point E). Personal saving equals $100 billion (point E′)—the vertical distance between the 45-degree line and the consumption function. At an income of $500 billion, consumption totals $700 billion (point B). The consumption function lies above the 45-degree line at this point; personal saving is

-$200 billion (point B'). A negative value for saving means that consumption exceeds disposable personal income; it must have come from saving accumulated in the past, from selling assets, or from borrowing.

Notice that for every $500 billion increase in disposable personal income, personal saving rises by $100 billion. Consider points C' and D' in Figure 28.3. When disposable personal income rises by $500 billion, personal saving rises by $100 billion. More generally, the slope of the saving function equals the change in personal saving divided by the change in disposable personal income. The ratio of the change in personal saving (ΔS) to the change in disposable personal income (ΔY_d) is the **marginal propensity to save** (*MPS*).

marginal propensity to save

The ratio of the change in personal saving (ΔS) to the change in disposable personal income (ΔY_d).

EQUATION 28.4

$$MPS = \frac{\Delta S}{\Delta Y_d}$$

In this case, the marginal propensity to save equals $100/$500 = 0.2. It can be interpreted as the fraction of an extra $1 of disposable personal income that people save. Thus, if a person with an *MPS* of 0.2 received an extra $1,000 of disposable personal income, that person's saving would rise by $0.20 for each extra $1 of disposable personal income, or $200. Since people have only two choices of what to do with additional disposable personal income—that is, they can use it either for consumption or for personal saving—the fraction of disposable personal income that people consume (*MPC*) plus the fraction of disposable personal income that people save (*MPS*) must add to 1:

EQUATION 28.5

$$MPC + MPS = 1$$

Current versus Permanent Income

The discussion so far has related consumption in a particular period to income in that same period. The **current income hypothesis** holds that consumption in any one period depends on income during that period, or current income.

current income hypothesis

Consumption in any one period depends on income during that period.

Although it seems obvious that consumption should be related to disposable personal income, it is not so obvious that consumers base their consumption in any one period on the income they receive during that period. In buying a new car, for example, consumers might base their decision not only on their current income but on the income they expect to receive during the three or four years they expect to be making payments on the car. Parents who purchase a college education for their children might base their decision on their own expected lifetime income.

Indeed, it seems likely that virtually all consumption choices could be affected by expectations of income over a very long period. One reason people save is to provide funds to live on during their retirement years. Another is to build an estate they can leave to their heirs through bequests. The amount people save for their retirement or for bequests depends on the income they expect to receive for the rest of their lives. For these and other reasons, then, personal saving (and thus consumption) in any one year is influenced by permanent income. **Permanent income** is the average annual income people expect to receive for the rest of their lives.

permanent income

The average annual income people expect to receive for the rest of their lives.

People who have the same current income but different permanent incomes might reach very different saving decisions. Someone with a relatively low current income but a high permanent income (a college student planning to go to medical school, for example) might save little or nothing now, expecting to save for retirement and for bequests later. A person with the same low income but no expectation of higher income later might try to save some money now to provide for retirement or bequests later. Because a decision to save a certain amount determines how much will be available for consumption, consumption decisions can also be affected by expected lifetime income. Thus, an alternative approach to explaining consumption behavior is the **permanent income hypothesis**, which assumes that consumption in any period depends on permanent income. An important implication of the permanent income hypothesis is that a change in income regarded as temporary will not affect consumption much, since it will have little effect on average lifetime

permanent income hypothesis

Consumption in any period depends on permanent income.

income; a change regarded as permanent will have an effect. The current income hypothesis, though, predicts that it does not matter whether consumers view a change in disposable personal income as permanent or temporary; they will move along the consumption function and change consumption accordingly.

The question of whether permanent or current income is a determinant of consumption arose in 1992 when President George H. W. Bush ordered a change in the withholding rate for personal income taxes. Workers have a fraction of their paychecks withheld for taxes each pay period; Mr. Bush directed that this fraction be reduced in 1992. The change in the withholding rate did not change income tax rates; by withholding less in 1992, taxpayers would either receive smaller refund checks in 1993 or owe more taxes. The change thus left taxpayers' permanent income unaffected.

President Bush's measure was designed to increase aggregate demand and close the recessionary gap created by the 1990–1991 recession. Economists who subscribed to the permanent income hypothesis predicted that the change would not have any effect on consumption. Those who subscribed to the current income hypothesis predicted that the measure would boost consumption substantially in 1992. A survey of households taken during this period suggested that households planned to spend about 43% of the temporary increase in disposable personal income produced by the withholding experiment.[2] That is considerably less than would be predicted by the current income hypothesis, but more than the zero change predicted by the permanent income hypothesis. This result, together with related evidence, suggests that temporary changes in income can affect consumption, but that changes regarded as permanent will have a much stronger impact.

Many of the tax cuts passed during the administration of President George W. Bush are set to expire at the end of 2012. The proposal to make these tax cuts permanent is aimed toward having a stronger impact on consumption, since tax cuts regarded as permanent have larger effects than do changes regarded as temporary.

Other Determinants of Consumption

The consumption function graphed in Figure 28.2 and Figure 28.3 relates consumption spending to the level of disposable personal income. Changes in disposable personal income cause movements *along* this curve; they do not shift the curve. The curve shifts when other determinants of consumption change. Examples of changes that could shift the consumption function are changes in real wealth and changes in expectations. Figure 28.4 illustrates how these changes can cause shifts in the curve.

FIGURE 28.4 Shifts in the Consumption Function

An increase in the level of consumption at each level of disposable personal income shifts the consumption function upward in Panel (a). Among the events that would shift the curve upward are an increase in real wealth and an increase in consumer confidence. A reduction in the level of consumption at each level of disposable personal income shifts the curve downward in Panel (b). The events that could shift the curve downward include a reduction in real wealth and a decline in consumer confidence.

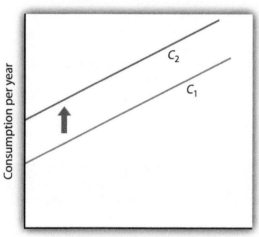

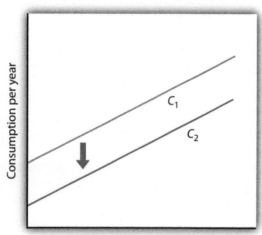

Changes in Real Wealth

An increase in stock and bond prices, for example, would make holders of these assets wealthier, and they would be likely to increase their consumption. An increase in real wealth shifts the consumption function upward, as illustrated in Panel (a) of Figure 28.4. A reduction in real wealth shifts it downward, as shown in Panel (b).

A change in the price level changes real wealth. We learned in an earlier chapter that the relationship among the price level, real wealth, and consumption is called the *wealth effect*. A reduction in the price level increases real wealth and shifts the consumption function upward, as shown in Panel (a). An increase in the price level shifts the curve downward, as shown in Panel (b).

Changes in Expectations

Consumers are likely to be more willing to spend money when they are optimistic about the future. Surveyors attempt to gauge this optimism using "consumer confidence" surveys that ask respondents to report whether they are optimistic or pessimistic about their own economic situation and about the prospects for the economy as a whole. An increase in consumer optimism tends to shift the consumption function upward as in Panel (a) of Figure 28.4; an increase in pessimism tends to shift it downward as in Panel (b). The sharp reduction in consumer confidence in 2008 and early in 2009 contributed to a downward shift in the consumption function and thus to the severity of the recession.

The relationship between consumption and consumer expectations concerning future economic conditions tends to be a form of self-fulfilling prophecy. If consumers expect economic conditions to worsen, they will cut their consumption—and economic conditions will worsen! Political leaders often try to persuade people that economic prospects are good. In part, such efforts are an attempt to increase economic activity by boosting consumption.

Key Takeaways

- Consumption is closely related to disposable personal income and is represented by the consumption function, which can be presented in a table, in a graph, or in an equation.
- Personal saving is disposable personal income not spent on consumption.
- The marginal propensity to consume is $MPC = \Delta C/\Delta Y_d$ and the marginal propensity to save is $MPS = \Delta S/\Delta Y_d$. The sum of the MPC and MPS is 1.
- The current income hypothesis holds that consumption is a function of current disposable personal income, whereas the permanent income hypothesis holds that consumption is a function of permanent income, which is the income households expect to receive annually during their lifetime. The permanent income hypothesis predicts that a temporary change in income will have a smaller effect on consumption than is predicted by the current income hypothesis.
- Other factors that affect consumption include real wealth and expectations.

Try It!

For each of the following events, draw a curve representing the consumption function and show how the event would affect the curve.

1. A sharp increase in stock prices increases the real wealth of most households.
2. Consumers decide that a recession is ahead and that their incomes are likely to fall.
3. The price level falls.

Case in Point: Consumption and the Tax Rebate of 2001

Source: © Shutterstock, Inc.

The first round of the Bush tax cuts was passed in 2001. Democrats in Congress insisted on a rebate aimed at stimulating consumption. In the summer of 2001, rebates of $300 per single taxpayer and of $600 for married couples were distributed. The Department of Treasury reported that 92 million people received the rebates. While the rebates were intended to stimulate consumption, the extent to which the tax rebates stimulated consumption, especially during the recession, is an empirical question.

It is difficult to analyze the impact of a tax rebate that is a single event experienced by all households at the same time. If spending does change at that moment, is it because of the tax rebate or because of some other event that occurred at that time?

Fortunately for researchers Sumit Agarwal, Chunlin Liu, and Nicholas Souleles, using data from credit card accounts, the 2001 tax rebate checks were distributed over 10 successive weeks from July to September of 2001. The timing of receipt was random, since it was based on the next-to-last digit of one's Social Security number, and taxpayers were informed well in advance that the checks were coming. The researchers found that consumers initially saved much of their rebates, by paying down their credit card debts, but over a nine-month period, spending increased to about 40% of the rebate. They also found that consumers who were most liquidity constrained (for example, close to their credit card debt limits) spent more than consumers who were less constrained.

The researchers thus conclude that their findings do not support the permanent income hypothesis, since consumers responded to spending based on when they received their checks and because the results indicate that consumers do respond to what they call "lumpy" changes in income, such as those generated by a tax rebate. In other words, current income does seem to matter.

Two other studies of the 2001 tax rebate reached somewhat different conclusions. Using survey data, researchers Matthew D. Shapiro and Joel Slemrod estimated an *MPC* of about one-third. They note that this low increased spending is particularly surprising, since the rebate was part of a general tax cut that was expected to last a long time. At the other end, David S. Johnson, Jonathan A. Parker, and Nicholas S. Souleles, using yet another data set, found that looking over a six-month period, the *MPC* was about two-thirds. So, while there is disagreement on the size of the *MPC*, all conclude that the impact was non-negligible.

Sources: *Based on Sumit Agarwal, Chunlin Liu, and Nicholas S. Souleles, "The Reaction of Consumer Spending and Debt to Tax Rebates—Evidence from Consumer Credit Data," NBER Working Paper No. 13694, December 2007; David S. Johnson, Jonathan A. Parker, and Nicholas S. Souleles, "Household Expenditure and the Income Tax Rebates of 2001," American Economic Review 96, no. 5 (December 2006): 1589–1610; Matthew D. Shapiro and Joel Slemrod, "Consumer Response to Tax Rebates," American Economic Review 93, no. 1 (March 2003): 381–96; and Matthew D. Shapiro and Joel Slemrod, "Did the 2001 Rebate Stimulate Spending? Evidence from Taxpayer Surveys," NBER Tax Policy & the Economy 17, no. 1 (2003): 83–109.*

Answers to Try It! Problems

1. A sharp increase in stock prices makes people wealthier and shifts the consumption function upward, as in Panel (a) of Figure 28.4.

2. This would be reported as a reduction in consumer confidence. Consumers are likely to respond by reducing their purchases, particularly of durable items such as cars and washing machines. The consumption function will shift downward, as in Panel (b) of Figure 28.4.

3. A reduction in the price level increases real wealth and thus boosts consumption. The consumption function will shift upward, as in Panel (a) of Figure 28.4.

28.3 The Aggregate Expenditures Model

Learning Objectives

1. Explain and illustrate the aggregate expenditures model and the concept of equilibrium real GDP.

2. Distinguish between autonomous and induced aggregate expenditures and explain why a change in autonomous expenditures leads to a multiplied change in equilibrium real GDP.

3. Discuss how adding taxes, government purchases, and net exports to a simplified aggregate expenditures model affects the multiplier and hence the impact on real GDP that arises from an initial change in autonomous expenditures.

aggregate expenditures model

Model that relates aggregate expenditures to the level of real GDP.

aggregate expenditures

The sum of planned levels of consumption, investment, government purchases, and net exports at a given price level.

The consumption function relates the level of consumption in a period to the level of disposable personal income in that period. In this section, we incorporate other components of aggregate demand: investment, government purchases, and net exports. In doing so, we shall develop a new model of the determination of equilibrium real GDP, the **aggregate expenditures model**. This model relates **aggregate expenditures**, which equal the sum of planned levels of consumption, investment, government purchases, and net exports at a given price level, to the level of real GDP. We shall see that people, firms, and government agencies may not always spend what they had planned to spend. If so, then actual real GDP will not be the same as aggregate expenditures, and the economy will not be at the equilibrium level of real GDP.

One purpose of examining the aggregate expenditures model is to gain a deeper understanding of the "ripple effects" from a change in one or more components of aggregate demand. As we saw in the chapter that introduced the aggregate demand and aggregate supply model, a change in investment, government purchases, or net exports leads to greater production; this creates additional income for households, which induces additional consumption, leading to more production, more income, more consumption, and so on. The aggregate expenditures model provides a context within which this series of ripple effects can be better understood. A second reason for introducing the model is that we can use it to derive the aggregate demand curve for the model of aggregate demand and aggregate supply.

To see how the aggregate expenditures model works, we begin with a very simplified model in which there is neither a government sector nor a foreign sector. Then we use the findings based on this simplified model to build a more realistic model. The equations for the simplified economy are easier to work with, and we can readily apply the conclusions reached from analyzing a simplified economy to draw conclusions about a more realistic one.

The Aggregate Expenditures Model: A Simplified View

To develop a simple model, we assume that there are only two components of aggregate expenditures: consumption and investment. In the chapter on measuring total output and income, we learned that real gross domestic product and real gross domestic income are the same thing. With no government or foreign sector, gross domestic income in this economy and disposable personal income would be nearly the same. To simplify further, we will assume that depreciation and undistributed corporate profits (retained earnings) are zero. Thus, for this example, we assume that disposable personal income and real GDP are identical.

planned investment

The level of investment firms intend to make in a period.

unplanned investment

Investment during a period that firms did not intend to make.

Finally, we shall also assume that the only component of aggregate expenditures that may not be at the planned level is investment. Firms determine a level of investment they intend to make in each period. The level of investment firms intend to make in a period is called **planned investment**. Some investment is unplanned. Suppose, for example, that firms produce and expect to sell more goods during a period than they actually sell. The unsold goods will be added to the firms' inventories, and they will thus be counted as part of investment. **Unplanned investment** is investment during a period that firms did not intend to make. It is also possible that firms may sell more than they had expected. In this case, inventories will fall below what firms expected, in which case, unplanned investment would be negative. Investment during a period equals the sum of planned investment (I_P) and unplanned investment (I_U).

EQUATION 28.6

$$I = I_P + I_U$$

We shall find that planned and unplanned investment play key roles in the aggregate expenditures model.

Autonomous and Induced Aggregate Expenditures

Economists distinguish two types of expenditures. Expenditures that do not vary with the level of real GDP are called **autonomous aggregate expenditures**. In our example, we assume that planned investment expenditures are autonomous. Expenditures that vary with real GDP are called **induced aggregate expenditures**. Consumption spending that rises with real GDP is an example of an induced aggregate expenditure. Figure 28.5 illustrates the difference between autonomous and induced aggregate expenditures. With real GDP on the horizontal axis and aggregate expenditures on the vertical axis, autonomous aggregate expenditures are shown as a horizontal line in Panel (a). A curve showing induced aggregate expenditures has a slope greater than zero; the value of an induced aggregate expenditure changes with changes in real GDP. Panel (b) shows induced aggregate expenditures that are positively related to real GDP.

autonomous aggregate expenditures

Expenditures that do not vary with the level of real GDP.

induced aggregate expenditures

Expenditures that vary with real GDP.

FIGURE 28.5 Autonomous and Induced Aggregate Expenditures
Autonomous aggregate expenditures do not vary with the level of real GDP; induced aggregate expenditures do. Autonomous aggregate expenditures are shown by the horizontal line in Panel (a). Induced aggregate expenditures vary with real GDP, as in Panel (b).

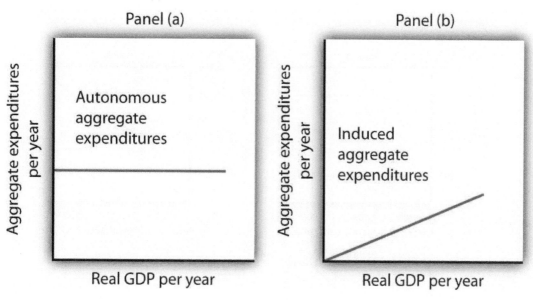

Autonomous and Induced Consumption

The concept of the marginal propensity to consume suggests that consumption contains induced aggregate expenditures; an increase in real GDP raises consumption. But consumption contains an autonomous component as well. The level of consumption at the intersection of the consumption function and the vertical axis is regarded as autonomous consumption; this level of spending would occur regardless of the level of real GDP.

Consider the consumption function we used in deriving the schedule and curve illustrated in Figure 28.2:

$$C = \$300 \text{ billion} + 0.8Y$$

We can omit the subscript on disposable personal income because of the simplifications we have made in this section, and the symbol Y can be thought of as representing both disposable personal income and GDP. Because we assume that the price level in the aggregate expenditures model is constant, GDP equals real GDP. At every level of real GDP, consumption includes $300 billion in autonomous aggregate expenditures. It will also contain expenditures "induced" by the level of real GDP. At a level of real GDP of $2,000 billion, for example, consumption equals $1,900 billion: $300 billion in autonomous aggregate expenditures and $1,600 billion in consumption induced by the $2,000 billion level of real GDP.

Figure 28.6 illustrates these two components of consumption. Autonomous consumption, C_a, which is always $300 billion, is shown in Panel (a); its equation is

EQUATION 28.7

$$C_a = \$300 \text{ billion}$$

Induced consumption C_i is shown in Panel (b); its equation is

EQUATION 28.8

$$C_i = 0.8Y$$

The consumption function is given by the sum of Equation 28.7 and Equation 28.8; it is shown in Panel (c) of Figure 28.6. It is the same as the equation $C = \$300$ billion + $0.8Y_d$, since in this simple example, Y and Y_d are the same.

FIGURE 28.6 Autonomous and Induced Consumption

Consumption has an autonomous component and an induced component. In Panel (a), autonomous consumption C_a equals $300 billion at every level of real GDP. Panel (b) shows induced consumption C_i. Total consumption C is shown in Panel (c).

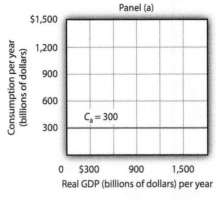

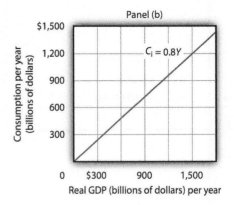

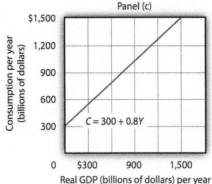

Plotting the Aggregate Expenditures Curve

In this simplified economy, investment is the only other component of aggregate expenditures. We shall assume that investment is autonomous and that firms plan to invest $1,100 billion per year.

EQUATION 28.9

$$I_P = \$1,100 \text{ billion}$$

The level of planned investment is unaffected by the level of real GDP.

Aggregate expenditures equal the sum of consumption C and planned investment I_P. The **aggregate expenditures function** is the relationship of aggregate expenditures to the value of real GDP. It can be represented with an equation, as a table, or as a curve.

aggregate expenditures function

The relationship of aggregate expenditures to the value of real GDP.

We begin with the definition of aggregate expenditures AE when there is no government or foreign sector:

EQUATION 28.10

$$AE = C + I_P$$

Substituting the information from above on consumption and planned investment yields (throughout this discussion all values are in billions of base-year dollars)

$$AE = \$300 + 0.8Y + \$1,100$$

or

EQUATION 28.11

$$AE = \$1,400 + 0.8Y$$

Equation 28.11 is the algebraic representation of the aggregate expenditures function. We shall use this equation to determine the equilibrium level of real GDP in the aggregate expenditures model. It is important to keep in mind that aggregate expenditures measure total planned spending at each level of real GDP (for any given price level). Real GDP is total production. Aggregate expenditures and real GDP need not be equal, and indeed will not be equal except when the economy is operating at its equilibrium level, as we will see in the next section.

In Equation 28.11, the autonomous component of aggregate expenditures is $1,400 billion, and the induced component is 0.8Y. We shall plot this aggregate expenditures function. To do so, we arbitrarily select various levels of real GDP and then use Equation 28.10 to compute aggregate expenditures at each level. At a level of real GDP of $6,000 billion, for example, aggregate expenditures equal $6,200 billion:

$$AE = \$1,400 + 0.8(\$6,000) = \$6,200$$

The table in Figure 28.7 shows the values of aggregate expenditures at various levels of real GDP. Based on these values, we plot the aggregate expenditures curve. To obtain each value for aggregate expenditures, we simply insert the corresponding value for real GDP into Equation 28.11. The value at which the aggregate expenditures curve intersects the vertical axis corresponds to the level of autonomous aggregate expenditures. In our example, autonomous aggregate expenditures equal $1,400 billion. That figure includes $1,100 billion in planned investment, which is assumed to be autonomous, and $300 billion in autonomous consumption expenditure.

FIGURE 28.7 Plotting the Aggregate Expenditures Curve

Values for aggregate expenditures *AE* are computed by inserting values for real GDP into Equation 28.10; these are given in the aggregate expenditures schedule. The point at which the aggregate expenditures curve intersects the vertical axis is the value of autonomous aggregate expenditures, here $1,400 billion. The slope of this aggregate expenditures curve is 0.8.

Point on curve	A	B	C	D	E	F
Y (billions)	$0	2,000	4,000	6,000	8,000	10,000
AE (billions)	$1,400	3,000	4,600	6,200	7,800	9,400

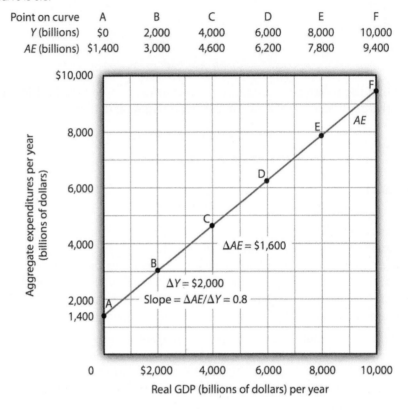

The Slope of the Aggregate Expenditures Curve

The slope of the aggregate expenditures curve, given by the change in aggregate expenditures divided by the change in real GDP between any two points, measures the additional expenditures induced by increases in real GDP. The slope for the aggregate expenditures curve in Figure 28.7 is shown for points B and C: it is 0.8.

In Figure 28.7, the slope of the aggregate expenditures curve equals the marginal propensity to consume. This is because we have assumed that the only other expenditure, planned investment, is autonomous and that real GDP and disposable personal income are identical. Changes in real GDP thus affect only consumption in this simplified economy.

Equilibrium in the Aggregate Expenditures Model

Real GDP is a measure of the total output of firms. Aggregate expenditures equal total planned spending on that output. Equilibrium in the model occurs where aggregate expenditures in some period equal real GDP in that period. One way to think about equilibrium is to recognize that firms, except for some inventory that they plan to hold, produce goods and services with the intention of selling them. Aggregate expenditures consist of what people, firms, and government agencies plan to spend. If the economy is at its equilibrium real GDP, then firms are selling what they plan to sell (that is, there are no unplanned changes in inventories).

Figure 28.8 illustrates the concept of equilibrium in the aggregate expenditures model. A 45-degree line connects all the points at which the values on the two axes, representing aggregate expenditures and real GDP, are equal. Equilibrium must occur at some point along this 45-degree line. The point at which the aggregate expenditures curve crosses the 45-degree line is the equilibrium real GDP, here achieved at a real GDP of $7,000 billion.

FIGURE 28.8 Determining Equilibrium in the Aggregate Expenditures Model

The 45-degree line shows all the points at which aggregate expenditures *AE* equal real GDP, as required for equilibrium. The equilibrium solution occurs where the *AE* curve crosses the 45-degree line, at a real GDP of $7,000 billion.

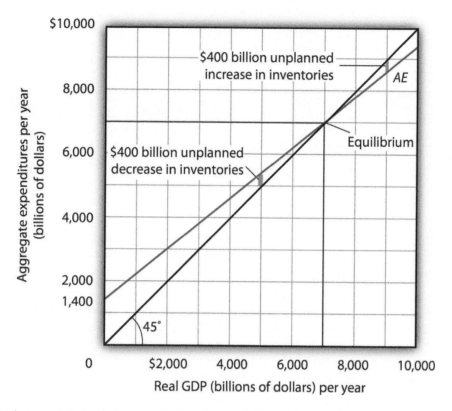

Equation 28.11 tells us that at a real GDP of $7,000 billion, the sum of consumption and planned investment is $7,000 billion—precisely the level of output firms produced. At that level of output, firms sell what they planned to sell and keep inventories that they planned to keep. A real GDP of $7,000 billion represents equilibrium in the sense that it generates an equal level of aggregate expenditures.

If firms were to produce a real GDP greater than $7,000 billion per year, aggregate expenditures would fall short of real GDP. At a level of real GDP of $9,000 billion per year, for example, aggregate expenditures equal $8,600 billion. Firms would be left with $400 billion worth of goods they intended to sell but did not. Their actual level of investment would be $400 billion greater than their planned level of investment. With those unsold goods on hand (that is, with an unplanned increase in inventories), firms would be likely to cut their output, moving the economy toward its equilibrium GDP of $7,000 billion. If firms were to produce $5,000 billion, aggregate expenditures would be $5,400 billion. Consumers and firms would demand more than was produced; firms would respond by reducing their inventories below the planned level (that is, there would be an unplanned decrease in inventories) and increasing their output in subsequent periods, again moving the economy toward its equilibrium real GDP of $7,000 billion. Figure 28.9 shows possible levels of real GDP in the economy for the aggregate expenditures function illustrated in Figure 28.8. It shows the level of aggregate expenditures at various levels of real GDP and the direction in which real GDP will change whenever *AE* does not equal real GDP. At any level of real GDP other than the equilibrium level, there is unplanned investment.

FIGURE 28.9 Adjusting to Equilibrium Real GDP

Each level of real GDP will result in a particular amount of aggregate expenditures. If aggregate expenditures are less than the level of real GDP, firms will reduce their output and real GDP will fall. If aggregate expenditures exceed real GDP, then firms will increase their output and real GDP will rise. If aggregate expenditures equal real GDP, then firms will leave their output unchanged; we have achieved equilibrium in the aggregate expenditures model. At equilibrium, there is no unplanned investment. Here, that occurs at a real GDP of $7,000 billion.

If real GDP is	Consumption expenditures will be	Planned investment will be	Aggregate expenditures will equal	Unplanned investment will be	Real GDP will
$9,000	$7,500	$1,100	$8,600	$400	Fall ↓
8,000	6,700	1,100	7,800	200	Fall ↓
7,000	5,900	1,100	7,000	0	Remain unchanged
6,000	5,100	1,100	6,200	−200	Rise ↑
5,000	4,300	1,100	5,400	−400	Rise ↑

Changes in Aggregate Expenditures: The Multiplier

In the aggregate expenditures model, equilibrium is found at the level of real GDP at which the aggregate expenditures curve crosses the 45-degree line. It follows that a shift in the curve will change equilibrium real GDP. Here we will examine the magnitude of such changes.

Figure 28.10 begins with the aggregate expenditures curve shown in Figure 28.8. Now suppose that planned investment increases from the original value of $1,100 billion to a new value of $1,400 billion—an increase of $300 billion. This increase in planned investment shifts the aggregate expenditures curve upward by $300 billion, all other things unchanged. Notice, however, that the new aggregate expenditures curve intersects the 45-degree line at a real GDP of $8,500 billion. The $300 billion increase in planned investment has produced an increase in equilibrium real GDP of $1,500 billion.

FIGURE 28.10 A Change in Autonomous Aggregate Expenditures Changes Equilibrium Real GDP

An increase of $300 billion in planned investment raises the aggregate expenditures curve by $300 billion. The $300 billion increase in planned investment results in an increase in equilibrium real GDP of $1,500 billion.

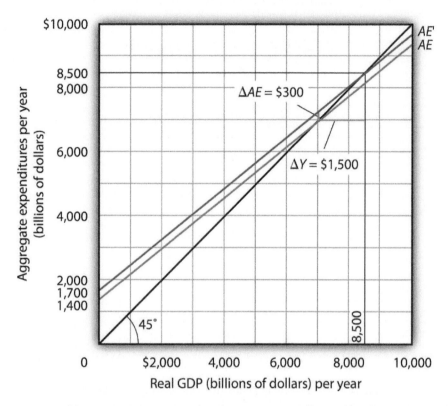

How could an increase in aggregate expenditures of $300 billion produce an increase in equilibrium real GDP of $1,500 billion? The answer lies in the operation of the multiplier. Because firms have increased their demand for investment goods (that is, for capital) by $300 billion, the firms that produce those goods will have $300 billion in additional orders. They will produce $300 billion in additional real GDP and, given our simplifying assumption, $300 billion in additional disposable personal income. But in this economy, each $1 of additional real GDP induces $0.80 in additional consumption. The $300 billion increase in autonomous aggregate expenditures initially induces $240 billion (= 0.8 × $300 billion) in additional consumption.

The $240 billion in additional consumption boosts production, creating another $240 billion in real GDP. But that second round of increase in real GDP induces $192 billion (= 0.8 × $240) in additional consumption, creating still more production, still more income, and still more consumption. Eventually (after many additional rounds of increases in induced consumption), the $300 billion increase in aggregate expenditures will result in a $1,500 billion increase in equilibrium real GDP. Table 28.1 shows the multiplied effect of a $300 billion increase in autonomous aggregate expenditures, assuming each $1 of additional real GDP induces $0.80 in additional consumption.

TABLE 28.1 The Multiplied Effect of an Increase in Autonomous Aggregate Expenditures

A $300 billion increase in autonomous aggregate expenditures initially increases real GDP and income by that amount. This is shown in the first round of spending. The increased income leads to additional consumption. The additional consumption boosts production and thus leads to even higher real GDP and income. Assuming each $1 of additional real GDP induces $0.80 in additional consumption, the multiplied effect of a $300 billion increase in autonomous aggregate expenditures leads to additional rounds of spending such that, in this example, real GDP rises by $1,500 billion.

Round of spending	Increase in real GDP (billions of dollars)
1	$300
2	240
3	192
4	154
5	123
6	98
7	79
8	63
9	50
10	40
11	32
12	26
Subsequent rounds	+103
Total increase in real GDP	$1,500

The size of the additional rounds of expenditure is based on the slope of the aggregate expenditures function, which in this example is simply the marginal propensity to consume. Had the slope been flatter (if the marginal propensity to consume were smaller), the additional rounds of spending would have been smaller. A steeper slope would mean that the additional rounds of spending would have been larger.

This process could also work in reverse. That is, a decrease in planned investment would lead to a multiplied decrease in real GDP. A reduction in planned investment would reduce the incomes of some households. They would reduce their consumption by the *MPC* times the reduction in their income. That, in turn, would reduce incomes for households that would have received the spending by the first group of households. The process continues, thus multiplying the impact of the reduction in aggregate expenditures resulting from the reduction in planned investment.

Computation of the Multiplier

In the context of an aggregate demand curve shift, the multiplier is the number by which we multiply an initial change in aggregate demand to get the full amount of the shift in the aggregate demand curve. Because the multiplier shows the amount by which the aggregate demand curve shifts at a given price level, and the aggregate expenditures model assumes a given price level, we can also use the aggregate expenditures model to derive the multiplier explicitly.

Let Y_{eq} be the equilibrium level of real GDP in the aggregate expenditures model, and let A be autonomous aggregate expenditures. Then the multiplier is

EQUATION 28.12

$$\text{Multiplier} = \frac{\Delta Y_{eq}}{\Delta \bar{A}}$$

In the example we have just discussed, a change in autonomous aggregate expenditures of $300 billion produced a change in equilibrium real GDP of $1,500 billion. The value of the multiplier is therefore $1,500/$300 = 5.

The multiplier effect works because a change in autonomous aggregate expenditures causes a change in real GDP and disposable personal income, inducing a further change in the level of aggregate expenditures, which creates still more GDP and thus an even higher level of aggregate expenditures. The degree to which a given change in real GDP induces a change in aggregate expenditures is given in this simplified economy by the marginal propensity to consume, which, in this case, is the slope of the aggregate expenditures curve. The slope of the aggregate expenditures curve is thus linked to the size of the multiplier. We turn now to an investigation of the relationship between the marginal propensity to consume and the multiplier.

The Marginal Propensity to Consume and the Multiplier

We can compute the multiplier for this simplified economy from the marginal propensity to consume. We know that the amount by which equilibrium real GDP will change as a result of a change in aggregate expenditures consists of two parts: the change in autonomous aggregate expenditures itself, $\Delta \bar{A}$, and the induced change in spending. This induced change equals the marginal propensity to consume times the change in equilibrium real GDP, ΔY_{eq}. Thus

EQUATION 28.13

$$\Delta Y_{eq} = \Delta \bar{A} + MPC \, \Delta Y_{eq}$$

Subtract the $MPC\Delta Y_{eq}$ term from both sides of the equation:

$$\Delta Y_{eq} - MPC \, \Delta Y_{eq} = \Delta \bar{A}$$

Factor out the ΔY_{eq} term on the left:

$$\Delta Y_{eq}(1 - MPC) = \Delta \bar{A}$$

Finally, solve for the multiplier $\Delta Y_{eq} \, \big/ \, \Delta \bar{A}$ by dividing both sides of the equation above by ΔA and by dividing both sides by $(1 - MPC)$. We get the following:

EQUATION 28.14

$$\frac{\Delta Y_{eq}}{\Delta \bar{A}} = \frac{1}{1 - MPC}$$

We thus compute the multiplier by taking 1 minus the marginal propensity to consume, then dividing the result into 1. In our example, the marginal propensity to consume is 0.8; the multiplier is 5, as we have already seen [multiplier = 1/(1 − MPC) = 1/(1 − 0.8) = 1/0.2 = 5]. Since the sum of the marginal propensity to consume and the marginal propensity to save is 1, the denominator on the right-hand side of Equation 28.13 is equivalent to the MPS, and the multiplier could also be expressed as 1/MPS.

EQUATION 28.15

$$Multiplier = \frac{1}{MPS}$$

We can rearrange terms in Equation 28.14 to use the multiplier to compute the impact of a change in autonomous aggregate expenditures. We simply multiply both sides of the equation by $\bar{A}$ to obtain the following:

EQUATION 28.16

$$\Delta Y_{eq} = \frac{\Delta \bar{A}}{1 - MPC}$$

The change in the equilibrium level of income in the aggregate expenditures model (remember that the model assumes a constant price level) equals the change in autonomous aggregate expenditures times the multiplier. Thus, the greater the multiplier, the greater will be the impact on income of a change in autonomous aggregate expenditures.

The Aggregate Expenditures Model in a More Realistic Economy

Four conclusions emerge from our application of the aggregate expenditures model to the simplified economy presented so far. These conclusions can be applied to a more realistic view of the economy.

1. The aggregate expenditures function relates aggregate expenditures to real GDP. The intercept of the aggregate expenditures curve shows the level of autonomous aggregate expenditures. The slope of the aggregate expenditures curve shows how much increases in real GDP induce additional aggregate expenditures.
2. Equilibrium real GDP occurs where aggregate expenditures equal real GDP.
3. A change in autonomous aggregate expenditures changes equilibrium real GDP by a multiple of the change in autonomous aggregate expenditures.
4. The size of the multiplier depends on the slope of the aggregate expenditures curve. The steeper the aggregate expenditures curve, the larger the multiplier; the flatter the aggregate expenditures curve, the smaller the multiplier.

These four points still hold as we add the two other components of aggregate expenditures—government purchases and net exports—and recognize that government not only spends but also collects taxes. We look first at the effect of adding taxes to the aggregate expenditures model and then at the effect of adding government purchases and net exports.

Taxes and the Aggregate Expenditure Function

Suppose that the only difference between real GDP and disposable personal income is personal income taxes. Let us see what happens to the slope of the aggregate expenditures function.

As before, we assume that the marginal propensity to consume is 0.8, but we now add the assumption that income taxes take ¼ of real GDP. This means that for every additional $1 of real GDP, disposable personal income rises by $0.75 and, in turn, consumption rises by $0.60 (= 0.8 × $0.75). In the simplified model in which disposable personal income and real GDP were the same, an additional $1 of real GDP raised consumption by $0.80. The slope of the aggregate expenditures curve was 0.8, the marginal propensity to consume. Now, as a result of taxes, the aggregate expenditures curve will be flatter than the one shown in Figure 28.7 and Figure 28.9. In this example, the slope will be 0.6; an additional $1 of real GDP will increase consumption by $0.60.

Other things the same, the multiplier will be smaller than it was in the simplified economy in which disposable personal income and real GDP were identical. The wedge between disposable personal income and real GDP created by taxes means that the additional rounds of spending induced by a change in autonomous aggregate expenditures will be smaller than if there were no taxes. Hence, the multiplied effect of any change in autonomous aggregate expenditures is smaller.

The Addition of Government Purchases and Net Exports

Suppose that government purchases and net exports are autonomous. If so, they enter the aggregate expenditures function in the same way that investment did. Compared to the simplified aggregate expenditures model, the aggregate expenditures curve shifts up by the amount of government purchases and net exports.[3]

Figure 28.11 shows the difference between the aggregate expenditures model of the simplified economy in Figure 28.8 and a more realistic view of the economy. Panel (a) shows an AE curve for an economy with only consumption and investment expenditures. In Panel (b), the AE curve includes all four components of aggregate expenditures.

FIGURE 28.11 The Aggregate Expenditures Function: Comparison of a Simplified Economy and a More Realistic Economy

Panel (a) shows an aggregate expenditures curve for a simplified view of the economy; Panel (b) shows an aggregate expenditures curve for a more realistic model. The AE curve in Panel (b) has a higher intercept than the AE curve in Panel (a) because of the additional components of autonomous aggregate expenditures in a more realistic view of the economy. The slope of the AE curve in Panel (b) is flatter than the slope of the AE curve in Panel (a). In a simplified economy, the slope of the AE curve is the marginal propensity to consume (MPC). In a more realistic view of the economy, it is less than the MPC because of the difference between real GDP and disposable personal income.

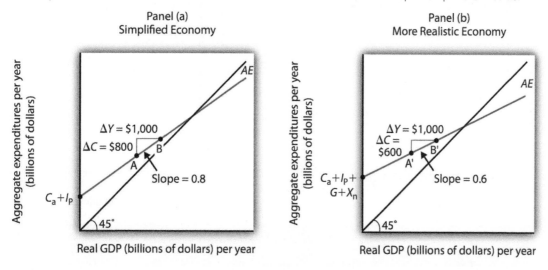

There are two major differences between the aggregate expenditures curves shown in the two panels. Notice first that the intercept of the AE curve in Panel (b) is higher than that of the AE curve in Panel (a). The reason is that, in addition to the autonomous part of consumption and planned investment, there are two other components of aggregate expenditures—government purchases and net exports—that we have also assumed are autonomous. Thus, the intercept of the aggregate expenditures curve in Panel (b) is the sum of the four autonomous aggregate expenditures components: consumption (C_a), planned investment (I_P), government purchases (G), and net exports (X_n). In Panel (a), the intercept includes only the first two components.

Second, notice that the slope of the aggregate expenditures curve is flatter for the more realistic economy in Panel (b) than it is for the simplified economy in Panel (a). This can be seen by comparing the slope of the aggregate expenditures curve between points A and B in Panel (a) to the slope of the aggregate expenditures curve between points A′ and B′ in Panel (b). Between both sets of points, real GDP changes by the same amount, $1,000 billion. In Panel (a), consumption rises by $800 billion, whereas in Panel (b) consumption rises by only $600 billion. This difference occurs because, in the more realistic view of the economy, households have only a fraction of real GDP available as disposable personal income. Thus, for a given change in real GDP, consumption rises by a smaller amount.

Let us examine what happens to equilibrium real GDP in each case if there is a shift in autonomous aggregate expenditures, such as an increase in planned investment, as shown in Figure 28.12. In both panels, the initial level of equilibrium real GDP is the same, Y_1. Equilibrium real GDP occurs where the given aggregate expenditures curve intersects the 45-degree line. The aggregate expenditures curve shifts up by the same amount—ΔA is the same in both panels. The new level of equilibrium real GDP occurs where the new AE curve intersects the 45-degree line. In Panel (a), we see that the new level of equilibrium real GDP rises to Y_2, but in Panel (b) it rises only to Y_3. Since the same change in autonomous aggregate expenditures led to a greater increase in equilibrium real GDP in Panel (a) than in Panel (b), the multiplier for the more realistic model of the economy must be smaller. The multiplier is smaller, of course, because the slope of the aggregate expenditures curve is flatter.

FIGURE 28.12 A Change in Autonomous Aggregate Expenditures: Comparison of a Simplified Economy and a More Realistic Economy

In Panels (a) and (b), equilibrium real GDP is initially Y_1. Then autonomous aggregate expenditures rise by the same amount, ΔI_P. In Panel (a), the upward shift in the AE curve leads to a new level of equilibrium real GDP of Y_2; in Panel (b) equilibrium real GDP rises to Y_3. Because equilibrium real GDP rises by more in Panel (a) than in Panel (b), the multiplier in the simplified economy is greater than in the more realistic one.

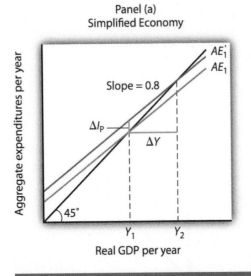
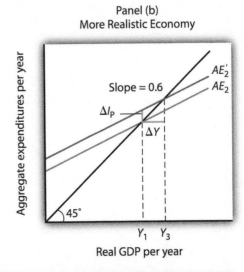

Key Takeaways

- The aggregate expenditures model relates aggregate expenditures to real GDP. Equilibrium in the model occurs where aggregate expenditures equal real GDP and is found graphically at the intersection of the aggregate expenditures curve and the 45-degree line.

- Economists distinguish between autonomous and induced aggregate expenditures. The former do not vary with GDP; the latter do.

- Equilibrium in the aggregate expenditures model implies that unintended investment equals zero.

- A change in autonomous aggregate expenditures leads to a change in equilibrium real GDP, which is a multiple of the change in autonomous aggregate expenditures.

- The size of the multiplier depends on the slope of the aggregate expenditures curve. In general, the steeper the aggregate expenditures curve, the greater the multiplier. The flatter the aggregate expenditures curve, the smaller the multiplier.

- Income taxes tend to flatten the aggregate expenditures curve.

Try It!

Suppose you are given the following data for an economy. All data are in billions of dollars. Y is actual real GDP, and C, I_P, G, and X_n are the consumption, planned investment, government purchases, and net exports components of aggregate expenditures, respectively.

Y	C	I_p	G	X_n
$0	$800	$1,000	$1,400	–$200
2,500	2,300	1,000	1,400	–200
5,000	3,800	1,000	1,400	–200
7,500	5,300	1,000	1,400	–200
10,000	6,800	1,000	1,400	–200

1. Plot the corresponding aggregate expenditures curve and draw in the 45-degree line.
2. What is the intercept of the AE curve? What is its slope?
3. Determine the equilibrium level of real GDP.
4. Now suppose that net exports fall by $1,000 billion and that this is the only change in autonomous aggregate expenditures. Plot the new aggregate expenditures curve. What is the new equilibrium level of real GDP?
5. What is the value of the multiplier?

Case in Point: Fiscal Policy in the Kennedy Administration

Walter Heller, Chief Economic Advisor to President John F. Kennedy

Source: Robert L. Knudsen [Public domain], via Wikimedia Commons

It was the first time expansionary fiscal policy had ever been proposed. The economy had slipped into a recession in 1960. Presidential candidate John Kennedy received proposals from several economists that year for a tax cut aimed at stimulating the economy. As a candidate, he was unconvinced. But, as president he proposed the tax cut in 1962. His chief economic adviser, Walter Heller, defended the tax cut idea before Congress and introduced what was politically a novel concept: the multiplier.

In testimony to the Senate Subcommittee on Employment and Manpower, Mr. Heller predicted that a $10 billion cut in personal income taxes would boost consumption "by over $9 billion."

To assess the ultimate impact of the tax cut, Mr. Heller applied the aggregate expenditures model. He rounded the increased consumption off to $9 billion and explained,

> *"This is far from the end of the matter. The higher production of consumer goods to meet this extra spending would mean extra employment, higher payrolls, higher profits, and higher farm and professional and service incomes. This added purchasing power would generate still further increases in spending and incomes. ... The initial rise of $9 billion, plus this extra consumption spending and extra output of consumer goods, would add over $18 billion to our annual GDP."*

We can summarize this continuing process by saying that a "multiplier" of approximately 2 has been applied to the direct increment of consumption spending.

Mr. Heller also predicted that proposed cuts in corporate income tax rates would increase investment by about $6 billion. The total change in autonomous aggregate expenditures would thus be $15 billion: $9 billion in consumption and $6 billion in investment. He predicted that the total increase in equilibrium GDP would be $30 billion, the amount the Council of Economic Advisers had estimated would be necessary to reach full employment.

In the end, the tax cut was not passed until 1964, after President Kennedy's assassination in 1963. While the Council of Economic Advisers concluded that the tax cut had worked as advertised, it came long after the economy had recovered and tended to push the economy into an inflationary gap. As we will see in later chapters, the tax cut helped push the economy into a period of rising inflation.

Source: *Based on Economic Report of the President 1964 (Washington, DC: U.S. Government Printing Office, 1964), 172–73.*

Answers to Try It! Problems

1. The aggregate expenditures curve is plotted in the accompanying chart as AE_1.

2. The intercept of the AE_1 curve is $3,000. It is the amount of aggregate expenditures ($C + I_P + G + X_n$) when real GDP is zero. The slope of the AE_1 curve is 0.6. It can be found by determining the amount of aggregate expenditures for any two levels of real GDP and then by dividing the change in aggregate expenditures by the change in real GDP over the interval. For example, between real GDP of $2,500 and $5,000, aggregate expenditures go from $4,500 to $6,000. Thus,

$$\frac{\Delta AE_1}{\Delta Y} = \frac{\$6,000 - \$4,500}{\$5,000 - \$2,500} = \frac{\$1,500}{\$2,500} = 0.6$$

3. The equilibrium level of real GDP is $7,500. It can be found by determining the intersection of AE_1 and the 45-degree line. At $Y = \$7,500$, $AE_1 = \$5,300 + 1,000 + 1,400 - 200 = \$7,500$.

4. A reduction of net exports of $1,000 shifts the aggregate expenditures curve down by $1,000 to AE_2. The equilibrium real GDP falls from $7,500 to $5,000. The new aggregate expenditures curve, AE_2, intersects the 45-degree line at real GDP of $5,000.

5. The multiplier is 2.5 [= (−$2,500)/(−$1,000)].

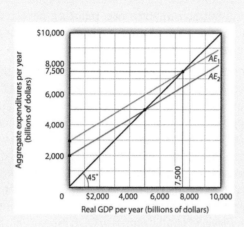

28.4 Aggregate Expenditures and Aggregate Demand

Learning Objectives

1. Explain and illustrate how a change in the price level affects the aggregate expenditures curve.
2. Explain and illustrate how to derive an aggregate demand curve from the aggregate expenditures curve for different price levels.
3. Explain and illustrate how an increase or decrease in autonomous aggregate expenditures affects the aggregate demand curve.

We can use the aggregate expenditures model to gain greater insight into the aggregate demand curve. In this section we shall see how to derive the aggregate demand curve from the aggregate expenditures model. We shall also see how to apply the analysis of multiplier effects in the aggregate expenditures model to the aggregate demand–aggregate supply model.

Aggregate Expenditures Curves and Price Levels

An aggregate expenditures curve assumes a fixed price level. If the price level were to change, the levels of consumption, investment, and net exports would all change, producing a new aggregate expenditures curve and a new equilibrium solution in the aggregate expenditures model.

A change in the price level changes people's real wealth. Suppose, for example, that your wealth includes $10,000 in a bond account. An increase in the price level would reduce the real value of this money, reduce your real wealth, and thus reduce your consumption. Similarly, a reduction in the price level would increase the real value of money holdings and thus increase real wealth and consumption. The tendency for price level changes to change real wealth and consumption is called the **wealth effect**.

Because changes in the price level also affect the real quantity of money, we can expect a change in the price level to change the interest rate. A reduction in the price level will increase the real quantity of money and thus lower the interest rate. A lower interest rate, all other things unchanged, will increase the level of investment. Similarly, a higher price level reduces the real quantity of money, raises interest rates, and reduces investment. This is called the **interest rate effect**.

wealth effect

The tendency for price level changes to change real wealth and consumption.

interest rate effect

The tendency for a higher price level to reduce the real quantity of money, raise interest rates, and reduce investment.

international trade effect

The impact of different price levels on the level of net exports.

Finally, a change in the domestic price level will affect exports and imports. A higher price level makes a country's exports fall and imports rise, reducing net exports. A lower price level will increase exports and reduce imports, increasing net exports. This impact of different price levels on the level of net exports is called the **international trade effect**.

Panel (a) of Figure 28.13 shows three possible aggregate expenditures curves for three different price levels. For example, the aggregate expenditures curve labeled $AE_{P=1.0}$ is the aggregate expenditures curve for an economy with a price level of 1.0. Since that aggregate expenditures curve crosses the 45-degree line at $6,000 billion, equilibrium real GDP is $6,000 billion at that price level. At a lower price level, aggregate expenditures would rise because of the wealth effect, the interest rate effect, and the international trade effect. Assume that at every level of real GDP, a reduction in the price level to 0.5 would boost aggregate expenditures by $2,000 billion to $AE_{P=0.5}$, and an increase in the price level from 1.0 to 1.5 would reduce aggregate expenditures by $2,000 billion. The aggregate expenditures curve for a price level of 1.5 is shown as $AE_{P=1.5}$. There is a different aggregate expenditures curve, and a different level of equilibrium real GDP, for each of these three price levels. A price level of 1.5 produces equilibrium at point A, a price level of 1.0 does so at point B, and a price level of 0.5 does so at point C. More generally, there will be a different level of equilibrium real GDP for every price level; the higher the price level, the lower the equilibrium value of real GDP.

FIGURE 28.13 From Aggregate Expenditures to Aggregate Demand
Because there is a different aggregate expenditures curve for each price level, there is a different equilibrium real GDP for each price level. Panel (a) shows aggregate expenditures curves for three different price levels. Panel (b) shows that the aggregate demand curve, which shows the quantity of goods and services demanded at each price level, can thus be derived from the aggregate expenditures model. The aggregate expenditures curve for a price level of 1.0, for example, intersects the 45-degree line in Panel (a) at point B, producing an equilibrium real GDP of $6,000 billion. We can thus plot point B′ on the aggregate demand curve in Panel (b), which shows that at a price level of 1.0, a real GDP of $6,000 billion is demanded.

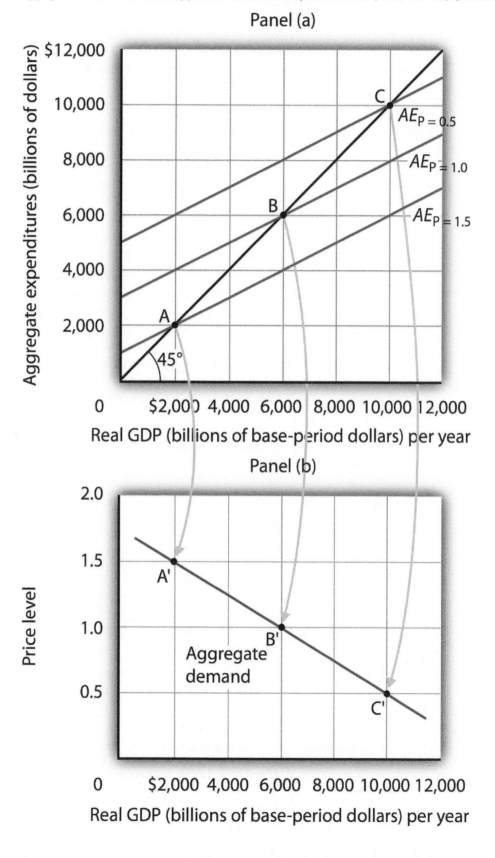

Panel (b) of Figure 28.13 shows how an aggregate demand curve can be derived from the aggregate expenditures curves for different price levels. The equilibrium real GDP associated with each price level in the aggregate expenditures model is plotted as a point showing the price level and the quantity of goods and services demanded (measured as real GDP). At a price level of 1.0, for example, the equilibrium level of real GDP in the aggregate expenditures model in Panel (a) is $6,000 billion at point B. That means $6,000 billion worth of goods and services is demanded; point B' on the aggregate demand curve in Panel (b) corresponds to a real GDP demanded of $6,000 billion and a price level of 1.0. At a price level of 0.5 the equilibrium GDP demanded is $10,000 billion at point C', and at a price level of 1.5 the equilibrium real GDP demanded is $2,000 billion at point A'. The aggregate demand curve thus shows the equilibrium real GDP from the aggregate expenditures model at each price level.

The Multiplier and Changes in Aggregate Demand

In the aggregate expenditures model, a change in autonomous aggregate expenditures changes equilibrium real GDP by the multiplier times the change in autonomous aggregate expenditures. That model, however, assumes a constant price level. How can we incorporate the concept of the multiplier into the model of aggregate demand and aggregate supply?

Consider the aggregate expenditures curves given in Panel (a) of Figure 28.14, each of which corresponds to a particular price level. Suppose net exports rise by $1,000 billion. Such a change increases aggregate expenditures at each price level by $1,000 billion.

A $1,000-billion increase in net exports shifts each of the aggregate expenditures curves up by $1,000 billion, to $AE'_{P=1.0}$ and $AE'_{P=1.5}$. That changes the equilibrium real GDP associated with each price level; it thus shifts the aggregate demand curve to AD_2 in Panel (b). In the aggregate expenditures model, equilibrium real GDP changes by an amount equal to the initial change in autonomous aggregate expenditures times the multiplier, so the aggregate demand curve shifts by the same amount. In this example, we assume the multiplier is 2. The aggregate demand curve thus shifts to the right by $2,000 billion, two times the $1,000-billion change in autonomous aggregate expenditures.

FIGURE 28.14 Changes in Aggregate Demand

The aggregate expenditures curves for price levels of 1.0 and 1.5 are the same as in Figure 28.13, as is the aggregate demand curve. Now suppose a $1,000-billion increase in net exports shifts each of the aggregate expenditures curves up; $AE_{P=1.0}$, for example, rises to $AE'_{P=1.0}$. The aggregate demand curve thus shifts to the right by $2,000 billion, the change in aggregate expenditures times the multiplier, assumed to be 2 in this example.

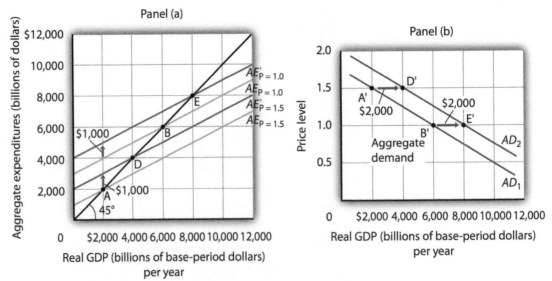

In general, any change in autonomous aggregate expenditures shifts the aggregate demand curve. The amount of the shift is always equal to the change in autonomous aggregate expenditures times the multiplier. An increase in autonomous aggregate expenditures shifts the aggregate demand curve to the right; a reduction shifts it to the left.

Key Takeaways

- There will be a different aggregate expenditures curve for each price level.
- Aggregate expenditures will vary with the price level because of the wealth effect, the interest rate effect, and the international trade effect. The higher the price level, the lower the aggregate expenditures curve and the lower the equilibrium level of real GDP. The lower the price level, the higher the aggregate expenditures curve and the higher the equilibrium level of real GDP.
- A change in autonomous aggregate expenditures shifts the aggregate expenditures curve for each price level. That shifts the aggregate demand curve by an amount equal to the change in autonomous aggregate expenditures times the multiplier.

Try It!

Sketch three aggregate expenditures curves for price levels of P_1, P_2, and P_3, where P_1 is the lowest price level and P_3 the highest (you do not have numbers for this exercise; simply sketch curves of the appropriate shape). Label the equilibrium levels of real GDP Y_1, Y_2, and Y_3. Now draw the aggregate demand curve implied by your analysis, labeling points that correspond to P_1, P_2, and P_3 and Y_1, Y_2, and Y_3. You can use Figure 28.13 as a model for your work.

Case in Point: Predicting the Impact of Alternative Fiscal Policies

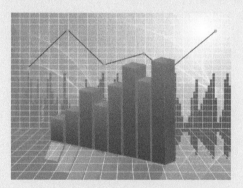

Source: © Shutterstock, Inc.

Using a large-scale model of the U.S. economy to simulate the effects of government policies, Princeton University professor Alan Blinder and Moody Analytics chief economist Mark Zandi concluded that the expansionary fiscal, monetary, and other policies aimed at relieving the financial crisis (such as the Troubled Asset Relief Program, or TARP) worked together from 2008 onward to effectively combat the Great Recession and probably kept it from turning into the Great Depression 2.0. Specifically, they estimated that U.S. GDP would have fallen about 12% peak-to-trough and that the unemployment rate would have hit 16.5% without these policies, instead of GDP declining about 4% and the unemployment rate reaching about 10%. While they attribute the bulk of the improvement to monetary and other financial policies, they found that fiscal policies also played a substantial role. For example, they concluded that fiscal stimulus added more than 3% to real GDP in 2010.

How much did the different components of the fiscal policies contribute? The following table provides estimates for the multiplied effects of various stimulus measures that were considered. In general, they estimate a stronger "bang for the buck," or multiplier, from spending increases than from tax cuts.

Tax cuts	Bang for the buck
Nonrefundable lump-sum tax rebate	1.01
Refundable lump-sum tax rebate	1.22
Temporary tax cuts	
Payroll tax holiday	1.24
Across-the-board tax cut	1.02
Accelerated depreciation	0.25
Permanent tax cuts	
Extend alternative minimum tax patch	0.51
Make Bush income tax cuts permanent	0.32
Make dividend and capital gains tax cuts permanent	0.32
Spending increases	
Extending UI benefits	1.61
Temporary increase in food stamps	1.74
General aid to state governments	1.41
Increased infrastructure spending	1.57

While Blinder and Zandy acknowledge that no one can know for sure what would have happened without the policy responses and that not all aspects of the programs were perfectly designed or implemented, they feel strongly that the aggressive policies were, overall, appropriate and worth taking.

Source: *Based on Alan S. Blinder and Mark Zandi, "How the Great Recession Was Brought to an End," Moody's Economy.com, July 27, 2010.*

Answer to Try It! Problem

The lowest price level, P_1, corresponds to the highest AE curve, $AE_{P} = P_1$, as shown. This suggests a downward-sloping aggregate demand curve. Points A, B, and C on the AE curve correspond to points A′, B′, and C′ on the AD curve, respectively.

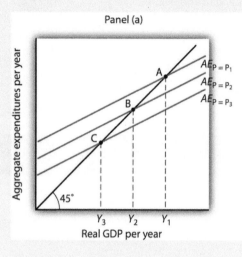

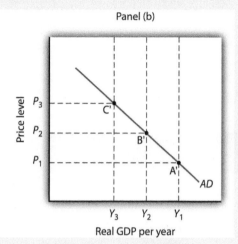

28.5 Review and Practice

Summary

This chapter presented the aggregate expenditures model. Aggregate expenditures are the sum of planned levels of consumption, investment, government purchases, and net exports at a given price level. The aggregate expenditures model relates aggregate expenditures to the level of real GDP.

We began by observing the close relationship between consumption and disposable personal income. A consumption function shows this relationship. The saving function can be derived from the consumption function.

The time period over which income is considered to be a determinant of consumption is important. The current income hypothesis holds that consumption in one period is a function of income in that same period. The permanent income hypothesis holds that consumption in a period is a function of permanent income. An important implication of the permanent income hypothesis is that the marginal propensity to consume will be smaller for temporary than for permanent changes in disposable personal income.

Changes in real wealth and consumer expectations can affect the consumption function. Such changes shift the curve relating consumption to disposable personal income, the graphical representation of the consumption function; changes in disposable personal income do not shift the curve but cause movements along it.

An aggregate expenditures curve shows total planned expenditures at each level of real GDP. This curve is used in the aggregate expenditures model to determine the equilibrium real GDP (at a given price level). A change in autonomous aggregate expenditures produces a multiplier effect that leads to a larger change in equilibrium real GDP. In a simplified economy, with only consumption and investment expenditures, in which the slope of the aggregate expenditures curve is the marginal propensity to consume (MPC), the multiplier is equal to $1/(1 - MPC)$. Because the sum of the marginal propensity to consume and the marginal propensity to save (MPS) is 1, the multiplier in this simplified model is also equal to $1/MPS$.

Finally, we derived the aggregate demand curve from the aggregate expenditures model. Each point on the aggregate demand curve corresponds to the equilibrium level of real GDP as derived in the aggregate expenditures model for each price level. The downward slope of the aggregate demand curve (and the shifting of the aggregate expenditures curve at each price level) reflects the wealth effect, the interest rate effect, and the international trade effect. A change in autonomous aggregate expenditures shifts the aggregate demand curve by an amount equal to the change in autonomous aggregate expenditures times the multiplier.

In a more realistic aggregate expenditures model that includes all four components of aggregate expenditures (consumption, investment, government purchases, and net exports), the slope of the aggregate expenditures curve shows the additional aggregate expenditures induced by increases in real GDP, and the size of the multiplier depends on the slope of the aggregate expenditures curve. The steeper the aggregate expenditures curve, the larger the multiplier; the flatter the aggregate expenditures curve, the smaller the multiplier.

Concept Problems

1. Explain the difference between autonomous and induced expenditures. Give examples of each.

2. The consumption function we studied in the chapter predicted that consumption would sometimes exceed disposable personal income. How could this be?

3. The consumption function can be represented as a table, as an equation, or as a curve. Distinguish among these three representations.

4. The introduction to this chapter described the behavior of consumer spending at the end of 2008. Explain this phenomenon in terms of the analysis presented in this chapter.

5. Explain the role played by the 45-degree line in the aggregate expenditures model.

6. Your college or university, if it does what many others do, occasionally releases a news story claiming that its impact on the total employment in the local economy is understated by its own employment statistics. If the institution keeps accurate statistics, is that possible?

7. Suppose the level of investment in a certain economy changes when the level of real GDP changes; an increase in real GDP induces an increase in investment, while a reduction in real GDP causes investment to fall. How do you think such behavior would affect the slope of the aggregate expenditures curve? The multiplier?

8. Give an intuitive explanation for how the multiplier works on a reduction in autonomous aggregate expenditures. Why does equilibrium real GDP fall by more than the change in autonomous aggregate expenditures?

9. Explain why the marginal propensity to consume out of a temporary tax rebate would be lower than that for a permanent rebate.

10. Pretend you are a member of the Council of Economic Advisers and are trying to persuade the members of the House Appropriations Committee to purchase $100 billion worth of new materials, in part to stimulate the economy. Explain to the members how the multiplier process will work.

Numerical Problems

1. Suppose the following information describes a simple economy. Figures are in billion of dollars.

Disposable personal income	Consumption
0	100
100	120
200	140
300	160

   a. What is the marginal propensity to consume?

   b. What is the marginal propensity to save?

   c. Write an equation that describes consumption.

   d. Write an equation that describes saving.

2. The graph below shows a consumption function.

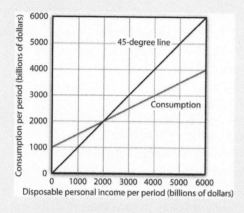

   a. When disposable personal income is equal to zero, how much is consumption?

   b. When disposable personal income is equal to $4,000 billion, how much is consumption?

   c. At what level of personal disposable income are consumption and disposable personal income equal?

   d. How much is personal saving when consumption is $2,500 billion?

   e. How much is personal saving when consumption is $5,000 billion?

   f. What is the marginal propensity to consume?

   g. What is the marginal propensity to save?

   h. Draw the saving function implied by the consumption function above.

3. For the purpose of this exercise, assume that the consumption function is given by $C = \$500$ billion $+ 0.8Y_d$. Construct a consumption and saving table showing how income is divided between consumption and personal saving when disposable personal income (in billions) is $0, $500, $1,000, $1,500, $2,000, $2,500, $3,000, and $3,500.

   a. Graph your results, placing disposable personal income on the horizontal axis and consumption on the vertical axis.

   b. What is the value of the marginal propensity to consume?

   c. What is the value of the marginal propensity to save?

4. The graph below characterizes a simple economy with only two components of aggregate expenditures, consumption and investment.

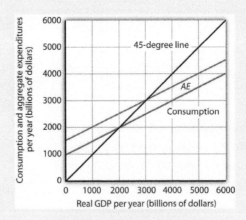

a. How much is planned investment? How do you know?

b. Is planned investment autonomous or induced? How do you know?

c. How much is autonomous aggregate expenditures?

d. What is the value of equilibrium real GDP?

e. If real GDP were $2,000 billion, how much would unplanned investment be? How would you expect firms to respond?

f. If real GDP were $4,000 billion, how much would unplanned investment be? How would you expect firms to respond?

g. Write an equation for aggregate expenditures based on the graph above.

h. What is the value of the multiplier in this example?

5. Explain and illustrate graphically how each of the following events affects aggregate expenditures and equilibrium real GDP. In each case, state the nature of the change in aggregate expenditures, and state the relationship between the change in *AE* and the change in equilibrium real GDP.

a. Investment falls.

b. Government purchases go up.

c. The government sends $1,000 to every person in the United States.

d. Real GDP rises by $500 billion.

6. Mary Smith, whose marginal propensity to consume is 0.75, is faced with an unexpected increase in taxes of $1,000. Will she cut back her consumption expenditures by the full $1,000? How will she pay for the higher tax? Explain.

7. The equations below give consumption functions for economies in which planned investment is autonomous and is the only other component of GDP. Compute the marginal propensity to consume and the multiplier for each economy.

a. $C = \$650 + 0.33Y$

b. $C = \$180 + 0.9Y$

c. $C = \$1,500$

d. $C = \$700 + 0.8Y$

8. Suppose that in Economies A and B the only components of aggregate expenditure are consumption and planned investment. The marginal propensity to consume in Economy A is 0.9, while in Economy B it is 0.7. Both economies experience an increase in planned investment, which is assumed to be autonomous, of $100 billion. Compare the changes in the equilibrium level of real GDP and the shifts in aggregate demand this will produce in the two economies.

9. Assume an economy in which people would spend $200 billion on consumption even if real GDP were zero and, in addition, increase their consumption by $0.50 for each additional $1 of real GDP. Assume further that the sum of planned investment plus government purchases plus net exports is $200 billion regardless of the level of real GDP.

      a. What is the equilibrium level of income in this economy?

      b. If the economy is currently operating at an output level of $1,200 billion, what do you predict will happen to real GDP in the future?

10. Suppose the aggregate expenditures curve in Numerical Problem 9 is drawn for a price level of 1.2. A reduction in the price level to 1 increases aggregate expenditures by $400 billion at each level of real GDP. Draw the implied aggregate demand curve.

Endnotes

1. J. R. Mc Culloch, *A Discourse on the Rise, Progress, Peculiar Objects, and Importance, of Political Economy: Containing the Outline of a Course of Lectures on the Principles and Doctrines of That Science* (Edinburgh: Archibald Constable, 1824), 103.

2. Matthew D. Shapiro and Joel Slemrod, "Consumer Response to the Timing of Income: Evidence from a Change in Tax Withholding," *American Economic Review* 85 (March 1995): 274–83.

3. An even more realistic view of the economy might assume that imports are induced, since as a country's real GDP rises it will buy more goods and services, some of which will be imports. In that case, the slope of the aggregate expenditures curve would change.

CHAPTER 29
Investment and Economic Activity

29.1 Start Up: Jittery Firms Slash Investment

In the recession that began in late 2007 in the United States, the first main element of GDP that faltered was the part of investment called residential structures. When housing prices started falling in 2006, new home construction slowed down. In 2008, this sector had shrunk by more than 40% from where it had been just a few years earlier.

In 2008, the part of investment that reflects business spending on equipment ranging from computers to machines to trucks also turned down. The only major part of investment left standing was business spending on structures—factories, hospitals, office buildings, and such. In late 2008, firms around the world seemed to be trying to outdo each other in announcing cutbacks.

Among automakers, it was not just the Detroit 3 cutting back. Toyota announced an indefinite delay in building a Prius hybrid sedan plant in Mississippi.[1] Walgreen's, which had been increasing drugstore locations by about 8% a year, said it would expand by only about 4% in 2009 and by less than 3% in 2010.[2] Package carrier FedEx announced a 20% decline in capital spending, on top of suspending pension contributions and cutting salaries.[3] Even hospitals began scaling back on construction.[4]

Companies around the world were announcing similar cutbacks. Consumer electronics maker Sony announced is was not only closing plants but also not moving forward in constructing an LCD television plant in Slovakia.[5] With the drop in oil prices, oil companies were also cancelling planned projects right and left.[6]

Choices about how much to invest must always be made in the face of uncertainty; firms cannot know what the marketplace has in store. Investment is a gamble; firms that make the gamble hope for a profitable payoff. And, if they are concerned that the payoff may not materialize, they will be quick to take the kinds of actions cited above—to slash investment spending.

Private investment plays an important role, not only in the short run, by influencing aggregate demand, but also in the long run, for it influences the rate at which the economy grows. That is, it influences long-run aggregate supply.

In this chapter, we will examine factors that determine investment by firms, and we will study its relationship to output in the short run and in the long run. One determinant of investment is public policy; we will examine the ways in which public policy affects investment.

Private firms are not the only source of investment; government agencies engage in investment as well. We examined the impact of the public sector on macroeconomic performance in the chapter devoted to fiscal policy. When we refer to "investment" in this chapter, we will be referring to investment carried out in the private sector.

29.2 The Role and Nature of Investment

How important is investment? Consider any job you have ever performed. Your productivity in that job was largely determined by the investment choices that had been made before you began to work. If you worked as a clerk in a store, the equipment used in collecting money from customers affected your productivity. It may have been a simple cash register, or a sophisticated computer terminal that scanned purchases and was linked to the store's computer, which computed the store's inventory and did an analysis of the store's sales as you entered each sale. If you have worked for a lawn maintenance firm, the kind of equipment you had to work with influenced your productivity. You were more productive if you had the latest mulching power lawn mowers than if you struggled with a push mower. Whatever the work you might have done, the kind and quality of capital you had to work with strongly influenced your productivity. And that capital was available because investment choices had provided it.

Investment adds to the nation's capital stock. We saw in the chapter on economic growth that an increase in capital shifts the aggregate production function outward, increases the demand for labor, and shifts the long-run aggregate supply curve to the right. Investment therefore affects the economy's potential output and thus its standard of living in the long run.

Investment is a component of aggregate demand. Changes in investment shift the aggregate demand curve and thus change real GDP and the price level in the short run. An increase in investment shifts the aggregate demand curve to the right; a reduction shifts it to the left.

Components of Investment

Additions to the stock of private capital are called Gross Private Domestic Investment (GPDI). GPDI includes four categories of investment:

1. Nonresidential Structures. This category of investment includes the construction of business structures such as private office buildings, warehouses, factories, private hospitals and universities, and other structures in which the production of goods and services takes place. A structure is counted as GPDI only during the period in which it is built. It may be sold several times after being built, but such sales are not counted as investment. Recall that investment is part of GDP, and GDP is the value of production in any period, not total sales.

2. Nonresidential Equipment and Software. Producers' equipment includes computers and software, machinery, trucks, cars, and desks, that is, any business equipment that is expected to last more than a year. Equipment and software are counted as investment only in the period in which they are produced.

3. Residential Investment. This category includes all forms of residential construction, whether apartment houses or single-family homes, as well as residential equipment such as computers and software.

4. Change in Private Inventories. Private inventories are considered part of the nation's capital stock, because those inventories are used to produce other goods. All private inventories are capital; additions to private inventories are thus investment. When private inventories fall, that is recorded as negative investment.

Figure 29.1 shows the components of gross private domestic investment from 1999 through 2015. We see that producers' equipment and software constitute the largest component of GPDI in the United States. Residential investment was the second largest component of GPDI for most of the period shown but it shrank considerably during the 2007–2009 recession and has yet to completely recover.

FIGURE 29.1 Components of Gross Private Domestic Investment, 1999–2015

This chart shows the levels of each of the four components of gross private domestic investment from 1999 through 2015. Nonresidential equipment and software is the largest component of GPDI and has shown the most substantial growth over the period.

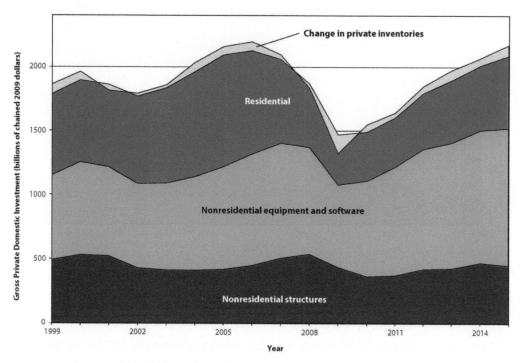

Source: Based on data from Bureau of Economic Analysis, NIPA Table 1.1.6 (revised November 29, 2016).

Gross and Net Investment

As capital is used, some of it wears out or becomes obsolete; it depreciates (the Commerce Department reports depreciation as "consumption of fixed capital"). Investment adds to the capital stock, and depreciation reduces it. Gross investment minus depreciation is net investment. If gross investment is greater than depreciation in any period, then net investment is positive and the capital stock increases. If gross investment is less than depreciation in any period, then net investment is negative and the capital stock declines.

In the official estimates of total output, gross investment (GPDI) minus depreciation equals net private domestic investment (NPDI). The value for NPDI in any period gives the amount by which the privately held stock of physical capital changed during that period.

Figure 29.2 reports the real values of GPDI, depreciation, and NPDI from 1990 to 2015. We see that the bulk of GPDI replaces capital that has been depreciated. Notice the sharp reductions in NPDI during the recessions of 1990–1991, 2001, and especially 2007–2009.

FIGURE 29.2 Gross Private Domestic Investment, Depreciation, and Net Private Domestic Investment, 1990–2015

The bulk of gross private domestic investment goes to the replacement of capital that has depreciated, as shown by the experience of the past two decades.

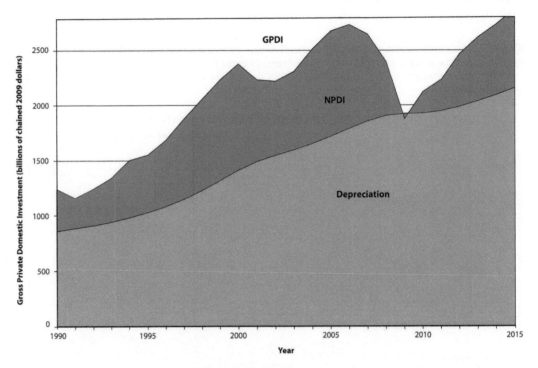

Source: Based on data from Bureau of Economic Analysis, NIPA Table 5.2.6 (revised November 29, 2016).

The Volatility of Investment

Investment, measured as GPDI, is among the most volatile components of GDP. In percentage terms, year-to-year changes in GPDI are far greater than the year-to-year changes in consumption or government purchases. Net exports are also quite volatile, but they represent a much smaller share of GDP. Figure 29.3 compares annual percentage changes in GPDI, personal consumption, and government purchases. Of course, a dollar change in investment will be a much larger change in percentage terms than a dollar change in consumption, which is the largest component of GDP. But compare investment and government purchases: their shares in GDP are comparable, but investment is clearly more volatile.

FIGURE 29.3 Changes in Components of Real GDP, 1990–2015

Annual percentage changes in real GPDI have been much greater than annual percentage changes in the real values of personal consumption or government purchases.

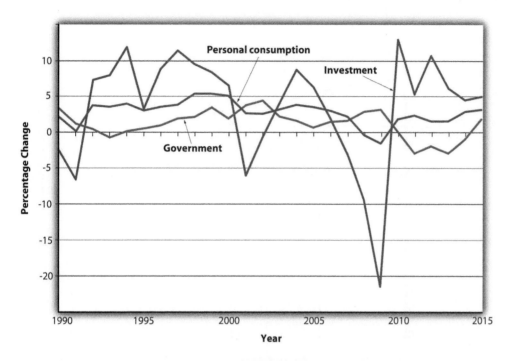

Source: Based on data from Bureau of Economic Analysis, NIPA Table 1.1.1 (revised November 29, 2016).

Given that the aggregate demand curve shifts by an amount equal to the multiplier times an initial change in investment, the volatility of investment can cause real GDP to fluctuate in the short run. Downturns in investment may trigger recessions.

Investment, Consumption, and Saving

Earlier we used the production possibilities curve to illustrate how choices are made about investment, consumption, and saving. Because such choices are crucial to understanding how investment affects living standards, it will be useful to reexamine them here.

Figure 29.4 shows a production possibilities curve for an economy that can produce two kinds of goods: consumption goods and investment goods. An economy operating at point A on PPC_1 is using its factors of production fully and efficiently. It is producing C_A units of consumption goods and I_A units of investment each period. Suppose that depreciation equals I_A, so that the quantity of investment each period is just sufficient to replace depreciated capital; net investment equals zero. If there is no change in the labor force, in natural resources, or in technology, the production possibilities curve will remain fixed at PPC_1.

FIGURE 29.4 The Choice between Consumption and Investment
A society with production possibilities curve PPC_1 could choose to produce at point A, producing C_A consumption goods and investment of I_A. If depreciation equals I_A, then net investment is zero, and the production possibilities curve will not shift, assuming no other determinants of the curve change. By cutting its production of consumption goods and increasing investment to I_B, however, the society can, over time, shift its production possibilities curve out to PPC_2, making it possible to enjoy greater production of consumption goods in the future.

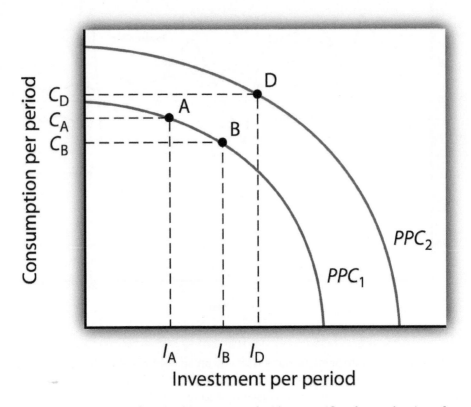

Now suppose decision makers in this economy decide to sacrifice the production of some consumption goods in favor of greater investment. The economy moves to point B on PPC_1. Production of consumption goods falls to C_B, and investment rises to I_B. Assuming depreciation remains I_A, net investment is now positive. As the nation's capital stock increases, the production possibilities curve shifts outward to PPC_2. Once that shift occurs, it will be possible to select a point such as D on the new production possibilities curve. At this point, consumption equals C_D, and investment equals I_D. By sacrificing consumption early on, the society is able to increase both its consumption and investment in the future. That early reduction in consumption requires an *increase* in saving.

We see that a movement along the production possibilities curve in the direction of the production of more investment goods and fewer consumption goods allows the production of more of both types of goods in the future.

Key Takeaways

- Investment adds to the nation's capital stock.
- Gross private domestic investment includes the construction of nonresidential structures, the production of equipment and software, private residential construction, and changes in inventories.
- The bulk of gross private domestic investment goes to the replacement of depreciated capital.
- Investment is the most volatile component of GDP.
- Investment represents a choice to postpone consumption—it requires saving.

Try It!

Which of the following would be counted as gross private domestic investment?

1. Millie hires a contractor to build a new garage for her home.
2. Millie buys a new car for her teenage son.
3. Grandpa buys Tommy a savings bond.
4. General Motors builds a new automobile assembly plant.

Case in Point: The Reduction of Private Capital in the Depression and in the Great Recession

Source: © Shutterstock, Inc.

Net private domestic investment (NPDI) has been negative during only three periods in the last 90 years. During one period, World War II, massive defense spending forced cutbacks in private sector spending. (Recall that government investment is not counted as part of net private domestic investment in the official accounts; production of defense capital thus is not reflected in these figures.) NPDI, shown in orange, was also negative during the Great Depression.

Aggregate demand plunged during the first four years of the Depression. As firms cut their output in response to reductions in demand, their need for capital fell as well. They reduced their capital by holding gross private domestic investment below depreciation beginning in 1931. That produced negative net private domestic investment; it remained negative until 1936 and became negative again in 1938. In all, firms reduced the private capital stock by more than $529.5 billion (in 2007 dollars) during the period.

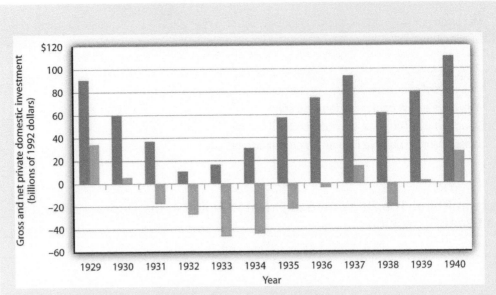

A third—very brief and very small—encounter with negative net private domestic investment, shown in red, occurred in 2009, when it fell by $47 billion (in 2009 dollars).

The two graphs in this case present a contrast between the Great Depression and the Great Recession. The Great Recession was bad, but the Great Depression was ever so much worse.

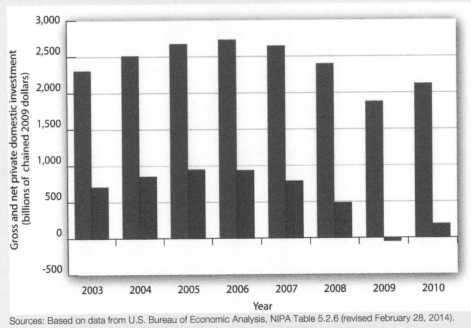

Sources: Based on data from U.S. Bureau of Economic Analysis, NIPA Table 5.2.6 (revised February 28, 2014).

Answers to Try It! Problems

1. A new garage would be part of residential construction and thus part of GPDI.

2. Consumer purchases of cars are part of the consumption component of the GDP accounts and thus not part of GPDI.

3. The purchase of a savings bond is an example of a financial investment. Since it is not an addition to the nation's capital stock, it is not part of GPDI.

4. The construction of a new factory is counted in the nonresidential structures component of GPDI.

29.3 Determinants of Investment

Learning Objectives

1. Draw a hypothetical investment demand curve, and explain what it shows about the relationship between investment and the interest rate.
2. Discuss the factors that can cause an investment demand curve to shift.

We will see in this section that interest rates play a key role in the determination of the desired stock of capital and thus of investment. Because investment is a process through which capital is increased in one period for use in future periods, expectations play an important role in investment as well.

Capital is one factor of production, along with labor and natural resources. A decision to invest is a decision to use more capital in producing goods and services. Factors that affect firms' choices in the mix of capital, labor, and natural resources will affect investment as well.

We will also see in this section that public policy affects investment. Some investment is done by government agencies as they add to the public stock of capital. In addition, the tax and regulatory policies chosen by the public sector can affect the investment choices of private firms and individuals.

Interest Rates and Investment

We often hear reports that low interest rates have stimulated housing construction or that high rates have reduced it. Such reports imply a negative relationship between interest rates and investment in residential structures. This relationship applies to all forms of investment: higher interest rates tend to reduce the quantity of investment, while lower interest rates increase it.

To see the relationship between interest rates and investment, suppose you own a small factory and are considering the installation of a solar energy collection system to heat your building. You have determined that the cost of installing the system would be $10,000 and that the system would lower your energy bills by $1,000 per year. To simplify the example, we shall suppose that these savings will continue forever and that the system will never need repair or maintenance. Thus, we need to consider only the $10,000 purchase price and the $1,000 annual savings.

If the system is installed, it will be an addition to the capital stock and will therefore be counted as investment. Should you purchase the system?

Suppose that your business already has the $10,000 on hand. You are considering whether to use the money for the solar energy system or for the purchase of a bond. Your decision to purchase the system or the bond will depend on the interest rate you could earn on the bond.

Putting $10,000 into the solar energy system generates an effective income of $1,000 per year—the saving the system will produce. That is a return of 10% per year. Suppose the bond yields a 12% annual interest. It thus generates interest income of $1,200 per year, enough to pay the $1,000 in heating bills and have $200 left over. At an interest rate of 12%, the bond is the better purchase. If, however, the interest rate on bonds were 8%, then the solar energy system would yield a higher income than the bond. At interest rates below 10%, you will invest in the solar energy system. At interest rates above 10%, you will buy a bond instead. At an interest rate of precisely 10%, it is a toss-up.

If you do not have the $10,000 on hand and would need to borrow the money to purchase the solar energy system, the interest rate still governs your decision. At interest rates below 10%, it makes sense to borrow the money and invest in the system. At interest rates above 10%, it does not.

In effect, the interest rate represents the opportunity cost of putting funds into the solar energy system rather than into a bond. The cost of putting the $10,000 into the system is the interest you would forgo by not purchasing the bond.

At any one time, millions of investment choices hinge on the interest rate. Each decision to invest will make sense at some interest rates but not at others. The higher the interest rate, the fewer potential investments will be justified; the lower the interest rate, the greater the number that will be justified. There is thus a negative relationship between the interest rate and the level of investment.

investment demand curve

A curve that shows the quantity of investment demanded at each interest rate, with all other determinants of investment unchanged.

Figure 29.5 shows an **investment demand curve** for the economy—a curve that shows the quantity of investment demanded at each interest rate, with all other determinants of investment unchanged. At an interest rate of 8%, the level of investment is $950 billion per year at point A. At a lower interest rate of 6%, the investment demand curve shows that the quantity of investment demanded will rise to $1,000 billion per year at point B. A reduction in the interest rate thus causes a movement along the investment demand curve.

FIGURE 29.5 The Investment Demand Curve

The investment demand curve shows the volume of investment spending per year at each interest rate, assuming all other determinants of investment are unchanged. The curve shows that as the interest rate falls, the level of investment per year rises. A reduction in the interest rate from 8% to 6%, for example, would increase investment from $950 billion to $1,000 billion per year, all other determinants of investment unchanged.

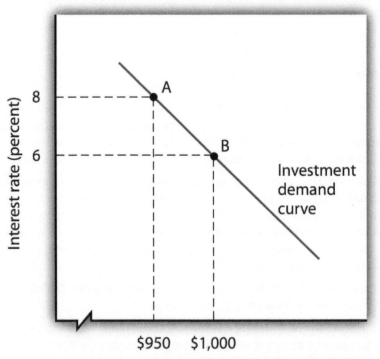

Heads Up!

To make sense of the relationship between interest rates and investment, you must remember that investment is an addition to capital, and that capital is something that has been produced in order to produce other goods and services. A bond is not capital. The purchase of a bond is not an investment. We can thus think of purchasing bonds as a financial investment—that is, as an alternative to investment. The more attractive bonds are (i.e., the higher their interest rate), the less attractive investment becomes. If we forget that investment is an addition to the capital stock and that the purchase of a bond is not investment, we can fall into the following kind of error: "Higher interest rates mean a greater return on bonds, so more people will purchase them. Higher interest rates will therefore lead to greater investment." That is a mistake, of course, because the purchase of a bond is not an investment. Higher interest rates increase the opportunity cost of using funds for investment. They reduce investment.

Other Determinants of Investment Demand

Perhaps the most important characteristic of the investment demand curve is not its negative slope, but rather the fact that it shifts often. Although investment certainly responds to changes in interest rates, changes in other factors appear to play a more important role in driving investment choices.

This section examines eight additional determinants of investment demand: expectations, the level of economic activity, the stock of capital, capacity utilization, the cost of capital goods, other factor costs, technological change, and public policy. A change in any of these can shift the investment demand curve.

Expectations

A change in the capital stock changes future production capacity. Therefore, plans to change the capital stock depend crucially on expectations. A firm considers likely future sales; a student weighs prospects in different occupations and their required educational and training levels. As expectations change in a way that increases the expected return from investment, the investment demand curve shifts to the right. Similarly, expectations of reduced profitability shift the investment demand curve to the left.

The Level of Economic Activity

Firms need capital to produce goods and services. An increase in the level of production is likely to boost demand for capital and thus lead to greater investment. Therefore, an increase in GDP is likely to shift the investment demand curve to the right.

To the extent that an increase in GDP boosts investment, the multiplier effect of an initial change in one or more components of aggregate demand will be enhanced. We have already seen that the increase in production that occurs with an initial increase in aggregate demand will increase household incomes, which will increase consumption, thus producing a further increase in aggregate demand. If the increase also induces firms to increase their investment, this multiplier effect will be even stronger.

The Stock of Capital

The quantity of capital already in use affects the level of investment in two ways. First, because most investment replaces capital that has depreciated, a greater capital stock is likely to lead to more investment; there will be more capital to replace. But second, a greater capital stock can tend to reduce investment. That is because investment occurs to adjust the stock of capital to its desired level. Given that desired level, the amount of investment needed to reach it will be lower when the current capital stock is higher.

Suppose, for example, that real estate analysts expect that 100,000 homes will be needed in a particular community by 2010. That will create a boom in construction—and thus in investment—if the current number of houses is 50,000. But it will create hardly a ripple if there are now 99,980 homes.

How will these conflicting effects of a larger capital stock sort themselves out? Because most investment occurs to replace existing capital, a larger capital stock is likely to increase investment. But that larger capital stock will certainly act to reduce net investment. The more capital already in place, the less new capital will be required to reach a given level of capital that may be desired.

Capacity Utilization

capacity utilization rate

A measure of the percentage of the capital stock in use.

The **capacity utilization rate** measures the percentage of the capital stock in use. Because capital generally requires downtime for maintenance and repairs, the measured capacity utilization rate typically falls below 100%. For example, the average manufacturing capacity utilization rate was 79.7% for the period from 1972 to 2007. In November 2008 it stood at 72.3.

If a large percentage of the current capital stock is being utilized, firms are more likely to increase investment than they would if a large percentage of the capital stock were sitting idle. During recessions, the capacity utilization rate tends to fall. The fact that firms have more idle capacity then depresses investment even further. During expansions, as the capacity utilization rate rises, firms wanting to produce more often must increase investment to do so.

The Cost of Capital Goods

The demand curve for investment shows the quantity of investment at each interest rate, all other things unchanged. A change in a variable held constant in drawing this curve shifts the curve. One of those variables is the cost of capital goods themselves. If, for example, the construction cost of new buildings rises, then the quantity of investment at any interest rate is likely to fall. The investment demand curve thus shifts to the left.

The $10,000 cost of the solar energy system in the example given earlier certainly affects a decision to purchase it. We saw that buying the system makes sense at interest rates below 10% and does not make sense at interest rates above 10%. If the system costs $5,000, then the interest return on the investment would be 20% (the annual saving of $1,000 divided by the $5,000 initial cost), and the investment would be undertaken at any interest rate below 20%.

Other Factor Costs

Firms have a range of choices concerning how particular goods can be produced. A factory, for example, might use a sophisticated capital facility and relatively few workers, or it might use more workers and relatively less capital. The choice to use capital will be affected by the cost of the capital goods and the interest rate, but it will also be affected by the cost of labor. As labor costs rise, the demand for capital is likely to increase.

Our solar energy collector example suggests that energy costs influence the demand for capital as well. The assumption that the system would save $1,000 per year in energy costs must have been based on the prices of fuel oil, natural gas, and electricity. If these prices were higher, the savings from the solar energy system would be greater, increasing the demand for this form of capital.

Technological Change

The implementation of new technology often requires new capital. Changes in technology can thus increase the demand for capital. Advances in computer technology have encouraged massive investments in computers. The development of fiber-optic technology for transmitting signals has stimulated huge investments by telephone and cable television companies.

Public Policy

Public policy can have significant effects on the demand for capital. Such policies typically seek to affect the cost of capital to firms. The Kennedy administration introduced two such strategies in the early 1960s. One strategy, accelerated depreciation, allowed firms to depreciate capital assets over a very short period of time. They could report artificially high production costs in the first years of an asset's life and thus report lower profits and pay lower taxes. Accelerated depreciation did not change the actual rate at which assets depreciated, of course, but it cut tax payments during the early years of the assets' use and thus reduced the cost of holding capital.

The second strategy was the investment tax credit, which permitted a firm to reduce its tax liability by a percentage of its investment during a period. A firm acquiring new capital could subtract a fraction of its cost—10% under the Kennedy administration's plan—from the taxes it owed the government. In effect, the government "paid" 10% of the cost of any new capital; the investment tax credit thus reduced the cost of capital for firms.

Though less direct, a third strategy for stimulating investment would be a reduction in taxes on corporate profits (called the corporate income tax). Greater after-tax profits mean that firms can retain a greater portion of any return on an investment.

A fourth measure to encourage greater capital accumulation is a capital gains tax rate that allows gains on assets held during a certain period to be taxed at a different rate than other income. When an asset such as a building is sold for more than its purchase price, the seller of the asset is said to have realized a capital gain. Such a gain could be taxed as income under the personal income tax. Alternatively, it could be taxed at a lower rate reserved exclusively for such gains. A lower capital gains tax rate makes assets subject to the tax more attractive. It thus increases the demand for capital. Congress reduced the capital gains tax rate from 28% to 20% in 1996 and reduced the required holding period in 1998. The Jobs and Growth Tax Relief Reconciliation Act of 2003 reduced the capital gains tax further to 15% and also reduced the tax rate on dividends from 38% to 15%. A proposal to eliminate capital gains taxation for smaller firms was considered but dropped before the stimulus bill of 2009 was enacted.

Accelerated depreciation, the investment tax credit, and lower taxes on corporate profits and capital gains all increase the demand for private physical capital. Public policy can also affect the demands for other forms of capital. The federal government subsidizes state and local government production of transportation, education, and many other facilities to encourage greater investment in public sector capital. For example, the federal government pays 90% of the cost of investment by local government in new buses for public transportation.

Key Takeaways

- The quantity of investment demanded in any period is negatively related to the interest rate. This relationship is illustrated by the investment demand curve.

- A change in the interest rate causes a movement along the investment demand curve. A change in any other determinant of investment causes a shift of the curve.
- The other determinants of investment include expectations, the level of economic activity, the stock of capital, the capacity utilization rate, the cost of capital goods, other factor costs, technological change, and public policy.

Try It!

Show how the investment demand curve would be affected by each of the following:

1. A sharp increase in taxes on profits earned by firms
2. An increase in the minimum wage
3. The expectation that there will be a sharp upsurge in the level of economic activity
4. An increase in the cost of new capital goods
5. An increase in interest rates
6. An increase in the level of economic activity
7. A natural disaster that destroys a significant fraction of the capital stock

Case in Point: Assessing the Impact of a One-Year Tax Break on Investment

Source: By FxJ (Own work) [Public domain], via Wikimedia Commons

The U.S. economy was expanding in 2004, but there was a feeling that it still was not functioning as well as it could, as job growth was rather sluggish. To try to spur growth, Congress, supported by President Bush, passed a law in 2004 called the American Jobs Creation Act that gave businesses a one-year special tax break on any profits accumulating overseas that were transferred to the United States. Such profits are called repatriated profits and were estimated at the time to be about $800 billion. For 2005, the tax rate on repatriated profits essentially fell from 25% to 5.25%.

Did the tax break have the desired effect on the economy? To some extent yes, though business also found other uses for the repatriated funds. There were 843 companies that repatriated $312 billion that qualified for the tax break. The Act thus generated about $18 billion in tax revenue, a higher level than had been expected. Some companies announced they were repatriating profits and continuing to downsize. For example, Colgate-Palmolive brought back $800 million and made known it was closing a third of its factories and eliminating 12% of its workforce. However, other companies' plans seemed more in line with the objectives of the special tax break—to create jobs and spur investment.

For example, the *Wall Street Journal* reported that spokesman Chuck Mulloy of Intel, which repatriated over $6 billion, said the company was building a $3-billion wafer fabrication facility and spending $345 million on expanding existing facilities. "I can't say dollar-for-dollar how much of the funding for those comes from off-shore cash," but he felt that the repatriated funds were contributing to Intel's overall investments. Spokeswoman Margaret Graham of Bausch and Lomb, which makes eye-care products and repatriated $805 million, said, "We plan to use that cash for capital expenditures, investment in research and development, and paying nonofficer compensation."

Analysts are skeptical, though, that the repatriated profits really contributed to investment. The *New York Times* reported on one study that suggested it had not. Rather, the repatriated funds were used for other purposes, such as stock repurchases. The argument is that the companies made investments that they were planning to make and the repatriated funds essentially freed up funding for other purposes.

Sources: *Based on Timothy Aeppel, "Tax Break Brings Billion to U.S., But Impact on Hiring Is Unclear," Wall Street Journal, October 5, 2005, p. A1; Lynnley Browning, "A One-Time Tax Break Saved 843 U.S. Corporations $265 Billion," New York Times, June 24, 2008, p. C3.*

Answers to Try It! Problems

1. The investment demand curve shifts to the left: Panel (b).
2. A higher minimum wage makes labor more expensive. Firms are likely to shift to greater use of capital, so the investment demand curve shifts to the right: Panel (a).
3. The investment demand curve shifts to the right: Panel (a).
4. The investment demand curve shifts to the left: Panel (b).
5. An increase in interest rates causes a movement along the investment demand curve: Panel (c).
6. The investment demand curve shifts to the right: Panel (a).
7. The need to replace capital shifts the investment demand curve to the right: Panel (a).

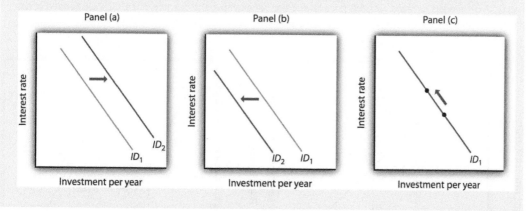

29.4 Investment and the Economy

1. Explain how investment affects aggregate demand.
2. Explain how investment affects economic growth.

We shall examine the impact of investment on the economy in the context of the model of aggregate demand and aggregate supply. Investment is a component of aggregate demand; changes in investment shift the aggregate demand curve by the amount of the initial change times the multiplier. Investment changes the capital stock; changes in the capital stock shift the production possibilities curve and the economy's aggregate production function and thus shift the long- and short-run aggregate supply curves to the right or to the left.

Investment and Aggregate Demand

In the short run, changes in investment cause aggregate demand to change. Consider, for example, the impact of a reduction in the interest rate, given the investment demand curve (*ID*). In Figure 29.6, Panel (a), which uses the investment demand curve introduced in Figure 29.5, a reduction in the interest rate from 8% to 6% increases investment by $50 billion per year. Assume that the multiplier is 2. With an increase in investment of $50 billion per year and a multiplier of 2, the aggregate demand curve shifts to the right by $100 billion to AD_2 in Panel (b). The quantity of real GDP demanded at each price level thus increases. At a price level of 1.0, for example, the quantity of real GDP demanded rises from $8,000 billion to $8,100 billion per year.

FIGURE 29.6 A Change in Investment and Aggregate Demand
A reduction in the interest rate from 8% to 6% increases the level of investment by $50 billion per year in Panel (a). With a multiplier of 2, the aggregate demand curve shifts to the right by $100 billion in Panel (b). The total quantity of real GDP demanded increases at each price level. Here, for example, the quantity of real GDP demanded at a price level of 1.0 rises from $8,000 billion per year at point C to $8,100 billion per year at point D.

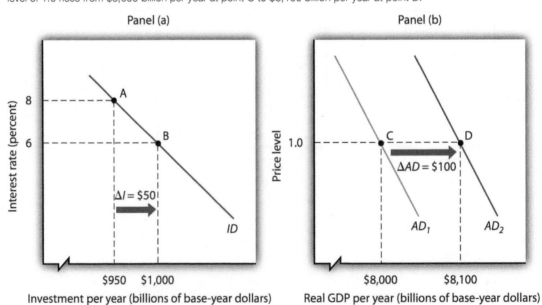

A reduction in investment would shift the aggregate demand curve to the left by an amount equal to the multiplier times the change in investment.

The relationship between investment and interest rates is one key to the effectiveness of monetary policy to the economy. When the Fed seeks to increase aggregate demand, it purchases bonds. That raises bond prices, reduces interest rates, and stimulates investment and aggregate demand as illustrated in Figure 29.6. When the Fed seeks to decrease aggregate demand, it sells bonds. That lowers bond prices, raises interest rates, and reduces investment and aggregate demand. The extent to which investment responds to a change in interest rates is a crucial factor in how effective monetary policy is.

Investment and Economic Growth

Investment adds to the stock of capital, and the quantity of capital available to an economy is a crucial determinant of its productivity. Investment thus contributes to economic growth. We saw in Figure 29.4 that an increase in an economy's stock of capital shifts its production possibilities curve outward. (Recall from the chapter on economic growth that it also shifts the economy's aggregate production function upward.) That also shifts its long-run aggregate supply curve to the right. At the same time, of course, an increase in investment affects aggregate demand, as we saw in Figure 29.6.

Key Takeaways

- Changes in investment shift the aggregate demand curve to the right or left by an amount equal to the initial change in investment times the multiplier.
- Investment adds to the capital stock; it therefore contributes to economic growth.

816 Principles of Economics

Try It!

The text notes that rising investment shifts the aggregate demand curve to the right and at the same time shifts the long-run aggregate supply curve to the right by increasing the nation's stock of physical and human capital. Show this simultaneous shifting in the two curves with three graphs. One graph should show growth in which the price level rises, one graph should show growth in which the price level remains unchanged, and another should show growth with the price level falling.

Case in Point: China's Growth "Miracle"

Source: © Shutterstock, Inc.

The world's most populous country—about 1.3 billion people and a fifth of the world's population—has had an incredibly successful economic run: For over 30 years, starting in the early 1980s, China's economy grew by an astounding rate of 10% per year on average. No other country has ever achieved such impressive growth for such a long period of time. These numbers translate into impressive improvements in the standard of living for Chinese people. For example, in 1980 China's real GDP per capita was about 5% of the U.S. level. Today, it is about 20%. This performance may also be considered the greatest anti-poverty program ever. Over the 30-year period, on the order of 600 million people have been lifted out of extreme poverty.

How did China do it? Starting in 1949, under the leadership of Mao Zedong and China's Communist Party, China became a socialist state. Firms were nationalized and land was redistributed. Similar to the former Soviet Union, China adopted five-year plans. Mao also launched some uniquely Chinese experiments, such as the Great Leap Forward in 1958. With the goal of turning China quickly into an industrialized country, households were encouraged to form their own, small, labor-intensive productive units under the slogan "An iron and steel foundry in every backyard." The period also saw the collectivization of agriculture. Farmers were organized into communes containing several thousand households in each. Small private plots were abolished. The Great Leap Forward was an economic disaster. Output plunged and famine ensued. The 1960s saw other experiments.

It was not until after Mao's death in 1976 that the country began to adopt more market-oriented reforms. In agriculture, the reforms entailed contracting individual households to farm the land again. Agricultural output soared. While China continues to have state-owned enterprises, there are also many private companies, both domestic and foreign. As a symbol of how far China has progressed, it entered the World Trade Organization in 2001.

What were the engines of China's economic growth? Federal Reserve Bank of San Francisco economist Zheng Liu analyzed the sources of Chinese growth in a recent study. He considered three broad categories to explain growth: Increases in labor adjusted for quality, capital accumulation (representing investment in the economy in physical capital), and productivity improvements (which we have referred to as representing technological improvement). The figure below shows that for the 30 years from 1980 to 2010, investment and productivity improvements explain most of the growth. Looking at just the last four years covered in the study, 2008 to 2011, investment is the main driver. Zheng speculates that this shift may have occurred due to the recession in many countries that started in 2008 which reduced demand for China's exports. To support the economy through this period, the Chinese government boosted investment but may not have directed it to the most productive places.

Accounting for China's growth

Source: Penn World Tables and author's calculations.

The Chinese economy has slowed in recent years to about 6-7% a year, well below the 10% it had become accustomed to but still high in comparison to most other countries. In response the Chinese government has announced a number of market-oriented reforms. Zheng believes that if these are implemented China's momentum will not stall.

Source: *Based on Zheng Liu, "Is China's Growth Miracle Over?" Federal Reserve Bank of San Francisco Economic Letter 2015-26, August 10, 2015 available at http://www.frbsf.org/economic-research/publications/economic-letter/2015/august/china-economic-growth-miracle-slowdown/.*

Answer to Try It! Problem

Panel (a) shows *AD* shifting by more than *LRAS*; the price level will rise in the long run.

Panel (b) shows *AD* and *LRAS* shifting by equal amounts; the price level will remain unchanged in the long run.

Panel (c) shows *LRAS* shifting by more than *AD*; the price level falls in the long run.

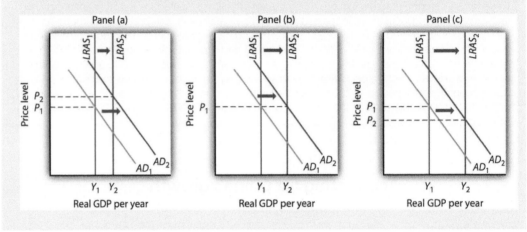

29.5 Review and Practice

Summary

Investment is an addition to the capital stock. Investment may occur as a net addition to capital or as a replacement of depreciated capital. The bulk of investment spending in the United States falls into the latter category. Investment is a highly volatile component of GDP.

The decision to save is linked directly to the decision to invest. If a nation is to devote a larger share of its production to investment, then it must devote a smaller share to consumption, all other things unchanged. And that requires people to save more.

Investment is affected by the interest rate; the negative relationship between investment and the interest rate is illustrated by the investment demand curve. The position of this curve is affected by expectations, the level of economic activity, the stock of capital, the price of capital, the prices of other factors, technology, and public policy.

Because investment is a component of aggregate demand, a change in investment shifts the aggregate demand curve to the right or left. The amount of the shift will equal the initial change in investment times the multiplier.

In addition to its impact on aggregate demand, investment can also affect economic growth. Investment shifts the production possibilities curve outward, shifts the economy's aggregate production function upward, and shifts the long-run aggregate supply curve to the right.

Concept Problems

1. Which of the following would be counted as gross private domestic investment?
    a. General Motors issues 1 million shares of stock.
    b. Consolidated Construction purchases 1,000 acres of land for a regional shopping center it plans to build in a few years.

c. A K-Mart store adds 1,000 T-shirts to its inventory.

d. Crew buys computers for its office staff.

e. Your family buys a house.

2. If saving dropped sharply in the economy, what would likely happen to investment? Why?

3. Suppose local governments throughout the United States increase their tax on business inventories. What would you expect to happen to U.S. investment? Why?

4. Suppose the government announces it will pay for half of any new investment undertaken by firms. How will this affect the investment demand curve?

5. White House officials often exude more confidence than they actually feel about future prospects for the economy. Why might this be a good strategy? Are there any dangers inherent in it?

6. Suppose everyone expects investment to rise sharply in three months. How would this expectation be likely to affect bond prices?

7. Suppose that every increase of $1 in real GDP automatically stimulates $0.20 in additional investment spending. How would this affect the multiplier?

8. If environmental resources were counted as part of the capital stock, how would a major forest fire affect net investment?

9. In the Case in Point on reducing private capital in the Great Depression, we saw that net investment was negative during that period. Could gross investment ever be negative? Explain.

10. The Case in Point on lowering the tax rate for one year for companies that repatriated profits suggests that investment did not increase, even though company representatives are quoted as saying that they were using the repatriated profits for investment. Explain this seeming contradiction.

11. Use the model of aggregate demand and aggregate supply to evaluate the argument that an increase in investment would raise the standard of living.

Numerical Problems

1. Suppose a construction company is trying to decide whether to buy a new nail gun. The table below shows the hypothetical costs for the nail gun and the amount the gun will save the company each year. Assume the gun will last forever. In each case, determine the highest interest rate the company should pay for a loan that makes purchase of the nail gun possible.

	Cost	Savings
a.	$1,000	$100
b.	$1,000	$200
c.	$1,000	$300

2. A car company currently has capital stock of $100 million and desires a capital stock of $110 million.

   a. If it experiences no depreciation, how much will it need to invest to get to its desired level of capital stock?

   b. If its annual depreciation is 5%, how much will it need to invest to get to its desired level?

   c. If its annual depreciation is 10%, how much will it need to invest to get to its desired level?

3. Burger World is contemplating installing an automated ordering system. The ordering system will allow Burger World to permanently replace five employees for an annual (and permanent) cost savings of $100,000.

a. If the automated system cost $1,000,000, what is the rate of return on the investment?

b. If the system cost $2,000,000, what would be its rate of return?

c. If the government were to introduce an investment tax credit that allows firms to deduct 10% of its investment from its tax liability, what would happen to the rate of return if the system costs $1,000,000?

d. If Burger World has to pay 8% to borrow the funds to purchase the system, what is the most it should pay for the system? Assume that there is no investment tax credit.

4. The table below shows a number of investment projects and their effective earned interest rates or returns. Given the market interest rates shown below, identify which projects will be undertaken and the total amount of investment spending that will ensue.

Project	Return on project	Cost
A	30%	$1,000
B	28	500
C	22	2,500
D	17	1,000
E	8	750
F	4	1,200

a. 20%

b. 15%

c. 10%

d. 5%

e. 3%

f. Sketch out the investment demand curve implied by these data.

5. The table below describes the amounts of investment for different interest rates.

Interest rate	Amount of investment (billions)
25%	$5
20	$10
15	$15
10	$20
5	$25

a. Draw the investment demand curve for this economy.

b. Show the effect you would expect a decrease in the cost of capital goods to have on this investment demand curve.

c. Show the effect you would expect an investment tax credit to have on this investment demand curve.

d. Show the effect you would expect a recession to have on this investment demand curve.

6. Suppose real GDP in an economy equals its potential output of $2,000 billion, the multiplier is 2.5, investment is raised by $200 billion, and the increased investment does not affect the economy's potential.

a. Show the short- and long-run effects of the change upon real GDP and the price level, using the graphical framework for the model of aggregate demand and aggregate supply.

b. Would real GDP rise by the multiplier times the change in investment in the short run? In the long run? Explain.

7. Use the information below to compute the levels of gross and net private domestic investment. Data are in billions of dollars.

   Change in business inventories $ 59.3

   Residential construction 369.6

   Producers' durable equipment 691.3

   Nonresidential structures 246.9

   Depreciation 713.9

8. Complete the table, which shows investment in the United States in billions of 2000 chained dollars.

	Year	Gross private domestic investment	Depreciation	Net private domestic investment
a.	2005	1,873.5	1,266.6	
b.	2006		1,216.1	696.4
c.	2007	1,809.7		546.7

Endnotes

1. Kate Linebaugh, "Toyota Delays Mississippi Prius Factor Amid Slump," *Wall Street Journal*, December 16, 2008, p. B1.
2. Amy Merrick, "Walgreen to Cut Back on Opening New Stores," *Wall Street Journal*, December 23, 2008, p. B1.
3. Darren Shannon, "FedEx Takes More Measures to Offset Fiscal Uncertainty," *Aviation Daily*, December 19, 2008, p. 6.
4. Reed Abelson, "Hurting for Business," *New York Times*, November 7, 2008, p. B1.
5. Bettina Wassener, "Sony to Cut 8,000 Workers and Shut Plants," *New York Times*, December 10, 2008, p. B8.
6. Steve LeVine, "Pullback in the Oil Patch," *Business Week*, December 8, 2008, p. 60.

CHAPTER 30

Net Exports and International Finance

30.1 Start Up: Currency Crises Shake the World

It became known as the "Asian Contagion," and it swept the world as the 20th century came to a close.

Japan, crippled by the threat of collapse of many of its banks, seemed stuck in a recessionary gap for most of the decade. Because Japan was a major market for the exports of economies throughout East Asia, the slump in Japan translated into falling exports in neighboring economies. Slowed growth in a host of economies that had grown accustomed to phenomenal growth set the stage for trouble throughout the world.

The first crack appeared in Thailand, whose central bank had successfully maintained a stable exchange rate between the baht, Thailand's currency, and the U.S. dollar. But weakened demand for Thai exports, along with concerns about the stability of Thai banks, put downward pressure on the baht. Thailand's effort to shore up its currency ultimately failed, and the country's central bank gave up the effort in July of 1997. The baht's value dropped nearly 20% in a single day.

Holders of other currencies became worried about their stability and began selling. Central banks that, like Thailand's, had held their currencies stable relative to the dollar, gave up their efforts as well. Malaysia quit propping up the ringgit less than two weeks after the baht's fall. Indonesia's central bank gave up trying to hold the rupiah's dollar value a month later. South Korea let the won fall in November.

Currency crises continued to spread in 1998, capped by a spectacular plunge in the Russian ruble. As speculators sold other currencies, they bought dollars, driving the U.S. exchange rate steadily upward.

What was behind the currency crises that shook the world? How do changes in a country's exchange rate affect its economy? How can events such as the fall of the baht and the ringgit spread to other countries?

We will explore the answers to these questions by looking again at how changes in a country's exchange rate can affect its economy—and how changes in one economy can spread to others. We will be engaged in a study of **international finance**, the field that examines the macroeconomic consequences of the financial flows associated with international trade.

We will begin by reviewing the reasons nations trade. International trade has the potential to increase the availability of goods and services to everyone. We will look at the effects of trade on the welfare of people and then turn to the macroeconomic implications of financing trade.

international finance

The field that examines the macroeconomic consequences of the financial flows associated with international trade.

30.2 The International Sector: An Introduction

Learning Objectives

1. Discuss the main arguments economists make in support of free trade.
2. Explain the determinants of net exports and tell how each affects aggregate demand.

How important is international trade?

Take a look at the labels on some of your clothing. You are likely to find that the clothes in your closet came from all over the globe. Look around any parking lot. You may find cars from Japan, Korea, Sweden, Britain, Germany, France, and Italy—and even the United States! Do you use a computer? Even if it is an American computer, its components are likely to have been assembled in Indonesia or in some other country. Visit the grocery store. Much of the produce may come from Latin America and Asia.

The international market is important not just in terms of the goods and services it provides to a country but also as a market for that country's goods and services. Because foreign demand for U.S. exports is almost as large as investment and government purchases as a component of aggregate demand, it can be very important in terms of growth. The increase in exports in 2011, for example, accounted for about half of the gain in U.S. real GDP in that year.

The Case for Trade

International trade increases the quantity of goods and services available to the world's consumers. By allocating resources according to the principle of comparative advantage, trade allows nations to consume combinations of goods and services they would be unable to produce on their own, combinations that lie outside each country's production possibilities curve.

A country has a comparative advantage in the production of a good if it can produce that good at a lower opportunity cost than can other countries. If each country specializes in the production of goods in which it has a comparative advantage and trades those goods for things in which other countries have a comparative advantage, global production of all goods and services will be increased. The result can be higher levels of consumption for all.

tariff

A tax imposed on imported goods and services.

quota

A ceiling on the quantity of specific goods and services that can be imported, which reduces world living standards.

If international trade allows expanded world production of goods and services, it follows that restrictions on trade will reduce world production. That, in a nutshell, is the economic case for free trade. It suggests that restrictions on trade, such as a **tariff**, a tax imposed on imported goods and services, or a **quota**, a ceiling on the quantity of specific goods and services that can be imported, reduce world living standards.

The conceptual argument for free trade is a compelling one; virtually all economists support policies that reduce barriers to trade. Economists were among the most outspoken advocates for the 1993 ratification of the North American Free Trade Agreement (NAFTA), which virtually eliminated trade restrictions between Mexico, the United States, and Canada, and the 2004 Central American Free Trade Agreement (CAFTA), which did the same for trade between the United States, Central America, and the Dominican Republic. They supported the 2007 free trade agreement with Peru and the 2011 agreements with Colombia, Panama, and South Korea. Most economists have also been strong supporters of worldwide reductions in trade barriers, including the 1994 ratification of the General Agreement on Tariffs and Trade (GATT), a pact slashing tariffs and easing quotas among 117 nations, including the United States, and the Doha round of World Trade Organization negotiations, named after the site of the first meeting in Doha, Qatar, in 2001 and still continuing. In Europe, member nations of the European Union (EU) have virtually eliminated trade barriers among themselves, and 17 EU nations now have a common currency, the euro, and a single central bank, the European Central Bank, established in 1999. Trade barriers have also been slashed among the economies of Latin America and of Southeast Asia. A treaty has been signed that calls for elimination of trade barriers among the developed nations of the Pacific Rim (including the United States and Japan) by 2010 (although this deadline was missed) and among all Pacific rim nations by 2020.

The global embrace of the idea of free trade demonstrates the triumph of economic ideas over powerful forces that oppose free trade. One source of opposition to free trade comes from the owners of factors of production used in industries in which a nation lacks a comparative advantage.

A related argument against free trade is that it not only reduces employment in some sectors but also reduces employment in the economy as a whole. In the long run, this argument is clearly wrong. The economy's natural level of employment is determined by forces unrelated to trade policy, and employment moves to its natural level in the long run.

Further, trade has no effect on real wage levels for the economy as a whole. The equilibrium real wage depends on the economy's demand for and supply curve of labor. Trade affects neither.

In the short run, trade does affect aggregate demand. Net exports are one component of aggregate demand; a change in net exports shifts the aggregate demand curve and affects real GDP in the short run. All other things unchanged, a reduction in net exports reduces aggregate demand, and an increase in net exports increases it.

Protectionist sentiment always rises during recessions. Unlike what happened during the great Depression of the 1930s, there was a lot of talk during the Great Recession about more protection, but most countries avoided imposing substantially increased trade restrictions. However in 2016 there were two events that could foreshadow an increase in trade barriers. The first was the vote in the United Kingdom, commonly referred to as Brexit, to leave the European Union. Its passage led to a process to negotiate withdrawal, which will take several years. While the main reason a majority of voters voted to leave was concern over immigration, how trade will look after the exit is currently unknown. The current government, headed by Prime Minister Theresa May, seems to favor an exit that would continue to allow free trade but limit immigration from other EU countries. The EU, however, may not agree to this. The other event was the election of Donald Trump as U.S. president. As a candidate, he favored renegotiating NAFTA and withdrawing from a trade agreement that the Obama administration had negotiated called the Trans-Pacific Partnership (TPP). In his first week in office, he signed an executive order stating that the U.S. would withdraw from the TPP. How NAFTA or other trade agreements will change is still unknown.

The Rising Importance of International Trade

International trade is important, and its importance is increasing. For example, from 1990 to 2010, world output growth was about 3% per year on average, while world export growth averaged about 6% per year.

While international trade was rising around the world, it was playing a more significant role in the United States as well. In 1960, exports represented just 3.5% of real GDP; by 2015, exports accounted for more than 13% of real GDP. Figure 30.1 shows the growth in exports and imports as a percentage of real GDP in the United States from 1960 to 2015.

Why has world trade risen so spectacularly? Two factors have been important. First, advances in transportation and communication have dramatically reduced the costs of moving goods around the globe. The development of shipping containerization that allows cargo to be moved seamlessly from trucks or trains to ships, which began in 1956, drastically reduced the cost of moving goods around the world, by as much as 90%. As a result, the numbers of container ships and their capacities have markedly increased.[1] Second, we have already seen that trade barriers between countries have fallen and are likely to continue to fall.

FIGURE 30.1 U.S. Exports and Imports Relative to U.S. Real GDP, 1960–2015
The chart shows exports and imports as a percentage of real GDP from 1960 through 2015.

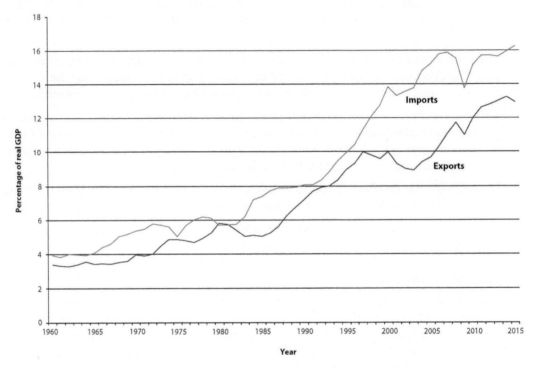

Source: Based on data from Bureau of Economic Analysis, NIPA Table 1.1.6 (revised November 29, 2016).

Net Exports and the Economy

As trade has become more important worldwide, exports and imports have assumed increased importance in nearly every country on the planet. We have already discussed the increased shares of U.S. real GDP represented by exports and by imports. We will find in this section that the economy both influences, and is influenced by, net exports. First, we will examine the determinants of net exports and then discuss the ways in which net exports affect aggregate demand.

Determinants of Net Exports

Net exports equal exports minus imports. Many of the same forces affect both exports and imports, albeit in different ways.

Income

As incomes in other nations rise, the people of those nations will be able to buy more goods and services—including foreign goods and services. Any one country's exports thus will increase as incomes rise in other countries and will fall as incomes drop in other countries.

A nation's own level of income affects its imports the same way it affects consumption. As consumers have more income, they will buy more goods and services. Because some of those goods and services are produced in other nations, imports will rise. An increase in real GDP thus boosts imports; a reduction in real GDP reduces imports. Figure 30.2 shows the relationship between real GDP and the real level of import spending in the United States from 1960 through 2015. Notice that the observations lie close to a straight line one could draw through them and resemble a consumption function.

FIGURE 30.2 U.S. Real GDP and Imports, 1960–2015

The chart shows annual values of U.S. real imports and real GDP from 1960 through 2015. The observations lie quite close to a straight line.

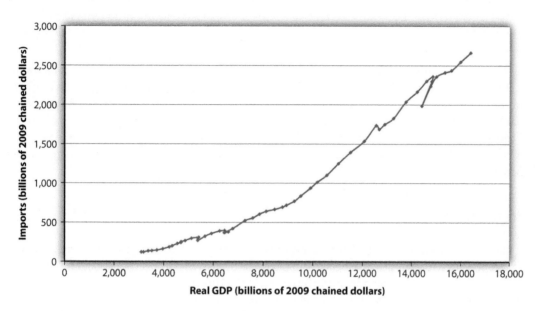

Source: Based on data from Bureau of Economic Analysis, NIPA Table 1.1.6 (revised November 29, 2016).

Relative Prices

A change in the price level within a nation simultaneously affects exports and imports. A higher price level in the United States, for example, makes U.S. exports more expensive for foreigners and thus tends to reduce exports. At the same time, a higher price level in the United States makes foreign goods and services relatively more attractive to U.S. buyers and thus increases imports. A higher price level therefore reduces net exports. A lower price level encourages exports and reduces imports, increasing net exports. As we saw in the chapter that introduced the aggregate demand and supply model, the negative relationship between net exports and the price level is called the international trade effect and is one reason for the negative slope of the aggregate demand curve.

The Exchange Rate

The purchase of U.S. goods and services by foreign buyers generally requires the purchase of dollars, because U.S. suppliers want to be paid in their own currency. Similarly, purchases of foreign goods and services by U.S. buyers generally require the purchase of foreign currencies, because foreign suppliers want to be paid in their own currencies. An increase in the exchange rate means foreigners must pay more for dollars, and must thus pay more for U.S. goods and services. It therefore reduces U.S. exports. At the same time, a higher exchange rate means that a dollar buys more foreign currency. That makes foreign goods and services cheaper for U.S. buyers, so imports are likely to rise. An increase in the exchange rate should thus tend to reduce net exports. A reduction in the exchange rate should increase net exports.

Trade Policies

A country's exports depend on its own trade policies as well as the trade policies of other countries. A country may be able to increase its exports by providing some form of government assistance (such as special tax considerations for companies that export goods and services, government promotional efforts, assistance with research, or subsidies). A country's exports are also affected by the degree to which other countries restrict or encourage imports. The United States, for example, has sought changes in Japanese policies toward products such as U.S.-grown rice. Japan banned rice imports in the past, arguing it needed to protect its own producers. That has been a costly strategy; consumers in Japan typically pay as much as 10 times the price consumers in the United States pay for rice. Japan has given in to pressure from the United States and other nations to end its ban on foreign rice as part of the GATT accord. That will increase U.S. exports and lower rice prices in Japan.

Similarly, a country's imports are affected by its trade policies and by the policies of its trading partners. A country can limit its imports of some goods and services by imposing tariffs or quotas on them—it may even ban the importation of some items. If foreign governments subsidize the manufacture of a particular good, then domestic imports of the good might increase. For example, if the governments of countries trading with the United States were to subsidize the production of steel, then U.S. companies would find it cheaper to purchase steel from abroad than at home, increasing U.S. imports of steel.

Preferences and Technology

Consumer preferences are one determinant of the consumption of any good or service; a shift in preferences for a foreign-produced good will affect the level of imports of that good. The preference among the French for movies and music produced in the United States has boosted French imports of these services. Indeed, the shift in French preferences has been so strong that the government of France, claiming a threat to its cultural heritage, has restricted the showing of films produced in the United States. French radio stations are fined if more than 40% of the music they play is from "foreign" (in most cases, U.S.) rock groups.

Changes in technology can affect the kinds of capital firms import. Technological changes have changed production worldwide toward the application of computers to manufacturing processes, for example. This has led to increased demand for high-tech capital equipment, a sector in which the United States has a comparative advantage and tends to dominate world production. This has boosted net exports in the United States.

Net Exports and Aggregate Demand

Net exports affect both the slope and the position of the aggregate demand curve. A change in the price level causes a change in net exports that moves the economy along its aggregate demand curve. This is the international trade effect. A change in net exports produced by one of the other determinants of net exports listed above (incomes and price levels in other nations, the exchange rate, trade policies, and preferences and technology) will shift the aggregate demand curve. The magnitude of this shift equals the change in net exports times the multiplier, as shown in Figure 30.3. Panel (a) shows an increase in net exports; Panel (b) shows a reduction. In both cases, the aggregate demand curve shifts by the multiplier times the initial change in net exports, provided there is no other change in the other components of aggregate demand.

FIGURE 30.3 Changes in Net Exports and Aggregate Demand

In Panel (a), an increase in net exports shifts the aggregate demand curve to the right by an amount equal to the multiplier times the initial change in net exports. In Panel (b), an equal reduction in net exports shifts the aggregate demand curve to the left by the same amount.

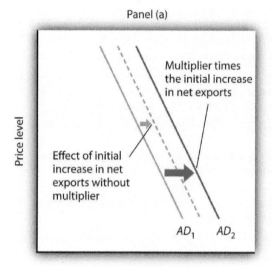

Changes in net exports that shift the aggregate demand curve can have a significant impact on the economy. The United States, for example, experienced a slowdown in the rate of increase in real GDP in the second and third quarters of 1998—virtually all of this slowing was the result of a reduction in net exports caused by recessions that staggered economies throughout Asia. The Asian slide reduced incomes there and thus reduced Asian demand for U.S. goods and services. We will see in the next section another mechanism through which difficulties in other nations can cause changes in a nation's net exports and its level of real GDP in the short run.

Key Takeaways

- International trade allows the world's resources to be allocated on the basis of comparative advantage and thus allows the production of a larger quantity of goods and services than would be available without trade.
- Trade affects neither the economy's natural level of employment nor its real wage in the long run; those are determined by the demand for and the supply curve of labor.
- Growth in international trade has outpaced growth in world output over the past five decades.
- The chief determinants of net exports are domestic and foreign incomes, relative price levels, exchange rates, domestic and foreign trade policies, and preferences and technology.
- A change in the price level causes a change in net exports that moves the economy along its aggregate demand curve. This is the international trade effect. A change in net exports produced by one of the other determinants of net exports will shift the aggregate demand curve by an amount equal to the initial change in net exports times the multiplier.

Try It!

Draw graphs showing the aggregate demand and short-run aggregate supply curves in each of four countries: Mexico, Japan, Germany, and the United States. Assume that each country is initially in equilibrium with a real GDP of Y_1 and a price level of P_1. Now show how each of the following four events would affect aggregate demand, the price level, and real GDP in the country indicated.

1. The United States is the largest foreign purchaser of goods and services from Mexico. How does an expansion in the United States affect real GDP and the price level in Mexico?
2. Japan's exchange rate falls sharply. How does this affect the price level and real GDP in Japan?
3. A wave of pro-German sentiment sweeps France, and the French sharply increase their purchases of German goods and services. How does this affect real GDP and the price level in Germany?
4. Canada, the largest importer of U.S. goods and services, slips into a recession. How does this affect the price level and real GDP in the United States?

Case in Point: Canadian Net Exports Survive the Loonie's Rise

Source: © Shutterstock, Inc.

Throughout 2003 and the first half of 2004, the Canadian dollar, nicknamed the loonie after the Canadian bird that is featured on its one-dollar coin, rose sharply in value against the U.S. dollar. Because the United States and Canada are major trading partners, the changing exchange rate suggested that, other things equal, Canadian exports to the United States would fall and imports rise. The resulting fall in net exports, other things equal, could slow the rate of growth in Canadian GDP.

Fortunately for Canada, "all other things" were not equal. In particular, strong income growth in the United States and China increased the demand for Canadian exports. In addition, the loonie's appreciation against other currencies was less dramatic, and so Canadian exports remained competitive in those markets. While imports did increase, as expected due to the exchange rate change, exports grew at a faster rate, and hence net exports increased over the period.

In sum, Canadian net exports grew, although not by as much as they would have had the loonie not appreciated. As Beata Caranci, an economist for Toronto Dominion Bank put it, "We might have some bumpy months ahead but it definitely looks like the worst is over. ... While Canadian exports appear to have survived the loonie's run-up, their fortunes would be much brighter if the exchange rate were still at 65 cents."

Source: *Based on Steven Theobald, "Exports Surviving Loonie's Rise: Study," Toronto Star, July 13, 2004, p. D1.*

Answers to Try It! Problems

1. Mexico's exports increase, shifting its aggregate demand curve to the right. Mexico's real GDP and price level rise, as shown in Panel (a).

2. Japan's net exports rise. This event shifts Japan's aggregate demand curve to the right, increasing its real GDP and price level, as shown in Panel (b).

3. Germany's net exports increase, shifting Germany's aggregate demand curve to the right, increasing its price level and real GDP, as shown in Panel (c).

4. U.S. exports fall, shifting the U.S. aggregate demand curve to the left, which will reduce the price level and real GDP, as shown in Panel (d).

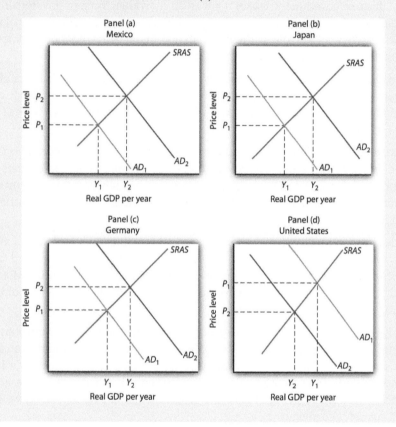

30.3 International Finance

Learning Objectives

1. Define a country's balance of payments, and explain what is included on the current and capital accounts.

2. Assuming that the market for a country's currency is in equilibrium, explain why the current account balance will always be the negative of the capital account balance.

3. Summarize the economic arguments per se against public opposition to a current account deficit and a capital account surplus.

There is an important difference between trade that flows, say, from one city to another and trade that flows from one nation to another. Unless they share a common currency, as some of the nations of the European Union do, trade among nations requires that currencies be exchanged as well as goods and services. Suppose, for example, that buyers in Mexico purchase silk produced in China. The Mexican buyers will pay in Mexico's currency, the peso; the manufacturers of the silk must be paid in China's currency, the yuan. The flow of trade between Mexico and China thus requires an exchange of pesos for yuan.

balance of payments

The balance between spending flowing into a country and spending flowing out.

This section examines the relationship between spending that flows into a country and spending that flows out of it. These spending flows include not only spending for a nation's exports and imports, but payments to owners of assets in other countries, international transfer payments, and purchases of foreign assets. The balance between spending flowing into a country and spending flowing out of it is called its **balance of payments**.

We will simplify our analysis by ignoring international transfer payments, which occur when an individual, firm, or government makes a gift to an individual, firm, or government in another country. Foreign aid is an example of an international transfer payment. International transfer payments play a relatively minor role in the international financial transactions of most countries; ignoring them will not change our basic conclusions.

A second simplification will be to treat payments to foreign owners of factors of production used in a country as imports and payments received by owners of factors of production used in other countries as exports. This is the approach when we use GNP rather than GDP as the measure of a country's output.

These two simplifications leave two reasons for demanding a country's currency: for foreigners to purchase a country's goods and services (that is, its exports) and to purchase assets in the country. A country's currency is supplied in order to purchase foreign currencies. A country's currency is thus supplied for two reasons: to purchase goods and services from other countries (that is, its imports) and to purchase assets in other countries.

We studied the determination of exchange rates in the chapter on how financial markets work. We saw that, in general, exchange rates are determined by demand and supply and that the markets for the currencies of most nations can be regarded as being in equilibrium. Exchange rates adjust quickly, so that the quantity of a currency demanded equals the quantity of the currency supplied.

Our analysis will deal with flows of spending between the domestic economy and the rest of the world. Suppose, for example, that we are analyzing Japan's economy and its transactions with the rest of the world. The purchase by a buyer in, say, Germany of bonds issued by a Japanese corporation would be part of the rest-of-world demand for yen to buy Japanese assets. Adding export demand to asset demand by people, firms, and governments outside a country, we get the total demand for a country's currency.

A domestic economy's currency is supplied to purchase currencies in the rest of the world. In an analysis of the market for Japanese yen, for example, yen are supplied when people, firms, and government agencies in Japan purchase goods and services from the rest of the world. This part of the supply of yen equals Japanese imports. Yen are also supplied so that holders of yen can acquire assets from other countries.

Equilibrium in the market for a country's currency implies that the quantity of a particular country's currency demanded equals the quantity supplied. Equilibrium thus implies that

EQUATION 30.1

$$\text{Quantity of currency demanded} = \text{quantity of currency supplied}$$

In turn, the quantity of a currency demanded is from two sources:

1. Exports
2. Rest-of-world purchases of domestic assets

The quantity supplied of a currency is from two sources:

1. Imports
2. Domestic purchases of rest-of-world assets

Therefore, we can rewrite Equation 30.1 as

EQUATION 30.2

Exports+(rest-of-world purchases of domestic assets) = imports+(domestic purchases of rest-of-world assets)

Accounting for International Payments

In this section, we will build a set of accounts to track international payments. To do this, we will use the equilibrium condition for foreign exchange markets given in Equation 30.2. We will see that the balance between a country's purchases of foreign assets and foreign purchases of the country's assets will have important effects on net exports, and thus on aggregate demand.

We can rearrange the terms in Equation 30.2 to write the following:

EQUATION 30.3

Exports−imports = − [(rest-of-world purchases of domestic assets) − (domestic purchases of rest-of-world assets)]

Equation 30.3 represents an extremely important relationship. Let us examine it carefully.

The left side of the equation is net exports. It is the balance between spending flowing from foreign countries into a particular country for the purchase of its goods and services and spending flowing out of the country for the purchase of goods and services produced in other countries. The **current account** is an accounting statement that includes all spending flows across a nation's border except those that represent purchases of assets. The **balance on current account** equals spending flowing into an economy from the rest of the world on current account less spending flowing from the nation to the rest of the world on current account. Given our two simplifying assumptions—that there are no international transfer payments and that we can treat rest-of-world purchases of domestic factor services as exports and domestic purchases of rest-of-world factor services as imports—the balance on current account equals net exports. When the balance on current account is positive, spending flowing in for the purchase of goods and services exceeds spending that flows out, and the economy has a **current account surplus** (i.e., net exports are positive in our simplified analysis). When the balance on current account is negative, spending for goods and services that flows out of the country exceeds spending that flows in, and the economy has a **current account deficit** (i.e., net exports are negative in our simplified analysis).

current account

An accounting statement that includes all spending flows across a nation's border except those that represent purchases of assets.

balance on current account

Spending flowing into an economy from the rest of the world on current account less spending flowing from the nation to the rest of the world on current account.

current account surplus

Situation that occurs when spending flowing in for the purchase of goods and services exceeds spending that flows out.

current account deficit

Situation that occurs when spending for goods and services that flows out of the country exceeds spending that flows in.

capital account

An accounting statement of spending flows into and out of the country during a particular period for purchases of assets.

balance on capital account

The balance between rest-of-world purchases of domestic assets and domestic purchases of rest-of-world assets.

capital account surplus

A positive balance on capital account.

capital account deficit

A negative balance on capital account.

A country's **capital account** is an accounting statement of spending flows into and out of the country during a particular period for purchases of assets. The term within the parentheses on the right side of the equation gives the balance between rest-of-world purchases of domestic assets and domestic purchases of rest-of-world assets; this balance is a country's **balance on capital account**. A positive balance on capital account is a **capital account surplus**. A capital account surplus means that buyers in the rest of the world are purchasing more of a country's assets than buyers in the domestic economy are spending on rest-of-world assets. A negative balance on capital account is a **capital account deficit**. It implies that buyers in the domestic economy are purchasing a greater volume of assets in other countries than buyers in other countries are spending on the domestic economy's assets. Remember that the balance on capital account is the term *inside* the parentheses on the right-hand side of Equation 30.3 and that there is a minus sign *outside* the parentheses.

Equation 30.3 tells us that a country's balance on current account equals the negative of its balance on capital account. Suppose, for example, that buyers in the rest of the world are spending $100 billion per year acquiring assets in a country, while that country's buyers are spending $70 billion per year to acquire assets in the rest of the world. The country thus has a capital account surplus of $30 billion per year. Equation 30.3 tells us the country must have a current account deficit of $30 billion per year.

Alternatively, suppose buyers from the rest of the world acquire $25 billion of a country's assets per year and that buyers in that country buy $40 billion per year in assets in other countries. The economy has a capital account deficit of $15 billion; its capital account balance equals -$15 billion. Equation 30.3 tells us it thus has a current account surplus of $15 billion. In general, we may write the following:

EQUATION 30.4

$$\text{Current account balance} = -(\text{capital account balance})$$

Assuming the market for a nation's currency is in equilibrium, a capital account surplus *necessarily* means a current account deficit. A capital account deficit *necessarily* means a current account surplus. Similarly, a current account surplus implies a capital account deficit; a current account deficit implies a capital account surplus. Whenever the market for a country's currency is in equilibrium, and it virtually always is in the absence of exchange rate controls, Equation 30.3 is an identity—it must be true. Thus, any surplus or deficit in the current account means the capital account has an offsetting deficit or surplus.

The accounting relationships underlying international finance hold as long as a country's currency market is in equilibrium. But what are the economic forces at work that cause these equalities to hold? Consider how global turmoil in 1997 and 1998, discussed in the chapter opening, affected the United States. Holders of assets, including foreign currencies, in the rest of the world were understandably concerned that the values of those assets might fall. To avoid a plunge in the values of their own holdings, many of them purchased U.S. assets, including U.S. dollars. Those purchases of U.S. assets increased the U.S. surplus on capital account. To buy those assets, foreign purchasers had to purchase dollars. Also, U.S. citizens became less willing to hold foreign assets, and their preference for holding U.S. assets increased. United States citizens were thus less willing to supply dollars to the foreign exchange market. The increased demand for dollars and the decreased supply of dollars sent the U.S. exchange rate higher, as shown in Panel (a) of Figure 30.4. Panel (b) shows the actual movement of the U.S. exchange rate in 1997 and 1998. Notice the sharp increases in the exchange rate throughout most of the period. A higher exchange rate in the United States reduces U.S. exports and increases U.S. imports, increasing the current account deficit. Panel (c) shows the movement of the current and capital accounts in the United States in 1997 and 1998. Notice that as the capital account surplus increased, the current account deficit rose. A reduction in the U.S. exchange rate at the end of 1998 coincided with a movement of these balances in the opposite direction.

FIGURE 30.4 A Change in the Exchange Rate Affected the U.S. Current and Capital Accounts in 1997 and 1998

Turmoil in currency markets all over the world in 1997 and 1998 increased the demand for dollars and decreased the supply of dollars in the foreign exchange market, which caused an increase in the U.S. exchange rate, as shown in Panel (a). Panel (b) shows actual values of the U.S. exchange rate during that period; Panel (c) shows U.S. balances on current and on capital accounts. Notice that the balance on capital account generally rose while the balance on current account generally fell.

Deficits and Surpluses: Good or Bad?

For the past quarter century, the United States has had a current account deficit and a capital account surplus. Is this good or bad?

Viewed from the perspective of consumers, neither phenomenon seems to pose a problem. A current account deficit is likely to imply a trade deficit. That means more goods and services are flowing into the country than are flowing out. A capital account surplus means more spending is flowing into the country for the purchase of assets than is flowing out. It is hard to see the harm in any of that.

Public opinion, however, appears to regard a current account deficit and capital account surplus as highly undesirable, perhaps because people associate a trade deficit with a loss of jobs. But that is erroneous; employment in the long run is determined by forces that have nothing to do with a trade deficit. An increase in the trade deficit (that is, a reduction in net exports) reduces aggregate demand in the short run, but net exports are only one component of aggregate demand. Other factors—consumption, investment, and government purchases—affect aggregate demand as well. There is no reason a trade deficit should imply a loss of jobs.

What about foreign purchases of U.S. assets? One objection to such purchases is that if foreigners own U.S. assets, they will receive the income from those assets—spending will flow out of the country. But it is hard to see the harm in paying income to financial investors. When someone buys a bond issued by Microsoft, interest payments will flow from Microsoft to the bond holder. Does Microsoft view the purchase of its bond as a bad thing? Of course not. Despite the fact that Microsoft's payment of interest on the bond and the ultimate repayment of the face value of the bond will exceed what the company originally received from the bond purchaser, Microsoft is surely not unhappy with the arrangement. It expects to put that money to more productive use; that is the reason it issued the bond in the first place.

A second concern about foreign asset purchases is that the United States in some sense loses sovereignty when foreigners buy its assets. But why should this be a problem? Foreign-owned firms competing in U.S. markets are at the mercy of those markets, as are firms owned by U.S. nationals. Foreign owners of U.S. real estate have no special power. What about foreign buyers of bonds issued by the U.S. government? Foreigners owned about 52% of these bonds at the end of December 2010; they are thus the creditors for about half the national debt. But this position hardly puts them in control of the government of the United States. They hold an obligation of the U.S. government to pay them a certain amount of U.S. dollars on a certain date, nothing more. A foreign owner could sell his or her bonds, but more than $100 billion worth of these bonds are sold every day. The resale of U.S. bonds by a foreign owner will not affect the U.S. government.

In short, there is no economic justification for concern about having a current account deficit and a capital account surplus—nor would there be an economic reason to be concerned about the opposite state of affairs. The important feature of international trade is its potential to improve living standards for people. It is not a game in which current account balances are the scorecard.

Key Takeaways

- The balance of payments shows spending flowing into and out of a country.
- The current account is an accounting statement that includes all spending flows across a nation's border except those that represent purchases of assets. In our simplified analysis, the balance on current account equals net exports.
- A nation's balance on capital account equals rest-of-world purchases of its assets during a period less its purchases of rest-of-world assets.
- Provided that the market for a nation's currency is in equilibrium, the balance on current account equals the negative of the balance on capital account.
- There is no economic justification for viewing any particular current account balance as a good or bad thing.

Try It!

Use Equation 30.3 and Equation 30.4 to compute the variables given in each of the following. Assume that the market for a nation's currency is in equilibrium and that the balance on current account equals net exports.

1. Suppose U.S. exports equal $300 billion, imports equal $400 billion, and rest-of-world purchases of U.S. assets equal $150 billion. What is the U.S. balance on current account? The balance on capital account? What is the value of U.S. purchases of rest-of-world assets?

2. Suppose Japanese exports equal ¥200 trillion (¥ is the symbol for the yen, Japan's currency), imports equal ¥120 trillion, and Japan's purchases of rest-of-world assets equal ¥90 trillion. What is the balance on Japan's current account? The balance on Japan's capital account? What is the value of rest-of-world purchases of Japan's assets?

3. Suppose Britain's purchases of rest-of-world assets equal £70 billion (£ is the symbol for the pound, Britain's currency), rest-of-world purchases of British assets equal £90 billion, and Britain's exports equal £40 billion. What is Britain's balance on capital account? Its balance on current account? Its total imports?

4. Suppose Mexico's purchases of rest-of-world assets equal $500 billion ($ is the symbol for the peso, Mexico's currency), rest-of-world purchases of Mexico's assets equal $700 billion, and Mexico's imports equal $550 billion. What is Mexico's balance on capital account? Its balance on current account? Its total exports?

Case in Point: Alan Greenspan on the U.S. Current Account Deficit

Source: By White House photo by Shealah Craighead (Whitehouse.gov (link)) [Public domain], via Wikimedia Commons

The growing U.S. current account deficit has generated considerable alarm. But, is there cause for alarm? In a speech in December 2005, former Federal Reserve Chairman Alan Greenspan analyzed what he feels are the causes of the growing deficit and explains how the U.S. current account deficit may, under certain circumstances, decrease over time without a crisis.

"In November 2003, I noted that we saw little evidence of stress in funding the U.S. current account deficit even though the real exchange rate for the dollar, on net, had declined more than 10% since early 2002. ... Two years later, little has changed except that our current account deficit has grown still larger. Most policy makers marvel at the seeming ease with which the United States continues to finance its current account deficit.

"Of course, deficits that cumulate to ever-increasing net external debt, with its attendant rise in servicing costs, cannot persist indefinitely. At some point, foreign investors will balk at a growing concentration of claims against U.S. residents ... and will begin to alter their portfolios. ... The rise of the U.S. current account deficit over the past decade appears to have coincided with a pronounced new phase of globalization that is characterized by a major acceleration in U.S. productivity growth and the decline in what economists call home bias. In brief, home bias is the parochial tendency of persons, though faced with comparable or superior foreign opportunities, to invest domestic savings in the home country. The decline in home bias is reflected in savers increasingly reaching across national borders to invest in foreign assets. The rise in U.S. productivity attracted much of those savings toward investments in the United States. ...

"Accordingly, it is tempting to conclude that the U.S. current account deficit is essentially a byproduct of long-term secular forces, and thus is largely benign. After all, we do seem to have been able to finance our international current account deficit with relative ease in recent years.

"But does the apparent continued rise in the deficits of U.S. individual households and nonfinancial businesses themselves reflect growing economic strain? (We do not think so.) And does it matter how those deficits of individual economic entities are being financed? Specifically, does the recent growing proportion of these deficits being financed, net, by foreigners matter? ...

"If the currently disturbing drift toward protectionism is contained and markets remain sufficiently flexible, changing terms of trade, interest rates, asset prices, and exchange rates will cause U.S. saving to rise, reducing the need for foreign finance, and reversing the trend of the past decade toward increasing reliance on it. If, however, the pernicious drift toward fiscal instability in the United States and elsewhere is not arrested and is compounded by a protectionist reversal of globalization, the adjustment process could be quite painful for the world economy."

Source: *Based on Alan Greenspan, "International Imbalances" (speech, Advancing Enterprise Conference, London, England, December 2, 2005), available at http://www.federalreserve.gov/ boarddocs/speeches/2005/200512022/default.htm.*

Answers to Try It! Problems

1. All figures are in billions of U.S. dollars per period. The left-hand side of Equation 30.3 is the current account balance

$$\text{Exports} - \text{imports} = \$300 - \$400 = -\$100$$

Using Equation 30.4, the balance on capital account is

$$-\$100 = -(\text{capital account balance})$$

Solving this equation for the capital account balance, we find that it is $100. The term in parentheses on the right-hand side of Equation 30.3 is also the balance on capital account. We thus have

$$\$100 = \$150 - \text{U.S. purchases of rest-of-world assets}$$

Solving this for U.S. purchase of rest-of-world assets, we find they are $50.

2. All figures are in trillions of yen per period. The left-hand side of Equation 30.3 is the current account balance

$$\text{Exports} - \text{imports} = ¥200 - ¥120 = ¥80$$

Using Equation 30.4, the balance on capital account is

$$¥80 = -(\text{capital account balance})$$

Solving this equation for the capital account balance, we find that it is –¥80. The term in parentheses on the right-hand side of Equation 30.3 is also the balance on capital account. We thus have

$$-¥80 = \text{rest-of-world purchases of Japan's assets} - ¥90$$

Solving this for the rest-of-world purchases of Japan's assets, we find they are ¥10.

3. All figures are in billions of pounds per period. The term in parentheses on the right-hand side of Equation 30.3 is the balance on capital account. We thus have

$$£90 - £70 = £20$$

Using Equation 30.4, the balance on current account is

$$\text{Current account balance} = -(£20)$$

The left-hand side of Equation 30.3 is also the current account balance

$$£40 - \text{imports} = -£20$$

Solving for imports, we find they are £60. Britain's balance on current account is –£20 billion, its balance on capital account is £20 billion, and its total imports equal £60 billion per period.

4. All figures are in billions of pesos per period. The term in parentheses on the right-hand side of Equation 30.3 is the balance on capital account. We thus have

$$\$700 - \$500 = \$200$$

Using Equation 30.4, the balance on current account is

$$\text{Current account balance} = -(\$200)$$

The left-hand side of Equation 30.3 is also the current account balance

$$\text{Exports} - \$550 = -\$200$$

Solving for exports, we find they are $350.

30.4 Exchange Rate Systems

Learning Objectives

1. Define the various types of exchange rate systems.
2. Discuss some of the pros and cons of different exchange rate systems.

Exchange rates are determined by demand and supply. But governments can influence those exchange rates in various ways. The extent and nature of government involvement in currency markets define alternative systems of exchange rates. In this section we will examine some common systems and explore some of their macroeconomic implications.

There are three broad categories of exchange rate systems. In one system, exchange rates are set purely by private market forces with no government involvement. Values change constantly as the demand for and supply of currencies fluctuate. In another system, currency values are allowed to change, but governments participate in currency markets in an effort to influence those values. Finally, governments may seek to fix the values of their currencies, either through participation in the market or through regulatory policy.

Free-Floating Systems

free-floating exchange rate system

System in which governments and central banks do not participate in the market for foreign exchange.

In a **free-floating exchange rate system**, governments and central banks do not participate in the market for foreign exchange. The relationship between governments and central banks on the one hand and currency markets on the other is much the same as the typical relationship between these institutions and stock markets. Governments may regulate stock markets to prevent fraud, but stock values themselves are left to float in the market. The U.S. government, for example, does not intervene in the stock market to influence stock prices.

The concept of a completely free-floating exchange rate system is a theoretical one. In practice, all governments or central banks intervene in currency markets in an effort to influence exchange rates. Some countries, such as the United States, intervene to only a small degree, so that the notion of a free-floating exchange rate system comes close to what actually exists in the United States.

A free-floating system has the advantage of being self-regulating. There is no need for government intervention if the exchange rate is left to the market. Market forces also restrain large swings in demand or supply. Suppose, for example, that a dramatic shift in world preferences led to a sharply increased demand for goods and services produced in Canada. This would increase the demand for Canadian dollars, raise Canada's exchange rate, and make Canadian goods and services more expensive for foreigners to buy. Some of the impact of the swing in foreign demand would thus be absorbed in a rising exchange rate. In effect, a free-floating exchange rate acts as a buffer to insulate an economy from the impact of international events.

The primary difficulty with free-floating exchange rates lies in their unpredictability. Contracts between buyers and sellers in different countries must not only reckon with possible changes in prices and other factors during the lives of those contracts, they must also consider the possibility of exchange rate changes. An agreement by a U.S. distributor to purchase a certain quantity of Canadian lumber each year, for example, will be affected by the possibility that the exchange rate between the Canadian dollar and the U.S. dollar will change while the contract is in effect. Fluctuating exchange rates make international transactions riskier and thus increase the cost of doing business with other countries.

Managed Float Systems

Governments and central banks often seek to increase or decrease their exchange rates by buying or selling their own currencies. Exchange rates are still free to float, but governments try to influence their values. Government or central bank participation in a floating exchange rate system is called a **managed float**.

Countries that have a floating exchange rate system intervene from time to time in the currency market in an effort to raise or lower the price of their own currency. Typically, the purpose of such intervention is to prevent sudden large swings in the value of a nation's currency. Such intervention is likely to have only a small impact, if any, on exchange rates. Roughly $1.5 trillion worth of currencies changes hands every day in the world market; it is difficult for any one agency—even an agency the size of the U.S. government or the Fed—to force significant changes in exchange rates.

Still, governments or central banks can sometimes influence their exchange rates. Suppose the price of a country's currency is rising very rapidly. The country's government or central bank might seek to hold off further increases in order to prevent a major reduction in net exports. An announcement that a further increase in its exchange rate is unacceptable, followed by sales of that country's currency by the central bank in order to bring its exchange rate down, can sometimes convince other participants in the currency market that the exchange rate will not rise further. That change in expectations could reduce demand for and increase supply of the currency, thus achieving the goal of holding the exchange rate down.

managed float

Government or central bank participation in a floating exchange rate system.

Fixed Exchange Rates

In a **fixed exchange rate system**, the exchange rate between two currencies is set by government policy. There are several mechanisms through which fixed exchange rates may be maintained. Whatever the system for maintaining these rates, however, all fixed exchange rate systems share some important features.

fixed exchange rate system

System in which the exchange rate between two currencies is set by government policy.

A Commodity Standard

In a **commodity standard system**, countries fix the value of their respective currencies relative to a certain commodity or group of commodities. With each currency's value fixed in terms of the commodity, currencies are fixed relative to one another.

For centuries, the values of many currencies were fixed relative to gold. Suppose, for example, that the price of gold were fixed at $20 per ounce in the United States. This would mean that the government of the United States was committed to exchanging 1 ounce of gold to anyone who handed over $20. (That was the case in the United States—and $20 was roughly the price—up to 1933.) Now suppose that the exchange rate between the British pound and gold was £5 per ounce of gold. With £5 and $20 both trading for 1 ounce of gold, £1 would exchange for $4. No one would pay more than $4 for £1, because $4 could always be exchanged for 1/5 ounce of gold, and that gold could be exchanged for £1. And no one would sell £1 for less than $4, because the owner of £1 could always exchange it for 1/5 ounce of gold, which could be exchanged for $4. In practice, actual currency values could vary slightly from the levels implied by their commodity values because of the costs involved in exchanging currencies for gold, but these variations are slight.

commodity standard system

System in which countries fix the value of their respective currencies relative to a certain commodity or group of commodities.

Under the gold standard, the quantity of money was regulated by the quantity of gold in a country. If, for example, the United States guaranteed to exchange dollars for gold at the rate of $20 per ounce, it could not issue more money than it could back up with the gold it owned.

The gold standard was a self-regulating system. Suppose that at the fixed exchange rate implied by the gold standard, the supply of a country's currency exceeded the demand. That would imply that spending flowing out of the country exceeded spending flowing in. As residents supplied their currency to make foreign purchases, foreigners acquiring that currency could redeem it for gold, since countries guaranteed to exchange gold for their currencies at a fixed rate. Gold would thus flow out of the country running a deficit. Given an obligation to exchange the country's currency for gold, a reduction in a country's gold holdings would force it to reduce its money supply. That would reduce aggregate demand in the country, lowering income and the price level. But both of those events would increase net exports in the country, eliminating the deficit in the balance of payments. Balance would be achieved, but at the cost of a recession. A country with a surplus in its balance of payments would experience an inflow of gold. That would boost its money supply and increase aggregate demand. That, in turn, would generate higher prices and higher real GDP. Those events would reduce net exports and correct the surplus in the balance of payments, but again at the cost of changes in the domestic economy.

Because of this tendency for imbalances in a country's balance of payments to be corrected only through changes in the entire economy, nations began abandoning the gold standard in the 1930s. That was the period of the Great Depression, during which world trade virtually was ground to a halt. World War II made the shipment of goods an extremely risky proposition, so trade remained minimal during the war. As the war was coming to an end, representatives of the United States and its allies met in 1944 at Bretton Woods, New Hampshire, to fashion a new mechanism through which international trade could be financed after the war. The system was to be one of fixed exchange rates, but with much less emphasis on gold as a backing for the system.

currency board arrangements

Fixed exchange rate systems in which there is explicit legislative commitment to exchange domestic currency for a specified foreign currency at a fixed rate.

In recent years, a number of countries have set up **currency board arrangements**, which are a kind of commodity standard, fixed exchange rate system in which there is explicit legislative commitment to exchange domestic currency for a specified foreign currency at a fixed rate and a currency board to ensure fulfillment of the legal obligations this arrangement entails. In its simplest form, this type of arrangement implies that domestic currency can be issued only when the currency board has an equivalent amount of the foreign currency to which the domestic currency is pegged. With a currency board arrangement, the country's ability to conduct independent monetary policy is severely limited. It can create reserves only when the currency board has an excess of foreign currency. If the currency board is short of foreign currency, it must cut back on reserves.

Argentina established a currency board in 1991 and fixed its currency to the U.S. dollar. For an economy plagued in the 1980s with falling real GDP and rising inflation, the currency board served to restore confidence in the government's commitment to stabilization policies and to a restoration of economic growth. The currency board seemed to work well for Argentina for most of the 1990s, as inflation subsided and growth of real GDP picked up.

The drawbacks of a currency board are essentially the same as those associated with the gold standard. Faced with a decrease in consumption, investment, and net exports in 1999, Argentina could not use monetary and fiscal policies to try to shift its aggregate demand curve to the right. It abandoned the system in 2002.

Fixed Exchange Rates Through Intervention

The Bretton Woods Agreement called for each currency's value to be fixed relative to other currencies. The mechanism for maintaining these rates, however, was to be intervention by governments and central banks in the currency market.

Again suppose that the exchange rate between the dollar and the British pound is fixed at $4 per £1. Suppose further that this rate is an equilibrium rate, as illustrated in Figure 30.5. As long as the fixed rate coincides with the equilibrium rate, the fixed exchange rate operates in the same fashion as a free-floating rate.

Now suppose that the British choose to purchase more U.S. goods and services. The supply curve for pounds increases, and the equilibrium exchange rate for the pound (in terms of dollars) falls to, say, $3. Under the terms of the Bretton Woods Agreement, Britain and the United States would be required to intervene in the market to bring the exchange rate back to the rate fixed in the agreement, $4. If the adjustment were to be made by the British central bank, the Bank of England, it would have to purchase pounds. It would do so by exchanging dollars it had previously acquired in other transactions for pounds. As it sold dollars, it would take in checks written in pounds. When a central bank sells an asset, the checks that come into the central bank reduce the money supply and bank reserves in that country. We saw in the chapter explaining the money supply, for example, that the sale of bonds by the Fed reduces the U.S. money supply. Similarly, the sale of dollars by the Bank of England would reduce the British money supply. In order to bring its exchange rate back to the agreed-to level, Britain would have to carry out a contractionary monetary policy.

Alternatively, the Fed could intervene. It could purchase pounds, writing checks in dollars. But when a central bank purchases assets, it adds reserves to the system and increases the money supply. The United States would thus be forced to carry out an expansionary monetary policy.

Domestic disturbances created by efforts to maintain fixed exchange rates brought about the demise of the Bretton Woods system. Japan and West Germany gave up the effort to maintain the fixed values of their currencies in the spring of 1971 and announced they were withdrawing from the Bretton Woods system. President Richard Nixon pulled the United States out of the system in August of that year, and the system collapsed. An attempt to revive fixed exchange rates in 1973 collapsed almost immediately, and the world has operated largely on a managed float ever since.

Under the Bretton Woods system, the United States had redeemed dollars held by other governments for gold; President Nixon terminated that policy as he withdrew the United States from the Bretton Woods system. The dollar is no longer backed by gold.

Fixed exchange rate systems offer the advantage of predictable currency values—when they are working. But for fixed exchange rates to work, the countries participating in them must maintain domestic economic conditions that will keep equilibrium currency values close to the fixed rates. Sovereign nations must be willing to coordinate their monetary and fiscal policies. Achieving that kind of coordination among independent countries can be a difficult task.

The fact that coordination of monetary and fiscal policies is difficult does not mean it is impossible. Eleven members of the European Union not only agreed to fix their exchange rates to one another, they agreed to adopt a common currency, the euro. The new currency was introduced in 1998 and became fully adopted in 1999. Since then, six other nations have joined. The nations that adopted it agreed to strict limits on their fiscal policies. Each continues to have its own central bank, but these national central banks operate similarly to the regional banks of the Federal Reserve System in the United States. The new European Central Bank conducts monetary policy throughout the area. Details of this revolutionary venture and the extraordinary problems it has encountered in recent years are provided in the accompanying Case in Point.

When exchange rates are fixed but fiscal and monetary policies are not coordinated, equilibrium exchange rates can move away from their fixed levels. Once exchange rates start to diverge, the effort to force currencies up or down through market intervention can be extremely disruptive. And when countries suddenly decide to give that effort up, exchange rates can swing sharply in one direction or another. When that happens, the main virtue of fixed exchange rates, their predictability, is lost.

Thailand's experience with the baht illustrates the potential difficulty with attempts to maintain a fixed exchange rate. Thailand's central bank had held the exchange rate between the dollar and the baht steady, at a price for the baht of $0.04. Several factors, including weakness in the

FIGURE 30.5 Maintaining a Fixed Exchange Rate Through Intervention
Initially, the equilibrium price of the British pound equals $4, the fixed rate between the pound and the dollar. Now suppose an increased supply of British pounds lowers the equilibrium price of the pound to $3. The Bank of England could purchase pounds by selling dollars in order to shift the demand curve for pounds to D_2. Alternatively, the Fed could shift the demand curve to D_2 by buying pounds.

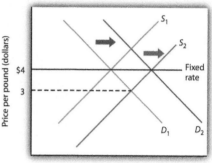

Japanese economy, reduced the demand for Thai exports and thus reduced the demand for the baht, as shown in Panel (a) of Figure 30.6. Thailand's central bank, committed to maintaining the price of the baht at $0.04, bought baht to increase the demand, as shown in Panel (b). Central banks buy their own currency using their reserves of foreign currencies. We have seen that when a central bank sells bonds, the money supply falls. When it sells foreign currency, the result is no different. Sales of foreign currency by Thailand's central bank in order to purchase the baht thus reduced Thailand's money supply and reduced the bank's holdings of foreign currencies. As currency traders began to suspect that the bank might give up its effort to hold the baht's value, they sold baht, shifting the supply curve to the right, as shown in Panel (c). That forced the central bank to buy even more baht—selling even more foreign currency—until it finally gave up the effort and allowed the baht to become a free-floating currency. By the end of 1997, the baht had lost nearly half its value relative to the dollar.

FIGURE 30.6 The Anatomy of a Currency Collapse

Weakness in the Japanese economy, among other factors, led to a reduced demand for the baht (Panel [a]). That put downward pressure on the baht's value relative to other currencies. Committed to keeping the price of the baht at $0.04, Thailand's central bank bought baht to increase the demand, as shown in Panel (b). However, as holders of baht and other Thai assets began to fear that the central bank might give up its effort to prop up the baht, they sold baht, shifting the supply curve for baht to the right (Panel [c]) and putting more downward pressure on the baht's price. Finally, in July of 1997, the central bank gave up its effort to prop up the currency. By the end of the year, the baht's dollar value had fallen to about $0.02.

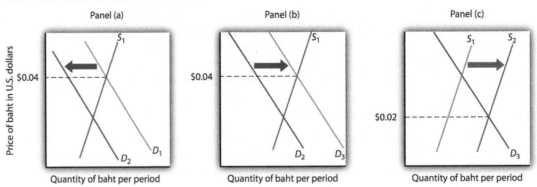

As we saw in the introduction to this chapter, the plunge in the baht was the first in a chain of currency crises that rocked the world in 1997 and 1998. International trade has the great virtue of increasing the availability of goods and services to the world's consumers. But financing trade—and the way nations handle that financing—can create difficulties.

Key Takeaways

- In a free-floating exchange rate system, exchange rates are determined by demand and supply.
- Exchange rates are determined by demand and supply in a managed float system, but governments intervene as buyers or sellers of currencies in an effort to influence exchange rates.
- In a fixed exchange rate system, exchange rates among currencies are not allowed to change. The gold standard and the Bretton Woods system are examples of fixed exchange rate systems.

Try It!

Suppose a nation's central bank is committed to holding the value of its currency, the mon, at $2 per mon. Suppose further that holders of the mon fear that its value is about to fall and begin selling mon to purchase U.S. dollars. What will happen in the market for mon? Explain your answer carefully, and illustrate it using a demand and supply graph for the market for mon. What action will the nation's central bank take? Use your graph to show the result of the central bank's action. Why might this action fuel concern among holders of the mon about its future prospects? What difficulties will this create for the nation's central bank?

Case in Point: The Euro

Source: © Shutterstock, Inc.

It was the most dramatic development in international finance since the collapse of the Bretton Woods system. A new currency, the euro, began trading among 11 European nations—Austria, Belgium, Finland, France, Germany, Ireland, Italy, Luxembourg, the Netherlands, Portugal, and Spain—in 1999. During a three-year transition, each nation continued to have its own currency, which traded at a fixed rate with the euro. In 2001, Greece joined, and in 2002, the currencies of the participant nations disappeared altogether and were replaced by the euro. In 2007, Slovenia adopted the euro, as did Cyprus and Malta in 2008, Slovakia in 2009, and Estonia in 2011. Notable exceptions are Britain, Sweden, Switzerland, and Denmark. Still, most of Europe now operates as the ultimate fixed exchange rate regime, a region with a single currency.

To participate in this radical experiment, the nations switching to the euro had to agree to give up considerable autonomy in monetary and fiscal policy. While each nation continues to have its own central bank, those central banks operate more like regional banks of the Federal Reserve System in the United States; they have no authority to conduct monetary policy. That authority is vested in a new central bank, the European Central Bank.

The participants also agreed in principle to strict limits on their fiscal policies. Their deficits could be no greater than 3% of nominal GDP, and their total national debt could not exceed 60% of nominal GDP.

The fact that many of the euro nations had disregarded these limits became a major problem for the new currency when the recession and financial crisis hit in 2008. The biggest "sinner" turned out to be Greece, but there were others, such as Italy, that also had not adhered to the agreement. The fiscal situation of other countries, such as Ireland, went sour as the recession and financial problems deepened. The countries that seemed most at risk of being unable to pay their sovereign (government) debts as they became due came to be known as the PIIGS—Portugal, Ireland, Italy, Greece, and Spain—but there was a period in 2011 when even the interest rate on French bonds was abnormally high. The whole world seemed to be waiting throughout most of 2011 to see if the euro would hold together and, in particular, if Greece would default on its debt.

Finally, in early 2012, the situation seemed to calm down. The European Union nations (excluding the United Kingdom and the Czech Republic, which are not part of the eurozone) agreed to a new treaty that again requires fiscal discipline but this time has more enforcement associated with it. The European Union was setting up the European Stability Mechanism: a fund to help out with short-term liquidity problems that nations might encounter. Greece agreed to tough demands to reduce its deficit and then became eligible for a second EU bailout. It also managed to negotiate a debt-restricting deal with its private-sector lenders.

The euro has been a mixed blessing for eurozone countries trying to get through this difficult period. For example, guarantees that the Irish government made concerning bank deposits and debt have been better received, because Ireland is part of the euro system. On the other hand, if Ireland had a floating currency, its depreciation might enhance Irish exports, which would help Ireland to get out of its recession. The euro exchange rate has probably benefited German exports, since a German currency would probably trade at a premium over the euro, but it has hurt exports from countries whose single-nation currencies would likely be weaker.

Also, even though there is a single currency, each country in the eurozone issues its own debt. The smaller market for each country's debt, each with different risk premiums, makes them less liquid, especially in difficult financial times. In contrast, the U.S. government is a single issuer of federal debt.

Even with general regulation of overall parameters, fiscal policy for the 17 nations is largely a separate matter. Each has its own retirement and unemployment insurance programs, for example. In the United States, if one state is experiencing high unemployment, more federal unemployment insurance benefits will flow to that state. But if unemployment rises in Portugal, for example, its budget deficit will be negatively impacted, and Portugal will have to undertake additional austerity measures to stay within the EU-imposed deficit limit.

The fate of the euro remains uncertain. Even with the restructuring and bailouts, will Greece be able to meet its debt obligations? In early 2017 there were renewed worries that Greece could default on debt payments due in the summer, and the interest rate on Greek bonds again spiked. Is Grexit, Greek exit from the eurozone, on the horizon? If that happens, what changes for the euro might follow? For example, the value of the currency might appreciate if Greece and possibly other weaker economies in the eurozone left the arrangement. Or might the whole experiment collapse? Agreements to get through crises have tended to form at the eleventh hour and this one may end in the same way, or maybe…

Answer to Try It! Problem

The value of the mon is initially $2. Fear that the mon might fall will lead to an increase in its supply to S_2, putting downward pressure on the currency. To maintain the value of the mon at $2, the central bank will buy mon, thus shifting the demand curve to D_2. This policy, though, creates two difficulties. First, it requires that the bank sell other currencies, and a sale of any asset by a central bank is a contractionary monetary policy. Second, the sale depletes the bank's holdings of foreign currencies. If holders of the mon fear the central bank will give up its effort, then they might sell mon, shifting the supply curve farther to the right and forcing even more vigorous action by the central bank.

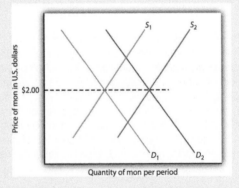

30.5 Review and Practice

Summary

In this chapter we examined the role of net exports in the economy. We found that export and import demand are influenced by many different factors, the most important being domestic and foreign income levels, changes in relative prices, the exchange rate, and preferences and technology. An increase in net exports shifts the aggregate demand curve to the right; a reduction shifts it to the left.

In the foreign exchange market, the equilibrium exchange rate is determined by the intersection of the demand and supply curves for a currency. Given the ease with which most currencies can be traded, we can assume this equilibrium is achieved, so that the quantity of a currency demanded equals the quantity supplied. An economy can experience current account surpluses or deficits. The balance on current account equals the negative of the balance on capital account. We saw that one reason for the current account deficit in the United States is the U.S. capital account surplus; the United States has attracted a great deal of foreign financial investment.

The chapter closed with an examination of floating and fixed exchange rate systems. Fixed exchange rate systems include commodity-based systems and fixed rates that are maintained through intervention. Exchange rate systems have moved from a gold standard, to a system of fixed rates with intervention, to a mixed set of arrangements of floating and fixed exchange rates.

Concept Problems

1. David Ricardo, a famous English economist of the 19th century, stressed that a nation has a comparative advantage in those products for which its efficiency relative to other nations is the highest. He argued in favor of specialization and trade based on comparative, not absolute, advantage. From a global perspective, what would be the "advantage" of such a system?

2. For several months prior to your vacation trip to Naples, Italy, you note that the exchange rate for the dollar has been increasing relative to the euro (that is, it takes more euro to buy a dollar). Are you pleased or sad? Explain.

3. Who might respond in a way different from your own to the falling value of the euro in Question 2?

4. Suppose a nation has a deficit on capital account. What does this mean? What can you conclude about its balance on current account?

5. Suppose a nation has a surplus on capital account. What does this mean? What can you conclude about its balance on current account?

6. The following analysis appeared in a newspaper editorial:

   "If foreigners own our businesses and land, that's one thing, but when they own billions in U.S. bonds, that's another. We don't care who owns the businesses, but our grandchildren will have to put up with a lower standard of living because of the interest payments sent overseas. Therefore, we must reduce our trade deficit."

   Critically analyze this editorial view. Are the basic premises correct? The conclusion?

7. In the years prior to the abandonment of the gold standard, foreigners cashed in their dollars and the U.S. Treasury "lost gold" at unprecedented rates. Today, the dollar is no longer tied to gold and is free to float. What are the fundamental differences between a currency based on the gold standard and one that is allowed to float? What would the U.S. "lose" if foreigners decided to "cash in" their dollars today?

8. Can there be a deficit on current account and a deficit on capital account at the same time? Explain.

9. Suppose the people of a certain economy increase their spending on foreign-produced goods and services. What will be the effect on real GDP and the price level in the short run? In the long run?

10. Now suppose the people of a certain economy reduce their spending on foreign-produced goods and services. What will be the effect on real GDP and the price level in the short run? In the long run?

11. Canada, Mexico, and the United States have a free trade zone. What would be some of the advantages of having a common currency as well? The disadvantages? Do you think it would be a good idea? Why or why not?

12. The text says that the U.S. capital account surplus necessarily implies a current account deficit. Suppose that the United States were to undertake measures to eliminate its capital account surplus. What sorts of measures might it take? Do you think such measures would be a good idea? Why or why not?

Numerical Problems

1. For each of the following scenarios, determine whether the aggregate demand curve will shift. If so, in which direction will it shift and by how much?

    a. A change in consumer preferences leads to an initial $25-billion decrease in net exports. The multiplier is 1.5.

    b. A change in trade policies leads to an initial $25-billion increase in net exports. The multiplier is 1.

    c. There is an increase in the domestic price level from 1 to 1.05, while the price level of the country's major trading partner does not change. The multiplier is 2.

    d. Recession in a country's trading partner lowers exports by $20 billion. The multiplier is 2.

2. Fill in the missing items in the table below. All figures are in U.S. billions of dollars.

	U.S. exports	U.S. imports	Domestic purchases of foreign assets	Rest-of-world purchases of U.S. assets
a.	100	100	400	
b.	100	200		200
c.	300		400	600
d.		800	800	1,100

3. Suppose the market for a country's currency is in equilibrium and that its exports equal $700 billion, its purchases of rest-of-world assets equal $1,000 billion, and foreign purchases of its assets equal $1,200 billion. Assuming it has no international transfer payments and that output is measured as GNP:

    a. What are the country's imports?

    b. What is the country's balance on current account?

    c. What is the country's balance on capital account?

4. Suppose that the market for a country's currency is in equilibrium and that its exports equal $400, its imports equal $500 billion, and rest-of-world purchases of the country's assets equal $100. Assuming it has no international transfer payments and that output is measured as GNP:

    a. What is the country's balance on current account?

    b. What is the country's balance on capital account?

    c. What is the value of the country's purchases of rest-of-world assets?

5. The information below describes the trade-weighted exchange rate for the dollar (standardized at a value of 100) and net exports (in billions of dollars) for an eight-month period.

Month	Trade-weighted exchange rate	Net exports
January	100.5	−9.8
February	99.9	−11.6
March	100.5	−13.5
April	100.3	−14.0
May	99.6	−15.6
June	100.9	−14.2
July	101.4	−14.9
August	101.8	−16.7

   a. Plot the data on a graph.

   b. Do the data support the expected relationship between the trade-weighted exchange rate and net exports? Explain.

6. The graph below shows the foreign exchange market between the United States and Japan before and after an increase in the demand for Japanese goods by U.S. consumers.

   a. If the exchange rate was free-floating prior to the change in demand for Japanese goods, what was its likely value?

   b. After the change in demand, the free-floating exchange rate would be how many yen per dollar?

   c. If the Japanese central bank wanted to keep the exchange rate fixed at its initial value, how many dollars would it have to buy?

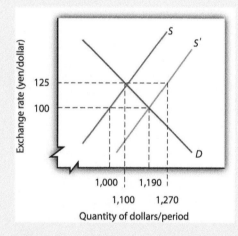

7. Suppose Japan relaxes its restrictions on imports of foreign goods and services and begins importing more from the United States. Illustrate graphically how this will affect the U.S. exchange rate, price level, and level of real GDP in the short run and in the long run. How will it affect these same variables in Japan? (Assume both economies are initially operating at their potential levels of output.)

8. Suppose U.S. investors begin purchasing assets in Mexico. Illustrate graphically how this will affect the U.S. exchange rate, price level, and level of real GDP in the short run and in the long run. How will it affect these same variables in Mexico? (Assume both economies are initially operating at their potential levels of output.)

9. Suppose foreigners begin buying more assets in the United States. Illustrate graphically how this will affect the U.S. exchange rate, price level, and level of real GDP in the short run and in the long run. (Assume the economy is initially operating at its potential output.)

Endnotes

1. For an interesting history of this remarkable development, see Marc Levinson, *The Box: How the Shipping Container Made the World Smaller and the World Economy Bigger* (Princeton: Princeton University Press, 2006).

Inflation and Unemployment

31.1 Start Up: The Inflation/Unemployment Conundrum

As the twentieth century drew to a close, the people of the United States could look back on a remarkable achievement. From 1992 through 2000, the unemployment rate *fell* every year. The inflation rate, measured as the annual percentage change in the implicit price deflator, was about 2% or less during this period. The dramatic reduction in the two rates provided welcome relief to a nation that had seen soaring unemployment early in the 1980s, soaring inflation in the late 1970s, and painful increases in both rates early in the 1970s.

Unemployment and inflation rates remained fairly low during the early 2000s. Following a brief recession in 2001, in which unemployment reached nearly 6% (though this actually occurred after the recession officially ended), it fell back to 4.6% in 2006 and 2007. Through 2007, inflation never exceeded 3.3%. With the start of the recession in December 2007, the unemployment rate began to rise. At first, though, it appeared that inflation was becoming a bigger problem, as rising gas and food prices until summer 2008 seemed to be driving up other prices and increasing inflationary expectations. Indeed, through much of 2008, a debate over the appropriate direction of monetary policy occurred over just this issue: should the Fed ease the federal funds rate in an attempt to reduce unemployment or at least to keep it from rising as much as it would otherwise have, or should it stem rising inflation and inflationary expectations by holding the federal funds rate constant or even increasing it? While the Fed voted during most of its 2008 meetings for easing, the year is notable in that there were often dissenters at the Federal Open Market Committee meetings. For example, the minutes of the March 18, 2008, meeting note that two members, Richard W. Fisher of the Dallas Fed and Charles I. Plosser of the Philadelphia Fed voted against the 0.75% point drop approved at that meeting. Their rationale was that the inflation risks were simply too great. The minutes state,

> *"Incoming data suggested a weaker near-term outlook for economic growth, but the Committee's earlier policy moves had already reduced the target federal funds rate by 225 basis points to address risks to growth, and the full effect of those rate cuts had yet to be felt. … Both Messrs. Fisher and Plosser were concerned that inflation expectations could potentially become unhinged should the Committee continue to lower the funds rate in the current environment. They pointed to measures of inflation and indicators of inflation expectations that had risen and Mr. Fisher stressed the international influences on U.S. inflation rates. Mr. Plosser noted that the Committee could not afford to wait until there was clear evidence that inflation expectations were no longer anchored, as by then it would be too late to prevent a further increase in inflation pressures."[1]*

But as the depth of the recession increased toward the latter part of 2008, with the unemployment rate reaching 7.2% in December and prices of both oil and other commodities falling back substantially, the inflation threat had dissipated. Unanimity had returned to the FOMC: the Fed should use all of its powers to fight the recession.

This chapter examines the relationship between inflation and unemployment. We will find that there have been periods in which a clear trade-off between inflation and unemployment seemed to exist. During such periods, the economy achieved reductions in unemployment at the expense of increased inflation. But there have also been periods in which inflation and unemployment rose together and periods in which both variables fell together. We will examine some explanations for the sometimes perplexing relationship between the two variables.

We will see that the use of stabilization policy, coupled with the lags for monetary and for fiscal policy, have at times led to a cyclical relationship between inflation and unemployment. The explanation for the fact that Americans enjoyed such a long period of falling inflation and unemployment in the 1990s lies partly in improved policy, policy that takes those lags into account. We will see that a bit of macroeconomic luck in aggregate supply has also played a role.

31.2 Relating Inflation and Unemployment

Learning Objectives

1. Draw a short-run Phillips curve and describe the relationship between inflation and unemployment that it expresses.
2. Describe the other relationships or phases that have been observed between inflation and unemployment.

It has often been the case that progress against inflation comes at the expense of greater unemployment, and that reduced unemployment comes at the expense of greater inflation. This section looks at the record and traces the emergence of the view that a simple trade-off between these macroeconomic "bad guys" exists.

Clearly, it is desirable to reduce unemployment and inflation. Unemployment represents a lost opportunity for workers to engage in productive effort—and to earn income. Inflation erodes the value of money people hold, and more importantly, the threat of inflation adds to uncertainty and makes people less willing to save and firms less willing to invest. If there were a trade-off between the two, we could reduce the rate of inflation or the rate of unemployment, but not both. The fact that the United States did make progress against unemployment and inflation through most of the 1990s and early 2000s represented a macroeconomic triumph, one that appeared impossible just a few years earlier. The next section examines the argument that once dominated macroeconomic thought—that a simple trade-off between inflation and unemployment did, indeed, exist. The argument continues to appear in discussions of macroeconomic policy today; it will be useful to examine it.

The Phillips Curve in the Short Run

short-run Phillips curve

A curve that suggests a negative relationship between inflation and unemployment.

In 1958, New Zealand–born economist Almarin Phillips reported that his analysis of a century of British wage and unemployment data suggested that an inverse relationship existed between rates of increase in wages and British unemployment.[2] Economists were quick to incorporate this idea into their thinking, extending the relationship to the rate of price-level changes—inflation—and unemployment. The notion that there is a trade-off between the two is expressed by a **short-run Phillips curve**, a curve that suggests a negative relationship between inflation and unemployment. Figure 31.1 shows a short-run Phillips curve.

The short-run Phillips curve seemed to make good theoretical sense. The dominant school of economic thought in the 1960s suggested that the economy was likely to experience either a recessionary or an inflationary gap. An economy with a recessionary gap would have high unemployment and little or no inflation. An economy with an inflationary gap would have very little unemployment and a higher rate of inflation. The Phillips curve suggested a smooth transition between the two. As expansionary policies were undertaken to move the economy out of a recessionary gap, unemployment would fall and inflation would rise. Policies to correct an inflationary gap would bring down the inflation rate, but at a cost of higher unemployment.

The experience of the 1960s suggested that precisely the kind of trade-off the Phillips curve implied did, in fact, exist in the United States. Figure 31.2 shows annual rates of inflation (computed using the implicit price deflator) plotted against annual rates of unemployment from 1961 to 1969. The points appear to follow a path quite similar to a Phillips curve relationship. The civilian unemployment rate fell from 6.7% in 1961 to 3.5% in 1969. The inflation rate rose from 1.1% in 1961 to 4.8% in 1969. While inflation dipped slightly in 1963, it appeared that, for the decade as a whole, a reduction in unemployment had been "traded" for an increase in inflation.

In the mid-1960s, the economy moved into an inflationary gap as unemployment fell below its natural level. The economy had already reached its full employment level of output when the 1964 tax cut was passed. The Fed undertook a more expansionary monetary policy at the same time. The combined effect of the two policies increased aggregate demand and pushed the economy beyond full employment and into an inflationary gap. Aggregate demand continued to rise as U.S. spending for the war in Vietnam expanded and as President Lyndon Johnson launched an ambitious program aimed at putting an end to poverty in the United States.

By the end of the decade, unemployment at 3.5% was substantially below its natural level, estimated by the Congressional Budget Office to be 5.6% that year. When Richard Nixon became president in 1969, it was widely believed that, with an economy operating with an inflationary gap, it was time to move back down the Phillips curve, trading a reduction in inflation for an increase in unemployment. President Nixon moved to do precisely that, serving up a contractionary fiscal policy by ordering cuts in federal government purchases. The Fed pursued a contractionary monetary policy aimed at bringing inflation down.

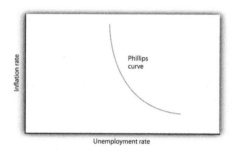

FIGURE 31.1 The Short-Run Phillips Curve

The relationship between inflation and unemployment suggested by the work of Almarin Phillips is shown by a short-run Phillips curve.

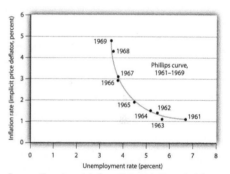

FIGURE 31.2 The Short-Run Phillips Curve in the 1960s

Values of U.S. inflation and unemployment rates during the 1960s generally conformed to the trade-off implied by the short-run Phillips curve. The points for each year lie close to a curve with the shape that Phillips's analysis predicted.

Source: Based on data from Economic Report of the President, 2011, Tables B-3 and B-42.

The Short-Run Phillips Curve Goes Awry

The effort to nudge the economy back down the Phillips curve to an unemployment rate closer to the natural level and a lower rate of inflation met with an unhappy surprise in 1970. Unemployment increased as expected. But inflation rose! The inflation rate rose to 5.3% from its 1969 rate of 4.8%.

The tidy relationship between inflation and unemployment that had been suggested by the experience of the 1960s fell apart in the 1970s. Unemployment rose substantially, but inflation remained the same in 1971. In 1972, both rates fell. The economy seemed to fall back into the pattern described by the Phillips curve in 1973, as inflation rose while unemployment fell. But the next two years saw increases in both rates. The negatively sloped Phillips curve relationship between inflation and unemployment that had seemed to hold true in the 1960s no longer prevailed.

Indeed, a look at annual rates of inflation and unemployment since 1961 suggests that the 1960s were quite atypical. Figure 31.3 shows the two variables over the period from 1961 through 2015. It is hard to see a negatively sloped Phillips curve lurking within that seemingly random scatter of points.

FIGURE 31.3 Inflation and Unemployment, 1961–2015

Annual observations of inflation and unemployment in the United States from 1961 to 2015 do not seem consistent with a Phillips curve.

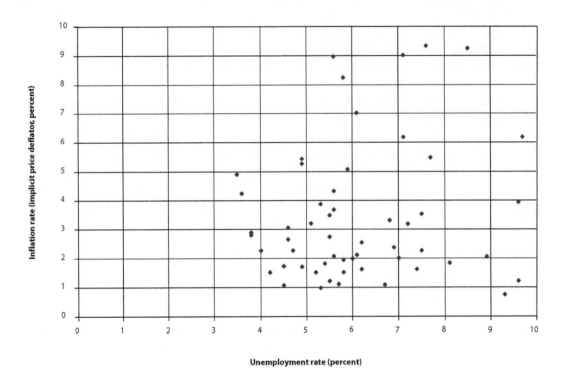

Sources: Based on data from Economic Report of the President, 2016, Tables B-3 and B-12.

Inflation and Unemployment Relationships Over Time

Although the points plotted in Figure 31.3 are not consistent with a negatively sloped, stable Phillips curve, connecting the inflation/unemployment points over time allows us to focus on various ways that these two variables may be related.

In Figure 31.4 we draw connecting lines through the sequence of observations. By doing so, we see periods in which inflation and unemployment are inversely related (as in the 1960s, late 1970s, late 1980s, the end of the twentieth century, and the first decade of the 2000s). We refer to a period when inflation and unemployment are inversely related as a **Phillips phase**.

During other periods, both inflation and unemployment were increasing (as from 1973 to 1975 or 1979 to 1981). A period of rising inflation and unemployment is called a **stagflation phase**. Finally, a **recovery phase** is a period in which both unemployment and inflation fall (as from 1975 to 1976, 1982 to 1984, and 1992 to 1998). Figure 31.5 presents a stylized version of these three phases.

Phillips phase

Period in which inflation and unemployment are inversely related.

stagflation phase

Period in which inflation remains high while unemployment increases.

recovery phase

Period in which inflation and unemployment both decline.

FIGURE 31.4 Connecting the Points: Inflation and Unemployment
Connecting observed values for unemployment and inflation sequentially suggests a cyclical pattern of clockwise loops over the 1961–2002 period, after which we see a series of inverse relationships.

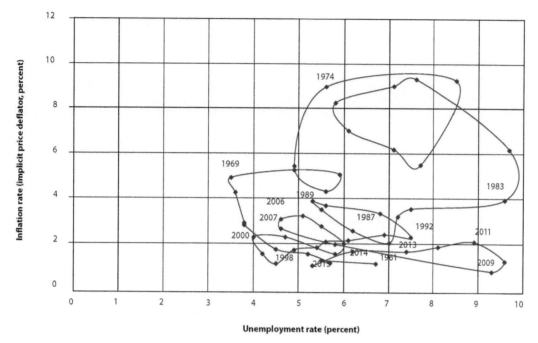

Sources: Based on data from Economic Report of the President, 2016, Tables B-3 and B-12.

Trace the path of inflation and unemployment as it unfolds in Figure 31.4. Starting with the Phillips phase in the 1960s, we see that the economy went through three clockwise loops, representing a stagflation phase, then a recovery phase, a Phillips phase, and so on. Each took the United States to successively higher rates of inflation and unemployment. Following the stagflation of the late 1970s and early 1980s, however, something quite significant happened. The economy suffered a very high rate of unemployment but also achieved very dramatic gains against inflation. The recovery phase of the 1990s was the longest since the U.S. government began tracking inflation and unemployment. Good luck explains some of that: oil prices fell in the late 1990s, shifting the short-run aggregate supply curve to the right. That boosted real GDP and put downward pressure on the price level. But one cause of that improved performance seemed to be the better understanding economists gained from some policy mistakes of the 1970s.

The 2000s look like a series of Phillips phases. The brief recession in 2001 brought higher unemployment and slightly lower inflation. Unemployment fell from 2003 to 2006 but with slightly higher inflation each year. The Great Recession, which began at the end of 2007, was characterized by higher unemployment and lower inflation. The unemployment rate reached almost 10% in 2010 with the inflation rate close to 1%. Since then, the unemployment rate has been falling while the inflation rate has remained at about 2% or less. The next section will explain these experiences in a stylized way in terms of the aggregate demand and supply model.

FIGURE 31.5 Inflation—Unemployment Phases
The figure shows the way an economy may move from a Phillips phase to a stagflation phase and then to a recovery phase.

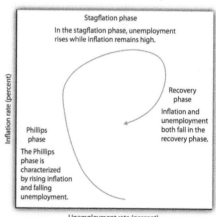

Key Takeaways

- The view that there is a trade-off between inflation and unemployment is expressed by a short-run Phillips curve.

- While there are periods in which a trade-off between inflation and unemployment exists, the actual relationship between these variables is more varied.
- In a Phillips phase, the inflation rate rises and unemployment falls. A stagflation phase is marked by rising unemployment while inflation remains high. In a recovery phase, inflation and unemployment both fall.

Try It!

Suppose an economy has experienced the rates of inflation and of unemployment shown below. Plot these data graphically in a grid with the inflation rate on the vertical axis and the unemployment rate on the horizontal axis. Identify the periods during which the economy experienced each of the three phases of the inflation-unemployment cycle identified in the text.

Period	Unemployment Rate (%)	Inflation Rate (%)
1	2.5	6.3
2	2.6	5.9
3	2.8	4.8
4	4.7	4.1
5	4.9	5.0
6	5.0	6.1
7	4.5	5.7
8	4.0	5.1

Case in Point: Some Reflections on the 1970s

Source: By Unknown or not provided (U.S. National Archives and Records Administration) [Public domain], via Wikimedia Commons

Looking back, we may find it difficult to appreciate how stunning the experience of 1970 and 1971 was. But those two years changed the face of macroeconomic thought.

Introductory textbooks of that time contained no mention of aggregate supply. The model of choice was the aggregate expenditures model. Students learned that the economy could be in equilibrium below full employment, in which case unemployment would be the primary macroeconomic problem. Alternatively, equilibrium could occur at an income greater than the full employment level, in which case inflation would be the main culprit to worry about.

These ideas could be summarized using a Phillips curve, a new analytical device. It suggested that economists could lay out for policy makers a menu of possibilities. Policy makers could then choose the mix of inflation and unemployment they were willing to accept. Economists would then show them how to attain that mix with the appropriate fiscal and monetary policies.

Then 1970 and 1971 came crashing in on this well-ordered fantasy. President Richard Nixon had come to office with a pledge to bring down inflation. The consumer price index had risen 4.7% during 1968, the highest rate since 1951. Mr. Nixon cut government purchases in 1969, and the Fed produced a sharp slowing in money growth. The president's economic advisers predicted at the beginning of 1970 that inflation and unemployment would both fall. Appraising the 1970 debacle early in 1971, the president's economists said that the experience had not been consistent with what standard models would predict. The economists suggested, however, that this was probably due to a number of transitory factors. Their forecast that inflation and unemployment would improve in 1971 proved wide of the mark—the unemployment rate rose from 4.9% to 5.9% (an increase of 20%), while the rate of inflation measured by the change in the implicit price deflator barely changed from 5.3% to 5.2%.

As we will see, the experience can be readily explained using the model of aggregate demand and aggregate supply. But this tool was not well developed then. The experience of the 1970s forced economists back to their analytical drawing boards and spawned dramatic advances in our understanding of macroeconomic events. We will explore many of those advances in the next chapter.

Source: *Based on Economic Report of the President, 1971, pp. 60–84.*

Answer to Try It! Problem

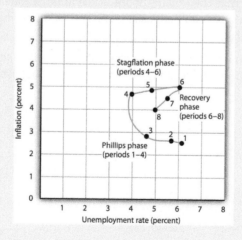

31.3 Explaining Inflation–Unemployment Relationships

Learning Objective

1. Use the model of aggregate demand and aggregate supply to explain a Phillips phase, a stagflation phase, and a recovery phase.

We have examined the inflation and unemployment experience in the United States during the past half century. Our task now is to explain it. We will apply the model of aggregate demand and aggregate supply, along with our knowledge of monetary and fiscal policy, to explain just why the economy performed as it did. We will find that the relationship between inflation and unemployment depends crucially on events, macroeconomic policy, and expectations.

The next three sections discuss the pattern that unfolded from the 1970s through the 1990s in which stagflation and then recovery followed Phillips phases. We will also look at the behavior of the economy in the first decade of the 21st century. Each phase results from a specific pattern of shifts in the aggregate demand and short-run aggregate supply curves.

It is important to be careful in thinking about the meaning of changes in inflation as we examine the cycle of inflation and unemployment. The rise in inflation during a Phillips phase does not simply mean that the price level rises. It means that the price level rises by larger and larger percentages. Rising inflation means that the price level is rising *at an increasing rate*. In a recovery phase, a falling rate of inflation does *not* imply a falling price level. It means the price level is rising, but by smaller and smaller percentages. Falling inflation means that the price level is rising more slowly, not that the price level is falling.

The Phillips Phase: Increasing Aggregate Demand

As we saw in the last section, the Phillips phase of the inflation-unemployment relationship conforms to the concept of a short-run Phillips curve. It is a period in which inflation tends to rise and unemployment tends to fall.

Figure 31.6 shows how a Phillips phase can unfold. Panel (a) shows the model of aggregate demand and aggregate supply; Panel (b) shows the corresponding path of inflation and unemployment.

FIGURE 31.6 A Phillips Phase

A Phillips phase is marked by increases in aggregate demand pushing real GDP and the price level up along the short-run aggregate supply curve $SRAS_{1,2,3}$. The result is rising inflation and falling unemployment. The points labeled in Panels (a) and (b) correspond to one another; point 1 in Panel (a) corresponds to point 1 in Panel (b), and so on.

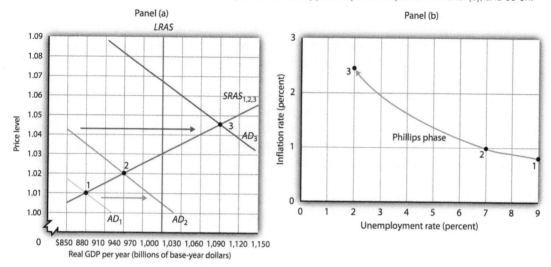

We shall assume in Figure 31.6 and in the next two figures that the following relationship between real GDP and the unemployment rate holds. In our example, the level of potential output will be $1,000 billion, while the natural rate of unemployment is 5.0%. The numbers given in the table correspond to the numbers used in Figure 31.6 through Figure 31.8. Notice that the higher the level of real GDP, the lower the unemployment rate. That is because the production of more goods and services requires more employment. For a given labor force, a higher level of employment implies a lower rate of unemployment.

Real GDP (Billions)	Unemployment Rate (%)
$880	9.0
910	8.0
940	7.0
970	6.0
1,000	5.0
1,030	4.0
1,060	3.0
1,090	2.0

Suppose that in Period 1 the price level is 1.01 and real GDP equals $880 billion. The economy is operating below its potential level. The unemployment rate is 9.0%; we shall assume the price level in Period 1 has risen by 0.8% from the previous period. Point 1 in Panel (b) thus shows an initial rate of inflation of 0.8% and an unemployment rate of 9.0%.

Now suppose policy makers respond to the recessionary gap of the first period with an expansionary monetary or fiscal policy. Aggregate demand in Period 2 shifts to AD_2. In Panel (a), we see that the price level rises to 1.02 and real GDP rises to $940 billion. Unemployment falls to 7.0%. The price increase from 1.01 to 1.02 gives us an inflation rate of about 1.0%. Panel (b) shows the new combination of inflation and unemployment rates for Period 2.

Impact lags mean that expansionary policies, even those undertaken in response to the recessionary gap in Periods 1 and 2, continue to expand aggregate demand in Period 3. In the case shown, aggregate demand rises to AD_3, pushing the economy well past its level of potential output into an inflationary gap. Real GDP rises to $1,090 billion, and the price level rises to 1.045 in Panel (a) of Figure 31.6. The increase in real GDP lowers the unemployment rate to 2.0%, and the inflation rate rises to 2.5% at point 3 in Panel (b). Unemployment has fallen at a cost of rising inflation.

The shifts from point 1 to point 2 to point 3 in Panel (b) are characteristic of the Phillips phase. It is crucial to note how these changes occurred. Inflation rose and unemployment fell, because increasing aggregate demand moved along the original short-run aggregate supply curve $SRAS_{1,2,3}$. We saw in the chapter that introduced the model of aggregate demand and aggregate supply that a short-run aggregate supply curve is drawn for a given level of the nominal wage and for a given set of expected prices. The Phillips phase, however, drives prices above what workers and firms expected when they agreed to a given set of nominal wages; real wages are thus driven below their expected level during this phase. Firms that have sticky prices are in the same situation. Firms set their prices based on some expected price level. As rising inflation drives the price level beyond their expectations, their prices will be too low relative to the rest of the economy. Because some firms and workers are committed to their present set of prices and wages for some period of time, they will be stuck with the wrong prices and wages for a while. During that time, their lower-than-expected relative prices will mean greater sales and greater production. The combination of increased production and lower real wages means greater employment and, thus, lower unemployment.

Ultimately, we should expect that workers and firms will begin adjusting nominal wages and other sticky prices to reflect the new, higher level of prices that emerges during the Phillips phase. It is this adjustment that can set the stage for a stagflation phase.

Changes in Expectations and a Stagflation Phase

As workers and firms become aware that the general price level is rising, they will incorporate this fact into their expectations of future prices. In reaching new agreements on wages, they are likely to settle on higher nominal wages. Firms with sticky prices will adjust their prices upward as they anticipate higher prices throughout the economy.

As we saw in the chapter introducing the model of aggregate demand and aggregate supply, increases in nominal wages and in prices that were sticky will shift the short-run aggregate supply curve to the left. Such a shift is illustrated in Panel (a) of Figure 31.7, where $SRAS_{1,2,3}$ shifts to $SRAS_4$. The result is a shift to point 4; the price level rises to 1.075, and real GDP falls to $970 billion. The increase in the price level to 1.075 from 1.045 implies an inflation rate of 2.9% ([1.075 − 1.045] / 1.045 = 2.9%); unemployment rises to 6.0% with the decrease in real GDP. The new combination of inflation and unemployment is given by point 4 in Panel (b).

FIGURE 31.7 A Stagflation Phase

In a stagflation phase, workers and firms adjust their expectations to a higher price level. As they act on their expectations, the short-run aggregate supply curve shifts leftward in Panel (a). The price level rises to 1.075, and real GDP falls to $970 billion. The inflation rate rises to 2.9% as unemployment rises to 6.0% at point 4 in Panel (b).

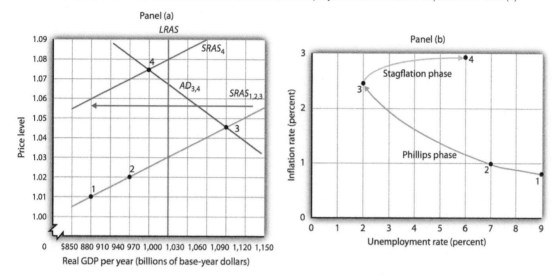

The essential feature of a stagflation phase is a change in expectations. Workers and firms that were blindsided by rising prices during a Phillips phase ended up with lower real wages and lower relative price levels than they intended. In a stagflation phase, they catch up. But the catching up shifts the short-run aggregate supply curve to the left, producing a reduction in real GDP and an increase in the price level.

A Recovery Phase

The stagflation phase shown in Figure 31.7 leaves the economy with a recessionary gap at point 4 in Panel (a). The economy is bumped into a recession by changing expectations. Policy makers can be expected to respond to a recessionary gap by boosting aggregate demand. That increase in aggregate demand will lead the economy into a recovery phase.

Figure 31.8 illustrates a recovery phase. In Panel (a), aggregate demand increases to AD_5, boosting the price level to 1.09 and real GDP to $1,060. The new price level represents a 1.4% ([1.09 − 1.075] / 1.075 = 1.4%) increase over the previous price level. The price level is higher, but the inflation rate has fallen sharply. Meanwhile, the increase in real GDP cuts the unemployment rate to 3.0%, shown by point 5 in Panel (b).

FIGURE 31.8 A Recovery Phase

Policy makers act to increase aggregate demand in order to move the economy out of a recessionary gap created during a stagflation phase. Here, aggregate demand shifts to AD_4, boosting the price level to 1.09 and real GDP to $1,060 billion at point 5 in Panel (a). The increase in real GDP reduces unemployment. The price level has risen, but at a slower rate than in the previous period. The result is a reduction in inflation. The new combination of unemployment and inflation is shown by point 5 in Panel (b).

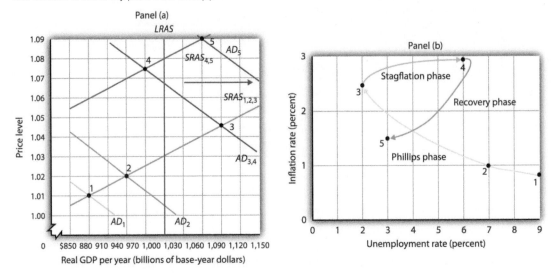

Policies that stimulate aggregate demand and changes in expected price levels are not the only forces that affect the values of inflation and unemployment. Changes in production costs shift the short-run aggregate supply curve. Depending on when these changes occur, they can reinforce or reduce the swings in inflation and unemployment. For example, Figure 31.4 shows that inflation was exceedingly low in the late 1990s. During this period, oil prices were very low—only $12.50 per barrel in 1998, for example. In terms of Figure 31.7, we can represent the low oil prices by a short-run aggregate supply curve that is to the right of $SRAS_{4,5}$. That would mean that output would be somewhat higher, unemployment somewhat lower, and inflation somewhat lower than what is shown as point 5 in Panels (a) and (b) of Figure 31.8.

The U.S. Economy in the 21st Century: A Series of Phillips Phases

Comparing the very late 1990s to the early 2000s, Figure 31.4 shows that both periods exhibit Phillips phases, but that the early 2000s has both higher inflation and higher unemployment. One way to explain these back-to-back Phillips phases is to look at Figure 31.6. Assume point 1 represents the economy in 2001, with aggregate demand increasing. At the same time, though, oil and other commodity prices were rising markedly—tripling between 2001 and 2007. Thus, the short-run aggregate supply curve was also shifting to the left of $SRAS_{1,2,3}$. This would mean that output would be somewhat lower, unemployment somewhat higher, and inflation somewhat higher than what is shown as points 2 and 3 in Panels (a) and (b) of Figure 31.6. The early 2000s Phillips curve would thus be above the late 1990s Phillips curve. While the Phillips phase of the early 2000s is farther from the origin than that of the late 1990s, it is noteworthy that the economy did not go through a severe stagflation phase, suggesting some learning about how to conduct monetary and fiscal policy.

The recession that began in late 2007 is largely seen as a shift to the left in aggregate demand due to the marked fall in housing prices and financial market stresses. As a result, the economy went through a Phillips phase of higher unemployment and lower inflation. The expansionary monetary and fiscal policies during and after the Great Recession were geared toward pushing the aggregate demand curve back toward the right, thereby cajoling the economy back up the negatively sloped short-run Phillips curve.

As you can see, though, in Figure 31.4, the rate of inflation stayed quite low through the years following the Great Recession. One contributor was the falling price of oil starting in the middle of 2014 and continuing over the period shown, which would lead to a rightward shift in the short-run aggregate supply curve. Also, even though the unemployment rate kept coming down, the labor force participation rate had not gone back to what it had been before the recession. This was partly due to shifting demographics, in particular the aging of the population. However, some of the reduction was likely due to people having given up on finding employment. The effect was to keep pressure off wage increases. Although fiscal policy was not used again, monetary policy remained loose and the Fed did not even begin to tighten until near the end of 2015.

We can conclude that policy efforts to change aggregate demand, together with changes in expectations and a wide variety of factors that cause the aggregate demand or aggregate supply curve to shift, have played an important role in generating the inflation-unemployment patterns we observe in the past half century.

Lags have played a crucial role in the cycle as well. If policy makers respond to a recessionary gap with an expansionary fiscal or monetary policy, then we know that aggregate demand will increase, but with a lag. Policy makers could thus undertake an expansionary policy and see little or no response at first. They might respond by making further expansionary efforts. When the first efforts finally shift aggregate demand, subsequent expansionary efforts can shift it too far, pushing real GDP beyond potential and creating an inflationary gap. These increases in aggregate demand create a Phillips phase. The economy's correction of the gap creates a stagflation phase. If policy makers respond to the stagflation phase with a new round of expansionary policies, the initial result will be a recovery phase. Sufficiently large increases in aggregate demand can then push the economy into another Phillips phase, and so on.

Key Takeaways

- In a Phillips phase, aggregate demand rises and boosts real GDP, lowering the unemployment rate. The price level rises by larger and larger percentages. Inflation thus rises while unemployment falls.
- A stagflation phase is marked by a leftward shift in short-run aggregate supply as wages and sticky prices are adjusted upwards. Unemployment rises while inflation remains high.
- In a recovery phase, policy makers boost aggregate demand. The price level rises, but at a slower rate than in the stagflation phase, so inflation falls. Unemployment falls as well.

Try It!

Using the model of aggregate demand and aggregate supply; sketch the changes in the curve(s) that produced each of the phases you identified in Try It! 16-1. Do not worry about specific numbers; just show the direction of changes in aggregate demand and/or short-run aggregate supply in each phase.

Case in Point: From the Challenging 1970s to the Calm 1990s

Source: See page for author [Public domain], via Wikimedia Commons

The path of U.S. inflation and unemployment followed a fairly consistent pattern of clockwise loops from 1961 to 2002, but the nature of these loops changed with changes in policy.

If we follow the cycle shown in Figure 31.4, we see that the three Phillips phases that began in 1961, 1972, and 1976 started at successively higher rates of inflation. Fiscal and monetary policy became expansionary at the beginnings of each of these phases, despite rising rates of inflation.

As inflation soared into the double-digit range in 1979, President Jimmy Carter appointed a new Fed chairman, Paul Volcker. The president gave the new chairman a clear mandate: bring inflation under control, regardless of the cost. The Fed responded with a sharply contractionary monetary policy and stuck with it even as the economy experienced its worse recession since the Great Depression.

Falling oil prices after 1982 contributed to an unusually long recovery phase: Inflation and unemployment both fell from 1982 to 1986. The inflation rate at which the economy started its next Phillips phase was the lowest since the Phillips phase of the 1960s.

The Fed's policies since then have clearly shown a reduced tolerance for inflation. The Fed shifted to a contractionary monetary policy in 1988, so that inflation during the 1986–1989 Phillips phase never exceeded 4%. When oil prices rose at the outset of the Persian Gulf War in 1990, the resultant swings in inflation and unemployment were much less pronounced than they had been in the 1970s.

The Fed continued its effort to restrain inflation in 1994 and 1995. It shifted to a contractionary policy early in 1994 when the economy was still in a recessionary gap left over from the 1990–1991 recession. The Fed's announced intention was to prevent any future increase in inflation. In effect, the Fed was taking explicit account of the lag in monetary policy. Had it continued an expansionary monetary policy, it might well have put the economy in another Phillips phase. Instead, the Fed has conducted a carefully orchestrated series of slight shifts in policy that succeeded in keeping the economy in the longest recovery phase since World War II.

To be sure, the stellar economic performance of the United States in the late 1990s was due in part to falling oil prices, which shifted the short-run aggregate supply curve to the right and helped push inflation and unemployment down. But it seems clear that a good deal of the credit can be claimed by the Fed, which paid closer attention to the lags inherent in macroeconomic policy. Ignoring those lags helped create the inflation-unemployment cycles that emerged with activist stabilization policies in the 1960s.

Answer to Try It! Problem

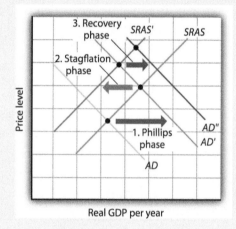

31.4 Inflation and Unemployment in the Long Run

Learning Objectives

1. Use the equation of exchange to explain what determines the inflation rate in the long run.
2. Explain why in the long run the Phillips curve is vertical.
3. Describe frictional and structural unemployment and the factors that may affect these two types of unemployment.
4. Describe efficiency wage theory and its predictions concerning cyclical unemployment.

In the last section, we saw how stabilization policy, together with changes in expectations, can produce the cycles of inflation and unemployment that characterized the past several decades. These cycles, though, are short-run phenomena. They involve swings in economic activity around the economy's potential output.

This section examines forces that affect the values of inflation and the unemployment rate in the long run. We shall see that the rates of money growth and of economic growth determine the inflation rate. Unemployment that persists in the long run includes frictional and structural unemployment. We shall examine some of the forces that affect both types of unemployment, as well as a new theory of unemployment.

The Inflation Rate in the Long Run

What factors determine the inflation rate? The price level is determined by the intersection of aggregate demand and short-run aggregate supply; anything that shifts either of these two curves changes the price level and thus affects the inflation rate. We have seen how these shifts can generate different inflation-unemployment combinations in the short run. In the long run, the rate of inflation will be determined by two factors: the rate of money growth and the rate of economic growth.

Economists generally agree that the rate of money growth is one determinant of an economy's inflation rate in the long run. The conceptual basis for that conclusion lies in the equation of exchange: $MV = PY$. That is, the money supply times the velocity of money equals the price level times the value of real GDP.

Given the equation of exchange, which holds by definition, we learned in the chapter on monetary policy that the sum of the percentage rates of change in M and V will be roughly equal to the sum of the percentage rates of change in P and Y. That is,

EQUATION 31.1

$$\%\Delta M + \%\Delta V \cong \%\Delta P + \%\Delta Y$$

Suppose that velocity is stable in the long run, so that $\%\Delta V$ equals zero. Then, the inflation rate ($\%\Delta P$) roughly equals the percentage rate of change in the money supply minus the percentage rate of change in real GDP:

EQUATION 31.2

$$\%\Delta P \cong \%\Delta M - \%\Delta Y$$

In the long run, real GDP moves to its potential level, Y_P. Thus, in the long run we can write Equation 31.2 as follows:

EQUATION 31.3

$$\%\Delta P \cong \%\Delta M - \%\Delta Y_P$$

There is a limit to how fast the economy's potential output can grow. Economists generally agree that potential output increases at only about a 2% to 3% annual rate in the United States. Given that the economy stays close to its potential, this puts a rough limit on the speed with which Y can grow. Velocity can vary, but it is not likely to change at a rapid rate over a sustained period. These two facts suggest that very rapid increases in the quantity of money, M, will inevitably produce very rapid increases in the price level, P. If the money supply grows more slowly than potential output, then the right-hand side of Equation 31.3 will be negative. The price level will fall; the economy experiences deflation.

Numerous studies point to the strong relationship between money growth and inflation, especially for high-inflation countries. For example, a recent study by John Thornton looked at the experiences of 116 countries from 1960 to 2007. His analysis, which used currency as the monetary aggregate because the definitions of M1 and M2 are not stable across such a wide sample of countries over long periods of time, concluded that when the annual inflation rate averages more than 10%, the relationship is particularly strong between money growth and inflation.

In the model of aggregate demand and aggregate supply, increases in the money supply shift the aggregate demand curve to the right and thus force the price level upward. Money growth thus produces inflation.

Of course, other factors can shift the aggregate demand curve as well. For example, expansionary fiscal policy or an increase in investment will shift aggregate demand. We have already seen that changes in the expected price level or in production costs shift the short-run aggregate supply curve. But such increases are not likely to continue year after year, as money growth can. Factors other than money growth may influence the inflation rate from one year to the next, but they are not likely to cause sustained inflation.

Inflation Rates and Economic Growth

Our conclusion is a simple and an important one. In the long run, the inflation rate is determined by the relative values of the economy's rate of money growth and of its rate of economic growth. If the money supply increases more rapidly than the rate of economic growth, inflation is likely to result. A money growth rate equal to the rate of economic growth will, in the absence of a change in velocity, produce a zero rate of inflation. Finally, a money growth rate that falls short of the rate of economic growth is likely to lead to deflation.

Unemployment and the Phillips Curve in the Long Run

Economists distinguish three types of unemployment: frictional unemployment, structural unemployment, and cyclical unemployment. The first two exist at all times, even when the economy operates at its potential. These two types of unemployment together determine the natural rate of unemployment. In the long run, the economy will operate at potential, and the unemployment rate will be the natural rate of unemployment. For this reason, in the long run the Phillips curve will be vertical at the natural rate of unemployment. Thus, the **long-run Phillips curve** is a vertical line at the natural rate of unemployment, showing that in the long run, there is no trade-off between inflation and unemployment. Figure 31.9 explains why. Suppose the economy is operating at Y_P on AD_1 and $SRAS_1$. Suppose the price level is P_0, the same as in the last period. In that case, the inflation rate is zero. Panel (b) shows that the unemployment rate is U_P, the natural rate of unemployment. Now suppose that the aggregate demand curve shifts to AD_2. In the short run, output will increase to Y_1. The price level will rise to P_1, and the unemployment rate will fall to U_1. In Panel (b) we show the new unemployment rate, U_1, to be associated with an inflation rate of π_1, and the beginnings of the negatively sloped short-run Phillips curve emerges. In the long run, as price and nominal wages increase, the short-run aggregate supply curve moves to $SRAS_2$ and output returns to Y_P, as shown in Panel (a). In Panel (b), unemployment returns to U_P, regardless of the rate of inflation. Thus, in the long-run, the Phillips curve is vertical.

long-run Phillips curve

A vertical line at the natural rate of unemployment, showing that in the long run, there is no trade-off between inflation and unemployment.

FIGURE 31.9 The Phillips Curve in the Long Run

Suppose the economy is operating at Y_P on AD_1 and $SRAS1$ in Panel (a) with price level of P_0, the same as in the last period. Panel (b) shows that the unemployment rate is U_P, the natural rate of unemployment. If the aggregate demand curve shifts to AD_2, in the short run output will increase to Y_1, and the price level will rise to P_1. In Panel (b), the unemployment rate will fall to U_1, and the inflation rate will be π_1. In the long run, as price and nominal wages increase, the short-run aggregate supply curve moves to $SRAS_2$, and output returns to Y_P, as shown in Panel (a). In Panel (b), unemployment returns to U_P, regardless of the rate of inflation. Thus, in the long-run, the Phillips curve is vertical.

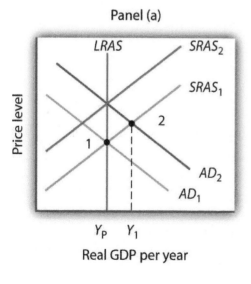

Panel (a)

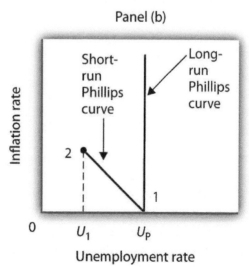

Panel (b)

An economy operating at its potential would have no cyclical unemployment. Because an economy achieves its potential output in the long run, an analysis of unemployment in the long run is an analysis of frictional and structural unemployment. In this section, we will also look at some new research that challenges the very concept of an economy achieving its potential output.

Frictional Unemployment

Frictional unemployment occurs because it takes time for people seeking jobs and employers seeking workers to find each other. If the amount of time could be reduced, frictional unemployment would fall. The economy's natural rate of unemployment would drop, and its potential output would rise. This section presents a model of frictional unemployment and examines some issues in reducing the frictional unemployment rate.

A period of frictional unemployment ends with the individual getting a job. The process through which the job is obtained suggests some important clues to the nature of frictional unemployment.

reservation wage

The lowest wage that an unemployed worker would accept, if it were offered.

By definition, a person who is unemployed is seeking work. At the outset of a job search, we presume that the individual has a particular wage in mind as he or she considers various job possibilities. The lowest wage that an unemployed worker would accept, if it were offered, is called the **reservation wage**. This is the wage an individual would accept; any offer below it would be rejected. Once a firm offers the reservation wage, the individual will take it and the job search will be terminated. Many people may hold out for more than just a wage—they may be seeking a certain set of working conditions, opportunities for advancement, or a job in a particular area. In practice, then, an unemployed worker might be willing to accept a variety of combinations of wages and other job characteristics. We shall simplify our analysis by lumping all these other characteristics into a single reservation wage.

A worker's reservation wage is likely to change as his or her search continues. One might initiate a job search with high expectations and thus have a high reservation wage. As the job search continues, however, this reservation wage might be adjusted downward as the worker obtains better information about what is likely to be available in the market and as the financial difficulties associated with unemployment mount. We can thus draw a reservation wage curve (Figure 31.10), that suggests a negative relationship between the reservation wage and the duration of a person's job search. Similarly, as a job search continues, the worker will accumulate better offers. The "best-offer-received" curve shows what its name implies; it is the best offer the individual has received so far in the job search. The upward slope of the curve suggests that, as a worker's search continues, the best offer received will rise.

FIGURE 31.10 A Model of a Job Search

An individual begins a job search at time t_0 with a reservation wage W_0. As long as the reservation wage exceeds the best offer received, the individual will continue searching. A job is accepted, and the search is terminated, at time t_c, at which the reservation and "best-offer-received" curves intersect at wage W_c.

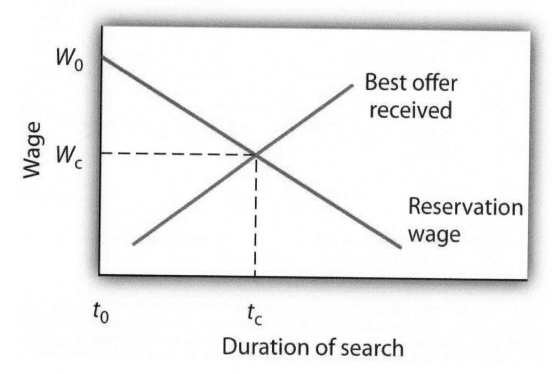

The search begins at time t_0, with the unemployed worker seeking wage W_0. Because the worker's reservation wage exceeds the best offer received, the worker continues the search. The worker reduces his or her reservation wage and accumulates better offers until the two curves intersect at time t_c. The worker accepts wage W_c, and the job search is terminated.

The job search model in Figure 31.10 does not determine an equilibrium duration of job search or an equilibrium initial wage. The reservation wage and best-offer-received curves will be unique to each individual's experience. We can, however, use the model to reach some conclusions about factors that affect frictional unemployment.

First, the duration of search will be shorter when more job market information is available. Suppose, for example, that the only way to determine what jobs and wages are available is to visit each firm separately. Such a situation would require a lengthy period of search before a given offer was received. Alternatively, suppose there are agencies that make such information readily available and that link unemployed workers to firms seeking to hire workers. In that second situation, the time required to obtain a given offer would be reduced, and the best-offer-received curves for individual workers would shift to the left. The lower the cost for obtaining job market information, the lower the average duration of unemployment. Government and private agencies that provide job information and placement services help to reduce information costs to unemployed workers and firms. They tend to lower frictional unemployment by shifting the best-offer-received curves for individual workers to the left, as shown in Panel (a) of Figure 31.11. Workers obtain higher-paying jobs when they do find work; the wage at which searches are terminated rises to W_2.

FIGURE 31.11 Public Policy and Frictional Unemployment
Public policy can influence the time required for job-seeking workers and worker-seeking firms to find each other. Programs that provide labor-market information tend to shift the best-offer-received (*BOR*) curves of individual workers to the left, reducing the duration of job search and reducing unemployment, as in Panel (a). Note that the wage these workers obtain also rises to W_2. Unemployment compensation tends to increase the period over which a worker will hold out for a particular wage, shifting the reservation wage (*RW*) curve to the right, as in Panel (b). Unemployment compensation thus boosts the unemployment rate and increases the wage workers obtain when they find employment.

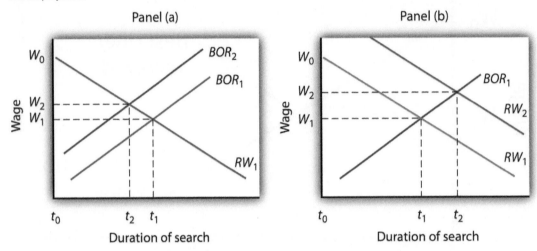

Unemployment compensation, which was introduced in the United States during the Great Depression to help workers who had lost jobs through unemployment, also affects frictional unemployment. Because unemployment compensation reduces the financial burden of being unemployed, it is likely to increase the amount of time people will wait for a given wage. It thus shifts the reservation wage curve to the right, raises the average duration of unemployment, and increases the wage at which searches end, as shown in Panel (b). An increase in the average duration of unemployment implies a higher unemployment rate. Unemployment compensation thus has a paradoxical effect—it tends to increase the problem against which it protects.

Structural Unemployment

Structural unemployment occurs when a firm is looking for a worker and an unemployed worker is looking for a job, but the particular characteristics the firm seeks do not match up with the characteristics the worker offers. Technological change is one source of structural unemployment. New technologies are likely to require different skills than old technologies. Workers with training to equip them for the old technology may find themselves caught up in a structural mismatch.

Technological and managerial changes have, for example, changed the characteristics firms seek in workers they hire. Firms looking for assembly-line workers once sought men and women with qualities such as reliability, integrity, strength, and manual dexterity. Reliability and integrity remain important, but many assembly-line jobs now require greater analytical and communications skills. Automobile manufacturers, for example, now test applicants for entry-level factory jobs on their abilities in algebra, in trigonometry, and in written and oral communications. Strong, agile workers with weak analytical and language skills may find many job openings for which they do not qualify. They would be examples of the structurally unemployed.

Changes in demand can also produce structural unemployment. As consumers shift their demands to different products, firms that are expanding and seeking more workers may need different skills than firms for which demand has shrunk. Similarly, firms may shift their use of different types of jobs in response to changing market conditions, leaving some workers with the "wrong" set of skills. Regional shifts in demand can produce structural unemployment as well. The economy of one region may be expanding rapidly, creating job vacancies, while another region is in a slump, with many workers seeking jobs but not finding them.

Public and private job training firms seek to reduce structural unemployment by providing workers with skills now in demand. Employment services that provide workers with information about jobs in other regions also reduce the extent of structural unemployment.

Cyclical Unemployment and Efficiency Wages

In our model, unemployment above the natural level occurs if, at a given real wage, the quantity of labor supplied exceeds the quantity of labor demanded. In the analysis we've done so far, the failure to achieve equilibrium is a short-run phenomenon. In the long run, wages and prices will adjust so that the real wage reaches its equilibrium level. Employment reaches its natural level.

Some economists, however, argue that a real wage that achieves equilibrium in the labor market may *never* be reached. They suggest that firms may intentionally pay a wage greater than the market equilibrium. Such firms could hire additional workers at a lower wage, but they choose not to do so. The idea that firms may hold to a real wage greater than the equilibrium wage is called **efficiency-wage theory**.

> **efficiency-wage theory**
>
> The idea that firms may hold to a real wage greater than the equilibrium wage.

Why would a firm pay higher wages than the market requires? Suppose that by paying higher wages, the firm is able to boost the productivity of its workers. Workers become more contented and more eager to perform in ways that boost the firm's profits. Workers who receive real wages above the equilibrium level may also be less likely to leave their jobs. That would reduce job turnover. A firm that pays its workers wages in excess of the equilibrium wage expects to gain by retaining its employees and by inducing those employees to be more productive. Efficiency-wage theory thus suggests that the labor market may divide into two segments. Workers with jobs will receive high wages. Workers without jobs, who would be willing to work at an even lower wage than the workers with jobs, find themselves closed out of the market.

Whether efficiency wages really exist remains a controversial issue, but the argument is an important one. If it is correct, then the wage rigidity that perpetuates a recessionary gap is transformed from a temporary phenomenon that will be overcome in the long run to a permanent feature of the market. The argument implies that the ordinary processes of self-correction will not eliminate a recessionary gap.[3]

Key Takeaways

- Two factors that can influence the rate of inflation in the long run are the rate of money growth and the rate of economic growth.
- In the long run, the Phillips curve will be vertical since when output is at potential, the unemployment rate will be the natural rate of unemployment, regardless of the rate of inflation.
- The rate of frictional unemployment is affected by information costs and by the existence of unemployment compensation.
- Policies to reduce structural unemployment include the provision of job training and information about labor-market conditions in other regions.
- Efficiency-wage theory predicts that profit-maximizing firms will maintain the wage level at a rate too high to achieve full employment in the labor market.

Try It!

Using the model of a job search (see Figure 31.10), show graphically how each of the following would be likely to affect the duration of an unemployed worker's job search and thus the unemployment rate:

1. A new program provides that workers who have lost their jobs will receive unemployment compensation from the government equal to the pay they were earning when they lost their jobs, and that this compensation will continue for at least five years.
2. Unemployment compensation is provided, but it falls by 20% each month a person is out of work.
3. Access to the Internet becomes much more widely available and is used by firms looking for workers and by workers seeking jobs.

Case in Point: Altering the Incentives for Unemployment Insurance Claimants

Source: © Shutterstock, Inc.

While the rationale for unemployment insurance is clear—to help people weather bouts of unemployment—especially during economic downturns, designing programs that reduce adverse incentives is challenging. A review article by economists Peter Fredriksson and Bertil Holmlund examined decades of research that looks at how unemployment insurance programs could be improved. In particular, they consider the value of changing the duration and profile of benefit payments, increasing monitoring and sanctions imposed on unemployment insurance recipients, and changing work requirements. Some of the research is theoretical, while some comes out of actual experiments.

Concerning benefit payments, they suggest that reducing payments over time provides better incentives than either keeping payments constant or increasing them over time. Research also suggests that a waiting period might also be useful. Concerning monitoring and sanctions, most unemployment insurance systems require claimants to demonstrate in some way that they have looked for work. For example, they must report regularly to employment agencies or provide evidence they have applied for jobs. If they do not, the benefit may be temporarily cut. A number of experiments support the notion that greater search requirements reduce the length of unemployment. One experiment conducted in Maryland assigned recipients to different processes ranging from the standard requirement at the time of two employer contacts per week to requiring at least four contacts per week, attending a four-day job search workshop, and telling claimants that their employer contacts would be verified. The results showed that increasing the number of employer contacts reduced the duration by 6%, attending the workshop reduced duration by 5%, and the possibility of verification reduced it by 7.5%. Indeed, just telling claimants that they were going to have to attend the workshop led to a reduction in claimants. Evidence on instituting some kind of work requirement is similar to that of instituting workshop attendance.

The authors conclude that the effectiveness of all these instruments results from the fact that they encourage more active job search.

Source: *Based on Peter Fredriksson and Bertil Holmlund, "Improving Incentives in Unemployment Insurance: A Review of Recent Research," Journal of Economic Surveys 20, no. 3 (July 2006): 357–86.*

Answer to Try It! Problem

The duration of an unemployed worker's job search increases in situation (1), as illustrated in panel (a) and decreases in situations (2) and (3), as illustrated in panels (b) and (c) respectively. Thus, the unemployment rate increases in situation (1) and decreases in situations (2) and (3).

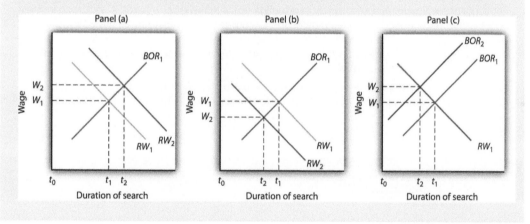

31.5 Review and Practice

Summary

During the 1960s, it appeared that there was a stable trade-off between the rate of unemployment and the rate of inflation. The short-run Phillips curve, which describes such a trade-off, suggests that lower rates of unemployment come with higher rates of inflation, and that lower rates of inflation come with higher rates of unemployment. But during subsequent decades, the actual values for unemployment and inflation have not always followed the trade-off script.

There has, however, been a relationship between unemployment and inflation over the four decades from 1961. Periods of rising inflation and falling unemployment were often followed by periods of rising unemployment and continued or higher inflation; those periods, in turn, were followed by periods in which both the inflation rate and the unemployment rate fell. These periods are defined as the Phillips phase, the stagflation phase, and the recovery phase. Following the recession of 2001, the economy returned quickly to a Phillips phase.

The Phillips phase is a period in which aggregate demand increases, boosting output and the price level. Unemployment drops and inflation rises. An essential feature of a Phillips phase is that the price increases that occur are unexpected. Workers thus experience lower real wages than they anticipated. Firms with sticky prices find that their prices are low relative to other prices. As workers and firms adjust to the higher inflation of the Phillips phase, they demand higher wages and post higher prices, so the short-run aggregate supply curve shifts leftward. Inflation continues, but real GDP falls. This is a stagflation phase. Finally, aggregate demand begins to increase again, boosting both real GDP and the price level. The higher price level, however, is likely to represent a much smaller percentage increase than had occurred during the stagflation phase. This is a recovery phase: inflation and unemployment fall together.

There is nothing inherent in a market economy that would produce the inflation-unemployment pattern we observed from 1961 until 2000. The cycle can begin if expansionary policies are launched to correct a recessionary gap, producing a Phillips phase. If those policies push the economy into an inflationary gap, then the adjustment of short-run aggregate supply will produce a stagflation phase. And, in the economy's first response to an expansionary policy launched to deal with the recession of the stagflation phase, the price level rises, but at a slower rate than before. The economy experiences falling inflation and falling unemployment at the same time: a recovery phase. The years since 2000 look more like a series of Phillips phases.

In the long run, the Phillips curve is vertical, and inflation is essentially a monetary phenomenon. Assuming stable velocity of money over the long run, the inflation rate roughly equals the money growth rate minus the rate of growth of real GDP. For a given money growth rate, inflation is thus reduced by faster economic growth.

Frictional unemployment is affected by information costs in the labor market. A reduction in those costs would reduce frictional unemployment. Hastening the retraining of workers would reduce structural unemployment. Reductions in frictional or structural unemployment would lower the natural rate of unemployment and thus raise potential output. Unemployment compensation is likely to increase frictional unemployment.

Some economists believe that cyclical unemployment may persist because firms have an incentive to maintain real wages above the equilibrium level. Whether this efficiency-wage argument holds is controversial.

Concept Problems

1. The Case in Point titled "Some Reflections on the 1970s" describes the changes in inflation and in unemployment in 1970 and 1971 as a watershed development for macroeconomic thought. Why was an increase in unemployment such a significant event?

2. As the economy slipped into recession in 1980 and 1981, the Fed was under enormous pressure to adopt an expansionary monetary policy. Suppose it had begun an expansionary policy early in 1981. What does the text's analysis of the inflation-unemployment cycle suggest about how the macroeconomic history of the 1980s might have been changed?

3. Suppose you read the following in the newspaper. In each case, identify the phase (Phillips, stagflation, or recovery) the economy is in, and suggest what change in aggregate demand or aggregate supply might have caused it.

   a. The president expressed much satisfaction with the performance of the economy last year. He said that with inflation and unemployment heading down, the nation is "on the right course."

b. The nation's inflation rate rose to a record high last month, the government reported yesterday. The consumer price index jumped 0.3% in January. Coupled with the announcement earlier this month that unemployment had risen by 0.5 percentage points, the reports suggested that the first month of the president's second term had gotten off to a rocky start.

c. The president expressed concern about reports of rising inflation but insisted the economy is on the right course. He pointed to recent reductions in unemployment as evidence that his economic policies are working.

4. The text notes that changes in oil prices can affect the inflation-unemployment outcome. Explain what effect changes in oil prices may have on these two variables.

5. The introduction to this chapter suggests that unemployment fell, and inflation generally fell, through most of the 1990s. What phase (Phillips, stagflation, or recovery) does this represent? Relative to U.S. experience from the 1960s until the 1990s, what was unusual about this?

6. Suppose that declining resource supplies reduce potential output in each period by 4%. What kind of monetary policy would be needed to maintain a zero rate of inflation at full employment?

7. The Humphrey–Hawkins Act of 1978 required that the federal government maintain an unemployment rate of 4% and hold the inflation rate to less than 3%. What does the inflation-unemployment relationship tell you about achieving such goals?

8. The American Economic Association publishes a newsletter (which is available on the AEA's Internet site at http://www.aeaweb.org/joe/) called *Job Openings for Economists* (JOE). Virtually all academic and many nonacademic positions for which applicants are being sought for economics positions are listed in the newsletter, which is quite inexpensive. How do you think that the publication of this journal affects the unemployment rate among economists? What type of unemployment does it affect?

9. Many people think that the process of putting computer technology to work and incorporating computers into the workplace is causing a massive restructuring of virtually every institution of modern life. If they are right, what are the implications for unemployment? What kind of unemployment would be affected?

10. The natural unemployment rate in the United States has varied over the last 50 years. According to the Congressional Budget Office, the natural rate was 5.5% in 1960, rose to about 6.5% in the 1970s, and had declined to about 4.8% by 2000. What do you think might have caused this variation?

11. Suppose the Fed begins carrying out an expansionary monetary policy in order to close a recessionary gap. Relate what happens during the next two phases of the inflation-unemployment cycle to the maxim "You can fool some of the people some of the time, but you can't fool all of the people all of the time."

Numerical Problems

1. Here are annual data for the inflation and unemployment rates for the United States for the 1948–1961 period.

Year	Unemployment Rate (%)	Inflation Rate (%)
1948	3.8	3.0
1949	5.9	−2.1
1950	5.3	5.9
1951	3.3	6.0
1952	3.0	0.8
1953	2.9	0.7
1954	5.5	−0.7
1955	4.4	0.4
1956	4.1	3.0
1957	4.3	2.9
1958	6.8	1.8
1959	5.5	1.7
1960	5.5	1.4
1961	6.7	0.7

    a. Plot these observations and connect the points as in Figure 31.5.

    b. How does this period compare to the decades that followed?

    c. What do you think accounts for the difference?

2. Here are hypothetical inflation and unemployment data for Econoland.

Time Period	Inflation Rate (%)	Unemployment Rate (%)
1	0	6
2	3	4
3	7	3
4	8	5
5	7	7
6	3	6

    a. Plot these points.

    b. Identify which points correspond to a Phillips phase, which correspond to a stagflation phase, and which correspond to a recovery phase.

3. Relate the observations in Numerical Problem 2 to what must have been happening in the aggregate demand–aggregate supply model.

4. Suppose the full-employment level of real GDP is increasing at a rate of 3% per period and the money supply is growing at a 4% rate. What will happen to the long-run inflation rate, assuming constant velocity?

Endnotes

1. Minutes of the Federal Open Market Committee March 18, 2008, https://www.federalreserve.gov/monetarypolicy/fomcminutes20080318.htm.

2. Almarin W. Phillips, "The Relation between Unemployment and the Rate of Change of Money Wage Rates in the United Kingdom, 1861–1957," *Economica* 25 (November 1958): 283–99.

3. For a discussion of the argument, see Janet Yellen, "Efficiency Wage Models of Unemployment," *American Economic Review, Papers and Proceedings* (May 1984): 200–205.

CHAPTER 32

A Brief History of Macroeconomic Thought and Policy

32.1 Start Up: Three Revolutions in Macroeconomic Thought

It is the 1930s. Many people have begun to wonder if the United States will ever escape the Great Depression's cruel grip. Forecasts that prosperity lies just around the corner take on a hollow ring.

The collapse seems to defy the logic of the dominant economic view—that economies should be able to reach full employment through a process of self-correction. The old ideas of macroeconomics do not seem to work, and it is not clear what new ideas should replace them.

In Britain, Cambridge University economist John Maynard Keynes is struggling with ideas that he thinks will stand the conventional wisdom on its head. He is confident that he has found the key not only to understanding the Great Depression but also to correcting it.

It is the 1960s. Most economists believe that Keynes's ideas best explain fluctuations in economic activity. The tools Keynes suggested have won widespread acceptance among governments all over the world; the application of expansionary fiscal policy in the United States appears to have been a spectacular success. But economist Milton Friedman of the University of Chicago continues to fight a lonely battle against what has become the Keynesian orthodoxy. He argues that money, not fiscal policy, is what affects aggregate demand. He insists not only that fiscal policy cannot work, but that monetary policy should not be used to move the economy back to its potential output. He counsels a policy of steady money growth, leaving the economy to adjust to long-run equilibrium on its own.

It is 1970. The economy has just taken a startling turn: Real GDP has fallen, but inflation has remained high. A young economist at Carnegie–Mellon University, Robert E. Lucas, Jr., finds this a paradox, one that he thinks cannot be explained by Keynes's theory. Along with several other economists, he begins work on a radically new approach to macroeconomic thought, one that will challenge Keynes's view head-on. Lucas and his colleagues suggest a world in which self-correction is swift, rational choices by individuals generally cancel the impact of fiscal and monetary policies, and stabilization efforts are likely to slow economic growth.

John Maynard Keynes, Milton Friedman, and Robert E. Lucas, Jr., each helped to establish a major school of macroeconomic thought. Although their ideas clashed sharply, and although there remains considerable disagreement among economists about a variety of issues, a broad consensus among economists concerning macroeconomic policy seemed to emerge in the 1980s, 1990s, and early 2000s. The Great Recession and the financial crisis in the late 2000s, though, set off another round of controversy.

In this chapter we will examine the macroeconomic developments of six decades: the 1930s, 1960s, 1970s, 1980s, 1990s, and 2000s. We will use the aggregate demand–aggregate supply model to explain macroeconomic changes during these periods, and we will see how the three major economic schools were affected by these events. We will also see how these schools of thought affected macroeconomic policy. Finally, we will see how the evolution of macroeconomic thought and policy influenced how economists design policy prescriptions for dealing with the recession that began in late 2007, which turned out to be the largest since the Great Depression.

In examining the ideas of these schools, we will incorporate concepts such as the potential output and the natural level of employment. While such terms had not been introduced when some of the major schools of thought first emerged, we will use them when they capture the ideas economists were presenting.

32.2 The Great Depression and Keynesian Economics

Learning Objectives

1. Explain the basic assumptions of the classical school of thought that dominated macroeconomic thinking before the Great Depression, and tell why the severity of the Depression struck a major blow to this view.
2. Compare Keynesian and classical macroeconomic thought, discussing the Keynesian explanation of prolonged recessionary and inflationary gaps as well as the Keynesian approach to correcting these problems.

It is hard to imagine that anyone who lived during the Great Depression was not profoundly affected by it. From the beginning of the Depression in 1929 to the time the economy hit bottom in 1933, real GDP plunged nearly 30%. Real per capita disposable income sank nearly 40%. More than 12 million people were thrown out of work; the unemployment rate soared from 3% in 1929 to 25% in 1933. Some 85,000 businesses failed. Hundreds of thousands of families lost their homes. By 1933, about half of all mortgages on all urban, owner-occupied houses were delinquent.[1]

The economy began to recover after 1933, but a huge recessionary gap persisted. Another downturn began in 1937, pushing the unemployment rate back up to 19% the following year.

The contraction in output that began in 1929 was not, of course, the first time the economy had slumped. But never had the U.S. economy fallen so far and for so long a period. Economic historians estimate that in the 75 years before the Depression there had been 19 recessions. But those contractions had lasted an average of less than two years. The Great Depression lasted for more than a decade. The severity and duration of the Great Depression distinguish it from other contractions; it is for that reason that we give it a much stronger name than "recession."

Figure 32.1 shows the course of real GDP compared to potential output during the Great Depression. The economy did not approach potential output until 1941, when the pressures of world war forced sharp increases in aggregate demand.

FIGURE 32.1 The Depression and the Recessionary Gap
The dark-shaded area shows real GDP from 1929 to 1942, the upper line shows potential output, and the light-shaded area shows the difference between the two—the recessionary gap. The gap nearly closed in 1941; an inflationary gap had opened by 1942. The chart suggests that the recessionary gap remained very large throughout the 1930s.

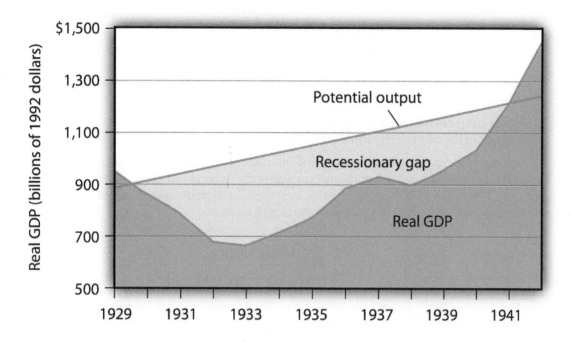

The Classical School and the Great Depression

The Great Depression came as a shock to what was then the conventional wisdom of economics. To see why, we must go back to the classical tradition of macroeconomics that dominated the economics profession when the Depression began.

Classical economics is the body of macroeconomic thought associated primarily with 19th-century British economist David Ricardo. His *Principles of Political Economy and Taxation*, published in 1817, established a tradition that dominated macroeconomic thought for over a century. Ricardo focused on the long run and on the forces that determine and produce growth in an economy's potential output. He emphasized the ability of flexible wages and prices to keep the economy at or near its natural level of employment.

According to the classical school, achieving what we now call the natural level of employment and potential output is not a problem; the economy can do that on its own. Classical economists recognized, however, that the process would take time. Ricardo admitted that there could be *temporary* periods in which employment would fall below the natural level. But his emphasis was on the long run, and in the long run all would be set right by the smooth functioning of the price system.

Economists of the classical school saw the massive slump that occurred in much of the world in the late 1920s and early 1930s as a short-run aberration. The economy would right itself in the long run, returning to its potential output and to the natural level of employment.

classical economics

The body of macroeconomic thought, associated primarily with 19th-century British economist David Ricardo, that focused on the long run and on the forces that determine and produce growth in an economy's potential output.

Keynesian Economics

In Britain, which had been plunged into a depression of its own, John Maynard Keynes had begun to develop a new framework of macroeconomic analysis, one that suggested that what for Ricardo were "temporary effects" could persist for a long time, and at terrible cost. Keynes's 1936 book, *The General Theory of Employment, Interest and Money*, was to transform the way many economists thought about macroeconomic problems.

Keynes versus the Classical Tradition

In a nutshell, we can say that Keynes's book shifted the thrust of macroeconomic thought from the concept of aggregate supply to the concept of aggregate demand. Ricardo's focus on the tendency of an economy to reach potential output inevitably stressed the supply side—an economy tends to operate at a level of output given by the long-run aggregate supply curve. Keynes, in arguing that what we now call recessionary or inflationary gaps could be created by shifts in aggregate demand, moved the focus of macroeconomic analysis to the demand side. He argued that prices in the short run are quite sticky and suggested that this stickiness would block adjustments to full employment.

Keynes dismissed the notion that the economy would achieve full employment in the long run as irrelevant. "In the long run," he wrote acidly, "we are all dead."

Keynes's work spawned a new school of macroeconomic thought, the Keynesian school. **Keynesian economics** asserts that changes in aggregate demand can create gaps between the actual and potential levels of output, and that such gaps can be prolonged. Keynesian economists stress the use of fiscal and of monetary policy to close such gaps.

Keynesian Economics and the Great Depression

The experience of the Great Depression certainly seemed consistent with Keynes's argument. A reduction in aggregate demand took the economy from above its potential output to below its potential output, and, as we saw in Figure 32.1, the resulting recessionary gap lasted for more than a decade. While the Great Depression affected many countries, we shall focus on the U.S. experience.

The plunge in aggregate demand began with a collapse in investment. The investment boom of the 1920s had left firms with an expanded stock of capital. As the capital stock approached its desired level, firms did not need as much new capital, and they cut back investment. The stock market crash of 1929 shook business confidence, further reducing investment. Real gross private domestic investment plunged nearly 80% between 1929 and 1932. We have learned of the volatility of the investment component of aggregate demand; it was very much in evidence in the first years of the Great Depression.

Other factors contributed to the sharp reduction in aggregate demand. The stock market crash reduced the wealth of a small fraction of the population (just 5% of Americans owned stock at that time), but it certainly reduced the consumption of the general population. The stock market crash also reduced consumer confidence throughout the economy. The reduction in wealth and the reduction in confidence reduced consumption spending and shifted the aggregate demand curve to the left.

Fiscal policy also acted to reduce aggregate demand. As consumption and income fell, governments at all levels found their tax revenues falling. They responded by raising tax rates in an effort to balance their budgets. The federal government, for example, doubled income tax rates in 1932. Total government tax revenues as a percentage of GDP shot up from 10.8% in 1929 to 16.6% in 1933. Higher tax rates tended to reduce consumption and aggregate demand.

Other countries were suffering declining incomes as well. Their demand for U.S. goods and services fell, reducing the real level of exports by 46% between 1929 and 1933. The Smoot–Hawley Tariff Act of 1930 dramatically raised tariffs on products imported into the United States and led to retaliatory trade-restricting legislation around the world. This act, which more than 1,000 economists opposed in a formal petition, contributed to the collapse of world trade and to the recession.

As if all this were not enough, the Fed, in effect, conducted a sharply contractionary monetary policy in the early years of the Depression. The Fed took no action to prevent a wave of bank failures that swept the country at the outset of the Depression. Between 1929 and 1933, one-third of all banks in the United States failed. As a result, the money supply plunged 31% during the period.

Keynesian economics

The body of macroeconomic thought that asserts that changes in aggregate demand can create gaps between the actual and potential levels of output, and that such gaps can be prolonged. It stresses the use of fiscal and monetary policy to close such gaps.

The Fed could have prevented many of the failures by engaging in open-market operations to inject new reserves into the system and by lending reserves to troubled banks through the discount window. But it generally refused to do so; Fed officials sometimes even applauded bank failures as a desirable way to weed out bad management!

Figure 32.2 shows the shift in aggregate demand between 1929, when the economy was operating just above its potential output, and 1933. The plunge in aggregate demand produced a recessionary gap. Our model tells us that such a gap should produce falling wages, shifting the short-run aggregate supply curve to the right. That happened; nominal wages plunged roughly 20% between 1929 and 1933. But we see that the shift in short-run aggregate supply was insufficient to bring the economy back to its potential output.

The failure of shifts in short-run aggregate supply to bring the economy back to its potential output in the early 1930s was partly the result of the magnitude of the reductions in aggregate demand, which plunged the economy into the deepest recessionary gap ever recorded in the United States. We know that the short-run aggregate supply curve began shifting to the right in 1930 as nominal wages fell, but these shifts, which would ordinarily increase real GDP, were overwhelmed by continued reductions in aggregate demand.

A further factor blocking the economy's return to its potential output was federal policy. President Franklin Roosevelt thought that falling wages and prices were in large part to blame for the Depression; programs initiated by his administration in 1933 sought to block further reductions in wages and prices. That stopped further reductions in nominal wages in 1933, thus stopping further shifts in aggregate supply. With recovery blocked from the supply side, and with no policy in place to boost aggregate demand, it is easy to see now why the economy remained locked in a recessionary gap so long.

Keynes argued that expansionary fiscal policy represented the surest tool for bringing the economy back to full employment. The United States did not carry out such a policy until world war prompted increased federal spending for defense. New Deal policies did seek to stimulate employment through a variety of federal programs. But, with state and local governments continuing to cut purchases and raise taxes, the net effect of government at all levels on the economy did not increase aggregate demand during the Roosevelt administration until the onset of world war.[2] As Figure 32.3 shows, expansionary fiscal policies forced by the war had brought output back to potential by 1941. The U.S. entry into World War II after Japan's attack on American forces in Pearl Harbor in December of 1941 led to much sharper increases in government purchases, and the economy pushed quickly into an inflationary gap.

FIGURE 32.2 Aggregate Demand and Short-Run Aggregate Supply: 1929–1933

Slumping aggregate demand brought the economy well below the full-employment level of output by 1933. The short-run aggregate supply curve increased as nominal wages fell. In this analysis, and in subsequent applications in this chapter of the model of aggregate demand and aggregate supply to macroeconomic events, we are ignoring shifts in the long-run aggregate supply curve in order to simplify the diagram.

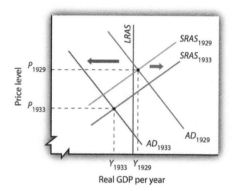

FIGURE 32.3 World War II Ends the Great Depression

Increased U.S. government purchases, prompted by the beginning of World War II, ended the Great Depression. By 1942, increasing aggregate demand had pushed real GDP beyond potential output.

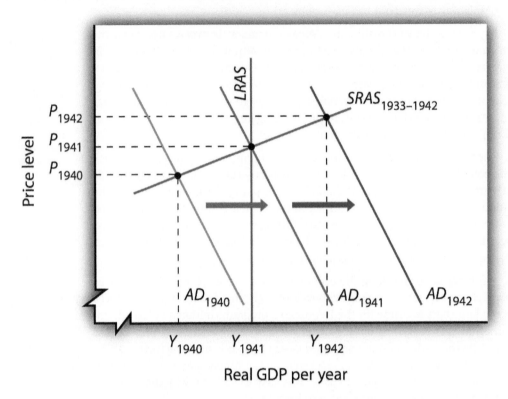

For Keynesian economists, the Great Depression provided impressive confirmation of Keynes's ideas. A sharp reduction in aggregate demand had gotten the trouble started. The recessionary gap created by the change in aggregate demand had persisted for more than a decade. And expansionary fiscal policy had put a swift end to the worst macroeconomic nightmare in U.S. history—even if that policy had been forced on the country by a war that would prove to be one of the worst episodes of world history.

Key Takeaways

- Classical economic thought stressed the ability of the economy to achieve what we now call its potential output in the long run. It thus stressed the forces that determine the position of the long-run aggregate supply curve as the determinants of income.

- Keynesian economics focuses on changes in aggregate demand and their ability to create recessionary or inflationary gaps. Keynesian economists argue that sticky prices and wages would make it difficult for the economy to adjust to its potential output.

- Because Keynesian economists believe that recessionary and inflationary gaps can persist for long periods, they urge the use of fiscal and monetary policy to shift the aggregate demand curve and to close these gaps.

- Aggregate demand fell sharply in the first four years of the Great Depression. As the recessionary gap widened, nominal wages began to fall, and the short-run aggregate supply curve began shifting to the right. These shifts, however, were not sufficient to close the recessionary gap. World War II forced the U.S. government to shift to a sharply expansionary fiscal policy, and the Depression ended.

Try It!

Imagine that it is 1933. President Franklin Roosevelt has just been inaugurated and has named you as his senior economic adviser. Devise a program to bring the economy back to its potential output. Using the model of aggregate demand and aggregate supply, demonstrate graphically how your proposal could work.

Case in Point: Early Views on Stickiness

Source: © Shutterstock, Inc.

Although David Ricardo's focus on the long run emerged as the dominant approach to macro-economic thought, not all of his contemporaries agreed with his perspective. Many 18th- and 19th-century economists developed theoretical arguments suggesting that changes in aggregate demand could affect the real level of economic activity in the short run. Like the new Keynesians, they based their arguments on the concept of price stickiness.

Henry Thornton's 1802 book, *An Enquiry into the Nature and Effects of the Paper Credit of Great Britain*, argued that a reduction in the money supply could, because of wage stickiness, produce a short-run slump in output:

> "The tendency, however, of a very great and sudden reduction of the accustomed number of bank notes, is to create an unusual and temporary distress, and a fall of price arising from that distress. But a fall arising from temporary distress, will be attended probably with no correspondent fall in the rate of wages; for the fall of price, and the distress, will be understood to be temporary, and the rate of wages, we know, is not so variable as the price of goods. There is reason, therefore, to fear that the unnatural and extraordinary low price arising from the sort of distress of which we now speak, would occasion much discouragement of the fabrication of manufactures."

A half-century earlier, David Hume had noted that an increase in the quantity of money would boost output in the short run, again because of the stickiness of prices. In an essay titled "Of Money," published in 1752, Hume described the process through which an increased money supply could boost output:

> *"At first, no alteration is perceived; by degrees the price rises, first of one commodity, then of another, till the whole at least reaches a just proportion with the new quantity of (money) which is in the kingdom. In my opinion, it is only in this interval or intermediate situation ... that the encreasing quantity of gold and silver is favourable to industry."*

Hume's argument implies sticky prices; some prices are slower to respond to the increase in the money supply than others.

Economists of the 18th and 19th century are generally lumped together as adherents to the classical school, but their views were anything but uniform. Many developed an analytical framework that was quite similar to the essential elements of new Keynesian economists today. Economist Thomas Humphrey, at the Federal Reserve Bank of Richmond, marvels at the insights shown by early economists: "Today economists and textbook writers perpetuate the myth by disseminating a caricature 'classical' macromodel in which money is always neutral... On the contrary, except for Ricardo and one or two others, the classicals believed that money had powerful temporary real effects and perhaps some residual permanent effects as well. In the view of the classicals, nonneutrality typified the short run and neutrality at best held approximately in the long run only."

Source: *Based on Thomas M. Humphrey, "Nonneutrality of Money in Classical Monetary Thought," Federal Reserve Bank of Richmond Economic Review 77, no. 2 (March/April 1991): 3–15, and personal interview.*

Answer to Try It! Problem

An expansionary fiscal or monetary policy, or a combination of the two, would shift aggregate demand to the right as shown in Panel (a), ideally returning the economy to potential output. One piece of evidence suggesting that fiscal policy would work is the swiftness with which the economy recovered from the Great Depression once World War II forced the government to carry out such a policy. An alternative approach would be to do nothing. Ultimately, that should force nominal wages down further, producing increases in short-run aggregate supply, as in Panel (b). We do not know if such an approach might have worked; federal policies enacted in 1933 prevented wages and prices from falling further than they already had.

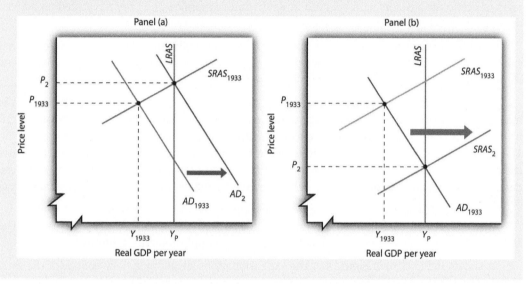

32.3 Keynesian Economics in the 1960s and 1970s

Learning Objectives

1. Briefly summarize the monetarist school of thought that emerged in the 1960s, and discuss how the experiences of the 1960s and 1970s seemed to be broadly consistent with it.
2. Briefly summarize the new classical school of thought that emerged in the 1970s, and discuss how the experiences of the 1970s seemed to be broadly consistent with it.
3. Summarize the lessons that economists learned from the decade of the 1970s.

The experience of the Great Depression led to the widespread acceptance of Keynesian ideas among economists, but its acceptance as a basis for economic policy was slower. The administrations of Presidents Roosevelt, Truman, and Eisenhower rejected the notion that fiscal policy could or should be used to manipulate real GDP. Truman vetoed a 1948 Republican-sponsored tax cut aimed at stimulating the economy after World War II (Congress, however, overrode the veto), and Eisenhower resisted stimulative measures to deal with the recessions of 1953, 1957, and 1960.

It was the administration of President John F. Kennedy that first used fiscal policy with the intent of manipulating aggregate demand to move the economy toward its potential output. Kennedy's willingness to embrace Keynes's ideas changed the nation's approach to fiscal policy for the next two decades.

Expansionary Policy in the 1960s

We can think of the macroeconomic history of the 1960s as encompassing two distinct phases. The first showed the power of Keynesian policies to correct economic difficulties. The second showed the power of these same policies to create them.

Correcting a Recessionary Gap

President Kennedy took office in 1961 with the economy in a recessionary gap. He had appointed a team of economic advisers who believed in Keynesian economics, and they advocated an activist approach to fiscal policy. The new president was quick to act on their advice.

Expansionary policy served the administration's foreign-policy purposes. Kennedy argued that the United States had fallen behind the Soviet Union, its avowed enemy, in military preparedness. He won approval from Congress for sharp increases in defense spending in 1961.

The Kennedy administration also added accelerated depreciation to the tax code. Under the measure, firms could deduct depreciation expenses more quickly, reducing their taxable profits—and thus their taxes—early in the life of a capital asset. The measure encouraged investment. The administration also introduced an investment tax credit, which allowed corporations to reduce their income taxes by 10% of their investment in any one year. The combination of increased defense spending and tax measures to stimulate investment provided a quick boost to aggregate demand.

The Fed followed the administration's lead. It, too, shifted to an expansionary policy in 1961. The Fed purchased government bonds to increase the money supply and reduce interest rates.

As shown in Panel (a) of Figure 32.4, the expansionary fiscal and monetary policies of the early 1960s had pushed real GDP to its potential by 1963. But the concept of potential output had not been developed in 1963; Kennedy administration economists had defined full employment to be an unemployment rate of 4%. The actual unemployment rate in 1963 was 5.7%; the perception of the time was that the economy needed further stimulus.

FIGURE 32.4 The Two Faces of Expansionary Policy in the 1960s
Expansionary fiscal and monetary policy early in the 1960s (Panel [a]) closed a recessionary gap, but continued expansionary policy created an inflationary gap by the end of the decade (Panel [b]). The short-run aggregate supply curve began shifting to the left, but expansionary policy continued to shift aggregate demand to the right and kept the economy in an inflationary gap.

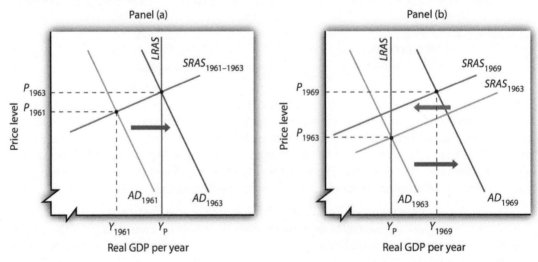

Expansionary Policy and an Inflationary Gap

Kennedy proposed a tax cut in 1963, which Congress would approve the following year, after the president had been assassinated. In retrospect, we may regard the tax cut as representing a kind of a recognition lag— policy makers did not realize the economy had already reached what we now recognize was its potential output. Instead of closing a recessionary gap, the tax cut helped push the economy into an inflationary gap, as illustrated in Panel (b) of Figure 32.4.

The expansionary policies, however, did not stop with the tax cut. Continued increases in federal spending for the newly expanded war in Vietnam and for President Lyndon Johnson's agenda of domestic programs, together with continued high rates of money growth, sent the aggregate demand curve further to the right. While President Johnson's Council of Economic Advisers recommended contractionary policy as early as 1965, macroeconomic policy remained generally expansionary through 1969. Wage increases began shifting the short-run aggregate supply curve to the left, but expansionary policy continued to increase aggregate demand and kept the economy in an inflationary gap for the last six years of the 1960s. Panel (b) of Figure 32.4 shows expansionary policies pushing the economy beyond its potential output after 1963.

The 1960s had demonstrated two important lessons about Keynesian macroeconomic policy. First, stimulative fiscal and monetary policy could be used to close a recessionary gap. Second, fiscal policies could have a long implementation lag. The tax cut recommended by President Kennedy's economic advisers in 1961 was not enacted until 1964—after the recessionary gap it was designed to fight had been closed. The tax increase recommended by President Johnson's economic advisers in 1965 was not passed until 1968—after the inflationary gap it was designed to close had widened.

Macroeconomic policy after 1963 pushed the economy into an inflationary gap. The push into an inflationary gap did produce rising employment and a rising real GDP. But the inflation that came with it, together with other problems, would create real difficulties for the economy and for macroeconomic policy in the 1970s.

The 1970s: Troubles from the Supply Side

For many observers, the use of Keynesian fiscal and monetary policies in the 1960s had been a triumph. That triumph turned into a series of macroeconomic disasters in the 1970s as inflation and unemployment spiraled to ever-higher levels. The fiscal and monetary medicine that had seemed to work so well in the 1960s seemed capable of producing only instability in the 1970s. The experience of the period shook the faith of many economists in Keynesian remedies and made them receptive to alternative approaches.

This section describes the major macroeconomic events of the 1970s. It then examines the emergence of two schools of economic thought as major challengers to the Keynesian orthodoxy that had seemed so dominant a decade earlier.

Macroeconomic Policy: Coping with the Supply Side

When Richard Nixon became president in 1969, he faced a very different economic situation than the one that had confronted John Kennedy eight years earlier. The economy had clearly pushed beyond full employment; the unemployment rate had plunged to 3.6% in 1968. Inflation, measured using the implicit price deflator, had soared to 4.3%, the highest rate that had been recorded since 1951. The economy needed a cooling off. Nixon, the Fed, and the economy's own process of self-correction delivered it.

Figure 32.5 tells the story—it is a simple one. The economy in 1969 was in an inflationary gap. It had been in such a gap for years, but this time policy makers were no longer forcing increases in aggregate demand to keep it there. The adjustment in short-run aggregate supply brought the economy back to its potential output.

FIGURE 32.5 The Economy Closes an Inflationary Gap
The Nixon administration and the Fed joined to end the expansionary policies that had prevailed in the 1960s, so that aggregate demand did not rise in 1970, but the short-run aggregate supply curve shifted to the left as the economy responded to an inflationary gap.

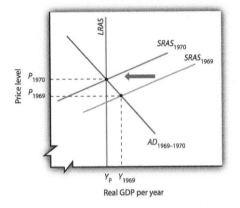

But what we can see now as a simple adjustment seemed anything but simple in 1970. Economists did not think in terms of shifts in short-run aggregate supply. Keynesian economics focused on shifts in aggregate demand, not supply.

For the Nixon administration, the slump in real GDP in 1970 was a recession, albeit an odd one. The price level had risen sharply. That was not, according to the Keynesian story, supposed to happen; there was simply no reason to expect the price level to soar when real GDP and employment were falling.

The administration dealt with the recession by shifting to an expansionary fiscal policy. By 1973, the economy was again in an inflationary gap. The economy's 1974 adjustment to the gap came with another jolt. The Organization of Petroleum Exporting Countries (OPEC) tripled the price of oil. The resulting shift to the left in short-run aggregate supply gave the economy another recession and another jump in the price level.

The second half of the decade was, in some respects, a repeat of the first. The administrations of Gerald Ford and then Jimmy Carter, along with the Fed, pursued expansionary policies to stimulate the economy. Those helped boost output, but they also pushed up prices. As we saw in the chapter on inflation and unemployment, inflation and unemployment followed a cycle to higher and higher levels.

The 1970s presented a challenge not just to policy makers, but to economists as well. The sharp changes in real GDP and in the price level could not be explained by a Keynesian analysis that focused on aggregate demand. Something else was happening. As economists grappled to explain it, their efforts would produce the model with which we have been dealing and around which a broad consensus of economists has emerged. But, before that consensus was to come, two additional elements of the puzzle had to be added. The first was the recognition of the importance of monetary policy. The second was the recognition of the role of aggregate supply, both in the long and in the short run.

The Monetarist Challenge

The idea that changes in the money supply are the principal determinant of the nominal value of total output is one of the oldest in economic thought; it is implied by the equation of exchange, assuming the stability of velocity. Classical economists stressed the long run and thus the determination of the economy's potential output. This meant that changes in the price level were, in the long run, the result of changes in the money supply.

monetarist school

The body of macroeconomic thought that holds that changes in the money supply are the primary cause of changes in nominal GDP.

At roughly the same time Keynesian economics was emerging as the dominant school of macroeconomic thought, some economists focused on changes in the money supply as the primary determinant of changes in the nominal value of output. Led by Milton Friedman, they stressed the role of changes in the money supply as the principal determinant of changes in nominal output in the short run as well as in the long run. They argued that fiscal policy had no effect on the economy. Their "money rules" doctrine led to the name *monetarists*. The **monetarist school** holds that changes in the money supply are the primary cause of changes in nominal GDP.

Monetarists generally argue that the impact lags of monetary policy—the lags from the time monetary policy is undertaken to the time the policy affects nominal GDP—are so long and variable that trying to stabilize the economy using monetary policy can be destabilizing. Monetarists thus are critical of activist stabilization policies. They argue that, because of crowding-out effects, fiscal policy has no effect on GDP. Monetary policy does, but it should not be used. Instead, most monetarists urge the Fed to increase the money supply at a fixed annual rate, preferably the rate at which potential output rises. With stable velocity, that would eliminate inflation in the long run. Recessionary or inflationary gaps could occur in the short run, but monetarists generally argue that self-correction will take care of them more effectively than would activist monetary policy.

While monetarists differ from Keynesians in their assessment of the impact of fiscal policy, the primary difference in the two schools lies in their degree of optimism about whether stabilization policy can, in fact, be counted on to bring the economy back to its potential output. For monetarists, the complexity of economic life and the uncertain nature of lags mean that efforts to use monetary policy to stabilize the economy can be destabilizing. Monetarists argued that the difficulties encountered by policy makers as they tried to respond to the dramatic events of the 1970s demonstrated the superiority of a policy that simply increased the money supply at a slow, steady rate.

Monetarists could also cite the apparent validity of an adjustment mechanism proposed by Milton Friedman in 1968. As the economy continued to expand in the 1960s, and as unemployment continued to fall, Friedman said that unemployment had fallen below its natural rate, the rate consistent with equilibrium in the labor market. Any divergence of unemployment from its natural rate, he insisted, would necessarily be temporary. He suggested that the low unemployment of 1968 (the rate was 3.6% that year) meant that workers had been surprised by rising prices. Higher prices had produced a real wage below what workers and firms had expected. Friedman predicted that as workers demanded and got higher nominal wages, the price level would shoot up and unemployment would rise. That, of course, is precisely what happened in 1970 and 1971. Friedman's notion of the natural rate of unemployment buttressed the monetarist argument that the economy moves to its potential output on its own.

Perhaps the most potent argument from the monetarist camp was the behavior of the economy itself. During the 1960s, monetarist and Keynesian economists alike could argue that economic performance was consistent with their respective views of the world. Keynesians could point to expansions in economic activity that they could ascribe to expansionary fiscal policy, but economic activity also moved closely with changes in the money supply, just as monetarists predicted. During the 1970s, however, it was difficult for Keynesians to argue that policies that affected aggregate demand were having the predicted impact on the economy. Changes in aggregate supply had repeatedly pushed the economy off a Keynesian course. But monetarists, once again, could point to a consistent relationship between changes in the money supply and changes in economic activity.

Figure 32.6 shows the movement of nominal GDP and M2 during the 1960s and 1970s. In the figure, annual percentage changes in M2 are plotted against percentage changes in nominal GDP a year later to account for the lagged effects of changes in the money supply. We see that there was a close relationship between changes in the quantity of money and subsequent changes in nominal GDP.

FIGURE 32.6 M2 and Nominal GDP, 1960–1980

The chart shows annual rates of change in M2 and in nominal GDP, lagged one year. The observation for 1961, for example, shows that nominal GDP increased 3.5% and that M2 increased 4.9% in the previous year, 1960. The two variables showed a close relationship in the 1960s and 1970s.

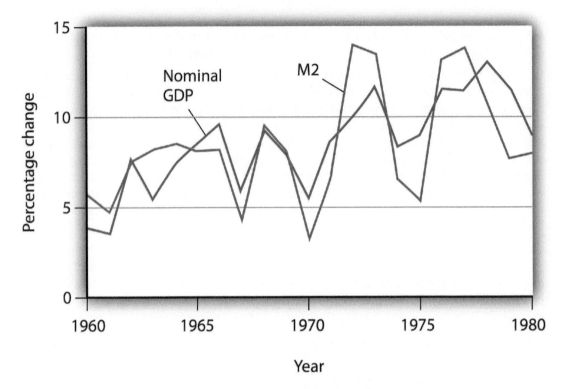

Monetarist doctrine emerged as a potent challenge to Keynesian economics in the 1970s largely because of the close correspondence between nominal GDP and the money supply. The next section examines another school of thought that came to prominence in the 1970s.

New Classical Economics: A Focus on Aggregate Supply

Much of the difficulty policy makers encountered during the decade of the 1970s resulted from shifts in aggregate supply. Keynesian economics and, to a lesser degree, monetarism had focused on aggregate demand. As it became clear that an analysis incorporating the supply side was an essential part of the macroeconomic puzzle, some economists turned to an entirely new way of looking at macroeconomic issues.

These economists started with what we identified at the beginning of this text as a distinguishing characteristic of economic thought: a focus on individuals and their decisions. Keynesian economics employed aggregate analysis and paid little attention to individual choices. Monetarist doctrine was based on the analysis of individuals' maximizing behavior with respect to money demand, but it did not extend that analysis to decisions that affect aggregate supply. The new approach aimed at an analysis of how individual choices would affect the entire spectrum of economic activity.

These economists rejected the entire framework of conventional macroeconomic analysis. Indeed, they rejected the very term. For them there is no macroeconomics, nor is there something called microeconomics. For them, there is only economics, which they regard as the analysis of behavior based on individual maximization. The analysis of the determination of the price level and real GDP becomes an application of basic economic theory, not a separate body of thought. The approach to macroeconomic analysis built from an analysis of individual maximizing choices is called **new classical economics**.

new classical economics

The approach to macroeconomic analysis built from an analysis of individual maximizing choices and emphasizing wage and price flexibility.

Like classical economic thought, new classical economics focuses on the determination of long-run aggregate supply and the economy's ability to reach this level of output quickly. But the similarity ends there. Classical economics emerged in large part before economists had developed sophisticated mathematical models of maximizing behavior. The new classical economics puts mathematics to work in an extremely complex way to generalize from individual behavior to aggregate results.

Because the new classical approach suggests that the economy will remain at or near its potential output, it follows that the changes we observe in economic activity result not from changes in aggregate demand but from changes in long-run aggregate supply. New classical economics suggests that economic changes don't necessarily imply economic problems.

New classical economists pointed to the supply-side shocks of the 1970s, both from changes in oil prices and changes in expectations, as evidence that their emphasis on aggregate supply was on the mark. They argued that the large observed swings in real GDP reflected underlying changes in the economy's potential output. The recessionary and inflationary gaps that so perplexed policy makers during the 1970s were not gaps at all, the new classical economists insisted. Instead, they reflected changes in the economy's own potential output.

Two particularly controversial propositions of new classical theory relate to the impacts of monetary and of fiscal policy. Both are implications of the **rational expectations hypothesis**, which assumes that individuals form expectations about the future based on the information available to them, and that they act on those expectations.

The rational expectations hypothesis suggests that monetary policy, even though it will affect the aggregate demand curve, might have no effect on real GDP. This possibility, which was suggested by Robert Lucas, is illustrated in Figure 32.7. Suppose the economy is initially in equilibrium at point 1 in Panel (a). Real GDP equals its potential output, Y_P. Now suppose a reduction in the money supply causes aggregate demand to fall to AD_2. In our model, the solution moves to point 2; the price level falls to P_2, and real GDP falls to Y_2. There is a recessionary gap. In the long run, the short-run aggregate supply curve shifts to $SRAS_2$, the price level falls to P_3, and the economy returns to its potential output at point 3.

rational expectations hypothesis

Individuals form expectations about the future based on the information available to them, and they act on those expectations.

FIGURE 32.7 Contractionary Monetary Policy: With and Without Rational Expectations
Panels (a) and (b) show an economy operating at potential output (1); a contractionary monetary policy shifts aggregate demand to AD_2. Panel (a) shows the kind of response we have studied up to this point; real GDP falls to Y_2 in period (2); the recessionary gap is closed in the long run by falling nominal wages that cause an increase in short-run aggregate supply in period (3). Panel (b) shows the rational expectations argument. People anticipate the impact of the contractionary policy when it is undertaken, so that the short-run aggregate supply curve shifts to the right at the same time the aggregate demand curve shifts to the left. The result is a reduction in the price level but no change in real GDP; the solution moves from (1) to (2).

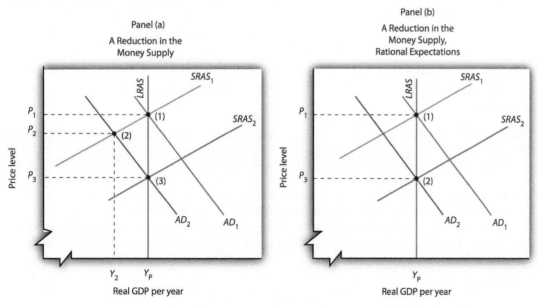

The new classical story is quite different. Consumers and firms observe that the money supply has fallen and anticipate the eventual reduction in the price level to P_3. They adjust their expectations accordingly. Workers agree to lower nominal wages, and the short-run aggregate supply curve shifts to $SRAS_2$. This occurs as aggregate demand falls. As suggested in Panel (b), the price level falls to P_3, and output remains at potential. The solution moves from (1) to (2) with no loss in real GDP.

In this new classical world, there is only one way for a change in the money supply to affect output, and that is for the change to take people by surprise. An unexpected change cannot affect expectations, so the short-run aggregate supply curve does not shift in the short run, and events play out as in Panel (a). Monetary policy can affect output, but only if it takes people by surprise.

The new classical school offers an even stronger case against the operation of fiscal policy. It argues that fiscal policy does not shift the aggregate demand curve at all! Consider, for example, an expansionary fiscal policy. Such a policy involves an increase in government purchases or transfer payments or a cut in taxes. Any of these policies will increase the deficit or reduce the surplus. New classical economists argue that households, when they observe the government carrying out a policy that increases the debt, will anticipate that they, or their children, or their children's children, will end up paying more in taxes. And, according to the new classical story, these households will reduce their consumption as a result. This will, the new classical economists argue, cancel any tendency for the expansionary policy to affect aggregate demand.

Lessons from the 1970s

The 1970s put Keynesian economics and its prescription for activist policies on the defensive. The period lent considerable support to the monetarist argument that changes in the money supply were the primary determinant of changes in the nominal level of GDP. A series of dramatic shifts in aggregate supply gave credence to the new classical emphasis on long-run aggregate supply as the primary determinant of real GDP. Events did not create the new ideas, but they produced an environment in which those ideas could win greater support.

For economists, the period offered some important lessons. These lessons, as we will see in the next section, forced a rethinking of some of the ideas that had dominated Keynesian thought. The experience of the 1970s suggested the following:

1. The short-run aggregate supply curve could not be viewed as something that provided a passive path over which aggregate demand could roam. The short-run aggregate supply curve could shift in ways that clearly affected real GDP, unemployment, and the price level.

2. Money mattered more than Keynesians had previously suspected. Keynes had expressed doubts about the effectiveness of monetary policy, particularly in the face of a recessionary gap. Work by monetarists suggested a close correspondence between changes in M2 and subsequent changes in nominal GDP, convincing many Keynesian economists that money was more important than they had thought.

3. Stabilization was a more difficult task than many economists had anticipated. Shifts in aggregate supply could frustrate the efforts of policy makers to achieve certain macroeconomic goals.

Key Takeaways

- Beginning in 1961, expansionary fiscal and monetary policies were used to close a recessionary gap; this was the first major U.S. application of Keynesian macroeconomic policy.
- The experience of the 1960s and 1970s appeared to be broadly consistent with the monetarist argument that changes in the money supply are the primary determinant of changes in nominal GDP.

- The new classical school's argument that the economy operates at its potential output implies that real GDP is determined by long-run aggregate supply. The experience of the 1970s, in which changes in aggregate supply forced changes in real GDP and in the price level, seemed consistent with the new classical economists' arguments that focused on aggregate supply.

- The experience of the 1970s suggested that changes in the money supply and in aggregate supply were more important determinants of economic activity than many Keynesians had previously thought.

Try It!

Draw the aggregate demand and the short-run and long-run aggregate supply curves for an economy operating with an inflationary gap. Show how expansionary fiscal and/or monetary policies would affect such an economy. Now show how this economy could experience a recession and an increase in the price level at the same time.

Case in Point: Tough Medicine Is Hard to Stomach: Macroeconomic Policy in the 1960s

Source: © Shutterstock, Inc.

The Keynesian prescription for an inflationary gap seems simple enough. The federal government applies contractionary fiscal policy, or the Fed applies contractionary monetary policy, or both. But what seems simple in a graph can be maddeningly difficult in the real world. The medicine for an inflationary gap is tough, and it is tough to take.

President Johnson's new chairman of the Council of Economic Advisers, Gardner Ackley, urged the president in 1965 to adopt fiscal policies aimed at nudging the aggregate demand curve back to the left. The president reluctantly agreed and called in the chairman of the House Ways and Means Committee, the committee that must initiate all revenue measures, to see what he thought of the idea. Wilbur Mills flatly told Johnson that he wouldn't even hold hearings to consider a tax increase. For the time being, the tax boost was dead.

The Federal Reserve System did slow the rate of money growth in 1966. But fiscal policy remained sharply expansionary. Mr. Ackley continued to press his case, and in 1967 President Johnson proposed a temporary 10% increase in personal income taxes. Mr. Mills now endorsed the measure. The temporary tax boost went into effect the following year. The Fed, concerned that the tax hike would be *too* contractionary, countered the administration's shift in fiscal policy with a policy of vigorous money growth in 1967 and 1968.

The late 1960s suggested a sobering reality about the new Keynesian orthodoxy. Stimulating the economy was politically more palatable than contracting it. President Kennedy, while he was not able to win approval of his tax cut during his lifetime, did manage to put the other expansionary aspects of his program into place early in his administration. The Fed reinforced his policies. Dealing with an inflationary gap proved to be quite another matter. President Johnson, a master of the legislative process, took three years to get even a mildly contractionary tax increase put into place, and the Fed acted to counter the impact of this measure by shifting to an expansionary policy.

The second half of the 1960s was marked, in short, by persistent efforts to boost aggregate demand, efforts that kept the economy in an inflationary gap through most of the decade. It was a gap that would usher in a series of supply-side troubles in the next decade.

Answer to Try It! Problem

Even with an inflationary gap, it is possible to pursue expansionary fiscal and monetary policies, shifting the aggregate demand curve to the right, as shown. The inflationary gap will, however, produce an increase in nominal wages, reducing short-run aggregate supply over time. In the case shown here, real GDP rises at first, then falls back to potential output with the reduction in short-run aggregate supply.

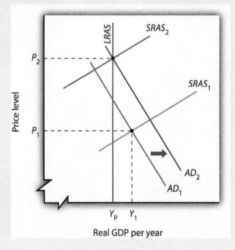

32.4 Macroeconomics for the 21st Century

Learning Objectives

1. Discuss how the Fed incorporated a strong inflation constraint and lags into its policies from the 1980s onwards.

2. Describe the fiscal policies that were undertaken from the 1980s onwards and their rationales.

3. Discuss the challenges that events from the 1980s onwards raised for the monetarist and new classical schools of thought.

4. Summarize the views and policy approaches of the new Keynesian school of economic thought.

Following the recession that ended in 1982, the last two decades of the 20th century and the early years of the 21st century have sometimes been referred to as the Great Moderation. Yes, there were recessions, but they were fairly mild and short-lived. Prematurely, economists began to pat themselves on the backs for having tamed the business cycle. There was a sense that macroeconomic theory and policy had helped with this improved performance. The ideas associated with macroeconomic theory and policy incorporated elements of Keynesian economics, monetarism, and new classical economics. All three schools of macroeconomic thought contributed to the development of a new school of macroeconomic thought: the new Keynesian school.

New Keynesian economics is a body of macroeconomic thought that stresses the stickiness of prices and the need for activist stabilization policies through the manipulation of aggregate demand to keep the economy operating close to its potential output. It incorporates monetarist ideas about the importance of monetary policy and new classical ideas about the importance of aggregate supply, both in the long and in the short run.

Another "new" element in new Keynesian economic thought is the greater use of microeconomic analysis to explain macroeconomic phenomena, particularly the analysis of price and wage stickiness. We saw in the chapter that introduced the model of aggregate demand and aggregate supply, for example, that sticky prices and wages may be a response to the preferences of consumers and of firms. That idea emerged from research by economists of the new Keynesian school.

New Keynesian ideas guide macroeconomic policy; they are the basis for the model of aggregate demand and aggregate supply with which we have been working. To see how the new Keynesian school has come to dominate macroeconomic policy, we shall review the major macroeconomic events and policies of the 1980s, 1990s, and early 2000s.

The 1980s and Beyond: Advances in Macroeconomic Policy

The exercise of monetary and of fiscal policy has changed dramatically in the last few decades.

The Revolution in Monetary Policy

It is fair to say that the monetary policy revolution of the last two decades began on July 25, 1979. On that day, President Jimmy Carter appointed Paul Volcker to be chairman of the Fed's Board of Governors. Mr. Volcker, with President Carter's support, charted a new direction for the Fed. The new direction damaged Mr. Carter politically but ultimately produced dramatic gains for the economy.

Oil prices rose sharply in 1979 as war broke out between Iran and Iraq. Such an increase would, by itself, shift the short-run aggregate supply curve to the left, causing the price level to rise and real GDP to fall. But expansionary fiscal and monetary policies had pushed aggregate demand up at the same time. As a result, real GDP stayed at potential output, while the price level soared. The implicit price deflator jumped 8.1%; the CPI rose 13.5%, the highest inflation rate recorded in the 20th century. Public opinion polls in 1979 consistently showed that most people regarded inflation as the leading problem facing the nation.

new Keynesian economics

A body of macroeconomic thought that stresses the stickiness of prices and the need for activist stabilization policies through the manipulation of aggregate demand to keep the economy operating close to its potential output. It incorporates monetarist ideas about the importance of monetary policy and new classical ideas about the importance of aggregate supply, both in the long run and in the short run.

FIGURE 32.8 The Fed's Fight Against Inflation

By 1979, expansionary fiscal and monetary policies had brought the economy to its potential output. Then war between Iran and Iraq caused oil prices to increase, shifting the short-run aggregate supply curve to the left. In the second half of 1979, the Fed launched an aggressive contractionary policy aimed at reducing inflation. The Fed's action shifted the aggregate demand curve to the left. The result in 1980 was a recession with continued inflation.

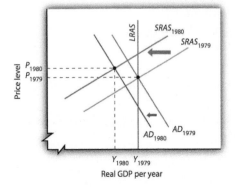

Chairman Volcker charted a monetarist course of fixing the growth rate of the money supply at a rate that would bring inflation down. After the high rates of money growth of the past, the policy was sharply contractionary. Its first effects were to shift the aggregate demand curve to the left. Continued oil price increases produced more leftward shifts in the short-run aggregate supply curve, and the economy suffered a recession in 1980. Inflation remained high. Figure 32.8 shows how the combined shifts in aggregate demand and short-run aggregate supply produced a reduction in real GDP and an increase in the price level.

The Fed stuck to its contractionary guns, and the inflation rate finally began to fall in 1981. But the recession worsened. Unemployment soared, shooting above 10% late in the year. It was, up to that point, the worst recession since the Great Depression. The inflation rate, though, fell sharply in 1982, and the Fed began to shift to a modestly expansionary policy in 1983. But inflation had been licked. Inflation, measured by the implicit price deflator, dropped to a 4.1% rate that year, the lowest since 1967.

The Fed's actions represented a sharp departure from those of the previous two decades. Faced with soaring unemployment, the Fed did not shift to an expansionary policy until inflation was well under control. Inflation continued to edge downward through most of the remaining years of the 20th century and into the new century. The Fed has clearly shifted to a stabilization policy with a strong inflation constraint. It shifts to expansionary policy when the economy has a recessionary gap, but only if it regards inflation as being under control.

This concern about inflation was evident again when the U.S. economy began to weaken in 2008, and there was initially discussion among the members of the Federal Open Market Committee about whether or not easing would contribute to inflation. At that time, it looked like inflation was becoming a more serious problem, largely due to increases in oil and other commodity prices. Some members of the Fed, including then Chairman Bernanke, argued that these price increases were likely to be temporary and the Fed began using expansionary monetary policy early on. By late summer and early fall, inflationary pressures had subsided, and all the members of the FOMC were behind continued expansionary policy. Indeed, at that point, the Fed let it be known that it was willing to do anything in its power to fight the current recession.

The next major advance in monetary policy came in the 1990s, under Federal Reserve Chairman Alan Greenspan. The Fed had shifted to an expansionary policy as the economy slipped into a recession when Iraq's invasion of Kuwait in 1990 began the Persian Gulf War and sent oil prices soaring. By early 1994, real GDP was rising, but the economy remained in a recessionary gap. Nevertheless, the Fed announced on February 4, 1994, that it had shifted to a contractionary policy, selling bonds to boost interest rates and to reduce the money supply. While the economy had not reached its potential output, Chairman Greenspan explained that the Fed was concerned that it might push past its potential output within a year. The Fed, for the first time, had explicitly taken the impact lag of monetary policy into account. The issue of lags was also a part of Fed discussions in the 2000s.

Fiscal Policy: A Resurgence of Interest

President Ronald Reagan, whose 1980 election victory was aided by a recession that year, introduced a tax cut, combined with increased defense spending, in 1981. While this expansionary fiscal policy was virtually identical to the policy President Kennedy had introduced 20 years earlier, President Reagan rejected Keynesian economics, embracing supply-side arguments instead. He argued that the cut in tax rates, particularly in high marginal rates, would encourage work effort. He reintroduced an investment tax credit, which stimulated investment. With people working harder and firms investing more, he expected long-run aggregate supply to increase more rapidly. His policy, he said, would stimulate economic growth.

The tax cut and increased defense spending increased the federal deficit. Increased spending for welfare programs and unemployment compensation, both of which were induced by the plunge in real GDP in the early 1980s, contributed to the deficit as well. As deficits continued to rise, they began to dominate discussions of fiscal policy. In 1990, with the economy slipping into a recession, President George H. W. Bush agreed to a tax increase despite an earlier promise not to do so. President Bill Clinton, whose 1992 election resulted largely from the recession of 1990–1991, introduced another tax increase in 1994, with the economy still in a recessionary gap. Both tax increases were designed to curb the rising deficit.

Congress in the first years of the 1990s rejected the idea of using an expansionary fiscal policy to close a recessionary gap on grounds it would increase the deficit. President Clinton, for example, introduced a stimulus package of increased government investment and tax cuts designed to stimulate private investment in 1993; a Democratic Congress rejected the proposal. The deficit acted like a straitjacket for fiscal policy. The Bush and Clinton tax increases, coupled with spending restraint and increased revenues from economic growth, brought an end to the deficit in 1998.

Initially, it was expected that the budget surplus would continue well into the new century. But, this picture changed rapidly. President George W. Bush campaigned on a platform of large tax cuts, arguing that less government intervention in the economy would be good for long-term economic growth. His administration saw the enactment of two major pieces of tax-cutting legislation in 2001 and 2003. Coupled with increases in government spending, in part for defense but also for domestic purposes including a Medicare prescription drug benefit, the government budget surpluses gave way to budget deficits. To deal with times of economic weakness during President Bush's administration, temporary tax cuts were enacted, both in 2001 and again in 2008.

As the economy continued to weaken in 2008, there was a resurgence of interest in using discretionary increases in government spending, as discussed in the Case in Point, to respond to the recession. Three factors were paramount: (1) the temporary tax cuts had provided only a minor amount of stimulus to the economy, as sizable portions had been used for saving rather than spending, (2) expansionary monetary policy, while useful, had not seemed adequate, and (3) the recession threatening the global economy was larger than those in recent economic history.

The Rise of New Keynesian Economics

New Keynesian economics emerged in the last three decades as the dominant school of macroeconomic thought for two reasons. First, it successfully incorporated important monetarist and new classical ideas into Keynesian economics. Second, developments in the 1980s and 1990s shook economists' confidence in the ability of the monetarist or the new classical school alone to explain macroeconomic change.

Monetary Change and Monetarism

Look again at Figure 32.6. The close relationship between M2 and nominal GDP in the 1960s and 1970s helped win over many economists to the monetarist camp. Now look at Figure 32.9. It shows the same two variables, M2 and nominal GDP, from the 1980s through 2015. The tidy relationship between the two seems to have vanished. What happened?

FIGURE 32.9 M2 and Nominal GDP, 1980–2015

The close relationship between M2 and nominal GDP a year later that had prevailed in the 1960s and 1970s seemed to vanish from the 1980s onward.

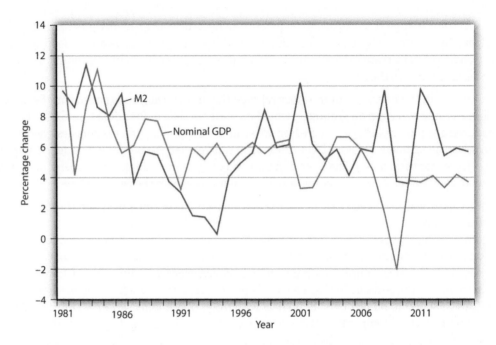

Source: Economic Report of the President 2017, Tables B-2 and B-26.

The sudden change in the relationship between the money stock and nominal GDP has resulted partly from public policy. Deregulation of the banking industry in the early 1980s produced sharp changes in the ways individuals dealt with money, thus changing the relationship of money to economic activity. Banks have been freed to offer a wide range of financial alternatives to their customers. One of the most important developments has been the introduction of bond funds offered by banks. These funds allowed customers to earn the higher interest rates paid by long-term bonds while at the same time being able to transfer funds easily into checking accounts as needed. Balances in these bond funds are not counted as part of M2. As people shifted assets out of M2 accounts and into bond funds, velocity rose. That changed the once-close relationship between changes in the quantity of money and changes in nominal GDP.

Many monetarists have argued that the experience of the 1980s, 1990s, and 2000s reinforces their view that the instability of velocity in the short run makes monetary policy an inappropriate tool for short-run stabilization. They continue to insist, however, that the velocity of M2 remains stable in the long run. But the velocity of M2 appears to have diverged in recent years from its long-run path. Although it may return to its long-run level, the stability of velocity remains very much in doubt. Because of this instability, in 2000, when the Fed was no longer required by law to report money target ranges, it discontinued the practice.

The New Classical School and Responses to Policy

New classical economics suggests that people should have responded to the fiscal and monetary policies of the 1980s in predictable ways. They did not, and that has created new doubts among economists about the validity of the new classical argument.

The rational expectations hypothesis predicts that if a shift in monetary policy by the Fed is anticipated, it will have no effect on real GDP. The slowing in the rate of growth of the money supply over the period from 1979 to 1982 was surely well known. The Fed announced at the outset what it was going to do, and then did it. It had the full support first of President Carter and then of President Reagan. But the policy plunged the economy into what was then its worst recession since the

Great Depression. The experience hardly seemed consistent with new classical logic. New classical economists argued that people may have doubted the Fed would keep its word, but the episode still cast doubt on the rational expectations argument.

The public's response to the huge deficits of the Reagan era also seemed to belie new classical ideas. One new classical argument predicts that people will increase their saving rate in response to an increase in public sector borrowing. The resultant reduction in consumption will cancel the impact of the increase in deficit-financed government expenditures. But the private saving rate in the United States *fell* during the 1980s. New classical economists contend that standard measures of saving do not fully represent the actual saving rate, but the experience of the 1980s did not seem to support the new classical argument.

The events of the 1980s do not suggest that either monetarist or new classical ideas should be abandoned, but those events certainly raised doubts about relying solely on these approaches. Similarly, doubts about Keynesian economics raised by the events of the 1970s led Keynesians to modify and strengthen their approach.

A Macroeconomic Consensus?

While there is less consensus on macroeconomic policy issues than on some other economic issues (particularly those in the microeconomic and international areas), surveys of economists generally show that the new Keynesian approach has emerged as the preferred approach to macroeconomic analysis. The finding that about 80% of economists agree that expansionary fiscal measures can deal with recessionary gaps certainly suggests that most economists can be counted in the new Keynesian camp. Neither monetarist nor new classical analysis would support such measures.During the period of the Great Moderation, however, most economists—about 70%—felt that discretionary fiscal policy should be avoided and that the business cycle should be managed by the Fed. A similar survey after the recession, however, showed that economists had become more sympathetic to using discretionary fiscal policy, as the percent saying it should be avoided fell to about 40%. It could be that economists generally feel that monetary policy should do the heaving lifting during typical recessions but that both fiscal and monetary policy should be used during severe recessions. [3] Just as the new Keynesian approach appears to have won support among most economists, it has become dominant in terms of macroeconomic policy. In the United States, the Great Recession was fought using traditional monetary and fiscal policies, while other policies were used concurrently to deal with the financial crisis that occurred at the same time.

Did the experience of the 2007–2009 recession affect economists' views concerning macroeconomic policy? One source for gauging possible changes in the opinions of economists is the twice-yearly survey of economic policy among the National Association for Business Economics (NABE).[4] According to the August 2010 survey of 242 members of NABE, almost 60% were supportive of monetary policy at that time, which was expansionary and continued to be so into 2014. Concerning fiscal policy, there was less agreement. Still, according to the survey taken at the time the 2009 fiscal stimulus was being debated, 22% characterized it as "about right," another third found it too restrictive, and only one third found it too stimulative. In the August 2010 survey, 39% thought fiscal policy "about right," 24% found it too restrictive, and 37% found it too stimulative. Also, nearly 75% ranked promotion of economic growth as more important than deficit reduction, roughly two thirds supported the extension of unemployment benefits, and 60% agreed that awarding states with federal assistance funds from the 2009 stimulus package was appropriate. Taken together, the new Keynesian approach still seems to reflect the dominant opinion.

Is the Great Moderation Over?

As did the Great Depression of the 1930s, the Great Recession of the late 2000s generated great fear. Even though it officially ended in the middle of 2009, the state of the economy was the major issue over which the 2012 U.S. presidential election was fought, as the two major political parties offered their competing visions. Unemployment was still high, the housing sector had still not recovered, and the European debt situation loomed in the background. During Obama's second term, the unemployment rate fell substantially, housing recovered, and the European debt problem faded somewhat, but GDP increased relatively slowly. During the 2016 election, this relatively slow rate of increase in GDP in the years following the Great Recession was a major issue, with Donald Trump arguing during the campaign that the policies he advocated would speed up the expansion considerably. Another lurking question was whether the experience of the recent deep recession, the related financial crisis, and the slow recovery from them would become the new "normal" or whether macroeconomic performance would return to being less volatile.

Economist Todd Clark at the Federal Reserve Bank of Kansas attempted to answer this question.[5] He first looked at the various explanations for the lower volatility of the U.S. economy during the 25-year period that preceded the Great Recession. Three broad reasons were given: structural changes, improved monetary policy, and good luck. While there is disagreement in the literature as to the relative importance of each of these, Clark argues that there is no reason to assume that the first two explanations for moderation will not continue to have moderating influences. For example, one positive structural change has been better inventory management, and he sees no reason why firms should become less able in the future to manage their inventories using the newly developed techniques. Similarly, in the future, monetary authorities should be able to continue to make the better decisions that they made during the Great Moderation. The element that can vary is luck. During the Great Moderation, the economy experienced fewer serious shocks. For example, oil prices were fairly stable. In contrast, during the recent recession, the price of oil rose from $54 per barrel in January 2007 to $134 per barrel in June 2008. The bursting of the housing price bubble and the ensuing crisis in financial markets was another major shock contributing to the depth and length of the recent recession. Clark says, "Accordingly, once the crisis subsides and the period of very bad luck passes, macroeconomic volatility will likely decline. In the future, the permanence of structural change and improved monetary policy that occurred in years past should ensure that low volatility is the norm."[6] Let's hope that he is correct.

Key Takeaways

- The actions of the Fed starting in late 1979 reflected a strong inflation constraint and a growing recognition of the impact lag for monetary policy.
- Reducing the deficit dominated much of fiscal policy discussion during the 1980s and 1990s.
- The events of the 1980s and early 1990s do not appear to have been consistent with the hypotheses of either the monetarist or new classical schools.
- New Keynesian economists have incorporated major elements of the ideas of the monetarist and new classical schools into their formulation of macroeconomic theory.

Try It!

Show the effect of an expansionary monetary policy on real GDP

1. according to new Keynesian economics
2. according to the rational expectations hypothesis

In both cases, consider both the short-run and the long-run effects.

Case in Point: Steering on a Difficult Course

Source: © Shutterstock, Inc.

Imagine that you are driving a test car on a special course. You get to steer, accelerate, and brake, but you cannot be sure whether the car will respond to your commands within a few feet or within a few miles. The windshield and side windows are blackened, so you cannot see where you are going or even where you are. You can only see where you have been with the rear-view mirror. The course is designed so that you will face difficulties you have never experienced. Your job is to get through the course unscathed. Oh, and by the way, you have to observe the speed limit, but you do not know what it is. Have a nice trip.

Now imagine that the welfare of people all over the world will be affected by how well you drive the course. They are watching you. They are giving you a great deal of often-conflicting advice about what you should do. Thinking about the problems you would face driving such a car will give you some idea of the obstacle course fiscal and monetary authorities must negotiate. They cannot know where the economy is going or where it is—economic indicators such as GDP and the CPI only suggest where the economy has been. And the perils through which it must steer can be awesome indeed.

One policy response that most acknowledge as having been successful was how the Fed dealt with the financial crises in Southeast Asia and elsewhere that shook the world economy in 1997 and 1998. There were serious concerns at the time that economic difficulties around the world would bring the high-flying U.S. economy to its knees and worsen an already difficult economic situation in other countries. The Fed had to steer through the pitfalls that global economic crises threw in front of it.

In the fall of 1998, the Fed chose to accelerate to avoid a possible downturn. The Federal Open Market Committee (FOMC) engaged in expansionary monetary policy by lowering its target for the federal funds rate. Some critics argued at the time that the Fed's action was too weak to counter the impact of world economic crisis. Others, though, criticized the Fed for undertaking an expansionary policy when the U.S. economy seemed already to be in an inflationary gap.

In the summer of 1999, the Fed put on the brakes, shifting back to a slightly contractionary policy. It raised the target for the federal funds rate, first to 5.0% and then to 5.25%. These actions reflected concern about speeding when in an inflationary gap.

But was the economy speeding? Was it in an inflationary gap? Certainly, the U.S. unemployment rate of 4.2% in the fall of 1999 stood well below standard estimates of the natural rate of unemployment. There were few, if any, indications that inflation was a problem, but the Fed had to recognize that inflation might not appear for a very long time after the Fed had taken a particular course. As noted in the text, this was also during a time when the once-close relationship between money growth and nominal GDP seemed to break down. The shifts in demand for money created unexplained and unexpected changes in velocity.

The outcome of the Fed's actions has been judged a success. While with 20/20 hindsight the Fed's decisions might seem obvious, in fact it was steering a car whose performance seemed less and less predictable over a course that was becoming more and more treacherous.

Since 2008, both the Fed and the government have been again trying to get the economy back on track. In this case, the car was already in the ditch. The Fed decided on a "no holds barred" approach. It moved aggressively to lower the federal funds rate target and engaged in a variety of other measures to improve liquidity to the banking system, to lower other interest rates by purchasing longer-term securities (such as 10-year treasuries and those of Fannie Mae and Freddie Mac), and, working with the Treasury Department, to provide loans related to consumer and business debt.

Continuing on smaller expansionary fiscal policy begun under President George W. Bush, the Obama administration for its part advocated and Congress passed a massive spending and tax relief package of more than $800 billion. Besides the members of his economic team, many economists seemed to be on board in using discretionary fiscal policy in this instance. The *New York Times* reported that the then Federal Reserve Bank of San Francisco President Janet Yellen put it this way: "The new enthusiasm for fiscal stimulus, and particularly government spending, represents a huge evolution in mainstream thinking." A notable convert to using fiscal policy to deal with this recession was Harvard economist and former adviser to President Ronald Reagan, Martin Feldstein. His spending proposal encouraged increased military spending and he stated, "While good tax policy can contribute to ending the recession, the heavy lifting will have to be done by increased government spending."

Predictably, not all economists jumped onto the fiscal policy bandwagon. Concerns included whether so-called shovel-ready projects could really be implemented in time, whether government spending would crowd out private spending, whether monetary policy alone was providing enough stimulus, and whether the spending would flow efficiently to truly worthwhile projects. As discussed elsewhere in this text, the controversy persists. But the fact that a variety of expansionary policies were used to ease the recession and spur the recovery is not in doubt.

Sources: *Based on Ben S. Bernanke, "The Crisis and the Policy Response" (speech, London School of Economics, January 13, 2009); Louis Uchitelle, "Economists Warm to Government Spending but Debate Its Form," New York Times, January 7, 2009, p. B1.*

Answer to Try It! Problem

Panel (a) shows an expansionary monetary policy according to new Keynesian economics. Aggregate demand increases, with no immediate reduction in short-run aggregate supply. Real GDP rises to Y_2. In the long run, nominal wages rise, reducing short-run aggregate supply and returning real GDP to potential. Panel (b) shows what happens with rational expectations. When the Fed increases the money supply, people anticipate the rise in prices. Workers and firms agree to an increase in nominal wages, so that there is a reduction in short-run aggregate supply at the same time there is an increase in aggregate demand. The result is no change in real GDP; it remains at potential. There is, however, an increase in the price level.

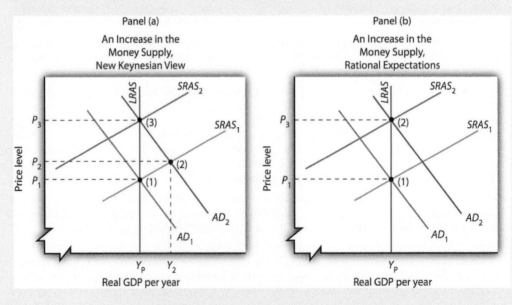

32.5 Review and Practice

Summary

We have surveyed the experience of the United States in light of the economic theories that prevailed or emerged during five decades. We have seen that events in the past century have had significant effects on the ways in which economists look at and interpret macroeconomic ideas.

Before the Great Depression, macroeconomic thought was dominated by the classical school. That body of theory stressed the economy's ability to reach full employment equilibrium on its own. The severity and duration of the Depression caused many economists to rethink their acceptance of natural equilibrating forces in the economy.

John Maynard Keynes issued the most telling challenge. He argued that wage rigidities and other factors could prevent the economy from closing a recessionary gap on its own. Further, he showed that expansionary fiscal and monetary policies could be used to increase aggregate demand and move the economy to its potential output. Although these ideas did not immediately affect U.S. policy, the increases in aggregate demand brought by the onset of World War II did bring the economy to full employment. Many economists became convinced of the validity of Keynes's analysis and his prescriptions for macroeconomic policy.

Keynesian economics dominated economic policy in the United States in the 1960s. Fiscal and monetary policies increased aggregate demand and produced what was then the longest expansion in U.S. history. But the economy pushed well beyond full employment in the latter part of the decade, and inflation increased. While Keynesians were dominant, monetarist economists argued that it was monetary policy that accounted for the expansion of the 1960s and that fiscal policy could not affect aggregate demand.

Efforts by the Nixon administration in 1969 and 1970 to cool the economy ran afoul of shifts in the short-run aggregate supply curve. The ensuing decade saw a series of shifts in aggregate supply that contributed to three more recessions by 1982. As economists studied these shifts, they developed further the basic notions we now express in the aggregate demand–aggregate supply model: that changes in aggregate demand and aggregate supply affect income and the price level; that changes in fiscal and monetary policy can affect aggregate demand; and that in the long run, the economy moves to its potential level of output.

The events of the 1980s and beyond raised serious challenges for the monetarist and new classical schools. New Keynesian economists formulated revisions in their theories, incorporating many of the ideas suggested by monetarist and new classical economists. The new, more powerful theory of macroeconomic events has won considerable support among economists today.

Concept Problems

1. Suppose you read the following: "For many years, the hands-off fiscal policies advocated by the classical economists held sway with American government. When times were hard, the prevailing response was to tough it out, awaiting the "inevitable" turnaround. The lessons of the Great Depression and a booming wartime economy have since taught us, however, that government intervention is sometimes necessary and desirable—and that to an extent, we can take charge of our own economic lives." Evaluate this statement based upon the discussion in this chapter. How would you classify the speaker in terms of a school of economic thought?

2. In his 1982 *Economic Report of the President*, Ronald Reagan said, "We simply cannot blame crop failures and oil price increases for our basic inflation problem. The continuous, underlying cause was poor government policy." What policies might he have been referring to?

3. Many journalists blamed economic policies of the Reagan administration for the extremely high levels of unemployment in 1982 and 1983. Given the record of the rest of the decade, do you agree that President Reagan's economic policies were a failure? Why or why not?

4. The day after the U.S. stock market crash of October 19, 1987, Federal Reserve Board Chairman Alan Greenspan issued the following statement: "The Federal Reserve, consistent with its responsibilities as the nation's central bank, affirmed today its readiness to serve as a source of liquidity to support the economic and financial system." Evaluate why the Fed chairman might have been prompted to make such a statement.

5. Compare the rationale of the Reagan administration for the 1981 tax reductions with the rationale behind the Kennedy–Johnson tax cut of 1964, the Bush tax cut of 2001, and the Bush tax cut of 2003.

6. If the economy is operating below its potential output, what kind of gap exists? What kinds of fiscal or monetary policies might you use to close this gap? Can you think of any objection to the use of such policies?

7. If the economy is operating above its potential output, what kind of gap exists? What kinds of fiscal or monetary policies might you use to close this gap? Can you think of any objection to the use of such policies?

8. In *General Theory*, Keynes wrote of the importance of ideas. The world, he said, is ruled by little else. How important do you think his ideas have been for economic policy today?

9. State whether each of the following events appears to be the result of a shift in short-run aggregate supply or aggregate demand, and state the direction of the shift involved.

   a. The price level rises sharply while real GDP falls.

   b. The price level and real GDP rise.

   c. The price level falls while real GDP rises.

   d. The price level and real GDP fall.

10. Explain whether each of the following events and policies will affect the aggregate demand curve or the short-run aggregate supply curve, and state what will happen to the price level and real GDP.

    a. Oil prices rise

    b. The Fed sells bonds

    c. Government purchases increase

    d. Federal taxes increase

    e. The government slashes transfer payment spending

    f. Oil prices fall

11. Using the model of aggregate demand and aggregate supply, illustrate an economy with a recessionary gap. Show how a policy of nonintervention would ultimately close the gap. Show the alternative of closing the gap through stabilization policy.

12. Using the model of aggregate demand and aggregate supply, illustrate an economy with an inflationary gap. Show how a policy of nonintervention would ultimately close the gap. Show the alternative of closing the gap through stabilization policy.

Endnotes

1. David C. Wheelock, "The Federal Response to Home Mortgage Distress: Lessons from the Great Depression," *Federal Reserve Bank of St. Louis Review* 90, no. 3 (Part 1) (May/June 2008): 133–48.
2. For a discussion of fiscal policy during the Great Depression, see E. Cary Brown, "Fiscal Policy in the 'Thirties: A Reappraisal," *American Economic Review* 46, no. 5 (December 1956): 857–79.
3. Dan Fuller and Doris Geide-Stevenson, "Consensus among Economists — An Update," *Journal of Economic Education* 45:2 (2014): 131–146.
4. National Association for Business Economics, Economic Policy Surveys, March 2009 and August 2010, available at http://www.nabe.com.
5. Todd E. Clark, "Is the Great Moderation Over? An Empirical Analysis," *Federal Reserve Bank of Kansas City Economic Review* 94, no. 4 (Fourth Quarter 2009): 5–42.
6. Ibid., 27.

CHAPTER 33

Appendix A: Graphs in Economics

A glance through the pages of this book should convince you that there are a lot of graphs in economics. The language of graphs is one means of presenting economic ideas. If you are already familiar with graphs, you will have no difficulty with this aspect of your study. If you have never used graphs or have not used them in some time, this appendix will help you feel comfortable with the graphs you will encounter in this text.

33.1 How to Construct and Interpret Graphs

Learning Objectives

1. Understand how graphs show the relationship between two or more variables and explain how a graph elucidates the nature of the relationship.
2. Define the slope of a curve.
3. Distinguish between a movement along a curve, a shift in a curve, and a rotation in a curve.

Much of the analysis in economics deals with relationships between variables. A variable is simply a quantity whose value can change. A **graph** is a pictorial representation of the relationship between two or more variables. The key to understanding graphs is knowing the rules that apply to their construction and interpretation. This section defines those rules and explains how to draw a graph.

graph

A pictorial representation of the relationship between two or more variables.

Drawing a Graph

To see how a graph is constructed from numerical data, we will consider a hypothetical example. Suppose a college campus has a ski club that organizes day-long bus trips to a ski area about 100 miles from the campus. The club leases the bus and charges $10 per passenger for a round trip to the ski area. In addition to the revenue the club collects from passengers, it also receives a grant of $200 from the school's student government for each day the bus trip is available. The club thus would receive $200 even if no passengers wanted to ride on a particular day.

The table in Figure 33.1 shows the relationship between two variables: the number of students who ride the bus on a particular day and the revenue the club receives from a trip. In the table, each combination is assigned a letter (A, B, etc.); we will use these letters when we transfer the information from the table to a graph.

FIGURE 33.1 Ski Club Revenues

The ski club receives $10 from each passenger riding its bus for a trip to and from the ski area plus a payment of $200 from the student government for each day the bus is available for these trips. The club's revenues from any single day thus equal $200 plus $10 times the number of passengers. The table relates various combinations of the number of passengers and club revenues.

Combination	Number of passengers	Club revenue
A	0	$200
B	10	300
C	20	400
D	30	500
E	40	600

We can illustrate the relationship shown in the table with a graph. The procedure for showing the relationship between two variables, like the ones in Figure 33.1, on a graph is illustrated in Figure 33.2. Let us look at the steps involved.

FIGURE 33.2 Plotting a Graph

Here we see how to show the information given in Figure 33.1 in a graph.

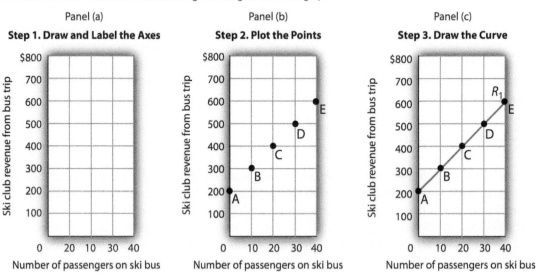

Step 1. Draw and Label the Axes

The two variables shown in the table are the number of passengers taking the bus on a particular day and the club's revenue from that trip. We begin our graph in Panel (a) of Figure 33.2 by drawing two axes to form a right angle. Each axis will represent a variable. The axes should be carefully labeled to reflect what is being measured on each axis.

It is customary to place the independent variable on the horizontal axis and the dependent variable on the vertical axis. Recall that, when two variables are related, the dependent variable is the one that changes in response to changes in the independent variable. Passengers generate revenue, so we can consider the number of passengers as the independent variable and the club's revenue as the dependent variable. The number of passengers thus goes on the horizontal axis; the club's revenue from a trip goes on the vertical axis. In some cases, the variables in a graph cannot be considered independent or dependent. In those cases, the variables may be placed on either axis; we will encounter such a case in the chapter that introduces the production possibilities model. In other cases, economists simply ignore the rule; we will encounter that case in the chapter that introduces the model of demand and supply. The rule that the independent variable goes on the horizontal axis and the dependent variable goes on the vertical usually holds, but not always.

The point at which the axes intersect is called the **origin** of the graph. Notice that in Figure 33.2 the origin has a value of zero for each variable.

In drawing a graph showing numeric values, we also need to put numbers on the axes. For the axes in Panel (a), we have chosen numbers that correspond to the values in the table. The number of passengers ranges up to 40 for a trip; club revenues from a trip range from $200 (the payment the club receives from student government) to $600. We have extended the vertical axis to $800 to allow some changes we will consider below. We have chosen intervals of 10 passengers on the horizontal axis and $100 on the vertical axis. The choice of particular intervals is mainly a matter of convenience in drawing and reading the graph; we have chosen the ones here because they correspond to the intervals given in the table.

We have drawn vertical lines from each of the values on the horizontal axis and horizontal lines from each of the values on the vertical axis. These lines, called gridlines, will help us in Step 2.

Step 2. Plot the Points

Each of the rows in the table in Figure 33.1 gives a combination of the number of passengers on the bus and club revenue from a particular trip. We can plot these values in our graph.

We begin with the first row, A, corresponding to zero passengers and club revenue of $200, the payment from student government. We read up from zero passengers on the horizontal axis to $200 on the vertical axis and mark point A. This point shows that zero passengers result in club revenues of $200.

The second combination, B, tells us that if 10 passengers ride the bus, the club receives $300 in revenue from the trip—$100 from the $10-per-passenger charge plus the $200 from student government. We start at 10 passengers on the horizontal axis and follow the gridline up. When we travel up in a graph, we are traveling with respect to values on the vertical axis. We travel up by $300 and mark point B.

Points in a graph have a special significance. They relate the values of the variables on the two axes to each other. Reading to the left from point B, we see that it shows $300 in club revenue. Reading down from point B, we see that it shows 10 passengers. Those values are, of course, the values given for combination B in the table.

We repeat this process to obtain points C, D, and E. Check to be sure that you see that each point corresponds to the values of the two variables given in the corresponding row of the table.

The graph in Panel (b) is called a scatter diagram. A **scatter diagram** shows individual points relating values of the variable on one axis to values of the variable on the other.

Step 3. Draw the Curve

The final step is to draw the curve that shows the relationship between the number of passengers who ride the bus and the club's revenues from the trip. The term "curve" is used for any line in a graph that shows a relationship between two variables.

origin

The point at which the axes of a graph intersect.

scatter diagram

A graph that shows individual points relating values of the variable on one axis to values of the variable on the other.

intercept

The point at which a curve intersects an axis.

We draw a line that passes through points A through E. Our curve shows club revenues; we shall call it R_1. Notice that R_1 is an upward-sloping straight line. Notice also that R_1 intersects the vertical axis at $200 (point A). The point at which a curve intersects an axis is called the **intercept** of the curve. We often refer to the vertical or horizontal intercept of a curve; such intercepts can play a special role in economic analysis. The vertical intercept in this case shows the revenue the club would receive on a day it offered the trip and no one rode the bus.

To check your understanding of these steps, we recommend that you try plotting the points and drawing R_1 for yourself in Panel (a). Better yet, draw the axes for yourself on a sheet of graph paper and plot the curve.

The Slope of a Curve

In this section, we will see how to compute the slope of a curve. The slopes of curves tell an important story: they show the rate at which one variable changes with respect to another.

slope

The ratio of the change in the value of the variable on the vertical axis to the change in the value of the variable on the horizontal axis measured between two points on the curve.

The **slope** of a curve equals the ratio of the change in the value of the variable on the vertical axis to the change in the value of the variable on the horizontal axis, measured between two points on the curve. You may have heard this called "the rise over the run." In equation form, we can write the definition of the slope as

EQUATION 33.1

$$\text{Slope} = \frac{\text{vertical change}}{\text{horizontal change}}$$

Equation 33.1 is the first equation in this text. Figure 33.3 provides a short review of working with equations. The material in this text relies much more heavily on graphs than on equations, but we will use equations from time to time. It is important that you understand how to use them.

FIGURE 33.3 Reading and Using Equations

Many equations in economics begin in the form of Equation 33.1, with the statement that one thing (in this case the slope) equals another (the vertical change divided by the horizontal change). In this example, the equation is written in words. Sometimes we use symbols in place of words. The basic idea though, is always the same: the term represented on the left side of the equals sign equals the term on the right side. In Equation 33.1 there are three variables: the slope, the vertical change, and the horizontal change. If we know the values of two of the three, we can compute the third. In the computation of slopes that follow, for example, we will use values for the two variables on the right side of the equation to compute the slope.

$$\text{Slope} = \frac{\text{vertical change}}{\text{horizontal change}}$$

Figure 33.4 shows R_1 and the computation of its slope between points B and D. Point B corresponds to 10 passengers on the bus; point D corresponds to 30. The change in the horizontal axis when we go from B to D thus equals 20 passengers. Point B corresponds to club revenues of $300; point D corresponds to club revenues of $500. The change in the vertical axis equals $200. The slope thus equals $200/20 passengers, or $10/passenger.

FIGURE 33.4 Computing the Slope of a Curve

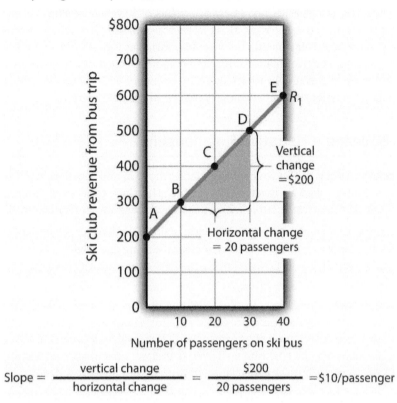

$$\text{Slope} = \frac{\text{vertical change}}{\text{horizontal change}} = \frac{\$200}{20 \text{ passengers}} = \$10/\text{passenger}$$

1. Select two points; we have selected points B and D.
2. The slope equals the vertical change divided by the horizontal change between the two points.
3. Between points B and D, the slope equals $200/20 passengers = $10/passenger.
4. The slope of this curve is the price per passenger. The fact that it is positive suggests a positive relationship between revenue per trip and the number of passengers riding the bus. Because the slope of this curve is $10/passenger between any two points on the curve, the relationship between club revenue per trip and the number of passengers is linear.

We have applied the definition of the slope of a curve to compute the slope of R_1 between points B and D. That same definition is given in Equation 33.1. Applying the equation, we have:

$$\text{Slope} = \frac{\text{vertical change}}{\text{horizontal change}} = \frac{\$200}{20 \text{ passengers}} = \$10 \big/ \text{passenger}$$

The slope of this curve tells us the amount by which revenues rise with an increase in the number of passengers. It should come as no surprise that this amount equals the price per passenger. Adding a passenger adds $10 to the club's revenues.

Notice that we can compute the slope of R_1 between any two points on the curve and get the same value; the slope is constant. Consider, for example, points A and E. The vertical change between these points is $400 (we go from revenues of $200 at A to revenues of $600 at E). The horizontal change is 40 passengers (from zero passengers at A to 40 at E). The slope between A and E thus equals $400/(40 passengers) = $10/passenger. We get the same slope regardless of which pair of points we pick on R_1 to compute the slope. The slope of R_1 can be considered a constant, which suggests that it is a straight line. When the curve showing the relationship between two variables has a constant slope, we say there is a **linear relationship** between the variable. A **linear curve** is a curve with constant slope.

linear relationship

Relationship that exists between two variables when the curve between them has a constant slope.

linear curve

A curve with constant slope.

positive relationship

Relationship that exists between two variables when both variables move in the same direction.

The fact that the slope of our curve equals $10/passenger tells us something else about the curve—$10/passenger is a positive, not a negative, value. A curve whose slope is positive is upward sloping. As we travel up and to the right along R_1, we travel in the direction of increasing values for both variables. A **positive relationship** between two variables is one in which both variables move in the same direction. Positive relationships are sometimes called direct relationships. There is a positive relationship between club revenues and passengers on the bus. We will look at a graph showing a negative relationship between two variables in the next section.

A Graph Showing a Negative Relationship

negative relationship

Relationship that exists between two variables when the variables move in opposite directions.

A **negative relationship** is one in which two variables move in opposite directions. A negative relationship is sometimes called an inverse relationship. The slope of a curve describing a negative relationship is always negative. A curve with a negative slope is always downward sloping.

As an example of a graph of a negative relationship, let us look at the impact of the cancellation of games by the National Basketball Association during the 1998–1999 labor dispute on the earnings of one player: Shaquille O'Neal. During the 1998–1999 season, O'Neal was the center for the Los Angeles Lakers.

O'Neal's salary with the Lakers in 1998–1999 would have been about $17,220,000 had the 82 scheduled games of the regular season been played. But a contract dispute between owners and players resulted in the cancellation of 32 games. Mr. O'Neal's salary worked out to roughly $210,000 per game, so the labor dispute cost him well over $6 million. Presumably, he was able to eke out a living on his lower income, but the cancellation of games cost him a great deal.

We show the relationship between the number of games canceled and O'Neal's 1998–1999 basketball earnings graphically in Figure 33.5. Canceling games reduced his earnings, so the number of games canceled is the independent variable and goes on the horizontal axis. O'Neal's earnings are the dependent variable and go on the vertical axis. The graph assumes that his earnings would have been $17,220,000 had no games been canceled (point A, the vertical intercept). Assuming that his earnings fell by $210,000 per game canceled, his earnings for the season were reduced to $10,500,000 by the cancellation of 32 games (point B). We can draw a line between these two points to show the relationship between games canceled and O'Neal's 1998–1999 earnings from basketball. In this graph, we have inserted a break in the vertical axis near the origin. This allows us to expand the scale of the axis over the range from $10,000,000 to $18,000,000. It also prevents a large blank space between the origin and an income of $10,500,000—there are no values below this amount.

FIGURE 33.5 Canceling Games and Reducing Shaquille O'Neal's Earnings
If no games had been canceled during the 1998–1999 basketball season, Shaquille O'Neal would have earned $17,220,000 (point A). Assuming that his salary for the season fell by $210,000 for each game canceled, the cancellation of 32 games during the dispute between NBA players and owners reduced O'Neal's earnings to $10,500,000 (point B).

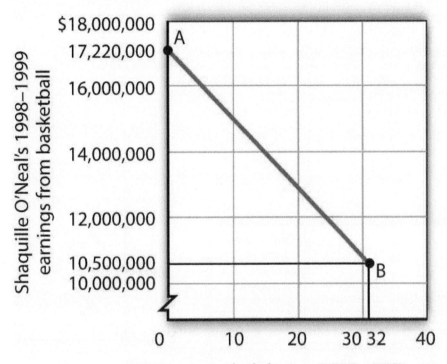

Games canceled during 1998–1999 season

What is the slope of the curve in Figure 33.5? We have data for two points, A and B. At A, O'Neal's basketball salary would have been $17,220,000. At B, it is $10,500,000. The vertical change between points A and B equals -$6,720,000. The change in the horizontal axis is from zero games canceled at A to 32 games canceled at B. The slope is thus

$$\text{Slope} = \frac{\text{vertical change}}{\text{horizontal change}} = \frac{-\$6,720,000}{32 \text{ games}} = -\$210,000 \Big/ \text{game}$$

Notice that this time the slope is negative, hence the downward-sloping curve. As we travel down and to the right along the curve, the number of games canceled rises and O'Neal's salary falls. In this case, the slope tells us the rate at which O'Neal lost income as games were canceled.

The slope of O'Neal's salary curve is also constant. That means there was a linear relationship between games canceled and his 1998–1999 basketball earnings.

Shifting a Curve

When we draw a graph showing the relationship between two variables, we make an important assumption. We assume that all other variables that might affect the relationship between the variables in our graph are unchanged. When one of those other variables changes, the relationship changes, and the curve showing that relationship shifts.

Consider, for example, the ski club that sponsors bus trips to the ski area. The graph we drew in Figure 33.2 shows the relationship between club revenues from a particular trip and the number of passengers on that trip, assuming that all other variables that might affect club revenues are unchanged. Let us change one. Suppose the school's student government increases the payment it makes to the club to $400 for each day the trip is available. The payment was $200 when we drew the original graph. Panel (a) of Figure 33.6 shows how the increase in the payment affects the table

shift in a curve

Change in the graph of a relationship between two variables that implies new values of one variable at each value of the other variable.

we had in Figure 33.1; Panel (b) shows how the curve shifts. Each of the new observations in the table has been labeled with a prime: A′, B′, etc. The curve R_1 shifts upward by $200 as a result of the increased payment. A **shift in a curve** implies new values of one variable at each value of the other variable. The new curve is labeled R_2. With 10 passengers, for example, the club's revenue was $300 at point B on R_1. With the increased payment from the student government, its revenue with 10 passengers rises to $500 at point B′ on R_2. We have a shift in the curve.

FIGURE 33.6 Shifting a Curve: An Increase in Revenues

The table in Panel (a) shows the new level of revenues the ski club receives with varying numbers of passengers as a result of the increased payment from student government. The new curve is shown in dark purple in Panel (b). The old curve is shown in light purple.

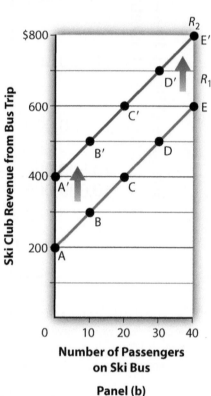

Combination	Number of passengers	Club revenue (with $400 payment from student government)
A′	0	$400
B′	10	500
C′	20	600
D′	30	700
E′	40	800

Panel (a)

Panel (b)

It is important to distinguish between shifts in curves and movements along curves. A **movement along a curve** is a change from one point on the curve to another that occurs when the dependent variable changes in response to a change in the independent variable. If, for example, the student government is paying the club $400 each day it makes the ski bus available and 20 passengers ride the bus, the club is operating at point C′ on R_2. If the number of passengers increases to 30, the club will be at point D′ on the curve. This is a movement along a curve; the curve itself does not shift.

Now suppose that, instead of increasing its payment, the student government eliminates its payments to the ski club for bus trips. The club's only revenue from a trip now comes from its $10/passenger charge. We have again changed one of the variables we were holding unchanged, so we get another shift in our revenue curve. The table in Panel (a) of Figure 33.7 shows how the reduction in the student government's payment affects club revenues. The new values are shown as combinations A″ through E″ on the new curve, R_3, in Panel (b). Once again we have a shift in a curve, this time from R_1 to R_3.

FIGURE 33.7 Shifting a Curve: A Reduction in Revenues
The table in Panel (a) shows the impact on ski club revenues of an elimination of support from the student government for ski bus trips. The club's only revenue now comes from the $10 it charges to each passenger. The new combinations are shown as A″ – E″. In Panel (b) we see that the original curve relating club revenue to the number of passengers has shifted down.

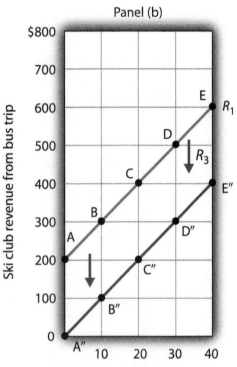

Panel (a)

Combination	Number of passengers	Club revenue (with no payment from student government)
A″	0	0
B″	10	100
C″	20	200
D″	30	300
E″	40	400

The shifts in Figure 33.6 and Figure 33.7 left the slopes of the revenue curves unchanged. That is because the slope in all these cases equals the price per ticket, and the ticket price remains unchanged. Next, we shall see how the slope of a curve changes when we rotate it about a single point.

Rotating a Curve

A **rotation of a curve** occurs when we change its slope, with one point on the curve fixed. Suppose, for example, the ski club changes the price of its bus rides to the ski area to $30 per trip, and the payment from the student government remains $200 for each day the trip is available. This means the club's revenues will remain $200 if it has no passengers on a particular trip. Revenue will, however, be different when the club has passengers. Because the slope of our revenue curve equals the price per ticket, the slope of the revenue curve changes.

Panel (a) of Figure 33.8 shows what happens to the original revenue curve, R_1, when the price per ticket is raised. Point A does not change; the club's revenue with zero passengers is unchanged. But with 10 passengers, the club's revenue would rise from $300 (point B on R_1) to $500 (point B′ on R_4). With 20 passengers, the club's revenue will now equal $800 (point C′ on R_4).

rotation of a curve

Change in a curve that occurs when its slope changes with one point on the curve fixed.

FIGURE 33.8 Rotating a Curve

A curve is said to rotate when a single point remains fixed while other points on the curve move; a rotation always changes the slope of a curve. Here an increase in the price per passenger to $30 would rotate the revenue curve from R_1 to R_4 in Panel (a). The slope of R_4 is $30 per passenger.

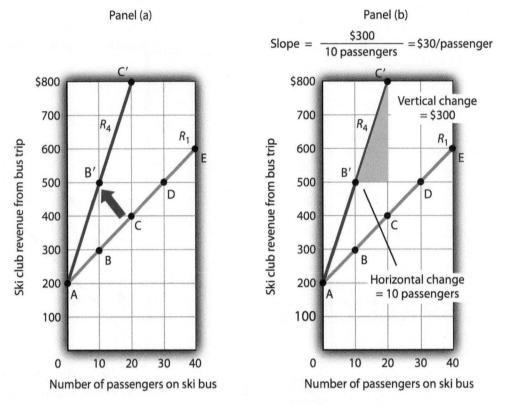

The new revenue curve R_4 is steeper than the original curve. Panel (b) shows the computation of the slope of the new curve between points B′ and C′. The slope increases to $30 per passenger—the new price of a ticket. The greater the slope of a positively sloped curve, the steeper it will be.

We have now seen how to draw a graph of a curve, how to compute its slope, and how to shift and rotate a curve. We have examined both positive and negative relationships. Our work so far has been with linear relationships. Next we will turn to nonlinear ones.

Key Takeaways

- A graph shows a relationship between two or more variables.
- An upward-sloping curve suggests a positive relationship between two variables. A downward-sloping curve suggests a negative relationship between two variables.
- The slope of a curve is the ratio of the vertical change to the horizontal change between two points on the curve. A curve whose slope is constant suggests a linear relationship between two variables.
- A change from one point on the curve to another produces a movement along the curve in the graph. A shift in the curve implies new values of one variable at each value of the other variable. A rotation in the curve implies that one point remains fixed while the slope of the curve changes.

Try It!

The following table shows the relationship between the number of gallons of gasoline people in a community are willing and able to buy per week and the price per gallon. Plot these points in the grid provided and label each point with the letter associated with the combination. Notice that there are breaks in both the vertical and horizontal axes of the grid. Draw a line through the points you have plotted. Does your graph suggest a positive or a negative relationship? What is the slope between A and B? Between B and C? Between A and C? Is the relationship linear?

Combination	Price per gallon	Number of gallons (per week)
A	$1.00	1,000
B	1.20	900
C	1.40	800

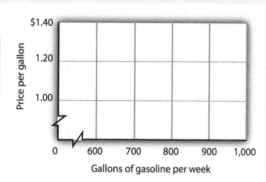

Now suppose you are given the following information about the relationship between price per gallon and the number of gallons per week gas stations in the community are willing to sell.

Combination	Price per gallon	Number of gallons (per week)
D	$1.00	800
E	1.20	900
F	1.40	1,000

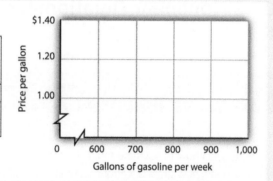

Plot these points in the grid provided and draw a curve through the points you have drawn. Does your graph suggest a positive or a negative relationship? What is the slope between D and E? Between E and F? Between D and F? Is this relationship linear?

Answer to Try It! Problem

Here is the first graph. The curve's downward slope tells us there is a negative relationship between price and the quantity of gasoline people are willing and able to buy. This curve, by the way, is a demand curve (the next one is a supply curve). We will study demand and supply soon; you will be using these curves a great deal. The slope between A and B is −0.002

(slope = vertical change/horizontal change = −0.20/100).

Here is the supply curve. Its upward slope tells us there is a positive relationship between price per gallon and the number of gallons per week gas stations are willing to sell. The slope between D and E is 0.002

(slope equals vertical change/horizontal change = 0.20/100).

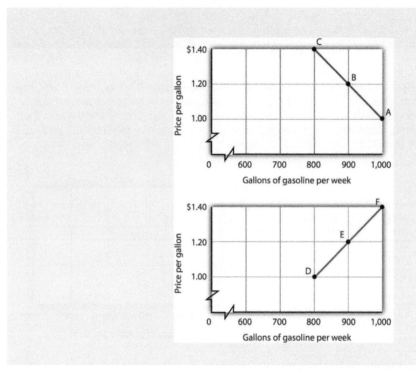

33.2 Nonlinear Relationships and Graphs without Numbers

1. Understand nonlinear relationships and how they are illustrated with nonlinear curves.
2. Explain how to estimate the slope at any point on a nonlinear curve.
3. Explain how graphs without numbers can be used to understand the nature of relationships between two variables.

In this section we will extend our analysis of graphs in two ways: first, we will explore the nature of nonlinear relationships; then we will have a look at graphs drawn without numbers.

Graphs of Nonlinear Relationships

In the graphs we have examined so far, adding a unit to the independent variable on the horizontal axis always has the same effect on the dependent variable on the vertical axis. When we add a passenger riding the ski bus, the ski club's revenues always rise by the price of a ticket. The cancellation of one more game in the 1998–1999 basketball season would always reduce Shaquille O'Neal's earnings by $210,000. The slopes of the curves describing the relationships we have been discussing were constant; the relationships were linear.

Many relationships in economics are nonlinear. A **nonlinear relationship** between two variables is one for which the slope of the curve showing the relationship changes as the value of one of the variables changes. A **nonlinear curve** is a curve whose slope changes as the value of one of the variables changes.

Consider an example. Suppose Felicia Alvarez, the owner of a bakery, has recorded the relationship between her firm's daily output of bread and the number of bakers she employs. The relationship she has recorded is given in the table in Panel (a) of Figure 33.9. The corresponding points are plotted in Panel (b). Clearly, we cannot draw a straight line through these points. Instead, we shall have to draw a nonlinear curve like the one shown in Panel (c).

nonlinear relationship

Relationship between two variables in which the slope of the curve showing the relationship changes as the value of one of the variables changes.

nonlinear curve

A curve whose slope changes as the value of one of the variables changes.

FIGURE 33.9 A Nonlinear Curve
The table in Panel (a) shows the relationship between the number of bakers Felicia Alvarez employs per day and the number of loaves of bread produced per day. This information is plotted in Panel (b). This is a nonlinear relationship; the curve connecting these points in Panel (c) (Loaves of bread produced) has a changing slope.

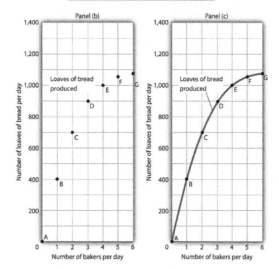

Inspecting the curve for loaves of bread produced, we see that it is upward sloping, suggesting a positive relationship between the number of bakers and the output of bread. But we also see that the curve becomes flatter as we travel up and to the right along it; it is nonlinear and describes a nonlinear relationship.

How can we estimate the slope of a nonlinear curve? After all, the slope of such a curve changes as we travel along it. We can deal with this problem in two ways. One is to consider two points on the curve and to compute the slope between those two points. Another is to compute the slope of the curve at a single point.

When we compute the slope of a curve between two points, we are really computing the slope of a straight line drawn between those two points. In Figure 33.10, we have computed slopes between pairs of points A and B, C and D, and E and F on our curve for loaves of bread produced. These slopes equal 400 loaves/baker, 200 loaves/baker, and 50 loaves/baker, respectively. They are the slopes of the dashed-line segments shown. These dashed segments lie close to the curve, but they clearly are not on the curve. After all, the dashed segments are straight lines. Our curve relating the number of bakers to daily bread production is not a straight line; the relationship between the bakery's daily output of bread and the number of bakers is nonlinear.

FIGURE 33.10 Estimating Slopes for a Nonlinear Curve

We can estimate the slope of a nonlinear curve between two points. Here, slopes are computed between points A and B, C and D, and E and F. When we compute the slope of a nonlinear curve between two points, we are computing the slope of a straight line between those two points. Here the lines whose slopes are computed are the dashed lines between the pairs of points.

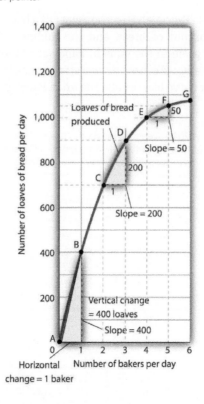

tangent line

A straight line that touches, but does not intersect, a nonlinear curve at only one point.

Every point on a nonlinear curve has a different slope. To get a precise measure of the slope of such a curve, we need to consider its slope at a single point. To do that, we draw a line tangent to the curve at that point. A **tangent line** is a straight line that touches, but does not intersect, a nonlinear curve at only one point. The slope of a tangent line equals the slope of the curve at the point at which the tangent line touches the curve.

Consider point D in Panel (a) of Figure 33.11. We have drawn a tangent line that just touches the curve showing bread production at this point. It passes through points labeled M and N. The vertical change between these points equals 300 loaves of bread; the horizontal change equals two bakers. The slope of the tangent line equals 150 loaves of bread/baker (300 loaves/2 bakers). The slope of our bread production curve at point D equals the slope of the line tangent to the curve at this point. In Panel (b), we have sketched lines tangent to the curve for loaves of bread produced at points B, D, and F. Notice that these tangent lines get successively flatter, suggesting again that the slope of the curve is falling as we travel up and to the right along it.

FIGURE 33.11 Tangent Lines and the Slopes of Nonlinear Curves

Because the slope of a nonlinear curve is different at every point on the curve, the precise way to compute slope is to draw a tangent line; the slope of the tangent line equals the slope of the curve at the point the tangent line touches the curve. In Panel (a), the slope of the tangent line is computed for us: it equals 150 loaves/baker. Generally, we will not have the information to compute slopes of tangent lines. We will use them as in Panel (b), to observe what happens to the slope of a nonlinear curve as we travel along it. We see here that the slope falls (the tangent lines become flatter) as the number of bakers rises.

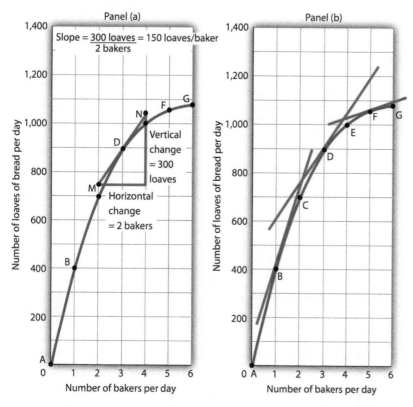

Notice that we have not been given the information we need to compute the slopes of the tangent lines that touch the curve for loaves of bread produced at points B and F. In this text, we will not have occasion to compute the slopes of tangent lines. Either they will be given or we will use them as we did here—to see what is happening to the slopes of nonlinear curves.

In the case of our curve for loaves of bread produced, the fact that the slope of the curve falls as we increase the number of bakers suggests a phenomenon that plays a central role in both microeconomic and macroeconomic analysis. As we add workers (in this case bakers), output (in this case loaves of bread) rises, but by smaller and smaller amounts. Another way to describe the relationship between the number of workers and the quantity of bread produced is to say that as the number of workers increases, the output increases at a decreasing rate. In Panel (b) of Figure 33.11 we express this idea with a graph, and we can gain this understanding by looking at the tangent lines, even though we do not have specific numbers. Indeed, much of our work with graphs will not require numbers at all.

We turn next to look at how we can use graphs to express ideas even when we do not have specific numbers.

Graphs Without Numbers

We know that a positive relationship between two variables can be shown with an upward-sloping curve in a graph. A negative or inverse relationship can be shown with a downward-sloping curve. Some relationships are linear and some are nonlinear. We illustrate a linear relationship with a curve whose slope is constant; a nonlinear relationship is illustrated with a curve whose slope changes. Using these basic ideas, we can illustrate hypotheses graphically even in cases in which we do not have numbers with which to locate specific points.

Consider first a hypothesis suggested by recent medical research: eating more fruits and vegetables each day increases life expectancy. We can show this idea graphically. Daily fruit and vegetable consumption (measured, say, in grams per day) is the independent variable; life expectancy (measured in years) is the dependent variable. Panel (a) of Figure 33.12 shows the hypothesis, which suggests a positive relationship between the two variables. Notice the vertical intercept on the curve we have drawn; it implies that even people who eat no fruit or vegetables can expect to live at least a while!

FIGURE 33.12 Graphs Without Numbers

We often use graphs without numbers to suggest the nature of relationships between variables. The graphs in the four panels correspond to the relationships described in the text.

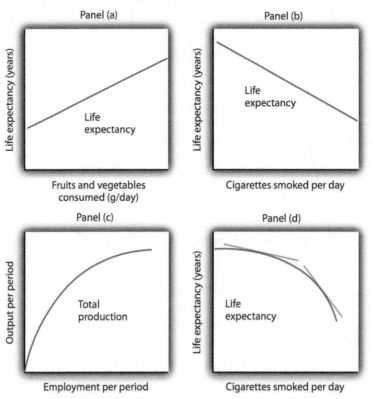

Panel (b) illustrates another hypothesis we hear often: smoking cigarettes reduces life expectancy. Here the number of cigarettes smoked per day is the independent variable; life expectancy is the dependent variable. The hypothesis suggests a negative relationship. Hence, we have a downward-sloping curve.

Now consider a general form of the hypothesis suggested by the example of Felicia Alvarez's bakery: increasing employment each period increases output each period, but by smaller and smaller amounts. As we saw in Figure 33.9, this hypothesis suggests a positive, nonlinear relationship. We have drawn a curve in Panel (c) of Figure 33.12 that looks very much like the curve for bread production in Figure 33.11. It is upward sloping, and its slope diminishes as employment rises.

Finally, consider a refined version of our smoking hypothesis. Suppose we assert that smoking cigarettes does reduce life expectancy and that increasing the number of cigarettes smoked per day reduces life expectancy by a larger and larger amount. Panel (d) shows this case. Again, our life expectancy curve slopes downward. But now it suggests that smoking only a few cigarettes per day reduces life expectancy only a little but that life expectancy falls by more and more as the number of cigarettes smoked per day increases.

We have sketched lines tangent to the curve in Panel (d). The slopes of these tangent lines are negative, suggesting the negative relationship between smoking and life expectancy. They also get steeper as the number of cigarettes smoked per day rises. Whether a curve is linear or nonlinear, a steeper curve is one for which the absolute value of the slope rises as the value of the variable on the horizontal axis rises. When we speak of the absolute value of a negative number such as -4, we ignore the minus sign and simply say that the absolute value is 4. The absolute value of -8, for example, is greater than the absolute value of -4, and a curve with a slope of -8 is steeper than a curve whose slope is -4.

Thus far our work has focused on graphs that show a relationship between variables. We turn finally to an examination of graphs and charts that show values of one or more variables, either over a period of time or at a single point in time.

Key Takeaways

- The slope of a nonlinear curve changes as the value of one of the variables in the relationship shown by the curve changes.
- A nonlinear curve may show a positive or a negative relationship.
- The slope of a curve showing a nonlinear relationship may be estimated by computing the slope between two points on the curve. The slope at any point on such a curve equals the slope of a line drawn tangent to the curve at that point.
- We can illustrate hypotheses about the relationship between two variables graphically, even if we are not given numbers for the relationships. We need only draw and label the axes and then draw a curve consistent with the hypothesis.

Try It!

Consider the following curve drawn to show the relationship between two variables, A and B (we will be using a curve like this one in the next chapter). Explain whether the relationship between the two variables is positive or negative, linear or nonlinear. Sketch two lines tangent to the curve at different points on the curve, and explain what is happening to the slope of the curve.

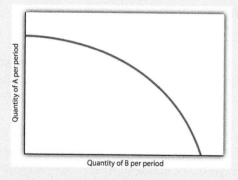

Answer to Try It! Problem

The relationship between variable A shown on the vertical axis and variable B shown on the horizontal axis is negative. This is sometimes referred to as an inverse relationship. Variables that give a straight line with a constant slope are said to have a linear relationship. In this case, however, the relationship is nonlinear. The slope changes all along the curve. In this case the slope becomes steeper as we move downward to the right along the curve, as shown by the two tangent lines that have been drawn. As the quantity of B increases, the quantity of A decreases at an increasing rate.

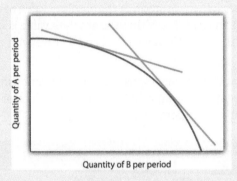

33.3 Using Graphs and Charts to Show Values of Variables

Learning Objective

1. Understand and use time-series graphs, tables, pie charts, and bar charts to illustrate data and relationships among variables.

You often see pictures representing numerical information. These pictures may take the form of graphs that show how a particular variable has changed over time, or charts that show values of a particular variable at a single point in time. We will close our introduction to graphs by looking at both ways of conveying information.

Time-Series Graphs

time-series graph

A graph that shows how the value of a particular variable or variables has changed over some period of time.

One of the most common types of graphs used in economics is called a time-series graph. A **time-series graph** shows how the value of a particular variable or variables has changed over some period of time. One of the variables in a time-series graph is time itself. Time is typically placed on the horizontal axis in time-series graphs. The other axis can represent any variable whose value changes over time.

The table in Panel (a) of Figure 33.13 shows annual values of the unemployment rate, a measure of the percentage of workers who are looking for and available for work but are not working, in the United States from 1998 to 2007. The grid with which these values are plotted is given in Panel (b). Notice that the vertical axis is scaled from 3 to 8%, instead of beginning with zero. Time-series graphs are often presented with the vertical axis scaled over a certain range. The result is the same as introducing a break in the vertical axis, as we did in Figure 33.5

FIGURE 33.13 A Time-Series Graph

Panel (a)

Year	Unemployment rate (percent)
1998	4.5
1999	4.2
2000	4.0
2001	4.7
2002	5.8
2003	6.0
2004	5.5
2005	5.1
2006	4.6
2007	4.6
2008	5.8
2009	9.3
2010	9.6

Panel (b)

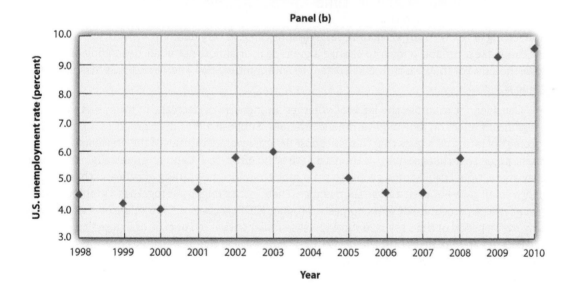

Panel (a) gives values of the U.S. unemployment rate from 1998 to 2010. These points are then plotted in Panel (b). To draw a time-series graph, we connect these points, as in Panel (c).

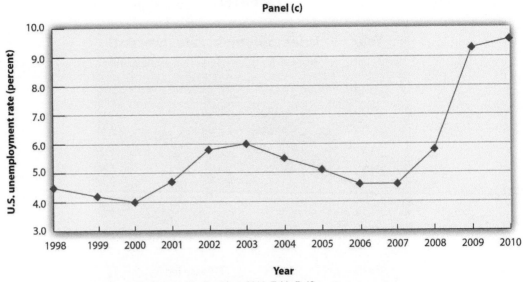

Panel (c)

Source: Based on data from Economic Report of the President, 2012, Table B-42.

The values for the U.S. unemployment rate are plotted in Panel (b) of Figure 33.13. The points plotted are then connected with a line in Panel (c).

Scaling the Vertical Axis in Time-Series Graphs

The scaling of the vertical axis in time-series graphs can give very different views of economic data. We can make a variable appear to change a great deal, or almost not at all, depending on how we scale the axis. For that reason, it is important to note carefully how the vertical axis in a time-series graph is scaled.

Consider, for example, the issue of whether an increase or decrease in income tax rates has a significant effect on federal government revenues. Suppose a president proposes an increase in income tax rates and argues that this will boost federal revenues. Critics of the president's proposal might argue that changes in tax rates have little or no effect on federal revenues. Higher tax rates, they argue, would cause some people to scale back their income-earning efforts and thus produce only a small gain—or even a loss—in revenues. These critics might put together a graph of federal revenues as a percentage of gross domestic product (GDP), a measure of total income in the economy, over a period of time, say 1960 through 1995, similar to that in Panel (a) of Figure 33.14. Labeling the tax cuts and tax hikes over the period, they would argue that tax changes have little effect on federal revenues relative to total income.

FIGURE 33.14 Two Tales of Taxes and Income
A graph of federal revenues as a percentage of GDP emphasizes the stability of the relationship when plotted with the vertical axis scaled from 0 to 100, as in Panel (a). Scaling the vertical axis from 16 to 21%, as in Panel (b), stresses the short-term variability of the percentage and suggests that major tax rate changes have affected federal revenues.

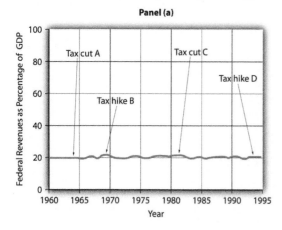
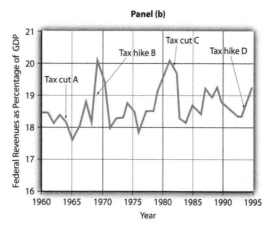

Supporters of the tax hike might argue that Panel (a) is misleading. By using a different scale, as shown in Panel (b), it appears that tax increases tend to increase federal revenues relative to income in the economy and that cuts in taxes reduce the federal government's share.

Which version is correct? Both are. Both graphs show the same data. In this example, it is certainly true that federal revenues, relative to economic activity, were remarkably stable over these years, as emphasized by the scaling in Panel (a). But it is also true that the federal share has varied between about 17 and 20%. And a small change in the federal share translated into a large amount of tax revenue.

It is easy to be misled by time-series graphs. Large changes can be made to appear trivial and trivial changes to appear large through an artful scaling of the axes. The best advice for a careful consumer of graphical information is to note carefully the range of values shown and then to decide whether the changes are really significant.

Testing Hypotheses with Time-Series Graphs

John Maynard Keynes, one of the most famous economists ever, proposed in 1936 a hypothesis about total spending for consumer goods in the economy. He suggested that this spending was positively related to the income households receive. One way to test such a hypothesis is to draw a time-series graph of both variables to see whether they do, in fact, tend to move together. Figure 33.15 shows the values of consumption spending and disposable income, which is after-tax income received by households. Annual values of consumption and disposable income are plotted for the period 1960–2007. Notice that both variables have tended to move quite closely together. The close relationship between consumption and disposable income is consistent with Keynes's hypothesis that there is a positive relationship between the two variables.

FIGURE 33.15 A Time-Series Graph of Disposable Income and Consumption
Plotted in a time-series graph, disposable income and consumption appear to move together. This is consistent with the hypothesis that the two are directly related.

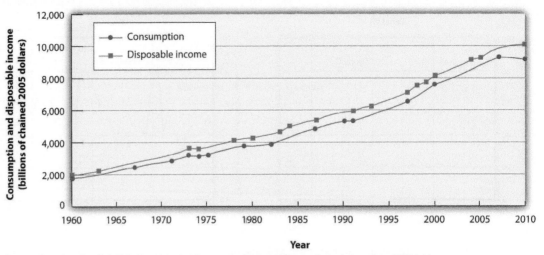

Source: Based on data from U.S. Department of Commerce, Bureau of Economic Analysis, various NIPA tables.

The fact that two variables tend to move together in a time series does not by itself prove that there is a systematic relationship between the two. Figure 33.16 shows a time-series graph of monthly values in 1987 of the Dow Jones Industrial Average, an index that reflects the movement of the prices of common stock. Notice the steep decline in the index beginning in October, not unlike the steep decline in October 2008.

FIGURE 33.16 Stock Prices and a Mystery Variable
The movement of the monthly average of the Dow Jones Industrial Average, a widely reported index of stock values, corresponded closely to changes in a mystery variable, X. Did the mystery variable contribute to the crash?

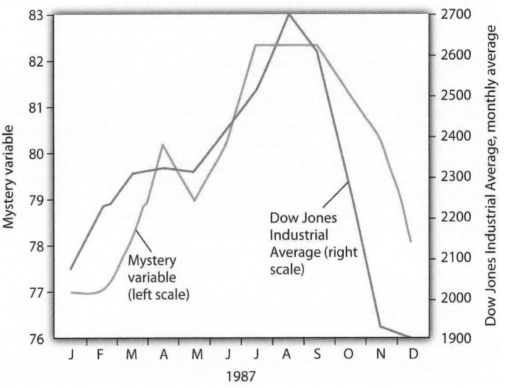

Source: Based on data from Dow Jones Industrial Averages historical data available at http://finance.yahoo.com/quote/^DJI/history?p=^DJI.

It would be useful, and certainly profitable, to be able to predict such declines. Figure 33.16 also shows the movement of monthly values of a "mystery variable," *X*, for the same period. The mystery variable and stock prices appear to move closely together. Was the plunge in the mystery variable in October responsible for the stock crash? The answer is: Not likely. The mystery value is monthly average temperatures in San Juan, Puerto Rico. Attributing the stock crash in 1987 to the weather in San Juan would be an example of the fallacy of false cause.

Notice that Figure 33.16 has two vertical axes. The left-hand axis shows values of temperature; the right-hand axis shows values for the Dow Jones Industrial Average. Two axes are used here because the two variables, San Juan temperature and the Dow Jones Industrial Average, are scaled in different units.

Descriptive Charts

We can use a table to show data. Consider, for example, the information compiled each year by the U.S. National Center for Education Statistics. The table in Panel (a) of Figure 33.17 shows the results of the 2009 survey. In the groupings given, economics is included among the social sciences.

FIGURE 33.17 Bachelor's Degrees Earned by Field, 2009

Panel (a)

Field of Study	Percentage of Bachelor's Degrees
Biological and biomedical sciences	5.0%
Business	21.7%
Communication, journalism, and related	5.2%
Engineering and engineering technologies	5.3%
Health professions and related clinical sciences	7.5%
Liberal arts and sciences, general studies, and humanities	2.9%
Psychology	5.9%
Social sciences and history	10.5%
Visual and performing arts	5.6%
Security and protective services	2.6%
Computer and information sciences	2.4%
Multi/interdisciplinary studies	2.3%
Parks, recreation, leisure, and fitness studies	2.0%
Other	21.0%

Panel (b)

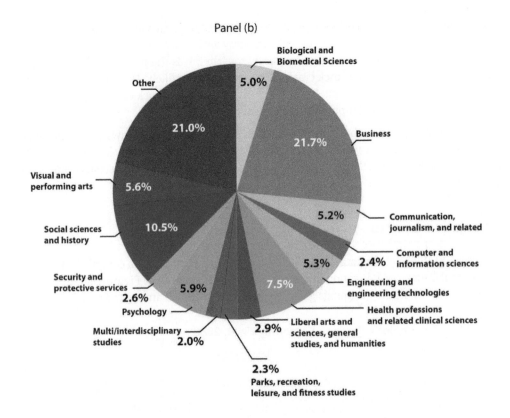

Panels (a), (b), and (c) show bachelor's degrees earned by field in 2009 in United States. All three panels present the same information. Panel (a) is an example of a table, Panel (b) is an example of a pie chart, and Panel (c) is an example of a vertical bar chart.

Panel (c)

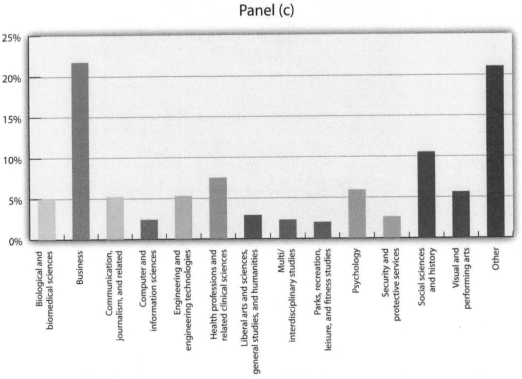

Source: Based on data from Statistical Abstracts of the United States, 2012, Table 302. Bachelor's Degrees Earned by Field, 1980 to 2009, based on data from U.S. National Center for Education Statistics, Digest of Educational Statistics. Percentages shown are for broad academic areas, each of which includes several majors.

Panels (b) and (c) of Figure 33.17 present the same information in two types of charts. Panel (b) is an example of a pie chart; Panel (c) gives the data in a bar chart. The bars in this chart are horizontal; they may also be drawn as vertical. Either type of graph may be used to provide a picture of numeric information.

Key Takeaways

- A time-series graph shows changes in a variable over time; one axis is always measured in units of time.
- One use of time-series graphs is to plot the movement of two or more variables together to see if they tend to move together or not. The fact that two variables move together does not prove that changes in one of the variables cause changes in the other.
- Values of a variable may be illustrated using a table, a pie chart, or a bar chart.

Try It!

The table in Panel (a) shows a measure of the inflation rate, the percentage change in the average level of prices below.[1] Panels (b) and (c) provide blank grids. We have already labeled the axes on the grids in Panels (b) and (c). It is up to you to plot the data in Panel (a) on the grids in Panels (b) and (c). Connect the points you have marked in the grid using straight lines between the points. What relationship do you observe? Has the inflation rate generally increased or decreased? What can you say about the trend of inflation over the course of the 1990s? Do you tend to get a different "interpretation" depending on whether you use Panel (b) or Panel (c) to guide you?

Panel (a)

Year	Inflation rate (percent)
1990	6.1
1991	3.1
1992	2.9
1993	2.7
1994	2.7
1995	2.5
1996	3.3
1997	1.7
1998	1.6

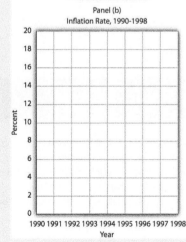

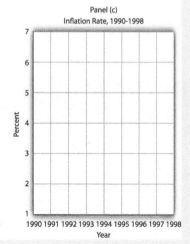

Answer to Try It! Problem

Here are the time-series graphs, Panels (b) and (c), for the information in Panel (a). The first thing you should notice is that both graphs show that the inflation rate generally declined throughout the 1990s (with the exception of 1996, when it increased). The generally downward direction of the curve suggests that the trend of inflation was downward. Notice that in this case we do not say negative, since in this instance it is not the slope of the line that matters. Rather, inflation itself is still positive (as indicated by the fact that all the points are above the origin) but is declining. Finally, comparing Panels (b) and (c) suggests that the general downward trend in the inflation rate is emphasized less in Panel (b) than in Panel (c). This impression would be emphasized even more if the numbers on the vertical axis were increased in Panel (b) from 20 to 100. Just as in Figure 33.14, it is possible to make large changes appear trivial by simply changing the scaling of the axes.

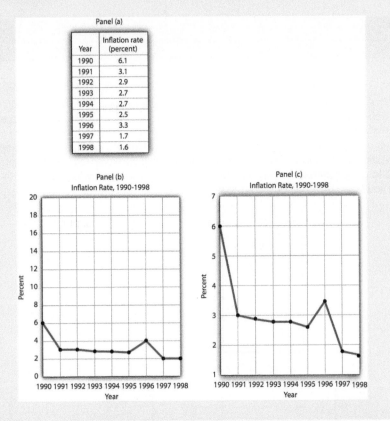

Numerical Problems

1. Panel (a) shows a graph of a positive relationship; Panel (b) shows a graph of a negative relationship. Decide whether each proposition below demonstrates a positive or negative relationship, and decide which graph you would expect to illustrate each proposition. In each statement, identify which variable is the independent variable and thus goes on the horizontal axis, and which variable is the dependent variable and goes on the vertical axis.

Panel (a)   Panel (b)

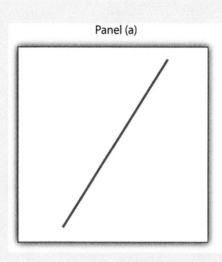

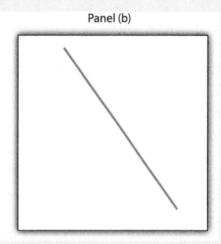

a. An increase in national income in any one year increases the number of people killed in highway accidents.

b. An increase in the poverty rate causes an increase in the crime rate.

c. As the income received by households rises, they purchase fewer beans.

d. As the income received by households rises, they spend more on home entertainment equipment.

e. The warmer the day, the less soup people consume.

2. Suppose you have a graph showing the results of a survey asking people how many left and right shoes they owned. The results suggest that people with one left shoe had, on average, one right shoe. People with seven left shoes had, on average, seven right shoes. Put left shoes on the vertical axis and right shoes on the horizontal axis; plot the following observations:

Left shoes	1	2	3	4	5	6	7
Right shoes	1	2	3	4	5	6	7

Is this relationship positive or negative? What is the slope of the curve?

3. Suppose your assistant inadvertently reversed the order of numbers for right shoe ownership in the survey above. You thus have the following table of observations:

Left shoes	1	2	3	4	5	6	7
Right shoes	7	6	5	4	3	2	1

Is the relationship between these numbers positive or negative? What's implausible about that?

4. Suppose some of Ms. Alvarez's kitchen equipment breaks down. The following table gives the values of bread output that were shown in Figure 33.9 It also gives the new levels of bread output that Ms. Alvarez's bakers produce following the breakdown. Plot the two curves. What has happened?

	A	B	C	D	E	F	G
Bakers/day	0	1	2	3	4	5	6
Loaves/day	0	400	700	900	1,000	1,050	1,075
Loaves/day after breakdown	0	380	670	860	950	990	1,005

5. Steven Magee has suggested that there is a relationship between the number of lawyers per capita in a country and the country's rate of economic growth. The relationship is described with the following Magee curve.

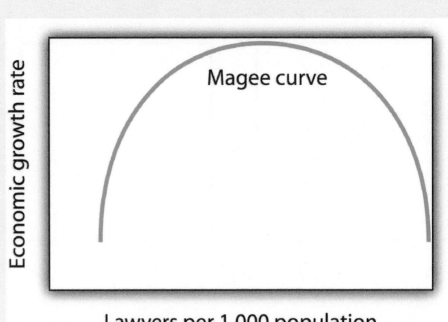

What do you think is the argument made by the curve? What kinds of countries do you think are on the upward- sloping region of the curve? Where would you guess the United States is? Japan? Does the Magee curve seem plausible to you?

6. Draw graphs showing the likely relationship between each of the following pairs of variables. In each case, put the first variable mentioned on the horizontal axis and the second on the vertical axis.

   a. The amount of time a student spends studying economics and the grade he or she receives in the course

   b. Per capita income and total expenditures on health care

   c. Alcohol consumption by teenagers and academic performance

   d. Household income and the likelihood of being the victim of a violent crime

Endnotes

1. Bureau of Labor Statistics, All Urban Consumers CPI-U, 1982-84 = 100, Dec.-Dec. inflation rate.

income ($1 in income minus $0.375 in taxes). Given a marginal propensity to consume of 0.8, this $1 increase in real GDP increases consumption by only $0.50 (= [$1 × (0.8 × 0.625)]). The new aggregate expenditures curve, AE_2 in Figure 34.3, shows the end result of the tax rate change in the aggregate expenditures model. Its slope is 0.5. The equilibrium of the level of real GDP in the aggregate expenditures model falls to $5,600 billion from its original level of $7,000. The $1,400-billion reduction in equilibrium real GDP in the aggregate expenditures model is equal to the $700-billion initial reduction in consumption (at the original equilibrium level of real GDP) times the new multiplier of 2. The tax rate increase has reduced aggregate expenditures and reduced the multiplier impact of this change (from 2.5 to 2). The aggregate demand curve will shift to the left by $1,400 billion, the new multiplier times the initial change in aggregate expenditures.

In the model of aggregate demand and aggregate supply, a tax rate increase will shift the aggregate demand curve to the left by an amount equal to the initial change in aggregate expenditures induced by the tax rate boost times the *new* value of the multiplier. Similarly, a reduction in the income tax rate rotates the aggregate expenditures curve upward by an amount equal to the initial increase in consumption (at the original equilibrium level of real GDP found in the aggregate expenditures model) created by the lower tax rate. It also increases the value of the multiplier. Aggregate demand shifts to the right by an amount equal to the initial change in aggregate expenditures times the new multiplier.

34.3 Review and Practice

Numerical Problems

1. Suppose an economy is characterized by the following equations. All figures are in billions of dollars.

$C = 400 + \frac{2}{3}(Y_d)$

$T = 300 + \frac{1}{4}(Y)$

$G = 400$

$= 200$

$= 100$

  a. Solve for the equilibrium level of income.
  b. Now let G rise to 500. What happens to the solution?
  c. What is the multiplier?

Consider the following economy. All figures are in billions of dollars.

$= 180 + 0.8(Y_d)$

$= 100 + 0.25Y$

300

$= 400$

$X_n = 200$

  a. Solve for the equilibrium level of real GDP.
  b. Now suppose investment falls to $200 billion. What happens to the equilibrium real GDP?
  c. What is the multiplier?

3. Suppose an economy has a consumption function $C = \$100 + \frac{2}{3} Y_d$. Autonomous taxes, T_a, equal 0, the income tax rate is 10%, and $Y_d = 0.9Y$. Government purchases, investment, and net exports each equal $100. Solve the following problems.

    a. Draw the aggregate expenditures curve, and find the equilibrium income for this economy in the aggregate expenditures model.

    b. Now suppose the tax rate rises to 25%, so $Y_d = 0.75Y$. Assume that government purchases, investments, and net exports are not affected by the change. Show the new aggregate expenditures curve and the new level of income in the aggregate expenditures model. Relate your answer to the multiplier effect of the tax change.

    c. Compare your result in the aggregate expenditures model to what the aggregate demand–aggregate supply model would show.

4. Suppose a program of federally funded public-works spending was introduced that was tied to the unemployment rate. Suppose the program was structured so that public-works spending would be $200 billion per year if the economy had an unemployment rate of 5% at the beginning of the fiscal year. Public-works spending would be increased by $20 billion for each percentage point by which the unemployment rate exceeded 5%. It would be reduced by $20 billion for every percentage point by which unemployment fell below 5%. If the unemployment rate were 8%, for example, public-works spending would be $260 billion. How would this program affect the slope of the aggregate expenditures curve?

Index

aggregate expenditures function for this representation of the economy. The aggregate expenditures function for the simplified economy that we presented in the chapter has a slope that was simply the marginal propensity to consume; there were no taxes in that model, and disposable personal income and real GDP were assumed to be the same. Notice that in using this more realistic aggregate expenditures function, the slope is less by a factor of $(1 - t)$.

We solve Equation 34.14 for Y:

$$Y - b(1 - t)(Y) = \bar{A}$$

$$Y[1 - b(1 - t)] = \bar{A}$$

EQUATION 34.15

$$Y = \frac{1}{1 - b(1 - t)}(\bar{A})$$

In Equation 34.15, $1/[1 - b(1 - t)]$ is the multiplier. Equilibrium real GDP is achieved at a level of income equal to the multiplier times the amount of autonomous spending. Notice that because the slope of the aggregate expenditures function is less than it would be in an economy without induced taxes, the value of the multiplier is also less, all other things the same. In this representation of the economy, the value of the multiplier depends on the marginal propensity to consume and on the tax rate. The higher the tax rate, the lower the multiplier; the lower the tax rate, the greater the multiplier.

For example, suppose the marginal propensity to consume is 0.8. If the tax rate were 0, then the multiplier would be 5. If the tax rate were 0.25, then the multiplier would be 2.5.

34.2 The Aggregate Expenditures Model and Fiscal Policy

In this appendix, we use the aggregate expenditures model to explain the impact of fiscal policy on aggregate demand in more detail than was given in the chapter on government and fiscal policy. As we did in the chapter, we will look at the impact of various types of fiscal policy changes. The possibility of crowding out was discussed in the fiscal policy chapter and will not be repeated here.

Changes in Government Purchases

All other things unchanged, a change in government purchases shifts the aggregate expenditures curve by an amount equal to the change in government purchases. A $200-billion increase in government purchases, for example, shifts the aggregate expenditures curve upward by $200 billion. A $75-billion reduction in government purchases shifts the aggregate expenditures curve downward by that amount.

Panel (a) of Figure 34.1 shows an economy that is initially in equilibrium at an income of $7,000 billion. Suppose that the slope of the aggregate expenditures function (that is, $b[1 - t]$) is 0.6, so that the multiplier is 2.5. An increase of $200 billion in government purchases shifts the aggregate expenditures curve upward by that amount to AE_2. In the aggregate expenditures model, real GDP increases by an amount equal to the multiplier times the change in autonomous aggregate expenditures. Real GDP in that model thus rises by $500 billion to a level of $7,500 billion.

FIGURE 34.1 An Increase in Government Purchases

The economy shown here is initially in equilibrium at a real GDP of $7,000 billion and a price level of P_1. In Panel (a), an increase of $200 billion in the level of government purchases shifts the aggregate expenditures curve upward by that amount to AE_2, increasing the equilibrium level of income in the aggregate expenditures model by $500 billion. In Panel (b), the aggregate demand curve thus shifts to the right by $500 billion to AD_2. The equilibrium level of real GDP rises to $7,300 billion, while the price level rises to P_2.

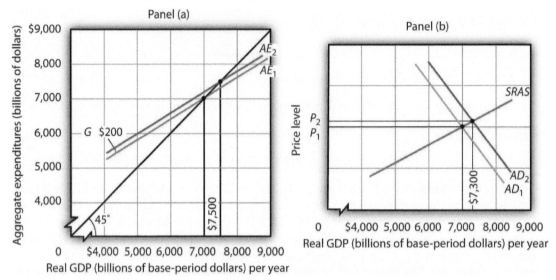

The aggregate expenditures model, of course, assumes a constant price level. To get a more complete picture of what happens, we use the model of aggregate demand and aggregate supply. In that model shown in Panel (b), the initial price level is P_1, and the initial equilibrium real GDP is $7,000 billion. That is the price level assumed to hold the aggregate expenditures model. The $200-billion increase in government purchases increases the total quantity of goods and services demanded, at a price level of P_1 by $500 billion. The aggregate demand curve thus shifts to the right by that amount to AD_2. The equilibrium level of real GDP, however, only rises to $7,300 billion, and the price level rises to P_2. Part of the impact of the increase in aggregate demand is absorbed by higher prices, preventing the full increase in real GDP predicted by the aggregate expenditures model.

A reduction in government purchases would have the opposite effect. All other things unchanged, aggregate expenditures would shift downward by an amount equal to the reduction in aggregate purchases. In the model of aggregate demand and aggregate supply, the aggregate demand curve would shift to the left by an amount equal to the initial change in autonomous aggregate expenditures times the multiplier. Real GDP and the price level would fall. The fall in real GDP is less than would occur if the price level stayed constant.

In the remainder of this appendix, we will focus on the shift in the aggregate expenditures curve. To determine what happens to equilibrium real GDP and the price level, we must look at the intersection of the new aggregate demand curve and the short-run aggregate supply curve, as we did in Panel (b) of Figure 34.1.

Change in Autonomous Taxes

A change in autonomous taxes shifts the aggregate expenditures in the opposite direction of the change in government purchases. If the autonomous taxes go up, for example, aggregate expenditures go down by a *fraction* of the change. Because the initial change in consumption is less than the change in taxes (because it is multiplied by the *MPC*, which is less than 1), the shift caused by a change in taxes is less than an equal change (in the opposite direction) in government purchases.

Now suppose that autonomous taxes fall by $200 billion and that the marginal propensity to consume is 0.8. Then the shift up in the aggregate expenditures curve is $160 billion (= 0.8 × $200). As we saw, a $200-billion increase in government purchases shifted the aggregate expenditures curve up by $200 billion. Assuming a multiplier of 2.5, the reduction in autonomous taxes causes equilibrium real GDP in the aggregate expenditures model to rise by $400 billion. This is less than the change of $500 billion caused by an equal (but opposite) change in government purchases. The impact of a $200-billion decrease in autonomous taxes is shown in Figure 34.2.

FIGURE 34.2 A Decrease in Autonomous Taxes
A decrease of $200 billion in autonomous taxes shifts the aggregate expenditures curve upward by the marginal propensity to consume of 0.8 times the changes in autonomous taxes of $200 billion, or $160 billion, to AE_2. The equilibrium level of income in the aggregate expenditures model increases by $400 billion to $7,400 billion. All figures are in billions of base-year dollars.

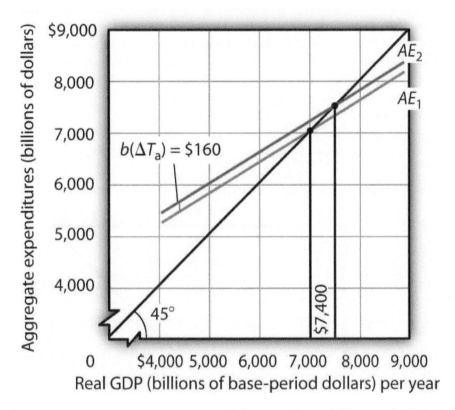

Similarly, an increase in autonomous taxes of, for example, $75 billion, would shift the aggregate expenditures curve downward by $60 billion (= 0.8 × $75) and cause the equilibrium level of real GDP to decrease by $150 billion (= 2.5 × $60).

Changes in Income Tax Rates

Changes in income tax *rates* produce an important complication that we have not encountered thus far. When government purchases or autonomous taxes changed, the aggregate expenditures curve shifted up or down. The new aggregate expenditures curve had the same slope as the old curve; the multiplier was the same before and after the change in government purchases or autonomous taxes. When income tax rates change, however, the aggregate expenditures curve will rotate, that is, its slope will change. As a result, the value of the multiplier itself will change.

We saw in the first section of this appendix that when taxes are related to income, the multiplier depends on both the marginal propensity to consume and the tax rate. An increase in income tax rates will make the aggregate expenditures curve flatter and reduce the multiplier. A higher income tax rate thus rotates the aggregate expenditures curve downward. Similarly, a lower income tax rate rotates the aggregate expenditures curve upward, making it steeper.

Suppose that an economy with an initial real GDP of $7,000 billion has an income tax rate of 0.25. To simplify, we will assume there are no autonomous taxes (that is, $T_a = 0$). So $T = tY$. Thus, disposable personal income Y_d is 75% of real GDP:

EQUATION 34.16

$$T = 0.25Y$$

EQUATION 34.17

$$Y_a = Y - T = 0.75Y$$

Suppose the marginal propensity to consume is 0.8. A $1 change in real GDP produces an increase in disposable personal income of $0.75, and that produces an increase in consumption of $0.60 (= 0.8 × 0.75 × $1). If the other components of aggregate expenditures are autonomous, then the multiplier is 2.5 (= 1 / [1 - 0.6]).

The impact of a tax rate change is illustrated in Figure 34.3. It shows the original aggregate expenditures curve AE_1 intersecting the 45-degree line at the income of $7,000 billion. The curve has a slope of 0.6. Now suppose that the tax rate is increased to 0.375. The higher tax rate will rotate this curve downward, making it flatter. The slope of the new aggregate expenditures curve AE_2 will be 0.5 (= 1 - 0.8[1 - 0.375]). The value of the multiplier thus falls from 2.5 to 2 (= 1 / [1 - 0.5]).

FIGURE 34.3 The Impact of an Increase in Income Tax Rates

An increase in the income tax rate rotates the aggregate expenditures curve downward by an amount equal to the initial change in consumption at the original equilibrium value of real GDP found in the aggregate expenditures model, $7,000 billion in this case, assuming no other change in aggregate expenditures. It reduces the slope of the aggregate expenditures curve and thus reduces the multiplier. Here, an increase in the income tax rate from 0.25 to 0.375 reduces the slope from 0.6 to 0.5; it thus reduces the multiplier from 2.5 to 2. The higher tax reduces consumption by $700 billion and reduces equilibrium real GDP in the aggregate expenditures model by $1,400 billion.

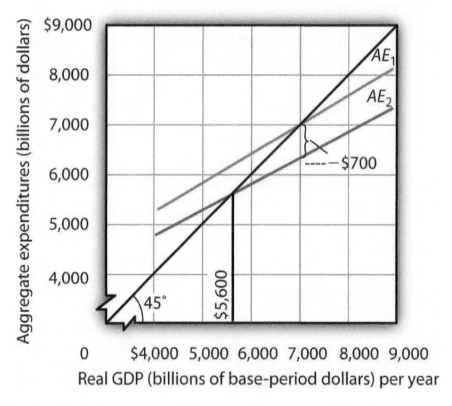

At the original level of income, $7,000 billion, tax collection equaled $1,750 billion (again, for this example, we assume T_a = 0, so T = 0.25 × $7,000). At the new tax rate and original level of income, they equal $2,625 billion (0.375 × $7,000 billion). Disposable personal income at a real GDP of $7,000 billion thus declines by $875 billion. With a marginal propensity to consume of 0.8, consumption drops by $700 billion (= 0.8 × $875 billion). The aggregate expenditures curve rotates down by this amount at the initial level of income of $7,000 billion, assuming no other changes in aggregate expenditures occur.

Before the tax rate increase, an additional $1 of real GDP induced $0.60 in additional consumption. At the new tax rate, an additional $1 of real GDP creates $0.625 in disposable personal